BFI FILM AND TELEVISION HANDBOOK 2001

 British Film Institute

Editor: Eddie Dyja
Production: Tom Cabot

Information Services
Statistics Manager: Peter Todd
Statistics Research: Erinna Mettler, Phil Wickham
Statistics Tabulation: Ian O'Sullivan

Additional Research/Editorial Assistance:
Sean Delaney, Allen Eyles, David Fisher,
Liz Heasman, Heidi Rasmussen, Laura Pearson,
Les Roberts, Heidi Rasmussen, Mandy Rosencrown,
David Sharp, Linda Wood
Database consultant: Lavinia Orton
Marketing: Rebecca Watts, Sarah Prosser
Cover design: DW Design

Advertisement Managers: TGP
4th Floor, 17 Shaftesbury Avenue,
Piccadilly, London W1V 7RL
Tel: 020 7439 3334
Fax: 020 7439 2935

With many thanks to those who assisted with
photographs: BBC, *bfi* Collections, Blue Light, Buena
Vista International, Carlton, Celador Productions,
Channel 4 Television, Columbia TriStar, Entertainment
Film Distributors, FilmFour Distributors, Granada,
Miramax, Pathé Distribution, Twentieth Century Fox,
Universal Pictures International, United International
Pictures (UK), The Walt Disney Company, Warner
Bros, Yorkshire Television

© **British Film Institute 2000**
21 Stephen Street
London W1T 1LN

Printed in Great Britain by Bath Press, Bath

A catalogue record for this book is available from the
British Library.

ISBN 0 85170 818 8

Price: £20.00

Contents

TWENTIETH CENTURY FOX

IS PROUD TO PRESENT IT'S LINE UP FOR 2001

QUILLS
DIGIMON
BOOTMEN
WOMAN ON TOP
DUDE WHERE'S MY CAR?
THE LEGEND OF BAGGER VANCE
SQUELCH
MEN OF HONOUR
MONKEYBONE
TIGERLAND
DR DOLITTLE 2
MOULIN ROUGE
PLANET OF THE APES
SAY IT ISN'T SO
FROM HELL
ANIMAL HUSBANDRY
KINGDOM COME
THE DUBBED ACTION MOVIE: ENTER THE FIST
FREDDY GOT FINGERED

A NEWS CORPORATION COMPANY

For further information please contact The Press Office
Twentieth Century Fox 31 Soho Square London W1V 6AP
Tel: 0207 437 7766 Fax: 0207 734 3187

ACKNOWLEDGMENTS

Sometimes putting the Handbook together feels like the refrain from that old Roger Daltrey song, *One Man Band*. Luckily, there are other times when I have felt more like a conductor with an orchestra of talented individuals who have supported the *bfi Film and Television Handbook* throughout the year, and helped me keep in tune with movements and changes within the industry.

My virtuoso soloist, Tom Cabot, ensured that the book's production values were note perfect and rightly receives my personal ovation.

Many thanks to the string section of the orchestra made up of Peter Todd and his team in the Information Service of the *bfi* – Phil Wickham, Erinna Mettler and Ian O'Sullivan. This quartet pulled together the statistical section of the Handbook.

Turning to the woodwind section special thanks go to the following for their excellent work on this year's bitter sweet symphony – Mark Batey and the Press Office, DW Design, Peter Duncan and TGP, Sean Delaney, Allen Eyles, David Fisher, Liz Heasman, Louise Johnston, Tina McFarling, Laura Pearson, Heidi Rasmussen, Les Roberts, Mandy Rosencrown, David Sharp and Linda Wood.

Elsewhere a nod of appreciation towards the percussion section, which also played its part in the success of this opus – Sophia Contento, Andrew Lockett, Sarah Prosser and Rebbeca Watts. All made sure that the book kept in time.

Special thanks go to the following vocalists for their support – Melissa Bromley, Christophe Dupin, Eugene Finn, Alan Gregory, Adrian Hughes, Matt Ker, Ed Lawrenson, Jonathan Morris, Ivan Mowse, Lavinia Orton, Markku Salmi, Sara Squire, Tise Vahimagi and Sophie Water.

Screen Finance, X25 Partnership and *Screen Digest* provided instruments by which we could compile the statistical sections and their continued support and co-operation is deeply appreciated.

Thanks also go to the brass section including the following organisations and individuals: The BBC, The British Film Commission (BFC), British Screen Finance, British Videogram Association (BVA), Central Statistical Office (CSO), Cinema Advertising Association (CAA), Entertainment Data Inc. (EDI), The Department for Culture, Media and Sport (DCMS), The Film Council, Independent Television Commission (ITC), Tim Adler, Roger Bennett at ELPSA, Lavinia Carey, Patrick Frater, Allan Hardy, Neil McCartney, Barrie MacDonald, Susan Pack and Steve Perrin.

Eddie Dyja, Handbook Editor, September 2000

FOREWORD

by Joan Bakewell CBE,
Chair of the British Film Institute

With the new century came a new structure for UK film. In April 2000 the Film Council, of whose Board I am a member, was inaugurated with a remit to develop coherent strategies for both a sustainable film industry and the wider promotion of film culture. The British Film Institute is devoted to the latter and receives funding from the Film Council to deliver greater understanding of the moving image throughout the UK.

Education, formal and informal, is the *bfi*'s priority. We deliver an impressive range of educational services relating to the moving image to many audiences. For instance, students and researchers may feast on our extensive filmographic database, collections of books and periodicals, and film viewing service which brings the holdings of our world-class Conservation Centre within easy reach. We offer workshops for school pupils and an array of resources for their teachers. For film-goers, we arrange programming beyond the mainstream at an increasing variety of local cinemas and festivals. And anyone interested in the moving image will find food for thought on our website and in our many publications, videos and DVDs.

This authoritative Handbook is another excellent example of the *bfi* at work. It brings together thousands of useful contacts from film and television, and records statistics and views on the past year. Like so many *bfi* initiatives, it would not be possible without the co-operation and support of many bfi staff and other organisations. I shall keep a copy of this 2001 edition close to hand, and urge you to do so too.

Films for Filmmakers

Kodak Vision 800T film 7289/5289

Tungsten-800 EI Daylight-500* EI

The world's fastest tungsten-balanced stock. Offers the sharpness and grain structure you would expect only in slower products.
Allows for increased creative flexibility in low light, fast action, anamorphic, super 35mm and other filming conditions, where systems speed is vitally important.

Kodak Vision 500T film 7279/5279

Tungsten-500 EI Daylight-320* EI

With improved grain and sharpness, this high speed tungsten balanced stock offers rich colours and excellent detail in low and very low light conditions.

Kodak Vision 320T film 7277/5277

Tungsten-320 EI Daylight-200* EI

This unique tungsten balanced stock offers a less saturated look with slightly lower contrast whilst providing superb shadow detail and clean white highlights.

Kodak Vision 250D film 7246/5246

Daylight-250 EI Tungsten-64**EI

A high speed daylight balanced film stock providing the highest image quality for its speed. It delivers a rich reproduction of blacks in natural and mixed lighting conditions.

Kodak Vision 200T film 7274/5274

Tungsten-200 EI Daylight-125* EI

A higher speed tungsten balanced stock with fine grain and outstanding sharpness, offering a wide exposure latitude and excellent colour reproduction. A very good all round stock that works very well in almost any lighting condition.

Eastman EXR 100T film 7248/5248

Tungsten-100 EI Daylight-64*EI

A medium speed tungsten balanced stock with wide exposure latitude. Very good grain and saturation producing excellent highlights and shadow detail.

Eastman EXR 50D film 7245/5245

Daylight-50 EI Tungsten-12**EI

A daylight balanced stock, extremely sharp and virtually grain free. This film offers a wide exposure latitude with rich, natural colours.
An excellent choice for bright exteriors.

Contact Numbers

To order film stock telephone the Order Services Department direct on 01442 845945, or fax us on 01442 844458.

Your order will be handled by Julie Jackson, Julie Carrington or Anne-Marie Masson.

*With Kodak Wratten 85 filter **With Kodak Wratten 80A filter.
Kodak, Eastman, Vision, EXR, T-grain and Wratten are trade marks.

Entertainment Imaging

http://www.Kodak.com/go/motion

INTRODUCTION

by Jon Teckman,
Director of the British Film Institute

The British Film Institute aims to promote the appreciation and enjoyment of film and television. Over the years, the expertise and dedication of our staff has deservedly secured for the *bfi* a reputation of authority and accuracy in moving image matters. We are usually at our most effective, and exert the greatest impact, when the various bfi departments come together to make the best of a particular programme. Examples from 2000 include:

Fritz Lang: A retrospective of his films at the bfi National Film Theatre; the re-release of *You Only Live Once* in UK cinemas; a new book from *bfi* Publishing; exclusive articles on our website and in *Sight and Sound* magazine.

A Midsummer Night's Dream: A 2-week exhibition of film stills and books in the NFT foyer; a gala showing of Max Reinhardt's lush 1935 film version of the play on midsummer's day with costume characters from our Museum Actors' Consultancy Service; a pre-film talk about Shakespeare on Screen.

bfi **TV 100:** A list of 100 'favourite' British television programmes of the 20th century, compiled from an industry poll, announced prior to the *bfi*'s annual television festival, TV2000; an exhibition of TV stills and materials; a special feature in *Sight and Sound*.

Typiquement British: The *bfi* has worked with the British Council in Paris to programme and present this five-month festival of British films at the Centre Pompidou, starting in October 2000, a month before our own 44th London Film Festival, sponsored by Regus, opened in London's Leicester Square.

Presentation of the 51st *bfi* Fellowship to Dame Elizabeth Taylor: As well as the presentation there was a series of her classic films at the NFT and available for booking by cinemas UK-wide.

We have other such large-scale initiatives planned for 2001. It is Walt Disney's centenary year and in the spring we are mounting a celebration of animation for children. I am pleased that the *bfi* also works with more than 100 partner organisations of many kinds, helping us to attract ever broader audiences to the diverse world of moving images.

Midsummer night dreams are made of this

Typiquement British c'est vrai

Looking ahead to the *bfi*'s 70th anniversary in 2003, we anticipate a digital universe. Not only film production (in which the bfi is no longer involved, our Production department having transferred to the Film Council in April 2000), but also film delivery and consumption, at home, in cinemas and other locations, are already undergoing a digital revolution. The *bfi* is embracing these changes with all the resources at its disposal.

In 2000-01, we are releasing more DVDs alongside video cassettes, and I am delighted that in the first three months of 2000 – the first full quarter after its relaunch – the *bfi*'s website attracted approximately half a million page hits. We are determined to build on this success and, where possible, to make much more of our extensive collections of film materials, information and resources available through the Internet.

We are currently preparing a new *bfi* Film Centre which, subject to planning permission and on-going consultation, will be constructed within the next few years on London's South Bank, close to the BA London Eye. Through the NFT, the *bfi* has had a home on the South Bank for almost 50 years and we are committed to the further development of the site. This new centre will offer the public state-of-the-art facilities for experiencing and discovering more about the world of film and television, as never before. It will be the UK's premier showcase for the moving image. Meanwhile, our long-established Conservation Centre in Hertfordshire will also be developed as a prestigious facility for film preservation and research.

How appropriate that the *bfi* should be embarking on such an engrossing and potentially rewarding odyssey as 2001 dawns. You can keep up to date with *bfi* news and services throughout the year via our ever expanding website: **www.bfi.org.uk.**

British Film Institute in 2000

Address: 21 Stephen Street
London W1T 1LN
Tel: +44 (0)20 7255 1444
Fax: +44 (0)20 7436 0439
email: discover@bfi.org.uk
Website: www.bfi.org.uk
24-hour *bfi* events line: 0870 240 40 50 (national call rate applies)

bfi Status

The British Film Institute is independently constituted as a Royal Charter body and a registered charity (number 287780), overseen by its Board of Governors.

The *bfi*'s annual grant-in-aid is awarded by the Film Council, the government-backed strategic agency inaugurated in April 2000 with a remit to develop the UK's film industry and promote its film culture. The *bfi* is the principal body delivering the Film Council's film education and cultural objectives.

The *bfi*'s Patron is HRH The Prince of Wales KG KT GCB.

The *bfi*'s various collections, amongst the largest in the world, include more than 275,000 feature films, dating from 1894; 200,000 television programmes; some seven million film stills, posters and designs; 41,000 reference books and annuals; 5,000 magazines; 2 million newspaper cuttings, mostly on microfiche; and 19,000 unpublished film scripts.

Essential cinema on the South Bank

British Film Institute's Highlights of 2000

We launched *bfi* at Odeon – a programming initiative to present the best of world cinema on selected Odeon screens UK-wide. We also began to programme three screens at the Warner Village Star City multiplex in Birmingham, which opened in July.

Amongst 27 new books, we published the 50th *bfi* Film Classic on Martin Scorsese's *Taxi Driver*, written by Amy Taubin. We also released *A Personal Journey with Martin Scorsese Through American Movies* on DVD, amongst other new DVD and video titles.

We re-released film classics in UK cinemas on brand new prints, including the original *Shaft, Singin' in the Rain, Once Upon A Time in the West, A Matter of Life and Death* and *Some Like It Hot*, which was the first in a slate of revivals enabled by an innovative sponsorship agreement .

We prepared and screened a newly tinted-and-toned restoration of Abel Gance's silent epic *Napoleon* (1927), in association with Photoplay Productions, and we hosted the 56th Annual Congress of the International Federation of Film Archives (FIAF) at the *bfi* National Film Theatre in June.

We presented the Regus London Film Festival (the 44th) from 1–16 November and the 14th London Lesbian and Gay Film Festival from 30 March – 13 April. Both were followed by tours of selected films to cinemas around the UK.

At the *bfi* London IMAX® Cinema in Waterloo, we presented Walt Disney Pictures' *Fantasia 2000* – The IMAX® Experience exclusively, and began an 'After Dark' season of classic feature films shown in 70mm.

We redesigned our authoritative magazine *Sight and Sound*, which enjoyed a monthly readership of 65,500.

We announced the *bfi* TV 100, a selection of the favourite British television programmes of the 20th century. The poll amongst members of the UK's TV industry was topped by the marvellous comedy *Fawlty Towers* (BBC, 1975 & 1979).

We developed a new strategy for Cultural Diversity at the *bfi* and circulated it to many interested parties for comments. Film lies at the heart of popular culture and the UK has many and diverse cultures and communities. We are committed to the principle of equality of opportunity to appreciate and enjoy all that the world of film has to offer.

BUENA VISTA INTERNATIONAL (UK) LTD
FORTHCOMING RELEASES

REMEMBER THE TITANS

PEARL HARBOR

UNBREAKABLE

THE EMPEROR'S NEW GROOVE

ATLANTIS

Buena Vista International (UK) Ltd. 3 Queen Caroline Street. London. W6 9PE.
Telephone. 020 8222 1000   Fax: 020 8222 2494   www.bvimovies.co.uk

CHRISTIE'S

A blue painted pine front door – represented
William Thackeray's (Hugh Grant) front door in the
1999 Working Title production "Notting Hill"

Sold for £5,750 on 9 December 1999

Film and Entertainment

costumes … props … scripts …autographed photographs … costume designs
… awards … Charlie Chaplin … Marilyn Monroe … Audrey Hepburn …
007/James Bond … Wizard of Oz … Aliens … Superman … Star Wars.

Auctions
Film Posters
London South Kensington,
11 September 2000 and March 2001

Film and Entertainment
London South Kensington
12 December 2000

Enquiries
Sarah Hodgson (020) 7321 3281
SHodgson@christies.com
Helen Bailey (020) 7321 3280
HBailey@christies.com
Carey Wallace (Consultant)

Catalogues
(020) 7389 2820

South Kensington
85 Old Brompton Road, London SW7 3LD

www.christies.com

UK FILM, TELEVISION AND VIDEO: OVERVIEW

by Eddie Dyja

By the late summer of 2000 it is already evident how the brave new digital world is having an important influence on interactive, multi-media technologies. No sooner had the chimes of Big Ben announced the start of the new millennium that we discovered that it wasn't simply a case of 'ring out the old, ring in the new' – but rather, 'ring in the new and bring the old along as well'.

Convergence

While the new media has been busy assimilating the traits of the old, the old media has recognised the need to embrace the new. This rapid acculturation of technologies has been the prevalent theme of the early 21st century. It seems that 'convergence' is the word tripping off most media executives' lips.

Mergers

The proposed AOL-Time Warner deal in America at the end of 1999, followed in June 2000 by the Vivendi and Seagram merger (forming Vivendi Universal based in Paris) were two significant examples of attempts at global domination of the mass media and communications markets.

It is no surprise that the convergence battleground is all about ownership and control. Cross-media monopolies loom large over the horizon, with new enterprises either being swallowed up by the giants or blocked to the point of withdrawal. It is already becoming clear that the notion of a digital Utopia where everyone can produce and distribute their own film/programmes/music is likely to remain just that – a Utopia.

Prompted by the rapid growth in convergence technologies, the Government announced its intention to publish a White Paper by the end of 2000, setting out proposals for the reform of broadcasting and communications legislation.

Come together, right now

In the UK the three main groups controlling ITV – Granada Media Group, Carlton Communications and United News & Media were embroiled in a power struggle. In November 1999, Carlton and United announced their intention to merge. To counter this the Granada Media Group declared it might propose a bid for Carlton or United. This prompted a Competitions Commission inquiry into the legality of the various bids. Until now the three companies could not combine, thanks to a rule that prevented them controlling more than a 25 per cent share of the advertising revenue. In July 2000, Trade and Industry Secretary Stephen Byers, scrapped that ruling, effectively allowing any of the three companies to consolidate into two. Carlton and United postponed their merger, leaving the field open again. Irrespective of who ends up merging with who, many predict the formation of a single ITV broadcaster within the next couple of years.

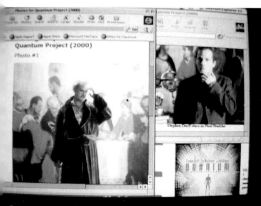

Quantum Project as seen on the Internet

The Internet

There is an advertisement on television at present where a man dashes upstairs to his son's bedroom to log on to the Internet to set up some car insurance thereby proving how fast and efficient the Internet is. He pauses to say "The Internet – it's great isn't it?"

The scope for access to information, infotainment, e-mail, e-commerce or B2B (Business to Business) is great indeed. It is already hard to imagine what life was like, say five years ago, before access to the world wide web was so readily available. It is also quite staggering how advances in technology have brought along changes enabling better access across more media platforms. Accessing the Internet via your mobile phone is commonplace now, and accessing it via your television as well as pre-programming your viewing for the week using EPG (electronic programme guides) will sound old hat by the time you read this.

In the short time since the last Handbook was last published Dot.coms have sprouted all over the new media landscapes. Some are finding their feet while others, such as online designer-wear retailer Boo.com, have already collapsed. However, e-commerce aside, there are interesting examples of how the marriage of old and the new can work.

Webcasts of events such as Sir Paul McCartney's return to the new Cavern in Liverpool, which was transmitted live on 14 December 1999 and shown (in slightly edited form on BBC1 the next day), were examples of the new media showing off its crowd-pulling potential.

The success of *The Blair Witch Project* demonstrated that with a little bit of imagination the Internet is a powerful marketing tool. This low-budget horror film, which has become the most profitable film ever made, brought together two first-time directors, Daniel Myrick and Eduardo Sanchez, and three unknown actors, who were given handheld cameras and sent into some woods to make a documentary. Before the film was released in America, the directors invented two centuries' worth of Blair Witch mythology for the website of the film – including interviews with police detectives and authentic looking archival material. The intention of teasing the audience into believing that the story might be true was the perfect curtain-raiser for the film – a case of light the blue touchpaper and watch it take off.

In the UK the film, which opened on Halloween, used TV commercials showing traumatised audiences as a powerful promotional tool. Added to the perfect marketing mix, the video/DVD release of the film continued to make full use of its medium, arguably more so, with the home-made video feel of the film translating well onto the small screen.

Quantum Project, directed by Eugenio Zanetti and starring Stephen Dorff, Fay Masterson, John Cleese and Russell Brown was billed as the first feature film made specifically for the Internet. The film, which was released in May 2000, lasts 32 minutes – downloading it probably took much longer. Therein lies the current problem: most home computers do not have the bandwidth to download more than a minute or two of video footage in a reasonable time-frame. However, the direct downloading of films from the Internet will become a real option once broadband Internet services achieve greater household penetration. At present distributors are happy to advertise their films via full online trailers.

The Blair Witch Project – a shining case of convergence

Yet, along with the advances in technology also come advances in the standard and availability of copying technology which encourage piracy. The inevitable growth in illegal copying on the Internet has led to understandable concern throughout the media industry. The Alliance Against Counterfeiting and Piracy was launched in July 1999 and consists of groups concerned with ownership of intellectual properties, whether it is from the world of music, film or design. Indeed, the Alliance has been trying to get legislation to outlaw theft over the Internet of intellectual property.

Interactive Films/Television

Running Time, which claimed to be the world's first interactive movie, was directed by Susie Halewood, with *The Full Monty* writer Simon Beaufoy as creative director. It developed on the Internet, growing in five minute sequences every four days after a public vote on what the viewers wanted to happen next. Once the vote was cast the outcome was then filmed on digital video and put on the site – www.itsyourmovie.com.

The concept of movies by consensus is by no means new. In fact, there are many examples of films (*Fierce Creatures* springs to mind) that have had to be re-shot after test screenings have left audiences unsatisfied at best or perplexed at worst. The novelty value of the audience choosing a set of options is obviously dictated by the choices the film-maker is prepared to offer the audience.

Convergence has also had a big effect on television. By the time you read this the *Big Brother* phenomenon may have died down or likely to have been replaced by the next interactive audience grabber. Love it or hate it, Channel 4's hit show, which merged docusoap with the game show, has performed across several media boundaries using the Internet (including six live camera feeds), television and the newspapers to promote itself. It is particularly interesting that 'the old media' – newspapers – have taken quite a lead in promoting the show, often in an almost Orwellian fashion. The tabloids seemed fascinated by the contestants (the Nasty Nick campaign wasn't that far removed from a version of Hate Week) and the broadsheets in turn couldn't resist carrying stories about who was evicted from the house.

So be prepared, come 2001 interactive television will be the new soap opera, the new quiz show and the new sit-com.

However, as with interactive film, the notion that "you, the viewer get to choose" implies a certain amount of control. The multi-channel landscape also purports to offer the viewer a choice of hundreds of channels, just as the multiplex and megaplexes offer a variety of screens. But with the media giants stampeding into the arena the concept of viewer empowerment increasingly carries a hollow ring. It's more of a case of "you the viewer will continue to be told what to watch and what to choose."

Film

In his book *Inconceivable* Ben Elton makes this observation: "It's an interesting thing about the Brit film industry (such as it is) that for all the gung-ho, Cool Britannia jingoism we spout about our cool new British talent, we judge our product exclusively on whether or not people in America go to see it."

There is indeed a great deal of rhetoric, if not nonsense, spoken about the British film industry. Added to Ben Elton's comments, and taking a leaf out of Nick Hornby's book *High Fidelity*, here is a list of some common themes that have already shaped the British film industry in 2000.

Top Five British Film Industry strengths in 2000

1. The success of films like *East is East* and *Ratcatcher*
The box-office success and critical acclaim accorded these two films (both set in the Seventies) proved several points about the quality of successful recent British films – they don't have to conform to type by being hip and trendy, they can reflect a British way of life and they can attract British audiences.

2. *Gladiator* being filmed at Shepperton Studios
Often the notion of British technical expertise and

You are watching Big Brother

Unlike Chicken Run, many UK films didn't take off

excellent facilities is rightly cited as one of the strengths of the British film industry. This point was emphasised by the big-budget *Gladiator* being filmed at Shepperton.

3. British Actors and Actresses

The success of the entire British film industry is often, wrongly, judged by how many nominations the Brits get at the Oscars. Nevertheless, Jude Law, Samantha Morton, Janet McTeer, (not to mention Michael Caine) serve to illustrate the continuing line of British bankable talent.

4. Sam Mendes directing *American Beauty*

Oscar-winning director Sam Mendes was the obvious toast of the British film industry. Other directors too, plied their trade in Hollywood such as Anthony Minghella with *The Talented Mr Ripley*, Stephen Frears with *High Fidelity*, and Peter Lord and Nick Park with *Chicken Run*

5. Cinema going is still on the increase

At the time of writing UK admissions between January and June 2000 had reached a 26-year high. Film, whether it is on a digital or celluloid format, is still as popular as ever in the UK.

Top Five British Film Industry weaknesses in 2000

1. *High Fidelity* being set in Chicago

If the British film industry was as buoyant and hip as we would sometimes like to believe, Stephen Frears' splendid adaptation of *High Fidelity* would have been set in North London rather than Chicago. After all, *Notting Hill* was set in London and did rather well didn't it?

2. British films struggling to get released

How great is a British film industry that shuns its own product? Even allowing for the recent spate of poor British films, (*Rancid Aluminum* and *Mad Cows* are just two films which were reviled by the press), British films struggle to find screen space, which seems exclusively reserved for Hollywood product.

3. Gangster movies – too many

Following the success of *Lock, Stock and Two Smoking Barrels* the British film industry seemed obsessed with similar crime capers. *Circus, Essex Boys, Gangster No 1, Honest, Love Honour and Obey, Sexy Beast, Snatch,* and *You're Dead* to name just a few (there were and still are more out there).

4. Waste of Lottery money

Not all Lottery money was wasted on dodgy British films but, like a parody of *Chicken Run*, there were too many turkeys out there trying to fly that should never have been allowed to get off the ground. The task of distributing Lottery funds has now been handed over to the Film Council and it is hoped that the fund managers will exercise some tough quality control over public money so that it isn't wasted on so much dross.

5. Foreign/arthouse films being marginalised.

There appears to be a dumbed-down approach to foreign language and arthouse films in the UK. A whole generation of cinema goers (therefore potential film-makers) have been brought up without the opportunities to see foreign language films. Had Quentin Tarantino never seen *City on Fire,* directed by Ringo Lam, he may have never made *Reservoir Dogs*. Sergei Eisenstein? Jean-Luc Godard? François Truffaut? Luis Buñuel? Roberto Rossellini? Vittorio De Sica? Ingmar Bergman? Krzysztof Kieslowski? Andrei Tarkovsky? Akira Kurosawa? Fritz Lang? Wim Wenders? Satyajit Ray? Who are they?

The Film Council

It is against this backdrop that the Film Council was launched on 1 April 2000. In May it announced Stage One of its strategy for creating a sustainable UK film industry with a package of £22 million production funds. The money was divided up via the following funds:

The Premiere Production Fund – £10 million per year set aside for the production of popular mainstream films.

The New Cinema Fund – £5 million per year devoted to new film-makers with an eye on new electronic production technologies.

A Film Development Fund – £5 million per year which is aimed at supporting the development of innovative and commercially attractive screenplays.

Some things you never get used to ... High Fidelity

The Film Training Fund – £1 million per year supporting training initiatives for scriptwriters, film development executives, business executives, producers and distributors.

First Movies – a £1 million pilot fund for children throughout the UK to make a first film using low-cost digital technology.

In addition, the Film Council pledged 20 per cent of the budget of each fund for European co-production. This was calculated at £4.2 million a year towards the Film Council's strategy of expanding business in Europe.

One of the points that the Film Council rightly recognised was the need to invest in project and script development. Many of the recently maligned British flops would undoubtedly have benefited from earlier script development and preparation. There is also a real need to not just rely on Lottery money for film production but to actively encourage investors to put money into film projects. However, investors generally want to see some return on their investments, and unfortunately box office success is never guaranteed, and therefore hits like *the Full Monty, Lock, Stock and Two Smoking Barrels* are difficult to predict.

However welcome the funds are, there was little in Stage One of the Film Council's plans to suggest the building of an infrastructure to support the films that are being made. Britain cannot compete with Hollywood at the moment by producing a string of homespun big blockbusters, the profits of which are poured back into the industry. The British film industry is dependent on

the likes of Hollywood and other co-productions to keep it afloat. It was noted in the Handbook last year that British film studios were losing out to competition from Canada, Australia and the Czech Republic. The battle for business is likely to be fierce – and some UK players have decided to bow out of the arena.

In February 2000 the Rank Group effectively pulled out of the film business when it sold Pinewood Studios, to an investment group led by Michael Grade and also sold its interest in the Odeon Group (thereby merging Odeon with ABC cinemas). Virgin also pulled the plug on its cinema operation by selling to French owned UGC. By August 2000 Michael Grade, now chairman of Pinewood, was working on a merger between Pinewood and Shepperton Studios.

It is within this context of mergers, consolidation and fierce competition that the Film Council is expected to deliver Stage Two of its strategy geared to creating real structural change to benefit the British film industry at the beginning of 2001.

It is likely that the problems of distribution, exhibition and marketing of British products will be addressed. It now remains to be seen how radical and innovative the new measures will be, in order to create a truly sustainable film industry in Britan.

Television

In September 2000 the *bfi* published the *bfi* TV 100, a list of all-time top British television programmes selected by members of the TV industry. The list, headed by *Fawlty Towers,* demonstrated a rich television heritage. Casting an eye over the top ten – *Cathy Come Home* (BBC), *Doctor Who* (BBC), *The Naked Civil Servant* (ITV), *Monty Python's Flying Circus* (BBC), *Blue Peter* (BBC) *Boys From The Blackstuff* (BBC), *Parkinson* (BBC), *Yes Minister/Yes Prime Minister* (BBC), *Brideshead Revisited* (ITV) – also served as a reminder of how poor television today seems in comparison to the hits of yesterday. Although lists shouldn't be taken too seriously, it is worth noting the absence in the *bfi* top 100 of any docusoaps, gardening/room make-overs, or cookery programmes, so prevalent on our screens today.

Since the Broadcasting Act of 1990, which succeeded in making television more competitive, the scramble for ratings and advertising revenue has taken precedence over everything else. It is no surprise therefore that quality, or rather a lack of it, became one of the issues of

Mr Fawlty, we're the top British TV programme!

the television's year. The Government, the Independent Television Commission, the press and even advertisers all voiced concern about the continuing slide in standards.

In the BBC's Annual Report for 1999/2000 the governors stated: "the average quality of programmes across the year on the channel is not good enough, particularly in the pre-watershed period...BBC1 is not held in the same degree of affection by the public as it once was." While they praised programmes like *Walking With Dinosaurs* and shows like *the Royle Family* there was a concern about the lack of consistency in output.

In February 2000 Chris Smith, Department of Culture Media and Sport minister, announced that the television licence fee would rise by 1.5 per cent over the rate of inflation each year for the next seven years. The award of £200 million was to help the BBC move towards digital television. However, he stressed that the money was to ensure that the BBC made more programmes and broadcast fewer repeats. At the time of writing the BBC schedule was full of classic comedies such as *Fawlty Towers, Whatever Happened to the Likely Lads* and *Only Fools and Horses,* which merely exposed the dearth of new sitcom material – on any of the channels.

At the same time pensioners over the age of 75 were able to get a free television licence from November 2000. It is ironic that 75-year-olds will get the benefit of a medium currently obsessed with youth. This comes at a time when the older population is increasing. According to the Office for National Statistics, the number of pensioners will overtake the number of children by the year 2008 – perhaps the programme-makers might take heed and alter their demographic analysis accordingly.

Meanwhile there was consternation in the press as the BBC continued to lose out to the highest bidder in its coverage of sporting events. The latest casualty was football. The three-year deal for the rights to Premier League matches remained with Sky but the rights to a highlights show of Premiership games went to ITV, leaving *Match of the Day* with crumbs of comfort in the form of the FA Cup and England matches.

While all this was going on Greg Dyke, Director General of the BBC, who began his regime in November 1999, was courting controversy by proposing a set of radical reforms designed to take the Corporation into the digital age. One idea was to abandon "mixed schedules" and divide BBC1 into an entertainment channel and turn BBC2 into a more high brow channel. He then announced the proposal of two digital channels, BBC 3, a youth-oriented channel, and BBC 4, an arts and politics channel, to counter allegations that the BBC had lost sight of its public service remit.

Turning over to ITV, the Carlton, United, Granada merger issue aside, the on-going row between the ITC and ITV about the decision to scrap *News at Ten* raged throughout the year. As audience figures dropped the

Past, present – Walking with Dinosaurs

Time for News at Ten again

ITC gave the ITV an ultimatum to improve its ratings for both the newly scheduled programmes and also the *Nightly News*. The demands for a return to News at Ten was given an almost surreal twist when Greg Dyke announced that the BBC were thinking of taking its news bulletin to the coveted/not so coveted 10 o'clock slot.

As has already been noted, Channel 4's *Big Brother* not only brought interactive television to the centre stage, it also amassed huge audiences. The channel was praised in a report by ITC for programmes such as innovative programmes such as *1900 House* and *Queer as Folk,* but in other quarters slated for shows such as *Ibiza/Greece/Caribbean Uncovered, the 11 O'Clock Show* and *Something for the Weekend.*

But the most constant criticism seemed to be levelled at Channel Five for its over-use of sex-based programmes, and the channel even earned a rebuke from the Government after a one-off nude game show entitled *Naked Jungle* had received complaints. The channel however, remained defiant that its mix of football, films and sex were ratings winners. Incidentally, no Channel Five programme made it into the *bfi* top 100.

While the terrestrial television channels battle for ratings raged on, there was a separate scrap over digital television. More than four million homes out of 22 million now have access to digital television. OnDigital and BSkyB have continued to entice their subscribers with free set-top boxes. Meanwhile, the Government pondered on how and when to achieve a shutdown of the analogue television broadcasting system – somewhere between 2006 and 2010. (BSkyB is planning to switch off its analogue satellite signal sooner than that.) The problem facing the Government is to persuade those people who have no intention of converting to digital that it is in their interests to do so. It is likely that the same sort of incentives offered by the competing digital TV companies may have to be offered to non-subscribers.

DVD Video

In the video industry the old and the new are engaged in a transitional relationship at present with VHS still occupying the front position but waiting for DVD to overtake it.

DVD sales have grown faster here than in the USA. However, according to the British Videogram Association (BVA), there are still in excess of 18 million VHS recorders, in 89 per cent of all British TV households – hardware penetration of DVDs is unlikely to be more than 1 million units by the end of this year. Nevertheless, the signs are that the British public are sold on the improved picture and sound quality and the extras (when available) of interviews, trailers and star biographies.

The DVD revolution is often compared to the introduction of CDs in the 1980s. However, the difference with DVD is that the format has the potential to expand. With a greater disk storage capacity DVDs can merge computer games, music and films – concept albums, which were the hallmark Sixties and early Seventies music, are likely to make a multi-media return.

It is unlikely that DVD video will become the casualty that some commentators predict. The view sometimes expressed is that once broadband is introduced on the Internet downloading films and programmes will become easier. And as has been noted earlier, there are concerns surrounding DVD piracy. The new threats lie in the sale of pre-released material over the Internet. This threat will increase once recordable DVD players become available.

However, once the teething problems associated with universal formats are overcome, it seems likely that DVD sales will go from strength to strength.

Film Production

UK film production finished the decade with a flourish by chalking up 100 films made in 1999 (Table 1). The total of 827 UK films produced during the 1990s surpassed that of the 1980s (427) and the 1970s (810). When you consider that 510 films have been made since 1995 it is easy to see why people like to talk about a resurgent British film industry. However, as in previous years, it is important to be able to put these figures into a proper perspective by dividing UK films into their respective categories. The bigger picture shows that the vast majority of money invested in British films comes from America (Tables 5&6).

The £549.2 million spent on UK films (Table 1), compared to £509.3 million in 1998, should be treated with caution. As we have seen in previous years, the figure gives a slightly unbalanced view of the state of film production in the UK.

In terms of a sustainable British film industry (which is the goal set for the Film Council) it is worth concentrating on Table 2 where the financial impetus derives solely from the UK. The first thing to note is that wholly-produced UK films accounted for nearly 50 per cent of the entire UK production output. However, only two films out of 47, *The House of Mirth* (£7.50 million) and *Whatever Happened to Harold Smith?* (£5.64 million) surpass the total overall average budget of £5.49 million for all UK films.

The average budget of wholly-produced UK films was £2.24 million, a slight decrease from 1998 (£2.49 million) when the figures were bolstered by *Notting Hill* and *Topsy-Turvy*. Roughly half of the 1999 films were made for budgets of £2 million or below and nearly 20 per cent of the films were made on budgets of less than £1 million.

While it is wrong to assume that low-budget or micro-budget films are unworthy of distribution – as we have already seen the success of *The Blair Witch Project* is evidence that it is possible, with the right kind of support, to make a blockbuster on a relative shoestring – it is more than likely that few of these films will make it onto the big screen (or any screen for that matter).

Sadly, evidence over the recent years has shown that at present, the UK produces too many films that do not ever get a theatrical release. By the winter of 2000/01 you might like to consider Table 2. How many of the 47 films

① Number and Value of UK Films* 1981–1999

Year	Titles produced	Current prices (£m)	Production cost (£m) (2000 prices)
1981	24	61.2	135.7
1982	40	141.1	288.4
1983	51	251.1	491.2
1984	53	270.4	469.5
1985	54	269.4	473.4
1986	41	165.8	281.8
1987	55	195.3	318.2
1988	48	175.2	274.8
1989	30	104.7	151.3
1990	60	217.4	283.5
1991	59	243.2	297.7
1992	47	184.9	217.9
1993	67	224.1	264.0
1994	84	455.2	525.1
1995	78	402.4	460.7
1996	128	741.4	820.4
1997	116	562.8	608.3
1998	88	509.3	532.6
1999	100	549.2	557.4

Source: Screen Finance/x25 Partnership/BFI

*UK films are defined here as films produced in the UK or with a UK financial involvement, they include majority and minority co-productions

House of Mirth – biggest budget for a UK production

UK Film Production 1999 – Category A

Feature films where the cultural and financial impetus is from the UK and where the majority of personnel are British.

Title	Production companies	Production cost (£m)
Another Life	Boxer Films/Arts Council of England	2.50
Between Two Women	Julie Woodcock Prods/North Country Pictures	5.00
Billy Elliot	Tiger Aspect/WT2/BBC/Arts Council of England	2.80
Blood	Cantor Markham/Loud Mouse/Yorkshire Media Production Agency	1.00
Breathtaking	September Films/Sky Pictures	3.40
Cold Fish	Opus Pictures	2.00
Complicity	Talisman Films/Carlton/Scottish Arts Council/British Screen	4.60
County Kilburn	Watermark Films	1.00
Creatures	Creatures Ltd/DNA/Arts Council of England	4.00
Dead Bolt Dead	It's Alright Ma Productions	1.00
Emotional Backgammon	Corazon	0.01
Essex Boys	Granada Films	3.00
Fed Rotten	Cake Media	0.20
Five Seconds to Spare	Scala/Wildgaze/BBC/Matrix Film and TV	3.00
The Ghost of Greville Lodge	Renown Pictures	0.75
Going off Big Time	KT Films/MIDA	1.50
Guest House Paradiso	Phil McIntyre Prods/House Films/Vision Video	4.00
Hard News Soft Money	Bolt on Media/Atlantic Celtic	1.00
House!	Wire Films/Arts Council of England/British Screen/CFI	2.00
The House of Mirth	Three Rivers/Film Four/Granada Films/Arts Council of England/ Scottish Arts Council/Glasgow Film Fund	7.50
The Inbetweeners	Britpack Films	1.00
Inside Outside Lydia's Head	Covent Garden Films	0.80
It was an Accident	Bukett Pictures/Litmus Pictures/Pathé/Arts Council of England	2.60
Kevin and Perry Go Large	Tiger Aspect/Fragile Films/	4.00
Lava	Sterling Pictures/Waking Point/Orange Top/Ernst and Young	1.00
London Blues	Prince World Ent.	1.00
Love, Honour and Obey	Fugitive/BBC	2.00
Love the One You're With	Palm Tree Prods/British Council/Big Issue Scotland	0.50
The Low Down	Oil Factory/Sleeper Films/Film Four/British Screen	1.00
Nasty Neighbours	Ipso Facto/Glenrinnes/MPCE/Northern Production Fund/ West Midland Support Agencies	1.50
New Year's Day	Imagine Films/Alchymie/Flashpoint/British Screen	2.50
One Life Stand	Elemental Films	0.50
Offending Angels	Pants Prods	1.00
Pandaemonium	Mariner Prods/BBC/Arts Council of England	3.76
Paradise Grove	Paradise Grove plc/Enterprise Investment Scheme	1.03
Paranoia	Trijbits Productions/Sky/Isle of Man Film Commission	3.14
Purely Belter	Mumbo Jumbo/Film Four	4.00
Saving Grace	Homerun/Wave Pictures/Sky Movies/Portman/Rich Pickings	3.00
Second Generation	Second Generation Films	1.00
Some Voices	Dragon Pictures/FilmFour/British Screen	2.00
Soul's Ark	Weston Union	0.03
Strictly Sinatra	Blue Orange/DNA	4.00
Strong Boys	Cowboy Films/Imagine Films	4.00
There's Only One Jimmy Grimble	Sarah Radclyffe/Impact/Pathe	3.00
The Truth Game	Screen Productions Associates	0.85
Warrior Sisters	Frank Scantori Films	0.01
Whatever Happened to Harold Smith?	West Eleven Films/Intermedia/Arts Council of England	5.64

TOTAL NUMBER OF FILMS   47
TOTAL COST   £105.12m
AVERAGE COST   £2.24m

Source: Screen Finance/X25 Partnership/BFI/British Council

3   ## UK Film Production 1999 – Category B

Majority UK Co-Productions. Films in which, although there are foreign partners, there is a UK cultural content and a significant amount of British finance and personnel.

Title	Production companies/participating countries	Production cost (£m)
Daybreak	Daybreak Films/FilmFour/Traumwerk/Scottish Arts Council/Scottish Screen	1.00
Gangster No.1	Pagoda Films/Road Movies/Film Four/Sky/British Screen (**Germany**)	4.15
Glory Glory	Peakviewing/Transatlantic (**South Africa**)	7.36
Honest	Honest Prods/Pathe/Pandora (**France**)	6.10
Hotel Splendide	Renegade Films/FilmFour/Canal +/British Screen (**France**)	3.20
Kin	Bard Entertainment/M-Net/Arts Council of England/British Screen (**South Africa**)	4.50
The Luzhin Defence	Renaissance/ICE/Egmond/Lantia (**France/Italy**)	5.50
The Man Who Cried	Adventure Films/Working Title/Canal + (**France**)	15.00
Maybe Baby	Phil McIntyre Prods/BBC/Pandora (**Luxembourg**)	3.25
The Nine Lives of Tomas Katz	Strawberry Vale/GFF (**Germany**)	0.40
Room to Rent	Renegade Films/Canal +/Ima/FilmFour/Arts Council of England/BFI (**France**)	2.20
Secret Society	Focus Film Prods/Ena Film/WDR/Filmstiftung/Isle of Man Film Commission/ Yorkshire Media Production Agency (**Germany**)	3.33
Shooters	Coolbeans Films/Catapault Prods (**Netherlands**)	1.20
That Girl From Rio	Casanova Films/Lola Films (**Spain**)	3.75
Very Annie Mary	Dragon Pictures/FilmFour/Canal +/Arts Council of England/ Arts Council of Wales (**France**)	3.09
Wild About Harry	Scala/BBC/Northern Ireland Film Commission/Medien Beteiligungs (**Germany**)	3.16

TOTAL NUMBER OF FILMS   16
TOTAL COST   £67.19m
AVERAGE COST   £4.20m

Screen Finance/X25 Partnership/BFI/British Council

4   ## UK Film Production 1999 – Category C

Minority UK Co-productions. Foreign (non US) films in which there is a small UK involvement in finance or personnel.

Title	Production companies/participating countries	Production cost (£m)
All About Adam	Exchequer Film Co/BBC/HAL/Venus/Irish Film Board (**Ireland**)	3.28
Aberdeen	Freeway Films/Norsk Films/Scottish Film Council (**Norway**)	3.80
Christie Malry's Own Double Entry	Movie Masters/Woodline (**Ireland**)	2.98
The Company Man	Studio Eight/Prophecy Pictures (**Canada**)	1.40
Deception	Studio Eight/GFT Kingsborough/Next Film (**Canada/France**)	3.60
The Intruder	Steve Walsh Prods/GFT Kingsborough (**Canada**)	2.90
The Little Vampire	Cometstone/First look/Filmstiftung (**Netherlands/Germany**)	13.94
Sabotage	Spice Factory/Cine B/Kinovision/Basque regional subsidies (**Spain/France**)	6.25
Saltwater	Treasure Films/BBC Films/Irish Film Board (**Ireland**)	2.08
Shaheed Udham Singh	Surjit Movies (**India**)	0.20
Sorted	Jovy Junior Enterprises/Advanced Medien (**Germany**)	4.00
When Brendan Met Trudy	Deadly Films/BBC/Irish Film Board (**Ireland**)	3.00

TOTAL NUMBER OF FILMS   12
TOTAL COST   £47.43m
AVERAGE COST   £3.94m

Source: Screen Finance/X25 Partnership/BFI/British Council

5   # UK Film Production 1999 – Category D

American financed or part-financed films made in the UK. Most titles have a British cultural content.

Title	Production company(ies)	Production cost (£m)
The Beach	Figment Films/Twentieth Century Fox	23.50
Birthday Girl	Portobello Pictures/Film Four/HAL/Miramax	10.00
Circus	Film Development Corp/Columbia	6.00
The Criminal	Christopher Johnson Company/Storm Entertainment/Palm Pictures	2.50
The Cup	Butchers Run/Eagle Beach/Seven Arts	4.00
The End of the Affair	Columbia	20.00
The Golden Bowl	Merchant Ivory/Miramax/TF1	9.62
Gladiator	Dreamworks SKG/Universal	92.00
Greenfingers	Boneyard Ent/Xingu Pictures/Motion Picture Partners	2.42
The Last Minute	Venom Entertainment/Summit Entertainment/Palm Pictures	1.82
Londinium	Sun-Lite Pictures	5.00
Love's Labour's Lost	Pathe/Miramax/Intermedia	8.50
Miss Julie	Red Mullet/Moonstone Entertainment	4.25
102 Dalmatians	Walt Disney	36.00
Quills	Charenton Prods/Fox Searchlight	9.00
Rat	Universal/Jim Henson Company/Ruby Films	5.20
Relative Values	Midsummer Films/Overseas FilmGroup/Isle of Man Film Commission	3.00
Sexy Beast	Recorded Picture Company/FilmFour/Fox Searchlight	4.38
Snatch	Ska Films/Sony Pictures	4.50
The Testimony Of Taliesin Jones	Frontier Features/Snake River/CPI/HTV/Arts Council of Wales	3.75
Thomas and the Magic Railway	Britt Allcroft Co/Destination Films/Icon	12.50
Women Talking Dirty	Rocket Pictures/Sweetland Films/Jean Doumanian Prods	3.00
The World is Not Enough	Eon Prods/United Artists	50.00

TOTAL NUMBER OF FILMS   23
TOTAL COST   £320.94m
AVERAGE COST   £13.95m

Source: Screen Finance/X25 Partnership/BFI

    # UK Film Production 1999 – Category E

US Films with some British financial involvement

Title	Production company(ies)	Production cost (£m)
In the Light of the Moon	Tartan Films/Flying High/Santelmo	3.68
Suspicious River	Tartan Films/Okulitch Pedersen	4.80

TOTAL NUMBER OF FILMS   2
TOTAL COST   £8.48m
AVERAGE COST   £4.24m

Source: Screen Finance/X25 Partnership/BFI

have you never heard of let alone seen? Without viewing the films it is impossible to know if there are some hidden gems that deserve to be screened. Perhaps more can be made of the idea of a statutory deposit of all UK films (to be held at the *bfi*'s national archive). The films which have no distribution deals a year after they have been completed could then be assessed by a specially designated film body, and either released re-edited or scrapped. Perhaps the films that are scrapped could then be used as training tools.

The number of major UK co-productions rose from 12 in 1998 to 16 in 1999 (Table 3). However, the average budget of these films of £4.20 million was lower than in 1998 (£5.46 million). This table is slightly unbalanced by *The Man Who Cried* with a budget of £15 million, which on its own accounts for 22 per cent of the total. A similar trend can be detected in the table of minority co-productions (Table 4). There was a rise in the total films co-produced from 8 in 1998 to 12 in 1999 – yet the average budget of £3.94 million was lower than the previous year's figure of £4.47 million. The £13.94 million spent on *The Little Vampire* distorts the general average cost of these films, which tends to be closer to £3 million than £4 million.

Despite having bigger budgets, majority and minority co-productions with foreign partners other than the USA also struggle to make an impact on the cinema screens of the UK. The whole question of the relationship of UK film with Europe was raised with the Film Council's decision to allocate 20 per cent of each of its newly created funds to European co-productions. With the Film Council sounding its intent to favour mainstream films for Friday night multiplex audiences, it will be interesting to see what kind of relationship the UK film industry will forge with its European neighbours.

It seems that the combination of 'foreign' and 'arthouse' does not chime well with the chinking sound of box office tills at your local multiplex. On the other hand, it is unlikely that British directors such as Ken Loach and Peter Greenaway will cease producing films with European partners.

When there is talk of a resurgence in the British film industry it usually refers to films that have been financed or part-financed by America partners (Table 5).

The £92 million budget of *Gladiator* alone is more than the total money spent on majority UK co-productions (£67.19 million), or minority UK co-productions

7	EU Film Production 1999	
Country	**No of films (inc Co-Prods)**	**Investment ($m)**
Austria	20	15.38
Belgium	14	38.05
Denmark	16	33.56
Finland	16	21.36
France	181	732.58
Germany	74	380.45
Greece	16	n/a
Ireland	23	98.92
Italy	108	171.10
Luxembourg	2	1.44
Netherlands	14	41.89
Portugal	10	3.22
Spain	97	168.46
Sweden	23	34.70
UK	100	356.98
TOTAL	**716**	

Source: Screen Digest

(£47.43 million) and certainly puts the £113.72 million invested in 47 wholly-UK made films into stunning perspective. It even makes the £50 million budget for *The World is Not Enough* look small by comparison. These two mega-budget films help boost the average cost of American co-productions up to £13.95 million. Needless to say this average figure is up on £12.44 million from 1998 when there were 21 films made. Taking Table 6 also into account, 60 per cent of the total budget of UK films come from American co-productions.

It is also worth noting that *The Beach*, *The End of the Affair*, *102 Dalmatians*, and *Thomas and the Magic Railroad* all had budgets of over £10 million – this being the figure the Film Council will distribute among its UK film-makers via its Premiere Production Fund. This observation is made again in reference to the intention of creating a sustainable film industry in the UK. If, for whatever reason, the Americans pulled out of the UK, our industry would effectively become a cottage industry overnight.

Maintaining close links with the USA is therefore vital to the UK film industry. It is no coincidence that the Film Council also announced the expansion of the British Film Office in Los Angeles in the hope of attracting more US films to be made in the UK, as well as acting as a base for promoting UK films.

8 Types of Release for UK films 1999

Proportion of films with a UK involvement which achieved;

a) Wide release. Opening or playing on 30 or more screens around the country within a year of production prior to 1 January 2000

b) Limited release, mainly in arthouse cinemas or a short West End run, prior to 1 January 2000.

c) Released or planned to be released during 2000

d) Unreleased with no plans to do so during 2000

Year	(a)%	(b)%	(c)%	(d)%
1997	15.5	19.0	22.4	43.1
1998	22.7	21.6	21.6	34.1

Source: ACNielsen EDI/BFI

Types of Release for UK films 1984–1999

Proportion of films with a UK involvement which achieved;

a) Wide release. Opening or playing on 30 or more screens around the country within a year of production

b) Limited release, mainly in art house cinemas or a short West End run

c) Unreleased a year after production

Year	(a)%	(b)%	(c)%
1984	50.00	44.00	6.00
1985	52.80	35.90	11.30
1986	55.80	41.90	2.30
1987	36.00	60.00	4.00
1988	29.50	61.20	9.30
1989	33.30	38.90	27.80
1990	29.40	47.10	23.50
1991	32.20	37.30	30.50
1992	38.30	29.80	31.90
1993	25.40	22.40	52.20
1994	31.00	22.60	46.40
1995	23.10	34.60	42.30
1996	19.00	14.00	67.00
1997	15.50	19.00	65.50
1998	22.70	21.60	55.70

Source: Screen Finance/X25 Partnership/ACNielsen EDI/BFI

Meanwhile back in Europe (Table 7), the UK (100) sits third behind France (181) and Italy (108) as a film producer. However, total investment in UK films works out at $356.98 million which is greater than the $171.10 million Italy spent on film production in 1999. Nevertheless, French investment of $732.5, nearly double that of the UK, kept them firmly at the top of the European league.

After a worrying drop in the small number of UK films which were given a wide release (defined as playing on 30 or more screens around the country within a year of production) there were reasons to be optimistic that the tide might have turned. Wide releases were up from 15.5 per cent in 1997 to 22.7 per cent in 1998. This is welcome news and brings to a halt a slide which began in 1995. But the UK film industry still has some way to go to achieve the 50 per cent mark achieved in the mid-1980s. It is also worth reiterating the point made in last year's Handbook about the number of screens now available. Perhaps it is no coincidence that there are now more opportunities than ever before to show films.

Croupier – the gamble paid off in the USA

9   # What Happened to 1998 UK Films?

Distribution of 1998 UK productions and foreign films made in the UK up to 1st July 2000

Released theatrically in 1998/9	Released theatrically in 2000	No distribution deal
(* signifies previous titles)		
Arlington Road	Best	No Distribution Deal
Beautiful People	**Chicken Run**	As of 1st July 2000
The Big Tease	The Closer you Get	
The Clandestine Marriage	The Darkest Light	Accelerator
The Debt Collector	The Escort (*The Wrong Blonde)	Anxiety
Dreaming of Joseph Lees	Grey Owl	Ashes to Ashes
East is East	I Could Read the Sky	Conquest
Eight and a Half Women	Janice Beard 45 wpm	Esther Kahn
Entrapment	The Last September	Freak Out
Fanny and Elvis	**Mansfield Park**	The German Undertaker
Felicia's Journey	Ordinary Decent Criminal	An Ideal Husband*
Following	Simon Magus	Lalla
Greenwich Mean Time	**Sleepy Hollow**	Lighthouse
Gregory's 2 Girls	Small Time Obsession	Mad About Mambo
Human Traffic	**Topsy Turvy**	Make Believe
Hold Back the Night	To Walk with Lions	Out of Depth
An Ideal Husband	Twenty Four Hours in London	Saintly
The Last Yellow	The Wedding Tackle	Soldier
The Lost Son	Wonderland	Straight Shooter
Mad Cows		Summer Rain
The Match		Texas Funeral
Mickey Blue Eyes	**Distribution deal but no**	Three Businessmen
The Mummy	**release date**	Three Days
Notting Hill		Trouble on Earth
Onegin	Alien Love Triangle Part One	Two Bad Mice
Rancid Aluminium	Being Considered	The Weekend
Ratcatcher	Elephant Juice	
A Room for Romeo Brass	Weak at Denise	* This is a different version of An Ideal
Shakespeare in Love		Husband to the one released in 1999
Still Crazy		
Swing	**Straight to TV or Video/DVD**	
Tea with Mussolini		**Films in bold signifiy opened or**
This Year's Love	Everybody Loves Sunshine	**played on 30 or more screens aroun**
The Trench	The Killing Zone	**the country within a year of**
Virtual Sexuality	Milk	**production prior to 1 January 2000**
The War Zone	Tube Tales	
The Winslow Boy		As of 1st July 2000
With or Without You		**Source: Screen Finance/**
(Northern Ireland only)		**ACNielsen EDI/BFI**

The worrying statistic remains that over half UK films (55.70 per cent) still remain unreleased a year after production. Breaking that figure down again shows that 34.1 per cent of films made in 1998 will remain unreleased in 2000. It is interesting to note that in the 1980s, when an average of 42 films were produced, the number of UK films unreleased was low. As film production practically doubled in the 1990s, so too did the numbers of films left on the shelf. Somewhere between the 1980s and the 1990s the balance was lost and it is understandable why many commentators cry out that there are too many UK films being made.

Whether fewer UK films will be made in the future remains to be seen.

Table 9 neatly breaks down the UK films made in 1998 into those that stood a chance of being seen and those which remain unseen. At the time of writing there are 23 UK films made in 1998 still waiting for a distribution deal, no doubt each film hoping that it somehow gets discovered. Indeed, Mike Hodges' film *Croupier,* which had a modest release in the UK in 1998, has since found favour within America. And once a film finds favour in America – well can you guess what the effect is likely to be in the UK?

10 Number of UK Feature Films Produced 1912–1999

Year	Number	Year	Number
1912	2	1960	122
1913	18	1961	117
1914	15	1962	114
1915	73	1963	113
1916	107	1964	95
1917	66	1965	93
1918	76	1966	82
1919	122	1967	83
		1968	88
1920	155	1969	92
1921	137		
1922	110	1970	97
1923	68	1971	96
1924	49	1972	104
1925	33	1973	99
1926	33	1974	88
1927	48	1975	81
1928	80	1976	80
1929	81	1977	50
		1978	54
1930	75	1979	61
1931	93		
1932	110	1980	31
1933	115	1981	24
1934	145	1982	40
1935	165	1983	51
1936	192	1984	53
1937	176	1985	54
1938	134	1986	41
1939	84	1987	55
		1988	48
1940	50	1989	30
1941	46		
1942	39	1990	60
1943	47	1991	59
1944	35	1992	47
1945	39	1993	67
1946	41	1994	84
1947	58	1995	78
1948	74	1996	128
1949	101	1997	116
		1998	88
1950	125	1999	100
1951	114		
1952	117	Source: Screen	
1953	138	Digest/Screen	
1954	150	Finance/BFI	
1955	110		
1956	108		
1957	138		
1958	121		
1959	122		

Double Oscar winner Topsy–Turvy

Money was set aside for Janice Beard 45 wpm

Billy Elliot packed a powerful punch

National Lottery

It is likely that if you have ever bought a Lottery ticket the thought of winning has crossed your mind. No matter how the odds are stacked against hitting the jackpot you are enticed into believing that 'it could be you'. A similar thought process must have gone through the minds of all the production companies that applied for, and received Lottery grants from the Arts Councils of England, Wales, Scotland and Northern Ireland. In both respects the Lottery is a gamble – certainly making a film in the UK and hoping for a return on the investment is a massive gamble. However, the outcome of playing the Lottery ought to be distinctly different. Whereas you can shrug your shoulders and hope for better luck next time, the consequences for the production company who squanders its Lottery grant should be devastating.

In May 1997 the Arts Council announced three National Lottery-funded commercial franchises – The Film Consortium (£30.25 million), Pathé Pictures (£33 million) and DNA Films (£29 million). The idea was to pool talent into three film studios in an attempt to make commercially successful films. After three years and very few box office hits, criticism of the three franchises is growing almost as loud as criticism of the entire film Lottery funding system.

The total amount of Lottery money allocated to film production in 1999 amounted to £27.8 million (Table 11) this was up by around £8 million from 1998. Of the three franchises, Pathé Pictures received the biggest amount – £7.2 million, and put money into five productions including Kenneth Branagh's *Love's Labour's Lost* and *There's Only One Jimmy Grimble* – while also setting aside six projects for development. The £2 million allocated to *Kingdom Come* represented the highest amount of Lottery cash for a film project. DNA Films stuck to three film projects, all with total budgets of around £4 million. The Film Consortium put money into four new film projects and eight projects received development funding. Interestingly, money was also allocated to prints and advertising of four films – *The Lost Son, Hold Back the Night, Fanny and Elvis, Janice Beard 45 wpm*. Unfortunately, none of this quartet took off at the box office.

The Arts Council of England ploughed £6.8 million into over 12 projects including *Billy Elliot*, which at the time of writing was receiving favourable reviews. The Arts Councils of Scotland, Wales and Northern Ireland allocated awards to 39 features/shorts/documentaries. Out of the 39 The Arts Council of Wales selected eight films for development.

Much of the criticism about Lottery funding has come from the low returns Lottery-funded films have yielded. With over £100 million disbursed to over 200 projects, less than £10 million has been repaid. Even given that film-making is a risk and some films are unlucky and fail, the distinct lack of success suggests that the whole film Lottery funding system should have a complete overhaul. On the other hand not every film has flopped; *This Year's Love, An Ideal Husband, Plunkett & Macleane* and *Hilary and Jackie* were among the Top 20 UK Films at the UK Box Office (see Table 18) in 1999. And when the press were wildly trumpeting the Brits at the Oscars, the fact that Mike Leigh's *Topsy-Turvy* (winner of Best Costume and Best Make-Up awards) had received Lottery money via the Arts Council of England was not mentioned at all.

Those who tend to criticise the allocation of Lottery funds almost seem to imply that it is the single biggest failure in an otherwise perfect film industry. However, they seem to forget that the Arts Councils were only required to invest money in films which wouldn't have been funded otherwise. The guess is that the crop of poor Lottery-funded British films would have failed anyway, regardless of Lottery cash – because, as have been seen throughout the recent years, with the exception of about half a dozen films, the majority of British films fail at the box office.

Enter the Film Council to take over Lottery funding from the Arts Council of England, with its plans to make mainstream popular films, clamp down on shabby half-baked scripts and treat film-making in a more business-like manner. The early talk is about putting an end to handing out money to small films that will struggle to find a distributor, let alone a screening in a multiplex. Instead, an ethos of value for money is being preached from the corridors of Little Portland Street, (headquarters of the Film Council) with the reasoning that bigger budget films are more likely to repay the money put into them. In a nutshell, the Film Council says that public money will be treated with the same reverence as private sector money. Three funds, the Premiere Production Fund, the New Cinema Fund and the Film Development Fund, have been set up to attempt to succeed in a way that the Arts Council was unable to.

In the meantime, the next time you buy your Lottery ticket, and in that moment when hope springs eternal, spare a thought for all those Lottery-funded films – after all you did help to make them.

11 Funding of Film Productions by National Lottery Awards 1999

Title	Amount of Award (£)	Total Budget (£)
THE FILM CONSORTIUM*		
Production		
Room To Rent	325,376	1,967,168
Journey to the Centre of the Brain	1,250,000	7,187,500
A Christmas Carol	1,182,500	6,846,000
Large	510,000	1,450,000
Post-Production		
Janice Beard 45 wpm	35,000	
Prints and Advertising		
The Lost Son	300,000	600,000
Hold Back the Night	175,000	350,000
Fanny and Elvis	400,000	800,000
Janice Beard 45 wpm	200,000	400,000
Development		
Me Again	18,000	47,250
A Christmas Carol	10,000	170,000
Gridlock	19,000	80,000
Spider	10,000	20,000
The Burning Hill	15,500	31,750
Normal Human Problems	15,000	35,000
See Under: Love	6,000	120,729
A Passionate Woman	44,500	115,000
TOTAL	**4,515,876**	
DNA FILMS*		
The Final Curtain	1,996,176	3,992,352
Strictly Sinatra	1,994,910	3,989,819
Night Creatures	2,000,000	4,000,000
TOTAL	**5,991,086**	
PATHÉ PICTURES*		
Production		
Love's Labour's Lost	1,057,000	8,500,000
Kingdom Come	2,000,000	12,500,000
There's Only One Jimmy Grimble	1,650,000	3,315,000
Miss Julie	900,000	4,250,000
It Was An Accident	1,382,000	2,765,000
Development		
White Merc with Fins	50,000	215,186
Simon Says	47,500	95,000
A Tale of Three Cities	40,740	81,481
Rebuilding Coventry	32,681	98,000
Snark	50,000	214,007
It Was An Accident	49,750	99,500
TOTAL	**7,259,671**	
ARTS COUNCIL OF ENGLAND		
Whatever Happened to Harold Smith?	500,000	5,640,000
State of the Party	275,000	1,132,660
Days Like This	1,000,000	5,100,000
Doctor Sleep	600,000	3,600,000
Billy Elliot	850,000	2,830,000
Pandemonium	617,935	3,359,900
Pornografia	350,000	3,400,000
Very Annie Mary	250,000	3,095,000
My Boy Jack	650,000	4,000,000
Cowboys Cywraeg	750,000	4,000,000
Raving Beauties	420,000	2,675,000
This Filthy Earth	598,648	1,198,648
TOTAL	**6,861,583**	

* Lottery franchise consortia

Title	Amount of Award (£)	Total Budget (£)

ARTS COUNCIL OF WALES

Features

Beautiful Mistake	100,000	500,000
Cowboys Cymraeg	250,000	3,800,000
One of the Hollywood Ten	200,000	3,000,000
The Testimony of Taliesin Jones	247,490	2,200,000
Very Annie Marie	275,000	3,405,701

Shorts

Black Dog	68,500	136,964
The Debt	80,364	155,569
Dune	8,487	(p and a)
Edith's Finger	40,613	81,440
The Letterbox	39,597	81,147
0 Little Town of Bethlehem	81,600	161,751
Suckerfish	43,295	89,590
Without a Song or Dance	31,065	89,590

Development

Beryl's List	15,000	30,010
Dead Long Enough	38,000	108,000
Dewis Teg	7,000	28,000
Headcases	15,000	30,000
I'm in Training, Don't Kiss Me	9,440	14,440
The King's Shadow	12,750	17,000
Spic n' Span	13,500	27,000
Tree of Crows	14,500	29,710

TOTAL	**1,591,201**	

SCOTTISH ARTS COUNCIL

Features

Late Night Shopping	400,000	800,000
Child of Air	250,000	500,000
The Last Great Wilderness	375,000	500,000
Daybreak	26,500	63,536

Shorts

Marathon 99	11,487	19,014
Next Stop Paradise	25,000	59,707
The Visual Purple	24,750	150,620
Daddy's Girl	20,000	41,980
Pastures New	11,080	36,503

TOTAL	**1,143,817**	

ARTS COUNCIL OF NORTHERN IRELAND

Features

A Little Piece of Earth	200,000	2,000,000
Wild About Harry	100,000	3,100,000

Shorts

Lladia	25,000	50,000
Do Armed Robbers have Love Affairs	24,000	59,000
Oh Superman	21,788	44,000
Mysterious Ways	14,000	28,000
The Furry Story	29,169	69,000

Documentary

Postcards from the Hedge	38,400	155,000
Rising Steps (YTV)	40,000	202,000

TOTAL	**492,357**	

TOTAL AWARD	**27,855,591**	

Source: Screen Finance/Scottish Arts Council/Arts Council of Wales/Arts Council of Northern Ireland

12 Cinema Admissions 1933–1999 (millions)

Year	Admissions	Year	Admissions
1933	903.00	1968	237.30
1934	950.00	1969	214.90
1935	912.33		
1936	917.00	1970	193.00
1937	946.00	1971	176.00
1938	987.00	1972	156.60
1939	990.00	1973	134.20
		1974	138.50
1940	1,027.00	1975	116.30
1941	1,309.00	1976	103.90
1942	1,494.00	1977	103.50
1943	1,541.00	1978	126.10
1944	1,575.00	1979	111.90
1945	1,585.00		
1946	1,635.00	1980	101.00
1947	1,462.00	1981	86.00
1948	1,514.00	1982	64.00
1949	1,430.00	1983	65.70
		1984	54.00
1950	1,395.80	1985	72.00
1951	1,365.00	1986	75.50
1952	1,312.10	1987	78.50
1953	1,284.50	1988	84.00
1954	1,275.80	1989	94.50
1955	1,181.80		
1956	1,100.80	1990	97.37
1957	915.20	1991	100.29
1958	754.70	1992	103.64
1959	581.00	1993	114.36
		1994	123.53
1960	500.80	1995	114.56
1961	449.10	1996	123.80
1962	395.00	1997	139.30
1963	357.20	1998	135.50
1964	342.80	1999	139.75
1965	326.60		
1966	288.80		
1967	264.80		

Source: Screen Digest/ Screen Finance/BFI

13 UK Box Office 1999

Admissions	139.75 m
Total Cinema Sites	692
Total Cinema Screens	2,758
Total Multiplex Sites	186
Total Multiplex Screens	1,727
Box Office Gross	£570.50 m
Average Ticket Price	£3.80

Source: Screen Finance/CAA/AC Nielsen/EDI

Cinema

The dip in cinema admissions in 1998 proved to be a blip on an otherwise upward trend which showed admissions rise to 139.75 million in 1999 (Table 12). This was the highest total since 1975. Indeed, the 1990s were significant in the resurgence of cinema going in the UK, compared to the fallow period of the 1980s. The reason for this is simple: the rise in admissions can be plotted to correspond to the introduction, development and expansion of multiplexes in the UK.

It is hard to remember the days of the flea-pit cinema. With more screens than ever before the cinema going audiences have never had it so good. Yet, with reports of oversaturation of multiplexes in some areas and the advent of digital technologies and their inherent costs, there is a real sense of uncertain consolidation as the cinema world opens its doors to the 21st century. However, at the present time the picture looks good.

UK cinemas took a total of £570.50 million (Table 13) at the box office, a rise of almost 10 per cent from 1998. Surprisingly, the average ticket price in the UK actually fell from £3.83 in 1998 to £3.80 in 1999.

Multiplexes and megaplexes continued to be built. In fact, the 30-screen Warner Village StarCity in Birmingham, which opened in June 2000, became the UK's largest multiplex complex. There were 186 multiplexes in 1999 compared with 167 in 1998. This helped to add an extra 194 screens to the total number of screens in the UK which stands at 2,758. Sixty two per cent of screens in the UK are now likely to be part of a multiplex.

So far, so good you may think. But there are areas for concern. There was a dramatic sudden fall from 759 to 692 in the number of sites available. Despite the

Dancers in the light – Shakespeare in Love

14   **UK Sites and Screens 1984–1999**

Year	Total Sites	Total Screens
1984	660	1,271
1985	663	1,251
1986	660	1,249
1987	648	1,215
1988	699	1,416
1989	719	1,559
1990	737	1,685
1991	724	1,789
1992	735	1,845
1993	723	1,890
1994	734	1,969
1995	743	2,019
1996	742	2,166
1997	747	2,383
1998	759	2,564
1999	692	2,758

Source: Screen Finance/X25 Partnership

Holy Smoke – at selected Odeons near you?

popularity of cinema, some regional ABCs, independent cinemas and small chains, such as Robins Cinemas, closed down. Fierce competition in the UK regions from multiplexes, contributed to the closure of the independents. Another notable closure was the IMAX at the Trocadero Centre, in London – evidence perhaps that there was only room for one IMAX in the capital.

There were signs that the multiplex operators were prepared, albeit cautiously, to experiment with lending some of their screens to less mainstream audiences, or specific niche audiences. In March 2000 the *bfi* joined forces with Odeon Cinemas in a pioneering move to schedule non-mainstream films (such as *Holy Smoke, Boys Don't Cry* and *Mansfield Park*) on one screen of eight selected Odeons (Birmingham, Liverpool, Ipswich,

Maidstone, Bournemouth, Cheltenham, Guildford and Epsom). This was a bold move, particularly in view of the fact that 'arthouse' or even 'non-mainstream' films have been regarded too risky to programme. The aforementioned 30-screen Warner Village StarCity in Birmingham also went against the grain when it announced that it would be setting aside six of its screens to show Bollywood films. It will be interesting to see in next year's Handbook how the two respective schemes have fared.

Both moves are interesting in that they set out to find new audiences for the cinema. As the Handbook records every year, the staple diet of the multiplex remains that of American mainstream movies aimed at 15–24 year-olds.

15   **Frequency of Cinema going 1999**

Age Group	7–14	15–24	25–34	35+	ABC1	C2DE	Male	Female
No.of People (m)	8.19	6.96	8.96	30.16	26.61	28.12	26.61	27.86
Once a month or more (%)	28 (%)	58 (%)	37 (%)	12 (%)	29 (%)	20 (%)	26 (%)	22 (%)
Less than once a month (%)	49 (%)	29 (%)	37 (%)	28 (%)	37 (%)	28 (%)	31 (%)	34 (%)
Once a year or less (%)	15 (%)	10 (%)	18 (%)	26 (%)	18 (%)	24 (%)	19 (%)	20 (%)
Total who ever go to the cinema (%)	92 (%)	96 (%)	91 (%)	66 (%)	84 (%)	72 (%)	77 (%)	79 (%)

Source: CAVIAR/Screen Finance

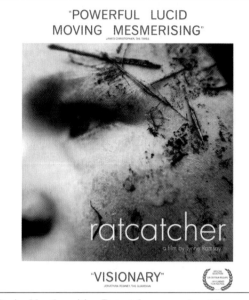

"POWERFUL LUCID
MOVING MESMERISING"
JAMES CHRISTOPHER, THE TIMES

ratcatcher
a film by Lynne Ramsay

"VISIONARY"
JONATHAN ROMNEY, THE GUARDIAN

Praised by the critics, Ratcatcher opened on 15 screens

East is East – as popular as popcorn

The demographic breakdown of cinemagoing remains constant (Table 15). The most pampered audiences are the 15-24-year-olds. The irony is that this represents the smallest demographic group of all. The largest demographic group, the 35+ brigade, which makes up over 75 per cent of the viewing public, is the least catered-for group. However, this group is likely to have more disposable income than the 15-24 age group. As the population gets older and perceptions of what constitutes 'old age' change, it is amazing that the trend still seems to be to target young people. Whether the exclusion of 35+ people (they don't go to films because the majority of releases are aimed at young people) is part of some self-fulfilling prophecy is a moot point.

Another demographic worth noting is the slightly higher percentage of women who go to the cinema. Although over a month men tend to go more regularly to the cinema, over the year there are slightly more women going to the cinema. While some might argue that the balance between male and females is more or less the same, others may reflect that a subtle shift has occurred in recent years, where film releases might actually appeal more to female audiences. Whichever is the case, it is definitely a trend that is worth looking out for.

On the surface 1999 was an excellent year for UK films. However, as has been noted with the film production statistics, it is important to give the statistics a sense of proportion in terms to the Britishness of the films on display. It is easy to reel off *Star Wars Episode 1: The Phantom Menace, Notting Hill, The World is Not Enough, Shakespeare in Love* and *Little Voice* (Table 16, 17, 18) and believe that there is a real resurgence in British films. (*Star Wars* is included as British only because it was filmed at Leavesden Studios – however, in every other respect it is a US film made with US money). Indeed, the top four films in that list would make up the most successful British films of all time at the UK box office (*The Full Monty* still leading the all-time list with a box office gross of £52,232,058). All these hit films are US/UK co-productions and, within the context of a sustainable British film industry, they flatter to deceive. The question always remains: how much money from these films is pumped back into the British film industry?

East is East was by far the top wholly-UK-produced film in 1999 (Table 16, 17, 18). Its relative success in UK film terms (the film won many plaudits and awards) demonstrated that there are British audiences for typically British films. The success of TV and radio sketch show *Goodness Gracious Me* and a growing fascination with Bollywood paved the way for audiences to accept this quirky cross-cultural comedy set in Salford. Based on Ayub Khan-Din's autobiographical play, the cultural mix was given a further twist by installing a relative newcomer from Dublin, Damien O'Donnell, to direct. The film was set in the Seventies, which also worked against the grain of most other British releases. However, *East is East* still may not have found its audience had it not been for FilmFour's aggressive marketing and faith in the quality of the film.

Last year the average budget for wholly-UK-made films was £2.49 million. Only three out of the 42 UK films in Table 16 managed to surpass that mark, but even then *Plunkett & Macleane* had a rather larger than average budget. *East is East* (£2.40 million budget), *This Year's Love* (£2.75 million budget), *Plunkett & Macleane* (£10.00 million budget). In fourth position *Human Traffic* (£2.20 million budget) just about managed to gross more than its production cost. The rest of the list (excluding the re-releases) is a sad reflection on the poor performance of UK films at the box office.

A similar tale can be told with the fate of other UK co-productions (Table 16) whose average production budget last year was around £5.00 million. Out of the 39 titles only *Waking Ned* (£3.10 million budget) took more at the box office than it cost to make. The big budget *Entrapment* (£51.60 million budget) could only bring £5.00 million in box office receipts, proof that a big budget does not always mean a big return. It is also a disappointment to see such a highly acclaimed film as *Ratcatcher* with such a low box office return. *Ratcatcher* opened on 15 screens in the UK and lasted three weeks in November 1999. Despite awards, rave reviews and recommendations from film critics, the film was not afforded a decent run. Contrast that with *Notting Hill* which opened on 457 screens and lasted 17 weeks.

However, on a less gloomy side, it is clear that when it comes to the UK/US co-productions (Table 16), the returns of money well-invested can be quite considerable. Out of the top five films in this section all but one (*The World is Not Enough* – budget of £50.00 million) doubled their budget to box office receipt ratios. Of the five, *Shakespeare in Love* (£8.40 million budget) had the most profitable return.

The success of these British films can be put into a proper perspective against the power of US product. Table 17 shows as many as seven UK (or UK co-productions) in the top 20 films of the year with *Star Wars* and *Notting Hill* in first and second position. Even in recent years the UK has struggled to get more than two films into the top 20.

It is not surprise that the key to a decent box office return is determined by a decent release (ie on over 200 screens) and an extended run (ie over 8 weeks). However, as has been noted earlier, the majority of UK films are lucky to get booked to over 30 screens, and luckier still if they can last over a fortnight. The scale of the struggle can be illustrated by comparing the UK box office fortunes of *Wild Wild West* (Table 17) and *Rogue Trader* (Table 18). *Rogue Trader* opened on 174 screens in June 1999 and lasted six weeks by which time it was on at just 15 screens – its box office gross was £1,024,860. *Wild Wild West* opened in

Notting Hill, the big box office hit – strangely enough set in London

16   **UK Box Office for UK Feature Films released in 1999 – UK Films**

Title	Distributor	Country of Origin	Box Office Gross (£m)
1 East is East (15)	FilmFour	UK	7,251,243
2 This Year's Love (18)	Entertainment	UK	3,600,636
3 Plunkett & Macleane (15)	Universal	UK	2,757,485
4 Human Traffic (18)	Metrodome	UK	2,271,369
5 Guest House Paradiso (15)	Universal	UK	1,492,963
6 Hilary & Jackie (15)	FilmFour	UK	1,040,788
7 Don't Go Breaking My Heart (PG)	Universal	UK	1,019,361
8 Virtual Sexuality (15)	Columbia TriStar	UK	749,714
9 Orphans (18)	Downtown	UKS	412,699
10 Mad Cows (15)	Entertainment	UK	291,147
11 The Acid House (18)	FilmFour	UK	242,829
12 The Third Man (re) (PG)	Optimum	UK	194,545
13 Get Carter (re) (18)	BFI	UK	124,296
14 The Debt Collector (18)	FilmFour	UK	107,970
15 Final Cut (18)	Downtown	UK	105,434
16 Beautiful People (15)	Alliance Releasing	UK	103,619
17 The Italian Job (re) (U)	UIP	UK	103,319
18 Parting Shots (12)	UIP	UK	101,041
19 Tichborne Claimant (PG)	Redbus	UK	88,988
20 Solomon & Gaenor (15)	Film Four	UKW	73,505
21 Among Giants (15)	20th C Fox	UK	68,992
22 Heart (18)	FFC	UK	34,272
23 Scrooge (re) (U)	FFC	UK	24,478
24 39 Steps (re) (U)	Winstone	UK	22,716
25 Cotton Mary (15)	UIP	UK	21,887
26 Following (15)	Alliance Releasing	UK	20,494
27 Captain Jack (PG)	FFC	UK	16,800
28 Yellow Submarine (re) (U)	UIP	UK	15,890
29 Kes (re) (U)	BFI	UK	15,538
30 The Clandestine Marriage (15)	Universal	UK	14,822
31 South (re) (U)	BFI	UK	13,907
32 Greenwich Mean Time (18)	Icon	UK	13,747
33 Julie & The Cadillacs (PG)	Capricorn	UK	13,640
34 Brylcreem Boys (15)	Guerilla	UK	7,045
35 Prometheus (15)	FilmFour	UK	5,956
36 A Kind Of Hush (15)	Metrodome	UK	5,864
37 All The Little Animals (15)	Entertainment	UK	3,376
38 The Man Who Knew Too Much (re) (PG)	BFI	UK	2,944
39 With Or Without You (18)	FilmFour	UK	2,156
40 Lucia (15)	Nepotism	UK	1,998
41 Darkness Falls (15)	Downtown	UK	1,133
42 A Quiet Day	Winstone	UK	239
42 Titles			**22,460,845**

UK Box Office for UK Feature Films released in 1999 – Other UK Co-productions

Title	Distributor	Country of Origin	Box Office Gross (£m)
1 Waking Ned (PG)	20th C Fox	UK/US/FR/IE	7,044,705
2 Entrapment (12)	20th C Fox	UK/US/GER	5,770,948
3 eXistenz (15)	Alliance	UK/CA	1,553,196
4 Tea With Mussolini (PG)	UIP	UK/IT	1,404,905
5 Hideous Kinky (15)	UIP	UK/FR	686,428
6 A Simple Plan (15)	UIP	UK/US/JP/GER/FR	561,629
7 The Straight Story (U)	FilmFour	UK/US/FR	299,877
8 Ratcatcher (15)	Pathé	UK/FR	299,113
9 Felicia's Journey (12)	Icon	UK/CA	263,207

10	Place Vendome (15)	Artificial Eye	UK/FR/BE	183,984
11	Fanny & Elvis (15)	UIP	UK/FR	148,229
12	Get Real (15)	UIP	UK/ZA	134,732
13	Gregory's 2 Girls (15)	FilmFour	UK/GER	128,396
14	Besieged (PG)	Alliance	UK/IT	103,332
15	The War Zone (18)	FilmFour	UK/IT	101,787
16	Bedrooms & Hallways (15)	Alliance	UK/FR/GER	86,183
17	The Trench (15)	Entertainment	UK/FR	86,012
18	Red Violin (15)	FilmFour	UK/CA/IT/US	84,473
19	The Lost Son (18)	UIP	UK/FR	49,302
20	Southpaw (15)	Downtown	UK/IE	34,246
21	Croupier (15)	BFI	UK/GER/ FR/IE	28,752
22	The Match (15)	Universal	UK/IE/US	28,429
23	Eight and a Half Women (15)	Pathé	UK/NL/LU/GER	22,828
24	Such A Long Journey (15)	Optimum	UK/CA	21,188
25	A Price Above Rubies (15)	FilmFour	UK/US/FR	14,690
26	Crush Proof (18)	Clarence	UK/NL/IE/GER	12,450
27	The Theory Of Flight (15)	Buena Vista	UK/ZA	8,699
28	Painted Angels (12)	Artificial Eye	UK/CA	7,816
29	The Secret Laughter of Women (12)	Optimum	UK/CA	7,121
30	Vigo – Passion For Life (15)	FilmFour	UK/JP/FR/ES/GER	5,479
31	Hold Back The Night (15)	UIP	UK/IT	5,236
32	The Last Yellow (15)	Metrodome	UK/GER	4,741
33	LA Without A Map (15)	United Media	UK/FR/FI/ LU	3,641
34	Misadventures of Margaret (15)	FFC	UK/FR	3,519
35	Kini & Adams (not submitted)	Sales	UK/FR/ZW/HV/CH	2,574
36	Appetite (not submitted)	ICA	UK/GER	2,176
37	Sweet Angel Mine (18)	Optimum	UK/CA	1,600
38	Food Of Love (15)	FilmFour	UK/FR	1,507
39	Skin Flick (not submitted)	Millivres	UK/GER/ CA/JP	958

39 Titles   **19,208,088**

UK Box Office for UK Feature Films released in 1999 – US/UK Co-productions

	Title	Distributor	Country of Origin	Box Office Gross (£m)
1	Star Wars Episode 1: The Phantom Menace (U)	20thC Fox	UK/US	50,928,328
2	Notting Hill (15)	Universal	UK/US	30,765,273
3	The World is Not Enough (12)	UIP	UK/US	23,375,037
4	Shakespeare In Love (15)	UIP	UK/US	20,407,662
5	Little Voice (15)	Buena Vista	UK/US	8,337,648
6	Eyes Wide Shut (18)	Warner	UK/US	5,244,320
7	Mickey Blue Eyes (15)	Universal	UK/US	5,172,636
8	An Ideal Husband (PG)	Pathé	UK/US	2,891,515
9	Arlington Road (15)	Universal	UK/US	1,864,927
10	Rogue Trader (15)	Pathé	UK/US	1,024,860
11	Muppets From Space (U)	Col/TriStar	UK/US	594,356
12	Onegin (12)	Entertainment	UK/US	583,527
13	Gods & Monsters (15)	Downtown	UK/US	454,733
14	Swing (15)	Entertainment	UK/US	399,301
15	Ravenous (18)	20th C Fox	UK/US	331,845
16	The Big Tease (15)	Warner	UK/US	79,798
17	Hi-Lo Country (15)	Universal	UK/US	57,903
18	Dreaming of Joseph Lees (12)	20th C Fox	UK/US	6,203

18 Titles   **152,519,872**

TOTAL 99 Titles   **194,188,805**

Source: AC Nielsen/EDI/Screen Finance/BFI

August 1999 on 425 screens and lasted five weeks by which time it was on at 178 screens – its box office gross was £6,845,175.

Once again films for the whole family dominate Table 17 with 11 out of the 20 carrying (PG), (12) or (U) certificates. This total should be compared to only five out of 33 (not counting re-releases) of wholly-UK titles (Table 16). On the one hand the UK film industry makes the majority of its films for the 15+ audience, and on the other hand bemoans the lack of box office success. When you consider that there is not a single 18 certificate film in the UK box office top 20 perhaps the conclusion is that the UK should concentrate the majority of its film-making on the lucrative (PG), (12), (U) certificate audience.

US influence can be seen in Table 19 with seven out of the top ten EU films a co-production with a German partner – and all these films were in English.

If the struggle to get UK films into cinemas is hard, then the battle for foreign language films is much harder. Nevertheless, foreign language films (Table 20) had a slightly better year than in 1998, boosted by Oscar winner *Life is Beautiful.* The table shows the influence of Asian films which make up almost half of the list and again reflects the small, but significant market for these films. As for the European films only *All About My Mother* made a big impact on box office receipts and this was in a year that brought the first of the Dogme 95 releases, *Festen,* to the screen, complete with shooting done on location using handheld cameras, natural light and sound and with no director's credit.

While the US still dominated the UK sector (Table 21) it was noticeable that US/UK productions accounted for over 26 per cent of the market. Whereas the number of titles didn't vary too much (there were 18 titles in 1999 compared to 14 in 1998) the box office receipts rose from £29 million in 1998 to over £152 million in 1999.

Not surprisingly, UK films (or to be precise US/UK co-productions) performed well in the US (Table 22). *The World is Not Enough* and *Notting Hill* took nearly $233 million between them. Both these films brought in more than last year's top total box office of $70 million. In fact, box office receipts for UK films rose by a dramatic 75 per cent in 1999.

Foreign language films do not even perform well in their own territories (Table 25). A massive 17 US films account for the top 20 admissions of films distributed in countries of the European Union.

And if that wasn't all, Festen had subtitles as well!

Taking US-only films away, *Notting Hill* proved to be the most popular European film in Europe (Table 24) and generally, UK films performed well. Including co-productions the table consists of eight French films, five each from UK and Germany, three each from Spain and Italy and one from Denmark.

Despite three consecutive years with the top films at the UK box office – *The Full Monty* (1997), *Titanic* (1998) and *Star Wars Episode 1: The Phantom Menace* (1999) – 20th Century Fox slipped to third position in the Distributors' table (Table 27). UIP (which distributed most films in the UK) took poll position with eight of its films in the top 20, including *The World is Not Enough, The Sixth Sense* and *Shakespeare in Love.* Buena Vista moved up one into second position with successes such as *A Bug's Life, Tarzan* and *Little Voice.*

Warner Bros remained in fourth position but distributed six fewer films than in 1998 while increasing its share of the box office, with *The Matrix* being its big hit in 1999. Meanwhile Universal's brief flurry into UK distribution (following the demise of Polygram Filmed Entertainment) ended when the US studio opted to stick with UIP as its main distribution outlet in the UK. Nevertheless, the brief encounter had a handsome reward with the success of *Notting Hill.* Columbia continued to lose ground on the other American majors.

17   ## Top 20 Films At The UK Box Office 1999

Film	Distributor	Country of Origin	Box Office Gross (£m)
1 Star Wars Episode 1: The Phantom Menace (U)	20th C Fox	US/UK	50,928,328
2 Notting Hill (15)	Universal	US/UK	30,765,273
3 A Bug's Life (U)	Buena Vista	US	29,310,536
4 Austin Powers 2: The Spy Who Shagged Me (12)	Entertainment	US	25,772,822
5 The World Is Not Enough (12)	UIP	US/UK	23,375,037
6 The Sixth Sense (15)	UIP	US	20,449,726
7 Shakespeare In Love (15)	UIP	US/UK	20,407,662
8 Tarzan (U)	Buena Vista	US	17,469,366
9 The Mummy (12)	UIP	US	17,439,339
10 The Matrix (15)	Warner	US	17,279,897
11 The Blair Witch Project (15)	Pathé	US	14,971,525
12 American Pie (15)	UIP	US	13,923,015
13 Rugrats: The Movie (U)	UIP	US	13,423,386
14 Little Voice (15)	Buena Vista	US/UK	8,337,648
15 The Deep Blue Sea (15)	Warner	US	8,139,940
16 Star Trek: Insurrection (PG)	UIP	US	7,572,978
17 Runaway Bride (PG)	UIP	US	7,562,023
18 East Is East (15)	FilmFour	UK	7,251,243
19 Waking Ned (PG)	20th C Fox	US/UK/FR/IE	7,044,705
20 Wild Wild West (12)	Warner	US	6,845,175

NB: Box Office Totals are for UK and Republic of Ireland for new releases from January 1st 1999 – Jan 5th 2000

Source: AC Nielsen/EDI/Screen Finance/BFI

 ## Top 20 UK Films At The UK Box Office 1999

Film	Distributor	Country of Origin	Box Office Gross (£m)
1 Star Wars Episode 1: The Phantom Menace (U)	20th C Fox	US/UK	50,928,328
2 Notting Hill (15)	Universal	US/UK	30,765,273
3 The World Is Not Enough (12)	UIP	US/UK	23,375,037
4 Shakespeare In Love (15)	UIP	US/UK	20,407,662
5 Little Voice (15)	Buena Vista	US/UK	8,337,648
6 East Is East (15)	FilmFour	UK	7,251,243
7 Waking Ned (PG)	20th C Fox	US/UK/FR/IE	7,044,705
8 Entrapment (12)	20th C Fox	US/UK/GER	5,770,948
9 Eyes Wide Shut (18)	Warner	US/ UK	5,244,320
10 Mickey Blue Eyes (15)	Universal	US/UK	5,172,636
11 This Year's Love (18)	Entertainment	UK	3,600,636
12 An Ideal Husband (PG)	Pathé	US/UK	2,891,515
13 Plunkett & Macleane (15)	Universal	UK	2,757,485
14 Human Traffic (18)	Metrodome	UK	2,271,369
15 Arlington Road (15)	Universal	US/UK	1,864,927
16 eXistenz (15)	Alliance	UK/CA	1,553,196
17 Guest House Paradiso (15)	Universal	UK	1,492,963
18 Tea With Mussolini (PG)	UIP	UK/IT	1,404,905
19 Hilary & Jackie (15)	FilmFour	UK	1,040,788
20 Rogue Trader (15)	Pathé	UK/US	1,024,860

Source: ACNielsen EDI/Screen Finance/BFI

19 ## Top 20 EU Films At The UK Box Office 1999

Film	Distributor	Country of Origin	Box Office Gross (£m)
1 Fight Club (18)	20th C Fox	GER/US	5,424,113
2 The General's Daughter (18)	UIP	GER/US	3,043,667
3 Life Is Beautiful (PG)	Buena Vista	IT	2,955,627
4 Madeline (U)	Col/TriStar	US/GER	2,497,577
5 Drop Dead Gorgeous (15)	Icon	US/GER	1,428,714
6 A Midsummer Night's Dream (PG)	20th C Fox	GER/US	1,399,806
7 Blue Streak (12)	Col/TriStar	US/GER	1,272,860
8 All About My Mother (15)	Pathé	ES/FR	1,038,387
9 Random Hearts (15)	Col/TriStar	US/GER	737,158
10 Buena Vista Social Club (U)	FilmFour	GER/CU	725,769
11 A Love Divided	Buena Vista	IE	614,252
12 This Is My Father	Buena Vista	CA/IE	508,184
13 Le Diner De Cons (15)	Pathé	FR	364,960
14 Run Lola Run (15)	Col/Tristar	GER	319,815
15 Agnes Browne (15)	UIP	US/IE	308,913
16 Festen (15)	Blue Light	DK	269,103
17 Romance (18)	Blue Light	FR	206,321
18 An Autumn Tale (U)	Artificial Eye	FR	190,777
19 Last Night (15)	FilmFour	CA/FR	183,673
20 Black Cat White Cat (15)	Artificial Eye	GER/FR/YU/AT/GR	172,575

NB: Box Office Totals are for UK and Republic of Ireland for new releases from January 1st 1999 – January 5th 2000

Source: ACNielsen EDI/ Screen Finance/BFI

20 ## Top 20 Foreign Language Films Released In The UK 1999

Title	Distributor	Country	Box Office (£)
1 Life Is Beautiful (PG)	Buena Vista	IT	2,955,627
2 All About My Mother (15)	Pathé	ES/FR	1,038,387
3 Buena Vista Social Club (U)	FilmFour	GER/CU	725,769
4 Central Station (15)	Buena Vista	BR	630,227
5 Hum Saath Saath Hain (U)	Eros	IN	622,909
6 Taal (U)	Eros	IN	604,800
7 This Is My Father	Buena Vista	CA/IE	508,184
8 Hum Aapke Dil Mein Rahte Hain	Eros	IN	455,257
9 Biwi No.1	Yash Raj	IN	385,936
10 Dil Kya Kare	Eros	IN	368,032
11 Le Diner De Cons (15)	Pathé	FR	364,960
12 Mann	Yash Raj	IN	353,082
13 Aa Ab Laut Chalen	UFDL	IN	350,604
14 Run Lola Run (15)	Col/TriStar	GER	319,815
15 Hum Dil De Chuck Sanam (PG)	Blue Star	IN	310,764
16 Baadshah	Stars Int.	IN	287,509
17 Festen (15)	Blue Light	DK	269,103
18 Romance (18)	Blue Light	FR	206,321
19 An Autumn Tale (U)	Artificial Eye	FR	190,777
20 Black Cat White Cat (15)	Artificial Eye	GER/FR/YU/AT/GR	172,575

Source: ACNielsen EDI/Screen Finance/BFI

21   ## Breakdown of UK Box Office by Country of Origin 1999

Territories	No Of Titles	Box Office	%
US	148	344,414,373	60.37
US/UK	18	152,519,872	26.73
UK	42	22,460,845	3.94
Other UK Co-productions	39	19,208,088	3.37
EU (including US and other non-EU co-productions)	75	25,397,293	4.51
Rest of world (foreign language)	64	6,400,251	1.12
Co-productions (rest of world)	2	62,621	0.01
Rest of world (English language)	4	42,020	0.00
Total	**393**	**570,505,363**	

Source: AC Nielsen EDI/BFI/ Screen Finance

Box Office for new releases in the UK and Irish Republic between January 1st 1999 and January 5th 2000

22   ## Top 10 US Box Office Revenue of UK Films Released in 1999

Title	Distributor US	Country	Box Office ($m)
1 The World is Not Enough (12)	MGM	US/UK	117,880,000
2 Notting Hill (15)	Universal	US/UK	116,090,000
3 Waking Ned (PG)	Fox Searchlight	US/UK	19,460,000
4 An Ideal Husband (PG)	Miramax	US/UK	18,540,000
5 Tea with Mussolini (PG)	MGM	UK/IT	14,400,000
6 Lock, Stock and Two Smoking Barrels (18)	Gramercy	UK	3,900,000
7 Mansfield Park (15)	Miramax	US/UK	2,470,000
8 Ravenous (18)	Fox Searchlight	US/UK	2,060,000
9 Get Real (15)	Paramount Classics	UK/SA	1,150,000
10 Felicia's Journey (12)	Artisan	UK/CA	760,000
Total			**296,710,000**

Source: AC Nielsen EDI

Life is Beautiful – top foreign language film in the UK   The World is Not Enough – top 'UK' film in the US

23   Top 20 of Admissions of Films Distributed in Europe in 1999

Based on an analysis of 80% of admissions in the European Union in 1999

	Title	Country	Admissions
1	Stars Wars Episode 1: The Phantom Menace (U)	US	38,843,453
2	Notting Hill (15)	UK	26,160,254
3	Tarzan (U)	US	23,647,493
4	A Bug's Life (U)	US	20,411,714
5	The Matrix (15)	US	19,895,760
6	The Mummy (12)	US	19,639,974
7	Asterix et Obelix contre Cesar (PG)	Fr/Ger/It	18,385,262
8	Shakespeare in Love (15)	US	16,032,558
9	The World is Not Enough (12)	US/UK	15,046,960
10	The Runaway Bride (PG)	US	14,091,519
11	Austin Powers 2: The Spy who Shagged Me (12)	US	10,063,323
12	You've Got Mail (PG)	US	9,875,293
13	Wild Wild West (12)	US	9,679,865
14	Enemy of the State (15)	US	9,513,749
15	Life is Beautiful (PG)	IT	8,621,872
16	Entrapment (12)	US	7,818,980
17	The Blair Witch Project (15)	US	7,331,121
18	Eyes Wide Shut (18)	US	7,286,222
19	American Pie (15)	US	7,148,576
20	The Sixth Sense (15)	US	7,008,462

Source: European Audiovisual Observatory/BFI

     Top 20 of Admissions of European Films
Distributed in the European Union in 1999

Data taken from data generated by 11 European countries. The data represents approximately 72% of admissions to cinemas in the European Union

	Title	Country	Admissions
1	Notting Hill (15)	UK	23,852,916
2	Asterix et Obelix contre Cesar (PG)	FR/GER/IT	17,288,501
3	The World is Not Enough (12)	UK/US	13,324,796
4	Life is Beautiful (PG)	IT	8,621,872
5	All About My Mother (15)	SP/FR	6,119,239
6	The Ninth Gate (15)	FR/SP	3,383,473
7	Joan of Arc (15)	FR	2,936,612
8	Werner –Volles Rooäää!!!	GER	2,755,103
9	Waking Ned (PG)	UK	2,586,346
10	Les Enfants du Marais (PG)	FR	2,220,558
11	Little Voice (15)	UK	2,208,023
12	Buena Vista Social Club (U)	GER/US/FR/CUBA	2,035,633
13	Cosi e la Vita	IT	1,932,683
14	Sonnennallee	GER	1,863,297
15	East is East (15)	UK	1,784,944
16	Quasimode d'el Paris	FR	1,706,110
17	Pünktchen und Anton	GER	1,716,478
18	Muertos de Risa	SP	1,668,594
19	Festen (15)	DEN	1,417,297
20	Ca commence aujourd'hui (12)	FR	1,329,284

Source: European Audiovisual Observatory/BFI

Yet again, Entertainment, which gave us *Austin Powers 2: The Spy Who Shagged Me*, was the top independent distributor and took overall sixth spot ahead of Columbia. Pathé was the second most successful independent and could boast a huge success with *The Blair Witch Project* while FilmFour stayed in third place boosted by the unexpected performance of *East is East*. Both Pathé and FilmFour made significant gains over the previous year, improving their market share by 85 per cent and 70 per cent respectively. The top three independents have stepped up their buying operations over the last year and have been rewarded for their dexterity.

The list of independents seems to grow longer each year. This year there are 48 compared with 42 in 1998. Many of these distributors appear on a one-off basis and are never heard of again. Nevertheless, distributors such as Redbus, Icon, Alliance and Metrodome look set to consolidate their own positions. No doubt all will be looking to see what kind of initiatives the Film Council might come up with to help the increasingly fragmented sector of the industry.

In October 1999 Virgin Entertainment sold its cinemas to France's Union Generale Cinematographique (UGC), and in February 2000 Odeon and ABC cinemas merged to form the biggest exhibitor in the UK. At the same time Hoyts, the Australian cinema chain, decided to pull out of the UK. Such frantic movement suggests that the building boom of new multiplexes may have reached its end (but then again this has been predicted every year for the last three years and it still hasn't happened). Problems of over–saturation of screens in areas such as Birmingham, Sheffield and Bristol have led to an increase in competition for audiences and led many small independent cinemas to the wall. However, with cinema attendances rising and advertising revenue reaching £123 million (Table 27) plus the interesting experiments with niche marketing, the exhibition sector is in a position to take stock of all the recent movements and mergers in the market. Cinemas in general may need some serious strategic thinking as digital technology becomes more prevalent and more films are delivered on disk rather than in film cans.

25 Breakdown of UK Box Office By Distributor in 1999

Distributor	Titles	Box office
UIP	39	133,206,947
Buena Vista	32	118,539,642
20thC Fox	22	86,423,946
Warner Brothers	19	68,558,266
Universal	14	45,605,281
Columbia TriStar	26	30,447,731
Total US Majors	**152**	**482,781,813**

Distributor	Titles	Box office
Entertainment	24	34,855,964
Pathé	11	21,048,407
FilmFour	19	17,364,907
Eros	17	2,799,177
Alliance	14	2,540,559
Icon	3	1,705,668
Artificial Eye	12	1,119,171
Downtown	11	1,071,162
Yash Raj	4	767,870
UFDL	5	659,569
Blue Light	4	617,926
Blue Star	6	513,772
BFI	12	353,362
Metro Tartan	6	304,233
Stars Int.	1	287,509
Metrodome	8	276,466
Shernwali	5	264,335
Optimum	4	224,454
Redbus	2	175,221
ICA	12	160,618
IFD	1	147,670
Feature Film Co	11	103,573
Gala	7	51,735
Monohill	3	43,054
Lucky Shamrock	1	40,104
1st Independent	4	35,728
Millivres	4	31,602
Contemporary	2	28,481
Winstone	3	24,055
Venus	4	20,240
Capricorn	1	13,640
Clarence	1	12,450
Manga	1	10,724
J Balfour	1	7,679
Guerilla	1	7,045
Celluloid	1	5,630
Arrow	2	4,750
Blue Dolphin	2	4,650
Barbican	2	4,228
United Media	1	3,641
City	1	2,762
Sales	1	2,574
GVI	1	2,064
Nepotism	1	1,998
Spark	1	1,948
Globe	1	1,752
Skillant	1	260
Bandit	1	163
Total (Independents)	**241**	**87,724,550**
Total	**393**	**570,506,363**

Source: ACNielsen EDI/BFI/Screen Finance/X25 Partnership

26

UK Cinema Circuits 1984–1999
s (sites) scr (screens)

Year	ABC		UGC *(ex-Virgin)		Cine UK		Odeon		Showcase		UCI		Warner Village		Small Chains		Independents	
	s	scr	s	scr	s	scr	s	scr	s	scr	s	scr	s	scr	s	scr	s	scr
1984	-	-	-	318*	-	-	-	205	-	-	-	-	-	-	-	-	-	-
1985	-	-	158	403*	-	-	76	194	-	-	3	17	1	5	-	-	-	-
1986	-	-	173	443*	-	-	74	190	-	-	3	17	1	5	-	-	-	-
1987	-	-	154	408*	-	-	75	203	-	-	5	33	1	5	-	-	-	-
1988	-	-	140	379*	-	-	73	214	7	85	12	99	1	5	-	-	-	-
1989	-	-	142	388*	-	-	75	241	7	85	18	156	3	26	-	-	-	-
1990	-	-	142	411*	-	-	75	266	7	85	21	189	5	48	-	-	-	-
1991	-	-	136	435*	-	-	75	296	8	97	23	208	6	57	-	-	-	-
1992	-	-	131	422*	-	-	75	313	9	109	25	219	7	64	-	-	-	-
1993	-	-	125	408*	-	-	75	322	10	127	25	219	9	84	-	-	-	-
1994	-	-	119	402*	-	-	76	327	11	141	26	232	10	93	-	-	437	631
1995	-	-	116	406*	-	-	71	320	11	143	26	232	12	110	-	-	469	716
1996	92	244	24	162*	2	24	73	362	14	181	26	232	16	143	58	139	437	679
1997	80	225	29	213*	5	66	73	362	15	197	26	263	17	152	68	166	434	739
1998	81	234	34	290*	10	116	79	415	15	199	29	287	22	200	73	100	416	633
1999	58	180	36	312	13	146	79	415	16	221	31	320	28	200	55	170	376	794

Source: Screen Finance   * figures from 1984 to 1998 indicate Virgin Cinemas

27

UK Cinema Advertising Revenue 1985–1999

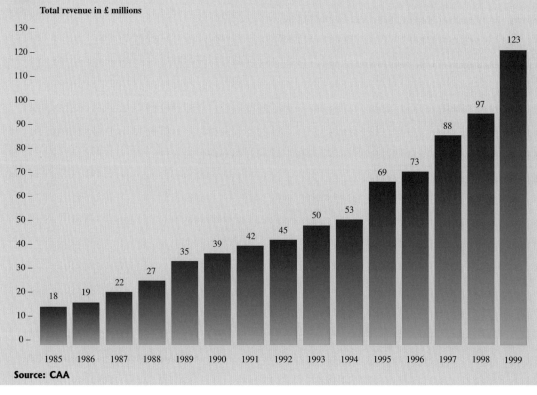

Total revenue in £ millions

Year	Revenue
1985	18
1986	19
1987	22
1988	27
1989	35
1990	39
1991	42
1992	45
1993	50
1994	53
1995	69
1996	73
1997	88
1998	97
1999	123

Source: CAA

28	**BBFC Censorship of Videos 1999**	
Certificate		**Number of Films passed after cuts**
U		4
PG		18
12		7
15		17
18		188
R18		11
Rejected		9
Source: BBFC		

Snug as a bug – A Bug's Life was the top retail video

DVD Video

No sooner had DVD slotted neatly into the lives of British people than controversies arose about UK release dates, DVD configurations and some DVDs not coming with all their unique extras. Despite teething problems the BVA has reported an exceptional take up of DVD players in the UK. Leading the charge are those (like film buffs) who love to purr over the crisp quality of image and sound that DVDs produce.

While DVD players stake their claim as the next essential consumable electrical item in UK households, old VTRs have not been tossed into skips up the length and breadth of the country. Retail transactions for DVDs accounted for four per cent of the market (Table 29). In this respect it is clear that the combined retail market for DVD and VHS remained the same in 1999 (100 transactions) as in 1998. The value of £950 million in 1999 was £10 million higher than the preceding year. Rental transactions fell by £12 million in 1999. It is unclear whether this signifies the beginning of a rental slump or merely a period of readjustment between VHS and DVD.

It is interesting to compare the retail and rental tables (Table 30 and Table 32) in terms of the type of videos on offer and then compare the two audiences to the new DVD retail table (Table 33). The easy generalisation to make is that the top 20 video rentals are largely made up of sci-fi, action, thriller or horror films aimed at a

29	The UK Video Market 1986–1999					
Year	**Retail Transactions (millions)**		**Value (£m)**		**Rental Transactions (millions)**	**Value (£m)**
1988	6		55		233	284
1987	12		110		251	326
1988	20		184		271	371
1989	38		345		289	416
1990	40		374		277	418
1991	45		440		253	407
1992	48		506		222	389
1993	60		643		184	350
1994	66		698		167	339
1995	73		789		167	351
1996	79		803		175	382
1997	87		858		161	369
1998	100		940		186	437
1999	96	(4)	882	(68)	174	408

DVD retail transactions in brackets

Source: BVA

30 Top 20 Rental Videos in the UK 1999

	Film	Distributor	Country
1	There's Something About Mary (15)	Fox Pathé	US
2	Armageddon (12)	Buena Vista	US
3	Saving Private Ryan (15)	CIC	US
4	Enemy of the State (15)	Buena Vista	US
5	Lock, Stock and Two Smoking Barrels (18)	UPV	UK
6	Blade (18)	EV	US
7	Lethal Weapon 4 (15)	Warner	US
8	The Truman Show (PG)	CIC	US
9	Payback (18)	Warner	US
10	Dr. Doolittle (PG)	Fox Pathé	US
11	Godzilla (PG)	Columbia	US
12	The Matrix (15)	Warner	US
13	Sliding Doors (15)	CIC	UK/US
14	Mercury Rising (15)	CIC	US
15	Notting Hill (15)	UPV	UK
16	Lost in Space (PG)	EV	US
17	The Siege (15)	Fox Pathé	US
18	Ronin (15)	MGM	US
19	Small Soldiers (PG)	CIC	US
20	Rush Hour (15)	EV	US

Source: Rental Monitor/BVA

There's Something About Mary – top video rental in 1999

31 Distributors Share of UK Rental Transactions 1999 (%)

	Distributor	% share
1	Warner/MGM	18.60
2	Buena Vista	16.80
3	CIC	15.80
4	Fox Pathé	12.80
5	Universal	11.50
6	EV	11.20
7	Columbia TriStar	8.80
8	FilmFour	1.90
9	High Fliers/Alliance	1.10
10	Mosaic	0.50

Source:Rental Monitor/BVA

predominantly male 15+ audience. So, with the striking exceptions of *There's Something About Mary* and *Sliding Doors,* the rental table conforms to type.

Retail demographics show a different story (Table 32). Here, the emphasis is on children's entertainment, and comedies with eight U certificate films in the top 20 – *A Bug's Life* leading a procession of other animated films. Also, the chart includes popular TV shows such as *Ali G, Innit* and *Friends.* However, this demographic is not repeated when we look at the top 20 retail DVD table (Table 33). Eleven of the DVD retail titles also appear in the video rental chart compared to only four DVD titles that appear in the video retail chart. The top film which announced the arrival of DVD onto the retail scene was *The Matrix* (which made third spot in the video retail chart and 12th spot in the rental chart). It will be interesting to see whether this trend continues when more households acquire DVD players, or whether 'family-orientated entertainment' will take over from 'action' as the prominent genre choice.

Warner/MGM had a particularly good year dominating both the retail and the rental share of the market (Tables 31 & 34), *The Matrix* and *Lethal Weapon 4* being two dominant titles (although the MGM portion of the partnership had significant pulling power). Universal scored three top 20 retail video entries which helped them ease past Buena Vista into second place in the retail market (Table 34). Despite having six films in the top 20 rental video chart (Table 32) including the top two, Buena Vista dropped to second place in the list of UK rental transactions by distributor.

The year was significant in that the British Board of Film Classification, under new director Robin Duval, courted controversy by granting certificates to so-called video nasties such as *The Texas Chainsaw Massacre* and *Driller Killer* and also issuing certificates to other controversial films such as *The Exorcist*, and in 2000 *A Clockwork Orange.* Not for the first time was the issue of censorship raised. The BBFC rejected 9 films in 1999 (including *Straw Dogs*) compared with 4 in 1998 (Table 28). Perhaps more controversial was the High Court ruling on censorship in May 2000 which allotted the R18 ratings to seven hardcore videos. This occurred after two distributors had challenged the BBFC's original decision not to grant the films with certificates. We wait and see whether the judgment will open the floodgates to similar developments in the video industry.

32 Top 20 Retail Videos in the UK 1999

	Title	Distributor	Country
1	A Bug's Life (U)	Buena Vista	US
2	The Lion King 2 – Simba's Pride (U)	Buena Vista	US
3	The Matrix (15)	Warner	US
4	Notting Hill (PG)	Universal	US
5	Saving Private Ryan (15)	CIC	US
6	Mulan (U)	Buena Vista	US
7	Lock, Stock and Two Smoking Barrels (18)	Universal	UK
8	Antz (U)	CIC	US
9	Dr Doolittle (U)	20th Century Fox	US
10	George of the Jungle (U)	Buena Vista	US
11	Godzilla (PG)	Columbia	US
12	Rugrats – The Movie (U)	CIC	US
13	Armageddon (12)	Buena Vista	US
14	Joseph and the Amazing Technicolor Dreamcoat	Universal	UK
15	Ali G, Innit	VCI	UK
16	Friends – Series 5 – Episodes 1–4	Warner	US
17	Billy Connolly Live	VVL	UK
18	The Royle Family - Complete Series 1	VCI	UK
19	The Prince of Egypt (U)	CIC	US
20	Friends – Series 5 – Episode 5–8	Warner	US

Source: BVA/CIN

34 Video Retail Company Market Share by Volume 1999 (%)

	Distributor	% share
1	Warner/MGM	24.20
2	Universal	17.80
3	Buena Vista	12.60
4	Columbia	12.30
5	CIC	11.40
6	Fox	8.60
7	EV	6.20
8	VCI	3.90
9	Carlton	0.50
10	MIA	0.30

Source: BVA/CIN

33 Top 20 Retail DVDs in the UK 1999

	Title	Distributor	Country
1	The Matrix (12)	Warner	US
2	Armageddon (15)	Buena Vista	US
3	Blade (18)	EV	US
4	Lock, Stock & Two Smoking Barrels (18)	Universal	UK
5	A Bug's Life (U)	Buena Vista	US
6	Enemy of the State (15)	Buena Vista	US
7	Notting Hill (15)	Universal	US
8	Lethal Weapon 4 (15)	Warner	US
9	The Exorcist (18)	Warner	US
10	Ronin (15)	MGM	US
11	Godzilla (PG)	Columbia	US
12	Payback (18)	Warner	UK
13	Shakespeare in Love (15)	Universal/Columbia	UK/US
14	Starship Troopers (15)	Buena Vista	US
15	Titanic (12)	20th Century Fox	US
16	The Mask of Zorro (PG)	Columbia	US
17	There's Something About Mary (PG)	20th Century Fox	US
18	The Negotiator (15)	Warner	US
19	Tomorrow Never Dies (12)	MGM	US/UK
20	The Faculty (15)	Buena Vista	US

Source: BVA/CIN

The Matrix topped video rental and DVD retail charts

35 The UK Video Games Market 1999 Computer Software Sales

Value	£969 million
Units	35.2 million

Source: Chartrack/Screen Digest/ELSPA

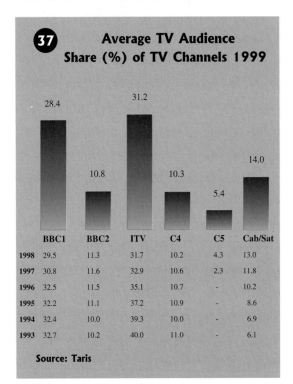

36 **Trends in Television Viewing 1999**

Average Daily Hours Viewing	3.65
Number of TV Households	24 million

Source: Taris/Taylor Nilson Sofres

37 **Average TV Audience Share (%) of TV Channels 1999**

	BBC1	BBC2	ITV	C4	C5	Cab/Sat
1999	28.4	10.8	31.2	10.3	5.4	14.0
1998	29.5	11.3	31.7	10.2	4.3	13.0
1997	30.8	11.6	32.9	10.6	2.3	11.8
1996	32.5	11.5	35.1	10.7	-	10.2
1995	32.2	11.1	37.2	10.9	-	8.6
1994	32.4	10.0	39.3	10.0	-	6.9
1993	32.7	10.2	40.0	11.0	-	6.1

Source: Taris

38 **Cable and Satellite Penetration 1999**

	cable	satellite
No.of subscribers	3.2m	4.1m
Penetration %	13.5*	17

* There is a 25.7 % TV take up in Cabled areas.
50% of TV households have been passed by broadband cable.

Source: ITC/Screen Digest/BSkyB

Television

With constant attacks on the quality of television on all channels, it is a wonder that anybody watches any television anymore. But while TV columnists were venting their spleens regarding the dearth of any decent new drama, comedy or documentary programmes, the TV viewer was seemingly unperturbed, and was actually watching more television. Much of the blame for the apparent decline in quality television has been the scramble for ratings above all else. It is an irony that enticing larger audiences somehow leads to poorer programmes. Average daily viewing figures rose by three minutes in 1999 to an average of three hours and 39 minutes (Table 36). Research published in May 2000 by NOP Solutions, a marketing research company, found that some people watched as much as 36 hours of television a week. What makes these statistics remarkable is that other distractions such as the Internet or computer games have yet to dent audience figures.

ITV continued to take the lion's share of audiences leading the field with 31.2 per cent (Table 37). Yet, ITV and both BBC channels saw their share drop. Indeed, since 1993 ITV has seen its share of the audience drop by almost 9 per cent, while BBC1's drop of around 4 per cent has indicated a slower decline. BBC2 fared poorly as well, with its audience share sliding over two years from 11.6 per cent in 1997 to 10.8 per cent in 1999. Channel 4 gained ground on BBC2 by more or less consolidating its position. Meanwhile the oft-maligned Channel 5 cheerfully continued its steady progress since its launch, by taking a 5.4 per cent share in the market.

Wonder what the million pound question is?

39 **ITV Companies' Programme Supply to the Network 1999**

Company	Hours of new programmes
Anglia	313
Border	–
Carlton	129
Central	100
Channel	–
Grampian	–
Granada	670
HTV	34
LWT	287
Meridian	53
STV	105
Tyne Tees	8
UTV	–
West Country	4
Yorkshire	177

Source: ITC

Coronation Street was the top TV programme again

Cable and satellite's continued rise in popularity (Table 37 & Table 38) is noteworthy in relation to the advent of digital television. By July 2000 four million homes had digital television via Sky and ONdigital: it will be interesting to see how much longer terrestrial broadcasters can keep their audience.

The future of ITV companies lies in the balance. The scramble for ownership looks likely to continue over the next couple years until there are two main owners. Table 39, may, for the penultimate time, show the new programme capacities of the ITV regions.

Despite all the speculation of mergers and the uneasy transitional period from analogue to digital broadcasting, ITV had a good year in 1999, claiming 14 out of the top 20 programmes including the top four (Table 40). *Coronation Street* continued its position as the nation's favourite programme, notching up 19.8 million viewers for its top episode. *Who Wants to be a Millionaire?* was narrowly behind in second place with an audience of 19.2 million viewers on the same evening. This new show, which was scheduled on consecutive evenings, proved addictive with audiences and introduced the now famous 'Can I phone a friend?' catchphrase, not to mention Chris Tarrant's earnest, tension-making enquiry – 'Is that your final answer?' On the same evening in March as ITV were racking up top ratings (a new series of *A Touch of Frost* followed *Who Wants to Be a Millionaire?*), BBC 1 offered The *Wildlife Specials* a

repeated programme, *Five Go Mad in the Kitchen,* a ten-minute Comic Relief recipe programme featuring Ruby Wax and Gary Rhodes, and *Love Town,* a docusoap about Gretna Green.

BBC1 had a miserable year. Its top soap *Eastenders,* which slipped from second position in 1998 to fifth in 1999, was BBC1's top show with an audience of 15.7 million. The much admired and innovative *Walking With Dinosaurs* gained a top audience figure of 15 million, while another crumb of comfort for the BBC was the Christmas edition of *The Vicar of Dibley* which was the only sitcom in the top 20.

The trend of popular ITV programmes eclipsing BBC1 shows continued in the original drama departments (Table 41). Again, *Coronation Street, Heartbeat* and *A Touch of Frost* proved to be the most popular programmes. *EastEnders* and *Casualty* were the top BBC shows but both slipped two places from 1998.

It is no surprise that the BBC governors called for improvements in the quality of BBC programmes and Director General Greg Dyke was keen to allocate money to the production of top quality original dramas. If the era leading up to the change over to digital television looks likely to be hard on ITV, it seems it will be harder for the BBC. With some notable exceptions, such as *Walking With Dinosaurs,* the BBC has gone down a slippery road by clogging its schedules with repeats or 'mut-

40   # Top 20 Programmes for all Terrestrial Channels 1999

Only top rated episodes of each series are included

	Title	Channel	TX date	Audience(m)
1	Coronation Street	ITV	07-Mar	19.8
2	Who Wants to be a Millionaire?	ITV	07-Mar	19.2
3	Heartbeat	ITV	28-Feb	17.0
4	A Touch of Frost	ITV	21-Mar	16.8
5	Eastenders	BBC1	07-Jan	15.7
6	Champions League Final: Man Utd v Bayern Munich	ITV	26-May	15.6
7	Walking with Dinosaurs	BBC1	04-Oct	15.0
8	Euro 2000 Play Off: England v Scotland	ITV	17-Nov	14.6
9	The Vicar of Dibley	BBC1	27-Dec	14.4
10	New You've Been Framed	ITV	07-Nov	13.9
11	Emmerdale	ITV	10-Jan	13.4
12	GoldenEye	ITV	10-Mar	13.2
13	TV Nightmares	ITV	09-Jan	13.1
14	Casualty	BBC1	13-Feb	13.1
15	Mission Impossible	BBC1	26-Dec	12.8
16	Neighbours From Hell	ITV	07-Jan	12.8
17	Before They Were Famous	BBC1	25-Dec	12.2
18	Lost for Words	ITV	03-Jan	12.2
19	Stars in Your Eyes	ITV	05-Jun	12.2
20	Police, Camera, Action	ITV	06-Jan	12.0

Source: BARB

     # Top Original Drama Productions 1999

Including soap operas, series, serials and UKTV Movies.
Audience figures are for highest rated episodes of each production

	Title	Producer/Sponsor	Tx Date	Audience (m)
1	Coronation Street	Granada	07-Mar	19.80
2	Heartbeat	Yorkshire	28-Feb	17.00
3	A Touch of Frost	Yorkshire	21-Mar	16.80
4	Eastenders	BBC	07-Jan	15.70
5	Emmerdale	Yorkshire	20-Jan	13.40
6	Casualty	BBC	13-Feb	13.10
7	Lost for Words	Bard Entertainment/Yorkshire	03-Jan	12.20
8	Forgotten	LWT	15-Feb	12.00
9	Coronation Street: sAfter Hours	Granada	13-Nov	12.00
10	Where the Heart Is	United/Anglia	18-Apr	11.70
11	Jonathan Creek	BBC	28-Dec	11.40
12	London's Burning	LWT	28-Feb	11.40
13	The Bill	Pearson/Carlton	05-Jan	11.20
14	Extremely Dangerous	North West One/Picture Palace/Carlton	11-Nov	11.10
15	Grafters	Coastal Prods/Granada	08-Nov	11.10
16	Midsomer Murders	Bentley Prods/Yorkshire	12-Sep	11.10
17	Rhinoceros	Coastal Prods/Granada	11-Apr	11.00
18	Peak Practice	Central	23-Feb	10.90
19	Harbour Lights	Valentine Prods/BBC	18-Feb	10.90
20	Silent Witness	BBC	31-May	10.90

Source: BARB

42 Television Advertising 1999

	£m
Net Terrestrial TV Advertising Revenue	2,777
ITV	1,874
C4	590
C5	187
S4C	9
GMTV	65
Programme Sponsorship	52
*Non-Terrestrial TV Revenue	2,145

*Figure to end of September 1999.
Includes Advertising Revenue, Sponsorship and Subscriptions.

Source : ITC

Lost For Words was the top UK TV Film

ton dressed up as lamb' programmes consisting of endless trawls through its admittedly glorious past. Radical reforms and an increase in revenue from the licence fee may be the tonic needed to persuade programme planners to actually make new programmes that might be worth repeating.

Overall advertising revenue for terrestrial TV advertising (Table 42) dropped by £171 million in 1999. The figure for non-terrestrial television, which also includes subscriptions, was £632 million behind terrestrial TV's total.

43 UK TV Films Premiered 1999

Title	Tx date	BARB Rating(m)	Title	Tx date	BARB Rating(m)
BBC1			**ITV**		
The Man	5th April	5.50	Lost For Words	3rd January	12.23
Split Second	26th August	5.97	Hornblower: The Duchess and		
All for Love	22nd October	6.16	the Devil	24th February	7.48
All the King's Men	14th November	9.67	Hunting Venus	31st March	8.70
Last Christmas	22nd December	6.13	Hornblower: Frogs and Lobsters	2nd April	5.95
The Greatest Store in the World	24th December	7.09	Rhinoceros	11th April	10.96
			Girls' Night*	14th April	8.36
			Bostock's Cup	25th May	6.26
BBC2			Trial by Fire	15th December	7.74
The Sixth Happiness*	21st March	0.71	The Flint Street Nativity	22nd December	9.33
Face*	5th April	3.68	The Turn of the Screw	26th December	6.08
Regeneration*	12th September	1.49			
My Son the Fanatic*	19th September	0.81	**Channel 4**		
I Went Down*	26th September	1.10	True Blue*	10th January	1.29
Sex 'n' Death	14th December	2.89	Bent*	23rd August	0.41
Jeffrey Bernard is Unwell	23rd December	0.75	Gallivant*	20th September	0.13
The Revenger's Comedies	30th December	3.10	The Slab Boys*	27th October	0.57
			Babymother*	19th December	0.93
			The Disappearance of Finbar*	23rd December	0.29
			The Woodlanders*	25th December	0.90

* denotes previous release in UK cinemas

Source: BARB/BFI

44   ## Top 20 Feature Films Shown on Terrestrial TV 1999

	Title	Country	Year	Channel	Audience (m)
1	GoldenEye	UK/US	1995	ITV	13.23
2	Mission Impossible	US	1996	BBC1	12.80
3	Tomorrow Never Dies	UK/US	1997	ITV	11.86
4	Jingle all the Way	US	1996	ITV	11.29
5	The Nutty Professor	US	1996	ITV	11.07
6	Twister	US	1996	ITV	10.67
7	The Specialist	US	1994	ITV	10.58
8	Never Say Never Again	UK/US	1983	ITV	10.13
9	Apollo 13	US	1995	BBC1	10.10
10	Dr. No	UK/US	1962	ITV	10.02
11	The Spy Who Loved Me	UK/US	1977	ITV	9.95
12	For Your Eyes Only	UK/US	1981	ITV	9.30
13	Home Alone 2	US	1992	ITV	9.28
14	The Man with the Golden Gun	UK/US	1974	ITV	9.28
15	Diamonds are Forever	UK/US	1971	ITV	9.23
16	K-9	US	1988	ITV	9.21
17	While You Were Sleeping	US	1995	ITV	9.20
18	Executive Decision	US	1996	ITV	9.09
19	In the Line of Fire	US	1993	ITV	9.06
20	Live and Let Die	UK/US	1973	ITV	9.01

Source: BARB

The top UK TV film in 1999 was Yorkshire TV's *Lost for Words,* based on the book by Deric Longden, about the relationship between a middle aged man and his elderly, eccentric mother. This attracted by far the biggest audience of 12.23 million. The BBC's top TV film was *All the King's Men*, about the fate of 147 workers on the Sandringham royal estate who fought at Gallipoli, which drew an audience of 9.67 million. Of the films that had previously been released in UK cinemas, *Girls' Night* starring Brenda Blethyn and Julie Walters, had the largest audience of 8.36 million.

ITV's season of James Bond films reaped rich viewing rewards with no fewer than 10 Bond films in the top 20, with GoldenEye proving the most popular attracting an audience of 13.23 million. *Mission Impossible* was the second most popular feature on terrestrial television, one of only two films shown by the BBC (*Apollo 13* being the other) to make it into the Top 20.

At present, the viewer has been offered more choice of channels than ever before. With interactive television proving already to be a ratings winner, the viewer is also likely to be persuaded more and more to control or contribute to the outcomes of programmes. However, one thing the TV executives of all the channels should bear before they devise their next 'sexy' interactive docusoap game show, is that the viewer also has the choice of turning their television off.

GoldenEye – Top of the James Bond films

45   ## UK General Statistics 1999

Population	59.1 million
Number of Households	24.3 million
Inflation	1.50%
Gross Domestic Product (Current Prices)	£843,725 million
Total TV Licences in Force	22.8 million
Licence Fee Income	£2,179.5 million

Source: ONS/BBC/Stationary Office

Further Reading

BRITISH BOARD OF FILM
CLASSIFICATION
Annual Report 1999.
BBFC, 2000.

BRITISH BROADCASTING
CORPORATION
Annual Report 1999/2000.
BBC, 2000.

BROADCASTING STANDARDS
COMMISSION
Annual Report 2000.
BSC, 2000.

BROWN, David
FT Focus on the BBC.
Informa (Previously FT Media &
Telecoms), 1999.

BVA YEARBOOK 2000
British Video Association, 2000.

CABLE & SATELLITE
YEARBOOK 2000
Informa, 2000.

CHANNEL FOUR TELEVISION
Annual Report 1999.

CINEMAGOING 8
Leicester: Dodona Research, 2000.

CULTURAL TRENDS
Issue 30 1998 Media.
London: Policy Studies Institute,
1999.

DOWNEY, Mike
The film finance handbook: volume
1: a practical guide to film financing
for European producers.
Madrid: Media Business School,
1999.

ELLIS, John
Seeing things: television in an age of
uncertainty.
London I.B. Tauris, 2000.

EUROPEAN CINEMA YEARBOOK
1999
Media Salles, 1999.

EUROPEAN VIDEO YEARBOOK
1999/2000
Screen Digest/International Video
Federation, 1999.

FILM COUNCIL
Towards a sustainable UK film
industry.
Film Council, 2000.

FILM EDUCATION WORKING
GROUP
Making Movies Matter: report of the
Film Education Working Group
BFI, 1999.

The FILM INDUSTRY: MARKET
REPORT
Key Note, 1998.

FILM POLICY REVIEW GROUP
A bigger picture: the report of the
Film Policy Review Group.
Department of Culture, Media and
Sport, 1998.

GB CINEMA EXHIBITORS
(Quarterly)
Office For National Statistics, 1999-
2000.

HAMILTON-DEELEY, Gavin (et.
al.)
The cost of making dreams:
accounting for the British film
industry.
Deloitte & Touche, 1999.

INDEPENDENT TELEVISION
COMMISSION
Annual Report 1999.
ITC, 2000.

MEDIA GUIDE 2000
London: 4TH Estate, 2000.

MEDIA MAP 2000
Exeter: CIT Publications, 2000.

MOLSKY, Norman
European public broadcasting in the
digital age.
Informa, 1999.

MORAN, Albert (ed)
Film Policy: international, national
and regional perspectives.
Routledge, 1996.

MURPHY, Robert (ed)
British cinema in the 1990s.
BFI, 2000.

OVERSEAS TRANSACTIONS OF
THE FILM & TV INDUSTRY 1997
Office for National Statistics, 1998.

PETRIE, Duncan
Screening Scotland
BFI, 2000

PRATTEN, Stephen & DEAKIN,
Simon
Competitiveness policy and economic
organisation: the case of the British
film industry (ERSC Centre working
paper no.127).
ESRC Centre for Business Research,
University of Cambridge, 1999.

STATISTICAL YEARBOOK:
CINEMA, TELEVISION, VIDEO
AND NEW MEDIA IN EUROPE
1999
Strasbourg: European Audiovisual
Observatory, 1999.

TaRIS UK TELEVISION & VIDEO
YEARBOOK 2000
London: Taylor Nelson Sofres, 2000.

The WORLD FILM & TELEVISION
MARKET 2000
(aka The IDATE report).
Montpellier: IDATE, 2000.

WORLD TELEVISION 2000
(Formerly known as TBI Yearbook).
Informa, 2000.

ARCHIVES AND FILM LIBRARIES

INTERNATIONAL ORGANISATIONS

FIAF
(International Federation of Film Archives)
1 Rue Defacqz
B-1000 Brussels
Belgium
Tel: 32 2 538 3065
Fax: 32 2 534 4774
email: info@fiafnet.org
Website: www.cinema.ucla.edu/FIAF
Christian Dimitziu
Founded in 1938, FIAF is a collaborative association of the world's leading film archives whose purpose is to ensure the proper preservation and showing of motion pictures. More than 100 archives in over 60 countries collect, restore, and exhibit films and cinema documentation spanning the entire history of film. It also publishes handbooks on film archiving practice which can be obtained from the above address

FIAT/IFTA
(International Federation of Television Archives)
Sveriges Television AB
Tevearkivet
RH-N2G
S-10510 Stockholm
Sweden
Tel: (+468) 784 5740
Fax: (+468) 660 4000
email: ifta@svt.se
Website: www.nb.no/fiat/fiat.html
Agneta Forsström, Administrative Coordinator
Lasse Nilsson (General Secretary)
FIAT membership is mainly made up of the archive services of broadcasting organisations. However, it also encompasses national archives and other television-related bodies. It meets annually and publishes its proceedings and other recommendations concerning television archiving

EUROPEAN ARCHIVES

Below are some European Film Archives of countries in the European Union. For more specialised information consult *Film and Television Collections in Europe – The MAP-TV Guide* published by Blueprint

Austria

Österreichisches Filmarchiv (Austrian Film Library)
Schaumburgergasse 11
1040 Wien
Tel: 43 1 512 99 36
Fax: 43 1 513 53 30
email: info@filmarchiv.org
Website: www.filmarchiv.org
Alexander V. Kammel

Belgium

Cinémathèque Royale/Koninklijk Filmarchief (Royal Film Archives)
Palais des Beaux Arts
Rue Ravenstein 23
1000 Bruxelles
Tel: 32 2 507 83 70
Fax: 32 2 513 12 72
email: filmarchive@ledoux.be
Gabrielle Claes
Every year the Film Museum grants 5 annual awards, each amounting to 250,000 BF, to assist the distribution of quality films in Belgium. These grants, funded with the help of the Ministry of the French Community of Belgium and of the Region of Brussels Capital, are presented to films which are unreleased in Belgium and have not yet been picked up by a distributor for the Belgian market. In addition, one film from among these five award winners is singled out by the jury for the Age d'Or Prize, a further 250,000 BF awarded to a film whose originality, marks a deliberate break with cinematographic conformity

Denmark

Det Danske Filmmuseum
Danske Filmminstitut/
Danish Film Institute
Vognmagerade 10
DK-1120 Copenhagen K
Tel: 45 33 74 34 00
Fax: 45 33 74 34 01

Finland

Suomen Elokuva-Arkisto (Finnish Film Archive)
PO Box 177
Fin 00151 Helsinki
Tel: 35 8 9 615 4 0 213
Fax: 35 8 9 615 40 242
email: sea@sea.fi
Website: www.sea.fi
Matti Lukkarila

France

Les Archives du Film du Centre National de la Cinématographie
7 bis rue Alexandre Turpault
78390 Bois D'Arcy Cedex
Tel: 33 1 30 14 80 00
Fax: 33 1 34 60 52 25
Eric Le Roy

Germany

Deutsche Rundfunkarchiv (DRA)/German Broadcast Archive
Standort Berlin
Rudower Chaussee 3
D12489 Berlin
Tel: 49 030 67 764 - 0
Fax: 49 030 67 764 - 100
email: info@dra.de
Website: www.dra.de
Sigrid Ritter

Greece

Teniothiki Tis Elladas (Greek Film Archives)
1 Canari Street
Athens 10761
Tel: 30 1 361 2046
Fax: 30 1 362 8468
Theodoros Adamopoulos, Director

Ireland

Irish Film Archive
Film Institute of Ireland
6 Eustace Street
Dublin 2
Tel: 353 1 679 5744
Fax: 353 1 677 8755
email: archive@ifc.ie
Website: www.fii.ie
Lar Joye, Head of Archive
Sunniva O'Flynn, Archive Curator
Liam Wylie, Keeper of Film &
Magnetic Collections
Emma Keogh, Librarian/Paper
Archivist

Italy

**Cineteca Nazionale
(National Film Archive)**
Centro Sperimentale di
Cinematografia
Via Tuscolana 1524
I-00173 Roma
Tel: 39 06 722 941
Fax: 39 06 722 3131
Angelo Libertini, General Director

Luxembourg

**Cinémathèque Municipale
de Luxembourg la Ville de
Luxembourg
(Luxembourg National Film
Archive City of Luxembourg)**
10 rue Eugène Ruppert
2453 Luxembourg
Tel: (352) 4796 2644
Fax: (352) 4075 19
Claude Bertemes

The Netherlands

**Nederlands Filmmuseum,
Stichting
(Netherlands Film Museum)**
Vondelpark 3
1071 AA Amsterdam
Tel: 31 20 589 1400
Fax: 31 20 683 3401
Peter Westervoorde, Head of
Cataloguing Department

Portugal

**Cinemateca Portuguesa -
Museu do Cinema
(Portuguese Film Archive -
Museum of Cinema)**
Rua Barata Salgueiro, No 39
1269-059 Lisboa

Tel: 351 21 546279
Fax: 351 21 3523180
email: cinemateca@cpmc.pt
João Bénard da Costa, Director
José Manuel Costa, Deputy Director
Rui Santana Brito, Deputy Director

Spain

**Filmoteca Española
(Spanish National FilmTheatre)**
Carretera de la Dehesa de la Villa s/n
28040
Madrid
Tel: 34 1 549 00 11
Fax: 34 1 549 73 48

Sweden

**Svenska Filminstitutet
(Swedish Film Institute)**
PO Box 27126
Borgvägen 1-5
S-102 52 Stockholm
Sweden
Tel: 46 8 665 11 00
Fax: 46 8 661 18 20
Rolf Lindfors, Head of Archive

NATIONAL ARCHIVES

**bfi Collections
(incorporating the
National Film and
Television Archive)**
21 Stephen Street
London W1T 1LN
Tel: 020 7255 1444
Fax: 020 7580 5830
Website: www.bfi.org.uk/collections
Caroline Ellis (Head of Collections)
Anne Fleming (Preservation)
Heather Stewart (Access)
bfi Collections contain more than
275,000 films and 200,000 TV
programmes, dating from 1895 to the
present. Related collections of stills,
posters, designs, scripts and printed
ephemera such as, marketing materials,
technology, props and costumes, have
been assembled alongside the software
to give added context and meaning

**Imperial War Museum Film
and Video Archive**
Lambeth Road
London SE1 6HZ
Tel: 020 7416 5000
Fax: 020 7416 5379
email: film@iwm.org.uk
Website: www.iwm.org.uk
Paul Sargent/Jane Fish
The national museum of modern
conflict, illustrating and recording all
aspects of modern war. The Archive
reflects these terms of reference with
an extensive collection of film and
video material, which is widely used
by historians and by film and
television companies

**Scottish Film and Television
Archive**
at Scottish Screen
1 Bowmont Gardens
Glasgow G2 9LR
Tel: 0141 337 7400
Fax: 0141 337 7413
email: info@scottishscreen.com
Website: www.scottishscreen.com
Janet McBain: Curator
Anne Docherty: Enquiries
Tel: 0141 337 7402
Almost exclusively non-fiction film,
the collection dates from 1896 to the
present day and concerns aspects of
Scottish social, cultural and industrial
history. Available to broadcasters,
programme makers, educational users
and researchers. Access charges and
conditions available on request

Wales Film and Television Archive

Unit 1, Aberystwyth Science Park
Cefn Llan, Aberystwyth
Dyfed SY23 3AH
Tel: 01970 626007
Fax: 01970 626008
email: wftva@aol.com
Director: Iola Baines
The Archive locates, preserves and catalogues film and video material relating to Wales. The collection is made accessible where possible for research and viewing. The Archive is part of Sgrín, Media Agency for Wales
Chief Executive: J Berwyn Rowlands

REGIONAL COLLECTIONS

East Anglian Film Archive

University of East Anglia
Norwich NR4 7TJ
Tel: 01603 592664
Fax: 01603 458553
email: eafa@uea.ac.uk
Website: www.uea.ac.uk/eafa/
David Cleveland, Director
Jane Alvey, Deputy Director
Preserving non-fiction films and videos, both amateur and professionally made, showing life and work in Bedfordshire, Cambridgeshire, Essex, Hertfordshire, Norfolk and Suffolk

North West Film Archive

Manchester Metropolitan University
Minshull House
47-49 Chorlton Street
Manchester M1 3EU
Tel: 0161 247 3097
Fax: 0161 247 3098
email: n.w.filmarchive@mmu.ac.uk
Website: www.nwfa.mmu.ac.uk
Maryann Gomes: Director
Enquiries: Lisa Ridehalgh
Preserves moving images showing life in the North West and operates as a public regional archive. Urban and industrial themes are particularly well illustrated. Online film and video catalogue at the Archive's website

Northern Region Film and Television Archive

Blandford House
Blandford Square
Newcastle upon Tyne NE1 4JA
Tel: 0191 232 6789 ext 456
Fax: 0191 230 2614
email: chris.galloway@dial.pipex.com
Chris Galloway, Project Director
The Northern Region Film and Television Archive is the recognised repository for moving image material covering the North of England (Cumbria, Northumberland, Teesside, Durham and Tyne and Wear). The Archive was created in 1998 and incorporates the collections of the North East Film and Television at Teesside University, Tyne and Wear Archives and the Northern Film and Television Archive formerly in Gateshead. BBC North East, Tyne Tees Television and Trade Films material is held by the Archive as well as substantial deposits of material from production companies and amateur film–makers within the region. A wide range of subject matter reflecting the social and industrial history of the region is held by the Archive

South East Film & Video Archive

University of Brighton
Grand Parade
Brighton BN2 2JY
Tel: 01273 643213
Fax: 01273 643214
email: sefva@brighton.ac.uk
Jane Pumford, Administrator
Established in 1992 the function of this regional film and video archive is to locate, collect, preserve and promote films and video tapes made in the four counties of Kent, Surrey, East Sussex, West Sussex and the unitary authorities of Brighton & Hove and Medway

TSW Film and Television Archive

New Cooperage
Royal William Yard
Stonehouse
Plymouth
Devon PL1 3RP
Tel: 01752 202650
Fax: 01752 205025
email: tsw@archive.fsnet.co.uk
Website: www.geocities.com/
Athens/Atlantis/1802/fta.htm
The official film archive for the South West of England. Holds south western film material and includes three television collections covering news coverage between 1961 to 1992 – Westward Television, Television South West and BBC South West

Wessex Film and Sound Archive

Hampshire Record Office
Sussex Street
Winchester SO23 8TH
Tel: 01962 847742
Fax: 01962 878681
email: sadedm@hants.gov.uk.
Website: www.hants.gov.uk/record-office/film.html
David Lee
Preserves and makes publicly accessible for research, films, video and sound recordings of local interest to central southern England

Yorkshire Film Archive

College of Ripon and York St John
College Road
Ripon HG4 2QX

Tel: 01765 696 264
Fax: 01765 606 267
email: s.howard@ucrysj.ac.uk
Website: www.yorkshire-media.co.uk
Sue Howard
The Yorkshire Film Archive exists to locate, preserve and show film about the Yorkshire region. Material dates from 1897 and includes newsreels, documentaries, advertising and amateur films

NEWSREEL, PRODUCTION AND STOCK SHOT LIBRARIES

Archive Film Agency
21 Lidgett Park Avenue
Roundhay
Leeds LS8 1EU
Tel: 0113 2662454
Fax: 0113 2662454/0113 2684761
email: info@archivefilmagency.co.uk
Website: www.archivefilmagency.com
Agnèse Geoghegan
Film from 1898 to present day, including a current worldwide stock shot library. Specialists in early fiction, newsreel, documentary, Music Hall, Midlands, Yorkshire, British 1930s stills. Cassette services

Associated Press Television News (APTN)
The Interchange
Oval Road
Camden Lock
London NW1 7DZ
Tel: 020 7410 5353
Fax: 020 7413 8327
email: info@aptnlibrary.com
Website: www.aptnlibrary.com
David Simmons
Newsfilm and video from 1896 – and adding every day up to 100 new items from around the world. Hard news, stock footage, features, personalities, annual compilations, background packages etc. Story details and shotlists are stored on full-text easy-to-search database. Database also available on CD-Rom and online (see website address above)

BBC Information & Archives - Television Archive
Reynard Mills Industrial Estate
Windmill Road
Brentford TW8 9NF
Tel: 020 8576 4964
Fax: 020 8740 8755
Paul Fiander, Head of Archive
The largest collection of broadcast programmes in the world reflecting the whole range of BBC output

bfi Archival Footage Sales
21 Stephen Street
London W1P 2LN
Tel: 020 7957 8934
Fax: 020 7580 5830
email: footage.films@bfi.org.uk
Website: www.bfi.org.uk
Jan Faull or Simon Brown
Material from the largest collection of film footage in Britain – the National Film and Television Archive. Television, films, documentaries, newsreels and animation are all covered with over 350,000 titles to choose from, including material dating back to 1895. First stop for serious research on subjects that have shaped the 20th century. Research facilities available

Boulton-Hawker Films
Hadleigh
near Ipswich
Suffolk IP7 5BG
Tel: 01473 822235
Fax: 01473 824519
Peter Boulton
Educational films produced over 50 years. Subjects include: health, biology, botany, geography, history, archaeology, and the arts

The British Defence Film Library
SSVC, Chalfont Grove
Narcot Lane
Chalfont St. Peter
Gerrards Cross
Bucks SL9 8TN
Tel: 01494 878278/878252
Fax: 01494 878007
email: robertd@ssvc.com
Robert Dungate: BDFL Librarian
SSVC has many years experience in providing both entertainment and support for the military. The British Defence Library (BDFL) is an independent department within SSVC which holds and distributes audio visual training materials for use by the armed forces which have been specifically commissioned by the Ministry of Defence. The Library also supplies this footage to the film and television industry offering a unique collection of British military material

British Movietonews
North Orbital Road
Denham
Middx UB9 5HQ
Tel: 01895 833071
Fax: 01895 834893
Barbara Heavens
One of the world's major film archives featuring high quality cinema newsreels from the turn of the century, with an emphasis on 1929-1979. The library now represents on

an exclusive basis the TV-AM News Library with over 1,100 hours of British and World news covering the period 1983-1991. This material is available on re-mastered digital tape

British Pathé Plc
60 Charlotte Street
London W1P 2AX
Tel: 020 7323 0407
Fax: 020 7436 3232
email: pathe@enterprise.net
Website: www.britishpathe.com/
search.html
Larry McKinna: Chief Librarian
50 million feet of newsreel and social documentary from 1896 to 1970. Rapid research and sourcing through computerised catalogue
Pinewood Studios
Pinewood Road
Iver, Bucks SL0 0NH
Tel: 01753 630 361
Fax: 01753 655 365
Ron Saunders

Canal + Image UK Ltd
Pinewood Studios
Pinewood Road, Iver
Bucks SL0 0NH
Tel: 01753 631111
Fax: 01753 655813
John Herron
Feature films, TV series, stock shot and stills, b/w and colour, 35mm, 1925 to present day

Central Office of Information Footage File
4th Floor
184-192 Drummond Street
London NW1 3HP
Tel: 0171 383 2292
Fax: 0171 383 2333
email: research@film-images.com
Website: www.film-images.com
Tony Dykes
40,000 Crown Copyright titles from the Government's News and Information archives spanning over 75 years of British social and business history. Most of the collection has been thoroughly shot listed and is available on VHS viewing cassettes

Chain Production Ltd
2 Clanricarde Gardens
London W2 4NA
Tel: 020 7229 4277
Fax: 020 7229 0861
email: films@chainproduction.co.uk
Website: www.chainproduction.co.uk
Specialist in European films and world cinema, cult classics, handling

European Film Libraries with all rights to over 1,000 films – also clip rights and clip search

Channel Four Clip Library
124 Horseferry Road
London SW1P 2TX
Tel: 020 7306 8490/8155
Fax: 020 7306 8362
email: caustin@channel4.co.uk
Website: www.channel4.com
Claire Austin/Eva Kelly
An ever growing portfolio of programmes and a diverse collection of library material. Also access to feature films when the copyright has been cleared with original copyright holders

The Cinema Museum
(See Ronald Grant Archive)

Clips & Footage
2nd Floor
80a Dean Street
London W1V 5AD
Tel: 020 7287 7287
Fax: 020 7287 0984
email: clipsetc@easynet.co.uk
Alison Mercer
Supplies historical and modern colour footage to broadcast, corporate and commercial producers. Special collections include B movies, feature film trailers, destinations, timelapse and lifestyle

Contemporary Films
24 Southwood Lawn Road
Highgate
London N6 5SF
Tel: 020 8340 5715
Fax: 020 8348 1238
email: contemporaryfilms@
compuserve.com
Website: www.contemporaryfilms. com
Documentaries on China, USSR, Cuba, Nazi Germany, South Africa. The library also covers areas like the McCarthy witch hunts in the '50s, the civil rights movements of the '60s, hippie culture, feminism

Editions Audiovisuel Beulah
66 Rochester Way
Crowborough TN6 2DU
Tel: 01892 652413
Fax: 01892 652413
email: iainlogan@enterprise.net
Website: www.homepages.enterprise.
net/beulah/library
Beulah publish the following videos
Vintage Music, Inland Waterways, Royal Navy, Military Transport, Yesterday's Britain. It also incorporates Film Archive Management (FAME)

Educational and Television Films (ETV)
247a Upper Street
London N1 1RU
Tel: 020 7226 2298
Fax: 020 7226 8016
email: zoe@etvltd.demon.co.uk
Documentaries on Eastern Europe, USSR, China, Vietnam, Cuba and British Labour movement, b/w and colour, 16mm and 35mm, 1896 to present day

Environmental Investigation Agency
69-85 Old Street
London EC1V 9HX
Tel: 020 7490 7040
Fax: 020 7490 0436
email: info@eia-international.org
Website: www.eia-international.org
Extensive and exclusive library of video and stills showing the exploitation of wildlife and the environment worldwide. Subjects include dolphin and whale slaughter, the bird trade, bear farms, animal products illegally on sale in shops and to undercover investigators, and other aspects of endangered species trade. All film sales help to fund future investigations and campaigns

Film Images
4th Floor
184-192 Drummond Street
London NW1 3HP
Tel: 020 7383 2288
Fax: 020 7383 2333
email: research@film-images.com
Website: www.film-images.com
Angela Saward
Thousands of hours of classic and contemporary film images from hundreds of different sources around the world. All fully catalogued and immediately available for viewing on VHS or U-Matic. Suppliers include Central Office of Information and Overseas Film and Television

Film Research & Production Services Ltd
Mitre House
177-183 Regent Street
London W1R 7SB
Tel: 020 7734 1525
Fax: 020 7734 8017
Amanda Dunne, James Webb
Film research and copyright clearance facilities, also third party clearance. Film holding of space footage

GB Associates

80 Montalt Road
Woodford Green
Essex IG8 9SS
Tel: 020 8505 1850
Fax: 020 8505 8094
email: filmview@aol.com
Malcolm Billingsley
An extensive collection, mainly on
35mm, of fact and fiction film from
the turn of the century. The collection
is particularly strong in vintage
trailers, the early sound era, early
colour systems and adverts

Fred Goodland Film, Video & Record Collections

81 Farmilo Road
Leyton
London E17 8JN
Tel: 020 8539 4412
Fax: 020 8539 4412
Fred Goodland MBKS
Diverse actuality and entertainment
material on film and disc (1890s-
1990s). Specialist collections include
early sound films and a wide range of
musical material. 100s of original 78
rpm discs in excellent condition
represent the authentic sounds of the
20th century, VHS tapes with
B.I.T.C. available to film researchers

Granada Media Clip Sales – London Weekend TV

London Television Centre
Upper Ground
London SE1 9LT
Tel: 020 7261 3690
Fax: 020 7261 3456
email: clips.london@granadamedia.com
Julie Lewis
Clips and stockshots available from
London Weekend Television's vast
programme library, dating from 1968.
Drama, entertainment, music, arts
and international current affairs. Plus
London's news, housing, transport,
politics, history, wildlife etc

Ronald Grant Archive

The Cinema Museum
The Master's House
The Old Lambeth Workhouse
2 Dugard Way
(off Renfrew Road, Kennington)
London SE11 4TH
Tel: 020 7840 2200
Fax: 020 7840 2299
email: martin@cinemamuseum.org.uk
Martin Humphries
15 million feet of fact and fiction
film, mainly 35mm, from 1896 on.
Also 1 million film stills, posters,

programmes, scripts and information.
The museum is a FIAF subscriber

Huntley Film Archives

78 Mildmay Park
Newington Green
London N1 4PR
Tel: 020 7923 0990
Fax: 020 7241 4929
email: films@huntleyarchives.com
Website: www.huntleyarchives.com
Amanda Huntley, John Huntley
Archive film library for broadcast,
corporate and educational purposes,
specialising in documentary footage
1900-1980. Phone to make an
appointment or write for brochure
detailing holdings. Now also 50,000
stills from films and film history

Index Stock Shots

12 Charlotte Mews
London W1P 1LN
Tel: 020 7631 0134
Fax: 020 7436 8737
email: index@msn.com
Website: www.index-stockshots.com
Philip Hinds
Unique stock footage on 35mm film
and tape. Including time-lapse and
aerial photography, cities, landmarks,
aviation, wildlife

ITN Archive

200 Gray's Inn Road
London WC1X 8XZ
Tel: 020 7430 4480
Fax: 020 7430 4453
email: archive.sales@itn.co.uk
Website: www.itnarchive.com
John Flewin
Worldwide TV news coverage on film
and video tape, from 1955 to the
present day. Complete library archive
on site including multi-format transfer
suite. Also an on-line stills from video
service, available via ISDN. A
newspaper cuttings reference library
with cuttings back to 1955 is available

London Film Archive

c/o 78 Mildmay Park
Newington Green
London N1 4PR
Tel: 020 7923 4074
Fax: 020 7241 4929
email: info@londonfilmarchive.org
Website: londonfilmarchive.org
Dedicated to the acquisition and
preservation of film relating to the
Greater London region. The collection
consists of material from 1895 to the
present day and represents
professional and amateur produced
features and documentary films

The Lux Centre

2-4 Hoxton Square
London N1 6NU
Tel: 020 7684 2782
Fax: 020 7684 1111
email: lea@easynet.co.uk
Website: www.lux.org.uk
Britain's national centre for video
and new media art, housing the most
extensive collection of video art in
the country. Artists' work dating from
the 1970s to the present

Medi Scene

32-38 Osnaburgh Street
London NW1 3ND
Tel: 020 7387 3606
Fax: 020 7387 9693
Aurora Salvador-Bennett
Wide range of accurately catalogued
medical and scientific shots available
on film and video. Part of the Medi
Cine Group

Moving Image Communications

61 Great Titchfield Street
London W1W 7PP
Tel: 020 7580 3300
Fax: 020 7580 2242
email: mail@milibrary.com
Website: www.milibrary.com
Michael Maloney
Over 12,000 hours of contemporary
and archive footage including:
Library Collection – WPA Film
Library (Representatives for the UK
& Ireland); RSPB Film Library; TV-
am Archive 1983-1992; Wild
Islands; Flying Through History;
The Lonely Planet; Shark Bay Films;
TIDA Public Information Films; Buff
Films; Drummer Films; Universal
Newsreels; The Freud Archive;
Natural World; Stockshots; Space
Exploration (NASA)
Access and Viewing – All
collections are logged shot by shot on
a research database for immediate
access. In house researchers service
all enquiries. Compilation preview
cassettes are tailored to the footage
brief. Alternatively, clients can view
on premises. Research services –
Internet online research database of
the Moving Image Library is
available on website. Alternatively, a
CD-ROM is provided to professional

Nova Film and Video Library

11a Winholme
Armthorpe
Doncaster DN3 3AF
Tel: 01302 833422

Fax: 08701 257917
email: library@novaonline.co.uk
Website: www.novaonline.co.uk/library
An extensive collection of unique archive material featuring a huge selection of amateur cine film documenting the changing social life of Britain, dating back to 1944 and has a dedicated collection of transport footage, from 1949 to the present day. The library also holds a wide selection of specially shot modern footage and interviews. A catalogue and showreel is available

The Olympic Television Archive Bureau
4th Floor Axis Centre
Burlington Lane
Chiswick
London W4 2TH
Tel: 020 8233 5353
Fax: 020 8233 5354
email: dwilliams@imgworld.com
Website: www.otab.com
David Williams
The International Olympic Committee owns a unique collection of film and television material covering the entire history of the Olympic Games from 1896 to 1994. Now it can be accessed via the Olympic Television Archive Bureau, which is administered by Trans World International

Oxford Scientific Films
Lower Road
Long Hanborough
Oxford OX8 8LL
Tel: 01993 881881
Fax: 01993 882808 or 01993 883969
email: jmulleneux@osf.uk.com
Website: www.osf.uk.com
Jane Mulleneux, Rachel Wakefield, Sandra Berry
Stock footage on 16mm, 35mm film and video. Wide range of wildlife, special fx, timelapse, slow motion, scenics, agriculture, traffic, macro, micro etc. Catalogue and showreel available. Extensive stills library

Pearson Television International Ltd
1 Stephen Street
London W1P 1PJ
Tel: 020 7691 6732/6733
Fax: 020 7691 6080
email: archive@pearsontv.com
Website: www.pearsontvarchive.com
Len Whitcher
Over 15,000 hours of a wide range of

TV programmes including all Thames, Grundy, Alomo, ACI and all American programming

Post Office Film and Video Library
PO Box 145
Sittingbourne
Kent ME10 1NH
Tel: 01795 426465
Fax: 01795 474871
email: poful@edist.co.uk
Barry Wiles, Linda Gates
Holds a representative selection of documentary programmes made under the GPO Film Unit, including the classic Night Mail. Catalogue available which also lists recent releases. New series of programmes on Millennium stamps now available

Reuters Television Library
(Managed and Distributed by ITN Archive)
200 Grays Inn Road
London WC1X 8XE
Tel: 020 7430 4480
Fax: 020 7430 4453
email: archive.sales@itn.co.uk
Website: www.itnarchive.com
Alwyn Lindsey, Sales Director
Original newsreel, television news and feature footage from 1896 to present day. Special Collections. Online database (free access) and expert researchers

RSPB Film and Video Unit
The Lodge
Sandy
Bedfordshire SG19 2DL
Tel: 01767 680551
Fax: 01767 692365
email: bird@rspb.demon.co.uk
Website: www.rspb.org.uk
Colin Skevington: Head of Film & Video
Producer: Mark Percival
Wildlife documentary filmmakers and corporate production. Over 500 hours of archive footage, mostly European birds and other animal and plant life including habitats and scenics

Sky News Library Sales
British Sky Broadcasting Ltd
6 Centaurs Business Park
Grant Way
Isleworth
Middlesex TW5 5QD
Tel: 020 7705 2872
Fax: 020 7705 3201
Sue Stewardson, Ben White
Extensive round the clock news and current affairs coverage since 1989. Entire library held on Beta SP on

site. Library operates 24 hours a day

TWI Archive
Trans World International
Axis Centre
Burlington Lane
Chiswick
London W4 2TH
Tel: 020 833 5500/5300
Fax: 020 8233 5301
Rita Costantinou
Includes golf, tennis, World Cup rugby, America's Cup, Test cricket, skating, snooker, gymnastics, yachting, motorsport, adventure sport, many minor and ethnic sports plus expanding catalogue of worldwide stockshots

Undercurrents Archive
16b Cherwell Street
Oxford OX4 1BG
Tel: 01865 230663
Fax: 08701 316103
email: underc@gn.apc.org
Website: www.undercurrents.org
Roddy Mansfield
Undercurrents video archive features grassroots dissent of the '90s and contains over 1500 hours of footage of protest

World Backgrounds Film Production Library
Imperial Studios
Maxwell Road
Borehamwood, Herts
Tel: 020 8207 4747
Fax: 020 8207 4276
Ralph Rogers
Locations around the world. Fully computerised. All 35mm including 3,000 back projection process plates. Numerous video masters held. Suppliers to TV commercials, features, pop promos, TV series, corporate videos etc

Photographic Libraries

BBC Photograph Library
B116 Television Centre
Wood Lane
London W12 7RJ
Tel: 020 8225 7193
Fax: 020 8746 0353
The BBC's unique archive of radio and television programme stills, equipment, premises, news and personalities dating from 1922. B/w and colour. Visits by appointment

bfi Stills, Posters and Designs
21 Stephen Street
London W1T
Tel: 020 7255 1444
Fax: 020 7323 9260
Website: www.bfi.org.uk/collections/
A visual resource of around seven million images, illustrating every aspect of the development of world cinema and television. The collection also holds approximately 15,000 film posters and 2,000 production and costume designs. Other material includes animation cels, storyboards, sketches and plans

The Bridgeman Art Library
17-19 Garway Road
London W2 4PH
Tel: 020 7727 4065
Fax: 020 7792 8509
email: info@bridgeman.co.uk
Website: www.bridgeman.co.uk
Tom Wynn
The Bridgeman Art Library is the world's most comprehensive source of fine art for reproduction. From Renaissance classics to Pop Art and beyond, all styles and periods are covered. Images can be viewed and ordered on the website and a free illustrated catalogue is available

Corbis Images
12 Regents Wharf
All Saints Street
London N1 9RL
Tel: 0800 731 9995
Fax: 020 7278 1408
email: info@corbisimages.com
Website: www.corbisimages.com
Photographic stills agency/library

Hulton Getty Picture Collection
10 Bayham Street
London NW1
Tel: 020 7266 2660
Fax: 020 7266 2414
email: ask@getty-images.com
Website: www.hultongetty.com
One of the world's largest stills archives with over 15 million photographs, prints and engravings covering the entire history of photojournalism

The Image Bank
17 Conway Street
London W1 6EE
Tel: 020 7312 0300
Fax: 020 7391 9111
Website: www.imagebank.co.uk
Ian Morris - Sales Director

Image Diggers Picture and Tape Library
618b Finchley Road
London NW11 7RR
Tel: 020 8455 4564
Fax: 020 8455 4564
email: zip@phancap.demon.co.uk
Neil Hornick
35mm slides, stills, postcards, sheet music, magazine and book material for hire. Cinema, theatre and literature clippings archive. Audio/visual tape resources in performing arts and other areas, plus theme research

image.net
18 Vine Hill
London EC1
Tel: 08701 522 333
Fax: 020 7216 9014
email: solutions@imagenet.co.uk
Website: www.imagenet.co.uk
Simon Townsley

Imperial War Museum
Photograph Archive
All Saints Annexe
Austral Street
London SE11 4SL
Tel: 020 7416 5333/8
Fax: 020 7416 5355
email: photos@iwm.org.uk
Website: www.iwm.org.uk
Bridget Kinally
A collection of some 6 million images illustrating all aspects of 20th century warfare. Film stills can also be made from material held by the IWM's Film & Video Archive, by prior arrangement

Institute of Contemporary History & Wiener Library
4 Devonshire Street
London W1W 5BH
Tel: 020 7636 7247
Fax: 020 7436 6428
email: lib@wl.u-net.com
Website: winerlibrary.co.uk
Rosemarie Nief: Head Librarian
Ben Barkow: Photo Archive,
Christine Patel: Video Collection
The Wiener Library is a private research library and institute specialising in contemporary European and Jewish history, especially the rise and fall of the Third Reich, Nazism and fascist movements, anit-Semitism, racism, the Middle East and post-war Germany. It holds Britain's largest collection of documents, testimonies, books and videos on the Holocaust. The photographic archive contains stills, postcards, posters and portraits, illustrated books, approx. 2,000 videos and recordings

Kobal Collection
4th Floor
184 Drummond Street
London NW1 3HP
Tel: 020 7383 0011
Fax: 020 7383 0044
David Ken
One of the world's leading film photo archives in private ownership. Film stills and portraits, lobby cards and posters, from the earliest days of the cinema to modern times

Mckenzie Heritage Picture Archive
Unit 226
Station House
Greenwich Commercial Centre
49 Greenwich High Road
London SE10 8JL
Tel: 020 8469 2000
Fax: 020 8469 2000
email: info@mckenziehpa.com
Website: www.mckenziehpa.com
Jeni Mckenzie
Mckenzie Heritage Picture Archive specialises in pictures of black communities from Britain and abroad. The images span the 19th and 20th centuries.

The Moviestore Collection Ltd
3 Jonathan Street
London SE11 5NH
Tel: 020 7820 3820
Fax: 020 7820 8420

Pearson Television Stills Library
Teddington Studios
Broom Road
Teddington TW11 9NT
Tel: 020 8781 2789

Fax: 020 8614 2250
Website: www.pearsontv.com/pages/
stillslibrary.htm
Colleen Kay
Stills from Thames TV, Alomo, Grundy

Museums

The Bill Douglas Centre for the History of Cinema and Popular Culture
University of Exeter
Queen's Building
Queen's Drive
Exeter EX4 4QH
Tel: 01392 264263
Fax: 01392 264361
Website: www.ex.ac.uk/bill.douglas/
The Centre's collection was assembled over many years by film-maker Bill Douglas and his friend Peter Jewell. It comprises a huge range of books, periodicals, programmes, posters, sheet music, cards, toys and games related to the cinema, in addition to 19th century pre-cinema artefacts such as zoetropes, magic lanterns, panoramas, peepshows and other optical toys and devices

The Cinema Museum
Ronald Grant Archive
The Master's House
The Old Lambeth Workhouse
2 Dugard Way
(off Renfrew Road, Kennington)
London SE11 4TH
Tel: 020 7840 2200
Fax: 020 7840 2299
email: martin@cinemamuseum.org.uk
Martin Humphries
The museum is a FIAF subscriber

Imperial War Museum Film and Video Archive
Lambeth Road
London SE1 6HZ
Tel: 020 7416 5000
Fax: 020 7416 5379
email: film@iwm.org.uk
Website: www.iwm.org.uk
Paul Sargent, Jane Fish
The national museum of modern conflict, illustrating and recording all aspects of modern war. The Archive reflects these terms of reference with an extensive collection of film and video material, which is widely used by historians and by film and television companies

Laurel and Hardy Museum
4C Upper Brook Street
Ulverston
Cumbria LA12 7BH
Tel: 01229 582292
Website: www.wwwebguides.com/
britain/cumbria/furness/laure.html
The museum is in Ulverston, Cumbria, Stan Laurel's birthplace. Open all year seven days a week for talks about Laurel and Hardy. It contains photos, letters, and memorabilia

National Museum of Photography, Film & Television
Pictureville
Bradford BD1 1NQ
Tel: 01274 202030
Fax: 01274 723155
Website: www.nmsi.ac.uk/nmpft
Bill Lawrence, Head of Cinema
The world's only museum devoted to still and moving pictures, their technology and history. Features Britain's first giant IMAX film system; the world's only public Cinerama; interactive galleries and 'TV Heaven', reference library of programmes and commercials

AWARDS

This section features some of the principal festival prizes and awards from January 1999 to December 1999. Compiled by Laura Pearson

Awards 1999

BAFTA FILM AWARDS
Awarded in London 11th April 1999

The Academy Fellowship: Elizabeth Taylor
The Michael Balcon Award for Outstanding British Contribution to Cinema: Michael Kuhn
The Alexander Korda Award for the Outstanding British Film of the Year: ELIZABETH (UK) Dir Shekhar Kapur
Best Film: SHAKESPEARE IN LOVE (US) Dir John Madden
The David Lean Award for Best Achievement in Direction: Peter Weir for The TRUMAN SHOW (US)
Best Original Screenplay: Andrew Niccol for The TRUMAN SHOW (US) Dir Peter Weir
Best Adapted Screenplay: Elaine May for PRIMARY COLORS (US) Dir Mike Nichols
Best Actress: Cate Blanchett for ELIZABETH (UK) Dir Shekhar Kapur
Best Actor: Roberto Benigni for La VITA É BELLA (Italy) Dir Roberto Benigni
Best Supporting Actress: Judi Dench for SHAKESPEARE IN LOVE (US) Dir John Madden
Best Supporting Actor: Geoffrey Rush for SHAKESPEARE IN LOVE (US) Dir John Madden
Best Film not in the English Language: CENTRAL DO BRASIL (Brazil/France/Spain/Japan) Dir Walter Salles
The Anthony Asquith Award for Achievement in Film Music: David Hirschfelder for ELIZABETH (UK) Dir Shekhar Kapur
The Carl Foreman Award for Most Promising Newcomer in British Film: Richard Kwietniowski
Best Cinematography: Remi Adefarasin for ELIZABETH (UK) Dir Shekhar Kapur
Best Production Design: Dennis Gassner for The TRUMAN SHOW (US) Dir Peter Weir
Best Costume Design: Sandy Powell for VELVET GOLDMINE (UK/US) Dir Todd Haynes
Best Editing: David Gamble for SHAKESPEARE IN LOVE (US) Dir John Madden
Best Sound: Gary Rydstrom, Ronald Judkins, Gary Summers, Andy Nelson, Richard Hymns for SAVING PRIVATE RYAN (US) Dir Steven Spielberg
Best Special Visual Effects: Stefen Fangmeier, Roger Guyett, Neil Corbould for SAVING PRIVATE RYAN (US) Dir Steven Spielberg
Best Make-Up/Hair: Jenny Shircore for ELIZABETH (UK) Dir Shekhar Kapur
Best Short Animated Film: The CANTERBURY TALES (UK Wales) Dir Dave Antrobus, Ashley Potter, Mic Graves, Joanna Quinn, Aida Zyablikova, Valeri Ugarov, Sergei Olifirenko, Damian Gascoigne

Best Short Film: HOME (UK) Prod: Hannah Lewis
Orange Audience Award: LOCK, STOCK AND TWO SMOKING BARRELS (UK) Dir Guy Ritchie

BAFTA TELEVISION AWARDS
Awarded in London 9th May 1999

The Academy Fellowship: Eric Morecambe and Ernie Wise
The Alan Clarke Award for Outstanding Creative Contribution to Television: Jimmy Mulville, Denise O'Donoghue
The Richard Dimbleby Award for Outstanding Personal Contribution to Factual Television: Trevor McDonald
The Dennis Potter Award: David Renwick
The Special Award: Richard Curtis
The Lew Grade Award for the Most Popular Television Programme: GOODNIGHT MR. TOM (Carlton Television for ITV)
Best Actress: Thora Hird for TALKING HEADS 2: WAITING FOR THE TELEGRAM (Slow Motion Limited for BBC2)
Best Actor: Tom Courtenay for A RATHER ENGLISH MARRIAGE (BBC/Wall to Wall Television for BBC2)
Best Light Entertainment Performance: Michael Parkinson for PARKINSON (BBC1)
Best Comedy Peformance: Dermot Morgan for FATHER TED (Hat Trick Productions for C4)
Best Single Drama: A RATHER ENGLISH MARRIAGE (BBC/Wall to Wall Television for BBC2)
Best Drama Series: The COPS (World Productions for BBC2)
Best Drama Serial: OUR MUTUAL FRIEND (BBC/Canadian Broadcasting Company for BBC2)
Best Soap: EASTENDERS (BBC1)
Best Factual Series: The HUMAN BODY (BBC Science/The Learning Channel for BBC1)
Best Light Entertainment Programme or Series: WHO WANTS TO BE A MILLIONAIRE? (Celador Productions for ITV)
Best Comedy: FATHER TED (Hat Trick Productions for C4)
The Huw Wheldon Award for Best Arts Programme or Series: The BRIAN EPSTEIN STORY (ARENA) (BBC2)
The Flaherty Documentary Award: SURVIVING LOCKERBIE (Scottish Television Enterprises for ITV)
Live Outside Broadcast Coverage: C4 RACING - DERBY DAY (Highflyer Productions for C4)
News and Current Affairs Journalism: DISPATCHES - INSIDE THE ANIMAL LIBERATION FRONT (C4)
Best Features (Programme or Series): BACK TO THE FLOOR (BBC2)
Originality: The HUMAN BODY (BBC Science/The Learning Channel for BBC1)
Best International Programme or Series: The LARRY SANDERS SHOW (Brillstein Grey/HBO)
Best Make-Up/Hair: Lisa Westcott for OUR MUTUAL

FRIEND (BBC/Canadian Broadcasting Company for BBC2)
Best Photography (Factual): George Jesse Turner for 42 UP (Granada Television for BBC1)
Best Photography and Lighting (Fiction/Entertainment): John Daly for FAR FROM THE MADDING CROWD (Granada Television/WGBH (Boston) for ITV)
Best Costume Design: Frances Tempest for A RESPECTABLE TRADE (BBC/Irish Screen Entertainment for BBC1)
Best Graphic Design: Tim Goodchild, David Haith for The HUMAN BODY (BBC Science/The Learning Channel for BBC1)
Best Sound (Factual): The LIFE OF BIRDS (BBC TV/Public Broadcasting Service for BBC1)
Best Sound (Fiction/Entertainment): Paul Hamblin, Catherine Hodgson, Graham Headicar, Richard Manton for OUR MUTUAL FRIEND (BBC/Canadian Broadcasting Company for BBC2)
Best Editing (Factual): Brian Tagg for LOCKERBIE: A NIGHT REMEMBERED (Castle Haven Digital for C4)
Best Editing (Fiction/Entertainment): Dave King for A RATHER ENGLISH MARRIAGE (BBC/Wall to Wall Television for BBC2)
Best Design: Malcolm Thornton for OUR MUTUAL FRIEND (BBC/Canadian Broadcasting Company for BBC2)
Best Original Television Music: Jim Parker for A RATHER ENGLISH MARRIAGE (BBC/Wall to Wall Television for BBC2)

4TH BAFTA CHILDREN'S AWARDS
Awarded in London 7 November 1999

Special Award: The Jim Henson Company
Writer's Award: Mark Haddon
Bafta Kid's Vote: ART ATTACK (The Media Merchants TV Company for ITV)
Drama: Andrew Rowley, Juliet May and Mark Haddon for MICROSOAP (Disney Channel UK/BBC Production for BBC1)
Entertainment: Martin Hughes, Lucy Bowden, Angela Sharp for LIVE & KICKING (BBC Production for BBC1)
Factual: Zoë Dobson, Stuart Bamforth and Kirsty Lyell for NICK NEWS (Nickelodeon/Wised-Up Productions)
Animation: Jackie Edwards and Graham Ralph for The FIRST SNOW OF WINTER (Hibbert/Ralph Entertainment for BBC1)
Pre-School: Lona Llewelyn Davies and Cliff Jones for TECWYN Y TRACTOR (S4C/Teledu Apollo)
Schools Drama: John Price, Marcus DF White and Barry Purchese for JUNK (Zenith North for BBC2)
Schools Factual - Primary: Roland Tongue and Susie Nott-Bower for RAT-TAT-TAT: BEANS ON TOAST AND KETCHUP ON YOUR CORNFLAKES (Open Mind Productions for C4)
Schools Factual - Secondary: Sara Feilden and Jonathan Hacker for TURNING POINTS: ALCOHOL MISUSE - EMMA'S STORY (BBC Education for BBC2)
International: Jonathan M Shiff for THUNDERSTONE (Disney Channel UK/Jonathan M Shiff Productions)
Children's Feature Film: Mark Gordon, Gary Levinsohn, Allison Lyon Segan and John Roberts for PAULIE (UIP/Dreamworks Pictures/Mutual Film Company)

49TH BERLIN INTERNATIONAL FILM FESTIVAL
Held in Berlin 10th-21st February 1999

Golden Berlin Bear: The THIN RED LINE (US) Dir Terrence Malick
Silver Berlin Bear (Jury Grand Prix): MIFUNES SIDSTE SANG - DOGME 3 (Denmark/Sweden) Dir Søren Kragh-Jacobsen
Silver Berlin Bear - Best Director: Stephen Frears for The HI-LO COUNTRY (US)
Silver Berlin Bear - Best Actress: Juliane Köhler and Maria Schrader for AIMÉE & JAGUAR (Germany) Dir Max Färberböck
Silver Berlin Bear - Best Actor: Michael Gwisdek for NACHTGESTALTEN (Germany) Dir Andreas Dresen
Silver Berlin Bear for Oustanding Single Achievement: Marc Norman and Tom Stoppard for their screenplay of SHAKESPEARE IN LOVE (US) Dir John Madden
Silver Berlin Bear for Outstanding Artistic Achievement: David Cronenberg for EXISTENZ (Canada/UK) Dir David Cronenberg
The Blue Angel: Yesim Ustaoglu for GÜNESE YOLCULUK (Turkey/Netherlands/Germany) Dir Yesim Ustaoglu
The Alfred Bauer Prize: KARNAVAL (Belgium/France/Germany/Switzerland) Dir Thomas Vincent
A Special Mention for his outstanding work as director of Photography: John Toll for The THIN RED LINE (US) Dir Terrence Malick
A Special Mention for the young actress: Iben Hjejle for MIFUNES SIDSTE SANG - DOGME 3 (Denmark/Sweden) Dir Søren Kragh-Jacobsen
A Special Mention for its subject matter: ÇA COMMENCE AUJOURD'HUI (France) Dir Bertrand Tavernier
Gay Teddy Bear - Best Feature: FUCKING ÅMÅL (Sweden) Dir Lukas Moodysson
Gay Teddy Bear - Best Documentary: The MAN WHO DROVE WITH MANDELA (UK) Dir Greta Schiller
Gay Teddy Bear Jury Award - Wieland Speck
Prizes for Short Films
Golden Berlin Bear: FARAON (Russia) Dir Sergej Ovtscharov and to MASKS (Germany/Poland) Dir Piotr Karwas
Silver Berlin Bear: DESSERTS (UK) Dir Jeff Stark
Gay Teddy Bear: LIU AWAITING SPRING (Australia) Dir Andrew Soo

BROADCASTING PRESS GUILD TELEVISION AND RADIO AWARDS 1998
Awarded in London 26th March 1999

Best Single Documentary: 42UP (Granada Television for BBC1)
Writer's Award: Caroline Aherne, Craig Cash and Henry Normal for The ROYLE FAMILY (Granada Television for BBC Manchester)
Best Documentary Series: The LIFE OF BIRDS (BBC TV/Public Broadcasting Service for BBC1)
Best Drama Series/Serial: OUR MUTUAL FRIEND (BBC TV/Canadian Broadcasting Corporation for BBC2)
Best Actress: Daniela Nardini for UNDERCOVER HEART (BBC1)
Best Actor: Timothy Spall for OUR MUTUAL FRIEND (BBC TV/Canadian Broadcasting Corporation for BBC2)

Best Entertainment: COLD FEET (Granada Television for ITV) and GOODNESS GRACIOUS ME (BBC2)
Best Single Drama: A RATHER ENGLISH MARRIAGE (Wall to Wall Productions for BBC2)
Best Performer: Michael Parkinson

52nd CANNES FESTIVAL
Held in Cannes 12th-23rd May 1999

Palme d'Or: ROSETTA (Belgium/France) Dir Luc and Jean-Pierre Dardenne
Grand Jury Prize: L'HUMANITÉ (France) Dir Bruno Dumont
Best Actress: Séverine Caneele for L'HUMANITÉ (France) Dir Bruno Dumont, and Emilie Dequenne for ROSETTA (Belgium/France) Dir Luc and Jean-Pierre Dardenne
Best Actor: Emmanuel Schotté for L'HUMANITÉ (France) Dir Bruno Dumont
Best Director: Pedro Almodovar for TODO SOBRE MI MADRE (Spain/France)
Best Screenplay: Yuri Arabov and Marina Koreneva for MOLOCH (Russia/Germany/France) Dir Alexandre Sokourov
Jury Prize for Daring and Originality: A CARTA (Portugal/France/Spain) Dir Manoel de Oliveira
Camera d'Or: MARANA SIMHASANAM (India/UK) Dir Murali Nair
Grand Prix Technique de la Commission Supèrieure Technique de L'image et du Son: JING KE CI QIN WANG (Japan/China/France) Dir Chen Kaige

Short Films
Palme d'Or: WHEN THE DAY BREAKS (Canada) Dir Wendy Tilby and Amanda Forbis
Grand Jury Prize: STOP (France) Dir Rodolphe Marconi, and SO-POONG (Republic of Korea) Dir Song Ilgon

24th CÉSARS
Awarded in Paris 6th March 1999

Best Film: La VIE RÊVÉE DES ANGES (France) Dir Erick Zonca
Best Director: Patrice Chéreau for CEUX QUI M'AIMENT PRENDRONT LE TRAIN (France)
Best Actress: Élodie Bouchez for La VIE R VÉE DES ANGES (France) Dir Erick Zonca
Best Actor: Jacques Villeret for Le DÎNER DE CONS (France) Dir Francis Veber
Best Foreign Film: La VITA È BELLA (Italy) Dir Roberto Benigni
Best First Film: DIEU SEUL ME VOIT (VERSAILLES-CHANTIERS) (France) Dir Bruno Podalydès
Best New Actress: Natacha Régnier for La VIE RÊVÉE DES ANGES (France) Dir Erick Zonca
Best New Actor: Bruno Putzulu for PETITIS DÉSORDRES AMOUREUX (France/Switzerland/Spain) Dir Olivier Péray
Best Sound: Vincent Tulli and Vincent Arnardi for TAXI (France/Italy) Dir Gérard Pirès
Best Sets: Jacques Rouxel for LAUTREC (France/Spain) Dir Roger Planchon
Best Costume Design: Jean-Pierre Larroque for LAUTREC (France/Spain) Dir Roger Planchon
Best Editing: Véronique Lange for TAXI (France/Italy)

Dir Gérard Pirès
Best Music: Tony Gatlif for GADJO DILO (France) Dir Tony Gatlif
Best Short Film: L'INTERVIEW (France) Dir Xavier Giannoli
Best Supporting Actress: Dominique Blanc for CEUX QUI M'AIMENT PRENDRONT LE TRAIN (France) Dir Patrice Chéreau
Best Supporting Actor: Daniel Prévost for Le DÎNER DES CONS (France) Dir Francis Veber
Best Screenplay: Francis Veber for Le DÎNER DES CONS (France) Dir Francis Veber
Best Photography: Eric Gautier for CEUX QUI M'AIMENT PRENDRONT LE TRAIN (France) Dir Patrice Chéreau
Honorary Césars:
Pedro Almodòvar
Jean Rochefort
Johnny Depp

53rd EDINBURGH INTERNATIONAL FILM FESTIVAL
Held 15th-29th August 1999, Edinburgh
88 Lothian Road
Edinburgh EH3 9BZ
Tel: (44) 131 229 2550
Fax: (44) 131 229 5501
Web site: www.edfilmfest.org.uk/

Best New British Feature: The WAR ZONE (UK/Italy) Dir Tim Roth
Pathé Best British Performance Award: Jeremy Northam for The WINSLOW BOY (US) Dir David Mamet
New Director's Award: Lynne Ramsay for RATCATCHER (UK/France)
Standard Life Audience Award: BUENA VISTA SOCIAL CLUB (Germany) Dir Wim Wenders
Best British Shorts: HOME (UKScotland) Dir Morag McKinnon, IN MEMORY OF DOROTHY BENNETT (UKScotland) Dir Martin Radich, and MY JOB (UKScotland) Dir Joern Utkilen
Best British Animation: The WOLF MAN (UK) Dir Tim Hope

EMMY AWARDS - 27TH INTERNATIONAL EMMY AWARDS GALA
Awarded in New York City 22nd November 1999
International Council for the National Academy of TV Arts & Sciences
142 West 57th Street
New York
NY 10019
Tel: (212) 489 6969
Fax: (212) 489 6557
Website: www.intlemmyawards.com/

Best Drama: LOST FOR WORDS (UK) (Yorkshire Television in association with Bad Entertainments)
Best Performing Arts: RODGERS & HAMMERSTEIN'S "OKLAHOMA!" (UK) (Richard Price Television Associates/Iambic Productions/Sky Productions) and KAREN KAIN: DANCING IN THE MOMENT (Canada) (Canadian Broadcasting Corporation)
Best Popular Arts: SMACK THE PONY (UK) (A Talkback Production for C4)

Best News Programme: DISPATCHES: A WITNESS TO MURDER (UK) (Hardcash Productions for C4)
Best Documentary: BORN IN THE USSR - 14 UP (UK) (Granada Television for BBC Television) and JUST LIKE ANYONE ELSE (Japan) (Mainichi Broadcasting System)
Best Arts Documentary: The PHIL - PART 3 (UK) (A Diverse Production for C4/NVC Arts/Ovation - The Arts Network) and LET IT COME DOWN: THE LIFE OF PAUL BOWLES (Canada) (Requisite Productions)
Best Programme for Children and Young People: TELL US ABOUT YOUR LIFE - BATTLEFIELD DOCTOR (Japan) (NHK/Japan Broadcasting Corporation)

EMMY AWARDS - NATIONAL ACADEMY FOR TELEVISION ARTS AND SCIENCES

5220 Lankershim Blvd
North Hollywood
CA 91601
Tel: (1) 818 754 2800
Fax: (1) 818 761 2827
Email: academy-info@emmys.org
Website: www.emmys.tv

51ST ANNUAL PRIME TIME EMMY AWARDS

(for nighttime programming USA)
Awards in 52 categories presented 28th August in Pasadena (selection)

Outstanding Cinematography for a Series: Robert Primes for FELICITY: TODD MULCAHY, PART 2 (Imagine Television in association with Touchstone Television)
Outstanding Individual Achievement in Non-Fiction Programming: Samuel Henriques and Bob Perrin for cinematography on INVESTIGATIVE REPORTS: THE FARM: LIFE INSIDE ANGOLA PRISON (A&E Television Networks)
Outstanding Cinematography for a Miniseries or a Movie: Robbie Greenberg for WINCHELL (Fried Films in association with HBO Pictures)
Outstanding Guest Actress in a Comedy Series: Tracey Ullman in ALLY McBEAL (David E. Kelley Productions in association with 20th Century Fox)
Outstanding Guest Actor in a Comedy Series: Mel Brooks in MAD ABOUT YOU (NBC)
Outstanding Guest Actress in a Drama Series: Debra Monk in NYPD BLUE (ABC)
Outstanding Guest Actor in a Drama Series: Edward Herrmann in The PRACTICE (David E. Kelley Productions in association with 20th Century Fox)
Outstanding Casting for a Series: Georgianne Walken and Sheila Jaffe for The SOPRANOS (Chase Films/Brillstein Grey Entertainment in association with HBO Original Programming)
Outstanding Casting for a Miniseries or a Made for Television Movie: Juel Bestrop for WINCHELL (Fried Films in association with HBO Pictures)
Outstanding Classical Music-Dance Program: ITZHAK PERLMAN: FIDDLING FOR THE FUTURE (Four Oaks Foundation/Thirteen/WNET for PBS) Dir Allan Miller
Outstanding Music Composition for a Series (Dramatic Underscore): Carl Johnson for INVASION AMERICA: FINAL MISSION (Dreamworks Animation)
Outstanding Music Composition for a Miniseries or a Movie (Dramatic Underscore): Richard Hartley for

ALICE IN WONDERLAND (Hallmark Entertainment in association with Babelsberg International Film Produktion)
Outstanding Music Direction: Mark Adler for The RAT PACK (Home Box Office/Neal H. Moritz/Original Film Production)
Outstanding Music and Lyrics: AFI'S 100 YEARS – 100 MOVIES (American Film Institute presentation in association with Smith Hemion Productions) song title: "A Ticket To Dream" by Marvin Hamlisch, Alan Bergman, Marilyn Bergman
Outstanding Choreography: Judith Jamison for DANCE IN AMERICA: A HYMN FOR ALVIN AILEY (GREAT PERFORMANCES) (Roja Productions/Thirteen WNET) and Marguerite Derricks for GOODWILL GAMES OPENING CELEBRATION (Tall Pony Productions in association with Warner Bros.)
Outstanding Costume Design for a Series: Melina Root for THAT 70S SHOW: THAT DISCO EPISODE (Carsey-Werner Productions)
Outstanding Costume Design for a Miniseries or a Movie: Charles Knode for ALICE IN WONDERLAND (Hallmark Entertainment in association with Babelsberg International Film Produktion)
Outstanding Costume Design for a Variety or Music Program: Jef Billings for The SNOWDEN RAGGEDY ANN AND ANDY HOLIDAY SHOW (A Smith-Hemion Production in association with Target Stores)
Outstanding Animated Program (For Programming More Than One Hour): TODD MCFARLANE'S SPAWN (Todd Mcfarlane Entertainment in association with HBO Original Programming)
Outstanding Animated Program (For Programming One Hour or Less): KING OF THE HILL: AND THEY CALL IT BOBBY LOVE (Deedle-Dee Productions/Judgemental Films/3Arts Entertainment in association with 20th Century Fox TV)
Outstanding Children's Program: THE TRUTH ABOUT DRINKING; THE TEEN FILES produced by Arnold Shapiro, Allison Grodner, Mike Rabb
Outstanding Art Direction for a Series: Thomas A. Walsh, Kim Hix and Leslie Frankenheimer for BUDDY FARO (CBS/Spelling Television)
Outstanding Art Direction for a Variety or Music Program: Roy Christopher and Steve Olson for 71ST ANNUAL ACADEMY AWARDS (ABC)
Outstanding Art Direction for a Miniseries or a Movie: Hilda Stark Manos, Kathleen M. McKernin and Linda Spheeris for The RAT PACK (HBO)
Outstanding Special Visual Effects for a Series: Dan Curry, Ronald B. Moore, Mitch Suskin and team for STAR TREK: VOYAGER: DARK FRONTIER (Paramount Pictures)
Outstanding Special Visual Effects for a Miniseries or a Movie: David Booth, Richard Conway, Bob Hollow and team for ALICE IN WONDERLAND (Hallmark Entertainment in association with Babelsberg International Film Produktion)
Outstanding Non-Fiction Series: The AMERICAN EXPERIENCE (WGBH Education Foundation for PBS) produced by Margaret Drain, Mark Samels, Austin Hoyt
Outstanding Non-Fiction Special: THUG LIFE IN D.C. (Blowback Prouductions for HBO) Dir Marc Levin
Outstanding Sound Editing for a Series: Walter Newman and team for ER: THE STORM, PART 2 (Constant Productions/Amblin Television/Warner Bros. Television for NBC)
**Outstanding Sound Editing for a Miniseries, Movie or

a Special: Richard Taylor and team for STEPHEN KING'S STORM OF THE CENTURY: PART 2 (Mark Carliner Productions/Greengrass Productions for ABC)

27 categories presented 12th September 1999

Outstanding Drama Series: The PRACTICE (David E. Kelley Productions in association with 20th Century Fox)
Outstanding Directing for a Drama Series: Paris Barclay for NYPD BLUE: HEARTS AND SOULS (Steven Bochco Productions)
Outstanding Writing for a Drama Series: James Manos, Jr. and David Chase for THE SOPRANOS: COLLEGE (Chase Films/Brillstein-Grey Entertainment)
Outstanding Lead Actress in a Drama Series: Edi Falco in The SOPRANOS (Chase Films/Brillstein Grey Entertainment/HBO Original Programming)
Outstanding Lead Actor in a Drama Series: Dennis Franz in NYPD BLUE (Steven Bochco Productions)
Outstanding Supporting Actress in a Drama Series: Holland Taylor in The PRACTICE (David E. Kelley Productions/20th Century Fox)
Outstanding Supporting Actor in a Drama Series: Michael Badalucco The PRACTICE (David E. Kelley Productions/20th Century Fox)
Outstanding Comedy Series: ALLY McBEAL (David E. Kelley Productions in association with 20th Century Fox)
Outstanding Directing for a Comedy Series: Thomas Schlamme for SPORTS NIGHT (Imagine Television/Touchstone Television)
Outstanding Writing for a Comedy Series: Jay Kogen for FRASIER: MERRY CHRISTMAS, MRS. MOSKOWITZ (Grub Street Productions/Paramount Pictures)
Outstanding Lead Actress in a Comedy Series: Helen Hunt in MAD ABOUT YOU (Infront Productions/Nuance Productions/TriStar Television)
Outstanding Lead Actor in a Comedy Series: John Lithgow in 3RD ROCK FROM THE SUN (Carsey-Werner Productions)
Outstanding Supporting Actor in a Comedy Series: David Hyde Pierce in FRASIER (Grub Street Productions/Paramount Pictures)
Outstanding Supporting Actress in a Comedy Series: Kristen Johnston in 3RD ROCK FROM THE SUN (Carsey-Werner Productions for NBC)
Outstanding Variety, Music or Comedy Special: 1998 TONY AWARDS (Tony Awards Productions for CBS)
Outstanding Variety, Music or Comedy Series: LATE SHOW WITH DAVID LETTERMAN (Worldwide Pants for CBS)
Outstanding Directing for a Variety or Music Program: Paul Miller for 1998 TONY AWARDS (Tony Awards Productions for CBS)
Outstanding Writing for a Variety or Music Program: Tom Agna, Vernon Chatman, Louis CK, Lance Crouther, Gregory Greenberg, Ali Leroi, Steve O'Donnell, Chris Rock, Frank Sebastiano, Chuck Sklar, Jeff Stilson, Wanda Sykes-Hall, Mike Upchurch for The CHRIS ROCK SHOW (Chris Rock Enterprises/3Arts Entertainment/HBO Downtown Productions)
Outstanding Performance in a Variety or Music Program: John Leguizamo for JOHN LEGUIZAMO'S FREAK (Lower East Side Films for HBO)
Outstanding Miniseries: HORATIO HORNBLOWER (United Productions/Meridian Broadcasting/A&E Networks)
Outstanding Directing for a Miniseries or a Movie:

Allan Arkush for The TEMPTATIONS (de Passe Entertainment/Babelsberg International Film Productions)
Outstanding Writing for a Miniseries or a Movie: Ann Peacock for A LESSON BEFORE DYING (A Spanky Pictures Production in association with Ellen M. Krass Productions)
Outstanding Lead Actress in a Miniseries or a Movie: Helen Mirren in The PASSION OF AYN RAND (SHO/Producers Entertainment Group)
Outstanding Lead Actor in a Miniseries or a Movie: Stanley Tucci in WINCHELL (Fried Films/HBO Pictures)
Outstanding Supporting Actress in a Miniseries or a Movie: Anne Bancroft in DEEP IN MY HEART (The Konigsberg Company for CBS)
Outstanding Supporting Actor in a Miniseries or a Movie: Peter O'Toole in JOAN OF ARC (Alliance Atlantis Production/CBS Television Network/the Canadian Broadcasting Corporation/Endemol Entertainment)
Outstanding Made for Television Movie: A LESSON BEFORE DYING (A Spanky Pictures Production in association with Ellen M. Krass Productions)

12TH EUROPEAN FILM AWARDS
4th December 1999, Berlin
European Film AcademyKurf͵rstendamm 225
10719 Berlin
Tel: 49 (30) 887 1670
Fax: 49 (30) 887 167 77
Website: www.europeanfilmacademy.org/

Best European Film: TODO SOBRE MI MADRE (Spain/France) Dir Pedro Almodòvar
Best European Actress: Cecilia Roth for TODO SOBRE MI MADRE (Spain/France) Dir Pedro Amodòvar
Best European Actor: Ralph Fiennes for A NAPFÉNY ÍZE (Hungary/Germany/Canada/Austria/UK) Dir István Szabó
Best European Screenwriter: István Szabò and Israel Horovitz for A NAPFÉNY ÍZE (Hungary/Germany/Canada/Austria/UK) Dir István Szabò
Best European Cinematographer: Lajos Koltai for La LEGGENDA DELL PIANISTA SULL'OCEANO (Italy/US) Dir Giuseppe Tornatore and for A NAPFÉNY ÍZE (Hungary/Germany/Canada/Austria/UK)
Screen International Award for a non-European Film: The STRAIGHT STORY (US) Dir David Lynch
European Critic's Award - Prix Fipresci: ADIEU PLANCHER DES VACHES (France/Switzerland/Italy) Dir Otar Iosseliani
European Documentary Award - Prix Arte: BUENA VISTA SOCIAL CLUB (Germany) Dir Wim Wenders
European Short Film: BENVENUTO IN SAN SALVARIO (Italy) Dir Enrico Verra
European Discovery - Fassbinder Award: Tim Roth for The WAR ZONE (UK/Italy)
European Achievement in World Cinema: Antonio Banderas and Roman Polanski
European Film Academy Lifetime Achievement Award: Ennio Morricone

THE PEOPLE'S CHOICE AWARDS
Best European Director: Pedro Almodòvar for TODO SOBRE MI MADRE (Spain/France)
Best European Actor: Sean Connery for ENTRAPMENT (US/Germany) Dir Jon Amiel
Best European Actress: Catherine Zeta Jones for ENTRAPMENT (US/Germany) Dir Jon Amiel

EVENING STANDARD BRITISH FILM AWARDS 1998
Awarded in London 7th February 1999

Best Film: The GENERAL (Ireland/UK) Dir John Boorman
Best Actress: Julie Christie for AFTERGLOW (US) Dir Alan Rudolph
Best Actor: Derek Jacobi for LOVE IS THE DEVIL STUDY FOR A PORTRAIT OF FRANCIS BACON (UK/France/Japan) Dir John Maybury
Best Screenplay: Eileen Atkins for MRS DALLOWAY (UK) Dir Marleen Gorris
Best Technical Achievement: Ashley Rowe for TWENTYFOURSEVEN (UK) Dir Shane Meadows, The WOODLANDERS (UK) Dir Phil Agland, STILL CRAZY (UK) Dir Brian Gibson, The GOVERNESS (UK) Dir Sandra Goldbacher
Most Promising Newcomer: Guy Ritchie for LOCK, STOCK AND TWO SMOKING BARRELS (UK) Dir Guy Ritchie
Peter Sellers Award for Comedy: Bill Nighy for STILL CRAZY (UK) Dir Brian Gibson
Special Awards:
Ken Loach
Michael Caine

56th GOLDEN GLOBE AWARDS
Awarded in Los Angeles 24th January 1999

FILM
Best Motion Picture (Drama): SAVING PRIVATE RYAN (US) Dir Steven Spielberg
Best Actress (Drama): Cate Blanchett for ELIZABETH (UK) Dir Shekhar Kapur
Best Actor (Drama): Jim Carrey for The TRUMAN SHOW (US) Dir Peter Weir
Best Motion Picture (Comedy or Musical): SHAKESPEARE IN LOVE (US) Dir John Madden
Best Actress (Comedy or Musical): Gwyneth Paltrow for SHAKESPEARE IN LOVE (US) Dir John Madden
Best Actor (Comedy or Musical): Michael Caine for LITTLE VOICE (UK/US) Dir Mark Herman
Best Foreign Language Film: CENTRAL DO BRASIL (Brazil/France/Spain/Japan) Dir Walter Salles
Best Supporting Actress: Lynn Redgrave for GODS AND MONSTERS (US/UK) Dir Bill Condon
Best Supporting Actor: Ed Harris for The TRUMAN SHOW (US) Dir Peter Weir
Best Director: Steven Spielberg for SAVING PRIVATE RYAN (US)
Best Screenplay: Marc Norman and Tom Stoppard for SHAKESPEARE IN LOVE (US) Dir John Madden
Best Original Score: Burkhard Dallwitz / additional music by Philip Glass for The TRUMAN SHOW (US) Dir Peter Weir
Best Original Song: David Foster and Carole Bayer Sager (Italian translation Alberto Testa and Tony Renis) for "The Prayer", QUEST FOR CAMELOT THE MAGIC SWORD (US) Dir Frederick Du Chau
Cecil B. deMille Award: Jack Nicholson

TELEVISION
Best TV Series (Drama): The PRACTICE (David E. Kelley/Twentieth Century-Fox Film Corporation)
Best Actress (Drama Series): Keri Russell for FELICITY (Imagine TV/Touchstone Television)
Best Actor (Drama Series): Dylan McDermott for The PRACTICE (David E. Kelley/Twentieth Century-Fox Film Corporation)
Best TV Series (Comedy or Musical): ALLY McBEAL (David E. Kelley Productions/20th Century Fox TV)
Best Actress (Musical or Comedy Series): Jenna Elfman for DHARMA AND GREG (Chuck Lorre/4 to 6 Productions/Fox Broadcasting Company)
Best Actor (Musical or Comedy Series): Michael J. Fox for SPIN CITY (UBU Productions/Lottery Hill/Dreamworks SKG)
Best Mini-Series or TV Movie: FROM THE EARTH TO THE MOON (HBO/Clavius Base/Imagine Entertainment)
Best Actress (Mini-Series or TV Movie): Angelina Jolie for GIA (Marvin Worth Productions/Citadel Entertainment/Kahn Power Pictures)
Best Actor (Mini-Series or TV Movie): Stanley Tucci for WINCHELL (Fried Films/HBO Pictures)
Best Supporting Actress (Series, Mini-Series or TV Movie): Camryn Manheim for The PRACTICE (David E. Kelley/Twentieth Century-Fox Film Corporation) and Faye Dunaway for GIA (Marvin Worth Productions/Citadel Entertainment/Kahn Power Pictures)
Best Supporting Actor (Series, Mini-Series or TV Movie): Don Cheadle for The RAT PACK (HBO Pictures/Moritz Original) and Gregory Peck for MOBY DICK (Whale Productions/Southern Whale/Nine Network/UK-Australian Co-Productions/USA Pictures)

39th GOLDEN ROSE OF MONTREUX
Held 22 April 1999, Montreux

Golden Rose: The LEAGUE OF GENTLEMEN (BBC2)
Silver Rose (Comedy): FIKTIV (Prime Productions)
Bronze Rose (Comedy): BIG TRAIN (Talkback for BBC2)
Comedy Special Mention: VENTIL (SF/DRS) (Switzerland) and SPANK! (Omer Productions) (Isr)
Silver Rose (Sitcom): FATHER TED (Hat Trick Productions for Channel 4)
Bronze Rose (Sitcom): THIRD ROCK FROM THE SUN (Carsey-Werner Productions) (US)
Sitcom Special Mention: KISS ME KATE (BBC1) and IN EXILE (Assembly Film & Television) (Isr)
Silver Rose (Music): NOBODY DOES IT BETTER: THE MUSIC OF JAMES BOND (NVC Arts for Channel 4) Silver Rose (Variety): WHATEVER YOU WANT (Hat Trick Productions for BBC1)
Bronze Rose (Variety): DIVA AND THE MAESTRO (The Multimedia Group of Canada) CA
Silver Rose (Game Shows): WHO WANTS TO BE A MILLIONAIRE? (Celador Productions for ITV)
Bronze Rose (Game Shows): BRING ME THE HEAD OF LIGHT ENTERTAINMENT (AngliaTelevision/United Film and Television Productions for Channel 5)
Special Prize of the City of Montreux: A HYMN FOR ALVIN ALLEY (Thirteen/WNET) (US)
Press Prize: DINNERLADIES (Good Fun/Pozzitive Television for BBC1)

GRIERSON AWARD 1998
Awarded in London 25 March 1999

Best Documentary: INSIDE STORY: TONGUE TIED (BBC1 Dir Olivia Lichtenstein)
Jury Commendation: BORN IN THE USSR - 14UP

(BBC1 Dir Sergei Miroshnichenko) and The NAZIS: A WARNING FROM HISTORY - THE ROAD TO TREBLINKA (BBC2 Dir Laurence Rees)
Special Award: Michael Apted

34th KARLOVY VARY INTERNATIONAL FILM FESTIVAL
Held 2nd-10th July 1999, Karlovy Vary
Panska 1
110 00 Prague 1
Czech Republic
Tel: (420) 224 23 54 13
Fax: (420) 224 23 34 08
Email: Foundation@iffkv.cz
Web site: www.iffkv.cz/

Crystal Globe: HACHAVERIM SHEL YANA (Israel) Dir Arik Kaplun
Best Director: Aleksandr Rogozhkin for BLOKPOST (Russia)
Best Actress: Evlyn Kaplun for HACHAVERIM SHEL YANA (Israel) Dir Arik Kaplun
Best Actor: Hilmar Thate for WEGE IN DIE NACHT (Germany) Dir Andreas Kleinert
FIPRESCI Jury Award: PELISKY (Czech Republic) Dir Jan Hrebejk
FIPRESCI Jury Special Mention: DROP DEAD GORGEOUS (US/Germany) Dir Michael Patrick Jann
Jury Special Mention: PELISKY (Czech Republic) Dir Jan Hrebejk
Audience Award: FUCKING ÅMÅL (Sweden/Denmark) Dir Lukas Moodysson
Town of Karlovy Vary Award: SIBIRSKII TSIRIULNIK (Russia/France/Italy/Czech Republic) Dir Nikita Mikhalkov
Outstanding Contribution to World Cinema: Karel Kachyna and Franco Zeffirelli
Special Prize of the Jury: FUCKING ÅMÅL (Sweden/Denmark) Dir Lukas Moodysson
Ecumenical Jury Award: A REASONABLE MAN (South Africa/UK) Dir Gavin Hood
Ecumenical Jury Special Mention: BEAUTIFUL PEOPLE (UK) Dir Jasmin Dizdar and HACHAVERIM SHEL YANA (Israel) Dir Arik Kaplun
Don Quijote Award: FUCKING ÅMÅL (Sweden/Denmark) Dir Lukas Moodysson
Don Quijote Special Mention: FILLE SUR LE PONT (France) Dir Patrice Leconte
Freedom Award: OKRAINA (Russia) Dir Pyotr Lutsik
Emil Radok Award: Z PEKLA STESTÍ (Czech Republic) Dir Zdenek Troska

52ND LOCARNO INTERNATIONAL FILM FESTIVAL
Held 4th-14th August 1999, Locarno
Via Luini 3a
CH-6601 Locarno
Tel: (41) 91 756 2121
Fax: (41) 91 756 2149
Email: info@pardo.ch

Golden Leopard: PEAU D'HOMME, COEUR DE B TE (France) Dir Hélène Angel
Silver Leopard (New Cinema): BARAK (Russia/Germany) Dir Valerij Ogorodnikov
Silver Leopard (Young Cinema): La VIE NE ME FAIT

PAS PEUR (France/Switzerland) Dir Noémie Lvovsky
Special Prize (Bronze Leopard): to the actress Véra Briole for MADELEINE (France) Dir Laurent Bouhnik
Special Prize (Bronze Leopard): to the actor Serge Riaboukine for PEAU D'HOMME, COEUR DE B TE (France) Dir Hélène Angel
Special Jury Prize (Crossair): El MEDINA (Egypt/France) Dir Yousry Nasrallah
Jury Special Mention: to El MILAGRO DE P. TINTO (Spain) Dir Javier Fesser

LONDON CRITICS' CIRCLE FILM AWARDS
Awarded at the Dorchester Hotel, London 1999

Director of the Year: Peter Weir for The TRUMAN SHOW (US)
Film of the Year: SAVING PRIVATE RYAN (US) Dir Steven Spielberg
Foreign Language Fim of the Year: SHALL WE DANSU? (Japan) Dir Masayuki Suo
Actress of the Year: Cate Blanchett for ELIZABETH (UK) Dir Shekhar Kapur
Actor of the Year: Jack Nicholson for AS GOOD AS IT GETS (US) Dir James L. Brooks
British Newcomer of the Year: Peter Mullan for MY NAME IS JOE (Germany/UK/France) Dir Ken Loach
Screenwriter of the Year: Andrew Niccol for The TRUMAN SHOW (US) Dir Peter Weir
British Film of the Year: LOCK, STOCK AND TWO SMOKING BARRELS (UK) Dir Guy Ritchie
British Producer of the Year: Alison Owen, Tim Bevan and Eric Fellner for ELIZABETH (UK) Dir Shekhar Kapur
British Screenwriter of the Year: Guy Ritchie for LOCK, STOCK AND TWO SMOKING BARRELS (UK) Dir Guy Ritchie
British Actress of the Year: Helena Bonham Carter for WINGS OF THE DOVE (US/UK) Dir Iain Softley
British Actor of the Year: Brendan Gleeson for The GENERAL (Ireland/UK) Dir John Boorman
British Director of the Year: John Boorman for The GENERAL (Ireland/UK)
British Supporting Actress of the Year: Minnie Driver for GOOD WILL HUNTING (US) Dir Gus Van Sant and Kate Beckinsale for The LAST DAYS OF DISCO (US) Dir Whit Stillman
British Supporting Actor of the Year: Nigel Hawthorne for The OBJECT OF MY AFFECTION (US) Dir Nicholas Hytner
The Dilys Powell Award: Albert Finney and John Hurt
Lifetime Achievement Award: John Boorman and John Box

43RD LONDON FILM FESTIVAL
Held 4th-19th November 1999
National Film Theatre
South Bank
Waterloo
London SE1 8XT
Tel: 44 020 7815 1322/1323
Fax: 44 020 7633 0786
Email: (contact Sarah Lutton, Festival Administrator) sarahlutton@bfi.org.uk
Website: www.lff.org.uk

Sutherland Trophy: RATCATCHER (UK/France) Dir

Lynne Ramsay
Special Mention: FUCKING ÅMÅL (Sweden/Denmark)
Dir Lukas Moodysson
Fipresci Award: BOYS DON'T CRY (US) Dir Kimberly
Peirce

39th MONTE CARLO TELEVISION FESTIVAL
Held 18th-24th February 1999, Monte Carlo

Special Prize of H.S.H. Prince Rainier III:
OPERATION HVIDVASK (DR TV) (Denmark)
Prize of the Monaco Red Cross: L'ENFANT DES
TERRES BLONDES (France 3) (France)
AMADE & UNESCO Prize: L'ENFANT DES TERRES
BLONDES (France 3) (France)
Prix Unda (Best Television Film): Le BONHEUR
D'AUTRUI (Télévision Polonaise) (Poland)
European Produce Award: Telfrance (France) for its
fiction productions over the last 2 years
FILMS FOR TV
Gold Nymph (Best Film): L'ENFANT DES TERRES
BLONDES (France 3) (France)
Silver Nymph (Best Script): Shin-Ichi Ichikawa for YU-
KON (Chubu-Nippon Broadcasting Co) (Japan)
Silver Nymph (Best Direction): Edouard Niermans for
L'ENFANT DES TERRES BLONDES (France 3) (France)
Silver Nymph (Best Actress): Amanda Burton for The
GIFT (Tetra Films for BBC1) (UK)
Silver Nymph (Best Actor): Neil Dudgeon for The GIFT
(Tetra Films for BBC1) (UK)
MINI-SERIES
Gold Nymph (Best Mini-Series): OPERNBALL (Atlas
International Film) (Germany)
Silver Nymph (Best Script): Sandro Petraglia and
Stefano Rulli for La VITA CHE VERRA (Rai Due) (Italy)
Silver Nymph (Best Direction): Urs Egger for
OPERNBALL (Atlas International Film) (Germany)
Silver Nymph (Best Actress): Lena Mossegard for The
WOMAN IN THE LOCKED ROOM (Sveriges
Television) (Sweden)
Silver Nymph (Best Actor): Tony Doyle for AMONGST
WOMEN (Parallel Film Productions for BBC Northern
Ireland) (UK)
Special Mention: VANITY FAIR (BBC1) (UK)
NEWS & CURRENT AFFAIRS PROGRAMMES
Gold Nymph: PROFESSION REPORTER: EMBARGO
(TF1) (France)
Silver Nymph: Les HOMMES EN NOIR (Télévision
Suisse Romande) (Switzerland)
Silver Nymph: CORRESPONDENT SPECIAL: THE
UNFINISHED WAR (BBC2) (UK)
Silver Nymph: VILLAGE HEAD ELECTION (China
Control TV) (China)
Special Mention: Les CRAMPONS DE LA LIBERTE
(Doc en Stock) (France)

71st OSCARS -ACADEMY OF MOTION PICTURE ARTS AND SCIENCES
Awarded 21st March 1999, Los Angeles

Best Film: SHAKESPEARE IN LOVE (US) Dir John
Madden
Best Director: Steven Spielberg for SAVING PRIVATE
RYAN (US)
Best Original Screenplay: Marc Norman and Tom

Stoppard for SHAKESPEARE IN LOVE (US) Dir John
Madden
Best Screenplay Adaptation: Bill Condon for GODS
AND MONSTERS (US/UK) Dir Bill Condon
Best Actress: Gwyneth Paltrow for SHAKESPEARE IN
LOVE (US) Dir John Madden
Best Actor: Roberto Benigni for La VITA é BELLA
(Italy) Dir Roberto Benigni
Best Supporting Actress: Judi Dench for
SHAKESPEARE IN LOVE (US) Dir John Madden
Best Supporting Actor: James Coburn for AFFLICTION
(US) Dir Paul Schrader
Best Cinematography: Janusz Kaminski for SAVING
PRIVATE RYAN (US) Dir Steven Spielberg
Best Original Song: Stephen Schwartz for "When You
Believe" The PRINCE OF EGYPT (US) Dir Brenda
Chapman
Best Costume Design: Sandy Powell for
SHAKESPEARE IN LOVE (US) Dir John Madden
Best Make-Up: Jenny Shircore for ELIZABETH (UK)
Dir Shekhar Kapur
Best Art Direction: Martin Childs and Jill Quertier for
SHAKESPEARE IN LOVE (US) Dir John Madden
Life Achievement Award: Elia Kazan
Best Documentary Feature: The LAST DAYS (US) Dir
Jim Moll
Best Documentary Short: The PERSONALS:
IMPROVISATIONS ON ROMANCE IN THE GOLDEN
YEARS (US) Dir Keiko Ibi
Best Visual Effects: Joel Hynek, Nicholas Brooks, Stuart
Robertson and Kevin Mack for WHAT DREAMS MAY
COME (US/NZ) Dir Vincent Ward
The Irving G. Thalberg Award: Norman Jewison
Best Editing: Michael Kahn for SAVING PRIVATE
RYAN (US) Dir Steven Spielberg
Best Original Dramatic Score: Nicola Piovani for La
VITA É BELLA (Italy) Dir Roberto Benigni
Best Original Musical or Comedy Score: Stephen
Warbeck for SHAKESPEARE IN LOVE (US) Dir John
Madden
Best Foreign Language Film: La VITAÉ BELLA (Italy)
Dir Roberto Benigni
Best Sound: Gary Rydstrom, Gary Summers, Andy
Nelson and Ronald Judkins for SAVING PRIVATE RYAN
(US) Dir Steven Spielberg
Best Sound Effects Editing: Gary Rydstrom and Richard
Hymns for SAVING PRIVATE RYAN (US) Dir Steven
Spielberg
Best Short Film (Animated): BUNNY (US) Dir Chris
Wedge
Best Short Film (Live Action): ELECTION NIGHT
(Denmark) Anders Thomas Jensen

ROYAL TELEVISION SOCIETY AWARDS
RTS PROGRAMME AWARDS
Awarded in London 29th March 1999

Single Drama: A RATHER ENGLISH MARRIAGE
(Wall to Wall Television for BBC2)
Drama Series: JONATHAN CREEK (BBC Production
for BBC1)
Drama Serial: A YOUNG PERSON'S GUIDE TO
BECOMING A ROCK STAR (Company TV for Channel 4)
Team: GOODNESS GRACIOUS ME (BBC Production
for BBC2)
Network Newcomer (Behind the Screen): Damien
O'Donnell for THIRTY FIVE ASIDE (Clingfilm

Productions for BBC2)

Network Newcomer (On Screen): Tony Maudsley for A LIFE FOR A LIFE (Celtic/Picture Palace for ITV)

Best Actress: Thora Hird for TALKING HEADS: WAITING FOR THE TELEGRAM (Slow Motion for BBC2)

Best Actor: Ray Winstone for OUR BOY (Wall to Wall Television for BBC1)

Regional Programme: A LIGHT IN THE VALLEY (BBC Wales)

Regional Documentary: PUT TO THE TEST (Brian Waddell Productions for BBC Northern Ireland)

Regional Presenter: Noel Thompson (BBC Northern Ireland)

Presenter: David Attenborough for LIFE OF BIRDS (BBC Production for BBC1)

Television Performance: Rory Bremner for RORY BREMNER WHO ELSE? (Vera Productions for Channel 4)

Writer's Award: Peter Berry for A LIFE FOR A LIFE (Celtic/Picture Palace for ITV)

Entertainment: WHO WANTS TO BE A MILLIONAIRE? (Celador Productions for ITV)

Situation Comedy and Comedy Drama: COLD FEET (Granada Television)

Children's Drama: MICROSOAP (BBC Production/Buena Vista Productions for BBC1)

Children's Entertainment: The FIRST SNOW OF WINTER (Hibbert Ralph Entertainment for BBC1)

Children's Factual: The FAME GAME (BBC Scotland for BBC1)

Documentary Series: WINDRUSH (BBC Production for BBC2)

Documentary Strand: The NATURAL WORLD (BBC Production for BBC2)

Single Documentary: MODERN TIMES: DRINKING FOR ENGLAND (Century Films for BBC2)

Features (Prime Time): TIME TEAM (Videotext/Picture House for Channel 4)

Features (Daytime): CITY HOSPITAL (Topical Television for BBC1)

Arts: CLOSE UP: THIS ENGLAND (BBC Production for BBC2)

Special Award: FATHER TED (Hat Trick Productions for Channel 4)

RTS EDUCATIONAL AWARDS
Awarded in London on 15th April 1999

SCHOOLS TELEVISION

Pre-School & Infants: RAT-A-TAT-TAT - WINNIE THE WITCH (Open Mind Productions for Channel 4)

Primary (Arts): MUSIC MAKERS: PROFESSOR ALLEGRO - IN THE FIELDS (BBC Education)

Primary (Humanities): ALL ABOUT US - KARL'S STORY (Television Junction for Channel 4)

Primary (Science): STAGE TWO SCIENCE - ACTION FORCES - PUSHING AND PULLING (Scottish Television for Channel 4)

Secondary (Arts): SPORTSBANK DANCE TV DANCE ATHLETES (BBC Education)

Secondary (Humanities): TURNING POINTS: EMMA'S STORY (BBC Education)

Secondary (Science): SHORT CIRCUIT: BLOOD (BBC Education)

ADULT EDUCATIONAL TELEVISION

Education and Training: STUDENT CHOICE '98 (Wobbly Picture Productions for BBC Education)

Personal Education: SMASHED - ALCOHOL SEASON - LAST ORDERS (Evans Woolfe for Channel 4)

General: The DROP DEAD SHOW (Granada Production for Channel 4)

Campaigns and Seasons: COMPUTERS DON'T BITE (BBC Education) RTS/NIACE: The DROP DEAD SHOW (Granada Production for Channel 4)

Multimedia Award: Dynamo Website (www.bbc.co.uk/education/parents/dynamo/) (BBC Education)

RTS TELEVISION SPORTS AWARDS
Awarded in London 29th April 1999

Live Outside Broadcast Coverage of the Year: The FIRST DIVISION PLAY-OFF (Sky Sports)

Sports Documentary: The MAN WHO JUMPED TO EARTH (BBC Wales for BBC1)

Sports News: NEWS AT TEN - WORLD CUP TROUBLE (ITN News on ITV)

Sports Commentator: Clive Tyldesley (ITV Sport)

Sports Presenter: Desmond Lynam (BBC Sport)

Sports Pundit: Martin Brundle

Regional Sports Documentary: BRED FOR THE RED: HOME TRUTHS (BBC Northern Ireland)

Regional Sports Programme (Actuality): GOODWOOD HISTORIC RACING (Meridian Broadcasting)

Regional Sports Programme (Entertainment): EXTREME (Westcountry Television)

Regional Sports Presenter or Commentator: Hazel Irvine (BBC Scotland)

Regional Sports News: MERIDIAN TONIGHT (Meridian Broadcasting)

Newcomer: Guy Mowbray (Eurosport)

Sports Innovation: CHELTENHAM - WIRE CAM (Channel 4)

Sports Programme of the Year (Entertainment): A QUESTION OF SPORT (BBC Production for BBC1)

Television Sports Award of the Year: Sky Sports Football Production Team

Judges Award: Jimmy Hill

RTS JOURNALISM AWARDS
Awarded in London 11th May 1999

News Award (International): NINE O'CLOCK NEWS - The Massacre at Drenica (BBC News)

News Award (Home): GMTV - Drumcree: Portadown Divided (GMTV/Reuters for ITV)

Regional Daily News Magazine: LONDON TONIGHT (London News Network)

Television Technician of the Year: Nikki Millard (BBC News)

Interview of the Year: Dermot Murnaghan (interview of Peter Mandelson) (ITN News on ITV)

Regional Current Affairs: The GHOST OF PIPER ALPHA (TV6 for BBC Scotland)

Current Affairs (International): The SERBS LAST STAND (BBC2)

Current Affairs (Home): DISPATCHES: INSIDE THE ALF (David Monaghan Productions)

Television Journalist of the Year: David Loyn (BBC News)

Young Journalist of the Year: Peter Lane (5 News ITN)

Programme of the Year: NEWS AT TEN (ITN News on ITV)

Judges' Award: WORLD IN ACTION (Granada Television for ITV)

56TH VENICE FILM FESTIVAL
Held 1st-11th September 1999, Venice
San Marco, 1364/a Ca'Giustinian
30124 Venice
Tel: 0039 41 5218711
Fax: 0039 41 5227539
Email: das@labiennale.com
Website: 194.185.28.38/

Golden Lion for Best Film: YE GE DOU BU NENG SHAO (China) Dir Zhang Yimou
Jury Gran Prix: Le VENT NOUS EMPORTERA (France/Iran) Dir Abbas Kiarostami
Special Prize for Best Director: Zhang Yuan for GUO NIAN HUI JIA (China/Italy)
Coppa Volpi for Best Actor: Jim Broadbent for TOPSY TURVY (UK/US) Dir Mike Leigh
Coppa Volpi for Best Actress: Nathalie Baye for Une LIAISON PORNOGRAPHIQUE (Belgium/France/Luxembourg/Switzerland) Dir Frédéric Fonteyne
Marcello Mastroianni Award for Best Young Emerging Actor or Actress: Nina Proll for NORDRAND (Austria/Germany/Switzerland) Dir Barbara Albert
Golden Medal of the Italian Senate: RIEN A'FAIRE (France) Dir Marion Vernoux
"Venezia Opera Prima-Luigi de Laurentiis" Award: QUESTO E'IL GIARDINO (Italy) Dir Giovanni Davide Maderna
Special Mention: BYE BYE AFRICA (France/Chad) Dir Mahamat Saleh Haroun
Corto-Cortissimo Silver Lion: PORTRAIT OF A YOUNG MAN DROWNING (South Africa) Dir Teboho Mahlatsi
Special Mention: SE-TONG (Australia/China) Dir Heng Tang

This section features some of the principal festival prizes and awards from January 2000 to June 2000. Compiled by Laura Pearson

Awards 2000 -

BAFTA FILM AWARDS

Awarded 9th April 2000, London
195 Piccadilly
London W1V OLN
Tel: 020 7734 0022
Fax: 020 7734 1792
Website: www.bafta.org

The Academy Fellowships: Michael Caine & Stanley Kubrick
The Michael Balcon Award for Outstanding British Contribution to Cinema: Joyce Herlihy
The Alexander Korda Award for Outstanding British Film of the Year: EAST IS EAST (UK) Dir Damien O'Donnell
Best Film: AMERICAN BEAUTY (US) Dir Sam Mendes
The David Lean Award for Best Achievement in Direction: Pedro Almodòvar for TODO SOBRE MI MADRE (Spain/France)
Best Original Screenplay: Charlie Kaufman for BEING JOHN MALKOVICH (US) Dir Spike Jonze
Best Adapted Screenplay: Neil Jordan for The END OF THE AFFAIR (US/Germany) Dir Neil Jordan
Best Actress: Annette Bening for AMERICAN BEAUTY (US) Dir Sam Mendes
Best Actor: Kevin Spacey for AMERICAN BEAUTY (US) Dir Sam Mendes
Best Supporting Actress: Maggie Smith for Un Té CON IL DUCE (Italy/UK) Dir Franco Zeffirelli
Best Supporting Actor: Jude Law for The TALENTED MR RIPLEY (US) Dir Anthony Minghella
Best Film not in the English Language: TODO SOBRE MI MADRE (Spain/France) Dir Pedro Almodòvar
The Anthony Asquith Award for Achievement in Film Music: Thomas Newman for AMERICAN BEAUTY (US) Dir Sam Mendes
The Carl Foreman Award for Newcomer in British Film: Lynne Ramsay for RATCATCHER (UK) Dir Lynne Ramsay
Best Cinematography: Conrad L. Hall for AMERICAN BEAUTY (US) Dir Sam Mendes
Best Production Design: Rick Heinrichs for SLEEPY HOLLOW (US/Germany) Dir Tim Burton
Best Costume Design: Colleen Atwood for SLEEPY HOLLOW (US/Germany) Dir Tim Burton
Best Editing: Tariq Anwar and Christopher Greenbury for AMERICAN BEAUTY (US) Dir Sam Mendes
Best Sound: David Lee, John Reitz, Gregg Rudloff, David Campbell and Dane A. Davis for The MATRIX (US/Australia) Dir Andy Wachowski
Best Achievement in Special Visual Effects: John Gaeta, Steve Courtley, Janek Sirrs and Jon Thum for The MATRIX (US/Australia) Dir Andy Wachowski
Best Makeup/Hair: Christine Blundell for TOPSY TURVY (UK/US) Dir Mike Leigh
Best Short Film: WHO'S MY FAVOURITE GIRL (Scotland) Dir Adrian McDowall
Best Short Animation: The MAN WITH BEAUTIFUL EYES (UK) Dir Jonathan Hodgson
The Orange Audience Award: NOTTING HILL (US/UK) Dir Roger Michell

BAFTA TELEVISION AWARDS

14th May 2000
195 Piccadilly
London W1V OLN
Tel: 020 7734 0022
Website: www.bafta.org

Best Actress: Thora Hird for LOST FOR WORDS (Yorkshire Television in association with Bard Entertainment for ITV)
Best Actor: Michael Gambon for WIVES & DAUGHTERS (WGBH (Boston)/BBC for BBC1)
Best Entertainment Performance: Graham Norton for SO GRAHAM NORTON (United Film & Television Production for C4)
Best Comedy Performance: Caroline Aherne for The ROYLE FAMILY (Granada Television for BBC Manchester, BBC1)
The Richard Dimbleby Award for Best Presenter (Factual, Features and News): Jeremy Paxman for NEWSNIGHT (BBC2)
Best Single Drama: Mark Redhead and Paul Greengrass for The MURDER OF STEPHEN LAWRENCE (Granada Television in association with Vanson Productions for ITV)
Best Drama Series: The COPS (World Productions for BBC2)
The Lew Grade Award (voted by readers of the Radio Times): A TOUCH OF FROST (Yorkshire TV for ITV)
Best Soap: Matthew Robinson for EASTENDERS (BBC1)
Best Drama Serial: Nigel Stafford-Clark, Peter Kosminsky and Leigh Jackson for WARRIORS (BBC Films in association with Deep Indigo Productions for BBC1)
Best Factual Series: Adam Curtis for The MAYFAIR SET (BBC2)
Best Entertainment (Programme or Series): ROBBIE THE REINDEER: HOOVES OF FIRE (BBC Animation Unit for BBC1)
Best Comedy (Programme or Series): The LEAGUE OF GENTLEMEN (BBC2)
Best Situation Comedy Award: Kenton Allen, Caroline Aherne and Craig Cash for The ROYLE FAMILY (Granada Television for BBC Manchester, BBC1)
Best Features: Robert Thirkell and Nick Mirsky for BLOOD ON THE CARPET (BBC2)
The Huw Wheldon Award for the Best Arts Programme or Series: Ian MacMillan and Matt Collings for THIS IS MODERN ART (Oxford Television Company for C4)
Best Sports Programme: Jeff Foulser and Gary Franses for TEST CRICKET (Sunset and Vine Productions for C4)
News and Current Affairs Journalism: John Simpson and the BBC News team for their coverage of the Kosovo conflict (BBC1)
Innovation: John Lynch, Tim Haines and Mike Milne for WALKING WITH DINOSAURS (BBC/Discovery Channel/TV Asahi in association with ProSieben and France 3 for BBC1)
The Flaherty Documentary Award: Kim Longinotto and Ziba Mir-Hosseini for TRUE STORIES - DIVORCE IRANIAN STYLE (20th Century Vixen Productions for C4)
The Academy Fellowship: Peter Bazalgette
The Dennis Potter Award: Tony Marchant
The Special Award: Honor Blackman, Joanna Lumley, Diana Rigg and Linda Thorson for The AVENGERS series (ABC Television)

BAFTA TELEVISION CRAFT AWARDS
(1st presentation)
Awarded in London 30th April 2000

Best Costume Design: Odile Dicks-Mireaux for GREAT EXPECTATIONS (WGBH (Boston)/BBC for BBC2)
Best Design: Gerry Scott for WIVES & DAUGHTERS (WGBH (Boston)/BBC for BBC1)
Best Editing (Factual): Malcolm Daniel for INSIDE STORY - CHILD OF THE DEATH CAMPS (BBC1)
Best Editing (Fiction/Entertainment): Tony Cranstoun for The ROYLE FAMILY (Granada Television for BBC Manchester, BBC1)
Best Graphic Design: Philip Dupee for The VICE (Carlton UK Television for ITV)
Best Hair & Makeup: Lisa Westcott for WIVES & DAUGHTERS (WGBH (Boston)/BBC for BBC1)
Best Original Television Music: Ben Bartlett for WALKING WITH DINOSAURS (BBC/Discovery Channel/TV Asahi in association with ProSieben and France 3 for BBC1)
Best Photography (Factual): Chip Houseman and Hugh Miles for WILDLIFE SPECIAL - TIGER (BBC Bristol/Mike Birkhead Associates for BBC1)
Best Photography & Lighting (Fiction/Entertainment): Fred Tammes for WIVES & DAUGHTERS (WGBH (Boston)/BBC for BBC1)
Best Sound (Factual): John Pritchard and Bob Jackson for MICHAEL PALIN'S HEMINGWAY ADVENTURE (Prominent Television for BBC1)
Best Sound (Fiction/Entertainment): David Old, Graham Headicar, Maurice Hillier, Danny Longhurst for WARRIORS (BBC Films in association with Deep Indigo Productions)

50TH BERLIN INTERNATIONAL FILM FESTIVAL
Held 9th-20th February 2000, Berlin
Internationale Filmfestspiele Berlin
Potsdamer Straße 5
D-10785 Berlin
Tel: (49) 030 25 920
Fax: (49) 030 25 920 299
Email: info@berlinale.de
Website: www.berlinale.de

INTERNATIONAL JURY
Golden Bear: MAGNOLIA (US) Dir Paul Thomas Anderson
Silver Bear (Grand Jury Prize): WO DE FU QIN MU QIN (China) Dir Zhang Yimou
Silver Bear - Best Actress: Bibiana Beglau and Nadja Uhl for Die STILLE NACH DEM SCHUSS (Germany) Dir Volker Schloendorff
Silver Bear - Best Actor: Denzel Washington for The HURRICANE (US) Dir Norman Jewison
Silver Bear - Best Director: Milos Forman for MAN ON THE MOON (US)
Silver Bear (Jury Prize): The MILLION DOLLAR HOTEL (Germany/US) Dir Wim Wenders
Silver Bear - Oustanding Artistic Achievement: to the entire cast of PARADISO - SIEBEN TAGE MIT SIEBEN FRAUEN (Germany) Dir Rudolf Thome
Golden Bear - Best Short Film: HOMMAGE ¿ ALFRED LEPETIT (France) Dir Jean Rousselot
Silver Bear - Best Short Film: MEDIA (Czech Republic) Dir Pavel Koutsky

Blue Angel (AGICOA Copyright) Prize for Best European Film: Die STILLE NACH DEM SCHUSS (Germany) Dir Volker Schloendorff
Alfred Bauer Prize for Debut Film: DOKURITSU SHONEN GASSHOUDAN (Japan) Dir Akira Ogata

OTHER AWARDS
FIPRESCI (International Critics) Prizes: Competition - La CHAMBRE DES MAGICIENNES (France) Dir Claude Miller
Forum - MONDAY (Japan) Dir Sabu
Panorama - PARAGRAPH 175 (US) Dir Rob Epstein and Jeffrey Friedman
Ecumenical Jury Prizes: Competition - WO DE FU QIN MU QIN (China) Dir Zhang Yimou
Short Film: - MEDIA (Czech Republic) Dir Pavel Koutsky
Panorama - BOTIN DE GUERRA (Argentina/Spain) Dir David Blaustein
Special Prize, Short Film - ECHO (Belgium) Dir Frédéric Roullier-Gall
Forum - De GROTE VAKANTIE (Netherlands) Dir Jan van der Keuken
Special Prize - CINÉ.MA VÉRITÉ: DEFINING THE MOMENT (Canada) Dir Peter Wintonick
Peace Film Prize: LONG DAY'S JOURNEY INTO DAY - SOUTH AFRICA'S SEARCH FOR TRUTH AND RECONCILIATION (US) Dir Deborah Hoffmann and Frances Reid
Wolfgang Staudte Prize: Forum - MARSAL (Croatia) Dir Vinco Bresan
Special Mention - TRUTHS: A STREAM (Japan) Dir Masahiro Tsuchi
Don Quixote Prize: Forum - I EARINI SYNAXIS TON AGROFYLAKON (Greece) Dir Dimos Avdeliodis
Special Mention - MONDAY (Japan) Dir Sabu
Special Mention - RUANG TALOK 69 (Thailand) Dir Pen-ek Ratanaruang
CICAE Prizes: Panorama - SALTWATER (Ireland) Dir Conor McPherson
Forum - I EARINI SYNAXIS TON AGROFYLAKON (Greece) Dir Dimos Avdeliodis
Guild of German Art House Cinemas Prize: The HURRICANE (US) Dir Norman Jewison
Caligari Prize: I EARINI SYNAXIS TON AGROFYLAKON (Greece) Dir Dimos Avdeliodis
Special Mention - MONDAY (Japan) Dir Sabu
NETPAC PRIZE: Forum - BARIWALI (India) Dir Rituparno Ghosh and NABBIE NO KOI (Japan) Dir Yuji Nakae
Special Mention - GOCHOO MALIGEE (Korea) Dir Jan Hee-Sun
International Jury, Children's Film Festival: MAN VAN STAAL (Belgium) Dir Vincent Bal and TSATSIKI, MORSAN OCH POLISEN (Sweden/Norway/Denmark) Dir Ella Lemhagen
Special Mention - MANOLITO GAFOTAS (Spain) Dir Miguel Albaladejo
Special Mention - DOKHTARI BA KAFSH-HAYE-KATANI (Iran) Dir Rassul Sadr Ameli
Best Short Film - KONGEN SOM VILLE HA MER EN KRONE (Norway) Dir Randall Meyers and Anita Killi and PUGALO (Russia) Dir Alexander Kott
Crystal Bear, Young People's Jury, Children's Film Festival: TSATSIKI, MORSAN OCH POLISEN (Sweden/Norway/Denmark) Dir Ella Lemhagen
Special Mention - MR. RICE'S SECRET (Canada) Dir Nicholas Kendall

Crystal Bear Best Short Film - En DJEVEL I SKAPET (Norway) Dir Lars Berg
Reader's Prize of the 'Berliner Morgenpost': MAGNOLIA (US) Dir Paul Thomas Anderson
Manfred Satzgeber Prize: El MAR (Spain) Dir Augusti Villaronga
Panorama Short Film Prize of the New York Film Academy: HARTES BROT (Germany) Dir Nathalie Percillier and HOP, SKIP & JUMP (Slovenia/Bosnia) Dir Srdjan Vuletic
Special Mention - SPARKLEHORSE (Canada) Dir Gariné Torossian
Special Mention - 2~3 (US) Dir Richard Press
New York Film Academy Scholarship: Gianluca Vallero for FINIMONDO (Germany)
Panorama Audience Prize: NATIONALE 7 (France) Dir Jean-Pierre Sinapi
Gay Teddy Bear for Best Feature: GOUTTES D'EAU SUR PIERRES BRÛLANTES Dir Franáois Ozon
Gay Teddy Bear for Best Documentary: PARAGRAPH 175 (US) Dir Rob Epstein and Jeffrey Friedman
Gay Teddy Bear for Best Short: HARTES BROT (Germany) Dir Nathalie Percillier
Gay Teddy Bear Jury Award: DR'LE DE FELIX (France) Dir Olivier Ducastel and Jacques Martineau and CHRISSY (Australia) Dir Jacqui North
Reader's Prize of the 'Siegessäule' [Berlin's gay/lesbian magazine]: DRÔLE DE FELIX (France) Dir Olivier Ducastel and Jacques Martineau
Reader's Prize of the 'Berliner Zeitung': LONG NIGHT'S JOURNEY INTO DAY - SOUTH AFRICA'S SEARCH FOR TRUTH AND RECONCILIATION (US) Dir Deborah Hoffman and Frances Reid
Special Mention - I EARINI SYNAXIS TON AGROFYLAKON (Greece) Dir Dimos Avdeliodis
Special Mention - BEAU TRAVAIL (France) Dir Claire Denis

BFI FELLOWSHIPS
London
British Film Institute
21 Stephen Street
London W1P
Tel: (44) 020 7255 1444
Fax: (44) 020 7436 0439
Web site: www.bfi.org.uk

Awarded 24th May 2000 to Dame Elizabeth Taylor

BROADCASTING PRESS GUILD AWARDS 1999
Held mid-April 2000, London
c/o Richard Last
Tiverton, The Ridge
Woking
Surrey GU22 7EQ
Tel: 01483 764895

Writer's Award: Stephen Poliakoff for SHOOTING THE PAST (Talkback for BBC Television, BBC2)
Harvey Lee Award: Cilla Black
Best Actress: Justine Waddell for WIVES AND DAUGHTERS (BBCTV in association with WGBH (Boston) for BBC1)
Best Actor: Tony Doyle for BALLYKISSANGEL (World Productions/BBC Northern Ireland for BBC1) and FOUR

FATHERS (Sally Head Productions for ITV)
Best Drama Serial: WIVES AND DAUGHTERS (BBC TV in association with WGBH (Boston) for BBC1)
Best Entertainment: BREMNER, BIRD AND FORTUNE (Vera Productions for C4)
Best Performer: Chris Tarrant for WHO WANTS TO BE A MILLIONAIRE? (Celador Productions for ITV)
Best Single Drama: WARRIORS (BBC TV in association with Deep Indigo Productions)

53rd CANNES FESTIVAL
10th-21st May 2000, Cannes
99 Boulevard Malesherbes
75008 Paris
Tel: (33) 1 45 61 66 00
Fax: (33) 1 45 61 45 88
Email: RDF@festival-cannes.fr
Website: www.festival-cannes.org

Feature Film Palme d'Or: DANCER IN THE DARK (Denmark/Sweden/France/Germany) Dir Lars von Trier
Grand Jury Prize: GUIZI LAI LE (China) Dir Jiang Wen
Best Actress: Björk for DANCER IN THE DARK (Denmark/Sweden/France/Germany) Dir Lars von Trier
Best Actor: Tony Leung Chiu-Wai for IN THE MOOD FOR LOVE (Hong Kong/France) Dir Wong Kar-Wai
Best Director: Edward Yang for YI YI (Taiwan/Japan)
Best Screenplay: Neil LaBute for NURSE BETTY (US) Dir Neil LaBute
Jury Prize: (co-winners) SÅNGER FRÅN ANDRA VÅNINGEN (Sweden/Denmark/Norway/France/Germany) Dir Roy Andersson and TAKHTÉ SIAH (Iran/Italy/Japan) Dir Samira Makhmalbaf
Camera d'Or: (co-winners) DJOMEH (Iran/France) Dir Hassan Yektapanah and ZAMANI BARAYE MASTI ASBHA (Iran) Dir Bahman Ghobadi
Grand Prix Technique de la Commission Supèrieure Technique de L'image et du Son: Christopher Doyle, Mark Li Ping Bing and William Chang Suk-Ping for IN THE MOOD FOR LOVE (Hong Kong/France) Dir Wong Kar-Wai
Short Films
Palme d'Or: ANINO (Philippines) Dir Raymond Red CineFondation
First Prize: FIVE FEET HIGH AND RISING (US) Dir Peter Sollett
Second Prize: (co-winners) KISS IT UP TO GOD (US) Dir Caran Hartsfield and KINU'ACH (Israel) Dir Amit Sakomski
Third Prize: (co-winners) INDIEN (Denmark) Dir Pernille Fisher Christensen and CUOC XE DEM (Vietnam/France) Dir Bui Thac Chuyên

25th CÉSARS
Awarded in Paris 19th February 2000
Césars du Cinéma Français
19 av.du Pdt Wilson
75116 Paris
Tel.01 47 23 72 33
Fax.01 40 70 02 91
Web site: www.césars.com

Best Film: VÉNUS BEAUTÉ (INSTITUT) (France) Dir Tonie Marshall
Best Actress: Karin Viard in HAUT LES COEURS!

(France/Belgium) Dir Solveig Anspach
Best Actor: Daniel Auteuil in La FILLE SUR LE PONT (France) Dir Patrice Leconte
Best Supporting Actress: Charlotte Gainsbourg in La BÛCHE (France) Dir Danièle Thompson
Best Supporting Actor: François Berléand in MA PETITE ENTREPRISE (France) Dir Pierre Jolivet
Best Female Newcomer: Audrey Tautou in VÉNUS BEAUTÉ (INSTITUT) (France) Dir Tonie Marshall
Best Male Newcomer: Eric Caravaca in C'EST QUOI LA VIE? (France) Dir FranÁois Dupeyron
Best Director: Tonie Marshall for VÉNUS BEAUTÉ (INSTITUT) (France)
Best Original Screenplay: Tonie Marshall for VÉNUS BEAUTÉ (INSTITUT) Dir Tonie Marshall
Best Foreign Film: TODO SOBRE MI MADRE (Spain/France) Dir Pedro Almodòvar
Best Music: Bruno Coulais for HIMALAYA, L'ENFANCE D'UN CHEF (France/China/UK/Nepal) Dir Eric Valli
Best Photography: Eric Guichard for HIMALAYA, L'ENFANCE D'UN CHEF (France/China/UK/Nepal)
Best First Film: VOYAGES (France/Poland/Belgium) Dir Emmanuel Finkiel
Best Editing: Emmanuelle Castro for VOYAGES (France/Poland/Belgium) Dir Emmanuel Finkiel
Best Sound: Vincent Tulli, FranÁois Grouli, Bruno Tarrière for JEANNE D'ARC (France) Dir Luc Besson
Best Costume Design: Catherine Leterrier for JEANNE D'ARC (France) Dir Luc Besson
Best Set Design: Philippe Chiffre for REMBRANDT (France) Dir Charles Matton
Best Short Film: SALE BATTARS (France) Dir Delphine Gleize
Césars d'Honneur: Jean-Pierre Léaud, Josiane Balasko, and Georges Cravenne

EVENING STANDARD BRITISH FILM AWARDS
Awarded 6th February 2000, Savoy Hotel, London

Best Film: EAST IS EAST (UK) Dir Damien O'Donnell
Best Actor: Jeremy Northam in IDEAL HUSBAND (UK/US) Dir Oliver Parker and also in WINSLOW BOY (US) Dir David Mamet
Best Actress: Samantha Morton in DREAMING OF JOSEPH LEES (US/UK) Dir Eric Styles
Best Screenplay: Tom Stoppard for SHAKESPEARE IN LOVE (US) Dir John Madden
Most Promising Newcomer: Peter Mullan for ORPHANS (UK)
Best Technical/Artistic Achievement: John de Borman for HIDEOUS KINKY (UK/France) Dir Gillies MacKinnon
Peter Sellers Award for Comedy: NOTTING HILL (US/UK) Dir Roger Michell
Special Award (Lifetime Achievement): Freddie Francis

57th GOLDEN GLOBE AWARDS
Awarded 23rd January 2000, Los Angeles
Hollywood Foreign Press Association
646 North Robertson Boulevard
West Hollywood
California 90069
Tel.(310) 657 1731
Fax.(310) 657 5576

Email: hfpa95@aol.com
Web site: www.hfpa.com

FILM
Best Motion Picture (Drama): AMERICAN BEAUTY (US) Dir Sam Mendes
Best Motion Picture (Comedy/Musical): TOY STORY 2 (US) Dir John Lasseter
Best Actor (Drama): Denzel Washington in The HURRICANE (US) Dir Norman Jewison
Best Actor (Comedy/Musical): Jim Carrey in MAN ON THE MOON (US) Milos Forman
Best Actress (Drama): Hilary Swank in BOYS DON'T CRY (US) Dir Kimberly Peirce
Best Actress (Comedy/Musical): Janet McTeer in TUMBLEWEEDS (US) Dir Gavin O'Connor
Best Supporting Actor: Tom Cruise in MAGNOLIA (US) Dir Paul Thomas Anderson
Best Supporting Actress: Angelina Jolie in GIRL, INTERRUPTED (US) Dir James Mangold
Best Director: Sam Mendes for AMERICAN BEAUTY (US)
Best Screenplay: Alan Ball for AMERICAN BEAUTY (US) Dir Sam Mendes
Best Original Song: Phil Collins for "You'll Be In My Heart" for TARZAN (US) Dir Kevin Lima
Best Original Score: Ennio Morricone for La LEGGENDA DEL PIANISTA SULL'OCEANO (Italy/US) Dir Giuseppe Tornature
Best Foreign Language Film: TODO SOBRE MI MADRE (Spain/France) Dir Pedro Almodòvar

TELEVISION
Best Actor in a TV-Series (Drama): James Gandolfini in The SOPRANOS (HBO Productions/Brillstein-Grey Entertainment)
Best Actor in a TV-Series (Comedy/Musical): Michael J. Fox in SPIN CITY (ABC TV)
Best Actor in a Mini-Series or Motion Picture Made for TV: Jack Lemmon in INHERIT THE WIND (Showtime)
Best Actress in a TV-Series (Drama): Edie Falco in The SOPRANOS (HBO Productions/Brillstein-Grey Entertainment)
Best Actress in a TV-Series (Comedy/Musical): Sarah Jessica Parker in SEX AND THE CITY (HBO)
Best Actress in a Mini-Series or Motion Picture Made for TV: Halle Berry in INTRODUCING DOROTHY DANDRIDGE (HBO) Dir Martha Coolidge
Best Supporting Actor in a Series, Mini-Series or Motion Picture Made for TV: Peter Fonda in The PASSION OF AYN RAND (Showtime) Dir Chris Menaul
Best Supporting Actress in a Series, Mini-Series or Motion Picture Made for TV: Nancy Marchand in The SOPRANOS (HBO Productions/Brillstein-Grey Entertainment)
Best TV Series (Comedy/Musical): SEX AND THE CITY (HBO)
Best TV Series (Drama): The SOPRANOS (HBO Productions/Brillstein-Grey Entertainment)
Best Mini-Series or Motion Picture Made for TV: RKO 281 (HBO Pictures) Dir Benjamin Ross
Cecil B. DeMille Award: Barbra Streisand

40th GOLDEN ROSE OF MONTREUX
Held 4th-9th May 2000, Montreux
Télévision Suisse Romande
Quai E. Anserment 20

P.O. Box 234
CH-1211 Geneva 8
Tel: (41) 22 708 89 98
Fax: (41) 22 781 52 49
Email: Sarah.Fanchini@tsr.ch
Website: www.rosedor.ch

Rose D'Or: The MOLE (VRT/Vlaamse Radio- en
Televisieomroep) (Belgium)
Silver Rose (Sitcoms): ALL STARS (Vara Television)
(Netherlands)
Bronze Rose (Sitcoms): WILL & GRACE (NBC
Enterprises/Everything Entertainment) (US)
Silver Rose (Music): JOSEPH AND THE AMAZING
TECHNICOLOR DREAMCOAT (Really Useful Picture
Company) (UK)
Bronze Rose (Music): ROBBIE WILLIAMS LIVE AT
SLANE CASTLE (Done & Dusted for Robert Williams
Productions) (UK)
Silver Rose (Variety): FRANCAMENTE...ME NE
INFISCHIO (Rai UNO) (Italy)
Bronze Rose (Variety): MICHAEL MOORE: THE
AWFUL TRUTH (Dog Eat Dog Films) (US/UK)
Silver Rose (Comedy): PEOPLE LIKE US (Talkback
Productions for BBC2) (UK)
Bronze Rose (Comedy): TRIGGER HAPPY TV
(Absolutely Productions for C4) (UK)
Silver Rose (Gameshows): The BIG CLASS REUNION
(Wegelius Television APS) (Denmark)
Bronze Rose (Gameshows): FRIENDS LIKE THESE
(BBC1) (UK)
Special Prize of the City of Montreux Egg: The ARTS
SHOW #101 (Thirteen/WNET) (US)
Press Prize: ALL STARS (Vara Television) (Netherlands)
UNDA Prize: The REST (Langteaux/A.D.D. Prod./TLN
Television (US)

GRIERSON AWARD 1999

Awarded 23rd March 2000, Savoy Hotel, London
The Grierson Memorial Trust
37 Gower Street
London WC1E 6HH
Tel: 020 7580 1502
Fax: 020 7580 1504
Email: john.chittock@which.net
Website: www.editor.net/griersontrust

Best Documentary: GULAG (ENEMY OF THE
PEOPLE) Dir Angus Macqueen (BBC2 Television)
Commended: TRUE STORIES: KOSOVO THE
VALLEY Dir Dan Reed (Mentorn Barraclough
Carey/Suspect Device for C4)
Commended: TRUE STORIES: DIVORCE IRANIAN
STYLE Dir Kim Longinotto and Ziba Mir-Hosseini
(Twentieth Century Vixen for C4)
Special Mention: TIMEWATCH: TALES OF THE
EIFFEL TOWER Dir Jonathan Gill (BBC2)
Trustees' Tribute: David Munro and Philip Donnellan

INTERNATIONAL INDIAN FILM AWARDS

**Awarded 24th June 2000 at the Millennium Dome,
London**

Best Film: HUM DIL DE CHUKE SANAM (India) Dir
Sanjay Leela Bhansali

Best Director: Sanjay Leela Bhansali for HUM DIL DE
CHUKE SANAM (India)
Best Story: Sanjay Leela Bhansali and Pratap Karvat for
HUM DIL DE CHUKE SANAM (India) Dir Sanjay Leela
Bhansali
Best Actress in a Leading Role: Aishwarya Rai for HUM
DIL DE CHUKE SANAM (India) Dir Sanjay Leela
Bhansali
Best Actor in a Leading Role: Sanjay Dutt for
VAASTAV (India) Dir Mahesh Manjrekar
Lifetime Achievement Award: Jackie Chan
Special Prize: EAST IS EAST (UK) Dir Damien
O'Donnell
Special Prize: ELIZABETH (UK) Dir Shekhar Kapur
Best Lyrics: Anand Bakshi for the song "Ishq Bina" from
TAAL (India) Dir Subhash Gai
Best Music Direction: AR Rehman for TAAL (India) Dir
Subhash Gai
Best Female Playback Singer: Alka Yagnik for the song
"Taal Se Taal" from TAAL (India) Dir Subhash Gai
Best Male Playback Singer: Udit Narayan for "Chand
Chupa" from HUM DIL DE CHUKE SANAM (India) Dir
Sanjay Leela Bhansali
Best Performance in a Negative Role: Naseeruddin Shah
for SARFAROSH (India) Dir John Mathew Matthan
Best Actor in a Supporting Role: Anil Kapoor for TAAL
(India) Dir Subhash Gai
Best Actress in a Supporting Role: Sushmita Sen for
BIWI NO.1 (India) Dir David Dhawan
Best Performance in a Comic Role: Anil Kapoor for
BIWI NO.1 (India) Dir David Dhawan

LONDON CRITICS' CIRCLE FILM AWARDS

Awarded 2nd March 2000, London

Best Actor: Kevin Spacey in AMERICAN BEAUTY (US)
Dir Sam Mendes
Best Actress: Annette Bening in AMERICAN BEAUTY
(US) Dir Sam Mendes
Best British Film: EAST IS EAST (UK) Dir Damien
O'Donnell
Best British Producer: Leslee Udwin for EAST IS EAST
(UK) Dir Damien O'Donnell
Best British Screenwriter: Ayub Khan-Din for EAST IS
EAST (UK) Dir Damien O'Donnell
Best Director: Sam Mendes for AMERICAN BEAUTY
(US)
Best English Language Film: AMERICAN BEAUTY
(US) Dir Sam Mendes
Best Foreign Language Film: TODO SOBRE MI
MADRE (Spain/France) Dir Pedro Almodòvar
Best Screenplay: Alan Ball for AMERICAN BEAUTY
(US) Dir Sam Mendes
Best British Supporting Actor: Michael Caine in
LITTLE VOICE (UK/US) Dir Mark Herman
Special Award: Mike Leigh

40th MONTE CARLO TELEVISION FESTIVAL

Held 17th-23rd February 2000, Monte Carlo
4 Boulevard de Jardin Exotique
98000 Monte Carlo
Monaco
Tel: (37) 793 10 40 60
Fax: (37) 793 50 70 14

Email: info@tvfestival.com
Website: www.tvfestival.com/

TELEVISION FILMS
Gold Nymphs:
Best Film: BONHOEFFER DIE LEZTE STUFE
(Germany/Canada) Dir Eric Till (Norflicks/NFP/Teleart
GmbH & Co.)
Best Script: Theo Hakola for The FAVOURITE
DAUGHTER (France) (M6 Droits Audiovisuels)
Best Direction: Daniel Alfredson for D÷DSKLOCKAN
(Sweden) (Sveriges Television)
Best Actor: Lino Banfi in VOLA SCIUSCIU, THE
SAVIOR OF SAN NICOLA (Italy) (Lux Vide)
Best Actress: Orla Brady in A LOVE DIVIDED (Ireland)
(Parallel Films Productions)

MINI-SERIES
Gold Nymphs:
Best Mini-Series: WARRIORS (UK) Dir Peter
Kosminsky (BBC Films in association with Deep Indigo
Productions)
Best Script: Tony Marchant for KID IN THE CORNER
(UK) (Tiger Aspect Production for C4)
Best Direction: Billie Eltringham for KID IN THE
CORNER (UK) (Tiger Aspect Production for C4)
Best Actor: Douglas Henshall in KID IN THE CORNER
(UK) (Tiger Aspect Production for C4)
Best Actress: Virna Lisi in BALZAC (France) (TF1)

NEWS PROGRAMMES
Gold Nymph (Best News Programme): ITN News
compilation of reports on the Kosovo conflict (UK) (ITN)
Silver Nymph (News Programme): NEWSNIGHT:
SOUTH AFRICA POLICE (UK) (BBC News)
Gold Nymph (Best Current Affairs Programme):
KOSOVO THE VALLEY (UK) (C4)
Silver Nymph (Current Affairs Programme):
RINJINTACHI NO SENSO KOSOVO: HAJDAR DUSHI
DORI NO HITOBITO (Japan) (NHK Japan Broadcasting
Corporation)
Special Mention: FMI - RUSSIE: L'ENJEU (France) (La
Sept Arte)

SPECIAL PRIZES
Special Prize of H.S.H. Prince Rainier III: L'OR VERT
(ENVOYE SPECIAL) (France) (France 2)
Prize of the Monaco Red Cross: BEHIND THE MASK
(US) (Pearson Television International)
AMADE & UNESCO Prize: DESSINE MOI UN JOUET
(France) (France 3)
Prix UNDA: NEWS: MAS ENLLA DEL DOLOR
(Spain) (TV3/Televisio de Catalunya S.A.)
European Producer Award: Zentropa Productions
(Denmark) for its fiction productions over the last two years

72ND OSCARS - ACADEMY OF MOTION PICTURE ARTS AND SCIENCES
Awarded 26th March 2000, Los Angeles
8949 Wilshire Boulevard
Beverly Hills
California 90211
Tel: (310) 247 3000
Fax: (310) 859 6919
Website: www.oscar.com and www.oscars.org

Best Film: AMERICAN BEAUTY (US) Dir Sam Mendes
Best Director: Sam Mendes for AMERICAN BEAUTY (US)
Best Actor: Kevin Spacey in AMERICAN BEAUTY (US)
Dir Sam Mendes
Best Actress: Hilary Swank in BOYS DON'T CRY (US)
Dir Kimberly Peirce
Best Supporting Actor: Michael Caine in The CIDER
HOUSE RULES (US) Dir Lasse Hallstr^m
Best Supporting Actress: Angelina Jolie in GIRL,
INTERRUPTED (US) Dir James Mangold
Best Screenplay: Alan Ball for AMERICAN BEAUTY
(US) Dir Sam Mendes
Best Adapted Screenplay: John Irving for The CIDER
HOUSE RULES (US) Dir Lasse Hallstr^m
Best Cinematography: Conrad L. Hall for AMERICAN
BEAUTY (US) Dir Sam Mendes
Best Editing: Zach Staenberg for The MATRIX
(US/Australia) Dir Andy Wachowski
Best Music (Original Score): John Corigliano for The
RED VIOLIN (Canada/Italy/US/UK) Dir FranÁois Girard
Best Music (Original Song): Phil Collins for "You'll Be
In My Heart" from TARZAN (US) Dir Kevin Lima
Best Art Direction: Rick Heinrichs for SLEEPY
HOLLOW (US/Germany) Dir Tim Burton
Best Costume Design: Lindy Hemming for TOPSY-
TURVY (UK/US) Dir Mike Leigh
Best Sound: John Reitz, Gregg Rudloff, David Campbell
and David Lee for The MATRIX (US/Australia) Dir Andy
Wachowski
Best Sound Effects Editing: Dane A. Davis for The
MATRIX (US/Australia) Dir Andy Wachowski
Best Visual Effects: John Gaeta, Janek Sirrs, Steve
Courtley and Jon Thum for The MATRIX (US/Australia)
Dir Andy Wachowski
Best Foreign Language Film: TODO SOBRE MI
MADRE (Spain/France) Dir Pedro Almodòvar
Best Make-up: Christine Blundell and Trefor Proud for
TOPSY-TURVY (UK/US) Dir Mike Leigh
Best Documentary Feature: ONE DAY IN
SEPTEMBER (UK) Dir Kevin MacDonald
Best Documentary Short Subject: KING GIMP (US)
Dir Susan Hannah Hadary and William A. Whiteford
Best Animated Short Film: The OLD MAN AND THE
SEA (Quebec/Japan/Russia) Dir Alexander Petrov
Best Live Action Short Film: MY MOTHER DREAMS
THE SATAN'S DISCIPLES IN NEW YORK (US) Dir
Barbara Schock

ROYAL TELEVISION SOCIETY AWARDS
Awarded in London March 2000
100 Gray's Inn Road
London WC1X 8AL
Tel: 020 7430 1000
Fax: 020 7430 0924
Email: info@rts.org.uk
Website: www.rts.org.uk/

RTS PROGRAMME AWARDS
Situation Comedy/Comedy Drama: PEOPLE LIKE US (BBC Production for BBC2)
Entertainment: The LEAGUE OF GENTLEMEN (BBC Production for BBC2)
Single Documentary: MALCOLM AND BARBARA: A LOVE STORY (Granada Television)
Documentary Series: The DECISION (A Windfall Film Production for C4)
Documentary Strand: HORIZON (BBC Production for BBC2)
Regional Documentary: SPINNERS AND LOSERS (Scottish Television)
Regional Programme: NUTS AND BOLTS (HTV)
Regional Presenter: Roy Noble for COMMON GROUND: THE SHED (Presentable Productions for BBC Wales)
Features - Daytime: SHOW ME THE MONEY (Princess Productions for C4)
Features - Primetime: 1900 HOUSE (Wall To Wall Television for C4)
Children's Drama: SEE HOW THEY RUN (BBC Production in association with ABC Australia for BBC1)
Children's Entertainment: SM:TV LIVE (Blaze Television for ITV)
Children's Factual: NICK NEWS (Wised Up Productions for Nickelodeon UK)
Presenter: Johnny Vaughan for The BIG BREAKFAST (Planet 24 for C4)
Arts: THIS IS MODERN ART (Oxford TV Productions for C4)
Network Newcomer - On Screen: Jamie Oliver for The NAKED CHEF (Optomen Television for BBC2)
Network Newcomer - Behind the Screen: David Wolstencroft for PSYCHOS (A Kudos Production for C4)
Television Performance: Rory Bremner for BREMNER, BIRD & FORTUNE (Vera for C4)
Single Drama: WARRIORS (BBC Films in association with Deep Indigo Productions for BBC1)
Drama Serial: SHOOTING THE PAST (Talkback Productions for BBC2)
Drama Series: The COPS (World Productions for BBC2)
Actor - Female: Thora Hird for LOST FOR WORDS (Yorkshire Television in association with Bard Entertainments for ITV)
Actor - Male: Michael Gambon for WIVES & DAUGHTERS (BBC Production for BBC1)
Writer: Caroline Aherne & Craig Cash for The ROYLE FAMILY (Granada Television for BBC1)
Team: WALKING WITH DINOSAURS (BBC Production for BBC1)
Cyril Bennett Award/Judges Award: Peter Symes
Gold Medal: BSkyB

RTS EDUCATIONAL AWARDS
SCHOOLS TELEVISION
Pre-School & Infants: TWEENIES (Blow Tell-Tale Productions for BBC Education)
Primary Numeracy & Literacy: NUMBER CREW (Sports Day Open Mind for C4)
Primary Arts & Humanities: ZIG ZAG: A WALK THROUGH TIME - WORK (BBC Education)
Primary & Secondary Science & Maths: SCIENTIFIC EYE: MATERIALS AND THEIR PROPERTIES - CHANGING STATE (Yorkshire Television for C4)
Primary & Secondary Multimedia & Interactive: RAINFOREST DEVELOPMENT: The AMAZONIA EXPERIENCE (Channel 4 Learning with InSignificant Productions for C4)
Secondary Arts & Language: ENGLISH FILE: ROOTS & WATER (BBC Education)
Secondary Humanities: PLACE & PEOPLE: LAND FORMS (Ice Flying Pictures for C4)
ADULT EDUCATIONAL TELEVISION
Campaigns & Seasons - RTS/NIACE Award: BROOKIE BASICS (C4)
Vocational Training: STUDENT CHOICE í99 (Wobbly Picture Productions for BBC Education)
Single Programme: EMBARASSING ILLNESSES: TESTICULAR CANCER (A Maverick Production for C4)
Educational Impact In The Prime Time Schedule: The SECOND WORLD WAR IN COLOUR (A TWI/Carlton Co-Production for ITV)
Judges Award: BBC Education Online

RTS TELEVISION SPORTS AWARDS
Live Outside Broadcast Coverage Of The Year: TEST CRICKET (A Sunset & Vine Production for C4)
Sports News: OLYMPIC CORRUPTION - CHANNEL 4 NEWS (ITN/Atlantic Television for Channel 4 News)
Sports Documentary: CLASH OF THE TITANS: BENN V EUBANK (BBC Television)
Regional Sports News: DOUGIE WALKER - REPORTING SCOTLAND (BBC Scotland Sport)
Regional Sports Documentary: WORKING CLASS HERO - NEIL JENKINS (BBC Wales)
Regional Sports Programme Of The Year - Entertainment: OFFSIDE (BBC Scotland Sport)
Regional Sports Programme Of The Year - Actuality: FRIDAY SPORTSCENE (BBC Scotland Sport
Regional Sports Presenter Or Commentator: Jonathan Wills (London News Network)
Sports Presenter: Jim Rosenthal (ISN/Carlton/MACh 1 for ITV)
Sports Commentator: Peter Alliss (BBC Sport)
Sports Pundit: Martin Brundle (Chrysalis Sport/United Productions for ITV)
Sports Innovation: SKY SPORTS ACTIVE/INTERACTIVE FOOTBALL (Sky Sports)
Television Image Of The Year: F1: BRITISH GRAND PRIX LIVE - MICHAEL SCHUMACHER CRASH (Chrysalis Sport/United Productions for ITV)
Sports Programme Of The Year - Entertainment: SPORTS PERSONALITY OF THE CENTURY (BBC Sport)
Sports Programme Of The Year - Actuality: SCOTLAND V ENGLAND (Sky Sports)
Television Sports Award Of The Year: TEST CRICKET (A Sunset & Vine Production for C4)
Judges' Award: Bill McLaren

RTS TELEVISION JOURNALISM AWARDS

News Award - International: NINE OíCLOCK NEWS - DILI INDONESIA (BBC News)
News Award - Home: CHANNEL 4 NEWS - The PADDINGTON CRASH & ITS CAUSES (ITN for C4)
Regional Daily News Magazine: LOOK NORTH (BBC North East and Cumbria)
News Event Award: SKY NEWS - KOSOVO LIBERATION DAY (Sky News)
Television Technician Of The Year: Miguel Gil (APTN)
Interviewer Of The Year: Tim Sebastian for BBC News
Regional Current Affairs: LONDON TONIGHT SPECIAL - SOHO BOMBING (London News Network)
Current Affairs - International: DISPATCHES - PRIME SUSPECTS (Hardcash for C4)
Current Affairs - Home: BLACK BRITAIN SPECIAL - WHY STEPHEN? (BBC News)
Production Award: CHANNEL 4 NEWS (ITN for C4)
Television Journalist Of The Year: John Simpson for BBC News
Young Journalist Of The Year: Matthew Price for BBC Newsround
Specialist Journalism: Susan Watts for BBC News
Programme Of The Year: TONIGHT WITH TREVOR McDONALD (Granada Television)
Judges Award: Michael Brunson

RTS CRAFT & DESIGN AWARDS
(Awarded in London 25 November 1999)

Production Design - Drama: Alice Normington for GREAT EXPECTATIONS (A BBC/WGBH Boston Co-Production for BBC2)
Production Design - Entertainment & Non-Drama: Simon Jago for CHANNEL 4 NEWS (Jago Design for C4)
Costume Design - Drama: Susannah Buxton for SHOOTING THE PAST (A Talkback Production for BBC2)
Make-Up - Drama: Ann Humphreys for GIRLS NIGHT (Granada Film)
Make-Up: Non-Drama: Helen Barrett for The GREATEST RORY EVER TOLD (Made By Vera for C4)
Graphic Design - Channel Idents: Jane Wyatt & Sean De Sparengo for CHRISTMAS ON BBC TWO (BBC2)
Graphic Design - Titles: Paul Baguley MAD FOR IT (Carlton Television)
Graphic Design - Programme Content Sequences: Sarah Grigg, Howard Jones & Marlon Griffin for SUPERNATURAL
(John Downer Productions for BBC1)
Lighting, Photography & Camera - Photography Drama: David Odd for GREAT EXPECTATIONS (BBC/WGBH (Boston) for BBC2)
Lighting, Photography & Camera - Photography Documentary & Factual & Non-Drama Production: Jacek Petrycki for KOSOVO - The VALLEY (Mentorn Barraclough Carey for C4)
Lighting, Photography & Camera - Lighting For Multicamera: Bernie Davis for MASTERWORKS - VAUGHAN WILLIAMS (BBC2)
Lighting, Photography & Camera - Multicamera Work: GLADIATORS Camera Team (London Weekend Television)
Tape & Film Editing - Drama: Beverley Mills Dalziel and Pascoe for BONES AND SILENCE (BBC1)
Tape & Film Editing - Documentary & Factual: Kim Horton Malcolm and Barbara for A LOVE STORY (Granada Television)
Tape & Film Editing - Entertainment & Situation Comedy: Tony Cranstoun for The ROYLE FAMILY (Granada Television for BBC2)
Sound - Drama: Richard Manton for GREAT EXPECTATIONS (BBC/WGBH (Boston) for BBC2)
Sound - Entertainment & Non-Drama: Patrick Boland for KOSOVO - The VALLEY (Mentorn Barraclough Carey for C4)
Music - Original Title Music: Hal Lindes for RECKLESS - The MOVIE (Granada Television)
Music - Original Score: Murray Gold for QUEER AS FOLK (Red Productions for C4)
Team Award: MASTERWORKS - SIX PIECES OF BRITAIN (BBC2)
Craft & Design Innovation: John Downer, Mark Brownlow, Rod Clarke, Steve Downer, Sarah Grigg, James Honeyborne, Howard Jones, Susan Macmillan & Tim Macmillan for SUPERNATURAL (BBC1)
Judges' Award: Cosgrove Hall Films

RTS TECHNOLOGY AWARDS
Innovative Applications: "Specter" Virtual DataCine - Philips Digital Video Systems
Research & Development: The Commute-Interactive Project ITC/ComTel/Convergence/DTI(RA)/Eurobell/GEC-Marconi/Sony/Thomson
Special Award: The Digital Television Group
Judges' Award: Digital Services - British Sky Broadcasting

RTS STUDENT TELEVISION AWARDS
Animation: Anwyn Beier for NIGHTLIFE (Edinburgh College of Art)
Factual: Talya Exrahi & Lewie Kerr for The JAHALIN (London College of Printing)
Non Factual: Adrian J McDowall, Kara Johnston, Joern Utkilen, Martin Radich & Monica Heilpern for WHO'S MY FAVOURITE GIRL? (Edinburgh College of Art)

British Successes in the Academy Awards 1927-1999

The following list chronicles British successes in the Academy Awards. It includes individuals who were either born, and lived and worked, in Britain into their adult lives, or those who were not born here but took on citizenship.
Compiled by Erinna Mettler

(1st) 1927/28 held in 1930

Charles Chaplin
- **Special Award (acting, producing, directing and writing):** THE CIRCUS

(2nd) 1928/29 held in 1930

Frank Lloyd
- **Best Direction:** THE DIVINE LADY

(3rd) 1929/30 held in 1930

George Arliss
- **Best Actor:** THE GREEN GODDESS

(6th) 1932/33 held in 1934

William S. Darling
- **Best Art Direction:** CAVALCADE
Charles Laughton
- **Best Actor:** THE PRIVATE LIFE OF HENRY VIII
Frank Lloyd
- **Best Direction:** CAVALCADE

(8th) 1935 held in 1936

Gaumont British Studios
- **Best Short Subject:** WINGS OVER MT. EVEREST
Victor Mclaglen
- **Best Actor:** THE INFORMER

(11th) 1938 held in 1939

Ian Dalrymple, Cecil Lewis & W.P. Lipscomb
- **Best Screenplay:** PYGMALION

(12th) 1939 held in 1940

Robert Donat
- **Best Actor:** GOODBYE MR. CHIPS
Vivien Leigh
- **Best Actress:** GONE WITH THE WIND

(13th) 1940 held in 1941

Lawrence Butler & Jack Whitney
- **Special Visual Effects:** THE THIEF OF BAGDAD
Vincent Korda
- **Best Colour Set Design:** THE THIEF OF BAGDAD

(14th) 1941 held in 1942

British Ministry of Information
- **Honorary Award:** TARGET FOR TONIGHT
Donald Crisp
- **Best Supporting Actor:** HOW GREEN WAS MY VALLEY
Joan Fontaine
- **Best Actress:** SUSPICION
Jack Whitney & The General Studios Sound Department
- **Best Sound:** THAT HAMILTON WOMAN

(15th) 1942 held in 1943

Noel Coward
- **Special Award:** IN WHICH WE SERVE
Greer Garson
- **Best Actress:** MRS. MINIVER

(16th) 1943 held in 1944

British Ministry of Information
- **Best Documentary:** DESERT VICTORY
William S. Darling
- **Best Art Direction:** THE SONG OF BERNADETTE

(18th) 1945 held in 1946

The Governments of the United States & Great Britain
- **Best Documentary:** THE TRUE GLORY
Ray Milland
- **Best Actor:** THE LOST WEEKEND
Harry Stradling
- **Best Cinematography (b/w):** THE PICTURE OF DORIAN GRAY

(19th) 1946 held in 1947

Muriel & Sydney Box
- **Best Original Screenplay:** THE SEVENTH VEIL
Clemence Dane
- **Best Original Story:** VACATION FROM MARRIAGE
Olivia de Havilland
- **Best Actress:** TO EACH HIS OWN
Laurence Olivier
- **Special Award:** HENRY V
Thomas Howard
- **Best Special Effects:** BLITHE SPIRIT
William S. Darling
- **Best Art Direction (b/w):** ANNA AND THE KING OF SIAM

(20th) 1947 held in 1948

John Bryan
- **Best Art Direction:** GREAT EXPECTATIONS
Jack Cardiff
- **Best Cinematography (col):** BLACK NARCISSUS

Ronald Colman
- **Best Actor:** A DOUBLE LIFE

Guy Green
- **Best Cinematography (b/w):** GREAT EXPECTATIONS

Edmund Gwen
- **Best Supporting Actor:** MIRACLE ON 34TH STREET

(21st) 1948 held in 1949

Carmen Dillon & Roger Furse
- **Best Art Direction (b/w):** HAMLET

Brian Easdale
- **Best Score:** THE RED SHOES

Roger Furse
- **Best Costume Design:** HAMLET

Laurence Olivier
- **Best Picture:** HAMLET

Laurence Olivier
- **Best Actor:** HAMLET

(22nd) 1949 held in 1950

British Information Services
- **Best Documentary:** DAYBREAK IN UDI

Olivia de Havilland
- **Best Actress:** THE HEIRESS

(23rd) 1950 held in 1951

George Sanders
- **Best Supporting Actor:** ALL ABOUT EVE

(24th) 1951 held in 1952

James Bernard & Paul Dehn
- **Best Motion Picture Story:** SEVEN DAYS TO NOON

Vivien Leigh
- **Best Actress:** A STREETCAR NAMED DESIRE

(25th) 1952 held in 1953

T.E.B. Clarke
- **Best Story & Screenplay:** THE LAVENDER HILL MOB

London Films Sound Dept.
- **Best Sound:** THE SOUND BARRIER

(26th) 1954 held in 1955

British Information Services
- **Best Documentary Short Subject:** THURSDAY'S CHILDREN

S. Tyne Jule
- **Best Song:** THREE COINS IN THE FOUNTAIN

Jon Whitely & Vincent Winter
- **Special Award (Best Juvenile Performances):** THE KIDNAPPERS

(29th) 1956 held in 1957

George K. Arthur
- **Best Short Subject:** THE BESPOKE OVERCOAT

(30th) 1957 held in 1958

Malcolm Arnold
- **Best Musical Score:** THE BRIDGE ON THE RIVER KWAI

Alec Guinness
- **Best Actor:** THE BRIDGE ON THE RIVER KWAI

Jack Hildyard
- **Best Cinematography:** THE BRIDGE ON THE RIVER KWAI

David Lean
- **Best Director:** THE BRIDGE ON THE RIVER KWAI

Pete Taylor
- **Best Editing:** THE BRIDGE ON THE RIVER KWAI

(31st) 1958 held in 1959

Cecil Beaton
- **Best Costumes:** GIGI

Wendy Hiller
- **Best Supporting Actress:** SEPARATE TABLES

Thomas Howard
- **Special Visual Effects:** TOM THUMB

David Niven
- **Best Actor:** SEPARATE TABLES

(32nd) 1959 held in 1960

Hugh Griffith
- **Best Supporting Actor:** BEN HUR

Elizabeth Haffenden
- **Best Costume Design (col.):** BEN HUR

(33rd) 1960 held in 1961

Freddie Francis
- **Best Cinematography (b/w):** SONS & LOVERS

James Hill
- **Best Documentary:** GIUSEPPINA

Hayley Mills
- **Special Award (Best Juvenile Performance):** POLLYANNA

Peter Ustinov
- **Best Supporting Actor:** SPARTACUS

(34th) 1961 held in 1962

Vivian C. Greenham
- **Best Visual Effects:** THE GUNS OF NAVARONE

(35th) 1962 held in 1963

John Box & John Stoll
- **Best Art Direction:** LAWRENCE OF ARABIA

Anne V. Coates
- **Best Editing:** LAWRENCE OF ARABIA

Jack Howells (Janus Films)
- **Best Documentary:** DYLAN THOMAS

David Lean
- **Best Director:** LAWRENCE OF ARABIA

Shepperton Studios Sound Dept. (John Cox Sound Director)
- **Best Sound:** LAWRENCE OF ARABIA

Freddie Young
- **Best Cinematography:** LAWRENCE OF ARABIA

(36th) 1963 held in 1964

John Addison
- **Best Score:** TOM JONES
John Osborne
- **Best Adapted Screenplay:** TOM JONES
Tony Richardson
- **Best Director:** TOM JONES
Tony Richardson (Woodfall Films)
- **Best Picture:** TOM JONES
Margaret Rutherford
- **Best Supporting Actress:** THE V.I.P.S

(37th) 1964 held in 1965

Julie Andrews
- **Best Actress:** MARY POPPINS
Cecil Beaton
- **Best Art Direction (col):** MY FAIR LADY
Cecil Beaton
- **Best Costume Design (col):** MY FAIR LADY
Rex Harrison
- **Best Actor:** MY FAIR LADY
Walter Lassally
- **Best Cinematography (b/w):** ZORBA THE GREEK
Harry Stradling
- **Best Cinematography (col):** MY FAIR LADY
Peter Ustinov
- **Best Supporting Actor:** TOPKAPI
Norman Wanstall
- **Best Sound Effects:** GOLDFINGER

(38th) 1965 held in 1966

Julie Christie
- **Best Actress:** DARLING
Robert Bolt
- **Adapted Screenplay:** DOCTOR ZHIVAGO
Frederic Raphael
- **Original Screenplay:** DARLING
Freddie Young
- **Colour Cinematography:** DOCTOR ZHIVAGO
John Box, Terence Marsh
- **Best Art Direction (colour):** DOCTOR ZHIVAGO
Julie Harris
- **Costume (b/w):** DARLING
Phyllis Dalton
- **Costume (col):** DOCTOR ZHIVAGO
John Stears
- **Special Visual Effects:** THUNDERBALL

(39th) 1966 held in 1967

John Barry
- **Best Original Score:** BORN FREE
John Barry & Don Black
- **Best Song:** BORN FREE
Robert Bolt
- **Best Adapted Screenplay:** A MAN FOR ALL SEASONS
Joan Bridge & Elizabeth Haffenden
- **Best Costume (col):** A MAN FOR ALL SEASONS
Gordon Daniel
- **Best Sound:** GRAND PRIX
Ted Moore
- **Best Cinematography (col):** A MAN FOR ALL SEASONS
Ken Thorne
- **Best Adapted Score:** A FUNNY THING HAPPENED ON THE WAY TO THE FORUM
Peter Watkins
- **Best Documentary Feature:** THE WAR GAME

(40th) 1967 held in 1968

Leslie Bricusse
- **Best Song:** DOCTOR DOLITTLE (TALK TO THE ANIMALS)
Alfred Hitchcock
- **Irving Thalberg Memorial Award**
John Poyner
- **Best Sound Effects:** THE DIRTY DOZEN

(41st) 1968 held in 1969

John Barry
- **Best Original Score:** THE LION IN WINTER
Vernon Dixon & Ken Muggleston
- **Best Art Direction:** OLIVER!
Carol Reed
- **Best Director:** OLIVER!
Shepperton Sound Studio
- **Best Sound:** OLIVER!
Charles D. Staffell
- **Scientific, Class I Statuett -**
for the development of a successful embodiement of the reflex background projection system for composite cinematography
John Woolf
- **Best Picture:** OLIVER!

(42nd) 1969 held in 1970

Margaret Furfe
- **Best Costume:** ANNE OF THE THOUSAND DAYS
Cary Grant
- **Honorary Award**
John Schlesinger
- **Best Director:** MIDNIGHT COWBOY
Maggie Smith
- **Best Actress:** THE PRIME OF MISS JEAN BRODIE

(43rd) 1970 held in 1971

The Beatles
- **Best Original Score:** LET IT BE
Glenda Jackson
- **Best Actress:** WOMEN IN LOVE
John Mills
- **Best Supporting Actor:** RYAN'S DAUGHTER

Freddie Young
- **Best Cinematography:** RYAN'S DAUGHTER

(44th) 1971 held in 1972

Robert Amram
- **Best Short:** SENTINELS OF SILENCE

Ernest Archer, John Box, Vernon Dixon & Jack Maxsted
- **Best Art Direction:** NICHOLAS & ALEXANDRA

Charles Chaplin
- **Honorary Award**

David Hildyard & Gordon K. McCallum
- **Best Sound:** FIDDLER ON THE ROOF

Oswald Morris
- **Best Cinematography:** FIDDLER ON THE ROOF

(45th) 1972 held in 1973

Charles Chaplin
- **Best Original Score:** LIMELIGHT

David Hildyard
- **Best Sound:** CABARET

Anthony Powell
- **Best Costume Design:** TRAVELS WITH MY AUNT

Geoffrey Unsworth
- **Best Cinematography:** CABARET

(46th) 1973 held in 1974

Glenda Jackson
- **Best Actress:** A TOUCH OF CLASS

(47th) 1974 held in 1975

Albert Whitlock
- **Special Achievement In Visual Effects:** EARTHQUAKE

(48th) 1975 held in 1976

Ben Adam, Vernon Dixon & Roy Walker
- **Best Art Direction:** BARRY LYNDON

John Alcott
- **Best Cinematography:** BARRY LYNDON

Bob Godfrey
- **Best Animated Short:** GREAT

Albert Whitlock
- **Special Achievement In Visual Effects:** THE HINDENBERG

(49th) 1976 held in 1977

Peter Finch
- **Best Actor:** NETWORK

(50th) 1977 held in 1978

John Barry, Roger Christians & Leslie Dilley
- **Best Art Direction:** STAR WARS

John Mollo
- **Best Costume Design:** STAR WARS

Vanessa Redgrave
- **Best Supporting Actress:** JULIA

John Stears
- **Best Visual Effects:** STAR WARS

(51st) 1978 held in 1979

Les Bowie, Colin Chilvers, Denys Coop, Roy Field & Derek Meddings
- **Special Achievement In Visual Effects:** SUPERMAN

Michael Deeley, John Peverall & Barry Spikings
- **Best Picture:** THE DEER HUNTER

Laurence Oilvier
- **Lifetime Achievement Award**

Anthony Powell
- **Best Costume Design:** DEATH ON THE NILE

Maggie Smith
- **Best Supporting Actress:** CALIFORNIA SUITE

(52nd) 1979 held in 1980

Nick Allder, Denis Ayling & Brian Johnson
- **Special Achievement In Visual Effects:** ALIEN

Alec Guinness
- **Honorary Award**

Tony Walton
- **Best Art Direction:** ALL THAT JAZZ

(53rd) 1980 held in 1981

Brian Johnson
- **Special Achievement In Visual Effects:** THE EMPIRE STRIKES BACK

Lloyd Phillips
- **Best Live Action Short:** THE DOLLAR BOTTOM

Anthony Powell
- **Best Costume Design:** TESS

David W. Samuelson
- **Scientific and Engineering Award -**
for the engineering and development of the Louma Camera Crane and remote control system for motion picture production

Jack Stevens
- **Best Art Direction:** TESS

Geoffrey Unsworth
- **Best Cinematography:** TESS

(54th) 1981 held in 1982

Leslie Dilley & Michael Ford
- **Best Art Direction:** RAIDERS OF THE LOST ARK

John Gielgud
- **Best Supporting Actor:** ARTHUR

Nigel Nobel
- **Best Documentary Short:** CLOSE HARMONY

David Puttnam
- **Best Picture:** CHARIOTS OF FIRE

Arnold Schwartzman
- **Best Documentary Feature:** CLOSE HARMONY

Colin Welland
- **Best Original Screenplay:** CHARIOTS OF FIRE

Kit West
- **Special Achievement In Visual Effects:** RAIDERS OF THE LOST ARK

(55th) 1982 held in 1983

Richard Attenborough
- **Best Picture:** GANDHI

Richard Attenborough
- **Best Director:** GANDHI

John Briley
- **Best Original Screenplay:** GANDHI

Stuart Craig, Bob Laing & Michael Seirton
- **Best Art Direction:** GANDHI

Ben Kingsley
- **Best Actor:** GANDHI

John Mollo
- **Best Costume Design:** GANDHI

Sarah Monzani
- **Best Achievement In Make Up:** QUEST FOR FIRE

Colin Mossman & Rank Laboratories
- **Scientific and Engineering Award -**
for the engineering and implementation of a 4,000
meter printing system for motion picture laboratories

Christine Oestreicher
- **Best Live Action Short:** A SHOCKING ACCIDENT

Ronnie Taylor & Billy Williams
- **Best Cinematography:** GANDHI

(56th) 1983 held in 1984

Gerald L. Turpin (Lightflex International)
- **Scientific And Engineering Award**
- for the design, engineering and development of an on-
camera device providing contrast control, sourceless fill
light and special effects for motion picture
photography

(57th) 1984 held in 1985

Peggy Ashcroft
- **Best Supporting Actress:** A PASSAGE TO INDIA

Jim Clark
- **Best Editing:** THE KILLING FIELDS

George Gibbs
- **Special Achievement In Visual Effects:** INDIANA
JONES AND THE TEMPLE OF DOOM

Chris Menges
- **Best Cinematography:** THE KILLING FIELDS

Peter Shaffer
- **Best Adapted Screenplay:** AMADEUS

(58th) 1985 held in 1986

John Barry
- **Best Original Score:** OUT OF AFRICA

Stephen Grimes
- **Best Art Direction:** OUT OF AFRICA

David Watkin
- **Best Cinematography:** OUT OF AFRICA

(59th) 1986 held in 1987

Brian Ackland-Snow & Brian Saregar
- **Best Art Direction:** A ROOM WITH A VIEW

Jenny Beavan & John Bright
- **Best Costume Design:** A ROOM WITH A VIEW

Michael Caine
- **Best Supporting Actor:** HANNAH & HER SISTERS

Simon Kaye
- **Best Sound:** PLATOON

Lee Electric Lighting Ltd.
- **Technical Achievement Award**

Chris Menges
- **Best Cinematography:** THE MISSION

Peter D. Parks
- **Technical Achievement Award**
**William B. Pollard & David W. Samuelson - Technical
Achievement Award**

John Richardson
- **Special Achievement In Visual Effects:** ALIENS

Claire Simpson
- **Best Editing:** PLATOON

Don Sharpe
- **Best Sound Effects Editing:** ALIENS

Vivienne Verdon-Roe
- **Best Documentary Short:** WOMEN - FOR AMERICA,
FOR THE WORLD

(60th) 1987 held in 1988

James Acheson
- **Best Costume Design:** THE LAST EMPEROR

Sean Connery
- **Best Supporting Actor:** THE UNTOUCHABLES

Mark Peploe
- **Best Adapted Screenplay:** THE LAST EMPEROR

Ivan Sharrock
- **Best Sound:** THE LAST EMPEROR

Jeremy Thomas
- **Best Picture:** THE LAST EMPEROR

(61st) 1988 held in 1989

James Acheson
- **Best Costume Design:** DANGEROUS LIAISONS

George Gibbs
- **Special Achievement In Visual Effects:** WHO
FRAMED ROGER RABBIT

Christopher Hampton
- **Best Adapted Screenplay:** DANGEROUS LIAISONS

(62nd) 1989 held in 1990

Phyllis Dalton
- **Best Costume:** HENRY V

Daniel Day-Lewis
- **Best Actor:** MY LEFT FOOT

Freddie Francis
- **Best Cinematography:** GLORY

Brenda Fricker
- **Best Supporting Actress:** MY LEFT FOOT

Anton Furst
- **Best Art Direction:** BATMAN

Richard Hymns
- **Best Sound Effects Editing:** INDIANA JONES AND
THE LAST CRUSADE

Jessica Tandy
- **Best Actress:** DRIVING MISS DAISY

James Hendrie
- **Best Live Action Short:** WORK EXPERIENCE

(63rd) 1990 held in 1991

John Barry
- **Best Original Score:** DANCES WITH WOLVES

Jeremy Irons
- **Best Actor:**REVERSAL OF FORTUNE

Nick Park
- **Best Animated Short:** CREATURE COMFORTS

(64th) 1991 held in 1992

Daniel Greaves
- **Best Animated Short:** MANIPULATION

Anthony Hopkins
- **Best Actor:** SILENCE OF THE LAMBS

(65th) 1992 held in 1993

Simon Kaye
- **Best Sound:** THE LAST OF THE MOHICANS

Tim Rice
- **Best Original Song:** ALADDIN (A WHOLE NEW WORLD)

Emma Thompson
- **Best Actress:** HOWARDS END

Ian Whittaker
- **Best Art Direction:** HOWARDS END

(66th) 1993 held in 1994

Richard Hymns
- **Best Sound Effects Editing:** JURASSIC PARK

Nick Park
- **Best Animated Short:** THE WRONG TROUSERS

Deborah Kerr
- **Career Achievement Honorary Award**

(67th) 1994 held in 1995

Ken Adam & Carolyn Scott
- **Best Art Direction:** THE MADNESS OF KING GEORGE

Peter Capaldi & Ruth Kenley-Letts
- **Best Live Action Short:** FRANZ KAFKA'S IT'S A WONDERFUL LIFE

Elton John & Tim Rice
- **Best Song:** THE LION KING (CAN YOU FEEL THE LOVE TONIGHT)

Alison Snowden & David Fine
-**Best Animated Short:** BOB'S BIRTHDAY

(68th) 1995 held in 1996

James Acheson
- **Best Costume Design:** RESTORATION

Jon Blair
- **Best Documentary Feature:** ANNE FRANK REMEMBERED

Lois Burwell & Peter Frampton
- **Special Achievement In Make Up:** BRAVEHEART

Emma Thompson
- **Best Adapted Screenplay:** SENSE & SENSIBILITY

Nick Park
- **Best Animated Short:** A CLOSE SHAVE

(69th) 1996 held in 1997

Anthony Minghella
- **Best Director:** THE ENGLISH PATIENT

Rachel Portman
- **Best Original Score Musical or Comedy:** EMMA

Tim Rice & Andrew Lloyd Webber
- **Best Original song:** EVITA (YOU MUST LOVE ME)

Stuart Craig & Stephanie McMillan
- **Best Art Direction:** THE ENGLISH PATIENT

(70th) 1997 held in 1998

Peter Lamont and Michael Ford
- **Best Achievement In Art Direction:** TITANIC

Anne Dudley
- **Best Original Score Musical or Comedy:** THE FULL MONTY

Jan Pinkava
- **Best Animated Short:** GERI'S GAME

(71st) 1998 held in 1999

David Parfitt
- **Best Film:** SHAKESPEARE IN LOVE

Judi Dench
- **Best Actress in a Supporting Role:** SHAKESPEARE IN LOVE

Tom Stoppard
- **Best Original Screenplay:** SHAKESPEARE IN LOVE

Martin Childs and Jill Quertier
- **Best Art Direction:** SHAKESPEARE IN LOVE

Sandy Powell
- **Best Costume Design:** SHAKESPEARE IN LOVE

Jenny Shircore
- **Best Make-up:** ELIZABETH

Stephen Warbeck
- **Best Original Score Musical or Comedy:** SHAKESPEARE IN LOVE

Andy Nelson
- **Best Sound:** SAVING PRIVATE RYAN

(72nd) 1999 held in 2000

Michael Caine
- **Actor in a Supporting Role:** CIDER HOUSE RULES

Peter Young
- **Art Direction:** SLEEPY HOLLOW

Lindy Hemming
- **Costume Design:** TOPSY-TURVY

Sam Mendes
- **Directing:** AMERICAN BEAUTY

Kevin MacDonald, John Battsek,
- **Documentary Feature:** ONE DAY IN SEPTEMBER

Christine Blundell, Trefor Proud
- **Make up:** TOPSY-TURVY

Phil Collins
- **Original Song:** TARZAN "You'll Be In My Heart"

BOOKS

Below is a selective list of books, in the English language, published in 1999 on the subject of film and television, all of which can be found at the bfi National Library. An ISBN has been provided where known. Compiled by Heidi Rasmussen

FILM – GENERAL

Alien identities: exploring differences in film and fiction.
Cartmell, Deborah et al.
Pluto Press, vi-ix. 197p. index.
ISBN 0745314058

Art museums & media: film, video, CD-ROM & interactive media in U.S. art museums: results of a 1993 survey...
Covert, Nadine.
Program for Art on Film, 55p. figs. appendices.

Cinematography.
Ettedgui, Peter.
RotoVision, 207p. gloss. index. col. illus.
ISBN 2880463564

Disaster and memory: celebrity culture and the crisis of Hollywood cinema.
Dixon, Wheeler Winston.
Columbia University Press, xi. 182p. bibliog. index.
ISBN 023111317X

Fifty years of the future: a chronicle of the Institute of Contemporary Arts 1947-1997.
Institute of Contemporary Arts.
Institute of Contemporary Arts, 48p. col illus.

Film and literature: an introduction and reader.
Corrigan, Timothy.
Prentice Hall, v-x. 374p. illus. bibliog. index.
ISBN 0135265428

Film and the anarchist imagination.
Porton, Richard.

Verso, 314p. illus. index.
ISBN 1859842615

 Identifying Hollywood's audiences: cultural identity and the movies.
Stokes, Melvyn and Maltby, Richard (eds.)
British Film Institute, iv-v. 209p. illus. index.
ISBN 0851707394

An introduction to visual culture.
Mirzoeff, Nicholas.
Routledge, i-xi. 274p. illus. bibliog. index.
ISBN 0415158761

The invisible art of film music: a comprehensive history.
MacDonald, Laurence E.
Ardsley House, vi-xvi. 431p. illus. bibliog. filmog. index.
ISBN 188015756X

Movie map: your guide to exploring Britain through film and tv.
Adams, Mark.
British Tourist Authority, 1 folded sheet. illus.

Movies: a crash course.
Naughton, John and Smith, Adam.
Watson-Guptill Publications, 144p. index. col. illus.
ISBN 0823009777

Paths of individuation in literature and film: a Jungian approach.
Kenevan, Phyllis Berdt.
Lexington Books, viii-x. 123p. bibliog. index.
ISBN 0739100165

A short guide to writing about film: 3rd ed.
Corrigan, Timothy.
Longman, v-viii. 182p. illus. bibliog. index.
ISBN 0321011104

FILM – GENRES

Alienation, animation: studies in East European experimentation.
Rogers, Ben.
46p. 7 plates. bibliog.

American science fiction and the Cold War: literature and film.
Seed, David.
Edinburgh University Press, 167p. illus.
ISBN 0953192601

Art in motion: animation aesthetics.
Furniss, Maureen.
John Libbey & Co, xi-x. 278p. illus. [16] col. plates. index.
ISBN 1864620390

A-Z of silent film comedy.
Mitchell, Glenn.
B.T. Batsford, 256p. illus. bibliog.
ISBN 0713479396

Back in the saddle: essays on Western film and television actors.
McFarland, vii. 216p. illus.
ISBN 078640566X

The big book of noir.
Server, Lee and Gorman, Ed and Greenberg, Martin H. (eds.)
Carroll & Graf, 386p. index.
ISBN 0786705744

 Bleeding images: Performance and the British gangster movie.
Swain, John.
British Film Institute/ Birckbeck College MA in Cinema and Television Studies, 52p. bibliog. filmog.

British crime cinema.
Chibnall, Steve and Murphy, Robert (eds.)
Routledge, vi-x. 251p. illus. filmog. index.
ISBN 0415168708

British science fiction cinema.
Hunter, I.Q.
Routledge, vi-x. 217p. illus. filmog. index.
ISBN 0415168686

Disaster movies:
information source pack.
Kerameos, Anastasia and Sharp,
David.
BFI National Library.
ISBN 0851706894

A distant technology: science
fiction film and the machine age.
Telotte, J.P.
University Press of New England,
vii-viii. 218p. illus. filmog. bibliog.
index.
ISBN 0819563455

The documentary film movement:
an anthology.
Aitken, Ian (ed.)
Edinburgh University Press, v-x.
261p. bibliog. index.
ISBN 0748609482

Documenting the documentary:
close readings of documentary film
and video.
Grant, Barry Keith and Sloniowski,
Jeanette (eds.)
Wayne State University Press, 488p.
illus. bibliog. index.
ISBN 0814326390

Drums of terror: voodoo in the
cinema.
Senn, Bryan
Midnight Marquee Press, 256p.
appendices. bibliog. index.
ISBN 1887664181

Eros in hell: sex, blood and
madness in Japanese cinema.
Hunter, Jack.
Creation Books, 288p. illus. indices.
ISBN 1871592933

Feminism and documentary.
Waldman, Diane and Walker, Janet
(eds.)
Minnesota University Press, vii-ix.
365p. illus. filmog. bibliog. index.
ISBN 0816630070

Femme Noir: bad girls of film.
Hannsberry, Karen Burroughs.
McFarland, vii-x. 633p. bibliog.
index.
ISBN 0786404299

Film cartoons: a guide to 20th
century American animated
features and shorts.
Mccall, Douglas L.
McFarland & Company, 261p.
appendix. bibliog. index.
ISBN 0786405848

Film follies: the cinema out of
order.
Klawans, Stuart.

Cassell, 188p. bibliog. index. [8]
plates.
ISBN 0304700541

 Film/ Genre.
Altman, Rick.
British Film Institute, v-x. 246p.
illus. bibliog. index.
ISBN 0851707181

For documentary.
Vaughan, Dai.
University of California Press, ix-xix.
215p. index.
ISBN 0520216954

Forward Soviet!: history and non-
fiction film in the USSR.
Roberts, Graham.
I.B.Tauris, 195p. [4]p. of plates.
filmog. bibliog. index.
ISBN 1860642829

A girl and a gun: the complete
guide to film noir on video.
Meyer, David N.
Avon Books, x-xv. 303p. illus.
ISBN 038079067X

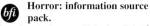 **A history of experimental**
film and video: from the
canonical avant-garde to
contemporary British practice.
Rees, A.L.
British Film Institute, x-viii. 152p.
[32] plates. bibliog. index.
ISBN 0851706819

Hollywood cartoons: American
animation in its golden age.
Barrier, Michael.
Oxford University Press, ix-xviii.
648p. illus. index.
ISBN 0195037596

Hollywood Hex: death and destiny
in the dream factory.
Brottman, Mikita.
Creation Books, 201p. illus. bibliog.
index.
ISBN 1871592852

 Horror: information source
pack.
Ormsby, Andrew and Mettler, Erinna
and Forbes, Tess.
BFI National Library, 23p. bibliog.
ISBN 0851706908

Imortal monster: the mythological
evolution of the fantastic beast in
modern fiction and film.
Andriano, Joseph D.
Greenwood Press, I-xix. 179p.
filmog. bibliog. index.
ISBN 0313306672

Jungian reflections within the
cinema: a psychological analysis of
sci-fi and fantasy archetypes.
Iaccino, James F.
Praeger, I-xx. 216p. filmog. bibliog.
index.
ISBN 0275950484

King Arthur on film: new essays on
Arthurian cinema.
Harty, Kevin J.
McFarland, I-xi. 275p. illus. filmog.
bibliog. index.
ISBN 0786401524

Meat is murder!: an illustrated
guide to cannibal culture.
Brottman, Mikita.
Creation Books, 213p. illus. filmog.
bibliog.
ISBN 1871592909

Millennium movies: end of the
world cinema.
Newman, Kim.
Titan, 272p. illus. bibliog. index.
ISBN 1840230606

 Modern noir: A-level guide.
Forbes, Tess and Sharp, David
and Waller, Fiona.
BFI National Library, 28p. bibliog.
ISBN 0851707699

Of gods and monsters: a critical
guide to Universal Studios' science
fiction, horror and mystery films,
1929-1939.
Soister, John T.
McFarland & Company, I-x. 395p.
illus. bibliog. appendices. indices.
ISBN 078640454X

The political film.
Genovese, Michael A.
Simon & Schuster, vii-viii. 139p.
bibliog.
ISBN 0536012504

Projections of war: Hollywod,
American culture and World War
II: Revised and updated.
Doherty, Thomas.
Columbia University Press, viii-x.
3382p. illus. appendices. indices.
ISBN 0231116357

The psychopath in film.
Wilson, Wayne.
University Press of America, i-vii.
311p. bibliog. indices.
ISBN 0761813179

Public enemies, public heroes:
screening the gangster from Little
Caesar to Touch of evil.
University of Chicago Press, vii-xii.
263p. illus. appendix. bibliog.

indices.
ISBN 0226550338

Saucer movies: a UFOlogical history of the cinema.
Meehan, Paul.
Scarecrow Press, 373p. filmog. bibliog. index.
ISBN 0810835738

Science fiction serials: a critical filmography of the 31 hard SF cliffhangers; with an appendix of the 37 serials with slight SF content.
Kinnard, Roy.
McFarland, vi. 217p. illus. bibliog. index.
ISBN 07864054567

Screams of reason: mad science and modern culture.
Skal, David J.
W.W. Norton, 368p. illus. appendix. index.
ISBN 039304582X

 Spectacular cinema and The Towering Inferno.
Lavender, Sam.
British Film Institute/ Birkbeck College MA in Cinema and Television Studies, 22p. illus. bibliog.

Tall in the saddle: great lines from classic westerns.
Thompson, Peggy and Usukawa, Saeko.
Chronicle Books, ix-xiii. 118p. illus. index.
ISBN 081181730X

Thrillers.
Rubin, Martin.
Cambridge University Press, ix-xiv. 319p. illus. bibliog. filmog. index.
ISBN 0521588391

Transcultural cinema.
MacDougall, David: Taylor, Lucien (ed.)
Princeton University Press, I-x. 318p. illus. filmog. bibliog. indices.
ISBN 0691012342

Understanding animation.
Wells, Paul.
Routledge, v-x. 265p. illus. bibliog. index. filmog.
ISBN 0415115973

Video nasties: from absurd to zombie flesh-eaters – a collector's guide to the most horrifying films ever banned!
Bryce, Allan.
Stray Cat Publishing, [158]p. col. illus.
ISBN 0953326101

Walt Disney and Europe: European influences on the animated feature films of Walt Disney.
Allan, Robin.
John Libbey, 304p. [48] col. plates. illus. appendices. bibliog. filmog. index.
ISBN 1864620412

 War films: A-level guide.
Delaney, Sean and Mettler, Erinna.
BFI National Library, 24p.
ISBN 0851707718

Western all'italiana: the specialists.
Piselli, Stefano.
Glittering Images, 141p. illus. bibliog. discog.
ISBN 8882750345

The western reader.
Kitses, Jim and Rickman, Gregg (eds.)
Limelight Editions, 407p. illus.
ISBN 0879102683

What is non-fiction cinema? On the very idea of motion picture communication.
Ponech, Trevor.
Westview, i-vii. 302p. bibliog. index.
ISBN 0813367034

Women in horror films, 1930s.
Mank, Gregory William.
McFarland, ix-xi. 403p. illus. appendix. index.
ISBN 0786405538

Women in horror films, 1940s.
Mank, Gregory William.
McFarland, ix-xi. 392p, illus. appendix. index.
ISBN 0786404647

FILM – SOCIAL ASPECTS

 Acting up: women, performance and self-representation.
Picken, Susan.
British Film Institute/ Brikbeck College MA in Cinema and Television Studies, 61p. illus. filmog. bibliog.

 The aesthetics of violence in films about Vietnam.
Evans, Ben.
British film Institute/ Birckbeck College MA in Cinema and Television Studies, 36p. bibliog.

American domesticity: from how-to manual to Hollywood melodrama.
Mchugh, Kathleen Anne.
Oxford University Press, x. 235p. illus. notes. bibliog. index.
ISBN 0195122615

 American movie audiences: from the turn of the century to the early sound era.
Stokes, Melvyn and Maltby, Richard (eds.)
British Film Institute, iv-vi. 186p. illus. index.
ISBN 0851707211

Asian America through the lens.
Xing, Jun.
Sage Publications, 122p. illus.

Babylon blue: an illustrated history of adult cinema.
Flint, David.
Creation Books, 188p. [8] col. plates. illus. bibliog. index.
ISBN 1840680024

Bad girls and sick boys: fantasies in contemporary art and culture.
Kauffman, Linda S.
University of California Press, ix-xii. 328p. illus. index.
ISBN 0520210328

"Banned in the USA": British films in the United States and their censorship, 1933-1960.
Slide, Anthony.
I.B. Taurus, vii-xi. 212p. appendices. bibliog. indices.
ISBN 1860642543

The body's perilous pleasures: dangerous desires and contemporary culture.
Aaron, Michelle (ed.)
Edinburgh University Press, v-vii.

232p. index.
ISBN 074860961X

Brave dames and wimpettes: what women are really doing on page and screen.
Isaacs, Susan.
Ballantine, 157p. index.
ISBN 0345422813

Captive bodies: postcolonial subjectivity in cinema.
Foster, Gwendolyn Audrey.
State University of New York Press, v-xii. 249p. illus. bibliog. index.
ISBN 0791441563

Cartoon crazy?: children's perceptions of 'action' cartoons.
Chambers, Sue and Karet, Nicki and Samson, Neil and Sancho-Aldridge, Jane.
Independent Television Commission, 64p. illus. appendices.
ISBN 0900485698

Cinema cinema: contemporary art and the cinematic experience.
Bloemheuvel, Marente and Guldemond, Jaap (eds.)
Stedelijk Van Abbemuseum, 128p. bibliog. col. illus.
ISBN 9070149710

Cinematic political thought: narrating race, nation and gender.
Shapiro, Michael J.
Edinburgh University Press, ix. 176p. illus. index.
ISBN 0748612890

Close up 1927-1933: cinema and modernism.
Donald, James and Friedberg, Anne and Marcus, Laura (eds,)
Princeton University Press, vi-x. 341p. illus. index.
ISBN 0691004633

Communication, cinema, development: from morosity to hope.
Roberge, Gaston.
Manohar, 216p. illus. index.
ISBN 8173041490

Dangerous dames: women and representation in the Weimar street film and film noir.
Ohio University Press, i-xvi. 159p. illus. index.
ISBN 0821412701

The de-voicing of society: why we don't talk to each other any more.
Locke, John L.
Simon & Schuster, 256p. index.
ISBN 0684843331

Entertainment-education: a communication strategy: a communication strategy for social change.
Singhal, Arvind and Rogers, Everett M.
Lawrence Erlbaum, vii-xiv. 265p. illus. tables. figs. gloss. bibliog. indices.
ISBN 0805833501

Film and the nuclear age: representing cultural anxiety.
Perrine, Toni.
Garland Publishing, i-xiv. 287pp. filmog. bibliog. index.
ISBN 0815329326

A fuller picture: the commercial impact of six British films with black themes in the 1990s.
Wambu, Onyekachi and Arnold, Kevin.
British Film Intitute, i-vi. 76p. appendix.
ISBN 0851707610

Gay signatures: gay and lesbian theory, fiction and film in France, 1945-1995.
Heathcote, Owen and Hughes, Alex and Williams, James S. (eds.)
Berg, i-x. 227p. bibliog. index.
ISBN 1859739873

Girl reporter: gender, journalism, and the movies.
Good, Howard.
Scarecrow Press, v-vii. 189p. illus. filmog. bibliog. index.
ISBN 0810833980

Hard core: power, pleasure, and the "frenzy of the visible": Expanded.
Williams, Linda.
University of California Press, ix-xviii. 380p. illus. bibliog. index.
ISBN 0520219430

Heroes in hard times: cop action movies in the U.S.
King, Neal.
Temple University Press, vii-xi. 282p. [8] plates. index.
ISBN 1566397022

A history of X: 100 years of sex in film.
Ford, Luke.
Prometheus Books, 252p. bibliog. index.
ISBN 1573926787

Hollywood's Latin lovers: Latino, Italian and French men who make the screen smolder.
Thomas, Victoria.
Angel City Press, 144p. illus.
ISBN 1883318416

Home, exile, homeland: film, media and the politics of place.
Naficy, Hamid.
Routledge, vii-xii. 248p. index.
ISBN 0415919460

Hyperreality and global culture.
Perry, Nick.
Routledge, i-xii. 194p. illus. bibliog. indices.
ISBN 0415105153

Inside the gaze: the fiction film and its spectator.
Casetti, Francesco; Andrew, Nell and O'Brien, Charles (transl.)
Indiana University Press, vii-xv. 174p. gloss. index.
ISBN 0253212324

In the company of women: contemporary female friendship in films.
Hollinger, Karen.
University of Minnesota Press, vii-viii. 275p. illus. index.
ISBN 0816631786

In the public good?: censorship in New Zealand.
Watson, Chris and Shuker, Roy.
Dunmore Press, 219p. illus. bibliog. index.
ISBN 0864693052

Life the movie: how entertainment conquered reality.
Gabler, Neal.
Alfred A. Knopf, 303p. bibliog. index.
ISBN 0679417524

Mythologies of violence in postmodern media.
Sharrett, Christopher.
Wayne State University, 453p. illus. bibliog. index.
ISBN 0814327427

National identity.
Cameron, Keith.
Intellect Books, iv. 155p. illus.
ISBN 1871516056

No go the bogeyman: scaring, lulling and making mock.
Warner, Marina.
Chatto & Windus, xi-xii. 435p. illus. [16] col. plates. index.
ISBN 0701165936

Not just race, not just gender: black feminist readings.
Smith, Valerie.
Routledge, i-xxiii. 166p. index.
ISBN 0415903262

Old wives' tales and other women's stories.
Modleski, Tania.
New York Univesity Press, vii-ix.
238p. illus. bibliog. index.
ISBN 0814755941

Open secret: gay Hollywood, 1928-1998.
Ehrenstein, David.
William Morrow, 371p. [8] plates.
index.
ISBN 0688153178

Out takes: essays on queer theory and film.
Hanson, Ellis (ed.)
Duke Univesity Press, vi. 364p. illus.
bibliog. index.
ISBN 0822323427

Postmodernism in the cinema.
Degli-Esposito, Cristina (ed.)
Berghahn Books, 264p. illus. index.
ISBN 1571811052

Redirecting the gaze: gender, theory and cinema in the third world.
Robin, Diana and Jaffe, Ira Sheldon (eds.)
State University of New York Press, i-xi. 377p. illus. bibliog. index.
ISBN 0791439941

Reelpolitik: political ideologies in '30s and '40s films.
Kelley, Beverly Merrill.
Praeger, ix-xvii. 194p. bibliog. index.
ISBN 0275960196

Renegade sisters: girl gangs on film.
Zalcock, Beverley.
Creation Books, 187p. illus.
appendix. bibliog. index.
ISBN 1871592925

Screening the past: film and the representation of history.
Barta, Tony (ed.)
Praeger, i-xi. 279p. illus. [8] plates.
index.
ISBN 0275954021

Sexual politics and narrative film: Hollywood and beyond.
Wood, Robin.
Columbia University Press, i-x. 352p.
ill.
ISBN 0231076053

Subject: cinema, object: woman: a study of the portrayal of women in Indian cinema.
Chatterji, Shoma a.
Parumita Publications, 298p. [6]p. of plates. bibliog. index.

The visible wall: Jews and other ethnic outsiders in Swedish film.

Wright, Rochelle.
Southern Illinois University Press, vii-xvi. 453p. illus. appendix. bibliog. index.
ISBN 0809321645

Western gunslingers in fact and on film: Hollywood's famous lawmen and outlaws.
Rainey, Buck.
McFarland, i-vii. 341p. illus. bibliog. index.
ISBN 0786403969

What it is... What is was!: the black film explosion of the '70s in words and pictures.
Martinez, Gerald and Martinez, Diana and Chavez, Andres.
Miramax Books/ Hyperion, 208p. illus. (many col.). filmog.
ISBN 0786883774

Widescreen dreams: growing up gay at the movies.
Horrigan, Patrick E.
University of Wisconsin Press, vii-xxii. 227p. illus. bibliog.
ISBN 0299161609

Women in Hollywood: from vamp to studio head.
Sova, Dawn B.
Fromm International Publishing Corporation, vii-xiii. 225p. illus. appendices. bibliog. index.
ISBN 0880642327

FILM STUDIES/ THEORY AND CRITICISM

Artists in the audience: cults, camp, and American film criticism.
Taylor, Greg.
Princeton University Press, 198p. illus. bibliog index.
ISBN 0691004218

Chick flicks: theories and memories of the feminist film movement.
Rich, Ruby.
Duke University Press, 419p. index.
ISBN 0822321211

 The cinema book: 2nd ed.
Cook, Pam and Bernink, Mieke (eds.)
British Film Institute, vii-x. 406p. illus. bibliog. index.
ISBN 0851707262

The essential Framework: classic film and TV essays.
Willemen, Paul and Pines, Jim (eds.)
EpiGraph, v-vi. 258p.
ISBN 1902458001

Feminist film theory: a reader.
Thornham, Sue.
New York University Press, vi. 361p. bibliog. index.
ISBN 0814782442

Film: an introduction.
Phillips, William H.
Bedford/St. Martin's, i-xxi. 599p. illus. tables. bibliog. index.
ISBN 0312178182

Film quarterly: forty years – a selection.
Henderson, Brian and Martin, Ann (eds.)
University of California Press, v-xii. 571p. illus. index.
ISBN 0520216032

An introduction to film studies. (2nd ed.)
Nelmes, Jill.
Routledge, i xviii. 522p. illus. bibliog. index.
ISBN 0415173108

 Landscapes of the mind: the idea of landscape in Patrick Keiller's London and Andrew Kotting's Gallivant.
Pichler, Barbara.
British Film Institute/ Birkbeck College MA in Cinema and Television Studies, September 1998.
Dissertation.

The memory of Tiresias: intertextuality and film.
Iampolski, Mikhail; Ram, Harsha (transl.)
University of California Press, ix. 326p. bibliog. index.
ISBN 0520085302

Negative space: Manny Farber on the movies. (expanded edition)
Farber, Manny and Walsh, Robert.
Da Capo, vii-xiv. 412p. index.
ISBN 0306808293

Post-traumatic culture: injury and interpretation in the nineties.
Farrell, Kirby.
Johns Hopkins University Press, vii-xv. 420p. index.
ISBN 0801857872

Screen histories: a Screen reader.
Kuhn, Annette and Stacey, Jackie (eds.); Screen.
Oxford University Press, 233p. appendix.
ISBN 0198159498

Sight, sound, motion: applied media aesthetics. (3rd ed.)
Zettl, Herbert.
Wadsworth, ix-xxvii. 407p. illus. gloss. bibliog. index.
ISBN 0534526772

Thinking about movies: watching, questioning, enjoying.
Lehman, Peter and Luhr, William.
Harcourt Brace College Publishers, vii-xi. 311p. [8] col. plates. illus. index.
ISBN 0155000012

Totally, tenderly, tragically: essays and criticism from a lifelong love affair with the movies.
Lopate, Phillip.
Anchor Press/ Doubleday, 384p. index.
ISBN 0385492502

The transparency of spectacle: meditations on the moving image.
Dixon, Wheeler Winston.
State University of New York Press, vii-xi. 223p. bibliog. index.
ISBN 0791437825

Understanding movies. (8th ed.)
Giannetti, Louis.
Prentice Hall, iii-ix. 529p. col. plates. illus. gloss. index.
ISBN 0136465633

Visual culture: the reader.
Evans, Jessica and Hall, Stuart (eds.)
Sage, vi-xviii. 478p. illus. index.
ISBN 0761962484

The voice in cinema.
Chion, Michel; Gorbman, Claudia (transl.)
Columbia University Press, vii-xiii. 183p. illus. index.
ISBN 0231108230

ECONOMICS/ PRODUCTION/ FILM INDUSTRY

The art of the storyboard: storyboarding for film. TV, and animation.
Hart, John.
Focal Press, vii-xii. 223p. illus. bibliog.
ISBN 0240803299

The big deal: Hollywood's million-dollar spec script market.
Taylor, Thom.
William Morrow, viii-xiii. 319p. appendix. index.
ISBN 0688161715

Communication from the Commission to the European Parliament and the Council of Ministers: audiovisual policy: next step.
Commission of the European Communities.
Office for Official Publications of the European Community, 20p.
ISBN 9278384194

The cost of making dreams: accounting for the British film industry.
Hamilton-Deeley, Gavin and Hussey, Roger and Sowinska, Monika.
Deloitte & Touche, 48p. illus. appendices. bibliog. gloss. index.

 A discussion of film production in Bombay and spectatorship in the South Asian diaspora.
Hines, Jessica.
British Film Institute/ Birkbeck College MA in Cinema and Television Studies, 33p. illus.

"Film Europe" and "Film America": cinema, commerce and cultural exchane 1920-1939.
Higson, Andrew and Maltby, Richard (eds.)
University of Exeter Press, x. 406p. figs. tables. index.
ISBN 0859895467

The filmmaker's handbook: a comprehensive guide for the digital age: Completely revised and updated.
Ascher, Steven and Pincus, Edward.
Plume, viii-x. 614p. illus. figs. appendices. bibliog. index.
ISBN 0452279577

The grammar of film-making.
Huston, John and Munn, Michael.
[s.n.], 7p.

**Guide to postproduction for TV
and film: managing the process.**
Clark, Barbara and Spohr, Susan J.
Focal Press, i-xv. 221p. tables. index.
ISBN 0240803221

**Keeping score: film and television
music, 1988-1997.**
Marill, Alvin H.
Scarecrow Press, v-ix. 358p. index.
ISBN 0810834162

The motion picture mega-industry.
Litman, Barry Russell.
Allyn & Bacon, v-xii. 321p. tables.
appendices. index.
ISBN 0205200265

**On actors and acting: essays by
Alexander Knox.**
Knox, Alexander; Slide, Anthony
(ed.)
Scarecrow Press, vii. 117p. illus.
filmog. index.
ISBN 081083499

**Playing to the camera: film actors
discuss their craft.**
Cardullo, Bert (ed.)
Yale University Press, v-xiv. 370p.
illus. bibliog. index.
ISBN 0300069839

**The sounds of commerce:
marketing popular film music.**
Smith, Jeff.
Columbia University Press, vii-x.
288p. illus. bibliog. index.
ISBN 023110863X

**The writer's journey: mythic
structure for storytellers and
screenwriters. (2nd rev. expanded
ed.)**
Vogler, Christopher.
Pan, i-xxiii. 326p. appendices.
ISBN 0330375911

HISTORIES – GENERAL

**Celebrating 1895: the centenary of
cinema.**
Fullerton, John (ed.)
John Libbey & Co, v-xv. 287p. illus.
index.
ISBN 1864620153

Collecting visible evidence.
Gaines, Jane M. and Renov, Michael
(eds.)
University of Minnesota Press, vii-ix.
339p. illus. index.
ISBN 0816631360

**Living pictures: the origins of the
movies.**
Rossell, Deac.
vii-xii. 188p. illus. bibliog. index.
ISBN 079143768X

The oral history reader.
Perks, Robert and Thomson, Alistair
(eds.)
Routledge, i-xiii. 479p. bibliog.
index.
ISBN 0415133521

**Projecting a nation: New Zealand
film and its reception in Germany.**
Jones, Stan.
Kakapo Books, 29p.
ISBN 0953017729

HISTORIES – AFRICA/ ASIA/ AUSTRALASIA

**Asian pop cinema: Bombay to
Tokyo.**
Server, Lee.
Chronicle Books, 132p. illus. bibliog.
ISBN 0811821196

**Dream makers on the Nile: a
portrait of Egyptian cinema.**
Darwish, Mustafa.
American University in Cairo Press,
43, [5]p. illus.
ISBN 977424429X

**Hong Kong: culture and politics of
disappearance.**
ABBAS, Ackbar.
University of Minnesota Press, v-vii.
155p. illus. index.

**Ideology of the Hindi film: a
historical contruction.**
Madhava Prasad, M.
Oxford University Press, ix. 258p.
illus. diagr. bibliog. index.
ISBN 019564218X

New Chinese cinema.
Tam, Kwok-kan and Dissanayake,
Wimal.
Oxford University Press, i-vii. 96p.
[18] col. plates. illus. filmog. bibliog.
index.
ISBN 0195906071

**One hundred acclaimed Tagalog
movies.**
Tobias, Mel C.
Peanut Butter, 255p. illus. bibliog.
gloss.
ISBN 0897168100

**The secret politics of our desires:
innocence, culpability and Indian
popular cinema.**
Nandy, Ashis (ed.)
Zed Books, i-ix. 259p filmog.
ISBN 1856495159

**Seeking the centre: the Australian
desert in literature, art and film.**
Haynes, Roslynn.
Cambridge University Press, vi-xvi.
347p. [30] col. plates. illus. bibliog.
index.
ISBN 0521571111

**Takarazuka: sexual politics and
popular culture in modern Japan.**
Robertson, Jennifer.
University of California Press, ix-xvi.
278p. bibliog. index.
ISBN 0520211510

The worlds of Japanese popular culture: gender, shifting boundaries and global cultures.
Martinez, D.P. (ed.)
Cambridge University Press, vii-xi. 212p. bibliog. index.
ISBN 0521637295

HISTORIES – EUROPE

The art of taking a walk flanerie, literature, and film in Weimar culture.
Gleber, Anke.
Princeton University Press, vii-xiii. illus. bibliog. index.
ISBN 069100239X

Belgian cinema = Le cinema belge = De belgische film.
Cinematheque royale de belgique.
Ludion, 992p. illus. bibliog. indices.
ISBN 9055442348

The cine goes to town: French cinema, 1896-1914. (Updated and expanded ed.)
Abel, Richard.
University of California Press, viii-xxiii. 568p. illus. bibliog. index.
ISBN 0520079361

Cinema greco/ Greek cinema.
Maraldi, Antonio and Martinin, Giacomo (eds.); Centro cinema citta di Cesena.
Il Ponte Vecchio, 60p. illus. filmog.

Deterritorializing the new German cinema.
Davidson, John.
University of Minnesota Press, xi. 201p. illus. notes. index.
ISBN 081662982X

Feminism, film, fascism: women's auto/ biographical film in postwar Germany.
Linville, Susan E.
University of Texas Press, ix-x. 196p. illus. filmog. bibliog. index.
ISBN 0292746970

The folklore of consensus: theatricality in the Italian cinema 1930-1943.
Landy, Marcia.
State University of New York Press, v-xxi. illus. bibliog. index.
ISBN 079143804X

Landscapes and loss: the national past in postwar French cinema.
Greene, Naomi.
Princeton University Press, vii. 234p. index.
ISBN 0691004757

The magic mirror: moviemaking in Russia 1908-1918.
Youngblood, Denise J.
The University of Wisconsin Press, i-xvii. 197p. [16] p. of plates. filmog.

bibliog. index.
ISBN 0299162346

Modes of representation in Spanish cinema.
Talens, Jenaro, and Zunzunegui, Santos (eds.)
Minnesota University Press, i-xxvi. 1-346p. index.
ISBN 0816629757

Russia on reels: the Russian idea in post-Soviet cinema.
Beumers, Birgit.
I.B. Tauris, vii-viii. 219p. appendices. filmog. bibliog. index.
ISBN 1860643906

Scratch book: 1983-1998.
Beauvais, Yann and Collin, Jean-Damien (eds.)
Light Cone/ Scratch, 411p. illus.
ISBN 2950325513

HISTORIES – GREAT BRITAIN

bfi **Analysis of a conflict of interests: origins, creation and first achievements of the British Film Institute, 1929-1936.**
Dupin, Christophe.
British Film Institute/ Birkbeck College MA in Cinema and Television Studies, 62p. viii. bibliog. appendices.

The beginnings of the cinema in England 1894-1901. Volume One: 1894-1896. (revised and updated).
Barnes, John; Maltby, Richard (ed.)
University of Exeter Press, vi-xv. 294p. illus. appendices. index.
ISBN 0859895645

Best of British: cinema and society from 1930 to the present.
Aldgate, Anthony and Richards, Jeffrey.
I.B. Tauris, vii-ix. 262p. illus. filmog. index.
ISBN 1860642888

The Black cinema of Sunderland: their circuits and their cinemas.
Manders, Frank.
Mercia Cinema Society, 24p. illus.
ISBN 0946406472

bfi **A brief history of the BFI Library and information service (1933 –1996).**
Hartnoll, Gillian.
BFI National Library, 52p.

British cinema in the 1980s: issues and themes.
Hill, John.
Clarendon Press, ix-xiv. 261p. illus. bibliog. index.
ISBN 0198742568

The Broadway super cinema and variety theatre, Stratford, London.
Jones, David.
Mercia Cinema Society, 12p. illus.
ISBN 0946406332

Cinemas of Ilfracombe.
Vernon, Chris and Hornsey, Brian.
Mercia Cinema Society, 32p. illus.
ISBN 1901425479

Cineplex Odeon: an outline history.
Turner, Philip.
Brantwood Books, ii. 30p. illus.
ISBN 0953102149

Distorted images: British national identity and film in the 1920s.
Bamford, Kenton.

I.B. Tauris, xii. 227p. 8 tables.
ISBN 1860863582

Eighth report of the Culture, Media and Sport Committee: report and accounts of the BBC for 1997/98: memorandum by the Department for Culture, Media & Sport.
Great Britain Department for Culture, Media and Sport;
The Stationary Office, 5p.
ISBN 0101425821

England is mine: pop life in Albion from Wilde to Goldie.
Bracewell, Michael.
Flamingo, 245p. index.
ISBN 0006550150

bfi **Entertaining the nation: Britain since 1930: education resource pack.**
Pearce, Hilary (ed.); British Film Institute Museum of the Moving Image.
British Film Institute Museum of the Moving Image, unpaged, bibliog. chronol.

bfi **Entertaining the Victorians: education resource pack.**
Pearce, Hilary (ed.); British Film Institute Museum of the Moving Image.
British Film Institute Museum of the Moving Image. unpaged. bibliog. chronolog.

The Essoldo circuit.
Hornsey, Brian.
Mercia Cinema Society, 28p. illus.
ISBN 0946406383

Filmed in Cornwall.
Craig, Sue and Fitzgerald, David.
Bossiney Books, 95p. col. illus.
ISBN 1899383271

Lanarkshire's legendary cinemas.
Peter, Bruce.
Stenlake, 48p. illus.
ISBN 1840330686

Magic in the dark: the cinemas of central Manchester and Ardwick Green: an affectionate tribute.
Southall, Derek J.
Neil Richardson, 63p. illus.
ISBN 1852161302

bfi **Making movies matter: report of the Film Education Working Group.**
Film Education Working Group.
British Film Institute, 94p. illus. appendices.
ISBN 08517707661

bfi **New British cinema: information source pack.**
Mettler, Erinna and Ormsby, Andrew.
BFI National Library, 24p. bibliog.
ISBN 0851706916

New links for the lottery: proposals for the new opportunities fund, presented to Parliament by the Secretary of State for Culture, Media and Sport by command of Her Majesty, November 1998.
Great Britain Department for Culture, Media and Sport.
The Stationary Office, 20p.
ISBN 0101416628

Ninety years of cinema in Bristol.
Hornsey, Brian.
44p. illus.
ISBN 190142538X

Ninety years of cinema in Montrose, Portobello and Kelso.
Hornsey, Brian.
[s.n.], 12. Illus.
ISBN 1901425509

Ninety years of cinema in Peterborough.
Hornsey, Brian.
[s.n.], 21p. illus.
ISBN 1873969279

Ninety years of cinema in Widnes & Runcorn.
Hornsey, Brian.
16p. illus.
ISBN 1901425266

bfi **Rogue reels: opositional film in Britain, 1945-1990.**
Dickinson, Margaret (ed.)
British Film Institute, vi. 330p. illus. bibliog. index.
ISBN 0851707270

Seats in all parts…: Mansfield's stage and screen history.
Orton, Leslie and Bradbury, David J. and Old Mansfield Society.
Old Mansfield Society, 40p. illus.
ISBN 0951794833

bfi **UK-wide cinema exhibition strategy consultation document, June 1999.**
Brett, Paul; British Film Institute and BFI Exhibition.
British Film Institute, 35p. appendices. maps.

A Victorian film enterprise: the history of the British Mutoscope and Biograph Company.
Brown, Richard and Anthony, Barry.
Flicks Books, vi-xiv. 344p. illus. appendices. bibliog. index.
ISBN 0948911271

HISTORIES – USA/ America

African-American blues, rhythm and blues, gospel and zydeco on film and video, 1926-1997.
Vernon, Paul.
Ashgate Publishing, vi-xvii. 421p.
filmog. bibliog. index.
ISBN 1840142944

Balboa Films: a history and filmography of the silent film studio.
Jura, Jean-Jacques and Bardin II, Rodney Norman.
McFarland, ix. 292p. filmog. bibliog. index.
ISBN 0786404965

Building a company: Roy O. Disney and the creation of an entertainment empire.
Thomas, Bob.
Hyperion, 359p. index. [16 plates].
ISBN 0786862009

The Bureau of Motion Pictures and its influence on film content during World War II: the reasons for its failure.
Myers, James M.
The Edwin Mellen Press, vi. 234p.
appendix. bibliog.
ISBN 0773483047

Celluloid soldiers: the Warner Bros. Campaign against Nazism.
Birdwell, Michael E.
New York University Press, i-xxi.
266p. illus. bibliog. index.
ISBN 0814713386

Contemporary Hollywood cinema.
Neale, Steve (ed.)
Routledge, i-xxii. 338p. illus. bibliog.
index.
ISBN 0415170085

The decade that shaped television news: CBS in the 1950s.
Mickelson, Sig.
Praeger, xviii. 242p. bibliog. index.
ISBN 0275955672

Destructing Disney.
Byrne, Eleanor and McQuillan, Martin.
Pluto Press, vii. 209p. index.
ISBN 0745314511

The Disney way: harnessing the management secrets of Disney in your company.
Capodagli, Bill and Jackson, Lynn.
McGraw Hill, xiv. 221p. illus.

bibliog. index.
ISBN 0070120641

Gendering the nation: Canadian women's cinema.
Armatage, Kay et al.
University of Toronto Press, x-xi.
329p. bibliog. index.
ISBN 0802079644

The gross: the hits, the flops – the summer that ate Hollywood.
Bart, Peter
St. Martin's Press, 311p.

Hollywood: hoopla and chutzpah, 1910-1940.
Jensen, Billie J. and Jensen, Reece C.
The Ghastly Gallimaufry, 248p. illus.
bibliog. index.
ISBN 1886278091

Hollywood hoopla: creating stars and selling movies in the golden age of Hollywood.
Sennett, Robert S.
Billboard Books, 191p. illus. bibliog.
index.
ISBN 0823083314

Hollywood on Lake Michigan: 100 years of Chicago and the movies.
Bernstein, Arnie.
Lake Claremont Press, x-xiii. 364p.
illus. appendices. bibliog. index.
ISBN 0964242621

Hollywood party: how communism seduced the American film industry in the 1930s and 1940s.
Billingsley, K.L.
Forum, i-xvii. 365p. [8]p. of plates.
appendices. index.
ISBN 0761513760

Hollywood rat race.
Wood, Edward D., Jr.
Four Walls Eight Windows, 138p.
ISBN 156858119X

Madcaps, screwballs, and con women: the female trickster in American culture.
Landay, Lori.
University of Pennsylvania Press, ix-xi. 258p. illus. bibliog. index.
ISBN 0812216512

Motion picture exhibition in Washington, D.C.: an illustrated history of parlors, palaces and multiplexes in the metropolitan area, 1894-1997.
Headland, Robert K.
McFarland, v-ix. 398p. illus.
appendices. bibliog. index.
ISBN 0786405449

The mouse that roared: Disney and the end of innocence.
Giroux, Henry A.
Rowman and Littlefield, xi, 186p.
ISBN 0847691098

The new American cinema.
Lewis, Jon (ed.)
Duke University Press, ix. 405p.
bibliog. index.
ISBN 0822321157

Nixon on stage and screen: the thirty-seventh president as depicted in films, television plays and opera.
Monsell, Thomas.
McFarland, v-vii. 239p. index.
ISBN 078640163X

Paramount in Paris: 300 films produced at the Joinville Studios, 1930-1033, with credits and biographies.
Waldman, Harry; Slide, Anthony (ed.).
Scarecrow Press, i-xix. 237p.
ISBN 0810834316

The Penguin book of Hollywood.
Silvester, Christopher (ed.)
Viking, vii-xxiii. 696p. index.
ISBN 0670880655

So close to the State/s the emergence of Canadian feature film policy.
Dorland, Michael.
University of Toronto Press, xi. 199p.
bibliog.
ISBN 080208043X

The sound of silence: conversations with 16 film and stage personalities who bridged the gap between silents and the talkies.
Ankerich, Michael G.
McFarland, vii-xii. 260p. index.
ISBN 078640504X

Team rodent: how Disney devours the world.
Hiaasen, Carl.
Ballantine, 83p.
ISBN 0345422805

Teenage confidential: an illustrated history of the American teen.
Barson, Michael and Heller, Steven.
Chronicle Books, 132p. col. illus.
bibliog.
ISBN 0811815846

Uncertain guardians: the news media as a political institution.
Sparrow, Bartholemew.
Johns Hopkins University Press, ix-xxi. 277p. illus. index.
ISBN 0801860369

INDIVIDUAL FILMS

The acid house.
Welsh, Irvine.
Methuen, vii-xii. 81p. [8] plates.
ISBN 0413724204

Adamah: a vanished film.
Tryster, Hillel.
Steven Spielberg Jewish Film
Archive, 20p. illus.

Amistad.
Gold, Claudia and Wall, Ian.
Film Education, 24p. illus. appendix.
bibliog. + 1 CD-ROM.

**An analytical guide to television's
Battlestar Galactica.**
Muir, John Kenneth.
McFarland, vii-x. 234p. illus. bibliog.
index.
ISBN 0786404418

The art of Mulan.
Kurtti, Jeff.
Hyperion, 189p. col. illus.
ISBN 0786863889

**Austin Powers: the spy who
shagged me: groovenir film
programme.**
Inside Film.
Inside Film, 18p. illus.

**The Bad and the beautiful: a
screenplay.**
Schnee, Charles; Bruccoli, Matthew
J. (ed.)
Southern Illinois University Press, i-
xix. 137p. illus. appendices.
ISBN 0809321823

**Before the Exorcist: William Peter
Blatty's own story of taking his
novel to film.**
Blatty, William Peter.
ScreenPress Books, 58p. illus.

Brief encounter.
Coward, Noel.
Faber and Faber, vii-xvi. 72p. illus.
ISBN 0571196802

 Caravaggio.
Bersani, Leo and Dutoit,
Ulysse.
British Film Institute, 86p. illus.
ISBN 0851707246

Central Station: screenplay.
Carneiro, Joao Emanuel and
Bernstein, Marcos; Gledson, John
(transl.)
Bloomsbury, v-ix. 115p. [8] col.
plates. illus.
ISBN 0747545022

**Charlie's family: an illustrated
screenplay.**
Van Bebber, Jim.
Creation Books, i-viii. 188p. illus.
filmog. bibliog. indices.
ISBN 1871592941

 **Crash: David Cronenberg's
post-mortem on J.G.
Ballard's "trajectory of fate".**
Sinclair, Iain.
British Film Institute, 128p. illus.
bibliog.
ISBN 085170719X

**David Lloyd George: the movie
mystery.**
Berry, David and Horrocks, Simon (eds.).
University of Wales Press, vii-xiv.
210p. illus. appendices. index.
ISBN 070831371X

Divorcing Jack.
Bateman, Colin.
HarperCollins, vii-xiii. 180p. illus.
credits.
ISBN 0006512747

**Get Carter: a screenplay by Mike
Hodges.**
Hodges, Mike.
ScreenPress Books, 61p.

Holy smoke.
Campion, Anna and Campion, Jane.
Bloomsbury, 259p. bibliog.
ISBN 0747531900

**The horse whisperer: an illustrated
companion to the major motion
picture.**
Ehrlich, Gretel.
Bantam, 157p. col. illus.
ISBN 0593044711

**Jack Arnold's final storyboards for
"The lost world" 1984.**
Arnold, Jack (illus.); Reemes, Dana
(comp.).
Photocopied reproduction of Jack
Arnold's storyboards for an
unrealised film project.
Ca. 300 leaves.

Jane Campion's The Piano.
Margolis, Harriet E.
Cambridge University Press, vii-xiv.
204p. filmog. bibliog. index.
ISBN 0521592585

**Jerry Maguire & a Jerry Maguire
journal.**
Crowe, Cameron.
Faber and Faber, 200p. illus.
ISBN 0571196721

The land girls.
Gold, Claudia and Wall, Ian.
Film Education, 11p. illus.

**Lawrence of Arabia: a film's
anthropology.**
Caton, Steven Charles.
University of California Press, ix-xv.
301p. illus. bibliog. index.
ISBN 0520210832

Life is beautiful: la vita e bella.
Benigni, Roberto and Cerami,
Vincenzo; Taruschio, Lisa (transl.).
Faber and Faber, 162p. illus.
ISBN 0571200346

Little Voice: a screenplay.
Herman, Mark.
Methuen, 113p. [8] plates.
ISBN 0413734900

**Luis Bunuel's The discreet charm
of the bourgeoisie.**
Kinder, Marsha.
Cambridge University Press, ix-xi.
224p. illus. bibliog. index.
ISBN 0521568315

 **Masquerade and fluidity in
Under the skin.**
Parker, Claire.
British Film Institute/ Birkbeck
College MA in Cinema and
Television Studies, 40, [32]p. col.
illus. bibliog. filmog. appendices.

North by northwest.
Lehman, Ernest.
Faber and Faber, 196p. illus.
ISBN 0571201849

Notting Hill.
Curtis, Richard; Coote, Clive (photo.)
Hodder and Stoughton, 207p. illus.
ISBN 0340738448

**Occupation in 26 pictures =
Okupacija u 26 slika.**
Goulding, Daniel J.
Flicks Books, 55p. bibliog. index.
ISBN 0948911646

Orphans: an original screenplay.
Mullan, Peter.
ScreenPress Books, viii. 130p. illus.
ISBN 1901680304

Out of sight.
Frank, Scott.
ScreenPress Books, ix-xxxii. 213p.
illus.
ISBN 1901680231

Pi.
Aronofsky, Darren.
Faber and Faber, 167p. illus.
ISBN 0571200427

**Planet of the apes as American
myth: race, politics and popular
culture: 2nd**
Greene, Eric.

University Press of New England, v-xvi. 248p. illus. filmog. bibliog. index.
ISBN 0819563293

The Prince of Egypt: a new vision in animation.
Solomon, Charles; Magee, rhion (designer)
Thames and Hudson, 192p. col. illus. bibliog.
ISBN 0500019134

Resurrecting The Mummy: the making of the movie.
Cadigan, Pat.
Ebury Press, 96p. col. illus.
ISBN 0091868300

Return of the Jedi: the illustrated screenplay.
Kasdan, Lawrence and Lucas, George.
Del Rey Book, 96p. illus.
ISBN 0752213482

Richard Wagner, Fritz Lang and The Nibelungen: the dramaturgy of disavowel.
Levin, David J.
Princeton University Press, vii-xi. 207p. illus. bibliog. index.
ISBN 0691026211

Robinson in space.
Keiler, Patrick.
Reaktion Books, 235p. col. illus.
ISBN 1861890281

Rounders: a screenplay.
Levien, David and Koppelman, Brian.
Miramax Books, 154p. illus. gloss.
ISBN 0786884223

Rushmore.
Anderson, Wes and Wilson, Owen.
Faber and Faber, vii-xvii. 137p. illus.
ISBN 0571200125

Sam Peckinpah's The Wild Bunch.
Prince, Stephen (ed.)
Cambridge University Press, ix-xii. 228p. illus. filmog. bibliog. index.
ISBN 0521586062

Saving Private Ryan: a film by Steven Spielberg.
James, David (phot.); Sunshine, Linda (ed.).
Del Rey Book/ Ballantine, 96p. illus.
ISBN 0752213482

The script of Elizabeth.
Hirst, Michael.
Boxtree, 127p. illus.
ISBN 0752224549

Shagadelically speaking: the words and world of Austin Powers.
Gould, Lance.
Ebury Press, v-vi. 154p. illus.
ISBN 0091871727

Shakespeare in love.
Norman, Marc and Stoppard, Tom.
Faber and Faber, 169p. illus.
ISBN 1861890281

Shooting to kill: how an independent producer blasts through the barriers to make movies that matter.
Vachon, Christine with Edelstein, David.
Avon Books, 335p. illus. index.
ISBN 0380798549

Star Wars encyclopedia.
Sansweet, Stephen J.
Virgin, ix-xxii. 354p. illus.
ISBN 185227736X

Still crazy.
Clement, Dick and La Frenais, Ian.
ScreenPress Books, vii-viii. 146p. illus.
ISBN 1901680215

Sunless = Sans soleil.
Kear, Jon.
Flicks Books, 59p. bibliog. index.
ISBN 0948911379

Sunset Boulevard.
Wilder, Billy.
University of California Press, vii-xvii. 126p.
ISBN 0520218558

Teaching aids to accompany the film "In the days of chivalry".
Glick, Annette.
Academy of Motion Picture Arts and Sciences, 20p.

Titanic: James Cameron's illustrated screenplay.
Cameron, James.
Boxtree, 153, 13p. col. illus.
ISBN 0752213202

Titanic: study guide.
Wall, Ian and Film Education.
Film Education, 16p. illus. Bibliog.

Titanic Town.
Devlin, Anne.
Faber and Faber, 127p. illus. credits.
ISBN 0571196756

The Truman show: the shooting script.
Niccol, Andrew.
Nick Hern Books, ix-xviii. 115p. [24] col. plates.
ISBN 1854594176

Visions of Armageddon.
Vaz, Mark Cotta.
Hyperion, 175p. col. illus.
ISBN 0786883472

Waking Ned Devine.
Jones, Kirk.
ScreenPress Books, ix-xv. 142p. illus.
ISBN 1901680290

Witness: the making of Schindler's list.
Palowski, Frranciszek; Ware, Anna and Ware, Robert G. (transl.)
Orion, ix-xix. 198p. [24] plates. index.
ISBN 0752817906

 WR – mysteries of the organism (WR mysterije organizma).
Durgnat, Raymond.
British Film Institute, 96p. col. illus. bibliog.
ISBN 0851707203

COLLECTED FILMS

Andrei Tarkovsky: collected screenplays.
Tarkovsky, Andrei; Powell, William and Synessios, Natasha (transl.)
Faber and Faber, ix-xxviii. 564p. illus. filmog.
ISBN 0571142664

The 50 greatest movies never made.
Gore, Chris.
St. Martin's Griffin, 233p. illus.
ISBN 031220082X

Great Christmas movies.
Thompson, Frank.
Taylor, xx. 220p. illus. [12] plates. index.
ISBN 0878332146

A guide to Charlie Chan films.
Mitchell, Charles P.
Greenwood Press, ix-xxx. 260p. illus. filmog. appendices. index.
ISBN 031330985X

Hamlet.
Hapgood, Robert (ed.); Shakespeare, William.
Cambridge University Press, v-xv. 296p. illus. bibliog. index.
ISBN 0521444381

Jane Austen in Hollywood.
Troost, Linda and Greenfield, Sayre (eds.)
University Press of Kentucky, 202p. [16] plates. bibliog. index.
ISBN 0813120845

Paper dreams: the art and artists of Disney storyboards.
Canemaker, John.
Hyperion, ix-xiv. 272p. col. illus. index.
ISBN 0786

The Poe cinema: a critical filmography of theatrical releases based on the works of Edgar Allan Poe.
Smith, Don G.
McFarland, vii. 307p. illus. filmog. bibliog. index.
ISBN 0786404531

Shakespeare on film.
Shaughnessy, Robert (ed.)
Macmillan, vii-xi. 205p. bibliog. index.
ISBN 0333720164

The Spanish prisoner and the Winslow boy.
Amet, David.
Faber and Faber, vii. 208p.
ISBN 0571200745

The unauthorized Star Wars compendium: the complete guide to the movies, comic books, novels, and more.
Edwards, Ted.
Little, Brown and Company, vii. 232p. illus. index.
ISBN 0316329290

Unspeakable ShaXXXspeares: queer theory and American kiddie culture.
Burt, Richard.
Macmillan, ix-xvii. 318p. illus. bibliog. filmog. index.
ISBN 0333753275

The worst movies of all time: or what were they thinking? (Rev. and updated ed.)
Sauter, Michael.
Greenwood Press, i-x. 358p. illus. index.
ISBN 0806520787

PERSONALITIES – COLLECTED STUDIES

 **Alfred Hitchcock: centenary essays.**
Allen, Richard and Ishii-Gonzales, S. (eds.)
British Film Institute, v-xviii. 362p. illus. bibliog. index.
ISBN 0851707351

Art directors in cinema: a worldwide biographical dictionary.
Stephens, Michael L.
McFarland & Company, i-ix. 350p. bibliog. index.
ISBN 0786403128

Contemporary cinematographers on their art.
Rogers, Pauline B.
Focal Press, i-xvi. 223p. tables.
ISBN 0240803094

Drama queens: wild women of the silver screen.
Stephens, Autumn.
Conari Press, vii-ix. 224p. illus. bibliog. index.
ISBN 1573241369

The film 100.
Smith, Scott.
Carol, 318p. index.
ISBN 0806519401

Hitchcock's notebooks: an authorized and illustrated look inside the creative mind of Alfred Hitchcock.
Auiler, Dan.
Avon Books, 567p. illus. bibliog. index.
ISBN 0380977834

Hollywood's maddest doctors.
Mank, Gregory William.
Midnight Marquee Press, 320p. illus. filmog. index.
ISBN 188766422X

Horror. Hero. Homo.: death, desire and subjectivity in Genet, Fassbinder and Haynes.
Tuttle, Tricia,
University of London, 44p. illus. bibliog.

Joel & Ethan Coen.
Korte, Peter and Seesslen, Georg (eds.); Mulholland, Jim (transl.)
Titan, 287p. illus. filmog. bibliog.
ISBN 1840230977

Lucid dreams: the films of Krzysztof Kieslowski.
Coates, Paul.
Flicks Books, 234p. index. filmog. bibliog.
ISBN 0948911638

Major film directors of the American and British cinema: (Revised Edition).
Phillips, Gene D.
Associated University Presses, 322p. bibliog. filmog. index. illus.
ISBN 0934223599

Mr. Bernds goes to Hollywood: my early life and career in sound recording at Columbia with Frank Capra and others.
Bernds, Edward.
Scarecrow Press, vii-xi. 319p. [16] plates. appendix. index.
ISBN 0810836025

National deconstruction: violence, identity, and justice in Bosnia.
Campbell, David.
University of Minnesota Press, ix-xv. 304p. index.
ISBN 0816629374

Orson Welles, Shakespeare and popular culture.
Anderegg, Michael A.
Columbia University Press, ix-xiv. 213p. illus. bibliog. index.
ISBN 0231112289

Phantasmagoria: pre-cinema to virtuality: Melies, Hegedus, Iwai, Oursler.
Callas, Peter, and Watson, David (curators).
Museum of Contemporary Art, 51p. col. illus. filmogs.
ISBN 187563245X

The power of glamour: the women who defined the magic of stardom.
Tapert, Annette.
Crown, 256p. illus. bibliog. index.
ISBN 0517703769

Projections 9: French film-makers on film-making.
Ciment, Michel and Herpe, Noel (eds.); Hodgson, Pierre (transl.)
Faber and Faber, vi-x. 193p. illus.
ISBN 0571193560

Screenwriters: America's storytellers in portrait.
Lumme, Helena; Manninen, Mika (phot)
Angel City Press, 127p. col. illus.
ISBN 1883318181

Time Out: interviews, 1968-1998.
Broughton, Frank (ed.)

Penguin, 320p. illus.
ISBN 0140279636

The ultimate directory of film technicians: a necrology of dates and places of brths and deaths of more than 9,000 producers, screenwriters, composers, cinematographers, art directors, costume designers, choreographers, executives, and publicists.
Doyle, Billy H.
Scarecrow Press, v-xv. 297p. bibliog.
ISBN 0810835460

Vixens, floozies and molls: 28 actresses of late 1920s and 1930s Hollywood.
Woolstein, Hans J.
McFarland & Company, viii. 274p illus. filmog.
ISBN 0786405651

Why we watch: the attractions of violent entertainment.
Goldstein, Jeffrey (ed.)
Oxford University Press, i-ix. 270p. illus. indices.
ISBN 0195118219

PERSONALITIES – INDIVIDUAL STUDIES

Absolutely… Goldie: the biography.
Wilson, Christopher.
HarperCollins, ix-xxiii. 232p. [16] plates (some colours). index.
ISBN 0002570181

The adventures of Roberto Rossellini.
Gallagher, Tag.
McFarland, i-x. 802p. illus. filmog. bibliog. indices.
ISBN 0306808730

Angela Lansbury: a life on stage and screen: Revised and updated.
Edelman, Rob and Kupferberg, Audrey E.
Citadel Press, vii-xii. 299p. [16] plates. filmog. bibliog. index.
ISBN 0806520760

Back lot: growing up with the movies.
Rapf, Maurice.
Scarecrow Press, xv. 211p. filmog. Illus. appendix. index.
ISBN 0810835835

Bedside manners: George Clooney and ER.
Keenleyside, Sam.
EXW Press, 224p. illus. [16] col. plates. filmog.
ISBN 1550223364

Bertrand Tavernier: fractured narrative and bourgeois values.
Zants, Emily.
Scarecrow Press, vi-xiii. 130p. illus. filmog. bibliog. index.
ISBN 0910836270

Between silk and cyanide: the story of SOE's code war.
Marks, Leo.
HarperCollins, viii. 613p. [8] plates. index.
ISBN 0002559447

Beyond terror: the films of Lucio Fulci.
Thrower, Stephen.
FAB Press, 311p. illus. filmogs. bibliog. indices.
ISBN 0952926067

Bombshell: the life and death of Jean Harlow.
Stenn, David.
Doubleday, x. 370p. [24] plates. filmog. index.
ISBN 0385421575

Bruce Lee anthology: films and fighting.
Crompton, Paul (comp.)
Pau H. Crompton, 208p. illus.
ISBN 1874250901

Cannibal Holocaust and the savage cinema of Ruggero Deodato.
Fenton, Howard and Grainger, Julian and Castoldi, Gian Luca.
FAB Press, 111p. filmog. bibliog. indices. col. illus.
ISBN 0952926040

Careless love: the unmaking of Elvis Presley.
Guralnick, Peter.
Little, Brown, xi-xv. 767p. illus. bibliog. index.
ISBN 0316644021

Cary Grant: a life in pictures.
Curtis, Jenny.
MetroBooks, 96p. illus. filmog. bibliog. index.
ISBN 1567995659

Cilla Black: Bobby's girl.
Thompson, Douglas.
Simon & Schuster, xiii. 300p. [8] plates. discog. index.
ISBN 0684840308

Cinema journeys of the man alone: the New Zealand and American films of Geoff Murphy.
Rayner, Jonathan.
Kakapo Books, 41p.
ISBN 0953017737

The cinema of Jean Cocteau.
Tolton, C.D.E. (ed.)
Legas, 200p. illus. bibliog.
ISBN 092125282X

Clint Eastwood: interviews.
Kapsis, Robert E. and Coblentz, Kathie (eds.)
University Press of Mississippi, vii-xiix. [8] plates. index.
ISBN 1578060702

Clint: the life and legend.
McGilligan, Patrick.
HarperCollins, ix-xi. 612p. [32] plates. filmog. index.
ISBN 000255528X

Coline Serreau.
Rollet, Brigitte.
Manchester University Press, vii-x. 166p. 6 plates. filmog. index.
ISBN 071905088X

The complete Hitchcock.
Condon, Paul and Sangster, Jim.
Virgin, 300p. [16] plates. filmog. bibliog.
ISBN 075350362X

The complete unauthorized Howard Stern.
Hoffman, Matthew.
Courage Books, 120p. col. Illus. bibliog. index.
ISBN 0762403772

Cue the bunny on the rainbow: tales from TV's most prolific sitcom director.
Rafkin, Alan.
Syracuse University Press, ix-xi. 179p. illus. appendix. index.
ISBN 0815605420

Dark knights and holy fools: the art and films of Terry Gilliam.
McCabe, Bob.
Orion, 192p. col. illus. filmog. bibliog.
ISBN 0752818279

Des Lynam: the biography.
Purcell, Steve.
Andre Deutsch, vii-xi. 209p. [12] plates.
ISBN 0233996613

Diane Kurys.
Tarr, Carrie.
Manchester University Press, vi-x. 162p. illus. filmog. bibliog. index.
ISBN 0719050952

Dorothy Dandridge: a biography.
Bogle, Donald.
Boulevard Books, i-xxiv. 611p. 32p. of plates. filmog. bibliog. index.
ISBN 1572972920

Down but not quite out in Hollow-weird: a documentary in letters of Eric Knight.
Gehman, Geoff.
Scarecrow Press, ix-xiii. 228p. illus. bibliog. index.
ISBN 0810834464

Duke: the life and image of John Wayne.
Davis, Ronald L.
University of Oklahoma Press, xvi. 377p. illus. filmog. index.
ISBN 0806130156

Eddie Izzard: dress to kill.
Izzard, Eddie and Quantick, David and Double, Steve.
Virgin, 160p. illus.
ISBN 1852277637

English Hitchcock.
Barr, Charles.
Cameron & Hollis, 255p. illus. filmog. bibliog.
ISBN 0906506131

Ewan McGregor.
Pendreigh, Brian.
Orion, v-x. 230p. [16] plates. filmog.

bibliog. index.
ISBN 0752817876

Ewan McGregor: from junkie to Jedi.
Robb, Brian J.
Plexus, 127p. illus. filmog.
ISBN 0859652769

Eyes wide open: a memoir of Stanley Kubrick.
Raphael, Frederic.
Ballantine, 190p.
ISBN 0345437764

The films of Lon Chaney.
Blake, Michael F.
Vestal Press, ix-xviii. 218p. illus. filmog. bibliog.
ISBN 1879511266

The films of Mack Sennett: credit documentation from the Mack Sennett collection at the Margaret Herrick Library.
Sherk, Warren (ed.)
Scarecrow Press, v-xxvi. 320p. [8] plates. appendices. index.
ISBN 081083443X

The films of Michelangelo Antonioni.
Brunette, Peter
Cambridge University Press, ix-xiii. 186p. illus. filmog. bibliog. index.
ISBN 0521380855

The films of Peter Greenaway.
Lawrence, Amy.
Cambridge University Press, vii-ix. 225p. bibliog. index. illus.
ISBN 0521479193

The films of Roger Corman: "shooting my way out of trouble".
Frank, Alan.
Batsford, 194p. illus. filmog. index.
ISBN 0713482729

Five rounds rapid!: the autobiography of Nicholas Courtney, Doctor Who's Brigadier.
Courtney, Nicholas; Nathan-Turner, John (ed.)
Virgin, 128p. illus. index.
ISBN 1852277823

Francis X. Bushman: a biography and filmography.
Maturi, Richard J. and Maturi, Mary Buckingham.
McFarland & Company, ix. 254p. illus. filmog. bibliog. appendix.
ISBN 078640485X

Frank Sinatra and popular culture: essays on an American icon.
Mustazza, Leonard (ed.)
Praeger, vi-xv. 311p. appendix. bibliog. index.
ISBN 0275964957

Get back: the Beatles' Let it be disaster.
Sulpy, Doug and Schweighardt, Ray.
Helter Skelter Publishing, 248p.
index.
ISBN 0900924129

Gilliam on Gilliam.
Christie, Ian (ed.)
Faber and Faber, vi-x. 294p. illus.
filmog. bibliog.
ISBN 0571191908

The good vibrations guide: adult videos.
Winks, Cathy.
Down There Press, 83p. bibliog.
index.
ISBN 0940208229

Hans Richter; activism, modernism and the avant-garde.
Foster, Stephen C. (ed.)
MIT Press, i-x. 329p. illus. [4] col.
plates. bibliog. appendix. index. 4p.
of col. plates.
ISBN 0262061961

The hidden screen: low-power television in America.
Hilliard, Robert L. and Keith, Michael C.
M.E. Sharpe, vii-x. 212p. figs.
appendices. bibliog. index.
ISBN 0765604191

Hollywood diva: a biography of Jeanette MacDonald.
Turk, Edward Baron.
University of California Press, i-xix.
467p. 24p. of plates. filmog. bibliog.
index.
ISBN 0520212029

Humphrey Bogart: a bio-bibliography.
Duchovnay, Gerald.
Greenwood Press, ix-xi. 344p.
bibliog. chronol. filmog. discog.
index.

I am Jackie Chan: my life in action.
Chan, Jackie and Yang, Jeff.
Pan Books; Macmillan, 356p. [8] . of
plates. filmog. [8] p. of col. plates.
ISBN 0330375903

In search of Donna Reed.
Fultz, Jay.
University of Iowa Press, ix. 236p.
illus. [16] plates. notes. index.
ISBN 0877456259

The incomparable Rex: a memoir of Rex Harrison in the 1980s.
Garland, Patrick.
Macmillan, xi. 259p. [8] plates.
index.
ISBN 0333717961

Jack Nicholson.
Shiach, Don.
B.T.Batsford, 176p. illus. index.
ISBN 0713484306

Jacques Tourneur: the cinema of nightfall.
Fujiwara, Chris.
McFarland, vii-xi. 328p. illus. filmog.
bibliog. index.
ISBN 0786404914

James Mason: a bio-bibliography.
Sweeney, Kevin.
Greenwood Press, ix-xiii. 299p.
chronol. bibliog. filmog. discog.
Index.
ISBN 0313284962

Jane Campion interviews.
Wexman, Virginia Wright.
University Press of Mississippi, i-
xxvii. 216p. [4] p. of plates. filmog.
index.
ISBN 1578060834

Jean-Luc Godard: interviews.
Sterritt, David (ed.)
University Press of Mississippi, vii-
xxxiii. [8] plates. chronol. filmog.
index.
ISBN 1578060818

John Barry: a sixties theme – from James Bond to Midnight cowboy.
Fiegel, Eddi.
Constable, v-x. 261p. discog. index.

John Ford: a bio-bibliography.
Levy, Bill.
Greenwood Press, ix-xiv. 352p.
filmog. bibliog. index.
ISBN 0313275149

John Sayles, filmmaker: a critical study of the independent writer-director; with a filmography and a bibliography.
Ryan, Jack.
McFarland, vii-viii. 271p. illus.
bibliog. index.
ISBN 0786405295

Joseph H. Lewis: overview, interview, and filmography.
Nevins, Francis M.
Scarecrow Press, ix-xiii. 125p. [8]
plates. filmog. bibliog. index.
ISBN 0810834073

A Kentish lad: the autobiography of Frank Muir.
Muir, Frank.
Corgi, 426p. [32] plates.
ISBN 0552141372

King pulp: the wild world of Quentin
Tarantino. (Revised and expanded ed.)

Woods, Paul A.
Plexus, 208p. filmog. col. illus.
ISBN 085965270X

The last days of Marilyn Monroe.
Wolfe, Donald H.
William Morrow, vi-xiii. 130p. illus.
filmog. bibliog. index.
ISBN 0810836270

The last mogul: Lew Wasserman, MCA, and the hidden history of Hollywood.
Crown Publishers, vii-xiii. 560p. [12]
plates. bibliog. index.
ISBN 0517704641

Lee Van Cleef: a biographical, film and television reference.
Malloy, Mike.
McFarland, vii. 196p. illus. filmog.
teleog. appendix. bibliog. index.
ISBN 078640437X

Lenya: the legend: a pictorial autobiography.
Farneth, David (ed.)
Thames and Hudson, 219p. illus.
bibliog. discog. index.
ISBN 050001888X

Leonardo: up close and personal.
Looseleaf, Victoria.
Ballantine, 127p. illus.
ISBN 0345432223

(bfi) **The Lepagian cinematic universe: time and space in the films of Robert Lepage.**
Sulick, Sarah.
British Film Institute/ Birkbeck
College MA in Cinema and
Television Studies, 53p. [21] p. col.
illus. bibliog. filmog.

Life's a scream: the autobiography of Ingrid Pitt.
Pitt, Ingrid.
William Heinemann, 292p. [16] p. of
plates. index.
ISBN 0434007625

Light and illusion: the Hollywood portraits of Ray Jones.
Zimmerman, Tom; Jones, John (ed.);
Jones, Ray (photo.)
Balcony Press, 120p. illus. bibliog.
index. stills.
ISBN 1890449008

Love is where it falls: an account of a passionate friendship.
Callow, Simon.
Nick Hern, 214p.
ISBN 1854592572

Marilyn, Hitler and me: the memoirs of Milton Shulman.

Shulman, Milton.
Andre Deutsch, ix. 386p. illus. index.
ISBN 0233994084

Mario Lanza: tenor in exile.
Bessette, Roland L.
Amadeus Press, 270p. [36] plates.
bibliog. discog. filmog. index.
ISBN 1574670441

Martin Scorsese.
Dougan, Andy.
Thunder's Mouth Press, 143p. illus.
(some col.).
ISBN 1560251611

Martin Scorsese: interviews.
Brunette, Peter (ed.)
University Press of Mississippi,
270p. [8] plates. index.
ISBN 1578060729

**Me and my shadows: a family
memoir.**
Luft, Lorna.
Pocket Books, ix-x. 417p. [16] plates.
index.
ISBN 067101899X

Memories of Eric.
Morecambe, Gary and Sterling,
Martin (eds.)
Andre Deutsch, 191p. illus. chronol.
ISBN 0233996699

Morecambe & Wise.
Mccann, Graham.
Fourth Estate, ix-xiv. 398p. [24]
plates. bibliog. index.
ISBN 1857027353

My autobiography.
Briggs, Johnny and Codd, Pat.
Blake, iii-vii. 279p. [24] plates.
ISBN 1857822064

 **Nanni Moretti:
autobiography as discourse.**
Fussell, Emily.
British Film Institute: Brikbeck
College MA in Cinema and
Television Studies, 1997-98, [60] p.
illus. filmog. bibliog.

**Narrative and stylistic patterns in
the films of Stanley Kubrick.**
Mainar, Luis M. Garcia.
Camden House, Inc., i-x. 257p. illus.
bibliog. index.
ISBN 1571132643

**Nicolas Cage: Hollywood's wild
talent.**
Robb, Brian J.
Plexus, 160p. illus. filmog.
ISBN 0859652645

**Notorious: Alfred Hitchcock and
contemporary art.**

Brougher, Kerry and Tarantino,
Michael and Bowron, Astrid (eds.)
Museum of Modern Art, 84p. col.
plates. biogs. bibliogs. list of works.
ISBN 1901352064

**Ol' Blue Eyes: a Frank Sinatra
encyclopedia.**
Mustazza, Leonard.
Greenwood, viii-xii. 436p. illus.
appendices. bibliog. index.
ISBN 0313304866

**On Sunset Boulevard: the life and
times of Billy Wilder.**
Sikov, Ed.
Hyperion, vi-ix. 675p. [16] plates.
bibliog. filmog. index.
ISBN 0786861940

**Oona: living in the shadows: a
biography of Oona O'Neill Chaplin.**
Scovell, Jane.
Waner Books, 354p. [16] plates.
bibliog. index.
ISBN 0446517305

**Our father: a tribute to Dermot
Morgan.**
Morgan, Don et al.
New Island, 206p. [16] plates.
ISBN 1874597960

**Out of tune: David Helfgott and
the myth of Shine.**
Gross, Tom and Helfgott, David.
Warner Books, 294p. [8] plates.
index.
ISBN 0446523836

**Over the limit: my secret diaries
1993-8.**
Monkhouse, Bob.
Century, 346p. [8] plates. index.
ISBN 071267707

Piaf: a passionate life.
Bret, David.
Robson Books, vii-x. 282p. [12]
plates. discog. filmog. index.
ISBN 1861052189

Pictures in my head.
Byrne, Gabriel.
Wolfhound Press, 160p. [16] plates.
ISBN 0863277098

**Plague years: a life in underground
movies.**
Hoolboom, Mike; Reinke, Steve (ed.)
YYZ Books, 209p. illus. filmog.
ISBN 0920397212

**Principal photography: interviews
with feature film cinematographers.**
Lobrutto, Vincent.
Praeger, ix-xii. 248p. gloss. bibliog.
index.
ISBN 0275949540

Quentin Tarantino: interviews.
Peary, Gerald (ed.)
University Press of Mississippi, vi-
xxiv. 215p. [8] plates. index.
ISBN 1578060516

**Rat pack confidential: Frank,
Dean, Sammy, Peter, Joey & the
last great showbiz party.**
Levy, Shawn.
Fourth Estate, 344p. [16] plates.
bibliog. index.
ISBN 1841150002

**Reconstructing Woody: art, love,
life in the films of Woody Allen.**
Nichols, Mary P.
Rowman and Littlefield, v-xiv. 255p.
illus. bibliog. index.
ISBN 0847689891

Reporting live.
Stahl, Lesley.
Simon & Schuster, 444p. 47 plates.
index.
ISBN 0684829304

**A retake please!:Night mail to
Western approaches.**
Jackson, Pat.
Liverpool University Press/ Royal
Naval Museum, v-vii. 308p. [32]
plates.
ISBN 0853239533

**Robert Siodmak: a biography, with
critical analyses of his film noirs
and a filmography of all his works.**
Alpi, Deborah Lazaroff.
McFarland & Company, xi. 406p,
illus. filmog. bibliog. notes.
ISBN 0786404892

Robin Williams.
Dougan, Andy.
Orion, i-ix. 326p. of plates. filmog.
index.
ISBN 0752826735

Rod Steiger: memoirs of a friendship.
Hutchinson, Tom.
Orion, 235p. [16] p. of plates. filmog.
bibliog.
ISBN 0752827278

**Ruby Keeler: a photographic
biography.**
Marlow-Trump, Nancy.
McFarland, vii-ix. 169p. illus. filmog.
index.
ISBN 0786405244

Saeed: an actor's journey.
Jaffrey, Saeed.
Constable, ix-xi. 290p. [20] plates.
index.
ISBN 009476770X

Satyajit Ray: an intimate master.
Das, Santi (ed.)
Allied Publishers, viii-xvii. 238p.
[67] plates. filmog. videog. discog.
bibliog. biog.
ISBN 8170237483

Schlock-o-rama: the films of Al Adamson.
Konow, David.
Lone Eagle, 160p. illus. filmog.
bibliog.
ISBN 1580650015

The secret art of Antonin Artaud.
Derrida, Jacques and Thevenin,
Paule; Caws, Mary Ann (transl.)
MIT Press, ix-xiv. 157p. illus.
ISBN 0262041650

September song: an intimate biography of Walter Huston.
Wed, John.
Scarecrow Press, ix-xviii. 231p.
filmog. index.
ISBN 0810834081

Seventy light years.
Young, Freddie and Busby, Peter.
Faber and Faber, v-xi. 164p. illus.
filmog. index.
ISBN 0571197930

Sex murder art: the films of Jorg Buttgereit.
Kerekes, David.
Headpress, 177p. illus. filmog. index.
ISBN 0952328844

🅑🅕🅘 **Shahrukh Khan – superstar.**
Mirza, Nahrein.
British Film Institute/ Birkbeck
College MA in Cinema and
Television Studies, 57p. illus. bibliog.
filmog.

Shaken but not stirred: my story.
Chegwin, Keith.
Hodder and Stoughton, 165p. [8]
plates. index.
ISBN 0340639784

🅑🅕🅘 **Shakespeare: A-level guide.**
Kerameos, Anastasia and
Ormsby, Andrew.
BFI National Library, 30p. bibliog.
ISBN 085170770X

Shirley Temple Black: a bio-bibliography.
Hammontree, Patsy Guy.
Greenwood Press, viii-xi. 290p.
bibliog. filmog. index.
ISBN 0313258481

Shooting from the lip.
Puckrik, Katie.
Headline, 339p.
ISBN 0747260168

Sinatra: an annotated bibliography, 1939-1998.
Mustazza, Leonard. (ed.)
Praeger, ix-xiii. 293p. bibliog.
appendix. index.
ISBN 0313308292

Sinatra: the artist and the man.
Lahr, John.
Phoenix, 64p. [64] pages of plates.
ISBN 0753808420

Sleeping where I fall: a chronicle.
Coyote, Peter.
Counterpoint, xi-xiv. 367p. [16]
plates.
ISBN 1887178678

So far, so funny: my life in show business.
Kanter, Hal.
McFarland, vii-xi. 308p. illus. index.
ISBN 0786404833

Speaking about Godard.
Silverman, Kaja and Farocki, Harun.
New York University Press, v-xiii.
243p. illus. bibliog.
ISBN 0814780660

Speaking for myself.
Day, Robin.
Ebury Press, 272p. index.
ISBN 0091867967

Stephen Sondheim: a life.
Secrest, Meryle.
Bloomsbury, 461p. illus. index.
ISBN 0747535353

They died too young: Rudolph Valentino.
Dempsey, Amy.
Parragon, 73p. illus.
ISBN 0752508369

Threading the needle: the PAX NET story.
Paxson, Lowell with Templeton,
Giuseppe.
HarperBusiness, vii. 183p.
ISBN 0887309488

🅑🅕🅘 **Tri-angle on Lee: in search of a geopolitical aesthetic in Ang Lee's films.**
Lim, Alice.
British Film Institute/ Birkbeck
College MA in Cinema and
Television Studies, 56p. illus. filmog.
bibliog. 24 col. plates.

A tribute to John Wayne.
Fryd, Peter R. A.
31p. illus. (some col.).

Valentino: a dream of desire.
Bret, David.
Robson Books, ix. 224p. [8] plates.

appendices. bibliog. index.
ISBN 1861051239

Weasels and wisemen: ethics and ethnicity in the work of David Mamet.
Kane, Leslie.
Macmillan, ix-xii. 404p. bibliog.
index.
ISBN 0333754700

Wes Craven: the art of horror.
Muir, John Kenneth.
McFarland, i-viii. 319p. illus. filmog.
bibliog. appendices. index.
ISBN 0786405767

When the wind changed: the life and death of Tony Hancock.
Goodwin, Cliff.
Century, viii-x. 580p. [16] plates.
chronol. index.
ISBN 0712676155

When you're smiling: the illustrated biography of Les Dawson.
Middles, Mick.
Chameleon Books, 127p. col. ill.
ISBN 0233996680

Wife of the life of the party.
Chaplin, Lita Grey and Vance,
Jeffrey.
Scarecrow Press, i-xxvi. 306p. [24] p.
of plates. index.
ISBN 0810834324

Winona Ryder: the biography.
Goodall, Nigel.
Blake, ix-xv. 240p. [16] plates.
filmog. index.
ISBN 1857822145

Woody Allen: a biography.
Baxter, John.
HarperCollins, ix-xi. 488p. [24]
plates. filmog. bibliog. index.
ISBN 0002557754

Work in progress.
Eisner, Michael with Schwartz, Tony.
Penguin, ix-xi. 450p. index.
ISBN 0140281983

SCRIPTWRITING

Good scripts, bad scripts: learning the craft of screenwriting through 25 of the best and worst films in history.
Pope, Thomas.
Three Rivers Press, v-xxii. 232p. diagrams.
ISBN 0609801198

Now that's funny!: writers on writing comedy.
Bradbury, David and McGrath, Joe.
Methuen, 191p.
ISBN 0413725200

Secrets of screenplay structure: how to recognize and emulate the structural frameworks of great films.
Cowgill, Linda J.
Lone Eagle, v-xv. 318p. index.
ISBN 158065004X

Story: substance, structure, style and the principles of screenwriting.
McKee, Robert.
Methuen, i-xi. 466p. filmog. bibliog. index.
ISBN 0413715507

Unfinished business: screenplays, scenarios and ideas.
Antonioni, Michelangelo; Di Carlo, Carlo and Tinazzi, Giorgio (eds.)
Marsilio, xi-xvii. 233p.
ISBN 156886051

TRAINING/ CAREERS/ MANUALS

Film studies.
Buckland, Warren.
Hodder and Stoughton, viii-ix. 162p. [8] plates. index.
ISBN 0340697687

Getting into films & television: how to spot the opportunities and find the best way in.
Angell, Robert.
How To Books, 173p. appendix. gloss. index.
ISBN 1857034139

Making movies on your own: practical talk from independent filmmakers.
Lindenmuth, Kevin J.
McFarland, 192p. illus. appendices. index.
ISBN 0786405171

Movies to manage by: lessons in leadership from great films.
Clemens, John K. and Wolff, Melora.
Contemporary Books, ix-xvi. 224p. illus. bibliog. index.
ISBN 0809227983

Teaching popular pedagogy.
Buckingham, David (ed.)
UCL Press, v-vi. 207p. index.
ISBN 1857287932

Teen spirits: music and identity in media education.
Richards, Chris.
UCL Press, vii-xiv. 215p. bibliog. index.
ISBN 1857288599

Writing and cinema.
Bignell, Jonathan (ed.)
Longman, i-xi. 268p. bibliog. index.
ISBN 0582357578

CATALOGUES

The American Film Institute catalog of motion pictures produced in the United States: feature films, 1941-1950: film entries. Feature films 1941-1950: indexes.
Hanson, Patricia King and Dunkleberger, Amy (eds.); American Film Institute.
University of California Press, 3v. (vii-xviii. 2876. ii-v. 1115p.). chronol. indices.
ISBN 0520215214

 Avant Garde: the holding of the National Film and Television Archive.
Finn, Eugene (compiler)
British Film Institute, 114p. bibliog. index.

 British silent comedy films: viewing copies in the National film and Television Archive.
Dixon, Bryony and Mckernan, Luke (eds.)
BFI Collections, 62p. indices.

 Ethnic; towards a cinema of cultural diversity.
Sulick, Sarah (ed.)
BFI films, 23p. illus.

Gramophone musicals good cd guide. (2nd ed.)
Walker, Mark (ed.)
Gramophone Publications Limited, 263p. index.
ISBN 0902470981

ImagineNative: aboriginally produced film & video.
Aboriginal film & Video Art Alliance and V/Tape.
V/Tape, i-v. 95p. illus. index.

Pop off: the regular 8 faction.
Kovacova, Milada (curator)
XYZ Artist's Outlet, 32p. illus.
ISBN 0920397190

DIRECTORIES

Director's A_Z: a concise guide to the art of 250 great film-makers.
Andrew, Geoff.
Prion, 252p. illus.
ISBN 1853753351

The LION handbook.
Broughton, Sue (ed.)
Library Association, 244p. index.
ISBN 1856041263

Writer's guide to Hollywood producers, directors, and screenweiter's agents 1999-2000.
Press, Skip.
Prima, x. 454p. gloss. bibliog. index.
ISBN 0761514848

DICTIONARIES/ ENCYCLOPEDIAS

The American musical film song encyclopedia.
Hischak, Thomas S.
Greenwood Press, ix-xv. 521p.
bibliog. index.
ISBN 0313307377

Encyclopedia of Chinese film.
Zhang, Yingjin and Xiao, Zhiwei;
Zhang, Yingjin (ed.)
Routledge, viii-xxiv. 475p. bibliog.
gloss. indices.
ISBN 0415151686

Encyclopedia of contemporary French culture.
Hughes, Alex and Reader, Keith
(eds.)
Routledge, v-xxii. 618p. index.
ISBN 0415131863

(bfi) **Encyclopedia of Indian cinema. (Rev. ed.)**
Rajadhyaksha, Ashish and Willemen,
Paul.
British Film Institute/ Oxford
University Press, 658p. illus. bibliog.
indices.
ISBN 085170669X

The encyclopedia of TV game shows: 3rd.
Schwartz, David and Ryan, Steve and
Wostbrock, Fred.
Facts On File, v-xxii. 377p. illus.
bibliog. index.
ISBN 0816038465

Hollywood stunt performers: a dictionary and filmography of over 600 men and women, 1922-1996.
Freese, Gene Scott.
McFarland & Company, v. 261p.
illus. appendix. bibliog. index.
ISBN 0786405112

Images in the dark: an encyclopedia of gay and lesbian film and video.
Murray, Raymond.
Titan, x-xviii. 622p. illus. index.
Revised and updated ed.
ISBN 1840230339

The Virgin encyclopedia of stage & film musicals.
Larkin, Colin; Martland, John (contr.)
Virgin, 680p. index.
ISBN 0753503751

FILMOGRAPHIES

African American films through 1959: a comprehensive illustrated filmography.
Richards, Larry.
McFarland, vii. 312p. illus.
ISBN 0786403071

American Movie Classics classic movie companion.
Moses, Robert.
Hyperion, v-xvi. 622p.
ISBN 0786883944

The Asian film library reference to Japanese film 1998: volume 1: films; volume 2: cast & staff.
Cremin, Stephen (ed./comp.)
Asian Film Library, vol1: ca. 270p.
vol2: ca. 350p.

Cinematherapy: the girl's guide to movies for every mood.
Peske, Nancy K. and West, Beverly.
Dell, ix-xiii. 258p. illus. index.
ISBN 0440508509

The classic 1000 videos to rent or buy.
Robertson, Sandy.
Foulsham, 367p. indices.
ISBN 0572023898

Cult TV: the comedies: the ultimate critical guide.
Lewis, Jon E. and Stempel, Penny.
Pavillion, 256p. illus. index.
ISBN 186205245X

Feature films, 1950-1959: a United States filmography.
Fetrow, Alan G.
McFarland, v. 712p. index.
ISBN 0786404272

Film and the American left: a research guide.
Ooker, M. Keith.
Greenwood Press, v-xvi. 622p.
ISBN 0786883944

Full-frontal: male nudity video guide. (2nd ed.)
Stewart, Steve (ed.)
Companion Press, 127p. indices.
ISBN 1889138118

The Greek filmography, 1914 through 1996.
Koliodimos, Dimitris.
McFarland, vii-x. 773p. illus.
appendices. indices.
ISBN 0786405465

The Guinness book of film: the ultimate guide to the best films ever.
Guiness.

Guiness, 360p. illus.
ISBN 0851120733

Radio Times guide to TV comedy.
Lewisohn, Mark.
BBC, 800p. chronol. bibliog. indices.
ISBN 0563369779

The reel middle ages: American, Western and Eastern European, Middle Eastern and Asian films about medieval Europe.
Harty, Kevin J.
McFarland, vii. 316p. illus. bibliog. index.
ISBN 0786405414

The republic pictures checklist: features, serials, cartoons, short subjects and training films of Republic Pictures Corporation, 1935-1959.
Martin, Len D.
McFarland & Company, i-vii. 383p. illus. bibliog. appendices. indices.
ISBN 0786404388

Serials and series: a world filmography, 1912-1956.
Rainey, Buck.
McFarland, ix. 321p. illus. bibliog. index.
ISBN 0786404493

The Universal silents: a filmography of the Universal Motion Picture Manufacturing Company, 1912-1929.
Braff, Richard E.
McFarland & Company, vii. 675p. index.
ISBN 0786402873

BROADCASTING

Basic studio directing.
Fairweather, Rod.
Focal Press, 192p. illus.
ISBN 0240515250

The broadcast television industry.
Walker, James R. and Ferguson, Douglas A.
Allyn & Bacon, iii-x. 228p. gloss. bibliog. index.
ISBN 0205189504

Building a global audience: British television in overseas markets.
David Graham and Associates.
Department for Culture, Media and Sport, Broadcasting Policy Division, 50p. figs.

Critical ideas in television studies.
Corner, John.
Oxford University Press, 139p. bibliog. index.
ISBN 0198742207

Death by television.
Johnston, Ian.
Pottersfield Press, 224p.
ISBN 1895900212

Dictionary of television and audiovisual terminology.
Moshkovitz, Moshe.
McFarland, vi-vii. 175p.
ISBN 078640440X

Don Quixote's art & television: seeing things in art & television.
Rushton, Dave.
Institute of Local Television, 48p. illus.
ISBN 189940502X

The essential TV director's handbook.
Jarvis, Peter.
Focal Press, i-xii. 209p. illus. appendix. index.
ISBN 024051503X

The Nationwide television studies.
Morley, David and Brunsdon, Charlotte.
Routledge, viii-ix. 326p. index. bibliog.
ISBN 0415148790

Seeing things: television in the age of uncertainty.
Ellis, John.
I.B.Tauris, 193p. bibliog. index.
ISBN 1860641253

Television and the press since 1945.
Negrine, Ralph.
Manchester University Press, x.

212p. index.
ISBN 0719049210

Television production. (13th ed.)
Millerson, Gerald.
Focal Press, vi-xiv. 635p. tables. figs. gloss. bibliog. index.
ISBN 0240514920

This business of television. (Rev. and updated 2nd ed.)
Blumenthal, Howard J. and Goodenough, Oliver R.
Billboard Books, v-xii. 666p. appendices. index.
Includes floppy disc containing legal documents, forms and contracts.
ISBN 0823077047

TV mania: a timeline of television.
Pavese, Edith and Henry, Judith.
Abrams, ca. 140p. col. illus.
ISBN 0810938928

Uses of television.
Hartley, John.
Routledge, v-x. 246p. illus. appendices. bibliog. index.
ISBN 0415085098

BROADCASTING AND SOCIETY

Bad language: what are the limits?
Hargrave, Andrea Millwood.
Broadcasting Standards Commission,
66p. tables. appendices.

Channeling violence: the economic market for violent television programming.
Hamilton, James T.
Princeton University Press, xix. 390p.
illus. bibliog.
ISBN 0691048487

 Children's television in Britain: history, discourse and policy.
Buckingham, David and Davies,
Hannah and Jones, Ken and Kelley,
Peter.
British Film Institute, vii. 200p.
tables. bibliog. index.
ISBN 085170686X

The chosen image: television's portrayal of Jewish themes and characters.
Pearl, Jonathan and Pearl, Judith.
McFarland & Company, vii-ix. 259p.
index.
ISBN 0786405228

Color by Fox: the Fox network and the revolution in black television.
Zook, Kristal Brent.
Oxford University Press, vii-ix. 148p.
[16] plates. refs. index.
ISBN 0195106121

Consuming environments: television and commercial culture.
Budd, Mike and Craig, Steve and
Steinman, Clay.
Rutgers University Press, i-xix. 225p.
illus. index.
ISBN 0813525926

Copycat television: globalisation, program formats and cultural identity.
Moran, Albert.
University of Luton Press, iv-xi.
204p. bibliog. index.
ISBN 1860205372

Deciding what we watch: taste, decency and media ethics in the UK and USA.
Shaw, Colin.
Oxford University Press, v-xii. 184p.
bibliog. index.
ISBN 0198159366

Defining violence: the search for understanding.
Morrison, David E.
University of Luton Press, iv-viii.
149p. appendices.
ISBN 1860205682

Defining visions: television and the American experience since 1945.
Watson, Mary Ann.
Harcourt Brace College Publishers,
303p. illus. bibliog. index.
ISBN 0155032011

 The eloquence of the vulgar: language, cinema and the politics of culture.
Maccabe, Colin.
British Film Institute, 66p. tables.
appendices.

Film versus drama: relative acceptability of the two genres on television.
Counterpoint Research and Hanley,
Pam.
Independent Television Commission,
36p. illus. appendices.
ISBN 0900485779

Get a life!: the little red book of the white dot anti-television campaign.
Burke, David and Lotus, Jean.
Bloomsbury, 257 [25]p. illus.
ISBN 0747536899

Making sense of television: the psychology of audience interpretation. (2nd. ed.)
Livingstone, Sonia.
Routledge, v-xi. 212p. bibliog.
indices.
ISBN 041518536X

Media, culture, & the religious right.
Kintz, Linda and Lesage, Julia (eds.)
Minnesota University Press, xi-xviii.
380p. index.
ISBN 0816630852

Men viewing violence.
Stirling Media Research Institute and
Violence Research Centre,
Manchester University.
Broadcsting Standards Commission,
77p. bibliog. tables.
ISBN 1872521339

Representing "race": ideology, identity and the media.
Ferguson, Robert.
Arnold, v-vi. 288p. filmog. bibliog.
index.
ISBN 0340692391

Saturday morning censors: television regulation before the V-chip.
Hendershot, Heather.

Duke University Press, vii-viii. 285p.
bibliog. index.
ISBN 0822322404

Television across the years: the British public's view.
Svennevig, Michael.
University of Luton Press, iv-v. 101p.
tables. figs.
ISBN 0900485787

Television and common knowledge.
Gripsrud, Jostein (ed.)
Routledge, i-x. 209p. illus. tables.
indices.
ISBN 0415189292

Television and culture: policies and regulations in Europe.
Machet, Emmanuelle and Robillard,
Serge.
European Institute for the Media,
182p. tables. bibliog.
ISBN 3929673290

Television and its viewers: cultivation theory and research.
Shanahan, James and Morgan,
Michael.
Cambridge University Press, i-xiii.
267p. tables. index.
ISBN 0521587557

Television and new media audiences.
Seiter, Ellen.
Clarendon Press, 154p. bibliog.
index.
ISBN 0198711417

Television violence and public policy.
Hamilton, James T.
University of Michigan Press, xiv.
394p. illus. index.
ISBN 0472109030

Television: what's on, who's watching, and what it means.
Comstock, George and Scharrer,
Erica.
Academic Press, v-xi. 388p. tables.
bibliog. indices.
ISBN 0121835804

A thousand screenplays: the French imagination in a time of crisis.
Chalvon-Demersay, Sabine.
University of Chicago Press, vii.
199p. appendices. bibliog. index.
ISBN 0226100693

Understanding society, culture and television.
Monaco, Paul.
Praeger, i-viii. 141p. bibliog. index.
ISBN 0275960579

While America watches: televising the Holocaust.
Shandler, Jeffrey.
Oxford University Press, v-xviii.
316p. illus. index.
ISBN 0195119355

TELEVISION – NATIONAL/ INTERNATIONAL

American television abroad: Hollywood's attempt to dominate world television.
Segrave, Kerry.
McFarland, 330p. appendices.
Bibliog. index.
ISBN 0786405821

Audio-visual communications and the regulation of broadcasting: minutes of evidence, Thursday 29 January 1998.
Great Britain House of Commons Culture, Media and Sport Committee;
Kaufman, Gerald (chairman).
The Stationary Office, 36p.
ISBN 010218898X

Audio-visual communications and the regulation of broadcasting: minutes of evidence, Thursday 5 February 1998.
Great Britain House of Commons Culture, Media and Sport Committee:
Kaufman, Gerald (chairman).
The Stationary Office, pp. 37-78.
ISBN 0102190984

Audio-visual communications and the regulation of broadcasting: minutes of evidence, Thursday 12 February 1998.
Great Britain House of Commons Culture, Media and Sport Committee;
Kaufman, Gerald (chairman).
The Stationary Office, pp. 79-115.
ISBN 0102227985

Audio-visual communications and the regulation of broadcasting: minutes of evidence, Thursday 19 February 1998.
Great Britain House of Commons Culture, Media and Sport Committee;
Kaufman, Gerald (chairman).
The Stationary Office, pp. 116-159.
ISBN 0102237980

Audio-visual communications and the regulation of broadcasting: minutes of evidence, Thursday 26 February 1998.
Great Britain House of Commons Culture, Media and Sport Committee;
Kaufman, Gerald (chairman).
The Stationary Office, pp. 160-195.
ISBN 0102255989

Audio-visual communications and the regulation of broadcasting: minutes of evidence, Thursday 5

March 1998.
Great Britain House of Commons Culture, Media and Sport Committee:
Kaufman, Gerald (chairman).
The Stationary Office, pp. 196-227.
ISBN 0102254982

Audio-visual communications and the regulation of broadcasting: minutes of evidence, Thursday 19 March 1998.
Great Britain House of Commons Culture, Media and Sport Committee;
Kaufman, Gerald (chairman).
The Stationary Office, pp. 228-275.
ISBN 0102282986

The BBC beyond 2000.
British Broadcasting Corporation.
British Broadcasting Corporation,

BBC producer choice: a case study.
Cloot, Peter.
Major Projects Association, 48p. figs.
bibliog.

British Film Institute television tracking study: third report – May 1999.
British Film Institute; Sheppard, Elaine (compiler).
British Film Institute, 54p. tables.
figs. appendices.

British Sky Broadcasting group plc and Manchester United plc: a report on the proposed merger: presented to parliament by the Secretary of State for Trade and Industry by command of Her Majesty, April 1999.
Great Britain Monopolies and Mergers Commission.
The Stationary Office, iii-v. 254p.
tables. appendices.
ISBN 0101430523

Broadcasting: the Broadcasting Act 1996 (commencement no.3) Order 1998.
Great Britain, Statutory Instruments.
The Stationary Office, [2]p.
ISBN 0110654862

Broadcasting: the Broadcasting (Local Delivery Services) Order 1998.
Great Britain, Statutory Instruments.
The Stationary Office, 3p.
ISBN 0110790456

Broadcasting: the broadcasting (restrictions on the holding of licenses) (amendment) order 1999.
Great Britain, Statuary Instruments.
The Stationary Office, [2]p.
ISBN 0110803868

Broadcasting: the Channel 4 (application of excess revenues) order 1998.
Great Britain, Statutory Instruments.
The Stationary Office, [2]p.
ISBN 0110798627

Broadcasting: the dissolution of the Broadcasting Complaints Commission and the Broadcasting Standards Council Order 1998.
Great Britain, Statutory Instruments.
The Stationary Office, [2]p.
ISBN 0110798821

Broadcasting: the foreign satellite service proscription (no.2) order 1998.
Great Britain, Statutory Instruments.
The Stationary Office, [2]p.
ISBN 0110799259

Broadcasting: the television broadcasting regulations 1998.
Great Britain, Statutory Instruments.
The Stationary Office, 7p.
ISBN 0110803280

Codes of guidance June 1998.
Broadcasting Standards Commission.
Broadcasting Standards Commission, 42p. index.
ISBN 1872521312

Communication, commerce and power: the political economy of America and the direct broadcast satellite, 1960-2000.
Comor, Edward A.
Macmillan, v-xii. 253p. bibliog. index.
ISBN 0333688236

Culture, Media and Sport Committee, eight report: report and accounts of the BBC for 1997-98: report, together with proceedings of the committee and minutes of evidence.
Great Britain House of Commons
Culture, Media and Sport Committee;
Kaufman, Gerald (chairman).
The Stationary Office, ii-xviii. 20p.
ISBN 0105550833

Culture, Media and Sport Committee: minutes of proceedings.
Great Britain House of Commons
Culture, Media and Sport Committee;
Kaufman, Gerald (chairman).
The Stationary Office, ii. [1]p.
ISBN 010209599X

Culture, Media and Sport Committee: minutes of proceedings.
Great Britain House of Commons
Culture, Media and Sport Committee;

Kaufman, Gerald (chairman).
The Stationary Office, ii-xxviii.
ISBN 0105551163

Culture, Media and Sport Committee, ninth report: the future of News at ten: report, together with proceedings of the committee, minutes of evidence and appendices.
Great Britain House of Commons
Culture, Media and Sport Committee;
Kaufman, Gerald (chairman).
The Stationary Office, ii-xv. 31p.
appendices.
ISBN 0105550868

A decade of EU broadcasting regulation: the directive "Television without frontiers".
Machet, Emmanuelle.
European Institute for the Media, iii-vii. 87, [24]p. bibliog. annex.

The decline and fall of public service broadcasting.
Tracey, Michael.
Oxford University Press, viii-xvii. 295p. bibliog. Index.
ISBN 0198159242

Delights, desires and dilemmas: essays on women and the media.
Hall, Ann C.
Praeger, ix-xxi. 168p. index.
ISBN 0275961567

The development of parliamentary broadcasting: minutes of evidence, Wednesday 15 July 1998.
Great Britain House of Commons.
HMSO, 26p. appendices.

Directing for television: conversations with American TV directors.
Rose, Brian G.
Scarecrow Press, iii-ix. 227p.
ISBN 0810835916

Do you remember TV? The book that takes you back.
Gitter, Michael and Anapol, Sylvie and Glazer, Erika.
Chronicle Books, 144p. virtually all col. plates. index.
ISBN 0811823059

Indigenous aesthetics: native art media and identity.
Leuthold, Steven.
University of Texas Press, ix-xiii. 238p. illus. filmog. bibliog. index.
ISBN 0292747039

The internationalization of television in China.
Hong, Junhao.
Praeger, xvii. 165p. bibliog. index.

The ITC code of advertising standards and practice, Autumn 1998.
Independent Television Commission.
ITC, iii-iv. 36p. appendices.

ITC rules on the amount and scheduling of advertising, autumn 1998.
Independent Television Commission.
Independent Television Commission, 20p.

Latin American television: a global view.
Sinclair, John.
Oxford University Press, i-vii. 187p.
indices.
ISBN 0198159293

Memories of Tyne Tees Television.
Phillips, Geoff.
G.P. Electronic Services, 144p. illus.
ISBN 0952248069

9th European Television and Film Forum 6-8 November 1997, Lisbon: new media strategies: convergence or competition?
Contamine, Claude and Whittle, Stephen and Deleville-McGuire, Sophie (eds.).
European Institute for the Media, 263p. index.
ISBN 3929673258

Perspectives of public service television in Europe.
Woldt, Runar and Dries, Josephine and Gerber, Arnaud and Konert, Bertram.
European Institute for the Media, 156p. bibliog.
ISBN 3929673320

Producing public television, producing public culture.
Dornfeld, Barry.
Princeton University Press, 240p.
illus. filmog. appendices. indices.
ISBN 0691044678

Public purposes in broadcasting: funding the BBC.
Graham, Andrew and Koboldt, Christian and Hogg, Sara (et al.)
University of Luton Press, i-vi. 159p.
index.
ISBN 1860205615

Scotland's parliament: devolution, the media and political culture.
Schlesinger, Philip.
ARENA, 23p.

Seducing America: how television charms the modern voter: 2nd rev. ed.
Hart, Roderick P.

Thousand Oaks, xi. 209p. bibliog. index.
ISBN 0761916237

Telegraphs: the wireless telegraphy (television licence fees) (amendment) regulations 1998.
Great Britain, Statutory Instruments. The Stationary Office, 3p.

Third communication from the Commission to the Council and the European Parliament on the application of Articles 4 and 5 of Directive 89/552/EEC "Television without Frontiers" for the period 1995-96 including an overall assessment of application over the period 1991-96.
Commission of the European Communities.
Office for Official Publications of the European Community, 73p. tables. figs.
ISBN 9278329193

TV or not TV: television, justice, and the courts.
Goldfarb, Ronald L.
New York University Press, ix-xxiv. 238p. [8] plates. appendices. index.
ISBN 0814731120

Worlds in common?: television discourse in a changing Europe.
Richardson, Kay and Meinhof, Ulrike Marie.
Routledge, i-vi, 197p. index.
ISBN 0415140617

TELEVISION – GENRES

American science fiction television series of the 1950s: episode guides and casts and credits for twenty shows.
Lucanio, Patrick and Colville, Gary.
Oxford University Press, i-vii. 252p. illus. bibliog. indices.
ISBN 0786404345

An analysis of racial stereotyping in SABC-TV commercials in the context of reform, 1978-1992.
Submitted in fulfillment of the requirements for the degree of Doctor of Philosophy. In the Centre for Cultural and Media Studies, University of Natal, Durban, December 1998. 2 vols, ii-v. 349p. bibliog. ii-iv. 260p.

Eurofiction: television fiction in Europe; second report 1998.
Buonanno, Milly (ed.)
European Audiovisual Observatory, i-xi. 212p. tables. figs.

Good times, bad times: soap operas and society in Western Europe.
O'Donnell, Hugh.
Leicester University Press, i-vii. 247p. bibliog. indices.
ISBN 0718500466

News and journalism in the UK: a textbook. (3rd ed.)
McNair, Brian.
Routledge, i-xvi. 240p. bibliog. index.
ISBN 0415199247

O.J.Simpson facts and fictions: news rituals in the construction of reality.
Hunt, Darnell M.
Cambridge University Press, i-xii. 350p. tables. appendices. index.
ISBN 0521624681

On television and journalism.
Bourdieu, Pierre; Ferguson, Patricia Parkhurst (transl.)
Pluto Press, 104p. appendix. bibliog. index.
ISBN 0745313337

Other worlds: society seen through soaap opera.
Anger, Dorothy C.
Broadview Press, 171p. appendix. bibliog.
ISBN 1551111039

Puppets, playboys & prisoners: your guide to the very best ITC series.
Rogers, Dave and Gillis, S.J.
Cult TV, 97p.

 Soap operas: information source pack.
Delaney, Sean and O'Sullivan, Ian.
BFI National Library, 39p. bibliog.
ISBN 0851706932

Soap operas worldwide: cultural and serial realities.
Matelski, Marily J.
McFarland, vii-xi. 220p. bibliog. index.
ISBN 0786405570

U.S. television news and cold war propaganda, 1947-1960.
Bernhard, Nancy E.
Cambridge Unviersity Press, xiv. 245p. illus. notes. bibliog. index.
ISBN 0521594154

Why docudrama?: fact-fiction on film and TV.
Rosenthal, Alan.
Southern Illinois University Press, viii-xxi. 387p. bibliog.
ISBN 0809321874

INDIVIDUAL TELEVISION PROGRAMMES

The Adam and Joe show book.
Buxton, Adam and Cornish, Joe.
Channel 4 Books, 94p. col. Illus.
ISBN 075221330X

Adventures in a TV nation.
Moore, Michael and Glynn, Kathleen.
Harper Perennial, i-x. 241p. illus.
appendices.
ISBN 0060988096

Ally McBeal: the official guide.
Appelo, Tim.
HarperCollins, 207p. illus.
ISBN 0002571196

Are you being served?: a celebration of twenty-five years.
Webber, Richard and Croft, David and Lloyd, Jeremy.
Orion, 181p.
ISBN 029772058

Are we there yet?: The Simpsons guide to Springfield.
Gimple, Scott M.; Morrison, Bill (ed.)
Boxtree, 127p. col. illus.
ISBN 0752224034

Babylon 5: season by season: signs and portents.
Del Rey Book/ Ballantine, 176p. [14] col. plates.
ISBN 0345424476

Battle on!: an unauthorized irreverent look at Xena: warrior princess.
Cox, Greg.
ROC, 238p. bibliog.
ISBN 0451457315

Behind the scenes at Time Team.
Taylor, Tim; Bennett, Chris (photo.)
Channel Four, 192p. index. col. plates.
ISBN 075221327X

The best of Frasier: fifteen complete scripts of the finest Frasier episodes.
Lloyd, Christopher (et al.)
Channel 4 Books, vii-x. 293p. [16] plates.
ISBN 0752213946

Blackadder: the whole damn dynasty.
Curtis, Richard and Elton, Ben and Atkinson, Rowan.
Michael Joseph, xv. 455p. illus.
ISBN 0718143728

The boy ain't right.
Aibel, Jonathan.
HarperCollins, ca. 100p. illus.
ISBN 0006531105

Buffy x-posed: the unauthorized biography of Sara Michelle Gellar and her on-screen character.
Edwards, Ted.
Prima, v-viii. 208p. illus. index.
ISBN 076151368X

The colour of justice: based on the transcripts of the Stephen Lawrence inquiry.
Norton-Taylor, Richard (ed.)
Oberon Books, 143p.
ISBN 1840021071

The complete guide to Ally McBeal.
Chunovic, Louis.
Boxtree, 192p. [4] col. plates.
ISBN 0752213326

Confessions of a late night talk show host: the autobiography of Larry Sanders with Rensin, David.
Simon & Schuster, 237p. illus.
ISBN 0684812045

A critical history of Doctor Who on television.
Muir, John Kenneth.
McFarland, vii-xi. 491p. illus.
appendices. bibliog. index.
ISBN 0786404426

Dad's army: a celebration.
Webber, Richard.
Virgin Publishing, 192p. illus.
ISBN 0753503077

Dad's army: the lost episodes.
Perry, Jimmy and Croft, David.
Virgin, 160p. illus.
ISBN 1852277572

Dawson's Creek: the official companion.
Crosdale, Darren.
Ebury Press, 159p. illus. [16] plates.
ISBN 0091868823

Days of our lives: a tour through Salem.
Zenka, Lorraine.
Dutton, ix-xi. 225p. col. Illus.
ISBN 1525943021

The double vision of Star Trek: half-humans, evil twins, and science fiction.
Hertenstein, Mike.
Cornerstone Press Chicago, ix-xiv. 284p. bibliog. indices.
ISBN 0940895420

Due South: the official guide.
Mouland, Michael.
Key Porter Books, 112p. illus. (col. and b&w).
ISBN 1550139665

bfi Eastenders: information source pack.
Delaney, Sean and O'Sullivan, Ian.
BFI Library and Information Services, 16p. bibliog.
ISBN 08517006673

Emmerdale: behind the scenes.
Hayward, Anthony.
Orion Media, 176p. illus. (col.).
index.
ISBN 0752817783

Father Ted: the Craggy Island parish magazines.
Mathews, Arthur and Linehan, Graham.
Boxtree, 88p. illus.
ISBN 0752224727

La femme Nikita x-posed: the unauthorized biography of Peta Wilson and her on-screen character.
Edwards, Ted.
Prima, 189p. index.
ISBN 0761514546

Homicide: life on the screen.
Hoffman, Tod.
ECW Press, 236p. [8] plates.
ISBN 1550223585

Homicide: life on the street: an episode guide.
Kytasaari, Dennis.
Ca. 50 leaves.

Inside The prisoner: radical television and film in the 1960s.
Rakoff, Ian.
B.T.Batsford, 192p. illus. bibliog. index.
ISBN 0713484136

Lost in space: the true story.
Shifres, Edward B.
Windsor House Publishing Group, i-xxviv. 365p. illus. tables. appendices. bibliog.
ISBN 1881636178

Lucy Lawless and Renee O'Connor: warrior stars of Xena.
Stafford, Nikki.
ECW Press, 350p. illus. [16] plates (col.). appendices.
ISBN 155022347X

The making of Hornblower: the official companion to the ITV series.
McGregor, Tom.
Boxtree, 121p. illus.
ISBN 0752211897

The making of The scarlet pimpernel: the official companion to the BBC Series.
Tibballs, Geoff.
Boxtree, 128p. illus.
ISBN 0752213016

bfi Mary Shelley's Frankenstein; Northern Exposure; the Vicar of Dibley: information source pack.
Delaney, Sean et al.
BFI Library and Information services, 26p. bibliog.

bfi Mmm... television!: narrative, form and television in The Simpsons.
Kinnear, Simon.
Presented as the author's dissertation for the MA in Cinema and Television Studies at the BFI/ Birkbeck College, University of London, 1997-98.
58p. appendix. bibliog.

Monty Python: a celebration.
Topping, Richard.
Virgin, 160p. illus.
ISBN 1852278250

Monty Python speaks!
Morgan, David.
Fourth Estate, vii-xi. 258p. illus. bibliog. index.
ISBN 1841151688

NYPD blue: an episode guide.
Kytassaari, Dennis.
Ca. 50 leaves.

Oliver Twist: the official companion to the ITV drama series.
McGregor, Tom.
Virgin, 160p. col. illus.
ISBN 1852278374

The Only fools and horses story.
Clark, Steve.
BBC, 92p. illus.
ISBN 0563384603

Resist or serve: the official guide to the X Files.
Meisler, Andy.
HarperCollins, 288p. illus.
ISBN 0061073091

Ringmaster!.
Springer, Jerry and Morton, Laura.
St. Martin's Press, xi-xii. 273p. illus.
ISBN 0312201885

The Rogers & Gillis guide to The Avengers.
Rogers, Dave and Gillis, S.J.
SJG Communications Services, 234p. credits.
ISBN 0952844141

The Royle family: the scripts: series 1.
Aherne, Caroline and Cash, Craig and Normal, Henry.
Granada Media, ix-xi. 180p. [8] plates.
ISBN 0233997210

The Seinfeld universe: the entire domain. (new and updated).
Gattuso, Greg.
BBC, v-x. 198p. illus.
ISBN 0563384336

Shooting the past.
Poliakoff, Stephen.
Methuen, 140p. [8] plates.
ISBN 0413731405

Sid and Marty Krofft: a critical study of Saturday morning children's television, 1969-1993.
Erickson, Hal.
McFarland, vii-x. 293p. appendices. index.
ISBN 078640518X

Talking heads 2.
Bennett, Alan.
BBC Worldwide, 92p. illus.
ISBN 0563384603

Tune in, log on: soaps, fandom, and online community.
Baym, Nancy K.
Sage, ix-x. 249p. appendices. bibliog. index.
ISBN 0761916490

Watching M*A*S*H, Watching America: a social history of the 1972-1983 television series.
Wittebols, James H.
McFarland & Company, 272p. index.
ISBN 0786404574

The world of Inspector Morse: a complete A-Z reference for the Morse enthusiast.
Bird, Christopher.
Boxtree, 160p. col. illus. bibliog.
ISBN 0752221175

The women of Coronation St.
Little, Daran.
Boxtree, 191p. illus. index.
ISBN 0752217429

MASS MEDIA/ COMMUNICATIONS

Advanced level media.
Bell, Angela and Joyce, Mark and Rivers, Danny.
Hodder and Stoughton, iv-x. 374p. illus. gloss. bibliog. index.
ISBN 0340674024

Advanced studies in media.
Nicholas, Joe and Price, John.
Nelson, iii-xii. 244p. illus. gloss. index.
ISBN 0174900473

Ad worlds: brands, media, audiences.
Myers, Greg.
Arnold, ix-xiii. 246p. gloss. bibliog. index.
ISBN 0340700076

Approaches to media literacy: a handbook.
Silverblatt, Art and Ferry, Jane and Finan, Barbara.
M.E. Sharpe, vii-xii. 280p. illus. bibliog. index.
ISBN 0765601850

Banned in the media: a reference guide to censorship in the press, motion pictures, broadcasting and the internet.
Foerstel, Herbert N.
Greenwood Press, xii. 252p. appendix. index.

Communication in history: technology, culture, society. (3rd ed.)
Crowley, David and Heyer, Paul.
Longman, i-xii. 347p. illus. index.
ISBN 0801331331

Controversies in media ethics. (2nd ed.)
Gordon, A. David and Kittross, John M.
Longman, v-xvii. 316p. bibliog. index.
ISBN 0801330254

Cultural diversity and the U.S. media.
Kamalipour, Yahya R. and Carilli, Theresa (eds.)
State University of New York Press, vii-xxii. 307p. figs. bibliog. index.
ISBN 0791439305

Deciphering violence: the cognitive structure of right and wrong.
Cerulo, Karen A.
Routledge, 189p. tables. bibliog. indices.
ISBN 0415917999

The entertainment economy: how mega-media forces are transforming our lives.
Wolf, Michael J.
Times Book/ Random House, ix-xxi. 314p. index.
ISBN 0812930428

Female stories, females bodies: narrative, identity and representation.
Curti, Lidia.
Macmillan, vii-xviii. 232p. bibliog. index.
ISBN 0333471652

Forging war: the media in Serbia, Croatia, Bosnia and Hercegovina.
Thompson, Mark.
University of Luton Press, iv-xvi. 388p. appendices. gloss. index.
ISBN 1860205526

From satellite to single market: new communication technology and European public service television.
Collins, Richard.
Routledge, i-xiv. 297p. tables. bibliog. index.
ISBN 041517970X

Get me a murder a day!: a history of mass communication in Britain.
Williams, Kevin.
Arnold, i-ix. 288p. indices.
ISBN 0340614668

Innovation and continuity: television and film on the brink of the 21st century: proceedings of the 10th European Television and Film Forum.
Contamine, Claude and Whittle, Stephen and Masius, Monique (eds.)
European Institute for the Media, 195p. index.
ISBN 39296673320

Interactions: critical studies in communication, media and journalism.
Hardt, Hanno.
Rowman and Littlefield, vii-xvii. 253p. bibliog. index.
ISBN 0847688887

McLuhan and Baudrillard: the masters of implosion.
Genosko, Gary.
Routledge, i-x. 140p. bibliog. indices.
ISBN 0415190622

Major principles of media law: 1999 ed.
Overbeck, Wayne.
Harcourt Brace. 537p. index.
ISBN 0155072935

Mayhem: violence as public entertainment.
Bok, Sissela.
Addison-Wesley, x. 194p. index.
ISBN 0201489791

Media, crime and criminal justice: images and realities: 2nd ed.
Surette, Ray.
Wadsworth, i-xiv. 318p. illus. appendices. index.
ISBN 0534508634

The media in American politics: contents and consequences.
Paletz, David L.
Longman, v-xxi. 394p. illus. appendices. index.
ISBN 0321029917

Media industry documentation.
Henry, Michael.
Butterworths, v-xxxiii. 1745p. index.
ISBN 0406905126

Media industry transactions.
Henry, Michael.
Butterworths, 463p. gloss. index.
ISBN 0406049777

Media policy: convergence, concentration and commerce.
Mcquail, Denis and Siune, Karen (eds.); Euromedia Research Group.
Sage Publications, i-vii. 231p. tables. index.
ISBN 0761959408

Media regulation, public interest and the law.
Feintuck, Mike.
Edinburgh University Press, v-ix. 230p. bibliog. index.
ISBN 0748609970

Media Studies: texts, institutions and audiences.
Taylor, Lisa and Willis, Andrew.
Blackwell Publishers, i-x. 262p. illus. bibliog. index.
ISBN 0631200274

Megamedia: how giant corporations dominate mass media, distort competition, and endanger democracy.
Alger, Dean.
Rowman and Littlefield, v-viii. 277p. illus. index.
ISBN 0847683893

Metholody, culture, audiovisuality.
Wilk, Eugeniusz (ed.)
Slask, 221p. index.
ISBN 8371640994

New media and American politics.
Davis, Richard and Owen, Diana.
Oxford University Press, 304p. notes. index.

ISBN 0195120612

A philosophy of mass art.
Carroll, Noel.
Clarendon Press, 425p. index.
ISBN 0198742371

Politics and the media: harlots and prerogatives at the turn of the millennium.
Seaton, Jean.
Blackwell, 135p. illus. index.
ISBN 0631209417

Regulating the media. (2nd ed.)
Gibbons, Thomas.
Sweet and Maxwell, vii-xix. 326p. index.
ISBN 0421606606

Remote & controlled: media politics in a cynical age: 2nd ed.
Kerbel, Matthew Robert.
Westview, i-xv. 172p. tables. index.
ISBN 0813368693

The search for a method: focus groups and the development of mass communication research.
Morrison, David E.
University of Luton Press, iv-xv. 294p. bibliog. index.
ISBN 1860205402

The silenced media: the propaganda war between Russian and the west in northern Europe.
Salminen, Esko; Kokkonen, Jyri (transl.)
Macmillan, v-xii. 198p. bibliog. index.
ISBN 0333724518

Sport, culture and the media.
Rowe, David.
Open University Press, viii-xii. 193p. illus. gloss. bibliog. index.
ISBN 0335202020

Tough girls: women warriors and wonder women in popular culture.
Inness, Sherrie.
University of Pennsylvania Press, vii. 228p. illus. bibliog. index.
ISBN 0812216733

War and the media: propaganda and persuasion in the Gulf War. (2nd ed.)
Taylor, Philip M.
Manchester University Press, xxvi. 340p. appendices. bibliog. index.
ISBN 0719055504

Whitewash: racialized politics and the media.
Gabriel, John.
Routledge, v-vii. 219p. notes. bibliog. index.
ISBN 0415149703

VIDEO/ NEW TECHNOLOGIES

Basics of video production (2nd ed.)
Lyver, Des and Swainson, Graham.
Focal Press, i-x. 150p. illus.
ISBN 0240515609

Cinema futures: Cain, Abel or cable?: the screen arts in the digital age.
Elsaesser, Thomas and Hoffmann, Kay
Amsterdam University Press, 312p. illus. bibliog. index.
ISBN 90553563121

Digital diversions: youth culture in the age of multimedia.
Sefton-Green, Julian (ed.)
UCL Press 179p. bibliogs. index.
ISBN 1857288572

Experimental ethnography: the work of film in the age of video.
Russell, Catherine.
Duke University Press, x-xvii. illus. bibliog. filmog. index.
ISBN 0822323192

From Barbie to Mortal kombat.
Cassell, Justine and Jenkins, Henry (eds.)
MIT Press, viii-xviii. 360p. illus. [12] plates. index.
ISBN 0262032589

Funding information and communications technology in the heritage sector: policy recommendtions to the Heritage Lottery fund, January 1998.
Humanities Advanced Technology & Information Institute, University of Glasgow.
University of Glasgow, 137p. illus. tables. indices.

The internet challenge to television.
Owen, Bruce M.
Harvard University Press, vi-xii. 372p. appendix. figs. gloss. bibliog. index.
ISBN 0674872991

Playing for success: a white paper on the UK leisure software industry.
ELSPA.
ELSPA, 28p. tables. figs. appendices.

Regulating communications: approaching convergence in the Information Age.
Great Britain Department of Trade and Industry and Department of Culture, Media and Sport.

The Stationary Office, 65p.
ISBN 0101402228

Remediation: understanding new media.
Bolter, David J. and Grusin, Richard.
MIT Press, viii-xi. 295p. [8] col. plates. illus. gloss. bibliog. index.
ISBN 0262024527

Single-camera video production. (2nd ed.)
Musburger, Robert B.
Focal Press, v-xi. illus. bibliog. gloss. index.
ISBN 0240803337

Techgnosis: myth, magic and mysticism in the age of information. Davis, Erik.
Harmony, ix-x. 353p. index.
ISBN 0517704153

bfi Tomb raider: exploration of space, the solving of puzzles and narrative in 3D videogames.
Cooper, Kimberley.
British Film Institute/ Birckbeck College MA in Cinema and Television Studies, 48p. col. illus. bibliog.

The V-chip debate: content filtering from television to the internet.
Price, Monroe E. (ed.)
Lawrence Erlbaum, xx-xxv. 363p. bibliog. indices.
ISBN 0805830626

Videojournalism: the definitive guide to multi-skilled television production.
Griffiths, Richard.
Focal Press, vi-xi. 142p. illus. gloss. index.
ISBN 0240515080

The view from Babylon: the notes of a Hollywood voyeur.
Rawley, Donald.
Warner Books, i-ix. 204p.
ISBN 0446524115

BOOKSELLERS

Stock

A   Books

B   Magazines

C   Posters

D   Memorabilia eg Stills

E   Cassettes, CDs, Records Videos and DVDs

F   Postcards and Greetings Cards

Arnolfini Bookshop
16 Narrow Quay
Bristol BS1 4QA
Tel: 0117 9299191
Fax: 0117 9253876
email: bookshop@arnolfini.demon.co.uk
Website: www.arnolfini.demon.co.uk
Peter Begen, Bookshop Manager
Open: 10.00-7.00 Mon-Sat, 12.00-6.30 Sun
Stock: A, B, F
Based in the Arnolfini Gallery, concentrating on the visual arts. No catalogues issued. Send requests for specific material with SAE

Blackwell's
48-51 Broad Street
Oxford OX1 3BQ
Tel: 01865 792792
Fax: 01865 794143
email: blackwells.extra@blackwell.co.uk
Website: www.bookshop.blackwell.co.uk
Open: 9.00-6.00 Mon, Wed-Sat, 9.30-6.00 Tue, 11.00-5.00 Sun
Stock: A
Literature department has sections on cinemas and performing arts, sociology department has a Media Studies section `and performing arts. International charge and send service available

Blackwell's Art & Poster Shop
27 Broad Street
Oxford OX1 2AS
Tel: 01865 792792
Open: 9.00-6.00 Mon, Wed-Sat, 9.30-6.00 Tues, 11.00-5.00 Sun
Stock: A, B, C, F
A wide selection of books, posters, cards, calendars and gift items, all available by mail order

Bookshop at Namara House
45-46 Poland Street
London W1
Tel: 020 7734 6768
Leonie Van Ness
produced three times a year

The Cinema Bookshop
13-14 Great Russell Street
London WC1B 3NH
Tel: 020 7637 0206
Fax: 020 7436 9979
Open: 10.30-5.30 Mon-Sat
Stock: A, B, C, D
Comprehensive stock of new, out-of-print and rare books. Posters, Pressbooks and stills etc. No catalogues are issued. Send requests for specific material with SAE

The Cinema Store
Unit 4B, Orion House
Upper Saint Martin's Lane
London WC2H 9NY
Tel: 020 7379 7838
(general enquiries)
Fax: 020 7240 7689
email: cinemastor@aol.com
Website: www.the-cinema-store.com
Tel: 020 7379 7865
(laserdiscs, mail order books, cd's)
Tel: 020 7379 7895
(trading cards, VHS)
Open: 10.00-6.00 Mon-Wed, Sat, 10.00-7.00 Thu-Fri
12-6 Sun
Stock: A, B, C, D, E, F
Mail order available worldwide. Latest and vintage posters/stills, magazines, models and laser discs, new/rare VHS, soundtracks and trading cards

Cornerhouse Books
70 Oxford Street
Manchester M1 5NH
Tel: 0161 228 7621
Fax: 0161 200 1506
Stock: A, B, F
Open: 12.00-8.30 daily
No catalogues issued. Send requests for specific material with SAE

Ray Dasilva Puppet Books
63 Kennedy Road
Bicester
Oxfordshire OX6 8BE
Tel: 01869 245793
email: dasilv@puppetbooks.co.uk
Website: puppetbooks.co.uk
Mail order (visitors by appointment). New and second hand books on puppetry and animation including film and television. Catalogue available

David Drummond at Pleasures of Past Times
11 Cecil Court
Charing Cross Road
London WC2N 4EE
Tel: 020 7836 1142
Open: 11.00-2.30, 3.30-5.45 Mon-Fri. First Sat in month 11.00-2.30
Stock: A, D, F
Extended hours and other times by arrangement. No catalogue

Decorum Books
24 Cloudsley Square
London N1 0HN
Tel: 020 7278 1838
Fax: 020 7837 6424
email: decorumbooks@lineone.net
Mail order only. Secondhand books on film and theatre; music and art. Also secondhand scores and sheet music

Dress Circle
57-59 Monmouth Street
Upper St Martin's Lane
London WC2H 9DG
Tel: 020 7240 2227
Fax: 020 7379 8540
Website: www.dresscircle.co.uk
Open: 10.00-7.00 Mon-Sat
Stock: A, B, C, D, E, F
Specialists in stage music and musicals. Catalogue of the entire stock issued annually with updates twice yearly. Send SAE for details

Everyman Cinema
5 Holly Bush Vale
Hampstead
London NW3 6TX
Tel: 020 7431 1818
Fax: 020 7435 2292
Website: www.everymancinema.com
Tomislav Terek
Stock: A, B, C, D, E, F
Based at the Pullman Everyman Cinema, offers wide range of materials for scholars and enthusiasts alike

Anne FitzSimons
62 Scotby Road
Scotby
Carlisle CA4 8BD
Tel: 01228 513815
Stock: A, B, C, D, F
Mail order only. Antiquarian and out-of-print titles on cinema, broadcasting and performing arts. A catalogue is issued twice a year. Send three first-class postage stamps for current issue

Flashbacks
6 Silver Place
Beak Street

London W1R 3LJ
Tel: 020 7437 8562
Fax: 020 7437 8562
email: shop@flashbacks.freeserve.co.uk
Website: www.dacre.simplenet.com/
Richard Dacre, Chris Voisey
Stock: C, D
Stockist of vintage and modern movie posters and stills. Shop and mail order service. Send SAE and 'wanted' list for stock details

Forbidden Planet
71-75 New Oxford Street
London WC1A 1DG
Tel: 020 7836 4179
Fax: 020 7240 7118
Open: 10.00-6.00 Mon-Wed, Sat, 10.00-7.00 Thur, Fri
Stock: A, B, C, D, E, F
Science fiction, horror, fantasy and comics specialists. Mail order service available on 0171 497 2150

Grant and Cutler
Language Booksellers
55-57 Great Marlborough Street
London W1V 2AY
Tel: 020 7734 2012
Fax: 020 7734 9272
email: postmaster@grant-c.demon.co.uk
Website: www.grant-c.demon.co.uk
Stock A,E
Foreign language book specialist. World cinema books and screenplays
Open 9:00 to 17:30 Mon to Sat. Thursdays, 9:00 to 19:00

Hay Cinema Bookshop (including Francis Edwards)
The Old Cinema
Castle Street
Hay-on-Wye
via Hereford HR3 5DF
Tel: 01497 820071
email: sales@haycinemabookshop.co.uk
Website: www.haycinemabookshop.co.uk
Large second hand stock. Open 9.00-7.00 Mon-Sat, 11.30-5.30 Sun
Includes an antiquira bookshop within the Cinema Bookshop:
Francis Edwards
email: sales@francisedwards.demon.co.uk
Website: francisedwards.co.uk

Heffers Booksellers
20 Trinity Street
Cambridge CB2 ITY
Tel: 01223 568568

Fax: 01223 568591
email: heffers@heffers.co.uk
Website: www.heffers.co.uk
Open: 9.00-5.30 Mon-Sat
11.00-5.00 Sun
Stock: A, E
Catalogues of videocassettes and spoken word recordings issued. Copies are available on request.

LV Kelly Books
6 Redlands
Blundell's Road
Tiverton
Devon EX16 4DH
Tel: 01884 256170
Fax: 01884 251063
email: lenkelly@topservice.com
Website: www.lvkellybooks.webjump.com
Stock: A, B, E
Principally mail order but visitors welcome by appointment. Catalogue issued regularly on broadcasting and mass communications. Occasional lists on cinema, music, journalism

Ed Mason
Room 301
Third Floor
River Bank House Business Centre
1, Putney Bridge Approach
London SW6 3JD
Tel: 020 7736 8511
Stock: A, B, C, D
Specialist in original film memorabilia from the earliest onwards. Also organises the Collectors' Film Convention six times a year
Office only - all memorabilia stock is re-located to Rare Discs (see entry)

National Museum of Photography, Film & Television
Pictureville
Bradford BD1 1NQ
Tel: 01274 202030
Fax: 01274 723155
Website: www.nmpft.org.uk
Bookshop run by A Zwemmer
Open: 10.00-6.00 Tue-Sun
Closed Mondays (except Bank Holidays and School Holidays)
Stock: A, C, D, F
Mail order available. Send SAE with requests for information

Offstage Theatre & Film Bookshop
37 Chalk Farm Road
London NW1 8AJ
Tel: 020 7485 4996
Fax: 020 7916 8046

email: offstage@btinternet.com
Brian Schwartz
Free cinema and media catalogues
available. Send SAE. Open seven
days a week

C D Paramor
25 St Mary's Square
Newmarket
Suffolk CB8 0HZ
Tel: 01638 664416
Fax: 01638 664416
Stock: A, B, C, F, E
Mail order only. Visitors welcome
strictly by appointment. Catalogues
and most of the performing arts
issued regularly free of charge

Rare Discs
18 Bloomsbury Street
London WC1B 3QA
Tel: 020 7580 3516
Open: 10.00-6.30 Mon-Sat
Stock: E
Retail shop with recorded mail order
service. Over 7,000 titles including
soundtracks, original cast shows,
musicals and nostalgia. Telephone for
information

Screenwriter's Store
10-11 Moor Street
London W1V 5LJ
Tel: 020 7287 9009
Fax: 020 7287 6009
Website: www.screenwritertore.co.uk
Sells screenplays and screenwriting
software

Spread Eagle Bookshop (Incorporates Greenwich Gallery)
9 Nevada Street
London SE10 9JL
Tel: 020 8305 1666
Fax: 020 8305 0447
email: antiques@spreadeagle.org.uk
Open: 10.00-5.30 daily
Stock: A, B, C, D
All second-hand stock. Memorabilia,
ephemera. Large stock of books on
cinema, theatre, posters and photos

Stable Books
Holm Farm
Coldridge
Crediton
Devon EX17 6BR
Tel: 01363 83227
Mail order (visitors by appointment
only). Second hand stock concerning
theatre, cinema and puppetry

Stage and Screen
34 Notting Hill Gate

London W11
Tel: 020 7221 3646

Stage Door Prints
9 Cecil Court
London WC2N 4EZ
Tel: 020 7240 1683
General stock of performing arts
titles including antiquarian prints,
ephemera and movie memorabilia.
Open 11.00-6.00 Mon-Fri,
11.30-6.00 Sat

H Terence Kaye
52 Neeld Crescent
London NW4 3RR
Tel: 020 8202 8188
Rare and collectable books.
Specialist in books about theatre,
cinema and performing arts.
Open 9.30-5.30 Mon-Sat

Treasure Chest
61 Cobbold Road
Felixstowe
Suffolk 1P11 7BH
Tel: 01394 270717
Second hand stock specialising in
cinema and literature.
Open 9.30-5.30 Mon-Sat

Vinmagco limited
39-43 Brewer Street
London W1R 9UD
Tel: 020 7439 8525
Fax: 0207 439 8527
email: vintage.soho@ndirect.co.uk
Website: vinmag.com
Open: 10.00-8.00 Mon-Sat,
12.00-7.00 Sun
Stock: B, C, D, F
247 Camden High Street,
London NW1
Tel: 020 7482 0587
Open: 10.00-6.00 Mon-Fri,
10.00-7.00 Sat, Sun
Stock: B,C,D,F
55 Charing Cross Road
London WC2H ONE
Open: 10.00-10.00
Tel: 0207 494 4064

Peter Wood*
20 Stonehill Road
Great Shelford
Cambridge CB2 5JL
Tel: 01223 842419
Stock: A, D, F
Mail order. Visitors are welcome by
appointment. A free catalogue is
available of all books in stock

A Zwemmer
80 Charing Cross Road
London WC2H 0BB

Tel: 020 7240 4157
Fax: 020 7240 4186
email: enquiries@zwemmer.co.uk
Website: www.zwemmer.co.uk
Claire de Rouen
Open: 9.30-6.00 Mon-Fri,
10.00-6.00 Sat
Stock: A, B
A catalogue of new and in-print titles
on every aspect of cinema is
available on request. Mail order
service for all books available
through Mail Order Department

CABLE, SATELLITE AND DIGITAL

Information in this section is provided by David Fisher, Editor of Screen Digest whose continuing support we gratefully acknowledge

As the number of channels and digital services expands, the number of companies involved in delivering multichannel television to UK homes is rapidly diminishing. In the satellite orbit there has been one dominant operator—British Sky Broadcasting (BSkyB)—for some years. The cable business is moving towards a comparable position now that the third largest operator, NTL, has taken over the domestic cable television operations of the biggest, Cable & Wireless Communications, leaving only two major multiple system operators (MSOs). The second largest MSO, Telewest, is widely expected to become part of one major cable company in due course through a merger with NTL. The cost to NTL of the CWC acquisition is £8.2 billion, whilst Cable & Wireless is paying £6.5 billion to take full ownership of CWC's business operations. These figures indicate the massive financial scale of cable investment and costs.

This process of merger and takeover has radically altered the structure of the UK's broadband cable industry as envisaged when the first franchises were awarded in November 1983. With 12.5m homes already passed by cable systems that are continuing to build—and only 4m homes outside franchise areas—a new phase is beginning as the exclusivity that operators enjoyed as part of their franchises is abandoned. Competition between cable companies is thus possible, although the prospect of operators spending huge sums of money on building competitive cable networks in the foreseeable future is remote.

MULTIPLE SYSTEM OPERATORS

Almost all franchises are held as part of groups of holdings. Such groups are called multiple system operators (MSOs). Extensive consolidation has taken place since 1995 and especially during the first half of 1998, which resulted in the emergence of three dominant groups: Cable & Wireless Communications, NTL and Telewest. However, in mid 1999 NTL agreed to acquire the cable operations of Cable & Wireless, a process that is now nearing completion.

AT&T
US telecom operator, which acquired Tele-Communications Inc (TCI), the largest US cable operator, holder of 50% share in TW Holdings, which owns 53% of Telewest [qv]

Atlantic Telecom Group
303 King Street
Aberdeen AB2 3AP
Tel: 01224 646644
Fax: 01224 644601
Website: www.atlantic-telecom.co.uk
Areas: Aberdeen

British Telecommunications (BT)
87-89 Baker Street
London W1M 2LP
Tel: 020 7487 1254
Fax: 020 7487 1259
Areas: as BT New Towns Cable TV Services: Milton Keynes
as Westminster Cable Company: Westminster LB.
Also upgrade systems at Barbican (London), Brackla, Martlesham, Walderslade, Washington
Note: From 1 January 2001 BT will be allowed to compete in delivery of television-related services with existing cable networks.

Cable & Telecoms (UK)
PO Box 319
Whipsnade
Dunstable
Bedfordshire LU6 2LT
Tel: 01582 873006

Fax: 01582 873003
Ownership: US Cable Corporation, McNicholas Construction, Morgan Cable
as Ayrshire Cable & Telecoms: Ayr
as Cumbria Cable & Telecoms: Carlisle; Cumbria, Central
as Northumberland Cable & Telecoms: Northumberland
as South Cumbria Cable & Telecoms: Cumbria, South

Cable & Wireless Communications
26 Red Lion Square
London WC1R 4HQ
Tel: 020 7528 2000
Website: www.cwcom.co.uk
Formed 1997 by merger of cable operators Bell Cablemedia (inc Videotron), Nynex Cablecomms and telecom operator Mercury
Ownership: NTL [qv, with whose brand it is being replaced]
Areas: Aylesbury/Amersham/Chesham, Bolton, Bournemouth/Poole/Christchurch, Brighton/Hove/Worthing, Bromley, Bury/Rochdale, Cheshire North, Chichester/Bognor, Dartford/Swanley, Derby/Spondon, Durham South /North Yorkshire, Ealing, Eastbourne/Hastings, Epping Forest/Chigwell/Loughton/Ongar, Fenland, Great Yarmouth/Lowestoft/Caister, Greater London East, Greenwich/Lewisham, Harrogate/Knaresborough, Harrow, Havering, Hertfordshire South, Kensington/Chelsea, Kent South East, Lambeth/Southwark, Lancashire East, Leeds, London North West, Macclesfield/Wilmslow, Manchester/Salford, Newham/Tower Hamlets, Norwich, Oldham/Tameside, Peterborough, Portsmouth/Fareham/Gosport/Havant, Southampton/Eastleigh, Stockport, Stoke-on-Trent/Newcastle, Surrey North, Surrey North East, Thamesmead, Totton/Hythe, Waltham Forest, Wandsworth, Wearside, Whittlesey/March/Wisbech, Winchester, The Wirral, York
CWC is being acquired by NTL [qv].

Convergence Group
Premiere House
3 Betts Way
Crawley, West Sussex RH10 2GB
Tel: 01293 540444
Fax: 01293 540900
Areas: East Grinstead, Haywards
Heath
50% in Taunton/Bridgewater, Yeovil
(with Orbis Trust (Guernsey))

Cox Communications
US cable operator
10% stake in Telewest (23% of
preference shares) [qv]

Eurobell (Holdings)
Multi-Media House
Lloyds Court, Manor Royal
Crawley, West Sussex RH10 2PT
Tel: 01293 400444
Fax: 01293 400440
Ownership: Detecon (Deutsche
Telepost Consulting)
Areas: Crawley/Horley/Gatwick,
Devon South, Kent West

Metro Cable
Areas: Irvine
Shareholder in Ayrshire Cable & Telecoms

NTL
Bristol House
1 Lakeside Road
Farnborough
Hampshire GU14 6XP
Tel 01252 402662
Fax 01252 402665
Website: www.cabletel.co.uk
HQ: **110 East 59th Street, New
York, NY 10022 USA**
Tel +1/212 906 8440
Fax +1/212 752 1157
Formerly: International CableTel
Ownership: Rockefeller family,
Capital Cities Broadcasting Company
(subsidiary of Walt Disney
Company), Microsoft, France
Télécom (eventually will be largest
shareholder with 25%)
NTL has acquired Cable & Wireless
Communications cable franchises and
is replacing that brand with its own.
Areas: former CableTel franchises
as CableTel Bedfordshire: Bedford
as CableTel Glasgow:
Bearsden/Milngavie, Glasgow
Greater, Glasgow North
West/Clydebank, Invercylde,
Paisley/Renfrew
as CableTel Herts & Bedfordshire:
Luton/South Bedfordshire
as CableTel Hertfordshire:
Hertfordshire Central, Hertfordshire
East,

as CableTel Kirklees:
Huddersfield/Dewsbury
as CableTel Northern Ireland:
Northern Ireland
as CableTel South Wales:
Cardiff/Penarth, Glamorgan West,
Glamorgan/Gwent,
Newport/Cwmbran/Pontypool
as CableTel Surrey: Guildford/West
Surrey
former Comcast UK franchises:
as Anglia Cable: Harlow/Bishops
Stortford/Stansted Airport
as Cambridge Cable:
Cambridge/Ely/Newmarket,
as Comcast Teesside: Darlington,
Teesside
as East Coast Cable:
Colchester/Ipswich/etc,
as Southern East Anglia Cable: East
Anglia South,
Sold its 50% stake in Cable London
to Telewest (qv) August 1999.
former ComTel franchises:
Andover/Salisbury/Romsey, Daventry,
Corby/Kettering/Wellingborough,
Hertfordshire West,
Litchfield/Burntwood/Rugeley,
Northampton,
Nuneaton/Bedworth/Rugby,
Oxford/Abingdon, Stafford/Stone,
Swindon, Tamworth/North
Warwickshire/Meriden, Thames
Valley, Warwick/Stratford-upon-
Avon/Kenilworth/Leamington Spa
former Diamond Cable franchises:
Bassetlaw, Burton-on-Trent, Coventry,
East Derbyshire, Grantham,
Grimsby/Immingham /Cleethorpes,
Hinckley/Bosworth,
Huddersfield/Dewsbury, Leicester,
Lincoln, Lincolnshire/South
Humberside, Loughborough/
Shepshed, Mansfield/Sutton/Kirkby-
in-Ashfield, Melton Mowbray,
Newark-on-Trent, Northern Ireland,
Nottingham, Ravenshead, Vale of
Belvoir

SBC International
Ownership: Southwestern Bell
Telecom [US telecom operator]
10% stake in Telewest (23% of
preference shares) [qv]

Telewest Communications
Unit 1, Genesis Business Park
Albert Drive
Woking, Surrey GU21 5RW
Tel: 01483 750900
Fax 01483 750901
Website: www.telewest.co.uk
Ownership: TW Holdings (= Tele-
Communications International
(TINTA) 50% and US West
International 50%) 53%, Microsoft

29.9%, Liberty Media (=AT&T), Cox
Communications 10%, SBC
International (= Southwestern Bell
Telecom) 10%
Acquired NTL's (formerly Comcast
UK's) half-share in Cable London in
August 1999.
Areas:
as Birmingham Cable:
Birmingham/Solihull, Wythall
as Cable Corporation:
Hillingdon/Hounslow, Windsor
as Cable London: Camden, Enfield,
Hackney & Islington, Haringey
as Telewest London & the South
East): Croydon, Kingston/Richmond,
Merton/Sutton, Thames Estuary
North, Thames Estuary South
as Telewest Midlands & the South
West: Avon, Black Country,
Cheltenham/Gloucester,
Taunton/Bridgewater, Telford,
Worcester
as Telewest North West):
Blackpool/Fylde, Lancashire Central,
Liverpool North/Bootle/Crosby,
Liverpool South, St
Helens/Knowsley, Southport, Wigan
as Telewest Scotland & North East:
Cumbernauld, Dumbarton, Dundee,
Edinburgh, Falkirk/West Lothian,
Fife, Glenrothes/Kirkaldy/Leven,
Motherwell/East
Kilbride/Hamilton/Wishaw/Lanark,
Perth/Scone, Tyneside
as Yorkshire Cable Communications:
Barnsley, Bradford, Calderdale,
Doncaster/Rotherham, Sheffield,
Wakefield/Pontefract/Castleford

US West International
50% share in TW Holdings, which
owns 53% of Telewest [qv]

CABLE FRANCHISES

All broadband cable franchises to date were granted by the Cable Authority (apart from 11 previously granted by the Department of Trade and Industry), the role of which was taken over by the Independent Television Commission (ITC) in January 1991, under the Broadcasting Act 1990.

The Act empowered the ITC to grant fifteen-year 'local delivery licences', which can include use of microwave distribution. Licences must be awarded to the highest bidder on the basis of an annual cash bid in addition to forecasts of the sums that will be paid to the Exchequer as a percentage of revenue earned in the second and third five-year periods of the licence.

The biggest change since the last edition of the Handbook is that the major operators, by agreement with the ITC, have each opted for a single non-exclusive local delivery service licence, thus allowing the possibility of competitive marketing and delivery on a potentially national basis. The individual franchise exclusive licences held by NTL were consequently revoked by the ITC on 31 December 1999 and those of Telewest on 31 May 2000.

The franchises are arranged in alphabetical order of area. Where appropriate the principal towns in the area are identified under the area name; cross references are provided for these and other principal towns at the appropriate alphabetical point.

'Homes in area' is the number of homes in the franchise area at the time of the last census before award of the franchise. 'Build completed' is indicated where all homes nominally in the area are passed by cable. 'Homes passed' is the number of homes to which a cable service is available and marketed. 'Subscribers' (abbreviated to 'Subs') are those taking at least the basic service, with the percentage this represents of homes passed. Unless stated, services have not yet begun.

In some towns an older cable system still exists. These are not franchised but are licensed by the ITC to provide limited services. They are gradually being superseded by new broadband networks

Aberdeen
Franchise holder: Aberdeen Cable Services = Atlantic Telecom Group (see MSOs)
Homes in area: 91,000 (build complete)
Awarded: 29 Nov 83
Service start: 1 May 85
Homes passed: 97,875 (1 Apr 2000)
Subs: 16,074 = 16.4% (1 Apr 2000)

Abingdon
see Oxford

Accrington
see Lancashire, East

Airdrie
see Cumbernauld

Alconbury
Narrowband upgrade system operated by Cablecom Investments (see MSOs)

Aldershot
see Guildford

Amersham
see Aylesbury

Andover/Salisbury/Romsey
Franchise holder: NTL (see MSOs)
Homes in area: 84,500
Awarded: Andover Apr 89, Salisbury/Romsey 6 Apr 90
Service start: Andover Mar 90, Salisbury/Romsey Jun 95
Homes passed: 50,912 (1 Apr 2000)
Subs: 12,174 = 23.9% (1 Apr 2000)
Franchises awarded separately but amalgamated

Ashford
see Kent, South-east

Avon
Bristol, Bath, Weston-super-Mare, Frome, Melksham etc
Franchise holder: Telewest (see MSOs)
Homes in area: 300,000 (build complete)
Awarded: 16 Nov 88
Service start: 14 Sept 90
Homes passed: 294,377 (1 Apr 2000)
Subs: 86,298 = 29.3% (1 Apr 2000)

Aylesbury/Amersham/ Chesham/Wendover
Franchise holder: Cable & Wireless Communications (see MSOs)
Homes in area: 89,000
Awarded: 31 May 90; acquired Jul 94
Service start: Apr 96
Homes passed: 37,891 (1 Apr 2000)
Subs: 5,549 = 14.6% (1 Apr 2000)

Ayr
Local delivery franchise holder: Cable & Telecoms (see MSOs)
Homes in area: 155,000
Awarded: July 1997
Area includes narrowband system in Irvine.

Baldock
see Hertfordshire, Central

Banstead
see East Grinstead

Barking/Dagenham, London Borough of
see Greater London East

Barnet, London Borough of
see London, North West

Barnsley
Franchise holder: Telewest (see MSOs)
Homes in area: 82,000
Awarded: 14 Jun 90; acquired Apr 93
Homes passed: 36,463 (1 Apr 2000)
Subs: 6,374 = 17.5% (1 Apr 2000)

Barrow in Furness
see Cumbria, South

Basildon
see Thames Estuary North

Basingstoke
see Thames Valley

Bassetlaw
Local delivery licence holder: NTL (see MSOs)
Homes in area: 32,800
Date awarded: 13 Jul 95

Bath
see Avon

Bearsden/Milngavie
Franchise holder: CableTel Glasgow (see MSOs)
Homes in area: 16,000
Awarded: 7 Jun 90
Homes passed: 13,577 (1 Apr 2000)
Subs: 5,053 = 37.2% (1 Apr 2000)

Bedford
Franchise holder: CableTel Bedfordshire (see MSOs)
Homes in area: 55,000 (build complete)
Awarded: 14 Jun 90
Service start: Nov 1994
Homes passed: 57,994 (1 Apr 2000)
Subs: 22,263 = 38.4% (1 Apr 2000)

Bedworth
see Nuneaton

Beith
Narrowband upgrade system operated by A Thomson (Relay)

Belfast
Franchise revoked from Ulster Cablevision
Homes in area: 136,000
Awarded: 29 Nov 83
see Northern Ireland

Belper
see Derbyshire, East

Berkhamsted
see Hertfordshire, West

Bexley, London Borough of
see Greater London East

Birmingham/Solihull
Franchise holder: Birmingham Cable
(see MSOs)
Homes in area: 465,000
Awarded: 19 Oct 88
Service start: Dec 89
Homes passed: 437,280 (1 Apr 2000)
Subs: 115,566 = 26.43% (1 Apr 2000)

Bishops Stortford
see Harlow

Black Country
Dudley, Sandwell, Walsall,
Wolverhampton, urban parts of
Bromsgrove, Cannock, Kidderminster
Franchise holder: Telewest (see MSOs)
Homes in area: 470,000
Awarded: 14 Jul 89
Service start: Sept 91
Homes passed: 469,766 (1 Apr 2000)
Subs: 120,822 = 25.7% (1 Apr 2000)

Blackburn
see Lancashire, East

Blackpool and Fylde
Local delivery franchise holder:
Telewest (see MSOs)
Homes in area: 101,000
Date awarded: Sept 94
Homes passed: 39,272 (1 Apr 2000)
Subs: 7,159 = 18.2% (1 Apr 2000)

Blaenau Ffestiniog
Narrowband upgrade system operated
by John Sulwyn Evans

Bognor
see Chichester

Bolsover
see Derbyshire, East

Bolton
Franchise holder: Cable & Wireless
Communications (see MSOs)
Homes in area: 135,000
Awarded: 13 Aug 85; acquired 22 Mar
93
Service start: Jul 90
Homes passed: 128,401 (1 Apr 2000)
Subs: 29,193 = 22.7% (1 Apr 2000)

Bootle
see Liverpool, North

Borehamwood
see Hertfordshire, South

Bosworth
see Hinkley

Bournemouth/Poole/Christc hurch
Franchise holder: Cable & Wireless

Communications (see MSOs)
Homes in area: 143,000
Awarded: 6 Apr 90
Service start: mid 94
Home passed: 120,569 (1 Apr 2000)
Subs: 35,904 = 29.8% (1 Apr 2000)

Bracknell
see Thames Valley

Bradford
Franchise holder: Telewest (see
MSOs)
Homes in area: 175,000
Awarded: 14 Jun 90
Service start: Jul 92
Homes passed: 143,551 (1 Apr 2000)
Subs: 28,556 = 19.9% (1 Apr 2000)

Braintree
see East Anglia, South

Brecon
Narrowband upgrade system operated
by Metro Cable

Brent, London Borough of
see London, North West

Brentwood
see Thames Estuary North

Brighouse
see Calderdale

Brighton/Hove/Worthing
Franchise holder: Cable & Wireless
Communications (see MSOs)
Homes in area: 160,000 (build complete)
Awarded: 20 Oct 89; acquired 22 Mar
93
Service start: Apr 1992
Homes passed: 159,658 (1 Apr 2000)
Subs: 43,636 = 27.3% (1 Apr 2000)
Separate upgrade system in Brighton
operated by CDA Communications

Bristol
see Avon

Broadstairs
see Thanet, Isle of

Bromley, London Borough of
Franchise holder: Cable & Wireless
Communications (see MSOs)
Homes in area: 117,000 (build complete)
Awarded: 16 Mar 90
Service start: Jan 93
Homes passed: 117,323 (1 Apr 2000)
Subs: 30,476 = 26.0% (1 Apr 2000)

Burgess Hill
see Haywards Heath

Burnley
see Lancashire, East

Burntwood
see Stafford

Bury St Edmunds
see East Anglia, South

Burton-on-Trent/ Swadlincote/Ashby-de-la Zouch/ Coalville/Uttoxeter
Local delivery franchise holder: NTL
(see MSOs)
Homes in area: 77,675
Awarded: Jun 95
Homes passed: 14,871 (1 Apr 2000)
Subs: 3,881 = 26.1% (1 Apr 2000)

Bury/Rochdale
Franchise holder: Cable & Wireless
Communications (see MSOs)
Homes in area: 143,000
Awarded: 17 May 90; acquired 4 May
93
Homes passed: 73,795 (1 Apr 2000)
Subs: 18,053 = 24.5% (1 Apr 2000)
Separate upgrade system in Rochdale
operated by CDA Communications

Bushey
see Hertfordshire, South

Calderdale
Halifax, Brighouse
Franchise holder: Telewest (see MSOs)
Homes in area: 75,000
Awarded: 14 Jun 90
Homes passed: 30,704 (1 Apr 2000)
Subs: 5,115 = 16.7% (1 Apr 2000)

Camberley
see Guildford

Cambridge and district
Cambridge, Newmarket, Ely, Saffron
Walden, Huntingdon, St Ives, St
Neots, Royston, etc
Franchise holder: Cambridge Cable =
Comcast Europe (see MSOs)
Homes in area: 132,000
Awarded: 4 Jun 89
Service start: Jul 91
Homes passed: 129,050 (1 Apr 2000)
Subs: 32,591 = 25.3% (1 Apr 2000)

Camden, London Borough of
Franchise holder: Telewest (see MSOs)
Homes in area: 70,000 (build complete)
Awarded: 1 Feb 86
Service start: Dec 89
Homes passed: 84,264 (1 Apr 2000)
Subs: 21,609 = 25.6% (1 Apr 2000)

Canterbury/Thanet
No applicants for local delivery
franchise (January 1997)
Upgrade systems in Canterbury and
Isle of Thanet operated by CDA
Communications

Cardiff/Penarth
Franchise holder: CableTel South
Wales (see MSOs)
Homes in area: 103,000
Awarded: 5 Feb 86
Service start: Sept 94
Homes passed: 100,452 (1 Apr 200)
Subs: 44,877 = 44.7% (1 Apr 2000)

Carlisle
Local delivery licence holder: Cable & Telecoms (UK) (see MSOs)
Homes in area: 35,000
Awarded: Nov 95
Original franchise surrendered by Carlisle Cablevision (awarded: 21 Jun 90)

Carmarthen
Narrowband upgrade system operated by Metro Cable

Castleford
see Wakefield

Chatham
see Thames Estuary South

Chelmsford
see Thames Estuary North

Cheltenham/Gloucester
Franchise holder: Telewest (see MSOs)
Homes in area: 90,000
Awarded: 13 Aug 85
Service start: Aug 94
Homes passed: 84,536 (1 Apr 2000)
Subs: 23,739 = 28.1% (1 Apr 2000)

Cheshire, North
Chester, Ellesmere Port, Warrington, Widnes, Runcorn
Franchise holder: Cable & Wireless Communications (see MSOs)
Homes in area: 175,000
Awarded: 12 Jan 90; acquired 21 Apr 93
Homes passed: 115,476 (1 Apr 2000)
Subs: 29,392 = 25.5% (1 Apr 2000)

Chesham
see Aylesbury

Cheshunt
see Hertfordshire, East

Chesterfield
see Derbyshire, East

Chichester/Bognor
Local delivery franchise holder: Cable & Wireless Communications (see MSOs)
Homes in area: 67,100
Awarded: Nov 95

Chigwell
see Epping Forest

Chorley
see Southport

Chorleywood
see Hertfordshire, South

Christchurch
see Bournemouth

Clacton on Sea
see East Anglia, South

Cleethorpes
see Grimsby

Clydebank
see Glasgow, North West

Coalville
see Burton-on-Trent

Coatbridge
see Cumbernauld

Colchester/Ipswich/ Felixstowe/Harwich/ Woodbridge
Franchise holder: East Coast Cable = Comcast Europe (see MSOs)
Homes in area: 126,000
Awarded: 21 Jul 89
Service start: late 94
Homes passed: 89,883 (1 Apr 2000)
Subs: 20,424 = 22.7% (1 Apr 2000)

Colne
see Lancashire, East

Consett/Stanley (Derwentside)
Local delivery franchise holder: Telewest (see MSOs)
Homes in area: 37,000
Awarded: 27 Jul 98

Corby
see Northampton, North-east

Coventry
Franchise holder: Coventry Cable = NTL (see MSOs)
Homes in area: 119,000 (build complete)
Awarded: 29 Nov 83
Service start: 1 Sept 85
Homes passed: 114,325 (1 Apr 2000)
Subs: 23,150= 20.2% (1 Apr 2000)

Crawley/Horley/Gatwick
Franchise holder: Eurobell (see MSOs)
Homes in area: 44,000 (build complete)
Awarded: 27 Apr 89
Service start: Jun 93
Homes passed: 44,078 (1 Apr 2000)
Subs: 10,511 = 23.8% (1 Apr 2000)

Crosby
see Liverpool, North

Croydon, London Borough of
Franchise holder: Telewest (see MSOs)
Homes in area: 115,000 (build complete)
Awarded: 1 Nov 83
Service start: 1 Sept 85
Homes passed: 122,397 (1 Apr 2000)
Subs: 28,912 = 23.6% (1 Apr 2000)

Cumbernauld/Kilsyth/ Airdrie/Coatbridge
Franchise holder: Telewest (see MSOs)
Homes in area: 55,000
Awarded: 27 Apr 89
Service start: May 95

Cumbria, Central
Local delivery franchise holder: Cable & Telecoms (UK) (see MSOs)

Homes in area: 84,000
Awarded: Oct 96

Cumbria, South
Barrow-in-Furness, South Lakeland District
Local delivery franchise holder: South Cumbria Cable & Telecoms = Cable & Telecoms (UK) (see MSOs)
Homes in area: 61,500
Awarded: May 97

Cwmbran
see Newport

Dagenham
see Greater London East

Darlington
Franchise holder: Comcast Teesside (see MSOs)
Homes in area: 34,000
Awarded: 21 Jun 90
Service start: Jun 95
Homes passed: 37,240 (1 Apr 2000)
Subs: 11,020 = 9.6% (1 Apr 2000)

Dartford/Swanley
Franchise holder: Cable & Wireless Communications (see MSOs)
Homes in area: 35,000
Awarded: 16 Mar 90
Service start: Dec 94
Homes passed: 23,474 (1 Apr 2000)
Subs: 4,746 = 20.2% (1 Apr 2000)

Daventry
Local delivery franchise holder: NTL (see MSOs)
Homes in area: 8,710
Awarded: Nov 96
Homes passed: 19,262 (1 Apr 99)
Subs: 4,355 = 22.6% (1 Apr 99)

Deal
see Kent, South East

Derby/Spondon
Franchise holder: Cable & Wireless Communications (see MSOs)
Homes in area: 83,000 (build complete)
Awarded: 16 Feb 90; acquired 22 Mar 93
Service start: Oct 91
Homes passed: 95,088 (1 Apr 2000)
Subs: 21,173 = 22.3% (1 Apr 2000)

Derbyshire, East
Chesterfield, Bolsover, Matlock, Belper
Local delivery franchise holder: NTL (see MSOs)
Homes in area: 89,000
Awarded: Jun 96

Devon, South
Exeter, Plymouth, Torbay, Totnes, Newton Abbot
Franchise holder: Eurobell (see MSOs)
Homes in area: 236,000
Awarded: 15 Dec 89

Service start: May 1996
Homes passed: 161,376 (1 Apr 2000)
Subs: 25,063 = 15.5% (1 Apr 2000)

Dewsbury
see Kirklees

Diss
see East Anglia, South

Doncaster/Rotherham
Franchise holder: Telewest(see MSOs)
Homes in area: 192,000
Awarded: 10 May 90
Homes passed: 69,284 (1 Apr 2000)
Subs: 11,954 = 17.3% (1 Apr 2000)

Dorset, West
Dorchester, Weymouth, Portland
Homes in area: 35,000
Awarded: 10 Feb 90
Franchise revoked from Coastal
Cablevision = Leonard
Communication (US)

Dover
see Kent, South East

Droitwich
see Worcester

Dudley
see Black Country

Dumbarton/Vale of Leven
Franchise holder: Telewest (see MSOs)
Homes in area: 17,000 (build complete)
Awarded: 27 Apr 89
Service start: Nov 96
Homes passed: 19,898 (1 Apr 2000)
Subs: 9,766 = 49.1% (1 Apr 2000)

Dumfries and Galloway
Local delivery franchise holder:
Dumfries and Galloway Cable &
Telecoms
Ownership: US Cable Group,
McNicholas Construction, Morgan
Cable
PO Box 319
Whipsnade
Bedfordshire LU6 2LT
Tel: 01582 873006
Fax: 01582 873003
Homes in area: 155,000
Awarded: Dec 97

**Dundee/Broughty
Ferry/Monifieth/Carnoustie**
Franchise holder: Telewest (see MSOs)
Homes in area: 95,000
Awarded: 19 Jan 90
Service start: Jan 91
Homes passed: 72,151 (1 Apr 2000)
Subs: 13,426 = 18.6% (1 Apr 2000)

Dunstable
see Luton

**Durham, South/North
Yorkshire**
Local delivery franchise holder: Cable

& Wireless Communications (see MSOs)
Homes in area: 155,000
Awarded: Apr 96

Durham
see Wearside

Ealing, London Borough of
Franchise holder: Cable & Wireless
Communications (see MSOs)
Homes in area: 105,000
Awarded: 8 Nov 83
Service start: 1 Nov 86
Homes passed: 101,045 (1 Apr 200)
Subs: 20,157 = 19.9% (1 Apr 2000)

East Anglia, South
Bury St Edmunds, Sudbury, Braintree,
Clacton on Sea, Stowmarket,
Thetford, Diss
Local delivery licence holder:
Southern East Anglia Cable =
Comcast Europe (see MSOs)
Homes in area: 205,000
Date awarded: Jan 95

East Grinstead
East Grinstead, Crowborough, parts of
Banstead and Reigate
Local delivery licence holder:
Convergence (East Grinstead) (see
MSOs)
Homes in area: 30,300
Date awarded: 11 Jul 96

East Kilbride
see Motherwell

Eastbourne/Hastings
Local delivery franchise holder: Cable
& Wireless Communications (see
MSOs)
Homes in area: 150,000
Awarded: Feb 96
Separate upgrade systems in
Eastbourne and Hastings operated by
CDA Communications

Eastleigh
see Southampton

East Lothian
see Lothian

Edinburgh
Franchise holder: Telewest (see MSOs)
Homes in area: 183,000 (build complete)
Awarded: 5 Feb 86
Service start: May 92
Homes passed: 247,182 (1 Apr 2000)
Subs: 72,581 = 29.4% (1 Apr 2000)
see also Lothian

Ellesmere Port
see Cheshire, North

Elmbridge
see Surrey, North

Elstree
see Hertfordshire, South

Enfield
Franchise holder: Telewest (see MSOs)
Homes in area: 105,000 (build complete)
Awarded: 31 May 90
Service start: Oct 91
Homes passed: 108,586 (1 Apr 2000)
Subs: 28,965 = 26.7% (1 Apr 2000)

**Epping Forest/Chigwell/
Loughton/Ongar**
Franchise holder: Cable & Wireless
Communications (see MSOs)
Homes in area: 45,000
Awarded: 3 May 90
Service start: Dec 94
Homes passed: 34,117 (1 Apr 2000)
Subs: 5,472 = 16.0% (1 Apr 2000)

Epsom
see Surrey, North East

Exeter
see Devon, South

Falkirk/West Lothian
Franchise holder: Telewest (see MSOs)
Homes in area: 30,000
Awarded: 21 Jun 90
Service start: Oct 94

Fareham
see Portsmouth

Farnborough
see Guildford

Faversham
Narrowband upgrade system operated
by CDA Communications (see MSOs)

Felixstowe
see Colchester

Fenland
Wisbech, March, Whittlesey
Franchise holder: Cable & Wireless
Communications (see MSOs)
Homes in area: 21,000
Awarded: 5 Jul 90
Service start: Apr 97
Homes passed: 12,648 (1 Apr 2000)
Subs: 2,938 = 23.2% (1 Apr 2000)

Fife
Kingdom of Fife excluding
Glenrothes and Kirkcaldy
Local delivery franchise holder:
Telewest (see MSOs)
Homes in area: 35,000
Awarded: Jul 97

Folkestone
see Kent, South East

Gateshead
see Tyneside

Gatwick
see Crawley

Gillingham
see Thames Estuary South

Glamorgan, West
Swansea, Neath, Port Talbot
Franchise holder: CableTel South
Wales (see MSOs)
Homes in area: 110,000
Awarded: 16 Nov 89
Service start: Dec 90
Homes passed: 107,693 (1 Apr 2000)
Subs: 52,547 = 48.8% (1 Apr 2000)
Separate narrowband upgrade systems
operated in parts of the area by Metro
Cable

Glamorgan/Gwent
Franchise holder: CableTel South
Wales (see MSOs)
Homes in area: 230,000
Awarded: Oct 95
Service start: Apr 97 on existing
network
Homes passed: 22,121 (1 Apr 2000)
Subs: 11,093 = 50.1% (1 Apr 2000)
Separate narrowband upgrade systems
operated in parts of the area by Metro
Cable

Glasgow, Greater
Franchise holder: CableTel Glasgow
(see MSOs)
Homes in area: 274,000
Awarded: 7 Jun 90
Homes passed: 103,224 (1 Apr 2000)
Subs: 41,708= 40.4% (1 Apr 2000)

Glasgow, North West/Clydebank
Franchise holder: CableTel Glasgow
(see MSOs)
Homes in area: 112,000; 16,000
business premises
Awarded: 29 Nov 83
Service start: 1 Oct 85
Homes passed: 120,250 (1 Apr 2000)
Subs: 37,278 = 31.0% (1 Apr 2000)

Glenrothes/Kirkcaldy/Leven/Buckhaven/Methil
Franchise holder: Telewest (see MSOs)
Homes in area: 60,000
Awarded: 21 Jun 90
Service start: Oct 91
Homes passed: 54,440 (1 Apr 2000)
Subs: 18,190 = 33.4% (1 Apr 2000)

Gloucester
see Cheltenham

Godalming
see Guildford

Gosport
see Portsmouth

Gourock
see Inverclyde

Grantham
Franchise holder: NTL (see MSOs)
Homes in area: 30,000
Awarded: 26 Apr 90
Service start: Oct 95

Homes passed: 14,102 (1 Apr 2000)
Subs: 3,548 = 25.2% (1 Apr 2000)

Gravesend
see Thames Estuary South

Great Yarmouth/Lowestoft/Caister
Franchise holder: Cable & Wireless
Communications (see MSOs)
Homes in area: 64,000
Awarded: 5 Jul 90
Service start: Jun 96
Homes passed: 20,665 (1 Apr 2000)
Subs: 4,785 = 23.2% (1 Apr 2000)

Greater London East
Boroughs of Barking/Dagenham,
Bexley, Redbridge
Franchise holder: Cable & Wireless
Communications (see MSOs)
Homes in area: 229,000
Awarded: 15 Dec 88
Service start: Dec 90
Homes passed: 203,306 (1 Apr 2000)
Subs: 42,609 = 21.0% (1 Apr 2000)

Greenock
see Inverclyde

Greenwich/Lewisham, London Boroughs of
Franchise holder: Cable & Wireless
Communications (see MSOs)
Homes in area: 175,000
Awarded: 7 Apr 89
Service start: Jan 91
Homes passed: 143,984 (1 Apr 2000)
Subs: 30,278 = 21.0% (1 Apr 2000)

Grimsby/Immingham/Cleethorpes
Franchise holder: NTL (see MSOs)
Homes in area: 63,000
Awarded: 5 Jul 90
Service start: Jun 95
Homes passed: 63,102 (1 Apr 2000)
Subs: 17,695 = 28.0% (1 Apr 2000)

Guildford/West Surrey/East Hampshire
Guildford, Aldershot, Farnborough,
Camberley, Woking, Godalming
Franchise holder: CableTel UK (see
MSOs)
Flagship House
Reading Road North
Surrey GU13 8XR
Tel: 01252 652000
Fax: 01252 652100
Homes in area: 22,000 + 115,000
Awarded: 29 Nov 83 + Aug 85
Service start: 1 Jul 87
Homes passed: 136,357 (1 Apr 2000)
Subs: 54,918 = 40.3% (1 Apr 2000)

Gwent
see Glamorgan/Gwent

Hackney/Islington, London Boroughs of
Franchise holder: Telewest (see MSOs)
Homes in area: 150,000
Awarded: 13 Apr 90
Service start: Apr 95
Homes passed: 120,050 (1 Apr 2000)
Subs: 30,951 = 25.8% (1 Apr 2000)

Halifax
see Calderdale

Hamilton
see Motherwell

Hammersmith and Fulham, London Borough of
see London, North West

Haringey, London Borough of
Franchise holder: Telewest (see MSOs)
Homes in area: 85,000
Awarded: Sept 89
Homes passed: 75,650 (1 Apr 2000)
Subs: 19,490 = 26.1% (1 Apr 2000)

Harlow/Bishops Stortford/Stansted Airport
Franchise holder: Anglia Cable =
Comcast Europe (see MSOs)
Homes in area: 43,000 (build complete)
Date awarded: 23 Mar 90
Service start: Jun 93
Homes passed: 47,466 (1 Apr 2000)
Subs: 14,864 = 31.3% (1 Apr 2000)

Harpenden
see Hertfordshire, West

Harrogate/Knaresborough
Franchise holder: Cable & Wireless
Communications (see MSOs)
Homes in area: 78,000
Awarded: 30 Mar 90, acquired Apr 94
Service start: Sep 95
Homes passed: 32,344 (1 Apr 2000)
Subs: 5,585 = 17.3% (1 Apr 2000)

Harrow
Franchise holder: Cable & Wireless
Communications (see MSOs)
Homes in area: 79,000
Awarded: 24 May 90
Service start: Dec 91
Homes passed: 70,043 (1 Apr 2000)
Subs: 17,699 = 25.3% (1 Apr 2000)

Hartlepool
see Teesside

Harwich
see Colchester

Hastings
see Eastbourne

Hatfield
see Hertfordshire, Central

Havant
see Portsmouth

Haverfordwest
Narrowband upgrade system operated by Metro Cable

Havering, London Borough of
Franchise holder: Cable & Wireless Communications (see MSOs)
Homes in area: 90,000
Awarded: 6 Apr 90
Service start: Sept 93
Homes passed: 80,770 (1 Apr 2000)
Subs: 14,668 = 18.2% (1 Apr 2000)

Haywards Heath
Local delivery franchise holder: Convergence Group (see MSOs)
Homes in area: 31,150
Original franchise revoked from N-Comm Cablevision

Heathrow
see Windsor

Hemel Hempstead
see Hertfordshire, West

Henley-on-Thames
see Thames Valley

Herne Bay
Narrowband upgrade system operated by CDA Communications (see MSOs)

Hertford
see Hertfordshire, East

Hertfordshire, Central
Stevenage, Welwyn, Hatfield, Hitchin, Baldock, Letchworth
Franchise holder: CableTel Hertfordshire (see MSOs)
Homes in area: 100,000
Awarded: 3 Nov 89
Homes passed: 91,224 (1 Apr 2000)
Subs: 50,348 = 55.2% (1 Apr 2000)
Separate upgrade system operated in Hatfield by Metro Cable

Hertfordshire, East
Hertford, Cheshunt, Ware, Lea Valley, Hoddesdon
Franchise holder: CableTel Bedfordshire (see MSOs)
Homes in area: 60,000
Awarded: 31 May 90
Homes passed: 49,795 (1 Apr 2000)
Subs: 18,002 = 36.2% (1 Apr 2000)

Hertfordshire, South
Watford, Chorleywood, Rickmansworth, Bushey, Radlett, Elstree, Borehamwood, Potters Bar
Franchise holder: Cable & Wireless Communications (see MSOs)
Homes in area: 95,000
Awarded: 3 Nov 89
Service start: Apr 92
Homes passed: 91,105 (1 Apr 2000)
Subs: 24,547 = 26.9% (1 Apr 2000)

Hertfordshire, West
Harpenden, Hemel Hempstead, St Albans, Berkhamsted, Tring, Redbourne
Franchise holder: NTL (see MSOs)
Homes in area: 100,000
Awarded: 3 Nov 89
Service start: Mar 91
Homes passed: 88,614 (1 Apr 2000)
Subs: 21,539 = 24.3% (1 Apr 2000)

High Wycombe
see Thames Valley

Hillingdon
see Middlesex

Hinckley/Bosworth
Local delivery franchise holder: NTL (see MSOs)
Homes in area: 31,200
Awarded: Jun 95
Homes passed: 18,358 (1 Apr 2000)
Subs: 4,144 = 22.6% (1 Apr 2000)

Hitchin
see Hertfordshire, Central

Hoddesdon
see Hertfordshire, East

Horley
see Crawley

Hounslow
see Middlesex

Hove
see Brighton

Huddersfield
see Kirklees

Hull
see Kingston upon Hull

Immingham
see Grimsby

Inverclyde
Greenock, Port Glasgow, Gourock, Kilmacolm
Franchise holder: CableTel Glasgow (see MSOs)
Homes in area: 32,000
Awarded: 5 Jul 90
Service start: 1995
Homes passed: 27,505 (1 Apr 2000)
Subs: 14,494 = 52.7% (1 Apr 2000)

Ipswich
see Colchester

Isle of Thanet
see Thanet, Isle of

Isle of Wight
Local delivery franchise holder: Isle of Wight Cable and Telephone
Company
Elm Farm, Elm Lane
Calbourne
Isle of Wight PO30 4JY
Ownership: Utility Cable, Fortuna Advanced Communications Networks
Homes on area: 43,000
Awarded: May 1997

Islington
see Hackney

Jersey
Franchise holder: Jersey Cable (not ITC licensed)
3 Colomberie
St Helier, Jersey
Channel Islands JE4 9SY
Tel: 01534 66477
Fax: 01534 66681
Ownership: Carveth 50.4%, Mattbrel 30%, others 19.6%
Homes in area: 28,000
Service start: 1987
Franchise renewed: Jan 94
Homes passed: 3,500 cable, 4,600 SMATV

Kenilworth
see Warwick

Kensington/Chelsea, London Borough of
Franchise holder: Cable & Wireless Communications (see MSOs)
Homes in area: 82,000
Awarded: 4 Feb 88
Service start: Sep 89
Homes passed: 75,400 (1 Apr 2000)
Subs: 14,731 = 19.5% (1 Apr 2000)

Kent, South East
Ashford, Deal, Dover, Folkestone
Local delivery franchise holder: Cable & Wireless Communications (see MSOs)
Homes in area: 116,300
Awarded: May 90
Service start: Sep 96
Homes passed: 43,755 (1 Apr 2000)
Subs: 5,796 = 13.2% (1 Apr 2000)
Separate upgrade system in Ashford operated by CDA Communications

Kent, West
Tunbridge Wells, Tonbridge, Sevenoaks
Local delivery franchise holder: Eurobell (see MSOs)
Homes in area: 90,600
Awarded: May 94
Homes passed: 24,662 (1 Apr 2000)
Subs: 3,611 = 14.6% (1 Apr 2000)

Kettering
see Northampton, North-east

Kidderminster
see Black Country

Kilbirnie
Narrowband upgrade system operated by A Thomson (Relay)

Kilsyth
see Cumbernauld

Kingston and Richmond, London Boroughs of
Franchise holder: Telewest (see MSOs)
Homes in areas: 124,000
Awarded: 6 May 89
Service start: Jan 91
Homes passed: 104,397 (1 Apr 2000)
Subs: 24,459 = 23.4% (1 Apr 2000)

Kingston upon Hull
Narrowband upgrade system operated
by Hull Cablevision = Atlantic
Telecom Group (see MSOs)

Kirkcaldy
see Glenrothes

Kirkby-in-Ashfield
see Mansfield

Kirklees
Huddersfield, Dewsbury
Franchise holder: CableTel Kirklees
(see MSOs)
Homes in area: 148,000
Awarded: 14 Jun 90
Service start: Jun 95
Homes passed: 95,961 (1 Apr 2000)
Subs: 36,539 = 38.1% (1 Apr 2000)

Knaresborough
see York

Knowsley
see St Helens

Lakenheath
Narrowband upgrade system operated
by Cablecom Investments (see MSOs)

Lambeth/Southwark, London Boroughs of
Franchise holder: Cable & Wireless
Communications (see MSOs)
Homes in area: 191,000
Awarded: 6 Jul 89
Service start: Jul 91
Homes passed: 140,656 (1 Apr 2000)
Subs: 28,257 = 20.1% (1 Apr 2000)

Lanark
see Motherwell

Lancashire, Central
Preston, Leyland
Franchise holder: Telewest (see MSOs)
Homes in area: 114,000
Awarded: 5 Feb 86
Build start: Jun 90
Homes passed: 96,773 (1 Apr 2000)
Subs: 16,518 = 17.1% (1 Apr 2000)

Lancashire, East
Blackburn, Burnley, Accrington,
Nelson, Colne, Rossendale Valley
Franchise holder: Cable & Wireless
Communications (see MSOs)
Homes in area: 168,000
Awarded: 9 May 88; acquired 21 Apr

93
Service start: 30 Nov 89
Homes passed: 118,838 (1 Apr 2000)
Subs: 25,203 = 21.2% (1 Apr 2000)
Narrowband upgrade system in
Burnley operated by Cablecom
Investments (see MSOs)

Lancaster/Morecambe
No applications
Homes in area: 40,000

Lancashire West
see Southport

Largs
Narrowband upgrade system operated
by Harris of Saltcoats (see MSOs)

Lea Valley
see Hertfordshire, East

Leamington Spa
see Warwick

Leeds
Franchise holder: Cable & Wireless
Communications (see MSOs)
Homes in area: 289,000
Awarded: Mar 90
Service Start: Jun 94
Homes passed: 214,681 (1 Apr 2000)
Subs: 49,231 = 22.9% (1 Apr 2000)

Leicester/ Loughborough/Shepshed
Franchise holder: NTL (see MSOs)
Homes in area: Leicester 170,670 +
Loughborough 30,000
Awarded: Leicester 22 Sept 89,
Loughborough 9 March 90
Service start: 1 Mar 91
Homes passed: 156,240 (1 Apr 2000)
Subs: 40,711 = 26.1% (1 Apr 2000)
Separate upgrade system in Leicester
operated by CDA Communications

Leighton Buzzard
see Luton

Letchworth
see Hertfordshire, Central

Lewes
Narrowband upgrade system operated
by CDA Communications (see MSOs)

Leyland
see Lancashire, Central

Lichfield
see Stafford

Lincoln
Franchise holder: NTL (see MSOs)
Homes in area: 42,000
Awarded: 5 Jul 90
Service start: Jul 95
Homes passed: 48,477 (1 Apr 2000)
Subs: 13,143 = 27.1% (1 Apr 2000)

Lincolnshire/South Humberside
Local delivery franchise holder: NTL
(see MSOs)
Homes in area: 144,000
Awarded: Jan 96
Homes passed: 28,248 (1 Apr 2000)
Subs: 8,845 = 31.3% (1 Apr 2000)

Liverpool, North/Bootle/Crosby
Franchise holder: Telewest (see MSOs)
Homes in area: 119,000 (build complete)
Awarded: 5 Jul 90
Homes passed: 120,963 (1 Apr 2000)
Subs: 47,519 = 39.3% (1 Apr 2000)

Liverpool, South (Merseyside)
Franchise holder: Telewest (see MSOs)
Homes in area: 125,000
Awarded: 29 Nov 83
Service start: Oct 90
Homes passed: 114,653 (1 Apr 2000)
Subs: 27,606 = 24.1% (1 Apr 2000)

Llandeilo
Narrowband system operated by John
Jones

London
see also Greater London East and
individual boroughs

London, North West
Boroughs of Barnet, Brent,
Hammersmith and Fulham
Franchise holder: Cable & Wireless
Communications (see MSOs)
Homes in area: 280,000
Awarded: 19 Jan 89
Service start: Jul 91
Homes passed: 123,613 (1 Apr 2000)
Subs: 25,348 = 20.5% (1 Apr 2000)
Separate upgrade system operated in
Brent by Sapphire

Lothian
East Lothian, Midlothian, parts of City
of Edinburgh
Local delivery franchise applicant:
Telewest (see MSOs)
Homes in area: 30,000

Loughborough
see Leicester

Loughton
see Epping Forest

Lowestoft
see Great Yarmouth

Luton/Dunstable/Leighton Buzzard
Franchise holder: CableTel
Bedfordshire (see MSOs)
Homes in area: 97,000
Awarded: Jul 86
Service start: Nov 86 on upgrade
system, Mar 90 on new build network

Homes passed: 116,733 (1 Apr 2000)
Subs: 43,299 = 37.1% (1 Apr 2000)

Macclesfield/Wilmslow
Franchise holder: Cable & Wireless
Communications (see MSOs)
Homes in area: 45,000
Awarded: 11 Jul 90; acquired 4 May
93
Homes passed: 41,175 (1 Apr 2000)
Subs: 10,154 = 24.7% (1 Apr 2000)

Maidenhead
see Windsor

Maidstone
see Thames Estuary South

Manchester/Salford/Trafford
Franchise holder: Cable & Wireless
Communications (see MSOs)
Homes in area: 363,000
Awarded: 17 May 90; acquired 22
Mar 93
Service start: Oct 94
Homes passed: 218,755 (1 Apr 2000)
Subs: 49,733 = 22.7% (1 Apr 2000)
Separate upgrade system in Salford
operated by CDA Communications

Mansfield/Sutton/Kirkby-in-Ashfield
Franchise holder: NTL (see MSOs)
Homes in area: 58,000 (build complete)
Awarded: 3 Mar 90
Homes passed: 76,069 (1 Apr 2000)
Subs: 25,790 = 33.9% (1 Apr 2000)

March
see Fenland

Margate
see Thanet, Isle of

Market Harborough
see Northampton, North-east

Marlow
see Thames Valley

Matlock
see Derbyshire, East

Melton Mowbray
Franchise holder: NTL (see MSOs)
Homes in area: 30,000
Awarded: 26 Apr 90
Service start: Oct 95

Meriden
see Stafford

Merton and Sutton, London Boroughs of
Franchise holder: Telewest (see MSOs)
Homes in area: 135,000 (build complete)
Awarded: 6 May 89
Service start: Mar 90
Homes passed: 133,196 (1 Apr 2000)
Subs: 31,206 = 23.4% (1 Apr 2000)

Middlesbrough
see Teesside

Middlesex
Hillingdon, Hounslow (franchises
awarded separately but since
combined)
Franchise holder: Telewest (see
MSOs)
Homes in area: 186,886
Awarded: 24 May 90
Service start: Nov 91
Homes passed: 169,169 (1 Apr 2000)
Subs: 28,290 = 16.7% (1 Apr 2000)

Midlothian
see Lothian

Mildenhall
Narrowband upgrade system operated
by Cablecom Investments (see MSOs)

Milford Haven
Narrowband upgrade system operated
by Metro Cable

Milton Keynes
Local delivery franchise holder: BT
New Towns Cable TV (see MSOs)
51 Alston Drive
Bradwell Abbey
Milton Keynes MK13 9HB
Tel: 01908 322522
Fax: 01908 319802
Homes in area: 114,000
Awarded: 29 May 1997
Homes passed: 52,969 (1 Apr 2000)
Subs: 41,961 = 79.2% (1 Apr 2000)

Mole Valley
see Surrey, North East

Monifieth
see Dundee

Morecambe
see Lancaster

Motherwell/East Kilbride/Hamilton/Wishaw/Lanark
Franchise holder: Telewest (see MSOs)
Homes in area: 125,000 (build complete)
Awarded: 27 Apr 89
Service start: Mar 92
Homes passed: 162,442 (1 Apr 2000)
Subs: 53,017 = 32.6% (1 Apr 2000)

Neath
see Glamorgan, West

Nelson
see Lancashire, East

Newark on Trent
Franchise holder: NTL (see MSOs)
Homes in area: 35,000
Awarded: 26 Apr 90
Service start: Sep 95
Homes passed: 19,059 (1 Apr 2000)
Subs: 4,569 = 24.0% (1 Apr 2000)

Newbury
see Thames Valley

Newcastle-under-Lyne
see Stoke-on-Trent

Newcastle-upon-Tyne
see Tyneside

Newham and Tower Hamlets, London Boroughs of
Franchise holder: Cable & Wireless
Communications (see MSOs)
Homes in area: 127,000
Awarded: 13 Aug 85
Service start: May 87
Homes passed: 114,971 (1 Apr 2000)
Subs: 16,858 = 14.7% (1 Apr 2000)

Newport/Cwmbran/Pontypool
Franchise holder: CableTel South
Wales (see MSOs)
Homes in area: 85,000
Awarded: 11 Jul 90
Homes passed: 49,483 (1 Apr 2000)
Subs: 24,163 = 40.6% (1 Apr 2000)

Newton Abbot
see Devon, South

Neyland
Narrowband upgrade system operated
by Metro Cable

Northampton
Franchise holder: NTL (see MSOs)
Homes in area: 72,000
Awarded: 19 Jan 89
Service start: 1988 on 13-channel
upgrade network (classified as
broadband), Mar 91 on new-build
network
Homes passed: 71,320 (1 Apr 2000)
Subs: 19,474 = 27.3% (1 Apr 2000)
Separate upgrade system operated by
CDA Communications

Northamptonshire, North-east
Corby, Kettering, Wellingborough,
Market Harborough
Franchise holder: NTL (see MSOs)
Homes in area: 90,000
Awarded: 21 Jun 90
Service start: Dec 94
Homes passed: 43,103 (1 Apr 2000)
Subs: 9,134 = 21.2% (1 Apr 2000)

Northern Ireland
Franchise holder: CableTel Northern
Ireland (see MSOs)
Homes in area: 428,000
Date awarded: May 95
Homes passed: 183,417 (1 Apr 2000)
Subs: 70,232= 38.3% (1 Apr 2000)

Northumberland
Local delivery franchise holder: Cable
& Telecoms
Homes in area: 125,000
Awarded: Oct 97

Norwich
Franchise holder: Cable & Wireless
Communications (see MSOs)
Homes in area: 83,000
Awarded: 21 Jul 89, acquired Jul 94
Service start: Jun 90
Homes passed: 68,681 (1 Apr 2000)
Subs: 14,418 =21.0 (1 Apr 2000)

Nottingham
Franchise holder: NTL (see MSOs)
Homes in area: 160,000
Awarded: 22 Sept 89
Service start: 10 Sept 90
Homes passed: 230,682 (1 Apr 2000)
Subs: 57,722 = 25.0% (1 Apr 2000)

Nuneaton/Bedworth/Rugby
Franchise holder: NTL (see MSOs)
Homes in area: Nuneaton 44,000 +
Rugby 23,000 (awarded as two
separate franchises)
Awarded: 6 Apr 90
Service start: Feb 96
Homes passed: 21,551 (1 Apr 2000)
Subs: 4,567 = 21.2% (1 Apr 2000)

Oldham/Tameside
Franchise holder: Cable & Wireless
Communications (see MSOs)
Homes in area: 172,000
Awarded: 17 May 90; acquired 4 May
93
Service start: Oct 94
Homes passed: 102,341 (1 Apr 2000)
Subs: 25,525 = 24.9% (1 Apr 2000)

Ongar
see Epping Forest

Oxford/Abingdon
Franchise holder: NTL (see MSOs)
Homes in area: 72,000 (build complete)
Awarded: 14 Jun 90
Service start: Sept 95
Homes passed: 110,887 (1 Apr 2000)
Subs: 16,704 = 15.1% (1 Apr 2000)

Paisley/Renfrew
Franchise holder: CableTel Glasgow
(see MSOs)
Homes in area: 67,000
Awarded: 7 Jun 90
Service start: Aug 94
Homes passed: 63,145 (1 Apr 2000)
Subs: 25,964 = 41.1% (1 Apr 2000)

Pembroke Dock
Narrowband upgrade system operated
by Metro Cable

Penarth
see Cardiff

Perth/Scone
Franchise holder: Telewest (see MSOs)
Homes in area: 18,000
Awarded: 19 Jan 90
Service start: 1997
Homes passed: 20,610 (1 Apr 2000)
Subs: 4,663 = 22.6% (1 Apr 2000)

Separate upgrade system operated in
Perth by Perth Cable TV

Peterborough
Franchise holder: Cable & Wireless
Communications (see MSOs)
Homes in area: 58,000
Awarded: 21 Jul 89
Service start: May 90
Homes passed: 55,893 (1 Apr 2000)
Subs: 14,073 = 25.2% (1 Apr 2000)

Plymouth
see Devon, South

Pontefract
see Wakefield

Pontypool
 see Newport

Poole
see Bournemouth

Port Glasgow
see Inverclyde

Port Talbot
see Glamorgan, West

**Portsmouth/Fareham/
Gosport/Havant/East
Hampshire**
Franchise holder: Cable & Wireless
Communications (see MSOs)
Homes in area: 213,000
Awarded: 2 Feb 90
Service start: Sept 91
Homes passed: 212,299 (1 Apr 2000)
Subs: 68,144 = 32.1% (1 Apr 2000)

Potters Bar
see Hertfordshire, South

Preston
see Lancashire, Central

Radlett
see Hertfordshire, South

Ramsgate
see Thanet, Isle of

Ravenshead
Local delivery licence holder: NTL
(see MSOs)
Homes in area: 2,500
Date awarded: 13 July 95

Reading
see Thames Valley

Redbourne
see Hertfordshire, West

Redbridge, London Borough of
see Greater London East

Reddish
see Worcester

Redhill
see Surrey, North East

Reigate
see Surrey, North East and East
Grinstead

Renfrew
see Paisley

Richmond, London Borough of
see Kingston

Rickmansworth
see Hertfordshire, South

Rochdale
see Bury

Rochester
see Thames Estuary South

Romsey
see Andover

Rossendale Valley
see Lancashire, East

Rotherham
see Doncaster

Rugby
see Nuneaton

Rugeley
see Stafford

Runcorn
see Cheshire, North

Runnymede
see Surrey, North

St Albans
see Hertfordshire, West

St Helens/Knowsley
Franchise holder: Telewest (see MSOs)
Homes in area: 121,000
Awarded: 5 Jul 90
Service start: Jun 92
Homes passed: 106,499 (1 Apr 2000)
Subs: 26,577 = 25.0% (1 Apr 2000)

Salford
see Manchester

Salisbury
see Andover

Saltcoats
Narrowband upgrade system operated
by Harris of Saltcoats (see MSOs)

Sandwell
see Black Country

Sefton
see Southport

Scone
see Dundee

Sheffield
Franchise holder: Telewest (see MSOs)
Homes in area: 210,000
Awarded: 31 May 90
Service start: Apr 94

Homes passed: 89,206 (1 Apr 2000)
Subs: 18,039= 20.2% (1 Apr 2000)

Shepshed
see Leicester

Shrewsbury
Local delivery licence holder: Cable
& Telecoms (see MSOs)
Homes in area: 90,000
Awarded: Jan 96
Licence revoked Dec 97

Sittingbourne
see Thames Estuary South

Skelmersdale
Narrowband upgrade system operated
by Tawd Valley Cable

Slough
see Windsor

Solihull
see Birmingham

South Ribble
see Southport

Southampton/Eastleigh
Franchise holder: Cable & Wireless
Communications (see MSOs)
Homes in area: 119,371
Awarded: 12 Sept 86
Service start: 1 Dec 90
Homes passed: 109,808 (1 Apr 2000)
includes Winchester
Subs: 29,278 = 26.7% (1 Apr 2000)
includes Winchester

Southport/Sefton/West Lancashire/South Ribble/Chorley
Local delivery licence holder:
Telewest
Homes in area: 90,000
Awarded: Jan 96
Service start: Jun 97

Southend
see Thames Estuary North

Southwark, London Borough of
see Lambeth

Stafford/Stone
Franchise holder: NTL (see MSOs)
Homes in area: 30,600
Awarded: 1 Dec 89
Service start: Sept 95
Awarded: Jun 95
Service start: Mar 97
Homes passed: 37,365 (1 Apr 2000)
Subs: 7,894 = 21.1% (1 Apr 2000)
operated in conjunction with
Lichfield/Burntwood/Rugeley
Homes in area: 39,290
Awarded: Jun 95
Service start: Mar 97
merged with local delivery licence for
Tamworth/North

Warwickshire/Meriden
Homes in area: 43,315
Awarded: Jun 95
Service start: Mar 97
Homes passed: 25,446 (1 Apr 2000)
Subs: 5,084= 20.0% (1 Apr 2000)

Staines
see Windsor

Stanley
see Consett

Stanwell
see Windsor

Stevenage
see Hertfordshire, Central

Stockport
Franchise holder: Cable & Wireless
Communications (see MSOs)
Homes in area: 113,000
Awarded: 17 May 90; acquired 4 May
93
Service start: Oct 94
Homes passed: 104,890 (1 Apr 2000)
Subs: 27,613 = 26.3% (1 Apr 2000)

Stockton
see Teesside

Stoke-on-Trent/Newcastle-under-Lyne
Franchise holder: Cable & Wireless
Communications (see MSOs)
Homes in area: 156,000
Awarded: 1 Dec 89; acquired 21 Apr
93
Homes passed: 125,342 (1 Apr 2000)
Subs: 27,597 = 22.0% (1 Apr 2000)

Stone
see Stafford

Stowmarket
see East Anglia, South

Stratford-upon-Avon
see Warwick

Sudbury
see East Anglia, South

Sunderland
see Wearside

Surrey, North/North East
Banstead, Caterham, Chertsey,
Cobham, Dorking, Elmbridge, Epsom,
Ewell, Leatherhead, Reigate, Redhill,
Sunbury, Weybridge etc
Franchise holder: Cable & Wireless
Communications (see MSOs)
Homes in area: 71,000 + 98,000
(awarded as two franchises)
Awarded: 21 Jun 90
Service start: Apr 93
Homes passed: 154,016 (1 Apr 2000)
Subs: 32,916 = 21.4% (1 Apr 2000)

Sutton
see Mansfield

Sutton, London Borough of
see Merton
Swansea see Glamorgan, West

Swindon
Franchise holder: Swindon Cable =
NTL (see MSOs)
Homes in area: 65,000 (build complete)
Service start: 1 Sep 84
Homes passed: 59,397 (1 Apr 2000)
Subs: 24,091 = 40.6% (1 Apr 2000)

Tameside
see Oldham

Tamworth
see Stafford

Taunton/Bridgwater
Local delivery licence holder:
Telewest
Homes in area: 71,300
Awarded: Feb 97

Teesside
Middlesbrough, Stockton, Hartlepool
Franchise holder: Comcast Teesside
(see MSOs)
Homes in area: 195,000
Awarded: 5 Jul 90
Service start: Jun 95
Homes passed: 204,438 (1 Apr 2000)
Subs: 64,874= 31.7% (1 Apr 2000)

Telford
Franchise holder: Telewest (see MSOs)
Homes in area: 55,000
Awarded: 26 Apr 90
Service start: May 92
Homes passed: 53,213 (1 Apr 99)
Subs: 15,152 = 28.5% (1 Apr 99)

Thames Estuary North
Southend, Basildon, Billericay,
Brentwood, Chelmsford etc
Franchise holder: Telewest (see MSOs)
Homes in area: 300,000
Awarded: 16 Nov 88
Service start: Jun 94
Homes passed: 202,545 (1 Apr 2000)
Subs: 69,345 = 34.2% (1 Apr 2000)
Separate upgrade system in Basildon
operated by CDA Communications

Thames Estuary South
Gravesend, Chatham, Rochester,
Gillingham, Maidstone, Sittingbourne
Franchise holder: Telewest (see MSOs)
Homes in area: 145,000
Awarded: 16 Nov 88
Homes passed: 109,062 (1 Apr 2000)
Subs: 25,853 = 23.7% (1 Apr 2000)
Separate upgrade systems in Chatham
and Sittingbourne operated by CDA
Communications

Thames Valley
Reading, Twyford, Henley-on-

Thames, Wokingham, High
Wycombe, Marlow, Bracknell,
Basingstoke, Ascot, Newbury,
Thatcham
Franchise holder: NTL (see MSOs)
Homes in area: 215,000
Awarded: 2 Dec 88
Service start: Dec 91
Homes passed: 174,444 (1 Apr 2000)
Subs: 42,730 = 24.5% (1 Apr 2000)

Thamesmead
Franchise holder: Cable & Wireless
Communications (see MSOs)
Homes in area: 11,000
Awarded: 31 May 90
Service start: Jul 91
Homes passed: 8,544 (1 Jul 98)
Subs: 2,577 = 30.2% (1 Jul 98)

Thanet, Isle of
Margate, Ramsgate, Broadstairs
Franchise revoked from Coastal
Cablevision = Leonard
Communications
Homes in area: 51,000
Awarded: 16 Feb 90
Separate narrowband upgrade system
operated CDA Communications (see
MSOs)

Thetford
see East Anglia, South

Torbay
see Devon, South

Totnes
see Devon, South

Totton/Hythe
Local delivery franchise holder: Cable
& Wireless Communications (see MSOs)
Homes in area: 25,200
Awarded: Sep 95
Service start: Apr 97

**Tower Hamlets, London
Borough of**
see Newham

Tring
see Hertfordshire, West

Twyford
see Thames Valley

Tyneside
Newcastle-upon-Tyne, Gateshead,
North and South Tyneside
Franchise holder: Telewest (see MSOs)
Homes in area: 325,000
Awarded: 14 Dec 89
Service start: Sept 90
Homes passed: 231,706 (1 Apr 2000)
Subs: 69,298 = 29.9% (1 Apr 2000)

Upper Heyford
Narrowband upgrade system operated
by Cablecom Investments (see MSOs)

Uttoxeter
see Burton-on-Trent

Vale of Belvoir
Local delivery franchise holder: NTL
(see MSOs)
Homes in area: 4,545
Awarded: Jul 96

**Wakefield/Pontefract/
Castleford**
Franchise holder: Telewest (see MSOs)
Homes in area: 94,000
Awarded: 2 Mar 90; acquired Apr 93
Homes passed: 45,158 (1 Apr 2000)
Subs: 6,019 = 13.3% (1 Apr 2000)

Walsall
see Black Country

**Waltham Forest, London
Borough of**
Franchise holder: Cable & Wireless
Communications (see MSOs)
Homes in area: 83,000
Awarded: 28 Sept 89
Service start: Feb 94
Homes passed: 80,991 (1 Apr 2000)
Subs: 17,818 = 22.0% (1 Apr 2000)

**Wandsworth, London
Borough of**
Franchise holder: Cable & Wireless
Communications (see MSOs)
Homes in area: 100,000
Awarded: 13 Aug 85
Service start: Aug 93
Homes passed: 71,858 (1 Apr 2000)
Subs: 12,913 = 18.0% (1 Apr 2000)

Ware
see Hertfordshire, East

Warrington
see Cheshire, North

**Warwick/Stratford-upon-
Avon/Kenilworth/
Leamington Spa**
Franchise holder: NTL (see MSOs)
Homes in area: 50,000 (build complete)
Awarded: 30 Mar 90
Homes passed: 102,915 (1 Apr 2000)
Subs: 19,912 = 19.3% (1 Apr 2000)

Watford
see Hertfordshire, South

Wearside
Sunderland, Durham, Washington
Franchise holder: Cable & Wireless
Communications (see MSOs)
Homes in area: 200,000
Awarded: 14 Jun 90
Service start: Aug 96
Homes passed: 63,050 (1 Apr 2000)
Subs: 14,235 = 22.6% (1 Apr 2000)

Wellingborough
see Northampton, North-east

Welwyn
see Hertfordshire, Central

Wendover
see Aylesbury

West Lothian
see Falkirk

**Westminster, London
Borough of**
Franchise holder: Westminster Cable
Company = British Telecom (see MSOs)
87-89 Baker Street
London W1M 1AG
Tel: 020 7935 6699
Fax: 020 7486 9447
Homes in area: 120,000
Awarded: 29 Nov 83
Service start: Sept 85
Homes passed: 92,750 (1 Apr 200)
Subs: 20,883 = 22.5% (1 Apr 2000)

Weymouth
see Dorset, West

Whittlesey
see Fenland

Widnes
see Cheshire, North

Wigan
Franchise holder: Telewest (see MSOs)
Homes in area: 110,000
Awarded: 17 May 90
Service start: Jun 92
Homes passed: 109,243 (1 Apr 200)
Subs: 24,491 = 22.4% (1 Apr 2000)

Wilmslow
see Macclesfield

Winchester
Franchise holder: Cable & Wireless
Communications (see MSOs)
Homes in area: 19,000
Awarded: 6 Apr 90
Service start: 1995
Homes passed: 13,035 (1 Apr 2000)
Subs: 2,576 = 19.8% (1 Apr 2000)

**Windsor/Slough/Maidenhead
/Ashford/Staines/Stanwell/
Heathrow/Iver**
Franchise holder: Telewest (see MSOs)
Homes in area: 110,000 (build complete)
Awarded: 1 Nov 83; Iver added
subsequently to create contiguity with
Middlesex
Service start: 1 Dec 85
Homes passed: 108,660 (1 Apr 2000)
Subs: 16,243 = 14.9% (1 Apr 2000)

Wirral, The
Franchise holder: Cable & Wireless
Communications (see MSOs)
Homes in area: 120,000
Awarded: 11 Jul 90
Homes passed: 78,579 (1 Apr 2000)
Subs: 18,025 = 22.9% (1 Apr 2000)

Separate upgrade system operated by CDA Communications

Wisbech
see Fenland

Wishaw
see Motherwell

Woking
see Guildford

Wokingham
see Thames Valley

Wolverhampton
see Black Country

Worcester/Redditch/ Droitwich
Franchise holder: Telewest (see MSOs)
Homes in area: 70,000
Awarded: 14 Jun 90
Service start: 1997
Homes passed: 27,396 (1 Apr 99)
Subs: 7,806 = 28.5% (1 Apr 99)

Worthing
see Brighton

Wythall
Local delivery franchise holder:
Birmingham Cable (see MSOs)
Homes in area: 4,000
Awarded: Sep 95
Service start: Apr 97

Yeovil
Local delivery licence holder:
Convergence Group
Ownership: Convergence Group (see MSOs), Orbis Trust (Guernsey)
Homes in area: 62,300
Awarded: Jul 96

York
Franchise holder: Cable & Wireless Communications (see MSOs)
Homes in area: 78,000
Homes passed: 3,925 (upgrade system)
Awarded: 30 Mar 90, acquired Apr 94
Service start: Sep 95
Homes passed: 30,517 (1 Apr 2000)
Subs: 5,421 = 17.8% (1 Apr 2000)

Yorkshire, North
see Durham, South

SATELLITE AND CABLE TELEVISION CHANNELS

All channels transmitting via cable or satellite within or to the UK, wholly or partly in the English language or intended for viewing by other linguistic groups within the UK. Services are licensed and monitored by the Independent Television Commission (ITC). Channels not intended for reception in the UK are excluded, as are those that are licensed but not actively broadcasting (many licensed channels never materialise).

The television standard and encrypting system used are indicated after the name of the satellite. Services for which a separate charge is made are marked 'premium' after the programming type.

The advent of digital television from the fourth quarter 1998 has already created several new channels, although initially most digital channels are conversions of services already available in analogue form.

MULTIPLE SERVICE PROVIDERS (MSP)

BBC Digital Programme Services
Broadcasting House
Portland Place
London W1A 1AA
Tel: 020 8752 5045
Services: BBC Knowledge

BBC Worldwide
Woodlands
80 Wood Lane
London W12 0TT
Tel: 0181 576 2000
Services: Animal Planet 50%, BBC News 24, UK Arena 50%, UK Gold 50%, UK Horizons 50%, UK Style 50%

British Sky Broadcasting (BSkyB)
6 Centaurs Business Park
Grant Way, Syon Lane
Isleworth
Middlesex TW7 5QD
Tel: 020 8782 3000
Fax: 020 8782 3030
Website: www.sky.co.uk
Ownership: News International Television 39.88 %, BSB Holdings (= Pathé 30.27%, Granada 36.22%, Pearson 4.29%) 12.82 %, Pathé 12.71 %, Granada Group 6.48 %
Services: The Computer Channel, The History Channel 50%, National Geographic Channel 50%, Nickelodeon 50%, QVC 20%, Sky Box Office, Sky Cinema, Sky MovieMax, Sky News, Sky One, Sky Premier, Sky Soap, Sky Sports1 , Sky Sports 2, Sky Sports 3, Sky Sports Extra, Sky Travel
40% stake in Granada Sky Broadcasting

Carlton Communications
45 Fouberts Street
London W1V 2DN
Tel: 020 7432 9000
Fax: 020 7432 3151
Services: Carlton Food Network, Carlton Select

Discovery Communications
160 Great Portland Street
London W1N 5TB
Tel: 020 7462 3600
Fax: 020 7462 3700
Services: Animal Planet, Discovery Channel Europe, TLC Europe

Flextech Television
160 Great Portland Street
London W1N 5TB
Tel: 020 7299 5000
Fax: 020 7299 5400
Ownership: Telewest (see MSOs)
Services: Bravo, Challenge TV,
Living, Trouble, UK Arena 50%, UK
Gold 50%, UK Horizons 50%, UK
Style 50%
Service management: Discovery,
Discovery Home & Leisure, Playboy
TV, Screenshop, TV Travel Shop

Granada Sky Broadcasting
Franciscan Court
16 Hatfields
London SE1 8DJ
Tel: 020 7578 4040
Fax: 020 7578 4176
Ownership: Granada Group 60%,
British Sky Broadcasting 40%
Services: Granada Breeze, Granada
Plus, Granada Men & Motors

Home Video Channel
Aquis House
Station Road
Hayes
Middlesex UB3 4DX
Tel: 020 8581 7000
Fax: 020 8581 7007
Ownership: Spice Entertainment
Companies
Services: The Adult Channel, HVC

Landmark Communications
64-66 Newman Street
London W1P 3PG
Tel: 020 7665 0600
Fax: 020 7665 0601
Ownership: Landmark
Communications Inc
Services: Travel Channel

Portland Enterprises
Portland House
Portland Place
London E14 9TT
Tel: 020 7308 5095
Services: Gay TV, Television X The
Fantasy Channel

Turner Broadcasting System (TBS)
CNN House
19-22 Rathbone Place
London W1P 1DF
Tel: 0171 637 6700
Fax: 0171 637 6768
Ownership: Time Warner
Services: Cartoon Network, CNN
International, Turner Network
Television

UK Channel Management
160 Great Portland Street
London W1N 5TB
Tel: 020 7765 1959
Ownership: BBC Worldwide,
Flextech [qqv]

CHANNELS

The Adult Channel
Ownership: Home Video Channel
[see MSP above]
Service start: Feb 1992
Satellite: Astra 1B (PAL/Videocrypt)
Programming: 'adult' entertainment
(premium)
E-mail: adultch@spicecos.com
Website: www.cyberspice.com

Animal Planet
Ownership: BBC Worldwide,
Discovery Communications [see
MSP above]
Service start: Sep 98
Satellite: Astra 1E, Hot Bird 1
(PAL/encrypted)
Programming: natural history
documentaries
Website: www.animal.discovery.com

Asianet
Unit 1, Endsleigh Industrial Estate
Endsleigh Road
Uxbridge
Middlesex UB2 5QR
Tel: 020 8930 0930
Fax: 020 8930 0546
Cable only from videotape
Programming: movies and
entertainment in Hindi, Punjabi and
other languages

BBC Choice
Ownership: BBC Worldwide [See
MSP above]
Programming: general entertainment
Digital

BBC Knowledge
Ownership: BBC Digital Programme
Services [See MSP above]
Programming: educational
Digital

BBC News 24
Ownership: BBC Worldwide [See
MSP above]
Programming: news

Bloomberg Television
City Gate House
39-45 Finsbury Square
London EC2A 1PQ
Tel: 020 7330 7500
Fax: 020 7256 5326
Service start: 1 Nov 1995
Satellite: Astra 1E, Eutelsat II-F1
Programming: business and finance
Website: www.bloomberg.co.uk

The Box
Imperial House

11-13 Young Street
London W8 5EH
Tel: 020 7376 2000
Fax: 020 7376 1313
Ownership: Emap
Service start: 2 Mar 1992
Satellite: Astra 1A (PAL/Videocrypt; cable only)
Programming: interactive pop music
Website: www.thebox.com

Bravo
Ownership: Flextech Television [see MSP above]
Service start: Sept 1985
Satellite: Astra 1C (PAL/Videocrypt)
Programming: old movies and television programmes
Website: www.bravo.co.uk

British Eurosport
55 Drury Lane
London WC2B 5SQ
Tel: 020 7 468 7777
Fax: 020 7468 0024
Ownership: ESO Ltd = TF1 34%, Canal Plus 33%, ESPN 33%
Service start: Feb 89
Satellite: Astra 1A, Hot Bird 1 (PAL/clear)
Programming: sport
Website: www.eurosport-tv.com
Also digital

Carlton Cinema
Ownership: Carlton Communications [see MSP above]
Service start: 2 Sep 1996
Website: www.carltoncinema.co.uk
Digital, included in ONdigital

Carlton Food Network
Ownership: Carlton Communications [see MSP above]
Service start: 2 Sep 1996
Satellite: Intelsat 601 (MPEG2 encrypted)
Programming: Food
Website: www.cfn,co.uk
Also digital

Carlton Kids
Ownership: Carlton Entertainment [see MSP above]
Programming: children's
Digital, included in ONdigital

Carlton Select
Ownership: Carlton Communications [see MSP above]
Service start: 1 Jun 1995
Satellite: Intelsat 601 (MPEG2 encrypted); cable exclusive
Programming: entertainment; classic TV shows
Website: www.carltonselect.co.uk
Also digital

Carlton World
Ownership: Carlton Entertainment [see MSP above]
Programming: documentary
Digital, included in ONdigital

Cartoon Network
1 Soho Square
London W1V 5FD
Tel: 020 7478 1000
Ownership: Turner Broadcasting [see MSP above]
Service start: Sept 93
Satellite: Astra 1C, Astra 1F (PAL/clear)
Programming: children's animation
Website: www.cartoonnetwork.co.uk
Also digital

Challenge TV
Ownership: Flextech [see MSP above]
Service start: 3 Feb 1997
Satellite: Astra 1C (PAL/Videocrypt)
Programming: general entertainment, game shows
Website: www.challengetv.co.uk

The Channel Guide
1a French's Yard
Amwell End
Ware, Herts SG12 9HP
Tel: 01920 469238
Fax: 01920 468372
Ownership: Picture Applications
Service start: May 1990
Cable only (text)
Programming: programme listings

Chinese News and Entertainment (CNE)
Marvic House
Bishops Road, Fulham
London SW6 7AD
Tel: 020 7610 3880
Fax: 020 7610 3118
email: chinesemarkets@ cnetv.demon.co.uk
Ownership: The CNT Group
Service start: Nov 92
Satellite: Astra 1C (PAL/Clear)
Programming: news, current affairs, films, dramas, lifestyle

Christian Channel Europe
Christian Channel Studios
Stonehills, Shields Road
Gateshead NE10 0HW
Tel: 0191 4952244
email: info@godnetwork.com
Service start: 1 Oct 1995
Satellite: Astra 1B
Programming: Christian
Website: www.indigo.ie/spugradio/cce.html

CNBC Europe
10 Fleet Place
London EC4M 7QS
Tel: 0181 653 9300
email: talkback@nbc.com
Website: www.cnbceurope.com
Ownership: NBC and Dow Jones
Service start: 11 Mar 1996
Satellite: Astra 1E
Programming: business news

CNN International
Ownership: Turner Broadcasting [see MSP above]
Service start: Oct 1985
Satellite: Astra 1B, Intelsat 605 (PAL/clear)
Programming: news
Website: www.europe.cnn.com

The Computer Channel
Ownership: British Sky Broadcasting (see MSP)
Satellite: Astra 1D
Programming: computer topics and programs

The Discovery Channel Europe
Ownership: Discovery Communications [see MSP above]
Service start: Apr 89
Satellite: Astra 1C, Hot Bird 1 (PAL/encrypted)
Programming: documentaries
Website: www.discovery.com/ digitnets/international/europe/europe.html

Discovery Home & Leisure
Ownership: Discovery Communications [see MSP above]
Service start: Mar 1992
Satellite: Astra 1C, Hot Bird 1 (PAL/encrypted)
Programming: lifestyle
Website: www.discovery.com/ digitnets/learning/learning.html

The Disney Channel UK
Beaumont House
Kensington Village
Avonmore Road
London W14 8TS
Tel: 020 8222 1000
Ownership: Walt Disney Company
Satellite: Astra 1B (PAL/Videocrypt)
Programming: children's (supplied as bonus with Sky Premier and Moviemax)
Website: www.disneychannel.co.uk

EBN: European Business News
10 Fleet Place

London EC4M 7RB
Tel: 020 7653 9300
Fax: 020 7653 9333
Website: www.ebn.co.uk
Ownership: Dow Jones & Co 70%,
Flextech 30%
Service start: 27 Feb 95
Satellite: Eutelsat II F6 (PAL/clear)
Programming: financial and business
news

EDTV (Emirates Dubai TV)
c/o Teleview Productions
7a Grafton Street
London W1X 3LA
Tel: 020 7493 2496
Fax: 020 7629 6207
Ownership: Dubai government
Service start: Dec 93
Satellite: Arabsat 2A, Intelsat K
Programming: news (from ITN),
entertainment, film, sports, children's
in Arabic and English
Website: www.edtv.com

Euronews
60 Chemin des Mouilles
69130 Ecully
France
Tel: (33) 4 72 18 80 00
Fax: (33) 4 73 18 93 71
Ownership: 18 European
Broadcasting Union members 51%,
Générale Occidentale 49%
Service start: 1 Jan 1993
Satellite: Hot Bird 3, Eutelsat II-F1
(PAL/clear)
Programming: news in English,
French, Spanish, German and Italian

FilmFour
124 Horseferry Road
London SW1P 2TX
Tel: 020 7396 4444
Ownership: Channel Four Television
Programming: feature and short films
[premium]
Website: www.channel4.com
Digital

Fox Kids Network
Ownership: Fox Television (managed
by BSkyB, see MSP above)
Satellite: Astra 1A (PAL/Videocrypt)
Programming: children's
Website: www.foxkids.co.uk

Front Row
Front Row Television
19 Newman Street
London W1P 3HB
Tel: 020 7307 2222
Ownership: NTL, Telewest
Programming: movies [pay-per-view]

Gay TV
Ownership: Portland Enterprises [see
MSP above]
Satellite: Astra 1C (PAL/encrypted)
Programming: erotic

GMTV2
The London Television Centre
Upper Ground
London SE1 9TT
Tel: 020 7827 7000
Programming: morning general
interest
Digital

Granada Breeze
Ownership: Granada Sky
Broadcasting [see MSP above]
Satellite: Astra 1E (PAL/encrypted)
Programming: lifestyle
Website: www.gsb.co.uk/breeze/
home.html
Also digital

Granada Men & Motors
Ownership: Granada Sky
Broadcasting [see MSP above]
Satellite: Astra 1A (PAL/Videocrypt)
Programming: male-oriented,
motoring
Website: www.gsb.co.uk/
men/home.html
Also digital

Granada Plus
Ownership: Granada Sky
Broadcasting [see MSP above]
Satellite: Astra 1A (PAL/Videocrypt)
Programming: classic TV
programmes
Website: www.gsb.co.uk/
plus/home.html
Also digital

The History Channel
Ownership: BSkyB 50%, A&E
Television Networks 50%
Service start: 1 Nov 1995
Satellite: Astra 1B (PAL/Videocrypt)
Programming: history
Website: www.thehistorychannel.
co.uk
Also digital

HVC: Home Video Channel
Ownership: Home Video Channel
[see MSP above]
Service start: Sept 1985
Satellite: Astra 1D (cable exclusive)
Programming: movies (premium)
Website: www.cyberspice.com

ITV2
200 Gray''s Inn Road
London WC1X 8HF
Tel: 020 7843 8000

Ownership: ITV companies
Website: www.itv.co.uk
Digital; also on analogue cable

Japan Satellite TV (JSTV)
Quick House
65 Clifton Street
London EC2A 4JE
Tel: 020 7426 7330
Fax: 020 7426 7333
Ownership: NHK, private Japanese
investors
Satellite: Astra 1E (PAL/Videocrypt)
Programming: Japanese news, drama,
documentary, entertainment, sport
Website: www.jstv.co.uk

The Landscape Channel
Landscape Studios
Hye House
Crowhurst, East Sussex TN33 9BX
Tel: 01424 83688
Fax: 01424 83680
E-mail: info@landscapetv.com
Service start: Nov 1988 (on
videotape); Apr 1993 (on satellite)
Satellite: Orion, Hispasat (PAL/clear)
Programming: music and visual
wallpaper
Website: www.landscapetv.com

Live TV
24th floor
1 Canada Square
Canary Wharf
London E14 5AP
Tel: 0171 293 3900
Fax: 0171 293 3820
email: cable@livetv.co.uk
Ownership: Mirror Group
Newspapers
Service start: 12 June 95
Programming: general entertainment
Website: www.livetv.co.uk

Living
Ownership: Flextech [see MSP
above]
Service start: Sept 93
Satellite: Astra 1C (PAL/Videocrypt)
Programming: daytime lifestyle,
evening general entertainment
Website: www.livingtv.co.uk

MBC: Middle East Broadcasting Centre
80 Silverthorne Road
Battersea
London SW8 3XA
Tel: 020 7501 1111
Fax: 020 7501 1110
Service start: Sept 91
Programming: general and news in
Arabic

MTV UK
180 Oxford Street
London W1N 0DS
Tel: 020 7478 6000
Ownership: Viacom
Service start: Aug 87
Satellite: Astra 1A (PAL/Videocrypt)
Programming: pop music
Website: www.mtv.co.uk
Also digital

Muslim TV Ahmadiyyah
16 Gressenhall Road
London SW18 5QL
Tel: 020 8870 8517
Fax: 020 8870 0684
email: mta/mtl@dial.pipex.com
Ownership: Al-Shirkatul Islamiyyah
Service start: Jan 94
Satellite: Intelsat 601
Programming: spiritual, educational,
training
Website: www.alislam.org/mta

MUTV
Manchester United Television
274 Deansgate
Manchester M3 4SB
Tel: 0161 834 1111
Ownership: Manchester United FC,
BSkyB, Granada
Programming: Manchester United FC
Website: www.manutd.com

Namaste Television
7 Trafalgar Business Centre
77-87 River Road
Barking
Essex IG11 0EZ
Tel: 0181 507 8292
Fax: 0181 507 8292
Service start: Sept 92
Satellite: Intelsat 601
Programming: Asian entertainment
Website: www.namastev.co.uk

National Geographic Channel
Ownership: British Sky Broadcasting
(see MSP), National Geographic
Telephone: 0181 847 4319
Service start: 1997
Satellite: Astra 1A (PAL/Videocrypt)
Programming: natural history
documentaries
Website: www.nationalgeographic.
com

Nickelodeon
15-18 Rathbone Place
London W1P 1DF
Tel: 0171 462 1000
Fax: 0171 462 1030
Ownership: British Sky Broadcasting
50% [see MSP above], MTV

Networks 50%
Service start: 1 Sept 93
Satellite: Astra 1C (PAL/Videocrypt)
Programming: children's
Website: www.nick.uk.com

The Paramount Comedy Channel
15-18 Rathbone Place
London W1P 1DF
Tel: 020 7462 1200
Fax: 020 7462 1030
Ownership: British Sky Broadcasting
[see MSP above], Viacom
Service start: 1 Nov 1995
Satellite: Astra 1C (PAL/Videocrypt)
Programming: comedy
Website: www.paramountcomedy.
com

The Parliamentary Channel
160 Great Portland Street
London W1N 5TB
Tel: 020 7299 5000
Fax: 020 7299 6000
Ownership: consortium of cable
operators
Service start: Jan 92
Satellite: Intelsat 601 (PAL/clear)
Programming: coverage of British
parliamentary debates
Website: www.parlchan.co.uk

Performance: The Arts Channel
60 Charlotte Street
London W1P 2AX
Tel: 0171 927 8808
Ownership: Arts & Entertainment
Service start: Oct 92
Cable only from videotape
Programming: opera, jazz and
classical concerts, drama

Playboy TV
Ownership: Flextech 51% [see MSP
above], BSkyB, Playboy
Service start: 1 Nov 1995
Satellite: Astra 1B (PAL/Videocrypt)
Programming: erotic (premium)
Website: www.playboytv.co.uk

QVC: The Shopping Channel
Marcopolo House, Chelsea Bridge
Queenstown Road
London SW8 4NQ
Tel: 020 7705 5600
Fax: 020 7705 5602
Ownership: QVC (= Comcast, TCI)
80%, BSkyB 20%
Satellite: Astra 1C (soft scrambled)
Service start: Oct 93
Programming: home shopping
Website: www.qvc.com

The Racing Channel
17 Corsham Street
London N1 6DR
Tel: 0171 253 2232
Fax: 0171 696 8681
email: info@satelliteinfo.co.uk
Service start: Nov 1995
Satellite: Astra 1D
Programming: horse racing

The Sci-Fi Channel Europe
77 Charlotte Street
London W1P 2DD
Tel: 020 7805 6100
Fax: 020 7805 6150
Service start: 1 Nov 1995
Satellites: Astra 1B, Hot Bird 1
(PAL/encrypted)
Programming: science fiction
Website: www.scifi.com/sfeurope/
index.html

S4C2
Sianel Pedwar Cymru
Parc Ty-Glas
Llanisien
Cardiff CF4 5DU
Wales
Tel: 01222 747 444
Fax: 01222 754 444
Programming: Coverage of the Welsh
Assembly in session initially, news
and general entertainment in Welsh
and English
Digital

Shop! The Home Shopping Channel
Sir John Moores Building
100 Old Hall Street
Liverpool
Merseyside L70 1AB
Tel: 0151 235 2055
Ownership: The Home Shopping
Channel Ltd
Digital

Sky Box Office
Ownership: British Sky Broadcasting
[see MSP above]
Service start: 1 Dec 97
Satellite: Astra 1E (PAL/Videocrypt)
Programming: movies, concerts,
events (pay-per-view)
Also digital

Sky Cinema
Ownership: British Sky Broadcasting
[see MSP above]
Service start: Oct 92
Satellite: Astra 1C (PAL/Videocrypt)
Programming: movies (premium)

Sky MovieMax
Ownership: British Sky Broadcasting
[see MSP above]

Service start: Feb 89
Satellite: Astra 1A (PAL/Videocrypt)
Programming: movies (premium)
Also digital

Sky News
Ownership: British Sky Broadcasting
[see MSP above]
Service start: Feb 89
Satellite: Astra 1A (PAL/Videocrypt)
Programming: news

Sky One
Ownership: British Sky Broadcasting
[see MSP above]
Service start: Feb 89
Satellite: Astra 1A (PAL/Videocrypt)
Programming: entertainment
Also digital

Sky Premier
Ownership: British Sky Broadcasting
[see MSP above]
Service start: Apr 91
Satellite: Astra 1B (PAL/Videocrypt)
Programming: movies (premium)
Also digital

Sky Soap
Ownership: British Sky Broadcasting
[see MSP above]
Satellite: Astra 1B (PAL/Videocrypt)
Programming: entertainment

Sky Sports 1
Ownership: British Sky Broadcasting
[see MSP above]
Service start: Apr 91
Satellite: Astra 1B (PAL/Videocrypt)
Programming: sport (premium)
Also digital

Sky Sports 2
Ownership: British Sky Broadcasting
[see MSP above]
Service start: Aug 94
Satellite: Astra 1C (PAL/Videocrypt)
Programming: sport (premium)
Also digital

Sky Sports 3
Ownership: British Sky Broadcasting
[see MSP above]
Service start: Aug 94
Satellite: Astra 1B (PAL/Videocrypt)
Programming: sport (premium)
Also digital

Sky Sports Extra
Ownership: British Sky Broadcasting
[see MSP above]
Service start: Aug 99
Satellite: Astra 1B (PAL/Videocrypt)
Programming: sport (bonus with
premium channels)
Digital

Sky Travel
Ownership: British Sky Broadcasting
[see MSP above]
Satellite: Astra 1C (PAL/Videocrypt)
Programming: travel documentaries

STEP-UP
University of Plymouth
Notte Street
Plymouth PL1 2AR
Tel: 01752 233635
Programming: educational and
business

Tara Television
The Forum
74-80 Camden Street
London NW1 0EG
Tel: 020 7383 3330
Fax: 020 7383 3450
Service start: 15 Nov 1996
Satellite: Intelsat 601 (MPEG-2
encrypted)
Programming: Irish entertainment
Website: http://www.tara-tv.co.uk

TCC
Ownership: Flextech [see MSP
above]
Service start: Sept 1984
Satellite: Astra 1C (PAL/Videocrypt)
Programming: children's
Website: www.tcc.flextech.co.uk/

Television X: The Fantasy
Channel
Portland House
Portland Place
Millharbour
London E14 9TT
Tel: 020 7987 5095
Service start: 2 Jun 1995
Satellite: Astra 1C (PAL/Videocrypt)
Programming: erotic (premium)
Website:www.televisionx.co.uk

TNT Classic Movies
1 Soho Square
London W1V 5FD
Tel: 020 7478 1000
Ownership: Turner Broadcasting [see
MSP above]
Service start: Sept 93
Satellite: Astra 1C, Astra 1F
(PAL/clear)
Programming: movies, entertainment

Travel Channel
66 Newman Street
London W1P 3LA
Tel: 020 7636 5401
Fax: 020 7636 6424
Ownership: Landmark
Communications [see MSP above]
Service start: 1 Feb 94

Satellite: Astra 1E
Programming: travel
Website: www.travelchannel.co.uk

Trouble
Ownership: Flextech Television [see
MSP above]
Service start: Sept 1985
Satellite: Astra 1C (PAL/Videocrypt)
Programming: teenagers
E-mail: webmaster@trouble.co.uk
Website: www.trouble.co.uk

[.tv]
96-97 Wilton Road
London SW1V 1DW
Tel: 0171 599 8938
Satellite: Astra 1E
Programming: computer-related
topics
Website: www.tvchannel.co.
uk/dottv/

TV Travel Shop
Satellite: Astra 1C
Website: www.tvtravelshop.co.uk

TVBS Europe
30-31 Newman Street
London W1P 3PE
Tel: 020 7636 8888
Satellite: Astra 1E (digital)
Programming: Chinese-language
Website: www.chinese-channel.co.uk

UK Arena
Ownership: UKTV = BBC
Worldwide, Flextech [see MSP
above]
Satellite: Astra 1E
Programming: arts
Also digital

UK Gold
Ownership: UKTV = BBC
Worldwide, Flextech [see MSP
above]
Service start: Nov 92
Satellite: Astra 1B (PAL/Videocrypt)
Programming: entertainment
Also digital

UK Horizons
Ownership: UKTV = BBC
Worldwide, Flextech [see MSP
above]
Satellite: Astra 1E
Programming: documentaries
Also digital

UK Play
Ownership: UKTV = BBC
Worldwide, Flextech [see MSP
above]
Programming: popular music, comedy
Digital

UK Style
Ownership: UKTV = BBC
Worldwide, Flextech [see MSP
above]
Satellite: Astra 1E
Programming: lifestyle
Also digital

VH-1
180 Oxford Street
London W1N 0DS
Tel: 020 7284 7777
Fax: 020 7284 7788
Ownership: MTV Networks =
Viacom (100%)
Satellite: Astra 1B (PAL/encrypted)
Programming: pop music
Website: www.vh1.com
Also digital

Zee TV Europe
Unit 7
Belvue Business Centre
Belvue Road
Northolt
Middlesex UB5 5QQ
Tel: 020 8839 4000
Fax: 020 8842 3223
Ownership: Asia TV Ltd
Service start: Mar 1995
Satellite: Astra 1E (PAL/Videocrypt)
Programming: films, discussions,
news, game shows in Hindi, Punjabi,
Urdu, Bengali, Tamil, English, etc
Website: www.zeetelevision.com/

DIGITAL TELEVISION

ONdigital
346 Queenstown Road
London SW8 4NE
Tel: 020 7819 8000
Fax: 020 819 8100
Website: www.ondigital.co.uk

Sky Digital
6 Centaurs Business Park
Grant Way
Syon Lane
Isleworth
Middlesex TW7 5QD
Tel: 020 8 782 3000
Fax: 020 8 782 3030
Website: www.skydigital.co.uk

CAREERS AND TRAINING

Careers

No one organisation gives individually-tailored advice about careers in the media industries, but it is an area much written about, and we have included in this section details of some books and other sources or contacts that may help. Compiled by David Sharp.

There is no doubt that the media industries are perceived as being "glamourous" and young people are attracted to them. Opportunities in television appear to be increasing as the number of companies and organisations continues to grow, boosted by the growth of digital delivery and the new technologies. The film sector too, continues to appear reasonably healthy.
Anyone wanting to work in these industries should expect to be open to the idea of working with new technologies and should anticipate the need to update their skills regularly. Offering a range of skills, rather than just one can be to an applicant's benefit.

Finally, it is important to recognise that this area of training and learning, like many others, has been undergoing shifts of emphasis that provide vocational alternatives to more traditional ways of obtaining qualifications and experience. Health warning! it is still the case that formal qualifications are only part of the picture. If you do get a foot in the door and show initiative and skill you can still get on.

For these reasons it is important that anyone considering a career in the industry takes care to investigate what courses are available that will help prepare the way, and if possible, although this is rarely easy, talks to someone already doing a job similar to the one they are interested in.

The Jobs

The media industry contains a wide range of jobs, some of which, usually of a support or administrative nature (eg librarian; accountant) have equivalents in many other areas, and some of which are quite specialised and have unique, though possibly misleading titles (eg best boy; gaffer).

The bibliography, below, will help guide you.

Bibliography
Below is a selected list, based on holdings at the BFI National Library. These will give you some guidance as to the range of jobs available, the structure of the industry, and they will offer some general guidance on preparing a CV. There are publications (and short courses) devoted to creating and presenting CVs, and you should check with your nearest library about these.

GETTING INTO FILMS & TELEVISION
Angell, Robert
How To Books, 6th ed., 1999
ISBN 1-85703-5453

HOW TO GET INTO THE FILM & TV BUSINESS
Gates, Tudor
Alma House, 1995
ISBN 0-415-15112-0

INSIDE BROADCASTING
Newby, Julian
Routledge, 1997
ISBN 0-415-15112-0

 LIGHTS, CAMERA, ACTION! CAREERS IN FILM, TELEVISION, VIDEO
Langham, Josephine
BFI, 2nd ed., 1996
ISBN 0-85170-573-1

MAKING ACTING WORK
Salt, Chrys
Bloomsbury, 1997
ISBN 0-74753-595-7

A WOMAN'S GUIDE TO JOBS IN FILM AND TELEVISION
Muir, Anne Ross
Pandora Press, 1987
ISBN 0-86358-061-0

WORKING IN TELEVISION, FILM & RADIO
Foster, Val et al
DCMS/Design Council/ACE, 1999

YOUR CREATIVE FUTURE
Burnside, Amanda
DfEE, 1997
ISBN 0-86111-0696-2

Courses
The following titles are recommended for information on courses. You will need to consider what balance between theory, practice and academic study you wish to undertake, and plan accordingly. Decide what qualifications and skills you want to acquire, check who validates the course, and for practical courses, what equipment is available to learn with.

 MEDIA COURSES UK
Orton, Lavinia
BFI, Annual.

MEDIA AND MULTIMEDIA SHORT COURSES
Orton, Lavinia
BFI/Skillset (3 issues per year)
This is also available on the BFI website; and at some Regional Arts Boards

FLOODLIGHT
(covers the Greater London region) and other local guides to courses may be worth checking at your local library

Courses Abroad
COMPLETE GUIDE TO AMERICAN FILM SCHOOLS AND CINEMA AND TELEVISION COURSES
Pintoff, Ernest
Penguin, 1994
ISBN 0-1401-7226-2

COMPLETE GUIDE TO ANIMATION AND COMPUTER GRAPHICS SCHOOLS
Pintoff, Ernest
Watson-Guptill, 1995
ISBN 0-8230-2177-7
Restricted to American courses only

VARIETY INTERNATIONAL FILM GUIDE
Cowie, Peter, ed.
This annual guide includes an international film schools section.

WHERE TO GET MULTIMEDIA TRAINING IN EUROPE
Institut National de L' Audiovisuel
4th edition CIDJ 1999
ISBN 2-86938-136-0

Bi-lingual guide online version on http//: www.inafr/guide

For courses abroad:

CILECT (Centre International de Liaison Ecoles de Cinema et de Télévision)
8 rue Theresienne
1000 Bruxelles
Belgique
Tel: 00 32 2 511 98 39
Fax: 00 32 2 511 00 35
Contact: Executive Secretary, Henry Verhasselt. email:
hverh.cilect@skynet.be

Training Organisations

All Regional Arts Boards and Media Development Agencies are involved with or have information on training. These are listed in the Funding section of the Handbook.

Media Skills Wales

Cyfle
Part of the same grouping, with MSW focusing on English speakers and Cyfle on Welsh speakers and reasonably advanced learners of Welsh. They support the training needs of the Welsh film and television industry
3rd Floor/3ydd Llawr
Crichton House/Ty Crichton
11-12 Mount Stuart Square/Sgwar Mount Stuart
Cardiff/Cardydd CF1 6EE
Tel: 029 20 465533
Fax: 029 20 463344
also at:
Gronant, Penrallt Isaf
Caernarfon, Gwynedd LL55 1NS
Tel: 01286 671000
Fax: 01286 678831
email: cyfle@cyfle-cyf.demon.co.uk
Website: www.cyfle-cyf.demon.co.uk

English & Media Centre
18 Compton Terrace
London N1 2UN
Tel: 020 7359 8080
Fax: 020 7354 0133
email: info@enlishandmedia.co.uk

Film Education
Alhambra House
27-31 Charing Cross Road
London WC2H 0AU
Tel: 020 7976 2291
Fax: 020 7839 5052
Website: www.filmeducation .org
Fact sheets about how to get ahead in film, describing some of the key jobs are located on their website. Film Education also produce packs for teachers on recently released films, which give some background on the production process

ft2 - Film & Television Freelance Training
4th Floor Warwick House
9 Warwick Street
London W1 R 5RA
Tel: 020 7734 5141
Fax: 020 7287 9899

Website: www.ft2.org.uk
FT2 is the only UK-wide provider of new entrant training for young people wishing to enter the freelance sector of the industry in the junior construction, production and technical grades. Funded by Skillset, Freelance Training Fund, European Social Fund, the AFVPA and Channel 4, ft2 is the largest industry training managed training provider in its field and has a 100% record of people graduating from the scheme and entering the industry

4FIT
Managed by ft2 (see above) this is Channel 4's training programme for people from ethnic minority backgrounds wishing to train as new entrants to junior production grades

Gaelic Television Training Trust
c/o Sabhal Mór Ostaig College
An Teanga
Isle of Skye, IV44 8RQ
Tel: 01471 844373
Fax: 01471 844383
Website: www.smo.uhi.ac.uk

Midlands Media Training Consortium
Birmingham office:
The Big Peg
120 Vyse Street
Birmingham B18 6NF
Tel: 0121 248 1515
Fax: 0121 248 1616
email: training@mmtc.co.uk
Website: www.mmtc.co.uk

Nottingham office: Studio 1
Nottingham Fashion Centre
Huntingdon Street
Nottingham NG1 3LH
Tel/Fax: 0115 993 0151
email: training@mmtc.co.uk
Midlands Media Training Consortium provides substantial funding to Midlands professional freelancers and broadcast staff to help them keep up with new technology, new working practices and new markets

National Film & Television School
National Short Course Training Programme
Beaconsfield Film Studios
Station Road
Beaconsfield
Bucks HP9 1LG
Tel:01494 677903
Fax: 01494 678708

Website: www.nifc.co.uk
Short course training for those
already working in the industry

Northern Ireland Film Commission
21 Ormeau Avenue
Belfast BT2 8HD
Tel: 028 90232444
Fax: 028 90239918
email: info@nifc.co.uk
Website: www.nifc.co.uk

Scottish Screen Training
249 West George Street
Glasgow G2 4QE
Tel: 0141 302 1700
Fax: 0141 302 1711

Skillnet South West
Regional Training Consortium for
the South West
59 Prince Street
Bristol BS1 4QH
Tel: 0117 925 4011
Fax: 0117 925 3511
email: skillnetsw@bfv.co.uk

Skillsbase
Part of the BECTU training and
career advice service aimed at
freelancers already working in the
industry. Limited places, reduced fees
for BECTU members. Application
forms available on the website or by
sending an A4 self-addressed
envelope plus 39p stamp to BECTU
HQ. (See Organisations section for
address).
Website: www.bectu.org.uk/
skillbase.html

Skillset
103 Dean Street
London W1V 5TA
Tel: 020 7534 5300
Fax: 020 7534 5333
email: info@skillset.org
Website: http://www.skillset.org
Skillset is the National Training
Organisation for broadcast, film,
video and multimedia. It takes an
overview but does not carry out
training itself. Enquiries relating to
N.E. England are being handled by
Skillset following closure of
Mediaskill and NW Media Training
Consortium. It produces a careers
handbook (send SAE with £1 stamp),
also available on the website . A
separate publication on TV for
14-17-year olds is available (send A4
sae with 66p 1st class postage)

Yorkshire Media Training Consortium
40 Hanover Square
Leeds LS3 1BQ
Tel: 0113 294 4410
Fax: 0113 294 4989
email: info@ymtc.co.uk
Website: www.ymtc.co.uk
A regional agency, YMTC is
concerned to develop a strategy to
identify, develop and provide training
for those who are already working
within the industry in the region
Paying Your Way

Paying Your Way

It is important to be clear on the cost
of any course you embark on and
sources of grants or other funding.
Generally speaking short courses do
not attract grants, but your local
authority or local careers office may
be able to advise on this, or your
nearest Training and Enterprise
Council. Find out where they are, and
check directories of sources for
grants at your local library. Learn
Direct may also be able to advise.
They are on 0800 100 900 with a
website at www.learndirect.co.uk
UK researchers over 19, not
receiving other government funding
for education may be eligible for an
Individual Learning Account (ILA)
towards costs if their course leads to
a recognised qualification such as an
NVQ. Contact them on 0800-072 -
5678
Website: my-ila.com

CINEMAS

Listed below are the companies who control the major cinema chains and multiplexes in the UK, followed by the cinemas themselves listed by county and town, and including seating capacities. The listing also includes disabled access information, where available. Compiled by Allen Eyles

KEY TO SYMBOLS

bfi *bfi* supported - either financial and/or programming assistance

P/T Part-time screenings
S/O Seasonal openings

DISABILITY CODES

West End/Outer London

E Hearing aid system installed. Always check with venue whether in operation
W Venue with unstepped access (via main or side door), wheelchair space and adapted lavatory
X Venue with flat or one step access to auditorium
A Venue with 2-5 steps to auditorium
G Provision for Guide Dogs

England/Channel Islands/Scotland/Wales/Northern Ireland

X Accessible to people with disabilities (advance arrangements sometimes necessary - please phone cinemas to check)
E Hearing aid system installed. Always check with venue whether in operation
The help of Artsline, London's Information and Advice Service for Disabled People on Arts & Entertainment, in producing this section, including the use of their coding system for venues in the Greater London area, is gratefully acknowledged. Any further information on disability access would be welcome.

CINEMA CIRCUITS

Apollo Leisure Group
7 Palatine Suite
Coppull Enterprises Centre
Mill Lane, Coppull
Lancs PR7 5AN
Tel: 01257 471012
Fax: 01257 794109
Operates 14 cinemas with 64 screens in the North West of England, Wales, Yorkshire and the Midlands and a 9 screen multiplex at Paignton, Devon

Artificial Eye Film Company
14 King Street
London WC2E 8HN
Tel: 020 7240 5353
Fax: 020 7240 5242
Film distributors operating the Chelsea Cinema and Renoir in London's West End

Caledonian Cinemas
1st Floor, Highland Rail House
Station Square
Inverness IV1 1LE
Tel: 01463 718888
Fax: 01463 718180
Operates 15 screens on 5 sites, all in Scotland

Cine-UK Ltd
Chapter House
22 Chapter Street
London SW1P 4NP
Tel: 020 7932 2200
Fax: 020 7932 2222
Operates 17 multiplexes (195 screens) in August 2000 with others under construction or planned for 15 further locations

City Screen
86 Dean Street
London W1V 5AA
Tel: 020 7734 4342
Fax: 020 7734 4027
Operates the Picture House cinemas in Clapham, Brighton (Duke of York's), Oxford (Phoenix), Exeter, Stratford upon Avon, Stratford East, London, East Grinstead, Southampton (Harbour Lights) York and Cambridge (Arts). The company also operates cinemas at Gosport,

Aberdeen and elsewhere and programmes or manages the Curzon group of cinemas in London's West End, Metro and others

Film Network
23 West Smithfield
London EC1A 9HY
Tel: 020 7489 0531
Fax: 020 7248 5781
Operates nine screens on two sites at Greenwich and Peckham in South East London

Mainline Pictures
37 Museum Street
London WC1A 1LP
Tel: 020 7242 5523
Fax: 020 7430 0170
Website: www.screencinemas.co.uk
Operates Screen cinemas at Baker Street, Haverstock Hill, Islington Green, Reigate, Walton-on-Thames and Winchester with a total of 10 screens

National Amusements (UK)
Showcase Cinema
Redfield Way
Lenton
Nottingham NG27 2UW
Tel: 0115 986 2508
Owners and operators of 16 Showcase cinemas with 211 screens in Nottingham, Derby, Peterborough, Leeds, Liverpool, Walsall, Birmingham, Coventry, Manchester, Stockton, Bristol, Wokingham (Reading), Newham (London), two in the Glasgow area near Coatbridge and Linwood, one near Cardiff (Nantgarw) and another announced for Dudley

Oasis Cinemas
20 Rushcroft Road
Brixton
London SW2 1LA
Tel: 020 7733 8989
Fax: 020 7733 8790
Owns the Gate Notting Hill and Cameo Edinburgh, and the Ritzy Brixton which is a five-screen multiplex

Odeon Cinemas/ABC Cinemas
54 Whitcomb Street
London WC2H 7DN

Tel: 0207 321 0404
Fax: 0207 321 0357
The combined ABC/Odeon chain
totalled 643 screens on 131 sites in
June 2000, with new multiplexes
opening at Dundee and elsewhere

Picturedrome Theatres
1 Duchess Street
London W1N 3DE
Tel: 01372 460 108
Independent chain of five cinemas at
Bognor, Bristol, Cannock,
Chippenham, and Ryde (Isle of
Wight)

Scott Cinemas
Alexandra
Newton Abbot
Devon
Tel: 01626 65368
West Country circuit with cinemas at
Bridgwater, Exmouth, Lyme Regis,
Newton Abbot, Sidmouth and
Teignmouth

UCI Cinemas
7th Floor, Lee House
90 Great Bridgewater Street
Manchester M1 5JW
Tel: 0161 455 4000
Fax: 0161 455 4076
Website: www.uci-cinemas.co.uk
Operators of 31 purpose-built
multiplexes with 320 screens in the
UK(in August 2000) plus the Empire
and Plaza in London's West End with
more multiplexes scheduled for
Manchester (Printworks) and
Maidenhead

UGC Cinemas
6th Floor, Adelaide House
626 High Road
Chiswick
London W4 5RY
Tel: 020 8987 5000
Fax: 020 8742 7984
Operates 34 multiplexes in UK with
309 screens and 4 traditional cinemas
in August 2000. Has further
multiplexes opening at Cardiff,
Glasgow, Enfield, and Parrs Wood
(Manchester)

Ward-Anderson Cinema Group
Film House
35 Upper Abbey Street
Dublin 1
Ireland
Tel: (353) 1 872 3422/3922
Fax: (353) 1 872 3687
Leading cinema operator in Northern
and Southern Ireland. Sites include
Ballymena, Belfast, Londonderry,
Lisburn and Newry

Warner Village Cinemas
Warner House
98 Theobald's Road
London WC1X 8WB
Tel: 020 7984 6600
Operating 28 multiplex cinemas in
the UK with 292 screens, including
the 9-screen Warner Village West
End in London's Leicester Square
and the 30-screen Birmingham
StarCity site. Village Roadshow
separately owns multiplexes at
Birkenhead and Carlisle, under
Warner Village management.
Numerous other sites are in
development

LONDON WEST END - PREMIERE RUN

BAKER STREET
Screen on Baker Street
Baker Street, NW1
Tel: 020 7935 2772
Seats: 1:95, 2:100

BAYSWATER
UCI
Whiteleys, Queensway, W2
WG
Tel: 08700 102030
Seats: 1:333, 2:281, 3:196, 4:178,
5:154, 6:138, 7:147, 8:125

BLOOMSBURY
Renoir
Brunswick Square, WC1
Tel: 020 7837 8402
Seats: 1:251, 2:251

CHELSEA
Chelsea Cinema
Kings Road, SW3
Tel: 020 7351 3742
Seats: 713

UGC Cinemas
Kings Road, SW3
Tel: 0870 907 0710
Seats: 1:220, 2:238, 3:122, 4:111

CITY OF LONDON
Barbican
Silk Street, EC2
WE
Tel: 020 7382 7000
Seats: 1:288, 2:255

FULHAM ROAD
UGC Cinemas
Fulham Road, SW10
Tel: 0870 907 0711
Seats: 1:348 X, 2:329 X, 3:173 X,
4:203 X, 5:218, 6:154

HAVERSTOCK HILL
Screen on the Hill
Haverstock Hill, NW3
A
Tel: 020 7435 3366/9787
Seats: 339

HAYMARKET
UGC Cinemas
Haymarket, SW1
Tel: 0870 907 0712
Seats: 1:448, 2:200, 3:201

Odeon
Haymarket SW1
A
Tel: 0870 505 0007
Seats: 566

ISLINGTON
The Lux Cinema
2-4 Hoxton Square, N1
Tel: 020 7684 0200/0201
Seats: 120

Screen on the Green
Upper Street, Islington, N1
A
Tel: 020 7226 3520
Seats: 280

KENSINGTON
Odeon
Kensington High Street, W8
Tel: 0870 505 0007
Seats: 1:520, 2:66, 3:91, 4:265 X,
5:171 X, 6:204 X

KILBURN
Tricycle Cinema
269 Kilburn High Road, NW6
EWG
Tel: 020 7328 1000/1900
Seats: 289

LEICESTER SQUARE
ABC Panton St
Panton Street, SW1
Tel: 020 7930 0631/2
Seats: 1:127 X, 2:144 X, 3:138, 4:136

ABC Swiss Centre
Swiss Centre, W1
Tel: 020 7439 4470/437 2096
Seats: 1:97, 2:101, 3:93, 4:108

Empire
Leicester Square, WC2
Tel: 020 7437 1234
Seats: 1:1,330 X, 2:353, 3:77

Odeon Leicester Square
Leicester Square, WC2
Tel: 0870 505 0007
Seats: 1,943 EX; Mezzanine: 1:60 W,
2:50, 3:60, 4:60, 5:60

Odeon West End
Leicester Square, WC2
E
Tel: 0870 505 0007
Seats: 1:503, 2:838

Prince Charles
Leicester Place, WC2
X
Tel: 020 7437 8181
Seats: 488

Warner Village West End
Cranbourne Street, WC2
Tel: 020 7437 4347/3484
Seats: 1:187, 2:126, 3:300, 4:298,
5:414, 6:264, 7:410, 8:180, 9:303

THE MALL
ICA Cinema
The Mall, SW1
AG
Tel: 020 7930 3647
Seats: 185, C'thèque: 45

MARBLE ARCH
Odeon
Edgware Road, W1
E
Tel: 0870 505 0007
Seats: 1:254, 2:126, 3:174, 4:229, 5:239

MAYFAIR
Curzon Mayfair
Curzon Street, W1
Tel: 020 7369 1720
Seats: 542

NOTTING HILL GATE
Coronet
Notting Hill Gate, W11
A
Tel: 020 7727 6705
Seats: 1: 388, 2:147

Gate
Notting Hill Gate, W11
X
Tel: 020 7727 4043
Seats: 240

PICCADILLY CIRCUS
ABC
Piccadilly, W1
Tel: 020 7437 3561
Seats: 1:124, 2:118

Metro
Rupert Street, W1
W
Tel: 020 7437 0757
Seats: 1:195, 2:84

Plaza
Lower Regent Street, W1
Tel: 0990 888990
Seats: 1:752, 2:370 X, 3:161, 4:187

UGC Cinemas
Trocadero Centre
Piccadilly Circus, W1
XE
Tel: 0870 907 0716
Seats: 1:548, 2:240, 3:146, 4:154,
5:122, 6:94, 7:89

PORTOBELLO ROAD
Electric
Portobello Road, W11
X
Seats: 400
(Scheduled to re-open late 2000)

SHAFTESBURY AVENUE
ABC
Shaftesbury Avenue, WC2
Tel: 020 7836 6279/8606
Seats: 1:616, 2:581

Curzon Soho
Shaftesbury Avenue, W1
Tel: 020 7734 2255
Seats: 1:249, 2:110, 3:130

SOUTH KENSINGTON
Ciné Lumière
French Institute
Queensberry Place, SW7
Tel: 020 7838 2144/2146
Seats: 350

Goethe Institute
50 Princes Gate,
Exhibition Rd, SW7
Tel: 020 7596 4000
Seats: 170

TOTTENHAM COURT ROAD
ABC
Tottenham Court Road, W1
Tel: 020 7636 6148/6749
Seats: 1:328, 2:145, 3:137

 WATERLOO
bfi London IMAX
Charlie Chaplin Walk, SE 1
Tel: 020 7902 1234
Seats: 482

National Film Theatre
South Bank, Waterloo, SE1
WE
Tel: 020 7928 3232
Seats: 1:450, 2:160, 3:135

Queen Elizabeth Hall
South Bank, Waterloo, SE1
X
Tel: 020 7928 3002
Seats: 906

Royal Festival Hall
South Bank, Waterloo, SE1
X
Tel: 020 7928 3002
Seats: 2,419

OUTER LONDON

ACTON
Warner Village
Royale Leisure Park, Park Royal
Tel: 020 8896 0099
Seats: 1:425, 2:159, 3:205, 4:274,
5:314, 6:274, 7:205, 8:159, 9:425

BARNET
Odeon
Great North Road
Tel: 0870 505 0007
Seats: 1:522 E, 2:178, 3:78, 4:190 W,
5:158

BECKENHAM
ABC
High Street
Tel: 020 8650 1171/658 7114
Seats: 1:478, 2:228 A, 3:127 A

Studio
Beckenham Road
Tel: 020 8663 0103
Seats: 84

BEXLEYHEATH
Cineworld
The Broadway
Tel: 020 8303 0015
Seats: 1:157, 2:128, 3:280, 4:244,
5:88, 6:84, 7:111, 8:168, 9:221

BOREHAMWOOD
Cinema
Leisure Centre
Shenley Road
WG
Tel: 020 8207 2028
Seats: 1:180, 2:144, 3:111, 4:108

BRENTFORD
Watermans Arts Centre
High Street
WEG
Tel: 020 8568 1176
Seats: 240

BRIXTON
Ritzy
Brixton Oval
Coldharbour Lane SW2
Tel: 020 7737 2121
Seats: 1:353, 2:179, 3:125, 4:108,
5:84

BROMLEY
Odeon
High Street
Tel: 0870 505 0007
Seats: 1:392, 2:129 X, 3:105 X,
4:273

CAMDEN TOWN
Odeon
Parkway
Tel: 0870 505 0007
Seats: 1:403, 2:92, 3:238, 4:90, 5:99

CATFORD
ABC
Central Parade SE6 2TF
Tel: 020 8698 3306/697 6579
Seats: 1:519 X, 2:259

CLAPHAM
Picture House
Venn Street, SW4
Tel: 020 7498 3323
Seats: 1:202, 2:153 X, 3:134 X,
4:115

CROYDON
Safari
London Road
Tel: 020 8688 3422
Seats: 1:650, 2:399 X, 3:187 X

David Lean Cinema
Clock Tower
Katherine St
X
Tel: 020 8253 1030
Seats: 68

Fairfield Halls/Ashcroft Theatre
Park Lane
Tel: 020 8688 9291
Seats: Fairfield: 1,552 WEG
Ashcroft: 750

Warner Village
Valley Park Leisure Complex, off
Purley Way
Tel: 020 8680 1968
Seats: 1:253, 2:205, 3:178, 4:396,
5:396, 6:178, 7:205, 8:253

DAGENHAM
Warner Village
Dagenham Leisure Park,
Cook Road
Tel: 020 8592 2211
Seats: 1:404, 2:146, 3:189, 4:252,
5:305, 6:252, 7:189, 8:146, 9:404

DALSTON
Rio
Kingsland High Street, E8
WEG
Tel: 020 7241 9410
Seats: 405

EALING
Gosai
Northfield Avenue, W13
Tel: 020 8567 1075
Seats: 1:155, 2:149

UGC Cinemas,
Uxbridge Road, W5
Tel: 0870 907 0719
Seats: 1:576, 2:371, 3:193

EAST FINCHLEY
Phoenix
High Road, N2
XG
Tel: 020 8444 6789
Seats: 308

EAST HAM
Boleyn
Barking Road
Tel: 020 8471 4884
Seats: 1:800, 2:250, 3:250

EDGWARE
Cinemax
Station Road
Tel: 020 8381 2556
Seats: 1:700, 2:200, 3:158

ENFIELD
UGC Cinemas
Seats: 1: 3,450 (15 screens)

FELTHAM
Cineworld
Leisure West, Browells Lane
Tel: 020 8867 0888
Seats: 1:104, 2:116, 3:132, 4:205,
5:253, 6:351, 7:302, 8:350, 9:265,
10:90, 11:112, 12: 137, 13:124, 14:99

FINCHLEY ROAD
Warner Village Cinemas
02 Centre
Tel: 020 7604 3066
Seats: 1:359, 2:324, 3:159, 4:261,
5:376, 6:258, 7:134, 8:86

GREENWICH
Greenwich Cinema
High Road, SE10
WEG
Tel: 01426 919 020
Seats: 1:350, 2:288, 3:144

HAMMERSMITH
UGC Cinemas
King Street, W6
Tel: 0870 907 0718
Seats: 1:322, 2:322, 3:268 A,
4:268 A

Riverside Studios
Crisp Road, W6
E
Tel: 020 8237 1111
Seats: 200

HAMPSTEAD
ABC
Pond Street, NW3
Tel: 020 7794 4000/6603
Seats: 1:476, 2:198 X, 3:193 X

Everyman
Holly Bush Vale, NW3
X
Tel: 020 7431 1777
Seats: 184

HARRINGEY
New Curzon
Frobisher Road
Tel: 020 8347 6664
Seats: 498

HARROW
Safari
Station Road
Tel: 020 8426 0606
Seats: 1:612, 2:133

Warner Village
St George's Centre,
St. Anne's Road
Tel: 020 8427 9900/9944
Seats: 1:347, 2:288, 3:424, 4:296,
5:121, 6:109, 7:110, 8:87, 9:96

HAYES
Beck Theatre
Grange Road
XE
Tel: 020 8561 8371
Seats: 518

HOLLOWAY
Odeon
Holloway Road, N7
Tel: 0870 505 0007
Seats: 1:243, 2:192, 3:223, 4:328,
5:301,6:78, 7:112, 8:124

ILFORD
Cinema
High Road
Seats: 650

Odeon
Gants Hill
Tel: 0870 505 0007
Seats: 1:768, 2:255 X, 3:290 X,
4:190, 5:62

KILBURN
Tricycle Cinema
High Road
Tel: 020 7328 1000
Seats: 280

KINGSTON
ABC Options
Richmond Road

Tel: 020 8546 0404/547 2860
Seats: 1:287 X, 2:273 X, 3:200

LAMBETH
Imperial War Museum
Lambeth Road, SE1
X
Tel: 020 7735 8922
Seats: 216

LEE VALLEY
UCI
Picketts Lock Lane
Meridian Way,
Edmonton
X
Tel: 08700 102030
Seats: 164 (6 screens), 206
(4 screens), 426 (2 screens)

MILE END
Genesis
Mile End Road
Tel: 020 7780 2000
Seats: 1:575, 2:159, 3:159, 4:101,
5:95

MUSWELL HILL
Odeon
Fortis Green Road, N10
Tel: 0870 505 0007
Seats: 1:568, 2:173 X, 3:169 X

NEWHAM
Showcase Cinemas
Jenkins Lane, off A13
X
Tel: 020 8477 4500
Seats: 3,664 (14 screens)

NORTH FINCHLEY
Warner Village
Great North Leisure Park, Chaplin
Square, N12
Tel: 020 8446 9977/9933
Seats: 1:377, 2:164, 3:219, 4:333,
5:333, 6:219, 7:164, 8:377

PECKHAM
Premier
Rye Lane
X
Tel: 020 7732 1010
Seats: 1:397, 2:255, 3:275, 4:197,
5:218, 6:112

PUTNEY
ABC
High Street, SW15
AWG
Tel: 020 8788 3003/785 3493
Seats: 1:433, 2:313, 3:147

RICHMOND
Filmhouse
Water Lane

WG
Tel: 020 8332 0030
Seats: 150

Odeon
Hill Street
Tel: 0870 505 0007
Seats: 1:412, 2:179 X, 3:179 X

Odeon Studio
Red Lion Street
Tel: 0870 505 0007
Seats: 1:81, 2:78, 3:78, 4:92

ROMFORD
Odeon Liberty 2
Mercury Gardens
Tel: 0870 505 0007
Seats: 1:412 W, 2:255, 3:150, 4:181,
5:181, 6:150, 7:331, 8:254

STAPLES CORNER
UGC Cinemas
Geron Way
WE
Tel: 0870 907 0717
Seats: 1:455, 2:362, 3:214, 4:210,
5:166, 6:166

STRATFORD
Picture House
Gerry Raffles Square
Salway Road E15
Tel: 020 8555 3311/66
Seats: 1:260, 2:242, 3:215, 4:151

STREATHAM
ABC
High Road, SW16
Tel: 020 8769 1928/6262
Seats: 1:630, 2:427 X, 3:227 X

Odeon
High Road, SW16
Tel: 0870 505 0007
Seats: 1:1,092, 2:231 X, 3:201 X,
4:253, 5:198

SURREY QUAYS
UCI Cinemas
Redriff Road, SE16
Tel: 0870 102030
Seats: 1:411, 2:401, 3:328, 4:200,
5:198, 6:198, 7:164, 8:164, 9:164

SUTTON
Secombe Centre
Cheam Road
XE
Tel: 020 8661 0416
Seats: 330

UCI
St Nicholas Centre
St Nicholas Way
X
Tel: 0870 010 2030

Seats: 1:305, 2:297, 3:234, 4:327,
5:261, 6:327

SWISS COTTAGE
Odeon
Finchley Road, NW3
Tel: 0870 505 0007
Seats: 1:715, 2:111, 3:220, 4:120,
5:154, 6:156

WALTHAMSTOW
ABC
Hoe Street, E17
Tel: 020 8520 7092
Seats: 1:592, 2:183 A, 3:174 A

WEST INDIA QUAY
UGC Cinemas
Hertsmere Road
Tel: 0207 517 7860
Seats: 1:111, 2:168, 3:216, 4: 275,
5:360, 6: 104, 7:164, 8: 216, 9:275,
10:359

WILLESDEN
Belle Vue
Willesden Green Library Centre,
NW10
Tel: 020 8830 0822
Seats: 204

WIMBLEDON
Odeon
The Broadway, SW19
Tel: 0870 505 0007
Seats: 1:662, 2:90, 3:190 X, 4:175,
5:226 X

WOODFORD
ABC
High Road, E18
Tel: 020 8989 3463/4066
Seats: 1:561, 2:199 X, 3:131 X

WOOD GREEN
Cineworld
Shopping City
High Road
Tel: 020 8829 1400
Seats: 1:267, 2:315, 3:106, 4:152,
5:185, 6:111, 7:180, 8:137, 9:172,
10:140, 11:162, 12:105

ENGLAND

ALDEBURGH - Suffolk
Aldeburgh Cinema
High Street
X
Tel: 01728 452996
Seats: 284

ALDERSHOT - Hants
ABC, High Street
Tel: 01252 317223/20355
Seats: 1:313, 2:187, 3:150

West End Centre, Queens Road
X
Tel: 01252 330040
Seats: 98

ALNWICK - Northumberland
Playhouse, Bondgate Without
(P/T)
Tel: 01665 510785
Seats: 272

ALTON - Hants
Palace, Normandy Street
Tel: 01420 82303
Seats: 111

AMBLESIDE - Cumbria
Zeffirelli's, Compston Road
X
Tel: 01539 431771
Seats: 1:205, 2:63

ANDOVER - Hants
Savoy, London Street
Tel: 01264 356356
Seats: 250

ARDWICK - Greater Manchester
Apollo, Ardwick Green (P/T)
X
Tel: 0161 273 6921
Seats: 2,641

ASHFORD - Kent
Cineworld
Eureka Leisure Park
Trinity Road
Tel: 01233 620568/622226
Seats: 1:344, 2:75, 3:63, 4:89, 5:156,
6:254, 7:254, 8:156, 9:89, 10:63,
11:215, 12:345

ASHTON-UNDER-LYNE - Greater Manchester
Metro, Old Street
Tel: 0161 330 1993
Seats: 987

AYLESBURY - Buckinghamshire
ABC, The Exchange
Tel: 01296 424 474
Seats: 1: 396, 2:283, 3:266, 4:230,
5:133, 6:205

BANBURY - Oxfordshire
ABC, Horsefair
Tel: 01295 262071
Seats: 1:431, 2:225

BARNSLEY - South Yorkshire
Odeon, Eldon Street
Tel: 0870 505 0007
Seats: 1:416, 2:619X

BARNSTAPLE - Devon
Astor, Boutport Street
Tel: 01271 42550
Seats: 360

BARROW - Cumbria
Apollo, Hollywood Park,
Hindpool Road
Tel: 01229 825354
Seats: 1:118, 2:103, 3:258, 4:258,
5:118, 6:118

BASILDON - Essex
Towngate (P/T)
Tel: 01268 532632
Seats: 552, (Mirren Studio) 158

UCI
Festival Leisure Park
Pipps Hill
Tel: 0870 010 2030
Seats: 2,909 (12 screens)

BASINGSTOKE - Hants
Anvil, Churchill Way (P/T)
X
Tel: 01256 844244
Seats: 70

Warner Village, Basingstoke
Leisure Park, Churchill Way West,
West Ham
XE
Tel: 01256 818739/818517
Seats: 1:427, 2:238, 3:223, 4:154,
5:157, 6:157, 7:154, 8:223, 9:238,
10:427

BATH - Avon
ABC, Beau Nash, Westgate Street
X
Tel: 01225 461730/462959
Seats: 727

Little Theatre, St Michael's Place
Tel: 01225 466822
Seats: 1:192, 2:74

Robins, St John's Place
Tel: 01225 461506
Seats: 1:151, 2:126 X, 3:49

BEDFORD - Bedfordshire
Civic Theatre, Horne Lane (P/T)
Tel: 01234 44813
Seats: 266

UGC Cinemas, Aspect Leisure
Park, Newnham Avenue
XE
Tel: 0541 555 130
Seats: 1:340, 2:300, 3:300, 4:300,
5:200, 6:200

BERWICK - Northumberland
Maltings Art Centre, Eastern Lane
(P/T)
Tel: 01289 330999/330661
Seats: 100

Playhouse, Sandgate
Tel: 01289 307769
Seats: 650

BEVERLEY - East Yorkshire
Playhouse, Market Place
Tel: 01482 881315
Seats: 310

BEXHILL - East Sussex
Curzon, Western Road
Tel: 01424 210078
Seats: 175

BIDEFORD - Devon
College Theatre (P/T)
Tel: 01237 428110
Seats: 181

BILLINGHAM - Cleveland
Forum Theatre,
Town Centre (P/T)
Tel: 01642 552663
Seats: 494

BIRKENHEAD - Merseyside
Warner Village Cinemas
Europa Boulevard
Conway Park,
Tel: 0151 649 8822
Seats: 1:298, 2:359, 3:164, 4:206,
5:433, 6:206, 7:164

BIRMINGHAM - West Midlands
Electric, Station Street
X
Tel: 0121 643 7277
Seats: 1:200, 2:100

UGC Cinemas,
Arcadian Centre, Hurst Street
XE

Tel: 0121 622 3323
Seats: 1:419, 2:299, 3:275, 4:240,
5:192, 6:222, 7:210, 8:196, 9:168

UGC Cinemas, Five Ways Leisure,
Tennant Street/Broad Street
Tel: 0121 643 0631
Seats: 1: 371, 2:330, 3:269, 4:181.
5:287, 6:434, 7:341, 8:185, 9:269,10:
240, 11: 263, 12:167

MAC
Cannon Hill Park
Tel: 0121 440 3838
Seats: 1:202, 2:144

Odeon, New Street
Tel: 0870 505 0007
Seats: 1:231, 2:390, 3:298, 4:229,
5:194, 6:180, 7:130, 8:80

Piccadilly, Stratford Road
Sparkbrook
Tel: 0121 773 1658

Showcase Cinemas,
Kingsbury Road
Erdington
Tel: 0121 382 9779
Seats: 3,599 (12 screens)

Warner Village Cinemas
StarCity, Watson Road
Tel: 0121 326 0264
Seats: 1:432, 2:126, 3112, 4:175,
5:245, 6:245, 7:179, 8:142, 9:142,
10:142, 11:142, 12:534, 13:135,
14:192, 15: 201, 16:135, 17:192,
18:201, 19:534, 20:128, 21:128,
22:120, 23:115, 24:146, 25:143,
26:181, 27: 245, 28:245, 29:159,
30:318

BISHOP'S STORTFORD - Herts
Cineworld, Anchor Street
Seats: 1100 (6 screens)
(Scheduled to open December 2000)

BLACKBURN - Lancashire
Apollo Five, King William Street
Tel: 01254 695979
Seats: 1:295, 2:205, 3:115, 4:100,
5:95

BLACKPOOL - Lancashire
ABC, Church Street
Tel: 01253 27207/24233
Seats: 1:714, 2:324, 3:225

Odeon, Rigby Road
Tel: 0870 505 0007
Seats: 1:422, 2:139, 3:346, 4:153,
5:200, 6:397, 7:159, 8:351, 9:381,
10:201

BLUEWATER - Kent
Hoyts
Tel: 0870 242 7070
Seats: 1:129, 2:197, 3:361, 4:464,
5:245, 6:176, 7:80, 8:139, 9:298,
10:379, 11:193, 12:132, Studio:86

BLYTH - Northumberland
Wallaw, Union Street
Tel: 01670 352504
Seats: 1:850, 2:150, 3:80

BOGNOR REGIS - West Sussex
Picturedrome, Canada Grove
Tel: 01243 841015
Seats: 1:399, 2:100

Odeon, Butlin's Southcoast World
Tel: 0870 841916
Seats: 1:240, 2:240

BOLDON - Tyne and Wear
UGC Cinemas, Boldon Leisure
Park, Boldon Colliery
Tel: 0541 550512
Seats: 1:284, 2:197, 3:80, 4:119,
5:263, 6:529, 7:263, 8:136, 9:119,
10:197, 11:284

BOLTON - Greater Manchester
Warner Village
Middlebrook Leisure Park,
Horwich
Tel: 01204 669668
Seats: 1:375, 2:124, 3:124, 4:166,
5:244, 6:269, 7:269, 8:244, 9:166,
10:124, 11:124, 12:368

UGC Cinemas
Eagley Brook Way
Tel: 01204 366200
Seats: 1: 143, 2:144, 3:118, 4:155,
5:230, 6:467, 7:635, 8:522, 9:233,
10:156, 11:156, 12:193, 13:193,
14:72, 15:72

BOSTON - Lincolnshire
Blackfriars Arts Centre,
Spain Lane (P/T)
Tel: 01205 363108
Seats: 237

Regal, West Street
Tel: 01205 350553
Seats: 182

BOURNEMOUTH - Dorset
ABC, Westover Road
Tel: 01202 558433
Seats: 1:652, 2:585, 3:223

Odeon, Westover Road
Tel: 0870 505 0007
Seats: 1:757, 2:359, 3:266, 4:120,
5:121, 6:146

BOWNESS-ON-WINDERMERE - Cumbria
Royalty, Lake Road
X
Tel: 01539 443364
Seats: 1:400, 2:100, 3:65

BRACKNELL - Berkshire
South Hill Park Arts Centre
X
Tel: 01344 427272/484123
Seats: 1:60, 2:200 m

UCI, The Point
Skimpedhill Lane
X
Tel: 0870 010 2030
Seats: 1:177, 2:205, 3:205, 4:177,
5:316, 6:316, 7:177, 8:205, 9:205,
10:177

BRADFORD - West Yorkshire
National Museum of Photography,
Film and Television,
Prince's View (P/T)
Tel: 01274 732277/727488
Seats: 340 (IMAX)

Odeon, Gallagher Leisure Park,
Thornbury
X
Tel: 0870 505 0007
Seats: 1:128, 2:217, 3:155, 4:231,
5:300, 6:443, 7:438, 8:215, 9:154,
10:159, 11:148, 12:142, 13:147

Pictureville Cinema,
NMPFTV, Pictureville, BD1 1NQ X
Tel: 01274 732277
Seats: 306

Priestley Centre for the Arts
Chapel Street
Little Germany BD1 5DL
XE
Tel: 01274 820666
Seats: 290

BRENTWOOD - Essex
ABC, Chapel High X
Tel: 020 8795 6405
Seats: 1:262, 2:165

BRIDGNORTH - Shropshire
Majestic, Whitburn Street
Tel: 01746 761815/761866
Seats: 1:500, 2:86, 3:86

BRIDGWATER - Somerset
Film Centre, Penel Orlieu
Tel: 01278 422383
Seats: 1:223, 2:232

BRIDLINGTON - Humberside
Forum, The Promenade
Tel: 01262 676767
Seats: 1:202, 2:103, 3:57

BRIDPORT - Dorset
Palace, South Street
(temporarily closed)
Seats: 420

BRIERLEY HILL - Staffordshire
UCI Merry Hill,
Shopping Centre 10
X
Tel: 0870 0102030
Seats: 1:350, 2:350, 3:274, 4:274,
5:224, 6:224, 7:254, 8:254, 9:178,
10:178

BRIGHTON - East Sussex
Cinematheque, Media Centre,
Middle Street
Tel: 01273 739970

Duke of York's Premier Picture
House, Preston Circus
Tel: 01273 626 261
Seats: 327

Gardner Arts Centre,
University of Sussex, Falmer (P/T)
Tel: 01273 685861
Seats: 354

UGC Cinemas, Brighton Marina
Tel: 0541 555 145
Seats: 1:351, 2:351, 3:251, 4:251,
5:223, 6:223, 7:202, 8:203

Odeon Kingswest, West Street
Tel: 0870 505 0007
Seats: 1:388, 2:883, 3:504, 4:273,
5:242, 6:103

BRISTOL - Avon
Arnolfini, Narrow Quay
XE
Tel: 0117 929 9191
Seats: 176

The Cube
King Square
X
Tel: 0117 907 4190/4191
Seats: 124

Cineworld
Hengrove Leisure Park,
Hengrove Way
Tel: 01275 831099
Seats: 1:97, 2:123, 3:133, 4:211,
5:264, 6:343, 7:312, 8:344, 9:262,
10:88, 11:113, 12:152, 13:123, 14:98

IMAX Canon's Marsh
Tel: 0117 915 5000 X
Seats: 250

Orpheus, Northumbria Drive,
Henleaze
Tel: 0117 962 1644
Seats: 1:186, 2:129, 3:125

ABC, Whiteladies Road, Clifton
Tel: 0117 973 0679/973 3640
Seats: 1:372, 2:252 X, 3:135 X

Odeon, Union Street
Tel: 0870 505 0007
Seats: 1:399, 2:244, 3:215

Showcase Cinemas, Avon Meads off
Albert Road, St Phillips Causeway
Tel: 0117 972 3800
Seats: 3,408 (14 screens)

bfi   Watershed, 1 Canon's Road,
BS1 5TX
XE
Tel: 0117 927 6444/925 3845
Seats: 1:200, 2:50

Warner Village Cinemas
The Venue, Cribbs Causeway
Leisure Complex, Merlin Road
Tel: 0117 950 0222
Seats: 1:385, 2:124, 3:124, 4:166,
5:239, 6:273, 7:273, 8:239, 9:166,
10:124, 11:124, 12:385

Warner Village Cinemas,
Aspects Leisure Park, Longwell
Green
Tel: 0117 960 0021
Seats: 1:382, 2:165, 3:122, 4:122,
5:165, 6:290, 7:342, 8:290, 9:165,
10:122, 11:122, 12:165, 13:382

BROADSTAIRS - Kent
Windsor, Harbour Street
Tel: 01843 865726
Seats: 120

BROMBOROUGH - Merseyside
Odeon,
Wirral Leisure Retail Park
Welton Road
X
Tel: 0870 505 0007
Seats: 1:465, 2:356, 3:248, 4:203,
5:338, 6:168, 7:168, 8:86, 9:135,
10:71, 11:122

BUDE - Cornwall
Rebel, off A39, Rainbow
Trefknic Cross
Tel: 01288 361442
Seats: 120

BURGESS HILL - West Sussex
Orion, Cyprus Road
Tel: 01444 232137/243300
Seats: 1:150, 2:121

BURNHAM-ON-CROUCH - Essex
Rio, Station Road
Tel: 01621 782027
Seats: 1:220, 2:60

BURNHAM-ON-SEA - Somerset
Ritz, Victoria Street
Tel: 01278 782871
Seats: 204

BURNLEY - Lancashire
Apollo, Hollywood Park,
Centenary Way, Manchester Road
Tel: 01282 456222/456333
Seats: 1:61, 2:238, 3:93, 4:339, 5:93,
6:339, 7:93, 8:238, 9:93

BURTON-ON-TRENT - Staffordshire
Cineworld, Guild Street
Seats: 1,600 (9 screens)

BURY - Greater Manchester
Warner Village, Park 66, Pilsworth
Road X
Tel: 0161 766 2440/1787
Seats: 1:559, 2:322, 3:278, 4:434,
5:208, 6:166, 7:166, 8:208, 9:434,
10:278, 11:322, 12:573

BURY ST EDMUNDS - Suffolk
ABC, Hatter Street
Tel: 01284 754477
Seats: 1:196, 2:117

CAMBERLEY - Surrey
ArtsLink, Knoll Road (P/T)
Tel: 01276 707600
Seats: 338

Robins, London Road
Tel: 01276 63909/26768
Seats: 1:420, 2:114, 3:94

Globe, Hawley (P/T)
Tel: 01252 876769
Seats: 200

CAMBRIDGE - Cambridgeshire
Arts Picture House
St Andrews Street
Tel: 01223 504444/578939
Seats: 1: 250, 2:150, 3:98

Warner Village,
Grafton Centre, East Road
XE
Tel: 01223 460442/460225
Seats: 1:162, 2:168, 3:182, 4:205,
5:166, 6:175, 7:321, 8:442

CANNOCK - Staffordshire
Picturedrome, Walsall Road
Tel: 01543 502226
Seats: 1:368, 2:185

CANTERBURY - Kent
bfi Cinema 3,
Cornwallis South
University of Kent CT2 7NX
Tel: 01227 769075/764000 x4017
Seats: 300

ABC, St Georges Place
Tel: 01227 462022/453577
Seats: 1:536, 2:404

CANVEY ISLAND - Essex
Movie Starr Cineplex
Eastern Esplandade
Tel: 01268 699799
Seats: 1:134, 2:122, 3:104, 4:73

CARLISLE - Cumbria
Lonsdale, Warwick Road
Tel: 01228 514654
Seats: 1:375, 2:216, 3:54

City Cinemas 4 & 5,
Mary Street
X
Tel: 01228 514654
Seats: 4:122, 5:112

Village Cinemas
Botchergate
X
Tel: 01228 819 104
Seats: 1:145, 2:242, 3:242, 4:145,
5:295, 6:295, 7:334

CHATHAM - Kent
ABC, High Street
Tel: 01634 846756/842522
Seats: 1:520, 2:360, 3:170

CHELMSFORD - Essex
Central Theatre
High Street (P/T)
Tel: 01634 403868

Odeon, Kings Head Walk
EX
Tel: 0870 505 0007
Seats: 1:338, 2:110, 3:160, 4:236,
5:174, 6:152, 7:131, 8:141

CHELTENHAM - Gloucestershire
Odeon, Winchcombe Street

Tel: 0870 505 0007
Seats: 1:252, 2:184, 3:184, 4:90,
5:129, 6:104, 7:177

CHESHAM - Buckinghamshire
New Elgiva Theatre, Elgiva Lane
(P/T)
XE
Tel: 01494 582900
Seats: 328

CHESHIRE OAKS - Cheshire
Warner Village Cinemas,
The Coliseum, Stannley Lane,
Ellesmere Port
Tel: 0151 356 2261
Seats: 1:345, 2:166, 3:124, 4:166,
5:239, 6:252, 7:345, 8:252, 9:239,
10: 166, 11: 124, 12:124, 13:166, 14:
345, Iwerks: 312

CHESTER - Cheshire
UGC Cinemas,
Chaser Court
Greyhound Park,
Sealand Road
XE
Tel: 01244 380459/380301/380155
Seats: 1:366, 2:366, 3:265, 4:232,
5:211, 6:211

Odeon, Northgate Street
Tel: 0870 505 0007
Seats: 1:408, 2:148, 3:148, 4:122,
5:122

CHESTERFIELD - Derbyshire
Cineworld,
Derby Road, Alma Leisure Park
Tel: 0246 229172/278000
SeatsL 1:245, 2:128, 3:107, 4:150,
5:291, 6:291, 7:150, 8: 107, 9:128,
10:237

CHICHESTER - West Sussex
Minerva Movies
Chichester Festival Theatre
Oaklands Park (S/O)
X
Tel: 01243 781312
Seats: 214

New Park Film Centre
New Park Road
X
Tel: 01243 786650
Seats: 120

CHIPPENHAM - Wiltshire
Astoria, Marshfield Road
Tel: 01249 652498
Seats: 1:215, 2:215

**CHIPPING NORTON -
Oxfordshire**
The Theatre, Spring Street (P/T)
Tel: 01608 642349/642350
Seats: 195

CHRISTCHURCH - Dorset
Regent Centre, High Street (P/T)
Tel: 01202 479819/499148
Seats: 485

**CIRENCESTER -
Gloucestershire**
Regal, Lewis Lane
Tel: 01285 658755
Seats: 1:100, 2:100

CLACTON - Essex
Flicks, Pier Avenue
Tel: 01255 429627/421188
Seats: 1:625, 2:135

CLEVEDON - Avon
Curzon, Old Church Road
Tel: 01275 871000
Seats: 392

CLITHEROE - Lancashire
Regal, York Street
Tel: 01200 423278
Seats: 400

COLCHESTER - Essex
Odeon, Crouch Street
Tel: 0870 505 0007
Seats: 1:480, 2:237, 3:118, 4:133,
5:126, 6:177

**COLEFORD -
Gloucestershire**
Studio, High Street
Tel: 01594 833331
Seats: 1:200, 2:80

CONSETT - Co Durham
Empire, Front Street
XE
Tel: 01207 506751
Seats: 535

COSHAM - Hants
ABC, High Street
Tel: 023 92376635
Seats: 1:441, 2:118, 3:107

**COVENTRY - West
Midlands**
Odeon, Sky Dome, Croft Road
X
Tel: 0870 505 0007
1: 228, 2:415, 3:180, 4:359, 5:174,
6:137, 7:115, 8:163, 9:172

Showcase Cinemas, Cross Point,
Hinckley Road
Tel: 01203 602111
Seats: 4,413 (14 screens)

Warwick Arts Centre,
University of Warwick, CV4 7AL
X
Tel: 024 76 524524/523060
Seats: 240

CRANLEIGH - Surrey
Regal, High Street
Tel: 01483 272373
Seats: 268

CRAWLEY - West Sussex
UGC Cinemas,
Crawley Leisure Park
London Road
Tel: 0870 902 0411
Seats: 1:236, 2:421, 3:186, 4:551,
5:186, 6:129, 7:129, 8:318, 9:173,
10:231, 11:184, 12:156, 13:173,
14:173, 15:70

CREWE - Cheshire
Apollo, High Street
Tel: 0870 444 3149
Seats: 1:107, 2:110, 3:91

Lyceum Theatre, Heath Street (P/T)
Tel: 01270 215523
Seats: 750

Victoria Film Theatre,
West Street l
Tel: 01270 211422
Seats: 180

CROMER - Norfolk
Regal, Hans Place
Tel: 01263 513311
Seats: 1:129, 2:136, 3:66, 4:55

CROOKHAM - Hants
Globe, Queen Elizabeth Barracks
Tel: 01252 876769
Seats: 340

CROSBY - Merseyside
Plaza, Crosby Road North, Waterloo
Tel: 0151 474 4076
Seats: 1:600, 2:92, 3:74

DARTFORD - Kent
Orchard Theatre
Home Gardens (P/T)
XE
Tel: 01322 220000
Seats: 930

**DARLINGTON - Co
Durham**
Arts Centre, Vane Terrace (P/T)
XE

Tel: 01325 483168/483271
Seats: 100

ABC, Northgate
Tel: 01325 462745/484994
Seats: 1:578, 2:201, 3:139

DARTINGTON - Devon
bfi Barn Theatre
Arts Society
The Gallery, TQ9 6DE
(P/T)
X
Tel: 01803 865864/863073
Seats: 208

DEAL - Kent
Flicks, Queen Street
Tel: 01304 361165
Seats: 1:162, 2:99

DERBY - Derbyshire
bfi Metro Cinema
Green Lane, DE1 1SA
XE
Tel: 01332 340170/347765
Seats: 128

Showcase Cinemas,
Foresters Park, Osmaston Park
Road at Sinfin Lane
X
Tel: 01332 270300
Seats: 2,557 (11 screens)

UCI Meteor Centre 10,
Mansfield Road
X
Tel: 0870 0102030
Seats: 1:191, 2:188, 3:188, 4:191,
5:276, 6:276, 7:191, 8:188, 9:188,
10:191

DEREHAM - Norfolk
Hollywood, Dereham,
Entertainment Centre,
Market Place
Tel: 01362 691133
Seats: 1:160, 2:90, 3:108

DEVIZES - Wiltshire
Palace, Market Place
Tel: 01380 722971
Seats: 253

**DONCASTER - South
Yorkshire**
Civic Theatre, Waterdale (P/T)
Tel: 01302 62349
Seats: 547

Odeon, Hallgate
X
Tel: 0870 505 0007
Seats: 1:1,003, 2:155, 3:158

Warner Village, Doncaster Leisure
Park, Bawtry Road
Tel: 01302 371313/371020
Seats: 1:224, 2:212, 3:252, 4:386,
5:252, 6:212, 7:224

DORCHESTER - Dorset
Plaza, Trinity Street
Tel: 01305 262488
Seats: 1:100, 2:320

DORKING - Surrey
Dorking Halls
Tel: 01306 881717
Seats: 198

DOUGLAS - Isle of Man
Palace Cinema
Tel: 01624 76814
Seats: 1:319, 2:120

Summerland Cinema
Tel: 01624 25511
Seats: 200

DOVER - Kent
Silver Screen, White Cliffs
Experience, Gaol Lane
Tel: 01304 228000
Seats: 110

DUDLEY - West Midlands
Limelight Cinema, Black Country
Living Museum
Tel: 0121 557 9643
Seats: 100

Showcase Cinemas
Seats: 2,850 (14 screens)
(Scheduled to open late 2000)

DURHAM - Co Durham
Robins, North Road
Tel: 0191 384 3434
Seats: 1:312 X, 2:98, 3:96, 4:74

EASTBOURNE - East Sussex
Curzon, Langney Road
Tel: 01323 731441
Seats: 1:530, 2:236, 3:236

UGC Cinemas, Crumbles Harbour
Village,
Pevensey Bay Road
XE
Tel: 0541 555159
Seats: 1:322, 2:312, 3:271, 4:254,
5:221, 6:221

EAST GRINSTEAD - West Sussex
King Street Picture House
Atrium Building, King Street
Tel: 01342 321666/321216
Seats: 1:240, 2:240

EASTLEIGH - Hants
Point Dance and Arts Centre
Town Hall Centre, Leigh Road (P/T)
Tel: 023 8065 2333
Seats: 264

ELLAND - North Yorkshire
Rex, Coronation Street
X
Tel: 01422 372140
Seats: 294

ELLESMERE PORT - Cheshire
Epic Cinema,
Epic Leisure Centre (P/T)
X
Tel: 0151 355 3665
Seats: 163

ELY - Cambridgeshire
The Maltings, Ship Lane (P/T)
Tel: 01353 666388
Seats: 200

Cineworld, Towerfields, Abbot's
Ripton Road
Tel: 01480 412255
Seats: 1:224, 2:126, 3:90, 4:125,
5:110, 6:317, 7:284, 8:208,
9:208,10:101

EPSOM - Surrey
Odeon, Upper High Street
Seats: 2,177 (8 screens)

Playhouse, Ashley Avenue (P/T)
XE
Tel: 01372 742555/6
Seats: 300

ESHER - Surrey
ABC, High Street
Tel: 020 8795 6410
Seats: 1:918 A, 2:117

EVESHAM - Hereford & Worcs
Regal, Port Street
Tel: 01386 446002
Seats: 540

EXETER - Devon
Northcott Theatre,
Stocker Road (P/T)
Tel: 01392 54853
Seats: 433

Odeon, Sidwell Street
Tel: 0870 505 0007
Seats: 1:740, 2:121, 3:106, 4:344

Picture House
51 Bartholomew Street West
Tel: 01392 251341
Seats: 1:220, 2:156

EXMOUTH - Devon
Savoy, Rolle Street
Tel: 01395 268220
Seats: 1:204, 2:100, 3:70

FAKENHAM - Norfolk
Hollywood Cinema,
The Market Place
Tel: 01328 856 466
Seats: 1:120, 2:60

FALMOUTH - Cornwall
Arts, Church Street
Tel: 01326 212300
Seats: 199

FARNHAM - Surrey
Redgrave Theatre, Brightwells
X
Tel: 01252 727 720
Seats: 362

FAVERSHAM - Kent
New Royal, Market Place
Tel: 01795 591211
Seats: 448

FAWLEY - Hants
Waterside, Long Lane
Tel: 023 80891335
Seats: 355

FELIXSTOWE - Suffolk
Palace, Crescent Road
Tel: 01394 282787
Seats: 1:150, 2:90

FOLKESTONE - Kent
Silver Screen, Guildhall Street
Tel: 01303 221230
Seats: 1:435, 2:106

FOREST GUERNSEY - Channel Islands
Mallard Cinema, Mallard Hotel
La Villiaze
Tel: 01481 64164
Seats: 1:154, 2:54, 3:75, 4:75

FROME - Somerset
Westway, Cork Street
Tel: 01373 465685
Seats: 304

GAINSBOROUGH - Lincolnshire
Trinity Arts Centre
Trinity Street (P/T)
X
Tel: 01427 810710
Seats: 210

GATESHEAD - Tyne and Wear
UCI Metro 11, Metro Centre
Tel: 0191 493 2022/3
Seats: 1:200, 2:200, 3:228, 4:256,
5: 370, 6:370, 7:256, 8:228, 9:200,
10:200, 11:520

GATLEY - Greater Manchester
Tatton, Gatley Road
Tel: 0161 491 0711/428 2133
Seats: 1:648, 2:247, 3:111

GERRARDS CROSS - Buckinghamshire
ABC, Ethorpe Crescent
Tel: 01753 882516/883024
Seats: 1:350, 2:212

GLOUCESTER - Gloucestershire
Guildhall Arts Centre,
Eastgate Street (P/T)
X
Tel: 01452 505086/9
Seats: 1:120, 2: 150

UGC Cinemas,
Peel Centre,
St. Ann Way, Bristol Road
XE
Tel: 0541 555 174
Seats: 1:354, 2:354, 3:238, 4:238,
5:219, 6:219

GODALMING - Surrey
Borough Hall (P/T)
Tel: 01483 861111
Seats: 250

GOOLE - Herts
The Gate, Dunhill Road
Tel: 01405 720219
Seats: 90

GOSPORT - Hants
St Vincent Cinema, Mill Lane
Tel: 02392 588311
Seats: 140

GRANTHAM - Lincolnshire
Paragon, St Catherine's Road
X
Tel: 01476 570046
Seats: 1:270, 2:160

GRAVESEND - Kent
ABC, King Street
Tel: 01474 356947/352470
Seats: 1:571, 2:296, 3:109

GRAYS - Essex
Thameside, Orsett Road (P/T)
Tel: 01375 382555
Seats: 303

GREAT YARMOUTH - Norfolk
Hollywood, Marine Parade
Tel: 01493 842043
Seats: 1:500, 2:296, 3:250, 4:250

GRIMSBY - Herts
ABC, Freeman Street
Tel: 01472 342878/349368
Seats: 1:393, 2:236, 3:126

Screen, Crosland Road, Willows
DN37 9EH (P/T)
X
Tel: 01472 240410
Seats: 206

GUILDFORD - Surrey
Odeon, Bedford Road
Tel: 0870 505 0007
Seats: 1:430, 2:361, 3:343, 4:273,
5:297, 6:148, 7:112, 8:130, 9:130

HAILSHAM - East Sussex
Pavilion, George Street (P/T)
Tel: 01323 841414
Seats: 203

HALIFAX - West Yorkshire
ABC, Ward's End
Tel: 01422 352000/346429
Seats: 1:670, 2:199, 3:172

HALSTEAD - Essex
Empire, Butler Road
Tel: 01787 477001
Seats: 320

HALTON - Buckinghamshire
Astra, RAF Halton (P/T)
Tel: 01296 623535
Seats: 570

HANLEY - Staffordshire
ABC, Broad Street
Tel: 01782 212320/268970
Seats: 1:572, 2:248, 3:171

Forum Theatre,
Stoke-on-Trent City Museum,
Bethesda Street (P/T)
Tel: 01782 232799
Seats: 300

HARLOW - Essex
UGC Cinemas, Queensgate Centre,
Edinburgh Way
XE
Tel: 0870 907 0713
Seats: 1:356, 2:260, 3:240, 4:234,
5:233, 6:230

Odeon, The High
Tel: 0870 505 0007
Seats: 1:450, 2:239, 3:200

Playhouse, The High (P/T)
XE
Tel: 01279 431945
Seats: 330

HARROGATE - North Yorkshire
Odeon, East Parade
Tel: 0870 505 0007
Seats: 1:532, 2:105 X, 3:78 X, 4:339

HARTLEPOOL - Cleveland
Warner Village Cinemas
The Lanyard, Marina Way
Tel: 01429 261 177/263 263
Seats: 1:295, 2:336, 3:160, 4:204,
5:430, 6:204, 7:160

HARWICH - Essex
Electric Palace,
King's Quay Street (P/T)
Tel: 01255 553333
Seats: 204

HASLEMERE - Surrey
Haslemere Hall, Bridge Road (P/T)
Tel: 01428 661793
Seats: 350

HASTINGS - East Sussex
ABC, Queens Road
Tel: 01424 420517/431180
Seats: 1:387, 2:176, 3:129

St Mary-in-the-Castle Arts Centre,
Pelham Crescent (P/T)
Tel: 01424 781624
Seats: 590

HATFIELD - Herts
UCI, The Galleria
Comet Way
Tel: 0870 010 2030
Seats: 1:172, 2:235, 3:263, 4:167,
5:183, 6:183, 7:260, 8:378, 9:172

HAVANT - Hants
Arts Centre, East Street (P/T)
X
Tel: 023 92472700
Seats: 130

HAVERHILL - Suffolk
Arts Centre, Town Hall,
High Street (P/T)
Tel: 01440 714140
Seats: 210

HAYLING ISLAND - Hants
Hiads Theatre, Station Road
Tel: 023 92462573
Seats: 150

HAYWARDS HEATH - West Sussex
Clair Hall, Perrymount Road (P/T)

Tel: 01444 455440/454394
Seats: 350

HEATON MOOR - Greater Manchester
Savoy, Heaton Moor Road
Tel: 0161 432 2114
Seats: 476

HEBDEN BRIDGE - West Yorkshire
Picture House, New Road
XE
Tel: 01422 842807
Seats: 498

HEMEL HEMPSTEAD - Herts
Odeon, Leisure World,
Jarmans Park
XE
Tel:0870 505 0007
Seats: 1:136, 2:187, 3:187, 4:320,
5:260, 6:435, 7:168, 8:168

HENLEY-ON-THAMES - Oxfordshire
Kenton Theatre, New Street (P/T)
X
Tel: 01491 575698
Seats: 240

Regal, Broma Way, off Bell Street
Tel: 01491 414150
Seats: 1:152, 2:101, 3:85

HEREFORD - Hereford & Worcs
ABC, Commercial Road
Tel: 01432 272554
Seats: 378

The Courtyard Theatre and Arts
Centre, Edgar Street (P/T)
X
Tel: 01432 359252
Seats: 1:364, (Studio) 124

HERNE BAY - Kent
Kavanagh, William Street
X
Tel: 01227 362228
Seats: 1:137, 2:95

HEXHAM - Northumberland
Forum, Market Place
Tel: 01434 601144
Seats: 207

HIGH WYCOMBE - Buckinghamshire
UCI Wycombe 6,
Crest Road, Cressex
X

Tel: 0870 010 2030
Seats: 1:388, 2:388, 3:284, 4: 284,
5:202, 6:202

HODDESDON - Herts
Broxbourne Civic Hall
High Street (P/T)
Tel: 01992 441946/31
Seats: 564

HOLLINWOOD - Greater Manchester
Roxy, Hollins Road
Tel: 0161 681 1441
Seats: 1:470, 2:130, 3:260, 4:260,
5:320, 6:96, 7:140

HOLMFIRTH - North Yorkshire
Picturedrome, Market Walk
Tel: 01484 689759
Seats: 200

HORDERN - Co Durham
WMR Film Centre,
Sunderland Road
Tel: 01783 864344
Seats: 1:156, 2:96

HORSHAM - West Sussex
Arts Centre (Ritz Cinema and
Capitol Theatre), North Street (P/T)
Tel: 01403 268689
Seats: 1:126, 2:450

HORWICH - Lancashire
Leisure Centre, Victoria Road
(P/T)
Tel: 01204 692211
Seats: 400

HUCKNALL - Notts
Byron, High Street
Tel: 0115 963 6377
Seats: 430

HUDDERSFIELD - West Yorkshire
Tudor, Queensgate, Zetland Street
Tel: 01484 530874
Two screens

UCI, McAlpine Stadium
Bradley Mills Road
Tel: 0870 0102030
Seats: 1:375, 2:296, 3:296, 4:268,
5:268, 6:176, 7:176, 8:148, 9:148

HULL - Herts
Odeon, Kingston Street
X
Tel: 0870 505 0007
Seats: 1:172, 2:172, 3:152, 4:174,
5:168, 6:275, 7:134, 8:152, 9:110,
10:91

 Screen, Central Library
Albion Street HU1 3TF
XE
Tel: 01482 226655
Seats: 247

UCI St Andrew's Quay
Clive Sullivan Way
X
Tel: 0870 0102030
Seats: 1:166, 2:152, 3:236, 4:292,
5:292, 6:236, 7:152, 8:166

UCG Cinemas, Kingswood
Leisure Park, Ennerdale Link
Road
Tel: 01482 835035
Seats: 1:165, 2:211, 3:253, 4:498,
5:253, 6:211, 7:165, 8:165, 9:98

HUNSTANTON - Norfolk
Princess Theatre, The Green (P/T)
Tel: 01485 532252
Seats: 467

HUNTINGDON - Cambridgeshire
Cromwell Centre, Princes Street
Tel: 01480 433499
Seats: 264

Cineworld, Towerfields, Abbot's
Ripton Road
Tel: 01480 412255
Seats: 1:224, 2:126, 3:90, 4:125,
5:110, 6:317, 7:284, 8:208, 9:208,
10:101

ILFRACOMBE - Devon
The Landmark Theatre
Wilder Road (P/T)
Tel: 01271 324242
Seats: 175

Pendle Stairway, High Street
X
Tel: 01271 863260
Seats: 460

ILKESTON - Derbyshire
Scala, Market Place
Tel: 0115 932 4612
Seats: 500

IPSWICH - Suffolk
 Film Theatre, Corn Exchange,
King Street, IP1 1DH
XE
Tel: 01473 433100
Seats: 1:220, 2:40

Odeon, St Margaret's Street
Tel: 0870 505 0007
Seats: 1:509, 2:320, 3:292, 4:220,
5:220

UGC Cinemas, Cardinal Park,
Greyfriars Road
Tel: 0870 907 0748
Seats: 1:168, 2:186, 3:168, 4:270,
5:179, 6:510, 7:238, 8:398, 9:186,
10:168, 11:83

KEIGHLEY - West Yorkshire
Picture House
Tel: 01535 602561
Seats: 1:364, 2:95

KENDAL - Cumbria
Brewery Arts Centre
Highgate, LA9 4HE (S/O)
XE
Tel: 01539 725133
Seats: 1:192, 2:115, Theatre (P/T)
250

KESWICK - Cumbria
Alhambra
St John Street (S/O)
Tel: 017687 72195
Seats: 313

KETTERING - Northants
Odeon, Pegasus Court,
Wellingborough Road
Tel: 0870 505 0007
Seats: 1:174, 2:125, 3:232, 4:349,
5:105, 6:83, 7:105, 8:310

KINGSBRIDGE- Devon
The Reel Cinema, Fore Street
Tel: 01548 856636
Seats: 190

KING'S LYNN - Norfolk
Arts Centre, King Street
Tel: 01553 774725/773578
Seats: 359

Majestic, Tower Street
Tel: 01553 772603
Seats: 1:450, 2:123, 3:400

KIRKBY-IN-ASHFIELD - Notts
Regent, Diamond Street/Kingsway
Tel: 01623 753866
Seats: 180

KNUTSFORD - Cheshire
Studio, Toft Road
X
Tel: 01565 633005
Seats: 400

LAKE - Isle of Wight
Screen De Luxe, Sandown Road
Tel: 01983 404050
Seats: 150

LANCASTER - Lancashire
ABC, King Street
Tel: 01524 64141/841149
Seats: 1:250, 2:244

The Dukes Playhouse,
Moor Lane, LA1 1QE (P/T)
XE
Tel: 01524 66645/67461
Seats: 307

Warner Village, Church Road
Seats: (6 screens)
(Scheduled to open March 2001)

LEAMINGTON SPA - Warwicks
Apollo, Portland Place
Tel: 0906 2943456/0870 444 3148
Seats: 1:309 X, 2:199 X, 3:138, 4: 112 X

Royal, Spa Centre,
Newbold Terrace
Tel: 01926 887726/888997
Seats: 208

LEEDS - West Yorkshire
Cottage Road Cinema
Headingley
Tel: 0113 230 2562
Seats: 468

Hyde Park Cinema
Brudenell Road
Tel: 0113 275 2045
Seats: 360

Lounge, North Lane, Headingley
Tel: 0113 275 1061/258932
Seats: 691

Odeon, The Headrow
Tel: 0870 505 0007
Seats: 1:975, 2:385 X, 3:198 X,
4:172, 5:110

Showcase Cinemas
Gelderd Road, Birstall
X
Tel: 01924 420622
Seats: 4,250 (16 screens)

Warner Village Cinemas
Cardigan Fields
Kirkstall Road
Tel: 0113 279 9855
Seats: 1: 345, 2: 124, 3:166, 4: 245,
5: 252, 6: 245, 7:166, 8:124, 9:345

LEICESTER - Leicestershire
Piccadilly, Abbey Street
Tel: 0116 262 0005
Seats: 1:250, 2:180

Bollywood, Melton Road
Tel: 0116 268 1422
Seats: 1:450, 2:150

Odeon, Aylestone Road,
Freemans Park
XE
Tel: 0870 505 0007
Seats: 1:128, 2:164, 3:154, 4;239,
5:210, 6:632, 7:332, 8:212, 9:329,
10:154, 11:164, 12:126

 Phoenix Arts
21 Upper Brown Street
LE1 5TE (P/T)
XE
Tel: 0116 255 4854/255 5627
Seats: 274

Piccadilly, Green Lane Road
Tel: 0116 251 8880
2 Screens

Warner Village,
Meridian Leisure Park,
Lubbesthorpe Way
Braunstone
Tel: 0116 282 7733/289 4001
Seats: 1:423, 2:158, 3:189, 4:266,
5:306, 6:266, 7:202, 8:158, 9:423

LEIGHTON BUZZARD - Bedfordshire
Theatre, Lake Street (P/T)
Tel: 01525 378310
Seats: 170

LEISTON - Suffolk
Film Theatre, High Street
Tel: 01728 830549
Seats: 288

LETCHWORTH - Herts
Broadway, Eastcheap
Tel: 01462 681 223
Seats: 1:488, 2:176 X, 3:174 X

LEYBURN - North Yorkshire
Elite, Railway Street (P/T)
Tel: 01969 624488
Seats: 173

LINCOLN - Lincolnshire
Odeon, Tritton Trading Estate,
Valentine Road
Tel: 0870 505 0007
Seats: 1:279, 2:164, 3:181, 4:138,
5:134, 6:138

LITTLEHAMPTON - West Sussex
Windmill Theatre, Church Street
(P/T)
Tel: 01903 722224
Seats: 252

LIVERPOOL - Merseyside
ABC, Allerton Road
Tel: 0151 724 3550/5095
Seats: 472

Odeon, London Road
Tel:0870 505 0007
Seats: 1:482, 2:154, 3:157, 4:149,
5:217, 6:134, 7:125, 8:194, 9:137

Philharmonic Hall, Hope Street (P/T)
X
Tel: 0151 709 2895/3789
Seats: 1,627

Showcase Cinemas, East
Lancashire Road, Norris Green
X
Tel: 0151 549 2021
Seats: 3,415 (12 screens)

UGC Cinemas, Edge Lane Retail
Park, Binns Road
XE
Tel: 0151 252 0544
Seats: 1:356, 2:354, 3:264, 4:264,
5:220, 6:220, 7:198, 8:200

Woolton, Mason Street
X
Tel: 0151 428 1919
Seats: 256

LONGRIDGE - Lancashire
Palace, Market Place
Tel: 01772 785600
Seats: 200

LOUGHBOROUGH - Leicestershire
Curzon, Cattle Market
Tel: 01509 212261
Seats: 1:420, 2:303, 3:199, 4:186,
5:140, 6:80

Stanford Hall Cinema at the
Co-operative College (P/T)
Tel: 01509 852333
Seats: 352

LOUTH - Lincolnshire
Playhouse, Cannon Street
Tel: 01507 603333
Seats: 1:215, 2:158 X, 3:78 X

LOWESTOFT - Suffolk
Hollywood, London Road South
Tel: 01502 564567
Seats: 1:200, 2:175, 3:65, 4:40

Marina Theatre, The Marina
(P/T)
Tel: 01502 573318
Seats: 751

LUDLOW - Shropshire
Assembly Rooms
Mill Street (P/T)
X
Tel: 01584 878141
Seats: 320

LUTON - Bedfordshire
ABC, George Street
Tel: 020 8795 6408
Seats: 1:562, 2:436, 3:272

Cineworld
The Galaxy, Bridge Street
Tel: 01582 401092/400705
Seats: 1:114, 2:75, 3:112, 4:284,
5:419, 6:212, 7:123, 8:217, 9:137,
10:213, 11:240

Artezium, Arts and Media Centre
Tel: 01582 707100
Seats: 96

St George's Theatre
Central Library (P/T)
Tel: 01582 547440
Seats: 238

LYME REGIS - Dorset
Regent, Broad Street
X
Tel: 01297 442053
Seats: 400

LYMINGTON - Hants
Community Centre, New Street (P/T)
Tel: 015907 2337
Seats: 110

LYTHAM ST. ANNES - Lancashire
Pleasure Island Cinemas,
South Promenade
Tel: 01253 780085
Seats: 1:170, 2:92, 3:117, 4:105

MABLETHORPE - Lincolnshire
Loewen, Quebec Road
Tel: 0150 747 7040
Seats: 1:203, 2:80

MAIDENHEAD - Berkshire
UCI, Grenfell Island
Tel: 0870 0102030
Seats: 1:319,
2:246, 3:139, 4:113, 5:201, 6:179,
7:87, 8:146

MAIDSTONE - Kent
Odeon, Lockmeadow
Tel: 0870 505 0007
Seats: 1:86, 2:89, 3:127, 4:111,
5:240, 6:240, 7:398, 8:347

MALVERN - Hereford & Worcs
Festival Cinema,
Winter Gardens Complex,
Grange Road
Tel: 01684 892277/892710
Seats: 407

MANCHESTER - Greater Manchester
Arena 7, Hunts Bank, Victoria
Station
X
Tel: 0161 839 0700
Seats: 1:138, 2:143, 3:287, 4:257,
5:221, 6:370, 7:156

Cine City, Wilmslow Road,
Withington
Tel: 0161 445 8181
Seats: 1:150, 2:130, 3:130

 Cornerhouse
70 Oxford Street M1 5NH
XE
Tel: 0161 228 2467/7621
Seats: 1:300, 2:170, 3:60

Odeon, Oxford Street
Tel: 0870 505 0007
Seats: 1:629 E, 2:346 E, 3:144 X,
4:97, 5:203 E, 6:143 X, 7:86

Showcase Cinemas
Hyde Road, Belle Vue
Tel: 0161 220 8765
Seats: 3,191 (14 screens)

UCI, Trafford Centre
The Dome, Dumplington
Tel: 0870 0102030
Seats: 1:427, 2:427, 3:371, 4:301,
5:243, 6:243, 7:181, 8:181, 9:181,
10:181, 11:181, 12:181, 13:152,
14:152, 15:140, 16:140, 17:112,
18:112, 19:112, 20:112

UCI, The Printworks X
Tel: 0870 0102030
Seats: 1 (IMAX) 368, 2: 217, 3:122,
4:140, 5:140, 6:140, 7:122, 8:214,
9:120, 10:138, 11:228, 12:371,
13:422, 14:164, 15:140, 16:140,
17:322, 18:564, 19:122, 20:122

MANSFIELD - Notts
ABC, Mansfield Leisure Park
Park Lane
Tel: 01623 422 462
Seats: 1:390, 2:390, 3:246, 4:246,
5:221, 6:221, 7:193, 8:193

MARGATE - Kent
Dreamland, Marine Parade
Tel: 01843 227822
Seats: 1:378, 2:376

MARPLE - Greater Manchester
Regent, Stockport Road
X
Tel: 0161 427 5951
Seats: 285

MARKET DRAYTON -
Shropshire
Royal Festival Centre (P/T)
Seats: 165

MELTON MOWBRAY -
Leicestershire
Regal, King Street
Tel:0116 267 3127
Seats: 226

MIDDLESBROUGH -
Cleveland
Odeon, Corporation Road
Tel: 0870 505 0007
Seats: 1:611, 2:129, 3:148, 4:254

MILLOM - Cumbria
Palladium, Horn Hill (S/O)
Tel: 01657 2441
Seats: 400

MILTON KEYNES -
Buckinghamshire
Cineworld
Xscape, Marlborough Gate
Tel: 01908 230 088
Seats: 1:137, 2:234, 3:205, 4:170,
5:214, 6:281, 7:304, 8:158, 9:158,
10:316, 11:281, 12: 214, 13:170, 14:
205, 15: 234, 16:135

UCI The Point 10
Midsummer Boulevard
Tel: 0870 010 2030
Seats: 1:156, 2:169, 3:250, 4:222,
5:222, 6:222, 7:222, 8:250, 9: 169,
10: 156

MINEHEAD - Somerset
Odeon, Butlin's Summerwest World
X
Tel: 0870 505 0007
Seats: 218

MONTON - Greater
Manchester
Princess, Monton Road
Tel: 0161 789 3426
Seats: 580

MORECAMBE - Lancashire
Apollo, Central Drive
Tel: 01524 426642
Seats: 1:207, 2:207, 3:106, 4:106

MORPETH -
Northumberland
Coliseum, New Market
Tel: 01670 516834
Seats: 66

NAILSEA - Avon
Cinema, Scotch Horn Leisure

Centre, Brockway (P/T)
Tel: 01275 856965
Seats: 250

NANTWICH - Cheshire
Civic Hall, Market Street (P/T)
Tel: 01270 628633
Seats: 300

NEWARK - Notts
Palace Theatre,
Appleton Gate (P/T)
Tel: 01636 671156
Seats: 351

NEWBURY - Berkshire
Corn Exchange,
Market Place (P/T)
X
Tel: 01635 522733
Seats: 370

NEWCASTLE-UNDER-LYME
- Staffordshire
Warner Village
(Opens Autumn 2000)

NEWCASTLE-UPON-TYNE
- Tyne and Wear
Odeon, Pilgrim Street
Tel: 0870 505 0007
Seats: 1:1,1171, 2:155, 3:250, 4:361

 Tyneside,
10-12 Pilgrim Street, NE1
6QG
XE
Tel: 0191 232 8289
Seats: 1:296, 2:122

Warner Village
New Bridge Street
Tel: 0191 221 0202/0222
Seats: 1:404, 2:398, 3:236, 4:244,
5:290, 6:657, 7:509, 8:398, 9:248

NEWPORT - Isle of Wight
Cineworld Coppins Bridge
Tel: 01983 550800
1:300, 2:96, 3:202, 4:178, 5:152,
6:101, 7:84, 8:132, 9:169, 10:195,
11:263
Seats: 1:900 (11 screens)

Medina Theatre, Mountbatten
Centre, Fairlee Road (P/T)
XE
Tel: 01983 527 020
Seats: 419

NEWTON ABBOT - Devon
Alexandra, Market Street
X
Tel: 01626 65368
Seats: 1:206, 2:127

NORTHAMPTON -
Northants
UGC Cinemas
Sixfields Leisure
Weeden Road, Upton
Tel: 0541 560564
Seats: 1:452, 2:287, 3:287, 4:207,
5:207, 6:147, 7:147, 8:147, 9:147

Forum Cinema, Lings
Forum, Weston Favell
Centre, NN3 4JR (P/T)
Tel: 01604 401006/ 402 833
Seats: 270

NORTH SHIELDS - Tyne
and Wear
UCI Cinemas, Silverlink
Tel: 0870 0102030
Seats: 1:326, 2:156, 3:185, 4:198,
5:410, 6:198, 7:185, 8:156, 9:326

NORTHWICH - Cheshire
Regal, London Road
Tel: 01606 43130
Seats: 1:797, 2:200

NORWICH - Norfolk
ABC, Prince of Wales Road
Tel: 01603 624677/623312
Seats: 1:523, 2:343, 3:186, 4:105

Cinema City,
St Andrew's Street NR2 4AD
X
Tel: 01603 625145/622047
Seats: 230

Odeon, Anglia Square
E
Tel: 0870 505 0007
Seats: 1:442, 2:197, 3:195 X

Ster Century, Castle Mall
Tel: 01603 221 900
Seats: 1: 170, 2: 143, 3:216, 4:324,
5:313, 6:294, 7:331, 8:126

UCI Cinemas, Riverside
Tel: 0870 010 2030
Seats: 1:168, 2:349, 3:123, 4:138,
5:157, 6:269, 7:464, 8:247, 9:157,
10:138, 11:138, 12:156, 13:247,
14:212

NOTTINGHAM - Notts
Broadway,
Nottingham Media Centre
14 Broad Street, NG1 3AL
Tel: 0115 952 6600/952 6611
Seats: 1:379 E, 2:155 XE

Odeon, Angel Row
Tel: 0870 505 0007
Seats: 1:903, 2:557, 3:150, 4:150,
5:113, 6:100

Royal Centre, Theatre Square (P/T)
Tel: 0115 989 5555
Seats: 1,000

Savoy, Derby Road
Tel: 0115 947 2580/941 9123
Seats: 1:386, 2:128, 3:168

Showcase Cinemas
Redfield Way, Lenton
Tel: 0115 986 6766
Seats: 3,307 (13 screens)

NUNEATON - Warwicks
Odeon, Bermuda Park
Tel: 0870 505 0007/0247 635 6256
Seats: 1:475, 2:390, 3:318, 4:318,
5:257, 6:257, 7:212, 8:212

OKEHAMPTON - Devon
Carlton, St James Street
Tel: 01837 52167
Seats: 380

OLDHAM - Lancashire
Roxy, Hollins Road
Tel: 0161 683 4759
Seats: 1:400, 2:300, 3:130

OXFORD - Oxfordshire
ABC, George Street
Tel: 01865 251998
Seats: 1:626, 2:327, 3:140

ABC, Magdalen Street
Tel: 01865 251998
Seats: 864

Phoenix Picture House,
57 Walton Street
X
Tel: 01865 512526/316570
Seats: 1:220, 2:105

Ultimate Picture Palace, Jeune Street
X
Tel: 01865 245288
Seats: 185

OXTED - Surrey
Plaza, Station Road West
X
Tel: 01883 712567
Seats: 442

PADSTOW - Cornwall
Cinedrome, Lanadwell Street
Tel: 01841 532344
Seats: 183

PAIGNTON - Devon
Apollo Cinemas, Esplanade
Tel: 0870 444 3140
Seats: 1:360, 2:184, 3: 184, 4:219,
5:360, 6:77, 7:86, 8:33, 9:97

PENISTONE - South Yorkshire
Paramount, Town Hall
Tel: 01226 762004
Seats: 348

PENRITH - Cheshire
Rhegel Discovery Centre
Tel: 01768 868000
Seats: 258 (large screen format)

PENRITH - Cumbria
Alhambra, Middlegate
Tel: 01768 62400
Seats: 1:170, 2:90

PENZANCE - Cornwall
Savoy, Causeway Head
Tel: 01736 363330
Seats: 1:200, 2:50, 3:50

PETERBOROUGH - Cambridgeshire
Showcase Cinemas
Mallory Road, Boon Gate
X
Tel: 01733 555636
Seats: 3,365 (13 screens)

PICKERING - North Yorkshire
Castle, Burgate
Tel: 01751 472622
Seats: 250

PLYMOUTH - Devon
Arts Centre, Looe Street
X
Tel: 01752 660060
Seats: 73

ABC, Derry's Cross
Tel: 01752 663300/225553
Seats: 1:582, 2:380, 3:115

Warner Village Cinemas
Barbican Leisure Park
Shapters Road, Coxside
Tel: 01752 223435
Seats: 1:175, 2:189, 3:153, 4:196,
5:188, 6:133, 7:292, 8:454, 9:498,
10:257, 11:215, 12:133, 13:127,
14:190, 15:187

PONTEFRACT - West Yorkshire
Crescent, Ropergate
Tel: 01977 703788
Seats: 412

POOLE - Dorset
Arts Centre, Kingland Road (P/T)
X
Tel: 01202 685222
Seats: 143

UCI Tower Park,
Mannings Heath
Tel: 0870 010 2030
Seats: 1:194, 2:188, 3;188, 4:194,
5:276, 6:276, 7:194, 8:188, 9:188,
10:194

PORTSMOUTH - Hants
Odeon, London Road, North End
Tel:0870 505 0007
Seats: 1:631, 2:225, 3:173, 4:259

Rendezvous
Lion Gate Building
University of Portsmouth (S/O)
Tel: 023 92833854
Seats: 90

UCI Port Way, Port Solent, Cosham
X
Tel: 0870 010 2030
Seats: 1:214, 2:264, 3:318, 4:264,
5:257, 6:190

POTTERS BAR - Herts
Wyllyotts Centre,
Darkes Lane (P/T)
X
Tel: 01707 645005
Seats: 345

PRESTON - Lancashire
Guild Hall, Lancaster Road (P/T)
X
Tel: 01772 258858

UCI Riversway
Ashton-on-Ribble
X
Tel: 0870 0102030
Seats: 1:194, 2:188, 3:188, 4:194,
5:276, 6:276, 7:194, 8:188, 9:188,
10:194

Warner, The Capitol Centre,
London Way, Walton-le-Dale
X
Tel: 01772 881100/882525
Seats: 1:180, 2:180, 3:412, 4:236,
5:236, 6:412, 7:192

QUINTON - West Midlands
ABC, Hagley Road West
Tel: 0121 422 2562/2252
Seats: 1:300, 2:236, 3:232, 4:121

RAMSEY - Cambridgeshire
Grand, Great Whyte (P/T)
Tel: 01487 710221
Seats: 173

RAMSGATE - Kent
Granville Premier, Victoria Parade
(P/T)
Tel: 01843 591750
Seats: 1:300, 2:240

READING - Berkshire
Film Theatre, Whiteknights (P/T)
Tel: 0118 986 8497
Seats: 409

The Hexagon, South Street (P/T)
Tel: 0118 960 6060
Seats: 450

Warner Village Cinemas,
Oracle Centre
Tel: 0118 956 0047
Seats: 1:134, 2:146, 3:264, 4:384,
5:212, 6:212, 7:246, 8:158, 9:113,
10:84

REDCAR - Cleveland
Regent, Newcomen Terrace
Tel: 01642 482094
Seats: 350

REDHILL - Surrey
The Harlequin
Warwick Quadrant (P/T)
X
Tel: 01737 765547
Seats: 494

REDRUTH - Cornwall
Regal Film Centre, Fore Street
Tel: 01209 216278
Seats: 1:171, 2:121, 3:600, 4:95

REIGATE - Surrey
Screen, Bancroft Road
Tel: 01737 223200
Seats: 1:139, 2:142

RICKMANSWORTH - Herts
Watersmeet Theatre
High Street (P/T)
Tel: 01923 771542
Seats: 390

ROCHDALE - Greater Manchester
ABC Sandbrook Way
Sandbrook Park
Tel: 01706 719 955
Seats: 1:474, 2:311, 3:311, 4:236,
4:236, 5:236, 6:208, 7:208, 8:165,
9:165

ROCHESTER - Kent
UGC Cinemas, Valley Park,
Chariot Way, Strood
Tel: 0541 560 568
Seats: 1:485, 2:310, 3:310, 4:217,
5:220, 6:199, 7:199, 8:92, 9:142

ROYSTON - Herts
Priory, Priory Lane
Tel: 01763 243133/248527
Seats: 305

RUBERY - West Midlands
UGC Cinemas, Great Park
Tel: 0870 907 0726
Seats: 1:165, 2:187, 3:165, 4:149,
5:288, 6:194, 7:523, 8:247, 9:400
10:149 11:187 12:165, 13:82

RUGBY - Warwicks
Cineworld,
Junction One Retail Park
Seats: 1,600 (9 screens)
(Scheduled to open February 2001)

RUNCORN - Cheshire
Cineworld
Trident Park,
Halton Lea
Tel: 01928 759811
Seats: 1:127, 2:121, 3:94, 4:87,
5:317, 6:283, 7:164. 8:184, 9:214

RYDE - Isle of Wight
Commodore Picturedrome,
Star Street
Tel: 01983 565609
Seats: 1:186, 2:184, 3:180

ST ALBANS - Herts
Alban Arena, Civic Centre (P/T)
XE
Tel: 01727 844488
Seats: 800

ST AUSTELL - Cornwall
Film Centre, Chandos Place
Tel: 01726 73750
Seats: 1:274, 2:134, 3:133, 4:70, 5:70

ST HELENS - Merseyside
Cineworld, Water Street
Seats: 2000 (11 screens)
(Scheduled to open December 2000)

ST HELIER JERSEY- Channel Islands
Odeon, Bath Street
Tel: 0870 505 0007
Seats: 1:412, 2:247, 3:184x, 4:162x

ST IVES - Cornwall
Royal, Royal Square
Tel: 01736 796843
Seats: 1:350, 2:150, 3:63

ST PETER PORT GUERNSEY - Channel Islands
Beau Sejour Centre
Tel: 01481 26964
Seats: 250

ST SAVIOUR JERSEY - Channel Islands
Cine Centre, St Saviour's Road
Tel: 01534 871611
Seats: 1:400, 2:291, 3:85

SALFORD QUAYS - Lancashire
UGC Cinemas
Clippers Quay
Tel: 0161 873 7279
Seats: 1:287, 2:265, 3:249, 4:249,
5:213, 6:213, 7:177, 8:177

SALISBURY - Wiltshire
Odeon, New Canal
Tel: 0870 505 0007
Seats: 1:471, 2:281 X, 3:128 X,
4:111 X, 5:70

SANDWICH - Kent
Empire, Delf Street
Tel: 01304 620480
Seats: 136

SCARBOROUGH - North Yorkshire
Futurist, Forshaw Road (P/T)
X
Tel: 01723 370742
Seats: 2,155

Hollywood Plaza
North Marine Road
Tel: 01723 365119
Seats: 275

Stephen Joseph Theatre,
Westborough (P/T)
XE
Tel: 01723 370541
Seats: 165 (McCarthy Auditorium)

YMCA Theatre, St Thomas Street
(P/T)
Tel: 01723 506750
Seats: 290

SCUNTHORPE - Herts
Majestic, Oswald Road
Tel: 01724 842352
Seats: 1:176, 2:155 X, 3:76 X,
4:55 X, 5:38

Screen, Central Library
Carlton Street, DN15 6TX (P/T)
X
Tel: 01724 860190/860161
Seats: 253

SEVENOAKS - Kent
Stag Theatre Majestic 1 & 2,
London Road
Tel: 01732 450175/451548
Seats: 1:126, 2:108

SHAFTESBURY - Dorset
Arts Centre, Bell Street (P/T)
Tel: 01747 854321
Seats: 160

SHEFFIELD - South Yorkshire

 The Showroom
Media and Exhibition
Centre
Paternoster Row, S1 2BX
X
Tel: 0114 275 7727
Seats: 1:83, 2:110, 3:178, 4:282

Odeon, Arundel Gate
Tel: 0870 505 0007
Seats: 1:253 XE, 2:231 X,
3:250 XE, 4:117 XE, 5:115 XE,
6:131, 7:170, 8:160, 9:161, 10:123

UCI Crystal Peaks 10
Eckington Way, Sothall
X
Tel: 0870 0102030
Seats: 1:202: 2:202, 3:230, 4:226,
5:316, 6:316, 7:226, 8:230, 9:202,
10:202

UGC Cinemas, Broughton Lane
Tel: 0114 242 1237
Seats: 1:143, 2:141, 3:164, 4:262,
5:262, 6:551, 7:691, 8:551, 9:262,
9:262, 10:262, 11:173, 12:193,
13:115, 14:197, 15:197, 16:197,
17:197, 18:93, 19:82, 20:82

Warner Village
Meadowhall Centre
X
Tel: 0114 256 9825
Seats: 1:200, 2:200, 3:97, 4:238,
5:200, 6:365, 7:195, 8:195, 9:73,
10:195, 11:323

SHEPTON MALLET - Somerset

Amusement Centre, Market Place
(P/T)
Tel: 01749 3444688
Seats: 270

SHERINGHAM - Norfolk

Little Theatre
Station Road (S/O)
Tel: 01263 822347
Seats: 198

SHREWSBURY - Shropshire

Cineworld
Old Potts Way
Tel: 01743 340726/240350
Seats: 1: 224, 2:157, 3:226, 4:280,
5:135, 6:100, 7:81, 8:222

The Film Theatre,
The Music Hall,
The Square, SY1 1LH
Tel: 01743 281281
Seats: 100

SIDMOUTH - Devon

Radway, Radway Place X
Tel: 01395 513085
Seats: 272

SITTINGBOURNE - Kent

New Century, High Street
Tel: 01795 423984/426018
Seats: 1:300, 2:110

SKEGNESS - Lincolnshire

Odeon, Butlins Family
Entertainment Resort
Roman Bank
Tel: 0870 505 0007
Seats: 1:120, 2:120

Tower, Lumley Road
Tel: 01754 3938
Seats: 401

SKELMERSDALE - Lancashire

Premiere Film Centre
Tel: 01695 25041
Seats: 1:230, 2:248

SKIPTON - North Yorkshire

Plaza, Sackville Street
X
Tel: 01756 793417
Seats: 320

SLEAFORD - Lincolnshire

Cinema, Southgate
Seats: 60
(Scheduled to re-open early 2001)

SLOUGH - Berkshire

UGC Cinemas,
Queensmere Centre
Tel: 0870 907 0715
Seats: 2,113 (10 screens)

SMETHWICK - West Midlands

Princes, High Street
Tel: 0121 565 5202
Seats: 600

SOLIHULL - West Midlands

UCI 8, Highlands Road, Shirley
X
Tel: 0870 010 2030
Seats: 286 (2 screens), 250 (2 screens),
214 (2 screens), 178 (2 screens)

SOUTH SHIELDS - Tyne and Wear

Customs House, Mill Dam
Tel: 0191 455 6655
Seats: 1:400, 2:160

SOUTH WOODHAM FERRERS - Essex

Flix, Market Street
Tel: 01245 329777
Seats: 1:249, 2:101

SOUTHEND - Essex

Odeon, Victoria Circus
XE
Tel: 0870 505 0007
Seats: 1:200, 2:264, 3:148, 4:224,
5:394, 6:264, 7:264, 8:200

SOUTHAMPTON - Hants

 The Gantry, Off
Blechynden Terrace, SO15
1GW
X
Tel: 023 8022 9319
Seats: 198

Harbour Lights Picture House
Ocean Village SO14 3TL
Tel: 023 8033 5533/8063 5335
Seats: 1:325, 2:144

Mountbatten Theatre
East Park Terrace (P/T)
Tel: 023 80221991
Seats: 515

Northguild Lecture Theatre
Guildhall (P/T)
XE
Tel: 023 80632601
Seats: 118

Odeon, Leisure World
West Quay Road
Tel: 0870 505 0007
Seats: 1:540, 2:495, 3:169, 4:111,
5:112, 6:139, 7:270, 8:318, 9:331,
10:288, 11:502, 12:102, 13:138

UGC Cinemas, Ocean Way
Ocean Village
Tel: 0541 555132
Seats: 1:421, 2:346, 3:346, 4:258,
5:258

SOUTHPORT - Merseyside

Arts Centre, Lord Street (P/T)
X
Tel: 01704 540004/540011
Seats: 400

ABC, Lord Street
X
Tel: 01704 530627
Seats: 1:504, 2:385

SPILSBY - Lincolnshire

Phoenix, Reynard Street
Tel: 01790 753 675
Seats: 264

STAFFORD - Staffordshire
Apollo, Newport Road
Tel: 0870 444 3150
Seats: 1:305, 2:170, 3:164

STAINES - Middlesex
ABC, Clarence Street
Tel: 020 8795 6411
Seats: 1:586, 2:363 X, 3:174 X

STALYBRIDGE - Greater Manchester
Palace, Market Street
Tel: 0161 330 1993
Seats: 414

STANLEY - Co Durham
Civic Hall (P/T)
Tel: 01207 32164
Seats: 632

STAMFORD - Lincolnshire
Arts Centre, St. Mary's Street
Tel: 01780 763203
Seats: 166

STEVENAGE - Herts
Gordon Craig Theatre
Lytton Way (P/T)
Tel: 01438 766 866
Seats: 507

Cineworld
Stevenage Leisure Park
Six Hills Way
Tel: 01438 740944/740310
Seats: 1:357, 2:289, 3:175, 4:148,
5:88, 6:99, 7:137, 8:112, 9:168,
10:135, 11:173, 12:286

STOCKPORT - Greater Manchester
UGC Cinemas, Grand Central
Square, Wellington Road South
XE
Tel: 08701 555 157
Seats: 1: 303, 2:255, 3:243, 4:243,
5:122, 6:116, 7:96, 8:120, 9:84, 10:90

STOCKTON - Cleveland
The Arc
Dovecot Street
Tel: 01642 666600/666606/666669
Seats: 130

Showcase Cinemas, Aintree Oval
Teeside Leisure Park
Tel: 01642 633111
Seats: 3,400 (14 screens)

STOKE-ON-TRENT - Staffordshire
 Film Theatre,
College Road, ST4 2DE
Tel: 01782 411188/413622
Seats: 212

Odeon, Festival Park, Etruria
Road
X
Tel: 0870 505 0007
Seats: 1:201, 2:216, 3:368, 4:162,
5:169, 6:185, 7:564, 8:162, 9:104,
10:75

STOURPORT - Hereford & Worcs
Civic Centre, Civic Hall,
New Street
Tel: 01562 820 505
Seats: 399

STOWMARKET - Suffolk
Regal, Ipswich Street (P/T)
Tel: 01449 612825
Seats: 234

STRATFORD-ON-AVON - Warwicks
Picture House, Windsor Street
X
Tel: 01789 415511
Seats: 1:208, 2:104

STREET - Somerset
 Strode Theatre, Strode
College, Church Road, BA16
0AB (P/T)
XE
Tel: 01458 442846/46529
Seats: 400

SUDBURY - Suffolk
Quay Theatre, Quay Lane
Tel: 01787 374745
Seats: 129

SUNNINGHILL - Berkshire
Novello Theatre, High Street (P/T)
Tel: 01990 20881
Seats: 160

SUTTON COLDFIELD - West Midlands
Odeon, Birmingham Road
Tel: 0870 505 0007
Seats: 1:590, 2:128 X, 3:110 X,
4:330 X

SWANAGE - Dorset
Mowlem, Shore Road
Tel: 01929 422239
Seats: 411

SWINDON - Wiltshire
Arts Centre, Devizes Road,
Old Town (P/T)
E
Tel: 01793 614 837
Seats: 228

Cineworld, Greenbridge Retail &
Leisure Park, Drakes Way
Tel: 01793 484322/420710
Seats: 1:327, 2:282, 3:170, 4:154,
5:94, 6:102, 7:134, 8:105, 9:139,
10:129, 11:137, 12:263

UGC Cinemas, Shaw Ridge
Leisure Park, Whitehill Way
XE
Tel: 0541 555134
Seats: 1:349, 2:349, 3:297, 4:297,
5:272, 6:166, 7:144

Wyvern, Theatre Square (P/T)
Tel: 01793 524481
Seats: 617

SWITCH ISLAND - Merseyside
Odeon, Dunnings Bridge Road,
Netherton
Tel: 0870 505 0007
Seats: 1:373, 2: 230, 3:132, 4:161,
5:245, 6:615, 7:343, 8:230, 9:132,
10:151, 11:245, 12:158

TADLEY - Hants
Cinema Royal, Boundary Road
(P/T)
Tel: 01734 814617

TAMWORTH - Staffordshire
Palace, Lower Gungate (P/T)
Tel: 01827 57100
Seats: 325

UCI, Bolebridge Street
X
Tel: 0870 010 2030
Seats: 203 (8 screens),
327 (2 screens)

TAUNTON - Somerset
Odeon, Heron Gate, Riverside
X
Tel: 0870 505 0007
Seats: 1:125, 2:126, 3:372, 4:258,
5:304

TAVISTOCK - Devon
The Wharf, Canal Street (P/T)
Tel: 01822 611166
Seats: 212

TELFORD - Shropshire
UCI Telford Centre 10,
Forgegate
X
Tel: 0870 010 2030
Seats: 1:194, 2:188, 3:188, 4:194,
5:276, 6:276, 7:194, 8:188, 9:188,
10:194

**TENBURY WELLS -
Hereford & Worcs**
Regal, Sun Street (P/T)
Tel: 01584 810971
Seats: 260

**TEWKESBURY -
Gloucestershire**
Roses Theatre (P/T)
Tel: 01684 295074
Seats: 375

THIRSK - North Yorkshire
Ritz
Tel: 01845 523484
Seats: 238

TIVERTON - Devon
Tivoli, Fore Street
Tel: 01884 252157
Seats: 364

TONBRIDGE - Kent
Angel Centre, Angel Lane (P/T)
Tel: 01732 359588
Seats: 306

TORQUAY - Devon
Central, Abbey Road
Tel: 0870 380001
Seats: 1:304, 2:333

TORRINGTON - Devon
Plough Arts Centre, Fore Street
Tel: 01805 622552/3
Seats: 108

TOTNESS - Devon
Dartington Arts Centre,
Dartington Hall (P/T)
Tel: 01803 863073
Seats: 185

TRURO - Cornwall
Plaza, Lemon Street
Tel: 01872 272 894
Seats: 1:300, 2:198, 3:135, 4:70

TUNBRIDGE WELLS - Kent
ABC, Mount Pleasant
Tel: 01892 541141/523135
Seats: 1:450 X, 2:402, 3:130

Odeon, Knights Way, Pembury
Tel: 0870 505 0007
Seats: 1:439, 2:272, 3;258, 4:221,
5:139, 6:272, 7:258, 8:221, 9:139

UCKFIELD - East Sussex
Picture House, High Street
Tel: 01825 763822/764909
Seats: 1:150, 2:100, 3:100

ULVERSTON - Cumbria
Laurel & Hardy Museum
Upper Brook Street (P/T) (S/O)

Tel: 01229 52292/86614
Seats: 50

Roxy, Brogden Street
Tel: 01229 53797/56211
Seats: 310

**URMSTON - Greater
Manchester**
Curzon, Princess Road
Tel: 0161 748 2929
Seats: 1:400, 2:134

UXBRIDGE - Middlesex
Odeon, High Street
Tel: 0870 505 0007
Seats: 1:236, 2:445

WADEBRIDGE - Cornwall
Regal, The Platt
Tel: 01208 812791
Seats: 1:224, 2:98

**WAKEFIELD - West
Yorkshire**
Cineworld
Westgate Leisure Centre
X
Tel: 01924 332114
Seats: 1:323, 2:215, 3:84, 4:114,
5:183, 6:255, 7:255, 8:183, 9:114,
10:84, 11:215, 12:323

**WALKDEN - Greater
Manchester**
Apollo, Ellesmere Centre,
Bolton Road
Tel: 0161 790 9432
Seats: 1:118, 2:108, 3:86, 4:94

**WALLINGFORD -
Oxfordshire**
Corn Exchange (P/T)
Tel: 01491 825000
Seats: 187

WALSALL - West Midlands
Showcase Cinemas,
Bentley Mill Way, Darlaston
X
Tel: 01922 22123
Seats: 2,870 (12 screens)

**WALTON ON THAMES -
Surrey**
Screen, High Street
Tel: 01932 252825
Seats: 1:200, 2:140

WANTAGE - Oxfordshire
Regent, Newbury Street
Tel: 01235 771 155
Seats: 1:110, 2:87

WAREHAM - Dorset
Rex, West Street
Tel: 01929 552778
Seats: 151

WARRINGTON - Cheshire
UCI 10, Westbrook Centre,
Cromwell Avenue
X
Tel: 08700 102030
Seats: 1:186, 2:180, 3:180, 4:186,
5:276, 6:276, 7:186, 8:180, 9:180,
10:186

**WASHINGTON - Tyne and
Wear**
Fairworld, Victoria Road
Tel: 0191 416 2711
Seats: 1:227, 2:177

WATFORD - Herts
Warner Village,
Woodside Leisure Park
Garston
Tel: 01923 682886/682244
Seats: 1:249, 2:233, 3:264, 4:330,
5:221, 6:208, 7:215, 8:306

**WELLINGBOROUGH -
Northants**
Castle,
Castle Way
Off Commercial Way (P/T)
Tel: 01933 270007
Seats: 500

WELLINGTON - Somerset
Wellesley, Mantle Street
Tel: 01823 666668/666880
Seats: 432

WELLS - Somerset
Film Centre, Princes Road
Tel: 01749 672036/673195
Seats: 1:116, 2:113, 3:82

**WELWYN GARDEN CITY -
Herts**
Campus West,
The Campus, AL8 6BX (P/T)
Tel: 01707 357117/357165
Seats: 300

**WEST BROMWICH - West
Midlands**
Kings, Paradise Street
X
Tel: 0121 553 0192
Seats: 1:450, 2:260

WESTGATE-ON-SEA - Kent
Carlton, St Mildreds Road
Tel: 01843 832019
Seats: Premiere: 297, Century: 56,
Bijou: 32

WESTON-SUPER-MARE - Avon
Odeon, The Centre
Tel: 0870 505 0007
Seats: 1:586, 2:109, 3:126, 4:268

Playhouse, High Street (P/T)
Tel: 01934 23521/31701
Seats: 658

WEST THURROCK - Essex
UCI Lakeside 10
Lakeside Retail Park
X
Tel: 0870 010 2030
Seats: 276 (2 screens), 194
(4 screens), 188 (4 screens)

Warner, Village Cinemas, Lakeside
Shopping Centre
X
Tel: 01708 860 393
Seats: 1:382, 2:184, 3:177, 4:237,
5:498, 6:338, 7:208

WETHERBY - West Yorkshire
Film Theater, Crossley Street
Tel: 01937 580544
Seats: 156

WEYMOUTH - Dorset
Cineworld,
New Bond Street
Tel: 01305 768798
Seats: 1:299, 2:218, 3:265, 4:102,
5:136, 6:187, 7:139, 8:132, 9:148

WHITEHAVEN - Cumbria
Gaiety
Tangier Street
Tel: 01946 693012
Seats: 330

Rosehill Theatre, Moresby (P/T)
X
Tel: 01946 694039/692422
Seats: 208

WHITLEY BAY - Tyne and Wear
Playhouse, Marine Avenue
Tel: 0191 252 3505
Seats: 746

WHITSTABLE - Kent
Imperial Oyster, The Horsebridge,
Horsebridge Road
Tel: 01227 770829
Seats: 144

WIGAN - Greater Manchester
UGC Cinemas,
Robin Park Road, Newtown
X

Tel: 08701 555 157
Seats: 1:554, 2:290, 3:290, 4:207,
5:207, 6:163, 7:163, 8:163, 9:163,
10:207, 11:129

WILMSLOW - Cheshire
Rex, Alderley Road (P/T)
Tel: 01625 522266
Seats: 838

WIMBORNE - Dorset
Tivoli, West Borough (P/T)
Tel: 01202 848014
Seats: 500

WINCANTON - Somerset
Plaza, South Street
Seats: 380

WINCHESTER - Hants
The Screen at Winchester,
Southgate Street
X
Tel: 01962 877007
Seats: 1:214, 2:170

Theatre Royal, Jewry Street (P/T)
Tel: 01962 842122
Seats: 405

WINDSOR - Berkshire
Arts Centre, St Leonards Road (P/T)
Tel: 01753 8593336
Seats: 108

WITNEY - Oxfordshire
Corn Exchange, Market Square
(P/T)
Tel: 01993 703646
Seats: 207

WOKING - Surrey
Ambassador Cinemas
Peacock Centre off Victoria Way
X
Tel: 01483 761144
Seats: 1:434, 2:447, 3:190, 4:236,
5:268, 6:89

WOKINGHAM - Berkshire
Showcase Cinemas, Loddon
Bridge, Reading Road,
Winnersh
X
Tel: 0118 974 7711
Seats: 2,980 (12 screens)

WOLVERHAMPTON - West Midlands
Cineworld, Wednesfield Way
Wednesfield
Tel: 01902 305418
Seats: 1:103, 2:113, 3:151, 4:205,
5:192, 6:343, 7:379, 8:343, 9:184,
10:89, 11:105, 12:162, 13:143, 14:98

Light House, Chubb Buildings,
Fryer Street
XE
Tel: 01902 716055
Seats: 1:242, 2:80

WOODBRIDGE - Suffolk
Riverside Theatre, Quay Street
Tel: 01394 382174/380571
Seats: 280

WOODHALL SPA - Lincolnshire
Kinema in the Woods
Coronation Road
Tel: 01526 352166
Seats: 1:290, 2:90

WORCESTER - Hereford & Worcs
Odeon, Foregate Street
Tel: 0870 505 0007
Seats: 1:306, 2:201, 3:125, 4:99,
5:68, 6:306, 7:131

Warner Village Cinemas
Friar Street
Tel: 01905 617806
Seats: 1,800 (6 screens)
(Scheduled to open Autumn 2000)

WORKINGTON - Cumbria
Rendezvous,
Murray Road
Tel: 01900 602505
Two screens

WORKSOP - Notts
Regal, Carlton Road
Tel: 01909 482896
Seats: 1:326 (P/T) , 2:154

WORTHING - West Sussex
Connaught Theatre, Union Place
(P/T)
Tel: 01903 231799/235333
Seats: 1:512, 2 (Ritz): 220

Dome, Marine Parade
Tel: 01903 200461
Seats: 425

WOTTON UNDER EDGE - Gloucestershire
Town Cinema
Tel: 01453 521666
Seats: 200

YEOVIL - Somerset
ABC, Court Ash Terrace
Tel: 01935 413333/413413
Seats: 1:602, 2:248, 3:246

YORK - North Yorkshire
Picture House
Coney Street

Tel: 01904 541144/612940
Seats: 1:226, 2:142, 3:135

**Film Theatre, City Screen,
Yorkshire Museum, Museum
Gardens, YO1 2DR (P/T)**
X
Tel: 01904 612940
Seats: City Screen 300,
Film Theatre 720

Odeon, Blossom Street
Tel: 0870 505 0007
Seats: 1:832, 2:115 X, 3:115 X

**Warner Village, Clifton Moor
Centre, Stirling Road**
X
Tel: 01904 691147/691094
Seats: 1:128, 2:212, 3:316, 4:441,
5:185, 6:251, 7:251, 8:185, 9:441,
10:316, 11:212, 12:128

SCOTLAND

A number of *bfi*-supported
cinemas in Scotland also
receive substantial central
funding and programming/
management support via
Scottish Screen

ABERDEEN - Grampian
The Belmont, Belmont Street
Tel: 01224 343536/343500
Seats 1:272, 2:146, 3:67

Odeon, Justice Mill Lane
Tel:0870 505 0007
Seats: 1:415, 2:123, 3:123, 4:225,
5:225

**UGC Cinemas, Queens Link,
Leisure Park, Links Road**
Tel: 01224 572228
Seats: 1:160, 2:86, 3:208, 4:290,
5:560, 6:280, 7:208, 8:160, 9:160

ANNAN - Dumfries & Gall
**Londsdale Cinemas, Lady Street
Leisure Centre, Moat Street**
Tel: 01461 202796
Seats: 1:107, 2:57

AVIEMORE - Highlands
Speyside, Aviemore Centre
X
Tel: 01479 810624/810627
Seats: 721

AYR - Strathclyde
Odeon, Burns Statue Square
Tel: 0870 505 0007
Seats: 1:388, 2:168, 3:135, 4:371

BRODICK, ARRAN - Strathclyde
Brodick, Hall Cinema
Tel: 01770 302065/302375
Seats:250

CAMPBELTOWN - Strathclyde
Picture House, Hall Street (P/T)
Tel: 01586 553899
Seats: 265

CASTLE DOUGLAS - Dumfries & Gall
Palace, St Andrews Street (S/O)
Tel: 01556 2141
Seats: 400

CLYDEBANK - Strathclyde
**UCI Clydebank 10, Clyde Regional
Centre, Britannia Way**

Tel: 0870 0102030
Seats: 1:202, 2:202, 3:230, 4:253,
5:390, 6:390, 7:253, 8:230, 9:202,
10:202

COATBRIDGE - Strathclyde
**Showcase Cinemas
Langmuir Road, Bargeddie,
Bailleston**
X
Tel: 01236 434 434
Seats: 3,664 (14 screens)

**Robert Burns Centre Film Theatre,
Mill Road (P/T)**
Tel: 01387 264808
Seats: 67

DUMFRIES - Dumfries & Gall
ABC, Shakespeare Street
Tel: 01387 253578
Seats: 526

**Robert Burns Centre, Mill Road
(P/T)**
Tel: 01387 264808

DUNDEE - Tayside
**Odeon, The Stack Leisure Park
Harefield Road**
X
Tel: 0870 505 0007
Seats: 1:574, 2:210, 3:216, 4:233,
5:192, 6:221

Odeon, Eclipse Leisure Park
Tel: 0870 505 0007
Seats: 2,500 (10 screens)
(Scheduled to open November 2000)

**Dundee Contemporary Arts,
Nethergate**
Tel: 01382 432000
Seats: 1:217, 2:77

**Steps Theatre
Central Library,
The Wellgate
Dundee DD1 1DB**
Tel: 01382 432082
Seats: 250

**UGC Cinemas,
Camperdown Park, Kingsway
West**
Tel: 01382 828793
Seats: 1: 263, 2: 180, 3:109, 4:224,
5:512, 6:224, 7:130, 8:109, 9:79

DUNFERMLINE - Fife
**Odeon, Whimbrel Place, Five
Leisure Park**
Tel: 0870 505 0007
Seats: 1: 268, 2:337, 3:268, 4:210,
5:139, 6:419, 7:268, 8:337, 9:210,
10:139

Robins, East Port
Tel: 01383 623535
Seats: 1:209, 2:156, 3:78

DUNOON - Strathclyde
Studio, John Street
Tel: 01369 704545
Seats: 1:188, 2:70

EAST KILBRIDE - Strathclyde
Arts Centre, Old Coach Road (P/T)
Tel: 01355 261000

UCI, Olympia Shopping Centre
Rothesay Street, Town Centre
Tel: 0870 0102030
Seats: 1:319, 2:206, 3:219, 4:207,
5:207, 6:219, 7:206, 8:206, 9:219

EDINBURGH - Lothian
Cameo, Home Street, Tollcross
X
Tel: 0131 228 4141
Seats: 1:253, 2:75, 3:66

Dominion, Newbattle Terrace,
Morningside
Tel: 0131 447 2660/4771
Seats: 1:586, 2:317, 322:47, 4:67

Filmhouse, 88 Lothian Road
EH3 9BZ
XE
Tel: 0131 228 2688/6382
Seats: 1:280, 2:97, 3:73

ABC, Lothian Road
Tel: 0131 228 1638/229 3030
Seats: 1:868, 2:730 X, 3:318 X

ABC, Westside Plaza,
Wester Hailes Road
Tel: 0131 442 2200
Seats: 1:416, 2:332, 3:332, 4:244,
5:228, 6:213, 7:192, 8:171

The Lumière, Royal Museum
Chambers Street,
Edinburgh EH1 1JF
Tel: 0131 247 4219
Seats: 280

Odeon, Clerk Street
Tel: 0870 505 0007
Seats: 1:675, 2:301 X, 3:203 X,
4:262, 5:173

UCI Kinnaird Park,
Newcraighall Road
Tel: 0870 0102030
Seats: 170 (6 screens), 208
(4 screens), 312 (2 screens)

UGC Cinemas, Fountain Park,
Dundee Street
Tel: 0131 228 8788

Seats: 1: (Iwerks) 298, 2:339, 3: 228,
4:208, 5: 174, 6:159, 7:527, 8:248, 9:
188, 10: 194, 11: 194, 12:177, 13:88

ELGIN - Grampian
Moray Playhouse, High Street
Tel: 01343 542680
Seats: 1:300, 2:250

FALKIRK - Central
ABC, Princess Street
Tel: 01324 631713/623805
Seats: 1:690, 2:140 X, 3:137

Cineworld
Seats: 2,300 (12 screens)
(Scheduled to open February 2001)

FTH Arts Centre, Town Hall,
West Bridge Street
Tel: 01324 506850

FORT WILLIAM - Highlands
Studios 1 and 2, Cameron Square
Tel: 01397 705095
Seats: 1:126, 2:76

GALASHIELS - Borders
Pavilion, Market Street
Tel: 01896 752767
Seats: 1:335, 2:172, 3:147, 4:56

GIRVAN - Strathclyde
Vogue, Dalrymple Street (S/O)
Tel: 01465 2101
Seats: 500

GLASGOW - Strathclyde
ABC, Clarkston Road, Muirend
X
Tel: 0141 637 2641
Seats: 1:482, 2:208, 3:90

Bombay Cinema, Lorne Road
Ibrox
Tel: 0141 419 0722

 Glasgow Film Theatre,
12 Rose Street, G3 6RB
XE
Tel: 0141 332 6535/8128
Seats: 1:404, 2:144

Grosvenor, Ashton Lane,
Hillhead
Tel: 0141 339 4298
Seats: 1:274, 2:252

Odeon, Springfield Quay,
Paisley Road
Tel:0870 505 0007
 X
Seats: 1:428, 2:128, 3:89, 4:201,
5:200, 6:277, 7:321, 8:128, 9:89,
10:194, 11:242, 12:256

Odeon, Renfield Street
X
Tel: 0870 505 0007
Seats: 1:555, 2:152, 3:113, 4:173,
5:196, 6:239, 7:247, 8:257, 9:222

UGC Cinemas, The Forge
Parkhead
XE
Tel: 0141 556 4282
Seats: 1:434, 2:434, 3:322, 4:262,
5:208, 6:144, 7:132

UGC Cinemas, Ranfield Street
Seats: 4,100 (18 screens)
(Scheduled to open January 2001)

GLENROTHES - Fife
Kingsway, Church Street
Tel: 01592 750980
Seats: 1:294, 2:223

GREENOCK - Strathclyde
Waterfront
off Container Way
Tel: 01475 732201
Seats: 1:258, 2:148, 3:106, 4:84

INVERNESS - Highlands
Eden Court Theatre
Bishops Road
Tel: 01463 234234
Seats: 84

La Scala, Strothers Lane
Tel: 01463 233302
Seats: 1:429, 2:250

Warner Village Cinemas
Inverness Business and Retail
Park, Eastfield Way
Tel: 01463 711 175/147
Seats: 1:314, 2:352, 3:160, 4:203,
5:430, 6:203, 7:160

IRVINE - Stathclyde
Magnum, Harbour Street
X
Tel: 01294 278381
Seats: 323

KELSO - Borders
Roxy, Horse Market
Tel: 01573 224609
Seats: 260

KILMARNOCK - Strathclyde
Odeon, Queens Drive
Tel: 0870 505 0007
Seats: 1:308, 2:308, 3: 145, 4:145,
5:185, 6:185, 7:437, 8:201

KIRKCALDY - Fife
Adam Smith Theatre
Bennochy Road, KY1 1ET
(P/T) XE

Tel: 01592 412929
Seats: 475

ABC, High Street
Tel: 01592 260143/201520
Seats: 1:546, 2:285 X, 3:235 X

KIRKWALL - Orkney
Cinema, Pickaquoy Centre
Seats: 240

LARGS - Strathclyde
Vikingar Cinema, Greenock Road
Tel: 01475 689777
Seats: 470

LOCKERBIE - Dumfries & Gall
Rex, Bridge Street (S/O)
Tel: 01576 202547
Seats: 195

MILLPORT - Strathclyde
The Cinema (Town Hall)
Clifton Street (S/O)
Tel: 01475 530741
Seats: 250

MOTHERWELL - Lanarkshire
Civic Theatre, Civic Centre (P/T)
Tel: 01698 66166
Seats: 395

NEWTON STEWART - Dumfries & Gall
Cinema, Victoria Street
Tel: 01671 403 333

OBAN - Strathclyde
Highland Theatre, Highland
Discovery Centre, George Street
(P/T)
Tel: 01631 563794
Seats: 1:277, 2:25

PAISLEY - Strathclyde
Showcase Cinemas,
Phoenix Business Park,
Linwood
Tel: 0141 887 0011
Seats: 3,784 (14 screens)

PERTH - Tayside
Playhouse, Murray Street
Tel: 01738 623126
Seats: 1:606, 2:56, 3:156, 4:144,
5:131, 6:113, 7:110

PETERHEAD - Grampian
Playhouse, Queen Street
Tel: 01779 471052
Seats: 731

PITLOCHRY - Tayside
Regal, Athal Road (S/O)
Tel: 01796 2560
Seats: 400

PORTREE
Aros Cinema, Viewfield Road
Tel: 01478 613750
Seats: 400

ROTHESAY - Isle of Bute
MBC Cinema, Winter Gardens,
Victoria Centre, Victoria Street
Tel: 01700 505462
Seats: 98

ST ANDREWS - Fife
New Picture House, North Street
Tel: 01334 473509
Seats: 1:739, 2:94

STIRLING - Central
Allanpark Cinema, Allanpark
Tel: 01786 474137
Seats: 1:399, 2:289

 MacRobert Arts Centre,
University of Stirling,
FK9 4LA (P/T)
XE
Tel: 01786 461081
Seats: 495

STORNOWAY - Western Isles
Twilights, Seaforth Hotel
James Street (P/T)
Tel: 01851 702740
Seats: 60

WISHAW - Strathclyde
Arrow Cinema
Wishaw Retail Park
Tel: 01698 371 000
Seats: 1:242, 2:82, 3:188, 4:80

WALES

ABERAMAN - Mid Glamorgan
Grand Theatre, Cardiff Road (P/T)
Tel: 01685 872310
Seats: 950

ABERCWMBOI - Mid Glamorgan
Capitol Screen
Tel: 01443 475766
Seats: 280

ABERDARE - Mid Glamorgan
Coliseum, Mount Pleasant Street
(P/T)
X
Tel: 01685 881188
Seats: 621

ABERYSTWYTH - Dyfed
Arts Centre, Penglais, Campus,
University of Wales (P/T)
Tel: 01970 623232
Seats:125

Commodore, Bath Street
Tel: 01970 612421
Seats: 410

BALA - Gwynedd
Neuadd Buddig (P/T)
Tel: 01678 520 800
Seats: 372

BANGOR - Gwynedd
Plaza, High Street
X
Tel: 01248 371080
Seats: 1:310, 2:178

Theatr Gwynedd, Deiniol Road
X
Tel: 01248 351707/351708
Seats: 343

BARRY - South Glamorgan
Theatre Royal, Broad Street
Tel: 01446 735019
Seats: 496

BETHESDA - Gwynedd
Ogwen, High Street (P/T)
Tel: 01286 676335
Seats: 315

BLACKWOOD - Gwent
Miners' Institute, High Street (P/T)
X
Tel: 01495 227206
Seats: 409

BLAENGARW - Mid Glamorgan
Workmen's Hall, Blaengarw Rd (P/T)
X
Tel: 01656 871911
Seats: 250

BRECON - Powys
Coliseum Film Centre
Wheat Street
Tel: 01874 622501
Seats: 1:164, 2:164

BRIDGEND - Mid Glamorgan
Odeon, McArthur Glen Designer Outlet
Tel: 0870 505 0007
Seats: 1:433, 2:329, 3:255, 4:248, 5:222, 6:179, 7:157, 8:165, 9:112

BRYNAMMAN - Dyfed
Public Hall, Station Road
Tel: 01269 823232
Seats: 838

BRYNMAWR - Gwent
Market Hall, Market Square
Tel: 01495 310576
Seats: 320

BUILTH WELLS - Powys
Wyeside Arts Centre, Castle Street
Tel: 01982 552555
Seats: 210

CARDIFF - South Glamorgan
bfi   Chapter, Market Road
        Canton, CF5 1QE
        X
Tel: 029 20304 400
Seats: 1:194, 2:68

Chapter Globe, Albany Road
Tel: 029 20304 400
Seats: 200

Monico, Pantbach Road, Rhiwbina
Tel: 029 20693426
Seats: 1:500, 2:156

Odeon, Capitol Shopping Centre
Station Terrace
Tel: 0870 505 0007
Seats: 1:433, 2:257, 3:220, 4:183, 5:158

St David's Hall, The Hayes (P/T)
Tel: 029 20371236/42611
Seats: 1,600

UCI, Hemingway Road
Atlantic Wharf, Cardiff Bay
Tel: 0870 010 2030
Seats: 1:520, 2:353, 3:351, 4:313,

5:267, 6:267, 7:200, 8:200, 9:153, 10:153, 11:147, 12:147

UGC Cinemas
Seats: 3,085 (16 screens)
(Scheduled to open February 2001)

CARDIGAN - Dyfed
Theatr Mwldan,
Bath House Road (P/T)
X
Tel: 01239 621200
Seats: 210

CARMARTHEN - Dyfed
Lyric
King's Street (P/T)
Tel: 01267 232632
Seats: 740

CROSS HANDS - Dyfed
Public Hall
Tel: 01269 844441
Seats: 300

CWMAMAN - Mid Glamorgan
Public Hall, Alice Place (P/T)
Tel: 01685 876003
Seats: 344

CWMBRAN - Gwent
Scene, The Mall
Tel: 016338 66621
Seats: 1:115, 2:78, 3:130

FERNDALE - Mid Glamorgan
Cinema, Hall, High Street (P/T)
Seats: 190

FISHGUARD - Dyfed
Theatr Gwaun, West Street
Tel: 01348 873421/874051
Seats: 252

HARLECH - Gwynedd
Theatr Ardudwy Coleg Harlech (P/T)
Tel: 01766 780667
Seats: 266

HAVERFORDWEST - Dyfed
Palace, Upper Market Street
Tel: 01437 767675
Seats: 500

HOLYHEAD - Gwynedd
Empire
Stanley Street
Tel: 01407 761458
Seats: 160

LLANDUDNO JUNCTION - Gwynedd
Cineworld

Seats: 1,600 (9 screens)
(Scheduled to open April 2001)

LLANELLI - Dyfed
Entertainment Centre, Station Rd
Tel: 07000 001234
Seats: 1:516, 2:310, 3:122

LLANTWIT MAJOR - Mid Glamorgan
St Donat's Arts Centre
St Donat's Castle
Tel: 01446 799099
Seats: 220

MAESTEG - Mid Glamorgan
Town Hall Cinema, Talbot Street
Tel: 01656 733269
Seats: 170

MERTHYR TYDFIL - Mid Glamorgan
Castle
Tel: 01685 386669
Seats: 1:98, 2:198

MILFORD HAVEN - Dyfed
Torch Theatre, St Peters Road
Tel: 01646 695267
Seats: 297

MOLD - Clwyd
Theatr Clwyd, County Civic Centre, CH7 1YA
X
Tel: 01352 756331/755114
Seats: 1:530, 2:129

MONMOUTH - Gwent
Savoy, Church Street
Tel: 01600 772467
Seats: 450

NANTGARW - Mid Glamorgan
Showcase Cinemas
Tel: 01443 846 908
Seats: 2,604 (12 screens)

NEWPORT - Gwent
UGC Cinemas,
Retail Park
Seven Styles Avenue
Tel: 0541 550516
Seats: 1:199, 2:178, 3:123, 4:187, 5:267, 6:405, 7:458, 8:287, 9:180, 10:123, 11:211, 12:156, 13:77

NEWTOWN - Powys
Regent, Broad Street
Tel: 01686 625917
Seats: 210

PONTARDAWE - West Glamorgan
Arts Centre, Herbert Street
Tel: 01792 863722
Seats: 450

PONTYPOOL - Gwent
Scala, Osborne Road
Tel: 0149 575 6038
Seats: 197

PONTYPRIDD - Mid Glamorgan
Muni Screen, Gelliwastad Rd (P/T)
XE
Tel: 01443 485934
Seats: 400

PORT TALBOT - West Glamorgan
Apollo, Hollywood Park
Aberavon Sea Front
Princess Margaret Way
Tel: 01639 895552
Seats: 1:118, 2:103, 3:258, 4:258, 5:118, 6:118

PORTHCAWL - Mid Glamorgan
Grand Pavilion (S/O) (P/T)
Tel: 01656 786996
Seats: 500

PORTMADOC - Gwynedd
Coliseum, Avenue Road
Tel: 01766 512108
Seats: 582

PRESTATYN - Clwyd
Scala, High Street
Tel: 01745 854365
Seats: 314

PWLLHELI - Gwynedd
Odeon, Butlin's Starcoast World
Tel: 0870 505 0007
Seats: 200

Town Hall Cinema (P/T)
Tel: 01758 613371
Seats: 450

RHYL - Clwyd
Apollo, Children's Village
West Promenade
Tel: 01745 353856
Seats: 1:206, 2:206, 3:117, 4:107, 5:107

SWANSEA - West Glamorgan
Taliesin Arts Centre, University College, Singleton Park, SA2 8PZ
XE
Tel: 01792 296883/295491
Seats: 328

UCI, Quay Parade, Parc Tawe
Tel: 01792 645005
Seats: 1:180, 2:188, 3:188, 4:194, 5:276, 6:276, 7:194, 8:188, 9:188, 10:180

TENBY - Dyfed
Royal Playhouse
White Lion Street
Tel: 01834 844809
Seats: 479

TREORCHY - Mid Glamorgan
Parc and Dare Theatre
Station Road
Tel: 01443 773112
Seats: 794

TYWYN - Gwynedd
The Cinema, Corbett Square
X
Tel: 01654 710260
Seats: 368

WELSHPOOL - Mid Glamorgan
Pola, Berriew Street
Tel: 01938 555715
Seats: 1:150, 2:40

WREXHAM - Clwyd
Odeon Plas Coch Retail Park
Plas Coch Road
Tel: 0870 505 0007
Seats: 1:354, 2:191, 3:148, 4:254, 5:112, 6:112, 7:112

YSTRADGYNLAIS - Mid Glamorgan
Miners' Welfare and Community Hall, Brecon Road (P/T)
X
Tel: 01639 843163
Seats: 345

NORTHERN IRELAND

ANTRIM - Antrim
Cineplex, Fountain Hill
Tel: 028 94 461 111
Seats: 1:312, 2:232, 3:132, 4:112

ARMAGH - Armagh
City Film House
Tel: 028 37 511033
Four screens

BALLYMENA - Antrim
IMC, Larne Link Road
Tel: 028 25 631111
Seats: 1:342, 2:261, 3:160, 4:160, 5:109, 6:112, 7:109

BANBRIDGE - Down
Iveagh, Hanratty Road
Tel: 01820 662423
Seats: 863

BANGOR - Down
Cineplex, Valentine's Road
Castlepark
Tel: 028 91454729
Seats: 1:287, 2:196, 3:164, 4:112

BELFAST - Antrim
Cineworld, Kennedy Centre
Falls Road E
Tel: 028 90 600988
Seats: 1:296, 2:190, 3:178, 4:178, 5:165

IMAX Queen's Quay
Seats: 380
(Scheduled to open late 2000)

Movie House,
Yorkgate Shopping Centre
X
Tel: 028 90 755000
Seats: 1:314, 2:264, 3:248, 4:181, 5:172, 6:97, 7:97, 8:332, 9:72, 10:67, 11:67, 12:83, 13:83, 14:475

Queen's Film Theatre,
25 College Gardens, BT9 6BS
X
Tel: 028 90 244857/667687
Seats: 1:250, 2:150

UGC Cinemas, Dublin Road
Tel: 028 90 245700
Seats: 1:436, 2:354, 3:262 X, 4:264 X, 5:252, 6:272, 7:187 X, 8:187 X, 9:169, 10:118 X

The Strand, Hollywood Road
Tel: 028 90 673500
Seats: 1:250, 2:193, 3:84, 4:98

CARRICKFERGUS - Antrim
Omniplex, Marina, Rogers Quay
Tel: 02893 351111
Seats: 1: 378, 2:232, 3:210, 4:153,
5:117, 6:128

COLERAINE - Londonderry
Jet Centre, Riverside Park
Tel: 01265 58011
Seats: 1:273, 2:193, 3:152, 4:104

COOKSTOWN - Tyrone
Ritz, Burn Road
Tel: 02886 765182
Five screens

DUNGIVEN - Londonderry
St Canice's Hall, Main Street
Seats: 300

ENNISKILLEN - Fermanagh
Ardhowen Theatre,
Dublin Road (P/T)
Tel: 028 66325440
Seats: 295

Omniplex, Factory Road
Tel: 02866 324777
Seats: 1:300, 2:126, 3:104, 4:154,
5:254, 6:165, 7:78

GLENGORMLEY - Antrim
Movie House, Glenville Road
Tel: 028 90 833424
Seats: 1:309, 2:243, 3:117, 4:110,
5:76, 6:51

KILKEEL - Down
Vogue, Newry Road
Tel: 016937 63092
Seats: 295

LARNE - Antrim
Regal, Curran Road
Tel: 028 28 277711
Seats: 1:300, 2:220, 3:120, 4:120

LISBURN - Antrim
Omniplex, Governors Road
Tel: 028 92 663664
Seats: 1:489, 2:219, 3:161, 4:112,
5:176, 6:234, 7:142, 8:112, 9:84,
10:66, 11:66, 12:84, 13:97, 14:148

LONDONDERRY -
Londonderry
Orchard, Orchard Street
Tel: 028 71 267789
Seats: 132, 700 m

Strand, Quayside Centre, Strand
Road
Tel: 028 71373939
Seats: 1:317, 2:256, 3:227, 4:227,
5:134, 6:124, 7:90

LURGAN - Armagh
Centre Point Cinemas
Portadown Road
Tel: 01762 324667
Seats: 1:281, 2:182, 3:142, 4:90

MAGHERA - Londonderry
Movie House, St Lurach's Road
Tel: 028 796 43872/42936
Seats: 1:221, 2:117, 3:95

MAGHERAFELT -
Londonderry
Queen Street
Tel: 028 796 33172
Seats: 1:230, 2:75

NEWRY - Down
Savoy 2, Merchant's Quay
Tel: 028 028 30260000
Seats: 1:197, 2:58

Omniplex, Quays Shopping Centre,
Albert Basin
Tel: 028 30256098
Seats: 1:470, 2:219, 3:168, 4:2003,
5:203, 6:168, 7:219, 8:333, 9:122

NEWTOWNARDS - Down
Movieland, Ards Shopping Centre
Tel: 028 9182 2000/01247 821000
Seats: 1:278, 2:238, 3:155, 4:155,
5:119, 6:119

OMAGH - Tyrone
Studios 1-6, Gillyhooley Road
Tel: 02882 242034
Six screens

PORTRUSH - Antrim
Playhouse, Mainstreet
Tel: 01265 823917
Seats: 1:299, 2:65

COURSES

Listed here is a selection of educational establishments which offer courses in film, television and media studies. (P) indicates where a course is mainly practical. Emphasis on the remaining courses is usually on theoretical study; some of these courses include minor practical components.

A wider range of courses and more detailed information can be found in two indispensable bfi publications, *Media Courses UK 2001* and *Media and Multimedia Short Courses* both edited by Lavinia Orton.

It is worth checking individual college websites for up to date course details.

Barking

Barking College
Dagenham Road
Romford RM7 0XU
Tel: 01708 766841
Fax: 01708 731067
(P) B/TEC National Diploma Media
This two year broad–based media course covers video, radio and sound recording, print and journalism. Facilities include: television studio; portable video; video editing suites; sound recording studio and DTP equipment. There is a practical and vocational emphasis and students are prepared for either a career in the media industries, or for entry to higher education. Applications from mature students are welcome
Access to Media
This one year evening class — two evenings a week – prepares students for Higher Education in Media Studies/Production and includes some practical work

Bath

University of Bath
School of Modern Languages and International Studies
Claverton Down
Bath BA2 7AY
Tel: 01225 826482
Fax: 01225 826099
BA (Hons) European Studies and Modern Languages
First year: Introduction to language, history, and theory of film.
Second year: Options on French, German, Italian, and Russian Film.
Final year: options include French New Wave; surrealist film; Russian and East European film; German and Italian film. Also an option in European Film
MA in European Cinema

Beaconsfield

National Film and Television School
Beaconsfield Studios
Station Road
Beaconsfield
Bucks HP9 1LG
Tel: 01494 671234
Fax: 01494 674042
email: admin@nftsfilm–tv.ac.uk
Website: www.nftsfilm–tv.ac.uk
Full–time professional training leading to an NFTS Associateship; it is expected that the NFTS will offer an MA in most Diploma Courses from January 2001. The 2–year Diploma Course develops creative and technical skills in people with some experience while the one–year, project–based Advanced Programme is designed for those with substantial experience in the media or a related field. Both Diploma and Advanced students train in one of the following specialisations: producing, screenwriting, animation, documentary or fiction direction, screen design, cinematography, editing, sound, screen music and television. In most departments, shortlisted applicants take part in a short course prior to final selection.

In addition, the National Short Course Training Programme runs a continuous programme of short courses for freelancers, while the Finishing School, a joint venture between the NFTS and the Lux Centre, in Shoreditch, offers industry–accredited training in digital post–production. The NFTS is funded by a partnership of Government and the screen industries. Its graduates occupy leading roles in all aspects of film, television and new media

Bedford

De Montfort University Bedford
Polhill Avenue
Bedford MK41 9EA
Tel: 01234 351967
Fax: 01234 217738
Website: www.dmu.ac.uk/Bedford
BA (Hons) English
Screening the Text. A module which examines the transposition of a range of texts, from Shakespeare to the postmodern novel, on to the screen

Belfast

University of Ulster at Belfast
School of Design & Communication
Faculty of Art and Design
York Street
Belfast BT15 1ED
Tel: 01232 328515
Fax: 01232 321048
DipHE/BA (Hons) Visual Communication
Practical and theoretical film/video/media studies available to all students plus a specialist pathway, Screen Based Imaging (SBI) which includes Video production, Animation and Multimedia Design
DipHE/BA (Hons) Combined Studies
Students choose from modules across all courses and many specialise in a combination of Visual/ Communication SBI and Fine Art Video plus media studies theory modules

MA courses in the following specialisations

Animation Direction, Cinematography, Documentary Direction, Editing, Fiction Direction, Producing, Screen Design, Screen Sound, Screen Music and Screenwriting
ALSO: One-year courses in Screenwriting; entry level depends on experience. One year courses do not lead to an MA

PLUS: 1-year project-led Advanced Programme

For further information contact:

National Film and Television School
Beaconsfield Studios
Station Road
Beaconsfield
Bucks HP9 1LG
Tel: 01494 671234 Fax: 01494 674042

e-mail: admin@nftsfilm-tv.ac.uk
website: www.nftsfilm-tv.ac.uk

National Short Course Training Programme
Updating and retraining for industry professionals.
Tel: 01494 677903
Fax: 01494 678708

Professional training and training for professionals

The NFTS operates an equal opportunities policy and positively welcomes applications from all sections of the community.

Birmingham

University of Birmingham
Cultural Studies Department
Faculty of Commerce and Social Science
PO Box 363
Birmingham B15 2TT
Tel: 0121 414 6060
Ann Gray
BA Media, Culture and Society
Full degree or combined half degree, looking at a range of contemporary social and cultural issues, in a cross–disciplinary way.

Bournemouth

The Arts Institute at Bournemouth School of Media
Wallisdown
Poole
Dorset BH12 5HH
Tel: 01202 363281
Fax: 01202 537729
B/TEC National Diploma in Moving Image (Media Production)
Jon Towlson
Tel: 01202 363289
Fax: 01202 537729

Two–year vocational course centred around the disciplines of video and audio production. These practical studies are supported by elements of design studies, drama, music, scriptwriting, animation, Contextual Studies, Business and Professional Studies. The course is recognised by BKSTS
(P) BA Hons Film and Animation Production
Nik Stratton
Tel: 01202 363269
Fax: 01202 537729
The course offers experience of film and video production for either live action or animation and, within this, the opportunity to specialise in either camera editing, producing, directing etc. It also encourages engagement with the history of the moving image of the relationship between contemporary media theory and practice. In 1998 the Arts Institute was awarded the Queen's Anniversary Prize for Higher Education in recognition of its achievements in education for the film and animation industries

Bournemouth University
School of Media Arts and Communication, Poole House,

Talbot Campus, Fern Barrow, Poole
Dorset BH12 5BB
Tel: 01202 595553
email: srose@bournemouth.ac.uk
Website: www.bournemouth.ac.uk
BA (Hons) New Media Production
A three year course covering the academic, practical, aesthetic, technical and professional aspects of work in the media. The course is divided equally between practical and theoretical studies. Students work in audio, video and interactive multimedia leading to a major project in Year 3 produced as an interactive CD Rom. In addition, students complete a piece of individual written research
BA (Hons) Scriptwriting for Film and Television
A comprehensive three year programme, taught by practising scriptwriters, comprising theoretical and practical work specifically designed to meet the needs of new writers in the industry. All graduates will have a thorough knowledge of the industry and a portfolio of work developed to a very high standard. Applications from mature students are encouraged.
(P) BA (Hons) Television and

Video Production
A three year degree course which enables students to work with broadcast–quality equipment to produce video and television programmes. There are supporting courses dealing with media, communication and film theories, professional studies, and the history of cinema and broadcasting

PGDip/MA in Television and Video Production
A one year full–time course for graduates or proven practitioners who seek ultimately to become directors or producers. Using Betacam SP, the course centres on practical productions on location and in the studio, supported by theoretical and professional studies. The MA element is a continuation period of 3–6 months part time study and includes a dissertation on a selected research topic

MA in Music Design for Film and Television
This course centres on composing for film and television. It offers tuition in and experience of the practical and theoretical aspects of combining music with moving pictures. The syllabus includes: Composition; Film Music Analysis; Film Theory; Production Theory; Law of Contract & Copyright; and Technology. Each composer spends the entire year based at his/her dedicated workstation which is designed to produce music at the highest broadcast standard

Bradford

University of Bradford
Department of Electronic Imaging and Media Communications
Richmond Road
Bradford BD7 1DP
Tel: 01274 234011
Fax: 01274 233727
email: p.e.dale@bradford.ac.uk
Website: www.eimc.brad.ac.uk
Paula Dale, Admissions Secretary

BSc Electronic Imaging and Media Communications
A three year, full–time course, developed by a group of staff with various specialities – electronics, art and design, digital music, sociology, photography and television. The breadth of the course is unusual and offers real advantages in preparing students for a career in the media. A Foundation Year is available

BSc Media Technology and Production
In this course high calibre candidates will be able to develop full media products in realistic environments

BSc Interactive Systems and Video Games Design
BSc Computer Animation and Special Effects
BSc Internet Product Design
Three new courses offering Bradford's successful new media background alongside the opportunity to specialise in these areas

Brighton

Brighton Film School
Admin Office
13 Tudor Close
Dean Court Road
Rottingdean, East Sussex BN2 7DF
Tel: 01273 302166
Fax: 01273 302163
email: brightonfilmschool@cwcom.net
Website: www.tbfs.8m.com
Franz von Habsburg MBKS, Senior Lecturer
Meryl von Habsburg MSc BSc Cert Ed, Admissions
The Brighton Film School is a member of the National Association for Higher Education in the Moving Image and fees include one year's student membership of the Moving Image Society (BKSTS)

Director's Foundation Course in Cinematography
This module is offered as a one–term part–time course (2 evenings per week over 13 weeks totalling 80 hours) designed for those who want to explore their own skills and interests in filmmaking. Our aim is to teach the cinematic skills which should be known by the competent director and include Camera, Film Stock, Lighting, Sound, Editing, Film Grammar, Scriptwriting, production skills such as budgeting and stagecraft skills such as makeup. Theoretical tuition by a variety of lecturers in all disciplines of film production followed by practical exercises is combined with film company and studio visits, including Pinewood and RADA, providing a route which may also be available as an Access Course to other establishments offering full–time degree courses

Director's Diploma Course in

Cinematography
This is planned to start soon and will be a one–year part–time course, ie three academic terms, the third being for practical assignments

Director's Full–time Course in Cinematography
These are planned for the future and will be announced when ready. All our courses are designed to meet industry needs and include coursework to assess competence. We are committed to gaining academic recognition and, *inter alia*, accreditation by the BKSTS, to which our students belong

Bristol

University of Bristol
Department of Drama
Cantocks Close
Woodland Road
Bristol BS8 1UP
Tel: 0117 928 9000
Fax: 0117 928 7832
email: mark.sinfield@bristol.ac.uk
Mark Sinfield

(P) BA Drama
Three year course with theatre, film and TV options. Alongside theatre–based Units, critical and theoretical approaches to film and TV are part of the core syllabus in year 1. Additional critical and practical options are offered in years 2 and 3. Practical work is group–based, extends and enriches critical study in a range of forms in fiction and non–fiction, and results in the production of original work. Theoretical work may be developed through individual dissertations as well as a range of seminar courses

(P) MA in Film and Television Production
This one–year course was the first of its kind in a British university and has produced numerous distinguished practitioners working internationally. It offers a broad grounding in practical skills in film and television production, regular consultation with professional practitioners, and a collective forum for the development of critical thinking and creative practice. Based around a core of group–based practical work, the course offers modular options in a range of practical and critical disciplines, leading to group–based production for public festival entry and/or broadcast, and individual

analysis. Production platforms include broadcast–standard video and 16mm film, as well as digital media. The course enjoys widespread support from film and television organisations and leading practitioners

Canterbury

Canterbury Christ Church University College
Dept of Radio, Film and Television
North Holmes Road
Canterbury CT1 1QU
Tel: 01227 767700
Fax: 01227 782914
email: n.burton@cant.ac.uk
Website: www.cant.ac.uk
Nick Burton
(P) BA in Radio, Film and Television Single Honours
Contact: Nick Burton
RFTV single honours is an integrated theory and practice course in these three media, with students having the option to specialise in one or two of them on the practical courses in year two and three. The basic ratio between theory and practice is 50:50, but there is some flexibility to weight the programme in either direction. This well resourced programme introduces students to an understanding and appreciation of radio, film and television as media of communication and creative expression, stressing their relevance to the individual and society, as well as offering an opportunity to develop and practice production skills in 16mm film and digital video and sound. The programme also includes an option in animation. There are strong links with the industry, and the BBC has a studio in the department. The BA/BSc Joint and Combined Honours offers the opportunity to study part of the above programme with fewer options and less practical work, but to combine it with Media and Cultural Studies, Art, American Studies, English, Music, Religious Studies, Science, Mathematics, Business Studies, Tourism, History or Geography
MA Media Production
Contact: Andy Birtwistle
A one year taught MA which concentrates on production in radio, film and television. Part I of the course introduces relevant production skills; in Part II members will fulfil a

measurable major role in a production project. Course members with practical experience can update their skills and concentrate on one medium in Part I. All course members attend theory seminars through the course. Assessment will be based on the major piece of practical work and an extended essay

University of Kent
Rutherford College
Canterbury
Kent CT2 7NX
Tel: 01227 764000
Fax: 01227 827846
BA Combined Hons
A Part 1 course on Narrative Cinema is available to all Humanities students in Year 1. The Part 2 component in Film Studies in Years 2 and 3 can vary from 25 per cent to 75 per cent of a student's programme. Courses include film theory, British cinema, non–narrative cinema, comedy, and sexual difference and cinema. The rest of a student's programme consists of courses from any other humanities subject. No practical component
BA Single Hons
This includes a practical film production option
MA, MPhil and PhD
An MA in Film is also available, which combines courses in film history and archiving, with courses in film criticism and film theory. An MA combining Film and Art History is also available. Students are also accepted for MA, MPhil and PhD by thesis

Cardiff

University of Wales, College of Cardiff
PO Box 908
French Section/German Section,
EUROS
Cardiff CF1 3YQ
Tel: 029 2087 4000
Fax: 029 2087 4946
BA French
Study of Francophone African cinema included as part of optional courses. Small practical component
BA German
Study of contemporary German cinema forms part of optional courses

Chislehurst

Ravensbourne College of Design & Communication
Broadcasting Department
Walden Road, Chislehurst
Kent BR7 5SN
Tel: 020 8289 4900
Fax: 020 8325 8320
email: info@rave.ac.uk
Website: www.rave.ac.uk
(P) Edexcel HND Professional
Broadcasting (Engineering Pathway)
Two year full–time vocational course designed in consultation with the broadcasting industry leading to employment opportunities as technician engineers. Students develop skills in installing, aligning and maintaining a wide range of professional broadcast equipment using analogue and digital technologies
Edexcel HND Professional Broadcasting (Technical Operations pathway)
Two year full–time vocational course designed in consultation with the TV broadcasting industry leading to employment opportunities in television and video production as members of programme making presentation and transmission teams. Students develop skills in budgeting, production management and lighting, camera operation, sound, video recording and editing, vision–mixing, Telecine, and audio–recording
BA (Hons) in Professional Broadcasting
90 week full–time vocational course designed in consultation with the broadcasting industry leading to employment opportunities for creative, team–centred individuals possessing a fundamental competence for working in the production process, business practice and technology of a changing and highly competitive industry
BSc (Hons) Communication and Technology
A two year course which explores the use of communication technology in both broadcast and non–broadcast environments. In doing so, it provides students with 3 main tool kits: technology (broadcast video and computer technology), design (especially for screen) and management (marketing, finance and project management).
(P) BEng Broadcast Engineering

This three year programme is offered in conjunction with the University of Sussex, Ravensbourne's partner institution. Exploring the application of electronic engineering and computing principles to television and broadcast technology, this course maximises the potential for employment

HNC Broadcast Post Production
A one year course which covers editing on both linear and non–linear systems in online and offline environments

Coleraine

University of Ulster at Coleraine
School of Media and Performing Arts, Coleraine
Co Londonderry
Northern Ireland BT52 1SA
Tel: 028 70324196
Fax: 028 70324964
Website: www.ulst.ac.uk
(P) BA (Hons) Media Studies
Three year course integrating theoretical, critical and practical approaches to film, television, photography, radio, the press and new technologies. Important practical component
MA Media Studies
A one–year full–time course designed to provide an opportunity to study the mass media (especially film, television, the press and the new technologies) in an international context. Students will also be provided with opportunities for undertaking media practice (in video, radio, photography and practical journalism). MA is awarded 40 per cent on coursework, 60 per cent on dissertation (which may incorporate a production element)
MPhil and DPhil
Students are accepted for MPhil and DPhil by thesis. Particular expertise is offered in the area of the media and Ireland, although supervision is provided in most areas of Media Studies

Coventry

Coventry University
Coventry School of Art and Design
Priory Street
Coventry CV1 5FB
Tel: 024 7683 8690
Fax: 024 7683 8667

BA (Hons) Communication, Culture and Media
Three year course which includes specialities in Cultural and Media Studies, and in Communication Management, built around a core of studies in communication, culture and media, with a range of other options from which students select. European exchange and work placement programmes are included; also options in journalism, photography and video. Projects enable students to combine theoretical and practical work according to their particular interests
Postgraduate Programme Communication, Culture and Media: MA or PgC/PgD
One full–time, two year part–time. The programme is a modular scheme with core theory and research elements, specialist options, and a selection of electives which include film theory and psychoanalysis, journalism, media policy, television culture and politics. Students may specialise in applied communications, or cultural policy, or media and culture for the MA qualification

Derby

University of Derby
School of Art and Design,
Green Lane,
Derby DE1 1RX
Tel: 01332 622282
Fax: 01332 622296
(P) BA (Hons) Film and Video
Specialist visual arts course designed to help develop film–makiing and video–making skills
BA Film and Television Studies
Theoretical course with no practical component

Doncaster

Nova Camcorder School
11a Winholme
Armthorpe
Doncaster DN3 3AF
Tel: 01302 833422
Fax: 08701 257917
email: ncs@novaonline.co.uk
Website: www.novaonline.co.uk/camcorder
Practical evening course for camcorder beginners
A 10 week course, one night a week

running throughout the year, for people who want to learn how to use their camcorders properly. The course explains all the features and functions of a camcorder before moving onto basic film–making techniques and home editing and titling. The course is specifically designed for beginners, and participants receive a worksheet every week which summarises the topics covered

Dover

South Kent College
DASH
Maison Dieu Road
Dover CT16 1DH
Tel: 01304 204573
Fax: 01304 204573
(P) B/TEC National Diploma Media Studies
Two year full–time course covering video, film, print/DTP, photography and radio. Students complete advertising, drama, news and documentary projects closely linked to community groups. The course is modular and work experience is offered

Edinburgh

Edinburgh College of Art
School of Visual Communication
Lauriston Place
Edinburgh EH3 9DF
Tel: 0131 221 6138
Fax: 0131 221 6100
These courses are strongly based on practical production work and run for three years.
BA (Hons) Visual Communications (Film and Television)
The course runs for three years and most applicants have done either a foundation course in art and design, or a further education course in video/audio–visual. Film/television students will generally combine individual projects with participation in group projects. All kinds of work can be tackled – drama, documentary and experimental. The course includes possibilities of cross–disciplinary projects with other departments in the school – animation, illustration, photography, and graphic design. All students are also encouraged to use the school's computer workshop
Masters Degree
A small number of postgraduates can

be accepted, studying either for a diploma (three terms) or a masters degree (four terms). In both cases there is no formal taught course – the programme is tailored to the practical production proposals of the individual student. Postgraduates must already have appropriate skills and experience to use the resources available. The masters degree is awarded on the strength of the practical work produced

Napier University
Department of Photography, Film and Television
61 Marchmont Road
Edinburgh EH9 1HU
Tel: 0131 466 7321
BA (Hons) Photography, Film and Television
With option of specialising in Film and Television production from the start of the 3rd year. At the end of the 2nd year students take either the still image stream or the moving image stream in this four year course
MPhil/PhD
A 2/3 year research programme with tutorial support facilitating opportunities for advanced study in creative practice in the moving image, including production of a major film or multimedia project

Exeter

University of Exeter
School of English,
Queen's Building,
The Queen's Drive
Exeter EX4 4QH
Tel: 01392 264263
Fax: 01392 264361
Website: www.ex.ac.uk/
BA (Hons) English Studies
Students can take up to a half of their degree in Film Studies, including courses on British Cinema, Hollywood and Europe and an introduction to Key Issues in Film Studies. No practical component.
MA Programme in the History of Cinema and Popular Culture
The core modules in this programme concentrate on key moments in cinema history and the relationship between cinema and 19th Century optical media and popular entertainment. Optical modules cover a variety of theoretical and historical topics including Cult Movies and Postcolonial Cinema.
Mphil and PhD

Applications for postgraduate study in British Cinema, Early and Pre–Cinema History, and Cinema and Cultural Theory will be particularly welcome

Farnborough

Farnborough College of Technology
Media and Visual Arts
Boundary Road, Farnborough
Hants GU14 6SB
Tel: 01252 407270
Fax: 01252 407271
email: A.Harding@Farnct.ac.uk
(P) BSc (Hons) Media Technology (Production)
Fundamental to this degree is practical use and knowledge of technical skills and theories of new media technologies

Farnham

Surrey Institute of Art and Design
Faculty of Arts and Media
Falkner Road, The Hart
Farnham, Surrey GU9 7DS
Tel: 01252 722441
Fax: 01252 732213
(P) BA (Hons) Film and Video
(P) BA (Hons) Animation
The approach in each course is essentially practical, structured to encourage a direct and fundamental appraisal of photography, film, video and animation through practice and by theoretical study. 70 per cent practical, 30 per cent theoretical. Courses are BECTU accredited

Glasgow

Glasgow Caledonian University
Division of Journalism & Media
Cowcaddens Road
Glasgow G4 0BA
Tel: 0141 331 3259
Fax: 0141 331 3264
email: hod@gcal.ac.uk
Website: www.gcal.ac.uk
Dr Hugh O'Donnell, Admissions Tutor
BA Communication and Mass Media
Four year course (unclassified and honours) examining the place of mass communication in contemporary society. Includes practical studies in television,

advertising and public relations

University of Glasgow
Department of Theatre,
Film and Television Studies
University of Glasgow
Glasgow G12 8QQ
Tel: 0141 330 5162
Fax: 0141 330 4142
email: tfts.office@arts.gla.ac.uk
Website: www.arts.gla.ac.uk/tfts/
Ian P. Craven
MA Joint Honours Film and Television Studies
Four year undergraduate course. Film/Television Studies represents 50 per cent of an Honours degree or 30 per cent of a non–Honours degree. Year 1 is concerned with Film and TV as 'languages', and with the institutional, industrial and technological contexts of cinema and television. Year 2 is structured under two headings; Film and Television: Theories and Methods and Film and Television: National and Cultural Identities. Years 3 and 4 consist of a range of Honours optional courses, seven to be taken over two years in addition to a dissertation. There is also a compulsory practical course, involving either the production of a video, a contractual work placement or an applied research project

Hull

The Hull School of Art and Design
University of Lincolnshire & Humberside
Queens Gardens
Kingston–upon–Hull HU1 3DQ
Tel: 01482 440550
Fax: 01482 462101
All courses in The Hull School of Art & Design are 80 per cent practice and 20 per cent theory and are provided with extensive facilities including: SVHS, DV, DAT, Digital, Analogue, 16mm; production and post production including non linear editing; and current professional programmes for Macs and PCs

Kingston–Upon–Thames

Kingston University
School of Three Dimensional Design, Knights Park
Kingston–Upon–Thames

Surrey KT1 2QJ
Tel: 020 8547 2000 ext 4165
School of Art and Design History
Tel: 020 8547 7112
Website: www.kingston.ac.uk
BA/BA (Hons) Combined Studies: History of Art, Architecture and Design
Five to six year part–time or three year full–time. Optional film strand: three Film Studies modules, each representing one sixth of a full–time student's yearly programme, one third of a part–time student's. Foundation level: concepts of 'Art' cinema. Intermediate level: photographic issues. Advanced level; the study of a selected artist
MA Design for Film and Television
One year MA Course in scenic design tailored to the needs of those who wish to enter the industry with the eventual aim of becoming production designers or art directors. The course is constructed as a series of design projects to cover different types of film and television production
School of Languages
Penrhyn Road
Kingston–Upon–Thames
Surrey KT1 2EE
Tel: 020 8547 2000
Fax: 020 8547 7392
BA (Hons) French Full and Half–field, Full and Part–time
Introduction to French Cinema. Year two on French Cinema. Year four special subject on New Wave Cinema

Leeds

Northern School of Film and Television
Leeds Metropolitan University
2 Queen Square
Leeds LS2 8AF
Tel: 0113 283 1900
Fax: 0113 283 1901
email: nsftv@lmu.ac.uk
Website: www.lmu.ac.uk/
This is run by Leeds Metropolitan University, with the support of Yorkshire Television, providing postgraduate level professional training in practical film production
(P) MA/PgD Scriptwriting for Film and TV (Fiction)
An intensive practical course running from February, one year full–time, and one year part–time (off site). Staffed largely by working professional writers, it covers the various forms of fiction scriptwriting for film and television – short film, feature film, television drama, soap opera, series etc.
(P) PgD Film Production (Fiction)
An intensive one year practical course running from October to October. Students are admitted into specialist areas: Direction (six students per year), Production (six), Camera (three), Art–Direction (six), Editing (three) and Sound (three). Students work in teams to produce six short films, in two batches of three. The resulting films may be broadcast on Yorkshire Television, which provide the base production funding and some facilities.
MA Film Production (Fiction)
Part–time course. Normally taken up by students who have completed the Postgraduate Diploma (see above),

Trinity and All Saints College
(A College of the University of Leeds)
Brownberrie Lane, Horsforth
Leeds LS18 5HD
Tel: 0113 283 7100
Fax: 0113 283 7200
email: j.foale@tasc.ac.uk
Website: www.tasc.ac.uk
Diploma/MA in BiMedia or Print Journalism
The course takes the form of a Postgraduate Diploma which, for suitable candidates, can be enhanced to Master's level. The Diploma consists of three taught modules: Basic Journalism, Journalism Skills (Bimedia or Print and Essential Knowledge. The Diploma courses run full–time for 39 weeks and include a minimum attatchment at a news organisation

Leicester

De Montfort University Leicester
School of Arts
The Gateway
Leicester LE1 9BH
Tel: 0116 255 1551 or 0116 257 8391
Fax: 0116 257 7199
Website: www.dmu.ac.uk/leicester
Dr Paul Wells/Tim O'Sullivan
BA (Hons) Media Studies (Single, Joint or Combined Honours Degrees)
As a Single Honours degree, Media Studies offers a range of courses which focus specifically on Film, Television/Video, Photography and Media institutions

University of Leicester
Centre for Mass Communication Research
104 Regent Road
Leicester LE1 7LT
Tel: 0116 252 3863
Fax: 0116 252 3874
email: cmcr@le.ac.uk
Website: www.le.ac.uk/cmcr/
BSc Communications and Society
A three–year social science based undergraduate course. The modules taught cover a wide range of areas including media institutions, research methods in mass communications, film and TV forms and television production. Students are assessed by a combination of continuous assessment and examination
MA Mass Communications
One year taught course studying the organisation and impact of the mass media both nationally and internationally and providing practical training in research methods
MA Mass Communications (by Distance Learning)
Two year part–time course by distance learning. Organized in 10 modules plus dissertation. Course materials include 60 course units, readers, set books, AV materials. Contributions from a team of international experts. The course covers media theories, history, regulation, media in global context, methodology, media industries, professional practices, audiences, texts and issues of representation. Options include media education, film. Day and weekend schools are voluntary but highly recommended

Liverpool

Liverpool John Moores University
School of Media, Critical and Creative Arts
Dean Walters Building
St James Road
Liverpool L1 7BR
Tel: 0151 231 5052
BA (Hons) Media and Cultural Studies
Three year, full–time or four–year, part–time course.
BA (Hons) Screen Studies
Course spans history of film and television

BA (Hons) Media Professional Studies
Brings together theoretical and vocational approaches to the study of television and related media.

University of Liverpool
School of Politics and Communication Studies
Roxby Building
PO Box 147
Liverpool L69 3BX
Tel: 0151 794 2890
Fax: 0151 794 3948
Website: www.liv.ac.uk
BA Combined Hons (Social and Environmental Studies)
BA Joint Hons (English and Communication Studies)
BA Joint Hons (Politics and Communication Studies)
In all these programmes, students combine work in the Communication Studies Department with largely non media–related work in other Departments; Communication Studies forms up to 50 per cent of their programme. Year 1: Communication: a programme of introductory work on communication and cultural analysis. Year 2: courses on Broadcasting, Film Studies and Drama. Year 3: courses available include Documentary, exploring a range of work in literature, photography, film and television. No practical component
MA Cultural Research and Analysis
The purpose of this degree is to introduce students to current work in the area of research on popular cultural institutions, forms and behaviours. Core courses look at the mass media and culture, at culture and national identity, and at city culture and urban life. There is a particular emphasis on research of a broadly ethnographic character, involving students in the field work within the Merseyside area

London

AFECT (Advancement of Film Education Charitable Trust)
4 Stanley Buildings
Pancras Road
London NW1 2TD
Tel: 020 7837 5473
Patron: Mike Leigh
Makes professional–level, practical film education available on a part–time basis to those who may have neither the means nor the time to attend a full–time film course
(P) Practical Part–time 16mm Film–making Course
Two year course integrating learning with production. Bias is traditional narrative; despite limitations of scale, students are enabled to realise personal, artistic, social and cultural expression in this medium. Term 1: Shoot 35mm stills storyboard. Instruction/practicals camera. Interior lit sequence. Editing. Term 2: Script/shoot/edit group mute film with individual sequences, rotating crewing jobs. Term 3: Individual shot–mute three minute films. Term 4: Obtaining and adding sound. Dubbing. Sync–sound intro. Term 5: Individual six minute sync–sound film each. Term 6: Completing these. Year 3: Advanced projects; semi–independent productions

AIU – London
Department of Media Production
110 Marylebone High Street
London W1M 3DB
Tel: 020 7467–5600
Fax: 0171935–8144
Website: www.aiulondon.ac.uk/
(American InterContinental University–formerly the American College in London)
Founded 1970
(P) BA in Media Production
The Bachelor of Fine Arts is a three– to four–year full time degree programme. Students can select classes from the areas of Videography, Audio and Electronic Music, Scriptwriting and Journalism, Photography, Multimedia, Production Management, Animation and Computer Graphics, and Post–production. The curriculum is a balance of theoretical and practical courses and focuses on preparing students for employment within the media industry. There are general education requirements for the degree. Equipment is digitally based utilising DVC–Pro, Sony Mini DV, Final cut Pro, and Avid. Class sizes are kept small and practical work is group based. Courses are designed as a modular format delivered over three to five academic terms per year. Students are expected to produce a major thesis project for public exhibition at the end of their academic career.
(P) AA in Media Production
Associate of Arts degree in Media Production is a two–year full time course in which students take foundation knowledge classes. The curriculum is a balance of theoretical and practical courses and focuses on preparing students for employment within the media industry. Equipment is digitally based utilising DVC–Pro, Sony Mini DV, Final cut Pro, and Avid. Courses are delivered in a modular format over three to five academic terms per year.

Birkbeck College University of London
Department of Media Studies
Centre for Extra–Mural Studies
26 Russell Square
London WC1B 5DQ
Tel: 020 7631 6667/6639
Fax: 020 7631 6683
Extra–Mural Certificate and Diploma in Media Studies
Part–time courses in film, television, journalism and in areas of media practice such as screenwriting, freelance journalism, video, radio, leading to the Certificate/Diploma in Media Studies or in Media Practice.
Contact: Manize Talukdar
BA Humanities
Four year part–time interdisciplinary course, including 4–6 media modules.
Contact: Cathy Moore

Goldsmiths College
University of London
Lewisham Way
London SE14 6NW
Tel: 020 7919 7171
Fax: 020 7919 7509
email: admissions@gold.ac.uk
Website: www.goldsmiths.ac.uk
BA Media and Communications
This course brings together theoretical analyses in social sciences and cultural studies with practical work in creative writing (fiction), electronic graphics and animation, photography, print journalism, radio, script writing or television (video and film) production. The practical element constitutes 50 per cent of the total degree course. The theoretical element includes media history and sociology, textual and cultural studies, anthropology and psychology and media management
BA Anthropology and Communication Studies
Half of this course constitutes Communication Studies. The course is mainly theoretical but does include

The London
International
Film School

- Training film makers for 40 years
- Graduates now working worldwide
- Located in Covent Garden in the heart of London
- 16mm documentary & 35mm studio filming
- Two year Diploma course in film making
- Commences three times a year: January, May, September

London International Film School

Department F23. 24 Shelton Street, London WC2H 9UB
Tel: 020 7836 9642 Fax: 020 7497 3718
e-mail: film.school@lifs.org.uk
web: http://www.lifs.org.uk

two short practical courses of ten weeks in length in two of the practice areas. These include television, videographics and animation, radio, print journalism, photography, creative writing and script writing. The theory component is concerned with media history, sociology, psychology, textual and cultural studies

BA Communication Studies/Sociology

Communication Studies constitutes half this course and is split into theoretical studies and two ten week practical courses. Practical options include television, videographics and animation, radio, print journalism, photography, creative writing and script writing. The theory component is concerned with psychology, media sociology, cultural studies, semiotics and media history

MA Image and Communication (Photography or Electronic Graphics)

One year full–time course combines theory and practice, specialising in either photography or electronic graphics. Practical workshops cover medium and large format cameras, flash, colour printing, lighting, computer and video graphics, design, desktop publishing, animation, animatics, two and three dimensional computer animation. Assessment by coursework, practical production and viva voce

MA Television

(TV Drama or Documentary) One year full–time course specialising in either documentary or drama modes, taught by practical and theoretical sessions. Course covers script writing, programme planning, camera work, studio and location work, interviewing, sound and post production. Assessment is by coursework, practical production and viva voce

MA Media and Communication Studies

This course offers an inter–disciplinary approach as well as the opportunity to specialise in media and communications. The course is based around a series of compulsory courses and options drawing on theoretical frameworks from cultural studies, political economy, sociology, anthropology, and psychology to develop a critical understanding of the role of the media and communications

industries in contemporary culture. Assessment is by coursework, written examinations and dissertation

MA Journalism

The course is essentially a practical introduction to journalism as a multi–media skill with the emphasis on print journalism. In addition, you will take a subsidiary course dealing, in the first term, with the Law and ethical issues and in the second term, with the history and changing structure of the media industry. There is also a course related to wide theoretical issues in the study of media and culture

MA Radio

This one year full time programme combines the acquisition and development of radio production skills with a subsidiary analytical course on the radio industry and a theoretical related to wider issues in media and culture. It provides an opportunity for postgraduates with some knowledge of radio to explore the medium in depth, both in theory and practice.

London College of Printing & Distributive Trades

Media School
Back Hill Road
Clerkenwell
London EC1R 5EN
Tel: 020 7514 6500

MA Screenwriting,
MA Documentary Research
MA Independent Film & Video

These are part–time (1 day a week), two years. Enquiries to the course leaders: Screenwriting – Phil Parker; Documentary Research – Michael Chanan; Independent Film & Video – Liz Wells

London Guildhall University

Sir John Cass Department of Art
133 Whitechapel High Street
London E1 7QA
Tel: 020 7320 3455/3456
Fax: 020 7320 3462
Website: www.lgu.ac.uk

(P) BA (Hons) Communication and Audio–Visual Production Studies (Early Specialisation)

This degree includes both practical and theoretical studies. Practical units include film television and video production, photo–journalism, radio journalism and writing for the media. Theoretical units include cultural history and cultural studies. The degree may be studied full–time or

part–time. Communication Studies may also be studied as half of a joint degree or as a minor component of a degree

London International Film School

Department F17
24 Shelton Street
London WC2H 9HP
Tel: 020 7836 9642
Fax: 020 7497 3718
Website: www.lifs.org.uk

(P) Diploma in Film Making

A two year full–time practical course teaching skills to professional levels. All students work on one or more films each term and are encouraged to interchange unit roles termly to experience different skill areas. Approximately half each term is spent in film making, half in practical instruction, seminars, workshops, tutorials, and script writing. Established for over 40 years, the school is constituted as an independent, non profit–making, educational charity and is a member of NAHEFV and CILECT – respectively the national and international federations of film schools. Graduates include Bill Douglas, Danny Huston, John Irwin, Mike Leigh, Michael Mann and Franc Roddam. The course is accredited by BECTU and widely recognised by local education authorities for grants. New courses commence each January, April and September

London School of Economics and Political Science

Department of Social Psychology
Media and Communications
Houghton Street
London WC2A 2AE
Tel: 020 7955 7710/7714
Fax: 020 7955 7565
Website: www.lse.ac.uk

MSc Media and Communications

One year MSc programme (two years part–time) provides an advanced understanding of the development and forms of media systems (eg text, audience, organisation, effects) in Britain and elsewhere. Students take two core courses, one inter–disciplinary theoretical approaches to media and communications, and one research methodology in media and communications. Additionally, students choose from a range of optional courses reflecting social science approaches to media and communications, and complete an original, supervised, research report on a subject of their choice

The Lux Centre
2–4 Hoxton Square
London N1 6NU
Tel: 020 7684 2787
Fax: 020 7684 2222
email: lux@lux.org.uk
Website: www.lux.org.uk
The training and education programme at the Lux Centre aims to broaden practical and theoretical understanding of film, video and digital art. From talks and events in the Lux Gallery to monthly open submissions screenings in the Lux Cinema, participation in the Lux's exhibition programme is encouraged. Lux Education also offers an extensive short course programme, approaching training both from a creative and technical angle. Courses cover everything from 16mm Film Production (from script to post–production) to multimedia authoring, and a host of specialised areas such as Super 8 editing, AVID editing, optical printing, rostrum animation and studies in film history and theory organised with Birkbeck college

Newham College of Further Education
East Ham Campus
High Street South
London E6 4ER
Tel: 020 8257 4000
Fax: 020 8257 4307
Offers part–time study up to level 4. Video Production, Photography and Digital Imaging

South Bank University
Education, Politics and Social Science
103 Borough Road
London SE1 1AA
Tel: 020 7928 8989
Fax: 020 7815 8273
email: registry@sbu.ac.uk
BSc (Hons) Media and Society
Three year full time course. Two thirds critical studies, one third practical work. This course combines units assessing the social and political significance of the mass media, together with units

introducing practical production skills. Critically, the course grows from studies of the media in the Britain during year one, to studies of European and global media in years two and three. Other units also address the understanding of media audiences, news forms and media law. Individual research leads to the completion of a dissertation thesis in year three. Practically, the course develops skills in audio, radio, video and multimedia production. These skills are then employed by students in the creation of their own final year projects

South Thames College
Department of Design and Media
Wandsworth High Street
London SW18 2PP
Tel: 020 8918 7043
(P) Bsc (Hons) Media and Society
Course run in conjunction with South Bank University. Practical areas include: television, radio, audio, photography, and computer–aided design

Thames Valley University, London
London College of Music and Media
St Mary's Road
Ealing
London W5 5RF
Tel: 020 8231 2304
Fax: 020 8231 2546
email: enquiries@elgar.tvu.ac.uk
Website: www.elgar.tvu.ac.uk
Carla Willis–Smith
BA (Combined Hons) Digital Arts with another subject
A Digital Arts major can be combined with a range of minor pathways including: Advertising, Multimedia Computing; Music; Photography; Sound and Music Recording and Video Production
BTEC Higher National Diploma and BSc in Media Technology
This course enables students to develop creative, technical, analytical and evaluative skills using a broad range of audio and visual media and their associated technology for application within the creative, cultural, leisure and business industries
MA in Film and the Moving Image
This three–year, full or part–time course comprises the study of: Film Theory; Cinemas of Places and Peoples (national and ethnic cinemas)

Genres; and Exhibition and Audiences
(P) MA in Digital Arts
This one–year, full–time or two–year, part–time programme is designed to extend the existing skills of those currently working within the creative and visual industries. (50–75% practical)

University of East London
Department of Cultural Studies
Longbridge Road, Dagenham
Essex RM8 2AS
Tel: 020 8590 7722 x 2741
Fax: 020 8849 3598
Website: www.uel.ac.uk
BA (Hons) Media Studies
Media Studies is offered as a single honours degree or as a major, minor or joint degree in combination with other subjects (eg Cultural Studies; History; Literature and Women's Studies)
Department of Innovation Studies
Maryland House, Manbey Park Road
London E15 1EY
Tel: 020 8590 7722 x 4216
Fax: 020 8849 3677
BSc (Hons) New Technology: Media & Communication
This degree examines the media industries in the context of a study of technological change in society. Covers the social relations of technology, the film, recording, newspaper, television, cable and satellite industries
BA (Hons) Moving Image Design
Using computer technology, the course combines live action video techniques with 3D animation to produce time–based imagery for the broadcast media, advertising and publicity
Faculty of Design Built Environment
Greengate Street
London E14 0BG
Tel: 020 8590 7722
Fax: 020 8849 3694
BA (Hons) Fine Art, Time Based Art
During the first year students can experiment with each of the disciplines that are available but can also specialise in film, video and video animation throughout the three years
School of Art and Design
Greengate House
Greengate Street
London E13 0BG
BA Visual Theories: Film Histories

A specialist pathway within the university's modular structure and the range of options is generally extensive with theoretical work on the history of cinema

University of North London
School of Literary and Media Studies
116–220 Holloway Road
London N7 8DB
Tel: 020 7753 5111
BA (Hons) Humanities
Film Studies may be taken as a major, joint or minor with one of 13 other subjects within BA (Hons) Humanities

University of Surrey
Roehampton
Faculty of Arts and Humanities
Digby Stuart College
Roehampton Lane
London SW15 5PU
Tel: 020 8392 3230
Fax: 020 8392 3289
email: j.ridgman@roehampton.ac.uk
BA Film and Television Studies
A three year modular degree programme, which may be combined with a variety of other subjects. Several core courses are available (Genre and Gender, Issues of Authorship, Hollywood, British Television Drama, French National Cinema etc) to which may be added selected topic modules. The course includes up to 35 per cent practical work in television and video, moving from principles of single camera production in year one to sustained, independent project work in the final year

University of Westminster
School of Communication and Creative Industries
Harrow Campus, Watford Road
Northwick Park HA1 3TP
Tel: 020 7911 5944
Fax: 020 7911 5943
email: cdm@wmin.ac.uk
Website: www.wmin.ac.uk/media
BA (Hons) Film and Television
A modular degree course for young and mature students interested in film–making (fiction, documentary and experimental), television drama and documentary, screenwriting and film and television theory and criticism. The course emphasises creative collaboration and encourages some specialisation. It aims to equip students with understanding and

competence in relevant critical ideas and the ability to work confidently and professionally in film and allied media using traditional and new technologies
BA (Hons) Media Studies
This degree studies the social context in which the institutions of mass communications operate, including film and television, and teaches the practice of print and broadcasting journalism and video production. On levels 2 and 3 students choose one of the following pathways: radio, journalism or video production. The course gives equal emphasis to theory/criticism and practice. The video pathway is accredited by BECTU
MA PgD Film and Television Studies
Advanced level part–time course taught in Central London (evenings and study weekends) concerned with theoretical aspects of film and television. Modular credit and accumulation scheme, with exemption for work previously done. The MA is normally awarded after three years' study (120 credits). A Postgraduate Certificate can be awarded after one year (45 credits) or a Diploma after two years (75 credits)
(P) BA (Hons) Contemporary Media Practice
A modular three year full–time course offering an integrated approach to photography, film, video and digital–imaging. Students are encouraged to use a range of photographic and electronic media and theoretical studies are considered crucial to the development of ideas. In Years 1 and 2, the taught programme covers basic and applied skills on a project basis; these are complemented by a range of options. In Year 3 students are given the opportunity to develop their own programme of study, resulting in the production of major projects in practice and dissertations

Wimbledon School of Art
Merton Hall Road
London SW19 3QA
Tel: 020 8540 0231
Fax: 020 8543 1750
(P) BA (Hons) Technical Arts: Design
Training of set designers for theatre, film and television

Maidstone

Kent Institute of Art and Design
School of Visual Communication
Maidstone College
Oakwood Park
Maidstone, Kent ME16 8AG
Tel: 01622 757286
Fax: 01622 692003
email: kiadmarketing@kiad.ac.uk
BA (Hons) Visual Communication Time Based Media
Explores all aspects of the moving image, including video, film, sound and animation. The emphasis is on personal authored work, mainly in video, but traditional production roles and values are also taught. The pathway encourages creative and investigative video production, and is a pioneer of the 'multi–skilled' approach used today in all aspects of professional and independent TV and Video production
Master of Arts in Visual Communication
This Master of Arts Programme has been developed for designers, illustrators, photographers, film/video makers, and theorists who wish to develop their practices either as a single discipline or combination of disciplines within an ethos of interdisciplinarity. Each application to the programme is determined by an individually proposed MA Project defined within the speculative framework of the programme. All graduates in Visual Communication are part of one programme but develop their Master of Arts projects within a negotiated study plan drawn from the School's principal study areas.
Time Based Media with Electronic Imaging
Time Based Media with Electronic Imaging (TBN) includes video/film production, conventional and digital animation, multi–media and sound.
Visual Theory
This aspect of the programme provides an introduction to a range of theoretical frameworks for understanding the role of visual media in contemporary society. For further information contact the Registrar on: 01622 757286 or Fax: 01622 692003
MPhil and PHd Study
Applicants for MPhil/PhD must demonstrate an understanding of research methodologies. These are

taught as part of MPhil study. Students wishing to register for PhD will normally be required to register for MPhil in the first instance. Conversion to PhD is dependent upon completion of MPhil requirements (two years) and evidence of sufficient aptitude and ability to sustain the research project through to the Doctoral award. The areas of expertise that the Institute is initially providing for research degree activity includes Electronic and Time–Based Media. For further information contact the Registrar on: 01622 757286 or Fax: 01622 692003

Manchester

The City College Manchester,
Arden Centre
Manchester M23 0DD
Tel: 0161 957 1749
Fax: 0161 935 3854
email: smarland@ccm.ac.uk
Website: www.manchester–city–coll. ac.uk
Steve Marland
B/TEC National Diploma Multimedia
Multi–disciplinary course bringing together video, photography, digital imaging and and design. Teaching practical production skills in analogue and new media, based on practical projects integrating theoretical studies

Manchester Metropolitan University
Department of Communication Media, Chatham Building
Cavendish Street
Manchester M15 6BR
Tel: 0161 247 1284
Fax: 0161 247 6393
(P) BA (Hons) Television Production
A three year, full–time course based around practical projects. Typically, these include dramas, documentaries, corporate productions and magazine programmes. Students work mainly in groups and are encouraged to experience different production roles. Emphasis is placed on development of original programme material through individually based research and scripting. Equipment includes a four–camera TV studio and non–linear editing. Complimentary studies include media history,

narrative studies and semiology. Subject to validation

University of Manchester
Department of Drama
Oxford Road, Manchester M13 9PL
Tel: 0161 275 3347
Fax: 0161 275 3349
Website: www.man.ac.uk
BA Single and Joint Honours Drama and BA in Drama and Screen Studies
Two film studies courses on Hollywood and European cinema compulsory in Year 1 and 2, with additional film studies and video production courses optional in Years 2 and 3.
MPhil/PhD
Opportunity for research theses on aspects of film and television and documentary

Middlesex

Brunel University
Department of Human Sciences
Uxbridge
Middx UB8 3PH
Tel: 01895 274000
Fax: 01895 232806
Ian Hurchby
BSc Media and Communications Studies
Four year interdisciplinary course which aims to give an understanding of the social, intellectual and practical dimensions of the communications media, with particular reference to the new information technologies
MA Communications and Technology
This course offers detailed study of the new communications and information technologies

Middlesex University
Faculty of Art, Design & Performing Arts
Cat Hill, Barnet
Herts EN4 8HT
Tel: 020 8362 5000
Fax: 020 8440 9541
email: admissions@mdx.ac.uk
Website: www.mdx.ac.uk
BA (Hons) Visual Culture
Modular system degree. Film studies develops from a first level in Art and Design History. Critical and theoretical approaches to film are covered, including production, distribution and reception. The set

allows detailed studies of different genres and modes of production in filmmaking, and raises issues of gender, nationality, representation and narrative
BA (Hons) Media and Cultural Studies
Students look at media as complex institutions involving its financial structures and also the subjective character of its consumers
(P) MA Video
A one year full–time course (45 wks) emphasising the creative aspects of professional video production in the independent sector. Intended for graduate students with considerable lo–band video experience. The course covers all aspects of the production cycle, with an emphasis on scriptwriting. 50 per cent practical; 50 per cent theoretical

Newcastle upon Tyne

University of Newcastle upon Tyne
Centre for Research into Film
Newcastle upon Tyne NE1 7RU
Tel: 0191 222 7492
Fax: 0191 222 5442
email: p.p.powrie@ncl.ac.uk
Website: www.ncl.ac.uk/ncrif
Diploma/MA in Film Studies
One year full–time; two year part–time course. Obligatory research training and introduction to the study of film, followed by 4 from 19 day–time and evening options, although not all are taught in every year: 6 on Hollywood cinema (the Biblical Epic; Lubitsch; romantic comedy; film noir; the Western; gender in the action film); 3 on British Cinema (pre–50s; post–60s; class and sex); on French cinema (New Wave; cinema and conflict since 1968; the contemporary nostalgia film & postmodern cinema (1960–1979; 1980–present) 2 on Spanish Cinema (60s–70s; 80s–90s); 4 on Media and Industry (Broadcasting in France; TV Comedy; Programming and Marketing; Financial Structures). Dissertation required for the MA
MLitt in Film Studies
Research–based course tailor–made for individual students. Three/four essays followed by a dissertation on negotiated topic in British, French, Hollywood, or Spanish cinemas.

PhD in Film Studies
Supervision offered in British, French, Hollywood, and Spanish cinemas. for current and suggested postgraduate projects
Department of Modern Languages
Newcastle upon Tyne NE1 7RU
Tel: 0191 222 7441
Fax: 0191 222 5442
Keith Reader
BA (Hons) French, French/Spanish, French/German
Optional modules in film studies.
Stage 1: introduction to the study of film. Stage 2: introduction to film theory. Stage 3: French Cinema in the 1980s

University of Northumbria at Newcastle
Faculty of Art & Design
Squires Building
Sandyford Road
Newcastle upon Tyne NE1 8ST
Tel: 0191 227 4935
Fax: 0191 227 3632
Website: www.unn.ac.uk
(P) BA (Hons) Media Production
Practical three year course with fully integrated theoretical and critical components in which students are

offered the opportunity to specialise in individual programmes of work.
BA (Hons) History of Modern Art, Design and Film
Offered as a three year full–time course. Film Studies is given equal weighting with painting and design in the first year. In the second year up to 60 per cent of a student's time can be devoted to Film Studies, with this rising to nearly 100 per cent in the third year
MPhil
There are possibilities for research degrees in either film theory or practice

Newport

University of Wales College, Newport
University Information Centre
Caerleon Campus
PO Box 101
Newport NP6 1YH
Tel: 01633 432432
Fax: 01633 432850
email: uic@newport.ac.uk
Website: www.newport.ac.uk
BA (Hons) Film and Video
The course is intended for students

wishing to explore the moving image in the broadest possible sense as an expressive and dynamic medium. It provides them with a programme of work designed to support and stimulate their personal development as creative and aware practitioners of film, regardless of their ultimate ambition. The practice of film is studied in a wider culture and intellectual context and students are encouraged to be analytical and critical. Their study acknowledges existing conventions in dominant cinema but seeks to extend them through experimentation and exploration
(P) BA (Hons) Animation
Intended for students wishing to use animation as part of a wider personal practice, as well as becoming professional animators working in independent production, advertising and design. The course is designed to develop students imaginations and ideas to explore and extend their animation technique. Therefore it is presented in a cultural context which promotes critical debate and rigorous analysis in terms of representation and expression. In Year 3 students

develop their own programme for the production of major pieces of animation on high quality production equipment to broadcast standards

BA (Hons) Media and Visual Culture

At a time when our culture seems dominated as never before by the presence of media systems and images, this stimulating programme critically examines issues relating to media and visual culture. Specialist courses in the theory and history of film, photography design and contemporary art complement the central study of media culture. Practical options in subjects such as film, photography and new media can be selected, leading to major work involving practice in the final year

(P) MA Film

This practical MA programme will offer an opportunity to: complete a short broadcast standard film explore and challenge the notions of the cinematic subject and language explore developing forms and changing technologies. The course will include: teaching through group and individual tutorials close links with the film and television industry and media agencies in Wales visiting masterclasses and facilities made available in professional production houses. The discursive and practical work on a short film wil be in one of the following areas; Fiction, Faction, Animation, Non–genre/experimental. Acceptance of the course will be based on interview including: the submission of a treatment of a proposed film to be made during the course, the screening of a previous film, some fees/production bursaries could be available

Norwich

University of East Anglia
School of English and American Studies
Norwich NR4 7TJ
Tel: 01603 456161
Undergraduate: Yvonne Tasker
01603 592283
Postgraduate: Lorraine Faith
01603 3262

BA (Hons) Film and English Studies

A Joint Major programme which integrates Film and Television history and theory with work on English literature, history and cultural

studies; the film work deals mainly with Hollywood, but also with British cinema. Course includes instruction in film and video production, and the option of submitting a practical project. All students submit an independent dissertation on a film or television topic

BA (Hons) Film and American Studies

A four year Joint Major programme which integrates Film and Television history and theory with work on American literature, history, cultural studies and politics. Course includes instruction in film and video production, and the option of submitting a practical project. All students spend a year at a University in the USA, and submit an independent dissertation on a film or television topic

BA (Hons) Modular System

Students admitted to the University to major in other subjects including Literature, Drama, American Studies etc have the option of taking one or more units in film and television study: together, these may comprise up to one third of the degree work. No practical element

MA Film Studies

One year full–time taught programme. MA is awarded 50 per cent on coursework and 50 per cent on dissertation. Within the School's modular system, it is possible to replace one or two of the four film seminars with others chosen from a range of topics in literary theory, creative writing, American studies and cultural studies. The film seminars deal with early cinema, British film history, film and narrative theory, screen costume and theories of the image, and research resources and methodology. Dissertation topics are freely chosen and may deal with television as well as cinema

MA Film Studies: Film Archive option

One year full–time taught programme, run in conjunction with the East Anglian Film Archive (located in the University). Students take two of the MA film seminars, plus two more that deal with the practical and administrative aspects of film archive work. Course includes visits to other archives, and a one–month placement at a chosen archive in Britain or overseas.

Assessment is based on two essays, a video production, a placement report, and an independent dissertation (counting 50 per cent)

MPhil and PhD

Students are accepted for research degrees. Areas of special expertise include early cinema, British film history, television history, gender and cinema, classical and contemporary Hollywood, and gender and authorship

Plymouth

Plymouth College of Art and Design
School of Media and Photography
Tavistock Place
Plymouth
Devon PL4 8AT
Tel: 01752 203434
Fax: 01752 203444

(P) B/TEC HND Media Production

(in partnership with the University of Plymouth). A two year modular course with pathways in film, video, animation and electronic imaging. All areas of film,video and television production are covered and the course is well supported by visiting lecturers and workshops. Strong links with the industry have been developed and work based experience forms an important part of the course. The course has BKSTS accreditation. Opportunities exist through the ERASMUS programme to undertake a programme of exchange with European universities or polytechnics during the course. In addition suitably qualified students can progress to third level modules for the award of a BA (Hons) PhotoMedia

Advanced Diploma Photography, Film and Television leading to the BIPP Professional Qualifying Exam

A one year course post HND and postgraduate. The photography, film and television option allows students to plan their own line of study, including practical work, dissertation and an extended period of work based experience. Students from both courses have had considerable success in film and video scholarships and competitions. Students on both courses have the opportunity for three month work placements in the media industry in

Europe
NCFE Foundation in Lens Based Media
A one year full time foundation course for those wishing to progress to Higher Education in one of the many exciting areas of lens based media. This practical course covers: photography, video, electronic imaging, multi–imaging and contextual studies. The course aims to help the student develop a portfolio which shows how the student has integrated technical skills with creative concepts and critical analysis. (This course may also be studied part time over two academic years)
National Diploma Programmes
ND Photography; ND MultiMedia, ND Media Studies

Portsmouth

University of Portsmouth
Department of Design
Lion Gate Building, Lion Terrace
Portsmouth PO1 3HF
Tel: 023 9287 43805
Fax: 023 9284 43808
email: lingardm@env2.enf.port.ac.uk
Website: www.port.ac.uk
BA (Hons) Art, Design and Media
Three year unitised programme has six specialist pathways. All are structured around historical, cultural and theoretical analysis which form an important part of the degree. Student placements in Europe and the UK and outside projects maintain the degree's links with industry and art practice
Media Arts – Moving Image Strand
In the first and second years, students undertake briefs around personal and cultural identity, gender, media arts practice, documentary as intervention etc. Students work in video, sound, multimedia and photography. In the third year students work on self–directed projects
Media Arts – Photography Strand
Encourages collaborative work with moving image and sound artists
Communication Design
Design for television, video graphics

and multimedia are central areas of concern
History and Cultural Theory
Aim to produce graduates with particular skills in research and communication
School of Social and Historical Studies, Milldam
Burnaby Road
Portsmouth PO1 3AS
Tel: 01705 876543
Fax: 01705 842174
BA (Hons) Cultural Studies
Year 3: options on British Cinema 1933–70, British television Drama, Avant–Garde Films and Feminism

Reading

University of Reading
Department of Film and Drama
Bulmershe Court
Woodlands Ave
Reading RG6 IHY
Tel: 0118 931 8878
Fax: 0118 931 8873
Website: www.reading.ac.uk
BA Film and Drama (Single Subject)
After the first two terms in which three subjects are studied (two being in film and drama), students work wholly in film and drama. The course is critical but with significant practical elements which are designed to extend critical understanding. It does not provide professional training
BA Film and Drama with English, German, Italian
Students in general share the same teaching as Single Subject students
MA Film and Drama
One year taught course, incorporating study of both film and drama, practical assignments and research methodologies
MPhil and PhD
Research applications for MPhil and PhD degrees are also invited in areas of cinema, television and twentieth century theatre
Department of English
Whiteknights
Reading RG6 6AA
Tel: 0118 931 8361
Fax: 0118 931 6561
BA (Hons) English
Second year optional course on film, television and literature. Third year optional course in media semiotics PhD Research can be supervised on the history of the BBC and other mass media topics

Department of French Studies
Whiteknights
Reading RG6 6AA
Fax: 0118 931 8122
BA (Hons) French
First year introductory course: detailed study of one film (one half–term). Final year: Two–term option: French cinema, with special emphasis on the 30s, 40s and the Nouvelle Vague. Includes introductory work on the principle of film study. Available also to students combining French with certain other subjects
Department of German Studies, University of Reading
Whiteknights
Reading RG6 6AA
Tel: 0118 931 8332
Fax: 0118 931 8333
email: j.e.sandford@reading.ac.uk
Website: www.rdg.ac.uk/german
Prof J. Sandford
BA (Hons) German
Two–term Finals option: The German Cinema. Course covers German cinema from the 1920s to the present, with special emphasis on the Weimar Republic, the Third Reich, and the 'New German Cinema'.
Department of Italian Studies
Whiteknights
Reading RG6 2AA
BA (Hons) Italian/French and Italian with Film Studies
First year introductory course: Post–War Italian Cinema (one half–term). Second year course: Italian Cinema (three terms). Final year course: Italian Cinema in its European and American context (two terms). Dissertation on an aspect of Italian cinema. These courses available to students reading other subjects in the Faculty.
MA Italian Cinema
One year full–time or two year part–time course on Italian cinema: compulsory theory course, options on film and literature, Bertolucci, Italian industry and genre – the Spaghetti Western.
MPhil and PhD
Research can be supervised on Italian cinema for degree by thesis

Salford

University of Salford
School of Media, Music and Performance
Adelphi, Peru Street
Salford, Manchester M3 6EQ

Tel: 0161 295 6026
Fax: 0161 295 6023
International Media Centre
Director and Head of School: Ron Cook
Adelphi House, The Crescent
Salford, Manchester M3 6EN
BA (Hons) Television and Radio
BA (Hons) Media and Performance
BA (Hons) Media, Language and Business
BSc (Hons) Media Technology
MA Television Feature and Documentary Production
MA Scriptwriting for Television and Radio (part–time)
Plus – degree courses in **Band Musicianship; Popular Music & Recording; Music, Acoustics & Recording; Composition; Performance**
Visiting Professor: David Plowright. Fellows: Richard Ellis, Ray Fitzwalter. Professional Patrons: Ken Russell, Ben Kingsley, Liz Forgan, Robert Powell, Gareth Morgan, Sir George Martin CBE, Jack Rosenthal CBE, Stuart Prebble, Leslie Woodhead OBE, Gillian Lynne. All courses are 50 per cent practical production/performance based. The Granada Education Awards are available to ethnic students. MA Documentary is supported by Channel 4, Avid Technology and Granada TV

Sheffield

Northern Media School
The Workstation
15 Paternoster Row
Sheffield S1 2BX
Tel: 0114 272 0994
Fax: 0114 275 6816
(P) PgDip Broadcast Journalism
Main focus is on practical work. Much of the teaching is conducted through workshops and practical exercises supplemented by seminars and lectures
(P) PgDip and MA in Screenwriting (Fiction)
Intensive practical course covering fiction scriptwriting for film and television
School of Cultural Studies
Psalter Lane
Sheffield S11 8UZ
Tel: 0114 253 2601/272 0911
Film and Media Studies Programme
BA (Hons) Film Studies
BA (Hons) Media Studies

The Film and Media Studies Programme consists of two degree routes. The courses provide opportunities for the study of film and a range of media (including television, radio and journalism from a variety of perspectives including historical development, social, political and economic contexts, and the artistic and aesthetic dimensions of film and media. The courses also provide a grounding in basic media production skills with units in film, video etc and scriptwriting
(P) BA (Hons) History of Art, Design and Film
Film studies is a major component of this course. Year 1: introduction to film analysis and history. Year 2: special study on Hollywood. Year 3: critical and theoretical studies in Art, Design and Film and Contemporary Film Theory and Practice
MA Film Studies
Two year part–time course; two evenings per week, plus dissertation to be written over two terms in a third year. Main areas of study: Problems of Method; The Classical Narrative Tradition; British Cinema 1927–45; Hollywood and Popular culture
BA (Hons) Fine Art (Combined and Media Arts)
After initial work with a range of media, students can specialise in film and/or video. Film productions range from short 8mm films to 16mm documentaries or widescreen features, to small 35mm productions

Sheffield Hallam University
Communications Subject Group
School of Cultural Studies
36 Collegiate Crescent
Sheffield S10 2BP
Tel: 0114 255 5555
Fax: 0114 253 2344
Website: www.shu.ac.uk
BA (Hons) Communication Studies
Course covers all aspects of human communication, one area being Mass Communication. Option course in Television Fictions in Year 3. Some practical work
MA/PgD/Certificate Communication Studies
Part–time course to gain certificate in three terms, Diploma in six terms, MA in 8 terms. Aims to develop theoretical understandings and analytical skills in relation to the processes and practices of

communication in modern society. Students attend for two sessions of 2+ hours each week. Full–time/route 12 months. 8 hours per week

University of Sheffield
Department of English Literature
Shearwood Mount
Shearwood Road
Sheffield S10 2TD
Tel: 0114 222 8480
Fax: 0114 282 8481
BA (Hons) English Literature
Students may study several Special Subjects in Film in their second and third years, and may take a Hollywood course in the first year

Southampton

University of Southampton
Research and Graduate School of Education
Faculty of Educational Studies
Southampton
Hants SO9 5NH
Tel: 01703 593387
Fax: 01703 593556
Website: www.soton.ac.uk
Certificate and Diploma Advanced Educational Studies – Media Education
Certificate is one year course involving 60 hours of contact time; the Diploma is taken over two years, with 120 hours of contact time. Both include a range of media courses. The Certificate is also available as a distance learning package, involving 240 hours of independent study
MA (Ed)
The MA in Education is run on a modular basis as a full– or part–time taught course. The course as a whole requires the completion of 12 x 15–hour units and a supervised dissertation. Included are Television, Media Education, Training
MPhil and PhD
Research degrees in any area of Media Education, Media Studies, Educational Broadcasting and Educational Technology are available
School of Research & Graduate Studies, Highfield
Southampton
Hants SO17 1BJ
Tel: 023 80 593406/592248
Fax: 023 80 593288/595437
email: srgs@soton.ac.uk
Website: www.soton.ac.uk/~srgs
Pam Cook, MA Coordinatior
MA Film Studies

The course aims to equip students with the capacity to engage intellectually with significant developments in film theory and history, together with the skills required to undertake contextual and textual analysis of films and critical writing. The weight given to European cinemas, including British cinema, and to transnational perspectives, is a unique feature, and Hollywood and American independent cinema represent core elements. Tutors include Tim Bergfelder, Caroline Blinder, Pam Cook, Deniz Göktürk, Sylvie Lindeperg, Bill Marshall, Lucy Mazdon, David Vilaseca and Linda Ruth Williams
Southampton University
New College
School of Culture and Language
The Avenue
Southampton SO17 1BG
Tel: 01703 597317
Fax: 01703 230944
BA (Hons) Humanities, Humanities (English Studies); Humanitites (English Studies and Historical Studies)
These degree courses offer a number of optional film modules eg American cinema, European Cinema, Film and History, Film and Political Metaphor

St Helens

St Helens College
School of Arts, Media and Design
Brook Street
St Helens
Merseyside WA10 1PZ
Tel: 01744 623322
(P) BA (Hons) Television and Video Production
Modular course in television, video, film and radio production skills

Staffordshire

Staffordshire University
School of Humanities & Social Sciences
Field of Media and Cultural Studies
PO Box 661, College Road
Stoke on Trent ST4 2XW
Tel: 01782 294413
Fax: 01782 294760
BA (Hons) Film, Television and Radio Studies
This single honours degree provides

a broad study of the media, with an emphasis on film, television and radio, but offering opportunities to consider new technologies, journalism and advertising, together with a strand of practical work in scriptwriting and production which runs throughout the degree.
After a foundation year in which students are introduced to key problems and issues of media study, there is a wide choice of options which enable students to construct a programme to suit their own interests. Students can, for instance, choosed to focus more strongly on one of the media offered – film, television or radio – or they might decide to spread their study evenly across the diversity of the media. By the final year it is possible to spend up to half their time on independent projects such as researching and writing a dissertation, producing a script, radio or video production, or developing and costing a project proposal for a media organisation or funding body
BA (Joint/Combined Hons) in Media Studies
The half degree in Media Studies begins with an introduction to ways of studying the media, with core modules on the British Press and Broadcasting History. It then goes on to explore the operation of the mass media in society through a focus on the broadcast media, together with consideration of the press, advertising and new technologies. Within this focus students are introduced to different theories and methodologies for analysing the relation between the media and society, including such issues as: the development of new technologies, their national and global implications, changing media audiences and patterns of consumption, and public debates about media policies and practices. As well as studying media problems and issues, a series of options offer modules in broadcasting history and different radio, television or journalistic forms. Students also have the opportunity to engage with media practices, formats and problems through practical work such as scriptwritng or audio/video production

Stirling

University of Stirling
Film and Media Studies
Stirling FK9 4LA
Tel: 01786 467520
Fax: 01786 466855
Website: www.stir.ac.uk
BA (Hons) Film and Media Studies (Single and Joint Hons)
Four year degree in the theory and analysis of all the principal media. All students take courses in the theories of mass communication and in cultural theories, as well as problems of textual analysis and then select from a range of options, including practical courses in the problems of news reporting in radio and television and in television documentary. As a joint honours degree Film and Media Studies can be combined with a variety of other subjects
BA General Degree
Students can build a component of their degree in film and media studies ranging from as much as eight units (approximately 50 per cent of their degree) if they take a major in the subject, down to as little as three if they wish merely to complete a Part 1 major. For the most part students follow the same units as do Film and Media Studies Honours students
MSc/Diploma Media Management
One year full–time programme consisting of two taught terms (Sept–May) followed by a dissertation (May–Aug). Internationally oriented and comparative in approach, the course offers media practitioners a wider analytical perspective on the key issues affecting their work and offers graduates a rigorous foundation for a career in the media industry. Areas covered include media policy and regulation, media economics, management and marketing, analytical methods and case studies and advanced media theory
MLitt and PhD
The specialist fields of the Stirling Media Research Institute: Media and National/Cultural identity; Political Communication and the Sociology of Journalism; Screen Interpretation; Media Management and Media Policy; Public Relations. Further details of the Institute's work are obtainable on request
Msc/Diploma Public Relations
Available in full time (12 months)

and distance learning (30 months) formats. The degree develops the key analytical and practical skills for a career in Public Relations. Areas covered incllude; Public Relations; management and organisational studies; research and evaluation; media and communication studies; marketing and political communication

Sunderland

The University of Sunderland
School of Arts, Design & Communications, Forster Building
Chester Road
Sunderland SR1 3RL
Tel: 0191 515 2125
Fax: 0191 515 2178
Website: www.sunderland.ac.uk
(P) BA (Hons) Photography, Video and Digital Imaging
Amalgamates three areas within a creative and fine art context
BA (Hons) Communication, Cultural Studies and Media Studies
Options include study of film, broadcasting and popular culture at each level. Up to 20 per cent practical study of the media is possible, including video, radio, photography, and broadcast and print journalism
MA Cultural and Textual Studies
One year full–time or two year part–time MA. Postgraduate courses are constructed from a wide range of modules. The compulsory module provides students with a flexible theoretical foundation, and a multi media and comparative study of verbal and visual forms of cultural communication, representing both 'high' and 'popular' culture. Students are then asked to choose three other modules, and to write a dissertation which allows them to specialise in film studies if they wish
MA Woman, Culture and Identity
One year full–time or two year part–time MA. The compulsory module introduces students to feminist theory and criticism in the areas of film and media studies, cultural studies, literary studies and philosophy. Students are then asked to choose three other specialist modules, and to write a dissertation, which allows them to specialise in feminist film and/or media studies if they wish

Sussex

University of Sussex
School of Cultural and Community Studies
Media Studies Co–Ordinator
Essex House, Falmer
Brighton BN1 9RQ
Tel: 01273 678019
Fax: 01273 678644
email: a.m.oxley@sussex.ac.uk
Website: sussex.ac.uk
BA (Hons) Media Studies
The degree course in Media Studies enables students to develop a critical understanding of the press, cinema, radio, television, new information technologies and of the particular character of media communications. The Major in Media Studies is taught in two Schools of Studies – Cultural and Community Studies (CCS) and European Studies (EURO): different School Courses accompany it according to the School. The course in EURO also involves study of a modern European language and an additional year abroad in Europe
BA English and Media Studies
BA Music and Media Studies
A three year full–time degree course which includes analysis of television, film and other media, together with some opportunity to be involved in practical television, video and radio production
MA in Media Studies
The MA comprises a two–term core course in media theory and research which students study the conceptual, methodological and policy related issues emerging from the study of the media. In addition, students choose, in each of the first two terms, an optional course from: European Media in Transition; Media Technology and Everyday Life; Media Audiences; The Political Economy of the New Communications Media; Promotional Culture; Queering Popular Culture; Sexual Difference; Theories of Representation; Memories of the Holocaust
MA in Digital Media
The course shares a core course, Media Theory and Research, with the MA in Media Studies. In addition, students take two dedicated courses: The Political Economy of the New Communications Media, and Theory and Practice of Interactive Multimedia. After two terms students either complete an academic dissertation, or undertake an industry placement and a multimedia project

Warrington

Warrington Collegiate Institute
**Faculty of Higher Education
(Affiliated to the University of
Manchester)
Media and Performing Arts
Padgate Campus
Crab Lane WA2 0DB**
Tel: 01925 494494
Fax: 01925 816077
email: media@warr.ac.uk
Website: www.warr.ac.uk
**(P) BA Hons Media and Cultural
Studies**
Students on this single honours
programme undertake wide–ranging
academic study in media and cultural
studies, extensive production work
chosen from television, radio,
commercial music production or
multimedia journalism, and a lengthy
period of work placement in the
media industry. They are eligible to
apply for the Granada TV internship
scheme.
**BA Hons Media (Television
Production)
BA Hons Media (Radio
Production)
BA Hons Media (Commercial
Music Production)
BA Hons Media (Multimedia
Journalism)**
These degrees are available as single
and joint honours programmes.
Students who take media as single
honours, or as a major or minor
subject within a joint honours
programme undertake academic
analysis of the media through core
modules in media forms, issues in
media representation, media
institutions and audiences, and media
professional issues, as well as
modules from a broad range of
optional units. Single honours and
major subject students undertake
extensive specialist production work
chosen from television, radio or
commercial music production and
multimedia journalism, and have an
extensive period of work experience
in the media industry. These students
are also eligible to apply for the
internship scheme run in association
with Granada TV. Production
modules are not available to students
who take media as a minor subject.
Students on joint honours
programmes can combine media with
other subjects such as leisure

management, performing arts,
business and sports studies
MA/PGDip Screen Studies
Offered on a one year full–time or
two year part–time basis. Students
take the same 3 core units as in the
**MA Media and Cultural Studies,
but** then choose 3 optional units
specifically related to aspects of
screen culture, including new media
technologies. To gain the award of
MA, students complete a 20,000
word dissertation
**(P) MA/PGDip Television
Production (in association with
Granada TV)**
Run in association with Granada TV,
this is a one year full–time fast track
vocational course for those with
serious aspirations to work in
television production. Following
intensive skills workshops, students
are expected to produce largely,
though not exclusively, factual–based
programming to professional
standards on Beta, using programme
budgets supplied by Granada TV. The
course includes 3–4 weeks work
experience at Granada or BBC North.
In addition to extensive production
work, students develop an
understanding of the contemporary
broadcasting, independent and
corporate sectors, and engage with
aspects of television theory. To gain
the award of MA, students complete
a written project, which can be a
conventional academic study, an
industrial study or an original script.
Granada TV bursaries are available
for successful applicants

Warwick

University of Warwick
**Department of Film and Television
Studies
Faculty of Arts
Coventry CV4 7AL**
Tel: 024 7652 3511
Fax: 024 7652 4757
Website:
www.warwick.ac.uk/fac/arts/film
**BA Joint Degree Film and
Literature**
Four courses offered each year, two
in film and two in literature. Mainly
film studies but some television
included.
BA in Film with Television Studies
Four courses offered each year, three
of which on film and, from year two,
television. Further options available

in film and/or television in year three
**BA French or Italian with Film
Studies**
This degree puts a particular
emphasis on film within and
alongside its studies of French or
Italian language, literature and
society
Various Degrees
Options in film studies can be taken
as part of undergraduate degrees in
other departments.
MA Film and Television Studies
Taught courses on Textual Analysis,
Methods in Film History, Modernity
and Innovation, and Issues of
Representation, Introduction to Film
and Television Studies for Graduates
**MA for Research in Film and
Television Studies**
Combination of taught course and
tailor–made programme of viewing
and reading for students with
substantial knowledge of film and
television studies at BA level. For
students wishing to proceed to PhD
research
MA, MPhil and PhD
Students are accepted for research
degrees

Watford

University of Hertfordshire
**Watford Campus, Wall Hall,
Aldenham
Watford
Herts WD2 8AT**
Tel: 01707 285643
Fax: 01707 285616
email: s.tegel@herts.ac.uk
Susan Tegel
BA (Hons) Humanities
Full– or part–time degree. Within the
History major/minor and single
honours there is a second year
option, Film and History, which
examines the inter–war period
through film and focuses on the
historian's use of film, and the
opportunity in the final year to
undertake a dissertation using films
as an historical source

West Yorkshire

Dewsbury College
**Batley School of Art & Design
Wheelwright Campus
Birkdale Road
Dewsbury, West Yorks WF13 4HQ**
Tel: 01924 451649
Fax: 01924 469491

(P) BA (Hons) Moving Image Design

This course provides an opportunity to study one of the most rapidly developing areas of design. Using computer technology, the course combines live action video techniques with 3D animation to produce time–based imagery for the broadcast media, advertising and publicity. The course demands an imaginative approach with an understanding of both 2D and 3D design

Weymouth

Weymouth College
Creative & Performing Arts
Cranford Avenue
Weymouth
Dorset DT4 7LQ
Tel: 01305 208856
Fax: 01305 208892
GNVQ Intermediate and Advanced Levels Media Communication and Production
Intermediate level: one year course designed to give a foundation in media theory and production across audio, video and print media.

Winchester

King Alfred's College Winchester (Affiliated to Southampton University)
School of Community and Performing Arts
Sparkford Road
Winchester SO22 4NR
Tel: 01962 841515
Fax: 01962 842280
Website: www.wkac.ac.uk
BA (Hons) Drama, Theatre and Television Studies
Three year course relating theories of contemporary television and drama to practical work in both media. The course looks at both the institutions and the practices of the two media from the perspectives of the ideology and aesthetic contexts in which work is produced together with critical ideologies of the Twentieth Century. It includes television projects in which students work in groups to produce documentaries or drama documentaries. These projects are community based
Media and Film Studies
Further details available from Dr Maggie Andrews: Head of Media Film School of Cultural Studies

Wolverhampton

University of Wolverhampton
School of Humanities and Social Sciences, Castle View, Dudley
West Midlands DY1 3HR
Tel: 01902 323400
Fax: 01902 323379
Website: www.wolverhampton.ac.uk
BA (Hons) Media and Cultural Studies
This is a modular programme which may be studied as a Specialist or Combined Award. Students follow a core programme covering key theoretical, historical and critical debates in both Media and Cultural Studies. A level 2 module in Research Methods prepares students for a final year project. Alongside the core students choose option modules drawn from the following themes: Film Studies; Video and Professional Communications (including Printand Broadcast Journalism, European Broadcasting and Organisational Communication); Gender and Representation (including Fashion, Style and Consumption). All students have the option of a Student Link, in which they undertake a small–scale research project in an organisation or company. This is not principally a practical programme but students taking the Video and Professional Communications Theme will undertake a range of practical work for assessment. This programme includes the option of studying a foreign language
BA (Hons) Applied Communications
This modular programme may be studied as a Specialist or Combined Award and is concerned with issues and problems of human communication in their professional or industrial context. It draws upon media studies and planned communication, including marketing, journalism, public relations, corporate communication and interactive multimedia. The programme offers a balance between the theory and practice of different forms of planned communications. Specialists take a professional placement within an appropriate sector of the communication industry as part of their final year. This programme combines theory and practice and on completion students will have acquired a range of communications skills in marketing,

journalism, design for interactive multimedia and public relations. This programme includes the options of studying a foreign language.
BA (Hons) Film Studies
This modular programme is available as a joint degree, which can be studied in combination with another subject. Students take a general foundation in Media Studies and then follow modules which introduce approaches to the analysis of films, studies of different genres (musicals, melodrama, film noir), theories of authorship, and the Hollywood studio system. The study of national cinemas includes options on British, French and Spanish cinema and special study of contemporary America. Film modules are taught at Wolverhampton's award–winning Light House Media Centre, which offers two purpose–built and fully equipped cinemas, library and exhibition facilities. The majority of films studied are screened in full cinema format. Additional library resources are housed on the Dudley and Wolverhampton campuses

York

College of Ripon and York St John
Faculty of Creative and Performing Arts
Lord Mayor's Walk
York 7EX
Tel: 01904 616672
Fax: 01904 616931
Website: www.ucrysj.ac.uk
Bill Pinner
(P) BA (Hons) Theatre, Film and Television
This degree programme embraces theoretical and practical aspects of theatre, film and television. 'Core' theories and concepts are taught alongside practical, production modules and all activity is focused on the development of both intellectual and practical skills. Emphasis is placed upon the interrelationship of the three areas alongside theories and skills specific to each. Workshops and specialist modules allow a focus of interests and skills, but students are expected to engage with all three areas of the degree. There are opportunities to study abroad in Europe or North America, and to undertake work placements and internships. There are excellent facilities for performance activity and video production

DISTRIBUTORS (NON-THEATRICAL)

Companies here control UK rights for non–theatrical distribution (for domestic and group viewing in schools, hospitals, airlines and so on).

For an extensive list of titles available non–theatrically with relevant distributors' addresses, see the *British National Film & Video Catalogue*, available for reference from the *bfi* National Library and major public libraries. Other sources of film and video are listed under Archives and Film Libraries and Workshops

Amber Films
5 Side
Newcastle upon Tyne NE1 3JE
Tel: 0191 232 2000
Fax: 0191 230 3217
email: amberside@btinternet.com

Arts Council Film and Video Library
Concord Video and Film Council
201 Felixstowe Road
Ipswich IP3 9BJ
Tel: 01473 726012
Fax: 01473 274531
email: concordvideo@btinternet.com
Website: www.btinternet.com/
~concordvideo
Lydia Vulliamy

BBC for Business
Woodlands
80 Wood Lane
London W12 0TT
Tel: 020 8576 2088
Fax: 020 8433 2867

bfi Films
21 Stephen Street
London W1T 1LN
Tel: 020 7957 8938
Fax: 020 7580 5830
email: bookings@bfi.org.uk
Website: www.bfi.org.uk/collections
Andrew Youdell
See *bfi* Bookings (Distributors Theatrical)

Big Bear Records
PO Box 944
Birmingham B16 8UT
Tel: 0121 454 7020/8100
Fax: 0121 454 9996
email: bigbearmusic@
compuserve.com
Website: www.bigbearmusic.com
Jim Simpson

Boulton–Hawker Films
Hadleigh
near Ipswich
Suffolk IP7 5BG
Tel: 01473 822235
Fax: 01473 824519
Educational films and videos: health education, social welfare, home economics, P.S.E., P.E., Maths, biology, physics, chemistry, geography

BUFVC (British Universities Film & Video Council)
77 Wells Street
London W1T 3QT
Tel: 020 7393 1500
Fax: 020 7393 1555
email: ask@bufvc.ac.uk
Videocassettes and videodiscs for sale direct from above address. Also off–air recording back–up service for education. Hire via Concord Video and Film Council

Carlton UK Television
Video Resource Unit
Lenton Lane
Nottingham NG7 2NA
Tel: 0115 964 5477
Fax: 0115 964 5202
email: sarah.hoyle@carltontv.co.uk
Sarah Hoyle

Chain Production Ltd
2 Clanricarde Gardens
London W2 4NA
Tel: 020 7229 4277
Fax: 020 7229 0861
email: films@chain.production.co.uk
Website: www.chain.production.
co.uk
Specialist in European films and world cinema, cult classics, handling European Film Libraries with all rights to over 1,000 films – also clip rights and clip search

Cinenova: Promoting Films by Women
113 Roman Road
Bethnal Green
London E2 0QN
Tel: 020 8981 6828
Fax: 020 8983 4441
email: admin@cinenova.org.uk
Website: www.cinenova.org.uk
Shona Barrett, Distribution
Laura Hudson: Development
Cinenova acts as a champion for the equality of women behind the camera, taking the diversity of women's voices to a global audience. It is committed to the acquisition, promotion, distribution and exhibition of films and videos directed by women and to provide the context to support women's film

Concord Video and Film Council
201 Felixstowe Road
Ipswich, Suffolk IP3 9BJ
Tel: 01473 726012
Fax: 01473 274531
email: concordvideo@btinternet.com
Website: www.btinternet.com/
~concordvideo
Lydia Vulliamy
Videos and films for hire/sale on domestic and international social issues – counselling, development, education, the arts, race and gender issues, disabilities, etc – for training and discussion. Also incorporates Graves Medical Audio Visual Library

CTVC Video
Hillside Studios
Merry Hill Road
Bushey
Watford WD2 1DR
Tel: 020 8950 4426
Fax: 020 8950 1437
email: ctvc@ctvc.co.uk
Website: www.ctvc.co.uk
Christian, moral and social programmes

Derann Film Services
99 High Street
Dudley
West Mids DY1 1QP
Tel: 01384 233191/257077
Fax: 01384 456488

Website: www.derann.com
D Simmonds, S Simmonds
8mm package movie distributors;
video production; bulk video
duplication; laser disc stockist

Education Distribution Service
Education House
Castle Road
Sittingbourne
Kent ME10 3RL
Tel: 01795 427614
Fax: 01795 474871
email: eds@edist.co.uk
Distribution library for many clients
including film and video releases.
Extensive catalogue available

Educational and Television Films
247A Upper Street
London N1 1RU
Tel: 020 7226 2298
Fax: 020 7226 8016
email: zoe@etvltd.demon.co.uk
Website: www.etvltd.demon.co.uk/
Zoe Moore, Jack Amos
Archive film library. Documentary films
from Eastern Europe, China, Vietnam,
Chile, Cuba, the former USSR and
the British Labour Movement

Educational Media, Film & Video
235 Imperial Drive
Rayners Lane
Harrow HA2 7HE
Tel: 020 8868 1908/1915
Fax: 020 8868 1991
email: edmedia@dircon.co.uk
Website: www. emf-v.com
Lynda Morrell
Distributors of British and overseas
educational, health, training/safety
video games as well as new
CD-ROM titles. Act as agent for the
promotion of British productions
overseas. Free catalogue

Euroview Management Services Limited
PO Box 80
Wetherby
Yorks LS23 7EQ
Tel: 01937 541010
Fax: 01937 541083
email: euroview@compuserve.com
Website: www.euroview.co.uk

Film Quest Ltd
Isabel House
46 Victoria Road
Surbiton
Surrey KT6 4JL

Tel: 020 8390 3677
Fax: 020 8390 1281
Booking agents for university, school
and private film societies

Filmbank Distributors
Grayton House
98 Theobalds Road
London WC1X 8WB
Tel: 020 7984 5950
Fax: 020 7984 5991
Bookings Department
Filmbank represents all of the major
film studios for the non-theatrical
market (group screenings) and
distributes titles on either 16mm film
or video

First Take Ltd
19 Liddell Road
London NW6 2EW
Tel: 020 7700 5060

Golds
The Independent Home
Entertainment Wholesaler
Gold House, 69 Flempton Road
Leyton
London E10 7NL
Tel: 020 8539 3600
Fax: 020 8539 2176
Contact: Garry Elwood, Sales &
Marketing Director
Gold product range ever increasing
multi-format selection including:
Audio cassettes, CD's, T-Shirts,
DVD, Spoken Word Cassettes and
CDs, Video, CD Rom, CDi, Video
CD, Laserdisc, computer games and
accessories to all formats. 42 years of
service and expertise. 32 years spent
in home entertainment market

Granada Learning/SEMERC
Granada Television
Quay Street
Manchester M60 9EA
Tel: 0161 827 2927
Fax: 0161 827 2966
email: info@granada-learning.com
Paula Warwick
Granada Learning Ltd is the UK's
leading publisher of educational
software. Its extensive range of
CD-ROMs spans the syllabus of
primary and secondary schools to
meet the requirements of learners of
all ages and abilities, including those
with special educational needs.
Granada Learning recently acquired
Letts Educational, the UK's leading
provider of educational textbooks and
revision guides for the home market,
and BlackCat, the UK's
market-leading supplier of

educational tools and applications for
younger children

IAC (Institute of Amateur Cinematographers)
63 Woodfield Lane
Ashstead
Surrey KT21 2BT
Tel: 013722 76358

Imperial War Museum
Film and Video Archive (Loans)
Lambeth Road
London SE1 6HZ
Tel: 020 7416 5000
Fax: 020 7416 5379
email: film@iwm.org.uk
Website: www.iwm.org.uk
Brad King/Toby Haggith
Documentaries, newsreels and
propaganda films from the Museum's
film archive on 16mm, 35mm and
video

IVN Entertainment
Centre 500
500 Chiswick High Road
London W4 5RG
Tel: 020 8956 2348
Fax: 020 8956 2339
Bob Burges

Leeds Animation Workshop (A Women's Collective)
45 Bayswater Row
Leeds LS8 5LF
Tel: 0113 248 4997
Fax: 0113 248 4997
email: law@leedsanimation.demon.
co.uk
Website: leedsanimation.demon.
co.uk
Milena Dragic
Producers and distributors of
animated films on social issues

The Lux Centre
2-4 Hoxton Square
London N1 6NU
Tel: 020 7684 2782
Fax: 020 7684 1111
email: dist@lux.org.uk
Website: www.lux.org.uk
The Lux Centre house the distribution
collections of the former London Film
Makers' Co-op and London
Electronic Arts, with over 3,500
artists' films, videos and works in new
media, ranging from 1920s animations
by Len Lye through classic avant
garde films by Maya Deren, Stan
Brakhage and others, to the latest
work by international artists such as
Sadie Benning and John Maybury

Melrose Film Productions
Dumbarton House
68 Oxford Street
London WIN OLH
Tel: 020 7637 7288
Fax: 020 7580 8103

National Educational Video Library
Arfon House
Bontnewydd
Caernarfon
Bangor
Gwynedd LL54 7UN
Tel: 01286 676001
Fax: 01286 676001
Supply of educational videotapes and loan of sponsored videotapes and film

National Film and Television School
Beaconsfield Studios
Station Road
Beaconsfield
Bucks HP9 1LG
Tel: 01494 671234
Fax: 01494 674042
email: h.jenkins@nftsfilm–tv.ac.uk
Website: www.nftsfilm–tv.ac.uk
Howard Jenkins

Open University Worldwide
The Berrill Building
3rd Floor North
Walton Hall
Milton Keynes MK7 6AA
Tel: 01908 858785
Fax: 01908 858787
email: d.m.Ruault@open.ac.uk

Post Office Video and Film Library
PO Box 145
Sittingbourne
Kent ME10 1NH
Tel: 01795 426465
Fax: 01795 474871
email: poful@edist.co.uk
Includes many video programmes and supporting educational material including curriculum guidelines. Also a comprehensive range of extension and other curriculum linked material. TV rights available

Royal Danish Embassy
55 Sloane Street
London SW1X 9SR
Tel: 020 7333 0200
Fax: 020 7333 0270

RSPCA
Causeway
Horsham
West Sussex RH12 1HG
Tel: 01403 264181
Fax: 01403 241048
email: webmail@rspca.org.uk
Website: www.rspca.org.uk
Michaela Miller

Sheila Graber Animation Limited
50 Meldon Avenue
South Shields
Tyne and Wear NE34 0EL
Tel: 0191 455 4985
Fax: 0191 455 3600
email: sheila@graber.demon.co.uk
Website: www.graber.demon.co.uk
Over 70 animated shorts available – 16mm, video and computer interactive featuring a range of 'fun' educational shorts on art, life, the universe and everything. Producers of interactive CD–Roms

The Short Film Bureau
47 Poland Street
London W1V 3DF
Tel: 020 7734 8708
Fax: 020 7734 2406
email: info@shortfilmbureau.com
Website: www.shortfilmbureau.com
Specialising in the promotion and distribution of short films for theatrical and non–theatrical release world wide

South West Arts
Bradninch Place
Gandy Street
Exeter EX4 3LS
Tel: 01392 218188
Fax: 01392 413554
email: info@swa.co.uk
Website: www.swa.co.uk
Clare Frank, Ruth Bint: Information Advisers
Sara Williams, Andrew Proctor: Visual Arts and Media Administrator

Team Video Productions
Canalot Studios
222 Kensal Road
London W10 5BN
Tel: 020 8960 5536
Fax: 020 8960 9784
Chris Thomas, Billy Ridgers
Producer and distributor of educational video resources

THE (Total Home Entertainment)
National Distribution Centre
Rosevale Business Park
Newcastle–under–Lyme
Staffs ST5 7QT
Tel: 01782 566566
Fax: 01782 568552
email: jed.taylor@the.co.uk
Website: www.the.co.uk
Jed Taylor
Exclusive distributors for Visual Corp, ILC, Quantum Leap, Mystique, Prime Time, IMS, Wardvision, Academy Media, Empire, RWP (over 6,000 titles) (see also Video Labels)

Training Services
Brooklands House
29 Hythegate
Werrington
Peterborough PE4 7ZP
Tel: 01733 327337
Fax: 01733 575537
email: tipton@training.services.demon.co.uk
Website: www.trainingservices.demon.co.uk/index.htm
C.Tipton
Distribute programmes from the following producers:
3E's Training
Aegis Healthcare
Angel Productions
Barclays Bank Film Library
John Burder Films
Career Strategies Ltd
CCD Product & Design
Easy–i Ltd
Flex Training
Flex Multi–Media Ltd
Grosvenor Career Services
Hebden Lindsay Ltd
Kirby Marketing Associates
McPherson Marketing
Promotions Sound & Vision
Schwops Productions
Touchline Training Group
Video Communicators Pty

TV Choice
22 Charing Cross Road
London WC2H 0HR
Tel: 020 7379 0873
Fax: 020 7379 0263

The University of Westminster
School of Communications and Creative Industries
Harrow Campus, Watford Road
Northwick Park HA1 3TP
Tel: 020 7911 5944
Fax: 020 7911 5943
email: cdm@wmin.ac
Website: www.wmin.ac.uk/media

Vera Media
30–38 Dock Street
Leeds LS10 1JF
Tel: 0113 242 8646
Fax: 0113 242 8739
email: vera@vera–media.co.uk

Website: www.vera.media.co.uk
Al Garthwaite
Catherine Mitchell

Video Arts
Dumbarton House
68 Oxford Street
London W1N 0LH
Tel: 020 7637 7288
Fax: 020 7580 8103
Video Arts produces and exclusively distributes the John Cleese training films; Video Arts also distributes a selection of meeting breaks from Muppet Meeting Films TM as well as Tom Peters programmes (produced by Video Publishing House Inc) and In Search of Excellence and other films from the Nathan/Tyler Business Video Library

Viewtech Film and Video
7–8 Falcons Gate
Northavon Business Centre
Dean Road Yate
Bristol BS37 5NH
Tel: 01454 858055
Fax: 01454 858056
email: info@viewtech.co.uk
Website: www.viewtech.co.uk
Safety films

Westbourne Film Distribution
1st Floor,
17 Westbourne Park Road
London W2 5PX
Tel: 020 7221 1998
Fax: 020 7221 1998
Agents for broadcasting/video sales for independent animators from outside the UK, particularly Central Eastern Europe. Classic children's film *The Singing Ringing Tree*

WFA
9 Lucy Street
Manchester M15 4BX
Tel: 0161 848 9782/5
Fax: 0161 848 9783
email:wfa@timewarp.com.uk

DISTRIBUTORS (THEATRICAL)

Alibi Communications plc
12 Maiden Lane
Covent Garden
London WC2E 7NA
Tel: 020 7845 0400
Fax: 020 7836 6919
email: info@alibifilms.co.uk
Website: www.alibifilms.co.uk
Roger Holmes
Alibi is active in the financing,
international sales and distribution of
theatrical feature films and the
production of feature films, television
drama and children's programming.
Titles include: *One More Kiss*
(1999); *One of the Hollywood Ten*
(2000)

Alliance Releasing & Momentum Pictures
2nd Foor
184–192 Drummond Street
London NW1 3HP
Tel: 020 7391 6900
Fax: 020 7383 0404

Arrow Film Distributors
18 Watford Road
Radlett
Herts WD7 8LE
Tel: 01923 858 306
Fax: 01923 859673
email: arrowfilms.co.uk
Website: www.arrowfilms.co.uk/

Artificial Eye Film Company
14 King Street
London WC2E 8HR
Tel: 020 7240 5353
Fax: 020 7240 5242
Website: www.artificial–eye.com
Robert Beeson, Sam Shinton

bfi Bookings
21 Stephen Street
London W1T 1LN
Tel: 020 7957 8905
Fax: 020 7580 5830
email: bookings@bfi.org.uk
Website: www.bfi.org.uk/collections
Christine Whitehouse
Handles theatrical and non–theatrical
16mm, 35mm and video. Catalogues
available online
Ultimate Hitchcock season at the
NFT: opening fim *The Ring*, closing
film *The Lodger*

First run: *The Man Who Knew Too
Much*
Robert Bresson season includes:
Mouchette; Au Hasard Balthazar
Akira Kurosawa season includes:
*Yojimbo; Seven Samurai; Throne of
Blood; The Hidden Fortress; Ikiru*
Releases 2000
*A Matter of Life and Death, Once
Upon a Time in the West, Shaft,
Sullivans Travels, Singin' in the Rain,
Vivre sa vie; Film en Douze
Tableaux, Bande à Par*

Blue Dolphin Film & Video
40 Langham Street
London W1N 5RG
Tel: 020 7255 2494
Fax: 020 7580 7670
Joseph D'Morais

Blue Light
231 Portobello Road
London W11 1LT
Tel: 020 7792 9791
Fax: 020 7792 9871
email: kevan@bluelight.co.uk
Website: www.bluelight.co.uk
Kevan Wilkinson
Alain De La Mata
(See Made in Hong Kong)

Buena Vista International (UK)
3 Queen Caroline Street
Hammersmith
London W6 9PE
Tel: 020 8222 1000
Fax: 020 8222 2795
Daniel Battsek

John Burder Films
7 Saltcoats Road
London W4 1AR
Tel: 020 8995 0547
Fax: 020 8995 3376
email: jburder@aol.com
Website: www.johnburder.co.uk

Carlton Film Distributors
35–38 Portman Square
London W1H 6NU
Tel: 020 7224 3339
Fax: 020 7612 7244
(Formerly Rank Film Distributors)

Chain Production Ltd
2 Clanricarde Gardens

London W2 4NA
Tel: 020 7229 4277
Fax: 020 7229 0861
email: films@chain.production.co.uk
Website: www.chain.production.
co.uk
Specialist in European films and
world cinema, cult classics, handling
European Film Libraries with all
rights to over 1,000 films – also clip
rights and clip search

Children's Film Unit
South Way
Leavesden
Herts WD2 7LZ
Tel: 01923 354656
email: cfilmunit@aol.com
Website: www.btinternet.com/~cfu
Carol Rennie

Cinenova: Promoting Films by Women
113 Roman Road
Bethnal Green
London E2 0QN
Tel: 020 8981 6828
Fax: 020 8983 4441
email: admin@cinenova.org.uk
Website: www.cinenova.org.uk
Shona Barrett, Distribution
Cinenova acts as a champion for the
equality of women behind the
camera, taking the diversity of
women's voices to a global audience.
It is committed to the acquisition,
promotion, distribution, and
exhibition of films and videos
directed by women and to provide
the context to support women's film

City Screen
86 Dean Street
London W1D 3SR
Tel: 020 7734 4342
Fax: 020 7734 4027

Columbia TriStar Films (UK)
Europe House
25 Golden Square
London W1R 6LU
Tel: 020 7533 1111
Fax: 020 7533 1105
Feature releases from Columbia,
TriStar, and Orion Pictures

Contemporary Films

24 Southwood Lawn Road
Highgate
London N6 5SF
Tel: 020 8340 5715
Fax: 020 8348 1238
email: contemporaryfilms@
compuserve.com
Website: www.contemporaryfilms.
com
Eric Liknaitzky
Strangers on a Train
Battleship Potemkin

Documedia International Films Ltd

Programme Sales/Acquisitions
19 Widegate Street
London E1 7HP
Tel: 020 7625 6200
Disbributors of award winning drama
specials, drama shorts and feature
films for theatrical release, also video
sales/Internet and video on demand.
Drama specials – *Soulscapes*;
Telemovies/Features – *Deva's Forest,
Leaves and Thorns*
International short drama for
theatrical release, also
educational/film club and non
theatrical release – *Pile of Clothes,
JoyRidden, The Cage, Nazdrovia,
Thin Lines, Late Fred Morse, The
Extinguisher, The Summer Tree, Arch
Enemy, Tea and Bullets, Isabelle,
Peregrine, Beyond Reach, Trauma,
Edge of Night, Something Wonderful*

Double: Take

21 St Mary's Grove
London SW13 0JA
Tel: 020 8788 5743
Fax: 020 8785 3050
Maya Kemp
Distributors and producers of
children's TV and video
The Clangers
Crystal Tipps and Alistair
Fred Basset
Ivor the Engine
Willo the Wisp

Downtown Pictures Ltd

4th Floor, Suite 2
St Georges House
14–17 Wells Street
London W1P 3FP
Tel: 020 7323 6604
Fax: 020 7636 8090
Martin McCabe, Alan McQueen,
Alan Latham, Anne Rigby

Entertainment Film Distributors

Eagle House

108–110 Jermyn Street
London SW1Y 6HB
Tel: 020 7930 7744
Fax: 020 7930 9399

Feature Film Company

68–70 Wardour Street
London W1V 3HP
Tel: 020 7734 2266
Fax: 020 7494 0309
Ulee's Gold
My Son the Fanatic
The Blackout
It's A Wonderful Life
Quadrophenia
Das Boot; the Director's Cut
Wild Man Blues
Gang Related

FilmFour Distributors

76–78 Charlotte Street
London W1P 1LX
Tel: 020 7868 7700
Fax: 020 7868 7767
Website: www.filmfour.com
The distribution arm of C4's
stand–alone film company FilmFour
Ltd. Handles the theatrical and video
distribution in the UK of all
FilmFour Productions and an
expanding slate of third party
acquisitions. Recent releases:
East is East
Holy Smoke
The Yards
Dancer in the Dark
Buena Vista Social Club
Dogma

GVI Distributors

1A Priory Way
Southall
Middlesex UB2 5EB
Tel: 020 8813 8059
Fax: 020 8813 8062

ICA Projects

12 Carlton House Terrace
London SW1Y 5AH
Tel: 020 7873 0056
Fax: 020 7930 9686
email: projects@ica.org.uk
Website: www.ica.org.uk/icaprojects
David Sin/Edward Fletcher
La vie de Jesus
Moment of Innocence
Hamam – The Turkish Bath
Afterlife
The Buttoners
Made in Hong Kong
Claire Dolan
The Wind Will Carry Us

Indy UK

Independent Feature Film
Distributors

13 Mountview
Northwood
Middlesex HA6 3NZ
Tel: 07000 Indyuk (463985)
Fax: 0870 161 7339
email: indyuk@realit.demo.co.uk
The Scarlet Tunic
The Usual Children

Brian Jackson Films Ltd

39/41 Hanover Steps
St George's Fields
Albion Street
London W2 2YG
Tel: 020 7402 7543
Fax: 020 7262 5736

Kino Kino!

24c Alexandra Road
London N8 OPP
Tel: 020 8881 9463
Fax: 020 8881 9463
email: vitaly@kinokino.u–net.com
Website: Kinokino.u–net.com
Hands (Dir Artur Aristakisyan)
released in 1998. *Brother* (Dir Alexei
Balabanov), *Happy Days* (Dir Alexei
Balabanov) released in 2000, *Maria*
(Dir Artur Aristakisyan) planned for
release 2000/2001

David Lamping Co

13 Berners Street
London W1P 3DE
Tel: 020 7580 0088
Fax: 020 7580 3468
email: tdlc@sovereignpix.com
David Lamping

Made in Hong Kong/Blue Light

231 Portobello Road
London W11 1LT
Tel: 020 7792 9791
Fax: 020 7792 9871
Website:
www.madeinhongkong.co.uk
Kevan Wilkinson
Made in Hong Kong releases the
finest in Hong Kong cinema
Bullet in the Head
Chinese Ghost Story
City on Fire
Days of Being Wild
Full Contact
Heroic Trio
The Killer
Saviour of the Soul
Blue Light distributes European and
other titles

Mainline Pictures

37 Museum Street
London WC1A 1LP
Tel: 020 7242 5523

Fax: 020 7430 0170
Website: www.screencinemas.co.uk

Medusa Communications & Marketing Ltd
Regal Chambers, 51 Bancroft
Hitchin
Herts SG5 1LL
Tel: 01462 421818
Fax: 01462 420393
email: steve@medusacom.co.uk
Website: www.getplayboy.co.uk
Stephen Rivers
Medusa Pictures, Odyssey, Playboy,
Adult Channel, Hong Kong Legends
Eastern Hero's, Jerry Springer,
Spawn Animation

Metro Tartan Distribution Ltd
Atlantic House
5 Wardour Street
London W1V 3HE
Tel: 020 7494 1400
Fax: 020 7439 1922
Laura DeCasto
Drifting Clouds
Tierra
Deep Crimson
Kissed
Prisoner of the Mountain
Un Air De Famille
Les Voleurs
JunkMail
Ponette
Dobermann
Funny Games
To Have and To Hold
The Last September
Slam
Billy's Hollywood Screen Kiss
Lovers of the Arctic Circle
The Idiots
Of Freaks and Men

Metrodome Distribution
110 Park Street
London W1Y 3RJ
Tel: 020 7408 2121
Fax: 020 7409 1935
Website: www.metrodomegroup.com
Metrodome Distribution is part of the
Metrodome Group. The distribution
arm was set up in order to distribute
films that Metrodome Films
produces, as well as to actively
acquire and release another 8–10
films per year.
Buffalo '66
The Real Blonde
The Daytrippers
Human Traffic
The Bride of Chucky
Tango
Taxi

Eye of the beholder
Sex – The Annabel Chong Story
Rage
Chuck & Buck
Elephant Juice

Millivres Multimedia
Ground Floor
Worldwide House
116–134 Bayham St
London NW1 0BA
Tel: 020 7482 2576

Miracle Communications
38 Broadhurst Avenue
Edgware
Middx HA8 8TS
Tel: 020 8958 8512
Fax: 020 8958 5112
email: martin@miracle63.freeserve.
co.uk
Martin Myers
Handles all First Independent titles

New Line International
4th Floor
25–28 Old Burlington Street
London W1X 1LB
Tel: 020 7440 1040
Fax: 020 7439 6118
Please see Entertainment Film
Distributors

Oasis Cinemas and Film Distribution
20 Rushcroft Road
Brixton
London SW2 1LA
Tel: 020 7733 8989
Fax: 020 7733 8790
email: mail@oasiscinemas.co.uk
Mike Ewin
at Winstone for all except *Dancehall*
Queen (Oasis)
Laws of Gravity
The Lunatic
The Secret Rapture
Dance Hall Queen
Gravesend

Optimum Releasing
1st Floor
143 Charing Cross Road
London WC2H OEE
Tel: 020 7478 4466
Fax: 020 7734 3044

Pathé Distribution
Kent House
14–17 Market Place
Great Titchfield Street
London W1N 8AR
Tel: 020 7323 5151
Fax: 020 7631 3568
Website: www.pathe.co.uk/

PD&B Films
c/o The Short Film Bureau
47 Poland Street
London W1V 3DF
Tel: 020 7734 8708
Fax: 020 7734 2406
email: info@pdbfilms.com
Website: www.pdbfilms.com
Distributors of short films
internationally

Poseidon Film Distributors
Hammer House
117 Wardour Street
London W1V 3TD
Tel: 020 7734 4441
Fax: 020 7437 0638
Autism
Dyslexia
Russian Composers – Writers
The Steal
Animation series *The Bears*
"The Odyssey"
The Night Witches

Redbus Film Distribution Plc
17–18 Henrietta Street
London WC2E 8QH
Tel: 020 7257 2000
Fax: 020 7257 2300
Website: www.films.redbus.co.uk

Sovereign Pictures
13 Berners Street
London W1P 3DE
Tel: 020 7580 0088
Fax: 020 7580 3468
email: sales@sovereignpix.com
David Lamping

Squirrel Films Distribution
119 Rotherhithe Street
London SE16 4NF
Tel: 020 7231 2209
Fax: 020 7231 2119

Supreme Film Distributors
3 Ferndown
Emerson Park
Hornchurch
Essex RM11 3JL
Tel: 01708 450352
Fax: 01708 470282

TKO Communications
PO Box 130
Hove, East Sussex BN3 6QU
Tel: 01273 550088
Fax: 01273 540969
email: jkruger02@aik,com
Gallavants (Gallavants)
3 Musketeers (Animated)
In Concert with Marvin Gaye
Jerry Lee Lewis – live in concert

Twentieth Century Fox Film Co

20th Century House
31–32 Soho Square
London W1V 6AP
Tel: 020 7437 7766
Fax: 020 7434 2170
Website: www.fox.co.uk/

UIP (United International Pictures (UK))

12 Golden Square
London W1A 2JL
Tel: 020 7534 5200
Fax: 020 7534 5201/5202
Website: www.uip.com/
Releases product from Paramount, Universal, MGM/UA and SKG DreamWorks

UK B4U Network (Europe) Limited

Unit 23
Sovereign Park
Off Coronation Road
London NW10 7PQ
Tel: 020 8963 8400
Fax: 020 8963 8445
email:b4u@b4utv.com
Website:www.b4utv.com

United Artists Corporation, Ltd (MGM/United Artists)

5 Kew Road
Richmond
Surrey TW9 2PR
Tel: 020 8939 9300
Fax: 020 8939 9411
Anke Folchert
Tomorrow Never Dies, Man in the Iron Mask

United Media

68 Berwick Street
London W1F 8SY
Tel: 020 7287 2396
Fax: 020 7287 2398
email: umedia@globalnet.co.uk
Website: united–media.co.uk
Lars Patterson

Warner Bros Distributors

98 Theobalds Road
London WC1X 8WB
Tel: 020 7984 5000
Fax: 020 7984 5001
Website: www.warnerbros.com/
Nigel Sharrocks

Westbourne Film Distribution

1st Floor
17 Westbourne Park Road
London W2 5PX
Tel: 020 7221 1998
Fax: 020 7221 1998
Agents for broadcasting/video sales for independent animators from outside the UK, particularly Central Eastern Europe. Classic children's film *The Singing Ringing Tree*

Winstone Film Distributors

18 Craignish Avenue
Norbury
London SW16 4RN
Tel: 020 8765 0240
Fax: 020 8765 0564
email: WinstoneFilmDis2aol.com
Mike G..Ewin, Sara Ewin
Sub–distribution for Canal + Image UK Ltd)– Library only

Yashraj Films International Limited

3rd Floor Wembley Point
1 Harrow Road
Middlesex HA9 6DE
Tel: 0870 7397345
Fax: 0870 7397346
email:ukoffice@yashrajfilms.com
Website: www.yashraj.com

FACILITES

Abbey Road Studios
3 Abbey Road
St John's Wood
London NW8 9AY
Tel: 020 7266 7000
Fax: 020 7266 7250
email: bookings@abbeyroad.co.uk
Website: www.abbeyroad.co.uk
Four studios; music to picture; 35mm
projection; film sound transfer
facilities; audio post–production and
DMM/Lacquer disc cutting. Sonic
Solutions computer sound
enhancement system; residential
accommodation, restaurant and bar.
Multimedia design and authoring,
DVD authoring

AFM Lighting Ltd
Waxlow Road
London NW10 7NU
Tel: 020 8233 7000
Fax: 020 8233 7001

Gary Wallace
Lighting equipment and crew hire;
generator hire

After Image Facilities
32 Acre Lane
London SW2 5SG
Tel: 020 7737 7300
Fax: 020 7326 1850
email: jane@arc.co.uk
Jane Thorburn
Full broadcast sound stage – Studio
A (1,680 sq ft, black, chromakey,
blue, white cyc) and insert studio
(730 sq ft hard cyc). Multiformat
broadcast on–line post production.
Special effects – Ultimatte/blue
screen

Air Studios
Lyndhurst Hall, Lyndhurst Road
Hampstead
London NW3 5NG
Tel: 020 7794 0660

Fax: 020 7794 8518
Alison Burton
Lyndhurst Hall: capacity – 500 sq m
by 18m high with daylight; 100 plus
musicians; four separation booths.
Full motion picture scoring facilities.
Neve VRP Legend 72ch console,
flying fader automation. LCRS
monitoring. Studio 1: capacity – 60
sq m with daylight. 40 plus
musicians. Neve/Focusrite 72ch
console; GML automation; LCRS
monitoring. Studio 2: Mixing Room;
SSL8000G plus series console with
Ultimation; ASM system. Film and
TV dubbing facilities; two suites
equipped with AMS Logic II
consoles; 16 output; AudioFile
spectra plus; LCRS monitoring.
Exabyte back–up. One suite equipped
with an AMS Logic III console.
Every tape machine format available

Alphabet Communications Ltd
Haig Road
Parkgate Estate
Knutsford
Cheshire WA16 8DX
Tel: 01565 755678
Fax: 01565 634164
email: info@alphabet.co.uk
Website: www.alphabet.co.uk
Simon Poyser
Digital Beta on line digital edit suites
Charisma DVE
Aston Motif caption generator
Sony 6000 vision switcher
Sony 9100 edit controller
Beta SP component edit suite
Avid 100OXL Media Composer online suite
Avid 800 offline 18Gbyte memory
2D Computer graphic Pixell Collage
3D Computer graphics Softimage 3D
Extreme Mental Ray render
Standards conversion
All tape formats available
Commentary recording and rostrum camera
1800sq ft drive in studio
Crews
Digital Beta DVW700P 16:9 & 4:3 camera
Beta SP
VHS Duplication
Authoring of Interactive DVD & CD ROM packages, Website building

Angel Recording Studios
311 Upper Street
London N1 2TU
Tel: 020 7354 2525
Fax: 020 7226 9624
email: angel@angelstudios.co.uk
Gloria Luck
Two large orchestral studios with Neve desks, and one small studio. All with facilities for recording to picture

Anvil Post Production Ltd
Denham Studios
North Orbital Road, Denham
Uxbridge
Middx UB9 5HL
Tel: 01895 833522
Fax: 01895 835006
email: *@anvil.nildram.co.uk
Sound completion service; re–recording, ADR, post–sync, Fx recording, transfers, foreign version dubbing; non–linear and film editing rooms, neg cutting, off–line editing, production offices

ARRI Lighting Rental
20a The Airlinks
Spitfire Way

Heston
Middx TW5 9NR
Tel: 020 8561 6700
Fax: 020 8569 2539
Tim Ross
Lighting equipment hire

Jim Bambrick and Associates
William Blake House
8 Marshall Street
London W1V 2AJ
Tel: 020 7434 2351
Fax: 020 7734 6362
6 x Avid Editing Suite with versions 6.5 software, 35mm Steinbeck

Barcud
Cibyn
Caernarfon
Gwynedd LL55 2BD
Tel: 01286 671671
Fax: 01286 671679
Video formats: 1"C, Beta SP, D2 OB
Unit 1: up to 7 cameras 4VTR OB
Unit 2: up to 10 cameras 6VTR, DVE, Graphics Betacam units.
Studio 1: 6,500 sq ft studio with audience seating and comprehensive lighting rig. Studio 2: 1,500 sq ft studio with vision/lighting control gallery and sound gallery. Three edit suites; two graphics suites, one with Harriet. DVE: three channels Charisma, two channels Cleo. Two Sound post–production suites with AudioFile and Screen Sound; BT lines. Wales' leading broadcast facility company can supply OB units, studios, Betamac Kits (all fully crewed if required) and full post production both on and off–line

Bell Digital Facilities
Lamb House
Church Street
Chiswick Mall
London W4 2PD
Tel: 020 8996 9960
Fax: 020 8996 9966
email: sales@bel–media.co
ProTools IV sound dubbing studio with non–linear picture. VocAlign & other ADR and outboard tools. Voice booth accessible from all suites. Extensive 3D animation & 2D graphics studio. Sound proofed, air–conditioned. 600 sq ft video studio available as 4–waller or with cameras. Avid off and on–line and After Effects

Blue Post Production
58 Old Compton Street
London W1V 5PA
Tel: 020 7437 2626

Fax: 020 7439 2477
Contact: Catherine Spruce, Director of Marketing
Digital Online Editing with Axial edit controllers, GVG 4000 digital vision mixers, Kaleidoscope DVEs, disc recorders, Abekas A72, digital audio an R–Dat
Quantel Edit Box 4000 with 2 hours non–compressed storage
Sound Studio with Avid Audio Vision, 32 input MTA fully automated desk
Offline Editing on Avid Media Composer 800
Telecine Ursa Diamond System, incorporating Pogle Platinium DCP with ESR & TWiGi

BUFVC
77 Wells Street
London W1P 3RE
Tel: 020 7393 1500
Fax: 020 7393 1555
email: ask@bufvc.ac.uk
16mm video steenbeck plus 35mm and 16mm viewing facilities.
Betacam 2 machine edit facility for low–cost assembly off–line work

Canalot Production Studios
222 Kensal Road
London W10 5BN
Tel: 020 8960 8580
Fax: 020 8960 8907
Nieves Heathcote
Media business complex housing over 80 companies, involved in TV, film, video and music production, with boardroom to hire for meetings, conferences and costings

Capital FX
21A Kingly Court
London W1R 5LE
Tel: 020 7439 1982
Fax: 020 7734 0950
Graphic design and production, laser subtitling, opticals effects and editing

Capital Studios
Wandsworth Plain
London SW18 1ET
Tel: 020 8877 1234
Fax: 020 8877 0234
Central London: 3,000 and 2,000 sq ft fully equipped broadcast standard television studios. 16x9/4x3 switchable, two on–line edit suites (D3, D2, D5, Digital Betacam & Beta SP). Avid on/off line editing. Multi track and digital sound dubbing facilities with commentary booth. 'Harriet' graphics suite. BT lines. All support facilities. Car park. Expert

team, comfortable surroundings, immaculate standards

Chromacolour International Ltd
11–16 Grange Mills
Weir Road
London SW12 0NE
Tel: 020 8675 8422
Fax: 020 8675 8499
Animation supplies/equipment

Cinebuild
Studio House
Rita Road
Vauxhall
London SW8 1JU
Tel: 020 7582 8750
Fax: 020 7793 0467
Special effects: rain, snow, fog, mist, smoke, fire, explosions; lighting and equipment hire. Studio: 200 sq m

Cinecontact
27 Newman Street
London W1P 4AR
Tel: 020 7323 0618
Fax: 020 7323 1215
Contact: Jacqui Timberlake
Documentary film–makers. Avid post production facilities

Cinesite (Europe) Ltd
9 Carlisle Street
London W1V 5RG
Tel: 020 7973 4000
Fax: 020 7973 4040
Website: www.cinesite.com
Utilising state–of–the–art technology, Cinesite provides expertise in every area of resolution–free digital imaging and digital special effects for feature films

Colour Film Services
10 Wadsworth Road
Perivale
Middx UB6 7JX
Tel: 020 8998 2731
Fax: 020 8997 8738
email: johnward@colourfilmservices.co.uk
Website: www.colourfilmservices.co.uk

Communicopia Ltd
The Old Town Hall
Albion Street
Southwick
West Sussex BN42 4AX
Tel: 01273 278575
Fax: 01273 416082
email: info@communicopia.co.uk

Website: www.communicopia.co.uk
Post production facility. Includes: Fast 601 non–linear video post production suite. Broadcast quality MPEG2 601. GEM WK4 music workstation. Voice–over sound suite. Digital sound mixer. Track laying and audio mixing to picture. Broadcast standard, non–linear editing. 3D effect/DVE. Unlimited layering, all with colour correction, keying and DVE. High–speed background rendering. 36 Gigabytes of media storage. Huge picture library. Lightwave 5 graphics system. 3D full–featured animation system. CD ROM, CD Burner and CD Players. DAT player/recorder. VHS and S–VHS recorders. Music and sound effects library. Zip drives. ISDN

Complete
Slingsby Place
Off Long Acre
London WC2E 9AB
Tel: 020 7379 7739
Fax: 020 7497 9305
email: info@complete.co.uk
Richard Ireland, Lucy Pye, Sarah Morgan, Lisa Sweet and Holly Ryan

Henry, Flame, Harriet. Digital editing. C–reality–Hires–Telecine. 3D Animation with Alias wave front and soft/maxDigital Ursa Diamond Telecine with Russell Square DI tape grading. Digital playouts and ISDN links. Award–winning creative team

Connections Communications Centre
Palingswick House
241 King Street
Hammersmith
London W6 9LP
Tel: 020 8741 1766
Fax: 020 8593 9134
email: info@cccmedia.demon.co.uk
Website: www.cccmedia.
demon.co.uk
Melanie Wiley (Training)
Bill Hammond (Facilities)
Production Equipment
BETA SP, DV, DVCPRO, SVHS cameras. Wide range of lighting and sound including SQN stereo mixer and portable D.A.T.
Post Production Equipment
Avid Xpress Deluxe Non–Linear Edit system. BETA SP 3 machine suite with computerised edit controller SVHS on–line and off–line editing

Fully Wheelchair Accessible

Corinthian Television Facilities (CTV)
87 St John's Wood Terrace
London NW8 6PY
Tel: 020 7483 6000
Fax: 020 7483 4264
Website: www.ctv.co.uk
OBs: Multi–camera and multi–VTR vehicles. Post Production: 3 suites, 1 SP component, 2 multi–format with 1", D2, D3, Abekas A64, A72, Aston and colour caption camera. Studios: 2 fully equipped television studios (1 in St John's Wood, 1, in Piccadilly Circus), 1–5 camera, multi–format VTRs, BT lines, audience seating. Audio: SSL Scrrensound digital audio editing and mixing system

Dateline Productions
79 Dean Street
London W1V 5HA
Tel: 020 7437 4510
Fax: 020 7287 1072
email: miranda@dircon.com
Miranda Watts
Avid non–linear editing

De Lane Lea Sound Centre
75 Dean Street

London W1V 5HA
Tel: 020 7439 1721
Fax: 020 7437 0913
email: dll@delanelea.com
Website: www.delanelea.com
2 high speed 16/35mm Dolby stereo dubbing theatres with Dolby SR; high speed ADR and FX theatre (16/35mm and NTSC/PAL video); Synclavier digital FX suite; digital dubbing theatre with Logic 2 console; 3 x AudioFile preparation rooms; sound rushes and transfers; video transfers to VHS and U–Matic; Beta rushes syncing. 24 cutting rooms/offices. See also under studios

Denman Productions
60 Mallard Place
Strawberry Vale
Twickenham TW1 4SR
Tel: 020 8891 3461
Fax: 020 8891 6413
Video and film production, including 3D computer animation and web design

Digital Audio Technology
134 Cricklewood Lane
London NW2 2DP
Tel: 020 8450 5665
Fax: 020 8208 1979

email: info@digitalauiotech.com
Website: digitalaudiotech.com
Ian Silvester
Providing a one–stop solution to all
your digital audio requirements for
music, film, television and DVD
productions

Diverse Production
6 Gorleston Street
London W14 8XS
Tel: 020 7603 4567
Fax: 020 7603 2148
Ray Nunney
TV post–production. Digital on–line
editing; off–line editing;
comprehensive graphic design
service; titles sequences, programme
graphics, generic packaging, sets and
printwork

Dolby Laboratories
Wootton Bassett
Wilts SN4 8QJ
Tel: 01793 842100
Fax: 01793 842101
email: info@dolby.co.uk
Website: www.dolby.com
Graham Edmondson
Cinema processors for replay of
Dolby Digital, Dolby Digital
Surround Ex and Dolby SR
(analogue) film soundtracks; audio
noise reduction equipment. Sound
consultancy relating to Dolby film
productions and Dolby Surround
productions for television

Dubbs
25–26 Poland Street
London W1V 3DB
Tel: 020 7629 0055
Fax: 020 7287 8796
email: customer_services@
dubbs.co.uk
Website: www.dubbs.co.uk
Videotape duplication: All digital
formats; BeatSP 1", BVU SP, SVHS,
VHS, U–matic, Hi–8 and Video 8.
Standards Conversion: Alchemist Ph
C, Adac, Tetra. Audio: Tascam DA88,
DAT, Audio cassette. Full labelling,
packing and despatch service
available

Edinburgh Film and Video Productions
Traquair House
Innelleithen
Peeblessairl EH44 6PW
Tel: 01896 831188
Fax: 01896 831198
Stage: 50 sq m; 16/Super 16/35mm
cutting rooms; preview theatre; edge
numbering; lighting grip equipment
hire; scenery workshops

Edinburgh Film Workshop Trust
56 Albion Road
Edinburgh EH7 5QZ
Tel: 0131 656 9123
email: post@efwt.demon.co.uk
Website: www.efwt.demon.co.uk
David Halliday, Angus Ferguson
Beta SP production; 16mm Arri,
6–plates and rostrum, broadcst
quality video animation and
non–linear editing; off–line editing.
Animation and video training,
consultancy and project development.
Specialists in enviornment, health
and welfare

Edric Audio–visual Hire
34–36 Oak End Way
Gerrards Cross
Bucks SL9 8BR
Tel: 01753 884646
Fax: 01753 887163
Audiovisual and video production
facilities

Elstree Light and Power
Millennium Studios
Elstree Way
Borehamwood
Herts WD6 1SF
Tel: 020 8236 1300
Fax: 020 8236 1333
Tony Slee
TV silent generators; Twin Sets HMI,
MSR and Tungsten Heads. Distribution
to BS 5550.Rigging Specialists

Faction Films
26 Shacklewell Lane
London E8 2EZ
Tel: 020 7690 4446
Fax: 020 7690 4447
email: faction@factionfilms.co.uk
Website: www.factionfilms.co.uk
Justine Faram
Avid MC1000 composer; Sony
VX1000 digi–cam; Sony Hi–8; HHB
Portadat; Nagra 4.2; Production
office space

The Film Factory at VTR
64 Dean Street
London W1V 5HG
Tel: 020 7437 0026
Fax: 020 7494 0059
email: alan.church@filmfactory.com
Website: www.filmfactory.com
Alan Church, Simon Giles
The Film Factory is one of London's
major feature film post–production
facilities specialising in
high–resolution digital effects.
Credits include *Deep Blue Sea, Tea*

*With Mussolini, Lost in Space, The
Wings of the Dove, Love is the Devil,
Gormenghast* and *Seven Years in
Tibet*. Produce visual effects, digital
opticals, titles, computer animation
and visual effects supervision. Title
sequences include: *The Adventures of
Pinocchio, Best Laid Plans,
Photographing Fairies, Bent, Saving
Grace, Cousin Bette, Up 'n' Under,
Tube Tales, I Want You* and
Pandaemonium. Company also has
tape–to–film transfer service and full
35mm digital scanning and recording
service

Film Work Group
Top Floor, Chelsea Reach
79–89 Lots Road
London SW10 0RN
Tel: 020 7352 0538
Fax: 020 7351 6479
Loren Squires, Nigel Perkins
Video and Film post–production
facilities. AVID on–line (2:1) and
off–line editing. 36 gigs storage,
Digital Animation Workstations
(draw, paint, image, modification,
edit). 3 machine Hi–Band SP and
mixed Beta SP/Hi–Band with DVE. 2
machine Lo–Band off–line with
sound mixing. 6 plate Steenbeck.
Special rates for grant aided,
self–funded and non–profit projects

FinePoint Broadcast
Furze Hill
Kingswood
Surrey KT20 6EZ
Tel: 0800 970 2020
Fax: 0800 970 2030
email: hire@finepoint.co.uk
Website: www.finepoint.co.uk
Broadcast equipment hire. Cameras,
lenses, control units, high speed
cameras, disc recorder, cables, VTRs,
edit controllers, digital video effects,
vision mixers, monitors, sound kit

Fisher Productions Europe Ltd
Studio House
Rita Road
Vauxhall
London SW8 1JU
Tel: 020 7582 8750
Fax: 020 7793 0467
(See Cinebuild)

FrameStore
9 Noel Street
London W1V 4AL
Tel: 020 7208 2600
Fax: 020 7208 2626
email: mandy.wells@framestore.

co.uk
Website: www.framestore.co.uk
Digital effects for film and video.
The latest technology, including Ursa
Diamond Telecine, 2x inferno/flame,
4x Henry, Digital Edit Suite, 3D
Computer Animation, Avid Editing
for commercials, broadcast and
graphic design projects. Plus digital
film opticals for feature effects,
repairs, pick–ups, restoration, titles
and tape to film transfers. Call
bookings or post–producers: Fiona,
Lottie, AJ and Drew for advice on
projects

Mike Fraser
Unit 6
Silver Road
White City Industrial Park
London W12 7SG
Tel: 020 8749 6911
Fax: 020 8743 3144
Mike Fraser, Rod Wheeler
Telecine transfer 35mm, 16mm and
S16; rushes syncing; non–linear edit
suites; film video list management,
post–production through OSC/R to
negative cutting. Storage

Frontline Television Services
44 Earlham Street
Covent Garden
London WC2H 9LA
Tel: 020 7836 0411
Fax: 020 7379 5210
Charlie Sayle
Extensive edit, duplication, computer
animation and multimedia facilities –
5 Avid Media Composers, Avid
Symphony, DS, Linear Digital
Betacam Suite. Low volume, low
cost, quick turnaround duplication.
2D and 3D animation and graphics.
Multimedia facilities including
encoding.

FX Projects
Studio House
Rita Road
Vauxhall
London SW8 1JU
Tel: 020 7582 8750
Fax: 020 7793 0467
(See Cinebuild)

Goldcrest Post Production Facilities Ltd
1 Lexington Street
London W1R 3HP
Tel: 020 7437 7972

Fax: 020 7437 5402
email:mailbox@goldcrest–post.co.uk
Alicja Syska, Raju Raymond
Theatre One with SSL5000 console,
Dolby SRD, film + video projection,
ADR & Effects recording, built in
Foley surfaces and extensive props;
Theatre Two with Otari Elite Plus
console, Dolby SRD, video
projection, ADR & Effects recording,
built in Foley surfaces & extensive
props; Theatre Three with Yamaha
O2R console, ADR & Effects
recording; Sound Transfer Bay for all
film and video formats with Dolby
SRD; Rank Cintel MKIIC Telecine
enhanced 4:2:2, Pogle and secondary
colour correction. Keycode and
Aaton readers, noise reduction, video
transfers to 1", Digibeta, Beta SP,
U–Matics, VHS and D2, ADAC
standards conversion. Non–linear
editing on and off line Avids and
Lightworks Turbo available. Cutting
rooms, production offices, duplex
apartments available

Hillside Studios
Merry Hill Road
Bushey
Herts WD2 1DR

Tel: 020 8950 7919
Fax: 020 8421 8085
email: enquiries@hillside-studios.co.uk
Website: www.hillside-studios.co.uk
David Hillier
Production and Post–Production facilities to Broadcast standards. 1500 sq ft studio with 16 x 9 switchable cameras and Digital Mixer. Smaller studio and single camera location units available. Sounds Studios and Dubbing Suite, Non–Linear and Digital Editing. Graphics, Set Design and Construction. Offices, restaurant and parking

Holloway Film & TV
68–70 Wardour Street
London W1V 3HP
Tel: 020 7494 0777
Fax: 020 7494 0309
Matt Stoddart
D5, D3, D2, Digital Betacam, 3 m/c Digital Betacam suite, AVID (AVRTT) on–line/Offline. Betacam SP, 1"C, BVU, Lo–Band Hi–8, Video–8, S–VHS, VHS, Standards Conversion, Audio Laybacks/Layoffs

Hull Time Based Arts
42 The High Street
Hull HU1 1PS
Tel: 01482 586340/216446
Fax: 01482 589952
email: lab@htba.demon.co.uk
Website: www.timebase.org
Jo Millett/Dan Van Heeswyk
Avid Media Composer 9000XL non–linear editing suite with 1:1 compression, digital I/O and Commotion 2.1 compositing software, Avid Media Composer 1000 editing suite with 2:1 compression, G4 with Final Cut Pro, ProTools Audio Suite, Multimedia authoring, DVC Pro, DVCam and DV cameras, DAT recorder, Data projector and all ancillary video equipment available. Special rates for non commercial projects

Humphries Video Services
Unit 2, The Willow Business Centre
17 Willow Lane
Mitcham
Surrey CR4 4NX
Tel: 020 8648 6111
Fax: 020 8648 5261
email: sales@hvs.bdx.co.uk
Website: www.hvs.co.uk
David Brown, Emma Lincoln
Video cassette duplication: all formats, any standard. Standards

convertors. Macrovision anti–copy process, labelling, shrink wrapping, packaging and mail out services, free collections and deliveries in central London. Committed to industrial and broadcast work

Interact Sound
160 Barlby Road
London W10 6BS
Tel: 020 8960 3115
Fax: 020 8964 3022
email: info@interact–sound.co.uk
Sandie Wirtz
Spacious digital and analogue dubbing theatres. Dolby stereo, SR–D. DTS compatible. Large screen film and video projection. 5 digital audio edit suites. Rooms available for production offices. Mixers: Aad Wirtz, Lee Taylor and John Falcini

ITN
200 Gray's Inn Road
London WC1X 8XZ
Tel: 020 7430 4134
Fax: 020 7430 4655
Martin Swain, Jenny Mazzey
2400 sq ft studio; live or recorded work; comprehensive outside source ability; audience 65; crews; video transfer; Westminster studio; graphics design service using Flash Harry, Paintbox etc; Training offered; Sound and dubbing; tape recycling; experienced staff

Terry Jones Post Productions Ltd
The Hat Factory
16–18 Hollen Street
London W1V 3AD
Tel: 020 7434 1173
Fax: 020 7494 1893
Terry Jones
Paul Jones or Matt Nutley
Lightworks V.I.P. online and Heavyworks editing suites. Plus computerised Beta offline and 35mm film editing facilities. Experiencd and creative, award winning editors handling commercials, documentaries, features and corporate work

Lee Lighting
Wycombe Road
Wembley
Middlesex HAO 1QD
Tel: 020 8900 2900
Fax: 020 8902 5500
Website: www.lee.co.uk
Film/TV lighting equipment hire

Light House Media Centre
The Chubb Buildings
Fryer Street
Wolverhampton WV1 1HT
Tel: 01902 716044
Fax: 01902 717143
Contact: Technical department
Three machine U–Matic edit suite (hi–band – BVE 900, lo–band BVE 600) VHS/U–Matic/Betacam/ENG kits, also animation and chroma keying

Lighthouse
9–12 Middle Street
Brighton BN1 1AL
Tel: 01273 384222
Fax: 01273 384233
email: info@lighthouse.org.uk
Website: www.lighthouse.org.uk
Technical Department
A training and production centre, providing courses, facilities and production advice. Avid off– and online edit suites. Apple Mac graphics and animation workstations. Digital video capture & manipulation. Output to/from Betacam SP. SVHS offline edit suite. Post Production and Digital Artists equipment bursaries offered three times a year

The Lux Centre – Lux Production Facilities
The Lux Centre for Film, Video and Digital Arts
2–4 Hoxton Square
London N1 6NU
Tel: 020 7684 0202
Fax: 020 7684 2222
email: lux@lux.org.uk
Website: www.lux.org.uk
Subsidised facilities for film, video and digital media production. 8mm & 16mm film cameras, digital video cameras, film and multi–format video editing, online and offline. Avids, Telecine and video transfer, digital audio editing, multimedia and Internet workstations, graphics, animation and much more. LCD video projectors, monitors and playback equipment for exhibition and events. Optical Printer for gauge transfers, colouring and all kinds of optical manipulation of film: Macs with Adobe Premiere for editing and Macromedia Director for interactive multimedia authoring: state of the art Avid editing suite: 16mm black and white film processing. Super 8, 16mm and Super 16 camera kits; Lighting including standard blonde

and redhead kits and the latest
Dedolight and Kino Flo Kits;
Analogue editing suites with
Steenbecks, plus a rare Super 8
Steenbeck; sound transfer room;
Rostrum Camera for animation, titles
and effects; broadcast quality Telecine

MAC Sound Hire
1–2 Attenburys Park
Park Road
Altrincham
Cheshire WA14 5QE
Tel: 0161 969 8311
Fax: 0161 962 9423
email: info@macsound.co.uk
Website: www.macsound.co.uk
Professional sound equipment hire

The Machine Room
54–58 Wardour Street
London W1V 3HN
Tel: 020 7734 3433
Fax: 020 7287 3773
email: david.atkinson@
machineroom.co.uk
Website: www.themachineroom.
co.uk
David Atkinson
2 wet/dry gate digital Telecine suites
with DVNR. VT viewing and sound
playback suite. Most digital and
analogue video tape formats in both

PAL and NTSC. Standards
conversion with Alchemist Phc and
Vector Motion Compensation
(VMC). Programme dubbing. VHS
duplication. Macrovision anti–piracy
system, 2 edit suites. FACT
accredited. Special rates for archive
film transfer. Full range of film
treatment services. See also Film
Treatment Centre under Laboratories.
Nitrate handling and nitrate storage
vaults. DVD Authoring and encoding

Mersey Film and Video (MFV)
13 Hope Street
Liverpool L1 9BQ
Tel: 0151 708 5259
Fax: 0151 707 8595
email: mfv@hopestreet.u–net.com
Website: www.mfv.merseyside.org
Julie Lau (Resource Manager)
Patrick Hall (Resource
Co–Ordinator)
Production facilities for: BETA SP,
DVCPro, Hi8, MiniDV, SVHS and
VHS – full shooting kits for all of the
above. Wide range of grip and
lighting equipment. All format tape
duplication and tape stock. Guidance
and help for funding, finance,
budgets production

Metro Broadcast
6–7 Great Chapel Street
London W1V 3AG
Tel: 020 7439 3494
Fax: 020 7437 3782
Mark Cox
Nayle Kemah
Broadcast Hire: Avid: MCO, Film
compsers, 9000,
Camera formats – Digital Beta, Beta
SX, Beta SP, DVC Pro, DV Cam,
Mini DV. VTRs, D2, D3, D5, DVW
A500 Broadcast crews available.
Duplication: Alchemist standards
conversion from/to all formats.
Technical assessment. Format
include: D1, D2, D3, Digital Beta,
Beta SX, DVC Pro DV Cam mini
DV. CD ROM, DVD

The Mill/Mill Film
40/41 Great Marlborough Street
London W1V 1DA
Tel: 020 7287 4041
Fax: 020 7287 8393
email: inb@mill.co.uk
Website: www.mill.co.uk
Emma Shield
Post Production for commercials and
feature films using Spirit, Ursa,
Inferno, Flame, Softimage, Henry,
Harry and digital editing

Millennium Studios
Elstree Way
Borehamwood
Herts WD6 1SF
Tel: 020 8236 1400
Fax: 020 8236 1444
Kate Tufano
Sound stage 80'x44'x24' with
6'x44'x11' balcony flying and cyc
grid. In house suppliers of: lighting;
generators; rigging; photography;
crew catering and fully licensed bar

Mister Lighting Studios Ltd
2 Dukes Road
Western Avenue
London W3 0SL
Tel: 020 8956 5600
Fax: 020 8956 5604
Steve Smith
Lighting equipment/studio hire

Molinare
34 Fouberts Place
London W1V 2BH
Tel: 020 7439 2244
Fax: 020 7734 6813
Video formats: Digital Betacam, D1,
D2, D3, 1", Beta SP, BVU, U–Matic,
VHS. NTSC: 1", Beta SP, U–Matic
& VHS. Editing: Editbox, three D1
serial digital suite; two component
multi–format; one composite
multi–format. DVEs: two A57, four
A53, DME, four ADO, Encore.
Storage: two A66, A64. Caption
Generators: Aston Motif, A72, Aston
Caption, Aston 3. Graphics: Harry
with V7 Paintbox, Encore and D1.
Harriet with V7 Paintbox, D1 and
Beta SP. 3D graphics with Silicon
Graphics and Softimage. Telecine:
Ursa Gold with Pogle + DCP, A57,
Rank Cintel 111 with 4.2.2 digital
links, wetgate, Pogle and DCP
controller and secondary colour
grading, 35mm, 16mm, S16mm/S8.
Audio: two digital studios, two 24
track and AudioFile studios,
track–laying studio with DAWN,
voice record studios, transfer room,
sound Fx libraries. Duplication,
standards conversion, Matrix camera,
BT landlines, satellite downlink

Mosiac Pictures Ltd
8–12 Broadwick Street
London W1V 1FH
Tel: 020 7437 6514
Fax: 020 7494 0595
email: info@mosaicfilms.com
Website: www.mosaicfilms.com
Emma Lewis, Facilities Manager
Avid Symphony, 6 Avid offline
suites, DV Camera Hire, Video

Transfer Suite, Final Cut Pro, DV
Post–Production expertise, Video
encoding for the Web,
Digibeta/16mm Aaton Cameramen,
meeting room, production offices

The Moving Picture Company
127 Wardour Street
London W1V 4AD
Tel: 020 7434 3100
Fax: 020 7437 3951/7287 5187
Video formats: D1, D2, Digital
Betacam, Betacam SP, 1" C format,
hi–/lo–band.
Editing: 3xD1/Disk based edit suites,
Sony 9100 and Abekas A84 (8
layers) A57 DVE, A64, A60 and A66
Disks; A72 and Aston Motif caption
generator. Video Rostrum and Colour
Caption Camera
Non Linear Offline Editing: 1 x Avid
4000 with Betacam SP. 35/16mm
cutting room
Telecine: 2 URSA Gold 4 x 4 with
Pogle DCP/Russell Square Colour
Correction Jump Free, Low
Speed/Silk Scan Options, Matchbox
Stills Store, Key Code, noise
reduction
SFX: Discreet Logic 2 x Flame, 1 x
Flint and Quantel 2 x Henry
3D: Hardware: 7 x SGI systems (3 x
High Impacts and 4 x Indigo 2
Extremes). Software: Alias
Poweranimator, Custom Programming
and Procedural Effects, Matador, 3D
Studio Paint, Elastic Reality and
Pandemonium. Rendering: SGI
Challenge and Onyx (x2). Digital
Film: High resolution 35mm digital
film post production, comprising 7 x
Kodak Cineon, 1 x Discreet Logic
Inferno and Matador. Filmtel TM
video tape to 35mm transfer. Mac:
Disk or ISDN input of artwork. File
transfer, Photoshop and Illustrator and
stills output to 35mm or high
resolution 5 x 4 transparencies.
Studio: 47' x 30' with L cyc

Northern Light
35/41 Assembly Street
Leith
Edinburgh EH6 7RG
Tel: 0131 553 2383
Fax: 0131 553 3296
Gordon Blackburn
Stage lighting equipment hire. Mains
distribution, staging, PA equipment
hire. Sale of colour correction
pyrotechnics etc

Oasis Television
6–7 Great Pulteney Street
London W1V 3LF
Tel: 020 7434 4133
Fax: 020 7494 2843
Helen Leicester
14 online suites (including digital
linear, analogue linear, Jaleo Digital,
Non–linear, Avid Online). 2 fully
digital audiodubbing suites. 11 Avid
and Lightworks offline services. 5
graphics suites C2D and 3D, including
illusion), standards conversion. Full
duplication facilities multimedia

Ocean Post
5 Upper James Street
London W1R 3HF
Tel: 020 7287 2297
Fax: 020 7287 0296
email: bookings@oceanpost.co.uk
Editbox suite, Avid online suites,
Avid offline suites

Omnititles
28 Manor Way
London SE3 9EF
Tel: 020 8297 7877
Fax: 020 8297 7877
email: Omnititles@compuserve.com
Spotting and subtitling services for
film, TV, video, satellite and cable.
Subtitling in most world languages

Oxford Film and Video Makers
The Stables
North Place
Headington
Oxford OX3 9HY
Tel: 01865 741682 or 01865 760074
(course enquiries)
Fax: 01865 742901
email: ofvm@ox39hy.demon.co.uk
Website: www.welcome.to/ofvm
Sue Evans, Office Administrator
Film and video equipment hire –
including Beta SP and non–linear
editing facility. FAST VM studio &
Adobe Premier. Wide range of
evening and weekend courses

Panavision Grips
5–11 Taunton Road
Metropolitan Centre
Greenford
Middx UB6 8UQ
Tel: 020 8578 2382
Fax: 020 8578 1536
email: pangrip.co.uk
Grip equipment and studio hire

The Pierce Rooms
Pierce House
Hammersmith Apollo
Queen Caroline Street

London W6 9QH
Tel: 020 8563 1234
Fax: 020 8563 1337
Deborah Cable
Complete surround sound facilities:
surround sound to picture recording.
Foley and mixing. Large and accurate
main control room – Neve VR 72–60
console with flying fader automation,
recall and digital surround
automation. Dynaudio M4–surround
sound monitoring. Separate digital
preproduction room. Permanent tie
lines to Apollo theatre for studio
quality live recordings. In house team
of engineers and programmers; 24
hour maintenance; private parking

Pinewood Studios
Sound Dept
Pinewood Road
Iver Heath
Bucks SL0 0NH
Tel: 01753 656301
Fax: 01753 656014
email: graham_hartstone
@pinewood–studios.co.uk
Graham Hartstone
Two large stereo dubbing theatres
with automated consoles, all digital
release formats. 35mm and digital
dubbing. Akai DD8 dubbers &
recorders, ADR & Foley recording.
Large ADR/Fx recording theatre,
35mm or AVID AUDIOVISION,
removable drives, ISDN Dolbyfax
with timecode in aux data. Digital
dubbing theatres with AMS/NEVE
Logic 2 and AudioFile Spectra 16.
Preview theatre 115 seats. Formats
35/70mm Dolby SR.D, DTS and
SDDS. Comprehensive transfer bay.
Stereo Optical Negative transfer
including Dolby SR.D, SDDS and
DTS. Cutting rooms

PMPP Facilities
69 Dean Street
London W1V 5HB
Tel: 020 7437 0979
Fax: 020 7434 0386
Website: www.pmpp.dircon.co.uk
Off–line editing: BVW SP, lo–band
and VHS. Non–linear editing: 5
custom built Avid suites either self
drive or with editor. On–line editing:
Digital Betacam, D3, D2, Beta SP,
1", BVU SP and Hi–8 formats. Three
suites with Charisma effects Aston or
A72 cap gen and GVG mixers.
Graphics: Matisse Painting,
Softimage 3D, Acrobat 3D,
animation and T–Morph morphing on
Silicon Graphics workstations. Sound
dubbing on Avid Audiovision or

AudioFile. Voiceover studio/A–DAT
digital multi–track recording. Full
transfer, duplication and standards
conversion service. Pack shot studio

Post Box
8 Lower James Street
London W1R 3PL
Tel: 020 7439 0600
Fax: 020 7439 0700
Jo Smith
Jo Beddington, Jason Elliott, Alice
Valdes–Scott
UK and international post
production. Offline, online, editbox,
Magnum and more – offering the
whole package for broadcasters

Red Post Production
Hammersley House
Hammersley House
London W1R 6JD
Tel: 020 7439 1449
Fax: 020 7439 1339
email: red–post@Demon.co.uk
email: redfx@demon.co.uk
Post production company specialising
in design and technical special effects
for commercials, video promos,
broadcast titles and idents, feature
film projects, broadcast projects
utilising computer animation
techniques. Motion capture, Flame,
Henry, Flash Harry. Full technical
supervision

Redapple
214 Epsom Road
Merrow
Guildford
Surrey GU1 2RA
Tel: 01483 455044
Fax: 01483 455022
Video formats: Beta SP, Beta Sx,
NTSC/PAL. Cameras: Sony DNW
90WSP 4:3016:9, IKEGAMI, V–55
Camcorders; Transport; VW
Caravelle and Volvo Camera Cars

Redwood Studios Recording & Film Post Production
1–6 Falconberg Court
London W1V 5FG
Andre Jacquemin – Managing
Director – Sound Designer
Post production for features including
large f/x library and digital audio
post work

Richmond Film Services
The Old School
Park Lane
Richmond

Surrey TW9 2RA
Tel: 020 8940 6077
Fax: 020 8948 8326
Sound equipment available for hire,
sales of tape and batteries, and UK
agent for Ursta recordists' trolleys
and Denecke timecode equipment

Salon Post–Productions
10 Livonia Street
London W1V 3PH
Tel: 020 7437 0516
Fax: 020 7437 6197
Website: www.salon.ndirect.co.uk
Editing Equipment rental –
non linear systems including Avid
Film Composer & Lightworks, hard
disk storage, BetaSP and DAT etc
Film equipment – including 35mm
and 16mm Steenbecks and all editing
accessories and supplies. Edit suites
in Soho or delivered to any location.
Digital sound editing systems include
Audiovision, AKAI, Protools

Sheffield Independent Film
5 Brown Street
Sheffield S1 2BS
Tel: 0114 272 0304
Fax: 0114 279 5225
email: admin.ympa@
workstation.org.uk
Colin Pons, Gloria Ward,
Alan Robinson
Aaton XTR + (S16/St 16). Vision 12
tripod S16/St 16. 6–plate Steenbeck.
Picsync. Nagra IS. SQN 45 mixer.
Microphones: 416, 816, ECM 55s.
SVHS edit suite. Avid MSP edit suite
Sony DXC537. UVW100
Betakit/Betacam (PVE
2800)/Hi–band SP (BVU 950)/Hi–8,
2 and 3 machine edit suite. Three
Chip cameras. Lighting equipment.
1,200 ft studio. Sony DVC Digital
Camcorder

Shepperton Sound
Shepperton Studios
Studios Road
Shepperton
Middx TW17 0QD
Tel: 01932 572676
Fax: 01932 572396
Three Dubbing Theatres (16mm,
35mm, video) Post–sync, and
footsteps; effects, theatre, in–house
sound transfers

Shepperton Studios
Studios Road
Shepperton
Middx TW17 0QD
Tel: 01932 562611
Fax: 01932 568989

email: sheppertonstudios@
dial.pipex.com
Cutting rooms; 16mm, 35mm
viewing theatres

Soho Images
8–14 Meard Street
London W1V 3HR
Tel: 020 7437 0831
Fax: 020 7734 9471
email: sohogroup.com
Website: www.sohoimages.com
Zahida Bacchus
Kodak endorsed laboratory offers full
processing of 16/35mm film, 24 hour
rushes, computerised in–house
negative cutting, cinema
commercials, broadcast and features
bulk prints, archive and restoration.
Facilities include: 8/16/35mm
Telecine transfers with Wet–Gate.
Spirit DataCine with POGAL
Platinum, URSA Gold with DCP,
Rank Cinitels' with up–grades.
Sound suite using Instant Sync,
InDaw and SADIE. Broadcast
standards conversions, aspect ratio
conversions, edit suites, Avid
Symphony Universal with 24P, 3D
and Animation. Flame, Henry and
Edit Box

Studo Pur
c/o Gargoyle Graphics
16 Chart St
London N1 6UG
Tel: 020 7490 5177
Fax: 020 7490 5177
email: sbayly@ich.ucl.ac.uk
Website: www.ace.mdx.ac.uk
/hyperhomes/houses/pur/index.htm
Simon Bayly, Lucy Thane
Media 100 & After Effects, Pro
Tools, Sony DSR–200 DVCAM
camcorder & tripod, Tascam portable
DAT, audio effects processing, 500
lumens video projector, multimedia
workstation, mics, lights & PA
equipment

SVC
142 Wardour Street
London W1V 3AU
Tel: 020 7734 1600
Fax: 020 7437 1854
Website: www.svc.co.uk
Catherine Langley
Video Post Production including the
following: Datacine, Inferno, Flame,
2 Infinitys; Henry, Computer
Animation and Motion Control

Tele–Cine
Video House

48 Charlotte Street
London W1P 1LX
Tel: 020 7208 2200
Fax: 020 7208 2250
email: telecine@telecine.co.uk
Website: www.telecine.co.uk
Wendy Bleazard
Digital linear and non linear editing;
telecine; audio post production; DVD
authoring; video compression; fibre
and satellite communications;
duplication

Tiny Epic Video Co
37 Dean Street
London W1V 5AP
Tel: 020 7437 2854
Fax: 020 7434 0211
Non–linear offlining on Avid, and
D/Vision. Tape offlining on Umatic
& VHS with and without shotlister.
Rushes dubbing. Tape transfers –
most formats including Hi–8 and
DAT. EDL Generation and
Translation

TVi
Film House
142 Wardour Street
London W1V 3AU
Tel: 020 7878 0000
Fax: 020 7878 7800
Website: www.tvi.co.uk
Mark Ottley, Joy Hancock
Post production; Telecine; sound
dubbing; copying and conversion.
Extensive integrated services
especially for film originated
programmes. Full digital compo–nent
environment. Wetgate digital Telecine
with Aaton and ARRI and full range
of gates including Super 16mm and
35mm wide aperture wetgate
transfers. Full film rushes transfer
service. Free film preparation service.
Wide range of VTRs including
Digital Betacam

TVMS, TV Media
420 Sauchiehall Street
Glasgow G2 3JD
Tel: 0141 331 1993
Fax: 0141 332 9040
Peter McNeill, Chas Chalmers
Media 100 off–line and on–line with
Beta SP and Digital facilities for
Broadcast, Commercials, and
Corporate Productions

TVP Videodubbing Ltd
2 Golden Square
London W1R 3AD
Tel: 020 7439 7138
Fax: 020 7434 1907
Jaqui Winston

Telecine transfer from 35mm, Super
16mm, 16mm and Super 8mm to all
video formats with full grading,
blemish concealment and image
restoration service. Video mastering,
reformatting and duplication to and
from any format; standards
conversion service including motion
compensation via the Alchemist Ph.
C. digital converter. Also landlines
for feeds to the BT Tower and
commercials playouts. Laserdisc
pre–mastering and full quality
assessment. Packaging

Twickenham Film Studios
St Margaret's
Twickenham
Middx TW1 2AW
Tel: 020 8607 8888
Fax: 020 8607 8889
Gerry Humphreys,
ISDN: 020 8744 1415
Gerry Humphreys, Caroline Tipple
Two dubbing theatres; ADR/Foley
theatre; 40 cutting rooms;
Lightworks, Avid, 16/35mm

Vector Television
Battersea Road
Heaton Mersey
Stockport
Cheshire SK4 3EA
Tel: 0161 432 9000
Fax: 0161 443 1325
Martin Tetlow
Vector Graphics; Vector Digital
Audio; Vector Digital editing; Vector
Studios; 2D/3D design and
visualisation consultancy

Video Film & Grip Company
23 Alliance Court
Alliance Road
London W3 0RB
Tel: 020 8993 8555
Fax: 020 8896 3941
Contact: G.Stubbings
Unit 9, Orchard Street Industrial
Estate, Salford
Manchester M6 6FL
Tel: 0161 745 8146
Fax: 0161 745 8161
Cardiff Studios, Culverhouse
Cross, Cardiff CF5 6XT
Tel: 029 2059 9777
Fax: 029 2059 7957
Suppliers of 35mm camera equipment.
16mm camera equipment for
documentaries, Digital SP and Beta SP
video equipment for broadcast, and
extensive range of cranes, dollies and
ancillary grip equipment

The Video Lab
Back West Crescent
St Annes on Sea
Lancs FY8 1SU
Tel: 01253 725499/712011
Fax: 01253 713094
Cintel Telecine 9.5/8/Super
8/16/35mm, slides and stills. Video
formats: 2", 1"C, BVU, U–Matic,
Beta SP. Cameras: Sony. Duplication,
standards conversion. Specialists in
transfer from discontinued videotape
formats. Library of holiday videos
(Travelogue), corporate and TV
production, TV and cinema
commercial production

Videola (UK)
162–170 Wardour Street
London W1V 3TA
Tel: 020 7437 5413
Fax: 020 7734 5295
Video formats: 1", U–Matic, Beta SP.
Camera: JVC KY35. Editing: three
machine Beta SP. Computer rostrum
camera. Lightworks offline

Videolondon Sound
16–18 Ramillies Street
London W1V 1DL
Tel: 020 7734 4811
Fax: 020 7494 2553
email: info@videolon.ftech.co.uk
Website: www.ftech.net/~videolon
Five sophisticated sound recording
studios with overhead TV projection
systems. 16mm, 35mm and video
post–sync recording and mixing. Two
Synclavier digital audio suites with
four further Synclaviers, five
AvidAudiovision, two StudioFrame
and one AudioFile assignable to any
of the studios. All sound facilities for
film or video post–production
including D3, DigiBetacam, Betacam
SP, 1" PAL and Dolby Surround for
TV with three Lightworks non–linear
editing systems

Videosonics Cinema Sound
68a Delancey Street
London NW1 7RY
Tel: 020 7209 0209
Fax: 020 7419 4470
2 x All Digital THX Film Dubbing
Theatres. Dolby Digital and SR 35
mm, 16mm and Super 16mm. All
aspect ratios, all speeds. Video
Projection if required Theatre I:
AMS–Neve Logic II console (112
channels) with 24track Audiofile.
Theatre II (Big Blue): AMS–Neve
DFC console (224 channels) with 2 x
24 track Audio files. 3 x additional
television Sound Dubbing Suites, 2

with AMS–Neve digital consoles, 1 x
SSL console. 6 x Digital Audio
Editing rooms, 35mm film editing,
Facilities for Lightworks and Avid 2
x Foley and ADR Studios. A total of
14 AMS Audiofiles. Parking by
arrangement. Wheelchair Access

VTR Ltd
64 Dean Street
London W1V 5HG
Tel: 020 7437 0026
Fax: 020 7439 9427
email: info@vtr.co.uk
Website: www.vtr.co.uk
Anthony Frend
VTR is one of London's major digital
non–linear post production facilities
specialising in commercials,
corporates and promos. Facilities
include: 2 x Spirit DataCines the
world's first real–time high resolution
film scanner for 35mm, 16mm and
super 16mm; Ursa Gold telecines
with Pogle Platinum and full range of
Ursa optical effects incl.
Kaleidoscope; Inferno and Flame for
resolution independent special effects
for TV and cinema. 3x Henry Infinity
for non–linear digital editing and
effects. 3D Computer Graphics and
Animation with Maya Software; Flint
RT, 3 x Macs; dubbing, ISDN and
playout facilities. Domino (digital
film effects) see under 'The Film
Factory at VTR.'

Windmill Lane Pictures
4 Windmill Lane
Dublin 2
Ireland
Tel: (353) 1 6713444
Fax: (353) 1 6718413
Liz Murphy
Telecine, digital on–line, AVID
off–line, Henry, Flame, Flint, EFP
Crews and number 4 Audio Studio

World Wide Sound
21–25 St Anne's Court
London W1V 3AW
Tel: 020 7434 1121
Fax: 020 7734 0619
email: sound@
worldwidegroup.ltd.uk
Website: www. worldwidegroup.
ltd.uk
Richard King
16/35mm, digital and Dolby
recording, track laying facilities,
specialising in post sync foreign
dubbing. Mixing for film – television
incl. Dolby Surround

Worldwide Television News (WTN Facilities)
The Interchange
Oval Road
Camden Lock
London NW1
Tel: 020 7410 5410
Fax: 020 7410 5335
Anne Marie Phelan
2 TV studios (full cyc and
component key); Digital Betacam
and Beta SP editing (PAL and
NTSC), Quantel Newsbox
Non–linear online editing; Vistek
VMC Digital standards conversion;
Soundstation Digital Audio dubbing;
UK and international satellite
delivery and crews

FESTIVALS

Listed below by country of origin are a selection of international film, television and video festivals with contact addresses and brief synopses

Australia

Melbourne International Film Festival
– July/August
PO Box 2206, Fitzroy Mail Centre
Fitzroy 3065
Victoria
Tel: (61) 3 417 2011
Fax: (61) 3 417 3804
Non–competitive showcase for Australian and International features, documentaries, animation together with an international short film competition

Sydney Film Festival
– June
PO Box 950
Glebe NSW 2037
Tel: (61) 2 9660 3844
Fax: (61) 2 9692 8793
email: sydfilm@ozonline.com.au
Website: www.sydfilm–fest.com.au/
A broad–based non–competitive Festival screening around 200 films not previously shown in Australia: features, documentaries, shorts, animation, video and experimental work. Competitive section for Australian short films only. Audience votes for best documentary, short and feature

Austria

Viennale – Vienna International Film Festival
– 13–25 October 2000
Siebensterngasse 2
A–1070
Vienna
Tel: (43) 1 526 5947
Fax: (43) 1 523 4172
email: office@viennale.at
Website: www.viennale.at
Non–competitive for features and documentaries. Additional categories:

Twilight Zone; Tributes; Historical Retrospective

Belgium

Brussels International Festival of Fantasy, Thriller and Science Fiction Films
– March
144 avenue de la Reine
1030 Brussels
Tel: (32) 2 201 17 13
Fax: (32) 2 201 14 69
Website: www.bifff.org/
Competitive for features and shorts (less than 20 mins)

Brussels International Film Festival
25 January 2001 – 3 February 2001
Chaussée de Louvain 30
B – 1210 Brussels
Tel: (32) 2 227 39 80
Fax: (32) 2 218 18 60
email: infoffb@netcity.be
Website: www.brusselsfilmfest.be
Christian Thomas
This is a competitive festival for European general interest films, annually showing about 100 features and 120 shorts. European features and shorts eligible to compete for Golden and Silver Iris Awards. Belgian shorts eligible to compete for Golden Iris Awards. Sections include European Competition, Kaleidoscope of the World Cinema, Belgian Focus with a National Competition for shorts and documentaries, 2001: Focus on New German directors, Special Events and Tributes. Feature entries should be over 60 minutes and shorts should be under 30 minutes. Formats accepted: 35mm, 16mm (Belgian films only). Deadline: 31st October. No entry fee

Flanders International Film Festival – Ghent
– October
1104 Kortrijksesteenweg
B–9051 Ghent
Tel: (32) 9 221 89 46
Fax: (32) 9 221 90 74
email: filmfestival@glo.be
Website: www.filmfestival.be

Contact: Jacques Dubrulle, Secretary–general, Walter Provo, Programme Executive Marian Ponnet, Guest Officer. Belgium's most prominent yearly film event. Competitive, showing 150 feature films and 80 shorts from around the world. Best film award $35,000. Deadline for entry forms mid August

Brazil

Gramado International Film Festival – Latin and Brazilian Cinema
– August
Avenida das Hortensias 2029
Grande 95670–000
Gramado – Rio do Sul
Tel: (55) 54 286 2335
Fax: (55) 54 286 2397
email: festival@via–rs.com.br
Website: www.viadigital.com.br/gramado
For exhibition of audiovisual products from Latin language speaking countries

Mostra Rio – Rio de Janeiro Film Festivals
– September
Rua Voluntários dá Pátria 97
CEP 22270–010
Rio de Janeiro RJ
Tel: (55) 21 539 1505
Fax: (55) 21 539 1247
Website: www.estacao.ignet.com.br/mostra/
Non–competitive, promoting films that would not otherwise get to Brazilian screens

São Paulo International Film Festival
20 October – 2 November 2000
Alameda 937, Cj 303
São Paulo SP 01424–001
Tel: (55) 11 3083 5137/3064 5819
Fax: (55) 11 3085 7936
email: info@mostra.org
Website: www.mostra.org
Renata de Almeida
Two sections, international selection (for features, shorts, documentary, animation) and a competitive section

for films of new directors (first, second or third feature), produced during two years preceding the festival

Burkina Faso

Panafrican Film and TV Festival of Ouagadougou
– February/March odd years
Secrétariat Général Permanent du
FESPACO
01 BP 2505
Ouagadougou 01
Tel: (226) 30 75 38
Fax: (226) 31 25 09
Competitive, featuring African diaspora and African film–makers, whose work has been produced during the three years preceding the Festival, and not shown before at FESPACO

Canada

The Atlantic Film Festival (Halifax)
– September
PO Box 36139
Halifax
Nova Scotia B3J 3S9
Tel: (1) 902 422 3456
Fax: (1) 902 422 4006
email: festival@atlanticfilm.com
Website: www.atlanticfilm.com
Gordon Whittaker – Executive Director
Lia Rinaldo – Program Director
Gregor Ash, Operations Manager
Entry Deadline: 9 June 2000
Located in coastal Halifax, Nova Scotia, the Atlantic Film Festival is a nine–day celebration of film known for its warm and festive atmosphere

Banff Television Festival
– June
1516 Railway Avenue
Canmore, Alberta, T1W 1P6
Tel: (1) 403 678 9260
Fax: (1) 403 678 9269
email: banff@banfftvfest.com
Website: www.banfftvfest.com
Competitive for programmes made for television, including short and long drama, limited and continuing series, arts and social and political documentaries, children's programmes, comedy, performance specials, information and animation programmes broadcast for the first time in the previous year and popular science programmes

Festival International du Film Sur L'Art (International Festival of Films on Art)
– March
640 rue St Paul Ouest
Bureau 406
Montreal, Quebec H3C 1L9
Tel: (1) 514 874 1637
Fax: (1) 514 874 9929
email: fifa@maniacom.com
Website: www.maniacom.com/fifa.html
The Festival encompasses all the arts, of any period or style. Films and videos must preferably be in French, otherwise in English, in their original, subtitled or dubbed version

Montreal International Festival of New Cinema and New Media
– October
Boulevard Saint–Laurent 3536
Montreal
Quebec H2X 2V1
Tel: (1) 514 847 9272
Fax: (1) 514 847 0732
email: montrealfest@fcmm.com
Website: www.fcmm.com
Claude Chamberlan
Discovery and promotion of outstanding international films, video and new media creations produced during previous two years, which have not been previously screened in Canada. Non–competitive (although some prizes in cash are awarded)

Montreal World Film Festival (+ Market)
– August/September
1432 de Bleury St
Montreal
Quebec H3A 2JI
Tel: (1) 514 848 3883
Fax: (1) 514 848 3886
Competitive festival recognized by the International Federation of Film Producers Associations. Categories: Official Competition; World Greats; World Cinema: Reflections of Our Time; Cinema of Tomorrow: New Trends; Latin American Cinema; Focus on Irish Cinema; Panorama Canada; Films for Television (documentaries and fiction films); Tributes

Ottawa International Animation Festival
– September
2 Daly Avenue
Ottawa

Ontario K1N 6E2
Tel: (1) 613 232 8769
Fax: (1) 613 232 6315
email: oiaf@ottawa.com
Website: www.awn.com/ottawa
Chris Robinson, Executive Director
Competitive. Next festival in 2002

Toronto International Film Festival
– September
Suite 1600 2 Carlton Street
Toronto
Ontario M5B IJ3
Tel: (1) 416 967 7371
Fax: (1) 416 967 9477
Non–competitive for feature films and shorts not previously shown in Canada. Also includes some American premieres, retrospectives and national cinema programmes. Films must have been completed within the year prior to the Festival to be eligible

Vancouver International Film Festival
– September/October
Suite 410, 1008 Homer Street
Vancouver
British Columbia V6B 2X1
Tel: (1) 604 685 0260
Fax: (1) 604 688 8221
email: viff@viff.org
Website: www.viff.org
Third largest festival in North America, with special emphasis on East Asian, Canadian and documentary films. Also British and European cinema and 'the Annual Film & Television Industry Trade Forum. Submission deadline mid–July

Croatia

World Festival of Animated Films – Zagreb
– June even years
Koncertna direkcija Zagreb
Kneza Mislava 18
10000 Zagreb
Tel: (385 – 1) 46 11 808/46 11 709/46 11 598
Fax: (385 – 1) 46 11 807/46 11 808
email: kdz@zg.tel.hr
Website: www.animafest.hr/
Competitive for animated films (up to 30 mins). Categories: a) films from 30 secs–6 mins, b) films from 6–15 mins, c) 15 min–30mins. Awards: Grand Prix, First Prize in each category (ABC), Best First Production (Film Debut) Best

Student Film, Five Special Distinctions. Films must have been completed in two years prior to the Festival and not have been awarded prizes

Cuba

International Festival of New Latin American Cinema
– December
Calle 23
1155 Vedado
Havana 4
Tel: (53) 7 552841 552849
Fax: (53) 7 33 30 78 /33 4273
Competitive for films and videos

Czech Republic

'Golden Prague' International TV Festival
– May
Czech Television
Kavci Hory
140 70 Prague 4
Tel: (42) 2 6113 4405/4028
Fax: (42) 2 6121 2891
Competitive for television music programmes and other types of serious music, dance, jazz and world music, music programmes. Entry forms must be submitted by 31st January and videos by 15th February

Karlovy Vary International Film Festival
– July
Film Servis Festival Karlovy Vary
Panská 1
110 00 Prague 1
Tel: (420) –2 2423 5412
Fax: (420) – 2 2423 3408
email: secretarial@iffkv.cz
Website: www.iffkv.cz/
Non–specialised international competition of feature films; international competition of full–length and short documentary films; non–competitive informational film programmes, retrospectives, homage profiles and other accompanying events approved by the Film Servis Festival Board. Works produced after 1st January 1999 can be included in competitive sections. It is obligatory that these films have not been previously shown in the competition section of another international film festival

Denmark

Balticum Film and TV Festival
– June
Skippergade 8
3740 Svaneke
Tel: (45) 7023 0024
Fax: (45) 7023 0025
Website: www.dk–web.com/bbf/
Competitive for documentaries from the countries around the Baltic Sea. Three categories: Best Film less than 35 minutes; Best film more than 35 minutes. Three prizes in each category in the Balticum competition: a special press juries prize. The Film School Competition: Only European Film Schools can enter new projects. 2 Prizes: Best film school documentary and best film school fiction

Copenhagen Film Festival
FSI
Vesterbrogade 35
1620 Copenhagen V
Tel: (45) 33 25 25 01
Fax: (45) 33 25 57 56
email: fside@datashopper.dk
Festival for the public. Previews of American, European and Danish films, both by established filmmakers and those less well known. Around 120 films, plus seminars and exhibition

International Odense Film Festival
– August
Vindegade 18
5100 Odense C
Tel: (45) 6613 1372 x4044
Fax: (45) 6591 4318
email: filmfestival@post.odkomm.dk
Website: www.filmfestival.dk/
Competitive for fairy–tale and experimental–imaginative films. Deadline for entries 1 April

Egypt

Cairo International Film Festival
November/December
17 Kasr El Nil Street
Cairo
Tel: (20) 2 392 3562/3962/393 3832
Fax: (20) 2 393 8979
Competitive for feature films, plus a film, television and video market

Cairo International Film Festival for Children
September
17 Kasr el El Nil Street
Cairo
Tel: (20) 2 392 3562/3962/393 3832
Fax: (20) 2 393 8979
Competitive for children's films: features, shorts, documentaries, educative, cartoons, television films and programmes for children up to 14 years

Finland

Midnight Sun Film Festival
June
Jäämerentie 9
99600 Sodankylä
Tel: (358) (0)16 614 524/614 522
Fax: (358) (0)16 618 646
Non–competitive for feature films, held in Finnish Lapland

Tampere 31st International Short Film Festival
7–11 March 2001
PO Box 305
33101 Tampere
Tel: (358) 3 213 0034
Fax: (358) 3 223 0121
email: office@tamperefilmfestival.fi
Website: www.tamperefilmfestival.fi
Competitive for short films, max. 30 mins. Categories for animated, fiction and documentary short films, completed on or after 1st January 1999. Videos (VHS) required for selection, only 16mm and 35mm screening prints. Extensive special programme of short films from all over the world, quality film market. Competition deadline 7 December 2000

France

20th Amiens International Film Festival
10–19 November 2000
MCA – 2 Place Léon Gontier
F–80000 Amiens
Tel: (33) 322 713570
Fax: (33) 322 92 53 04
email: amiensfilmfestival@burotec.fr
Films completed after 15 September 1998, and which make a contribution to the identity of people or an ethnic minority, are eligible for entry. They may be either full–length or short, fiction or documentary films

Annecy International Festival of Animation (+ Market)
– May
JICA/MIFA
BP 399
74013 Annecy Cédex
Tel: (33) 04 50 10 09 00
Fax: (33) 04 50 10 09 70
Competitive for animated short films, feature–length films, TV films, commercials, produced in the previous 26 months

Cannes International Film Festival – Festival International du Film de Cannes 54 ème édition
– May
99 Boulevard Malesherbes
75008 Paris
Tel: (33) 1 45 61 66 00
Fax: (33) 1 45 61 97 60
email: festival@festival–cannes.fr
Website: www.festival–cannes.org
Helene Lecomte
Competitive section for feature films and shorts (up to 15 mins) produced in the previous year, which have not been screened outside country of origin nor been entered in other competitive festivals, plus non–competitive section: Un Certain Regard & Cinefondation. Other non–competitive events: Directors Fortnight (Quinzaine des Réalisateurs)
14, rue Alexandre Parodi
75010 Paris
Tel: (33) 1 44 89 99 99
Fax: (33) 1 44 89 99 60
Critic's Week (Semaine de la Critique)
52 rue Labrouste
75015 Paris
Tel: (33) 1 56 08 18 88
Fax: (33) 1 56 08 18 28

Cinéma du Réel, (International Festival of Visual Anthropology)
Bibliothèque Publique
d'Information
25 rue du Renard
75197 Paris Cedex 04
Tel: (33) 1 44 78 44 21/45 16
Fax: (33) 1 44 78 12 24
email: cinereel@bpi.fr
Website: www.bpi.fr
Suzette Glenadel
Documentaries only (film or video). Competitive – must not have been released commercially or been awarded a prize at an international

festival in France. Must have been made in the year prior to the Festival

Cognac International Thriller Film Festival
– April
Le Public Systeme
36 rue Pierret
92200 Neuilly–sur–Seine
Tel: (33) 1 46 40 55 00
Fax: (33) 1 46 40 55 39
email: cognac@pobox.com
Competitive for thriller films, which have not been commercially shown in France or participated in festivals in Europe (police movies, thrillers, 'film noirs', court movies, investigations etc)

Deauville Festival of American Film
– September
36 rue Pierret
92200 Neuilly–sur–Seine
Tel: (33) 1 46 40 55 00
Fax: (33) 1 46 40 55 39
email: deauville@pobox.com
Studio previews (non competitive) Independent Films Competition and panorama. US productions only

Festival Cinématographique d'Automne de Gardanne
27 October – 7 November 2000
Cinéma 3 Casino
11 cours Forbin
13120 Gardanne
Tel: (33) (0)442 51 44 93
Fax: (33) (0) 442 58 17 86
email: festival.cinema.gardanne@wanadoo.fr
Includes European Competition of Shorts. Aims to discover high quality European cinema. Also junior section and retrospectives. All films for competition to be submitted on VHS, and to have been produced in the year prior to the Festival

Festival des Trois Continents
– November
BP 43302
44033 Nantes Cedex 1
Tel: (33) 2 40 69 74 14
Fax: (33) 2 4073 55 22
Feature–length fiction films from Africa, Asia, Latin and Black America. Competitive section, tributes to directors and actors, panoramas

Festival du Film Britannique de Dinard
– September

47 boulevard Féart
35800 Dinard
Tel: (33) 99 88 19 04
Fax: (33) 99 46 67 15
Competitive, plus retrospective and exhibition; tribute meeting between French and English producers

Festival International de Films de Femmes
– April
Maison des Arts
Place Salvador Allende
94000 Créteil
Tel: (33) 1 49 80 38 98
Fax: (33) 1 43 99 04 10
email: filmsfemme@wanadoo.fr
Website: www.gdebussac.fr/filmfem
Jacki Buet
Competitive for feature films, documentaries, shorts, retrospectives directed by women and produced in the previous 23 months and not previously shown in France

FIFREC (International Film and Student Directors Festival)
– June
16 chemin de Pommier
69330 Jons/Lyon
Tel: (33) 72 02 48 64
Fax: (33) 72 02 20 36
Official film school selections (three per school) and open selection for directors from film schools, either students or recent graduates. Categories include fiction, documentaries and animation. Also best film school award. Films to be under 40 mins

French–American Film Workshop
– June
10 Montée de la Tour
30400 Villeneuve–les–Avignon
Tel: (04) 90 25 93 23
Fax: (04) 90 25 93 24
198 Avenue of the Americas
New York, NY 10013
USA
Tel: (212) 343 2675
Fax: (212) 343 1849
email: JHR2001@AOL
Contact: Jerome Henry Rudes, General Director
The Workshop brings together independent filmmakers from the United States and France at the Avignon/New York Film Festival and Rencontres Cinématographiques Franco–Américanes d'Avignon (see below). French and American

independent film is celebrated with new films, retrospectives, round–tables on pertinent issues and daily receptions

Avignon/New York Film Festival
(April)
Alliance Française/French Institute, 22 East 60th Street, New York, NY – with 'the 21st Century Filmmaker Awards'
Rencontres Cinématographiques Franco–Américanes d'Avignon
(June)
Cinéma Vox, Place de l'Horloge, Avignon, France – with 'The Tournage Awards'

Gérardmer–Fantastic Arts International Fantasy Film Festival
– January
36 rue Pierret
92200 Neuilly–sur–Seine
Tel: (33) 1 46 40 55 00
Fax: (33) 1 46 40 55 39
email: fantasticarts@pdox.com
Competitive for international fantasy feature films (science–fiction, horror, supernatural etc)

International Festival of European Cinema La Boule
– October
97 Rue Raumur
75002 Paris
Tel: (33) 1 4041 0454
Fax: (33) 1 4026 5478
Categories for European feature, short film, animation and documentary. Prizes for best director, actor and actress

MIP–TV
– April
Reed MIDEM Organisation
179 avenue Victor Hugo
75116 Paris
Tel: (33) 1 44 34 44 44
Fax: (33) 1 44 34 44 00
International television programme market, held in Cannes

MIPCOM
– October
Reed MIDEM Organisation
179 avenue Victor Hugo
75116 Paris
Tel: (33) 1 44 34 44 44
Fax: (33) 1 44 34 44 00
International film and programme market for television, video, cable and satellite, held in Cannes

Germany

Berlin International Film Festival
– February
Internationale Filmfestspiele Berlin
Budapester Strasse 50
10787 Berlin
Tel: (49) 30 254 890
Fax: (49) 30 254 89249
Website: www.berlinale.de/
Competitive for feature films and shorts (up to 10 mins), plus a separate competition for children's films – feature length and shorts – produced in the previous year and not entered for other festivals. Also has non–competitive programme consisting of forum of young cinema, panorama, film market and New German films

Feminale, 10th International Women's Film Festival
– October
Feminale
Maybachstr, 111
50670 Cologne
Tel: (0049) 221 1300225
Fax: (0049) 221 1300281
email: info@feminale.de
Website: www.feminale.de
Katja Mildenberger, Carla Despineux
Biannual festival for films and videos by women directors only produced in 1999/2000, all genres, formats, lengths. Sections are Euro Pool, Horizons, Zoo, in Queer Looks and Portrait

Femme Totale – International Women's Film Festival
28 March – 1 April 2001
c/o Kulturbüro der Stadt Dortmund
Kleppingstr 21–23
44122 Dortmund
Tel: (49) 231 50 25 162
Fax: (49) 231 50 25 734
email: info@femmetotale.de
Website: www.femmetotale.de
Silke Johanna Räbiger
Held every two years. Women Film–makers' Festival screens features, short films, documentaries and videos. Workshops and seminars

Filmfest Hamburg
– September
Friedensallee 1
22765 Hamburg
Tel: (49) 40 398 26 210
Fax: (49) 40 398 26 211
Non–competitive, international features and shorts for cinema release (fiction, documentaries), presentation of one film country/continent, premieres of Hamburg–funded films, and other activities

International Festival of Animated Film Stuttgart
– April
Festivalbüro
Teckstrasse 56 (Kulturpark Berg)
70190 Stuttgart
Tel: (49) 711/925460
Fax: (49) 711/9254615
Competitive for animated short films of an artistic and experimental nature, which have been produced in the previous two years and not exceeding 35 mins. Animation, exhibitions and workshops. DM 139.000 worth of prizes

International Film Festival Mannheim – Heidelberg
9-18 November 2000
Collini–Center, Galerie
68161 Mannheim
Tel: (49) 621 10 29 43
Fax: (49) 621 29 15 64
email:
ifmh@mannheim–filmfestival.com
Website:
www.mannheim–filmfestival.com
Dr Michael Koetz, Director
Competition for young directors from all over the world. (Deadline for submission of films 25 August). Former participants were Truffaut, Fassbinder, Jarmusch, Egoyan, Vinterberg. Additional parts of the annual event are the "Co–Production Meetings" for producers seeing co–production opportunities/partners (deadline for submission of projects: 31 July) and the "New Film Market" for buyers

International FilmFest Emden
– May/June
An der Berufsschule 3
26721 Emden
Tel: (49) 4921 915 535
Fax: (49) 4921 915 591
email: filmfest@filmfest–emden.de
Website: www.filmfest–emden.de
Harald Tobermann, Thorsten Hecht
Established 1989. Germany's only fest focussing on British films, including a tribute to a British director. Audience awarded prizes for best feature film (DM20,0000) and best short film/animation (DM8,000)

made in Northwest Europe and German–speaking countries, and trade union sponsored jury award (DM7,500). British feature submissions to: Harald Tobermann Tel 0131 554 7391 **email:** harald@britishfilms.cjb.net

Internationales Filmwochenende Würzburg
– January
Gosbertsteige 2
97082 Würzburg
Tel: (49) 931 414 098
Fax: (49) 931 416 279
Competitive section for recent European and international productions, plus non–competitive section including tributes to directors as well as panoramas. Videos accepted for selection only

Internationales Leipziger Festival für Dokumentar– und Animationsfilm
– October/November
Grosse Fleischergasse 11
04109 Leipzig
Tel: (49) 341 9 80 39 21
Fax: (49) 341 9 80 61 41
email: dok–leipzig@t–online.de
Website: www.dokfestival–leipzig.de
Competition, special programmes, retrospective, international juries and awards

Munich Film Festival
– April/May
Internationale Münchner Filmwochen
Kaiserstrasse 39
80801 Munich
Tel: (49) 89 38 19 04 0
Fax: (49) 89 38 19 04 26
Non–competitive for feature films, shorts and documentaries which have not previously been shown in Germany

Munich International Documentary Festival
– May
Troger Strasse 46
Munich D–81675
Tel: (49) 89 470 3237
Fax: (49) 89 470 6611
email: filmstadt@t–online.de
Website: www.artechock.de/dokfestival
Gudrun Geyer
Ulla Wessler

Nordic Film Days Lübeck
– 2–5 November 2000
23539 Lübeck

Tel: (49) 451 122 41 05
Fax: (49) 451 122 41 06
email: info@filmtage.luebeck.de
Website: www.filmtage.luebeck.de
Festival of Scandinavian and Baltic films. Competitive for feature, children's, documentary, and Nordic countries' films

Oberhausen International Short Film Festival
– April
Grillostrasse 34
46045 Oberhausen
Tel: (49) 208 825 2652
Fax: (49) 208 825 5413
email: info@kurzfilmtage.de
Website: www.shortfilm.de
Competitive for documentaries, animation, experimental, short features and videos (up to 35 mins), produced in the previous 28 months; international competition and German competition; international symposia

Prix Europa
– October
Sender Freies Berlin
D–14046 Berlin
Tel: (0049 30) 3031 1610
Fax: (0049 30) 3031 1619
email: prix–europa@t–online.de
Website: www.prix–europa.de
Susanne Hoffmann
Competitive for fiction, non–fiction, current affairs, multicultural matters (Prix Iris) in television; documentary, drama, marketplace for young ears in radio. Open to all broadcasting organisations and producers in Europe

Prix Jeunesse International
– June
Bayerischer Rundfunk
80300 Munich
Tel: (49) 89 5900 2058
Fax: (49) 89 5900 3053
email: ubz@prixjeunesse.de
Website: www.prixjeunesse.de
Competitive for children's and youth television programmes (age groups up to 7, 7–12 and 12–17), in fiction and non–fiction, produced in the previous two years. (In odd years: seminars in children's and youth television)

Greece

International Thessaloniki Film Festival
– November

36 Sina Street
10672 Athens
Tel: (30) 1 645 36 69
Fax: (30) 1 644 81 43
email: filmfestival@magnet.gr
Dedicated to the promotion of independent cinema from all over the world. International Competition for first or second features (Golden Alexander worth approx. $43,000, Silver Alexander $27,000). Official non–competitive section for Greek films produced in 2000, informative section with the best independent films of the year, retrospectives, exhibitions, special events etc

Hong Kong

Hong Kong International Film Festival
– April
Level 7, Admin Building, Hong Kong Cultural Centre
10 Salisbury Road, Tsimshatsui Kowloon
Tel: (852) 2734 2892
Fax: (852) 2366 5206
email: hkiff@hkiff.org.hk
Website: hkiff.org.hk
Richie Lam
Non–competitive for feature films, documentaries and invited short films, which have been produced in the previous two years. Also a local short film and video competition, and a FIPRESCI Award for Young Asian cinema

Hungary

Hungarian Film Week
– February
Magyar Filmunio
Varosligeti fasor 38
H – 1068 Budapest
Tel: (361) 351 7760
Fax: (361) 351 7766
Competitive festival for Hungarian features, shorts and documentaries

India

International Film Festival of India (IFFI)
– January
Directorate of Film Festivals
Fourth Floor, Lok Nayak Bhavan
Khan Market,
New Delhi 110 003
Tel: (91) 11 4615953/4697167
Fax: (91) 11 4623430

Malti Sahai (Director)
Organised from January 10–20, each year and recognised by FIAPF. It is held in different Indian Film Cities by rotation including New Delhi, Bangalore, Bombay, Calcutta, Hyderbad and Trivandrum. IFFI'98 was organised in New Delhi and featured a specialised competition section for Asian film makers

International Film Festival of Kerala
– April
Kerala State Chalachitra Academy
Elankom Gardens
Vellyambalam
Trivandrum 695 010
Kerala
Tel: (91) 471 330994
Fax: (91) 471 325627
William Siepmann
Asian Cinema. Retrospectives of European, African and Japanese Cinema. International advertising films

Mumbai International Film Festival for Documentary, Short and Animation Films
– February
Films Division, Ministry of Information and Broadcasting
Government of India
24–Dr G Deshmukh Marg
Bombay 400 026
Tel: (91) 22 3864633/3873655/3861421/3861461
Fax: (91) 22 3800308
email: filsd@bom4.vsnl.net.in
Website: www.filmsdivision.org
Ramaswamy Babu
Competitive for fiction, non–fiction and animation films, plus Golden/Silver Conch and cash awards and Information Section

Iran

Tehran International Market (TIM)
c/o CMI
53 Koohyari Street
Fereshteh Avenue, Tehran 19658
Tel: (98) 21 254 8032
Fax: (98) 21 255 1914
The fourth Tehran International Market is designed to provide major producers from the West a personalised arena to target regional program buyers and theatrical distributors in the lucrative Middle East market and surrounding areas. Buyers will also represent the Persian

Gulf States, Asia and the Indian subcontinent, Central and Eastern Europe. More than 1,500 hours of programming was brought by Iranian TV alone during TIM'96

Ireland

Cork International Film Festival
– October
Hatfield House, Tobin Street
Cork
Tel: (353) 21 271711
Fax: (353) 21 275945
email: ciff@indigo.ie
Non–competitive, screening a broad range of features, shorts and documentaries from over 40 countries. Films of every category welcomed for submission.
Competitive: short films

Dublin Film Festival
– March
1 Suffolk Street
Dublin 2
Tel: (353) 1 679 2937
Fax: (353) 1 679 2939

Israel

Haifa International Film Festival
– October
142 Hanassi Avenue
Haifa 34633
Tel: (972) 4 8353530/8353521
Fax: (972) 4 8384327
email: haifaff@netvision.net.il
Website: www.haifaff.co.il
Pnina Blayer
The biggest annual meeting of professionals associated with the film industry in Israel. Competitions: 1. 'Golden Anchor' award $25,000 for mediterranean cinema. 2. Israeli Film Competition award $30,000

Jerusalem Film Festival
– July
PO Box 8561, Wolfson Gardens
Hebron Road
91083 Jerusalem
Tel: (972) 2 672 4131
Fax: (972) 2 673 3076
email: jer–cin@jer–cin.org.il
Website: www.jer–cin.org.il
Lia Van Leer
Finest in recent international cinema, documentaries, animation, avant garde, retrospectives, special tributes and homages, Mediterranean and

Israeli cinema, retrospectives, restored class Best Israeli Screenplay. Three international awards: Wim van Leer In Spirit of Freedom focus on human rights; Mediterranian Cinema; Jewish Theme Awards

Italy

Da Sodoma a Hollywood
– April
Turin Lesbian and Gay Film Festival, Associazione Culturale L'Altra Communicazione
Piazza San Carlo 161
10123 Turin
Tel: (39) 11 534 888
Fax: (39) 11 534 796
email:glfilmfest@assioma.com
Specialist lesbian/gay themed festival. Competitive for features, shorts and documentaries. Also retrospectives and special showcases for both cinema and television work

Europa Cinema & TV Viareggio, Italy
– September
Via XX Settembre Mo 3
Tel: (39) 6 42011184 (39) 6 42000211
Fax: (39) 6 42010599
An international competition of European Films

Festival dei Popoli – International Review of Social Documentary Films
– November
Borgo Pinti 82r
50121 Firenze
Tel: (39) 55 244 778
Fax: (39) 55 241364
email: fespopol@dadait
Mario Simondi (Secretary General)
Patricia Baroni (Assistant)
Franco Lucchesi (President)
Competitive and non–competitive sections for documentaries on sociological, historical, political, anthropological subjects, as well as music, art and cinema, produced during the year preceding the festival. The films for the competitive section should not have been screened in Italy before

Giffoni Film Festival
– July/August
Piazza Umberto I
84095 Giffoni Valle Piana
Tel: (39) 89 868 544
Fax: (39) 89 866 111

Competitive for full–length fiction for children 12–14 and 12–18 years. Entries must have been produced within two years preceding the festival

MIFED
29 October – 2 November 2000
Largo Domodossola 1
20145 Milan
Tel: (39) 2 480 12912 –48012920
Fax: (39) 2 499 77020
email: mifed@fmd.it
Website: fmd.it/mifed
Euena Lloyd
International market for companies working in the film and television industries

Mystery & Noir Film Festival
– December
Via Tirso 90
00198 Rome
Tel: 39 6 8848030 – 8844672
Fax: 39 6 8840450
Giorgio Gosetti
Competitive for thrillers between 30–180 mins length, which have been produced in the previous year and not released in Italy. Festival now takes place at Courmayeur (at the foot of Mount Blanc)

Pesaro Film Festival (Mostra Internazionale del Nuovo Cinema)
– June & October
Via Villafranca 20
00185 Rome
Tel: (39) 6 4456643/491156
Fax: (39) 6 491163
email: pesarofilmfest@mclink.it
Non–competitive. Particularly concerned with the work of new directors and emergent cinemas, with innovation at every level. In recent seasons the festival has been devoted to a specific country or culture

Pordenone Silent Film Festival (Le Giornate del Cinema Muto)
– October
c/o La Cineteca del Friuli
Via G. Bini, Palazzo Gurisatti
33013 Gemona (Udine)
Tel: (39) 0432 980458
Fax: (39) 0432 970542
email:
info.gcm@cinetecadelfriuli.org
Website: www.cinetecadel
friuli.org/gcm/
David Robinson, Director
The 2000 programme of the Giornate

will include a major retrospective of the films of Louis Feuillade, master of the thriller, the fourth instalment of 'The Griffith Project' (a long–term commitment to show every extant film from the huge output of D.W. (Griffith) and a retrospective on the German Avant–garde

The Pordenone Film Fair
– October
email: filmfair.gcm@
cinetecadelfriuli.org
An exhibition of books and journals, collectibles and ephemera presented by the Giornate del Cinema Muto. Authors attending the festival are invited to discuss their latest works

Prix Italia
– September
RAI Radiotelevisione Italiana
Borgo Sant Angelo, 23
00193 Rome
Tel: (39) 06 68889016–7
Fax: (39) 06 68889172–3
Competitive for television and radio productions from national broadcasting organisations. Radio categories: music, fiction (single plays and serials), documentary (factual and cultural). A maximum of four programmes can be submitted to the Radio competition. TV categories: performing arts, fiction (single plays and serials), documentary (factual and cultural). Only one programme can be submitted to each category

Salerno International Film Festival
– October
PO Box 137
84100 Salerno
Tel: (39) 89 223 632
Fax: (39) 89 223 632
All films – feature, documentaries, experimental and animated films – which are entered in the competitive section are eligible for the "Gran Premio Golta di Salerno"

Taormina International Film Festival
– July
Palazzo Firenze
Via Pirandello 31
98039 Taormina
Sicily
Tel: (39) 942 21142
Fax: (39) 942 23348
Competitive for features. Recognised by FIAPF, category B. Emphasis on new directors and cinema from developing countries

Torino Film Festival
17–25 November 2000
Via Monte di Pietà 1
10121 Torino
Tel: (39) 011 5623309
Fax: (39) 011 5629796
email: info@torinofilmfest.org
Website: www.torinofilmfest.org
Mara Signori
Competitive sections for feature and short films. Italian Space section (videos and films) open solely to Italian work. All works must be completed during 13 previous months, with no prior release in Italy

Venice Film Festival
– September
Mostra Internazionale d'Arte
Cinematografica
La Biennale di Venezia
Ca' Giustinian
San Marco, 30124 Venice
Tel: (39) 41 5218711
Fax: (39) 41 5227539
Website: www.labiennale.it
Competitive for feature films competitive for shorts (up to 30 mins); has competitive sections, perspectives, night and stars, Italian section; retrospective. Non–participation at other international festivals and/or screenings outside country of origin. Submission by 30 June

Japan

The 9th International Animation Festival in Japan, Hiroshima 2001
– August
4–17 Kako–machi
Naka–ku
Hiroshima 730–0812
Tel: (81) 82 245 0245
Fax: (81) 82 245 0246
email: hiroanim@urban.ne.jp
Website: www.urban.ne.jp/
home/hiroanim/
Sayoko Kinoshita, Festival Director
Competitive biennial festival. Also retrospective, symposium, exhibition etc. For competition, animated works under 30 mins, and completed during preceding two years are eligible on either 16mm, 35mm, 3/4" videotape (NTSC, PAL, SECAM) or Betacam (only NTSC)

Tokyo International Film Festival
– October

Organising Committee
3F, Landic Ginza Bldg II
1–6–5 Ginza, Chuo–Ku
Tokyo 104–0061
Tel: (81) 3 3563 6305
Fax: (81) 3 3563 6310
Website: www.tokyo–filmfest.or.jp
Competitive for Young Cinema
sections. Also special screenings,
cinema prism, Nippon cinema now,
symposium, no film market

Tokyo Video Festival
– January
c/o Victor Co of Japan Ltd
1–7–1 Shinbashi
Victor Bldg, Minato–ku
Tokyo 105
Tel: (81) 3 3289 2815
Fax: (81) 3 3289 2819
Competitive for videos; compositions
on any theme and in any style
accepted, whether previously
screened or not, but maximum tape
playback time must not exceed 20
minutes

Malta

Golden Knight International Amateur Film & Video Festival
– November
PO Box 450
Valletta CMR,01
Tel: (356) 222345/236173
Fax: (356) 225047
Three classes: amateur, student,
professional – maximum 30 mins

Martinique

Festival du Film Caribéen Cinéma, Vidéo: Images Caraïbes
– June even years
77 route de la Folie
97200 Fort–de–France
Tel: (596) 69 10 12/70 23 81
Fax: (596) 69 21 58/62 23 93
Competitive for all film and video
makers native to the Caribbean
Islands – features, shorts and
documentary

Monaco

Monte Carlo Television Festival and Market
– February
4, boulevard du Jardin Exotique
Monte–Carlo 98000 Monaco

Tel: 337 93 10 40 60
Fax: 337 93 50 70 14
Contact: David Tomatis
Annual festival and market, includes
awards for television films,
mini–series and news categories. In
1996 joined with Imagina conference

The Netherlands

Cinekid
– October
Korte Leidesedwarsstraat 12
1017 RC Amsterdam
Tel: (31) 0 20 5317890
Fax: (31) 0 20 5317899
email: engel2x2xsyall.nl
Website: www.cinekid.nl
Director: Sannette Naeyé
International children's film and
television festival. Winning film is
guaranteed distribution in the
Netherlands

Dutch Film Festival
– September/October
Stichting Nederlands Film Festival
PO Box 1581
3500 BN Utrecht
Tel: (31) 30 2322684
Fax: (31) 30 2313200
email: ned.filmfest@inter.nl.net
Website: www.nethlandfilm.nl/
Annual screening of a selection of
new Dutch features, shorts,
documentaries, animation and
television drama. Retrospectives,
seminars, talkshows, Cinema
Militans Lecture, Holland Film
Meeting, outdoor programme.
Presentation of the Grand Prix of
Dutch Film: the Golden Calf Awards

International Documentary Filmfestival Amsterdam
– November/December
Kleine–Gartmanplantsoen 10
1017 RR Amsterdam
Tel: (31) 20 6273329
Fax: (31) 20 6385388
Website: www.idfa.nl/
Competition programme: competitive
for documentaries of any length,
35mm or 16mm, produced in 15
months prior to the festival;
retrospectives; Joris Ivens award; Top
10 selected by well–known
filmmaker; competitive
video–programme; forum for
international co–financing of
European documentaries. Workshop,
seminar and debates

International Film Festival Rotterdam
24 January – 4 February 2001
PO Box 21696
3001 AR Rotterdam
Tel: (31) 10 890 9090
Fax: (31) 10 890 9091
email: tiger@iffrotterdam.nl
Website: www.filmfestivalrotterdam.com
Carlie Janszen
Addition to Tiger Award competition:
three premiums, each 10,000 Euro
cash, as well as guaranteed theatrical
distribution in The Netherlands, and a
broadcasting commitment from
Dutch public broadcaster VPRO

Le Nombre d'Or, International Widescreen Festival, Amsterdam
14–18 September 2001
IBC Office
Aldwych House, 81 Aldwych
London WC2B 4EL
Tel: (44) 020 7611 7511
Fax: (44) 020 7611 7530
email: joconnell@ibc.org
Website: www.ibc.org
Jarlath O'Connell, Festival Director
Competitive television Festival
celebrating widescreen production in
all genres and held as part of IBC in
Amsterdam. Programmes must have
been broadcast or have a broadcast
date scheduled. The focus is on
mainstream programming with
documentaries, dramas and music
programmes making up the bulk of
the entries. Programmes must have
been shot on widescreen video
(including HD) or in Super 16 or
35mm. Around 35 programmes are
screened before an International Jury
over five days of screenings.
Winning programmes are
re–screened with Q&A sessions with
the producers. IBC also includes
Masterclasses, Panel Discussions and
Workshops aimed at the production
community. The recent Festival
attracted 105 entries from 18
countries. Deadline for entries is late
May each year

New Zealand

Auckland International Film Festival
– July
PO Box 9544
Te Aro

Wellington 6035
Tel: (64) 4 385 0162
Fax: (64) 4 801 7304
Festival includes feature films, short
films, documentaries, video and
animation

Wellington Film Festival

– July
C/o New Zealand Film Festival
PO Box 9544
Te Aro
Wellington
Tel: (64) 4 385 0162
Fax: (64) 4 801 7304
email: enzedff@actrix.gen.nz
Festival includes feature films, short
films, documentaries, video and
animation

Norway

Norwegian International Film Festival

– August – September
PO Box 145
5501 Haugesund
Tel: (47) 52 73 44 30
Fax: (47) 52 73 44 20
email: info@filmfestivalen.no
Website: www.filmfestivalen.no
Gunnar J. Lovvik
Non–competitive film festival,
highlighting a selection of films for
the coming theatrical season. New
Nordic films – a market presenting
Nordic films with a potential outside
the Nordic Countries (27–29 Aug)

Poland

International and National Documentary and Short Film Festival in Kraków

– May/June
c/o PIF 'Apollo Film'
ul. Pychowicka 7
30–364 Kraków
Tel: (48) 12 267 13 55
Fax: (48) 12 267 23 40
email:festival@apollo.pl
Website: www.shortfilm.apollo.pl
Krzysztof Gierat, Festival Director
Competitive for short film (up to 60
mins), including documentaries,
fiction, animation, popular science
and experimental subjects, produced
in the previous 15 months

Portugal

Cinanima (International Animated Film Festival)

– November
Apartado 743
Rua 62, 251
4500–901 Espinho Codex
Tel: (351) 22 734 4611/734 1621
Fax: (351) 22 734 6015
email: cinanima@mail.telepac.pt
Website: www.cinanima.pt
Organising Committee
Competitive for animation short
films, features, series, first films,
didactic and educational, publicity,
title sequences and information.
Entries must have been completed
after 1st January 2000

Encontros Internacionais de Cinema Documental

– November
Centro Cultural Malaposta
Rua Angola, Olival Basto
2675 Odivelas
Tel: (351) 9388570/407
Fax: (351) 9389347
email: amascultura@mail.telepac.pt
Director: Manuel Costa e Silva
Two categories: film and video
(competition). Only event dedicated
to documentary in Portugal, to
increase awareness of the form and
show work from other countries

Fantasporto – 21st Oporto International Film Festival

– February/March
Cinema Novo – Multimedia Centre
Rua da Constituição 311
4200 Porto
Tel: (351) 2 5073880
Fax: (351) 2 5508210
email: fantas@caleida.pt
Website: www.caleida.pt.fantasporto
Mario Dorminsky
Competitive section for feature films
and shorts, particularly fantasy and
science fiction films. Includes 11th
New Directors week with an official
competition. The Festival runs now in
8 theatres (2,700 seats altogether)
and screens nearly 300 feature films
each year. Also includes, in
conjunction with the Portugese Film
Institute, a programme of Potuguese
film

Festival Internacional de Cinema da Figueira da Foz

– August/September
Apartado de Correios 5407
1709 Lisbon Codex

Tel: (351) 1 812 62 31
Fax: (351) 1 812 62 28
email: jose.marques@ficff.pt
Website: www.ficff.pt
Competitive for fiction and
documentary films, films for
children, shorts and video. Some cash
prizes. Special programmes on
different directors and countries. Also
retrospective of Portuguese cinema.
Entries must have been produced
during 20 months preceding Festival

International Film Festival of Troia

– June
International Film Festival of Troia
Forum Luisa Todi
Av. Luisa Todi, 61–65
2900–461 Setúbal
Tel: (351) 265 52 59 08 – 53 40 59
Fax: (351) 265 52 56 81
email: festroia@mail.teleweb.pt
Website: www.festroia.pt
Fernanda Silva, Director
Four categories: Official Section,
First Works, American Independents,
Man and His Environment. The
Official Section is devoted to films
coming from those countries which
have a limited production (less than
21 features per year). Films must not
have been screened previously in
Portugal and must have been
produced during 12 months
preceding the Festival. Also film
market, retrospectives in the
information section, Gay and Lesbian
section. Jury selection

Puerto Rico

Puerto Rico International Film Festival

– November
70 Mayagüez Street, Suite B1
Hato Rey PR 00918
Tel: (1) 809 764 7044
Fax: (1) 809 753 5367
Non–competitive international,
full–length feature event with
emphasis on Latin American, Spanish
and women directors. FIPRESCI jury
for the Latin American selection

Russia

International Film Festival of Festivals

– June
10 Kamennoostrovsky Avenue
St Petersburg 197101
Tel: (7) 812 237 0304

Fax: (7) 812 233 2174
Non–competitive, aimed at
promoting films from all over the
world that meet the highest artistic
criteria, and the distribution of
non–commercial cinema

Moscow International Film Festival
– July
**Interfest, General Management of
International Film Festivals
10 Khokholski Per
Moscow 109028**
Tel: (7) 95 917 9154
Fax: (7) 95 916 0107

Serbia

Belgrade International Film Festival
– January/February
**Sava Centar
Milentija Popovica 9
11070 Novi Beograd**
Tel: (38) 11 222 49 61
Fax: (38) 11 222 11 56
Non–competitive for features
reflecting high aesthetic and artistic
values and contemporary trends

Singapore

Singapore International Film Festival
– April
**29A Keong Saik Road
Singapore 089136**
Tel: (65) 738 7567
Fax: (65) 738 7578
email: filmfest@pacific.net.sg
Specialised competitive festival for
Best Asian Film. Non–competitive
includes panorama of international
film. 8mm, 16mm, 35mm and video
are accepted. Films must not have
been shown commercially in
Singapore

Slovakia

Forum – Festival of First Feature Films
– October
**Brectanova
833 14 Bratislava 1**
Tel: (42) 7 378 8290
Fax: (42) 7 378 8290
International competition for first
feature films at least 50 minutes long,
and made or first shown in the 16
months preceding the Festival

South Africa

Cape Town International Film Festival
**3 – 26 November 2000
University of Cape Town
Private Bag
Rondebosch 7700
Cape Town**
Tel: (27) 21 423 8257
Fax: (27) 21 423 8257
email: filmfest@hiddingh.uct.ac.za
Trevor Steele Taylor, Director
Steve Drake, Programme
Co–ordinator
Oldest film festival in South Africa.
Screen Features, Documentaries and
Short Films on 35mm, 16mm or
Video. Emphasis on the independent,
the transgressive and the iconoclastic.
Major profile of South African
production

Durban International Film Festival
**University of Natal
Centre for Creative Arts
4014 Durban**
Tel: (27) 31 260 2506
Fax: (27) 31 260 3074
The Festival aims to showcase films
of quality to local audiences,
including screenings in peri–urban
areas of the city

Spain

Festiva Internacional de Cine Independente de Ourense/International Independent Film Festival
**4–10 November 2000
Rua Arcediagos 3–2 dta
32005 Ourense**
Tel: (34) 988 224127
Fax: (34) 988 249561
email: oufest@ourencine.com
Website: www.ourencine.com
Fifth international festival for
independent cinema. Competitive
sections for every independent short
or long length film

Bilbao International Festival of Documentary & Short Films
– November/December
**Colón de Larreátegui 37, 4o drcha
48009 Bilbao**
Tel: (34) 4 248698/247860
Fax: (34) 4 245624
Competitive for animation, fiction
and documentary

Donostia–San Sebastian International Film Festival
**Plaza Oquendo S/N
20004 San Sebastian**
– September
Tel: (34) 943 48 12 12
Fax: (34) 943 48 12 18
email:
ssiff@sansebastianfestival.com
Website:
www.sansebastianfestival.com
Diego Galan
Competitive for feature films
produced in the previous year and not
released in Spain or shown in any
other festivals. Also retrospective
sections

International Film Festival For Young People of Gijón
– November/December
**Maternidad 2–20
33207 Gijón**
Tel: (34) 8 5343739
Fax: (34) 8 5354152
Competitive for features and shorts.
Must have been produced during 18
months preceding the festival and not
awarded a prize at any other major
international film festival

International Short Film Contest 'Ciudad de Huesca'
– June
**C/Del Parque 1,2
(Circulo Oscense)
Huesca 22002**
Tel: (34) 974 212582
Fax: (34) 974 210065
email: huescafest@tsai.es
Website: www.huesca–filmfestival.
com
Competitive for short films (up to 30
mins) on any theme except tourism
and promotion

L'Alternativa – VII Independent Film Festival of Barcelona
**17th–25th November 2000
Centre de Cultura Contemporania
de Barcelona
C/Montalegre 5
08001 Barcelona**
Tel: (34) 93 306 41 00
Fax: (34) 93 306 41 04
email: alternativa@cccb.org
Tessa Renaudo
International competitive for shorts,
animation, documentary and features.
Accept films made on 35mm, 16mm,
8mm, Beta SP and DV with
screening copy on 35mm, 16mm or
Beta SP (PAL)

Mostra de Valencia/Cinema del Mediterrani

– October
Pza del Arzobispo 2 bajo
46003 Valencia
Tel: (34) 6 392 1506
Fax: (34) 6 391 5156
Competitive official section.
Informative section, special events section, 'mostra' for children, and International Congress of Film Music

Sitges International Film Festival of Catalonia

– October
Av Josep Tarradellas
135 ESC A, 3r. 2a.
08029 Barcelona
Tel: (34) 3 93 419 3635
Fax: (34) 3 93 439 7380
email: cinsit@sitgestur.com
Website: www.sitges.com/cinema
Roc Villas (Director)
Two official sections. One for fantasy films and another for all–genre films. Also shorts, retrospectives, animation, video, exhibitions, etc

Valladolid International Film Festival

– October
Teatro Calderón
C/Leopoldo Cano, s/n
47003 Valladolid
Tel: (34 983) 30 57 00/77/88
Fax: (34 983) 30 98 35
email: festvalladolid@seminci.com
Website: www.seminic.com
Fernando Lara, Director
Denise O'Keeffe, Coordinator
Competitive for 35mm features and shorts, plus documentaries, entries not to have been shown previously in Spain. Also film school tributes, retrospectives and selection of new Spanish productions

Sweden

Göteborg Film Festival

26 January/5 February 2001
Box 7079
402 32 Gothenburg
Tel: (46) 31 41 05 46
Fax: (46) 31 41 00 63
email: goteborg@filmfestivl.org
Website: www.goteborg.filmfestival. org
Agneta Green, Program Coordinator
Non–competitive for features, documentaries and shorts not released in Sweden

Stockholm International Film Festival

– November
PO Box 7673
103 95 Stockholm
Tel: (46) 8 67 75 000
Fax: (46) 8 20 05 90
Competitive for innovative current feature films, focus on American Independents, a retrospective, summary of Swedish films released during the year, survey of world cinema. Around 100 films have their Swedish premiere during the festival. FIPRESCI jury, FIAPF accredited. 'Northern Lights' – Critics Week

Umea International Film Festival

– September
PO Box 43
S 901 02
Umea
Tel: (46) 90 13 33 88
Fax: (46) 90 77 79 61
email: film.festival@ff.umea.se
Thom Palmen
Non–competitive festival with focus mainly on features but does except shorts and documentaries. About 150 films are screened in several sections. The festival also organises seminars

Uppsala International Short Film Festival

– October
Box 1746
S–751 47 Uppsala
Tel: (46) 18 12 00 25
Fax: (46) 18 12 13 50
email: uppsala@shortfilmfestival. com
Website: www.shortfilmfestival.com
Competitive for shorts (up to 60 mins), including fiction, animation, experimental films, documentaries, children's and young people's films. 16 and 35mm only

Switzerland

19th Vevey International Comedy Film Festival

– September/October
CP 421
1800 Vevey
Tel: (41) 21 925 80 31
Fax: (41) 21 925 80 35
Competitive for medium and short films, hommage and retrospective

Biennale de l'image en movement/Biennial of Moving Images

– November odd years
Saint Gervais Gèneve, Centre pour l'image contemporaire
5 rue du Temple
1201 Geneva
Tel: (41) 22 908 20 60
Fax: (41) 22 908 20 01
email: cic@sgg.ch
Website: www.centreimage.ch/bim
Lysianne Léchottlirt, PR
Competition with international entries; seminars and conferences; retrospectives; special programmes; installations; Swiss art school programme

Festival International de Films de Fribourg

– March
Rue de Locarno 8
CH –1700 Fribourg
Tel: (41) (26) 322 22 32
Fax: (41) (26) 322 79 50
email: info@fiff.ch
Website: www.fiff.ch
Martial Knoebel
Competitive for films from Africa, Asia and Latin America (16/35mm, video). Films (16/35mm) may be circulated throughout Switzerland after the Festival

Golden Rose of Montreux TV Festival

– April
Télévision Suisse Romande
PO Box 234
1211 Geneva 8
Tel: (41) 22 708 8599
Fax: (41) 22 781 5249
email: gabrielle.bucher@tsr.ch
Competitive for television productions (24–60 mins) of light entertainment, music and variety, first broadcast in the previous 14 months

International Film – Video – Multimedia Festival Lucerne

– October
PO Box 4929
6002 Lucerne
Tel: (41) 41 362 17 17
Fax: (41) 41 362 17 18
email: info@viper.ch
Website: www.viper.ch
The festival presents new international innovative, experimental and artistic media productions: Film, Video, CD–ROM, internet–projects. Two competitions:

International competition for Film and Video (award sum SFR 10.000) and national competition for Film and Video (award sum SFR 5.000 plus material assets). VIPER also includes the "Videogallery", an outstanding selection of film and video work which is run by co–operating European festivals

Locarno International Film Festival

Via della Posta 6
CP 844
6601 Locarno
Tel: (41) 91 751 02 32
Fax: (41) 91 751 74 65
email: info@pardo.ch
Website: www.pardo.ch
Programme includes: a) Competition reserved for fiction features representative of Young Cinema (first or second features) and New Cinema (films by more established filmmakers who are innovating in film style and content and works by directors from emerging film industries. b) A (non–competitive) selection of films with innovative potential in style and content. c) A retrospective designed to enlarge perspectives on film history

Nyon International Documentary Film Festival – Visions du Réel

– May
PO Box 593
CH–1260 Nyon
Tel: (41) 22 361 60 60
Fax: (41) 22 361 70 71
International competition

Tunisia

Carthage Film Festival

– October/November
The JCC Managing Committee
5 Avenue Ali Belahouane
2070 La Marsa
Tel: (216) 1 745 355
Fax: (216) 1 745 564
Official competition open to Arab and African short and feature films. Entries must have been made within two years prior to the festival, and not have been awarded first prize at any previous international festival in an African or Arab country. Also has an information section, an international film market (MIPAC) and a workshop

Turkey

International Istanbul Film Festival

– April
Istanbul Foundation for Culture and Arts
Istiklal Cad Luvr
Apt No: 146
80070 Beyoglu
Istanbul
Tel: (90) 1 212 293 3133
Fax: (90) 1 212 249 7771
Two competitive sections, international and national. The International Competition for feature films on art (literature, theatre, cinema, music, dance and plastic arts) is judged by an international jury and the 'Golden Tulip Award' is presented as the Grand Prix. Entry by invitation

United Kingdom

Bath Film Festival

– October 13–5 November 2000
7 Terrace Walk
Bath BA1 1LN
Tel: 01225 401149
Fax: 01225 401149
Chris Baker, co–ordinator
Non–competitive, screening c30, preview, current, recent and classic features. 'Events Programme' of workshops, seminars, courses, film with other art forms especially music, screenings of the work of emergent filmmakers, and one or two 'keystone' events each year aimed at attracting national interest

BBC British Short Film Festival

Room A214
BBC Centre House
56 Wood Lane
London W12 7SB
Tel: 020 8743 8000 ext 62222/62052
Fax: 020 8740 8540
Competitive for short film in all categories (up to 40 mins). Thematic and specialised programmes and special events. Prizes awarded include Best British and International Productions. Closing date for entries is early June

Birmingham International Film and TV Festival

9 Margaret Street
Birmingham B3 3BS
Tel: 0121 212 0777

Fax: 0121 212 0666
email: info@film–tv–festival.org.uk
Non–competitive for features and shorts, plus retrospective and tribute programmes. The Festival hosts conferences debating topical issues in film and television production

Bite the Mango

– September
National Museum of Photography, Film & Television
Pictureville, Bradford BD1 1NQ
Tel: 01274 203311/203308
Fax: 01274 770217
email: i.ajeeb.nmsi.ac.uk
Website: www.nmpft.org
Lisa Kavanagh, Irfan Ajeeb
Europe's only annual festival for South Asian and Black film and television. Entries accepted from South Asian and Black film and video–makers. Provisional deadline for entries July 2001

Black Sunday – The British Genre Film Festival

51 Thatch Leach Lane
Whitefield
Manchester M25 6EN
Tel: 0161 766 2566
Fax: 0161 766 2566
Non–competitive for horror, thriller, fantasy, science–fiction and film noir genres produced in the previous year. First choice festival for UK premieres of many of the above genre films. Special guests and retrospective programmes

Blackpool Film Festival

– June/July
20 Glen Eldon Road
St Anne's–on–Sea
Lancashire FY8 2AU
Tel: 0253 721800
Fax: 0253 721800
Peter Stamford

Bradford Animation Festival

National Museum of Photography Film and Television
Pictureville
Bradford BD1 1NQ
Tel: 01274 203320/203308
Fax: 01274 770217
Website: www.nmpft.org.uk
Lisa Kavanagh
Competitive festival for animated shorts in 8 categories: under 16s non–professional, professional, experimental. Features closing awards night, interviews with animators, and international animation

Bradford Film Festival

– March
**National Museum of Photography,
Film & Television
Pictureville
Bradford BD1 1NQ**
Tel: 01274 203320/203308
Fax: 01274 770217
email: a.earnshaw@nmsi.ac.uk
Website: www.nmpft.co.uk
Tony Earnshaw, Lisa Kavanagh
Non–competitive for feature films.
Strands include widescreen with
world's only Cinerama Screen and
IMAX. Focus on national cinema of
selected European countries.
Provisional deadline November 2001

Brief Encounters – Bristol Short Film Festivals

**PO Box 576
Bristol BS99 2BD**
Tel: 0117 9224628
Fax: 0117 9222906
email:
brief.encounters@dial.pipex.com
Competitive for short film in all
categories (up to 30 mins). Thematic
and specialised programmes and
special events. Audience award.
Closing date for entries end of July

British Animation Awards

– March 2002
**c/o 219 Archway Rd
London N6 5BN**
Tel: 020 8340 4563
A bi–annual event

Cambridge Film Festival

– July
**Arts Cinema
8 Market Passage
Cambridge CB2 3PF**
Tel: 01223 504444
Fax: 01223 578956
email: festival@cambarts.co.uk
Non–competitive; new world cinema
selected from international festivals.
Also featuring director retrospectives,
short film programmes, thematic
seasons and revived classics.
Conference for independent
exhibitors and distributors. Public
debates and post–screening
discussions

Chichester Film Festival

– August/September
**Chichester Cinema at New Park
New Park Road
Chichester
West Sussex PO19 1XN**
Tel: 01243 784881/786650
Fax: 01243 539853

Roger Gibson
This is a non–competitive festival
that focuses on previews,
retrospectives, with a special
emphasis on UK and other European
productions. There is also an
International Short Film Competition
with a first prize sponsored by Anita
Roddick (deadline 31 May)

Cinemagic – International Film Festival for Young People

– December
**3rd Floor, Fountain House
17–21 Donegall Place
Belfast BT1 5AB**
Tel: (028) 90311900
Fax: (028) 90319709
email: info@cinemagic.org.uk
Website: www.cinemagic.org.uk
Frances Cassidy
Competitive for international short
and feature films aimed at 4–18
year–olds. The next festival will
include the usual charity premieres,
educational workpacks, practical
workshops, directors talks and
masterclasses with industry
professionals

CineWomen

**Cinema City
St. Andrew's Street
Norwich NR2 4AD**
Tel: 01603 632366
Fax: 01603 7678238
email: j.h.morgan@uea.ac.uk
Jayne Hathor Morgan, Festival
Director

Edinburgh Fringe Film and Video Festival

– February
**29 Albany Street
Edinburgh EH1 3QN**
Tel: 0131 556 2044
Fax: 0131 557 4400
Competitive for
low–budget/independent/innovative
works from Britain and abroad. All
submissions welcome

Edinburgh International Film Festival

– August
**Filmhouse
88 Lothian Road
Edinburgh EH3 9BZ**
Tel: 0131 228 4051
Fax: 0131 229 5501
email: info@edfilmfest.org.uk
Website: www.edfilmfest.org.uk
Cathy Ferrett, Production Facilities
Administrator

Patron: Sean Connery
Chairman: John McCormick
Director: Lizzie Francke
Managing Director: Ginnie Atkinson
Longest continually running film
festival in the world. Unique
showcase of new international
cinema with a special focus on the
British film sector. Programme
sections: Focus on British Film;
Retrospective; Gala (World,
European, British premieres);
Rosebud (first and second time
directors); Director's Focus; Reel
Life (illustrated lectures by
filmmakers); Documentary;
Mirrorball (music video); short films;
animation. Industry office, including
British film market place. Awards for
British feature, British director,
British short film, British animation.
Submissions deadline April

European Short Film Festival

– November
**11 Holbein House
Holbein Place
London SW1 8NH**
Tel: 020 7460 3901
Fax: 020 7259 9278
email: info@pearlproductions.co.uk
Website: www.pearlproductions.
co.uk
Festival organiser: Fritz Kohle
This festival is open to all, it serves
as a platform to students, newcomers
and filmmakers engaging in the
production of the short–film format
to present their work to the public
and professionals alike. Films should
be no longer than 20 minutes in
duration. The audience is encouraged
to participate in this event and awards
the 'Audience Award'.
Recommendations are made in the
following areas: Direction,
Production, Screenplay.
Documentary, Best Experimental.
Deadline 30 September.

Festival of Fantastic Films

– September
**33 Barrington Road
Altrincham
Cheshire WA14 1H2**
Tel: 0161 929 1423
Fax: 0161 929 1067
email: 101341.3352@
compuserve.com
Festival celebrates science fiction and
fantasy film. Features guests of honour,
interviews, signing panels, dealers,
talks and over 30 film screenings

Filmstock: Luton Film Festival

– June
c/o Zero Balance Ltd
24 Guildford Street
Luton
Beds LU1 2NR
Tel: 07957 336474
email: neil.fox@ntl.com
Justin Doherty
A two week event including submitted short film work from around the world, and some selected features. Submissions accepted from amateur, professional and educational groups. Outdoor screenings, guest speakers, premiere of a new documentary and a series of themed screenings throughout the festival period

Foyle Film Festival

– November
The Nerve Centre
2nd Floor
Northern Counties Building
8 Custom House Street
Derry BT48 6AE
Tel: 01504 267432
Fax: 01504 371738
email: s.kelpie@nerve–centre.org.uk
Shauna Kelpie (Festival Director)
Northern Ireland's major annual film event celebrated its 10th year in 1996. The central venue is the Orchard cinema in the heart of Derry city centre

French Film Festival

– November
13 Randolph Crescent
Edinburgh EH3 7TX
Tel: 0131 225 5366
Fax: 0131 220 0648
The UK's only festival devoted solely to French cinema including feature films and shorts. Section on first or second films qualifies for the Hennessy Audience Award. Retrospectives, panorama of new productions, and debates. Based at venues in three cities: Filmhouse, Edinburgh, Glasgow Film Theatre and Aberdeen Belmont Centre

Green Screen (London's International Environmental Film Festival)

– November
45 Shelton Street
London WC2H 9JH
Tel: 020 7379 7390
Fax: 020 7379 7197
Non–competitive selection of international environmental films, question and answer sessions following every film showing with well known environmentalists, film–makers, media personalities and celebrities with environmental clout

The Guardian Edinburgh International Television Festival

– August
2nd Floor
24 Neal Street
London WC2H 9PS
Tel: 020 7379 4519
Fax: 020 7836 0702
email: info@geitf.co.uk
Website: www.geitf.co.uk
Fran Barlow, Festival Director
The Guardian Edinburgh International Television Festival (GEIFT) is the key television industry forum where current creative practice is celebrated and assessed by all levels of the industry and where industry concerns can be debated collectively and objectively. Held over four days, GEITF uses debate and presentation to talk about the skill and business of television through a varied programme of sessions, workshops, lectures, screenings, demonstrations and networking parties

International Animation Festival, Cardiff

– June
18 Broadwick Street
London W1V 1FG
Tel: 020 7494 0506
Fax: 020 7494 0807

International Celtic Film and Television Festival

– March
The Library
Farraline Park
Inverness IV1 1LS
Tel: 01463 226 189
Fax: 01463 716 368
Competition for films whose subject matter has particular relevance to the Celtic nations

Italian Film Festival

– April
82 Nicolson Street
Edinburgh EH8 9EW
Tel: 0131 668 2232
Fax: 0131 668 2777
A unique UK event throwing an exclusive spotlight on il cinema italiano over ten days in Edinburgh (Filmhouse) Glasgow (Film Theatre); and London (Riverside). Visiting guests and directors, debates, first and second films, plus a broad range of current releases and special focuses on particular actors or directors

IVCA Awards

– October
IVCA
Bolsover House
5–6 Clipstone Street
London W1P 8LD
Tel: 020 7580 0962
Fax: 020 7436 2606
email: info@ivca.org
Website: www.ivca.org
Competitive for non–broadcast industrial/training films and videos, covering all aspects of the manufacturing and commercial world, plus categories for educational, business, leisure and communications subjects. Programme, Special and Production (Craft) Awards, and industry award for effective communication. Closing date for entries December

KinoFilm

– October/November
Manchester International Short Film and Video Festival
42 Edge Street
Manchester M4 1HN
Tel: 0161 288 2494
Fax: 0161 281 1374
email: john.kino@good.co.uk
Website: www.kinofilm.org.uk
John Wojowski
Kinofilm is dedicated to short films and videos from every corner of the world. Emphasis is placed on short innovative, unusual and off–beat productions. Films on any subject or theme can be submitted providing they are no longer than 30 minutes and were produced within the last two years and have not been previously submitted. All sections of film/video making community are eligible. Particularly welcome are applications from young film–makers and all members of the community who have never had work shown at festivals. Special categories include: Gay and Lesbian, Black Cinema, New Irish Cinema, New American Underground, Eastern European Work, Super 8 Film. Closing date for submissions for 2000 is August 2000 Please telephone or fax for an application form. Entry fee £3.50 National, £5.00 or $10 US International. Application forms can

be downloaded from the Kino website. Competitive strand was introduced for 1999

Leeds International Film Festival

– October
Town Hall
The Headrow
Leeds LS1 3AD
Tel: 0113 247 8398
Fax: 0113 247 8397
email: filmfestival@leeds.gov.uk
Website: www.leedsfilm.com
Charlotte Fergusson
Competitive for features by new directors, short films and animation (Louis le Prince Awards). Over 10 strands including 'evolution' (interactive and online), Eureka, Film Festival Fringe, Voices of Cinema and Fanomenon
Leeds Children's Film Festival
– October
Town Hall
The Headrow
Leeds LS1 3AD
Tel: 0113 247 8398
Fax: 0113 247 8397
email: filmfestival@leeds.gov.uk
Website: www.leedsfilm.com
Charlotte Fergusson
Non–competitive for features, short films and animation

London Latin American Film Festival

– September
Metro Pictures
79 Wardour Street
London W1V 3TH
Tel: 020 7434 3357
Fax: 020 7287 2112
Non–competitive, bringing to London a line up of contemporary films from Latin America and surveying current trends

London Lesbian and Gay Film Festival

Festivals Office
National Film Theatre
South Bank
London SE1 8XT
Tel: 020 7815 1323/1324
Fax: 020 7633 0786
Website: www.llgff.org.uk
Carol Coombes
Non–competitive for film and videos of special interest to lesbian and gay audiences. Some entries travel to regional film theatres as part of a national tour from April to June

Raindance Ltd

81 Berwick Street
London W1V 3PF
Tel: 020 7287 3833
Fax: 020 7439 2243
email: info@raindance.co.uk
Website: www.raindance.co.uk
Daniel Fellows
Britain's only film market for independently produced features, shorts and documentaries. Deadline 1 September

44th Regus London Film Festival

– November
National Film Theatre
South Bank
London SE1 8XT
Tel: 020 7815 1322/1323
Fax: 020 7633 0786
email: sarah.lutton@bfi.org.uk
Website: www.lff.org.uk
Sarah Lutton
Non–competitive for international feature films, shorts and video, by invitation only, which have not previously been screened in Great Britain. Some entries travel to regional film theatres as part of a national tour from November to December

Sheffield International Documentary Festival

– October
The Workstation
15 Paternoster Row
Sheffield S1 2BX
Tel: 0114 276 5141
Fax: 0114 272 1849
email: info@sidf.co.uk
Website: www.sidf.co.uk
The only UK festival dedicated to excellence in documentary film and television. The week long event is both a public film festival and an industry gathering with sessions, screenings and discussions on all the new developments in documentary. The festival is non–competitive

Shots in the Dark – Crime, Mystery and Thriller Festival

– June
Broadway
14–18 Broad Street
Nottingham NG1 3AL
Tel: 0115 952 6600/6611
Fax: 0115 952 6622
Non–competitive for all types of mysteries and thrillers. Includes previews of new movies,

retrospectives, television events, special guests. Honorary Patron: Quentin Tarantino

Television and Young People (TVYP)

– August
24 Neal Street
London WC2H 9PS
Tel: 020 7379 4519
Fax: 020 7836 0702
email: info@tvyp.co.uk
Website: www.tvyp.co.uk
Varsha Patel
Television and Young People (TVYP) is the educational arm of the Guardian Edinburgh International Television Festival (GEITF) and the UK's leading forum for young people aspiring to work in television. Taking place over five days, TVYP offers new entrants a unique insight into the television industry through a programme of masterclasses, workshops, screenings and career surgeries. Successful delegates will have the unique opportunity to meet, work with and learn from the leading creative talent in the industry. Each year, 150 places are offered to young people aged 18–21 from across the UK – other than their travel to and from Edinburgh, all expenses are covered by TVYP

Video Positive

– March/April
International Biennale of Video and Electronic Media Art
Foundation for Art and Creative Technology (FACT)
Bluecoat Chambers
School Lane
Liverpool L1 3BX
Tel: 0151 709 2663
Fax: 0151 707 2150
Non–competitive for video and electronic media art produced worldwide in the two years preceding the festival. Includes community and education programmes, screenings, workshops and seminars. Some commissions available

Welsh International Film Festival, Aberystwyth

– November
c/o Premiere Cymru Wales Cyf
Unit 6G, Cefn Llan
Aberystwyth
Dyfed SY23 3AH
Tel: 01970 617995
Fax: 01970 617942
email: wff995@aber.ac.uk
Non–competitive for international

feature films and shorts, together with films from Wales in Welsh and English. Also short retrospectives, workshops and seminars. D M Davies Award (£25,000) presented to the best short film submitted by a young film maker from Wales

Wildscreen
– October
PO Box 366, Deanery Road
College Green
Bristol BS99 2HD
Tel: 0117 909 6300
Fax: 0117 909 5000
email: info@wildscreen.org.uk
International festival of moving images from the natural world. Competitive: Panda Awards include Conservation, Revelation, Newcomer, Children's, Outstanding Achievement, Craft and multimedia

Uruguay

International Children's Film Festival
– March/April
Cinemateca Uruguaya
Carnelli 1311,
Casilla de Correo 1170
11200 Montevideo
Tel: (598) 2 408 24 60
Fax: (598) 2 409 45 72
Competitive for fiction international films, documentaries and animation for children

International Film Festival of Uruguay
– April
Cinemateca Uruguaya
Carnelli 1311,
Casilla de Correo 1170
11200 Montevideo
Tel: (598) 2 48 24 60
Fax: (598) 2 49 45 72
Competitive for fiction and Latin American videos

USA

36th Chicago International Film Festival
– October
32 West Randolph Street
Suite: 600
Chicago
Illinois 60601 USA
Tel: (1) 312 425 9400
Fax: (1) 312 425 0944
email: filmfest@wwa.com
Website: www.chicago.ddbn.com/

filmfest/
Contact: Michael Kutza
Founder & Artistic director
Competitive for feature films, documentaries, shorts, animation, student and First and Second Features

AFI Los Angeles International Film Festival
– 19–26 October 2000
2021 N Western Avenue
Los Angeles
CA 90027
Tel: (1) 323 856 7709
Fax: (1) 323 462 4049
email: afifest@afionline.org
Website: www.afifest.com
Julianna Brannum, Festival Coordinator
Official competition, New Directions (American Independents), European Film Showcase, Latin Cinema Series, Shorts, Documentaries. Final deadline for entries 17 July

AFI National Video Festival
– October
2021 N Western Avenue
Los Angeles
CA 90027
Tel: (1) 323 856 7707
Fax: (1) 323 462 4049
Non–competitive. Screenings in Los Angeles, Washington. Accepts: 1" U–Matic, NTSC/PAL/SECAM (No Beta, no 1"

AFM (American Film Market)
9th Floor, 10850 Wiltshire Blvd,
Los Angeles
CA 90024
Tel: (1) 310 446 1000
Fax: (1) 310 446 1600
Annual market for film, television and video

Asian American International Film Festival
– July
c/o Asian CineVision
32 East Broadway, 4th Floor
New York, NY 10002
Tel: (1) 212 925 8685
Fax: (1) 212 925 8157
Non–competitive, all categories and lengths. No video–to–film transfers accepted as entries. Films must be produced, directed and/or written by artists of Asian heritage

Chicago International Children's Film Festival
– October

Facets Multimedia
1517 West Fullerton Avenue
Chicago IL 60614
Tel: (1) 773 281 9075
Fax: (1) 773 929 5437 or 773 929 0266
email: kidsfest@facets.org
Competitive for entertainment films, videotapes and television programmes for children

Cleveland International Film Festival
Cleveland Film Society
2510 Market Avenue
Cleveland, OH 44113
Tel: (1) 216 623 3456
Fax: (1) 216 623 0103
email: cfs@clevelandfilm.org
Website: www.clevelandfilm.org
William Frank Guentzler
Non–competitive for feature, narrative, documentary, animation and experimental films. Competitive for shorts, with $2,500 prize money

Columbus International Film and Video Festival (a.k.a. The Chris Awards)
– October
5701 High Street
Suite 200
Worthington
Ohio 43085
Fax: (1) 614 841 1666
email: chrisawd@infinet.com
Website: www.infinet.com/~chrisawd
The Chris Awards is one of the longest–running competitions of its kind in North America, specialising in honouring documentary, education, business and information films and videos, as well as categories for the arts and entertainment. Entrants compete within categories for the first place Chris statuette, second place Bronze plaque and third place Certificate of Honorable Mention Expanded public screenings. Entry deadline 1 July

Denver International Film Festival
– October
1430 Larimer Square, Suite 201
Denver
CO 80202
Tel: (1) 303 595 3456
Fax: (1) 303 595 0956
email: dfs@denverfilm.org
Non–competitive. New international features, tributes to film artists, independent features, documentaries,

shorts, animation, experimental
works, videos and children's films

Florida Film Festival

8–17 June 2001
1300 South Orlando Avenue
Maitland
FL 32751
Tel: (1) 407 629 1088
Fax: (1) 407 629 6870
email: filmfest@enzian.org
Website: www.enzian.org
Matthew Curtis
A 10–day event involving over 100
films, several seminars and social
events. Highlights include an
American Independent Film
Competition with three categories
(Dramatic, Documentary and Shorts)
a Kodak cinematography award, an
International Showcase for features
and shorts, Midnight Movies,
"Spotlight Films", and special
screenings and tributes

Fort Lauderdale International Film Festival

– October/November
1314 East Las o Las, Blvd 007
Fort Lauderdale
FL 33301
Tel: (1) 954 760 9898
Fax: (1) 954 760 9099
email: brofilm@aol.com
Website: www.ftlaudfilmfest.com
Bonnie Adams
The festival typically features
40 – 50 full length features, plus
documentaries, an art on film series,
short subjects, as well as animation.
Awards are presented for Best Film,
Best Foreign Language Film,
Documentary, Short, Director, Actor,
Actress and an Audience Award. The
Festival also features an international
student film competition with $5,000
in product grants from Kodak

Hawaii International Film Festival

3–12 November 2000 in Honolulu on
Oahu
14–19 November on Maui, Kauai,
the Big Island, Molokai and Lanai
1001 Bishop Street
Pacific Tower, Suite 745
Honolulu, Hawaii 96813
Tel: (1) 808 528 3456
Fax: (1) 808 528 1410
email: info@hiff.org
Website: www.hiff.org
Chuck Boller, Managing Director
For 20 years the Hawaii International
Film Festival has been dedicated to
promoting cross–cultural

understanding among the people of
Asia, North America, and the Pacific
region. HIFF is a competitive festival
with awards for best feature,
documentary, short and an audience
award. The festival is committed to
presenting artistic, political and
commercial works from around the
world with an emphasis on Pacific
Rim filmmakers

Houston International Film and Video Festival

– 34th Annual Worldfest (+ Market)
20–29 April 2001
PO Box 56566
Houston
TX 77256–6566
Tel: (1) 713 965 9955
Fax: (1) 713 965 9960
email: worldfest@aol.com
Website: www.worldfest.org
Competitive for features, shorts,
documentary, television production
and television commercials.
Independent studios, experimental
and video. Worldfest Discovery
Programme where winners are
introduced to organisers of top 200
international festivals. Screenplay
category. Winning screenplays
submitted to top 100 US creative
agencies

Independent Feature Film Market

– September
12th Floor
104 West 29th Street
New York
NY 10001–5310
Tel: (1) 212 465 8200
Fax: (1) 212 465 8525
email: marketinfo@ifp.org
Website: www.ifp.org
The Independent Feature Film
Market is the longest running market
devoted to new, emerging American
independent film talent seeking
domestic and foreign distribution. It
is the market for discovering projects
in development, outstanding
documentaries, and startling works of
fiction. Domestic and foreign
filmmakers, distributors, and feature
films. Sales agents, producers,
festival representatives and casting
directors attend to acquire and
evaluate both completed films and
projects in development

Miami Film Festival

– January/February
Film Society of Miami
444 Brickell Avenue, Suite 229

Miami FL 33131
Tel: (1) 305 377 3456
Fax: (1) 303 577 9768
Non–competitive; screenings of
25–30 international films; all
categories considered, 35mm film
only. Entry deadline 1 November

Mobius Advertising Awards Competition

– February
841 North Addison Avenue
Elmhurst, IL 60126–1291
Tel: (1) 630 834 7773
Fax: (1) 630 834 5565
email: mobiusinfo@
mobiusawards.com
Website: www.mobiusawards.com
J.W. Anderson
International awards competition for
television and radio commercials
produced or released in the 12
months preceding the annual 1
October entry deadline. Founded in
1971

National Educational Media Network (formerly National Educational Film & Video Festival)

– November
655 Thirteenth Street
Oakland
CA 94612
Tel: (1) 510 465 6885
Fax: (1) 510 465 2835
email: nemn@nemm.org
Website: www.nemn.org
National Educational Media Network
is the only US media organisation
dedicated to recognising and
supporting excellence in educational
media, ranging from documentaries
to moving image media designed
especially for classroom and training
programs. NEMN's internationally
acclaimed annual Apple Awards
competition is the largest in the US,
with over 1,000 entrants yearly. The
competition recognises excellence
and innovation in educational film,
video, television and multimedia
works intended for national and
international distribution. Awards are
given to media programs
demonstrating technical and artistic
skill that educate, inform and
empower the end–user. MEM's
annual media market each spring is
the nation's primary gathering where
distributors can view and acquire
newly released educational
productions. NEM's biannual
Conference offers producers and

distributors the latest on industry trends in educational and interactive media through workshops, panel discussions, and exhibits of media hardware, software and services

New York Film Festival
Film Society of Lincoln Center
70 Lincoln Center Plaza, 4th Floor
New York NY 10023
Tel: (1) 212 875 5610
Fax: (1) 212 875 5636
Website: www.filmlinc.com
Non–competitive for feature films, shorts, including drama, documentary, animation and experimental films. Films must have been produced one year prior to the Festival and must be New York premieres

Nortel Palm Springs International Film Festival
– August
PO Box 2230
Palm Springs
California
CA 92263
Tel: (1) 760 322 2930
Fax: (1) 760 322 4087
At each festival world premieres mix with social functions, cultural events, industry seminars, student activities and directors workshops

Portland International Film Festival
– February
Northwest Film Center
1219 SW Park Avenue
Portland, OR 97205
Tel: (503) 221 1156
Fax: (503) 294 0874
email: info@nwfilm.org
Website: www.nwfilm.org
Invitational survey of New World cinema. Includes over 100 features, documentary and short films from more than two dozen countries. Numerous visiting artists. Attendance for the 23rd Festival is expected to be 35,000, drawn from throughout the North West of America

San Francisco International Film Festival
– April/May
1521 Eddy Street
San Francisco
CA 94115–4102
Tel: (1) 415 929 5014
Fax: (1) 415 921 5032
Feature films, by invitation, shown non–competitively. Shorts, documentaries, animation,

experimental works and television productions eligible for Golden Gate Awards competition section. Deadline for Golden Gate Awards entries early December

San Francisco International Lesbian & Gay Film Festival
– June
Frameline
346 Ninth Street
San Francisco CA 94103
Tel: (1) 415 703 8650
Fax: (1) 415 861 1404
Largest lesbian/gay film festival in the world. Features, documentary, experimental, short film and video. Deadline for entries 15 February

Seattle International Film Festival
– May/June
911 Pine St, 6th Floor
Seattle
WA 98101
Tel: (1) 206 464 5830
Fax: (1) 206 264 7919
email: mail@seattlefilm.com
Website: www.seattlefilm.com
Darryl Macdonald, Festival Director
Jury prize for new director and American independent award. Golden Space Needle awards voted by audience. Submissions accepted 1 Jan to 15 March

Sundance Film Festival
– January
PO Box 16450
Salt Lake City
UT 84116
Tel: (1) 801 328 3456
Fax: (1) 801 575 5175
Competitive for American independent dramatic and documentary feature films. Also presents a number of international and American premieres and short films, as well as sidebars, special retrospectives and seminars

Telluride Film Festival
– September
PO Box B–1156
53 South Main Street, Suite 212
Hanover NH 03755
Tel: (1) 603 643 1255
Fax: (1) 603 643 5938
email: tellufilm@aol.com
Website: www.elluridemm.
com/filmfest.htm
Non–competitive. World premieres, archival films and tributes. Entry deadline 31 July

US International Film & Video Festival
– June
841 North Addison Avenue
Elmhurst
IL 60126–1291
Tel: (1) 630 834 7773
Fax: (1) 630 834 5565
email: filmfestinfo@ filmfestawards.com
Website: www.filmfestawards.com
J.W. Anderson
International awards competition for business, television, documentary, industrial and informational productions, produced or released in the 18 months preceding the annual 1 March entry deadline. Formerly the US Industrial Film and Video Festival, founded 1968

FUNDING

For a more comprehensive look at UK funding *Lowdown The Low Budget Funding Guide 2000/2001* published by the Film Council is highly recommended. Website: www.filmcouncil.org.uk /filmmakers/lowdown

ADAPT (Access for Disabled People to Arts Premises Today)
The ADAPT Trust
8 Hampton Terrace
Edinburgh EH12 5JD
Tel: 0131 346 1999
Fax: 0131 346 1991
email: adapt.trust@virgin.net
Website: www.adapttrust.co.uk
Director: Stewart Coulter
Charitable trust providing advice and challenge funding to arts venues - cinemas, concert halls, libraries, heritage and historic houses, theatres, museums and galleries - throughout Great Britain. ADAPT also provides a consultancy service and undertakes access audits and assessments. Grants and Awards for 2000 advertised as available

Arts Council of England
Visual Arts Department
14 Great Peter Street
London W1P 3NQ
Tel: 020 7333 0100
Fax: 020 7973 6581
email: gary.thomas@ artscouncil.org.uk
Website: www.artscouncil.org.uk
Gary Thomas
The Visual Arts Department works with national agencies for artists' film and video. The National Touring Programme offers opportunities for organisations to commission and tour work; guidelines can be requested on 020 7973 6517. Project funding, including production funding for individual artists, is primarily the responsibility of the regional arts boards (or media development agencies).

Animate!
A collaboration with Channel 4 to commission innovative and experimental animation for television from individual animators and artists (including those living in Northern Ireland, Scotland and Wales).
Deadline: January 2001

BBC 10x10
Bristol Television Features
Whiteladies Road
Bristol BS8 2LR
Tel: 0117 974 6746
Fax: 0117 974 7452
email: 10x10@BBC.co.uk
Series Producer: Jeremy Howe
Produces 10 ten-minute films per series, documentary or fiction films for broadcast on BBC2. It is an initiative to encourage and develop new and innovative filmmaking talent in all genres, through the provision of modest production finance combined with practical guidance. The scheme is open to any director with no commissioned broadcast UK Network directing credit. All applications must include a showreel with their proposals - which should be treatments for documentary, scripts for drama

British Council
11 Portland Place
London W1B 1EJ
Tel: 020 7930 8466
Fax: 020 7389 3041
Website: www.britcoun.org/
Assists in the co-ordination and shipping of films to festivals, and in some cases can provide funds for the film-maker to attend when invited. A limited amount of fundraising is available for UK filmmakers to attend European seminars/workshops such as Arista, Eave, Sources etc

British Screen Finance Limited
14-17 Wells Mews
London W1P 3FL
Tel: 020 7323 9080
Fax: 020 7323 0092
email: BS@cd-online.co.uk
Invests in British feature films including, through the European Co-

production Fund Limited, films made under co-production treaties with other countries. Scripts should be submitted with full background information. All scripts are read. Scripts submitted by producers with a fully developed production package are given priority, and projects must have commercial potential in the theatrical market. British Screen's contribution is capped at £500,000, and is never more than 30 per cent of a film's budget

Channel 4/MOMI Animators
Professional Residencies
Museum of the Moving Image
South Bank
London SE1 8XT
Tel: 020 7815 1376
Louise Spraggon
Professional residencies are awarded to animators who have graduated within the last 5 years. Animators receive a fee, plus budget towards materials. At the end of the residencies projects will be considered for commission by Channel 4
British Animation Training Scheme
Museum of the Moving Image
Southbank
Waterloo
London SE1 8XT
Tel: 020 7815 1376
Contact: Louise Spraggon
The assisting in animation course for professionals in animation offers comprehensive training in all aspects of assisting in drawn animation. The course is delivered by professional animators working in the industry. Vocational over 30 weeks

Cineworks
Glasgow Media Access Centre
3rd Floor
34 Albion Street
Glasgow G1 1LH
Tel: 0141 553 2620
Fax: 0141 553 2660
email: cineworks9@aol.com
Website: www.g-mac.co.uk
Cordelia Stephens
Cineworks is a Scottish short film production scheme which produces

original and innovative films from emergent talent in the disciplines of drama, documentary and animation. It is run by the Glasgow Medias Access Centre in partnership with the Film and Video Access Centre, Edinburgh and in association with Scottish Screen. Cineworks develops 12 projects each year through script editing, producer training, workshops, masterclasses and mentoring and funds five projects on awards of £10,000 or £15,000. There are also £5,000 completion awards available. The five films are premiered at the Edinburgh International Film Festival and are distributed by Scottish Screen.

Glasgow Film Fund
249 West George Street
Glasgow G2 4RB
Tel: 0141 302 1757
Fax: 0141 302 1714
Contact: Judy Anderson
The Glasgow Film Fund (GFF) provides production funding for companies shooting films in the Glasgow area or produced by Glasgow-based production companies. Applications are accepted

for films intended for theatrical release and with a budget of at least £500,000. The maximum investment made by the GFF in any one project is normally £150,000, however, where there is an exceptionally high level of economic benefit the GFF may consider raising its maximum investment to £250,000. GFF application forms, meeting dates, submission deadlines and further information are available from the GFF office. Production credits include, *Shallow Grave, Small Faces, Carla's Song, Regeneration, Orphans, My Name Is Joe, The Acid House* and *House of Mirth*

Kraszna-Krausz Foundation
122 Fawnbrake Avenue
London SE24 0BZ
Tel: 020 7738 6701
Fax: 020 7738 6701
email: k-k@dial.pipex.com
Website: www.editor.net/k-k
Andrea Livingstone
The Foundation offers small grants to assist in the development of new or unfinished projects, work or literature where the subject specifically relates to the art, history, practice or technology of photography or the

moving image (defined as film, television, video and related screen media). Annual awards, with prizes for books on the moving image (film, television, video and related media), alternating with those for books on still photography. Books, to have been published in previous two years, can be submitted from publishers in any language. Prize money around £10,000, with awards in two categories. The 2000 awards are for books on photography

National Disability and Video Project (NDVP)
West Midlands Disability Arts Forum
Unit 009, The Custard Factory,
Gibb Street
Digbeth
Birmingham B9 4AA
Tel: 0121 242 2248
Fax: 0121 242 2268
Funded by the Arts Council of England, the NDFVP supports the production of film, video and digital media projects by disabled people. Awards are available for research and development (up to £2,000) and production (up to £19,000). Two

production awards are available for projects of up to 10 minutes with budgets of up to £25,000, the balance of funding to be obtained from other sources

Nicholl Fellowships in Screenwriting
Academy of Motion Picture Arts and Sciences
8949 Wilshire Boulevard
Beverly Hills, CA 90211-1972
USA
Tel: (1) 310 247 3000
email: nicoll@oscars.org
Website: www.oscars.org/nicholl
Annual Screenwriting Fellowship Awards
Up to five fellowships of US$25,000 each to new screenwriters. Eligible are writers in English who have not earned money writing for commercial film or television. Collaborations and adaptations are not eligible. A completed entry includes a feature film screenplay approx 100-130 pages long, an application form and a US$30 entry fee. for rules and application form, visit the website or request the information via mail or email, including your mailing address

Northern Ireland Film Commission
21 Ormeau Avenue
Belfast BT2 8HD
Tel: 01232 232444
Fax: 01232 239918
email: info@nifc.co.uk
Website: www.nifc.co.uk
The Northern Ireland Film Development Fund offers loans to production companies for the development of feature films or television drama series or serials that are intended to be produced primarily in Northern Ireland. NIFDF offers interest-free loans of up to 50 per cent of the cost of developing projects. Loans are unlikely to exceed £40,000 for a television drama series or serial or £15,000 for a single feature film

The Prince's Trust,
18 Park Square East
London NW1 4LH
Tel: 0207 543 1234
Fax: 0207 543 1200
The Prince's Trust aims to help young people to succeed by providing opportunities which they would otherwise not have. This is achieved through a nationwide network which delivers training,

personal development, support for business start ups, development awards and educational support. Richard Mills Travel Fellowship in association with the Gulbenkian Foundation and the Peter S Cadbury Trust, offers three grants of £1,000 for people working in community arts, in the areas of housing, minority arts, special needs, or arts for young people, especially the unemployed. The Fellowships are applicable to people under 35

Scottish Screen
Second Floor
249 West George Street
Glasgow G2 4QE
Tel: 0141 302 1700
Fax: 0141 302 1711
email: info@scottishscreen.com
Website: www.scottishscreen.com
Chief Executive: John Archer
Scottish Screen is responsible to the Scottish Parliament for developing all aspects of screen industry and culture in Scotland through script and company development, short film production, distribution of National Lottery film production finance, training, education, exhibition funding, the Film Commission locations support and the Scottish

Film and Television Archive.
Short Film Schemes
Cineworks in partnership with
Glasgow Media Access Centre
(Production Awards up to £10k and
£15k and completion funding up to
£5k). Tartan Shorts in partnership
with BBC Scotland (£60,000). New
Found Land in partnership with
Scottish Media Group (£45,000).
Antonine's 8.5 in partnership with
Antonine Films and others. New
Gaelic-language short film scheme to
be supported by the Comataidh
Craolaidh Gaidhlig is currently being
finalised
Script Development
Advice and Finance for the
development of feature films
(Development Awards of up to
£20,000, Small Discretionary Awards
of up to £5,000, Writers' Awards of
up to £5,000)
MEDIA
At Scottish Screen MEDIA Antenna
Scotland can help you access
MEDIA II and other European
support programmes
(See also entry for National Lottery)

Sgrîn, Media Agency for Wales

The Bank, 10 Mount Stuart Square
Cardiff Bay
Cardiff CF10 5EE
Tel: 029 20 333300
Fax: 029 20 333320
email: sgrin@sgrin.co.uk
Website: www.sgrin.co.uk
Production coordinator: Gaynor
Messer Price
Sgrîn, Media Agency for Wales, is
the primary organisation for film,
television and new media in Wales.
Sgrîn operates an independent filmmakers' fund, offering grants for
development, production and
completion of short films. It also
provides funding support for cinema
venues, both public and private,
cultural and interpretive printed and
audiovisual material which
complements and promotes
exhibition programmes, and events.
Guidelines and deadlines are
available on request

National Lottery

On 1 April 2000, the Film
Council came into existence. To
create the Film Council, the
DCMS merged the personnel
and functions of three bodies:
what was formerly BFI
Production (now the Film
Council Production
Department); what was
formerly the Arts Council of
England's (ACE) Lottery Film
Department (now the Film
Council Lottery Department);
and the British Film
Commission (BFC). The new
organisation will receive all
DCMS grant-in-aid for film
(with the exception of the grant
to the National Film and
Television School). In turn, it
will be a Lottery distributor
and be the main funder of film
organisations such as the *bfi*.
ACE however, retains
responsibility for other Arts
Lottery funds.

In Scotland, responsibility for
Lottery production support
transferred from the Scottish
Arts Council (SAC) to Scottish
Screen at the start of April.

The Arts Council of Wales and
the Arts Council of Northern
Ireland will continute to
distribute Lottery funds for
film projects.

Arts Council of Northern Ireland

Lottery Department
MacNeice House
Belfast BT9 6AQ
Fax: 01232 664766
Lottery Director: Tanya Greenfield

Arts Council of Wales

Lottery Unit
Holst House
9 Museum Place
Cardiff CF1 3NX
Tel: 029 2037 6500
Fax: 029 2039 5284/221 447
email: information@ccc-acw.org.uk
Website: www.ccc.acw.org.uk
Lottery Director: Robert Edge

Film Council

10 Little Portland Street
London W1N 5DF
Tel: 020 7861 7861
Fax: 020 7861 7862/3//4/5/6
Website: www.filmcouncil.org.uk
Tina McFarling
The Film Council is the new strategic
agency for developing the film
industry and film culture in the UK.
The Film Council is responsible for
channeling £55 million of public
money per year into the film industry
derived from the National Lottery
and government grant support
funding. It has two aims of equal
importance: developing a sustainable
UK film industry; developing film
culture in the UK by improving
access to, and education about the
moving image. The Film Council
officially came into existence on 1
April 2000 taking responsibility for a
number of organisations: the British
Film Commission; the Arts Council
of England's Lottery Film
Department; and the British Film
Institute's Production Department.
British Screen Finance, a publicly
supported film investment company
will become incorporated into the
Film Council in the latter part of
2000 and the British Film Institute
will operate as an independent body
funded by the Film Council to deliver
cultural and education opportunities
for the public

Scottish Screen

Second Floor
249 West George Street
Glasgow G2 4QE
Tel: 0141 302 1700
Fax: 0141 302 1711
email: info@scottishscreen.com
Website: www.scottishscreen.com
From 7 April 2000, Scottish Screen
assumed full responsibility for
allocating National Lottery funds for
all aspects of film production in
Scotland. There are currently seven
funding programmes:
**1. Feature Film Production
Funding**
Funding is available up to £500,000
per project for feature films
(including feature length
documentaries) aimed at theatrical
distribution
2. Short Film Production Funding
Applications for under £25,000 are
accepted on a continuous basis, and
will be decided on by the appropriate
monthly officers' meeting

3. Project Development Funding
Funding up to £75,000 is available
for second-stage development of
feature films. This is aimed at
projects already at a relatively
advanced stage. It will support
elements such as script polish,
preparation of schedule and budget,
casting, etc

4. Distribution and Exploitation Support
Funding of up to £25,000 is available
for completed feature films to
support Print and Advertising costs.

5. Company Development Programme
Finance of up to £75,000 is available
as working capital funding into
companies to support a slate of film,
television and multimedia.

6. Short Film Award Schemes
On an annual basis, Scottish Screen
will consider applications, of up to
£60,000, from outside bodies to
operate short film production
schemes.

7. Twenty First Films - Low Budget Film Scheme
This scheme offers support for low
budget features (including feature
documentaries) with budgets up to
around £600,000.

Regional Arts Boards and Regional Schemes

Croydon Film & Video Awards
Croydon Clocktower
Katharine Street
Croydon CR9 1ET
Tel: 020 8760 5400 ext 1048
email: paul-
johnson@croydon.gov.uk
Co-ordinator: Paul Johnson
The Croydon Film & Video Awards
are an ongoing production initiative
co-funded by the LFVDA and the
London Borough of Croydon. The
£10,000 scheme was established in
1997 to support local film and video
makers to make fictional,
documentary or experimental shorts.
Completed films will be premiered at
the David Lean Cinema

East Midlands Arts Board
Mountfields House
Epinal Way
Loughborough
Leics LE11 0QE
Tel: 01509 218292
Fax: 01509 262214
email: carol.clarke@em-arts.co.uk
Website: www.arts.org.uk
Suzanne Alizar, Film and Digital
Media Production Officer
New work and commissions, script
research and development awards,
production awards and distribution
awards

Eastern Arts Board
Cherry Hinton Hall
Cherry Hinton Road
Cambridge CB1 8DW
Tel: 01223 215355
Fax: 01223 248075
email: cinema@eastern-arts.co.uk
Website: www.eab.org.uk/
Cinema and Broadcasting Officer:
Martin Ayres
Media Assistant: Helen Dixon
Eastern Arts Board is the regional
arts development and funding agency
for the counties of Bedfordshire,
Cambridgeshire, Essex,
Hertfordshire, Norfolk and Suffolk,
and the unitary authorities of Luton,
Peterborough, Rochford and
Thurrock. The new East of England
Regional Arts Lottery Programme
and Small Scale Capital Scheme
includes priority support for film,
video, cinema and multimedia

activity. EAB Open Access schemes
will offer support for individuals.
EAB assists a network of agencies
and venues, including first take (see
entry for first take) with Anglia
Television. Policy, information,
development services and funding for
Cinema & Broadcasting covers five
interlocking areas: Collections,
Education & Training, Exhibition,
Production, and Artists Film & Video
& Multimedia. From Autumn 1999
EAB specialist film and video
production, scriptwriting, co-
commissioning funding and
development services will be
delivered through first take (see entry
for first take).

East of England Regional Production Fund
Launched in Autumn 1999, this fund
seeks to assist innovative practice and
creative experimentation in a range of
genres, styles and formats. It offers
seed funding for the realisation,
development and production of one-
off moving image projects

English Regional Arts Board
5 City Road
Winchester
Hampshire SO23 8SD
Tel: 01962 851063
Fax: 01962 842033
email: info@erab.org.uk
Website: www.arts.org.uk
Carolyn Nixson, Administrator

First Stop Media Production Awards
Media Arts
Town Hall Studios
Regent Circus
Swindon SN1 1QF
Tel: 01793 463226
Fax: 01793 463223
Contact: Steve Chapman
The scheme exists to encourage new
and creative projects, particularly the
work of first-time film or video
makers. First Stop is open to all who
live and work in the Swindon area
and people from other areas who
would like to involve local people or
whose project can benefit Swindon.
Funding is not available for student
or commercial productions. Grants
are available of up to £3,000 in
equipment hire credits and £500 cash
towards production expenses. The
scheme may also be able to help with
script development, budgeting,
production management, crewing,
casting and technical training.

first take films
Anglia Television Limited
Anglia House
Norwich
Norfolk NR1 3JG
Tel: 01603 615151
Fax: 01603 767191
email: cnorbury@angliatv.co.uk
Executive Producer: Caroline
Norbury
Administrator: Annette Culverhouse
Marketing & Distribution: Kate
Gerova
first take films is a joint initiative set
up by Eastern Arts Board and Anglia
Television. It is a regional cultural
production agency whose principal
function is to facilitate, encourage
and promote the creative arts of film,
video and moving image in the East
of England. The first take series is
Anglia TV's annual showcase for up
and coming new directors, and
submissions are usually accepted in
February

London Arts Board
Elme House
133 Long Acre
Covent Garden
London WC2E 9AF
Tel: 020 7240 1313
Fax: 020 7670 2400
email: firstname.surname@
lonab.co.uk
Website: www.arts.org.uk/lab
Chief Executive: Sue Robertson
The London Arts Board has no
dedicated funds for Film and Video.
However, it does offer awards to
individual artists working in the
medium of film and video and New
Media. Write to LAB at the above
address for funding guidelines. For
all other film and video enquiries,
call the London Film and Video
Development Agency (qv)

London Film and Video Development Agency
114 Whitfield Street
London W1P 5RW
Tel: 020 7383 7755
Fax: 020 7383 7745
email: lfvda@lfvda.demon.co.uk
Website: www.lfvda.demon.co.uk
Chief Executive: Gill Henderson
Provides funding to a range of
production, training facilities and
exhibition organisations
Project Funding
Support for training courses, film and
video exhibition and festivals in
London

The LFVDA is the assessing body
for London film and video
applications to all Lottery funding
streams. The LFVDA runs the
London Production Fund (q.v.)

London Production Fund
114 Whitfield Street
London W1T 5EF
Tel: 020 7383 7766
Fax: 020 7383 7745
Production Advisor: Maggie Ellis
The London Production Fund aims to
support and develop film, video and
television projects by independent
film-makers living/working in the
London region. It is run by the
London Film and Video Development
Agency and receives financial
support from Carlton Television,
Channel 4 and the LFVDA. It has an
annual budget of approximately
£200,000
Development Awards
Support of up to £3,000 each to assist
in the development of scripts,
storyboards, project packages, pilots
Production and Completion Awards
Offers support of up to £15,000 each
for production or part-production
costs. Awards will be made on the
basis of written proposals and
applicants' previous work. The Fund
is interested in supporting as diverse
a range of films and videos as
possible

North West Arts Board
Manchester House
22 Bridge Street
Manchester M3 3AB
Tel: 0161 834 6644
Fax: 0161 834 6969
email: jleather@nwarts.co.uk
Website: www.arts.org.uk/nwab
Julie Leather, Administrator
Information
NWAB offers a range of funding
schemes covering Production,
Exhibition, Training and Media
Education for those resident in the
NWAB region

Northern Arts
Ground Floor
Central Square
Forth Street
Newcastle-upon-Tyne NE1 3PJ
Tel: 0191 255 8500
Fax: 0191 230 1020
email: info@northernarts.org.uk
Website: www.arts.org.uk
Head of Film Media and Literature:
Mark Robinson
Northern Production Fund (NPF)

The aim of NPF is to support the
production of short and long form
drama, for film, television and radio,
animation, creative documentaries,
and all forms of experimental film-
making, including work for gallery
exhibition. The foremost concern of
NPF is for the quality of the
production. NPF to support
productions which are imaginative,
innovative, thoughtful, courageous
and powerful. NPF normally holds
three meetings per year to consider
applications under the small scale
production, development and feature
film development headings.
Production
Support of up to £30,000 for
production or part-production costs
or completion costs.
Development
Support of up to £5,000 to assist in
the development of scripts,
storyboards, full treatments, pilot
production, etc. This includes
research and development for feature
films, short drama for film or radio,
animation, documentary projects and
innovative television drama.
Feature Film Developments
A maximum of £10,000 awards for
feature film development will be
available for projects each year.
These awards will normally be made
to production companies, working
with a Northern-based writer, who
are able to demonstrate their ability
to match the Northern Arts
contribution. Matching funding may
include the cost of feature film
development expertise and/or the
contribution of another funding
partner.
Company Support
Support for companies is available to
assist in the development of a
programme of work. Company
support will normally be awarded to
support several projects rather than
production costs.
Broadcaster Partnership Schemes
The Northern Production Fund also
works in partnership with
broadcasters to offer production
schemes for short drama and
documentary production

South East Arts
Union House
Eridge Road
Tunbridge Wells
Kent TN4 8HF
Tel: 01892 507200
Fax: 01892 549383
email: info.sea@artsfb.org.uk

Website: www.arts.org.uk
Production Grants
Offers grants of up to £10,000 for
full or part-funding of films or videos
for more experienced filmmakers.
Grants of up to £1,000 are available
to newcomers or those with little
production experience

South West Arts
Bradninch Place
Gandy Street
Exeter EX4 3LS
Tel: 01392 218188
Fax: 01392 413554
email: info@swa.co.uk
Website: www.swa.co.uk
John Prescott Thomas
Chief Executive: Nick Capaldi

South West Media
Development Agency
59 Prince Street
Bristol BS1 4QH
Tel: 0117 927 3226
Fax: 0117 927 6216
Website: www.swmediadevagency.
co.uk
Director: Judith Higginbottom
The South West Media Development
Agency is the funding and
development body for film, video and
television in the south west. It
provides advice and financial support
for: low budget and independent
production, animation, script
development, artists' film and video
commissioning, exhibition of
independent art-house, historic and
experimental cinema. Applicants for
financial support must be resident in
the South West Media Development
region. For details of available
funding, please contact Sarah-Jane
Meredith

Southern Arts Board
13 St Clement Street
Winchester
Hants SO23 9DQ
Tel: 01962 855099
Fax: 01962 861186
email: info@southernarts.co.uk
Website: www.arts.org.uk
Film and Video production grants
available in two categories:
production (up to £5,000) and
completion (up to £3,000). Co-
production funding is strongly
encouraged. First Cut (with Central)
and Taped Up (with Meridian) are
both broadcast schemes to support
filmmakers new to television to make
short films for broadcast. The David
Alsthul Award is a competitive award

for creative achievement in film and
video production available to those
who live or work in the Southern
region including students. Annual
prize money of £1,000. Exhibition
Development Fund supports
programming, marketing, training
and research and includes support for
artists working with digital
technology and installation work.
Media Education Development Fund
supports strategic development of
regional media education. Full details
on all the above on application

Wandsworth Film and
Video Making Award
Wandsworth Arts Office
Room 224a, Town Hall
Wandsworth High Street
London SW18 2PU
Tel: 020 8871 7380
Fax: 020 8871 8712
Principal Arts Officer: Charlie
Catling
Annual award for film and video
makers arranged by Wandsworth
Borough Council and the LFVDA.
The maximum award for any one
film is £5,000 and the minimum
number of awards made each year is
two. The scheme is open to those
who live, work or study in the
London Borough of Wandsworth

West Midlands Arts Board
82 Granville Street
Birmingham B1 2LH
Tel: 0121 631 3121
Fax: 0121 643 7239
email: info@west-midlands-
arts.co.uk
Media Officer: Film and Video:
Laurie Hayward
email: laurie.hayward.@west-
midlands-arts.co.uk
"First Cut" Film and Video
Production Scheme.
A broadcast initiative supported by
West Midlands Arts, Birmingham
City Council, the Media
Development Agency for the West
Midlands (MDAWM), Central
Broadcasting, BBC Resources
Midlands and East, and the Midland
Media Training Consortium. The aim
is to produce a range of diverse
programmes for regional television.
Recipients of the award work with a
Production Co-ordinator based at
(MDAWM) to develop a project
through training, production support
and access to the broadcast industry.
A minimum of five awards are made
with budgets of up to £7,500. The

scheme results in the Central
Television 'First Cut' programme
which will be broadcast in the
Autumn of 2000. Application
deadline January 2000.
New Work and Commissions
Offer artist film and video makers an
opportunity to produce new work in
film, video and new technology. The
scheme seeks proposals which
demonstrate innovation and
experimentation. Awards are made
for pieces up to ten minutes with a
maximum budget of £5,000. The
scheme favours work for screening in
conventional, sites specific and other
contexts. Application deadlines
February/September.
Research and Development Awards
Enables makers to develop their
proposals for future productions.
Research and Development Awards
are expected to range between £200 to
£1,000. Deadline February/September

Yorkshire Arts
21 Bond Street
Dewsbury
West Yorks WF13 1AX
Tel: 01924 455555
Fax: 01924 466522
email: tony.dixon.yha@artsfb.org.uk
Short Film and Video Production
Awards 2000
More information will be available
later in the year regarding the
deadline and details for the Short
Film & Video Production Fund,
following implementation of the
restructure of Yorkshire Arts, and in
the light of major changes in the
national structure for funding moving
image work. The deadline is unlikely
to be before the end of March 2000.
Contact: Yorkshire Arts directly for
details
Development Awards 1999
Awards of £500 are available for
projects to be developed to a stage
where applications can be made to
YHA for short film production
funding. An award can be used in any
way which advances the project. For
example: scriptwriting, research,
fees. Applications will be accepted
from writers, producers, directors etc

European and Pan-European Sources

Eurimages
Council of Europe
Palais de l'Europe
67075 Strasbourg Cédex
France
Tel: (33) 3 88 41 26 40
Fax: (33) 3 88 41 27 60
Website:
www.culture.coe.fr/eurimages
Provides financial support for
feature-length fiction films,
documentaries, distribution and
exhibition. Applications from the UK
can only be accepted if a UK
producer is a fourth co-producer in a
tripartite co-production or the third in
a bipartite, provided his/her share
does not exceed 30 per cent of the
co-production

European Co-production Association
c/o France 2
22 Avenue Montaigne
75387 Paris
Cédex 08
France
Tel: (33) 1 4421 4126
Fax: (49) 1 4421 5179
Secretariat: Claire Heinrich
A consortium of European public
service TV networks for the co-
production of TV fiction series. Can
offer complete finance. Development
funding is also possible. Proposals
should consist of full treatment,
financial plan and details of proposed
co-production partners. Projects are
proposed directly to Secretariat or to
member national broadcasters
(Channel 4 in UK)

European Co-production Fund
c/o British Screen Finance
14-17 Wells Mews
London W1P 3FL
Tel: 020 7323 9080
Fax: 020 7323 0092
email: info@britishscreen.co.uk
The Fund's aim is to enable UK
producers to collaborate in the
making of films which the European
market demonstrably wishes to see
made but which could not be made
without the Fund's involvement. The
ECF offers commercial loans, up to
30 per cent of the total budget capped
at £500,000, for full length feature
films intended for theatrical release.

The film must be a co-production
involving at least two production
companies, with no link of common
ownership established in separate EU
states

FilmFörderung Hamburg
Friedensallee 14-16
22765 Hamburg
Germany
Tel: (49) 40 398 370
Fax: (49) 40 398 3710
email: filmfoerderung@ffhh.de
Website: www.ffhh.de
Eva Hubert
Producers of cinema films can apply
for a subsidy amounting to at most
50 per cent of the overall production
costs of the finished film. Foreign
producers can also apply for this
support. We recommend to co-
produce with a German partner. It is
necessary to spend at least 150 per
cent of the subsidy in Hamburg. Part
of the film should be shot in
Hamburg. Financial support provided
by the FilmFörderung Hamburg can
be used in combination with other
private or public funding, including
that of TV networks

MEDIA Programme

On 14 December 1999, the European
Commission adopted its proposal for
a programme in support of the
audiovisual industry called **Media
Plus** (2001-2005), to be introduced in
2001 as a follow-up to the Media II
programme which ends on 31
December 2000. MEDIA II was a
programme of the European Union,
managed by the European
Commission in Brussels. MEDIA II,
which followed on from MEDIA I,
started in 1996

European Commission
Directorate General X:
Information, Communication,
Culture, Audio-visual
200, rue de la Loi
1049 Brussels, Belgium
Tel: (32) 2 299 11 11
Fax: (32) 2 299 92 14
Website: www.europa.eu.int/comm
Head of MEDIA Unit: Jacques
Delmoly
MEDIA II is a programme of the
European Union, managed by the
European Commission in Brussels.
MEDIA II, which follows on from
MEDIA I, started in 1996 and will
conclude in the year 2000
Who is eligible?
All member states of the European
Unin and countries belonging to the
European Economic Area are eligible
for MEDIA II. The Programme is
also open to Cyprus, Malta, Central
and Eastern European countries
subject to special agreements with
the Commission
Objectives
The Commission publishes in the
Official Journal of the European
Commission calls for projects and
deadlines for submission for the
following areas of support: Training,
Development and
Distribution/Promotion
Media Contacts
As part of a network of 29 Desks and
Antennae throughout Europe, the
members of the UK MEDIA team
listed below should be the first point
of contact for UK companies seeking
information and advice of the
MEDIA Programme. Guidelines and
application forms for al the MEDIA
II schemes are available from them.
They produce regular newsletters and
other printed information detailing
upcoming deadlines, training courses
and markets

MEDIA Services England

249 West George Street
Glasgow G2 4QE
Tel: 0870 0100 791
Fax: 0141 302 1778
Website: www.mediadesk.co.uk
Chris Miller
This is a temporary contact until a
new MEDIA Desk is set up in
London in 2001
email: media.england@
scottishscreen.com
Website: www.mediadesk.co.uk

MEDIA Antenna Scotland

249 West George Street
Glasgow G2 4RB
Tel: 0141 302 1776/7
Fax: 0141 302 1778
email:
media.scotland@scottishscreen.com
Website: www.mediadesk.co.uk
Louise Scott
Rosie Ellison

MEDIA Antenna Wales

c/o Sgrîn: The Media Agency for
Wales
The Bank, 10 Mount Stuart Square
Llantrisant Road
Cardiff CF10 5EE
Tel: 01222 333 304
Fax: 01222 333 320
email: antenna@
scrwales.demon.co.uk
Website:
www.sgrin.wales.demon.co.uk
Contact: Gwarr Hughes

MEDIA Northern Ireland

MEDIA Services Northern Ireland
c/o Northern Ireland Film
Commission
21 Ormeau Avenue
Belfast BT2 8HD
Tel: 02890 232 444
Fax: 02890 239 918
email: media@nifc.com
Website: www.mediadesk.co.uk
Heike Meyer-Döring
Training Support
Support is available for training
institutions or bodies which provide
initial and continuous vocational
training courses in: Screenplay
techniques, economic and
commercial management, new
technologies
Development Support
MEDIA Development offers support
in the form of interest free oans in
two main areas: Project development:
fiction and creative documentary,
animation, multimedia projects, state
funding.

Company development: business
plans, company development
Distribution and Promotional Support
The MEDIA Distribution scheme
aims at improving the transnational
distribution of European audio-visual
works. The areas of support are:
Cinema distribution, Video and
multimedia publishing, TV
distribution, Marketing of licensing
rights
Support is also given to organisations
which: facilitate access by
independent producers and
distributors of European markets
Organise thematic markets or
specialist events
Film Festival Support
Networking and exchange of ideas,
experience, good practice and
product is encouraged between
festivals and events. Support is given
for:
activities organised by networks of
audio-visual events, audio-visual
festivals carried out in partnership
MEDIA also support two specialist
sectors: animation and exhibition

CARTOON (European Association of Animation Film)

314 Boulevard Lambermont
B-1030 Brussels
Belgium
Tel: (32) 2 245 12 00
Fax: (32) 2 245 46 89
email: cartoon@skynet.be
Website: www.cartoon-media.be
Contact: Corinne Jenart, Marc
Vandeweyer
CARTOON, based in Brussels, is a
European animation network which
organises the annual CARTOON
FORUM, co-ordinates the grouping of
European animation studios and runs
specialist training courses in animation

Europa Cinemas

54, rue Beaubourg
F-75 003 Paris, France
Tel: (33) 1 42 71 53 70
Fax: (33) 1 42 71 47 55
email: europacinema@magic.fr
Website: www.europa-cinemas.org
Contact: Claude-Eric Poiroux, Fatima
Djoumer
This project encourages screenings
and promotion of European films in a
network of cinemas in European
cities. It offers a financial support for
screening European films, for
promotional activities and for special
events

MEDIA Salles

Via Soperga, 2
1-20 127 Milan, Italy
Tel: (39) 02 66 98 4405
Fax: (39) 02 669 1574
email: infocinema@mediasalles.it
Website: www.mediasalles.it/
Elisabetta Brunella, Secretary
General
MEDIA Salles with Euro Kids
Network is an initiative aimed at
consolidating the availability of
'cinema at the cinema' for children
and young people in Europe, and at
raising the visibility of European film
to a younger audience

INTERNATIONAL SALES

Below is a selection of companies which acquire rights to audiovisual products for sale to foreign distributors in all media – see also Distributors (Non–Theatrical) and (Theatrical)

Action Time
Wrendal House
2 Whitworth Street West
Manchester M1 5WX
Tel: 0161 236 8999
Fax: 0161 236 8845
Specialises in international format sales of game shows and light entertainment

Alibi Films International
12 Maiden Lane
Covent Garden
London WCZE 7NA
Tel: 020 7845 0400
Fax: 020 7836 6919
email: info@alibifilms.co.uk
Website: www.alibifilms.co.uk
Gareth Jones
Alibi is active in the financing, international sales and distribution of theatrical feature films and the production of feature film, television drama and children's programming. Titles include: *One More Kiss* (1999); *One of the Hollywood Ten* (2000)

Associated Press Television News
The Interchange
32 Oval Road, Camden Lock
London NW1 7DZ
Tel: 020 7410 5200
Fax: 020 7413 8327 (Library)
Gerry O'Reilly, David Simmons
International TV news, features, sport, entertainment, documentary programmes and archive resources. Camera crews in major global locations, plus in–house broadcasting and production facilities

Australian Film Commission
Level 4, 150 William Street
Woolloomooloo 201
Australia

Tel: (61) 2 9321 6444
Fax: (61) 2 9357 3631
email: marketing@afc.gov.au
Website: www.afc.gov.au
Sabina Finnern
Australian government–funded body set up to assist in development, production and promotion of Australian film, television, video and interactive product

BBC Worldwide
Woodlands
80 Wood Lane
London W12 0TT
Tel: 020 8576 2000
Fax: 020 8 749 0538
Website: www.bbc.worldwide.com
Programme, Sales and Marketing – the sales and licensing of BBC programmes and international broadcasters, and the generation of co–production business; Channel Marketing – the development of new cable and satellite delivered television channels around the world

Beyond Films
3rd Floor
22 Newman Street
London W1V 3HB
Tel: 020 7636 9613
Fax: 020 7636 9614
email: dee-emerson@beyond.com.au
Website: www.Beyond.com
Dee Emerson
Films: *Strictly Ballroom, Love & Other Catastrophes, Love Serenade, Kiss or Kill, Heaven's Burning, SLC Punk, Orphans, Two Hands, Paperback Hero, Kick, Fresh Air, In a Savage Land, Cut*

bfi
21 Stephen Street
London W1T 1LN
Tel: 020 7957 8927
Fax: 020 7580 5830
email: sales.films@bfi.org.uk
Website: www.bfi.org.uk
John Flahive, Film Sales Manager, Laurel Warbrick–Keay, Film Sales Co–Ordinator
Sales of *bfi* Production and *bfi* TV features, shorts and documentaries, archival and acquired titles including: *Love is the Devil, Under the Skin,*

Speak Like a Child, early Peter Greenaway and Derek Jarman features and shorts, *Lee Marvin a Personal Portrait* by John Boorman, *South* and *Silent Shakespeare.* Catalogue available on request

bfi Archival Footage Sales
21 Stephen Street
London W1P 2LN
Tel: 020 7957 8934
Fax: 020 7580 5830
email: footage.films@bfi.org.uk
Website: www.bfi.org.uk
Jan Faull or Simon Brown
Material from the largest collection of film footage in Britain – the National Film and Television Archive. Television, films, documentaries, newsreels and animation are all covered with over 350,000 titles to choose from, including material dating back to 1895. First stop for serious research on subjects that have shaped the 20th century. Research facilities available.

The Box Office
3 Market Mews
London W1Y 7HH
Tel: 020 7499 3968
Fax: 020 7491 0008
email: paul@box–office.demon. co.uk
International film and television consultancy

British Home Entertainment
5 Broadwater Road
Walton–on–Thames
Surrey KT12 5DB
Tel: 01932 228832
Fax: 01932 247759
email: clivew@bhe.prestel.co.uk
Clive Williamson
Video distribution/TV marketing. *An Evening with the Royal Ballet, Othello, The Mikado, The Soldier's Tale, Uncle Vanya, King and Country, The Hollow Crown, The Merry Wives of Windsor*

Capitol Films
23 Queensdale Place
London W11 4SQ
Tel: 020 7471 6000

Fax: 020 7471 6012
email: films@capitolfilms.com
Simon Radcliffe
Recent productions include: *Beautiful Joe, House of Mirth, Drowning Mona, Wilde* and *Among Giants*

Carlton International
35–38 Portman Square
London W1H 0NU
Tel: 020 7224 3339
Fax: 020 7486 1707
Director of Sales: Louise Sexton
International TV programme and film sales agent, now representing Carlton Television, Central Television, HTV, ITN Productions and Meridian Broadcasting as well as a growing number of independent production companies.
The ITC Collection
The ITC Library was acquired in 1999 by Carlton International. The library includes such celebrated films as *The Eagle Has Landed,The Big Easy,The Boys from Brazil, On Golden Pond, Farewell My Lovely, Sophie's Choice* and *The Last Seduction*. It also features a huge array of classic series including *The Saint, The Prisoner, Randall and Hopkirk (Deceased)* and *Space 1999* and some of the most popular children's programmes including Gerry Anderson's *Thunderbirds, Joe 90* and *Captain Scarlet*

Cascade Worldwide Distribution
3 Waterhouse Square
138–142 Holborn
London EC1N 2NY
Tel: 020 7882 1000
Fax: 020 7882 1020
email: adrian.howells@
scottishmediagroup.com
Adrian Howells, Head of Sales
Tim Mutimer, Anne–Marie Scholey, Julie Norman.
International distribution of STV, Grampian and Third Party programming in the following genres: Drama, factual, children's and animation. Titles include:
Taggart, Rebus, The Last Musketeer, McCallum, Harry and the Wrinklies, Celtic America

CBC International Sales
43–51 Great Titchfield Street
London W1P 8DD
Tel: 020 7412 9200
Fax: 020 7323 5658
Susan Hewitt, Michelle Payne, Janice Russell

The programme sales division of Canadian Broadcasting Corporation and Société Radio–Canada

Chatsworth Television Distributors
97–99 Dean Street
London W1V 5RA
Tel: 020 7734 4302
Fax: 020 7437 3301

Cine Electra
National House
60–66 Wardour Street
London W1V 3HP
Tel: 020 7287 1123
Fax: 020 7722 4251

CTVC
Hillside Studios
Merry Hill Road
Bushey
Watford WD2 1DR
Tel: 020 8950 4426
Fax: 020 8950 1437
email: ctvc@ctvc.co.uk
Website: www.ctvc.co.uk
Ann Harvey
International programme sales and co–productions in documentary, music, children's, drama and arts programmes

DLT Entertainment UK Ltd
10 Bedford Square
London WC1B 3RA
Tel: 020 7631 1184
Fax: 020 7636 4571
John Reynolds; John Bartlett, Mike Taylor
Specialising in entertainment programming. Recent titles include: *As Time Goes By*, series eight for BBC Television; *Bloomin' Marvellous*, eight–part comedy series for BBC Television

Documedia International Films Ltd
19 Widegate Street
London E1 7HP
Tel: 020 7625 6200
Fax: 020 7625 7887
Distributors of innovative and award winning drama specials, drama shorts, serials, tele–movies and feature films; documentary specials and series; for worldwide sales and co–production

EVA Entertainment
74 Langley Street
Covent Garden
London WC2H 9JA
Tel: 020 7386 3000
Fax: 0207 836 3300

FilmFour International
76–78 Charlotte Street
London W1P 2TX
Tel: 020 7868 7700
Fax: 020 7868 7769
Website: www.filmfour.com
Susan Bruce–Smith, Director of Worldwide Sales and Marketing
The international sales arm of C4's stand–alone film company FilmFour Ltd. Recent titles represented by FFI include *East is East, Sexy Beast, Gangster No 1, The Filth and The Fury*

Goldcrest Films International
65/66 Dean Street
London W1D 4PR
Tel: 020 7437 8696
Fax: 020 7437 4448
Thierry Wase–Bailey
Major feature film production, sales and finance company. Recent films include *All Dogs Go to Heaven, Black Rainbow, Rock–A–Doodle, The Harvest, Me and Veronica, Painted Heart*

Grampian Television
Queen's Cross
Aberdeen AB15 4XJ
Tel: 01224 846846
Fax: 01224 846800
Alistair Gracie (Controller) Hilary I. Buchan (Head of Public Relations)
North Scotland ITV station producing a wide range of programming including documentaries, sport, children's, religion and extensive daily news and current affairs to serve ITV's largest region

Granada Media International
Dominican Court
17 Hatfields
London SC1 8DJ
Website: www.brite.tv.co.uk
Nadine Nohr
International programme sales and distribution for Granada Television, London Weekend Television and Yorkshire–Tyne Tees Television. Leading titles include *Cracker, Prime Suspect*

Hollywood Classics
8 Cleveland Gardens
London W2 6HA
Tel: 020 7262 4646
Fax: 020 7262 3242
email: hollywoodclassicsuk@
compuserve.com

Website: www.hollywoodclassics.com
Melanie Tebb
Hollywood Classics has offices in
London and Los Angeles and sells
back catalogue titles from major
Hollywood studios for theatrical
release in all territories outside North
America. Also represents an
increasing library of European and
independent American titles and has
all rights to catalogues from various
independent producers.

Icon Entertainment International
The Quadrangle, 4th Floor
180 Wardour Street
London W1V 3AA
Tel: 020 7494 8100
Fax: 020 7494 8151
Ralph Kamp: Chief Executive
Jamie Carmichael: Head of Sales
Caroline Johnson: Marketing
Manager

ITC Library
33 Foley Street
London W1P 7LB
Tel: 020 7306 7763
Fax: 306 7750
(See Carlton International)

J & M Entertainment
2 Dorset Square
London NW1 6PU
Tel: 020 7723 6544
Fax: 020 7724 7541
Julia Palau, Michael Ryan
Specialise in sales of all media,
distribution and marketing of
independent feature films

Kushner–Locke International
83 Marylebone High Street
London W1M 3DE
Website: www.kushner–locke.com
Company led by Donald Kushner and
Peter Locke has expanded its existing
television production and distribution
activities into international theatrical
feature films

Link Entertainment
7 Baron's Gate
33–35 Rothschild Road
Chiswick
London W4 5HT
Tel: 020 8996 4800
Fax: 020 8747 9452
email: info@linklic.demon.co.uk
Website: linkenterainment.com
Claire Derry, David Hamilton, Jo
Kavanagh–Payne
Specialists in children's programmes

for worldwide distribution and
character licensing. New properties
include: *Chatterhappy Ponies; The
Forgotten Toys Series; Pirates Series
III; Caribou Kitchen Series III; The
First Snow of Winter*

London Films
71 South Audley Street
London W1Y 5FF
Tel: 020 7499 7800
Fax: 020 7499 7994
Website: www.londonfilms.com
Andrew Luff
Founded in 1932 by Alexander
Korda, London Films is renowned for
the production of classics.
Co–productions with the BBC
include *Poldark* and *I Claudius*. More
recent series include *Lady Chatterley*
directed by Ken Russell and *The
Scarlet Pimpernell* starring Richard
E.Grant

London Television Service
21–25 St Anne's Court
London W1F OBJ
Tel: 020 7434 1121
Fax: 020 7734 0619
email: lts@londontv.com
Website: www.londontv.com
LTS is a specialist production and
distribution organisation that handles
the promotion and marketing of
British documentary and magazine
programmes worldwide to television,
cable, satellite and non–broadcast
outlets. The flagship science and
technology series *Perspective* has
sold to television in over 100
countries

National Film Board of Canada
Canada House
Trafalgar Square
London SW1Y 5BJ
Tel: 020 7258 6480
Fax: 020 7258 6532
Jane Taylor
European sales office for
documentary, drama and animation
productions from Canada's National
Film Board

NBD Television
Unit 2, Royalty Studios
105 Lancaster Road
London W11 1QF
Tel: 020 7243 3646
Fax: 020 7243 3656
Nicky Davies Williams, Charlotte
Felia, Carolyne Waters
Company specialising in music and
light entertainment

Orbit Media Ltd
7–11 Kensington High Street
London W8 5NP
Tel: 020 7287 4264
Fax: 020 7727 0515
Website: www.orbitmedia.co.uk
Chris Ranger, Jordan Reynolds
Specialises in vintage product from
the first decade of American TV: The
Golden Years of Television and 65 x
30 mins Series NoireTV series

Paramount Television
49 Charles Street
London W1X 8LU
Tel: 020 7318 6400
Fax: 020 7491 2086
Stephen Tague

PD&B Films
c/o The Short Film Bureau
47 Poland Street
London W1V 3DF
Tel: 020 7734 8708
Fax: 020 7734 2406
email: info@pdbfilms.com
Website: www.pdbfilms.com
PD&B Films is an international sales
agent for short films

Pearson Television International
1 Stephen Street
London W1P 1PJ
Tel: 020 7691 6000
Fax: 020 7691 6060
Website: www.pearsontv.com
Managing Director: Brian Harris
Executive Vice President: Joe Abrams
Pearson Television International is
one of the world's premier developers
and distributors of entertainment
programming. Highlights of PTI's
extensive catalogue include: 11
volumes of ACI television movies –
most recently Robert B Parker's *Thin
Air* starring Joe Mantegna, The
Golden *Spiders* with Timothy Hutton,
and *Stolen from the Heart* starring
Tracey Gold and Barbara Mandrell.
Sitcoms – *Mr Bean* to Simon Nye's
Beast and *Men Behaving Badly* and
Marks and Gran's *Birds of a Feather*.
Serial drama – *Neighbours, Shortland
Street* and *Family Affairs*. Drama –
highlights include Francis Ford
Coppola's sci–fi series *First Wave,
Baywatch Hawaii, The Bill* and
Homicide: Life on the Street.
Documentaries – *Secrets of War,
Destination Space, Fame and Fortune*
and *Final Day*. Comedy legends
including Benny Hill, Tommy Cooper
and Morecombe and Wise

Photoplay Productions
21 Princess Road
London NW1 8JR
Tel: 020 7722 2500
Fax: 020 7722 6662
Kevin Brownlow, David Gill, Patrick Stanbury
European dealer for the Blackhawk 16mm library of silent and early sound films

Portman Entertainment
167 Wardour Street
London W1V 3TA
Tel: 020 7468 3443
Fax: 020 7468 3469
email: sales@port-ent.co.uk
Tristan Whalley (Portman Film)
Gary Mitchell (Portman Television)
Saving Grace (feature), *Paranoid* (feature), *Stickmen* (feature), *Snakeskin* (feature), *Dark Knight* (TV series), *Urban Gothic* (TV series), *20:13 Thou Shalt Not Kill* (TVM)

Reuters Television
85 Fleet Street
London EC4P 4AJ
Tel: 020 7250 1122
Fax: 020 7542 4995
Distribution of international TV news and sports material to broadcasters around the world

RM Associates
46 Great Marlborough Street
London W1V 1DB
Tel: 020 7439 2637
Fax: 020 7439 2316
email: rma@rmassociates.co.uk
Neil Mundy: Director of Programmes
Sally Fairhead: Head of Publicity
In addition to handling the exclusive distribution of programmes produced/co–produced by RM Arts, RM Associates works closely with numerous broadcasters and independent producers to bring together a comprehensive catalogue of music and arts programming

S4C
Parc Ty Glas
Llanishen
Cardiff CF4 5DU
Tel: 029 2074 7444
Fax: 029 2074 4444
email: s4c@s4c.co.uk
Website: www.s4c.co.uk
Gwydion Griffiths
Distribute programmes plus co–productions commissioned by S4C from independent producers – animation, drama, documentaries

Safir Films Ltd
49 Littleton Rd
Harrow
Middx HA1 3SY
Tel: 020 8423 0763
Fax: 020 8423 7963
email: Safir@ibm.net
Lawrence Safir
Hold rights to numerous Australian, US and UK pictures, including Sam Spiegel's *Betrayal*

The Sales Company
62 Shaftesbury Avenue
London W1D 6LT
Tel: 020 7434 9061
Fax: 020 7494 3293
Alison Thompson, Rebecca Kearey and Joy Wong. The Sales Company is owned by British Screen, BBC Worldwide, Zenith Productions and The Film Consortium handles international sales for their films, for all rights. Recent films include: *The Snapper, Priest, Butterfly Kiss, Antonia's Line, Stonewall, Land and Freedom,The Van, I Went Down, My Name is Joe* and *Hideous Kinky*. Also occasionally handles product from the international arena including *Safe, La Seconda Volta, Jerusalem* and *Private Confessions*

The Samuel Goldwyn Company
St George's House
14–17 Wells Street
London W1P 3FP
Tel: 020 7436 5105
Fax: 020 7580 6520
Betsy Spanbock, Katerina Mattingley
Acquisition, development, sales, distribution and marketing of films and television product worldwide. Recent film titles include *The Perez Family, The Madness of King George, Napoleon, Go Fish, Suture, Oleanna, Angels and Insects.* Television product includes: *Flipper, Camp Gladiators*

Sanctuary Group Limited
A29 Barwell Business Park
Leatherhead Road
Chessington
Surrey KT9 2NY
Tel: 020 8974 1021
Fax: 020 8974 3707
Brian Leafe
Buddy's Song, The Monk, That Summer of White Roses, Conspiracy

Screen Ventures
49 Goodge Street
London W1P 1FB
Tel: 020 7580 7448
Fax: 020 7631 1265
email: sales@screenventures.com
Website: www.screenventures.com
Michael Evans
Christopher Mould
Specialise in international film, TV and video licensing of music, drama and arts featuring such artists as John Lennon, Bob Marley, Nirvana. Worldwide sales representation for international record companies and independent producers. Screen Ventures is also an independent producer of television documentaries and music programming

Smart Egg Pictures
11&12 Barnard Mews
Barnard Road
London SW11 1QU
Tel: 020 7350 4554
Fax: 020 7924 5650
Tom Sjoberg, Judy Phang
Independent foreign sales company. Titles include *Spaced Invaders, Dinosaurs, Montenegro, The Coca–Cola Kid, Rave Dancing to a Different Beat, Phoenix* and the *Magic Carpet* and *Evil Ed*

Sony Pictures Europe
Sony Pictures, Europe House
25 Golden Square
London W1R 6LU
Tel: 020 7533 1000
Fax: 020 7533 1246
European TV production and network operations and international distribution of Columbia TriStar's feature films and TV product

Southern Star Sales
45–49 Mortimer Street
London W1N 7TD
Tel: 020 7636 9421
Fax: 020 7436 7426
Circle is an international television rights group. Based in the UK, and trading in all the major territories of the world, Circle provides a range of services for producers and broadcasters. Circle comprises distinct businesses principally engaged in the creation, acquisition, marketing and licensing of visual entertainment rights. The companies within Circle Communications are:
Carnival (Films & Theatre)
Pavilion International
Delta Ventures
Production Finance & Management
Independent Wildlife
Harlequin Films & Television

Oxford Scientific Films
La Plante International

Stranger Than Fiction Film Sales Ltd
23 West Smithfield
London EC1A 9HY
Tel: 020 7751 0088
email:cinechix@aol.com
Grace Carley
Boutique–style sales agency dealing primarily in arthouse features from the UK, US and Ireland. Recent titles include: *Final Cut* from Fugitive Films, *Urban Ghost Story*, from Living Spirit Productions and the award–winning documentary feature *Southpaw*

Trans World International
TWI House
23 Eyot Gardens
London W6 9TR
Tel: 020 8233 5400
Fax: 020 8233 5401
Eric Drossart, Bill Sinrich, Buzz Hornett
The world's largest independent producer and distributor of sports programmes, TWI is owned by Mark McCormack's IMG Group and specialises in sports and arts programming. Titles include: *Trans World Sport, Futbol Mundial, PGA European Tour productions, ATP Tour highlights, West Indies Test Cricket, Oddballs, A–Z of Sport, Goal!, The Olympic Series, Century* and *The Whitbread Round The World Race*

Turner International Television Licensing
CNN House
19 Rathbone Place
London W1P 1DF
Tel: 020 7637 6900
Fax: 020 7637 6925
Ross Portugeis
US production and distribution company of films and programmes from Hanna–Barbera (animation), Castle Rock, New Line, Turner Pictures Worldwide, World Championship Wrestling, Turner Original Productions (non–fiction), plus a library of over 2,500 films, 1,500 hours of television programmes and 1,000 cartoons from the MGM (pre–1986) and Warner Bros (pre–1950) studios

Twentieth Century Fox Television
31–32 Soho Square

London W1D 3AP
Tel: 020 7437 7766
Fax: 020 7439 1806/434 2170
Website: www.fox.co.uk/
Stephen Cornish, Vice President
Randall Broman, Director of Sales
TV sales and distribution. A News Corporation company

Tyne Tees Television
City Road
Newcatle–upon–Tyne NE1 2AL
Tel: 0191 261 0181
Fax: 0191 261 2302
Tyne Tees TV

United Artists
10 Stephen Mews
London W1P 1PP
Tel: 020 7333 8877
Fax: 020 7333 8878
Wendy Palmer
Established in 1992, CiBy Sales is responsible for the international multi–media exploitation of films produced by French production company Ciby 2000 and other independent producers. Titles include: *Muriel's Wedding, The Piano, Secrets and Lies*

Universal International Television
5–7 Manderville Place
London W1U 3AR
Tel: 020 7535 3700
Fax: 020 7535 3771
Website: www.universalstudios.com
Roger Cordjohn, Penny Craig
UK operation for the major US corporation which owns Universal Pictures

VCI Programme Sales
VCI
76 Dean Street
London W1D 3SQ
Tel: 020 7396 8888
Fax: 020 7396 8890
Paul Hembury
A wholly owned subsidiary of VCI PLC, responsible for all overseas activities. Distributes a wide variety of product including music, sport, children's, fitness, documentary, educational, special interest and features

Victor Film Company Ltd
39/43 Brewer Street
London W1R 3FD
Tel: 020 7494 4477
Fax: 020 7494 4488
email:
post@victor–film–co.demon.co.uk

Website: www.victor-film-co.demon.co.uk
Alasdair Waddell
Vic Bateman, Calliste Lelliott
International sales agent for independent producers of commercial films. Recent titles include: *House! 24 Hours in London, Pasty Faces.* Forthcoming titles include: *Dog Soldiers, Father Figure, My Sister in Law*

Vine International Pictures
Astoria House
62 Shaftesbury Avenue
London W1V 7DE
Tel: 020 7437 1181
Fax: 020 7494 0634
Website: www.vineinternational. co.uk

The Walt Disney Television International
3 Queen Caroline Street
Hammersmith
London W6 9PA
Tel: 020 8222 1000
Fax: 020 8222 2795
MD: Etienne de Villiers
VP, Sales & Marketing: Keith Legoy
International television arm of a major US production company

Warner Bros International Television
98 Theobalds Road
London WC1X 8WB
Tel: 020 7494 3710
Fax: 020 7287 9086
Richard Milnes, Donna Brett, Tim Horan, Ian Giles
TV sales, marketing and distribution. A division of Warner Bros Distributors Ltd, A Time Warner Entertainment Company, LP

Yorkshire Television
Kirkstall Road
Leeds LS3 1JS
Tel: 0113 243 8283
Fax: 0113 244 5107
International sales division of Yorkshire TV

LABORATORIES

Bucks Laboratories Ltd
714 Banbury Avenue
Slough
Berks SL1 4LR
Tel: 01753 501500
Fax: 01753 691762
Website: www.bucks.co.uk
Darren Fagg
Comprehensive lab services in Super
35mm and 35mm, Super 16mm and
16mm, starting Sunday night. West
End rushes pick up unit 10.30 pm.
Also day bath. Chromakopy: 35mm
low–cost overnight colour reversal
dubbing prints. Photogard: European
coating centre for negative and print
treatment. Chromascan: 35mm and
16mm video to film transfer

Colour Film Services Group
10 Wadsworth Road
Perivale
Middx UB6 7JX
Tel: 020 8998 2731
Fax: 020 8997 8738
Website: www.colourfilmservices.
co.uk
Film Laboratory: full 16mm and
35mm colour processing laboratory,
with Super 16mm to 35mm blow up
a speciality. Video Facility: broadcast
standard wet gate telecines and full
digital edit suite. Video duplication,
CD mastering and archiving to
various formats. Superscan: unique
tape to film transfer system in both
Standard Resolution and High
Resolution. Sounds Studios: analogue
and digital dubbing, track laying,
synching, voice overs and optical
transfer bay

Colour–Technique
Cinematograph Film Laboratories
Finch Cottage, Finch Lane
Knotty Green
Beaconsfield HP9 2TL
Tel: 01494 672757
Specialists in 8mm, Super 8mm and
9.5mm blown up to 16mm with wet
gate printing. Stretch printing 16 and
18 Fps to 24, 32 and 48 Fps. 16mm to
16mm optical copies with wet gate
and stretch printing. World leader for
archival film copying for 8mm, Super
8mm, 9.5mm and 16mm with wet
gate printing from old shrunk films,
B/w dupe negs and colour internegs.
Also Super 8mm blown up to Super
16mm wet gate printing and stretch
printing. 16mm to Super 16mm wet
gate and stretch printing. Colour
internegs and B&W dupe negatives.
Super 8mm blown to 35 mm

Deluxe Laboratories Limited
North Orbital Road
Denham, Uxbridge
Middlesex UB9 5HQ
Tel: 01895 832323
Fax: 01895 833617
David Dowler
Deluxe London, together with sister
laboratories Deluxe Hollywood and
Deluxe Toronto, is a subsidiary of
Deluxe Entertainment Services. The
laboratories offer comprehensive
worldwide services to the Motion
Picture, Commercials and Television
industries. Deluxe London and
Toronto also include video transfer
suites. Deluxe Toronto includes
complete sound mixing and dubbing
suites. The well–known special
effects and optical house, General
Screen Enterprises, is also part of the
London operation

East Anglian Film Archive
University of East Anglia
Norwich NR4 7TJ
Tel: 01603 592664
Fax: 01603 458553
Specialises in blow–up printing of
Std 8mm, Super 8mm, 9.5 mm, and
17.5mm b/w or colour, onto 16mm film

Film and Photo Ltd
13 Colville Road
South Acton Industrial Estate
London W3 8BL
Tel: 020 8992 0037
Fax: 020 8993 2409
email: info@film–photo.co.uk
Website: www.film–photo.co.uk
Managing Director: Tony Scott
Post production motion picture
laboratory. 16/35mm Colour & B/W
reversal dupes. 16/35mm b/w
neg/pos. 35mm E6 camera reversal
processing. Tape to film transfers.
Nitrate restoration/preservation

Film Lab North Ltd
Croydon House
Croydon Street
Leeds LS11 9RT
Tel: 0113 243 4842
Fax: 0113 2434323
email: fin@filmlabnorth.free–online.
co.uk
Mike Varley, Peter Wright
Full service in 16mm colour
Negative Processing, 16mm colour
printing, 35mm colour printing video
transfer. Super 16mm a speciality –
Plus 35mm colour grading and
printing

Hendersons Film Laboratories
18–20 St Dunstan's Road
South Norwood
London SW25 6EU
Tel: 020 8653 2255
Fax: 020 8653 9773
Preserves nitrate film footage. A total
black and white Laboratory Service
in 35mm and 16mm. Printing and
processing black and white stocks

The Lux Centre
2–4 Hoxton Square
London N1 6NU
Tel: 020 7684 0202
Fax: 020 7684 2222
Website: www.lux.org.uk
Paul Murray
16mm b/w printing and processing

Metrocolor London
91–95 Gillespie Road
Highbury
London N5 1LS
Tel: 020 7226 4422
Fax: 020 7359 2353
Len Brown, Terry Lansbury,
Alan Douglas
Offers complete service for features,
commercials, television productions
and pop promos for 16mm, Super
16mm, 35mm and Super 35mm. Day
and night processing and printing
colour, b/w and vnf. Overnight
rushes and sound transfer. Overnight
'best–light' and 'gamma' Telecine
rushes transfer and sync sound.
Computerised logging and negative
matching. Sound transfer to optical
negative – Dolby stereo, Dolby SRD

Digital stereo and DTS Timecode.
Specialist Super 16mm services
include: 35mm fully graded blow–up
prints; 35mm fully graded blow–up
immediates; fully graded prints
re–formatted to standard 16mm
retaining 1.66:1 aspect ratio

Soho Images
8–14 Meard Street
London W1V 3HR
Tel: 020 7437 0831
Fax: 020 7734 9471
email: sohogroup.com
Website: www.sohoimages.com
Soho Laboratories offer day and
night printing and processing of
16mm (including Super 16mm) and
35mm colour or b/w film

Technicolor Film Services
Technicolor Ltd
Bath Road
West Drayton
Middx UB7 0DB
Tel: 020 8759 5432
Fax: 020 8759 6270
West End pick–up and delivery point:
Goldcrest Ltd
1 Lexington Street
London W1R 3HP
Tel: 020 7439 4177
A 'Technicolor' logo in the end
credits has always been synonymous
with high quality film processing. For
almost 60 years Technicolor has been
at the forefront of film handling
technology. A 24 hours–a–day service
in all film formats; Europe's leading
65/70m laboratory facility (with
specialist support for large 'space
theatre' formats) and a comprehensive
sound transfer service, are highlights
of Technicolor's broad based package.
The laboratory is fully equipped to
make SRD, SDDS and DTS prints
too

Todd–AO UK
13 Hawley Crescent
London NW1 8NP
Tel: 020 7284 7900
Fax: 020 7284 1018
Roger Harlow
Complete 35mm, Super 16 and
16mm film processing laboratory and
sound transfer service with full video
post–production facility including
Digital Wet Gate Telecines, D3,
Digital Betacam, Betacam SP and
other video formats. On–line editing,
duplication and standards conversion.
Sync sound and A+B roll negative to
tape transfer, neg cutting service

LEGISLATION

This section of the Handbook has a twofold purpose, first to provide a brief history of the legislation relating to the film and television in the United Kingdom, and second to provide a short summary of the current principal instruments of legislation relating to film, television and video industries in the United Kingdom and in the European Community. Current legislation is separated into four categories: cinema and broadcasting; finance; copyright and European Union legislation.

Legislative History

Cinema

Legislation for the cinema industry in the United Kingdom goes back to 1909, when the Cinematograph Act was passed providing for the licensing of exhibition premises, and safety of audiences. The emphasis on safety has been maintained through the years in other enactments such as the Celluloid and Cinematograph Film Act 1922, Cinematograph Act 1952 and the Fire Precautions Act 1971, the two latter having been consolidated in the Cinemas Act 1985.

The Cinematograph Films (Animals Act) 1937 was passed to prevent the exhibition and distribution of films in which suffering may have been caused to animals. The Cinematograph (Amendment) Act 1982 applied certain licensing requirements to pornographic cinema clubs. Excluded from licensing were the activities of bona fide film societies and 'demonstrations' such as those used in shops, as well as exhibitions intended to provide information, education or instruction. Requirements for licensing were consolidated in the Cinemas Act 1985.

The Sunday Entertainments Act 1932

as amended by the Sunday Cinema Act 1972 and the Cinemas Act 1985 regulated the opening and use of cinema premises on Sundays.

The Sunday Entertainments Act 1932 also established a Sunday Cinematograph Fund for 'encouraging the use and development of cinematograph as a means of entertainment and instruction'. This was how the British Film Institute was originally funded.

Statutory controls were imposed by the Cinematograph Films Act 1927 in other areas of the film industry, such as the booking of films, quotas for the distribution and renting of British films and the registration of films exhibited to the public. This Act was modified by the Cinematograph Films Acts of 1938 and 1948 and the Film Acts 1960, 1966, 1970 and 1980 which were repealed by the Films Act 1985.

The financing of the British film industry has long been the subject of specific legislation. The National Film Finance Corporation was established by the Cinematograph Film Production (Special Loans) Act 1949. The Cinematograph Film Production (Special Loans) Act 1952 gave the National Film Finance Corporation the power to borrow from sources other than the Board of Trade. Other legislation dealing with film finance were the Cinematograph Film Production (Special Loans) Act 1954 and the Films Acts 1970 and 1980. The Cinematograph Films Council was established by the Cinematograph Films Act 1948, but like the National Film Finance Corporation, the Council was abolished by the Films Act 1985.

The Cinematograph Films Act 1957 established the British Film Fund Agency and put on a statutory footing the formerly voluntary levy on exhibitors known as the 'Eady levy'. Eady money was to be paid to the British Film Fund Agency, which in turn was responsible for making pay-

ments to British film-makers, the Children's Film Foundation, the National Film Finance Corporation, the British Film Institute and towards training film-makers. The Film Levy Finance Act 1981 consolidated the provisions relating to the Agency and the exhibitors' levy. The Agency was wound up in 1988 pursuant to a statutory order made under the Films Act 1985.

The British Film Institute used to obtain its funding from grants made by the Privy Council out of the Cinematograph Fund established under the Sunday Entertainments Act 1932 and also from the proceeds of subscriptions, sales and rentals of films. The British Film Institute Act 1949 allows for grants of money from Parliament to be made to the British Film Institute as the Lord President of the Privy Council thinks fit.

Broadcasting

The BBC first started as the British Broadcasting Company (representing the interests of some radio manufacturers) and was licensed in 1923 by the Postmaster General under the Wireless Telegraphy Act 1904 before being established by Royal Charter. The company was involved in television development from 1929 and in 1935 was licensed to provide a public television service.

The Independent Television Authority was established under the Television Act 1954 to provide additional television broadcasting services. Its existence was continued under the Television Act 1964 and under the Independent Broadcasting Act 1973, although its name had been changed to the Independent Broadcasting Authority by the Sound Broadcasting Act 1972 (which also permitted it to provide local sound broadcasting services).

The Broadcasting Act 1981 amended and consolidated certain provisions contained in previous legislation including the removal of the prohibition on certain specified people from broadcasting opinions expressed in proceedings of Parliament or local authorities, the extension of the IBA's functions to the provision of programmes for Channel 4 and the establishment of the Broadcasting Complaints Commission.

Cable programme services and satellite broadcasts were the subject of the Cable and Broadcasting Act 1984. This Act and the Broadcasting Act 1981 were repealed and consolidated by the Broadcasting Act 1990 which implemented proposals in the Government's White Paper Broadcasting in the 1990's: Competition Choice and Quality (Cm 517, November 1988). Earlier recommendations on the reform of the broadcasting industry had been made in the Report of the Committee on Financing the BBC (the Peacock Report) (Cmnd 9824, July 1986) and the Third Report of the Home Affairs Committee's inquiry into the Future of Broadcasting (HC Paper 262, Session 1987-88, June 1988).

Current UK/EU Legislation

BROADCASTING AND CINEMAS

Broadcasting Act 1996
The Broadcasting Act 1996 makes provision for digital terrestrial television broadcasting and contains provisions relating to the award of multiplex licences. It also provides for the introduction of radio multiplex services and regulates digital terrestrial sound broadcasting. In addition, the Act amends a number of provisions contained in the Broadcasting Act 1990 relating to the funding of Channel Four Television Corporation, the funding of Sianel Pedwar Cymru, and the operation of the Comataidh Craolidgh Gaialig (the Gaelic Broadcasting Committee). The Act also dissolves the Broadcasting Complaints Commission and Broadcasting Standards Council and replaces these with the Broadcasting Standards Commission. The Act also contains other provisions relating to the transmission network of the BBC and television coverage of listed events.

Broadcasting Act 1990
The Broadcasting Act 1990 established a new framework for the regulation of independent television and radio services, and for satellite television and cable television. Under the Act, the Independent Broadcasting Authority (IBA) and the Cable Authority were dissolved and replaced by the Independent Television Commission. The Radio Authority was established in respect of independent radio services. The Broadcasting Standards Council was made a statutory body and the Act also contains provisions relating to the Broadcasting Complaints Commission. Besides reorganising independent broadcasting, the Act provided for the formation of a separate company with responsibility for effecting the technical arrangements relating to independent television broadcasting - National Transcommunications Limited ñ as a first step towards the privatisation of the former IBA's transmission functions.

The Broadcasting Act 1990 repealed the Broadcasting Act 1981 and the Cable and Broadcasting Act 1984, amended the Wireless Telegraphy Act 1949, the Wireless Telegraphy Act 1967, the Marine [&c] Broadcasting (Offences) Act 1967, and the Copyright, Designs and Patents Act 1988, and also implements legislative provisions required pursuant to Directive 89/552 - see below.

The Broadcasting Act 1990 requires the British Broadcasting Corporation, all Channel 3 Licensees, the Channel Four Television Corporation, S4C (the Welsh Fourth Channel Authority) and the future Channel 5 Licensee to procure that not less than 25 per cent of the total amount of time allocated by those services to broadcasting "qualifying programming" is allocated to the broadcasting of a range and diversity of "independent productions". The expressions "qualifying programming" and "independent productions" are defined in the Broadcasting (Independent Productions) Order 1991.

Cinemas Act 1985
The Cinemas Act 1985 consolidated the Cinematographic Acts 1909 to 1952, the Cinematographic (Amendment) Act 1982 and related enactments. The Act deals with the exhibition of films and contains provisions for the grant, renewal and transfer of licences for film exhibition. There are special provisions for Greater London.

The Cinemas Act specifies the conditions of Sunday opening, and provides for exempted exhibition in private dwelling houses, and for noncommercial shows in premises used only occasionally.

Video Recordings Act 1984
The Video Recordings Act 1984 controls the distribution of video recordings with the aim of restricting the depiction or simulation of human sexual activity, gross violence, human genital organs or urinary or excretory functions. A system of classification and labelling is prescribed. The supply of recordings without a classification certificate, or the supply of classified recordings to persons under a certain age or in certain premises or in breach of labelling regulations, is prohibited subject to certain exemptions.

Classification certificates are issued by the British Board of Film

Classification. It is an offence to supply or offer to supply, or to have in possession for the purposes of supplying, an unclassified video recording. Supplying recordings in breach of classification, supplying certain classified recordings otherwise than in licensed sex shops, supplying recordings in breach of labelling requirements and supplying recordings with false indications as to classification, are all offences under the Act. The Video Recordings Act provides for powers of entry, search and seizure and for the forfeiture of video recordings by the court.

Telecommunications Act 1984

The Telecommunications Act 1984 prohibits the running of a telecommunications system within the United Kingdom subject to certain exceptions which include the running of a telecommunication system in certain circumstances by a broadcasting authority. A broadcasting authority means a person who is licensed under the Wireless Telegraphy Act 1949 (see below) to broadcast programmes for general reception. Telecommunications systems include, among other things, any system for the conveyance of speech, music, other sounds and visual images by electric, magnetic, electro-magnetic, electro-chemical or electro-mechanical energy.

Wireless Telegraphy Acts 1967 and 1949

The 1967 Act provides for the Secretary of State to obtain information as to the sale and hire of television receiving sets. The Act allows the Secretary of State to prohibit the manufacture or importation of certain wireless telegraphy apparatus and to control the installation of such apparatus in vehicles.

The 1949 Act provides for the licensing of wireless telegraphy and defines "wireless telegraphy" as the sending of electro-magnetic energy over paths not provided by a material substance constructed or arranged for that purpose. The requirements to hold a licence under the Wireless Telegraphy Act 1949 or the Telecommunications Act 1984 are separate from the television and radio

broadcast licensing provisions and cable programme source licensing provisions contained in the Broadcasting Act 1990.

Marine [&c] Broadcasting (Offences) Act 1967

The making of broadcasts by wireless telegraphy (as defined in the Wireless Telegraphy Act 1949) intended for general reception from ships, aircraft and certain marine structures is prohibited under this Act.

The Cinematograph Films (Animals) Act 1937

The Cinematograph Films (Animals) Act 1937 provides for the prevention of exhibiting or distributing films in which suffering may have been caused to animals.

Celluloid and Cinematograph Film Act 1922

This Act contains provisions which are aimed at the prevention of fire in premises where raw celluloid or cinematograph film is stored or used. Silver nitrate film which was in universal use until the 1950s and was still used in some parts of the world (notably the former USSR) until the 1970s, is highly inflammable and becomes unstable with age. The purpose of the legislation was to protect members of the public from fire risks.

FINANCE

Finance (No 2) Act 1997

Section 48 Finance (No 2) Act 1997 introduced new rules for writing-off production and acquisition expenditure of British qualifying films costing £15 million or less to make. The relief applies to expenditure incurred between 2 July 1997 and 1 July 2000. Section 48 allows 100 per cent write-off for production or acquisition costs when the film is completed.

A British qualifying film is one certified as such by the Department of Culture Media and Sport under the Films Act 1985. In order to be certified a number of criteria must be met. These include the requirement for the maker of the film to be a UK/European Economic Area ("EEA") company and the requirement for a certain percentage of labour costs to be spent on UK/EEA nationals. The prohibition on using a

foreign studio was relaxed in 1999.

The Inland Revenue made an announcement on 25 March 1998 that the Government intends to extend the time limit for relief under section 48 from 3 years to 5 years in a future Finance Bill. The relief will then apply to expenditure incurred between 2 July 1997 and 1 July 2002. The Film Review Group issued a report on 25 March 1998 which sets out an action plan for delivery by April 1999.

The Finance Act 1990, Capital Allowances Act 1990 and Finance (No 2) Act 1992

Section 80 and Schedule 12 to the Finance Act 1990 deals with the tax issues relating to the reorganisation of independent broadcasting provided for in the Broadcasting Act 1990.

Section 68 of the Capital Allowances Act 1990 replaces Section 72 of the Finance Act 1982 providing for certain expenditure in the production of a film, tape or disc to be treated as expenditure of a revenue nature.

Sections 41-43 of the Finance (No 2) Act 1992 amend the tax regime to provide accelerated relief for pre-production costs incurred after 10 March 1992 and production expenditure on films completed after that date. Section 69 of the Act makes certain consequential amendments to Section 68 of the Capital Allowances Act 1990.

Films Act 1985

The Films Act 1985 dissolved the British Film Fund Agency, ending the Eady levy system established in 1951. The Act also abolished the Cinematograph Film Council and dissolved the National Film Finance Corporation, transferring its assets to British Screen Finance Limited. The Act repealed the Films Acts 1960 - 1980 and also repealed certain provisions of the Finance Acts 1982 and 1984 and substituted new provisions for determining whether or not a film was 'British' film eligible for allowances. Under the Finance Acts 1997 (No 2), 1992 (No2) and 1990. These provisions have been further amended to relax the prohibition on using a foreign studio

National Film Finance Corporation Act 1981

The National Film Finance Corporation Act 1981 repealed the Cinematograph Film Production (Special Loans) Acts of 1949 and 1954 and made provisions in relation to the National Film Finance Corporation which has since been dissolved by the Films Act 1985. The National Film Finance Corporation Act 1981 is, however, still on the statute book.

Film Levy Finance Act 1981

Although the British Film Fund Agency was dissolved by the British Film Fund Agency (Dissolution) Order 1988, SI 1988/37, the Film Levy Act itself is still in place.

COPYRIGHT

Copyright, Designs and Patents Act 1988

This Act is the primary piece of legislation relating to copyright in the United Kingdom. The Act provides copyright protection for original literary, dramatic, musical and artistic works, for films, sound recordings, broadcasts and cable programmes, and for typographical arrangements of published editions.

The Act repeals the Copyright Act 1956 which in turn repealed the Copyright Act 1911, but the transitional provisions of the Copyright, Designs and Patents Act 1988 apply certain provisions of the earlier legislation for the purpose of determining ownership of copyright, type of protection and certain other matters. Because the term of copyright for original literary, dramatic and/or musical works is the life of the author plus 50 years, the earlier legislation will continue to be relevant until well into the next century. The provisions of the Act have been amended by EU harmonisation provisions contained in Directive 93/98 extending the term of copyright protection in relation to literary, dramatic, musical and artistic works originating in countries within the European Economic Area or written by nationals of countries in the EEA, to the duration of the life of the author or last surviving co-author plus, 70 years calculated from 31 December in the relevant year of decrease.

The Act provides a period of copyright protection for films and sound recordings which expires 50 years from the end of the calendar year in which the film or sound recording is made, or if it is shown or played in public or broadcast or included in a cable programme service, 50 years from the end of the calendar year in which this occurred.

The provisions of the Act have been amended by EU harmonisation provisions contained in Directive 93/98 extending the term of copyright protection for films, to a period equal to the duration to the lifetime of the last to die of the persons responsible for the making of the film, plus 70 years calculated from 31 December in the relevant year of decrease.

The Act introduced three new moral rights into United Kingdom legislation. In addition to the right not to have a work falsely attributed to him or her, an author (of a literary dramatic musical or artistic work) or director (of a film) has the right to be identified in relation to their work, and the right not to permit their work to suffer derogatory treatment. A derogatory treatment is any addition, deletion, alteration or adaptation of a work which amounts to a distortion or mutilation of the work, or is otherwise prejudicial to the honour or reputation of the author or director. A person who commissions films or photographs for private and domestic purposes enjoys a new right of privacy established by the Act.

Another new development is the creation of a statutory civil right for performers, giving them the right not to have recordings of their performances used without their consent. United Kingdom copyright legislation was amended following a decision in Rickless -v- United Artists Corporation ñ a case which was brought by the estate of Peter Sellars and involved The Trail of the Pink Panther. The legislation is retrospective and protects performances given 50 years ago, not just in the United Kingdom, but in any country if the performers were "qualifying persons" within the meaning of the relevant Act. The performances which are covered include not only dramatic and musical performances, but readings of literary works, variety programmes and even mime.

Numerous other provisions are contained in the Copyright, Designs and Patents Act including sections which deal with the fraudulent reception of programmes, the manufacture and sale of devices designed to circumvent copy-protection, and patent and design law.

EUROPEAN COMMUNITY LEGISLATION

Directive 89/552 – on television without frontiers

The objective of the Directive is to eliminate the barriers which divide Europe with a view to permitting and assuring the transition from national programme markets to a common programme production and distribution market. It also aims to establish conditions of fair competition without prejudice to the public interest role which falls to be discharged by television broadcasting services in the EC.

The laws of all Member States relating to television broadcasting and cable operations contain disparities which may impede the free movement of broadcasts within the EC and may distort competition. All such restrictions are required to be abolished.

Member States are free to specify detailed criteria relating to language etc. Additionally, Member States are permitted to lay down different conditions relating to the insertion of advertising in programmes within the limits set out in the Directive. Member States are required to provide where practicable that broadcasters reserve a proportion of their transmission time to European works created by independent producers. The amount of advertising is not to exceed 15 per cent of daily transmission time and the support advertising within a given one hour period shall not exceed 20 per cent.

Directive 92/100 – on rental rights

Authors or performers have, pursuant to the Directive, an unwaivable right to receive equitable remuneration. Member States are required to provide a right for performers in relation to the fixation of their performances, a right for phonogram and film producers in relation to their phonograms and first fixations of their films and a right for broadcasters in relation to the fixation of broadcasts and their broadcast and cable transmissions. Member States must also provide a 'reproduction right' giving performers, phonogram producers, film producers and broadcasting organisations the right to authorise or prohibit the direct or indirect reproduction of their copyright works. The Directive also requires Member States to provide for performers, film producers, phonogram producers and broadcasting organisations to have exclusive rights to make available their work by sale or otherwise ñ known as the 'distribution right'.

Directive 93/83 on Satellite Transmission and Cable Retransmission

This Directive is aimed at eliminating uncertainty and differences in national legislation governing when the act of communication of a programme takes place. It avoids the cumulative application of several national laws to one single act of broadcasting.

The Directive provides that communication by satellite occurs in the member state where the programming signals are introduced under the control of a broadcaster into an uninterrupted chain of communication, leading to the satellite and down towards earth. The Directive also examines protection for authors, performers and producers of phonograms and broadcasting organisations, and requires that copyright owners may grant or refuse authorisation for cable retransmissions of a broadcast only through a collecting society.

Directive 98/98 on harmonising the term of protection of copyright and certain related rights

This Directive is aimed at harmonising the periods of copyright throughout the European Union where different states provide different periods of protection. Although the minimum term established by the Berne Convention on Copyright is 50 years post mortem auctoris, a number of states have chosen to provide for longer periods. In Germany the peri-

od of literary dramatic musical and artistic works is 70 years pma, in Spain 60 years (or 80 years for copyrights protected under the Spanish law of 1879 until its reform in 1987). In France the period is 60 years pma or 70 years for musical compositions.

In addition to the differences in the term of rights post mortem auctoris, further discrepancies arise in protection accorded by different member states through wartime extensions. Belgium has provided a wartime extension of 10 years, Italy 12 years, France six and eight years respectively in relation to the First and Second World Wars. In France, a further period of 30 years is provided in the case of copyright works whose authors were killed in action - such as Antoine de Saint-ExupÈry.

The Directive also provides that rights of performers shall run from 50 years from the date of performance or if later, from the point at which the fixation of the performance is lawfully made available to the public for the first time, or if this has not occurred from the first assimilation of the performance. The rights of producers of phonograms run 50 years from first publication of the phonogram, but expire 50 years after the fixation was made if the phonogram, but expire 50 years after the fixation was made if the phonogram has not been published during that time. A similar provision applies to the rights of producers of the first fixations of cinematographic works and sequences of moving images, whether accompanied or not by sound. Rights of broadcasting organisations run from 50 years from the first transmission of the broadcast.

The Directive provides that the person who makes available to the public a previously unpublished work which is in the public domain, shall have the same rights of exploitation in relation to the work as would have fallen to the author for a term of 25 years from the time the work was first made available to the public. The Directive applies to all works which are protected by at least one member state on 1 July 1995 when the Directive came into effect. As a result of the differing terms in European states, many works which were treated as being in the 'public

domain' in the United Kingdom will have their copyright revived. Works by Beatrix Potter, James Joyce and Rudyard Kipling are all works which will benefit from a revival of copyright. The provisions relating to the term of protection of cinematographic films are not required to be applied to films created before 1 July 1994. Each member state of the European Union's required to implement the Directive. The precise manner of implementation and the choice of transitional provisions, are matters which each state is free to determine.

Directive 93/98 was implemented in the United Kingdom by the Rights in Performances Regulations 1995/3297 which took effect from 1 January 1996. The term of copyright protection for literary dramatic musical or artistic works expires at the end of the period of 70 years from the last day of the calendar year in which the author dies. Copyright in a film expires 70 years from the end of the calendar year in which the death occurs of the last to die of the principal director, the author of the screenplay, the author of the dialogue or the composer of the music specially created for and used for the film. The period of copyright previously applying to films under the Copyright, Designs and Patents Act 1988 ended 50 years from the first showing or playing in public of a film, and the effect of the implementation of Directive 93/98 is to create a significant extension of the period in which a film copyright owner has the exclusive economic right to exploit a film. If, as anticipated, the United States of America also extends the duration of the copyright period applying to films, the value of intellectual property rights in audiovisual productions may increase significantly.

LIBRARIES

This section provides a directory of libraries which have collections of books, periodicals and papers covering film and television. It includes the libraries of colleges and universities with graduate and post-graduate degree courses in the media. Most of these collections are intended for student and teaching staff use: permission for access should always be sought from the Librarian. Where possible a breakdown of types of resources is provided

bfi National Library
21 Stephen Street
London WIT 1LN
Tel: 020 7255 1444
020 7436 0165 (Information)
Fax: 020 7436 2338
The *bfi*'s own library is extensive and holds the world's largest collection of documentation on film and television. It includes both published and unpublished material ranging from books and periodicals to news cuttings, press releases, scripts, theses, and files of festival material.
Reading Room opening hours
Monday   10.30am - 5.30pm
Tuesday   10.30am - 8.00pm
Wednesday   01.00pm - 8.00pm
Thursday   10.30am - 8.00pm
Friday   10.30am - 5.30pm
Institutional pass: £50.00
Library pass: £33.00
NFT Members pass: £25.00
Discount passes   £20.00*
Day pass   £06.00**
*Available to Senior Citizens, Registered Disabled and Unemployed upon proof of eligibility. Students may also apply for a discounted library pass.
**Available to anyone. Spaces may be reserved by giving 48 hours notice.
Enquiry Lines
The Enquiry Line is available for short enquiries. Frequent callers subscribe to an information service. The line is open from 10.00am to 5.00pm Monday to Friday - 020 7255 1444
Research Services:
For more detailed enquiries, users should contact Information Services by fax or mail

Key to Resources

A   Specialist sections
B   Film/TV journals
C   Film/TV/CD ROMS
D   Video loan service
E   Internet access
F   Special collections

Aberdeen

Aberdeen University Library
Queen Mother Library,
Meston Walk, Aberdeen
Grampian AB24 3UE
Tel: 01224 272579
Fax: 01224 487048
email: library@abdn.ac.uk
Website: www.abdn.ac.uk/library/
Contact: University Librarian

Bangor

Normal College
Education Library
Bangor
Gwynedd LL57 2P
Tel: 01248 370171
Fax: 01248 370461
Contact: Librarian

Barnet

Middlesex University Cat Hill Library
Cat Hill, Barnet
Herts EN4 8HT
Tel: 020 8362 5042
Fax: 020 8440 9541
Contact: Art and Design Librarian

Bath

Bath University Library
Claverton Down
Bath BA2 7AY
Tel: 01225 826084
Fax: 01225 826229
Contact: University Librarian

Belfast

Belfast Central Library
Royal Avenue
Belfast
Co. Antrim BT1 1EA
Tel: 028 9033 332819
Fax: 028 9033 312886
Contact: Chief Librarian

Northern Ireland Film Commission
21 Ormeau Avenue
Belfast BT2 8HD
Tel: 028 9023 232444
Fax: 028 9023 239918
email: info@nifc.co.uk
Website: www.nifc.co.uk
Contact: Information Officer
Resources: B, D

Queen's Film Theatre
25 College Gardens
Belfast BT9 6BS
Tel: 028 9066 7687 ext. 33
Fax: 028 9066 3733
email:m.open@qub.ac.uk
Website: www.qub.uk/qft
Contact: Administrator/Programmer
Resources: B, C, E, F

Birmingham

BBC Pebble Mill
Information Research Library
Pebble Mill Road
Birmingham B5 7QQ
Tel: 0121 432 8922
Fax: 0121 432 9589
Contact: Information Research Librarian
Resources: B, C, E

Birmingham University Library
Edgbaston
Birmingham B15 2TT
Tel: 0121 414 5817
Fax: 0121 471 4691
email: library@bham.ac.uk
Website: www.is.bham.ac.uk
Contact: Librarian, Arts and Humanities

Central Broadcasting Ltd
Broad Street

Birmingham B1 2JP
Tel: 0121 643 9898
Contact: Reference Librarian

Information Services
Franchise Street
Perry Barr
Birmingham B42 2SU
Tel: 0121 331 5300
Fax: 0121 331 6543
Contact: Dean of Information
Services

University of Central England
Birmingham Institute of Art & Design
Gosta Green
Birmingham B4 7DX
Tel: 0121 331 5860
Contact: Library staff

Vivid - Birmingham's Centre for Media Arts
Unit 311 The Big Peg
120 Vyse Street
Birmingham B18 6ND
Tel: 0121 233 4061
Fax: 0121 212 1784
email:vivid@waveriden.co.uk
Website: www.wavespace.waverider.co.uk
Contact: Head of Service: Yasmeen Baig
Resources: A, B, D, E,

Brighton

University of Brighton Faculty of Art, Design and Humanities
St Peter's House Library
16-18 Richmond Place
Brighton BN2 2NA
Tel: 01273 643221
Contact: Librarian

University of Sussex Library
Falmer
Brighton
East Sussex BN1 9QL
Tel: 01273 678163
Fax: 01273 678441
email: library@sussex.ac.uk
Website: www.sussex.ac.uk/library
Contact: Janice Parlett, Enquiries and Information Services

Bristol

Bristol City Council
Leisure Services
Central Library, Reference
Library, College Green

Bristol BS1 5TL
Tel: 0117 927 6121
Fax: 0117 922 6775
Contact: Head of Reference & Information Services

University of Bristol
University Library
Tyndall Avenue
Bristol BS8 1TJ
Tel: 0117 928 9017
Fax: 0117 925 5334
Website: www.bris.ac.uk/depts/library
Contact: Librarian
Resources: A, B, C, E

University of Bristol Theatre Collection
Department of Drama
Cantocks Close
Bristol BS8 1UP
Tel: 0117 928 7836
Fax: 0117 928 7832
email: theatre-collection@bris.ac.uk
Website: www.bris.ac.uk/depts/drama
Contact: Keeper

West of England University at Bristol
Library, Faculty of Art, Media & Design
Bower Ashton Campus
Clanage Road
Bristol BS3 2JU
Tel: 0117 966 0222 x4750
Fax: 0117 976 3946
Contact: Steve Morgan,
Campus/Subject Librarian, Art,
Media and Design

Canterbury

Canterbury Christ Church University College Library
North Holmes Road
Canterbury
Kent CT1 1QU
Tel: 01227 767700
Fax: 01227 767530
email: lib1@cant.ac.uk
Website: www.cant.ac.uk./depts/services/ library/library1.html
Contact: Director of Library Services
Resources: A, B, C, D, E

Kent Institute of Art & Design at Canterbury
New Dover Road
Canterbury
Kent CT1 3AN
Tel: 01227 769371
Fax: 01227 817500
Website: www.kiad.ac.uk
Kathleen Godfrey: Campus Librarian

Templeman Library
University of Kent at Canterbury
Canterbury, Kent CT2 7NU
Tel: 01227 764000
Fax: 01227 459025
Contact: Librarian

Cardiff

Cardiff University
Bute Resource Centre
PO Box 430
Cardiff CF10 3XT
Tel: 029 2087 4611
Fax: 029 2087 4192
email: buteliby@cardiff.ac.uk
Website: www.cardiff.ac.uk
Contact: Librarian

Coleg Glan Hafren
Trowbridge Road
Rumney
Cardiff CF3 1XZ
Tel: 029 20 25 0250
Fax: 029 20 25 0339
Website: www.glan-hafren.ac.uk
Contact: Learning Resources
Development Manager

Carlisle

Cumbria College of Art and Design Library
Brampton Road
Carlisle
Cumbria CA3 9AY
Tel: 01228 25333 x206
Contact: Librarian

Chislehurst

Ravensbourne College of Design and Communication Library
Walden Road, Chislehurst
Kent BR7 5SN
Tel: 020 8289 4900
Fax: 020 8325 8320
email: library@rave.ac.uk
Website: www.rave.ac.uk
Contact: Librarian

Colchester

University of Essex
The Albert Sloman Library
Wivenhoe Park
Colchester CO4 3SQ
Tel: 01206 873333
Contact: Librarian

Coleraine

University of Ulster
Library
Coleraine
Northern Ireland BT52 1SA
Tel: 028 7032 4345
Fax: 028 7032 4928
Contact: Pro-Librarian
Resources: A, B, C, D

Coventry

Coventry City Library
Smithford Way
Coventry CV1 1FY
Tel: 024 7683 2314
Fax: 024 7683 2440
email: covinfo@discover.co.uk
Contact: Librarian - Karen Berry

Coventry University, Art & Design Library
Priory Street
Coventry CV1 5FB
Tel: 024 7683 8546
Fax: 024 7683 8686
Website: www.coventry.
ac.uk./ibrary/
Contact: Sub-Librarian, Art & Design

Warwick University Library
Gibbet Hill Road
Coventry CV4 7AL
Tel: 024 7652 4103
Fax: 024 7652 4211
Contact: Librarian
Resources: A, B, C, D, E, F*
* Collection of German film
programme from the 1930s

Derby

Derby University Library
Kedleston Rd
Derby DE3 1GB
Tel: 01332 622222 x 4061
Fax: 01332 622222 x 4059
Contact: Librarian

University of Derby
Library and Learning Resources
Derby DE1 1RX
Tel: 01332 622222 Ext 3001
Website: www.derby.ac.uk
/library/homelib.html
Contact: Subject Adviser, Art & Design
Resources: A, B, C, D, E

Doncaster

Nova Productions
11a Winholme
Armthorpe

Doncaster DN3 3AF
Tel: 01302 833422
Fax: 08701 257917
email: library@novaonline.co.uk
Website: www.novaonline.
co.uk/library
Contact: The Administrator

Dorking

Surrey Performing Arts Library
Vaughan Williams House
West Street
Dorking, Surrey RH4 1BY
Tel: 01306 887509
Fax: 01306 875074
email: p.arts@dial.pipex.com
Website: www.surreycc.
gov.uk/libraries/direct/perfarts.html
Senior Librarian: G.Muncy
Contact: Librarian
Resources: A, B, C, D, E, F
 Scripts

Douglas

Douglas Corporation
Douglas Public Library
Ridgeway Street
Douglas
Isle of Man
Tel: 01624 623021
Fax: 01624 662792
Contact: Borough Librarian

Dundee

Library Duncan of Jordanstone College
University of Dundee
13 Perth Road
Dundee DD1 4HT
Tel: 01382 345255
Fax: 01382 229283
Contact: College Librarian
Resources: A, B, C, D, E, F
 Few scripts

Egham

Royal Holloway University of London Library
Egham Hill
Egham
Surrey TW20 OEX
Tel: 01784 443330
Fax: 01784 477670
Website: www.lb.rhbnc.ac.uk
Contact: Librarian
Resources: A, B, C, D, E

Exeter

Exeter University Library
Stocker Road
Exeter
Devon EX4 4PT
Tel: 01392 263869
Fax: 01392 263871
Website: www.exe.ac.uk
/@JACrawle/lib.film.html
Contact: Librarian
Resources: A, B, C, D, E, F
 The Bill Douglas Centre for the
History of Cinema and Popular Culture

Farnham

Surrey Institute of Art & Design, University College
Falkner Road
The Hart
Farnham
Surrey GU9 7DS
Tel: 01252 722441
Fax: 01252 892616
Contact: Institute Librarian
Resources: A, B, C, D , E
 Registered users only

Gateshead

Gateshead Libraries and Arts Department
Central Library
Prince Consort Road
Gateshead
Tyne and Wear NE8 4LN
Tel: 0191 477 3478
Fax: 0191 477 7454
Contact: The Librarian

Glasgow

Glasgow Caledonian University Library
Cowcaddens Road
Glasgow G4 0BA
Tel: 0141 331 3858
Fax: 0141 331 3005
Website: www.gcal.ac.uk/
library/index.html
Contact: Assistant Academic Liaison
Librarian for Language and Media
Resources: A, B, C, D, E

Glasgow City Libraries
Mitchell Library
North Street
Glasgow G3 7DN
Tel: 0141 287 2933
Fax: 0141 287 2815
Contact: Departmental Librarian, Art
Department

Glasgow School of Art Library
167 Renfrew Street
Glasgow G3 6RQ
Tel: 0141 353 4551
Fax: 0141 332 3506
Contact: Principal Librarian

Scottish Council for Educational Technology
Dowanhill
74 Victoria Crescent Road
Glasgow G12 9JN
Tel: 0141 337 5000
Fax: 0141 337 5050
Website: www.sect.com
Contact: Librarian
Resources: D

Scottish Screen
Second Floor
249 West George Street
Glasgow G2 4QE
Tel: 0141 302 1700
Fax: 0141 302 1711
email: info@scottishscreen.com
Website: www.scottishscreen.com
Chief Executive: John Archer
Resources: D, F
Scottish Screen is responsible to the Scottish Parliament for developing all aspects of screen industry and culture in Scotland through script and company development, short film production, distribution of National Lottery film production finance, training, education, exhibition funding, the Film Commission locations support and the Scottish Film and Television Archive
   Access to the Shiach Script library with over 100 feature and short film scripts, Video, publications resource. Internet site, National Archive collection of factual documentary material reflecting Scotland's social and cultural history. Available to broadcasters, programme makers, educational users and researchers. Distribution of Scottish shorts with back catalogue

University of Glasgow
The Library
Hillhead Street
Glasgow G12 8QQ
Tel: 0141 330 6704/5
Fax: 0141 330 4952
Contact: Librarian

Gravesend

VLV - Voice of the Listener and Viewer
101 King's Drive
Gravesend
Kent DA12 5BQ
Tel: 01474 352835
Fax: 01474 351112
Contact: Information Officer
In addition to its own VLV holds archives of the former independent Broadcasting Research Unit (1980-1991) and the former British Action for Children's Television (BACTV) (1988-1994) and makes these available for a small fee together with its own archives and library. VLV represents the citizen and consumer interest in broadcasting
Resources: A, E, F

Huddersfield

Kirklees Cultural Services
Central Library
Princess Alexandra Walk
Huddersfield HD1 2SU
Tel: 01484 221967
Fax: 01484 221974
Contact: Reference Librarian
Resources: C, D, E

Hull

Hull University Brynmor Jones Library
Cottingham Road
Hull
North Humberside HU6 7RX
Tel: 01482 465440
Fax: 01482 466205
Contact: Librarian

Humberside

Humberside University
School of Art, Architecture and Design Learning Support Centre
Guildhall Road
Hull HU1 1HJ
Tel: 01482 440550
Fax: 01482 449627
Contact: Centre Manager

Keele

Keele Information Services
Keele University
Keele
Staffs ST5 5BG
Tel: 01782 583239
Fax: 01782 711553
Contact: Visual Arts Department
Resources: B, C, D, E

Kingston upon Thames

Kingston Museum & Heritage Service
North Kingston Centre
Richmond Road
Kingston upon Thames
Surrey KT2 5PE
Tel: 020 8547 6738 or 6755
Website: www.kingston.ac.uk/muytexto.htm
Contact: T. Everson, Local History Officer
Resources: E, F
 Eadweard Maybridge Collection

Kingston University Library Services
Art and Design Library
Knights Park
Kingston upon Thames
Surrey KT1 2QJ
Tel: 020 747 2000 x 4031
Fax: 020 7547 8039
email: library@kingston.ac.uk
Website: www.king.ac.uk/library_media/index.html
Contact: Faculty Librarian (Design)

Kingston University Library
Library and Media Services
Penrhyn Road
Kingston Upon Thames
Surrey KT1 2EE
Tel: 020 8547 7101
Fax: 020 8547 7111
email: library@kingston.ac.uk
Website: www.king.ac.uk/library_media/index.html
Contact: Head of Library and Media Services

Leeds

Leeds City Libraries
Central Library
Municipal Buildings
Calverley Street
Leeds, West Yorkshire LS1 3AB
Tel: 0113 247 8265
Fax: 0113 247 8268
Contact: Director of Library Services

Leeds Metropolitan University
City Campus Library
Calverley Street
Leeds, West Yorkshire LS1 3HE
Tel: 0113 283 2600 x3836
Fax: 0113 242 5733
Contact: Tutor Librarian, Art & Design

Trinity and All Saints College Library

Brownberrie Lane
Horsforth
Leeds, West Yorkshire LS18 5HD
Tel: 0113 283 7100
Fax: 0113 283 7200
Website: www.tasc.ac.uk
Contact: Librarian
Resources: A, B, D, E

Leicester

Centre For Mass Communication Research

104 Regent Road
Leicester LE1 7LT
Tel: 0116 2523863
Fax: 0116 2523874
email: cmcr@le.ac.uk
Website: www.le.ac.uk/cmcr/
Contact: Director

De Montfort University Library

Kimberlin Library
The Gateway
Leicester LE1 9BH
Tel: 0116 255 1551
Fax: 0116 255 0307
Contact: Senior Assistant Librarian
(Art and Design)

Leicester Central Lending Library

54 Belvoir Street
Leicester LE1 6QL
Tel: 0116 255 6699
Contact: Area Librarian
Resources: D, E,

Leicester University Library

PO Box 248
University Road
Leicester LE1 9QD
Tel: 0116 252 2042
Fax: 0116 252 2066
Website: www.le.ac.uk
Contact: Librarian
Resources: A, B, E

Liverpool

Aldham Robarts Learning Resource Centre

Liverpool John Moores University
Mount Pleasant
Liverpool L3 5UZ
Tel: 0151 231 3104
Contact: Senior Information Officer
(Media, Critical and Creative Arts)

Liverpool City Libraries

William Brown Street

Liverpool L3 8EW
Tel: 0151 225 5429
Fax: 0151 207 1342
Contact: Librarian

Liverpool Hope University College

Hope Park
Liverpool L16 9LB
Tel: 0151 291 2000
Fax: 0151 291 2037
Website: www.hope.ac.uk
Contact: Director of Learning Resources
Resources: A, B, C, D, E

London

Barbican Library

Barbican Centre
London EC2Y 8DS
Tel: 020 7638 0569
Fax: 020 7638 2249
Contact: Librarian

BKSTS - The Moving Image Society

63-71 Victoria House
Vernon Place, London WC1B 4DA
Tel: 020 7242 8400
Fax: 020 7405 3560
email: movimage@
bksts.demon.co.uk
Contact: John Graham

British Universities Film & Video Council Library

77 Wells Street
London W1T 3QT
Tel: 020 7393 1508
Fax: 020 7393 1555
Website: www.bufvc.ac.uk
Contact: Head of Information
Resources: B, C, D* , E, F**
* Film loans
** British Universities Newsreel
Project database

Brunel University

Twickenham Campus
300 St Margarets Road
Twickenham TW1 1PT
Tel: 020 8891 0121
Fax: 020 8891 0240
Contact: Director of Library Services
Resources: A, B, C, E

Camberwell College of Arts Library

London Institute
Peckham Road
London SE5 8UF
Tel: 020 7514 6349
Fax: 020 7514 6324
Contact: College Librarian
Resources: A, B, E

Camden Public Libraries

Swiss Cottage Library
88 Avenue Road
London NW3 3HA
Tel: 020 7974 6522
Contact: Librarian
Resources: A, B, D, E

Carlton Screen Advertising Ltd

127 Wardour Street
London W1V 4NL
Tel: 020 7439 9531
Fax: 020 7439 2395
Contact: Secretary

Cinema Theatre Association

44 Harrowdene Gardens
Teddington, Middlesex TW11 0DJ
Tel: 020 8977 2608
Website: www.cinema-theatre.org.uk
Contact: Secretary

Independent Television Commission Library

33 Foley Street
London W1P 7LB
Tel: 020 7306 7763
Fax: 020 7306 7750
Contact: Librarian
Resources: A, B, C, E, F*
* Press cuttings

Institute of Education Library (London)

20 Bedford Way
London WC1H 0AL
Tel: 020 7612 6080
Fax: 020 7612 6093
email: lib.enquiries@ioe.ac.uk
Contact: Librarian

International Institute of Communications

Library and Information Service
3rd Floor, Westcott House
35 Portland Place
London W1N 3AG
Tel: 020 7323 9622
Fax: 020 7323 9623
email: enquiries@iicom.org
Website: www.iicom.org
Contact: Information & Library
Manager

London Borough of Barnet Libraries

Hendon Library
The Burroughs
Hendon, London NW4 4BQ
Tel: 020 8359 2628
Fax: 020 8359 2885
Contact: Librarian

London College of Printing & Distributive Trades
Media School
Backhill
Clerkenwell EC1R 5EN
Tel: 020 7514 6500
Fax: 020 7514 6848
Contact: Head of Learning Resources

London Guildhall University
Academic Services
Calcutta House
Old Castle Street
London E1 7NT
Tel: 020 7320 1000
Fax: 020 7320 1177
email: kelso@lgu.ac.uk
Website: www.lgu.ac.uk
Contact: Ian Kelso, Head of TV Services

Middlesex University Library
Bounds Green Road
London N11 2NQ
Tel: 020 8362 5240
Contact: University Librarian

The College of North East London Learning Resource Centre
High Road
Tottenham
London N15 4RU
Tel: 020 8442 3013
Fax: 020 8442 3091
Contact: Head of Learning Resources

Royal College of Art
Kensington Gore
London SW7 2EU
Tel: 020 7590 4224
Fax: 020 7590 4500
email: info@rca.ac.uk
Website: www.rca.ac.uk
Contact: Library Desk

Royal Television Society, Library & Archive
Holborn Hall
100 Grays Inn Road
London WC1X 8AL
Tel: 020 7430 1000
Fax: 020 7430 0924
Contact: Archivist

Slade/Duveen Art Library
University College London
Gower Street
London WC1E 6BT
Tel: 020 7504 2594
Fax: 020 7380 7373
email: r.dar@ucl.ac.uk
Contact: Art Librarian: Ruth Dar
Resources: A, B, C, E*
* For UCL staff and students

Thames Valley University
St Mary's Road
Learning Resources Centre
Walpole House, Ealing
London W5 5RF
Tel: 020 8231 2248
Fax: 020 8231 2631
Website: www.tvu.ac.uk
Contact: Humanities Librarian

University of East London
Greengate House Library
School of Art & Design
89 Greengate Street
London E13 0BG
Tel: 020 8590 7000 x 3434
Contact: Site Librarian

University of London: Goldsmiths' College Library
Lewisham Way
London SE14 6NW
Tel: 020 7919 7168
Fax: 020 7919 7165
email: lbslpm@gold.ac.uk
Website: www.gold.ac.uk
Contact: Subject Librarian: Media & Communications
Resources: A, B, C, D

University of North London
The Learning Centre
236-250 Holloway Road
London N7 6PP
Tel: 020 7607 2789 x 2720
Fax: 020 7753 5079
email: c.partridge@unl.ac.uk
Website: www.unl.ac.uk/library/aishums/film.shtml
Crispin Partridge
Resources: B, C, D, E

University of Surrey Roehampton
Information Services
Learning Resources Centre
Digby Stuart College
Roehampton Lane
London SW15 5SZ
Tel: 020 8392 3251
Fax: 020 8392 3259
email: edesk@roehampton.ac.uk
Website: www.roehampton.ac.uk
Contact: Information Adviser (Performing Arts)
Resources: B, C, E

University of Westminster
Harrow Learning Resources Centre
Watford Road
Northwick Park
Harrow HA1 3TP
Tel: 020 7911 5885
Fax: 020 7911 5952

Website: www.wmin.ac.uk/harlib
Contact: Communications Creative Industries Co-ordinator
Resources: A, B, C, D, E

Westminster Reference Library
35 St Martins Street
London WC2H 7HP
Tel: 020 7641 4636
Fax: 020 7641 4640
Contact: Margaret Girvan, Arts Librarian
Resources: A, B, C, E

Loughborough

Loughborough University Pilkington Library
Loughborough University
Loughborough LE11 3TU
Tel: 01509 222360
Fax: 01509 234806
Contact: Assistant Librarian

Luton

University of Luton Library
Park Square
Luton LU1 3JU
Tel: 01582 734111 Ext 2093
email: alan.bullimore@luton.ac.uk
Contact: Alan Bullimore
Humanities Academic Liaison Librarian

Maidstone

Kent Institute of Art & Design at Maidstone
Oakwood Park
Maidstone
Kent ME16 8AG
Tel: 01622 757286
Fax: 01622 692003
Contact: College Librarian

Manchester

John Rylands University Library
Oxford Road
Manchester M13 9PP
Tel: 0161 275 3751/3738
Fax: 0161 273 7488
Contact: Lending Services Librarian

Manchester Arts Library
Central Library
St Peters Square
Manchester M2 5PD
Tel: 0161 234 1974
Fax: 0161 234 1961
email: arts@libraries.

manchester.gov.uk
Website: www. manchester.gov.
uk/mccdlb/libguide/arts/home.htm
Contact: Arts Librarian
Resources: A, B, D, E

Manchester Metropolitan University Library
All Saints Building
Grosvenor Square
Oxford Road
Manchester M15 6BH
Tel: 0161 247 6104
Fax: 0161 247 6349
Contact: Senior Subject Librarian

North West Film Archive
Manchester Metropolitan
University
Minshull House
47-49 Chorlton Street
Manchester M1 3EU
Tel: 0161 247 3097
Fax: 0161 247 3098
email: n.w.filmarchive@mmu.ac.uk
Website: www.nwfa.mmu.ac.uk
Director: Maryann Gomes
Enquiries: Lisa Ridehalgh
Resources: D, E, F*
* Ephemera

Newcastle upon Tyne

Newcastle upon Tyne University Robinson Library
Newcastle upon Tyne NE2 4HQ
Tel: 0191 222 7662
Fax: 0191 222 6235
Website: www.ncl.ac.uk/library
Contact: The Librarian
Resources: A, B, C, D, E

University of Northumbria at Newcastle Library Building
Ellison Place
Newcastle Upon Tyne NE1 8ST
Tel: 0191 227 4132
Fax: 0191 227 4563
Website: www.unn.ac.uk
Contact: Jane Shaw, Senior Officer, Information Services Department

Newport

University of Wales College Newport
Caerleon
Newport NP6 1XJ
Tel: 01633 430088
Fax: 01633 432108
Contact: Art and Design Librarian

Northumberland

Northumberland Central Library
The Willows
Morpeth
Northumberland NE61 1TA
Tel: 01670 511156
Fax: 01670 518012
Website: www.amenities
@northumberland.gov.uk
Contact: The Librarian
Resources: A, B, C, D, E

Norwich

East Anglian Film Archive
Centre for East Anglian Studies
University of East Anglia
Norwich NR4 7TJ
Tel: 01603 592664
Fax: 01603 458553
Contact: Assistant Archivist

University of East Anglia
University Library
Norwich NR4 7TJ
Tel: 01603 592421
Fax: 01603 259490
email: library@uea.ac.uk
Website: www.lib.uea.ac.uk
Contact: Film Studies Librarian

Nottingham

Nottingham Central Library
Angel Row
Nottingham NG1 6HP
Tel: 0115 941 2121
Fax: 0115 953 7001
Contact: Librarian

Nottingham Trent University Library
The Boots Library
Goldsmith Street
Nottingham NG1 5LS
Tel: 0115 848 2110
Fax: 0115 848 2286
Website: www.ntu.ac.uk
Contact: Faculty Liaison Officer (Art & Design)
Resources: A, B, C, D, E

University of Nottingham Library
Hallward Library, University Park
Nottingham NG7 2RD
Tel: 0115 951 4584
Fax: 0115 951 4558
Website: www.nottingham.
ac.uk/library
Contact: Humanities Librarian
Resources: A, B, C, E

Plymouth

College of St Mark and St John Library
Derriford Road
Plymouth
Devon PL6 8BH
Tel: 01752 636700
Fax: 01752 636712
email: agress@marjon.ac.uk
Website: www.marjon.ac.uk
Contact: Resources Librarian
Resources: B, C, E

Plymouth College of Art & Design Library
Tavistock Place
Plymouth
Devon PL4 8AT
Tel: 01752 203412
Fax: 01752 203444
Contact: Librarian
Resources: A, B, C, D, E

Pontypridd

University of Glamorgan
Learning Resources Centre
Pontypridd
Rhondda Cynon Taff CF37 1DL
Tel: 01443 482625
Fax: 01443 482629
email: pjatkins@glam.ac.uk
Website: www.itc.glam.ac.uk/lrc.
Contact: Head of Learning Resources Centre

Poole

Bournemouth & Poole College of Art & Design
Fern Barrow
off Wallisdown Road, Poole
Dorset BH12 5HH
Tel: 01202 533011
Fax: 01202 537729
Contact: University Librarian

Bournemouth University Library
Dorset House, Talbot Campus
Fern Barrow, Poole
Dorset BH12 5BB
Tel: 01202 595011
Fax: 01202 595475
email: dbath@bournemouth.ac.uk
Website: www.bournemouth.ac.uk
Contact: David Ball, Librarian

Portsmouth

Highbury College Library
Cosham

Portsmouth
Hants PO6 2SA
Tel: 023 9231 3213
Fax: 023 9232 5551
email: library@highbury.ac.uk
Website: www.highbury.ac.uk
Contact: College Librarian

Portsmouth University Library
Frewen Library
Cambridge Road
Portsmouth
Hampshire PO1 2ST
Tel: 023 9284 3222
Fax: 023 9284 3233
Website: www.libr.port.ac.uk
Contact: University Librarian
Resources: A, B, C, D, E

Preston

University of Central Lancashire Library
St Peter's Square
Preston
Lancashire PR1 2HE
Tel: 01772 201201 x 2266
Fax: 01772 892937
Contact: Senior Subject Librarian

Reading

Reading University Library
Woodlands Avenue
Reading RG6 1HY
Tel: 0118 931 8651
Fax: 0118 931 8651
Website: www.rdg.ac.uk/
libweb/Lib/Bulm/bul.html
Contact: Faculty Team Manager
(Education & Community Studies)

Rochdale

Rochdale Metropolitan Borough Libraries
Wheatsheaf Library
Wheatsheaf Centre
Baillie Street, Rochdale
Lancashire OL16 1AQ
Tel: 01706 864914
Fax: 01706 864992
Contact: Librarian

Salford

University of Salford, Academic Information Services (Library)
Adelphi Campus
Peru Street
Salford

Greater Manchester M3 6EQ
Tel: 0161 295 6183/6185
Fax: 0161 295 6083
Website: www.salford.ac.uk
/ais/homepage.html
Contact: Sue Slade (Faculty co-ordinator)
Contact: Andy Callen (Information Officer, Music & Media Productions)
Resources: A, B, C, D, E, F*
* Scripts

Sheffield

Sheffield Hallam University Learning Centre
Psalter Lane Campus
Sheffield
South Yorkshire S11 8UZ
Tel: 0114 225 2721
Fax: 0114 225 2717
email: c.abson@shu.ac.uk
Website: www.shu.ac.uk
/services/lc/people/psalter1.htm
Contact: Claire Abson, Information Specialist, School of Cultural Studies
Resources: A, B, C, D, E

Sheffield Libraries & Information Services
Arts and Social Sciences Section
Central Library, Surrey Street
Tel: 0114 273 4747/8
Fax: 0114 273 5009
Contact: Librarian

Sheffield University Library
Main Library
University of Sheffield
Western Bank
Sheffield
South Yorkshire S10 2TN
Tel: 0114 222 7200/1
Fax: 0114 273 9826
Contact: Head of Reader Services

Solihull

Solihull College
Chelmsley Campus
Partridge Close
Chelmsley Wood
Solihull B37 6UG
Tel: 0121 770 5651
Contact: Librarian

Southampton

Periodical Office, Hartley Library
University of Southampton
University Road, Highfield
Southampton

Hants SO17 1BJ
Tel: 023 8059 3521
Fax: 023 8059 3007
Contact: Assistant Librarian, Arts
Resources: B, D, E, F*
* Personal papers, pressbooks

Southampton Institute, Mountbatten Library
East Park Terrace
Southampton
Hampshire SO17 1BJ
Tel: 023 8031 9000
Fax: 023 8031 6161
Website: www.solent.ac.uk/library/
Contact: Information Librarian (Communications)
Resources: D*, E*
* For existing Institute staff and students

University of Southampton New College
The Avenue
Southampton SO17 1BG
Tel: 023 8021 6220
Fax: 023 8021 0944
Contact: Librarian

Stirling

University of Stirling Library
Stirling FK9 4LA
Tel: 01786 467 235
Fax: 01786 51335
Contact: Librarian

Stoke-on-Trent

Staffordshire University Library and Information Service
College Road
Stoke-on-Trent
Staffordshire ST4 2DE
Tel: 01782 294770/294809
Fax: 01782 744035
Contact: Art & Design Librarian

Sunderland

City Library and Art Centre
Fawcett Street
Sunderland SR1 1RE
Tel: 0191 514 1235
Fax: 0191 514 8444
Contact: Librarian

Sunderland University Library
Langham Tower
Ryhope Road

Sunderland SR2 7EE
Tel: 0191 515 2900
Fax: 0191 515 2423
Contact: Librarian

Sutton

Sutton Central Library
Music and Arts Department
St Nicholas Way, Sutton
Surrey SM1 1EA
Tel: 020 8770 4764/5
Fax: 020 8770 4777
Contact: Information Manager (Recreation)

Swansea

Swansea Institute of Higher Education Library
Townhill Road
Swansea SA2 0UT
Tel: 01792 481000
Fax: 01792 298017
email: enquiry@sihe.ac.uk
Website: www.sihe.ac.uk
Contact: Librarian
Resources: B, C, E

Warrington

Warrington Collegiate Institute
Faculty of Higher Education
The Library
Padgate Campus
Crab Lane
Warrington WA2 0DB
Tel: 01925 494284
email: l.crewe@warr.ac.uk
Website: www.warr.ac.uk
Lorna Crewe, Deputy College Librarian

Wellingborough

Tresham Institute of Further and Higher Education Library
Church Street
Wellingborough
Northamptonshire NN8 4PD
Tel: 01933 224165
Fax: 01933 441832
Contact: Librarian

Winchester

King Alfred's College Library
Sparkford Road, Winchester
Hampshire SO22 4NR
Tel: 01962 827306
Fax: 01962 827443

Website: www.kc.wkac.ac.uk
Contact: Librarian

Winchester School of Art
Park Avenue, Winchester
Hampshire SO23 8DL
Tel: 02380 597015
Fax: 02380 597016
email: wsaenq@soton.ac.uk
Website: www.soton.ac.uk/
Contact: Head of Learning Resources
Resources: B, E

Wolverhampton

Light House
Media Reference Library
The Chubb Buildings
Fryer Street
Wolverhampton WV1 1HT
Tel: 01902 716055
Fax: 01902 717143
email: lighthse@waverider.co.uk
Contact Library: Librarian
Exhibitions/Cultural Events: Evelyn Wilson
Chief Executive: Frank Challenger
Resources: A, B, E, F*
* Scripts, pressbooks

Wolverhampton Libraries and Information Services
Central Library
Snow Hill
Wolverhampton WV1 3AX
Tel: 01902 312 025
Fax: 01902 714 579
Contact: Librarian
Resources: B, D

Wolverhampton University
Art and Law Library
54 Stafford Street
Wolverhampton WV1 3AX
Tel: 01902 321597
Fax: 01902 322668
Contact: Art and Design Librarian

Wolverhampton University
Dudley Learning Centre
University of Wolverhampton
Castle View
Dudley
West Midlands DY1 3BQ
Tel: 01902 323 560
Fax: 01902 323 354
Website: www.wlr.ac.uk.lib
Learning Centre Manager
Resources: A, B, C, D, E

York

University College of Ripon and York St John Library
Lord Mayors Walk

York YO3 7EX
Tel: 01904 616700
Fax: 01904 612512
Website: www.ucrysj.ac.uk/
services/library/index.htm
Contact: Librarian
Resources: B, C, D, E, F*
* Ripon campus of college houses - Yorkshire Film Archive

ORGANISATIONS

Listed below are the main trade/government organisations and bodies relevant to the film and television industries in the UK. This is followed by a separate list of Regional Film Commissions. Finally, a small selection of organisations from the US concludes this section

ABC (Association of Business Communicators)
1 West Ruislip Station
Ruislip
Middx HA4 7DW
Tel: 01895 622 401
Fax: 01895 631 219
Roger Saunders
Trade association of professionals providing the highest standards of audiovisual/video equipment/services for use in corporate communication

ACCS (Association for Cultural and Communication Studies)
Dept of Literature & Languages
Nottingham Trent University
Clifton Site
Nottingham NG11 8NS
Tel: 0115 941 8418 x3289
Fax: 0115 948 6632
Georgia Stone
Provides a professional forum for teachers and researchers in Media, Film, Television and Cultural Studies in both further and higher education. Its Executive Committee is drawn from the college and university sectors. Organises an Annual Conference, seeks to facilitate the exchange of information among members and liaises with various national bodies including 'sister' organisations: AME, NAHEFV and BUFVC

Advertising Association
Abford House
15 Wilton Road
London SW1V 1NJ
Tel: 020 7828 2771/4831
Fax: 020 7931 0376
email: aa@adassoc.org.uk

Website: www.adassoc.org.uk
Andrew Brown
A federation of 26 trade associations and professional bodies representing advertisers, agencies, the advertising media and support services. It is the central organisation for the UK advertising business, on British and European legislative proposals and other issues of common concern, both at national and international levels, and as such campaigns actively to maintain the freedom to advertise and to improve public attitudes to advertising. It publishes UK and European statistics on advertising expenditure, instigates research on advertising issues and organises seminars and courses for people in the communications business. Its Information Centre is one of the country's leading sources for advertising and associated subjects

Advertising Film and Videotape Producers' Association (AFVPA)
26 Noel Street
London W1V 3RD
Tel: 020 7434 2651
Fax: 020 7434 9002
email: afvpa@easynet.co.uk
Website: www.afvpa@easynet.co.uk
Cecilia Garnett
Represents most producers of TV commercials. It negotiates with recognised trade unions, with the advertisers and agencies and also supplies a range of member services

Advertising Standards Authority (ASA)
Brook House
2 Torrington Place
London WC1E 7HW
Tel: 020 7580 5555
Fax: 020 7631 3051
Website: www.asa.org.uk

AFMA Europe
49 Littleton Road
Harrow
Middx HA1 3SY
Tel: 020 8423 0763
Fax: 020 8423 7963
Chairman: Lawrence Safir

Hold rights to numerous Australian, US and UK pictures, including Sam Spiegel's *Betrayal*

AIM (All Industry Marketing for Cinema)
22 Golden Square
London W1R 3PA
Tel: 020 7437 4383
Fax: 020 7734 0912
email: sfd@sfd.demon.co.uk
John Mahony
Unites distribution, exhibition and cinema advertising in promoting cinema and cinema–going. Funds film education, holds Cinema Days for regional journalists, markets cinema for sponsorship and promotional ventures and is a forum for cinema marketing ideas

Amalgamated Engineering and Electrical Union (AEEU)
Hayes Court
West Common Road
Bromley
Kent BR2 7AU
Tel: 020 8462 7755
Fax: 020 8315 8234
Website: www.aeeu.org.uk
Trade union representing – among others – people employed in film and TV lighting/electrical/electronic work

AMPS (Association of Motion Picture Sound)
28 Knox Street
London W1H 1FS
Tel: 020 7723 6727
Fax: 020 7723 6727
email: ampsoffice@tinyonline.co.uk
Website: www.amps.net
Brian Hickin
Promotes and encourages science, technology and creative application of all aspects of motion picture sound recording and reproduction, and seeks to promote and enhance the status of those therein engaged

APRS – The Professional Recording Association
PO Box 111
Uckfield
TN22 5WQ
Tel: 01803 868600

Fax: 01803 868444
email: info@aprs.co.uk
Website: www.aprs.co.uk
Mark Broad – Chief Executive
Represents the interests of the professional sound recording industry, including radio, TV and audio studios and companies providing equipment and services in the field. The Recording Technology exhibition ran at the Business Design Centre in June 2000

Arts Council of England
14 Great Peter Street
London SW1P 3NQ
Tel: 020 7333 0100
Fax: 020 7973 6590
email: enquiries@artscouncil.org.uk
Website: www.artscouncil.org.uk
David Curtis, Gary Thomas
ACE has lead responsibility in England for artists' film and video and for large scale capital projects relating to film

Arts Council of Wales
9 Museum Place
Cardiff CF10 3NX
Tel: 029 2037 6500
Fax: 029 2039 5284
email: information@ccc–acw.org.uk
Website: www.ccc.acw.org.uk
Joanna Weston, Chief Executive

ASIFA
International Animated Film Association
94 Norton Gardens
London SW16 4TA
Tel: 020 8681 8988
Fax: 020 8688 1441
Pat Raine Webb
A worldwide association of individuals who work in, or make a contribution to, the animation industry, including students. Activities include involvement in UK and international events and festivals, an Employment Databank, Animation Archive, children's workshops. The UK group provides an information service to members and a news magazine

Association for Media Education in Scotland (AMES)
c/o Scottish Screen
249 West George Street
Glasgow G2 4QE
Tel: 01224 481976
email: d@murphy47.freeserve.co.uk
Website: www.ames.org.uk
Robert Preece

Audio Visual Association
Herkomer House
156 High Street
Bushey
Herts WD2 3DD
Tel: 020 8950 5959
Fax: 020 8950 7560
email: multimedia@visual–arena.co.uk
Website: www.visual–arena.co.uk
Mike Simpson FBIPP
The Audio Visual Association is a Special Interest Group within the British Institute of Professional Photography. With the Institute's current thinking of lateral representation within all categories of imaging and imaging technology, the AVA represents those individuals involved in the various disciplines of audiovisual

Australian Film Commission (AFC)
Level 4, 150 William Street
Woolloomooloo 201
Australia
Tel: (61) 2 9321 6444
Fax: (61) 2 9357 3631
email: marketing@afc.gov.au
Website: www.afc.gov.au/
Pressanna Vasudevan
The AFC is a statutory authority established in 1975 to assist the development, production and distribution of Australian films. The European marketing branch services producers and buyers, advises on co–productions and financing, and promotes the industry at markets and through festivals

Authors' Licensing & Collecting Society
Marlborough Court
14–18 Holborn
London EC1N 2LE
Tel: 020 7395 0600
Fax: 020 7395 0660
email: alcs@alcs.co.uk
Website: www.alcs.co.uk
The ALCS is the British collecting society for all writers. Its principal purpose is to ensure that hard–to–collect revenues due to authors are efficiently collected and speedily distributed. These include the simultaneous cable retransmission of the UK's terrestrial and various international channels, educational off–air recording and BBC Prime. Contact the ALCS office for more information

BAFTA (British Academy of Film and Television Arts)
195 Piccadilly
London W1V 0LN
Tel: 020 7734 0022
Fax: 020 7734 1792
Website: www.bafta.org/
John Morrell
BAFTA was formed in 1946 by Britain's most eminent filmmakers as a non–profit making company. It aims to advance the art and technique of film and television and encourage experiment and research. Membership is available to those who have worked, or have been working actively within the film and/or television industries for not less than three years. BAFTA has facilities for screenings, conferences, seminars and discussion meetings and makes representations to parliamentary committees when appropriate. Its Awards for Film and Television are annual televised events. There are also Awards for Children's films and programmes and for Interactive Entertainment. The Academy has branches in Liverpool, Manchester, Glasgow, Cardiff, Los Angeles and New York. See also under Awards and Preview Theatres

BARB (Broadcasters' Audience Research Board)
2nd Floor
18 Dering Street
London W1R 9AF
Tel: 020 7529 5531
Fax: 020 7529 5530
Website: www.barb.co.uk
The main source of television audience research in the United Kingdom is supplied by BARB (Broadcasters' Audience Research Board Limited). The company represents the major UK broadcasters, the British Broadcasting Corporation (BBC), the Independent Television Association (ITVA), Channels 4 and 5, BSkyB and The Institute of Practitioners in Advertising (IPA). BARB was created in August 1980 when the BBC and ITV decided to have a mutually agreed source of television audience research. BARB became operational in August 1981

BECTU (Broadcasting Entertainment Cinematograph and Theatre Union)
111 Wardour Street
London W1V 4AY

Tel: 020 7437 8506
Fax: 020 7437 8268
email: info@bectu.org.uk
Website: www.bectu.org.uk
General Secretary: Roger Bolton
Press Officer: Janice Turner
BECTU is the UK trade union for
workers in film, broadcasting and the
arts. Formed in 1991 by the merger
of the ACTT and BETA, the union is
30,000 strong and represents
permanently employed and freelance
staff in television, radio, film,
cinema, theatre and entertainment.
BECTU provides a comprehensive
industrial relations service based on
agreements with the BBC, ITV
companies, Channel 4, PACT,
AFVPA and MFVPA, Odeon, MGM,
Apollo, Society of Film Distributors,
National Screen Services,
independent exhibitors and the *bfi*
itself. Outside film and television, the
union has agreements with the
national producing theatres and with
the Theatrical Management
Association, the Society of London
Theatres and others

BECTU History Project
111 Wardour Street
London W1V 4AY
Fax: 0207 437 8506
email: histproj@bectu.org.uk
The Project seeks to record and
preserve the history of film and
television in the UK, and the
influence of personnel from the UK
working abroad, by interviewing
those who have been involved

BKSTS – The Moving Image Society
5 Walpole Court
Ealing Studios
Ealing Green
London W5 5ED
Tel: 020 8584 5220
Fax: 020 8584 5230
email: movimage@bksts.demon.
co.uk
Website: www.bksts.com
Executive Director: Anne Fenton
Formed in 1931, the BKSTS is the
technical society for film, television
and associated industries. A wide
range of training courses and
seminars are organised with special
rates for members. The society
produces many publications
including a monthly journal *Image
Technology* and a quarterly *Cinema
Technology* both free to members.
Corporate members must have
sufficient qualifications and

experience, however student and
associate grades are also available.
Biennial conference has become a
platform for new products and
developments from all over the
world. The BKSTs also has a college
accreditation scheme and currently
accredits nine courses within the HE
+ FE sector

BREMA (British Radio & Electronic Equipment Manufacturers' Association)
Landseer House
19 Charing Cross Road
London WC2H 0ES
Tel: 020 7930 3206
Fax: 020 7839 4613
email: information@brema.org.uk
Website: www.brema.org.uk
Trade association for British
consumer electronics industry

British Academy of Composers and Songwriters
2nd Floor
British Music House
26 Berners Street
London W1P 3DB
Tel: 020 7636 2929
Fax: 020 7636 2212
email: info@britishacademy.com
Website: www.britishacademy.com
Rosemary Dixson
(Formerly the Association of
Professional Composers (APC), the
Composers' Guild of Great Britain,
and the British Academy of
Songwriters, Composers and Authors
(BASCA))
The Academy represents the interests
of composers and songwriters across
all genres, providing advice on
professional and artistic matters. The
Academy publishes a quarterly
magazine and administers a number
of major awards and events including
the Ivor Novello Awards

British Actors Equity Association
Guild House
Upper St Martin's Lane
London WC2H 9EG
Tel: 020 7379 6000
Fax: 020 7379 7001
email: info@equity.org.uk
Website: www.equity.org.uk
General Secretary: Ian McGarry
Equity was formed in 1930 by
professional performers to achieve
solutions to problems of casual
employment and short–term
engagements. Equity has 40,000
members, and represents performers

(other than musicians), stage
managers, stage directors, stage
designers and choreographers in all
spheres of work in the entertainment
industry. It negotiates agreements on
behalf of its members with
producers' associations and other
employers. In some fields of work
only artists with previous
professional experience are normally
eligible for work. Membership of
Equity is treated as evidence of
professional experience under these
agreements. It publishes *Equity
Journal* four times a year

British Amateur Television Club (BATC)
Grenehurst
Pinewood Road
High Wycombe
Bucks HP12 4DD
Tel: 01494 528899
email: memsec@batc.org.uk
Website: www.batc.org.uk
Non–profit making organisation run
entirely by volunteers. BATC publish
a quarterly technical publication
CQ–TV which is available via
subscription

British Board of Film Classification (BBFC)
3 Soho Square
London W1D 3HD
Tel: 020 7440 1570
Fax: 020 7287 0141
Website: www.bbfc.co.uk
The 1909 Cinematograph Films Act
required public cinemas to be
licensed by their local authority.
Originally this was a safety
precaution against fire risk but was
soon interpreted by the local
authorities as a way of censoring
cinema owners' choice of films. In
1912, the British Board of Film
Classification was established by the
film industry to seek to impose a
conformity of view–point: films
cannot be shown in public in Britain
unless they have the BBFC's
certificate or the relevant local
authorisation. The Board finances
itself by charging a fee for the films
it views. When viewing a film, the
Board attempts to judge whether a
film is liable to break the law, for
example by depraving and corrupting
a significant proportion of its likely
audience. It then assesses whether
there is material greatly and
gratuitously offensive to a large
number of people. The Board seeks
to reflect contemporary public

attitudes. There are no written rules but films are considered in the light of the above criteria, previous decisions and the examiners' personal judgement. It is the policy of the Board not to censor anything on political grounds. Five film categories came into effect in 1982, with the introduction of a '12' category in August 1989:

In questions of classification, the Board is primarily concerned with the protection of children, and the category system was changed in 1982 so as to provide clear and concise information to parents and the public generally. Only if a film fails to fall naturally into one of the following categories will cuts be considered.

'U' – UNIVERSAL. Suitable for all.
'PG' – PARENTAL GUIDANCE. Some scenes may be unsuitable for young children.
'12' – Suitable only for persons of twelve years and over (introduced on video 1st July 1994)
'15' – Suitable only for persons of fifteen years and over.
'18' – Suitable only for persons of eighteen years and over.
'R18' – FOR RESTRICTED DISTRIBUTION ONLY, through specially licensed cinemas or sex shops to which no one under eighteen is admitted.

The '12', '15' and '18' categories are subject to age bars at the cinema box office and at the counters of video shops. The video industry has asked for an additional category, to be used for works to be stocked on the children's shelves of video shops:
'Uc' – UNIVERSAL. Particularly suitable for young children.

The final decision, however, still lies with the local authority. In 1986 the GLC ceased to be the licensing authority for London cinemas, and these powers devolved to the Borough Councils. Sometimes films are passed by the BBFC and then banned by local authorities (*Straw Dogs, Caligula*). Others may have their categories altered (*Monty Python's Life of Brian, 9 and a half Weeks, Mrs Doubtfire*). Current newsreels are exempt from censorship

British Broadcasting Corporation (BBC)
Television Centre
White City

201 Wood Lane
London W12 7TS
Tel: 020 8752 5252
Website: www.bbc.co.uk
The BBC provides two national television networks, five national radio networks, as well as local radio and regional radio and television services. They are funded through the Licence Fee. The BBC is a public corporation, set up in 1927 by Royal Charter. Government proposals for the future of the BBC were published in a White Paper in July 1994. The BBC also broadcasts overseas through World Service Radio and Worldwide Television, but these are not funded through the Licence Fee

British Copyright Council
29–33 Berners Street
London W1P 4AA
Tel: 01986 788 122
Fax: 01986 788847
Janet Ibbotson
Provides liaison between societies which represent the interest of those who own copyright in literature, music, drama and works of art, making representation to Government on behalf of its member societies

The British Council
Films and Television Department
11 Portland Place
London W1B 1EJ
Tel: 020 7389 3065
Fax: 020 7389 3041
Website: www.britfilms.com
The British Council is Britain's international network for education, culture and technology. It is an independent, non–political organisation with offices in over 100 countries. Films and Television Department acts as a clearing house for international festival screenings of British short films and videos, including animation and experimental work. Using its extensive 16mm library, and 35mm prints borrowed from industry sources, it also ensures British participation in a range of international feature film events. The department arranges seminars overseas on themes such as broadcasting freedom and the future of public service television. It publishes the *International Directory of Film and Video Festivals* (biennial) and the annual *British Films Catalogue*. a 15–seat Preview Theatre (16mm, 35mm, video) is available for daytime use by UK filmmakers

British Design & Art Direction (D&AD)
9 Graphite Square
Vauxhall Walk
London SE11 5EE
Tel: 020 7840 1111
Fax: 020 7840 0840
email: info@dandad.co.uk
Website: www.dandad.org
Marcelle Johnson, Marketing Director
A professional association, registered as a charity, which publishes an annual of the best of British and international design, advertising, television commercials and videos, and organises travelling exhibitions. Professional awards, student awards, education programme, lectures. Membership details are available on request

British Federation of Film Societies (BFFS)
BFFS
c/o 13 Oaklands Terrace
Mount Pleasant
Swansea SA1 6JJ
Tel: 01792 481170
Fax: 01792 476857
David Phillips
email: info: bffs.org.uk
Website: www.bffs.org.uk
The BFFS exists to promote the work of some 300 film societies in the UK

British Film Commission
10 Little Portland Street
London W1N 5DF
Tel: 020 7224 5000
Fax: 020 7224 1013
email: info@britfilmcom.co.uk
Website: www.britfilmcom.co.uk
The British Film Commission is funded by central Government to promote the UK as an international production centre and to encourage the use of British locations, services, facilities and personnel. It provides information services at no charge to enquirers and on all matters relevant to overseas producers contemplating production in the UK. For more details on area and city film commissions in the UK, see end of section

British Film Institute
21 Stephen Street
London W1T 1LN
Tel: 020 7255 0439
Fax: 020 7436 7950
email: discover@bfi.org.uk
Website: www.bfi.org.uk

Founded in 1933, the *bfi* offers the public UK–wide opportunities to experience, enjoy and discover more about the world of film and television. It is a Royal Charter body and a registered charity.
Approximately half the *bfi*'s income is received as a grant–in–aid from the Film Council, the remainder is generated by the *bfi* itself through its various activities.

British Institute of Professional Photography

Fox Talbot House
Amwell End
Ware
Herts SG12 9HN
Tel: 01920 464011
Fax: 01920 487056
Website: www.bipp.com
Company Secretary: Alex Mair
The qualifying body for professional photography and photographic processing. Members represent specialisations in the fields of photography, both stills and moving images

British Interactive Multimedia Association Ltd

5/6 Clipstone Street
London W1P 7EB
Tel: 020 7436 8250
Fax: 020 7436 8251
email: enquiries@bima.co.uk
Website: www.bima.co.uk
Janice Cable, Administrator

British Phonographic Industry Ltd (BPI), The

25 Savile Row
London W1X 1AA
Tel: 020 7851 4000
Fax: 020 7851 4010
email: general@bpi.co.uk
Website: www.bpi.co.uk
Andrew Yeates, Director General
BPI is the industry association for record companies in the UK. It provides professional negotiating skills, legal advice, information and other services for its 220 members. It protects rights, fights piracy and promotes export opportunities. Organises the BRIT Awards. Information service available

British Recording Media Association

Ambassador House
Brigstock Road
Thornton Heath CR7 7JG
Tel: 020 8665 5395
Fax: 020 8665 6447

email: rma@admin.co.uk
Trade association for the manufacturers of blank audio and videotape

British Screen Advisory Council (BSAC)

13 Manette Street
London W1D 4AW
Tel: 020 7287 1111
Fax: 020 7287 1123
email:bsac@bsacouncil.co.uk
Director: Fiona Clarke–Hackston,
Chairman: David Elstein
Events & Communications Officer: Anna Pottle
BSAC is an independent, advisory body to government and policy makers at national and European level. It is a source of information and research for the screen media industries. BSAC provides a unique forum for the audio visual industry to discuss major issues which effect the industry. Its membership embraces senior management from all aspects of television, film, and video. BSAC regularly commissions and oversees research on the audio visual industry and uses this research to underpin its policy documents. In addition to regular monthly meetings, BSAC organises conferences, seminars, industry briefings and an annual reception in Brussels. BSAC is industry funded

British Screen Development (BSD)

14–17 Wells Mews
London W1P 3FL
Tel: 020 7323 9080
Fax: 020 7323 0092
Head of Development: Jenny Borgours
BSD makes loans for the development of British and European cinema feature films. Films such as *Photographing Fairies; Wilde; Before the Rain; Antonia's Line; Land and Freedom; Rob Roy; House of America; The Tango Lesson; Jilting Joe*. It has a two–tier loan system: screenplay loans for new writers; development loans for production companies to pay writers, and ancillary costs. BSD also part–finances, administers and oversees the production of a variety of short films around the country. In 1999 some 15 short films will be commissioned with budgets of around £25,000. In Europe, BSD supports and sponsors candidates through the SOURCES, ACE and ARISTA programmes

British Screen Finance

14–17 Wells Mews
London W1P 3FL
Tel: 020 7323 9080
Fax: 020 7323 0092
email: BS@cd–online.co.uk
Since January 1986, British Screen, a private company aided by Government grant, has taken over the role and the business of the National Film Finance Corporation which was dissolved following the Films Act 1985. British Screen exists primarily to support new talent in commercially viable productions for the cinema which might find difficulty in attracting mainstream commercial funding. Between 1986 and 1998 it invested in more than 140 productions. Recent successful films include, *Sliding Doors* and *Hiliary and Jackie*. Through British Screen Development it also runs programmes of short films made in Northern Ireland and English regions

British Society of Cinematographers (BSC)

11 Croft Road
Chalfont St Peter
Gerrards Cross
Bucks SL9 9AE
Tel: 01753 888052
Fax: 01753 891486
email: britcinematographers@compuserve.com
Website: www.bscine.com
Frances Russell
Promotes and encourages the pursuit of the highest standards in the craft of motion picture photography. Publishes a Newsletter and the BSC Directory

Broadcasting Press Guild

Tiverton
The Ridge
Woking
Surrey GU22 7EQ
Tel: 01483 764895
Fax: 01483 765882
Secretary: Richard Last
An association of journalists who specialise in writing about the media in the national, regional and trade press. Membership by invitation. Monthly lunches with leading industry figures as guests. Annual Television and Radio Awards voted for by members

Broadcasting Research Unit

VLV Librarian
101 King's Drive
Gravesend

Kent DA12 5BQ
Tel: 01474 352835
Fax: 01474 351112
The Broadcasting Research Unit was an independent Trust researching all aspects of broadcasting, development and technologies, which operated from 1980–1991. Its publications and research are now available from the above address

Broadcasting Standards Commission
7 The Sanctuary
London SW1P 3JS
Tel: 020 7233 0544
Fax: 020 7233 0397
email: bsc@bsc.org.uk
Website: www.bsc.org.uk
Vikki Lomas, Communications Director
Deputy Chairs: Jane Leighton and Lady Warner
Director: Stephen Whittle
The Broadcasting Standards Commission is the statutory body for both standards and fairness in broadcasting. It is the only organisation within the regulatory framework of UK broadcasting to cover all television and radio. This includes BBC and commercial broadcasters as well as text, cable, satellite and digital services. As an independent organisation representing the interests of the consumer, the Broadcasting Standards Commission considers the portrayal of violence, sexual conduct and matters of taste and decency. As an alternative to a court of law, it provides redress for people who believe they have been unfairly treated or subjected to unwarranted infringement of privacy. The Commission has three main tasks which are set out in the 1996 Broadcasting Act: – produces codes of practice relating to standards and fairness; considers and adjudicates on complaints; monitors, researches and reports on standards and fairness in broadcasting. The Commission does not have the power to preview or to censor broadcasting

BUFVC (British Universities Film and Video Council)
77 Wells Street
London W1T 3QJ
Tel: 020 7393 1500
Fax: 020 7393 1555
email: ask@bufvc.ac.uk
Website: www.bufvc.ac.uk

Luke McKernan, Head of Information
An organisation, funded via the Open University, with members in many institutions of higher education. It provides a number of services to support the production and use of film, television and other audiovisual materials for teaching and research. It operates a comprehensive Information Service, produces a regular magazine *Viewfinder*, catalogues and other publications such as the *Researchers' Guide to British Film and Television Collections* and t*he BUFVC Handbook for Film and Television in Education*, organises conferences and seminars and distributes specialised film and video material. It runs a preview and editing facility for film (16mm) and video (Betacam and other formats). Researchers in history and film and programme researchers come to the Council's offices to use the Slade Film History Register, with its information on British newsreels. BUFVC's off–air recording back–up service records the five UK terrestrial channels between 10.00am and 2.10am each day. The recordings are held indefinitely allowing educational establishments to request copies if they have failed to record the material locally under ERA licence

BVA (British Video Association)
167 Great Portland Street
London W1W 5PE
Tel: 020 7436 0041
Fax: 020 7436 0043
Website: www.bva.org.uk/
Represents, promotes and protects the collective rights of its members who produce and/or distribute video cassettes for rental and sale to the public

Campaign for Press and Broadcasting Freedom
8 Cynthia Street
London N1 9JF
Tel: 020 7278 4430
Fax: 020 7837 8868
email: cpbf@arcitechs.com
Website: www.architechs.com/cpbf
A broad–based membership organ–isation campaigning for more diverse, accessible and accountable media in Britain, backed by the trade union movement. The CPBF was established in 1979. The mail order catalogue is regularly updated and

includes books on all aspects of the media from broadcasting policy to sexism; its bi–monthly journal *Free Press* examines current ethical, industrial and political developments in media policy and practice. CPBF acts as a parliamentary lobby group on censorship and media reform.

Celtic Film and Television Festival Company
249 West George Street
Glasgow G2 4QE
Tel: 0141 302 1737
Fax: 0141 302 1738
email: mail@celticfilm.co.uk
Website: www.celticfilm.co.u
Frances Hendron
Organises an annual competitive festival/conference, itinerant Scotland, Ireland, Cornwall, Wales and Brittany in March/April. Supports the development of television and film in Celtic nations and indigenous languages

Central Office of Information (COI)
Films and Video
Hercules Road
London SE1 7DU
Tel: 020 7261 8495
Fax: 020 7261 0942
Ian Hamilton
COI Films and Video is responsible for government filmmaking on informational themes. The COI organises the production of a wide range of TV commercials and trailers, documentary films, video programmes and CD ROMs. It uses staff producers, and draws on the film and video industry for production facilities

Chart Information Network
3rd Floor
Century House
100 Oxford Street
London W1N 9FB
Tel: 020 7436 3000
Fax: 020 7436 8000
Supplies BVA members with detailed sales information on the sell–through video market. Markets and licenses the Official Retail Video Charts for broadcasting and publishing around the world

Children's Film and Television Foundation (CFTF)
Elstree Film Studios
Borehamwood
Herts WD6 1JG

Tel: 020 8953 0844
Fax: 020 8953 1113
Anna Home, Head of Production and Development
In 1944 Lord Rank founded the Children's Entertainment Film Division to make films specifically for children. In 1951 this resulted in the setting up of the Children's Film Foundation (now CFTF), a non–profit making organisation which, up to 1981, was funded by an annual grant from the BFFA (Eady money). The CFTF no longer makes films from its own resources but, for suitable children's/family cinema/television projects, is prepared to consider financing script development for eventual production by commercial companies. Films from the Foundation's library are available for hiring at nominal charge in 35mm, 16mm and video format

Church of England Communications Unit
Church House
Great Smith Street
London SW1P 3NZ
Tel: 020 7898 1456
Fax: 020 7222 6672
Rev Jonathan Jennings
(Out of office hours: 020 7222 9233)
Responsible for liaison between the Church of England and the broadcasting and film industries. Advises the C of E on all matters relating to broadcasting

Cinema Advertising Association (CAA)
12 Golden Square
London W1F 9LE
Tel: 020 7534 6363
Fax: 020 7534 6464
Website: www.adassoc.org.uk
Bruce Koster
The CAA is a trade association of cinema advertising contractors operating in the UK and Eire. First established as a separate organisation in 1953 as the Screen Advertising Association, its main purpose is to promote, monitor and maintain standards of cinema advertising exhibition including the pre–vetting of commercials. It also commissions and conducts research into cinema as an advertising medium, and is a prime sponsor of the CAVIAR annual surveys

Cinema & Television Benevolent Fund (CTBF)
22 Golden Square

London W1F 9AD
Tel: 020 7437 6567
Fax: 020 7437 7186
The CTBF is the trade fund operating in the UK for retired and serving employees (actors have their separate funds) who have worked for two or more years in any capacity, in the cinema, film or independent television industries'. The CTBF offers caring help, support and financial assistance, irrespective of age, and the Fund's home in Wokingham, Berkshire offers full residential and convalescent facilities

Cinema and Television Veterans
Elanda House
9 The Weald
Ashford
Kent TN24 8RA
Tel: 01233 639967
An association open to all persons employed in the United Kingdom or by United Kingdom companies in the cinema and/or broadcast television industries in any capacity other than as an artiste, for a total of at least thirty years

Cinema Exhibitors' Association (CEA)
22 Golden Square
London W1R 3PA
Tel: 020 7734 9551
Fax: 020 7734 6147
email: cea@cinemauk.ftech.co.uk
John Wilkinson
The first branch of the CEA in the industry was formed in 1912 and consisted of cinema owners. Following a merger with the Association of Independent Cinemas (AIC) it became the only association representing cinema exhibition. CEA members account for the vast majority of UK commercial cinemas, including independents, Regional Film Theatres and cinemas in local authority ownership. The CEA represents members' interests – within the industry and to local, national and European Government. It is closely involved with legislation (current and proposed) emanating from the UK Government and the European Commission which affects exhibition

Cinema Theatre Association
44 Harrowdene Gardens
Teddington
Middx TW11 0DJ
Tel: 020 8977 2608

Website: www.cinema–theatre.org.uk
Adam Unger
The Cinema Theatre Association was formed in 1967 to promote interest in Britain's cinema building legacy, in particular the magnificent movie palaces of the 1920s and 1930s. It is the only major organisation committed to cinema preservation in the UK. It campaigns for the protection of architecturally important cinemas and runs a comprehensive archive. The CTA publishes a bi–monthly bulletin and the magazine *Picture House*

Comataidh Craolaidh Gaidhlig (Gaelic Broadcasting Committee)
4 Harbour View, Cromwell Street
Stornoway
Isle of Lewis HS1 2DF
Tel: 01851 705550
Fax: 01851 706432
The Gaelic Television Fund and Comataidh Telebhisein Gaidhlig was set up under the provisions of the Broadcasting Act 1990. Funds made available by the Government were to be paid to the ITC for the credit of the fund to be known as the Gaelic Television Fund. The Fund was to be managed by the body known as the Gaelic Television Committee. Under the Broadcasting Act 1996 the Gaelic Television Fund was redesignated as the Gaelic Broadcasting Fund and the Gaelic Television Committee became the Gaelic Broadcasting Committee

Commonwealth Broadcasting Association
17 Fleet Street
London ECHY 1AA
Tel: 020 7583 5550
Fax: 020 7583 5549
email: cba@cba.org.uk
Website: www.org/cba
Elizabeth Smith, Secretary General
An association of 94 public service broadcasting organisations in 54 Commonwealth countries, supporting quality broadcasting through training, consultancies, conferences, magazine and the exchange of information

Critics' Circle
4 Alwyne Villas
London N1 2HQ
Tel: 020 7226 2726
Fax: 020 7354 2574

Deaf Broadcasting Council
70 Blacketts Wood Drive
Chorleywood, Rickmansworth

Herts WD3 5QQ
Tel: 01923 284538
Typetalk: 0800 515152
Fax: 01923 283127
email: rmyers@waitrose.com
Website: deafbroadcastingcouncil.
org.uk
Ruth Meyers
An umbrella organisation working to
ensure TV broadcasters are aware of
the needs of deaf and hard of hearing
people

Defence Press and Broadcasting Advisory Committee
Room 2235
Ministry of Defence
Main Building
Whitehall
London SW1A 2HB
Tel: 020 7218 2206
Fax: 020 7218 5857
Website: www.btinternet.com
/~d.a.notices
Secretary: Rear Admiral Nick
Wilkinson
The Committee is made up of senior
officials from the Ministry of
Defence, the Home Office and the
Foreign & Commonwealth Office and
representatives of the media. It issues
guidance, in the form of DA Notices,
on the publication of information
which it regards as sensitive for
reasons of national security

Department for Culture, Media and Sport – Media Division (Films)
2–4 Cockspur Street
London SW1Y 5DH
Tel: 020 7721 6000
Fax: 020 7711 6249
Website: www.culture.gov.uk
Contacts:
For BFI, British Screen Finance
(BSF), European Co–production fund
(ECPF): Aidan McDowell
Tel: 020 7211 6429
For enquiries concerning film which
might be made under UK
Co–production Agreements: Diana
Brown
Tel: 020 7211 6433
For MEDIA Programme, British
Film Commission (BFC), National
Film and Television School (NFTS)
and Audiovisual Eureka (AVE): Peter
Wright
Tel: 020 7211 6435
Statistics and Social Policy Unit
Tracy Dalby
Tel: 020 7211 6395

The Department for Culture Media
and Sport is responsible for
Government policy on film, relations
with the film industry and
Government funding for: the British
Film Institute, British Screen
Finance, the European
Co–Production Fund (administered
by British Screen Finance), the
British Film Commission and the
National Film and Television School.
It is also responsible for Government
policy on and contribution to, the EC
Media Programme and Audiovisual
Eureka. It also acts as the UK
competent authority for administering
the UK's seven bilateral
co–production agreements and the
European Co–production Convention

Department for Education and Employment (DFEE)
Sanctuary Buildings
Great Smith Street
London SW1P 3BT
Tel: 020 7925 5000
Fax: 020 7925 6000
email: info@dfee.gov.uk
Website: www.dfee.gov.uk
Public enquiries: 020 7925 5555
The DFE is responsible for policies
for education in England and the
Government's relations with
universities in England, Scotland and
Wales

The Directors' and Producers' Rights Society
Victoria Chambers
16–18 Strutton Ground
London SW1P 2HP
Tel: 020 7227 4757
Fax: 020 7227 4755
email: dprs@dial.pipex.com
Suzan Dormer
The Directors' and Producers' Rights
Society is a collecting society which
administers authorials rights
payments on behalf of British film
and television Directors

Directors' Guild of Great Britain
Acorn House
314–320 Gray's Inn Road
London WC1X 8DP
Tel: 020 7278 4343
Fax: 020 7278 4742
email: guild@dggb.co.uk
Website: www.dggb.co.uk
Sarah Wain
Represents interests and concerns of
directors in all media. Publishes
regular magazine DIRECT

Educational Television and Media Association (ETMA)
(See Learning on Screen)

Euroview Management Services Limited
PO Box 80
Wetherby
Yorks LS23 7EQ
Tel: 01937 541010
Fax: 01937 541083
email: euroview@compuserve.com
Website: www.euroview.co.uk
CFL Vision is one of the oldest
established video library operations
in the UK. It is part of the Central
Office of Information and distributes
their video and CD ROM productios,
as well as programmes acquired from
both public and private sectors. Over
200 titles are available for loan or
purchase by small businesses,
industry, local authorities and schools

Federation Against Copyright Theft (FACT)
7 Victory Business Centre
Worton Road
Isleworth
Middx TW7 6DB
Tel: 020 8568 6646
Fax: 020 8560 6364
David Lowe & Robert Melrose,
co–directors
FACT, Federation Against Copyright
Theft, is an investigative organisation
funded by its members to combat
counterfeiting, piracy and misuse of
their products. The members of
FACT are major companies in the
British and American film, video and
television industries. FACT is a
non–profit making company limited
by guarantee. FACT assists all
statutory law enforcement authorities
and will undertake private criminal
prosecutions wherever possible

Federation of Entertainment Unions (FEU)
1 Highfield
Twyford
Nr Winchester
Hants SO21 1QR
Tel: 01962 713134
Fax: 01962 713134
email: harris@interalpha.co.uk
Steve Harris
The FEU represents 140,000 people
working across the media and
entertainment industries in the UK. It
is a lobbying and campaigning group
and meets regularly with statutory
bodies and pressure groups ranging
from the BBC, the ITC, the Film

Council and the British Film Commission through to the Parliamentary All Party Media Committee and the Voice of the Listener and Viewer. The Federation comprises British Actors' Equity Association, Broadcasting Entertainment Cinematograph and Theatre Union, Musicians' Union, National Union of Journalists, Writers' Guild of Great Britain and Amalgamated Engineering & Electrical Union (Electricians Section). It has three standing committees covering Film and Electronic Media, European Affairs and Training

The Feminist Library
5a Westminster Bridge Road
London SE1 7XW
Tel: 020 7928 7789
The Feminist Library provides information about women's studies, courses, and current events. It has a large collection of fiction and non–fiction books, pamphlets, papers etc. It holds a wide selection of journals and newsletters from all over the world and produces its own quarterly newsletter. Social events are held and discussion groups meet every other Tuesday. The library is run entirely by volunteers. Membership library. Open Tuesday (11.00am–8.00pm) Wednesday (3.00pm –5.00pm) and Saturday (2.00–5.00pm)

Film Artistes' Association (FAA)
111 Wardour Street
London W1V 4AY
Tel: 020 7437 8506
Fax: 020 7437 1221
email: smacdonald@bectu.org.uk
Spencer MacDonald
The FAA represents extras, doubles, stand–ins. Under an agreement with PACT, it supplies all background artistes in the major film studios and within a 40 mile radius of Charing Cross on all locations

The Film Council
10 Little Portland Street
London W1N 5DF
Tel: 020 7861 7861
Fax: 020 7861 7862/3//4/5/6
Website: www.filmcouncil.org.uk
John Woodward, Chief Executive
The Film Council is the new strategic agency for developing the film industry and film culture in the UK. The Film Council is responsible for channelling £55 million of public money per year into the film industry derived from the National Lottery and government grant support funding. It has two aims of equal importance: developing a sustainable UK film industry; developing film culture in the UK by improving access to, and education about the moving image. The Film Council officially came into existence on 1 April 2000 taking responsibility for a number of organisations: the British Film Commission; the Arts Council of England's Lottery Film Department; and the British Film Institute's Production Department. British Screen Finance, a publicly supported film investment company will become incorporated into the Film Council in the latter part of 2000 and the British Film Institute will operate as an independent body funded by the Film Council to deliver cultural and education opportunities for the public

Film Education
Alhambra House
27–31 Charing Cross Road
London WC2H 0AU
Tel: 020 7976 2291
Fax: 020 7839 5052
email: postbox@filmeducation.org
Website: www.filmeducation.org
Ian Wall
Film Education is a registered charity supported by the UK film industry. For over a decade it has been at the forefront of the development of Film and Media Studies in schools and colleges and now has more than 20,000 named primary and secondary teacher contacts on its unique database. The main aims of Film Education are to develop the use of film in the school curriculum and to facilitate the use of cinemas by schools. To this end it publishes a variety of free teaching materials, produces BBC Learning Zone programmes, organises Inset and runs a range of workshops and school screenings. All Film Education resources are carefully researched and written by teachers for teachers

The Film Office
Unit 107
134–146 Curtain Road
London EC2A 3AR
Tel: 020 7729 9644
Website: www.filmoffice.co.uk
Works in association with local authorities in London to assist with filming in London locations

Film & Television Commission
109 Mount Pleasant
Liverpool L3 5TF
Tel: 0151 330 6666
Fax: 0151 330 6611
FTC north west is the official film commission for the north west of England, working in partnership with the film offices of Liverpool, Manchester, Lancashire, Isle of Man and Cheshire

Film Unit Drivers Guild
136 The Crossways
Heston
Middlesex TW5 OJR
Tel: 020 8569 5001
Fax: 020 8569 5002
B. Newell
FUDG represents its freelance members in the Film and Television industry when they are not on a production. It supplies them with work, such as pick ups and drops to any destination the client wishes to travel. Guild members are made up of professional film unit drivers and will look after all transportation needs

First Film Foundation
9 Bourlet Close
London W1P 7PJ
Tel: 020 7580 2111
Fax: 020 7580 2116
email: info@firstfilm.demon.co.uk
Website: www.firstfilm.co.uk
First Film Foundation is a charity that exists to help new British writers, producers and directors make their first feature film by providing a range of unique, educational and promotional programmes. FFF also provides impartial practical advice on how to develop a career in the film industry

FOCAL International Ltd (Federation of Commercial Audio–Visual Libraries)
Pentax House
South Hill Avenue
Middx HA2 0DU
Tel: 020 8423 5853
Fax: 020 8933 4826
email: info@focalint.org
Website: www. focalint.org
Commercial Manager: Anne Johnson
An international, non–profit making professional trade association representing commercial film/audiovisual libraries and interested individuals. Among other

activities, it organises regular meetings, maximises copyright information, and produces a directory of libraries and quarterly journal

German Federal Film Board and Export Union of German Cinema
Top Floor
113–117 Charing Cross Road
London W2H 0DT
Tel: 020 7437 2047
Fax: 020 7439 2947
Iris Kehr
UK representative of the German Federal Film Board (Filmförderungsanstalt), the government industry organisation, and the German Film Export Union (Export Union des Deutschen Films), the official trade association for the promotion of German films abroad.

Grierson Memorial Trust
c/o Ivan Sopher & co
5 Elstree Gate
Elstree Way
Borehamwood
Herts WD6 1JD
Tel: 020 8207 0602
Fax: 020 8207 6758
email: accountants@ivansopher.co.uk
Website: www.editor.net/griersontrust
John Chittock, Chairman

Guild of British Animation
26 Noel Street
London W1V 3RD
Tel: 020 7434 2651
Fax: 020 7434 9002
Stephen Davies
Represents interests of producers of animated films. AFVPA acts as secretariat for this association

Guild of British Camera Technicians
5–11 Taunton Road
Metropolitan Centre
Greenford
Middx UB6 8UQ
Tel: 020 8578 9243
Fax: 020 8575 5972
Office manager: Maureen O'Grady
Magazine Editors, *Eyepiece*: Charles Hewitt and Kerry–Anne Burrows
The Guild exists to further the professional interests of technicians working with film or video motion picture cameras. Membership is restricted to those whose work brings them into direct contact with these cameras and who can demonstrate competence in their particular field of

work. By setting certain minimum standards of skill for membership, the Guild seeks to encourage its members, especially newer entrants, to strive to improve their art. Through its publication, Eyepiece: disseminates information about both creative and technical developments, past and present, in the film and television industry

Guild of British Film Editors
Travair, Spurlands End Road
Great Kingshill , High Wycombe
Bucks HP15 6HY
Tel: 0149 712313
Fax: 0149 712313
email: cox.gbfe@btinternet.com
To ensure that the true value of film and sound editing is recognised as an important part of the creative and artistic aspects of film production

Guild of Stunt and Action Co–ordinators
72 Pembroke Road
London W8 6NX
Tel: 020 7602 8319
Sally Fisher
To promote the highest standards of safety and professionalism in film and television stunt work

Guild of Television Cameramen
1 Churchill Road
Whitchurch, Tavistock
Devon PL19 9BU
Tel: 01822 614405
Fax: 01822 615785
Sheila Lewis
The Guild was formed in 1972 'to ensure and preserve the professional status of the television cameramen and to establish, uphold and advance the standards of qualification and competence of cameramen'. The Guild is not a union and seeks to avoid political involvement

Guild of Vision Mixers
147 Ship Lane
Farnborough
Hants GU14 8BJ
Tel: 01252 514953
Fax: 01252 656756
Peter Turl
The Guild aims to represent the interests of vision mixers throughout the UK and Ireland, and seeks to maintain the highest professional standards in vision–mixing

IAC (Institute of Amateur Cinematographers)
24c West Street
Epsom
Surrey KT18 7RJ
Tel: 01372 739672
Fax: 01372 739672
email: iacfilmvideo@compuserve.com
Website: www.theiac.org.uk
Janet Smith, Admin Secretary
Encouraging amateurs interested in the art of making moving pictures and supporting them with a variety of services

Imperial War Museum Film and Video Archive
Lambeth Road
London SE1 6HZ
Tel: 020 7416 5000
Fax: 020 7416 5379
email: film@iwm.org.uk
Website: www.iwm.org.uk
See entry under Archives and Film Libraries

Incorporated Society of British Advertisers (ISBA)
44 Hertford Street
London W1Y 8AE
Tel: 020 7499 7502
Fax: 020 7629 5255
Website: www.isba.org.uk
Deborah Morris
The ISBA was founded in 1900 as an association for advertisers, both regional and national. Subscriptions are based on advertisers' expenditure and the main objective is the protection and advancement of the advertising interests of member firms. This involves organised representation, co–operation, action and exchange of information and experience, together with conferences, workshops and publications. ISBA offer a communications consultancy service for members on questions as varied as assessment of TV commercial production quotes to formulation of advertising agency agreements

Incorporated Society of Musicians (ISM)
10 Stratford Place
London W1C 1AA
Tel: 020 7629 4413
Fax: 020 7408 1538
email: membership@ism.org
Website: www.ism.org
Chief Executive: Neil Hoyle
Professional association for all

musicians: teachers, performers and composers. The ISM produces various publications, including the monthly Music Journal, and gives advice to members on all professional issues

Independent Television Commission (ITC)
33 Foley Street
London W1W 7TH
Tel: 020 7255 3000
Fax: 020 7306 7800
email: publicaffairs@itc.org.uk
The ITC is the public body responsible for licensing and regulating commercially funded television services. These include Channel 3 (ITV), Channel 4, Channel 5, public teletext and a range of cable, local delivery and satellite services and digital television services

Institute of Practitioners in Advertising (IPA)
44 Belgrave Square
London SW1X 8QS
Tel: 020 7235 7020
Fax: 020 7245 9904
Website: www.ipa.co.uk
The representative body for UK advertising agencies. Represents the collective views of its member agencies in negotiations with Government departments, the media and industry and consumer organisations

International Arts Bureau
4 Baden Place
Crosby Row
London SE1 1YW
Tel: 020 7403 7001
Fax: 020 7403 2009
email:
enquiry@international–arts.org
Website: www.international–arts.org
Information Service
The International Arts Bureau specialises in providing information and advice on a range of international arts issues, including cultural policies, networks and funding programmes from around the world. It offers a free enquiry service; monthly one–to–one funding advice 'surgeries'; a range of publications including a bi–monthly journal called International Arts Navigator; it also runstraining seminars on European policies, structures and funding opportunities, and undertakes research and consultancy for national, regional and local cultural agencies

International Association of Broadcasting Manufacturers (IABM)
Broad Oaks
Parish Lane
Farnham Common
Slough SL2 3JW
Tel: 01753 645682
Fax: 01753 645682
email: info@iabm.org.uk
Website: www.iabm.org.uk
Secretariat: Brenda White
IABM aims to foster the interests of manufacturers of broadcast equipment from all countries. Areas of membership include liaison with broadcasters, standardisation, other technical information, an annual product Award for design and innovation and exhibitions. All companies active in the field of broadcast equipment manufacturing are encouraged to join

International Federation of the Phonographic Industry (IFPI) IFPI Secretariat
54–62 Regent Street
London W1B 5RE
Tel: 020 7878 7900
Fax: 020 7878 7950
Director General: Nicholas Garnett
An international association of 1,300 members in 71 countries, representing the copyright interests of the sound recording and music video industries

International Institute of Communications
3rd Floor
Westcott House
35 Portland Place
London W1B 1AE
Tel: 020 7323 9622
Fax: 020 7323 9623
The IIC promotes the open debate of issues in the communications field worldwide. Its current interests cover legal and policy, economic and public interest issues. It does this via its: bi–monthly journal Intermedia; through its international communications library; annual conference; sponsored seminars and research forums

ITV Network Ltd
200 Gray's Inn Road
London WC1X 8HF
Tel: 020 7843 8000
Fax: 020 7843 8158
Director of Programmes: David Liddiment

A body wholly owned by the ITV companies which independently undertakes the commissioning and scheduling of those television programmes which are shown across the ITV Network. It also provides a range of services to the ITV companies where a common approach is required

IVCA (International Visual Communication Association)
19 Pepper Street
Glengall Bridge
London E14 9RP
Tel: 020 7512 0571
Fax: 020 7512 0591
email: info@ivca.org
Chief Executive: Wayne Drew
The IVCA is the largest European Association of its kind, representing a wide range of organisations and individuals working in the established and developing technologies of visual communication. With roots in video, film and business events industries, the Association has also developed significant representation of the new and fast growing technologies, notably business television, multimedia, interactive software and the internet. It provides business services for its members: legal help, internet service, insurance, arbitration etc. and holds events/seminars for training, networking and for all industry related topics

Kraszna–Krausz Foundation
122 Fawnbrake Avenue
London SE24 0BZ
Tel: 020 7738 6701
Fax: 020 7738 6701
email: k–k@dial.pipex.com
Website: www.editor.net/k–k
Andrea Livingstone, Administrator
The Foundation offers small grants of up to £5,000 to assist in the development of new or unfinished projects, work or literature where the subject specifically relates to the art, history, practice or technology of photography or the moving image (defined as film, television, video and related screen media)

Learning on Screen (the Society for Screen–based learning)
9 Bridge Street
Tadcaster LS24 9AW
Tel: 01937 530 520

Fax: 01937 530 520
email: josie.key@learningonscreen.
u–net.com
Website: www.learningonscreen.
org.uk
Learning on Screen is an organisation
providing support and assistance to
those involved in any form of
screen–based learning. It is the new
identity of the Educational Television
and Media Association (ETmA). This
is part of the continuing evolution of
the Association from an organisation
set up in 1967 to support those in the
new technology of closed–circuit
television. 2001 annual conference
8–11 April 2001. 2001 Annual
Production Awards. Membership
details from the Administrator.

London Film Commission
20 Euston Centre
Regent's Place
London NW1 3JH
Tel: 020 7387 8787
Fax: 020 7387 8788
email: lfc@london–film.co.uk
Website: london–film.co.uk
Dominic Reid, Film Commissioner
Julia Willis, Production Co–ordinator
The London Film Commission
encourages and assists film and
television production in London and
holds databases of locations,
personnel and facilities. Funded by
Government, the film industry and
other private sector sponsors, it
works to promote London as a first
choice destination for overseas
film–makers. It collaborates with the
Local Authorities, the police and
other services to create a film
friendly atmosphere in the capital

London Jewish Cultural Centre
The Old House
c/o King's College London
Kidderpore Avenue
Lonon NW3 7SZ
Tel: 020 7431 0345
Fax: 020 7431 0361
email: admin.ljcc.org.uk
Website: www.ljcc.org.uk
The LJCC is an educational
organisaion with an extensive library
of feature, documentary and Israeli
film containing rare and previously
unseen documentary footage,
educational compilation tapes, and a
vast archive of material on the
Holocaust. It offers some consultancy
services to researchers and producers
working in this field and organises

regular showings of films from the
collection. The Centre also uses
documentary and feature film widely
in all its academic programmes and
teaches a variety of film courses

Mechanical–Copyright Protection Society (MCPS)
29/33 Berner Street
London W1P 4AA
Tel: 020 8664 4400
Fax: 020 8378 7300
email: info@mcps.co.uk
Website: www.mcps.co.uk
Contact: Non–retail Licensing
Department
MCPS is an organisation of music
publishers and composers, which
issues licences for the recording of its
members' copyright musical works in
all areas of television, film and video
production. Free advice and further
information is available on request

Media, Communication and Cultural Studies Association (MeCCA)
The Surrey Institute of Art and
Design University College
Falkner Road
Farnham
Surrey GU9 7DS
Tel: 01252 892806
email: hdavies@surrart.ac.uk
Website: www.surrat.ac.
uk/meida/meccsa
Dr Helen Davies
MeCCSA is the leading subject
association for the field of Media,
Communication and Cultural Studies
in UK higher education. It represents
the interests of individual academics
and HEIs across the field

Medialex – Legal & Business Training
15 Sandycombe Road
Kew
Richmond
Surrey TW9 2EP
Tel: 020 8940 7039
Fax: 020 8758 8647
email: info@medialex.co.uk
Industry approved Media Law
seminars designed for the film and
television industry including
copyright, contracts, industry
agreements, music copyright, internet
and new media

Mental Health Media
356 Holloway Road
London N7 6PA
Tel: 020 7700 8171

Fax: 020 7686 0959
email: info@mhmedia.com
Website: www.mhmedia.com
An independent charity founded in
1965, MHM provides information,
advice and consultancy on film/video
and multimedia production relevant
to mental health and learning
difficulties. Resource lists on
audiovisual materials. Producers of
video and broadcast programmes

Metier
Glyde House
Glydegate
Bradford BD5 0BQ
Tel: 01274 738 800
Fax: 01274 391 566
Chief Exec: Duncan Sones
A National Training Organisation,
developing National and Scottish
Vocational Qualifications for
occupations in performing and visual
arts, arts administration,
front–of–house, arts development &
interpretation and technical support
functions in the arts and
entertainment sector. It is responsible
for strategic action to improve the
quality, availability and effectiveness
of vocational training within its
industrial sector

Music Video Producers' Association (MVPA)
26 Noel Street
London W1V 3RD
Tel: 020 7434 2651
Fax: 020 7434 9002
Stephen Davies
The MVPA was formed in 1985 to
represent the interests of pop/music
promo production companies. It
negotiates agreements with bodies
such as the BPI and BECTU on
behalf of its members. Secretariat
support is run through AFVPA

Music Publishers Association Ltd
3rd Floor, Strandgate
18/20 York Buildings
London WC2N 6JU
Tel: 020 7839 7779
Fax: 020 7839 7776
email: info@mpaonline.org.uk
Website: www.mpaoline.org.uk
Alex Webb, Communications
Manager
The only trade association
repre–senting UK music publishers.
List of members available at £10.00

Musicians' Union (MU)
60–62 Clapham Road

London SW9 0JJ
Tel: 020 7582 5566
Fax: 020 7793 9185
email: info@musiciansunion.org.uk
Website: www.musiciansunion.
org.uk
Media Department Contacts: Howard
Evans, Marilyn Stoddart
Represents the interests of virtually
all professional musicians in the UK.
The media department deals with all
music related issues involving film
and TV: day to day working and
interpretation of the MU/PACT
agreement, synchronisation of audio
recordings and advertisements and
film and rights clearances. Queries
regarding video, DVD, promotional
filming, EPK's, contractors,
musicians, composers and arrangers

National Association for Higher Education in Film and Video (NAHEFV)

c/o London International Film
School
24 Shelton Street
London WC2H 9HP
Tel: 020 7836 9642/7240 0168
Fax: 020 7497 3718
The Association's main aims are to
act as a forum for debate on all
aspects of film, video and TV
education and to foster links with
industry, the professions and
Government bodies. It was
established in 1983 to represent all
courses in the UK which offer a
major practical study in film, video
or television at the higher educational
level

National Campaign for the Arts

Pegasus House
37–43 Sackville Street
London W1X 1DB
Tel: 020 7333 0375
Fax: 020 7333 0660
Director: Victoria Todd
Deputy Director: Anna Leatherdale
The NCA is the only independent
lobbying organisation that represents
all the arts. The campaign is funded
entirely by its members to ensure its
independence. It gives a voice for the
arts world in all its diversity. The
NCA meets, lobbies and influences
decision makers – ministers, shadow
ministers, officials, council leaders,
peers, journalists and influential back
benchers. It discusses policy and
proposals in detail with major arts
funders on a regular basis

National Council for Educational Technology (NCET)

Milburn Hill Road
Science Park
University of Warwick
Coventry CV4 7JJ
Tel: 024 7641 6994
Fax: 024 7641 1418
Formerly the National Council for
Educational Technology (NCET), the
new remit will be to ensure that
technology supports the DfEE's
objectives to drive up standards, in
particular to provide the professional
expertise the DfEE needs to support
the future development of the
National Grid for Learning. BECTA
will also have a role in the further
education sector's developing use of
ICT, in the identification of ICT
opportunities for special educational
needs, and in the evaluttion of new
technologies as they come on stream

National Film and Television School

Beaconsfield Studios
Station Road
Beaconsfield
Bucks HP9 1LG
Tel: 01494 671234
Fax: 01494 674042
email: admin@nftsfilm–tv.ac.uk
Website: www.nftsfilm–tv.ac.uk
Director: Stephen Bayly
The National Film and Television
School provides advanced training
and retraining in all major disciplines
to professional standards. Graduates
are entitled to BECTU membership
on gaining employment. It is an
autonomous non–profit making
organisation funded by the
Department for Culture, Media and
Sport and the film and television
industries. See also under Courses

National Film Trustee Company (NFTC)

14–17 Wells Mews
London W1P 3FL
Tel: 020 7580 6799
Fax: 020 7636 6711
An independent revenue collection
and disbursement service for
producers and financiers. The NFTC
has been in business since 1971. It is
a subsidiary of British Screen Finance

National Museum of Photography Film & Television

Pictureville

Bradford BD1 1NQ
Tel: 01274 202030
Fax: 01274 723155
Website: www.nmsi.ac.uk/nmpft
Bill Lawrence, Head of Cinema
The world's only museum devoted to
still and moving pictures, their
technology and history. Features
Britain's first giant IMAX film
system; the world's only public
Cinerama; interactive galleries and
'TV Heaven', reference library of
programmes and commercials

National Screen Service

Unit 10
Westpoint Trading Estate
Alliance Road
West Acton
London W3 0RA
Tel: 020 8992 3237
Fax: 020 8752 0593
Paul Logan, Head of Client Service
Formed in 1926 as a subsidiary of a
US corporation and purchased by its
present British owner/directors in
1998. It distributes trailers, posters
and other publicity material to UK
cinemas and carries out related
printing activity

National Union of Journalists

314 Gray's Inn Road
London WC1X 8DP
Tel: 020 7278 7916
Fax: 020 7837 8143
Deputy General Secretary: John Fray
Direct line to Broadcasting Office:
020 7843 3726
Represents nearly 5,000 journalists
working in broadcasting in the areas
of news, sport, current affairs and
features. It has agreements with all
the major broadcasting companies
and the BBC. It also has agreements
with the main broadcasting agencies,
WTN, Reuters Television and PACT

National Viewers' & Listeners' Association (NVALA)

3 Willow House
Kennington Road
Ashford
Kent TN24 0NR
Tel: 01233 633936
Fax: 01233 633836
email: info@nvala.org
Director: John C Beyer
Founder & President Emeritus: Mary
Whitehouse CBE
Concerned with moral standards in
the media

NESTA (The National Endowment for Science, Technology and the Arts)
Fishmongers' Chambers
110 Upper Thames Street
London, EC4R 3TJ
Tel: 0207 645 9500
Fax: 0207 645 9501
email: nesta@nesta.org.uk
Website: www.nesta.org.uk
Chief Executive: Jeremy Newton
Chairman: Lord Puttnam
NESTA was set up in July 1998 under the National Lottery Act 1998 and launched on June 30th 1999. £200 million of National Lottery money was committed to Britain's first ever national endowment. The work falls into three main areas: fellowships – helping exceptional individuals so they can pursue their ideas and fulfil their potential; invention and innovation – helping people develop ideas that can be exploited for commercial and social benefit; education – helping to communicate the importance of creativity in all our lives.

New Producers Alliance (NPA)
9 Bourlet Close
London W1W 7BP
Tel: 020 7580 2480
Fax: 020 7580 2484
email: queries@npa.org.uk
Website: newproducer.org.uk
Established in 1993 by a group of young producers building upon their shared desire to make commercial films for an international audience, NPA has now grown to a membership of more than 1,300. NPA is an independent networking organisation providing members with access to contacts, information, free legal advice and general help regarding film production. NPA publishes a monthly newsletter and organises meetings, workshops and seminars. Membership is available to producers, directors and writers affiliates (individuals other than the above) and corporate bodies

Northern Ireland Film Commission
21 Ormeau Avenue
Belfast BT2 8HD
Tel: 028 9023 2444
Fax: 028 9023 9918
email: info@nifc.co.uk
Website: www.nifc.co.uk
The Northern Ireland Film Commission promotes the growth of film and television culture and the industry in Northern Ireland

Office for National Statistics
1 Drummond Gate
London SW1V 2QQ
Tel: 020 7533 5725

Office of Fair Trading
Field House
15–25 Bream's Buildings
London EC4A 1PR
Tel: 020 7242 2858
Fax: 020 7269 8800
The Director General of Fair Trading has an interest in the supply of films for exhibition in cinemas. Following a report by the Monopolies and Mergers Commission (MMC) in 1994, the Director General has taken action to ensure that the adverse public interest findings of the MMC are remedied. Under the Broadcasting Act 1990, he also has two specific roles in relation to the television industry. In his report published in December 1992 he assessed the Channel 3 networking arrangement and from 1 January 1993 he had to monitor the BBC's progress towards a statutory requirement to source 25 per cent of its qualifying programming from independent producers

PACT (Producers Alliance for Cinema and Television)
45 Mortimer Street
London W1N 7TD
Tel: 020 7331 6000
Fax: 020 7331 6700
email: enquiries@pact.co.uk
Website: www.pact.co.uk
Chief Executive: Shaun Williams
Membership Officer: David Alan Mills
PACT exists to serve the feature film and independent television production sector. Currently representing 1,400 companies, PACT is the UK contact point for co–production, co–finance partners and distributors. Membership services include a dedicated industrial relations unit, legal documentation and back–up, a varied calendar of events, courses and business advice, representation at international film and television markets, a comprehensive research programme, publication of a monthly magazine, an annual members' directory, a number of specialist guidebooks, affiliation with European and international producers' organisations, plus extensive information and production advice. PACT works for participants in the industry at every level and operates a members' regional network throughout the UK with a divisional office in Scotland. PACT lobbies actively with broadcasters, financiers and governments to ensure that the producer's voice is heard and understood in Britain and Europe

Pearl & Dean
3 Waterhouse Square
138–142 Holborn
London EC1N 2NY
Tel: 020 7882 1100
Fax: 020 7882 1111

Performing Right Society (PRS)
29–33 Berners Street
London W1T 3AB
Tel: 020 7580 5544
Fax: 020 7306 4455
Website: www.prs.co.uk
PRS is a non–profit making association of composers, authors and publishers of musical works. It collects and distributes royalties for the use, in public performances, broadcasts and cable programmes, of its members' copyright music and has links with other performing right societies throughout the world

Phonographic Performance (PPL)
1 Upper James Street
London W1F 9DE
Tel: 020 7534 1000
Fax: 020 7534 1111
Head of External Affairs: Colleen Hue
Controls public performance and broadcasting rights in sound recordings on behalf of approximately 2,000 record companies in the UK. The users of sound recordings licensed by PPL range from BBC and independent TV and Radio, pan–European satellite services, night clubs and juke boxes, to pubs, shops, hotels etc

The Production Guild of Great Britain
Pinewood Studios
Pinewood Road
Iver Heath
Bucks SL0 0NH
Tel: 01753 651767
Fax: 01753 652803

email: admin@productionguild.com
Website: www.productionguild.com
Angela Pyle, Secretariat
President: Michael O'Sullivan
Organisation for senior management
employed within the British Film and
Television industry. The guild strives
to be the first port of call for both the
studios and production companies
looking for experienced management
teams but more importantly and
additionally, will become a
meaningful point of consultation for
Government and Industry bodies
when planning new legislation etc.

Production Managers Association (PMA)
Ealing Studios
Ealing Green
Ealing
London W5 5EP
Tel: 020 8758 8699
Fax: 020 8758 8658
email: pma@pma.org.uk
Website: www.pma.org.uk
C. Fleming
Represents over 140 broadcast
production managers who all have at
least three years experience and six
broadcast credits. Provides a network
of like–minded individuals

Radio, Electrical and Television Retailers' Association (RETRA)
Retra House
St John's Terrace
1 Ampthill Street
Bedford MK42 9EY
Tel: 01234 269110
Fax: 01234 269609
Fred Round
Founded in 1942, RETRA represents
the interests of electrical retailers to
all those who make decisions likely
to affect the selling and servicing of
electrical and electronic products

The Royal Photographic Society
Milsom Street
Bath, Avon BA1 1DN
Tel: 01225 462841
Fax: 01225 448688
email: rps@rps.org
Website: www.rps.org
A learned society founded for the
promotion and enjoyment of all
aspects of photography. Contains a
specialist Film and Video Group,
secretary John Tarby, FRPS, with a
regular journal, meetings and the
opportunity to submit productions for

the George Sewell Trophy and the
Hugh Baddeley Trophy; and an
Audiovisual group, secretary Brian
Jenkins, LRPS, offering an extensive
programme of events, seminars and
demonstrations, and the bi–monthly
magazine *AV News*. Membership
open to both amateur and
professional photographers

Royal Television Society
Holborn Hall
100 Grays Inn Road
London WC1X 8AL
Tel: 020 7430 1000
Fax: 020 7430 0924
email: info@rts.org.uk
Website: www.rts.org.uk
Dep. Exec. Director: Claire Price
The RTS, founded in 1927, has over
4,000 members in the UK and
overseas, which are serviced by the
Society's 17 regional centres. The
Society aims to bring together all the
disciplines of television by providing
a forum for debate on the technical,
cultural and social implications of the
medium. This is achieved through the
many lectures, conferences, symposia
and workshops and master classes
organised each year. The RTS does
not run formal training courses. The
RTS publishes a journal ten times a
year, *Television*. The RTS organises
awards for journalism, sports, craft
and design, education, general
programmes and student television

Scottish Arts Council
12 Manor Place
Edinburgh EH3 7DD
Tel: 0131 226 6051
Fax: 0131 225 9833
Website: sac.org.uk
Director: Tessa Jackson
See entry for Scottish Film Council,
the lead body for film in Scotland

Scottish Screen
Second Floor
249 West George Street
Glasgow G2 4QE
Tel: 0141 302 1700
Fax: 0141 302 1711
email: info@scottishscreen.com
Website: www.scottishscreen.com
Chief Executive: John Archer
(See Regional Film Commissions)
Scottish Screen is responsible to the
Scottish Parliament for developing all
aspects of screen industry and culture
in Scotland through script and
company development, short film
production, distribution of National
Lottery film production finance,

training, education, exhibition
funding, the Film Commission
locations support and the Scottish
Film and Television Archive

The Script Factory
Linton House
24 Wells Street
London W1P 3FG
Tel: 020 7323 1414
Fax: 020 7323 9464
email: general@
scriptfactory.freeserve.co.uk
Website: www.scriptfactory.com
Nadia Ward

Sgrîn (Media Agency for Wales)
The Bank, 10 Mount Stuart Square
Cardiff Bay
Cardiff CF1 6EE
Tel: 029 2033 3300
Fax: 029 2033 3320
email: sgrin@sgrin.co.uk
Website: www.sgrin.co.uk
Chief Executive: J. Berwyn
Rowlands
Sgrîn is the primary organisation for
film, television and new media in
Wales. Sgrîn promotes production,
education and exhibition, and is the
home to the Wales Film and
Television Archive and Media
Antenna Cymru Wales.

The Short Film Bureau
47 Poland Street
London W1V 3DF
Tel: 020 7734 8708
Fax: 020 7734 2406
email: info@shortbureau.com
Website: www.shortfilmbureau.com
Patrons: Sir Sydney Samuelson OBE,
Steve Woolley, Brian Cox, Kenneth
Branagh
The Bureau has two goals: To help
new filmmakers find audiences for
their work and to raise the profile and
acceptance of short films in general.
This is done by offering advice and
support on funding, production,
marketing and distribution. The
website offers professional and
practical advice on all aspects of
short film making. The Cinema
Programme provides an opportunity
for filmmakers to have their work
assessed for potential theatrical
release by UK distributors and
exhibitors.

SKILLSET
**The National Training
Organisation for Broadcast, Film,
Video and Multimedia**

103 Dean Street
London W1V 5RA
Tel: 020 7534 5300
Fax: 020 7534 5333
email: info@skillset.org
Website: www.skillset.org
Chief Executive: Dinah Caine
Director of Development: Kate
O'Connor
Communications Director: Gary
Townsend
Founded and managed by the key
employers and unions within the
industry, SKILLSET operates at a
strategic level providing relevant
labour market and training
information, encouraging higher
levels of investment in training and
developing and implementing
occupational standards and the
National and Scottish Vocation
Qualifications based upon them. It
seeks to influence national and
international education and training
policies to the industry's best
advantage, strives to create greater
and equal access to training
opportunities and career development
and assists in developing a healthier
and safer workforce. SKILLSET is a
UK–wide organisation

Society for the Study of Popular British Cinema

**Department of Media and Cultural
Production**
**Faculty of Humanities and Social
Science**
Gateway House
De Montfort University
Leicester LE1 9BH
Fax: 0116 2577199
Contact: Alan Burton, Secretary
Society which produces a newsletter
and the *Journal of Popular British
Cinema* and encourages an interest in
British films

Society of Authors' Broadcasting Group

84 Drayton Gardens
London SW10 9SB
Tel: 020 7373 6642
Fax: 020 7373 5768
email: authorsoc@writer.org.uk
Specialities: Radio, television and
film scriptwriters

Society of Cable Telecommunication Engineers (SCTE)

Fulton House Business Centre
Fulton Road, Wembley Park
Middlesex HA9 0TF

Tel: 020 8902 8998
Fax: 020 8903 8719
email: office@scte.org.uk
Website: www.scte.org.uk
Mrs Beverley K Allgood FSAE
Aims to raise the standard of cable
telecommunication engineering to the
highest technical level, and to elevate
and improve the status and efficiency
of those engaged in cable
telecommunication engineering

Society of Film Distributors (SFD)

22 Golden Square
London W1F 9JW
Tel: 020 7437 4383
Fax: 020 7734 0912
D C Hunt, Chief Executive, A.F.
Pearce, President
SFD was founded in 1915 and
membership includes all the major
distribution companies and several
independent companies. It promotes
and protects its members' interests
and co–operates with all other film
organisations and Government
agencies where distribution interests
are involved

Society of Television Lighting Directors

4 The Orchard
Aberthin
Cowbridge
South Glamorgan CF7 7HU
The Society provides a forum for the
exchange of ideas in all aspects of
the TV profession including
techniques and equipment. Meetings
are organised throughout the UK and
abroad. Technical information and
news of members' activities are
published in the Society's magazine

TAC (Welsh Independent Producers)

Gronant
Caernarfon
Gwynedd LL55 1NS
Tel: 01286 671123
Fax: 01286 678890
email: tac@taccyf.demon.co.uk
Website: www.taccyf.demon.co.uk
Dafydd Hughes
TAC is the trade association
representing the 95 production
companies working for Welsh
broadcasters. It offers a full IR
service and conducts negotiations on
standard terms of trade with the
broadcasters

Variety Club of Great Britain

Variety Club House
93 Bayham Street
London NW1 0AG
Tel: 020 7428 8100
Fax: 020 7428 8111
email: info@varietyclub.org.uk
Website: www.varietyclub.org.uk
Ginny Martin
Charity dedicated to helping disabled
and disadvantaged children
throughout Great Britain

Videola (UK)

Paramount House
162/170 Wardour Street
London W1V 3AT
Tel: 020 7437 2136
Fax: 020 7437 5413

VLV – Voice of the Listener and Viewer

101 King's Drive
Gravesend
Kent DA12 5BQ
Tel: 01474 352835
Fax: 01474 351112
email: vlv@btinternet.com
Website: www.vlv.org.uk
Linda Forbes
An independent non–profit making
society which represents the citizen
and consumer interest in broadcasting
and which supports the principle of
public service in broadcasting.
Founded in 1983, by Jocelyn Hay,
VLV is the only consumer body
speaking for listeners and viewers on
the full range of broadcasting issues.
VLV has over 2,000 members, more
than 20 corporate members (most of
which are registered charities) and
over 50 colleges and university
departments in academic
membership. VLV is funded by its
members and free from any sectarian,
commercial or political links. Holds
public lectures, conferences and
seminars and arranges exclusive
visits for its members to broadcasting
centres in different parts of the
country. Publishes a quarterly
newsletter and briefings on
broadcasting developments. Has
responded to all parliamentary and
public inquiries on broadcasting since
1984 and to consultations by the ITC,
Radio Authority, BBC and
Broadcasting Standards Council since
1990. Is in frequent touch with MPs,
civil servants, the BBC and
independent broadcasters, regulators,
academics and relevant consumer

bodies at UK and European level. Holds the archive of the former independent Broadcasting Research Unit and of the former British Action for Children's Television (BACTV) and makes these available for a small fee together with its own archives and library. Set up the VLV Forum for Children's Broadcasting in 1994

Women in Film and Television (UK)
6 Langley Street
London WC2H 9JA
Tel: 020 7240 4875
Fax: 020 7379 1625
email: info@wftv.org.uk
Director: Kate Norrish
Administrator: Donna Coyle
A membership organisation for women working in the film and television industries. WFTV aims to provide information and career support through a monthly programme of events that are free to members. In addition WFTV safeguards the interests of the members through its lobbying and campaigning. WFTV exists to protect and enhance the status, interests and diversity of women working at all levels in both film and television.

Writers' Guild of Great Britain
430 Edgware Road
London W2 1EH
Tel: 020 7723 8074
Fax: 020 7706 2413
email: postie@wggb.demon.co.uk
Website: www.writers.org.uk/guild
The Writers' Guild is the recognised TUC–affiliated trade union for writers working in film, television, radio, theatre and publishing

Regional film commissions and film offices

Bath Film Office
Abbey Chambers
Abbey Churchyard
Bath BA1 1LY
Tel: 01225 477711
Fax: 01225 477221
email: bath_filmoffice@bathnes.gov.uk
Maggie Ainley, Film Commissioner
As a member of the UK Screen Commission Network, the Bath Film Office offers a free service for TV, film and commercials in Bath and North East Somerset. This covers a wide range of city and country locations, together with access to a comprehensive database of experienced local crew and facilities based in the region

Central England Screen Commission
2/2 Broad Street
Birmingham B15 1AY
Tel: 0121 643 9309
Fax: 0121 643 9064
Website: www.central–screen.co.u

East Midlands Arts Board
Mountfields House
Epinal Way
Loughborough
Leicestershire LE11 0QE
Tel: 01509 218292
Fax: 01509 262214
email: info@em–arts.co.uk
Website: www.arts.org.uk
Chief Executive: John Buston
Caroline Pick, Film, Video and Broadcasting Officer, Suzanne Alizart – Officer (Film, Digital Arts and Broadcasting) Derbyshire (excluding High Peak District), Leicestershire, Northamptonshire, Nottinghamshire, Rutland, Lincolnshire

East Midlands Screen Commission
Broadway
14–18 Broad Street
Nottingham NG1 3AL
Tel: 0115 910 5564
Fax: 0115 910 5563
email: emsc@org.uk
Website: www.emsc.org.uk
Phil Nodding/Sarah Eccleston
Covers Nottinghamshire, Northamptonshire, Derbyshire, Leicestershire, Rutland and Lincolnshire

Eastern Arts Board
Cherry Hinton Hall
Cherry Hinton Road
Cambridge CB1 8DW
Tel: 01223 215355
Fax: 01223 248075
email: info@eastern–arts.co.uk
Website: www.arts.org.uk
Chief Executive: Andrea Stark
Arts Development Officer (Broadcasting): Martin Ayres
Bedfordshire, Essex, Cambridgeshire, Hertfordshire, Norfolk and Suffolk

Eastern Screen
Anglia House
Norwich NR1 3JG
Tel: 01603 767077
Fax: 01603 767191
Website: easternscreen.com
The Film Commission for the East of England offering free help and advice on locations, facilities companies local services and crew to anyone intending to film within the region

Edinburgh Film Focus
Castlecliff
25 Johnston Terrace
Edinburgh EH1 2NH
Tel: 0131 622 7337
Fax: 0131 622 7338
email: edinfilm@ednet.co.uk
Website: www.elas.hw.ac.uk/film/html
George Carlaw, Ros Davis
The Film Commission for the City of Edinburgh and the coastline, countryside and counties of Lothian and the Scottish Borders. Free advice on locations, crews, facilities and liaison with local authorities

English Regional Arts Boards
5 City Road
Winchester, Hants SO23 8SD
Tel: 01962 851063
Fax: 01962 842033
email: info@erab.org.uk
Website: www.arts.org.uk
Carolyn Nixson, Administrator
Chief Executive: Christopher Gordon
Liaison, lobbying, information and support for Regional Arts Boards

Film Dundee
Dept of Economic Development
Dundee City Council
3 City Square
Dundee DD1 3BA
Tel: 01382 434 914
Fax: 01382 434 650
email: vlynch@dundeecity.gov.uk
Website: www.dundeecity.gov.uk

Covers the City of Dundee, Angus and perth and Kinross

Glasgow Film Office
City Chambers
George Square
Glasgow G2 1DU
Tel: 0141 287 0424
Fax: 0141 287 0311
Website: www.glasgowfilm.org.uk

Herts Film Link
South Way
Leavesden
Hertfordshire WD2 7LZ
Tel: 01923 495 051
Fax: 01923 333007
email: hfl@herts–filmlink.co.uk
Website: www.hertsfilmlink.com
Roger Harrop

Isle of Man Film Commission
Illiam Dhone House
2 Circular Road
Douglas
Isle of Man 1M1 1PJ
Tel: 01624 685864
Fax: 01624 685454
email: filmcomm@dti.gov.im
Website: www.gov.im/dti/iomfilm
Hilary Dugdale, Project Manager
Nick Cain, Contracts Manager
Kim Fletcher, Film Officer

Lancashire Film and Television Office
Unit G14
Preston Technology Management Centre
Marsh Lane
Preston
Lancashire PR1 8UD
Tel: 01772 889090
Fax: 01772 889091
email: lftvo@hotmail.com
David Nelson
Lynda Banister

Lanarkshire Screen Locations
Dept of Planning & Environment
Economic Development Unit,
North Lanarkshire Council
Fleming House, Tryst Road
Cumbernaultd G67 1JW
Tel: 01236 812 387
Fax: 01236 431 068
email: leslie@northlan.gov.uk
Covers North Lanarkshire, South Lanarkshire

Liverpool Film Office
Pioneer Buildings
67 Dale Street

Liverpool L2 2NS
Tel: 0151 291 9191
Fax: 0151 291 9199
email: ifo@dial.pipex.com
Lynn Saunders, Film Commissioner
Information and Liaison: Tracy Riley
Provides a free film liaison service, and assistance to all productions intending to use locations, resources, services and skills in the Merseyside area. Undertakes research and location scouting, liaises with local agencies and the community. Offers access to the best range of locations in the UK through its extensive locations library. Eleven years experience of providing a quality one–stop shop service

London Arts Board
Elme House
133 Long Acre
Covent Garden
London WC2E 9AF
Tel: 020 7240 1313
Fax: 020 7670 2400
email: firstname.surname@lonab.co.uk
Website: www.arts.org.uk/lab
The London Arts Board has no dedicated funds for Film and Video. However, it does offer awards to individual artists working in the medium of film and video and New Media. Write to LAB at the above address for funding guidelines. For all other film and video enquiries, call the London Film and Video Development Agency (qv)

London Film and Video Development Agency (LFVDA)
2nd Floor
25 Gosfield Street
London WIP 7HB
Tel: 020 7637 3577
Fax: 020 7637 3578
Chief Executive: Steve McIntyre
Education and Training Officer: Tricia Jenkins
The area of the 32 London Boroughs and the City of London

Media Development Agency for the West Midlands incorporating Central England Screen Commission
Broad Street House
3rd Floor, 212 Broad Street
Birmingham B15 IAY
Tel: 0121 643 9309
Fax: 0121 643 9064
email: info@mda–wm.org.uk

Website: www.cesc–online.org.uk
Media Development Agency for the West Midlands and Central England Screen Commission, Directory & Database of local production facilities, crews and talents; location finding and liaison: low budget production funding including First Cut Production scheme; information resources and counselling service; legal surgeries; seminars and masterclasses; media business development support; copyright registration scheme

Mid Wales Film Commission
6G Science Park Cefn Llan,
Aberystwyth
Ceredigion SY23 3AH
Tel: 01970 617995
Fax: 01970 617942
email: info@midwalesfilm.com
Website: www.midwalesfilm.com
Mid Wales Film Commission seeks to promote the use of Mid Wales facilities and locations for the production of films, television programmes and commercial

North Wales Film Commission
Mentee, Deiniol Road
Bangor
Gwynedd LL57 2UP
Tel: 01286 679685
Fax: 01286 673324
email: fil@gwynedd.gov.uk
Hugh Edwin Jones, Peter Lowther
Area film liaison office for information on filming in the county of Gwynedd and Anglesey. Information provided on locations, facilities and crew

North West Arts Board
Manchester House
22 Bridge Street
Manchester M3 3AB
Tel: 0161 834 6644
Fax: 0161 834 6969
email: jleather@nwarts.co.uk
Website: www.arts.org.uk/nwab
Julie Leather, Administrator
Information
Chief Executive: Sue Harrison
Howard Rifkin: Director of Visual and Media Arts
Arts development organisation for the North West – Cheshire, Greater Manchester, Lancashire, Merseyside, High Peak of Derbyshire

North West England Film & Television Commission
Pioneer Buildings

65–67 Dale Street
Liverpool L2 2NS
Tel: 0151 330–6666
Fax: 0151 330–6611
email: ftc@nwengland.co.uk
Andrew Patrick: Chief Executive
Helen Bingham: Director of
Marketing & Information

Northern Arts
Ground Floor
Central Square
Forth Street
Newcastle upon Tyne NE1 3PJ
Tel: 0191 255 8500
Fax: 0191 230 5566
email: info@northernarts.org.uk
Website: www.arts.org.uk
Chief Executive: Andrew Dixon
Head of Film, Media and Literature:
Mark Robinson
Teesside, Cumbria, Durham,
Northumberland, Tyne and Wear

Northern Screen Commission (NSC)
Bio Science Centre
International Centre For Life
Times Square
Newcastle upon Tyne NE1 4EP
Tel: 0191 233 9234
Fax: 0191 233 9233
email: nsc@filmhelp.demon.co.uk
Website: www.nsc.org.uk
Peter Spark
Seeking to attract film, video and
television production to the North of
England, NSC can provide a full
liaison service backed by a network
of local authority contacts and public
organisations. Available at no cost is
a locations library, a database on
local facilities and services as well as
a full list of local crew or talent

Scottish Highlands and Islands Film Commission
Coimisean Fiolm na
Gaidhealtachd's nan Eilean Alba
Inverness Castle
Inverness IV2 3EG
Tel: 01463 710221
Fax: 01463 710848
email: trish@scotfilm.org
Website: www.scotfilm.org
Trish Shorthouse, Gordon Ireland,
Anne Wilson
The Scottish Highlands and Islands
Film Commission provides a free,
comprehensive liaison service to the
film and television industry, including
information and advice on locations,
permissions, crew and services etc.
We cover Argyll and Bute, Highland,
Moray, Orkney, Shetland and the

Western Isles, and have a network of
local film liaison officers able to
provide quick and expert local help

Scottish Screen
Second Floor
249 West George Street
Glasgow G2 4QE
Tel: 0141 302 1700
Fax: 0141 302 1711
email: info@scottishscreen.com
Website: www.scottishscreen.com
Chief Executive: John Archer
Scottish Screen promotes Scotland as
an international filming destination
and encourages incoming production
by co–ordinating locations enquiries.
Working in partnership with area
offices Scottish Screen provides
detailed support on locations,
crewing and facilities and has a
library of 35,000 stills covering 4,000
locations, all on database

South East Arts Board
Union House
Eridge Road
Tunbridge Wells
Kent TN4 8HF
Tel: 01892 507200
Fax: 01892 549383
email: info@seab.co.uk
Website: www.arts.org.uk
Chief Executive: Felicity Harvest
East Sussex, Kent, Surrey and West
Sussex

South Wales Film Commission
The Media Centre
Culverhouse Cross
Cardiff Cf5 6XJ
Tel: 029 2059 0240
Fax: 029 2059 0511
email: southwalesfilm@
compuserve.com
Website: www.southwalesfilm.com
Yvonne Cheal, Commissioner
A member of the British Film
Commission and AFCI, providing
information on locations, media
facilities and services across south
Wales for film and television
productions

South West Film Commission (South)
18 Belle Vue Road
Saltash
Cornwall PL12 6ES
Tel: 01752 841199
Fax: 01752 841254
email: infosouth@swfilm.co.uk
Website: www.swfilm.co.uk
Film Commissioner: Sue Dalziel

Offers professional assistance to
productions shooting in Devon,
Cornwall, Somerset, Dorset, Bristol
City, Gloucestershire, Wiltshire
South West Film Commission
(North)
59 Prince Street
Bristol B51 4QH
Tel: 0117 907 4315
Fax: 0117 907 4384
email: infonorth@swfilm.co.uk

South West Media Development Agency
59 Prince Street
Bristol BS1 4QH
Tel: 0117 9273226
Fax: 0117 9226216
email: swmda@eurobell.co.uk
Website: swmediadevagency.co.uk
Chief Executive: Judith
Higginbottom
Projects and Clients Manager:
Sarah–Jane Meredith
Cornwall, Devon,Somerset, Bristol,
Gloucestershire. All of Dorset except
Christchurch, Bournemouth and
Poole and The Unitary Authorities of
South Gloucestershire, North
Somerset, Bath and North East
Somerset, Plymouth and Torbay

South West Scotland Screen Commission
Gracefield Arts Centre
28 Edinburgh Road
Dumfries DG1 1NW
Tel: 01387 263666
Fax: 01387 263666
email: screencom@dumgal.gov.uk
Selle Doyle
An unrivalled variety and wealth of
locations to suit any style of shoot or
budget, plus a free location finding
and film liaison service for South
West Scotland

Southern Arts Board
13 St Clement Street
Winchester
Hampshire SO23 9DQ
Tel: 01962 855099
Fax: 01962 861186
email: info@southernarts.co.uk
Website: www.arts.org.uk
Chief Executive: Robert Hutchison
Film, Video and Broadcasting
Officer: Jane Gerson
Berkshire, Buckinghamshire, South
East Dorset, Hampshire, Isle of
Wight, Oxfordshire and Wiltshire

Southern Screen Commission
Town Hall

Bartholomew Square
Brighton BN1 1JP
Tel: 01273 384211
Fax: 01273 384212
email: southernscreen@
pavilion.co.uk
Sarah Bayliss, Project Co–ordinator
Southern Screen promotes and
markets locations, personnel and
services in the South East to the film
and television industries

West Midlands Arts Board

82 Granville Street
Birmingham B1 2LH
Tel: 0121 631 3121
Fax: 0121 643 7239
Website: www.west–midlands.arts.
org.uk
Chief Executive: Sally Luton
Media Officer (Film & Video):
Laurie Hayward
Herefordshire, Worcestershire,
Shropshire, The Wrekin and Telford,
Staffordshire, Stoke on Trent,
Warwickshire, and the Metropolitan
Districts of the West Midlands

Yorkshire and Humberside Arts Board

21 Bond Street
Dewsbury
West Yorks WF13 1AX
Tel: 01924 455555
Fax: 01924 466522
Website: www.arts.org.uk
Chief Executive: Roger Lancaster
Film and Broadcasting Officer: Terry
Morden
Yorkshire and The Humber

Yorkshire Screen Commission

The Workstation
15 Paternoster Row
Sheffield S1 2BX
Tel: 0114 279 9115
Fax: 0114 279 8593
email: ysc@workstation.org.uk
Website: www.ysc.co.uk
Liz Rymer, Commissioner
Alison Ollivent – Crew & Facilities
Manager
Kaye Elliott – Film Liaison Officer
YSC facilitates film and tv
production in the Yorkshire and
Humber region and operates a
location–finding and crewing service
in addition to negotiating location use
and securing permissions

US Organisations

American Film Institute

P.O. Box 27999/ 2021
North Western Avenue
Los Angeles, CA 90027
Tel: (323) 856–7600
Fax: Fax (323) 467–4578
Website: www.afionline.org/
The John F. Kennedy Center for the
Performing Arts
Washington, D.C. 20566
Tel: (202) 828–4000
Fax (202) 659–1970
Organisation dedicated to preserving
the heritage of film and television

AMPAS (Academy of Motion Picture Arts & Sciences)

8949 Wilshire Boulevard
Beverly Hills
CA 90211
Tel: (1) 310 247 3000
Fax: (1) 310 859 9619
Organisation of producers, actors and
others which is responsible for
widely promoting and supporting the
film industry, as well as awarding the
annual Oscars

Hollywood Foreign Press Association

292 S.LaCienega Blvd, 316
Beverly Hills
CA 90211
Tel: (1) 310 657 1731
Fax: (1) 310 657 5576
Journalists reporting on the
entertainment industry for non–US
media. Annual event; Golden Globe
Awards – awarding achievements in
motion pictures and television

Museum of Television and Radio

25 West 52 Street
New York
NY 10019
Tel: (1) 212 621 6600/6800
Fax: (1) 212 621 6715
The Museum (formerly The Museum
of Broadcasting) collects and preserves
television and radio programmes and
advertising commercials, and makes
them available to the public. The
collection, which now includes nearly
60,000 programmes, covers 70 years
of news, public affairs programmes,
documentaries, performing arts,
children's programming, sports, and
comedy. The Museum organises
exhibitions, and screening and
listening series

ORGANISATIONS (EUROPE)

The following is a list of some of the main pan–European film and television organisations, entries for countries of the European Union and the various MEDIA II projects instigated by the European Commission

Pan–European Organisations

ACE (Ateliers du Cinéma Européen/European Film Studio)
68 rue de Rivoli
75004 Paris
France
Tel: (33) 1 44 61 88 30
Fax: (33) 1 44 61 88 40
email: ace@pelnet.com
Director: Sophie Bourdon
ACE is a year–long training–through–projects and development programme designed for independent European cinema producers who have already produced at least one feature film. The selected producers then remain part of the ACE Producers' Network

AGICOA (Association de Gestion Internationale Collective des Oeuvres Audio–Visuelles)
rue de St–Jean 26
1203 Geneva
Switzerland
Tel: (41) 22 340 32 00
Fax: (41) 22 340 34 32
Rodolphe Egli, Luigi Cattaneo
AGICOA ensures the protection of the rights of producers worldwide when their works are retransmitted by cable. By entering their works in the AGICOA Registers, producers can claim royalties collected for them

Audio–Visual EUREKA
Permanent Secretariat
rue de la Bonté 5–7
1000 Brussels,
Belgium
Tel: (32) 2 543 76 60
Fax: (32) 2 538 04 39
email: secretariat@aveureka.be
Website: www.aveureka.be
Director: Sylivie Forbin
Audiovisual Eureka is a Pan–European Intergovernmental Organisation for the promotion of cooperation in the European Audiovisual Sector. Membership consists of the 35 members including the European Commission (member) and the Council of Europe (associate member). From 1996–1998 Audiovisual Eureka concentrated on Training (1996), Development (1997) and Distribution (1998). Currently Audiovisual Eureka is focusing on consolidation of the works undertaken so far and accomplishing an external evaluation of the actions and initiatives launched since 1996

Bureau de Liaison Européen du Cinéma
74 avenue Kliber
75016 Paris
Tel: (33) 1 42 66 05 32
Fax: (33) 1 42 66 96 92
email: film.paris@wanaduu.fr
Gilbert Grégoire
Umbrella grouping of cinema trade organisations in order to promote the cinema industry, including CICCE, FEITIS, FIAD, FIAPF, FIPFI and UNIC

Centre for Cultural Research
Am Hofgarten 17
53113 Bonn
Germany
Tel: (49) 228 211058
Fax: (49) 228 217493
Scharfschwerdtstr. 10
16540 Hohen Neuendorf
c/o IKM, Karlsplatz 2
1010 Vienna, Austria
Prof Andreas Johannes Wiesand
Research, documentation, and advisory tasks in all fields of the arts and media, especially with 'European' perspectives. Participation in arts and media management courses at university level. Produces publications and is founding seat of the European Institute for Comparative Cultural Policy and the Arts (ERIC Arts) with members in 21 European countries

EURIMAGES
Council of Europe
Palais de l'Europe
avenue de l'Europe
67075 Strasbourg Cédex, France
Tel: (33) 88 41 26 40
Fax: (33) 88 41 27 60
Website: www.culture.coe.
fr/eurimages
Contact: Executive Secretary
Founded in 1988 by a group of Council of Europe member states. Its objective is to stimulate film and audio–visual production by partly financing the co–production, distribution and exhibition of European cinematographic and audio–visual works. Eurimages now includes 24 member state

Eurocréation Media
rue Debelleyme 3
75003 Paris, France
Tel: (33) 1 44 59 27 01
Fax: (33) 1 40 29 92 46
Jean–Pierre Niederhauser,
Anne–Marie Autissier (Consultant)
Eurocréation Media develops consultation and expertise in the field of European audio–visual and cinema (research, support for the organisation and conception of European events, training activities)

European Academy for Film & Television
rue Verte 69
1210 Brussels, Belgium
Tel: (32) 2 218 66 07
Fax: (32) 2 217 55 72
Permanent Secretary: Dimitri Balachoff
The purpose of the Academy, a non–profit making association, is the research, development and disclosure of all matters relating to cinema and television chiefly in the European continent, and also in other continents, taking into account artistic, commercial, cultural, economic, financial, historical, institutional, pedagogical, trade union and technical aspects. Quarterly newsletter, *ACANEWS*

European Audio–visual Observatory

76 allée de la Robertsau
67000 Strasbourg, France
Tel: (33) 3 88 144400
Fax: (33) 3 88 144419
Website: www.obs.coe.int/
Executive Director: Nils Klevjer
AAS. A Pan–European institution
working in the legal framework of
the Council of Europe. The
Observatory is a public service centre
providing information on the
European television, film and video
industries, aimed at the audio–visual
industry, and available in English,
French and German. It provides
legal, economic and market, and film
and television funding related
information and counselling, and is
working with a network of partner
organisations on the developing
harmonisation of data covering the
whole of Europe. The Observatory
also publishes a monthly newsletter
(*IRIS*) on legal development in all of
its 33 member States, as well as an
annual *Statistical Yearbook on Film,
Television, Video and New Media* and
a *Legal Guide to Audiovisual Media*
in Europe. The internet site of the
Observatory provides a substantial
number of additional reports

European Broadcasting Union (EBU)

Ancienne Route 17a
1218 Grand–Saconnex
Geneva, Switzerland
Tel: (41) 22 717 2111
Fax: (41) 22 717 2200
Website: www.ebu.ch/
Jean–Pierre Julien
The EBU is a professional
association of national broadcasters
with 117 members in 79 countries.
Principal activities: daily exchange of
news, sports and cultural
programmes for television
(Eurovision) and radio (Euroradio);
Tv coproductions; technical studies
and legal action in the international
broadcasting sphere

European Coordination of Film Festivals

64 rue Philippe le Bon
1000 Bruxelles
Tel: (32) 2 280 13 76
Fax: (32) 2 230 91 41
email: cefc@skypro.be
Website: www.eurofilmfest.org
Marie José Carta

A network of 150 audio–visual
festivals in Europe to promote the
diversity of the European moving
image through collaboration projects
such as touring programmes, staff
exchanges, research and conferences
on the socio–economic impact of
film festivals, electronic subtitling
and sponsorship, the quarterly
newsletter (*EuroFilmFest*). The
Coordination is funded by MEDIA

European Co–production Association

c/o France 2
22 avenue Montaigne
75387 Paris Cedex 08
France
Tel: (33) 1 4421 4126
Fax: (33) 1 4421 5179
A consortium of, at present, six
European public service television
networks for the co–production of
television programmes. Can offer
complete finance. Proposals should
consist of full treatment, financial
plan and details of proposed
co–production partners. Projects are
proposed to the ECA Secretariat or to
member national broadcasters

European Film Academy (EFA)

Kurfurstendamm 225
D–10719 Berlin
Germany
Tel: (49) 30 88 71 67 – 0
Fax: (49) 30 88 71 67 77
Chairman: Nik Powell,
Director: Marion Döring
Promotes European cinema
worldwide to strengthen its
commercial and artistic position, to
improve the knowledge and
awareness of European cinema and to
pass on the substantial experience of
the Academy members to the
younger generation of film
professionals. The European Film
Academy presents the annual
European Film Awards

European Institute for the Media (EIM)

Kaistrasse 13
40221 Düsseldorf, Germany
Tel: (49) 211 90 10 40
Fax: (49) 211 90 10 456
Head of Research: Runar Woldt
Head of East–West: Dusoun Rejic
Acting Head of Library,
Documentation and Statistics Centre:
Helga Schmid
A forum for research and
documentation in the field of media

in Europe. Its activities include:
research into the media in Europe
with a political, economic and
juridicial orientation; the organisation
of conferences and seminars such as
the annual European Television and
Film Forum; East–West
Co–operation Programme; the
development of an advanced studies
programme for students and media
managers. Publication of the Bulletin
in English/French/German, quarterly
on European media development, and
of the Ukrainian and Russian Bulletin
as well as research reports. Officers
in Kiev and Moscow. Organises the
European Media Summer School, an
annual course on media development
for advanced students and
professionals, and facilitates an
information request service

EUTELSAT (European Telecommunications Satellite Organisation)

Tour Maine–Montparnasse
avenue du Maine 33
75755 Paris Cédex 15, France
Tel: (33) 1 45 38 47 47
Fax: (33) 1 45 38 37 00
Website: www.eutelsat.org/
Vanessa O'Connor
EUTELSAT operates a satellite
system for intra–European
communications of all kinds. Traffic
carried includes Television and Radio
channels, programme exchanges,
satellite newsgathering, telephony
and business communications

Fédération Européenne des Industries Techniques de l'Image et du Son (FEITIS)

avenue Marceau 50
75008 Paris
France
Tel: (33) 1 47 23 07 45
Fax: (33) 1 47 23 70 47
A federation of European professional
organisations representing those
working in film and video services
and facilities in all audio–visual and
cinematographic markets

Federation Internationale de la Press et Cinématographique (International Federation of Film Critics) (FIPRESCI)

Schleissheimer Str 83
D–80797 Munich
Tel: (49) 89 18 23 03
Fax: (49) 89 18 47 66
Klaus Eder, General Secretary

Fédération Internationale des Producteurs de Films Indépendants (FIPFI)

avenue Marceau 50
75008 Paris
France
Tel: (33) 1 47 23 70 30
Fax: (33) 1 47 20 78 17
Federation of independent film producers, currently with members in 21 countries. It is open to all independent producers, either individual or groups, provided they are legally registered as such. FIPFI aims to promote the distribution of independent films, to increase possibilities for co–production, to share information between member countries and seeks to defend freedom of expression

FIAD (Fédération Internationale des Associations de Distributeurs de Films)

74 avenue Kliber
75016 Paris
Tel: (33) 1 42 66 05 32
Fax: (33) 1 42 66 96 92
email: film.paris@wanaduu.fr
Président: Gilbert Grégoire
Président d'honneur: Luc Hemelaer
Vice Président: Stephan Hutter
Secrétaire Général: Antoine Virenque
Represents the interests of film distributors

FIAPF (Fédération Internationale des Associations de Producteurs de Films)

avenue des Champs–Elysées 33
75008 Paris, France
Tel: (33) 1 42 25 62 14
Fax: (33) 1 42 56 16 52
An international level gathering of national associations of film producers (23 member countries). It represents the general interests of film producers in worldwide forums (WIPO, UNESCO, WCO, GATT) and with European authorities (EC, Council of Europe, Audio–visual EUREKA), it lobbies for better international legal protection for film and audio–visual producers

FIAT/IFTA (International Federation of Television Archives)

Tevearkivet
Sveriges Television AB RH–N2G
S–105 10 Stockholm
Sweden
Tel: (+468) 784 5740
Fax: (+468) 660 4000
FIAT membership is mainly made up of the archive services of broadcasting organisations. However it also encompasses national archives and other television–related bodies. It meets annually and publishes its proceedings and other recommendations concerning television archiving

IDATE (Institut de l'audio–visuel et de télécommunications en Europe)

BP 4167
34092 Montpelier Cédex 5
France
Tel: (33) 4 67 14 44 44
Fax: (33) 4 67 14 44 00
email: info@idate.fr
Website: www.idate.fr
Jean–Dominique Séval: Marketing and Commercial Manager

Institut de Formation et d'Enseignement pour les Métiers de l'Image et du Son (FEMIS)

rue Francoeur 6
75018 Paris
France
Tel: (33) 1 42 62 20 00
Fax: (33) 1 42 62 21 00
High level technical training in the audio–visual field for French applicants and those from outside France with a working knowledge of French. Organises regular student exchanges with other European film schools

Institut de Journalisme Robert Schuman – European Media Studies

rue de l'Association 32–34
1000 Brussels
Belgium
Tel: (32) 2 217 2355
Fax: (32) 2 219 5764
Anne de Boeck
Postgraduate training in journalism. Drawing students from all over Europe, it offers nine months intensive training in journalism for press, radio and television

International Cable Communications Council

boulevard Anspach 1, Box 34
1000 Brussels
Belgium
Tel: (32) 2 211 94 49
Fax: (32) 2 211 99 07
International body gathering European, Canadian, North American and Latin American cable television organisations

International Federation of Actors (FIA)

Guild House
Upper St Martin's Lane
London WC2H 9EG
Tel: 020 7379 0900
Fax: 020 7379 8260
Trade union federation founded in 1952 and embracing 60 performers' trade unions in 44 countries. It organises solidarity action when member unions are in dispute, researches and analyses problems affecting the rights and working conditions of film, television and theatre actors as well as singers, dancers, variety and circus artistes. It represents members in the international arena on issues such as cultural policy and copyright and publishes twice yearly newsheet *FOCUS*

ISETU/FISTAV

(International Secretariat for Arts, Mass Media and Entertainment Trade Unions/International Federation of Audio–Visual Workers)
IPC, boulevard Charlemagne 1
PO Box 5
1040 Brussels, Belgium
Tel: (32) 2 238 09 51
Fax: (32) 2 230 00 76
General Secretary: Jim Wilson
Caters to the special concerns of unions and similar associations whose members are engaged in mass media, entertainment and the arts. It is a clearing house for information regarding multi–national productions or movement of employees across national borders, and acts to exchange information about collective agreements, legal standards and practices at an international level. It organises conferences, has opened a campaign in support of public service broadcasting, and has begun initiatives ranging from defending screen writers to focusing on the concerns of special groups

The Prince's Trust Partners in Europe

8 Bedford Row
London WC1R 4BA
Tel: 020 7405 5799

Contact: Anne Engel
Offer 'Go and See' grants (max
£500) towards partnership projects in
Europe to people under 26 out of full
time education

Telefilm Canada/Europe
5 rue de Constantine
Paris 75007
Director: Sheila´de La Varende
Canadian government organisation
financing film and television
productions. European office
provides link between Canada, UK
and other European countries

UK EUREKA Unit
Department of Trade and Industry
3rd Floor, Green Core
151 Buckingham Palace Road
London SW1W 9SS
Tel: 020 7215 1618
Fax: 020 7215 1700
For Advanced Broadcasting
Technology: Brian Aldous
Tel: 020 7215 1737
A pan–European initiative to
encourage industry–led,
market–driven collaborative projects
aimed at producing advanced
technology products, processes and
services

UNIC (Union Internationale des Cinémas)
15 Rue de Berri
75008 Paris
France
Tel: (33) 1 53 93 76 76
Fax: (33) 1 45 53 29 76
Defends the interests of cinema
exhibitors worldwide, particularly in
matters of law and economics. It
publishes *UNIC News* and a Bulletin.
Also provides statistical information
and special studies concerning the
exhibition sector, to members and
others

URTI (Université Radiophonique et Télévisuelle Internationale)
General Secretariat
116, avenue du Président Kennedy
75786 Paris Cedex 16
France
Tel: (33) 1 42 30 39 98
Fax: (33) 1 40 50 89 99
President: Roland Faure
A non–governmental organisation
recognised by UNESCO and founded
in 1949, URTI is an association of
professionals in the audio–visual
field from all over the world.

Promotes cultural programmes and
organisation of projects including the
International Grand Prix for Creative
Documentaries, the Young Television
Prize at the Monte Carlo
International Television Festival, the
Grand Prix for Radio (since 1989)

Austria

Animation Studio for Experimental Animated Films
University of Applied Arts
Vienna
A – 1010 Wien Salzgries 14
Tel: (43) 1 7120392/71133–521
Fax: (43) 1 7120392
Hubert Sielecki

Association of Audio–visual and Film Industry
Wiedner Haupstrasse 63
1045 Wien
PO Box 327
Tel: (43) 1 50105/3010
Fax: (43) 1 50105/276
email: film@fafo.at
Dr Elmar Peterlunger

Austrian Film Commission
Stiftgasse 6
A–1070 Vienna
Tel: (43) 1 526 33 23–0
Fax: (43) 1 526 68 01
email: afilmco@magnet.at
Website: www.afc.at
The Austrian Film Commission is an
export and promotion agency. The
organisation, financed by public
funds, offers a wide variety of
services for Austrian producers and
creative artists, it acts as consultant
whenever its productions are
presented in international festivals,
and it provides members of the
profession in all sectors with
comprehensive information as to
current activity in the Austrian film
industry. It is the aim of all activities
to enhance the perception of Austrian
film–making abroad. In addition to
the major festivals in Berlin, Cannes,
Venice and Toronto, the Austrian
Film Commission currently provides
support for more than 300
international film festivals and
markets. The catalogue *Austrian
Films* published annually, offers an
overview, divided in sections, of
current Austrian film–making.
Otherpublications: the *Austrian Film
Guide* designed to provide quick
access to the Austrian film industry
and the newsletter *Austrian Film
News*

Austrian Film Institute
Spittelberggasse 3
A–1070 Wien
Tel: (43) 1 526 97 30
Fax: (43) 1 526 97 30/440

email: oefi@filminstitut.or.at
Website: www.filminstitut.or.at
Film funding, Eurimages and
MEDIA II

Filmakademie Wien
National Film School
Vienna Hochschule für Musik und
darstellende Kunst
Metternichgasse 12
A–1030 Wien
Tel: (43) 1 713 52 12 0
Fax: (43) 1 713 52 12 23

Wiener Film Fonds (Vienna Film Fund)
Stiftgasse 6
A –1070 Vienna
Tel: (43) 1 526 50 88
Fax: (43) 1 526 50 88 - 20
email: wff@wff.at
Website: www.wff.at/wff
Dr Peter Zawrel
The Vienna Film Fund supports
professional film making in Vienna
and is the key agency contributing to
the growth of the national film
industry which reflects Austrian
society and culture. The Vienna Film
Fund works with new and established
film makers with a commitment to
the film and culture and industry in
Vienna. The principal funding
categories are Development schemes,
Production funding for audiovisual
products of all genres and formats
and Distribution and marketing
schemes. Applicants agree to spend
at least twice the investment made by
the Vienna Film Fund in their
production. Financial support takes
either the form of an interest free
loan, to be repaid of the net profits
when the film is subsequently
completed and distributed or the form
of a non–repayable subsidy

Belgium

Cinémathèque Royale de Belgique/Royal Film Archive
Rue Ravenstein 23
1000 Brussels
Tel: (32) 2 507 83 70
Fax: (32) 2 513 12 72
email: filmarchive@ledoux.be
Gabrielle Claes
Film preservation. The collection can
be consulted on the Archive's
premises for research purposes. Edits
the Belgian film annual

Commission de Sélection de Films
Ministère de la Culture et des
Affaires Sociales
Direction de l'Audio–visuel
Boulevard Léopold II 40
1080 Brussels
Tel: (32) 2 413 22 39
Fax: (32) 2 413 22 42
Christiane Dano, Serge Meurant
Assistance given to the production of
short and long features, as well as
other audio–visual production by
independent producers

Commission du Film
Ministère de la Culture et des
Affaires Sociales
Direction de l'Audiovisuel
Boulevard Léopold II 44
1080 Brussels
Tel: (32) 2 413 22 21
Fax: (32) 2 413 20 68
Gives official recognition to Belgian
films; decides whether a film has
sufficient Belgian input to qualify as
Belgian

Film Museum Jacques Ledoux
Rue Baron Horta 9
1000 Brussels
Tel: (32) 2 507 83 70
Fax: (32) 2 513 12 72
email: filmmuseum@ledoux.be
Gabrielle Claes
Permanent exhibition of the prehistory
of cinema. Five screenings per day –
three sound, two silent. Organises one
double festival a year: L'Age d'Or
Prize and prizes for the distribution of
quality films in Belgium

IDEM
227 Chaussee D'ixelles
1050 Brussels
Tel: (32) 2 640 77 31
Fax: (32) 2 640 98 56
Trade association for television
producers

Radio–Télévision Belge de la Communauté Française (RTBF)
Blvd Auguste Reyers 52
1044 Brussels
Tel: (32) 2 737 21 11
Fax: (32) 2 737 25 56
Administrateur Général: Jean–Louis
Stalport
Public broadcaster responsible for
French language services

VRT
Auguste Reyerslaan 52

1043 Brussels
Tel: (32) 2 741 3111
Fax: (32) 2 734 9351
Managing Director: Bert De Graeve
Television: Piet Van Roe
Radio: Chris Cleeren
Public television and radio station
serving Dutch speaking Flemish
community in Belgium

Denmark

Danish Film Institute/Archive and Cinematheque
Gothersgade 55
DK – 1123 Copenhagen K
Tel: (45) 3374 3400
Fax: (45) 3374 3599
email: museum@dfi.dk
Website: www.dfi.dk
Dan Nissen, Director
The Archive and Cinematheque,
founded in 1941, is one of the
world's oldest film archives. It has a
collection of 25,000 titles from
almost every genre and country, and
has daily screenings. There is also an
extensive library of books and
pamphlets, periodicals, clippings,
posters and stills

Danmarks Radio (DR)
Morkhojvej 170
2860 Soborg
Tel: (45) 35 20 30 40
Fax: (45) 35 20 26 44
Public service television and radio
network

DFI (Danish Film Institute)
Vognmagergade 10
DK – 1120 Copenhagen
Tel: (45) 33 74 34 00
Fax: (45) 33 74 34 01
An autonomous self–governing body
under the auspices of the Ministry of
Culture, financed through the state
budget. Provides funding for the
production of Danish feature films,
shorts and documentaries, and also
supports distribution and exhibition
of feature films. Promotes Danish
films abroad and finances two
community access workshops.
Furthermore, DFI purchases and
rents out shorts and documentaries on
16mm and video to educational
institutions/Libraries and private
persons

Film–og TV
Arbejderforeningen
Danish Film and Television

Workers Union
Kongens Nytorv 21
Baghuset 3. sal
1050 Copenhagen K
Tel: (45) 33 14 33 55
Fax: (45) 33 14 33 03
Trade union which organises film, video and television workers, and maintains the professional, social, economic and artistic interests of its members. Negotiates collective agreements for feature films, documentaries, commercials, negotiating contracts, copyright and authors' rights. Also protection of Danish film production

Producenterne
Kronprinsensgade 9B
1114 Copenhagen K
Tel: (45) 33 14 03 11
Fax: (45) 33 14 03 65
The Danish Producers' Association of Film, Television, Video and AV

Finland

AVEK – The Promotion Centre for Audio–visual Culture in Finland
Hietaniemenkatu 2
FIN – 00100 Helsinki
Tel: (358) 9 43152350
Fax: (358) 9 43152388
email: avek@avek.kopiosto.fi
Website: www.kopiostofi/avek
AVEK was established in 1987 to promote cinemas, video and television culture. It is responsible for the management of funds arising from authors' copyright entitlements and is used for authors' common purposes (the blank tape levy). AVEK's support activities cover the entire field of audio–visual culture, emphasis being on the production support of short films, documentaries and media art. The other two activity sections are training of the professionals working in the audio–visual field and audiovisual culture in general

Finnish Film Archive/Suomen Elokuva–arkisto
Pursimiehenkatu 29–31 A
PO Box 177
FIN–00151
Helsinki
Tel: (358) 9 615 40 246
Fax: (358) 9 615 40 242
email: sea@sea.fi

Website: www.sea.fi
Matti Lukkarila
Stock: 10,000 feature film titles; 30,000 shorts and spots; 18,000 video cassettes; 20,000 books and scripts; 330,000 different stills, 110,000 posters; and 40,000 documentation files. The archive arranges regular screenings in Helsinki and other cities. Documentation, database, publications (Finnish national filmography). Publications

Finnish Film Foundation
Kanavakatu 12
Fin–Helsinki
Tel: (358) 0 6220 300
Fax: (358) 0 6220 3050
Film funding for script, development and production of feature film and documentaries. Audio post production and auditorio services. Distribution and screening support. International activities (cultural export and promotion of Finnish Film)

France

Bibliothèque du Film (BIFI)
100 rue du Faubourg
Saint–Antoine
75012 Paris
Tel: (33–1) 53 02 22 30
Fax: (33–1) 53 02 22 39
Website: www.bifi.fr
Contact: Laurent Billia
Documentation
Contact: Marc Vernet
Head Manager

Centre National de la Cinématographie (CNC)
rue de Lübeck 12
75016 Paris
Tel: (33) 1 45 05 1440
Fax: (33) 1 47 55 04 91
Website: www.cnc.fr/
Director–General: Dominique Wallon, Press, Public & Internal Relations: Patrick Ciercoles
A government institution, under the auspices of the Ministry of Culture. Its areas of concern are: the economics of cinema and the audio–visual industries; film regulation; the promotion of the cinema industries and the protection of cinema heritage. Offers financial assistance in all aspects of French cinema (production, exhibition, distribution etc). In 1986, the CNC was made responsible for the system of aid offered to the production of

films made for television. These include fiction films, animated films and documentaries. The aim here corresponds to one of the principal objectives of public sector funding, where support is given to the French television industry while the development of a high standard of television is encouraged

Cinémathèque Française – Musée du Cinéma
4, rue de Longchamp
75016 Paris
Tel: (33) 1 53 65 74 57
Fax: (33) 1 53 65 74 97
Marianne de Fleury
Founded in 1936 by Henri Langlois, Georges Franju and Jean Mitry to save, conserve and show films. Now houses a cinema museum, screening theatres, library and stills and posters library

Fédération de la Production Cinématographique Française
rue du Cirque 5
75008 Paris
Tel: (33) 1 42 25 70 63
Fax: (33) 1 42 25 94 27
Alain Poiré, Pascal Rogard
National federation of French cinema production

Fédération Nationale des Distributeurs de Films
74 avenue Kliber
75016 Paris
Tel: (33) 1 42 66 05 32
Fax: (33) 1 42 66 96 92
email: film.paris@wanaduu.fr
Antoine Virenque
President: Nicolas Seyilouse, Délégué général: Antoine Virenque
National federation of film distributors

Fédération Nationale des Industries Techniques du Cinéma et de l'Audio–visuel
(FITCA)
avenue Marceau 50
75008 Paris
Tel: (33) 1 47 23 75 76
Fax: (33) 1 47 23 70 47
A federation of technical trade associations which acts as intermediary between its members and their market. Maintains a database on all technical aspects of production, and helps French and European companies find suitable

partners for research and development or commercial ventures

Forum des images (ex Vidéothèque de Paris)
Forum des Halles
2, Grande Galerie
Porte Saint–Eustache
75001 Paris
Tel: 01 44 76 62 00
Website: www.vdp.fr/

France 2
avenue Montaigne 22
75008 Paris
Tel: (33) 1 44 21 42 42
Fax: (33) 1 44 21 51 45
France's main public service terrestrial television channel

Institut National de l'Audiovisuel (INA)
4, avenue de l'Europe
94366 Bry–sur–Marne Cédex
Tel: (33) 1 49 83 20 00
Fax: (33) 1 49 83 25 80
Website: www.ina.fr/
Television and radio archive; research into new technology; research and publications about broadcasting; production of over 130 first works for television and 15 major series and collections. INA initiates major documentaries and cultural series involving partners from Europe and the rest of the world

Les Archives du Film du Centre National de la Cinématographie
7 bis rue Alexandre Turpault
78390 Bois d'Arcy
Tel: (33) 1 30 14 80 00
Fax: (33) 1 34 60 52 25
Michelle Aubert
The film collection includes some 131,000 titles, mostly French features, documentaries and shorts from 1895 to date through the new legal deposit for films which includes all categories of films shown in cinemas including foreign releases. Since 1991, a special pluriannual programme for copying early films, including nitrate film, has been set up. So far, some 8,000 titles have been restored including the whole of the Lumière brothers film production from 1895 to 1905 which covers 1,400 short titles. A detailed catalogue of the Lumiére production is available in print and CD–Rom. Enquiries and viewing facilities for film are available on demand

TF1
1 Quai du Point du Jour
92656 Boulogne, Cédex
Tel: (33) 1 41 41 12 34
Fax: (33) 1 41 41 29 10
Privatised national television channel

Germany

ARD (Arbeitsgemeinschaft der öffentlich rechtlichen Rundfunkanstalten der Bundesrepublik Deutschland)
Programme Directorate of Deutsches Fernsehen
Arnulfstrasse 42
Postfach 20 06 22
80335 Munich
Tel: (49) 89 5900 01
Fax: (49) 89 5900 32 49
One of the two public service broadcasters in Germany, consisting of 10 independent broadcasting corporations

Beauftragtr der Bundersregierung für Anglelegesheiten der Kulter und de Mediar
Postfach 170290
53108 Bonn
Tel: (49) 228 681 5566
Fax: (49) 228 681 5504
Friedrich–Wilhelm Moog
Awards prizes, grants funds for the production and distribution of German feature films, short films, films for children and young people and documentaries. Promotes film institutes, festivals and specific events. Supervisory body of the Federal Archive for national film production

BVDFP (Bundesverband Deutscher Fernseh – produzenten)
Widenmayerstrasse 32
80538 Munich
Tel: (49) 89 21 21 47 10
Fax: (49) 89 228 55 62
Trade association for independent television producers

Deutsches Filminstitut–DIF
Schaumainkai 41
60596 Frankfurt/Main
Tel: (49) 69 9612200
Fax: (49) 69 620 060
email: deutsches.filminstitut@ em.uni–frankfurt.de
Website: www.filminstitut.de

Raimar Wiegand
The German Institute for Film Studies is a non–profit making organisation, and its remit includes amassing culturally significant films and publications and documents about film; to catalogue them and make them available for study and research. It also supports and puts on screenings of scientific, cultural and art films

Deutsches Filmmuseum
Schaumainkai 41
60596 Frankfurt/Main
Tel: (49) 69 21 23 33 69
Fax: (49) 69 21 23 78 81
email:filmmuseum@ stadt–frankfurt.de
Permanent and temporary exhibitions, incorporates the Cinema, the municipally administered cinémathéque. Film archive and collections of equipment, documentation, stills, posters and designs, music and sound. Library and videothéque

Export–Union des Deutschen Films (EXU)
Türkenstrasse 93
80799 München
Tel: (49) 89–390095
Fax: (49) 89–395223
Board of Directors: Jochem Strate, Antonio Excoustos, Rolf Bahr, Michel Weber
Managing Director: Christian Dorsch
PR Manager: Susanne Reinker
The Export–Union des Deutschen Films (EXU) is the official trade association for the promotion of the export of German films, with overseas offices located in London, Paris, Rome, Madrid, Buenos Aires, Tokyo, Hong Kong, New York and Los Angeles. The EXU maintains a presence at all major film and TV festivals (ie Berlin, Cannes, Montreal, Toronto, Locarno, Venice, MIP–TV, MIPCOM and MIFED). It has a switchboard function for German film companies working abroad as well as for foreign companies and buyers looking for media outlets and coproduction facilities in Germany

FFA (Filmförderungsanstalt)
Budapester Strasse 41
10787 Berlin
Tel: (49) 30 254090–0
Fax: (49) 30 254090–57
Rolf Bahr, Dr. Karl Guhlke – Directors General

The German Federal Film Board (FFA), incorporated under public law, is the biggest film funding institution in the country. Its mandate is the all–round raising of standards of quality in German film and cinema and the improvement of the economic structure of the film industry. The annual budget of about 60 million Deutschmarks is granted by a levy raised from all major German cinemas and video providers. The administrative council of 29 members is a representative cross section of the German film industry including members of the government's upper and lower house as well as public and private TV stations. Funding is offered in the following areas: full–length features, shorts, screenplays, marketing, exhibition, additional prints and professional training. The Export–Union des Deutschen Films e.V. largely represents the FFA's interests abroad

Film Förderung
Hamburg GmbH
Friedensalle14–16
22765 Hamburg
Tel: (49) 40 39837–0
Fax: (49) 40 39837–10
email: filmforderung@ffhh.de
Website: www.ffhh.de
Managing director: Eva Hubert
Subsidies available for: script development; pre–production; co–production and distribution

Filmmuseum Berlin – Deutsche Kinemathek
Potsdamer Strasse 2
10785 Berlin
Tel: (49) 030 300 903
Fax: (49) 030 300 903–13
Hans Helmut Prinzler
German Film Archive with collection of German and foreign films, cine–historical documents and equipment (approx. 10,000 films, over a million photographs, around 20,000 posters, 15,000 set–design and costume sketches, projectors, camera and accessories from the early days of cinema to the 80s). Member of FIAF

FSK (Freiwillige Selbstkontrolle der Filmwirtschaft)
Kreuzberger Ring 56
65205 Wiesbaden
Tel: (49) 611 77 891 0

Fax: (49) 611 77 891 39
email: fsk@spio–fsk.de
Website: www.spio–fsk.de
Film industry voluntary self–regulatory body. Activities are: to examine together with official competent representatives which films can be shown to minors under 18 year olds and under; to discuss the examination of films with youth groups; to organise seminars on the study of film, videos and new media

Kunsthochschule für Medien Köln (Academy of Media Arts)
Peter–Welter–Platz 2
50676
Cologne
Tel: (49) 221 201890
Fax: (49) 221 2018917
The first academy of Arts in Germany to embrace all the audio–visual media. It offers an Audio–visual Media graduate programme concentrating on the areas of Television/Film, Media Art, Media Design and Art and Media Science

ZDF (Zweites Deutsches Fernsehen)
ZDF–Strasse
PO Box 4040
55100 Mainz
Tel: (49) 6131 702060
Fax: (49) 6131 702052
A major public service broadcaster in Germany

Greece

ERT SA (Hellenic Broadcasting Corporation)
Messoghion 402
15342 Aghia Paraskevi
Athens
Tel: (30) 1 639 0772
Fax: (30) 1 639 0652
National public television and radio broadcaster, for information, education and entertainment

Greek Film Centre
10 Panepistimiou Avenue
10671 Athens
Tel: (30) 1 361 7633/363 4586
Fax: (30) 1 361 4336
Governmental organisation under the auspices of the Ministry of Culture. Grants subsidies for production, promotion and distribution

Ministry of Culture
Cinema Department
Boulinas Street 20
10682 Athens
Tel: (30) 1 322 4737

Ireland

An Chomhairle Ealaíon/The Arts Council
70 Merrion Square
Dublin 2
Tel: (353) 1 6180200
Fax: (353) 1 6761302
The Arts Council/An Chomhairle Ealaion is the principal channel of Government funding for the arts in Ireland. In the area of film the Council focuses its support on the development of film as an art form and on the individual film–maker as artist. With a budget for film of £975,000 in 1998 the Council supports a national film centre and archive, four film festivals and a number of film resource organisations. It administers an awards scheme for the production of short dramas, experimental films and community video. It also co–operates with the Irish Film Board and RTE Television in Frameworks, an animation awards scheme

Bord Scannán na hÉireann/Irish Film Board
Rockfort House
St. Augustine Street
Galway
Tel: (353) 91 561398
Fax: (353) 91 561405
email: info@filmboard.ie
Website: www.filmboard.ie
Chief Executive: Rod Stoneman
Business Manager: Andrew Lowe
Applications Officer: Lara de Roiste
Information Co–ordinator: Anna O'Sullivan
Bord Scannán na hÉireann promotes the creative and commercial elements of Irish film–making and film culture for a home and international audience. Each year it supports a number of film projects by providing development and production loans. Normally three submission deadlines annually. Dates and application procedures available from the office

Film Censor's Office
16 Harcourt Terrace
Dublin 2
Tel: (353) 1 676 1985
Fax: (353) 1 676 1898

Sheamus Smith
The Official Film Censor is
appointed by the Irish Government to
consider and classify all feature films
and videos distributed in Ireland

Film Institute of Ireland
Irish Film Centre
6 Eustace Street, Temple Bar
Dublin 2
Tel: (353) 1 679 5744/677 8788
Fax: (353) 1 677 8755
email: info@ifc.ie
The Film Institute promotes film
culture through a wide range of
activities in film exhibition and
distribution, film/media education,
various training programmes and the
Irish Film Archive. Its premises, the
Irish Film Centre in Temple Bar, are
also home to Film Base, MEDIA
Desk, The Junior Dublin Film
Festival, The Federation of Irish Film
Societies, and Hubbard Casting. The
Building has conference facilities, a
bar cafe and a shop as well as 2
cinemas seating 260 and 115

RTE (Radio Telefis Eireann)
Donnybrook
Dublin 4
Tel: (353) 1 208 3111
Fax: (353) 1 208 3080
Public service national broadcaster

Italy

ANICA (Associazione Nazionale Industrie Cinematografiche e Audiovisive)
Viale Regina Margherita 286
00198 Rome
Tel: (39) 06 442 31 480
Fax: (39) 06 442 31 296/6 440 41 28
Gino de Dominicis
Trade association for television and
movie producers and distributors,
representing technical industries
(post–production
companies/dubbing/studios/labs);
home video producers and
distributors; television and radio
broadcasters

Fininvest Television
Viale Europa 48
20093 Cologno Monzese, Milan
Tel: (39) 2 251 41
Fax: (39) 2 251 47031
Adriano Galliani
Major competitor to RAI, running
television channels Canale 5, Italia
Uno and Rete Quattro

Fondazione Cineteca Italiana
Via Palestro 16
20121 Milan
Tel: (39) 2 76022847
Fax: (39) 2 798289
email: cinetecaitaliana@digibank.it
Film Museum
Palazzo Dugnani
Via D Manin 2/b
Milan
Tel: (39) 2 6554977
Gianni Comencini
Film archive, film museum. Set up to
promote the preservation of film as
art and historical document, and to
promote the development of cinema
art and culture

Fondazione Scuola Nazionale Di Cinema – Cineteca Nazionale
Via Tuscolana 1524
00173 Rome
Tel: (39) 06 72 2941
Fax: (39) 06 72 1619
email: snccn@tin.it
Website: snc.it

Istituto Luce S.p.A
Via Tuscolana 1055
00173 Rome
Tel: (39) 06 722931/729921
Fax: (39) 06 7222493/7221127
Presiolente e Administratore
Delegato: Angelo Guglieluni Diretore
Ufficio Stampa e Pubblicità: Patrizia
de Cesari
Diretiore Commerciale: Leonardo
Tiberi
Created to spread culture and
education through cinema. It invests in
film, distributes films of cultural
interest and holds Italy's largest
archive

Museo Nazionale del Cinema
Via Montebello 15
10124 Turin
Tel: (39) 11 8154230
Fax: (39) 11 8122503
Giuliano Soria, Paolo Bertetto,
Sergio Toffetti, Donata Pesenti
Campagnoni, Luciana Spina. The
museum represents photography,
pre–cinema and cinema history. Its
collections include films, books and
periodicals, posters, photographs and
cinema ephemera

RAI (Radiotelevisione Italiana)
Viale Mazzini 14
00195 Rome

Tel: (39) 06 361 3608
Fax: (39) 06 323 1010
Italian state broadcaster

Surproduction S.A.S
Via del Rosso Fiorentiono 2/b
50142 Firenze
Tel: (39) 055 712127
Fax: (39) 055 712127
Nicola Melloni

Luxembourg

Cinémathèque Municipale – Ville de Luxembourg
rue Eugène Ruppert 10
2453 Luxembourg
Tel: (352) 4796 2644
Fax: (352) 40 75 19
Official Luxembourg film archive,
preserving international film heritage.
Daily screenings every year 'Live
Cinema' performances – silent films
with music. Member of FIAF,
(13,000 prints/35mm, 16mm, 70mm)

CLT Multi Media
Blvd Pierre Frieden 45
1543 Luxembourg
Tel: (352) 42 1 42 2170
Fax: (352) 42 1 42 2756
Director of Corporate
Communications: Karin Schintgen
Radio, television;
co–production/distribution; press;
rights aquisitions

The Netherlands

Filmmuseum
PO Box 74782
1070 BT Amsterdam
Tel: (31) 20 589 1400
Fax: (31) 20 683 3401
email: filmmuseum@nfm.nl
Website: www.nfm.nl/filmmuseum
Film museum with three public
screenings each day, permanent and
temporary exhibitions, library, film
café and film distribution

Ministry of Education, Culture and Science (OCW)
Film Department
PO Box 25.000
2700LZ Zoetermeer
Tel: (31) 79–3234368
Fax: (31) 79–3234959
Rob Docter, Séamus Cassidy
The film department of the Ministry
is responsible for the development
and maintenance of Dutch film
policy. Various different
organisations for production,

distribution, promotion and conservation of film are subsidised by this department

Nederlandse Omroep Stichting (NOS)
Postbus 26444
1202 JJ Hilversum
Tel: (31) 35 6779 222
Fax: (31) 35 6773 586
Louis Heinsman
Public corporation co–ordinating three–channel public television

Vereniging van Onafhankelijke Televisie Producenten (OTP)
Sumatralaan 45
PO Box 27900
1202 KV Hilversum
Tel: (31) 35 6231166
Fax: (31) 6280051
Director: Andries M. Overste
Trade association for independent television producers (currently 14 members)

Portugal

Cinemateca Portuguesa – Museu do Cinema (Portuguese Film Archive – Museum of Cinema)
Rua Barata Salgueiro, No 39
1200–059 Lisboa
Portugal
Tel: (351) 21 546279
Fax: (351) 21 3523180
email: cinemateca@cpmc.pt
João Bénard da Costa
President: João Bénard da Costa, vice President: José Manuel Costa
National film museum and archive, preserving, restoring and showing films. Includes a public documentation centre, a stills and posters archive

Instituto Português da Arte Cinematográfica e Audiovisual (IPACA)
Rua S Pedro de Alcântara 45–1o
1250 Lisbon
Tel: (351) 1 346 66 34
Fax: (351) 1 347 27 77
President: Zita Seabra,
Vice–Presidents: Paulo Moreira, Salvato Telles de Menezes
Assists with subsidies, improvement, regulation and promotion of the television and film industry

RTP (Radiotelevisão Portuguesa)
Avenida 5 de Outubro 197
1094 Lisbon Cedex
Tel: (351) 1 793 1774
Fax: (351) 1 793 1758
Maria Manuela Furtado
Public service television with two channels: RTP1 – general, TV2 – cultural and sports. One satellite programme, RTP International, covering Europe, USA, Africa, Macau

Spain

Academia de las Artes y de las Ciencias Cinematográficas de España
General Oraá 68
28006 Madrid
Tel: (34) 1 563 33 41
Fax: (34) 1 563 26 93

Filmoteca Española
Carretera de la Dehesa de la Villa s/n, 28040 Madrid
Tel: (34) 1 549 00 11
Fax: (34) 1 549 73 48
Director: José Maria Prado; Deputy Director: Catherine Gautier;
Documentation: Dolores Devesa
National Film Archive, member of FIAF since 1958. Preserves 26,000 film titles including a large collection of newsreels. Provides access to researchers on its premises. The library and stills departments are open to the public. Publishes and co–produces various books on film every year. Five daily public screenings with simultaneous translation or electronic subtitles are held at the restored Cine Doré, C/Santa Isabel 3, in the city centre, where facilities include a bookshop and cafeteria

ICAA (Instituto de la Cinematografia y de las Artes Audio–visuales)
Ministerio de Cultura
Plaza del Rey No1
28071 Madrid
Tel: (34) 1 532 74 39
Fax: (34) 1 531 92 12
Enrique Balmaseda Arias–Dávila
The promotion, protection and diffusion of cinema and audiovisual activities in production, distribution and exhibition. Gives financial support in these areas to Spanish companies. Also involved in the

promotion of Spanish cinema and audio–visual arts, and their influence on the different communities within Spain

RTVE (Radiotelevision Española)
Edificio Prado del Rey – 3a planta
Centro RTVE, Prado Del Rey,
22224 Madrid
Tel: (34) 1 5 81 70 00
Fax: (34) 1 5 81 77 57
Head of International Sales RTVE: Teresa Moreno
National public service broadcaster, film producer and distributor

Sweden

Oberoende Filmares Förbund(OFF)/ Independent Film Producers Association
Box 27 121
102 52 Stockholm
Tel: (46) 8 665 12 21
Fax: (46) 8 663 66 55
email: off.se
OFF is a non–profit organisation, founded 1984, with some 300 members. OFF promotes the special interests of filmmakers and independent Swedish producers of documentaries, short and feature films. Their purpose is twofold: to raise the quality of Swedish audiovisual production and to increase the quantity of domestic production. OFF works on many levels. The organisation partakes in public debate, organises seminars, publishes a quarterly newsletter, does lobby–work on a national level besides Nordic and international networking. OFF aids its producers with legal counsel as well as copyright, economic and insurance policy advisement

Statens biografbyrå
Box 7728
103 95 Stockholm
Tel: (46) 8 24 34 25
Fax: (46) 8 21 01 78
email: registrator@statensbiografbyra.se
Website: www.statensbiografbyra.se
The Swedish National Board of Film Classification (Statens biografbyrå) was founded in 1911. Films and videos must be approved and classified by the Board prior to showing at a public gathering or

entertainment. For videos intended for sale or hire, there is a voluntary system of advance examination

Svenska Filminstitutet (Swedish Film Institute)
Box 27 126
Filmhuset
Borgvägen 1–5
S–10252 Stockholm
Tel: (46) 8 665 11 00
Fax: (46) 8 661 18 20
email: janerik.billinger@sfi.se
Jan–Erik Billinger: Head of the Information Department
The Swedish Film Institute is the central organisation for Swedish cinema. Its activities are to: support the production of Swedish films of high merit; promote the distribution and exhibition of quality films; preserve films and materials of interest to cinematic and cultural history and promote Swedish cinematic culture internationally

Sveriges Biografägareförbund
Box 1147
S 171 23 Solna
Tel: (946) 8 735 97 80
Fax: (946) 8 730 25 60
The Swedish Exhibitors Association is a joint association for Swedish cinema owners

Sveriges Filmuthyrareförening upa
Box 23021
S–10435 Stockholm
Tel: (946) 8 441 55 70
Fax: (946) 8 34 38 10
Kay Wall
The Swedish Film Distributors Association is a joint association for film distributors

Swedish Women's Film Association
Po Box 27182
S–10251 Stockholm
Visitors address: Filmhuset,
Borgvägen 5
Tel: (46) 8 665 1100/1293
Fax: (46) 8 666 3748
Anna Hallberg
Workshops, seminars, festivals and international exchange programme

MEDIA Programme

On 14 December 1999, the European Commission adopted its proposal for a programme in support of the audiovisual industry called **Media Plus** (2001-2005), to be introduced in 2001 as a follow-up to the Media II programme which ends on 31 December 2000. MEDIA II was a programme of the European Union, managed by the European Commission in Brussels. MEDIA II, which followed on from MEDIA I, started in 1996

European Commission
Directorate General X:
Information, Communication,
Culture, Audio–visual
rue de la Loi, 200
1040 Brussels,
Tel: (32) 2 299 11 11
Fax: (32) 2 299 92 14
Head of Programme: Jacques Delmoly

MEDIA Contacts
As part of a network of 29 Desks and Antennae throughout Europe, the members of the UK MEDIA team listed below should be the first point of contact for UK companies seeking information and advice of the MEDIA Programme. Guidelines and application forms for all the MEDIA schemes are available from them. They produce regular newsletters and other printed information detailing upcoming deadlines, training courses and markets

MEDIA Services England
c/o Scottish Screen
249 West George Street
Glasgow G2 4QE
Tel: 0870 0100 791
Fax: 0141 302 1778
email: media.england@
scottishscreen.com
Website: www.mediadesk.co.uk
This is a temporary contact until a new MEDIA Desk is set up in London in 2001
Chris Miller

MEDIA Antenna Scotland
c/o Scottish Screen
249 West George Street
Glasgow G2 4RB
Tel: 0141 302 1776/7
Fax: 0141 302 1778
email: media.scotland@
scottishscreen.com

Rosie Ellison
Website: www.mediadesk.co.uk

MEDIA Antenna Cymru Wales
c/o Sgrîn,
The Bank, 10 Mount Stuart Square
Cardiff CF10 5EE
Tel: 029 2033 3303/06
Fax: 029 2033 3320
email: antenna@sgrin.co.uk
Website: www.sgrin.co.uk
Contact: Gwawr Hughes,
Co–ordinator
Jason Tynan, Assistant
MEDIA Antenna Wales is the Welsh information office for the European Media II Programme. The Media II Programme (1996–2000) offers grants and loans for development, training and distribution, in film TV and multimedia as well as subsidised places to industry professionals on European training courses and at international markets

MEDIA Northern Ireland
MEDIA Services Northern Ireland
c/o Northern Ireland Film Commission
21 Ormeau Avenue
Belfast BT2 8HD
Tel: 01232 232 444
Fax: 01232 239 918
email: media@nifc.com
Heike Meyer–Döring

The Intermediary Organisations
The MEDIA II Programme contracted three companies to act as Intermediary Organisations (IOs) for the five year period of MEDIA II to assist Brussels in administering and processing applications in each of the three areas of support (Training, Development and Distribution) and dealing with payments.

TRAINING

Media Research and Consultancy Spain
(MRC) Madrid
Claudio Coello 43 – 2OD
E–28001 Madrid, Spain
Tel: (34) 1 577 94 04
Fax: (34) 1 575 71 99
email: mrc@mad.servicom.es
Head of office: Fernando Labrada
Training

DEVELOPMENT

MEDIA II Pilots
Pau Claris 115, 5è, 4a

E–8009 Barcelona
Tel: (34) 93 487 37 73
Fax: (34) 93 487 39 52
email: pilots@intercom.es
Website: www.acpilots.com
Roger Gregory, UK Contact
Tel: 01926 491934
Fax: 01926 491212
Workshops on script development for writers and producers of TV drama. Projects are developed working with specialists from Europe and America. Skillset bursaries available
PILOTS is an initiative of the MEDIA Programme of the European Union

Euroscript
Screenwriters' Centre
Suffolk House
1–8 Whitfield Place
London W1P 5SF
Tel: 020 7387 5880
Fax: 020 7387 6900
email: euroscript@netmatters.co.uk
Website: www.euroscript.co.uk
Paul Gallagher, Director
Euroscript is a project of the European Union's MEDIA II programme. Euroscript offers support and distance learning material to help EU screenwriters develop scripts and run screenwriters' groups. Euroscript is a continuous distance training project to develop and promote EU scripts.

DISTRIBUTION

CARTOON (European Association of Animation Film)
418 Boulevard Lambermont
1030 Brussels
Tel: (32) 2 245 12 00
Fax: (32) 2 245 46 89
email: cartoon@skynet.be
Website: www.cartoon–media.be
Contact: Corinne Jenart, Marc Vandeweyer
CARTOON, based in Brussels, is a European animation network which organises the annual CARTOON FORUM, co–ordinates the grouping of European animation studios and runs specialist training courses in animation

D&S Media Services
Brussels, Munich and Dublin
Rue Pere Deken 33
B – 1040 Brussels
Tel: (32) 2 743 22 44
Fax: (32) 2 743 22 45
Head of office: John Dick
Distribution

EXHIBITION NETWORKS

Europa Cinemas
54, rue Beaubourg
F–75 003 Paris, France
Tel: (33) 1 42 71 53 70
Fax: (33) 1 42 71 47 55
email: europacinema@magic.fr
Website: www.europa–cinemas.org
Claude–Eric Poiroux, Fatima Djoumer
Exhibition Networks
This project encourages screenings and promotion of European films through a network of cinemas in European cities. It offers financial support for screening European films, for promotional activities and for special events

MEDIA Salles
Via Soperga, 2
20127 Milan, Italy
Tel: (39) 02 66 98 44 05
Fax: (39) 02 669 15 74
email: infocinema@mediasalles.it
Website: www.mediasalles.it/
Elisabetta Brunella
MEDIA Salles with Euro Kids Network is an initiative aimed at consolidating the availability of 'cinema at the cinema' for children and young people in Europe, and at raising the visibility of European film to a younger audience

PR COMPANIES

These are a selection of companies which handle aspects of publicity and promotion for film and video production companies and/or individual productions

The Associates
34 Clerkenwell Close
London EC1R OAU
Tel: 020 7608 2204
Fax: 020 7250 1756
Catherine Flynn, Alison Marsh

Avalon Publicity Limited
4a Exmoor Street
London W10 6BD
Tel: 020 7598 7222
Fax: 020 7598 7223
email: edt@avalonuk.com
Edward Thomson
Specialist entertainment based PR agency providing services from PR and unit publicity to transmission publicity and media launches

Blue Dolphin PR and Marketing
40 Langham Street
London W1 5Rg
Tel: 020 7255 2494
Fax: 020 7580 7670
email: traceyhislop@bluedolphinfilms.com
PR and marketing company that specialises in key areas, such as film, video, television and music

Byron Advertising, Marketing and PR
Byron House
Wallingford Road
Uxbridge
Middx UB8 2RW
Tel: 01895 252131
Fax: 01895 252137
Les Barnes

Jacquie Capri Enterprises
3rd Floor
46/47 Chancery Lane
London WC21 1JB
Tel: 020 7831 4545
Fax: 020 7831 2557

Emma Chapman Publicity
2nd Floor
18 Great Portland Street
London W1N 5AB
Tel: 020 7637 0990
Fax: 020 7637 0660
email: emma@ecpub.com
Contact: Emma Chapman

CJP Public Relations Ltd
Park House
8 Grove Ash
Mount Farm
Milton Keynes MK 1B2
Tel: 01908 275271
Fax: 01908 275272
email: cajardine@cjppr.co.uk
Carolyn Jardine

Max Clifford Associates
109 New Bond Street
London W1Y 9AA
Tel: 020 7408 2350
Fax: 020 7409 2294
Max Clifford

Corbett and Keene
122 Wardour Street
London W1V 3LA
Tel: 020 7494 3478
Fax: 020 7734 2024
Ginger Corbett, Sara Keene, Charlotte Tudor

Dennis Davidson Associates (DDA)
Royalty House
72-74 Dean Street
London W1V 5HB
Tel: 020 7439 6391
Fax: 020 7437 6358
email: info@ddapr.com
Dennis Davidson, Stacy Wood, Chris Paton

FEREF Associates
14-17 Wells Mews
London W1A 1ET
Tel: 020 7580 6546
Fax: 020 7631 3156
Peter Andrews, Ken Paul, Robin Behling, David Kemp, Brian Bysouth, Gareth Shepherd

Soren Fischer
67 Parkway Drive
Queens Park
Bournemouth BH8 9JS
Tel: 01202 393033
Fax: 01202 301516
email: Sorenfischer@Compuserve.com
Soren Fischer
PR co-ordinator and British representative, Berlin Film Festival

Lynne Franks PR
327-329 Harrow Road
London W9 3RB
Tel: 020 7724 6777
Fax: 020 7724 8484
Julian Henry

HPS-PR Ltd
Park House
Desborough Park Road
High Wycombe
Bucks HP 123 DJ
Tel: 01494 684353
Fax: 01494 440952
email: r.hodges@hps-pr.co.uk
Ms Ray Hodges, MCam MIPR

Sue Hyman Associates
70 Chalk Farm Road
London NW1 8AN
Tel: 020 7485 8489/5842
Fax: 020 7267 4715
email: sue.hyman@btinternet.com
Sue Hyman

JAC Publicity
1st Floor, Playhouse Court
64 Southwark Bridge Road
London SE1 0AS
Tel: 020 7261 1211
Fax: 020 7261 1214
Claire Forbes

Richard Laver Publicity
3 Troy Court
Kensington High Street
London W8 7RA
Tel: 020 7937 7322
Fax: 020 7937 5976
email: richard@lavpub.u-net.com
Richard Laver

McDonald and Rutter
14-18 Ham Yard
Gt. Windmill Street
London W1P 7PD
Tel: 020 7734 9009
Fax: 020 7734 1151
email: mcdonaldrutter@btinternet.com
Charles McDonald, Jonathan Rutter

Optimum Communications
34 Hanway Street
London W1P 9DE
Tel: 020 7580 5352
Fax: 020 7636 3945
Nigel Passingham

Porter Frith Publicity & Marketing
26 Danbury Street
London N1 8JU
Tel: 020 7359 3734
Fax: 020 7226 5897
Sue Porter, Liz Frith

S.S.A. Public Relations
Suite 323/324
The Linen Hall
162-168 Regent Street
London W1R 5TB
Tel: 020 7494 2755
Fax: 020 7494 2833
Website: www.ssapr.com
Andrew O'Driscoll
S.S.A Public Relations is a full
service public relations firm that
provides trade and consumer
publicity for a wide range of
corporate and entertainment clients.
The company specialises in key
areas, representing television and
theatrical film production and
distribution companies

Peter Thompson Associates
134 Great Portland Street
London W1N 5PH
Tel: 020 7436 5991/2
Fax: 020 7436 0509
Peter Thompson, Amanda Malpass

Town House Publicity
45 Islington Park Street
London N1 1QB
Tel: 020 7226 7450
Fax: 020 7359 6026
email: townhouse@lineone.net
Mary Fulton

UpFront Television Ltd
39-41 New Oxford Street
London WC1A 1BH
Tel: 020 7836 7702
Fax: 020 7836 7701
email: upfront@binternet.com
Claire Nye
Richard Brecker

Warren Cowan/Phil Symes Associates
35 Soho Square
London W1V 6AX
Tel: 020 7439 3535
Fax: 020 7439 3737
Phil Symes, Warren Cowan

Stella Wilson Publicity
130 Calabria Road
London N5 1HT
Tel: 020 7354 5672
Fax: 020 7354 2242
email: stella@starmaker.
demon.co.uk
Stella Wilson

PRESS CONTACTS

6degrees.co.uk
39 King Street
London WC2E 8JS
Tel: 020 7420 6315
Fax: 020 7420 6314
email: publisher@6degrees.co.uk
Website: www.6degrees.co.uk
Publisher: Justin Bowyer
Editor: Nick Walker
6degrees is the online UK independent
film magazine, covering independ, art
house and world cinema news, reviews
and article - plus free weekly newsletter

19
(Monthly)
IPC Magazines
King's Reach Tower
Stamford Street
London SE1 9LS
Tel: 020 7261 6410
Fax: 020 7261 7634
Film: Corrine Barraclough
Magazine for young women
Lead time: 8 weeks
Circulation: 187,740

Arena
(Bi-monthly)
Third Floor, Block A
Exmouth House
Pine Street
London EC1R 0JL
Tel: 020 7689 2266
Fax: 020 7689 0900
Magazine for men covering general
interest, film, literature, music and
fashion
Lead time: 6-8 weeks
Circulation: 100,000

Ariel
(Weekly, Tues)
Room 123, Henry Wood House
3 and 6 Langham Place
London W1A 1AA
Tel: 020 7765 3623
Fax: 020 7765 3646
Editor: Robin Reynolds
BBC staff magazine
Lead time: Tuesday before
publication
Circulation: 26,000

Art Monthly
Britannia Art Publications,
Suite 17

26 Charing Cross Road
London WC2H 0DG
Tel: 020 7240 0389
Fax: 020 7497 0726
email: info@artmonthly.co.uk
Website: www.artmonthly.co.uk
Editor: Patricia Bickers
Aimed at artists, art dealers, teachers,
students, collectors, arts
administrators, and all those inter-
ested in contemporary visual art
Lead time: 4 weeks
Circulation: 4,000 plus

Asian Times
(Weekly, Tues)
138-148 Cambridge Heath Road
London E1 5QJ
Tel: 020 7702 8012
Fax: 020 7702 7937
Editor: Sanjay Gohil
National, weekly newspaper for
Britain's English-speaking, Asian
community
Press day: Thurs
Circulation: 30,000

The Big Issue
(Weekly, Mon)
236-240 Pentonville Road
Kings Cross
London N1 9JY
Tel: 020 7418 0418
Fax: 020 7418 0427
email: london@bigissue.com
Website: www.bigissue.com
Editor: Becky Gardiner
Arts: Tina Jackson
Film editor: Xan Brooks
General interest magazine, with
emphasis on homelessness. Sold by
the homeless
Lead time: Tues, 3 weeks before
Circulation: ABC figure 142,937

British Film
(Quarterly)
Arts and Entertainment
Publishing Ltd
24 Sandyford Place
Glasgow G3 7NG
Tel: 0141 221 4241
Fax: 0141 221 4247
Editor: Robert McColl
British Film covers Film making and
broadcasting within the UK.
Primarily a trade magazine

distributed to all production
companies and facility houses within
the UK
Circulation: 20,000

British Film and TV Facilities Journal
Gullimanor Ltd
Argyle House
1 Dee Road
Richmond on Thames
Surrey TW9 2JN
Tel: 020 8334 1159
Fax: 020 8334 1161
email: editorial@dial.pipex.com
Editor: Colin Lenthall
Journal for those working in British
film, TV and video industry

Broadcast
(Weekly, Fri)
EMAP Media
33-39 Bowling Green Lane
London EC1R 0DA
Tel: 020 7505 8014
Fax: 020 7505 8050
Publisher/Editor: Jon Baker
Broadcasting industry news magazine
with coverage of TV, radio, cable and
satellite, corporate production and
international programming and
distribution. Press day: Wed. Lead
time: 2 weeks. Circulation: 13,556

The Business of Film
(Monthly)
Suite 3
2a New Cavendish Street
London W1M 7RP
Tel: 020 7486 1996
Fax: 020 7486 1969
Publisher/executive editor: Elspeth
Tavares
Aimed at film industry professionals
- producers, distributors, exhibitors,
investors, financiers
Lead time: 2 weeks

Cable and Satellite Communications International
(Monthly)
104 City View
463 Bethnal Green Road
London E2 9QY
Tel: 020 7613 5553
Fax: 020 7729 7723

email: de81@dial.pipex.com
Editor: Joss Armitage
Business magazine for professionals
in the cable and satellite television
industry
Circulation: 4,029

Capital Gay
(Weekly, Thur)
1 Tavistock Chambers
Bloomsbury Way
London WC1A 2SE
Tel: 020 7242 2750
Fax: 020 7242 3334
Film editor: Pas Paschal
TV editor: Michael Mason
Newspaper for lesbians and gay men
in the South East combining news,
features, arts and entertainment,
what's on guide
Lead time: 1 week (Mon)
Circulation: 22,000

[handwritten: Gay UK, Fairchild St EC2, 0207 247 8558]

Caribbean Times
incorporating **African Times**
(Weekly, Mon)
138-148 Cambridge Heath Road
London E1 5QJ
Tel: 020 7702 8012
Fax: 020 7702 7937
Editor: Clive Morgan
Tabloid dealing with issues pertinent
to community it serves
Press day: Fri
Circulation: 25,000

City Life
(Fortnightly)
164 Deansgate
Manchester M60 2RD
Tel: 0161 839 1416
Fax: 0161 839 1488
Website: www.poptel.org.uk/citylife/
Editor: Chris Sharratt
Film editor: Melanie Dakin
What's on in and around Greater
Manchester
Circulation: 20,000

COIL (journal of the moving image)
PO Box 14649
London EC2A 3RD
Tel: 07711 069569
Fax: 020 7613 0378
email: probascis@easynet.co.uk
Website: www.easyweb.easynet.
co.uk /~probascis
Frequency: two issues per year
Editor: Giles Lane
Project Manager: Joan Johnston

Company
(Monthly)
National Magazine House

72 Broadwick Street
London W1V 2BP
Tel: 020 7439 5000
Fax: 020 7439 5117
Glossy magazine for women aged
18-30
Lead time: 10 weeks
Circulation: 272,160

Cosmopolitan
(Monthly)
National Magazine House
72 Broadwick Street
London W1V 2BP
Tel: 020 7439 5000
Fax: 020 7439 5101
Editor: Mandi Norwood
Arts/General: Sarah Kennedy
For women aged 18-35
Lead time: 12 weeks
Circulation: 461,080

Creation
(Monthly)
MDI Ltd
3 St Peters Street
London N1 8JD
Tel: 020 7226 8585
Fax: 020 7226 8586
Editor: James Hamilton
Film, television, new media
publication
Circulation: 14,000

Creative Review
(Monthly)
St. Giles House
50 Poland Street
London W1V 4AX
Tel: 020 7439 4222
Fax: 020 7734 6748
Editor: Lewis Blackwell
Publisher: Morag Arman-Addey
Trade paper for creative people
covering film, advertising and design.
Film reviews, profiles and technical
features
Lead time: 4 weeks
Circulation: 15,206

Daily Mail
[handwritten: Theatre Michael Coveney]
Northcliffe House
2 Derry Street
London W8 5TT
Tel: 020 7938 6000
Fax: 020 7937 4463
Chief showbusiness writer: Baz
Bamigboye
Film: Christopher Tookey
TV: Peter Paterson
National daily newspaper
Circulation: 2,163,676

The Daily Star
Ludgate House
245 Blackfriars Road

London SE1 9UX
Tel: 020 7928 8000
Fax: 020 7922 7962
Film: Sandro Monetti
TV: Pat Codd
Video: Sandro Monetti and Pat Codd
National daily newspaper
Circulation: 654,866

Daily Telegraph
1 Canada Square
Canary Wharf
London E14 5DT
Tel: 020 7538 5000
Fax: 020 7538 6242
Film critic: Quentin Curtis
Arts Editor: Sarah Crompton
TV: Marsha Dunstan
National daily newspaper
Lead time: 1 week
Circulation: 1,117,439

Diva
(Monthly)
Ground Floor
Worldwide House
116-134 Bayham Street
London NW1 0BA
Tel: 020 7482 2576
Fax: 020 7284 0329
email: diva@gaytimes.co.uk
Website: www.gaytimes.co.uk
Editor: Gillian Rodgerson
Lesbian news and culture
Lead times: 4-6 weeks
Circulation: 35,000

Eclipse
[handwritten: NO]
(Monthly)
Phoenix Magazines Limited
PO Box 33, Liskeard
Cornwall PL14 4YX
Tel: 01579 344313 *[handwritten: wrong no!]*
Fax: 01579 344313
email: phoenixmgs@aol.com
Editor: Simon Clarke
Magazine covering the entire
spectrum of science fiction in books,
cinema, television and comics, along
with role playing and computer
games. News, reviews, interviews,
competitions, features, profiles, etc.
Lead time: six weeks
Circulation: 15,000

The Economist
(Weekly)
25 St James's Street
London SW1A 1HG
Tel: 020 7830 7000
Fax: 020 7839 2968
Website: www.economist.com
Film/video/television
(cultural): Tony Thomas;
(business): Frances Cairncross

International coverage of major political, social and business developments with arts section
Press day: Wed
Circulation: 327,689

Elle
(Monthly)
Endeavour House
189 Shaftesbury Avenue
London WC2H 8JG
Tel: 020 7208 3458
Fax: 020 7208 3599
Editor: Fiona McIntosh
Arts Ed: Jenny Dyson
Glossy magazine aimed at 18-35 year old working women
Lead time: 3 months
Circulation: 205,623

Empire
(Monthly)
Mappin House
4 Winsley Street
London W1N 4AR
Tel: 020 7436 1515
Fax: 020 7312 8249
email: empire@ecm.emap.com
Website: www.empireonline.co.uk
Quality film monthly incorporating features, interviews and movie news as well as reviews of all new movies and videos
Lead time: 3 weeks
Circulation: 161,503

The European
(Weekly, Thurs)
200 Gray's Inn Road
London WC1X 8NE
Tel: 020 7418 7777
Fax: 020 7713 1840/1870
Arts Editor: Andrew Harvey
Editor in Chief: Andrew Neil
In-depth coverage of European news, politics and culture
Press day: Thurs
Circulation: 160,511

Evening Standard
(Mon-Fri)
Northcliffe House
2 Derry Street
London W8 5EE
Tel: 020 7938 2648
Fax: 020 7937 3193
Film: Alexander Walker, Neil Norman
Media editor: Victor Sebestyen
London weekday evening paper
Circulation: 438,136

Everywoman
(Monthly)
9 St Alban's Place

London N1 0NX
Tel: 020 7704 8440
Fax: 020 7226 9448
Arts editor: Nina Rapi
Feminist magazine covering mainstream issues
Lead time: 6 weeks
Circulation: 15,000

The Express
Ludgate House
245 Blackfriars Road
London SE1 9UX
Tel: 020 7928 8000
Fax: 020 7620 1654
Showbusiness editor: Annie Leask
Film: Jason Solomons
TV/Theatre critic: Robert Goe-Langton
Showbusiness Correspondent: David Wigg
National daily newspaper
Circulation: 1,227,971

The Express on Sunday
Ludgate House
245 Blackfriars Road
London SE1 9UX
Tel: 020 7928 8000
Fax: 020 7620 1656
Film: Chris Peachment
TV: Nigel Billen
National Sunday newspaper
Circulation: 1,159,759

The Face
(Monthly)
Second Floor, Block A
Exmouth House
Pine Street
London EC1R 0JL
Tel: 020 7689 9999
Fax: 020 7689 0300
Film: Charles Gant, Adam Higginbotham
Visual-orientated youth culture magazine: emphasis on music, fashion and films
Lead time: 4 weeks
Circulation: 100,744

FHM
(Monthly)
Mappin House
London W1N 7AR
Tel: 020 7312 8707
Fax: 020 7312 8191
Editor: Anthony Noguera
Deputy Editor: Ed Halliwell
Assistant Editor: Richard Galpin
Men's lifestyle magazine
Lead time: 6 weeks
Circulation: 755,000

Film
(Quarterly)
Suite 210
29 Great Pulteney Street
London W1R 3DD
Tel: 020 7734 9300
Fax: 020 7734 9093
Editor: Tom Brownlie
Thematically-based journal with information for Film Societies and other film exhibitors
Lead time: 2 weeks
Circulation: 2,000

Film Guide
(Monthly - Free)
Film Guide Ltd
30 North End Road
London W14 0SH
Tel: 020 7602 9790
Fax: 020 7602 2063
Editor: Alan Jones
Film news, features and interviews
Circulation: 125,000

Film Review
(Monthly + 4 specials)
Visual Imagination
9 Blades Court, Deodar Road
London SW15 2NU
Tel: 020 8875 1520
Fax: 020 8875 1588
email: filmreview@visimag.com
Website: www.visimag.com/filmreview
Editor: Neil Corry
Reviews of films on cinema screen and video; star interviews and profiles; book and CD reviews
Lead time: 1 month
Circulation: 50,000

Financial Times
1 Southwark Bridge
London SE1 9HL
Tel: 020 7873 3000
Fax: 020 7873 3076
Website: www.ft.com
Arts: Annalena McAfee
Film: Nigel Andrews
TV: Christopher Dunkley
National daily newspaper
Circulation: 316,578

Flicks
(Monthly)
25 The Coda Centre
189 Munster Road
London SW6 6AW
Tel: 020 7381 8811
Fax: 020 7381 1811
email: nick@flicks.co.uk
Website: www.flicks.co.uk
Editor: Nick Thomas
Managing Director: Val Lyon

Magazine of the film industry, for sale in cinemas and retail outlets throughout the UK, or by subscription
Lead time: 6 weeks
Circulation: 70,000

Gay Times
(Monthly)
Ground Floor
Worldwide House
116-134 Bayham Street
London NW1 0BA
Tel: 020 7482 2576
Fax: 020 7284 0329
email: edit@gaytimes.co.uk
Arts editor: James Cary Parkes
Britain's leading lesbian and gay magazine. Extensive film, television and arts coverage. Round Britain guide
Lead time: 6-8 weeks
Circulation: 65,000

The Guardian
119 Farringdon Road
London EC1R 3ER
Tel: 020 7278 2332
Fax: 020 7837 2114
Website: www.guardian.co.uk
Film: Derek Malcolm, Johnathan Romney
TV critic: Nancy Banks-Smith
Media editor: John Mulholland
Arts editor: Claire Armitstead
Head of Press, PR & Corporate Affairs: Camilla Nicholls
Weekend editor: Deborah Orr
National daily newspaper
Circulation: 407,870

Harpers & Queen
(Monthly)
National Magazine House
72 Broadwick Street
London W1V 2BP
Tel: 020 7439 5000
Fax: 020 7439 5506
Arts & Films: Anthony Quinn
Glossy magazine for women
Lead time: 12 weeks
Circulation: 93,186

Heat
4th Floor, Mappin House
4 Winsley Street
London W1N 7AR
Tel: 020 7436 1515
Fax: 020 7817 8847
email: heat@ecm.emap.com

The Herald
195 Albion Street
Glasgow G1 1QP
Grays Inn House
127 Clerkenwell Road
London EC1R 5DB

Tel: 020 7405 2121
Fax: 020 7405 1888
Film critic: William Russell (London address)
TV editor: Ken Wright
Scottish daily newspaper
Circulation: 107,527

The Hollywood Reporter
(daily; weekly international, Tues)
23 Ridgmount Street
London W1CE 7AH
Tel: 020 7332 6686
Fax: 020 7323 5513
email: cdunkley@hollywoodreporter.com
European bureau chief: Ray Bennett
Deputy bureau chief/European News Editor: Cathy Dunkley
Showbusiness trade paper
Circulation: 39,000

i-D Magazine
(Monthly)
Universal House
251-255 Tottenham Court Road
London W1P 0AE
Tel: 020 7813 6170
Fax: 020 7813 6179
Film & TV: David Sandhu
Youth/fashion magazine with film features
Lead time: 8 weeks
Circulation: 45,000

Illustrated London News
(2 pa)
20 Upper Ground
London SE1 9PF
Tel: 020 7805 5555
Fax: 020 7805 5911
Editor: Alison Booth
News, pictorial record and commentary, and a guide to coming events
Lead time: 8-10 weeks
Circulation: 30,000

In Camera
(Quarterly)
Professional Motion Imaging
PO Box 66, Hemel Hempstead
Herts HP1 1JU
Tel: 01442 844875
Fax: 01442 844987
Editor: Josephine Ober
Business editor: Giosi Gallotli
Journal for motion picture industry, primarily for cinematographers, but also for other technicians and anyone in the industry
Lead time: 4 weeks
Circulation: 45,000

The Independent
1 Canada Square
Canary Wharf
London E14 5DL
Tel: 020 7293 2000
Fax: 020 7293 2047
Film: Sam Taylor
TV: Tom Sutcliffe, Gerard Gilbert
Media: Rob Brown
National daily newspaper
Circulation: 257,594

The Independent on Sunday
1 Canada Square
Canary Wharf
London E14 5DL
Tel: 020 7293 2000
Fax: 020 7293 2027
Film critic: Kevin Jackson
TV: Robin Boss
National Sunday newspaper
Lead time: 2 weeks
Circulation: 275,000

International Connection
25 South Quay
Gt Yarmouth
Norfolk NR30 2RG
Tel: 01493 330565
Fax: 01493 330565
email: film@bnw.demon.co.uk
Website: www.filmtvdir.co.uk
Susan Fester
Film and TV industry business magazine

Interzone
(Monthly)
217 Preston Drove
Brighton BN1 6FL
Tel: 01273 504710
Editor: David Pringle
Film: Nick Lowe
Science-fiction magazine
Lead time: 8 weeks
Circulation: 10,000

Jewish Chronicle
(Weekly, Friday)
25 Furnival Street
London EC4A 1JT
Tel: 020 7405 9252
Editor: Edward J Temko
Film critic: Alan Montague
TV critic: Helen Jacobus
Lead time: 2 days
Press day: Wed
Circulation: 47,273

The List
(Fortnightly, Thur)
14 High Street
Edinburgh EH1 1TE
Tel: 0131 558 1191
Fax: 0131 557 8500

email: editor@list.co.uk
Editor: Mark Fisher
Film editor: Miles Fielder
TV: Brian Donaldson
Glasgow/Edinburgh events guide
Lead time: 1 week
Circulation: 18,000

Mail on Sunday
Northcliffe House
2 Derry Street
London W8 5TS
Tel: 020 7938 6000
Fax: 020 7937 3829
Film: Sebastian Faulks
TV critic: Jaci Stephen
National Sunday newspaper
Press day: Fri/Sat
Circulation: 2,325,618

Marie Claire
(Monthly)
2 Hatfields
London SE1 9PG
Tel: 020 7261 5240
Fax: 020 7261 5277
Film: Anthony Quinn
Arts: Louise Clark
Women's magazine
Lead time: 3 months
Circulation: 457,034

Media Week
(Weekly, Thur)
Quantum House
19 Scarbrook Road
Croydon CR9 1LX
Tel: 020 8565 4317
Fax: 020 8565 4394
email: mweeked@media.emap.co.uk
Editor: Susannah Richmond
News magazine aimed at the
advertising and media industries
Press day: Wed
Circulation: 13,209 ABC

Melody Maker
(Weekly, Weds)
26th Floor
King's Reach Tower
Stamford Street
London SE1 9LS
Tel: 020 7261 6229
Fax: 020 7261 6706
Editor: Mark Sutherland
Film: Ben Knowles/Colin Kennedy
Pop/rock music newspaper
Press day: Fri
Circulation: 40,349

Midweek
(Weekly, Thur/West End, Mon/City)
7-9 Rathbone Street
London W1P 1AF
Tel: 020 7636 6651

Fax: 020 7255 2352
Editor: Bill Williamson
Film editor: Derek Malcolm
General interest male/female London
living and arts oriented
18-35 target age readership
Lead time: 2 weeks
Circulation: 100,000

The Mirror
1 Canada Square
Canary Wharf
London E14 5DP
Tel: 020 7293 3000
Fax: 020 7293 3409
Film: Simon Rose
TV: Tony Purnell
National daily newspaper with
daily/weekly film and television
column
Circulation: 2,355,285
incorporating The Daily Record
(Scottish daily newspaper)

Morning Star
1-3 Ardleigh Road
London N1 4HS
Tel: 020 7254 0033
Fax: 020 7254 5950
Film/TV: Mike Parker
The only national daily owned by its
readers as a co-operative. Weekly
film and TV reviews
Circulation: 9,000

Movie Plus
(Monthly)
Inside Publications
16 Brand Street
Hitchin, Herts SG5 1JE
Tel: 01462 436785
Fax: 01462 436806
Editor: Carole Childs

Moving Pictures
(Monthly)
151-153 Wardour Street
London W1V 3TB
Tel: 020 7287 0070
Fax: 020 7287 9637
Editor: Christian de Schutter
Worldwide coverage of television,
film, video and new media
Circulation: 8,500

Ms London
(Weekly, Mon)
7-9 Rathbone Street
London W1P 1AF
Tel: 020 7636 6651
Fax: 020 7255 2352
Films: Dee Pilgrim
Free magazine with drama, video,
film and general arts section
Lead time: 2 weeks

Press day: Thurs
Circulation: 94,100

New Musical Express
(Weekly, Wed)
25th Floor
King's Reach Tower
Stamford Street
London SE1 9LS
Tel: 020 7261 5723
Fax: 020 7261 5185
Website: www.nme.com
Film/TV editor: John Mulvey
Rock music newspaper
Lead time: Mon, 1 week before press
day
Circulation: 121,001

New Scientist
(Weekly, Sat avail Thur)
151 Wardour Street
London W1V 4BN
Tel: 020 7331 2701
Fax: 020 7331 2772
email: news@newscientist.com
Website: www.newscientist.com
Editor: Alun Anderson
Contains articles and reports on the
progress of science and technology in
terms which the non-specialist can
understand
Press day: Mon
Circulation: 120,744

New Statesman and Society
(Weekly, Fri)
7th Floor
Victoria Station House
191 Victoria Street
London SW1E 5NE
Tel: 020 7828 1232
Fax: 020 7828 1881
email: info@newstatesman.co.uk
Website: www.newstatesman.co.uk
Editor: Peter Wilby
Arts films: Frances Stonor Saunders
Independent radical journal of
political, social and cultural comment
Press day: Mon
Circulation: 26,000

News of the World
News International
1 Virginia Street
London E1 9XR
Tel: 020 7782 1000
Fax: 020 7583 9504
Editor: Phil Hall
Films: Johnathon Ross
TV critic: Charles Catchpole
National Sunday newspaper
Press day: Sat
Circulation: 4,434,856

midweek@indmags.co.uk
Attn: Val Tumner
Ms.

9-5, GAT Ms, London.

Nine to Five
(Weekly, Mon)
7-9 Rathbone Street
London W1P 1AF
Tel: 020 7636 6651
Fax: 020 7255 2352
Film: Bill Williamson
Free London magazine
Press day: Wed
Circulation: 160,000

The Observer
(Weekly, Sun)
119 Farringdon Road
London EC1R 3ER
Tel: 020 7278 2332
Fax: 020 7713 4250
Arts editor: Jane Ferguson
Film critic: Philip French
TV: Mike Bradley
National Sunday newspaper
Lead time: 1 week
Press day: Fri
Circulation: 450,831

Observer Life Magazine
(Weekly, Sun)
119 Farringdon Road
London EC1R 3ER
Tel: 020 7278 2332
Fax: 020 7239 9837
Supplement to The Observer

Options
(Monthly)
King's Reach Tower
Stamford Street
London SE1 9LS
Tel: 020 7261 5000
Fax: 020 7261 7344
Film: Susy Feag
TV: Stuart Husband
Women's glossy magazine
Lead time: 3 months
Circulation: 146,692

The PACT Magazine
Producers Alliance for Cinema and
Television
published by MDI Ltd
30/31 Islington Green
London N1 8DU
Tel: 020 7226 8585
Fax: 020 7226 8586
Editor: Clare Mount
PACT members' monthly
Circulation: 2,000

The People
(Weekly, Sun)
1 Canada Square
Canary Wharf
London E14 5AP
Tel: 020 7510 3000
Fax: 020 7293 3810

Films: Jane Simon
TV: Rachel Lloyd
National Sunday newspaper
Press day: Sat
Circulation: 1,932,237

Picture House
(Annual)
Cinema Theatre Association
5 Coopers Close
Burgess Hill
West Sussex RH15 8AN
Tel: 01444 246893
Documents the past and present
history of cinema buildings
Lead time: 8 weeks
Circulation: 2,000

The Pink Paper
(Weekly, Thur)
Cedar House
72 Holloway Road
London N7 8NZ
Tel: 020 7296 6210
Fax: 020 7957 0046
Editor: Alistair Pegg
Film/TV: Neil Edwards
Britain's national lesbian and gay
newspaper
Lead time: 14 days
Circulation: 53,780

Attn: Anthony Cod Arts section

Premiere
(Monthly)
37-39 Millharbour
London E14 9TZ
Tel: 020 7972 6791
Fax: 020 7972 6791
Editor: Matt Mueller
A 16-page UK film supplement in
issues of American Premiere sold in
the UK, containing personality profiles,
on the set reports, news and reviews
Lead time: 3 months
Circulation: 40,000

Press Gazette
19 Scarbrook Road
Croydon
Surrey CR9 1LX
Tel: 020 8565 4200
Fax: 020 8565 4395
email: pged@qpp.co.uk
Website: www.pressgazette.co.uk
Editor: Philippa Kennedy
Weekly magazine covering all
aspects of the media industry:
journalism; advertising; broadcast;
freelance
Press day: Thurs
Circulation: 8,500

Q
(Monthly)
1st Floor

Mappin House
4 Winsley Street
London W1N 7AR
Tel: 020 7312 8182
Fax: 020 7312 8247
Website: www.qonline.co.uk
Editor: Andy Pemberton
Specialist music magazine for 18-45
year olds. Includes reviews of new
albums, films and books
Lead time: 2 months
Circulation: 212,607

Radio Times
(Weekly, Tues)
Woodlands
80 Wood Lane
London W12 0TT
Tel: 020 8576 3999
Fax: 020 8576 3160
Website: www.rtguide.beeb.com
Editor: Sue Robinson
Films: Barry Norman
Features: Kim Newson
Listings: Caroline Meyer
Weekly guide to UK television, radio
and satellite programmes
Lead time: 14 days
Circulation: 1,406,152

Regional Film & Video
(Monthly)
Flagship Publishing
164-165 North Street
Belfast BT1 1GF
Tel: 028 9031 9008
Fax: 028 9031 9101
Editor: Steve Preston
Film and Video Trade Newspaper
Circulation: 12,000

Satellite TV Europe
531-533 King's Road
London SW10 0TZ
Tel: 020 7351 3612
Website: www.satellite-tv.co.uk/

The Scotsman
108 Holyrood Road
Edinburgh EH8 8AS
Tel: 0131 620 8620
Fax: 0131 620 8620
email: online@scotsman.com
Website: www.scotsman.com
Arts Editor: Andrew Burnet
Film critic: Damien Love
Scottish daily newspaper
Circulation: 77,057

Scotland on Sunday
20 North Bridge
Edinburgh EH1 1YT
Tel: 0131 225 2468
Fax: 0131 220 2443
email: spectrum_sos@scotsman.com

Film: Allan Hunter
Arts and Features: Adrian Turpin
TV: Stewart Hennessey
Scottish Sunday newspaper
Lead time: 10 days
Circulation: 110,000

Scottish Film
(Quarterly)
Arts and Entertainment
Publishing Ltd
24 Sandyford Place
Glasgow G3 7NG
Tel: 0141 221 4241
Fax: 0141 221 4247
Editor: Robert McColl
Filmmaking and broadcasting within
Scotland. Scottish Film is distributed
throughout Scotland to all the
production companies, facility houses
and broadcasters
Circulation: 20,000

Screen
(Quarterly)
The Gilmorehill Centre
University of Glasgow
Glasgow G12 8QQ
Tel: 0141 330 5035
Fax: 0141 330 3515
email: screen@arts.gla.ac.uk
Website: www.arts.gla.ac.uk/tfs/
screen.html
Caroline Beven
Journal of essays, reports, debates
and reviews on film and television
studies. Organises the annual Screen
Studies Conference
Circulation: 1,400

Screen Digest
(Monthly)
Lyme House Studios
38 Georgiana Street
London NW1 0EB
Tel: 020 7482 5842
Fax: 020 7580 0060
email: screendigest@
compuserve.com
Managing director: Allan Hardy
Editor: David Fisher
Executive editor: Ben Keen
Deputy editor: Mark Smith
International industry news digest
and research report covering film,
television, cable, satellite, video and
other multimedia information. Has a
centre page reference system every
month on subjects like law, statistics
or sales. Now also available on a
computer data base via fax at 020
7580 0060 under the name Screenfax
(see entry under Screenfax)

Screen Finance
(Fortnightly)
Informa Media Group
40 Berners Street
London W1P 3AA
Tel: 020 7453 2800
Fax: 020 7453 2802
email: info.media@informa.com
Editor: Tim Adler
Detailed analysis and news coverage
of the film and television industries
in the UK and Europe
Lead time: 1-3 days

Screen International
(Weekly, Thur)
EMAP Media
33-39 Bowling Green Lane
London EC1R 0DA
Tel: 020 7505 8056/8080
Fax: 020 7505 8117
email: leo.barraclough@media.emap.
co.uk
Website: screendaily.com
Managing Editor: Leo Barraclough
International trade magazine for the
film, television, video, cable and
satellite industries. Regular news,
features, production information from
around the world
Press day: Tue
Features lead time: 3 months
Circulation: 10,000

Screenfax (Database)
Screen Digest
Lyme House Studios
38 Georgiana Street
London NW1 0EB
Fax: 020 7580 0060
Available on-line via Dialog, Profile,
Data-Star, MAID and most other online databases, or by fax: 020 7580
0060. Provides customised print-outs
on all screen media subjects with
summaries of news developments,
market research.

SFX
Future Publishing
30 Momouth Street
Bath BA1 2BW
Tel: 01225 442244
Fax: 01225 480696
email: sfx@futurenet.co.uk
Website: www.sfx.co.uk
Editor: Dave Golder

Shivers
(Monthly)
Visual Imagination
9 Blades Court
Deodar Road
London SW15 2NU
Tel: 020 8875 1520

Fax: 020 8875 1588
Editor: David Miller
Horror film reviews and features
Lead time: 1 month
Circulation: 30,000

Sight and Sound
(Monthly)
British Film Institute
21 Stephen Street
London W1P 2LN
Tel: 020 7255 1444
Fax: 020 7436 2327
Editor: Nick James
Deputy Editor: Edward Lawrenson
Includes regular columns, feature
articles, a book review section and
review/synopsis/credits of feature
films theatrically released, plus a
brief listing of every video
Copy date: 4th of each month
Circulation: 26,000

South Wales Argus
Cardiff Road
Newport
Gwent NP9 1QW
Tel: 01633 810000
Fax: 01633 462202
Film & TV editor: Lesley Williams
Regional evening newspaper
Lead time: 2 weeks
Circulation: 32,569

The Spectator
(Weekly, Thur)
56 Doughty Street
London WC1N 2LL
Tel: 020 7405 1706
Fax: 020 7242 0603
Arts editor: Elizabeth Anderson
Film: Mark Steyn
TV: James Delingpole and Simon
Hoggart
Independent review of politics,
current affairs, literature and the arts
Press day: Wed
Circulation: 56,313

The Stage
(incorporating Television Today)
(Weekly, Thurs)
Stage House
47 Bermondsey Street
London SE1 3XT
Tel: 020 7403 1818
Fax: 020 7357 9287
Website: www.thestage.co.uk
Editor: Brian Attwood
Weekly trade paper covering all
aspects of entertainment
Circulation: 39,258

Stage Screen & Radio
(10 issues a year)

111 Wardour Street
London W1V 4AY
Tel: 020 7437 8506
Fax: 020 7437 8268
Editor: Janice Turner
Journal of the film, broadcasting,
theatre and entertainment union
BECTU. Reporting and analysis of
these industries and the union's
activities plus coverage of
technological developments
Lead time: 4 weeks
Circulation: 34,600

Starburst
*(Monthly + 4 Specials + German
language version)*
Visual Imagination
9 Blades Court
Deodar Road
London SW15 2NU
Tel: 020 8875 1520
Fax: 020 8875 1588
email: star@cix.compulink.co.uk
Website: www.wisimag.com
Editor: Stephen Payne
Science fiction, fantasy and horror
films, television and video
Lead time: 1 month
Circulation: 45,000

Subway Magazine
The Attic
62 Kelvingrove Street
Glasgow G3 7SA
Tel: 0141 332 9088
Fax: 0141 331 1477
Editor: Gill Mill

The Sun
PO Box 481
1 Virginia Street
London E1 9XP
Tel: 020 7782 4000
Fax: 020 7488 3253
Films: Nick Fisher
Showbiz editor: Dominic Mohan
TV editor: Danny Buckland
TV News: Sarah Crosbie
National daily newspaper
Circulation: 3,875,329

Sunday Express Magazine
Ludgate House
245 Blackfriars Road
London SE1 9UX
Tel: 020 7922 7150
Fax: 020 7922 7599
Editor: Katy Bravery
Supplement to The Express on Sunday
Lead time: 6 weeks

Sunday Magazine
1 Virginia Street
London E1 9BD

Tel: 020 7782 7000
Fax: 020 7782 7474
Editor: Judy McGuire
Deputy Editor: Jonathan Worsnop
Supplement to News of the World
Lead time: 6 weeks
Circulation: 4,701,879

Sunday Mirror
1 Canada Square
Canary Wharf
London E14 5AP
Tel: 020 7293 3000
Fax: 020 7293 3939
Film critic: Quentin Falk
TV: David Rowe, Pam Francis
National Sunday newspaper
Circulation: 2,268,263

Sunday Telegraph
1 Canada Square
Canary Wharf
London E14 5DT
Tel: 020 7538 7391
Fax: 020 7538 7872
email: starts@telegraph.co.uk
Arts: Anna Murphy
Film: Anne Billson
TV: John Preston
National Sunday newspaper
Circulation: 886,377

Sunday Times
1 Virginia Street
London E1 9BD
Tel: 020 7782 5000
Fax: 020 7782 5731
Film: Tom Shone
TV reviews: A A Gill
Video: George Perry
National Sunday newspaper
Press day: Wed
Circulation: 1,314,576

Sunday Times Magazine
Admiral House
66-68 East Smithfield
London E11 9XW
Tel: 020 7782 7000
Fax: 020 7867 0410
Editor: Robin Morgan
Supplement to Sunday Times
Lead time: 4 weeks
Circulation: 1,314,576

Talking Pictures
(Quarterly)
34 Darwin Crescent
Laira
Plymouth PL3 6DX
Tel: 01752 347200
Fax: 020 7737 4720
email: stntpublishingltd@
btinternet.com
Website: www.filmcentre.co.uk

Editor: Nigel Watson
Devoted to a serious yet entertaining
look at film, computer entertainment,
television and video
Lead time: 2 months
Circulation: 500

Tatler
(Monthly)
Vogue House
1 Hanover Square
London W1R 0AD
Tel: 020 7499 9080
Fax: 020 7409 0451
Website: www.tatler.co.uk
Editor: Jane Procter
Arts: Celia Lyttleton
Smart society magazine favouring
profiles, fashion and the arts
Lead time: 3 months
Circulation: 88,235

The Teacher
(8 p.a.)
National Union of Teachers
Hamilton House
Mabledon Place
London WC1H 9BD
Tel: 020 7380 4708
Fax: 020 7387 8458
Editor: Mitch Howard
Circulation: 250,000 mailed direct to
all NUT members and to educational
institutions

Telegraph Magazine
1 Canada Square
Canary Wharf
London E14 5AU
Tel: 020 7538 5000
Fax: 020 7513 2500
TV films: Jessamy Calkin
Supplement to Saturday edition of
the Daily Telegraph
Lead time: 6 weeks
Circulation: 1,300,000

Television
(10 p.a.)
Royal Television Society
Holborn Hall
100 Gray's Inn Road
London WC1X 8AL
Tel: 020 7430 1000
Fax: 020 7430 0924
email: info@rts.org.uk
Website: www.rts.org.uk
Editor: Peter Fiddick
Television trade magazine
Lead time: 2 weeks
Circulation: 5,000

Televisual
(Monthly)
St. Giles House

50 Poland Street
London W1V 4AX
Tel: 020 7970 6666
Fax: 020 7970 6733
Editor: Mundy Ellis
Assistant Editor; Keely Winstone
Monthly business magazine for
production professionals in the
business of moving pictures
News lead time: 1 month
Features lead time: 2 months
Circulation: 8,040

Time Out
(Weekly, Tues)
Universal House
251 Tottenham Court Road
London W1P 0AB
Tel: 020 7813 3000
Fax: 020 7813 6028
Website: www.timeout.co.uk
Film: Geoff Andrew, Tom Charity
Video: Derek Adams
TV: Alkarim Jivani
London listings magazine with
cinema and television sections
Listings lead time: 8 days
Features lead time: 1 week
Circulation: 100,000 plus

The Times
1 Pennington Street
London E1 9XN
Tel: 020 7782 5000
Fax: 020 7488 3242
Website: www.the-times.co.uk
Film/video critic: Geoff Brown
Film writer: David Robinson
TV: Matthew Bond
National daily newspaper
Circulation: 747,054

The Times Educational Supplement
(Weekly, Fri)
Admiral House
66-68 East Smithfield
London E1 9XY
Tel: 020 7782 3000
Fax: 020 7782 3199
Editor: Caroline St John-Brooks
Review editor, Friday magazine:
Geraldine Brennan
Press day: Monday
Lead time for reviews: copy 14-21
days
Circulation: 157,000

The Times Educational Supplement Scotland
(Weekly, Fri)
Scott House
10 South St Andrew Street
Edinburgh EH2 2AZ
Tel: 0131 557 1133

Fax: 0131 558 1155
email: scoted@tes.co.uk
Website: www.tes.co.uk/scotland
Editor: Willis Pickard
Press day: Wed
Circulation: 10,000

The Times Higher Educational Supplement
(Weekly, Fri)
Admiral House
66-68 East Smithfield
London E1 9XY
Tel: 020 7782 3000
Fax: 020 7782 3300
Film/TV editor: Sean Coughlan
Press day: Wed
Lead time for reviews: copy 10 days
before publication
Circulation: 26,666

The Times Literary Supplement
(Weekly, Fri)
Admiral House
66-68 East Smithfield
London E1 9XY
Tel: 020 7782 3000
Fax: 020 7782 3100
Arts editor: Will Eaves
Press day: Tues
Lead time: 2 weeks
Circulation: 34,044

Top Review
England House
25 South Quay
Gt Yarmouth
Norfolk NR30 2RG
Tel: 01493 330565
Fax: 01493 330565
email: bnw@planetmail.com
Website: www.review.uk.com
Lauren Courtney
Film, video, car, computer book,
travel and DIY reviews
Circulation: 60,000

Total Film
Future Publishing
99 Baker Street
London W1M 1FB
Tel: 020 7317 2600
Fax: 020 7317 2644
email: totalfilm@futurenet.co.uk
Website: www.futurenet.co.uk
Editor: Emma Cochrane

Tribune
(Weekly, Fri)
308 Gray's Inn Road
London WC1X 8DY
Tel: 020 7278 0911
Fax: 020 7833 0385
email: george@tribpub.demon.co.uk

Website: tribuneuk.co.uk
Joe Handy
Editor: Max Seddon
Review editor: Caroline Rees
Political and cultural weekly
Lead time: 14 days
Circulation: 10,000

TV Quick
(Weekly, Mon)
25-27 Camden Road
London NW1 9LL
Tel: 020 7284 0909
Fax: 020 7284 0593
Editor: Jon Gower
Mass market television magazine
Lead time: 3 weeks
Circulation: 799,000

TV Times
(Weekly, Tues)
10th Floor
King's Reach Tower
Stamford Street
London SE1 9LS
Tel: 020 7261 7000
Fax: 020 7261 7777
Editor: Liz Murphy
Film editor: David Quinlan
Weekly magazine of listings and
features serving viewers of
independent TV, BBC TV, satellite
and radio
Lead time: 6 weeks
Circulation: 981,311

TV Zone
(Monthly + 4 specials)
Visual Imagination Limited
9 Blades Court
Deodar Road
London SW15 2NU
Tel: 020 8875 1520
Fax: 020 8875 1588
email: tvzone@visimag.com
Website: www.visimag.com/tvzone
Editor: Jan Vincent-Rudzki
Magazine of cult television, past,
present and future, with emphasis on
science fiction and fantasy
Lead time: 1 month
Circulation: 45,000

Uncut
IPC Magazines Ltd
King's Reach Tower
Stamford Street
London SE1 9LS
Tel: 020 7261 6992
Fax: 020 7261 5573
Website: www.uncut.net
Editor: Allan Jones

Variety
(Weekly, Mon) and Daily (Mon-Fri)

6 Bell Yard
London WC2A 2JR
Tel: 020 7520 5222
Fax: 020 7520 5220
email: adam.dawtrey@rbi.co.uk
Website: www.variety.com
European editor: Adam Dawtrey
International showbusiness
newspaper
Press day: Thurs
Circulation: 36,000

Video Home Entertainment
(Weekly, Fri)
Strandgate
18-20 York Buildings
London WC2 6JU
Tel: 020 7839 7774
Fax: 020 7839 4393
Editor: John Ferguson
Video trade publication for rental and
retail
Lead time: Monday before
publication
Circulation: 7,613

View
Oakwood House
422 Hackney Road
London E2 7SY
Tel: 020 7729 6881
Fax: 020 7729 0988
Editor: Branwell Johnson
A weekly trade magazine for the
video industry covering news relevant
to the business from a retail to
distributor level. It carries a complete
listing of the month's rental releases
and a highlighted sell through list.
Regular features include coverage
from the US and interviews with
leading industry figures
Circulation: 8,000

Viewfinder
(3 p.a.)
BUFVC
77 Wells Street
London W1P 3RE
Tel: 020 7393 1511
Fax: 020 7393 1555
email: suren@bufvc.ac.uk
Website: www.bufvc.ac.uk
Suren Rajeswaran, Editor
Periodical for people in higher
education and research, includes
articles on the production, study and
use of film, television and related
media. Deadlines: 10th Jan, 1st Apr,
1st Oct
Lead time: 6 weeks
Circulation: 5,000

Vision
Cinram UK Limited

Lee House, 2nd Floor
109-111 Hammersmith Road
Hammersmith
London W14 0QH
Tel: 020 7471 7800
Fax: 020 7471 7801
email: vision@cinram.com
Bob Thomson
Magazine which provides articles and
information on trends in media
manufacturing, distribution and retail

Vogue
(Monthly)
Vogue House
Hanover Square
London W1R 0AD
Tel: 020 7408 0559
Fax: 020 7493 1345
Website: www.vogue.co.uk
Editor: Alexandra Shulman
Films: Susie Forbes
Glossy magazine for women
Lead time: 12 weeks
Circulation: 201,187

The Voice
(Weekly, Monday)
370 Coldharbour Lane
London SW9 8PL
Tel: 020 7737 7377
Fax: 020 7274 8994
Editor in chief: Mike Best
Arts: Lee Pinkerton
Britain's leading black newspaper
with mainly 18-35 age group
readership. Regular film, television
and video coverage
Press day: Friday
Circulation: 52,000

The Web
Media House, Adlington Park
Macclesfield SK10 4NP
Tel: 01625 878888
Fax: 01625 879967
email: web@idg.co.uk
Editor: Mike Cowley
Focusing on lifestyle and culture on
the Net, film and television is
extensively covered with features,
leaders and listing
Lead time: 2 weeks

Western Mail
Thomson House
Cardiff CF1 1WR
Tel: 029 20223333
Fax: 029 20583652
Film: Carolyn Hitt
Daily newspaper
Circulation: 60,251

What DVD?
Future Publishing

Beauford Court
30 Monmouth Street
Bath BA1 2BW
Tel: 01225 442244
Fax: 01225 732282
Website: www.futurenet.com/

What's On In London
(Weekly, Tues)
180 Pentonville Road *Oliver Jones*
London N1 9LB
Tel: 020 7278 4393
Fax: 020 7837 5838
Editor: Michael Darvell
Films & Video: David Clark
London based weekly covering
cinema, theatre, music, arts, books,
entertainment and video
Press day: Mon
Lead time: 10 days *whatson@Globalnet.co.uk*
Circulation: 42,000

What's On TV
(Weekly, Tues)
King's Reach Tower
London SE1 9LS
Tel: 020 7261 7769
Fax: 020 7261 7739
Editor: Mike Hollingsworth
TV listings magazine
Lead time: 3 weeks
Circulation: 1,676,000

Yorkshire Post
Wellington Street
Leeds
West Yorkshire LS1 1RF
Tel: 0113 238 8536
Fax: 0113 244 3430
TV editor: Angela Barnes
Regional daily morning newspaper
Deadline: 10.00 pm
Circulation: 100,126

BBC Radio

BBC
Broadcasting House
Portland Place
London W1A 1AA
Tel: 020 7580 4468
Fax: 020 7637 1630

BBC CWR (Coventry & Warwickshire)
25 Warwick Road
Coventry CV1 2WR
Tel: 01203 559911
Fax: 01203 520080

BBC Essex
198 New London Road
Chelmsford
Essex CM2 9XB
Tel: 01245 262393
Fax: 01245 492983

BBC GMR Talk
PO Box 951
Oxford Road
Manchester M60 1SD
Tel: 0161 200 2000
Fax: 0161 228 6110

BBC Hereford & Worcester
Hylton Road
Worcester WR2 5WW
Tel: 01905 748485
Fax: 01905 748006

BBC Radio Bristol
Broadcasting House
Whiteladies Road
Bristol BS8 2LR
Tel: 0117 974 1111
Fax: 0117 923 8323

BBC Radio Cambridgeshire
Broadway Court, Broadway
Peterborough PE1 1RP
Tel: 01733 312832
Fax: 01733 343768

BBC Radio Cleveland
PO Box 95FM
Broadcasting House
Newport Road
Middlesbrough TS1 5DG
Tel: 01642 225211
Fax: 01642 211356

BBC Radio Cornwall
Phoenix Wharf
Truro TR1 1UA
Tel: 01872 275421
Fax: 01872 240679

BBC Radio Cumbria
Hartington Street
Barrow-in-Furness

Cumbria LA14 5SC
Tel: 01228 835252
Fax: 01228 870008

BBC Radio Derby
PO Box 269
Derby DE1 3HL
Tel: 01332 361111
Fax: 01332 290794
email: radio.derby@bbc.co.uk
Website: www.bbc.co.uk/radioderby

BBC Radio Devon
PO Box 5
Broadcasting House
Seymour Road, Mannamead
Plymouth PL3 5YQ
Tel: 01752 260323
Fax: 01752 234599

BBC Radio Foyle
8 Northland Road
Londonderry BT48 7JD
Tel: 01504 378 600
Fax: 01504 378666

BBC Radio Guernsey
Commerce House, Les Banques
St Peter Port
Guernsey GY1 2HS
Tel: 01481 728977
Fax: 01481 713557

BBC Radio Humberside
9 Chapel Street
Hull HU1 3NU
Tel: 01482 323232
Fax: 01482 226409

BBC Radio Jersey
18 Parade Road
St Helier
Jersey JE2 3PL
Tel: 01534 87000
Fax: 01534 32569

BBC Radio Lancashire
Darwen Street
Blackburn
Lancs BB2 2EA
Tel: 01254 262411
Fax: 01254 680821

BBC Radio Leeds
Broadcasting House
Woodhouse Lane
Leeds LS2 9PN
Tel: 0113 244 2131
Fax: 0113 242 0652

BBC Radio Leicester
Epic House
Charles Street
Leicester LE1 3SH
Tel: 0116 251 6688
Fax: 0116 251 1463

BBC Radio Lincolnshire
PO Box 219
Newport
Lincoln LN1 3XY
Tel: 01522 511411
Fax: 01522 511058

BBC Radio Merseyside
55 Paradise Street
Liverpool L1 3BP
Tel: 0151 708 5500
Fax: 0151 794 0909
Film and video reviewer: Ramsey
Campbell

BBC Radio Newcastle
Broadcasting Centre
Fenham
Newcastle Upon Tyne NE99 1RN
Tel: 0191 232 4141
Fax: 0191 232 5082

BBC Radio Norfolk
Norfolk Tower
Surrey Street
Norwich NR1 3PA
Tel: 01603 617411
Fax: 01603 633692

BBC Radio Northampton
Broadcasting House
Abington Street
Northampton NN1 2BH
Tel: 01604 239100
Fax: 01604 230709

BBC Radio Nottingham
PO York House
Mansfield Road
Nottingham NG1 3JB
Tel: 0115 955 0500
Fax: 0115 955 0501

BBC Radio Oxford
269 Banbury Road
Oxford OX2 7DW
Tel: 01865 311444
Fax: 01865 311996

BBC Radio Sheffield
Ashdell Grove
60 Westbourne Grove
Sheffield S10 2QU
Tel: 0114 268 6185
Fax: 0114 266 4375

BBC Radio Solent
PO Box 900
Dorchester DT1 1TP
Tel: 01305 269654
Fax: 01305 250910

BBC Radio Stoke
Cheapside
Hanley
Stoke-on-Trent ST1 1JJ

Tel: 01782 208080
Fax: 01782 289115

BBC Radio Sussex & Surrey
Broadcasting House
Guildford
Surrey GU2 5AP
Tel: 01483 306306
Fax: 01483 304952

BBC Radio WM
PO Box 206
Birmingham B5 7SD
Tel: 0121 414 8484
Fax: 0121 414 8817

BBC Somerset Sound
14-16 Paul Street
Taunton TA1 3PF
Somerset
Tel: 01823 251641
Fax: 01823 332539

BBC Southern Counties
Broadcasting Centre
Guildford GU2 5AP
Tel: 01483 306306
Fax: 01483 304952

BBC Three Counties Radio
PO Box 3CR, Hastings Street
Luton
Bedfordshire LU1 5XL
Tel: 01582 441000
Fax: 01582 401467

BBC Wiltshire Sound
Broadcasting House
Prospect Place
Swindon SN1 3RN
Tel: 01793 513626
Fax: 01793 513650

BBC World Service
Bush House
Strand
London WC2B 4PH
Tel: 020 7257 2171
Fax: 020 7240 3938

Independent Radio

Classic FM
Academic House
24-28 Oval Road
London NW1 7DQ
Tel: 020 7284 3000
Fax: 020 7713 2630

GLR
35c Marylebone High Street
London W1A 4LG
Tel: 0171 224 2424
Fax: 0171 487 2908

Longwave Radio
Atlantic 252
74 Newman Street
London W1P 3LA
Tel: 020 7637 5252
Fax: 020 7637 3925
Trim, Co Meath, Ireland
Tel/Fax: 00353 463655

Virgin 1215 AM
1 Golden Square
London W1R 4DJ
Tel: 020 7434 1215
Fax: 020 7434 1197

Television

Anglia Television
Anglia House
Norwich NR1 3JG
Tel: 01603 615151
Fax: 01603 615032
Website: www.anglia.tv.co.uk

BBC Television Centre
Wood Lane
London W12 7RJ
Tel: 020 8743 8000

Border Television
Television Centre
Carlisle CA1 3NT
Tel: 01228 525101
Fax: 01228 541384

Carlton Television
35-38 Portman Square
London W1H 0NU
Tel: 020 7486 6688
Fax: 020 7486 1132

Central Independent Television (East)
Carlton Studios
Lenton Lane
Nottingham NG7 2NA
Tel: 0115 986 3322
Fax: 0115 964 5018

Central Independent Television (South)
9 Windrush Court
Abingdon Business Park
Abingdon
Oxon OX14 1SA
Tel: 01235 554123
Fax: 01235 524024

Channel Five Broadcasting
22 Long Acre
London WC2E 9LY
Tel: 020 7550 5555
Fax: 020 7550 5554

Channel Four Television
124 Horseferry Road
London SW1P 2TX
Tel: 020 7396 4444
Fax: 020 7306 8353

Channel Television
Television House
Bulwer Avenue
St Sampsons
Guernsey GY2 4LA
Tel: 01481 41888
Fax: 01481 41889
The Television Centre
La Pouquelaye
St Helier

Jersey JE1 3ZD
Tel: 01534 816816
Fax: 01534 816689

GMTV
London Television Centre
Upper Ground
London SE1 9TT
Tel: 020 7827 7000
Fax: 020 7827 7249
email: malcolm.douglas@gmtv.co.uk
Website: www.gmtv.co.uk
Malcolm Douglas, Terry O'Sullivan

Grampian Television
Queen's Cross
Aberdeen AB15 4XJ
Tel: 01224 846846
Fax: 01224 846802
North Tonight; Crossfire; Telefios;
Walking Back to Happiness; Top
Club; We the Jury; The Art Sutter
Show

Granada Television
Quay Street
Manchester M60 9EA
Tel: 0161 832 7211
Fax: 0161 827 2324
Albert Dock
Liverpool L3 4BA
Tel: 0151 709 9393
White Cross
Lancaster LA1 4XQ
Tel: 01524 606688
36 Golden Square
London W1R 4AH
Tel: 020 7734 8080
Bridgegate House
5 Bridge Place
Lower Bridge Street
Chester CH1 1SA
Tel: 01244 313966

HTV Wales
Television Centre
Culverhouse Cross
Cardiff CF5 6XJ
Tel: 01222 590590
Fax: 01222 590759

HTV West
Television Centre
Bath Road
Bristol BS4 3HG
Tel: 0117 972 2722
Fax: 0117 972 3122
HTV News; The West This Week,
West Eye View

Independent Television News (ITN)
200 Gray's Inn Road
London WC1X 8XZ
Tel: 020 7833 3000

Meridian Broadcasting
TV Centre
Northam Road
Southampton SO14 0PZ
Tel: 023 8022 2555
Fax: 023 8033 5050
Website: www.meridiantv.com
TV Weekly

S4C
Parc Ty Glas
Llanishen
Cardiff CF4 5DU
Tel: 029 2074 7444
Fax: 029 2074 4444
email: s4c@s4c.co.uk
Website: www.s4c.co.uk
Head of Press and Public Relations:
David Meredith

Scottish TV
Cowcaddens
Glasgow G2 3PR
Tel: 0141 300 3000
Fax: 0141 332 9274

Tyne Tees Television
The Television Centre
City Road
Newcastle upon Tyne NE1 2AL
Tel: 0191 261 0181
Fax: 0191 232 7017

Ulster Television
Havelock House
Ormeau Road
Belfast BT7 1EB
Tel: 028 9032 8122
Fax: 028 9024 6695

Westcountry Television
Western Wood Way
Language Science Park
Plymouth PL7 5BQ
Tel: 01752 333333
Fax: 01752 333033

Yorkshire Television
The Television Centre
Kirkstall Road
Leeds LS3 1JS
Tel: 0113 243 8283
Fax: 0113 243 3655

News and Photo Agencies

Associated Press
12 Norwich Street
London EC4A 1BP
Tel: 020 7353 1515
Fax: 020 7583 0196

Bridge News
78 Fleet Street
London EC4Y 1HY
Tel: 020 7842 4000
Fax: 020 7583 5032
Business Information Service

Central Office of Information
Hercules Road
London SE1 7DU
Tel: 020 7928 2345
Fax: 020 7928 5037

Central Press Features
20 Spectrum House
32-34 Gordon House Road
London NW5 1LP
Tel: 020 7284 1433
Fax: 020 7284 4494
Film/TV: Chris King

Fleet Street News Agency
68 Exmouth Market
London EC1R 4RA
Tel: 020 7278 5661
Fax: 020 7278 8480

London News Service
68 Exmouth Market
London EC1R 4RA
Tel: 020 7278 5661
Fax: 020 7278 8480

Press Association
292 Vauxhall Bridge Road
London SW1V 1AE
Tel: 020 7963 7000
Fax: 020 7963 7192
email: www@padd.press.net
Website: www.pa.press.net/

Reuters Ltd
85 Fleet Street
London EC4P 4AJ
Tel: 020 7250 1122
Fax: 020 7542 7921
Website: www.reuters.com
Media: Mary Ellen-Barker

United Press International
408 The Strand
London WC2R 0NE
Tel: 020 7333 0990
Fax: 020 7333 1690

PREVIEW THEATRES

BAFTA
195 Piccadilly
London W1V 0LN
Tel: 020 7465 0277
Fax: 020 7734 1009
Website: www.bafta.org
Formats: Twin 35mm all aspect
ratios. Dolby A, SR, SRD, DTS
sound. 35 Double head mono,
twin/triple track stereo plus Dolby
Matrix. Twin 16mm and super
16mm, 16 double head stereo plus
Dolby Matrix. BARCO 9200 Data
Video Projector VHS, Lo Band/Hi
Band U-matic, Beta, Beta SP, Digi
Beta. Interfaces for most PC outputs,
SVGA, MAC etc. 35mm slides
single, twin and disolve multi-wau
control, Audio, RGB Video Tie Lines
in Theatre. ISDN 2. Catering by
Roux Fine Dining. Seats: Princess
Anee Theatre, 213 Run Run Shaw
Theatre, 30 (not all formats
available), Function Room, up to 200

British Film Institute
21 Stephen Street
London W1T 1LN
Tel: 020 7957 8976
Fax: 020 7580 5830
email: roger.young@bfi.org.uk
Website: www.bfi.org.uk
Formats: 35mm Dolby Opt/Mag
Stereo A/SR, Std 16mm Opt, Super
16 Mag Stereo A/SR, Large Screen
Video Projection PAL VHS, SVHS,
U-MATIC hi/lo band Triple Standard,
BETA SP, DVD (PAL/NTSC) Stereo
Large Screen Video Projection.
Disabled Access
Seats: 1: 36, 2: 36

BUFVC
77 Wells Street
London W1P 3RE
Tel: 020 7393 1500
Fax: 020 7393 1555
email: ask@bufvc.ac.uk
Formats: Viewing rooms equipped
with 16mm double-head, Betacam,
SVHS, VHS, lo-band and hi-band U-
Matic, Betamax, Phillips 1500
Seats: 20-30 max

Century Preview Theatres
31-32 Soho Square
London W1V 6AP

Tel: 020 7753 7135
Fax: 020 7753 7138
email: projection@foxinc.com
Nick Ross
Picture Formats: 1.1:33, 1.1:66,
1.1:85, Super 35, Scope
Sound Formats: (CP 500) Mono,
Dolby A, SR, SR-D+EX. DTS.
Double Head (Magnetic) 2000 ft.
Also: Spotlighting, microphones,
lecturns, for conventions. Video on
request
Seating Capacity: 73

Chapter Cinema
Market Road
Canton
Cardiff CF5 1QE
Tel: 029 2031 1050
Fax: 029 2031 3431
email: chaptercinema@easynet.co.uk
Formats: 35mm optical, 16mm
optical/sep mag, high quality video
projection, U-Matic/VHS - all
standards. Beta SP PAL2 Channel
infra-red audio amplification/
simultaneous translation system in
both screens. Reception space, bars
and restaurant
Seats: 1:194, 2:68

Columbia TriStar Films UK
Sony Pictures Europe House
25 Golden Square
London W1R 6LU
Tel: 020 7533 1095
Fax: 020 7533 1105
Formats: 35mm optical (SDDS,
Dolby "SR" + "A" type)/double head,
SVA Mag, 16mm optical (Mono),
Super 16 and Super 35. BETA SP,
BVU/U-Matic, VHS, High Definition
Video. Large reception area. Seats:
80

Computer Film Company
19-23 Wells Street
London W1P 3FB
Picture Formats: 1.1:33, 1.1:66,
1.1:85, Super 35, Scope. Variable
speeds, reverse projection if required.
Sound Formats: Mono, Dolby A, SR,
SRD. Video on request. Bar area
Seating: 64

The Curzon Minema
45 Knightsbridge

London SW1X 7NL
Tel: 020 7235 4226
Fax: 020 7235 3426
email:info@minema.com
Website: www.minema.com
Formats: 35mm and 16mm, video
and AV presentations

Curzon Soho
93-107 Shaftesbury Avenue
London W1V 7AE
Tel: 020 7734 9209
Fax: 020 7734 1977
email: joe@curzon-
soho.demon.co.uk
Joe Bateman
Picture Formats: 1.1:33, 1.1:66, 1.1:85,
Scope. 35mm Kodak slide projection
Video Projection: Beta SP, Digi-Beta,
Powerpoint Capable, Analogue
Projector. PA on request, all theatres to
THX standard
Sound Formats: Mono, Dolby, A+SR,
SRD, Double headed (magnetic) 3 and
6 Track. Six channel A type and SR
Reduction
Large lounge/reception area available
for hire. In-house Catering: breakfast,
canape and buffet menus available on
request
Seats: 1:249 2: 130 3: 110

De Lane Lea
75 Dean Street
London W1V 5HA
Tel: 020 7432 3800
Fax: 020 7432 3838
email: dll@delanelea.com
Website: www.delanelea.com
Picture Formats: 35mm. 1.1:33,
1.1:66, 1.1:85. Super 35, Scope
Sound Formats: Mono, Dolby, A +
SR with double-head capacity
(magnetic) 6,4,3 track stereo
Video: VHS, U-Matic, DVD, Beta sp.
Bar and catering available.
Seating Capacity: 37

Edinburgh Film & TV
Studios
Nine Mile Burn
Penicuik EH26 9LT
Tel: 01968 672131
Fax: 01968 672685
Formats: 16mm and 35mm double-
head stereo, U-Matic, VHS
Seats: 100

Eon Theatre
Eon House
138 Piccadilly
London W1V 95H
Tel: 020 7493 7953
Fax: 020 7408 1236
email: Nikki.Hunter@eon.co.uk
Ray Aguilar
Projection 35mm. Picture Formats:
1.1:33 & 1.1:85 Scope. D Head
Sound Formats: Mono, Dolby, A&S-R
Video Projection: Video, VHS, BETA
SP, DVD, U-Matic & Laserdisc
Hospitality Suite
Seating: 22

FilmFour Ltd
77-78 Charlotte Street
London W1P 1X
Tel: 020 7868 7700
Fax: 020 7868 7767
Website: www.filmfour.com
Picture Formats: 35mm, 16mm,
16mm super. 1.1:33. 1.1:66, 1.1:85,
Scope
Sound Formats: Mono, Dolby, A+SR,
SRD, Double headed (magnetic) (3
Track)
Seating Capacity: 30

ICA
12 Carlton House Terrace
London SW1Y 5AH
Tel: 020 7930 0493
Fax: 020 7873 0051
Formats:
Cinema 1: 185 seats 35mm com-
opt, Dolby CP, 16mm com-opt, + Sep
Mag; video projection Super 16mm
Cinema 2: 45 seats, 35mm com-opt,
16mm com-opt, Super 8, video
projection all formats.
Both Cinemas available up to 4.30pm
weekdays, 2pm at the weekend.
Two regency reception rooms also
available, level access to cinemas.
Cafe bar available exclusively till
noon

Imperial War Museum
(Corporate Hospitality)
Lambeth Road
London SE1 6HZ
Tel: 020 7416 5394
Fax: 020 7416 5392/020 7416 5374
email: film@iwm.org.uk
Website: www.iwm.org.uk
Formats: 35mm and 16mm; Betacam,
U-Matic, SVHS and VHS. Catering
by arrangement. Large Exhibit Hall,
capacity: 1,000 Disabled access
Seats: Cinema: 200

King's Lynn Arts Centre
27/29 King Street

King's Lynn
Norfolk PE30 1HA
Tel: 01553 765565
Fax: 01553 762141
Formats: 16mm, 35mm
Seats: 349

The Lux Cinema
2-4 Hoxton Square
London N1 6NU
Tel: 020 7684 2855
Fax: 020 7684 2222
email: lux@lux.org.uk
The Lux Cinema opens onto
fashionable Hoxton Square with a
distinctive lobby dominated by a
back-projection wall and video floor,
available for promotional use. The
cinema has a polished, semi-sprung
wooden floor with stylish,
upholstered and fully removable
seating. It can be adapted from an
auditorium to a 126 square meter
shell for master-classes, live music,
performance and studio production of
film and video. All major projection
formats are available, including data
projection, with variable and fully
programmable electronic screen,
lighting and acoustic qualities. Full
disabled access throughout, with
lower level counter and induction loop
Seats 120

Mr Young's
14 D'Arblay Street
London W1V 3FP
Tel: 020 7437 1771
Fax: 020 7734 4520
Contact: Reuben/Andy/Derry
Formats: 35mm, Super 35mm, U-
Matic, VHS, Betacam SP, Dolby
stereo double-head optical and
magnetic Dolby SR. Large screen
video projection. Bar area, catering
by request. Theatres non-smoking
Seats: 1: 42, 2: 25, 3:45

Pinewood Studios
Pinewood Road
Iver Heath
Bucks SL0 0NH
Tel: 01753 656296
Fax: 01753 656014
email: helen_wells@pinewood-
studios.co.uk
Contact: Helen Wells
Formats: 35mm, 70mm, Dolby SR,
SR.D, DTS, SDDS, Comopt,
Commag, Sepmag. Separate
timecode digital sound screening by
arrangement. Screen width 34ft.
Disabled access. Lounge available.
Seats: 115

Planet Hollywood
13 Coventry Street
London W1
Tel: 020 7437 7827
Fax: 020 7439 7827
Formats: 35mm, 70mm, SVHS/VHS,
U-Matic, Laser Disc, Lucasfilm Ltd
THX Sound Sytem, Dolby CP200 +
SRD/DTS digital stereo. Super
35mm with separate magnetic tracks
and remote volume control.
Microphone facilities. Lifts for the
disabled available
Seats: Cinema: 75, Dining area: 85,
120 (standing)

Prominent Facilities THX
68a Delancey Street
London NW1 7RY
Tel: 020 7284 1020
Fax: 020 7284 1202
Formats: 35mm Dolby optical and
magnetic, 2,000' double-head, rock
'n' roll. All aspect ratios, and Super
35, 24-25 30fps, triple-track,
interlock, Dolby A + SR stereo,
16mm double-head married. Fully air
conditioned, kitchen and reception
area. Wheelchair access. Seats: 26

RSA
8 John Adam Street
London WC2N 6EZ
Tel: 020 7839 5049
Fax: 020 7321 0271
email: Conference@rsa-
uk.demon.co.uk
Website: www.rsa.org.uk
The Great Room
Video Formats: SVHS, Beta SP.
Other formats by arrangement.
Barcographics 8100 Projector for
Video and Data Projection. Loop
system for hard of hearing, disabled
access to all rooms. Full catering
available: Seats: 202
Durham House Street Auditorium
Video Formats: SVHS, Low band U-
matic. Other formats by arrangement.
Sony 1252 Projector for Video and
Data Projection. Loop system for
hard of hearing, disabled access to all
rooms. Full catering available. Seats:
60

Screen West
John Brown Publishing
136-142 Bramley Road
London W10 6SR
Tel: 020 7565 3181
Jess Tully
Enquiries: Sarah Alliston
Technical Enquiries/bookings: Peter
Spence
State of the art preview theatre with

luxury seating for 74 people.
Formats: 35mm, 16mm, Super
35mm, Double Head, Beta, VHS, PC.
Surround Sound: Optical, Magnetic,
Digital (SRD and DTS). and full
catering facilities in the adjoining
function room.

The Screening Room
The Moving Picture Company
127 Wardour Street
London W1V 4NL
Tel: 020 7494 7879
Fax: 020 7287 9698
email: screening@moving-
picture.co.uk
Website: www.moving-picture.co.uk
Matt Bristowe, Chief Film
Technician (AMPS)
Mark Wiseman, Senior Film
Technician
Picture Formats: 35mm Projection,
1.1:37, 1.1:66, 1.1:85, Scope, Super
35.
Speeds: 0-50 FPS Forwards/Reverse
High Speed Shuttling @ 250 FPS
Xenon Lamps with controlled colour
temperature
Sound Formats: Optical; Mono,
Dolby A, Dolby SR, Dolby Digital
SRD, DTS. Magnetic; 6 track, 3
track, 1 track, with/without
Reduction.
Video: High Quality 5GV Digital
Projection. VHS (PAL, NTSC,
SECAM), SVHS, U-Matic
(High/Low Band), Digi-Beta,
Betacam-SP, D1, DVD (All
regions/5.1), VGA, SVGA, XGA.
Powerpoint PA System: CD,
Cassette, Stage with Lecturn,
Autocue (By Arrangement)
Self catering bar/reception area up to
75 people. Fully air conditioned,
wheelchair accessible
Seating capacity: 75

Shepperton Studios
Studios Road
Shepperton
Middx TW17 0QD
Tel: 01932 562611/572350
Fax: 01932 568989
email: sheppertonstudios@
dial.pipex.com
Formats: 35mm double-head and
married, Dolby A + SR, Video U-
Matic, NTSC, PAL, SECAM, VHS.
Seats: (35mm) 17

Total Film
99 Baker Street
London W1M 1FB
Tel: 020 7317 2600
Fax: 020 7486 5676

Graham Singleton
Fully air conditioned screening room
facility with Crestron touch screen
remote for computer generated
presentations and adjacent boardroom
facilities. Format: 35mm print,
Betacam and VHS through an
overhead CRT with line doubler.
Ernemann 15-laser audio projector
with both scope and flat lenses. Sony
Betacam SP player and professional
JVC HRH 507MS VCR with
overhead CRT projector. Sound
delivery by Sony Digital Camera
System with Dolby SR set-up &
installed by Dolby Laboratories
Seats: 24

Twentieth Century Fox
31-32 Soho Square
London W1V 6AP
Tel: 020 7735 7135
Fax: 020 7735 7138
email: projection@foxinc.com
Nick Ross
Picture formats: 1.1:85, 1:1:66
Scope, Super 35
Sound formats (CP500) Mono, Dolby
A, SR, SR-D-EX
Double Head (magnetic) 2000ft
Also microphones, video on request
Seating: 37

Twickenham Film Studios
St Margaret's
Twickenham
Middx TW1 2AW
Tel: 020 8607 8888
Fax: 020 8607 8889
Formats: 16mm, 35mm.
Seats: 31

UIP International Theatre
UIP House
45 Beardon Road
Hammersmith
London
Tel: 020 8741 9041
Picture Formats: 1.1:33, 1.1:66,
1.1:85, Scope
Sound Formats: Mono, Dolby, A+SR,
SRD +EX, DTS, SDDS, Double head
(magnetic). Mono, SVA, 6 Track
Video: VHS, U-Matic, Beta SP
Seating capacity: 43

Warner Bros
98 Theobalds Road
London WC1X 8WB
Tel: 020 7984 5272

Watershed Media Centre
1 Canons Road
Bristol BS1 5TX
Tel: 0117 9276444

Fax: 0117 9213958
email: watershed@online.
redirect.co.uk
Formats: Super 8mm, 16mm double-
head, 35mm, VHS U-Matic lo-band,
Betacam SP, Dolby A + SR. Lift
access, for wheelchair spaces each
theatre (prior notification for C2
required)
Seats: 1: 200. 2: 55

PRODUCTION COMPANIES

Listed below is a selection of UK companies currently active in financing and/or making audio visual product for the UK and international media markets. Not generally listed are the numerous companies making television commercials, educational and other non-broadcast material.

Check Book is a useful guide to all aspects of film production in the UK. Two other reference works *PACT Directory of UK Movie Producers* and *British Films Catalogue 2001* both give useful contact information for both feature and short film production in the UK

Lottery film production franchises

On 15 May 1997 The Arts Council announced three National Lottery-funded commercial feature film production franchises. Each franchise will extend over a six year period. All franchise funds offered will serve as funding pre-allocations over that period and will be drawn down conditional upon Arts Council approval of individual film proposals

Pathé Pictures
Kent House
Market Place
London W1N 8AR
Tel: 020 7323 5151
Fax: 020 7636 7594
Lottery award: £33 million
Number of films: 35
Contact: Peter Scott
Consists of: Thin Man Films and Imagine Films, Allied Filmmakers and Allied Films Ltd, NFH, Pandora Productions, Sarah Radclyffe Productions, Fragile Films and MW Entertainment

The Film Consortium
6 Flitcroft Street
London WC28H 8DJ
Tel: 020 7691 4440
Fax: 020 7691 4445
Lottery award: £30.25 million
Number of films: 39
Contact: Linda Gamble
Consists of: Greenpoint Films, Parallax Pictures, Scala and Skreba

DNA Films
3rd Floor
75-77 Margaret Street
London W1N 7HB
Tel: 020 7291 8010
Fax: 020 7291 8020
email: info@dnafilms.com
Lottery award: £29 million
Number of films: 16
Contact: Joanne Smith

A19 Film and Video
21 Foyle Street
Sunderland
Tel: 0191 565 5709
Fax: 0191 565 6288
Documentary programmes for television. Education/training material for distribution. Low budget fiction work. Production support offered to local and regionally based filmmakers, schools, community groups etc

Aardman Animations
Gas Ferry Road
Bristol BS1 6UN
Tel: 0117 984 8485
Fax: 0117 984 8486
Website: www.aardman.com
Award winning character led model animation studio producing films, commercials and television series. Aardman's first theatrical feature film, *Chicken Run* was released in 2000

ABTV
From July 99 Agran Barton Television (ABTV) has operated under the name of Harbour Pictures. Harbour Pictures is a subsidiary of Agran Barton Television (ABTV)

Acacia Productions Ltd

80 Weston Park
London N8 9TB
Tel: 020 8341 9392
Fax: 020 8341 4879
email: acacia@dial.pipex.com
Website: www.acaciaproductions.
co.uk
Recent productions: *Last Plant
Standing*, international series of
programmes about the global
conservation of plant genetic
resources (4x50mins) *Seeds of Hope
for Rwanda* (25 mins); *A Future for
Forests* (25 mins); *The Wokabout
Somil* (25 mins); *Spirit of Trees* (8 x
30 min, C4). Current project: *Under
Mount Fuji* (2x50 mins on the future
of Japanese Society)

Action Time

Wrendal House
2 Whitworth Street
West Manchester M15WX
Tel: 0161 236 8999
Fax: 0161 236 8845
Entertainment programme devisors
and producers in UK and Europe.
Recent productions: *Mr & Mrs With
Julian Clary* (ITV); *Catchphrase* (ITV)

Addictive TV

The Old House
39a North Road
London N7 9DP
Tel: 020 7700 0333
Fax: 020 7700 0303
email: mail@addictive.com
Nick Clarke
Recent productions include:
Transambient (6 part music series,
C4); *The Short Show* (Short film
showcase, LWT); *Nightshift* (Late
night series, ITV)

Adventure Pictures

6 Blackbird Yard
Ravenscroft Street
London E2 7RP
Tel: 020 7613 2233
Fax: 020 7256 0842
email: mail@adventurepictures.co.uk
Produced Sally Potter's *The Man
Who Cried, Orlando* and *The Tango
Lesson* with other features in
development. Television
documentaries include: *Death of a
Runaway* (RTS award nomination
1992); *Child's Eye* (RTS award
nomination 1995); *Looking for Billy;
Let Me See My Children; Our House;
Searching for Susan; Child's Eye;
Home Alone; Stepfamilies; The Test;
Men Who Pay For Sex; Footballer's
Wives; The End is Nigh*

After Image Ltd

32 Acre Lane
London SW2 5SG
Tel: 020 737 7300
Fax: 020 7326 1850
email: jane@arc.co.uk
Currently developing dramas

Agenda Film

Castell Close
Enterprise Park
Swansea SA7 9FH
Tel: 01792 410510
Fax: 01792 775469
Wales' largest independent
production company. Entertainment,
drama, features for S4C, C4, BBC,
corporate sector. Co-producer of
Welsh-based feature films, like
TwinTown

Alibi Productions

12 Maiden Lane
Covent Garden
London WCZE 7NA
Tel: 020 7845 0400
Fax: 020 7836 6919
email: info@alibifilms.co.uk
Website: www.alibifilms.co.uk
Linda James
Alibi is active in the financing,
international sales and distirbution of
theatrical feature films and the
production of feature film, television
drama and children's programming.
Production titles include: *Another Life*
(1999) - feature film. *Without Motive*
(2000) - 6 part television drama

Alive Productions

37 Harwood Road
London SW6 4QP
Tel: 020 7384 2243
Fax: 020 7384 2026
TV programme production company
including *Star Test* and *Star Chamber*
(both for C4)

Allied Films Ltd

Kent House
Market Place
London W1N 8AR
Tel: 020 7323 5151
Fax: 020 7631 3568
(See Pathé Productions - Lottery
Film Production Franchises)

Alomo Productions Ltd

45 Fouberts Place
London W1V 2DN
Tel: 020 7434 3060
Television comedy and drama:
*Goodnight Sweetheart; Birds of a
Feather; Love Hurts*. A Pearson
Company

Angelic Pictures

21 & 22 Colebrooke Row
Angel
Islington
London N1 8AP
Tel: 020 7359 9514
Fax: 020 7359 9153
email: rslw@hotmail.com
Website: www.angelicpictures.co.uk
Angelic Pictures supports a broad
range of individual productions -
both broadcast and non-broadcast,
including the full production of
corporate films, and multi-media
packages for companies

Anglia Television Limited

Anglia House
Norwich NR1 3JG
Tel: 01603 615151
Fax: 01603 631032
Website: www.anglia.tv.co.uk

The Animation Station

Leisure and Tourism Department
Cherwell District Council
Bodicote House
Bodicote, Banbury
Oxon OX15 4AA
Tel: 01295 252535
Fax: 01295 263155
Dex Mugan
A specialist arts education producer,
distributor and trainer. Works in
collaboration with innovative artists
and performers from across the
world, selecting and commissioning a
broad range of high quality work

Animha Productions

121 Roman Road
Linthorpe
Middlesbrough TS5 5QB
Tel: 01642 813 137
Fax: 01642 813 137
email: animha@awn.com
Website: www.awn.com/animha

Antelope

29B Montague Street
London WC1B 5BH
Tel: 020 7209 0099
Fax: 020 7209 0098
email: antelope@antelope.co.uk
Mick Csaky, Krishan Aróra
Dramas and documentaries for
broadcast TV in UK, USA, Europe
and Japan.

Arcane Pictures

46 Wetherby Mansions
Earl Court Square
London SW5 9DI
Tel: 020 7244 6590
Fax: 020 7565 4495

email: duffield@dircon.co.uk
Philippa Green
Producers: Meg Thomson, George
Duffield
Recent productions: *Milk*

Archer Street Ltd
Studio 5
10/11 Archer Street
London W1V 7HG
Tel: 020 7439 0540
Fax: 020 7437 1182
email: films@archerstreet.com
Andy Paterson, Producer
Feature film production company
owned by Frank Cottrell Boyce,
Anand Tucker and Andy Paterson,
the writer/director/producer team
behind the Oscar-nominated *Hilary
and Jackie*. Backed by FilmFour and
Intermedia

Ariel Productions Ltd
Ealing Studios
Ealing Green
Ealing
London W5 5EP
Tel: 0208 567 6655
Otto Plashkes
Production and development of
outsider projects through the National
Film Development Fund

Arlington Productions Ltd
Pinewood Studios
Iver Heath
Bucks SL0 ONH
Tel: 01753 651700
Fax: 01753 656050
TV filmmaker (previously as Tyburn
Productions Ltd): *The Masks of
Death; Murder Elite; Peter Cushing:
A One-Way Ticket to Hollywood*

Assembly Film & Television Ltd
Riverside Studios
Crisp Road, Hammersmith
London W6 9RL
Tel: 020 8741 2251
Fax: 020 8846 8083
William Burdett-Coutts
Television services and feature film
development

Richard Attenborough Productions
Twickenham Studios
St Margaret's
Twickenham TW1 2AW
Tel: 020 8607 8873
Fax: 020 8744 2766
Judy Wasdell

Avalon Television
4a Exmoor Street
London W10 6BD
Tel: 020 7598 7280
Fax: 020 7598 7281
The Frank Skinner Show (BBC1); *Harry
Hill* (Channel 4); *Quiz Ball* (BBC1)

Bandung
Block H
Carkers Lane
53-79 Highgate Road
London NW5 1TL
Tel: 020 7482 5045
Fax: 020 7284 0930
email: bandung@gn.apc.org

Peter Batty Productions
Claremont House
Renfrew Road
Kingston
Surrey KT2 7NT
Tel: 020 8942 6304
Fax: 020 8336 1661

Bazal
46-47 Bedford Square
London WC1B 3DP
Tel: 020 7462 9000
Fax: 020 7462 9998
Productions include: *Changing
Rooms* (BBC1); *Food & Drink*
(BBC2); *Ground Force* (BBC1)

BBC Films Ltd
Television Centre
302 Union House
London W12 7RJ
Tel: 020 7743 8000

Berwin and Dempsey Productions Ltd
37 Arteslan Road
London W2
Tel: 020 7792 5152
Dorothy Berwin, Ceci Dempsey
Recent production: *Bedrooms and Hallways*

The Big Group
91 Princedale Road
London W11 4HS
Tel: 020 7229 8827
Fax: 020 7243 146
email: ed.riseman@biggroup.co.uk
Website: www.biggroup.co.uk
Ed Riseman
Services for television and film (PR/Marketing)

Black & White Pictures
Teddington Studios
Teddington TW11 9NT
Tel: 020 8614 2344
Fax: 020 8614 2500
email: production@
blackandwhitepictures.co.uk

Blue Dolphin Film & Video
40 Langham Street
London W1N 5RG
Tel: 020 7255 2494
Fax: 020 7580 7670

Blue Heaven Productions Ltd
45 Leather Lane
London EC1N 7TJ
Tel: 020 7404 4222
Fax: 020 7404 4266
Producer of *The Ruth Rendell Mysteries* for Meridian/ITV Network

Braunarts
The Beehive
226a Gipsy Road
London SE27 9RB
Tel: 020 8670 9917
Fax: 020 8670 9917
email: terry@braunarts.com & gabi@braunarts.com
Website: www.braunarts.com
Contact: Gabi Braun & Terry Braun
Braunarts (previously known as Illuminations Interactive) works as both broadcast television and multimedia producers with a strong emphasis on the production of digital media. Braunarts focuses on three interconnected areas of work:
* The Performing Arts
* Education
* Creative Consultancy
The common link across these areas of interest is embodied in Braunarts commitment to the commissioning and production of new collaborations in the Digital Arts and Media. Complementing this commitment is our vision for a more challenging use of new media to broaden the understanding of and access to The Arts, Science and Learning

British Lion Film Corporation
Pinewood Studios
Iver Heath
Bucks SLO 0NH
Tel: 01753 651700
Fax: 01753 656391

The Britt Allcroft Company PLC
3 Grosvenor Square
Southampton SO15 2BE
Tel: 01703 331661
Fax: 01703 332206
Recent productions: *Thomas the Tank Engine and Friend*s, 104 stories filmed in live-action animation

Bronco Films
The Producer's Centre
61 Holland Street
Glasgow G2 4NJ
Tel: 0141 287 6817
Fax: 0141 287 6815
email: broncofilm@btinternet.com
Peter Broughan

Buena Vista Productions
Centre West
3 Queen Caroline Street
Hammersmith
London W4 9PE
Tel: 020 8222 1000
Fax: 020 8222 2795
International television production arm of The Walt Disney Studios

John Burder Films
7 Saltcoats Road
London W4 1AR
Tel: 020 8995 0547
Fax: 020 8995 3376
email: jburder@aol.com
Website: www.johnburder.co.uk
Corporate and broadcast worldwide, productions for many leading sponsors

Buxton Raven Productions Ltd
159-173 St. John Street
London EC1V 4QJ
Tel: 020 7296 0012
Fax: 020 7296 0014
email: jb@buxtonraven.
demon.co.uk
Website: buxtonraven.com
Jette Bonnevie, Jens Ravn
Founded in 1988, Buxton Raven focuses on feature film development and production

Capitol Films
23 Queensdale Place
London W11 4SQ
Tel: 020 7471 6000
Fax: 020 7471 6012
email: films@capitolfilms.com
Simon Radcliffe, Director of Acquisitions and Development
Recent productions include: *Beautiful Joe, House of Mirth, Drowning Mona, Wilde* and *Among Giants*

Carlton Select
45 Fouberts Place
London W1V 2DN
Tel: 020 7434 3060
Fax: 020 7494 1421
Owned by Carlton Communications

Carnival (Films and Theatre) Ltd
12 Raddington Road
Ladbroke Grove
London W10 5TG
Tel: 020 8968 1818
Fax: 020 8968 0155
email: info@carnival-films.co.uk
Website: www.carnival-films.co.uk
Recent productions: Films - *Firelight; Up on the Roof; The Mill on the Floss; Shadowlands; Under Suspicion;* Television - *The Tenth Kingdom; Agatha Christie's Poirot; Lucy Sullivan is Getting Married; Every Woman Knows A Secret; Oktober; BUGS; Crime Traveller; Jeeves & Wooster; Fragile Heart; Porterhouse Blue*

Cartwn Cymru
Screen Centre
Llantrisant Road
Cardiff CF5 2PU
Tel: 029 2057 5999
Fax: 029 2057 5919
email: production@cartwn-
cymru.demon.co.uk
Animation production. Recent productions: *Turandot: Operavox* (BBC2/S4C Animated Operas): *Testament: The Bible in Animation*; (S4C/BBC2). *The Miracle Maker* (S4C/BBC/British Screen/Icon); 90 minute theatrical feature. In

production: *The Mabinogi* (S4C/BBC); animated feature of medieval epic; *Faeries* (HIT Entertainment): 75 minute TV feature for Tx on CITV Christmas '99

Catalyst Television
Brook Green Studios
186 Shepherd's Bush Road
London W6 7LL
Tel: 020 7603 7030
Fax: 020 7603 9519
Gardeners World (BBC)

Celador Productions
39 Long Acre
London WC2E 9JT
Tel: 020 7240 8101
Fax: 020 7836 1117
Paul Smith
Television: primarily entertainment programming for all broadcast channels. Includes *Who Wants to be a Millionaire?* plus other game shows, variety, with selected situation comedy, drama and factual output

Chain Production Ltd
2 Clanricarde Gardens
London W2 4NA
Tel: 020 7229 4277
Fax: 020 7229 0861
email: films@chain.production.co.uk
Website: www.chain.production.
co.uk
Garwin Davison, Roberta Licurgo
Development and Co-Production
Feature Films, Previous
Co–production with India, Italy and
USA,

Channel X Communications
22 Stephenson Way
London NW1 2HD
Tel: 020 7387 3874
Fax: 020 7387 0738
email: mail@channelx.co.uk
XYZ; Jo Brand Through the Cakehole; The Smell of Reeves and Mortimer; The Unpleasant World of Penn and Teller; Funny Business, Phil Kay Feels..., Food Fight, Barking . Turning Tricks with Paul Zenon, Families at War, The Cooler, Bang, Bang It's Reeves and Mortimer, Leftfield, All Back to Mine series 1 and series 2; Johnny Meets Madonna, Comedy Cafe, Vic Reeves Explains, The Daren Saint Show, Celebrities...The Truth

Chapter One Ltd
Elstree Film Studios
Borehamwood
Hertforshire WD6 1JG

Tel: 020 8324 2744
Fax: 020 8324 2773
David Macmahon
Television production company credits include *The Real Holiday Show* for Channel Four

Charisma Films
507 Riverbank House
1 Putney Bridge Approach
London SW6 3JD
Tel: 020 7610 6830
Fax: 020 7610 6836
email: charismafi@aol.com
Alan Balladur, Head of Development

Chatsworth Television
97-99 Dean Street
London W1V 5RA
Tel: 020 7734 4302
Fax: 020 7437 3301
email: television@chatsworth-tv.co.uk
Sister company to Chatsworth distribution and merchandising companies. Producers of light entertainment and drama. Best known for the long running *Treasure Hunt* and *The Crystal Maze* (C4)

The Children's Film Unit
South Way
Leavesden
Herts WD2 7LZ
Tel: 01923 354656
Fax: 01923 354656
email: cfilmunit@aol.com
Website: www.btinternet.com/~cfu
Carol Rennie, Administrator
A registered Educational Charity, the CFU makes low-budget films for television and PR on subjects of concern to children and young people. Crews and actors are trained at regular weekly workshops in Putney. Work is in 16mm and video, and membership is open to children from 8-18. Latest films for C4: *The Gingerbread House; Awayday*

Chrysalis Visual Entertainment
The Chrysalis Building
13 Bramley Road
London W10 6SP
Tel: 020 7221 2213
Fax: 020 7465 6159
Website: www.chrysalis.co.uk
Charlotte Boundy
The following are all part of Chrysalis Visual Entertainment: Assembly Film and Television; Bentley Productions; Cactus TV, Chrysalis Television (includes Chrysalis Sport, Chrysalis Sport

USA, Mach1, Chrysalis TV, Chrysalis Television North, Chrysalis Creative). Lucky Dog, Red Rooster, Tandem Television,. Watchmaker Production, Chrysalis Television International, Chrysalis Distribution, IDTV (The Netherlands), South Pacific Pictures (New Zealand)

Circus Films Ltd
Shepperton Studios
Shepperton
Middlesex TW17 0QD
Tel: 01932 572680/1
Fax: 01932 568989
Film Development Corporation Ltd
St Georges House
14-17 Wells Street
London W1P 3FP
Tel: 020 7323 6603
Fax: 020 7636 9350

Claridge Pictures
Shepperton Studios
Shepperton
Middx TW17 0QD
Tel: 01932 562611
Fax: 01932 568989
Peter Claridge
Film and TV production, commercials, promos, corporate videos, interactive and film titles

Clark Television Production
Cavendish House
128-134 Cleveland Street
London W1P 5DN
Tel: 020 7388 7700
Fax: 020 7388 3366
Dispatches; The Black Bag

The Comedy House
6 Bayley Street
London WC1B 3HB
Tel: 020 7304 0047
Fax: 020 7304 0048
John Goldstone, Producer
Set up in 1990 to develop comedy films with British talent

The Comic Strip Ltd
Dean House
102 Dean Street
London W1V 5RA
Tel: 020 7734 1166
Fax: 020 7734 1105
Recent productions: *Four Men in a Car* - a one-off 30 minute comedy for C4

Company Pictures
184-192 Drummond Street
London NW1 3HP
Tel: 020 7388 9277
Fax: 020 7388 8107

Produces and develops feature films and drama for television. Recent productions include: *Titanic Town*

Connections Communications Centre Ltd

Palingswick House
241 King Street
Hammersmith
London W6 9LP
Tel: 020 8741 1767
Fax: 020 8563 1934
email: @cccmedia.demon.co.uk
Website: www.cccmedia.demon.co.uk
Jacqueline Davis
A registered charity producing promotional and educational videos for the voluntary and statutory sectors. Also able to provide training for such groups in video production. Fully wheelchair accessible

Contrast Films

311 Katherine Road
London E7 8PJ
Tel: 020 8472 5001
Fax: 020 8472 5001
Produce documentaries and feature films.

Cosgrove Hall Films

8 Albany Road
Chorlton-cum-Hardy
Manchester M21 0AW
Tel: 0161 882 2500
Fax: 0161 882 2555
Award-winning animation company
Producer of drawn and model animation. Creators of:
Dangermouse; The Wind in the Willows; Count Duckula; The B.F.G.; Noddy; Discworld, Foxbusters

Judy Couniham Films Ltd

12a Newburgh Street
London W1V 1LG
Tel: 020 7287 4329
Fax: 020 7287 2303
Previous productions include:
Antonia's Line, Before The Rain, Before the Rain, Time to Love, Janice Beard 45 wpm. See Dakota Films

Dakota Films

12a Newburgh Street
London W1V 1LG
Tel: 020 7287 4329
Fax: 020 7287 2303
Previous productions: *Let Him Have It; Othello; Janice Beard 45wpm*
In development: *Fade to Black; Me Without You; Mother of Pearl; Garnethill*

Dan Films Ltd

32 Maple Street
London W1P 5GD
Tel: 020 7916 4771
Fax: 020 7916 4773
email: office@danfilms.com
Website: www.danfilms.com
Cilla Ware (Director)
Julie Baines (Producer); Sarah Daniel (Producer); Sara Sutton (Producer's Assistant); Jason Newmark (Head of Development);
Recent productions: *LA Without a Map* (feature); *The Rise & Fall of Studio 54* (documentary)

De Warrenne Pictures

121 Free Trade Wharf
340 The Highway
London E1W 3EU
Tel: 020 7790 8068
Fax: 020 7790 6850
email: info@dewarrenne.com
Website: www.dewarrenne.com
Tom Waller
Feature film production company.
Recent projects include *Monk Dawson* based on award winning novel by Piers Paul Read. In Production: *Butterfly Man*, by Kaprice Kea

Dirty Hands

c/o Propaganda
2nd Floor
6-10 Lexington Street
London W1R 3HS
Tel: 020 7478 3207
Fax: 020 7734 7131

Diverse Productions

Gorleston Street
London W14 8XS
Tel: 020 7603 4567
Fax: 020 7603 2148
Established in 1982, Diverse is one of Britain's leading independent factual programme makers, and has recently expanded into Interactive media

DLT Entertainment UK Ltd

10 Bedford Square
London WC1B 3RA
Tel: 020 7631 1184
Fax: 020 7636 4571
John Reynolds; John Bartlett, Mike Taylor

DNA Films

3rd Floor
75-77 Margaret Street
London W1N &HB
Tel: 020 7291 8010
Fax: 020 7291 8020

email: info@dnafilms.com
Joanne Smith
(See DNA Film Ltd - Lottery Film Production Franchises)
Projects in production: *Creatures, Strictly Sinatra* (working title), *The Final Curtain*

Documedia International Films Ltd

Production Office
19 Widegate Street
London E1 7HP
Tel: 020 7625 6200
Fax: 020 7625 7887
Producers and distributors of documentary and drama programming; corporate and Internet adaptations

Domino Films

7 King Harry Lane
St Albans AL3 4S
Tel: 01727 750153
Fax: 01727 750153
email: jo@dominofilms.co.uk
Well-established company producing wide range of factual programmes

Double Exposure

Unit 22-23
63 Clerkenwell Road
London EC1M 5PS
Tel: 020 7490 2499
Fax: 020 7490 2556
Production and distribution of broadcast and educational documentaries in the UK and abroad

Downtown Pictures Ltd

4th Floor, Suite 2
St Georges House
14-17 Wells Street
London W1P 3FP
Tel: 020 7323 6604
Fax: 020 7636 8090
Martin McCabe, Alan McQueen, Alan Latham, Anne Rigby

Ecosse Films

12 Quayside Lodge
Watermeadow Lane
London SW6 2UZ
Tel: 020 7371 0290
Fax: 020 7736 3436
email: info@ecossefilms.com
Website: www.ecossefilms.com
Alexandra McIntosh
Mrs. Brown, The Ambassador, Unsuitable Job for a Woman, Monarch of the Glen

Edinburgh Film & Video Productions

Traquair House
Innelleithen

Peeblessairl EH44 6PW
Tel: 01896 831188
Fax: 01896 831198
Robin Crichton
Major Scottish production company
established in 1961

Elmgate Productions
Shepperton Studios, Studios Road
Shepperton
Middx TW17 0QD
Tel: 01932 562611
Fax: 01932 569918
Feature films, television films and
series

Eon Productions
138 Piccadilly
London W1Z 9FH
Tel: 020 7493 7953
Fax: 020 7408 1236
Producers of James Bond films

Equilibrium Films
28 Sheen Common Drive
Richmond TW10 5BN
Tel: 020 8898 0150/ 07980 622964
Fax: 020 8898 0150
Titles include: *The Tribe That Time
Forgot* - an Equilibrium Film
production in association with
WGBH Boston/Nova for PBS;
*Jaguar People;Yemen's Cultural
Drug: Dream or Nightmare;Yemen's
Jambiya Cult;Sudan's Slave Trade;
First Contact - Last Rites* - a Bare
Faced Production for BBC; *Egypt
Powerplays, Burma's Final Solution,
Conquering The Mountain of Fire,
Barefoot Among The Tame Tigers,
Dispatches* C4

Extreme International
The Coach House
Ashford Lodge
Halstead
Essex C09 2RR
Tel: 01787 479000
Fax: 01787 479111
email: xdream@xdream.co.uk
Website: www.extremeinternational.
com
Alistair Gosling
Specialises in the production and
distribution of extreme sports, travel,
technology, nature and wildlife and
children's programmes.
Extreme Sports Channel
A cable/satellite channel currently
broadcasting across Europe and
shortly going worldwide
email: al@extreme.com
Website: www.extreme.com
Extreme Interactive
International distribution and

production of Interactive Narrow and
Broadband Video Content and
Internet Broadcast Channels
email: xdream@xdream.co.uk
Website: www.extremeineractice.net

Festival Film and Television Ltd
Festival House
Tranquil Passage
Blackheath Village
London SE3 0BJ
Tel: 020 8297 9999
Fax: 020 8297 1155
email: info@festivalfilm.com
Website: www.festivalfilm.com
Ray Marshall
The company concentrates mainly on
popular television drama and
continues production of its Catherine
Cookson mini-series for ITV. Recent
completed productions include: *The
Round Tower, Colour Blind,Tilly
Trotter and the Secret.* A six-part
adaptation of Cookson's novel, *A
Dinner of Herbs* will air early in
2001. Series in development include
Decline and Fall by Evelyn Waugh,
Mrs Pargeter, based on the books by
Simon Brett and *Lily Josephine* based
on the best selling novel by Kate
Saunders

Fidelity Films Ltd
34-6 Oak End Way
Gerrards Cross
Buckinghamshire SL9 8BR
Tel: 01753 884646
Fax: 01753 887163
Graham Harris
Feature films

Figment Films Ltd
3rd Floor
75-77 Margaret Street
London W1N 7HB
Tel: 020 7291 8030
Fax: 020 7291 8040
email: figment@globalnet.co.uk
Website: www.figmentfilms.com
Productions include: *Shallow Grave;
Trainspotting, Twin Town, A Life Less
Ordinary, The Beach*
(See DNA Film - Lottery Film
Production Franchises)

The Film Consortium
6 Flitcroft Street
London WC2H 6DJ
Tel: 020 7691 4440
Fax: 020 7691 4445
Contact: Linda Gamble
Consists of: Greenpoint Films,
Parallax Pictures, Scala and Skreba
(See The Film Consortium - Lottery

Film Production Franchises)

Film Form Productions
64 Fitzjohn's Avenue
London NW3 5LT
Tel: 020 7794 6967
Fax: 020 7794 6967
Film/video production, drama and
documentary for television and video
distribution. Full crewing, writers,
producers and directors

FilmFair Animation
Unit 8
Silver Road
White City Industrial Park
London W12 7SG
Tel: 020 8735 1888
Fax: 020 8743 9591
email: info@filmfair.co.uk
Producers of model animation series,
special effects and commercials.
Productions include: *The Wombles;
Paddington Bear; Huxley Pig;
Gingerbread Man; Astro Farm; The
Dreamstone; Brown Bear's Wedding;
White Bear's Secret; The Legend of
Treasure Island*

FilmFour Ltd
76-78 Charlotte Street
London W1P 1LX
Tel: 020 7868 7700
Fax: 020 7868 7769
Website: www.filmfour.com
Paul Webster, Chief Executive
FilmFour Ltd is Channel 4
Television's wholly owned Film
Company and operates in the areas of
film development, production, sales
and distribution. FilmFour
Productions funds around 15-20 films
a year, many of them with co-finance
from other partners and some fully
funded. The FilmFour Lab
champions the spirit and practice of
creative low-budget filmmaking and
aims for a slate of around four films
a year. Recent productions:
*East is East; Purely Belter; Some
Voices; Gangster No 1; Sexy Beast;
Birthday Girl*

Fine Line Features
25-28 Old Burlington Street
London W1X 1LB
Tel: 020 7440 1000
Fax: 020 7439 6105
European film production
*Shine; Sweet Hereafter;
Deconstructing Harry*

The First Film Company
38 Great Windmill Street
London W1V 7PA

Tel: 020 7439 1640
Fax: 020 7437 2062
Feature film and television production.

Flashback Television Ltd
11 Bowling Green Lane
London EC1R OBD
Tel: 020 7490 8996
Fax: 020 7490 5610
Award-winning producers of a wide range of factual programming including lifestyle, history, natural history and sport documentaries

Focus Films Ltd
The Rotunda Studios
Rear of 116-118 Finchley Road
London NW3 5HT
Tel: 020 7435 9004
Fax: 020 7431 3562
email: focus@pupix.demon.co.uk
David Pupkewitz
Marsha Levin, Lisa Nicholson, Malcolm Kohll, Lucinda Van Rie
Feature Film Production and Financing Company. Recent productions Janet Suzman's *Othello*, *Crimetime* directed by George Sluizer starring Stephen Baldwin and Pete Postlethwaite, *Secret Society* directed by Imogen Kimmel starring Charlotte Britain and Lee Ross. In Development: *The 51st State* to be directed by Ronnie Yu starring Samuel L.Jackson, Mutant, Barry, *On the Frontline*, *Peaches Goes West*, *90 Minutes*

Mark Forstater Productions
27 Lonsdale Road
London NW6 6RA
Tel: 020 7624 1123
Fax: 020 7624 1124

Fox Searchlight Pictures
(see Twentieth Century-Fox Productions Ltd)
Twentieth Century-Fox Film Co Ltd
Twentieth Century House
31-32 Soho Square
London W1V 6AP
Tel: 020 7437 7766
Fax: 020 7734 3187
Website: www.fox.co.uk/
Recent productions: *Smilla's Feeling for Snow; Cousin Bette; Oscar and Lucinda*

Fragile Films
95-97 Dean Street
London W1N 3XX
Tel: 020 7287 6200
Fax: 020 7287 0069
email: fragile@fragilefilms.com
(See Pathé Productions - Lottery

Film Production Franchises)
An Ideal Husband

Front Page Films
507 Riverbank House
1 Putney Bridge Approach
London SW6 3JD
Tel: 020 7736 4534
Fax: 020 7610 6836
email: charismafi@aol.com
Alan Balladur, Head of Development

Fulcrum TV
254 Goswell Road
London EC1V 7RE
Tel: 020 7253 0353
Fax: 020 7490 0206
email: info@fulcrumTV.com
Website: www.fulcrumTV.com
Richard Belfield, Producer/Director
Most recent productions include, for Channel 4: *Can You Live Without, The Channel 4 Hate Commission*, *Dispatches* (Gayhurst Crescent Goes Surfing, A Matter of Life and Death, The No Car Challenge), *The Sick List*, *To The Ends of the Earth - Death*, *Deceit and the Nile*, *Power List*, *Pulp*, *Scottish Power*, and *Fusion - Looking For Dad*; for ITV: *Diana - The Paris Crash - A Special Enquiry*; for Channel 5 - *First on Five*

Gainsborough (Film & TV) Productions
The Groom Cottage
Pinewood Studios
Pinewood Lane
Iver Heath
Iver Bucks SLO ONH
Tel: 020 7409 1925
Fax: 020 7408 2042
In development: *Dangerous Love; Bewitched; A Heart in the Highlands*

Noel Gay Television
1 Albion Court
Gelene Road
Hammersmith
London W6 OQT
Tel: 020 8600 5200
Fax: 020 8600 5222
TV Drama and TV entertainment. Associate companies: Grant Naylor Production. Noel Gay Motion Picture Company, Noel Gay Scotland, Rose Bay Film Productions, Sunbeam Productions, Pepper Productions

General Entertainment Investments
Bray Film Studios
Down Place
Windsor Road
Windsor

Berkshire SL4 5UG
Tel: 01628 22111
Fax: 01628 770381
Feature film producers/financiers

Global Vision Network
Elstree Film Studios
Borehamwood
Hertfordshire WD6 1JG
Tel: 020 8324 2333
Fax: 020 8324 2700
email: info@gvn.co.uk
Website: www.gvn.co.uk

Bob Godfrey Films
199 Kings Cross Road
London WC1X 9DB
Tel: 020 7278 5711
Fax: 020 7278 6809
Prominent studio, with productions: *Small Talk*, entertainment short, Oscar nomination 1993;

Goldcrest Films International
65-66 Dean Street
London W1V 6PL
Tel: 020 7437 8696
Fax: 020 7437 4448
Major feature film production, sales and finance company. Recent productions: *No Way Home; Bring Me The Head of Mavis Davis; Clockwatchers; Annabelle's Wish*

Granada Film
The London Television Centre
Upper Ground
London SE1 9LT
Tel: 020 7737 8681
Fax: 020 7737 8682
email: granada.film@granadamedia.com
Mark Finlay
Head of Film: Pippa Cross
Established in 1989 - a subsidiary of the Granada Media Group. Feature films: *The Heart; Up On the Roof; Some Kind of Life; August; Jack & Sarah; The Field; My Left Foot; The Fruit Machine; Essex Boys; The Weekend; The Misadventures of Margaret; Captain Jack; Rogue Trader*

Greenpoint Films Ltd
27-29 Union Street
London SE1 1SD
Tel: 020 7357 9924
Fax: 020 7357 9920
A loose association of ten filmmakers: Simon Relph, Christopher Morahan, Ann Scott, Richard Eyre, Stephen Frears, Patrick Cassavetti, John Mackenzie, Mike Newell, David Hare and Christopher

Hampton
(See The Film Consortium - Lottery
Film Production Franchises)

Griffin Productions
Global House
96-108 Great Suffolk Street
London WC1
Tel: 020 7620 1620
Fax: 020 7578 4390
Current productions: *Human Bomb*
(Showtime), *Place of Lions* (Universal),
Pimpernel (Showtime), *Prince of Mars*
(Universal), *Week to Remember* (BBC),
Quintessial Verse (BBC)

Gruber Films
1st Floor
74 Margaret Street
London W1N 7HA
Tel: 020 7436 3413
Fax: 020 7436 3402
Neil Peplow
Recent productions: *Walking Ned,
Shooting Fish, Dead Babies*
In development: *Raving Beauties,
Snookered, Trilogy, The Abduction
Club*

HAL Films Ltd
45a Brewer Street
London W1R 3FD
Tel: 020 7434 4408
Recently founded British subsidiary
of Miramax Films UK. *Mansfield
Park*

Halas & Batchelor
The Halas & Batchelor Collection
Ltd
67 Southwood Lane
London N6 5EG
Tel: 020 8348 9696
Fax: 020 8348 3470
email: vivien@haba.demon.co.uk
Animation films from 1940

Hammer Film Productions
92 New Cavendish Street
London W1M 7FA
Tel: 020 7637 2322
Fax: 020 7323 2307
Website: www.hammerfilms.com
Terry Ilott
The company responsible for many
classic British horror films

Harbour Pictures
The Yacht Club
Chelsea Harbour
London SW10 0XA
Tel: 020 7351 7070
Fax: 020 7352 3528
email: username@harbourpictures.
com
Website: www.harbourpictures.com

Nick Barton, Suzanne Mackie, Cathy
Haslam
Productions in development: *The Next
Big Thing* (BBC Films); *Calendar
Girls* (BVI); *Kinky Boots* (Feature
Film); *Sculpture* (Documentary);
Genius (Documentary). Recent
productions as ABTV: *Great
Excavations* (C4); *Righteous Babes*
(C4); *Brimful of Asia* (C4). Previous
productions as ABTV: *The Vanishing
Man* (ITV); *Byzantium - The Lost
Empire* (TLC C4); *The Wimbledon
Poisoner* (BBC); *Boswell and
Johnson* (BBC); *Moving Story* (ITV);
Bye Bye Baby (FilmFour).

Harcourt Films
58 Camden Square
London NW1 9XE
Tel: 020 7267 0882
Fax: 020 7267 1064
Producer of documentaries and arts
programmes. Recent productions: 90
minute TV special *The Capeman* for
HBO, One hour music docs

Hartswood Films
Twickenham Studios
The Barons
St Margarets
Twickenham
Middx TW1 2AW
Tel: 020 8607 8736
Fax: 020 8607 8744
Kate Cotter
Border Café (8x45 min drama);
Coupling (6x30 min sitcom);
Wonderful You (7x60min drama);
Men Behaving Badly (6 series and 4
Christmas Specials, sitcom); *Is it
Legal?* (3 series, sitcom); *In Love
With Elizabeth* (1x60min,
documentary); *Officers and
Gentlemen* (1x60min, documentary);
The Red Baron (1x60min,
documentary); *Going to Chelsea*
(1x60min, documentary); *My Good
Friend* (2 series, comedy drama); *The
English Wife* (drama); *A Woman's
Guide to Adultery* (drama); *Code
Name Kyril* (drama)

Hat Trick Productions
10 Livonia Street
London W1V 3PH
Tel: 020 7434 2451
Fax: 020 787 9791
Denise O'Donoghue
Jimmy Mulville, Mary Bell, Hilary
Strong
Specialising in comedy, light
entertainment and drama.
Productions include: *Father Ted;
Drop the Dead Donkey; Have I Got*

*News For You; Confessions;
Whatever You Want; Game On; The
Peter Principle; If I Ruled the World;
Clive Anderson All Talk; Room 101*
and *Whose Line is it Anyway?* The
company's drama output includes: *A
Very Open Prison; Boyz Unlimited;
Eleven Men Against Eleven; Lord of
Misrule; Crossing the Floor; Gobble*
and *Underworld*

Jim Henson Productions
30 Oval Road, Camden
London NW1 7DE
Tel: 020 7428 4000
Fax: 020 7428 4001
Producers of high quality
children's/family entertainment for
television and feature films, usually
with a puppetry or fantasy
connection. Recent productions:
Muppet Treasure Island - feature

Holmes Associates
38-42 Whitfield Street
London W1P 5RF
Tel: 020 7813 4333
Fax: 020 7637 9024
Long-established UK independent
production company for broadcast
television

Michael Hurll Television
5th Floor
Avon House
Kensington Village
Avonmore Road
London W14 8TS
Tel: 020 7371 5354
Fax: 020 7371 5355

Iambic Productions
89 Whiteladies Road
Bristol BS8 2NT
Tel: 0117 923 7222
Fax: 0117 923 8343

Icon Entertainment International Ltd
The Quadrangle , 4th Floor
180 Wardour Street
London W1V 3AA
Tel: 020 7494 8100
Fax: 020 7494 8151
Recent productions: *Hamlet;
Immortal Beloved; Braveheart; Anna
Karenina.* In development: *Farenheit
451*

Idealworld Productions Ltd
St George's Studios
93-97 St George's Road
Glasgow G3 6JA
Tel: 0141 353 3222
Fax: 0141 353 3221
Film and television production

Illuminations Films/Koninck Studios
19-20 Rheidol Mews
Rheidol Terrace
London N1 8NU
Tel: 020 7226 0266
Fax: 020 7359 1151
email: griff@illumin.co.uk
Producers of fiction films for
television and theatric release

Illuminations Interactive
(See entry for Braunarts)

Illuminations Television
19-20 Rheidol Mews
Rheidol Terrace
London N1 8NU
Tel: 020 7226 0266
Fax: 020 7359 1151
email: illuminations@illumin.co.uk
Website: www.illumin.co.uk
Producers of cultural programmes for
C4, BBC and others

imaginary films
19 Ainsley St
London E2 0DL
Tel: 020 7613 5882
Fax: 020 7729 9280
email: brady@imagfilm.demon.co.uk
Website: www.imagfilm.co.uk
Ray and Deba Brady
An independent feature film
production company, films include
Boy Meets Girl (94), *Little England*
(96) and *Kiss Kiss Bang Bang* (99)
all directed by Ray Brady. In
pre-production and development with
Boudicca Films are the features films
Day of the Sirens (2000) thriller,
Daddy (2000) romantic comedy, *Fate*
a psychological horror film,
Adrenaline - black comedy/action.

Imagine Films Ltd
53 Greek Street
London W1V 5LR
Tel: 020 7287 4667
Fax: 020 7287 4668
(See Pathé Productions - Lottery
Film Production Franchises)
Producers: Simon Channing-
Williams; Stephanie Faugher;
Finance Director: Eddie Kane

Impact Pictures Ltd
12 Devonhirst Place
Heathfield Terrace
London W4 4JB
Tel: 020 734 9650
Fax: 020 7734 9652
email: impactpix.@aol.com
Jeremy Bolt
Productions include: *Shopping*,

directed by Paul Anderson and *Stiff
Upper Lips*, directed by Gary Sinyor,
Mortal Kombat, directed by Paul
Anderson, *Event Horizon* also
directed by Paul Anderson, *VIGO*,
directed by Julien Temple with
Nitrate Film/Channel 4, also *Soldier*,
directed by Paul Anderson, with
Gerry Weintraub. Most recently
There's Only One Jimmy Grimble
with Pathé, *Shadows* (for TV), with
20th Century Fox/BskyB. Up and
coming projects are *The Hole*, with
Pathé, *Death Race 3000*, to be
directed by Paul Anderson, with
Paramount and Stonehenge with
Constantin Film.

International Broadcasting Trust (IBT)
2 Ferdinand Place
London NW1 8EE
Tel: 020 7482 2847
Fax: 020 7284 3374
email: mail@ibt.org.uk
Website: www.ibt.org.uk
An independent, non-profit television
production company and educational
charity, specialising in making
programmes on development,
environment and human rights issues
for UK and international broadcast.
Recent productions include: a four-
part series for BBC2 from young
European directors on anti-racism
and cultural diversity; a two-part fly-
on-the-wall documentary series
inside the World Bank, for Channel
4; a 30 minute documentary for
Channel 4 following a VSO mental
health worker to Zanzibar; a ten-part
series on globalisation for BBC
Education and a five-part series on
China for Channel 4 Schools
Television

J&M Entertainment Ltd
2 Dorset Square
London NW1 6PX
Tel: 020 7723 6544
Fax: 020 7724 7541
email: sales@jment.com
Website: www.jment.com
Julia Palau
Recent productions: *Forever Mine,
The Guilty Complicity, A Texas
Funeral, History is Made at Night,
Bruno*

Jagged Films
Cheyne Walk
Chelsea
London SW3
Titles include: *Enigma*

Kai Film & TV Productions
1 Ravenslea Road
London SW12 8SA
Tel: 020 8673 4550
Fax: 020 8675 4760
email: mkwallington@cwcom.net
Recent productions: *The Unbearable
Shiteness of Being; Leopoldville*

Bill Kenwright Films
BKC House
106 Harrow Road
London W2 1RR
Tel: 020 7446 6200
Fax: 020 7446 6222
email: info@kenwright.com
Website: www.kenwright.com
Liz Holford
Recent productions: *Don't Go
Breaking My Heart, Zoe*

King Rollo Films
Dolphin Court
High Street
Honiton
Devon EX14 1HT
Tel: 01404 45218
Fax: 01404 45328
email: admin@kingrollofilms.co.uk
Clive Juster
Produce top quality animated
entertainment for children. In autumn
1993 the company's highly acclaimed
line of Spot films was launched under
licence by Disney for the North
American home video market and now
world sales of these titles approach
two million cassettes. Producers of the
animated series: *Mr Benn; King Rollo;
Victor and Maria; Towser; Watt the
Devil; The Adventures of Spot; The
Adventures of Ric; Anytime Tales; Art;
Play It Again; It's Fun to Learn with
Spot; Buddy and Pip, Spot's Magical
Christmas, Little Mr Jakob; Philipp;
Happy Birthday; Good Night, Sleep
Tight; Spot and his Grandparents go
to the Carnival, Maisy*

Kismet Film Company Ltd
27-29 Berwick Street
London W1V 3RF
Tel: 020 7734 9978
Fax: 020 7734 9871
Rosie Bridge
Titles include: *Photographing
Fairies; This Year's Love;
Wonderland; Born Romantic*

Landseer Film & Television Productions
140 Royal College Street
London NW1 0TA
Tel: 020 7485 7333
Fax: 020 7485 7573

email: mail@landseerfilms.com
Website: www.landseerfilms.com
Documentary, music arts, dance and children's programming. Recent prouductions: *Petula Clark - South Bank Show* (LWT), *Routes of Rock* (Carlton), *Death of a Legend - Frank Sinatra* (LWT), *The Judas Tree* (Channel Four), *Benjamin Zander - Living on One Buttock* (BBC), *Zeffirelli - South Bank Show* (LWT), *Gounods Faust* (Channel Four), *Hear My Chanson - South Bank Show* (LWT), *Swinger* (BBC2)

Large Door Productions
3 Shamrock Street
London SW4 6FF
Tel: 020 7627 4218
Fax: 020 7627 2469
email: ldoor@demon.co.uk
John Ellis
Founded in 1982 to specialise in documentaries about cinema and popular culture with an international emphasis. Now concerned with consultancy work

Little Bird Co
9 Grafton Mews
London W1P 5LG
Tel: 020 7380 3980
Fax: 020 7380 3981
email: info@littlebird.co.uk
Website: www.littlebird.ie
James Mitchell, Jonathan Cavendish
Feature films: *Nothing Personal; December Bride; Into the West; All Our Fault; A Man of No Importance; My Mother's Courage, Ordinary Decent Criminal. TV: The Hanging Gale; Divine Magic, Relative Strangers, All For Love,*
(Documentary: *Waiting for Harvey, In the Footsteps of Bruce Chatwin*)

Little Dancer Avonway
Naseby Road
London SE19 3JJ
Tel: 020 8653 9343
Fax: 020 8653 9343
Recent productions in development: *Adios* by Sue Townsend; *Wilderness Years* by Sue Townsend.

London Films
35 Davies Street
London W1Y 1FN
Tel: 020 7499 7800
Fax: 020 7499 7994
Founded in 1932 by Alexander Korda. Many co-productions with the BBC, including *Scarlet Pimpernel* starring Richard E. Grant for BBC TV/A+E Network, *Lady Chatterley,*

Resort to Murder; I, Claudius, Poldark and *Testament of Youth.* Produced *The Country Girls* for C4.

Malachite Productions
East Kirkby House
Spilsby
Lincolnshire PE23 4BX
Tel: 01790 763538
Fax: 01790 763409
email: malachite Ltd@csi.com
London Office: 020 7487 5451
Charles Mapleston, Nancy Thomas, Nikki Crane
Producers of people-based documentary programmes on music, design, painting, photography, arts, anthropology and environmental issues for broadcast television

Malone Gill Productions Ltd
27 Campden Hill Road
London W8 7DX
Tel: 020 7937 0557
Fax: 0207 376 1727
email: ikonic@compuserve.com
Georgina Denison
Recent productions: *The Face of Russia* (PBS); *Vermeer* (ITV); *Highlanders* (ITV); *Storm Chasers* (C4/Arts and Entertainment Network); *Nature Perfected* (C4/NHK/ABC/Canal Plus/RTE); *The Feast of Christmas* (C4/SBS); *Nomads* (C4/ITEL)

Jo Manuel Productions Ltd
11 Keslake Road
London NW6 6DG
Tel: 020 8930 0777
Fax: 020 8933 5475
Recent productions: *The Boy From Mercury* directed by Martin Duffy with Hugh O'Conor, Rita Tushingham and Tom Courtenay. *Widow's Peak* (Rank, Fineline, British Screen), directed by John Irvin with Mia Farrow, Joan Plowright, Natasha Richardson, *Mattie* starring Mia Farrow

Maya Vision International Ltd
43 New Oxford Street
London WC1A 1BH
Tel: 020 7836 1113
Fax: 020 7836 5169
email: info@mayavisionint.com
Website: www.mayavisionint.com
John Cranmer

Media Legal (Originations)
Media Legal
83 Clarendon Road
Sevenoaks

Kent TN13 1ET
Tel: 01732 460592
Production arm of Media Legal developing legal projects for film and TV

Meditel Productions
4a Hollybush Place
London E2 9QX
Tel: 020 7613 5266
Fax: 020 7613 5398
Provides medical, science-based and factual documentaries for television

Mentorn Barraclough Carey
43 Whitfield Street
London W1P 67G
Tel: 020 7258 6800
Fax: 020 7258 6888
Website: www.mentorn.co.uk
Entertainment, drama, entertainment news, documentaries, news and current affairs, children's and features

Merchant Ivory Productions
46 Lexington Street
London W1R 3LH
Tel: 020 7437 1200/7439 4335
Fax: 020 7734 1579
email: miplondon@merchantivory.demon.co.uk
Website: www.merchantivory.com
Paul Bradley
Merchant Ivory Productions is the collaboration of Ismail Merchant, James Ivory and Ruth Prawer Jhabvala, the screenwriter. The company is the longest, prolific filmmaking partnership in the world having made over 42 films over the last 30 years including: *Shakespeares Wallah, Savages, Roseland, The Europeans, Heat and Dust, A Room With a View, Maurice, Mr. and Mrs. Bridges, Jefferson in Paris, Howards End* and recently *Cotton Mary* with Greta Scaacchi and Madhur Jaffrey and *The Golden Bowl* with Uma Thurman, Nick Nolte and Angelica Houston. *The Mystic Masseur* and Dan Leno and *The Limehouse Golem* are among forthcoming projects planned for 2000/2001

The Mersey Television Company
Campus Manor
Childwall Abbey Road
Liverpool L16 0JP
Tel: 0151 722 9122
Fax: 0151 722 1969
Independent production company responsible for C4 series, *Brookside*

Miramax International (London)/Miramax Films UK Ltd
45a Brewer Street
London W1R 3FD
Tel: 020 7434 4408
David Aukin
Major US independent. Recent productions: *Shakespeare in Love; Little Voice; Velvet Goldmine*

Momentum Productions
90 York Road
Teddington TW11 8SN
Tel: 020 8977 7333
Fax: 020 8977 6999
Guy Meyer/Tam Derrick
email: production@momentum.co.uk
Specialists in on-screen marketing and promotion of feature films - film trailers, promos and commercials. Producers of corporate films

Mosaic Films Ltd
2nd Floor
8-12 Broadwick Street
London W1V 1FH
Tel: 020 7437 6514
Fax: 020 7494 0595
email: info@mosaicfilms.com
Website: www.mosaicfilms.com
Contact: Colin Luke
The Old Butcher's Shop
St Briavels
Glos. GL15 6TA
Tel: 01594 530708
Fax: 01594 530094
email: adam@mosaicfilms.com
Contact: Adam Alexander
Recent productions: *Return to Wonderland* - a series for BBC2; *Think of England* for BBC *Modern Times; Unholy Land* - a series for C4; *Vyvan's Hotel* - for BBC *Picture This; Patriarchs, Presidents and Profits* - BBC Correspondent Special

MW Entertainments
48 Dean Street
Soho
London W1V 5HL
Tel: 020 7734 7707
Fax: 020 7734 7727
(See Pathé Productions - Lottery Film Production Franchises)

New Realm Entertainments Ltd
2nd Floor, 25 Margaret Street
London W1
Tel: 020 7436 7800
Fax: 020 7436 0690

Nova Productions
11a Winholme
Armthorpe
Doncaster DN3 3AF
Tel: 01302 833422
Fax: 08701 257917
email: info@novaonline.co.uk
Website: www.novaonline.co.uk
Andrew White, Maurice White, Gareth Atherton
Film, television and graphics production company, specialising in documentary, entertainment, special event and music promo production

Nunhead Films plc
Pinewood Studios
Pinewood Road
Iver Heath
Bucks SL0 0NH
Tel: 01753 650075
Fax: 01753 655 700
email: info@nunheadfilms.com
Website: nunheadfilms.com
Carol Lemon, John Stewart
Released in 2000: *The Asylum*, a feature film produced by Carol Lemon, written and directed by John Stewart

Orbit Media Ltd
7/11 Kensington High Street
London W8 5NP
Tel: 020 7287 4264
Fax: 020 7727 0515
Website: www.orbitmedia.co.uk
Jordan Reynolds
Currently producing Richard O'Brien's *Midnight Matinee, History of Television*

Orlando TV Productions
Up-the-Steps
Little Tew
Chipping Norton
Oxon OX7 4JB
Tel: 01608 683218
Fax: 01608 683364
email: orlando.tv@btinternet.com
Producers of TV documentaries: *Nova* (WGBH-Boston); *Horizon* (BBC); *QED* (BBC)

Oxford Film and Video Makers
The Stables
North Place
Headington
Oxford OX3 9HY
Tel: 01865 741682 or 01865 760074
(course enquiries)
Fax: 01865 742901
email: ofvm@ox39hy.demon.co.uk
Website: www.welcome.to/ofvm
Oxford Film and Video Makers supports a broad range of individual productions

Oxford Film Company
6 Erskine Road
London NW3 3AJ
Tel: 020 7483 3637
Fax: 020 7483 3567
email: mail@oftv.co.uk
Released *Hilary and Jackie* starring Emily Watson, directed by Anand Tucker and *Restoration* directed by Micahel Hoffman

Oxford Scientific Films
Lower Road
Long Hanborough
Oxford OX8 8LL
Tel: 01993 881881
Fax: 01993 882808
email: enquiries@osf.uk.com
Website: www.osf.uk.com
Film Library: Sandra Berry, Jane Mulleneux
Photo Library: Suzanne Aitzetmuller
Commercials Production: Nicholas Unsworth
Natural History Production: Sean Morris

Pagoda Film & Television Corporation Ltd
Twentieth Century House
31-32 Soho Square
London W1V 6AP
Tel: 020 7534 3500
Fax: 020 7534 3501
email: pag@pagodafilm.co.uk
Head of Development
In development: *Mary Stuart; That Funny Old Thing; The Corsican Sisters; Blaz Getting Paid; Welcome to America; Hardcore Pornography*

Paladin Pictures
22 Ashchurch Grove
London W12 9B7
Tel: 020 8740 1811
Fax: 020 8740 7220
Quality documentary, drama, music and arts programming

Parallax Pictures
7 Denmark Street
London WC2H 8LS
Tel: 020 7836 1478
Fax: 020 7497 8062
Sally Hibbin
Recent productions: Ken Loach's *Ladybird, Ladybird, Land and Freedom; Carla's Song*; Les Blair's *Jump the Gun; Bad Behaviour, Bliss*; Philip Davis's *ID*; Christopher Monger's *The Englishman Who Went Up the Hill, But Came Down a Mountain*, Phil Davies' *Hold Back the Night*
(See The Film Consortium - Lottery Film Production Franchises)

Partridge Films
The Television Centre
Bath Road
Bristol BS4 3HG
Tel: 0117 972 3777
Fax: 0117 971 9340
email: wildlife@partridge.co.uk
Michael Rosenberg (Director of
Programmes), Andrew Buchanan
(Head of Development), Jayne Clark
(Director of Operations), Kate
Edmondson (Library)
Makers of wildlife documentaries
and videos for television and
educational distribution

Pathé Pictures
Kent House
Market Place
London W1N 8AR
Tel: 020 7323 5151
Fax: 020 7636 7594
Contact: Peter Scott
Consists of: Thin Man Films and
Imagine Films, Allied Filmmakers
and Allied Films Ltd, NFH, Pandora
Productions, Sarah Radclyffe
Productions, Fragile Films and MW
Entertainment
(See Pathé Productions - Lottery
Film Production Franchises)

Pearl Productions Ltd
11 Holbein House
London SW1 8NH
email: info@pearlproductions.co.uk
Website: www.pearlproductions.
co.uk
Camilla Doege-Kohle
Film production company. Also
involved in the European Short Film
Festival

Persistent Vision Productions
299 Ivydale Road
London SE15 3DZ
Tel: 020 7639 5596
Carol Lemon, John Stewart
In distribution: *Crash; The Gaol; The Break-In*

Photoplay Productions
21 Princess Road
London NW1 8JR
Tel: 020 7722 2500
Fax: 020 7722 6662
Kevin Brownlow, David Gill, Patrick
Stanbury
Producers of documentaries and
television versions of silent feature
films

Picture Palace Films Ltd
13 Egbert Street

London NW1 8LJ
Tel: 020 7586 8763
Fax: 020 7586 9048
email: picpalace@compuserve.com
Website: www.picturepalace.com
Malcolm Craddock, Alex Usborne
Specialise in feature film and TV
drama
Rebel Heart (4x1 hour TV drama,
BBC Northern Ireland, Irish Film
Board, Irish Screen), *Large* (feature
film for FilmFour & The Film
Consortium), *Extremely Dangerous*
(4x1 hour series for ITV, with
Northwest One Films starring Sean
Bean), *The Acid House* (feature film
for FilmFour); *A Life for a Life - The
True Story of Stefan Kiszko* starring
Olympia Dukakis (1 x 2hr film, co-
production with Celtic Films),
Sharpe (5 series (14 x2 hrs, Carlton),
starring Sean Bean set in the
Peninsular War. *Little Napoleons* (4 x
1 hr, C4).

Planet 24 Productions
The Planet Building, Thames Quay
195 Marsh Wall
London E14 9SG
Tel: 020 7345 2424/512 5000
Fax: 020 7345 9400
Recent productions: *The Big
Breakfast* (C4); *Gaytime TV* (BBC2)

Portman Productions
167 Wardour Street
London W1V 3TA
Tel: 020 7468 3400
Fax: 020 7468 3499
Major producer in primetime drama
and feature films worldwide

Praxis Films
PO Box 290
Market Rasen
Lincs LN3 6BB
Tel: 01472 399976
Fax: 01472 399976
email: info@praxisfilms.com
Website: www.praxisfilms.com
Sue Waterfield
Internet, new media, film, tv
production company. Documentaries,
current affairs, educational
programming for UK and
international broadcasters. Extensive
archive of sea, fishing, rural material

Presence Films
66a Great Titchfield Street
London W1P 7AE
Tel: 020 7636 8477
Fax: 020 7636 8722
email: news@presencefilms.com
Alan Dewhurst, Tessa Schneider

In production: *The Ship*, directed by
Lucy Lee, the first British animated
IMAX film. In development: several
other large format projects; and
Bertolt Brecht's *War Primer*
(television arts feature)

Prominent Features
34 Tavistock Street
London WC2E 7PB
Tel: 020 7497 1100
Fax: 020 7497 1133
Steve Abbott
Company owned by Steve Abbott,
John Cleese, Terry Gilliam, Anne
James, Terry Jones and Michael Palin
which has produced six feature films
to date

Prominent Television
34 Tavistock Street
London WC2E 7PB
Tel: 020 7497 1100
Company formed by Steve Abbott,
John Cleese, Terry Gilliam, Eric Idle,
Anne James, Terry Jones and
Michael Palin to produce in-house
television programmes

Sarah Radclyffe Productions
5th Floor
83-84 Berwick Street
London W1V 3PJ
Tel: 020 7437 3128
Fax: 020 7437 3129
email: srpltd@globalnet.co.uk
Sarah Radclyffe, Bill Godfrey
Sarah Radclyffe previously founded
and was co-owner of Working Title
Films and was responsible for,
amongst others, *My Beautiful
Laundrette*, *Wish You Were Here*, and
A World Apart. Sarah Radclyffe
Productions was formed in 1993 and
productions to date are: *Second Best*,
dir Chris Menges; *Sirens*, dir. John
Duigan; *Cousin Bette*, dir. Des
McAnuff; *Bent*, dir. Sean Mathias;
Les Misérables, dir Bille August; *The
War Zone*, dir Tim Roth *There's Only
One Jimmy Grimble*, dir John Hay
(See Pathé Productions - Lottery
Film Production Franchises)

Ragdoll Productions
Pinewood Studios
Pinewood Road
Iver Heath
Bucks SL0 0NH
Tel: 01753 631800
Fax: 01753 631831
Specialist children's television
producer of live action and
animation, currently producing long-
running series *Teletubbies, Tots TV,*

Rosie and Jim (for ITV); *Teletubbies; Brum and Open A Door* (for BBC)

Raw Charm
Ty Cefn
Rectory Road
Cardiff CF1 1QL
Tel: 029 2064 1511
Fax: 029 2066 8220
email: pam@rawcharm.demon.co.uk
Website: rawcharm.co.uk
Pamela Hunt
Kate Jones-Davies
Documentary, music, entertainment.
Recent productions: *King of Discount* (BBC), *Bad Boys* (Channel 5), *Wings* (HTV/Meridian)

Recorded Picture Co
24 Hanway Street
London W1P 9DD
Tel: 020 7636 2251
Fax: 020 7636 2261
Jocelyn Jones
Chairman: Jeremy Thomas
Films produced include: *Brother* (1999 Dir Takeshi Kitano), *Sexy Beast* (1999 Dir Jonathan Glazer), *Gohatto* (1999 Exec Prod - Dir Nagisa Oshima), *The Cup* (1999 Exec Prod - Dir Khyentse Norbu) *All the Little Animals* (1997 Dir Jeremy Thomas), *The Brave* (1997 Exec Prod - Dir Johnny Depp), *Victory* (1997 Exec Prod - Dir Mark Peploe), *Blood and Wine* (1996 Dir - Bob Rafelson), *Crash* (1995 Exec Prod - Dir David Cronenberg)

Red Rooster Film & Television Entertainment
29 Floral Street
London WC2E 9DP
Tel: 020 7379 7727
Fax: 020 7379 5756
Grainne Marmion, Sarah Williams, Tim Vaughan, Julia Ouston
The Chrysalis Group has bought the remaining 50 per cent holding in the company, and continues to maintain a £1m fund to develop television programmes and feature films.
Recent productions: *Wilderness* (ITV); *Beyond Fear* (Channel 5)

Redwave Films (UK) Ltd
31-32 Soho Square
London W1V 6AP
Tel: 020 7753 7200
Fax: 020 7753 7201
Uberto Pasolini, Polly Leys, Rachel Bennette

The Reel Thing
Airport House

Purley Way
Croydon
Surrey CRO 0XZ
Tel: 020 8395 7665
Fax: 020 8688 2598
Film and television production company providing broadcast and non-broadcast production services across all delivery media

Reeltime Pictures
70-72 Union Street
London SE1 0NW
Tel: 020 7620 3102
Fax: 020 7620 3104
Formed in 1984, Reeltime specialises in the production of drama and documentaries connected with cult film and television for theatrical and non-theatrical release

Regent Productions
The Mews
6 Putney Common
Putney
London SW15 1HL
Tel: 020 8789 5350
Fax: 020 8789 5332
Current productions: three new series of the C4 quiz series *Fifteen-to-One* (188 programmes). In development: quiz shows; a seven-part drama series; a current affairs project

Renaissance Films
34-35 Berwick Street
London W1V 3RF
Tel: 020 7287 5190
Fax: 020 7287 5191
email: info@renaissance-films.com
Website: www.renaissance-films.com
Angus Finney
Film development, production, finance and sales company. Films include: *Wings of the Dove, The Luzhin Defence, Disco Pigs*

Renegade Films
3rd Floor, Bolsover House
5/6 Clipstone Street
London W1P 8LD
Tel: 020 7637 0957
Fax: 020 7637 0959
email: renprism@dircon.co.uk
Robert Buckler, Amanda Mackenzie Stuart, Ildiko Kemeny
Productions include: *Brothers in Trouble, Pressure, The Last Place on Earth, Facts of Life, Midnight Expresso, The Star, The Sin Eater Hotel Splendide* and (as Prisma Communications) *The Financial Times Business Toolkit*. Development projects include: *The Go Kart, Room*

To Rent, Hotel Sordide, The Thought Gang

Revolution Films
10 Little Turstile
London WC1V 7DX
Tel: 020 7242 0372
Fax: 020 7242 0407
Recent productions: *Old New Borrowed Blue*

Richmond Light Horse Productions Ltd
3 Esmond Court
Thackeray Street
London W8 5HB
Tel: 020 7937 9315
Fax: 020 7938 4024
Euan Lloyd

Riverchild Films
2nd Floor, 26 Goodge St
London W1P 1FG
Tel: 020 7636 1122
Fax: 020 7636 1133
email: riverchild@riverchild.demon.co.uk
Features and short film production

Riverfront Pictures
Dock Cottages, Peartree Lane
Glamis Road
Wapping
London E1 9SR
Tel: 020 7481 2939
Fax: 020 7480 5520
Specialise in music, arts and drama-documentaries. Independent productions for television. Recent productions for C4 *Cutting Edge* and BBC Arts

RM Associates
46 Great Marlborough Street
London W1V 1DB
Tel: 020 7439 2637
Fax: 020 7439 2316
email: rma@rmassociates.co.uk
Neil Mundy (Director of Programmes)
Sally Fairhead (Head of Publicity)
RM Associates produces and distributes a broad range of music, arts and documentary programming for international television, videogram, and educational release, coproducing widely with major broadcasters and media companies world-wide, including BBC, LWT, ARD and ZDF, NOS, SVT, ABC Australia, PBS America, YLE Finland, ARTE and RAI

Rocket Pictures
7 King Street Cloisters
Clifton Walk

London W6 oGY
Tel: 020 8741 9009
Fax: 020 8741 9097
Recent productions include: *Women Talking Dirty*

Rodney Read
45 Richmond Road
Twickenham
Middx TW1 3AW
Tel: 020 8891 2875
Fax: 020 8744 9603
email: rodney_read@
Compuserve.com
R.J.D. Read
Film and video production offering experience in factual and entertainment programming. Also provides a full range of back-up facilities for the feature and television industries, including 'making of' documentaries, promotional programme inserts, on air graphics and title sequences, sales promos, trailers and commercials. Active in production for UK cable and satellite

RSPB Film and Video Unit
The Lodge, Sandy
Beds SG19 2DL
Tel: 01767 680551
Fax: 01767 692365
Producers of *Osprey, Kingfisher, Where Eagles Fly, Barn Owl, The Year of the Stork and Flying for Gold*. Recent productions: *The Flamingo Triangle; Skydancer*. The unit also acts as an independent producer of environmental films and videos

Samuelson Productions
4th Floor, 9 Hanover Street
London W1P 7LJ
Tel: 020 7495 3414
Fax: 020 7495 3415
Arlington Road dir Mark Pellington, starring Tim Robbins, Jeff Bridges, Joan Cusack and Hope Davis; *Wilde* dir Brian Gilbert, starring Stephen Fry, Jude Law, Vanessa Redgrave and Jennifer Ehle

Sands Films
119 Rotherhithe Street
London SE16 4NF
Tel: 020 7231 2209
Fax: 020 7231 2119
Recent productions: *A Midsummer Night's Dream, Nursery Rhymes, Cathedrals, Colla-Verdi*

Scala Productions Limited
15 Frith Street
London W1V 5TS

Tel: 020 7734 7060
Fax: 020 7437 3248
email: scalaprods@aol.com
Nik Powell, Amanda Posey, Rachel Wood, Finola Dwyer, Laurie Borg, Jonathan Karlsen
Recent productions: Shane Meadows' *Twentyfourseven* starring Bob Hoskins.
Mark Herman's *Little Voice* starring Michael Caine, Brenda Blethyn, Ewan McGregor, Jane Horrocks
Chris Menges' *The Lost Son* starring Daniel Auteuil and Nastassja Kinski
Kay Mellor's *Fanny & Elvis* starring Kerry Fox and Ray Winstone
Deborah Warner's *The Last September* starring Maggie Smith and Michael Gambon
Julian Fariono's *The Last Yellow* starring Mark Addy; Charlie Creed-Miles and Samantha Morton
Tom Connolly's *Five Seconds to Spare* starring Max Beesley
Declan Lowney's *Wild About Harry* starring Brendan Gleeson and Amanda Donohoe
Projects in development
The Brian Jones Project; Single Shot; Jonathan Wild; Last Orders Shang-A-Lang; Money

Scottish Television Enterprises
Cowcaddens
Glasgow G2 3PR
Tel: 0141 300 3000
Fax: 0141 300 3030
Darrel James, Managing Director
Producers of: *Taggart* (drama), *Inspector Rebus* (drama), *Sherlock Holmes in the 22nd Century* (animation), *How 2* (teenage/education), *Fun House* (children's game show), *Get Wet* (children's gameshow), *The Last Musketeer* (drama)

Screen Ventures
49 Goodge Street
London W1P 1FB
Tel: 020 7580 7448
Fax: 020 7631 1265
email: screenventures@easynet.co.uk
Christopher Mould, Jack Bond, Caroline Furness
Production and television sales company. Producing music, drama and documentaries

September Films
Silver House
35 Beak Street
London W1R 3LD
Tel: 020 7494 1884

Fax: 020 7439 1194
David Green, Elaine Day, Sally Miles
TV includes: *The Final Day; The Lookalikes Agency; Eddie Irvine: The Inside Track; Geri's World Walkabout; We Can Rebuild You*
Feature films: *House of America; Solomon and Gaenor*

Siren Film and Video Ltd
5 Charlotte Square
Newcastle-upon-Tyne NE1 4XF
Tel: 0191 232 7900
Fax: 0191 232 7900
email: sirenfilms@aol.com
Film and television production company specialising in work for and about children

Siriol Productions
Phoenix Buildings
3 Mount Stuart Square
Butetown
Cardiff CF1 6RW
Tel: 029 2048 8400
Fax: 029 2048 485962
email: siriol@baynet.co.uk
Formerly Siriol Animation. Producers of high quality animation for television and the cinema. Makers of: *SuperTed; The Princess and the Goblin; Under Milk Wood; Santa and the Tooth Fairies; Santa's First Christmas; Tales of the Tooth Fairies, The Hurricanes; Billy the Cat; The Blobs; Rowland the Reindeer*

Skreba
Union Hall
27-28 Union Street
London SE1 1SC
Tel: 020 7357 9924
Fax: 020 7357 9920
Ann Skinner, Simon Relph
(See The Film Consortium - Lottery Film Production Franchises)

Sky Pictures
Centaurs Park
Grant Way, Syon Lane
Isleworth
Middlesex TW7 5QD
Tel: 020 7705 3000
Titles include: *Milk; Saving Grace; Best*

Skyline Films
PO Box 821U
London W41 1WH
Tel: 07836 275584
Fax: 020 8354 2219
Steve Clark-Hall, Mairi Bett
Recent productions: *The Winter Guest* (with Ed Pressmann), *Love*

and Death on Long Island, Small Faces, Margaret's Museum, Still Crazy (for Margot Tandy)

Smoking Dogs Films
21b Brooksby Street
Islington
London N1 1EX
Tel: 020 7697 0747
Fax: 020 7697 0757
email: info@smokingdogsfilms.
demon.co.uk
John Akomfrah, Lina Gopaul, David Lawson
Independent films
The Call of Mist (BBC Arts)
Goldie - When Saturn Returnz (C4)
The Wonderful World of Louis Armstrong (BBC Omnibus)
Riot (Channel Four)

Soho Communications
2 Percy Street
London W1P 9FA
Tel: 020 7637 5825
Fax: 020 7436 9740
email: staton@dircon.co.uk
Website: sohocommunications.com
Jon Staton/Tony Coggans

Sony Pictures Europe UK Ltd
Sony Pictures Europe House
25 Golden Square
London W1R 6LU
Tel: 020 7533 1111
Fax: 020 7533 1105
Recent productions: *Virtual Sexuality*

Southern Star Primetime Limited
Southern Star Sales (UK) Limited
45-49 Mortimer Street
London W1N 7TD
Tel: 020 7636 9431
Fax: 020 7436 7426
Simon Willock: General Manager, Wild & Real
Victoria Ryan, Head of European Sales, Southern Star Primetime
Catherine Neubauer: Head of European Sales, Southern Star Kids Production and Distribution

Specific Films
25 Rathbone Street
London W1P 1AG
Tel: 020 7580 7476
Fax: 020 7494 2676
Michael Hamlyn
Recent productions: *The Last Seduction 2*, dir Terry Marcel; *PAWS* (exec. prod) dir Carl Zwicky; *The Adventures of Priscilla, Queen of the Desert*, directed by Stephan Elliott;

Mr Reliable dir by Nadia Tass. Developing a number of feature film projects

Spice Factory
81 The Promenade
Peacehaven
Brighton
East Sussex BN10 8LS
Tel: 01273 585275
Fax: 01273 585304
email: sfactory@fastnet.co.uk
Michael L.Cowan
Films, Games & Television Production Company. Productions: *Killer Tongue* (1997), *Dying to Go Home* (1997), *Ricky 6* (1998), *New Blood* (1998), *Pilgrim* (1999), *Sabotage* (1999). In development: *Fry; Crush Hour; The Void; Breaking the Code; Our Game; Bat Out of Hell.* Television project in development: *Kremlin Contact*; Paramount/BBC/Bavaria based on best selling book by Donald James. In production: *Heist* and *Sambaland*

Stagescreen Productions
12 Upper St Martin's Lane
London WC2H 9DL
Tel: 020 7497 2510
Fax: 020 7497 2208
email: stgescreen@aol.com
Film, television and theatre company

Talent Television
2nd Floor Regent House
235 Regent Street
London W1R 7AG
Tel: 020 7434 1677
Fax: 020 7434 1577
John Kaye Cooper, Managing Director

Talisman Films Limited
5 Addison Place
London W11 4RJ
Tel: 020 7603 7474
Fax: 020 7602 7422
email: email@talismanfilms.com
Richard Jackson
Neil Dunn, Caroline Oulton
Production of theatric features and the whole range of television drama. Recent productions: *Complicity* (feature) starring Jonny Lee Miller, Brian Cox and Keeley Hawes: *The Secret Adveutures of Jules Verne* (22 part tv series) starring Michael Praed and Francesca Hunt; *Remember Me?* (Imelda Staunton; *Rob Roy* (feature for United Artists) starring Liam Neeson, Jessica Lange, John Hurt, Tim Roth; *Just William* (series I & II, BBC): *The Rector's Wife* (4x60 mins, C4) drama serial starring Lindsay Duncan

TalkBack Productions
36 Percy Street
London W1P 0LN
Tel: 020 7323 9777
Fax: 020 7637 5105
Productions include: *Smith and Jones* (+ 5 previous series, BBC1); *They Think It's All Over* (+3 previous series, BBC1); *Never Mind The Buzzcocks* (+ 1 previous series, BBC2)

Telescope Pictures Ltd
Twickenham Film Studios
Saint Margarets
Twickenham
Middlesex TW1 2AW
Tel: 020 8607 8888
Fax: 020 8607 8889
Recent productions: *Princess Caraboo*, dir Michael Austin; *The Revengers' Comedies* (dir Malcolm Mowbrary); In development: *Red Right Hand, Slow Train to Milan*

Teliesyn
Chapter Arts Centre
Market Road
Cardiff CF5 1QE
Tel: 029 2030 0876
Fax: 029 2030 0877
email: ebost:tv@teliesyn.demon.
co.uk
Website: www.teliesyn.co.uk
Involved in feature film, television drama and television documentary/feature. In production: *Reel Truth*, docu/drama for S4C and C4; *Cyber Wales* and *Answering Back* for BBC Wales; *Dragon's Song* for C4. In development: *Video Pirates* (6 x 30 min drama) Coron yr Wythnons plus a number of feature film and drama series

Tempest Films
33 Brookfield
Highgate West Hill
London N6 6AT
Tel: 020 8340 0877
Fax: 020 8340 9309
In development: *The York Mysteries* with YTV. *Stop Press* - 6 part TV series; *The Actresses* - 3 part mini-series; *Mallory Short* and *the Very Big Bass* - feature film

Testimony Films
12 Great George Street,
Bristol BS1 5RS
Tel: 0117 925 8589
Fax: 0117 925 7668
Steve Humphries
Specialists in social history documentaries

Thin Man Films
9 Greek Street
London W1V 5LE
Tel: 020 7734 7372
Fax: 020 7287 5228
Simon Channing-Williams, Mike Leigh
Recent productions: *Career Girls; Secrets & Lies, Topsy–Turvy*
(See Pathé Productions - Lottery Film Production Franchises)

Tiger Aspect Productions
5 Soho Square
London W1V 5DE
Tel: 020 7434 0672
Fax: 020 7287 1448
Harry Enfield and Chums (2 series BBC); *The Vicar of Dibley* (BBC1) *The Thin Blue Line* (BBC1) *The Village* (7 series for Meridian) *Howard Goodall's Organ Works* (Ch4) *Hospital* (Ch5) *Deacon Brodie* (Screen One for BBC 1)

TKO Communications
PO Box 130, Hove
East Sussex BN3 6QU
Tel: 01273 550088
Fax: 01273 540969
email: jskruger@tkogroup.com
A division of the Kruger Organisation, making music programmes for television, satellite and video release worldwide as well as co-producing various series and acquiring rights to full length feature films for distribution

Toledo Pictures
3rd Floor
75-77 Margaret Street
London W1N 7HB
Tel: 020 7291 8050
Fax: 020 7291 8060
email: adam.tudhope@dnafilms.com
Adam Tudhope, Assistant to Duncan Kenworthy
(See DNA Films - Lottery Film Production Franchises)

Topaz Productions Ltd
Manchester House
46 Wormholt Road
London W12 0LS
Tel: 020 8749 2619
Fax: 020 8749 0358
email: prints@topazprods. freeserve.co.uk
In production: ongoing corporate productions

Trademark Films
5 Sherwood Street
London W1V 7RA
Tel: 020 7287 5944
Fax: 020 7287 1786
email: mail@trademarkfilms.co.uk
Liz Barron, Irena Brignull, Cleone Clarke, David Parfitt

Trans World International
TWI House
23 Eyot Gardens
London W6 9TR
Tel: 020 8233 5400
Fax: 020 8233 5401
Television and video sports production and rights representation branch of Mark McCormack's International Management Group, TWI produces over 2,500 hours of broadcast programming and represents the rights to many leading sports events including Wimbledon, British Open, US Open, and World Matchplay golf. Productions include: *Trans World Sport; Futbol Mundial; PGA European Tour; ATP Tour Highlights; West Indies, Indian and Pakistan Test cricket; Oddballs; A-Z of Sport; High 5; The American Big Match and Blitz; The Olympic Collection* and *The Whitbread Round The World Race*

Transatlantic Films
Studio 1
3 Brackenbury Road
London W6 0BE
Tel: 020 8735 0505
Fax: 020 8735 0605
email: mail@transatlanticfilms.com
Revel Guest, Justin Albert
Recent Programming: *Horse Tales* 13x30 mins stories about the special bond between people and horses, for *Animal Planet; Amazing Animal Adaptors* - 1x60 mins special for Discovery Channel; *History's Turning Point* - 26x30 mins about decisive moments in history, for Discovery Europe
Current Production:
Trailblazers - 13x60 mins, travel and adventure series for Discovery Europe, Travel Channel; *Three Gorges* - 2x60 mins, the building of the World's biggest dam in China, for Discovery Channel/TLC

Try Again Limited
Leigh Grove Farmhouse
Leigh Grove
Bradford on Avon
Wilts BA15 2RF
Tel: 01225 862 705
Fax: 01225 862 205
Michael Darlow, Rod Taylor, Chris Frederick

Produces drama, music, arts, documentary programmes

Turn On TV
1st Floor
77 Leonard Street
London EC2A 4QS
Alison Higgins

TV Cartoons
39 Grafton Way
London W1P 5LA
Tel: 020 7388 2222
Fax: 020 7383 4192
John Coates, Norman Kauffman

TV Choice
22 Charing Cross Road
London WC2H 0HR
Tel: 020 7379 0873
Fax: 020 7379 0263
Chris Barnard, Norman Thomas
Producer and distributor of dramas and documentaries about business, technology and finance.

Twentieth Century-Fox Productions Ltd
20th Century House
31-31 Soho Square
London W1V 6AP
Tel: 020 7437 7766
Fax: 020 7734 3187
Recent productions: *The Full Monty, Braveheart, Stealing Beauty; Titanic*

Twenty Twenty Television
Suite 2, Grand Union House
29 Kentish Town Road
London NW1 9NX
Tel: 020 7284 2020
Fax: 020 7284 1810
The company continues to produce programmes exclusively for broadcast television, specialising in worldwide investigative journalism, documentaries, productions, factually based drama, science and childrens programmes

Tyburn Film Productions Ltd
Pinewood Studios
Iver Heath
Bucks SL0 0NH
Tel: 01753 651700
Fax: 01753 656050
Filmmaker: *The Creeping Flesh; Persecution; The Ghoul; Legend of the Werewolf*

UBA (United British Artists)
21 Alderville Road
London SW6 3RL
Tel: 01984 623619

Fax: 01984 623733
Production company for cinema and
TV projects. Past productioninclude:
Keep the Aspidistra Flying for OFE;

Uden Associates
Chelsea Wharf
Lots Road
London SW10 0QJ
Tel: 020 7351 1255
Fax: 020 7376 3937
Film and television production
company for broadcast through C4,
BBC and corporate clients

Union Pictures
36 Marshall Street
London W1V 1LL
Tel: 020 7287 5110
Fax: 020 7287 3770
Recent productions include: *The
Crow Road; Deadly Voyage;
Masterchef; Junior Masterchef; The
Roswell Incident*

United Artists Films (an MGM company)
10 Stephen Mews
London W1P 1PP
Tel: 020 7333 8877
Fax: 020 7333 8878
Formerly Goldwyn Films

Universal Pictures International
Oxford House
76 Oxford Street
London W1N 0HQ
Tel: 020 7307 1300
Fax: 020 7307 1301

Universal Pictures Ltd
1 Hamilton Mews
London W1V 9FF
Tel: 020 7491 4666
Fax: 020 7493 4702
Recent productions: *The Jackal,
DragonHeart, Fierce Creatures*

UpFront Television Ltd
39-41 New Oxford Street
London WC1A 1BH
Tel: 020 7836 7702
Fax: 020 7836 7701
email: upfront@btinternet.com
Claire Nye
Richard Brecker

Vera Productions Ltd
3rd Floor
66/68 Margaret Street
London W1N 7FL
Tel: 020 7436 6116
Fax: 020 7436 6117/6016
Contact: Elaine Morris

Victor Film Company Ltd
39/43 Brewer Street
London W1R 3FD
Tel: 020 7494 4477
Fax: 020 7494 4488
email: post@victor-film-co.demon.co.uk
Website: www.victor-film-co.demon.co.uk
Alasdair Waddell
Forthcoming titles include: *Dog
Soldiers, Father Figure, My Sister in
Law*

Videotel Productions
84 Newman Street
London W1P 3LD
Tel: 020 7299 1800
Fax: 020 7299 1818
Producers of educational and training
packages for television and video
distribution

Vine International Pictures
21 Great Chapel Street
London W1V 3AQ
Tel: 020 7437 1181
Fax: 020 7494 0634
Marie Vine, Barry Gill
Sale of feature films such as
*Rainbow, The Pillow Book, The Ox
and the Eye, Younger and Younger,
The Prince of Jutland, Erik the
Viking, Let Him Have It, Trouble in
Mind*

Vixen Films
13 Aubert Park
Highbury
London N5 1TL
Tel: 020 7359 7368
Fax: 020 7359 7368
email: tg@tgraham.demon.co.uk
Film/video production and
distribution, mainly feature
documentaries. Recent projects:
Gaea Girls - a film about Japanese
women wrestlers

Wall To Wall Television
8-9 Spring Place
Kentish Town
London NW5 3ER
Tel: 020 7485 7424
Fax: 020 7267 5292
Alex Graham, Jane Root
Producers of quality innovative
programming

Walsh Bros Ltd
24 Redding House
Harlinger Street
King Henry's Wharf
London SE18 5SR
Tel: 020 8858 6870/020 8854 5557

Fax: 020 8858 6870
email: walshbros@lycosmail.com
John Walsh
Founded in 1993 by John Walsh.
Projects include feature films and
documentary programmes: *Monarch*,
acclaimed feature film on the death
of King Henry VIII. *Nu Model Armi*
10x30min (Channel Four) *Cowboyz
& Cowgirlz* 15x30min (Channel
Five). Other projects include: *Ray
Harryhausen*, Oscar winning
documentary profile of th eanimating
legend. *HRH Elizabeth II*; *The
Comedy Store, The Sleeper, The
Sceptic & The Psychic*

Warner Bros International Television
98 Theobalds Road
London WC1X 8WB
Tel: 020 7494 3710
Fax: 020 7287 9086
Richard Milnes, Donna Brett, Tim
Horan, Ian Giles
TV sales, marketing and distribution.
A division of Warner Bros
Distributors Ltd, A Time Warner
Entertainment Company, LP

Warner Bros Productions Ltd
98 Theobalds Road
London WC1X 8WB
Tel: 020 7494 3710
Fax: 020 7287 9086
Recent productions: *Eyes Wide Shut,
The Avengers*

Warner Sisters Film & TV Ltd, Cine Sisters Ltd
The Cottage
Pall Mall Deposit
124 Barlby Road
London W10 6BL
Tel: 020 8960 3550
Fax: 020 8960 3880
email: sisters@warnercine.com
Directors: Lavinia Warner, Jane
Wellesley, Anne-Marie Casey and
Dorothy Viljoen
Founded 1984. Drama, Comedy. TV
and Feature Films. Output includes *A
Village Affair; Dangerous Lady;
Dressing for Breakfast; The Spy Who
Caught a Cold; Capital Sins; The
Bite; The Jump; Lady Audley's Secret*
- and feature film *Jilting Joe*.
Developing a wide range of TV and
feature projects

David Wickes Productions
169 Queen's Gate
London SW7 5HE
Tel: 020 7225 1382

Fax: 020 7589 8847
email: wickesco@aol.com
David Wickes, Heide Wilsher

Winchester Entertainment plc
29/30 Kingly Street
London W1R 5LB
Tel: 020 7434 4374
Fax: 020 7287 4334
Chief Executive: Gary Smith
Recent productions: *Shooting Fish; Stiff Upper Lips; Divorcing Jack*

Working Title Films
Oxford House
76 Oxford Street
London W1N 9FD
Tel: 020 7307 3000
Fax: 020 7307 3001/2/3
Tim Bevan, Eric Fellner
Recent film productions: *The Hudsucker Proxy; Four Weddings and a Funeral; French Kiss; Loch Ness; Moonlight and Valentino; Fargo; Dead Man Walking*

Working Title Television
Oxford House
76 Oxford Street
London W1N 9FD
Tel: 020 7307 3000
Fax: 020 7307 3001/2/3
Simon Wright, Tim Bevan
Recent productions: *Edward II; Amnesty - The Big 30; Further Tales of the Riverbank; TV Squash; The Borrowers* (series 1 & 2); *Tales of the City; The Baldy Man, Land and Woodley*

The Worldmark Production Company Ltd
7 Cornwall Crescent
London W11 1PH
Tel: 020 7792 9800
Fax: 020 7792 9801
David Wooster
Current productions: *Swimming with Sharks* 1x52min for MNET South Africa

Zenith Entertainment plc
43-45 Dorset Street
London W1H 4AB
Tel: 020 7224 2440
Fax: 020 7224 3194
email: general@zenith.tv.co.uk
Film and television production company. Recent feature films: Todd Haynes' *Velvet Goldmine*; Nicole Holofcener's *Walking and Talking*; Hal Hartley's *Amateur*. Recent television drama: *The Uninvited* (ITV); *Bodyguards* (Carlton); *Hamish Macbeth* (3 series, BBC Scotland); *Rhodes* (BBC1), *Bomber* (ITV) *SMTV:CDUK* (ITV)

Zenith North
11th Floor
Cale Cross House
156 Pilgrim Street
Newcastle upon Tyne NE1 6SU
Tel: 0191 261 0077
Fax: 0191 222 0271
email: zenithnorth@dial.pipex.com
Ivan Rendall, Peter Mitchell (Managing Director), John Coffey

Zooid Pictures Limited
66 Alexander Road
London N19 5PQ
Tel: 020 7281 2407
Fax: 020 7281 2404
email: postmaster@zooid.co.uk
Website: www.zooid.co.uk
Producers of experimental and television documentaries, various shorts; documentaries; Anglo-Brazilian-German co-productions

PRODUCTION STARTS

These are feature-length films intended for theatrical release with a significant British involvement (whether creative, financial or UK-based) which went into production between January and December 1999. The production start date is given where known. Single television dramas in production for the same period are indicated with *
Compiled by Laura Pearson

1999 UK PRODUCTION STARTS

1999
The FILTH AND THE FURY
HOUSE!
ONE DAY IN SEPTEMBER
ONE MORE KISS
SACRED FLESH

JANUARY
The BEACH
4   BROTHERLY LOVE
4   WHY DID BOBBY DIE?
11 The WORLD IS NOT ENOUGH
12 PIRATE'S TALE
16 The INTRUDER
23 SUBTERFUGUE
25 KIN
28 The HOUSE ON HAUNTED HILL

FEBRUARY
1   GLADIATOR
1   HOTEL SPLENDIDE
3   BLOOD
5   COMPLICITY
6   COMPANY MAN
8   BEST
8   The GUILTY
15 END OF THE AFFAIR
15 NEW YEAR'S DAY
15 *TRIAL BY FIRE
20 NASTY NEIGHBOURS
24 LOVE'S LABOURS LOST
28 ANNA AND THE KING
28 ESSEX BOYS

MARCH
1   The NINE LIVES OF TOMAS KATZ
2   The CRIMINAL
8   DEAD BOLT DEAD
8   MISS JULIE
9   COUNTY KILBURN
14 15 MOMENTS
14 WOMEN TALKING DIRTY
17 ALL ABOUT ADAM
19 WHATEVER HAPPENED TO HAROLD SMITH?
20 COLD FISH
22 SALTWATER
25 SOUL'S ARK
26 MY MOTHER FRANK

APRIL
FOREVER MINE
5   FIVE SECONDS TO SPARE
5   THOUSANDS LIKE US [a.k.a. LOVE THE ONE YOU'RE WITH]
12 GUEST HOUSE PARADISO
12 WHEN THE SKY FALLS
18 SHADOW OF THE VAMPIRE
26 LOVE, HONOUR AND OBEY
26 WHAT'S COOKING?
27 ABERDEEN
28 CIRCUS
29 HIGH FIDELITY

MAY
1   SEXY BEAST
2   PARANOIA
4   SAVING GRACE
10 ONE LIFE STAND
10 SKELETON WRECK
16 The TESTIMONY OF TALIESIN JONES
17 BIRTHDAY GIRL
23 NORA
29 DUNGEONS AND DRAGONS
31 The INBETWEENERS

JUNE
RAGE
WARRIOR SISTERS
2   LONDINIUM
7   The HOUSE OF MIRTH
7   The LAST MINUTE
10 GANGSTER NO.1
15 EMOTIONAL BACKGAMMON
15 Die KLEINE VAMPIR [a.k.a. The LITTLE VAMPIRE]
25 BETWEEN TWO WOMEN (a.k.a. MOTHER AND SON)

28 BEAUTIFUL JOE
28 GREEN FINGERS
28 PAVAROTTI IN DAD'S ROOM
28 SECRET SOCIETY

JULY
25 The CUP (a.k.a. ROAD TO GLORY)
26 PARADISE GROVE
28 HONEST
30 MAYBE BABY
31 RELATIVE VALUES

AUGUST
*JOSEPH AND THE AMAZING TECHNICOLOR DREAMCOAT
LONDON BLUES
2   KEVIN & PERRY GO LARGE
3   THOMAS AND THE MAGIC RAILROAD
9   The LOW DOWN
9   QUILLS
9   SECOND GENERATION
16 STRONG BOYS
22 The GOLDEN BOWL
23 The GUV'NOR
23 OFFENDING ANGELS
25 The CLOSER YOU GET
23 DANCER
29 LAVA
30 THANKS FOR THE MEMORIES
31 DEAD BABIES

SEPTEMBER
4   The MAN WHO CRIED
5   ANOTHER LIFE
5   PEACHES
7   FED ROTTEN
7   INSIDE LYDIA'S HEAD
12 SOME VOICES
13 *CINDERELLA
13 PANDAEMONIUM

OCTOBER
BREAD AND ROSES
BREATHTAKING
SEASON TICKET
1   ROOM TO RENT
4   The LUZHIN DEFENSE
17 STRICTLY SINATRA
18 DAYBREAK
18 SNATCH
18 THERE'S ONLY ONE JIMMY GRIMBLE
18 The TRUTH GAME
21 YOUNG BLADES
24 CREATURES

25 The MOST FERTILE MAN IN
   IRELAND
25 RAT
25 SORTED
26 WHEN BRENDAN MET
   TRUDY

NOVEMBER

6 SHOOTERS
8 GLORY GLORY
14 GOING OFF BIG TIME
16 SUSPICIOUS RIVER
19 20:13 THOU SHALT NOT KILL
21 BROTHER
27 DANCING AT THE BLUE
   IGUANA
27 DECEPTION
30 The COMPANY MAN

DECEMBER

9 An EVERLASTING PIECE
12 CHRISTIE MALRY'S OWN
   DOUBLE ENTRY

ABERDEEN
27 April
Production Companies: Norsk
Films [Norway], Freeway Films [UK]
Locations/Studios: Scotland, Norway
Exec Prod: Tom Remlov
Producers: Peter Borgli
Director: Hans Petter Moland
Screenplay: Hans Petter Moland
Director of Photography: Philip
Ogaard
Cast: Ian Hart, Charlotte Rampling,
Stellan Skarsgaard, Lena Headey

ALL ABOUT ADAM
17 March
Production Companies: Venus
Productions, presented by HAL
Films, BBC Films, in association
with Bord Scannán na hÉireann
Locations/Studios: Ireland
Exec Prod: Harvey Weinstein, David
M Thompson, David Aukin, Trea
Leventhal, Rod Stoneman
Producers: Anna Devlin, Marina
Hughes
Director: Gerry Stembridge
Screenplay: Gerry Stembridge
Director of Photography: Bruno De
Keyzer
Editor: Mary Finlay
Cast: Stuart Townsend, Kate
Hudson, Frances O'Connor,
Charlotte Bradley, Tommy Tiernan

ANNA AND THE KING
28 February
Production Companies: Farang
Films, ©Twentieth Century Fox Film
Corporation, presented by Fox 2000
Pictures
Locations/Studios: Malaysia, London
Exec Prod: Terence Chang
Producers: Lawrence Bender, Ed
Elbert
Director: Andy Tennant
Screenplay: Steve Meerson, Peter
Krikes
Director of Photography: Caleb
Deschanel
Cast: Jodie Foster, Chow Yun-Fat,
Bai Ling, Tom Felton, Alwi Syed

ANOTHER LIFE
5 September
Production Companies: Boxer
Films funded by Lucida Investments,
Arts Council of England
Locations/Studios: London, Three
Mills Island Studios
Exec Prod: Gary Smith, Chris Craib,
Alexander Harakis, Fabio
Quaradeghini, Danny Passi
Producers: Angela Hart
Director: Philip Goodhew

Screenplay: Philip Goodhew
Director of Photography: Simon
Archer
Editor: Jamie Trevill
Cast: Natasha Little, Nick Moran,
Ioan Gruffudd, Imelda Staunton,
Rachael Stirling

The BEACH
January
Production Companies: Figment
Films, ©/presented by Twentieth
Century Fox Film Corporation
Locations/Studios: Thailand,
Australia, Maya Beach in Thailand
Producers: Andrew Macdonald,
John Hodge
Director: Danny Boyle
Screenplay: John Hodge
Director of Photography: Darius
Khondji
Editor: Masahiro Hirakubo
Cast: Leonardo DiCaprio, Tilda
Swinton, Virginie Ledoyen,
Guillaume Canet, Robert Carlyle

BEAUTIFUL JOE
28 June
Production Companies: Capitol
Films
Locations/Studios: Vancouver
Producers: Steven Haft, Fred Fuchs,
Jane Barclay, Sharon Havel, Hannah
Leader
Director: Stephen Metcalfe
Screenplay: Stephen Metcalfe
Director of Photography: Thomas
Ackerman
Editor: Nick Moore
Cast: Sharon Stone, Billy Connolly,
Jurnee Smollett, Dillon Moen, Ian
Holm

BEST
8 February
Production Companies: Best Films
Ltd, presented by IAC Film, Sky
Pictures, Isle of Man
Film Commission, presented in
association with Smoke & Mirrors,
Pembridge Productions
Locations/Studios: Isle of Man,
London
Exec Prod: John Lynch, Mary
McGuckian, Chris Roff, Michael
Ryan
Producers: Chris Roff, Mary
McGuckian
Director: Mary McGuckian
Screenplay: John Lynch, Mary
McGuckian
Director of Photography: Witold
Stok
Cast: John Lynch, Ian Bannen, Patsy
Kensit, Roger Daltry

BETWEEN TWO WOMEN
(a.k.a. MOTHER AND SON)
25 June
Production Companies: North Country Pictures
Locations/Studios: West Yorkshire, Greater Manchester
Exec Prod: Julie Woodcock
Producers: Steven Woodcock
Director: Steven Woodcock
Screenplay: Steven Woodcock
Director of Photography: Gordon Hickie
Cast: Barbara Marten, Andrew Dunn, Andrina Carroll, Frank Windsor, Eileen O'Brien

BIRTHDAY GIRL
17 May
Production Companies: Portobello Pictures, FilmFour, HAL Films
Locations/Studios: Australia, UK
Producers: Eric Abraham, Stephen Butterworth, Diana Phillips
Director: Jez Butterworth
Screenplay: Tom Butterworth, Jez Butterworth
Director of Photography: Oliver Stapleton
Editor: Chris Tellefsen
Cast: Nicole Kidman, Ben Chaplin, Vincent Cassel, Mathieu Kassovitz

BLOOD
3 February
Production Companies: Cantor Markham Productions, Loud Mouse Productions, Yorkshire Media Production Agency
Producers: Simon Markham
Director: Charly Cantor
Screenplay: Charly Cantor
Director of Photography: Katie Swain
Film **Editor**: Nick Packer
Cast: Adrian Rawlins, Lee Blakemore, Phil Cornwell, Paul Herzberg, Amelda Brown

BREAD AND ROSES
October
Production Companies: Parallax Pictures funded by FilmFour, BSkyB, Tornasol
Locations/Studios: Los Angeles
Producers: Rebecca O'Brien
Director: Ken Loach
Screenplay: Paul Laverty
Director of Photography: Barry Ackroyd
Editor: Jonathan Morris
Cast: Pilar Padilla, Adrien Brody, Elpidia Carrillo

BREATHTAKING
October
Production Companies: September Films, Sky Pictures
Locations/Studios: London
Exec Prod: Sally Miles
Producers: Rachel Brown
Director: David Green
Editor: Kant Pan
Cast: Joanne Whalley-Kilmer, Lorraine Pilkington, Jamie Foreman, Cal Macaninch, Neil Dudgeon

BROTHER
21 November
Production Companies: Office Kitano, Recorded Picture Co funded by Bandai Visual, Tokyo FM
Locations/Studios: Tokyo, Los Angeles
Producers: Masayuki Mori, Jeremy Thomas
Director: Takeshi Kitano
Screenplay: Takeshi Kitano
Cast: Takeshie Kitano, Omar Epps, Claude Maki

BROTHERLY LOVE
4 January
Production Companies: Causeway Films
Locations/Studio: Guildford, London
Director: Con O'Neill
Screenplay: Con O'Neill
Cast: Nick Moran, Jason Issacs

CHRISTIE MALRY'S OWN DOUBLE ENTRY
12 December
Production Companies: Woodline Films
Locations/Studios: London, Luxembourg
Exec Prod: Denis Wigman, Bob Hubar, Terry Glinwood
Producers: Kees Kasander
Director: Paul Tickell
Screenplay: Simon Bent
Director of Photography: Reinier van Brummelen
Cast: Nick Moran, Shirley Anne Field, Kate Ashfield, Neil Stuke

*CINDERELLA
13 September
Production Companies: Projector Productions funded by Channel Four, Channel Four International, Isle of Man Film Commission
Locations/Studios: Isle Of Man, Rugby
Producers: Simon Johnson, Trevor Eve
Director: Beeban Kidron
Screenplay: Nick Dear
Director of Photography: Alexei

Rodionov
Editor: Colin Monie
Cast: Kathleen Turner, David Warner, Marcella Plunkett, Katrin Cartlidge, Lucy Punch

CIRCUS
28 April
Production Companies: Columbia Pictures, Bridge
Locations/Studios: Brighton, Shepperton Studios
Producers: Alan Latham, James Gibb
Director: Rob Walker
Screenplay: David Logan
Director of Photography: Ben Seresin
Editor: Norrie Ottey
Cast: John Hannah, Famke Janssen, Eddie Izzard, Peter Stormare, Frederic Forrest

The CLOSER YOU GET
25 August
Production Companies: Redwave Films, Fox Searchlight Pictures
Producers: Uberto Pasolini
Director: Aileen Ritchie
Screenplay: William Ivory
Director of Photography: Robert Alazraki
Editor: Sue Wyatt
Cast: Ian Hart, Sean McGinley, Niamh Cusack, Ruth McCabe, Ewan Stewart

COLD FISH
20 March
Production Companies: Orion Pictures
Locations/Studios: London, Oxford
Producers: John Morrey, David Fairman
Director: David Fairman
Screenplay: Graham Cristie, PJ Swinburne
Director of Photography: Roger Eaton
Cast: Jon-Paul Gates, Stephen Yardley, Nadia Straham, Christopher Biggins, David Bowen

COMPANY MAN
6 February
Production Companies: InterMedia Film Equities, GreeneStreet Films
Locations/Studios: Los Angeles
Exec Prod: Guy East, Nigel Sinclair
Producers: Rick Leed, John Penotti
Director: Douglas McGrath, Peter Askin
Screenplay: Douglas McGrath, Peter Askin
Cast: Sigourney Weaver, John Turturro, Anthony LaPaglia, Ryan Phillippe, Alan Cumming

The COMPANY MAN
30 November
Production Companies: Studio Eight Productions, Prophecy Pictures
Locations/Studios: Vancouver
Exec Prod: John Curtis, Petros Tsaparas, Gary Howsam
Producers: Jamie Brown, John Curtis, Evan Taylor
Director: Robert Lee
Screenplay: Paul Birkett
Director of Photography: Dave Peltier
Editor: Gord Rempel
Cast: Brian Bosworth, Rachel Clark, Jenny Hayward

COMPLICITY
5 February
Production Companies: Talisman Films, Developed with the assistance of British Screen Finance, preproduction finance by Free Wheel Productions, Wallflower Ltd, presented by Carlton Films, presented in association with Scottish Arts Council Lottery Fund
Locations/Studios: Scotland
Exec Prod: Julia Palau, Michael Ryan
Producers: Richard Jackson, Neil Dunn
Director: Gavin Millar
Screenplay: Bryan Elsley
Director of Photography: David Odd
Editor: Angus Newton
Cast: Jonny Lee Miller, Brian Cox, Keeley Hawes, Paul Higgins, Bill Paterson

COUNTY KILBURN
9 March
Production Companies: Watermark Films
Locations/Studios: London
Exec Prod: Magnus Macintyre
Producers: Nick Heyworth
Director: Elliot Hegarty
Screenplay: Elliot Hegarty
Director of Photography: John Lynch
Cast: Ciaran McMenamin, Rick Warden, John Bowe, Georgia Mackenzie, Simon Sherlock, Tony Bluto

CREATURES
24 October
Production Companies: Creatures Ltd, DNA Film funded by Arts Council of England
Locations/Studios: Glasgow
Producers: Alan J Wands, Simon Donald

Director: Bill Eagles
Screenplay: Simon Donald
Director of Photography: James Welland
Cast: Rachel Weisz, Susan Lynch, Iain Glen, Maurice Roîves, Alex Norton

The CRIMINAL
2 March
Production Companies: ©Palm Pictures Limited, ©Criminal Pictures Limited, presented in association with Storm Entertainment, Christopher Johnson Company
Locations/Studios: London
Exec Prod: H Michael Heuser, Dan Genetti, Suzette Newman
Producers: Christopher Johnson, David Chapman, Mark Aarons
Director: Julian Simpson
Screenplay: Julian Simpson
Director of Photography: Nic Morris
Editor: Mark Aarons
Cast: Steven Mackintosh, Natasha Little, Eddie Izzard, Holly Aird, Yves Attal

The CUP
(a.k.a. ROAD TO GLORY)
25 July
Production Companies: Butcher's Run Films [US], Eagle Beach Productions [US]
Locations/Studios: Glasgow in Scotland
Exec Prod: Denis O'Neill
Producers: Rob Carliner, Robert Duvall, Michael Corrente
Director: Michael Corrente
Screenplay: Denis O'Neill
Director of Photography: Alex Thomson
Editor: David Ray
Cast: Brian Cox, Owen Coyle, Robert Duvall, Elaine M Ellis, Cole Hauser

DANCER
23 August
Production Companies: Tiger Aspect, WT2
Producers: Greg Brenman, Jon Finn
Director: Stephen Daldry
Screenplay: Lee Hall
Cast: Julie Walters, Jamie Bell, Jamie Draven, Gary Lewis, Stuart Wells

DANCING AT THE BLUE IGUANA
27 November
Production Companies: Moonstone

Entertainment
Locations/Studios: Los Angeles
Producers: Michael Radford, Sheila Kelly, Damian Jones, Graham Broadbent, Ernst Stroh, Ram Bergman, Dana Lustig
Director: Michael Radford
Screenplay: David Linter
Cast: Daryl Hannah, Jennifer Tilly, Sandra Oh, Sheila Kelly, Charlotte Ayanna

DAYBREAK
18 October
Production Companies: Daybreak Films funded by Scottish Arts Council, FilmFour
Locations/Studios: Edinburgh
Producers: James Mackay, Jim Hickey
Director: Bernard Rudden
Screenplay: Bernard Rudden
Director of Photography: Jean-Jacques Bouhon
Cast: Jim Cunningham, Diane Bell, Gaynor Purvis, Jean-Philippe Ecoffey

DEAD BABIES
31 August
Production Companies: Gruber Brothers
Locations/Studios: London, Hertfordshire
Producers: Richard Holmes, Neil Peplow
Director: William Marsh
Screenplay: William Marsh
Director of Photography: Danny Cohen
Editor: Eddie Hamilton
Cast: Charlie Condou, Paul Bettany, Katy Carmichael, Alexandra Gilbreath, Olivia Willimans

DEAD BOLT DEAD
8 March
Production Companies: It's Alright Ma Productions
Locations/Studios: London
Exec Prod: Etienne and Anita de Villiers
Producers: Paul de Villiers, Jon Harman
Director: James Rogan
Screenplay: Paul de Villiers
Director of Photography: Tom Wright
Cast: Ariyon Bakare, James Laurenson, Ronnie McCann, Neil Stuke, Monique de Villiers

DECEPTION
27 November
Production Companies: Studio Eight Productions, GFT,

Kingsborough Films, Next Films
Locations/Studios: Montreal and Quebec
Exec Prod: Gary Howsam
Producers: Jamie Brown, Pieter Kroonenburg, Marc Bikindou
Director: Max Fischer
Screenplay: Max Fischer
Director of Photography: Sylvain Brault
Cast: Daniel Pilon, Tom Rack, Marc Lavoine, Debi Mazar, Karina Lombard

DUNGEONS AND DRAGONS
29 May
Production Companies: Sweetpea Entertainment, Silver Pictures
Locations/Studios: Prague at Studios Barrandov
Exec Prod: Joel Silver
Producers: Courtney Solomon, Tom Hammel, Kia Jam
Director: Courtney Solomon
Screenplay: Topper Lilien, Carrol Cartwright
Director of Photography: Doug Milsome
Cast: Justin Whalen, Thora Birch, Kristen Wilson, Marlon Wayans, Jeremy Irons

EMOTIONAL BACKGAMMON
15 June
Production Companies: Corazon Productions
Producers: Ossie Smith
Director: Leon Herbert
Screenplay: Matthew Hope, Herbert Leon
Director of Photography: Koutaiba Al Janabi
Cast: Wil Johnson, Daniela Lavender, Jacqueline De Peza, Leon Herbert

END OF THE AFFAIR
15 February
Production Companies: ©Global Entertainment Productions GmbH, presented by Columbia Pictures Corporation
Locations/Studios: London, Brighton, Shepperton Studios
Producers: Stephen Woolley, Neil Jordan
Director: Neil Jordan
Screenplay: Neil Jordan
Director of Photography: Roger Pratt
Editor: Tony Lawson
Cast: Ralph Fiennes, Julianne Moore, Stephen Rea, Ian Hart, Jason Isaacs

ESSEX BOYS
28 February
Production Companies: Granada Films
Locations/Studios: Essex
Exec Prod: Pippa Cross
Producers: Jeff Pope
Director: Terry Winsor
Screenplay: Jeff Pope
Director of Photography: John Daly
Editor: Edward Mansell
Cast: Sean Bean, Alex Kingston, Charlie Creed-Miles, Tom Wilkinson

An EVERLASTING PIECE
9 December
Production Companies: Everlasting Productions
Locations/Studios: Dublin and Northern Ireland
Exec Prod: Patrick McCormick
Producers: Mark Johnson, Barry Levinson, Paula Weinstein, Louis DiGiamo, Jerome O'Connor
Director: Barry Levinson
Screenplay: Barry McEvoy
Director of Photography: Seamus Deasey
Editor: Stu Linder
Cast: Barry McEvoy, Bri·n F O'Byrne, Anna Friel, Billy Connolly

FED ROTTEN
7 September
Production Companies: Cake Media
Locations/Studios: South London
Producers: Mal Woolford
Director: Johnny Brunel
Screenplay: Mal Woolford

15 MOMENTS
14 March
Production Companies: Alliance/Atlantis, Serendipity Point Films
Locations/Studios: Montreal, Paris, London
Producers: Denise Robert, Robert Lantos
Director: Denys Arcand
Screenplay: Denys Arcand, Jacob Potashnik
Director of Photography: Guy Dufaux
Cast: Jessica Pare, Dan Aykroyd, Frank Langella, Thomas Gibson, Charles Berling

The FILTH AND THE FURY
Production Companies: Jersey Shore, Nitrate Film Ltd, ©Sex Pistols Residuals, presented by Film Four Ltd, presented in association with Sex Pistols
Exec Prod: Eric Gardner, Jonathan

Weisgal
Producers: Anita Camarata, Amanda Temple
Director: Julien Temple
Editor: Niven Howie
With: Paul Cook, Steve Jones, Glen Matlock, John Lydon, Sid Vicious

FIVE SECONDS TO SPARE
5 April
Production Companies: Scala Productions, Wave Pictures, Winchester Films
Locations/Studios: Three Mills Studio
Exec Prod: Nik Powell, Stephen Woolley
Producers: Amanda Posey
Director: Tom Connolly
Screenplay: Jonathan Coe
Director of Photography: Ashley Rowe
Editor: Caroline Biggerstaff
Cast: Max Beesley, Ray Winstone, Anastasia Hille, Valentina Cervi, Andy Serkis

FOREVER MINE
April
Production Companies: Moonstar Entertainment, Forever Mine Productions, presented by J&M entertainment
Locations/Studios: St Petersburg, Toronto
Exec Prod: Julia Palau, Matthew Payne
Producers: Damita Nikapota, Amy Kaufman, Kathleen Haase
Director: Paul Schrader
Screenplay: Paul Schrader
Director of Photography: John Bailey
Editor: Kristina Doden
Cast: Joseph Fiennes, Ray Liotta, Gretchen Mol, Vincent Laresca, Mik Watford

GANGSTER NO.1
10 June
Production Companies: Pagoda Films, Road Movies Vierte Produktion funded by Film Four, British Screen, BSkyB
Locations/Studios: London, Elstree Studios
Exec Prod: Peter Bowles
Producers: Norma Heyman, Jonathan Cavendish
Director: Paul McGuigan
Screenplay: Johnny Ferguson
Director of Photography: Peter Sova
Editor: Andrew Hulme
Cast: Malcolm McDowell, David

Thewlis, Paul Bettany, Saffron Burrows, Ken Cranham

GLADIATOR

1 February
Production Companies: DreamWorks SKG, Universal-International
Locations/Studios: Surrey, Morocco, Shepperton Studios
Exec Prod: Branko Lustig
Director: Ridley Scott
Screenplay: David H Franzoni, John Logan
Director of Photography: John Mathieson
Editor: Pietro Scalia
Cast: Russell Crowe, Djimon Hounsou, Ralph Moeller, Connie Nielsen, Joaquin Phoenix

GLORY GLORY

8 November
Production Companies: Peakviewing Productions
Locations/Studios: Johannesburg, South Africa and Nash's Farm in Gauteng South Africa
Exec Prod: Elizabeth Matthews
Producers: Paul Matthews
Director: Paul Matthews
Screenplay: Paul Matthews
Director of Photography: Vincent G Cox
Editor: Peter Davies
Cast: Chantelle Stander, Paul Johansson, David Dukas, Amanda Donohoe, Gary Busey

GOING OFF BIG TIME

14 November
Production Companies: KT Films
Locations/Studios: Liverpool
Producers: Ian Brady
Director: Jim Doyle
Screenplay: Neil Anthony
Director of Photography: Damian Bromley
Editor: Julian Day
Cast: Neil Anthony, Sarah Alexander, Del Henny, Bernard Hill, Stan Boardman

The GOLDEN BOWL

22 August
Production Companies: Merchant Ivory Productions
Locations/Studios: Suffolk, Lincolnshire in the UK, and Italy
Producers: Ismail Merchant, James Ivory
Director: James Ivory
Screenplay: Ruth Prawer Jhabvala
Director of Photography: Tony Pierce-Roberts

Cast: Anjelica Huston, Nick Nolte, Uman Thurman, Kate Beckinsale, Jeremy Northam

GREEN FINGERS

28 June
Production Companies: Boneyard Entertainment, Xingu Films, WestGrip, Wild Flowers
Locations/Studios: Cotswolds and Surrey
Exec Prod: Daniel Victor, Trudie Styler
Producers: Daniel Victor, Travis Swords
Director: Joel Hershman
Screenplay: Joel Hershma
Director of Photography: John Daly
Editor: Justin Krish
Cast: Helen Mirren, Clive Owen, David Kelly, Natasha Little, Warren Clarke

GUEST HOUSE PARADISO

12 April
Production Companies: House Films, © Vision Video Ltd, presented by Universal Pictures
Locations/Studios: Isle of Wight, Ealing Studios
Exec Prod: Helen Parker, Marc Samuelson, Peter Samuelson
Producers: Philip McIntyre
Director: Adrian Edmondson
Screenplay: Rik Mayall, Adrian Edmondson
Director of Photography: Alan Almond
Editor: Sean Barton
Cast: Rik Mayall, Adrian Edmondson, Vincent Cassel, Helene Mahieu, Bill Nighy

The GUILTY

8 February
Production Companies: J&M Entertainment (UK), Dogwood Pictures (US)
Locations/Studio: British Columbia
Exec Prod: Michael Prupas, Julia Palau, Michael Ryan
Producers: Thomas Hedman, Lisa Richardson
Director: Anthony Waller
Screenplay: Will Davies
Director of Photography: Tobias Schliessller
Cast: Bill Pullman, Devon Sawa, Gabrielle Anwar

The GUV'NOR

23 August
Production Companies: Impasse Productions
Locations/Studios: London and New

York, Roof Top Studios, Three Mills
Producers: Simon Brooks, Paul Brooks
Director: Andy Morahan
Screenplay: Joe Ainsworth, Craig Fairbrass, Danny Dyer
Cast: Craig Fairbrass, Martine McCutcheon, Danny Dyer

HIGH FIDELITY

29 April
Production Companies: presented by/© Touchstone Pictures, Working Title Films in association with Dogstar Films, New Crime Productions
Locations/Studios: Chicago
Exec Prod: Mike Newell, Alan Greenspan, Lisa Chasin
Producers: Tim Bevan, Rudd Simmons
Director: Stephen Frears
Screenplay: D.V.DeVincentis, Steve Pink, John Cusack, Scott Rosenberg
Director of Photography: Seamus McGarvey
Editor: Mick Audsley
Cast: John Cusack, Iben Hjejle, Todd Louiso, Jack Black, Lisa Bonet

HONEST

28 July
Production Companies: Honest Productions, Pandora Cinema
Locations/Studios: London
Producers: Michael Peyser, Eileen Gregory
Director: Dave Stewart
Screenplay: Dave Stewart, Dick Clement, Ian La Frenais
Director of Photography: David Johnson
Editor: David Martin
Cast: Nicola Appleton, Natalie Appleton, Melanie Blatt, Peter Facinelli, James Cosmo

HOTEL SPLENDIDE

1 February
Production Companies: Renegade Films, Channel Four, Canal Plus, British Screen
Locations/Studio: Northern Ireland, Three Mills Studio
Exec Prod: Charles Gassot, Robert Buckler
Producers: Ildiko Kemeny
Director: Terence Gross
Screenplay: Terence Gross
Director of Photography: Gyula Pados
Film Editor: Mike Ellis
Cast: Toni Collette, Daniel Craig, Katrin Cartlidge, Stephen Tompkinson, Hugh O'Conor

HOUSE!

Production Companies: House Film Ltd
Exec Prod: Christopher Figg, Adam Sutcliffe
Producers: Michael Kelk
Director: Julian Kemp
Screenplay: Jason Sutton
Director of Photography: Kjell Vassdal
Editor: Jonathan Rudd
Cast: Kelly MacDonald, Gwenllian Davies, Sue Hopkins, Eileen Edwards, Marlene Griffiths

The HOUSE OF MIRTH

7 June
Production Companies: Three Rivers funded by Arts Council of England, Film Four, Scottish Arts Council, Glasgow Film Fund
Locations/Studios: Scotland, France
Exec Prod: Bob Last, Pippa Cross, Olivia Stewart
Director: Terence Davies
Screenplay: Terence Davies
Director of Photography: Remi Adefarasin
Editor: Michael Patner
Cast: Gillian Anderson, Eric Stoltz, Dan Aykroyd, Laura Linney, Anthony Lapaglia

The HOUSE ON HAUNTED HILL

28 January
Production Companies: Dark Castle Entertainment, Warner Bros.
Locations/Studios: Los Angeles
Exec Prod: Dan Cracchiolo, Steve Richards
Producers: Joel Silver, Robert Zemeckis, Gil Adler
Director: William Malone
Screenplay: Dick Beebe
Director of Photography: Rick Bota
Editor: Anthony Adler
Cast: Geoffrey Rush, Famke Janssen, Taye Diggs, Ali Larter, Bridgette Wilson

The INBETWEENERS

31 May
Production Companies: The Britpack Film Company
Locations/Studios: North London
Exec Prod: Anil Dave, John Hair, Marion Gaskin
Producers: Darren Fisher
Director: Darren Fisher
Screenplay: Darren Fisher
Director of Photography: Matthew Woolf
Cast: Finlay Robertson, Kate Loustau, Lynn Edmonstone, Sarah Vandenbergh, Anthea Turner

INSIDE LYDIA'S HEAD

7 September
Production Companies: Convent Garden Films
Locations/Studios: London, Winchester, Dungeness
Producers: Simon Foster
Director: Dominick Rentiyens
Screenplay: Dominick Rentiyens
Director of Photography: Jo Say
Cast: Natasha Milkovich, Tom Bushe, John O'Byrne, Brett James, Goran Kostic

The INTRUDER

16 January
Production Companies: Kingsborough Greenlight Pictures, Steve Walsh Productions
Locations/Studio: Montreal
Exec Prod: Gary Howsam, Steve Walsh, Thierry Wase-Bailey
Producers: Jamie Brown, Pieter Kroonenburg
Director: David Bailey
Screenplay: Jamie Brown
Director of Photography: Jean Lepine
Film **Editor:** Angelo Corrao
Cast: Charlotte Gainsbourg, Charles Powell, Nastassja Kinski, John Hannah, Molly Parker

*JOSEPH AND THE AMAZING TECHNICOLOR DREAMCOAT

August
Production Companies: Really Useful Picture Company
Locations/Studios: Pinewood Studios
Director: David Mallet
Director of Photography: Nic Knowland
Cast: Maria Freidman, Robert Torti, Richard Attenborough, Ian McNeice, Joan Collins

KEVIN & PERRY GO LARGE

2 August
Production Companies: Tiger Aspect Productions in association with Icon Productions and Fragile Films, presented by Icon Entertainment International
Locations/Studios: London, Ibiza, Shepperton Studios
Exec Prod: Bruce Davey, Ralph Kamp, Barnaby Thompson
Producers: Peter Bennett-Jones, Jolyon Symonds, Harry Enfield
Director: Ed Bye
Screenplay: Harry Enfield, David Cummings
Director of Photography: Alan Almond
Editor: Mark Wybourn
Cast: Harry Enfield, Kathy Burke, Rhys Ifans, Laura Fraser, James Fleet

KIN

25 January
Production Companies: Bard Entertainments
Locations/Studio: Namibia
Exec Prod: Miles Donnelly
Producers: Margaret Matheson
Director: Elaine Proctor
Screenplay: Elain Proctor
Director of Photography: Amelia Vincent
Film **Editor:** Nicholas Gaster
Cast: Miranda Otto, Isaiah Washington, Chris Chameleon

Die KLEINE VAMPIR [a.k.a. The LITTLE VAMPIRE]

15 June
Production Companies: Comet Film, Filmstiftung Nordrhein-Westfalen Filmf˜rderungsanstalt
Locations/Studios: Scotland and the Warner Bros. Studios, Bottrop (Germany)
Exec Prod: Anthony Waller, Larry Wilson, Alexander Buchman
Producers: Richard Claus
Director: Ulrich Edel
Screenplay: Larry Wilson, Karey Kirkpatrick, Nicholas Waller
Director of Photography: Bill Wages
Cast: Jonathan Lipnicki, Rollo Weeks, Jim Carter, Alice Krige, Richard E Grant

The LAST MINUTE

7 June
Production Companies: Summit Entertainment, Venom Entertainment
Locations/Studios: Soho London, Iceland, Three Mills Island Studio
Producers: Matthew Justice
Director: Stephen Norrington
Screenplay: Stephen Norrington
Director of Photography: James Welland
Editor: Stephen Norrington
Cast: Maxton Gig Beesley, Emily Corrie, Tom Bell, Jason Isaacs, Kate Ashfield

LAVA

29 August
Production Companies: Sterling Pictures, Orangetop, Walking Point
Locations/Studios: London

Exec Prod: Andreas Lehmann
Producers: Michael Riley, Gregor Truter
Director: Joe Tucker
Screenplay: Joe Tucker
Director of Photography: Sam McCurdy
Editor: St John O'Rorke
Cast: Tom Bell, Nicola Stapleton, Joe Tucker, James Holmes, Leslie Grantham

LONDINIUM
2 June
Production Companies: Sun Lite Pictures
Locations/Studios: London
Producers: Jack Binder
Director: Mike Binder
Screenplay: Mike Binder
Director of Photography: Sue Gibson
Cast: Mike Binder, Mariel Hemingway, Irene Jacob, Colin Firth, Jack Dee

LONDON BLUES
August
Production Companies: Prince World Entertainment
Locations/Studios: London
Producers: Prince D
Director: Prince D, Godfrey Otudeko
Screenplay: Prince D
Cast: Prince D, Charmain Sinclair, Sandra Bee, Izu Ndefo, Flash, Baby D

LOVE, HONOUR AND OBEY
26 April
Production Companies: Fugitive Features, presented by BBC Films, © LH & O Ltd,
Locations/Studios: London
Exec Prod: David Thompson, Jane Tranter, Jim Beach
Producers: Dominic Anciano, Ray Burdis
Director: Dominic Anciano, Ray Burdis
Screenplay: Dominic Anciano, Ray Burdis
Director of Photography: John Ward
Editor: Rachel Meyrick
Cast: Jude Law, Rhys Ifans, Sadie Frost, Jonny Lee Miller, Ray Winstone

LOVE'S LABOURS LOST
24 February
Production Companies:
Shakespeare Film Company, Lost Films, ©Kenneth Branagh,

©InterMedia Film Equities, presented by PathÈ Pictures, presented in association with the Arts Council of England, Studio Canal Plus, Miramax Films, supported by the National Lottery through the Arts Council
Locations/Studios: Shepperton Studios
Producers: David Barron, Kenneth Branagh
Director: Kenneth Branagh
Screenplay: Kenneth Branagh
Director of Photography: Alex Thomson
Editor: Neil Farrell
Cast: Kenneth Branagh, Alicia Silverstone, Natasha McElhone, Carmen Ejogo, Nathan Lane

The LOW DOWN
9 August
Production Companies: Oil Factory, Sleeper Films funded by Film Four, British Screen Finance
Locations/Studios: London
Producers: John Stewart, Sally Llewellyn
Director: Jamie Thraves
Screenplay: Jamie Thraves
Director of Photography: Igor Jadue-Lillo
Editor: Lucia Zucchetti
Cast: Aidan Gillen, Kate Ashfield, Dean Lennox Kelly, Tobias Menzies, Rupert Proctor

The LUZHIN DEFENSE
4 October
Production Companies:
Renaissance Films
Locations/Studios: Italy, Hungary
Producers: Caroline Wood, Stephen Evans, Louis Becker, Philippe Guez
Director: Marleen Gorris
Screenplay: Peter Barry
Director of Photography: Bernard Lutic
Editor: Michiel Reichwein
Cast: Emily Watson, Geraldine James, Stuart Wilson, Simon McBurney, Anna Galiena

The MAN WHO CRIED
4 September
Production Companies: Adventure Pictures, Working Title Films, Canal Plus
Locations/Studios: UK, France, Pinewood Studios
Exec Prod: Tim Bevan, Eric Fellner
Producers: Sally Potter, Christopher Sheppard
Director: Sally Potter
Screenplay: Sally Potter
Director of Photography: Sacha

Vierny
Cast: Johnny Depp, Christina Ricci, Cate Blanchett, John Turturro, Harry Dean Stanton

MAYBE BABY
30 July
Production Companies: Phil McIntyre Promotions, © Inconceivable Films Ltd, funded by BBC Films, presented by Pandora Cinema, BBC Films
Locations/Studios: London, Dorset, Shepperton Studios
Exec Prod: Ernst Goldschmidt, David M Thompson
Producers: Phil McIntyre
Director: Ben Elton
Screenplay: Ben Elton
Director of Photography: Roger Lanser
Editor: Peter Hollywood
Cast: Hugh Laurie, Joely Richardson, Adrian Lester, James Purefoy, Tom Hollander

MISS JULIE
8 March
Production Companies: Red Mullet Productions, presented by Moonstone Entertainment
Locations/Studios: Elstree Studios
Exec Prod: Annie Stewart, Etchie Stroh, Willi Baer
Producers: Harriet Cruickshank, Mike Figgis
Director: Mike Figgis
Screenplay: Helen Cooper, Mike Figgis
Director of Photography: Benoit Delhomme
Editor: Matthew Woods
Cast: Saffron Burrows, Peter Mullan, Maria Doyle Kennedy

The MOST FERTILE MAN IN IRELAND
25 October
Production Companies: Samson Films funded by Sky Pictures, Bord Scannán na hÉireann, Northern Ireland Film Commission
Producers: Stephen Collins
Director: Dudi Appleton
Screenplay: Jim Keeble
Director of Photography: Ronan Fox
Editor: Emer Reynolds
Cast: Kris Marshall, James Nesbitt, Bronagh Gallagher, Kathy Kiera Clarke, Pauline McLynn

MY MOTHER FRANK
26 March
Production Companies: Intrepid Pictures, Premium Movie

Partnerships, presented by Australian Film Finance Corporation in association with Showtime (Australia) with the support of New South Wales Film & TV, Australian Film Commission, Channel Four
Locations/Studios: Sydney
Producers: Phaedon Vass, Susan Vass
Director: Mark Lamprell
Screenplay: Mark Lamprell
Director of Photography: Brian Breheny
Editor: Nicholas Beauman
Cast: SinÈad Cusack, Sam Neill, Sacha Horler, Lynette Curran, Celia Ireland

NASTY NEIGHBOURS
20 February
Production Companies: Ipso Facto Films in association with Glenrinnes Film Partnership and MPCE
Locations/Studio: Birmingham, Australia
Exec Prod: Adam Page, Nadine Marsh-Edwards, Terje Gaustad, Lukas Erni
Producers: Christine Alderson
Director: Debbie Isitt
Screenplay: Debbie Isitt
Director of Photography: Simon Reeves, Sam McCurdy
Film Editor: Nicky Ager
Cast: Ricky Tomlinson, Marion Bailey, Phil Daniels, Rachel Fielding, Hywell Bennett

NEW YEAR'S DAY
15 February
Production Companies: Imagine Films, Alchymie, presented by Flashpoint Pictures with the participation of the European Co-Production Fund, Liberator Productions S.a.r.l., Canal Plus
Locations/Studios: London, Buckinghamshire, Hertfordshire, the Isle of Wight, France
Exec Prod: Beau Rodgers, David Forrest, Pippa Cross, Cameron McCracken
Producers: Simon Channing-Williams, Stephen Cleary
Director: Suri Krishnamma
Screenplay: Ralph Brown
Director of Photography: John de Borman
Editor: Adam Ross
Cast: Marianne Jean-Baptiste, Anastasia Hille, Jacqueline Bisset, Andrew Lee Potts, Bobby Barry

The NINE LIVES OF TOMAS KATZ
1 March
Production Companies: Strawberry Vale Film & TV Productions
Locations/Studios: London
Producers: Caroline Hewitt
Director: Ben Hopkins
Screenplay: Ben Hopkins
Director of Photography: Julian Court
Editor: Alan Levy
Cast: Thomas Fisher, Ian McNeice, Tim Barlow, Trevor Jones, Janet Henfrey

NORA
23 May
Production Companies: Volta Films, Metropolitan Films, Road Movies Vierte Produktionen, GAM Film, Bord Scannán na hÉireann
Locations/Studios: Dublin, Hamburge, Trieste
Exec Prod: Guy Collins
Producers: Bradley Adams, Damon Bryant, Tracey Seaward
Director: Pat Murphy
Screenplay: Pat Murphy, Gerry Stembridge
Director of Photography: Jean-Francois Robin
Editor: Pia Di Ciaula
Cast: Ewan McGregor, Susan Lynch, Donal Donnelly, Veronica Duffy, Peter McDonald

OFFENDING ANGELS
23 August
Production Companies: Pants Productions
Locations/Studios: England, Scotland
Producers: Andrew Rajan
Director: Andrew Rajan
Screenplay: Andrew Rajan
Director of Photography: Alvin Leong
Cast: Susannah Harker, Andrew Lincoln, Shaun Parkes, Andrew Rajan, Marion Bailey

ONE DAY IN SEPTEMBER
Production Companies: Passion Pictures
Exec Prod: Lillian Birnbaum
Producers: John Battsek, Arthur Cohn
Director: Kevin Macdonald
Director of Photography: Alwin K¸chler, Neve Cunningham
Editor: Justine Wright
Cast: Ankie Spitzer, Jamal Al Gashey, Gerald Seymour, Alex Springer, Gad Zabari

ONE LIFE STAND
10 May
Production Companies: Elemental Films
Locations/Studios: Glasgow
Producers: Karen M Smyth
Director: May Miles Thomas
Screenplay: May Miles Thomas
Cast: Maureen Carr, Gary Lewis, John Kielty, Archie Lal

ONE MORE KISS
Production Companies: Mob Film Company in association with Jam Pictures, Freewheel Productions, developed by Metrodome Films, European Script Fund, ©One More Kiss Ltd
Locations/Studios: Berwick-on-Tweed
Exec Prod: Sara Giles, Derek Roy
Producers: Vadim Jean, Paul Brooks
Director: Vadim Jean
Screenplay: Suzie Halewood
Director of Photography: Mike Fox
Editor: Joe McNally
Cast: Gerard Butler, James Cosmo, Valerie Edmond, Valerie Gogan, Carl Proctor

PANDAEMONIUM
13 September
Production Companies: Mariner Films Production funded by BBC Films, BBC Worldwide, Arts Council of England
Locations/Studios: Somerset, Cornwall, the Lakes District, London
Exec Prod: David M Thompson, Mike Phillips
Producers: Nick O'Hagan, Michael Kustow
Director: Julien Temple
Screenplay: Frank Cottrell-Boyce
Director of Photography: John Lynch
Editor: Niven Howe
Cast: Linus Roache, John Hannah, Emily Woof, Samantha Morton, William Scott-Masson

PARADISE GROVE
26 July
Production Companies: Paradise Grove
Locations/Studios: London
Producers: David Castro
Director: Charles Harris
Screenplay: Charles Harris
Director of Photography: Miles Cook
Editor: John Hackney
Cast: Ron Moody, Rula Lenska, Lee Blakemore, Leyland O'Brien, Andy Lucas

PARANOIA

2 May
Production Companies: Sky Pictures, Isle of Man Film Commission, Portman Entertainment
Locations/Studios: Isle of Man, London
Producers: Paul Trijbits, Gareth Neame
Director: John Duigan
Screenplay: John Duigan
Director of Photography: Slawomir Idziak
Cast: Jessica Alba, Iain Glen, Jeanne Tripplehorn, Ewen Bremner, Kevin Whately

PAVAROTTI IN DAD'S ROOM

28 June
Production Companies: Dragon Pictures, Film Four International, Le Studio Canal Plus funded by Arts Council of England, Arts Council of Wales
Locations/Studios: South Wales
Producers: Graham Broadbent, Damian Jones
Director: Sara Sugarman
Screenplay: Sara Sugarman
Director of Photography: Barry Ackroyd
Editor: Robin Sales

PEACHES

5 September
Production Companies: Stone Ridge Entertainment
Locations/Studios: Dublin, London
Exec Prod: Nicholas O'Neill
Producers: Ronan Glennane
Director: Nick Grosso
Screenplay: Nick Grosso
Director of Photography: Brendan Galvin
Cast: Matthew Rhys, Kelly Reilly, Matthew Dunster, Justin Salinger, Sophie Okonedo

PIRATE'S TALE

12 January
Production Companies: Mercury Productions
Locations/Studios: Scotland, Los Angeles
Producers: Bruçe Mercury, Gretchen Janke
Director: Bruce Mercury
Screenplay: Bruce Mercury, Gretchen Janke
Editor: Duncan Burns
Cast: Bruce Mercury, Gretchen Janke, Patrick Lambke, RJ Jordan, Bo Jordan

QUILLS

9 August
Production Companies: Charenton Productions
Locations/Studios: Pinewood Studios
Producers: Peter Kaufman, Julia Chasman, Nick Wechsler
Director: Philip Kaufman
Screenplay: Doug Wright
Director of Photography: Rogier Stoffers
Cast: Geoffrey Rush, Kate Winslet, Joaquin Phoenix, Michael Caine

RAGE

June
Production Companies: Granite FilmWorks
Producers: Newton I Aduaka, Maria Elena L'Abbate
Director: Newton I Aduaka
Screenplay: Newton I Aduaka
Director of Photography: Carlos Arango
Editor: Marcela Cuneo
Cast: Fraser Ayres, Shaun Parkes, John Pickard, Alison Rose, Shango Baku

RAT

25 October
Production Companies: Universal Pictures International, Ruby Pictures, The Jim Henson Organisation
Locations/Studios: Dublin
Producers: Alison Owen, Steve Barron
Director: Steve Barron
Director of Photography: Brendan Galvin
Cast: Imelda Staunton, Peter Postlethwaite, David Wilmot, Frank Kelly, Ed Byrne

RELATIVE VALUES

31 July
Production Companies: Midsummer Films funded by Overseas Film Group, Isle of Man Film Commission
Locations/Studios: Isle of Man
Producers: Chris Milburn
Director: Eric Styles
Screenplay: Paul Rattigan, Michael Walker
Cast: Julie Andrews, Billy Baldwin, Colin Firth, Stephen Fry, Sophie Thompson

ROOM TO RENT

1 October
Production Companies: Renegade Films funded by The Film Consortium, Arts Council of England,FilmFour
Locations/Studios: London
Exec Prod: Robert Buckler, Georges Benayoun
Producers: Ildiko Kemeny
Director: Khaled Al-Haggar
Screenplay: Khaled Al-Haggar
Director of Photography: Romain Winding
Editor: John Richards
Cast: Said Taghmaoui, Juliette Lewis, Rupert Graves, Anna Massey

SACRED FLESH

Production Companies: Gothica, presented by Salvation Films in association with 400 Company
Locations/Studios: Knebworth House (UK)
Exec Prod: Mark Sloper
Producers: Louise Ross
Director: Nigel Wingrove
Screenplay: Nigel Wingrove
Editor: Chris Shaw, Jake West
Cast: Sally Tremaine, Moyna Cope, Simon Hill, Kristina Bill, Rachael Taggart

SALTWATER

22 March
Production Companies: Treasure Films, Dyehouse, presented by Bord Scannán na hÉireann, Bord Scannán na hÉireann BBC Films
Locations/Studios: Ireland
Exec Prod: David M Thompson, Rod Stoneman, Clare Duigan
Producers: Robert Walpole
Director: Conor McPherson
Screenplay: Conor McPherson
Director of Photography: Oliver Curtis
Editor: Emer Reynolds
Cast: Peter McDonald, Brian Cox, Brendan Gleeson, Conor Mullen, Hugh O'Conor

SAVING GRACE

4 May
Production Companies: Homerun, presented by Portman Entertainment in association with Sky Pictures, Wave Pictures
Locations/Studios: Cornwall and London, Elstree Studios
Exec Prod: Cat Villiers, Xavier Marchand
Producers: Mark Crowdy
Director: Nigel Cole
Screenplay: Craig Ferguson, Mark Crowdy
Director of Photography: John De Borman
Editor: Alan Strachan

Cast: Brenda Blethyn, Craig Ferguson, Martin Clunes, Tcheky Karyo, Jamie Forman

SEASON TICKET
October
Production Companies: Mumbo Jumbo Productions, FilmFour International
Exec Prod: Stephen Woolley
Producers: Elizabeth Karlsen
Director: Mark Herman
Screenplay: Mark Herman
Director of Photography: Andy Collins
Editor: Mike Ellis
Cast: Chris Beattie, Greg McLane, Tim Healy, Kevin Whately, Charlie Hardwick

SECOND GENERATION
9 August
Production Companies: Second Generation Films
Locations/Studios: London
Producers: Jack Kellett, Shane O'Sullivan
Director: Shane O'Sullivan
Screenplay: Shane O'Sullivan
Director of Photography: Mark Duffield
Cast: Hanayo, Shigetomo Yutani, Saeed Jaffrey, Nitin Ganatra, Mari Wilson

SECRET SOCIETY
28 June
Production Companies: Focus Films, Ena Film funded by CLT-UFA, Filmstiftung Nordrhein-Westfalen, Isle of Man Film Commission, Westdeutscher Rundfunk
Locations/Studios: Isle of Man
Producers: David Pupkewitz, Vesna Jovanoska
Director: Immogen Kimmel
Screenplay: Catriona McGowan, Immogen Kimmel
Cast: Lee Ross, Charlotte Brittain

SEXY BEAST
1 May
Production Companies: Recorded Picture Company [UK], Kanzaman SA [Sp]
Locations/Studios: Spain, UK
Producers: Jeremy Thomas, Denise O'Dell
Director: Jonathan Glazer
Screenplay: Louis Mellis, David Scinto
Director of Photography: Ivan Bird
Cast: Ben Kingsley, Ray Winstone, Amanda Redman

SHADOW OF THE VAMPIRE
18 April
Production Companies: Saturn Films [US], Delux Productions [Lux], Long Shot Films [UK], BBC Films [UK]
Exec Prod: Paul Brooks, Alan Howden
Producers: Nicolas Cage, Jeff Levine
Director: Elias Merhige
Screenplay: Stephen Katz
Director of Photography: Lou Bogue
Cast: John Malkovich, Willem Dafoe, Catherine McCormack, Udo Kier, Cary Elwes

SHOOTERS
6 November
Production Companies: Coolbeans Films, Catapult Productions funded by Feature Finance, Dutch Film Finance Scheme
Locations/Studios: London
Exec Prod: Jan Bruinstroop
Producers: Margery Bone
Director: Colin Teague
Screenplay: Gary Young, Andrew Howard, Louis Dempsey
Cast: Adrian Dunbar, Melanie Lynskey, Emma Fielding, Ioan Gruffudd, Andrew Howard

SKELETON WRECK
10 May
Production Companies: Dog Day Pictures
Locations/Studios: London
Exec Prod: Andreas Lambis
Producers: Dan Andrews
Director: Keith Robinson
Screenplay: Keith Robinson
Director of Photography: Dan Andrews
Editor: Keith Robinson
Cast: Dan O'Brian, Sally Burgess, Jack Burt, Phillip Inns, Andrew James

SNATCH
18 October
Production Companies: SKA Films, Columbia Pictures Corporation
Locations/Studios: London
Producers: Matthew Vaughn
Director: Guy Ritchie
Screenplay: Guy Ritchie
Director of Photography: Tim Maurice-Jones, Hugo Luczyc-Wyhowski
Cast: Brad Pitt, Jason Statham, Stephen Graham, Vinnie Jones, Ewan Bremner

SOME VOICES
12 September
Production Companies: Dragon Pictures funded by British Screen
Locations/Studios: West London, Hastings
Producers: Damian Jones, Graham Broadbent
Director: Simon Cellan Jones
Screenplay: Joe Penhall
Director of Photography: David Odd
Editor: Ellen Pierce Lewis
Cast: Daniel Craig, David Morrissey, Kelly Macdonald, Julie Graham, Peter McDonald

SORTED
25 October
Production Companies: Jovy Junior Productions
Locations/Studios: London, Elstree Studios
Exec Prod: Steve Clark-Hall
Producers: Mark Crowdy, Fabrizio Chiesa
Director: Alexander Jovy
Screenplay: Nick Villiers
Director of Photography: Mike Southon
Cast: Matthew Rhys, Sienna Guillory, Jason Donovan, Tim Curry, Louise Lombard

SOUL'S ARK
25 March
Production Companies: Amboseli/Weston Union Productions
Locations/Studios: Somerset
Exec Prod: Colin Stansfield
Producers: Ian Burgess
Director: Nik Harding
Screenplay: Nik Harding
Director of Photography: Steve Skitt
Cast: Colin Baker, Wendy Padbury, Steve Dineen, Paul Bryan, Carole Anne Ford

STRONG BOYS
16 August
Production Companies: Cowboy Films, Imagine Films funded by Flashpoint Films
Locations/Studios: London
Exec Prod: Beau Rogers, David Forrest
Producers: Charles Steel, Lisa Bryer, Simon Channing-Williams
Director: Nick Love
Screenplay: Nick Love, Dominic Eames
Director of Photography: Tony Imi
Editor: Patrick Moore
Cast: Paul Nicholls, Roland

Manookian, David Thewlis, Phil
Daniels, Jamie Foreman

STRICTLY SINATRA

17 October
Production Companies: DNA Film,
Blue Orange Films, Saracen Street
Productions funded by
Arts Council of England
Locations/Studios: Glasgow
Exec Prod: Duncan Kenworthy,
Andrew Macdonald
Producers: Ruth Kenley-Letts
Director: Peter Capaldi
Screenplay: Peter Capaldi
Director of Photography: Stephen
Blackman
Editor: Rodney Holland
Cast: Ian Hart, Kelly MacDonald,
Ian Bannen, Brian Cox, Ian
Cuthbertson

SUBTERFUGUE

23 January
Production Companies: Tempo
Productions
Locations/Studio: Central London
Producers: Piers Tempest, Tom Fox
Director: Richard Johnson
Screenplay: Christopher Warrack
Director of Photography: Franz
Pagot
Film **Editor:** James Canty
Cast: Kate Orr, Jan De Villeneueve

SUSPICIOUS RIVER

16 November
Production Companies: Tartan
Films, Okulitch Pedersen
Locations/Studios: Vancouver,
British Columbia
Producers: Hamish McAlpine,
Michael Okulitch, Erik Stensrud
Director: Lynne Stopkewich
Cast: Molly Parker, Callum Keith
Rennie

The TESTIMONY OF TALIESIN JONES

16 May
Production Companies: Frontier
Pictures, Tal Jones, HTV
Locations/Studios: Cardiff
Exec Prod: Michael Ryan, Helena
Mackenzie
Producers: Ben Goddard, Dominic
Berger
Director: Martin Duffy
Screenplay: Maureen Tilyou
Director of Photography: Tony Imi
Editor: John Victor Smith
Cast: Jonathan Pryce, Griff Rhys
Jones, Geraldine James, Matthew
Rhys, Ian Bannen

THANKS FOR THE MEMORIES

30 August
Production Companies: Scala
Productions funded by BBC Northern
Ireland, BBC Films, Arts
Council of Northern Ireland Lottery
Fund, Northern Ireland Film
Commission Production Fund,
MBP, WAVEpictures
Locations/Studios: Northern Ireland
Exec Prod: Nik Powell, David
Thompson
Producers: Laurie Borg, Robert
Cooper
Director: Declan Lowney
Screenplay: Colin Bateman
Director of Photography: Ron
Fortunato
Cast: Brendan Gleeson, Amanda
Donahoe, James Nesbitt, Adrian
Dunbar, Bronagh Gallagher

THERE'S ONLY ONE JIMMY GRIMBLE

18 October
Production Companies: Sarah
Radclyffe Productions, Impact Film
& Television Productions
funded by Pathe Pictures UK, Arts
Council of England
Locations/Studios: Manchester
Exec Prod: Alexis Lloyd, Andrea
Calderwood, Bill Godfrey
Producers: Sarah Radclyffe, Jeremy
Bolt, Alison Jackson
Director: John Hay
Screenplay: John Hay, Rik
Carmichael
Director of Photography: John de
Borman
Editor: Norrie Ottey
Cast: Robert Carlyle, Ray Winstone,
Lewis Mackenzie, Gina McKee

THOMAS AND THE MAGIC RAILROAD

3 August
Production Companies: Magic
Railroad Company
Locations/Studios: Isle of Man,
Pennsylvania, Canada
Exec Prod: Steve Stabler, Brent
Baum, Barry London, Charles Falzon
Producers: Britt Allcroft
Director: Britt Allcroft
Screenplay: Britt Allcroft
Director of Photography: Paul Ryan
Editor: Ron Wiseman
Cast: Alec Baldwin, Mara Wilson,
Peter Fonda, Didi Conn, Russell
Means

THOUSANDS LIKE US
[a.k.a. LOVE THE ONE YOU'RE
WITH]
5 April
Production Companies: Palm Tree
Productions, Big Issue Scotland
Locations/Studios: Glasgow
Producers: Mairi Fraser Sutherland,
Robbie Moffat
Director: Robbie Moffat
Screenplay: Robbie Moffat
Director of Photography: David Byrne
Editor: Fiona Macdonald
Cast: Hazel Ann Crawford, Steven
Duffy, Tomas Skene, Barry
Campbell, Paul Cunningham

*TRIAL BY FIRE

15 February
Production Companies: Arrowhead
Productions WB, funded by ITV
Producers: Alan Wright
Director: Patrick Lau
Screenplay: Trevor Bowen
Director of Photography: Simon
Kossoff
Editor: Jeremy Strachan
Cast: Juliet Stevenson, Jim Carter,
Anton Lesser, Emily Joyce, Jane
Gurnett

The TRUTH GAME

18 October
Production Companies: Screen
Production Associates
Locations/Studios: London
Exec Prod: Doug Abbott, John Jaquiss
Producers: Piers Jackson, Simon
Rumley
Director: Simon Rumley
Screenplay: Simon Rumley
Director of Photography: Alistair
Cameron
Editor: Colin Sherman
Cast: Paul Blackthorne, Tania
Emery, Tom Fisher, Selina Giles,
Stuart Laing

20:13 THOU SHALT NOT KILL

19 November
Production Companies: Trijbits
Productions, Gemini Films
Locations/Studios: London, Cologne
Exec Prod: Paul Trijbits
Producers: Peter Paulich, Anton Moho
Director: John Bradshaw
Cast: Thomas Heinze, Natacha
Lindinger

WARRIOR SISTERS

June
Production Companies: Scantori
Films
Producers: Frank Scantori

Director: Frank Scantori
Screenplay: Frank Scantori
Director of Photography: Anthony Holmes
Cast: Wendy Cooper, Helena Drake, Ana Diego, Hugo Simpson

WHATEVER HAPPENED TO HAROLD SMITH?
19 March
Production Companies: West Eleven Films, Yorkshire Media Production Agency, presented by InterMedia Film Equities, October Films in association with Arts Council of England, part funded by European Regional Development Fund
Locations/Studios: Sheffield
Exec Prod: Guy East, Nigel Siclair
Producers: Ruth Jackson, David Brown
Director: Peter Hewett
Screenplay: Ben Steiner
Director of Photography: David Tattersall
Editor: Martin Walsh
Cast: Tom Courtenay, Stephen Fry, Michael Legge, Laura Fraser, Lulu

WHAT'S COOKING?
26 April
Production Companies: Stagescreen Productions [UK], Hope & Glory Inc [US], presented by Flashpoint Pictures
Locations/Studios: Los Angeles
Producers: Jeffrey Taylor
Director: Gurinder Chadha
Screenplay: Gurinder Chadha, Paul Mayeda Berges
Director of Photography: Lin Jong
Editor: Janice Hampton
Cast: Julianna Marguilles, Mercedes Ruehl, Kyra Sedgwick, Alfre Woodard, Maury Chaykin

WHEN BRENDAN MET TRUDY
26 October
Production Companies: Collins Avenue Films, Deadly Films funded by BBC Films, BBC Worldwide, Bord Scann·n an h»ireann, RTE
Locations/Studios: Dublin
Exec Prod: David Thompson, Rod Stoneman, Clare Duigan, Mike Phillips
Producers: Lynda Myles
Director: Kieron J Walsh
Screenplay: Roddy Doyle
Director of Photography: Ashley Rowe
Editor: Scott Thomas
Cast: Peter McDonald, Flora Montgomery

WHEN THE SKY FALLS
12 April
Production Companies: Irish Screen, Sky Pictures
Locations/Studio: Dublin
Exec Prod: Kevin Menton, Peter Newman
Producers: Michael Wearing, Nigel Warren-Green
Director: John Mackenzie
Screenplay: Colum McCann, Ronan Gallagher
Editor: Graham Walker
Cast: Joan Allen, Patrick Bergin, Liam Cunningham, Peter Postlethwaite, Jimmy Smallhorne

WHY DID BOBBY DIE?
4 January
Production Companies: Can Productions, Quantum Entertainment
Locations/Studio: Los Angeles
Exec Prod: Karl Grafzu Ortenburg, Jurgen L. Reich
Producers: Larry Jenkins, Pamela Vlastas
Screenplay: Loni Kaye Harkless, Frank Glass
Cast: Larry Jenkins, Margaret Avery, Alex Rocco

WOMEN TALKING DIRTY
14 March
Production Companies: Petunia Productions (UK), Jean Doumanian Productions (US) in association with Rocket Pictures
Locations/Studios: Shepperton Studios
Exec Prod: Elton John, J E Beaucaire, Jean Doumanian
Producers: David Furnish, Polly Steele
Director: Coky Giedroyc
Screenplay: Isla Dewar
Director of Photography: Brian Tufano
Editor: Budge Tremlett
Cast: Helena Bonham-Carter, Gina McKee, James Purefoy, Jimmy Nesbitt, Richard Wilson

The WORLD IS NOT ENOUGH
11 January
Production Companies: Eon Productions (UK), United Artists (US)
Locations/Studio: London, Millennium Dome, Turkey, Spain, French Alps, Azerbaijan, the Bahamas, Pinewood Studios
Producers: Michael Wilson, Barbara Broccoli
Director: Michael Apted
Screenplay: Neil Purvis, Robert Wade, Dana Stevens, Bruce Feirstein
Director of Photography: Adrian Biddle
Film Editor: Jim Clark
Cast: Pierce Brosnan, Denise Richards, Sophie Marceaux, Dame Judi Dench, Samantha Bond

YOUNG BLADES
21 October
Production Companies: Le Sabre in association with Prosperity Pictures
Locations/Studios: Auvergne, South of France
Exec Prod: David Forrest, Beau Rogers, Rick Mischel, Jon Vein
Producers: Gwen Field, Georges Campana
Director: Mario Andreacchio
Screenplay: John Goldsmith
Director of Photography: Guillaume Schiffman
Cast: Ben Cross, Hugh Dancy, Sarah Jane Potts, Scott Hickman, Anthony Strachman

RELEASES

Listed here are feature-length films, both British and foreign which had a theatrical release in the UK between January and December 1999. Entries quote the title, distributor, UK release date, certificate, country of origin, director/s, leading players, production company/ies, duration, gauge (other than 35 mm), the Sight and Sound reference. Compiled by Laura Pearson

Films Released in the UK in 1999

* denotes re-release

1999

JANUARY
1 STAR TREK INSURRECTION
1 The ACID HOUSE
2 SEX LIFE IN L.A.
8 LITTLE VOICE
8 PI
8 PSYCHO
8 The SIEGE
8 SITCOM
8 TENSHI NO KUZU/ANGEL DUST
8 *TO HAVE AND HAVE NOT
15 AA AB LAUT CHALEN
15 DOBERMANN
15 HUM AAPKE DIL MEIN REHTE HAIN
15 KNOFLíKÀRI/BUTTONERS
15 MEET JOE BLACK
15 The OPPOSITE OF SEX
15 SOUR GRAPES
15 SOUTHPAW
22 BULWORTH
22 La CLASSE DE NEIGE/CLASS TRIP
22 54
22 *Der HÄNDLER DER VIER JAHRESZEITEN/The MERCHANT OF FOUR SEASONS
22 HILARY AND JACKIE
22 Le POLYGRAPHE/The POLYGRAPH

22 PRACTICAL MAGIC
29 *Un HOMME ET UNE FEMME/A MAN AND A WOMAN
29 SHAKESPEARE IN LOVE
29 STEPMOM
29 TWO GIRLS AND A GUY
29 VERY BAD THINGS

FEBRUARY
5 ANO NATSU, ICHIBAN SHIZUKANA UMI/A SCENE AT THE SEA
5 A BUG'S LIFE
5 HIDEOUS KINKY
5 HOW STELLA GOT HER GROOVE BACK
5 LIVING OUT LOUD
5 PECKER
12 DON'T GO BREAKING MY HEART
12 *Hô TEL DU NORD
12 I THINK I DO
12 JACK FROST
12 MADELINE
12 MY GIANT
12 SHAHEED-E-MOHABBAT BOOTA SINGH/MARTYR-IN-LOVE,
12 BOOTA SINGH
12 SWITCHBLADE SISTERS
12 TERRA ESTRANGEIRA/FOREIGN LAND
12 La VITA » BELLA/LIFE IS BEAUTIFUL
12 YOUR FRIENDS & NEIGHBOURS
16 HOLY MAN
19 AFFLICTION
19 DES NOUVELLES DU BON DIEU/NEWS FROM THE GOOD LORD
19 THIS YEAR'S LOVE
26 LOVED
26 PERDITA DURANGO
26 *Der RADFAHRER/The CYCLIST
26 The THIN RED LINE
26 TITANIC TOWN
26 URBAN LEGEND
26 YOU'VE GOT MAIL

MARCH
5 BELOVED
5 FESTEN

5 KINI & ADAMS
5 LAAWARIS
5 LAL BAADSHAH
5 *The 39 STEPS
12 CENTRAL DO BRASIL/CENTRAL STATION
12 The CLOCKWATCHERS
12 EYE OF GOD
12 4 LITTLE GIRLS
12 NIAGARA, NIAGARA
12 PATCH ADAMS
12 PLEASANTVILLE
12 SCHIZOPOLIS
12 The STICKY FINGERS OF TIME
19 AARZOO
19 APRILE
19 ARLINGTON ROAD
19 A NIGHT AT THE ROXBURY
19 SEUL CONTRE TOUS/I STAND ALONE
19 WAKING NED
26 AMERICAN HISTORY X
26 CONTE D'AUTOMNE/An AUTUMN TALE
26 GODS AND MONSTERS
26 INTERNATIONAL KHILADI
26 MIGHTY JOE
26 PAYBACK
26 La PROMESSE
26 The RUGRATS MOVIE

APRIL
2 JAANAM SAMJHA KARO
2 BLAST FROM THE PAST
2 JENSEITS DER STILLE/BEYOND SILENCE
2 MIZU NO NAKA NO HACHIGATSU/AUGUST IN THE WATER
2 *The NIGHT OF THE HUNTER
2 PLUNKETT & MACLEANE
2 TE CON IL DUCE/TEA WITH MUSSOLINI
9 BEDROOMS AND HALLWAYS
9 A CIVIL ACTION
9 The FACULTY
9 HIGH ART
9 Nô
9 ORGAZMO
9 The RED VIOLIN/Il VIOLINO ROSSO
9 SLAM
16 ACTRIUS/ACTRESSES
16 HAPPINESS
16 An IDEAL HUSBAND

16 PROMETHEUS
16 RETURN TO PARADISE
16 SILSILA HAI PYAR KA
16 ZULMI
23 L'ASSEDIO/BESIEGED
23 The BRYLCREEM BOYS
23 DANCE WITH ME
23 8MM
23 LEVEL FIVE
23 MESSAGE IN A BOTTLE
23 The MISADVENTURES OF
MARGARET/Les
MÉSAVENTURES DE
    MARGARET
23 ORPHANS
23 OUT OF THE PRESENT
23 SIDE STREETS
26 PAINTED ANGELS
30 AT FIRST SIGHT
30 The HONEST COURTESAN
30 IN DREAMS
30 KNOCK OFF
30 *The NINTH CONFIGURATION
30 SARFAROSH
30 SOLOMON AND GAENOR
30 The WATERBOY

MAY

7 ARTEMISIA
7 BLACK CAT WHITE CAT
7 CRUSH PROOF
7 FORCES OF NATURE
7 HOGI PYAR KI JEET
7 I STILL KNOW WHAT YOU
    DID LAST SUMMER
7 KARTOOS
7 LAST NIGHT
7 SWING
14 BEST LAID PLANS
14 ETERNITY AND A DAY
14 GET REAL
14 IDIOTERNE/IDIOTS
14 PARTING SHOTS
14 A PRICE ABOVE RUBIES
14 *SHATRANJ KE KHILARI/The
    CHESS PLAYERS
14 SHUANGLONG HUI/TWIN
    DRAGONS
14 TRUE CRIME
21 APT PUPIL
21 CAPTAIN JACK
21 The CORRUPTOR
21 The IMPOSTORS
21 NOTTING HILL
21 RAJAJI
21 SHE'S ALL THAT
21 A SIMPLE PLAN
21 SOORYAVANSHAM
21 *YA CUBA/SOY CUBA/I AM
    CUBA
28 BIWI NO.1
28 The KING AND I
28 The MAN WHO DROVE WITH
    MANDELA

28 MY FAVORITE MARTIAN
28 Die SIEBTELBAUERN/The
    INHERITORS
30 EXISTENZ

JUNE

1 PERFECT BLUE
4 *CITIZEN KANE
4 The DEEP END OF THE
    OCEAN
4 HUMAN TRAFFIC
4 *JEAN DE FLORETTE
4 VIGO PASSION FOR LIFE
4 VIRUS
4 WITHOUT LIMITS
11 AMERICAN PERFEKT
11 AMONG GIANTS
11 The DEBT COLLECTOR
11 FINDING NORTH
11 *GET CARTER
11 HEART
11 *MANON DES
    SOURCES/MANON OF THE
    SPRINGS
11 The MATRIX
11 OTHER VOICES OTHER
    ROOMS
11 SAFARI
11 SIRF TUM
11 Un 32 AOÛT SUR TERRE
11 WO SHI SHUI/WHO AM I?
18 BRIDE OF CHUCKY
18 CELEBRITY
18 CROUPIER
18 CRUEL INTENTIONS
18 GLORIA
18 HUM DIL DE CHUKE SANAM
18 JUST THE TICKET
18 TOUCH OF EVIL
18 VÉNUS BEAUTÉ
    (INSTITUT)/VENUS BEAUTY
23 The HI-LO COUNTRY
25 The BIG HIT
25 HASEENA MAAN JAYEGI
25 The LOST SON
25 The MUMMY
25 ROGUE TRADER
25 SIMON BIRCH
25 WING COMMANDER
25 XIANGGANG ZHIZAO/MADE
    IN HONG KONG

JULY

2 BELLY
2 Le DÓNER DE CONS
2 ENTRAPMENT
2 HOTE HOTE PYAAR HO GAYA
2 VIRTUAL SEXUALITY
2 WINTERSCHLÄFER/WINTER
    SLEEPERS
9 ALL THE LITTLE ANIMALS
9 BILLY'S HOLLYWOOD
    SCREEN KISS
9 MANN

9 TANGO
9 TEN THINGS I HATE ABOUT
    YOU
9 *O THIASSOS/The
    TRAVELLING PLAYERS
16 L'ARCHE DU DÉSERT
16 De POOLSE BRUID/The
    POLISH BRIDE
16 STAR WARS EPISODE I THE
    PHANTOM MENACE
16 *The THIRD MAN
23 «A COMMENCE
    AUJOURD'HUI/IT ALL
    STARTS TODAY
23 HINDUSTAN KI KASAM
23 *KOYAANISQATSI
23 *Le NOTTI DI CABIRIA/Les
    NUITS DE CABIRIA/NIGHTS
    OF CABIRIA
23 WEST BEYROUTH/WEST
    BEIRUT
30 AUSTIN POWERS THE SPY
    WHO SHAGGED ME
30 MOTEL SEONINJANG/MOTEL
CACTUS

AUGUST

6 HASARDS OU
    COïNCIDENCES/CHANCE OR
    COINCIDENCE
6 DOUG'S 1ST MOVIE
6 GOODBYE LOVER
6 The MATCH
6 PLACE VENDÔME
6 PLAYING BY HEART
13 ANOTHER DAY IN PARADISE
13 DISTURBING BEHAVIOR
13 KOHRAM
13 *STRANGERS ON A TRAIN
13 TAAL
13 WILD WILD WEST
20 ARJUN PANDIT
20 COOKIE'S FORTUNE
20 FIN AOûT, DÉBUT
    SEPTEMBRE/LATE AUGUST,
    EARLY SEPTEMBER
20 JULIE AND THE CADILLACS
20 *The MAN WHO KNEW TOO
    MUCH
20 MICKEY BLUE EYES
20 PASSION IN THE DESERT
20 REGARDE LA MER/SEE THE
    SEA
20 RUSHMORE
20 The THOMAS CROWN AFFAIR
27 BAADSHAH
27 The BIG TEASE
27 DARKNESS FALLS
27 LIFE
27 NEVER BEEN KISSED
27 SOUTH PARK BIGGER
    LONGER & UNCUT
27 TODO SOBRE MI
    MADRE/ALL ABOUT MY

MOTHER
30 PYAAR KOI KHEL NAHIN

SEPTEMBER
3 GO
3 PAPERBACK HERO
3 SANGHARSH
3 The 13TH WARRIOR
3 The WAR ZONE
3 *YELLOW SUBMARINE
10 The ALARMIST
10 EARTH
10 EYES WIDE SHUT
10 HELLO BROTHER
10 *The ITALIAN JOB
10 A KIND OF HUSH
10 *MOUCHETTE
10 RAVENOUS
10 SKIN FLICK
10 STOP MAKING SENSE
10 VARSITY BLUES
12 FIGHT CLUB
17 ÀLA PLACE DU COEUR
17 BEAUTIFUL PEOPLE
17 BUENA VISTA SOCIAL CLUB
17 DROP DEAD GORGEOUS
17 The GENERAL'S DAUGHTER
17 INSTINCT
17 LA WITHOUT A MAP
17 SWEET ANGEL MINE
17 The TRENCH
17 UNIVERSAL SOLDIER THE
   RETURN
24 ANALYZE THIS
24 DIL KYA KARE
24 ELECTION
24 FELICEÉ FELICEÉ
24 GIRL
24 The HAUNTING
24 HUM TUM PE MARTE HAIN
24 A MIDSUMMER NIGHT'S
   DREAM
24 The THEORY OF FLIGHT

OCTOBER
1 G:MT GREENWICH MEAN
  TIME
1 BIG DADDY
1 FINAL CUT
1 *KES
1 The LOVE LETTER
1 LUCIA
1 MIFUNE/MIFUNES SIDSTE
  SANG
1 PRAISE
1 WANDAFURU RAIFU/AFTER
  LIFE/WONDERFUL LIFE
1 YOU'RE DEAD...
8 AMERICAN PIE
8 FELICIA'S JOURNEY
8 GODMOTHER
8 The LAST DAYS
8 ROMANCE
8 RUNAWAY BRIDE

8 TARZAN
10 SAR ANKHON PAR
15 DEEP BLUE SEA
15 GREGORY'S TWO GIRLS
15 G‹NESE
   YOLCULUK/JOURNEY TO
   THE SUN
15 HEAD ON
15 MAST
15 SUCH A LONG JOURNEY
15 VAASTAV
22 The BLAIR WITCH PROJECT
22 BOWFINGER
22 Le CIEL, LES OISEAUX
   ETÉTA M»RE!/BOYS ON THE
   BEACH
22 DETROIT ROCK CITY
22 FOOD OF LOVE
22 LOLA RENNT/RUN LOLA
   RUN
22 SIMPLY IRRESISTIBLE
28 *CAT PEOPLE
28 *CURSE OF THE CAT PEOPLE
29 LUCKY PEOPLE CENTER
   INTERNATIONAL
29 MAD COWS
29 PUSHING TIN
29 VAMPIRES/JOHN
   CARPENTER'S VAMPIRES
29 The WINSLOW BOY

NOVEMBER
5 EAST IS EAST
5 FOLLOWING
5 HISTOIRE D'O/GESCHICHTE
  DER O/The STORY OF O
5 HUM SAATH-SAATH HAIN
5 IDLE HANDS
5 JAKOB THE LIAR
5 The OUT-OF-TOWNERS
5 RIDE WITH THE DEVIL
5 The SIXTH SENSE
12 GAIR
12 RATCATCHER
12 The TICHBORNE CLAIMANT
19 BROKEDOWN PALACE
19 EDtv
19 FANNY & ELVIS
19 ONEGIN
19 The OTHER SISTER
19 PHÖRPA/The CUP
19 The RAGE CARRIE 2
19 RANDOM HEARTS
19 A WALK ON THE MOON
26 The ASTRONAUT'S WIFE
26 DREAMING OF JOSEPH LEES
26 Les ENFANTS DU
   MARAIS/CHILDREN OF THE
   MARSHLAND
26 KHOOBSOORAT
26 *NRAN GOUYNE/The
   COLOUR OF
   POMEGRANATES
26 *SCROOGE

26 The SECRET LAUGHTER OF
   WOMEN
26 TAXI
26 The WORLD IS NOT ENOUGH

DECEMBER
3 HAPPY TEXAS
3 GUEST HOUSE PARADISO
3 ALICE ET MARTIN
3 ANYWHERE BUT HERE
3 The CLANDESTINE
  MARRIAGE
3 The STRAIGHT STORY
3 THAKSHAK
3 WITH OR WITHOUT YOU
10 8$^1/_2$ WOMEN
10 END OF DAYS
10 The FIVE SENSES
10 The LAST YELLOW
10 The LIMEY
10 The MUSE
10 OCTOBER SKY
17 ANNA AND THE KING
17 COTTON MARY
17 HOLD BACK THE NIGHT
17 INSPECTOR GADGET
17 The IRON GIANT
17 La LEGGENDA DEL PIANISTA
   SULL'OCEANO/The LEGEND
   OF 1900
17 *NUOVO CINEMA PARADISO
24 BLUE STREAK
24 Les CACHETONNEURS/The
   MUSIC FREELANCERS
24 DOGMA
24 JAANWAR
24 MUPPETS FROM SPACE
24 MYSTERY MEN
24 SHAHEED UDHAM SINGH
31 FANTASIA 2000

AA AB LAUT CHALEN
UFDL - 15 January
India, Dir Rishi Kapoor
with Aishwarya Rai, Akshaye
Khanna, Suman Ranganathan, Rajesh
Khanna, Paresh Rawal
R.K. Films
No S&S reference

AARZOO
Shernwali - 19 March
India, Dir Lawrence D'Souza
with Madhuri Dixit, Akshay Kumar,
Saif Ali Khan, Aruna Irani, Paresh
Rawal
Dayavanti Pictures
No S&S reference

The ACID HOUSE
FilmFour Distributors - 1 January
(18) UK, Dir Paul McGuigan
with Stephen McCole, Maurice
RoÍves, Garry Sweeney, Jenny
McCrindle, Simon Weir
© **Channel 4 Television
Corporation**
A Picture Palace North/Umbrella
Productions film for Channel 4 in
association with the Yorkshire
Media
Production Agency, part funded by
the European Regional
Development Fund/The Scottish
Arts Council National Lottery
Fund/The Glasgow Film Fund
110 minutes 54 seconds
S&S January 1999 p40

ACTRIUS/ACTRESSES
Downtown Pictures - 16 April
(15) Spain, Dir Ventura Pons
with Núria Espert, Rosa María Sard‡,
Anna Lizaran, Mercè Pons
© **Els Films de la Rambla, S.A.
(Barcelona)**
An Els Films de la Rambla, S.A.
production with the participation
of TVE Televisión Española with
the participation of Canal+ España
with the collaboration of
Department de Cultura/Generalitat
de Catalunya
87 minutes 32 seconds
S&S May 1999 p36

AFFLICTION
**Artificial Eye Film Company - 19
February**
(15) USA, Dir Paul Schrader
with Nick Nolte, James Coburn,
Sissy Spacek, Willem Dafoe, Mary
Beth Hurt
© **Largo Entertainment Inc**
Largo Entertainment presents a
Reisman/Kingsgate production

114 minutes 2 seconds
S&S March 1999 p36

À LA PLACE DU COEUR
**Artificial Eye Film Company - 17
September**
(15) France, Dir Robert Guédiguian
with Ariane Ascaride, Christine
Brücher, Jean-Pierre Darroussin,
Gérard Meylan, Alexandre Ogou
© **Agat Films & Cie/Diaphana/La
Sept Cinéma/France 2 Cinéma/Le
Studio Canal+**
Agat Films & Cie presents a La
Sept Cinéma/France 2 Cinéma/Le
Studio Canal+/Diaphana co-
production with the participation
of Canal+/Soficas Studio Images 4
and Sofinergie 4/Centre National
de la Cinématographique, an Agat
Films & Cie [Gilles Sandoz]
production
112 minutes 19 seconds
subtitles
S&S October 1999 p36

The ALARMIST
**Columbia Tristar Films (UK) - 10
September**
(15) USA, Dir Evan Dunsky
with David Arquette, Stanley Tucci,
Mary McCormack, Kate Capshaw,
Tricia Vessey
© **Life During Wartime LLC**
Key Entertainment in association
with Bandeira Entertainment
presents a Dan Stone,
Flynn/Simchowitz production
91 minutes 4 seconds
S&S November 1999 p38

ALICE ET MARTIN
**Artificial Eye Film Company - 3
December**
(15) France/Spain/USA, Dir André
Téchiné
with Juliette Binoche, Alexis Loret,
Mathieu Amalric, Carmen Maura,
Jean-Pierre Lorit
© **Les Films Alain Sarde/Vertigo
Films/France 2 Cinéma/France 3
Cinéma**
Alain Sarde presents a co-
production of Les Films Alain
Sarde/Vertigo Films/France 2
Cinéma/France 3 Cinéma with the
participation of Canal+/Studio
Images 4, associate producer Kuzui
Enterprises
124 minutes 19 seconds
subtitles
S&S November 1999 p36

ALL THE LITTLE ANIMALS
Entertainment Film Distributors

Ltd - 9 July
UK, Dir Jeremy Thomas
with John Hurt, Christian Bale,
Daniel Benzali, James Faulkner, John
O'Toole
© **RPC Animals Limited**
Recorded Picture Company
presents in association with British
Screen/J&M Entertainment/Isle of
Man Film Commission/BBC
Films/Entertainment Film
Distributors, developed with the
support of the European Script
Fund and the assistance of Indigo
112 minutes 15 seconds
Anamorphic
S&S September 1998 p36

AMERICAN HISTORY X
**Entertainment Film Distributors
Ltd - 26 March**
(18) USA, Dir Tony Kaye
with Edward Norton, Edward
Furlong, Fairuza Balk, Stacy Keach,
Jennifer Lien
© **New Line Productions, Inc**
New Line Cinema presents a
Turman-Morrissey Company
production
118 minutes 42 seconds
S&S May 1999 p36

AMERICAN PERFEKT
**Blue Dolphin Film & Video - 11
June**
(15) USA, Dir Paul Chart
with Fairuza Balk, Robert Forster,
Amanda Plummer, Paul Sorvino,
David Thewlis
© **Mondofin B.V.**
Nu Image
99 minutes 59 seconds
S&S June 1999 p34

AMERICAN PIE
**United International Pictures (UK)
Ltd - 8 October**
(15) USA, Dir Paul Weitz
with Jason Biggs, Chris Klein,
Natasha Lyonne, Thomas Ian
Nicholas, Tara Reid
© **Universal Studios**
Universal Pictures presents a
Zide/Perry production
95 minutes 32 seconds
S&S October 1999 p37

AMONG GIANTS
20th Century Fox (UK) - 11th June
(15) UK, Dir Sam Miller
with Pete Postlethwaite, Rachel
Griffiths, James Thornton, Lennie
James, Andy Serkis
© **Among Giants Ltd**
Capitol Films presents with the

participation of British Screen/the Arts Council of England/BBC Films and the Yorkshire Media Production Agency a Kudos production, developed with the assistance of British Screen Finance Ltd supported by the National Lottery through the Arts Council of England
93 minutes 36 seconds
S&S June 1999 p34

ANALYZE THIS
Warner Bros Distributors (UK) - 24 September
(15) USA, Dir Harold Ramis
with Robert De Niro, Billy Crystal, Lisa Kudrow, Joe Viterelli, Chazz Palminteri
© Warner Bros. (US, Canada, Bahamas & Bermuda) and Village Roadshow Films (BVI) Limited (all other territories)
Warner Bros. presents in association with Village Roadshow Pictures and NPV Entertainment a Baltimore/Spring Creek Pictures/Face/Tribeca production
103 minutes 17 seconds
S&S August 1999 p40

ANNA AND THE KING
20th Century Fox (UK) - 17 December
(12) USA, Dir Andy Tennant
with Jodie Foster, Chow Yun-Fat, Bai Ling, Tom Felton, Syed Alwi
© Twentieth Century Fox Film Corporation
Fox 2000 Pictures presents a Lawrence Bender production
147 minutes 59 seconds
Anamorphic [Panavision]
S&S February 2000 p41

ANO NATSU, ICHIBAN SHIZUKANA UMI/A SCENE AT THE SEA
ICA - shown at the ICA on 5 February
(not submitted) Japan, Dir Takeshi Kitano
with Kurodo Maki, Hiroko Oshima, Sabu Kawahara, Toshizo Fujiwara, Susumu Terajima
© Office Kitano/Totsu
Office Kitano/Totsu
102 minutes
subtitles
S&S April 1999 p57

ANOTHER DAY IN PARADISE
Metrodome Distribution Ltd - 13 August

(18) USA, Dir Larry Clark
with James Woods, Melanie Griffith, Vincent Kartheiser, Natasha Gregson Wagner, James Otis
© Another Day, Inc
Chinese Bookie Pictures presents a Larry Clark film
101 minutes 17 seconds
S&S August 1999 p38

ANYWHERE BUT HERE
20th Century Fox (UK) - 3 December
(12) USA, Dir Wayne Wang
with Susan Sarandon, Natalie Portman, Bonnie Bedelia, Shawn Hatosy, Hart Bochner
© Twentieth Century Fox Film Corporation
Fox 2000 Pictures presents a Laurence Mark production
113 minutes 45 seconds
S&S January 2000 p42

APRILE
Metro Tartan Distributors - 19 March
(15) Italy/France, Dir Nanni Moretti
with Nanni Moretti, Silvio Orlando, Silvia Nono, Pietro Moretti, Agata Apicella Moretti
© Sacher Film/BAC Films
BAC Films/Sacher Film present a Sacher Film (Rome)/BAC Films (Paris) co-production with the participation of RAI and Canal+
77 minutes 54 seconds
subtitles
S&S April 1999 p36

APT PUPIL
Columbia Tristar Films (UK) - 21 May
(15) USA/France, Dir Bryan Singer
with Ian McKellen, Brad Renfro, Bruce Davison, Elias Koteas, Joe Morton
© Phoenix Pictures Inc
Phoenix Pictures presents a Bad Hat Harry production in association with Canal+ D.A.
111 minutes 3 seconds
Super 35
S&S June 1999 p35

L'ARCHE DU DÉSERT
Downtown Pictures - 16 July
(12)
Algeria/France/Germany/Switzerland, Dir Mohamed Chouikh
with Myriam Aouffen, Messaouda Adami, Hacen Abdou, Shyraz Aliane, Amin Chouikh
An Atlas-Films (Algeria)/K-Films Production (France)/E.N.P.A.

(Algeria)/Vulkan Kultur GmbH (Germany) co-production & Le Ministère de la Culture et de la Communication (Algeria)/Fond Sud: Ministère des Affaires Etrangères/Ministère de la Coopération/Centre National de la Cinématographie (France)/U.N.E.S.C.O. & la contribution de la Fondation Montecinemaverit‡ (Locarno) & la DDA: Direction de la coopération au développement et de l'aide humanitaire (Switzerland)
subtitles
89 minutes 39 seconds
S&S August 1999 p38

ARJUN PANDIT
Blue Star - 20 August
India, Dir Rahul Rawail
with Sunny Deol, Juhi Chawla, Mukesh Rishi, Shahbaaz Khan, Saurabh Shukla
Ratan International
No S&S reference

ARLINGTON ROAD
PolyGram Filmed Entertainment - 19 March
(15) USA/UK, Dir Mark Pellington
with Jeff Bridges, Tim Robbins, Joan Cusack, Hope Davis, Robert Gossett
© Lakeshore Entertainment Corp.
PolyGram Filmed Entertainment presents in association with Lakeshore Entertainment a Gorai/Samuelson production
117 minutes 32 seconds
S&S April 1999 p36

ARTEMISIA
Gala Film Distributors - 7 May
(18) France/Germany/Italy, Dir Agnès Merlet
with Michel Serrault, Valentina Cervi, Miki Manojlovic, Luca Zingaretti, Brigitte Catillon
© Première Heure/France 3 Cinéma/Schlemmer Film/3 Emme Cinematografica
Première Heure Long Métrage presents a co-production of Première Heure/Schlemmer Film/France 3 Cinéma/3 Emme Cinematografica with the support of Fonds Eurimages and with participation of Canal+/Centre National de la Cinématographie in association with Sofygram/Sofinergie 4/Cofimage 8 and the support of La Procirep, screenplay developed in collaboration with Equinoxe
95 minutes 52 seconds

subtitles
S&S May 1999 p37

L'ASSEDIO/BESIEGED
Alliance Releasing (UK) - 23 April
(PG) Italy, Dir Bernardo Bertolucci
with Thandie Newton, David
Thewlis, Claudio Santamaria, John C.
Ojwang, Massimo De Rossi
© **Fiction s.r.l. Rome**
A Fiction and Navert Film in co-production with Mediaset presentation
93 minutes 35 seconds
S&S May 1999 p40

The ASTRONAUT'S WIFE
Entertainment Film Distributors Ltd - 26 November
(18) USA, Dir Rand Ravich
with Johnny Depp, Charlize Theron,
Joe Morton, Clea Duvall, Samantha
Eggar
© **New Line Productions, Inc**
New Line Cinema presents a Mad Chance production
109 minutes 1 seconds
S&S December 1999 p36

AT FIRST SIGHT
United International Pictures (UK) Ltd - 30 April
(12) USA, Dir Irwin Winkler
with Val Kilmer, Mira Sorvino, Kelly
McGillis, Steven Weber, Bruce Davison
© **Metro-Goldwyn-Mayer Pictures Inc**
Metro-Goldwyn-Mayer Pictures presents an Irwin Winkler film
128 minutes 52 seconds
S&S June 1999 p36

AUSTIN POWERS THE SPY WHO SHAGGED ME
Entertainment Film Distributors Ltd - 30 July
(12) USA, Dir Jay Roach
with Mike Myers, Heather Graham,
Michael York, Robert Wagner, Seth
Green
© **New Line Productions, Inc.**
New Line Cinema presents an Eric's Boy/Moving Pictures and Team Todd production
95 minutes 4 seconds
S&S August 1999 p39

BAADSHAH
Stars International - 27 August
India, Dir Abbas-Mustan
with Shah Rukh Khan, Twinkle
Khanna, Raakhee, Johny Lever,
Shashikala
United Seven Combines
No S&S reference

BEAUTIFUL PEOPLE
Warner Bros Distributors (UK) - 17 September
(15) UK, Dir Jasmin Dizdar
with Rosalind Ayres, Linda Bassett,
Charlotte Coleman, Edin
Dzandzanovic, Nicholas Farrell
© **Beautiful Stories Ltd.**
The British Film Institute and Channel Four present a Tall Stories production in association with the Arts Council of England and the Merseyside Film Production Fund with the participation of BskyB and British Screen Screenplay developed by BFI Production and Channel Four supported by the proceeds of the National Lottery through the Arts Council of England
107 minutes 52 seconds
S&S September 1999 p41

BEDROOMS AND HALLWAYS
Alliance Releasing (UK) - 9 April
(15) UK/France/Germany, Dir Rose
Troche
with Kevin McKidd, Hugo Weaving,
James Purefoy, Tom Hollander,
Christopher Fulford
© **Berwin & Dempsey Productions**
Pandora Cinema presents in association with ARP/Pandora Film and BBC Films a Berwin and Dempsey production
96 minutes 9 seconds
S&S May 1999 p38

BELLY
Alliance Releasing (UK) - 2 July
(18) USA, Dir Hype Williams
with Nas, DMX, Taral Hicks, Tionne
'T-Boz' Watkins, Method Man
© **Artisan Pictures, Inc**
Artisan Entertainment presents a Big Dog Films production
95 minutes 35 seconds
S&S August 1999 p40

BELOVED
Buena Vista International (UK) - 5 March
(15) USA, Dir Jonathan Demme
with Oprah Winfrey, Danny Glover,
Thandie Newton, Kimberly Elise,
Beah Richards
© **Touchstone Pictures**
A Harpo Pictures/Clinica Estetico production
171 minutes 33 seconds
S&S March 1999 p36

BEST LAID PLANS
20th Century Fox (UK) - 14 May
(15) USA, Dir Mike Barker
with Alessandro Nivola, Reese
Witherspoon, Josh Brolin, Rocky
Carroll, Michael G. Hagerty
© **Twentieth Century Fox Film Corporation**
Fox 2000 Pictures presents a Dogstar Films production
93 minutes 13 seconds
S&S June 1999 p38

BIG DADDY
Columbia Tristar Films (UK) - 1 October
(12) USA, Dir Dennis Dugan
with Adam Sandler, Joey Lauren
Adams, Jon Stewart, Allen Covert,
Rob Schneider
© **Columbia Pictures Industries, Inc**
Columbia Pictures presents an Out of the Blue Entertainment/Jack Giarraputo production
92 minutes 59 seconds
S&S October 1999 p38

The BIG HIT
Columbia Tristar Films (UK) - 25 June
(18) USA, Dir Che-Kirk Wong
with Mark Wahlberg, Lou Diamond
Phillips, Christina Applegate, Avery
Brooks, Bokeem Woodbine
© **TriStar Pictures Inc**
TriStar Pictures presents an Amen Ra Films/Zide-Perry/Lion Rock production
91 minutes 15 seconds
S&S July 1999 p36

The BIG TEASE
Warner Bros Distributors (UK) - 27 August
(15) USA/UK, Dir Kevin Allen
with Craig Ferguson, Frances Fisher,
Mary McCormack, Donal Logue,
Larry Miller
© **Warner Bros.**
Warner Bros. presents a Crawford P. Inc. production in association with Should Coco Films
86 minutes 16 seconds
S&S January 2000 p43

BILLY'S HOLLYWOOD SCREEN KISS
Metro Tartan Distributors - 9 July
(15) USA, Dir Tommy O'Haver
with Sean P. Hayes, Brad Rowe,
Richard Ganoung, Meredith Scott
Lynn, Matthew Ashford
© **Revolutionary Eye LLC.**
A Revolutionary Eye production
92 minutes 41 seconds
S&S July 1999 p36

BIWI NO.1
Yash Raj - 28 May
India, Dir David Dhawan
with Salman Khan, Karishma
Kapoor, Sushmita Sen, Anil Kapoor,
Tabu
Puja Films
No S&S reference

BLACK CAT WHITE CAT
**Artificial Eye Film Company - 7
May**
(15) Germany/France/Yugoslavia/
Austria/Greece, Dir Emir Kusturica
with Bajram Severdzan, Srdan
Todorovic, Branka Katic, Florijan
Ajdini, Ljubica Adzovic
© **Pandora Film GmbH & Co
KG/CiBy 2000/France 2 Cinéma
CiBy 2000/Pandora
Film/Komuna/France 2 Cinéma
with the support of
Canal+/Bayerischer
Rundfunk/Filmförderung
Hamburg/Filmstiftung
NRW/österreichischer
Rundfunk/Stefi S.A.**
128 minutes 56 seconds
subtitles
S&S May 1999 p41

The BLAIR WITCH
PROJECT
Pathé Distribution - 22 October
(15) USA, Dir Daniel Myrick,
Eduardo Sanchez
Heather Donahue, Michael Williams,
Joshua Leonard, Bob Griffith, Jim
King, Sandra S‡nchez, Ed Swanson,
Patricia Decou
© **Haxan Films, Inc.
An Artisan release of a Haxan
Films presentation**
80 minutes 57 seconds
aspect ratio 1.33:1
S&S November 1999 p38

BLAST FROM THE PAST
**Entertainment Film Distributors
Ltd - 2 April**
(12) USA, Dir Hugh Wilson
with Brendan Fraser, Christopher
Walken, Sissy Spacek, Alicia
Silverstone, Dave Foley
© **New Line Cinema Corporation
New Line Cinema presents a
Midnight Sun Pictures production**
108 minutes 38 seconds
S&S April 1999 p38

BLUE STREAK
**Columbia TriStar Films (UK) - 24
December**
(12) USA, Dir Les Mayfield
with Martin Lawrence, Luke Wilson,

Dave Chappelle, Peter Greene,
Nicole Ari Parker
© **Global Entertainment
Productions GmbH & Co. Movie KG
Columbia Pictures presents a Neal
H. Moritz/IndieProd/Jaffe
production**
93 minutes 58 seconds
S&S January 2000 p44

BOWFINGER
**United International Pictures (UK)
Ltd - 22 October**
(12) USA, Dir Frank Oz
with Steve Martin, Eddie Murphy,
Heather Graham, Christine Baranski,
Jamie Kennedy
© **Universal Studios
Universal and Imagine
Entertainment present a Brian
Grazer production**
97 minutes 10 seconds
S&S November 1999 p39

BRIDE OF CHUCKY
**Metrodome Distribution Ltd - 18
June**
(18) USA, Dir Ronny Yu
with Jennifer Tilly, Katherine Heigl,
Nick Stabile, John Ritter, Alexis
Arquette
© **Universal City Studios, Inc
Universal Pictures presents a David
Kirschner production**
88 minutes 45 seconds
S&S July 1999 p37

BROKEDOWN PALACE
**20th Century Fox (UK) - 19
November**
(12) USA, Dir Jonathan Kaplan
with Claire Danes, Bill Pullman,
Kate Beckinsale, Lou Diamond
Phillips, Jacqueline Kim
© **Twentieth Century Fox Film
Corporation
Fox 2000 Pictures presents an
Adam Fields production**
100 minutes 36 seconds
Super 35 [2.35:1]
S&S December 1999 p37

The BRYLCREEM BOYS
Downtown Pictures - 23 April
(15) UK, Dir Terence Ryan
with Bill Campbell, William
McNamara, Angus MacFadyen,
Gordon Sinclair, Oliver Tobias
**Sherwood Limited, Rough Magic
Films developed in association with
Freewheel Productions, developed
with the assistance of Ealing
Studios Productions**
106 minutes
S&S August 1998 p34

BUENA VISTA SOCIAL
CLUB
**FilmFour Distributors - 17
September**
(U) Germany, Dir Wim Wenders
with Joachim Cooder, Ry Cooder,
Ibrahim Ferrer, Juan de Marcos
González, Rubén González
© **Road Movies Produktion, Berlin
A Road Movies production in
association with Kintop Pictures
and ARTE**
104 minutes 42 seconds
some subtitles
S&S October 1999 p40

A BUG'S LIFE
**Buena Vista International (UK) - 5
February**
(U), USA, Dir John Lasseter
with character voices by Dave Foley,
Kevin Spacey, Julia Louis-Dreyfus,
Hayden Panettiere, Phyllis Diller
© **Disney Enterprises Inc/Pixar
Animation Studios
Walt Disney Pictures presents a
Pixar Animation Studios film**
94 minutes 49 seconds
S&S February 1999 p39

BULWORTH
**20th Century Fox (UK) - 22
January**
(18) USA, Dir Warren Beatty
with Warren Beatty, Halle Berry, Don
Cheadle, Oliver Platt, Paul Sorvino
© **Twentieth Century Fox Film
Corporation
Twentieth Century Fox presents a
Warren Beatty film**
108 minutes 6 seconds
S&S February 1999 p40

Les CACHETONNEURS/
The MUSIC FREELANCERS
Winstone - 24 December
(PG) France, Dir Denis Dercourt
with Pierre Lacan, Marc Citti,
Philippe Clay, Henri Garcin, Marie-
Christine Laurent
**Films ‡ un Dollar/Idea
Productions/Cine Classic**
91 minutes
No S&S reference

«A COMMENCE
AUJOURD'HUI/IT ALL
STARTS TODAY
**Artificial Eye Film Company - 23
July**
(12) France, Dir Bertrand Tavernier
with Philippe Torreton, Maria
Pitarresi, Nadia Kaci, Véronique
Ataly, Nathalie Bécue
© **Les Films Alain Sarde/Little**

Bear/TF1 Films Production
Alain Sarde & Frédéric
Bourboulon present a co-
production of Les Films Alain
Sarde/Little Bear/TF1 Films
Production with the participation
of Canal+/CRRAV/Sofica Studio
Images 5, made with the support of
La Région Nord Pas-de-Calais
subtitles
118 minutes 23 seconds
S&S August 1999 p46

CAPTAIN JACK
Feature Film Company - 21 May
(PG) UK, Dir Robert Young
with Bob Hoskins, Sadie Frost,
Gemma Jones, Anna Massey, Peter
McDonald
© Captain Jack Films Limited
Granada and Baltic Media present
in association with the Arts Council
of England a Granada Film/John
Goldschmidt production supported
by the National Lottery through
the Arts Council of England,
produced by Viva Films Limited
for Granada Film and Baltic
Media
100 minutes 24 seconds
S&S June 1999 p39

*CAT PEOPLE
BFI Collections - 28 October [NFT
First Run 28 Oct-3 Nov]
(PG) USA, Dir Jacques Tourneur
with Simone Simon, Kent Smith,
Tom Conway, Jane Randolph, Jack
Holt
RKO Radio Pictures
73 minutes
MFB March 1943 p27

CELEBRITY
Buena Vista International (UK) -
18 June
(18) USA, Dir Woody Allen
with Hank Azaria, Kenneth Branagh,
Judy Davis, Leonardo DiCaprio,
Melanie Griffith
© Magnolia Productions Inc and
Sweetland Films BV
A Jean Doumanian production
113 minutes 26 seconds
S&S July 1999 p38

CENTRAL DO BRASIL/CENTRAL STATION
Buena Vista International (UK) -
12 March
(15) Brazil/France/Spain/Japan, Dir
Walter Salles
with Fernanda Montenegro, Marilia
Pîra, Vinícius de Oliveira, Sôia Lira,

Othon Bastos
© Videofilmes/Mact Productions
Martine and Antoine de Clermont-
Tonnerre/Jack Gajos/Elisa
Tolomelli present a
Videofilmes/Mact
Productions/Riofilme co-
production with the participation
of Canal+/The French Ministry of
Culture and the Ministry of
Foreign Relations/Sogepaq with the
support of the Sundance Institute
and of N.H.K. This film was
produced with the support of the
Brazilian Ministry of Culture
through the Audiovisual
Development Bureau/The Rouanet
Law for Cultural Tax Incentives,
co-produced and concluded with
funds from Rio de Janeiro City
Hall/The Municipal Bureau of
Culture, through Riofilme,
institutional support from São
Paulo City Hall
110 minutes 10 seconds
subtitles
S&S March 1999 p38

Le CIEL, LES OISEAUX ETÉTA M»RE!/BOYS ON THE BEACH
Gala Film Distributors - 22
October
(15) France, Dir Djamel Bensalah
with Jamel Debbouze, Julien
Courbey, Lorant Deutsch, Stéphane
Soo Mongo, Olivia Bonamy
© Extravaganza/Orly
Films/Sédif/France 2 Cinéma
Extravaganza & Orly Films
present a co-production of
Extravaganza/Orly
Films/Sédif/France 2 Cinéma/sofica
Sofinergie 4/sofica Gimages with
the participation of Canal+/Centre
National de la Cinématographie
90 minutes 25 seconds
subtitles
S&S November 1999 p47

*CITIZEN KANE
PolyGram Filmed Entertainment -
4 June
(U) USA, Dir Orson Welles
with Joseph Cotten, Dorothy
Comingore, Agnes Moorehead, Ruth
Warrick, Ray Collins
RKO Radio Pictures, Mercury
Productions
119 minutes
black & white
MFB December 1941 p164

A CIVIL ACTION
United International Pictures (UK)

Ltd - 9 April
(15) USA, Dir Steven Zaillian
with John Travolta, Robert Duvall,
James Gandolfini, Dan Hedaya, John
Lithgow
© Paramount Pictures
Corporation/Touchstone Pictures
Paramount Pictures and Touchstone
Pictures present a Wildwood
Enterprises/Scott Rudin production
115 minutes 2 seconds
S&S April 1999 p39

The CLANDESTINE MARRIAGE
United International Pictures (UK)
Ltd - 3 December
(15) UK, Dir Christopher Miles
with Nigel Hawthorne, Joan Collins,
Timothy Spall, Tom Hollander, Paul
Nicholls
© Stanway Films Ltd
Portman Entertainment and BBC
Films present a Portman
production with the participation
of British Screen, the Gunner and
Stables Group and Milesian Films
90 minutes 45 seconds
S&S December 1999 p40

La CLASSE DE NEIGE/CLASS TRIP
Blue Light - 22 January
(15) France, Dir Claude Miller
with Clément Van Den Bergh,
Lokman Nalcakan, François Roy,
Yves Verhoeven, Emmanuelle Bercot
© Les Films de la Boissière
presents a co-production: Films de
la Boissière/P.E.C.F./France 3
Cinéma/Rhône-Alpes Cinéma, with
the support/participation of Centre
National de la Cinématographie,
with the participation of
Canal+/Région Rhône-Alpes
97 minutes 40 seconds
subtitles
S&S January 1999 p41

The CLOCKWATCHERS
Feature Film Company - shown as
part of the 'American
Independence' tour from 12 March
US, Dir Jill Sprecher
with Toni Collette, Parker Posey, Lisa
Kudrow, Alanna Ubach, Stanley
DeSantis
Goldcrest Films
105 minutes
No S&S reference

CONTE D'AUTOMNE/An AUTUMN TALE
Artificial Eye Film Company - 26
March

(U) France, Dir Eric Rohmer
with Marie Rivière, Béatrice
Romand, Didier Sandre, Alain Libolt,
Alexia Portal
© Les Films du Losange/La Sept
Cinéma
Margaret Ménégoz/Les Films du
Losange/La Sept Cinéma with the
participation of
Canal+/Sofilmka/Rhônes-Alpes
Cinéma present
111 minutes 30 seconds
subtitles
S&S April 1999 p37

COOKIE'S FORTUNE
Alliance Releasing (UK) - 20
August
(12) USA, Dir Robert Altman
with Glenn Close, Julianne Moore,
Liv Tyler, Chris O'Donnell, Charles
S.Dutton
© Kudzu Productions, Inc
October Films presents a
Sandcastle 5 and Elysian Dreams
production
117 minutes 47 seconds
S&S September 1999 p44

The CORRUPTOR
Entertainment Film Distributors
Ltd - 21 May
(18) USA, Dir James Foley
with Chow Yun-Fat, Mark Wahlberg,
Ric Young, Paul Ben-Victor, Andrew
Pang
© New Line Productions, Inc
New Line Cinema presents an
Illusion Entertainment Group
production
109 minutes 59 seconds
S&S June 1999 p40

COTTON MARY
United International Pictures (UK)
Ltd - 17 December
(15) UK, Dir Ismail Merchant
with Greta Scacchi, Madhur Jaffrey,
James Wilby, Sarah Badel, Riju Bajaj
© Cotton Productions Limited
Merchant Ivory Productions presents
a film by Ismail Merchant
123 minutes 26 seconds
S&S January 2000 p46

CROUPIER
BFI Films - 18 June [NFT First
Run 18-24 June]
(15) Ireland/Germany/France/UK,
Dir Mike Hodges
with Clive Owen, Kate Hardie, Alex
Kingston, Gina McKee, Nicholas
Ball
© Little Bird/Tatfilm/Compagnie
des Phares & Balises/La Sept

Cinéma/Channel Four Television
Corporation
Channel Four Films presents in
association with Filmstiftung
NRW/WDR/La Sept
Cinéma/ARTE/Canal+ a Little
Bird/Tatfilm production in
association with Compagnie des
Phares & Balises, produced in
association with La Sept
Cinéma/ARTE/Westdeutscher
Rundfunk/Canal+, supported by
Filmstiftung NRW
94 minutes 14 seconds
July 1999 p39

CRUEL INTENTIONS
Columbia Tristar Films (UK) - 18
June
(15) USA, Dir Roger Kumble
with Sarah Michelle Gellar, Ryan
Phillippe, Reese Witherspoon, Selma
Blair, Louise Fletcher
© Cruel Productions, LLC
Columbia Pictures presents in
association with Original Film and
Newmarket Capital Group a Neal
H. Moritz production
97 minutes 20 seconds
S&S June 1999 p42

CRUSH PROOF
Clarence Pictures - 7 May
(18)
UK/Netherlands/Ireland/Germany,
Dir Paul Tickell
with Darren Healy, Viviana Verveen,
Jeff O'Toole, Mark Dunne, Michael
McElhatton
© Woodline Productions Limited,
Movie Masters BV, Liquid Films
Limited and Continent Film
GmbH
Woodline Productions/Movie
Masters/Liquid Films/Continent
Film present a Kees Kasander
production, produced with the
participation of The European Co-
production Fund (U.K.) with the
assistance of Bord Scannán na
hÉireann/The Irish Film Board in
association with Vara and the
CoBO Fund, produced with the
support of investment incentives
for the Irish Film Industry by the
Government of Ireland
93 minutes 21 seconds
S&S May 1999 p42

*CURSE OF THE CAT PEOPLE
BFI Collections - 28 October [NFT
First Run 28 Oct-3 Nov]
(PG) USA, Dir Gunther V. Fritsch
with Simone Simon, Kent Smith,

Jane Randolph, Ann Carter, Eve
March
RKO Radio Pictures
70 minutes
MFB September 1944 p102

DAHEK
Eros Video (Electronics) Ltd - 17
December
India, Dir Lateef Binny
with Akshaye Khanna, Sonali
Bendre, Danny Denzongpa, Dalip
Tahil, Anjana Mumtaz
M.J. Films
No S&S reference

DANCE WITH ME
Entertainment Film Distributors
Ltd - 23 April
(PG) USA, Dir Randa Haines
with Vanessa L. Williams, Chayanne,
Kris Kristofferson, Jane Krakowski,
Beth Grant
© Mandalay Entertainment
Mandalay Entertainment presents
a Weissman/Egawa production
126 minutes 18 seconds
S&S May 1999 p44

DARKNESS FALLS
Downtown Pictures - 27 August
(15) UK, Dir Gerry Lively
with Sherilyn Fenn, Ray Winstone,
Tim Dutton, Anita Dobson, Bryan
Pringle
© Hoseplace Ltd
Alberto Ardissone and Film
Development Corporation present
in association with The Isle of Man
Film Commission and Vine
International Pictures Ltd,
developed in association with Jo
Gilbert
91 minutes 29 seconds
S&S January 1999 p42

The DEBT COLLECTOR
FilmFour Distributors - 11 June
(18) UK, Dir Anthony Neilson
with Billy Connolly, Ken Stott,
Francesca Annis, Iain Robertson,
Annette Crosbie
© FilmFour Limited
FilmFour presents in association
with the Glasgow Film Fund a
Dragon Pictures production
109 minutes 45 seconds
S&S June 1999 p43

DEEP BLUE SEA
Warner Bros Distributors (UK) -
15 October
(15) USA, Dir Renny Harlin
with Saffron Burrows, Thomas Jane,
LL Cool J, Jacqueline McKenzie,

Michael Rapaport
© **Warner Bros. (US, Canada, Bahamas & Bermuda) and Village Roadshow Films (BVI) Limited (all other territories)**
Warner Bros presents in association with Village Roadshow Pictures - Groucho III Film Partnership an Alan Riche-Tony Ludwig/Akiva Goldsman production
104 minutes 52 seconds
Super 35 [2.35:1]
S&S November 1999 p42

The DEEP END OF THE OCEAN
Entertainment Film Distributors Ltd - 4 June
(12) USA, Dir Ulu Grosbard
with Michelle Pfeiffer, Treat Williams, Jonathan Jackson, John Kapelos, Ryan Merriman
© **Mandalay Entertainment**
Mandalay Entertainment presents a Via Rosa production
108 minutes 13 seconds
S&S August 1999 p41

DES NOUVELLES DU BON DIEU/NEWS FROM THE GOOD LORD
ICA - shown at the ICA (London) from 19 February
(not submitted)
France/Switzerland/Portugal, Dir Didier Le Pecheur
with Marie Trintignant, Christian Charmetant, Isabelle Candelier, Florence Thomassin, Maria de Medeiros
M6 Films, Program 33, Grupo de Estudos e Realizacoes
100 minutes
No S&S reference

DETROIT ROCK CITY
Entertainment Film Distributors Ltd - 22 October
(15) USA, Dir Adam Rifkin
with Edward Furlong, Giuseppe Andrews, James DeBello, Sam Huntington, Gene Simmons
© **New Line Productions, Inc.**
New Line Cinema presents a Takoma Entertainment/Base-12 Productions/Kissnation production
94 minutes 38 seconds
S&S November 1999 p42

DIL KYA KARE
Eros Video (Electronics) Ltd - 24 September
India, Dir Veena Devgan
with Ajay Devgan, Mahima

Chaudhary, Kajol, Chandrachur Singh, Laxmikant Berde
Devgan Arts
No S&S reference

Le DÓNER DE CONS
Pathé Distribution - 2 July
(15) France, Dir Francis Veber
with Jacques Villeret, Thierry Lhermitte, Francis Huster, Alexandra Vandernoot, Daniel Prévost
© **Gaumont/Efve/TF1 Films Production**
A Gaumont/Efve/TF1 Films Production co-production with the participation of TPS Cinéma
79 minutes 54 seconds
S&S July 1999 p40

DISTURBING BEHAVIOR
Columbia Tristar Films (UK) - 13 August
(15) USA/Australia, Dir David Nutter
with James Marsden, Katie Holmes, Nick Stahl, Steve Railsback, Bruce Greenwood
© **Metro-Goldwyn-Mayer Pictures Inc (US, Canada & their territories), and Village Roadshow Pictures Worldwide Inc (rest of the world)**
Metro-Goldwyn-Mayer presents in association with Village Roadshow - Hoyts Film Partnership a Beacon Communications production
83 minutes 56 seconds
S&S October 1999 p41

DOBERMANN
Metro Tartan Distributors - 15 January
(18) France, Dir Jan Kounen
with Vincent Cassel, Monica Bellucci, Tchéky Karyo, Antoine Basier, Dominique Bettenfeld
© **Le Studio Canal+/PolyGram Audiovisuel/France 3 Cinéma/Noé Productions/La Chauve-Souris**
La Chauve-Souris & Noé Productions present a co-production of Le Studio Canal+/PolyGram Audiovisuel/France 3 Cinéma/Comstock/La Chauve-Souris/Noé Productions and Tawak Pictures, with the participation of Canal+/Sofinergie 4/Sofygram/Canal+ Écriture, with the participation of Centre National de la Cinématographie
103 minutes 6 seconds
Subtitles
S&S January 1999 p44

DOGMA
FilmFour Distributors - 24 December
(15) USA, Dir Kevin Smith
with Ben Affleck, George Carlin, Matt Damon, Linda Fiorentino, Salma Hayek
© **Miramax Film Corp.**
A View Askew production
128 minutes 22 seconds
Super 35 [2:35:1]
S&S January 2000 p47

DON'T GO BREAKING MY HEART
PolyGram Filmed Entertainment - 12 February
(PG) UK, Dir Willi Patterson
with Anthony Edwards, Jenny Seagrove, Charles Dance, Jane Leeves, Tom Conti
© **Bill Kenright Films Ltd**
PolyGram Filmed Entertainment presents a Bill Kenright Films production
93 minutes 40 seconds
S&S April 1999 p40

DOUG'S 1ST MOVIE
Buena Vista International (UK) - 6 August
(U) USA, Dir Maurice Joyce
with the character voices of Thomas McHugh, Fred Newman, Chris Phillips, Constance Shulman, Frank Welker
© **Jumbo Pictures, Inc**
Walt Disney Pictures presents a Jumbo Pictures production
77 minutes 13 seconds
S&S August 1999 p42

DREAMING OF JOSEPH LEES
20th Century Fox (UK) - 26 November
(12) USA/UK, Dir Eric Styles
with Samantha Morton, Lee Ross, Miriam Margolyes, Frank Finlay, Nick Woodeson
© **Twentieth Century Fox Film Corporation**
Fox Searchlight Pictures presents a Christopher Milburn production in association with the Isle of Man Film Commission
91 minutes 49 seconds
S&S December 1999 p42

DROP DEAD GORGEOUS
Icon Film Distribution - 17 September
(15) USA/Germany, Dir Michael Patrick Jann
with Kirstie Alley, Ellen Barkin,

Kirsten Dunst, Denise Richards,
Allison Janney
© **New Line Productions Inc**
New Line presents in association
with Capella/KC Medien a
Hofflund/Palone production
98 minutes 7 seconds
S&S October 1999 p42

EARTH
Pathé Distribution - 10 September
1999
(15) Canada, Dir Deepa Mehta
with Aamir Khan, Nandita Das,
Rahul Khanna, Maia Sethna, Kitu
Gidwani
© **Cracking the Earth Films Inc**
David Hamilton and Jhamu
Sughand present a Deepa Mehta
film
105 minutes 57 seconds
subtitles
S&S June 2000 p40

EAST IS EAST
FilmFour Distributors - 5
November
(15) UK, Dir Damien O'Donnell
with Om Puri, Linda Bassett, Jordan
Routledge, Archie Panjabi, Emil
Marwa
© **FilmFour Limited**
FilmFour presents an Assassin
Films production for FilmFour in
association with the BBC and
developed with the support of the
MEDIA Programme
96 minutes 22 seconds
S&S November 1999 p43

EDtv
United International Pictures (UK)
Ltd - 19 November
(12) USA, Dir Ron Howard
with Matthew McConaughey, Jenna
Elfman, Woody Harrelson, Sally
Kirkland, Martin Landau
© **Universal Studios**
Universal Pictures and Imagine
Entertainment present a Brian
Grazer production
123 minutes 16 seconds
S&S December 1999 p44

8¹/₂ WOMEN
Pathé Distribution Ltd - 10
December
(15) Netherlands/UK/
Luxembourg/Germany, Dir Peter
Greenaway
with John Standing, Matthew
Delamere, Vivian Wu, Shizuka Inoh,
Barbara Sarafian
© **Movie Masters BV/Woodline**
Productions Ltd/Delux Productions

s.a./Continent Films GmbH
Woodline Productions Ltd/Movie
Masters/Delux Productions
s.a./Continent Films GmbH present a
Kees Kasander production with the
support of Eurimages/Dutch Film
Fund/Luxembourg Audiovisual Tax
Credit Scheme
120 minutes 35 seconds
S&S January 2000 p48

8MM
Columbia Tristar Films (UK) - 23
April
(18) USA/Germany, Dir Joel
Schumacher
with Nicolas Cage, Joaquin Phoenix,
James Gandolfini, Peter Stormare,
Anthony Heald
© **Global Entertainment**
Productions GmbH & Co Medien
KG
Columbia Pictures present a
Hofflund/Polone production
123 minutes 8 seconds
S&S May 1999 p45

ELECTION
United International Pictures (UK)
Ltd - 24 September
(15) USA, Dir Alexander Payne
with Matthew Broderick, Reese
Witherspoon, Chris Klein, Jessica
Campbell, Mark Harelik
© **Paramount Pictures Corporation**
Paramount Pictures presents an
MTV Films production in
association with Bona Fide
Productions
102 minutes 49 seconds
Super 35
S&S October 1999 p43

END OF DAYS
Buena Vista International (UK) -
10 December
(18) USA, Dir Peter Hyams
with Arnold Schwarzenegger, Gabriel
Byrne, Kevin Pollak, Robin Tunney,
C.C.H. Pounder
© **Beacon Communications, LLC**
A Beacon Pictures presentation
121 minutes 53 seconds
Super 35 [2.35:1]
S&S February 2000 p45

Les ENFANTS DU MARAIS/CHILDREN OF THE MARSHLAND
Gala Film Distributors - 26
November
(PG) France, Dir Jean Becker
with Jacques Villeret, Jacques
Gamblin, André Dussollier, Michel
Serrault, Isabelle Carré

© **Films Christian**
Fechner/UGCF/France 2
Cinéma/UGC Images/Rhône Alpes
Cinéma/K.J.B.Production
Christian Fechner presents a
UGC/Fechner production with the
participation of soficas Sofinergie 4
& Sofinergie 5/Region Rhône
Alpes/Centre National de la
Cinématographie/Canal+
115 minutes 10 seconds
subtitles
Anamorphic [Panavision]
S&S December 1999 p38

ENTRAPMENT
20th Century Fox (UK) - 2 July
(12) USA/Germany, Dir Jon Amiel
with Sean Connery, Catherine Zeta-
Jones, Ving Rhames, Will Patton,
Maury Chaykin
© **Twentieth Century Fox Film**
Corporation/Monarchy Enterprises
B.V. and Regency Entertainment
(USA), Inc
Twentieth Century Fox and
Regency Enterprises present a
Fountainbridge Films and a
Michael Hertzberg production in
association with Taurus Film
112 minutes 51 seconds
S&S July 1999 p41

ETERNITY AND A DAY
Artificial Eye Film Company - 14
May
(PG) Greece/France/Italy/Germany,
Dir Theo Angelopoulos
with Vassilis Seimenis, Bruno Ganz,
Fabrizio Bentivoglio, Isabelle
Renauld, Ahilleas Skevis
© **Theo Angelopoulos**
Theo Angelopoulos/Eric
Heumann/Giorgio
Silvagni/Amedeo Pagani and the
Elliniko Kentro Kinimatographou
present a Theo
Angelopoulos/E.K.K./ETI/Paradis
Films Srl/Intermedias S.A./La Sept
Cinéma production with the
assistance of Canal+/Classic
Srl/Istituto Luce and with W.D.R.
and Arte with the support of
Eurimages
132 minutes 57 seconds
subtitles
S&S June 1999 p44

EXISTENZ
Alliance Releasing (UK) - 30 April
(15) Canada/UK, Dir David
Cronenberg
with Jennifer Jason Leigh, Jude Law,
Ian Holm, Don McKellar, Callum
Keith Rennie

© Screenventures XXIV
Productions Ltd, an Alliance
Atlantis company and Existence
Productions Limited
Alliance Atlantis and Serendipity
Point Films present in association
with Natural Nylon a Robert
Lantos production, produced with
the participation of Telefilm
Canada/Canadian Television Fund,
created by the Government of
Canada and the Canadian Cable
Industry CTF: License Fee
program/the Canadian film or
Video Production Tax Credit/the
Movie Network and the Harold
Greenberg Fund/le Fonds Harold
Greenberg
96 minutes 51 seconds
S&S May 1999 p46

EYE OF GOD
Feature Film Company - shown as
part of the 'American
Independence' tour from 12 March
US, Dir Tom Blake Nelson
with Martha Plimpton, Kevin
Anderson, Hal Holbrook, Nick Stahl,
Richard Jenkins
Minnow Pictures, Cyclone Film
84 minutes
No S&S reference

EYES WIDE SHUT
**Warner Bros. Distributors (UK) -
10 September**
USA/UK, Dir Stanley Kubrick
with Tom Cruise, Nicole Kidman,
Sydney Pollack, Marie Richardson,
Rade Sherbedgia
© **Warner Bros.**
**Warner Bros. presents a Pole Star
production made by Hobby Films
Ltd**
158 minutes 48 seconds
S&S September 1999 p45

The FACULTY
**Buena Vista International (UK) - 9
April**
(15) USA, Dir Robert Rodriguez
with Jordana Brewster, Clea Duvall,
Laura Harris, Josh Hartnett, Shawn
Hatosy
© **Miramax Film Corp.**
**Dimension Films presents a Los
Hooligans production**
104 minutes 7 seconds
S&S April 1999 p41

FANNY & ELVIS
**United International Pictures (UK)
Ltd - 19 November**
(15) UK/France, Dir Kay Mellor
with Kerry Fox, Ray Winstone, Ben

Daniels, David Morrissey, Jennifer
Saunders
© **Scala (Fanny) Limited/The Film
Consortium Limited/IMA Films SA
Production finance arranged
through Cofiloisirs S.A.**
110 minutes
S&S December 1999 p45

FANTASIA 2000
**Buena Vista International (UK) -
31 December (IMAX version)**
(U) USA, Dir Pixote Hunt, Hendel
Butoy, Eric Goldberg, James Algar,
Francis Glebas, Gaĩtan Brizzi, Don
Hahn
with hosts Steve Martin, Itzhak
Perlman, Quincy Jones, Bette Midler,
James Earl Jones, Penn & Teller,
James Levine, Angela Lansbury
© **Disney Enterprises, Inc
Walt Disney Pictures**
74 minutes 32 seconds
IMAX
S&S June 2000 p41

FELICEÉ FELICEÉ
**ICA - shown at the ICA on 24
September**
(not submitted) Netherlands, Dir
Peter Delpeut
with Johan Leysen, Toshie Ogura,
Rina Yasima, Noriko Sasaki, Kumi
Nakamura
Ariel Film/KRO
99 minutes
No S&S reference

FELICIA'S JOURNEY
Icon Film Distribution - 8 October
(12) UK/Canada, Dir Atom Egoyan
with Bob Hoskins, Elaine Cassidy,
Claire Benedict, Brid Brennan, Peter
McDonald
© **Marquis Films
Limited/Screenventures XLIII
Productions Limited, an Alliance
Atlantis company
A co-production between Marquis
Films Limited and Alliance Atlantis
Icon Entertainment International
presents an Icon production in
association with Alliance Atlantis
pictures produced with the
participation of The Movie
Network TMN/CAVCO,
production financing provided by
Newmarket Capital Group, L.P.**
115 minutes 54 seconds
Anamorphic [Panavision]
S&S October 1999 p44

FESTEN
Blue Light - 5 March
(15) Denmark, Dir Thomas

Vinterberg
with Ulrich Thomsen, Henning
Moritzen, Thomas Bo Larsen,
Paprika Steen, Birthe Neumann
© **Nimbus Film ApS
Nimbus Film presents a Nimbus
Film production in collaboration
with DR TV with support from
Nordisk Film & TV-Fond**
105 minutes 38 seconds
subtitles
S&S March 1999 p39

54
**Buena Vista International (UK) -
22 January**
(15) USA, Dir Mark Christopher
with Ryan Phillipe, Salma Hayek,
Sela Ward, Breckin Meyer, Sherry
Stringfield
© **Miramax Film Corp
Miramax presents a Redeemable
Features/Dollface/FilmColony
production**
93 minutes 12 seconds
S&S February 1999 p42

FIGHT CLUB
**20th Century Fox (UK) - 12
November**
(18) USA/Germany, Dir David
Fincher
with Brad Pitt, Edward Norton,
Helena Bonham Carter, Meat Loaf
Aday, Jared Leto
© **Twentieth Century Fox Film
Corporation/Monarchy Enterprises
B.V./Regency Entertainment (USA)
Inc
Fox 2000 Pictures and Regency
Enterprises present a Linson Films
production in association with
Taurus Film**
138 minutes 56 seconds
Super 35 [2.35:1]
S&S December 1999 p45

FINAL CUT
Downtown Pictures - 1 October
(18) UK, Dir Dominic Anciano and
Ray Burdis
with Ray Winstone, Jude Law, Sadie
Frost, Holly Davidson, John Beckett
© **Segma Limited
Fugitive Features presents**
92 minutes 50 seconds
S&S September 1999 p45

FIN AOûT, DÉBUT SEPTEMBRE/LATE AUGUST, EARLY SEPTEMBER
Artificial Eye Film Company - 20
August
(15) France, Dir Olivier Assayas

with Mathieu Amalric, Virginie Ledoyen, François Cluzet, Jeanne Balibar, Alex Descas
© Dacia Films/Cinéa
Dacia Films and Cinéa present with the participation of Canal+/Centre National de la Cinématographie/soficas Sofinergie & Sofygram
111 minutes 12 seconds
subtitles
S&S September 1999 p48

FINDING NORTH
Millivres Multimedia - 11 June
(15) USA, Dir Tanya Wexler
with Wendy Makkena, John Benjamin Hickey, Anne Bobby, Rebecca Creskoff, Angela Pietropinto
© SoNo Pictures, Inc
SoNo Pictures, Inc. presents a film by Tanya Wexler
94 minutes 40 seconds
S&S June 1999 p45

The FIVE SENSES
Alliance Releasing (UK) - 10 December
(15) Canada, Dir Jeremy Podeswa
with Mary Louise Parker, Pascale Bussières, Richard Clarkin, Brendan Fletcher, Marco Leonardi
© Five Senses Productions, Inc.
Alliance Atlantis presents a Five Senses production in association with Alliance Atlantis Pictures, produced with the participation of Telefilm Canada/the Canadian Television Fund/the Harold Greenberg Fund/TMN - The Movie Network/Viewer's Choice Canada, produced in association with Canadian Broadcasting Corporation, produced with the assistance of the Canadian Film or Video Production Tax Credit, developed with the assistance of the Sundance Institute/Canada Council for the Arts: Media Arts
104 minutes 52 seconds
S&S January 2000 p49

FOLLOWING
Alliance Releasing (UK) - 5 November
(15) UK, Dir Christopher Nolan
with Jeremy Theobald, Alex Haw, Lucy Russell, John Nolan, Dick Bradsell
© Christopher Nolan
A Syncopy Films production Next Wave Films
69 minutes 48 seconds
black & white
S&S December 1999 p47

FOOD OF LOVE
FilmFour Distribution - 22 October
(15) UK/France, Dir Stephen Poliakoff
with Richard E. Grant, Nathalie Baye, Joe McGann, Juliet Aubrey, Lorcan Cranitch
© Channel Four Television Corporation/MP Productions
Channel Four Films presents in association with the Arts Council of England and MP Productions with the support of Canal+ an Intrinsica Films production supported by the National Lottery through the Arts Council of England
108 minutes 51 seconds
S&S December 1999 p47

FORCES OF NATURE
United International Pictures (UK) Ltd - 7 May
(12) USA, Dir Bronwen Hughes
with Sandra Bullock, Ben Affleck, Maura Tierney, Steve Zahn, Blythe Danner
© DreamWorks LLC
DreamWorks Pictures presents a Roth/Arnold production
106 minutes 5 seconds
S&S May 1999 p47

4 LITTLE GIRLS
Feature Film Company - shown as part of the 'American Independence' tour from 12 March
US, Dir Spike Lee
Home Box Office, 40 Acres and a Mule Filmworks
102 minutes
No S&S reference

GAIR
Venus - 12 November
India, Dir Ashok Gaikwad
with Ajay Devgan, Raveena Tandon, Amrish Puri, Reena Roy, Ajinkya Deo
Prakash Chitralaya
No S&S reference

The GENERAL'S DAUGHTER
United International Pictures (UK) Ltd - 17 September
(18) USA/Germany, Dir Simon West
with John Travolta, Madeleine Stowe, James Cromwell, Timothy Hutton, Clarence Williams III
© Paramount Pictures
Paramount Pictures presents a Mace Neufeld and Robert Rehme production, a Jonathan D.Krane production in association with MFP Munich Film Partners GmbH

& Co 1 Produktions KG
116 minutes 27 seconds
Anamorphic [Panavision]
S&S October 1999 p44

*GET CARTER
BFI Collections - 11 June [NFT First Run 11-24 June]
(18) UK, Dir Mike Hodges
with Michael Caine, Britt Ekland, John Osborne, Ian Hendry, Bryan Mosley
Metro-Goldwyn-Mayer
112 minutes
MFB April 1971 p73

GET REAL
United International Pictures (UK) Ltd - 14 May
(15) UK/South Africa, Dir Simon Shore
with Ben Silverstone, Brad Gorton, Charlotte Brittain, Stacy A. Hart, Kate McEnery
© Graphite Films (Get Real) Ltd & Distant Horizon Ltd
Distant Horizon presents a Graphite Film with the participation of British Screen and the Arts Council of England supported by the National Lottery through the Arts Council of England, receipts collected & distributed by National Film Trustee Company Ltd, a Graphite Films production
S&S May 1999 p48

GIRL
Feature Film Company - 24 September
(15) USA, Dir Jonathan Kahn
with Dominique Swain, Sean Patrick Flanery, Summer Phoenix, Tara Reid, Selma Blair
© The Kusner-Locke Company
The Kusner-Locke Company presents an HSX films, Muse/Jeff Most/Brad Wyman production
99 minutes 32 seconds
S&S August 1999 p43

GLORIA
Entertainment Film Distributors Ltd - 18 June
(15) USA, Dir Sidney Lumet
with Sharon Stone, Jeremy Northam, Cathy Moriarty, Jean-Luke Figueroa, Mike Starr
© Mandalay Entertainment
Mandalay Entertainment presents an Eagle Point production
107 minutes 45 seconds
S&S August 1999 p44

GO

Columbia Tristar Films (UK) - 3 September
(18) USA, Dir Doug Liman
with Desmond Askew, Taye Diggs, William Fichtner, J.E.Freeman, Katie Holmes
© Columbia Pictures Industries, Inc
Columbia Pictures presents a Banner Entertainment production in association with Saratoga Entertainment
101 minutes 47 seconds
S&S September 1999 p46

GODMOTHER

Yash Raj - 8 October
India, Dir Vinay Shukla
with Shabana Azmi, Milind Gunaji, Nirmal Pandey, Raima Dev Sen, Ashwin Kumar
Gramophone Company of India
124 minutes
No S&S reference

GODS AND MONSTERS

Downtown Pictures - 26 March
(15) USA/UK, Dir Bill Condon
with Ian McKellen, Brendan Fraser, Lynn Redgrave, Lolita Davidovich, David Dukes
© Spike Productions Inc.
Flashpoint presents in association with BBC Films a Regent Entertainment production in association with Gregg Fienberg, produced in association with BBC Films
105 minutes 14 seconds
S&S April 1999 p42

GOODBYE LOVER

Warner Bros Distributors (UK) - 6 August
(15) USA/Germany, Dir Roland Joffé
with Patricia Arquette, Dermot Mulroney, Ellen DeGeneres, Mary-Louise Parker, Don Johnson
© Monarchy Enterprises B.V. and Regency Entertainment (USA), Inc
Regency Enterprises presents an Arnon Milchan/Gotham Entertainment Group/Lightmotive production in association with Taurus Film
100 minutes 54 seconds
Super 35
S&S October 1999 p45

G:MT GREENWICH MEAN TIME

Icon Film Distribution - 1 October
(18) UK, Dir John Strickland
with Alec Newman, Melanie Gutteridge, Georgia MacKenzie,
Chiwetel Ejiofor, Steve John Shepherd
© Anvil/GMT Films Ltd
Icon Entertainment International presents an Anvil Films production
117 minutes 37 seconds
S&S October 1999 p46

GREGORY'S TWO GIRLS

FilmFour Distributors - 15 October
(15) UK/Germany, Dir Bill Forsyth
with John Gordon-Sinclair, Dougray Scott, Maria Doyle Kennedy, Kevin Anderson, Martin Schwab
© FilmFour Ltd
FilmFour in association with the Scottish Arts Council National Lottery Fund and Kinowelt Filmproduktion present a Young Lake production for FilmFour
116 minutes 9 seconds
S&S December 1999 p48

GUEST HOUSE PARADISO

United International Pictures (UK) Ltd - 3 December
(15) UK, Dir Adrian Edmondson
with Rik Mayall, Adrian Edmondson, Vincent Cassel, Hélène Mahieu, Bill Nighy
© Vision Video Limited
Universal Pictures presents a Phil Mcintyre production
89 minutes 49 seconds
Anamorphic [Arriscope]
S&S January 2000 p50

GÜNESE YOLCULUK/JOURNEY TO THE SUN

Celluloid Dreams - 15 October [NFT First Run 15-21 October]
(not submitted)
Turkey/Netherlands/Germany, Dir Yesim Ustaoglu
with Nazmi Qirix, Newroz Bas, Mizgin Kapazan, Ara Güler, Berceste Akgün
© Istisnai Filmer/Film Company/Medias Res
Presented by Istisnai Filmer in association with Film Company/Medias Res in collaboration with Zweites Deutsches Fernsehen/Arte Deutschland supported by Fonds Eurimages du Conseil de l'Europe with the financial support of Filmfonds Rotterdam with the contribution of Montecinemaverità Foundation/United Colors of Benetton/Fabrica/Mediterranean Film Festival of Montpelier/EKD
105 minutes
No S&S reference

*Der HÄNDLER DER VIER JAHRESZEITEN/The MERCHANT OF FOUR SEASONS

BFI Collections - 22 January [NFT First Run 22-28 January]
(18) Germany, Dir Rainer Werner Fassbinder
with Hans Hirschmüller, Irm Hermann, Hanna Schygulla, Klaus Löwitsch, Karl Scheydt
Tango-Film (Munich)
89 minutes
MFB August 1975 p175

HAPPINESS

Entertainment Film Distributors Ltd - 16 April
(18) USA, Dir Todd Solondz
with Jane Adams, Elizabeth Ashley, Dylan Baker, Lara Flynn Boyle, Ben Gazzara
© October Films, Inc. and Livingston Pictures, Inc.
October Films presents a Good Machine/Killer Films production
139 minutes 9 seconds
S&S April 1999 p44

HAPPY TEXAS

Buena Vista International (UK) - 3 December
(12) USA, Dir Mark Illsley
with Jeremy Northam, Steve Zahn, Ally Walker, Illeana Douglas, William H. Macy
© Happy Texas Investors, LLC
Miramax International presents in association with Marked Entertainment an Illsley/Stone production
98 minutes 35 seconds
S&S January 2000 p51

HASARDS OU COÏNCIDENCES/CHANCE OR COINCIDENCE

Gala Film Distributors - 6 August [NFT First Run 6-19 August]
(PG) France/Canada, Dir Claude Lelouch
with Alessandra Martines, Pierre Arditi, Marc Hollogne, Laurent Hilaire, Véronique Moreau
© Les Films 13/TF1 Films Productions/SDA Productions/UGC Images/Neuilly Productions/FCC
Les Films 13 present a Les Films 13/TF1 Films Production/UGC Images/Neuilly Productions/SDA Productions co-production with the support of FCC and sofica Sofinergie 4 and the participation

of Canal+ Québec and Canada sequences produced by SDA Productions Inc with the participation of Téléfilm Canada/SODEC Société de développement des entreprises culturelles/Gouvernement du Québec (programme de crédits d'impôt du Québec)/ Gouvernement du Canada (programme de crédits d'impôt pour production cinématographique ou magnétoscopique Canadienne)/Le Bureau du Cinéma et de la Télévision de la Ville de Montréal
121 minutes 22 seconds
subtitles
S&S June 1999 p39

HASEENA MAAN JAYEGI
Eros Video (Electronics) Ltd - 25 June
India, Dir David Dhawan
with Sanjay Dutt, Govinda, Kader Khan, Karishma Kapoor, Pooja Batra
Rahul Productions
No S&S reference

The HAUNTING
United International Pictures (UK) Ltd - 24 September
(12) USA, Dir Jan De Bont
with Liam Neeson, Catherine Zeta-Jones, Owen Wilson, Lili Taylor, Bruce Dern
© Dream Works LLC
Dream Works Pictures presents a Roth/Arnold production
112 minutes 44 seconds
Anamorphic [Panavision]
S&S November 1999 p44

HEAD ON
Millivres Multimedia - 15 October
(18) Australia, Dir Ana Kokkinos
with Alex Dimitriades, Paul Capsis, Julian Garner, Elena Mandalis, Tony Nikolakopoulos
© Australian Film Finance Corporation Limited/Head On Productions Pty Ltd/Film Victoria
Australian Film Finance Corporation presents a Great Scott production developed and produced with the assistance of Film Victoria
104 minutes 28 seconds
some subtitles
S&S November 1999 p46

HEART
Feature Film Company - 11 June
(18) UK, Dir Charles McDougall
with Christopher Eccleston, Saskia Reeves, Kate Hardie, Rhys Ifans, Anna Chancellor
© Granada Film
Granada in association with The Merseyside Film Production Fund presents a Granada Film production
84 minutes 51 seconds
S&S June 1999 p46

HELLO BROTHER
IFD - 10 September
India, Dir Sohail Khan
with Salman Khan, Arbaz Khan, Rani Mukherjee, Neeraj Vohra, Razak Khan
G.S. Entertainment
No S&S reference

HIDEOUS KINKY
United International Pictures (UK) Ltd - 5 February
(15) UK/France, Dir Gillies MacKinnon
with Kate Winslet, Saïd Taghmaoui, Bella Riza, Carrie Mullan, Pierre Clémenti
© The Film Consortium/L Films
The Film Consortium and BBC Films present in association with The Arts Council of England a Greenpoint film, co-produced with L Films and AMLF, developed with the assistance of BBC Films/Greenpoint Films and with the support of the European Script Fund, supported by the National Lottery through the Arts Council of England
98 minutes 53 seconds
S&S February 1999 p43

HIGH ART
Blue Light - 9 April
(18) USA, Dir Lisa Cholodenko
with Ally Sheedy, Radha Mitchell, Tammy Grimes, Patricia Clarkson, Gabriel Mann
© High Art Pictures, LLC
October Films presents in association with 391 a Dolly Hall production
101 minutes 39 seconds
S&S April 1999 p45

HILARY AND JACKIE
FilmFour Distributors - 22 January
(15) UK, Dir Anand Tucker
with Emily Watson, Rachel Griffiths, James Frain, David Morrissey, Charles Dance
© Intermedia Film Equities Limited and FilmFour Ltd
FilmFour and Intermedia Films
present with the participation of British Screen and the Arts Council of England an Oxford Film Company production, supported by the National Lottery Through the Arts Council of England, developed with the support of the European Script Fund, developed in association with the BBC
122 minutes 10 seconds
S&S February 1999 p44

The HI-LO COUNTRY
PolyGram Filmed Entertainment - 23 July
(15) UK/USA, Dir Stephen Frears
with Woody Harrelson, Billy Crudup, Patricia Arquette, Cole Hauser, Penelope Cruz
© PolyGram Filmproduktion GmbH
PolyGram Filmed Entertainment presents in association with Martin Scorsese a Working Title production with Cappa/De Fina productions
114 minutes 25 seconds
S&S August 1999 p44

HINDUSTAN KI KASAM
Eros Video (Electronics) Ltd - 23 July
India, Dir Veeru Devgan
with Amitabh Bachchan, Ajay Devgan, Manisha Koirala, Sushmita Sen, Prem Chopra
Devgan Films
No S&S reference

HISTOIRE D'O/GESCHICHTE DER O/The STORY OF O
Arrow Film Distributors Ltd - 5 November
(not submitted) France/Germany, Dir Just Jaeckin
with Corinne Cléry, Udo Kier, Anthony Steel, Jean Gaven, Christian Minazzoli
© S.N.Prodis Paris
Gérard Lorin - S.N.Prodis, Eric Rochat - Yang Films present a co-production of S.N.Prodis/Yang Films/A.D.Création/Terra Filmkunst GmbH
106 minutes
S&S December 1999 p57

HOGI PYAR KI JEET
Monohill - 7 May
India, Dir P. Vasu
with Arshad Warsi, Mayuri Kango, Ajay Devgan, Neha, Prithvi
Shweta Arts International
No S&S reference

HOLD BACK THE NIGHT
United International Pictures (UK)
Ltd - 17 December
(15) UK/Italy, Dir Phil Davis
with Christine Tremarco, Stuart
Sinclair Blyth, Sheila Hancock,
Richard Platt, Julie Ann Watson
© The Film Consortium Ltd
The Film Consortium and Film on
Four present in association with
the Arts Council of England/BIM
and WavePictures a Parallax
Picture supported by the National
Lottery through the Arts Council
of England, developed by Sarah
McCarthy with Swingbridge Video
and Parallax Pictures Ltd, with the
support of the Film Consortium
Limited and the National Lottery
103 minutes 52 seconds
S&S January 2000 p52

HOLY MAN
Buena Vista International (UK) -
19 February
(PG) USA, Dir Stephen Herek
with Eddie Murphy, Jeff Goldblum,
Kelly Preston, Robert Loggia, Jon
Cryer, Eric McCormack
© Touchstone Pictures
Touchstone Pictures presents in
association with Caravan Pictures
a Roger Birnbaum production
113 minutes 36 seconds
S&S March 1999 p40

*Un HOMME ET UNE FEMME/A MAN AND A WOMAN
Gala Film Distributors - 29
January
(PG) France, Dir Claude Lelouch
with Anouk Aimée, Jean-Louis
Trintignant, Pierre Barouh, Valérie
Lagrange, Simone Paris
Films 13, Paris
102 minutes
MFB March 1967 p42

The HONEST COURTESAN
20th Century Fox (UK) - 30 April
(15) USA, Dir Marshall Herskovitz
with Catherine McCormack, Rufus
Sewell, Oliver Platt, Moira Kelly,
Fred Ward
© Monarchy Enterprises B.V. and
Regency Entertainment (USA) Inc
Regency Enterprises presents an
Arnon Milchan/Bedford Falls
production
111 minutes 49 seconds
Super 35
[US release title: DANGEROUS
BEAUTY]
S&S May 1999 p48

HOTE HOTE PYAAR HO GAYA
Eros Video (Electronics) Ltd -2
July
India, Dir Feroze Irani and Adi Irani
with Jackie Shroff, Kajol, Atul
Agnihotri, Ayesha Julka, Aruna Irani
Inega International
No S&S reference

*Hô TEL DU NORD
Gala Film Distributors - 12
February
(PG) France, Dir Marcel Carné
with Annabella, Arletty, Louis
Jouvet, Jean-Pierre Aumont, Jeanne
Marken
Impérial Film
96 minutes 27 seconds
black and white
subtitles
S&S March 1999 p41
MFB June 1939 p119

HOW STELLA GOT HER GROOVE BACK
20th Century Fox (UK) - 5
February
(15) USA, Dir Kevin Rodney
Sullivan
with Angela Bassett, Whoopi
Goldberg, Regina King, Suzzanne
Douglas, Taye Diggs
© Twentieth Century Fox Film
Corporation
Twentieth Century Fox presents a
Deborah Schindler production
124 minutes 30 seconds
S&S February 1999 p45

HUM AAPKE DIL MEIN REHTE HAIN
Eros Video (Electronics) Ltd - 15
January
India, Dir Satish Kaushik
with Anil Kapoor, Kajol, Anupam
Kher, Parmeet Sethi, Sudha
Chandran
Suresh Productions
No S&S reference

HUMAN TRAFFIC
Metrodome Distribution Ltd - 4
June
(18) UK/Ireland, Dir Justin Kerrigan
with John Simm, Lorraine Pilkington,
Shaun Parkes, Danny Dyer, Nicola
Reynolds
© Fruit Salad Films Ltd
Metrodome/Irish Screen presents a
Fruit Salad Films production of a
Justin Kerrigan film
99 minutes 21 seconds
S&S June 1999 p46

HUM DIL DE CHUKE SANAM
Blue Star - 18 June
India, Dir Sanjay Leela Bhansali
with Salman Khan, Aishwarya Rai,
Ajay Devgan, Zohra Segal, Vikram
Gokhale
Bhansali Productions
187 minutes
No S&S reference

HUM SAATH-SAATH HAIN
Eros Video (Electronics) Ltd - 5
November
India, Dir Sooraj Barjatya
with Salman Khan, Karishma
Kapoor, Saif Ali Khan, Tabu, Sonali
Bendre
Rajshri Pictures
No S&S reference

HUM TUM PE MARTE HAIN
Blue Star - 24 September
India, Dir Navkumar Raju
with Govinda, Urmila Matondkar,
Dimple Kapadia, Paresh Rawal,
Nirmal Pandey
C.Y. Films
No S&S reference

An IDEAL HUSBAND
Pathé Distribution - 16 April
(PG) UK/USA, Dir Oliver Parker
with Cate Blanchett, Minnie Driver,
Rupert Everett, Julianne Moore,
Jeremy Northam
© The Ideal Film Company Ltd
Icon Entertainment International
and Pathé Pictures in association
with the Arts Council of England
present a Fragile Film in
assocation with Icon Productions
and Miramax Films supported by
the National Lottery through the
Arts Council of England
97 minutes 43 seconds
S&S May 1999 p49

IDIOTERNE/IDIOTS
Metro Tartan Distributors - 14
May
(18)
Denmark/France/Italy/Netherlands/G
ermany/Sweden, Dir Lars von Trier
[uncredited]
with Bodil Jørgensen, Jens Albinus,
Anne Louise Hassing, Troels Lyby,
Nikolaj Lie Kaas
© Zentropa Entertainments2 ApS
and La Sept Cinéma
Produced by Zentropa
Entertaiments2 ApS and DR TV in
co-production with Liberator

Productions, S.a.r.l./La Sept
Cinéma/Argus Film
Produktie/VPRO Television,
Holland/ZDF-ARTE with the
support of Nordic Film and
Television Fund/CoBO Fund,
Holland in collaboration with SVT
Drama/Canal+ (France)/RAI
Cinema Fiction/3 Emme
Cinematografica
subtitles
S&S May 1999 p50

IDLE HANDS
**Columbia Tristar Films (UK) - 5
November**
(18) USA/Germany, Dir Rodman
Flender
with Devon Sawa, Seth Green, Elden
Henson, Jessica Alba, Steve Van
Wormer
© **Global Entertainment
Productions GmbH & Co. Medien
KG**
**Columbia Pictures presents a
Licht/Mueller Film
Corporation/Team Todd
production**
92 minutes 1 second
S&S June 2000 p45

The IMPOSTORS
20th Century Fox (UK) - 21 May
(15) USA, Dir Stanley Tucci
with Stanley Tucci, Oliver Platt,
Teagle F. Bougere, Elizabeth Bracco,
Steve Buscemi
© **Twentieth Century Fox Film
Corporation**
**Fox Searchlight presents a First
Cold Press production**
100 minutes 32 seconds
S&S January 1999 p47

IN DREAMS
**United International Pictures (UK)
Ltd - 30 April**
(18) USA, Dir Neil Jordan
with Annette Bening, Katie Sagona,
Aidan Quinn, Robert Downey Jr,
Stephen Rea
© **DreamWorks LLC and Amblin
Entertainment, Inc**
**A DreamWorks Pictures
presentation**
99 minutes 35 seconds
Super 35
S&S May 1999 p50

INSPECTOR GADGET
**Buena Vista International (UK) -
17 December**
(U) USA, Dir David Kellogg
with Matthew Broderick, Rupert
Everett, Joely Fisher, Michelle

Trachtenberg, Andy Dick
© **Disney Enterprises, Inc.**
**Walt Disney Pictures presents in
association with Caravan Pictures**
78 minutes 16 seconds
S&S January 2000 p52

INSTINCT
**Buena Vista International (UK) -
17 September**
(15) USA, Dir Jon Turteltaub
with Anthony Hopkins, Cuba
Gooding Jr, Donald Sutherland,
Maura Tierney, George Dzundza
© **Spyglass Entertainment Group,
L.P.**
**A Touchstone Pictures/Spyglass
Entertainment presentation**
123 minutes 46 seconds
Anamorphic [Panavision]
S&S October 1999 p47

INTERNATIONAL KHILADI
**Eros Video (Electronics) Ltd - 26
March**
India, Dir Umesh Mehra
with Akshay Kumar, Twinkle
Khanna, Rajat Bedi, Vivek Shauq,
Gulshan Grover
D.M.S. Films
No S&S reference

The IRON GIANT
**Warner Bros Distributors (UK) -
17 December**
(U) USA, Dir Brad Bird
with the character voices of Jennifer
Aniston, Harry Connick Jr, Vin
Diesel, James Gammon, Cloris
Leachman
© **Warner Bros**
**Warner Bros presents a Brad Bird
film**
86 minutes 31 seconds
S&S January 2000 p54

I STILL KNOW WHAT YOU DID LAST SUMMER
**Columbia Tristar Films (UK) - 7
May**
(18) USA/Germany, Dir Danny
Cannon
with Jennifer Love Hewitt, Freddie
Prinze Jr, Brandy, Mekhi Phifer,
Muse Watson
© **Global Entertainment
Productions GmbH & Co Medien
KG**
**Columbia Pictures presents in
association with Mandalay
Entertainment a Neal H. Moritz
production**
100 minutes 26 seconds
S&S May 1999 p51

*The ITALIAN JOB
**United International Pictures (UK)
Ltd - 10 September**
(PG) UK, Dir Peter Collinson
with Michael Caine, Noîl Coward,
Benny Hill, Raf Vallone, Tony
Beckley
**Paramount Pictures/Oakhurst
Productions**
99 minutes 20 seconds
MFB July 1969 p147

I THINK I DO
**Millivres Multimedia - 12
February**
(15) USA, Dir Brian Sloan
with Alexis Arquette, Guillermo
Diaz, Jamie Harrold, Christian
Maelen, Marni Nixon
© **I Think I Do LLC**
**Strand Releasing presents in
association with Robert
Miller/House of Pain Productions
& Danger Filmworks/Sauce
Entertainment & Daryl Roth
Productions a Lane Janger
production**
93 minutes 56 seconds
S&S April 1999 p45

JACK FROST
**Warner Bros Distributors (UK) -
12 February**
(PG) USA, Dir Troy Miller
with Michael Keaton, Kelly Preston,
Mark Addy, Joseph Cross, Andy
Lawrence
© **Warner Bros.**
**Warner Bros. presents an Azoff
Entertainment/Canton Company
production**
101 minutes 12 seconds
S&S March 1999 p44

JAKOB THE LIAR
**Columbia Tristar Films (UK) - 5
November**
(12) USA, Dir Peter Kassovitz
with Robin Williams, Alan Arkin,
Bob Balaban, Hannah Taylor
Gordon, Michael Jeter
© **Global Entertainment
Productions GmbH & Co., Film
KG**
**Columbia Pictures presents a Blue
Wolf Productions with Kasso Inc.
production**
119 minutes 57 seconds
S&S December 1999 p48

JAANAM SAMJHA KARO
Shernwali - 2 April
India, Dir Andalib Sultanpuri
with Salman Khan, Urmila
Matondkar, Monica Bedi, Shakti

Kapoor, Sadashiv Amrapurkar
Karishma Movies
No S&S reference

JAANWAR
Yash Raj - 24 December
India, Dir Suneel Darshan
with Akshay Kumar, Karishma
Kapoor, Ashish Vidyarthi, Malay
Chakraborty, Ashutosh Rana
Shree Krishna International
No S&S reference

*JEAN DE FLORETTE
Pathé Distribution - 4 June
(PG) France/Italy/Switzerland, Dir
Claude Berri
with Yves Montand, Gérard
Depardieu, Daniel Auteuil, Elisabeth
Depardieu, Margarita Lozano
**Renn Productions, Films A2,
Raidue, D.D. Films, Antenne 2,
Télévision Suisse Romande with
the participation of Centre
National de la Cinématograph,
Ministère Français de la Culture**
121 minutes
MFB July 1987 p208

JENSEITS DER STILLE/BEYOND SILENCE
Gala Film Distributors - 2 April
(12) Germany/Switzerland, Dir
Caroline Link
with Sylvie Testud, Howie Seago,
Emmanuelle Laborit, Sibylle
Canonica, Matthias Habich
**© Claussen-Wöbke
Filmproduktion GmbH/Roxy Film
GmbH & Co. KG - Luggi
Waldleitner
Bavaria Film International/Buena
Vista International presents a
Claussen-Wöbke Filmproduktion
and Roxy Film - Luggi Waldleitner
production co-produced by
Bayerischer
Rundfunk/Süddeutscher
Rundfunk/Arte/Schweizer
Fernsehen - DRS, supported by
Bayerischen Landesanstalt für
Aufbaufinanzierung,
LfA/Filmboard Berlin-
Brandenburg
GmbH/Bundesministerium des
Innern, BMI**
113 minutes 3 seconds
subtitles
S&S May 1999 p40

JULIE AND THE CADILLACS
Capricorn Communications Ltd -
20 August
(PG) UK, Dir Bryan Izzard

with Toyah Willcox, Victor Spinetti,
Peter Polycarpou, Thora Hird, James
Grout
**© Parker Mead Productions
Limited
A Parker Mead production**
106 minutes 40 seconds
S&S October 1999 p48

JUST THE TICKET
First Independent Films Ltd - 18
June
(15) USA, Dir Richard Wenk
with Andy Garcia, Andie
MacDowell, Richard Bradford,
Elizabeth Ashley, Fred Asparagus
**© CineSon Productions, Inc
From United Artists**
115 minutes 12 seconds
S&S June 1999 p47

KARTOOS
Shernwali - 7 May
India, Dir Mahesh Bhatt
with Jackie Shroff, Sanjay Dutt,
Manisha Koirala, Gulshan Grover,
Jaspal Bhatti
Base Industries Group
No S&S reference

*KES
BFI Collections - 1 October [NFT
First Run 1-7 October]
(PG) UK, Dir Ken Loach
with David Bradley, Freddie Fletcher,
Lynne Perrie, Colin Welland, Brian
Glover
**Woodfall Film Productions/Kestrel
Films**
113 minutes
MFB April 1970 p74

KHOOBSOORAT
Blue Star - 26 November
India, Dir Sanjay Chhel
with Sanjay Dutt, Urmila Matondkar,
Farida Jalal, Om Puri, Anjan
Srivastava
Friends India
No S&S reference

A KIND OF HUSH
Metrodome Distribution Ltd - 10
September
(15) UK, Dir Brian Stirner
with Harley Smith, Marcella
Plunkett, Nathan Constance, Ben
Roberts, Paul Williams
**© A Kind of Hush Limited
A First Film Company production
with the participation of British
Screen in association with the Arts
Council of England, developed with
the support of Tim White Film
Productions Ltd and with the**

assistance of British Screen
Finance Limited, supported by the
National Lottery through the Arts
Council of England
95 minutes 21 seconds
S&S October 1999 p49

The KING AND I
Warner Bros Distributors (UK) -
28 May
(U) USA, Dir Richard Rich
with the character voices of Miranda
Richardson, Christiane Noll, Martin
Vidnovic, Ian Richardson, Darrell
Hammond
**© Morgan Creek Productions, Inc
James G. Robinson presents a
Morgan Creek production in
association with Rankin/Bass
Productions and Nest
Entertainment**
88 minutes 36 seconds
S&S July 1999 p42

KINI & ADAMS
The Sales Company - 5 March
[NFT First Run 5-11 March]
(not submitted)
France/UK/Zimbabwe/Switzerland/B
urkina Faso, Dir Idrissa Ouédraogo
with Vusi Kunene, David Mohloki,
Nthati Moshesh, John Kani, Netsayi
Chigwendere
**Presented by Noé Production and
Films de la Plaine, Polar
Productions and Framework
International (Zimbabwe) co-
production with the participation
of European Union, European Co-
Production Fund, Canal+, Films de
l'Avenir, Ministère Français de la
Culture, Ministère Français de la
Coopération, Agence de
Coopération Culturelle, Stanley
Thomas Johnson Stiftung**
93 minutes
No S&S reference

KNOCK OFF
Columbia Tristar Films (UK) - 30
April
(18) USA/Hong Kong, Dir Tsui Hark
with Jean-Claude Van Damme, Rob
Schneider, Lela Rochon, Michael
Fitzgerald Wong, Paul Sorvino
**© TriStar Pictures Industries, Inc.
and Knock Film, A.V.V.
A Knock Films, A.V.V./MDP
Worldwide presentation of a Film
Workshop Company
Ltd/Val'd'Oro Entertainment
production**
Super 35
91 minutes 10 seconds
S&S July 1999 p43

KNOFLÍKÀRI/BUTTONERS
ICA - shown at the ICA on 15 January
(not submitted) Czech Republic, Dir Petr Zelenka
with Pavel Zajícek, Jan Haubert, Seisuke Tsukahara, Motohiro Hosoya, Junzo Inokuchi
© Ceská televize
Ceská televize Cestmir Kopecky Creative Group presents a film by Petr Zelenka and his friends
subtitles
108 minutes
S&S March 1999 p37

KOHRAM
Venus - 13 August
India, Dir Mehul Kumar
with Amitabh Bachchan, Nana Patekar, Jayapradha, Tabu, Danny Denzongpa
Mehul Movies P. Ltd
No S&S reference

*KOYAANISQATSI
Blue Dolphin Film & Video - 23 July
(U) USA, Dir Godfrey Reggio
Institute for Regional Education
86 minutes
MFB August 1983 p217

LAAWARIS
UFDL - 5 March
India, Dir Shreekant Sharma
with Akshaye Khanna, Manisha Koirala, Jackie Shroff, Dimple Kapadia, Govind Namdeo
Lama Productions
No S&S reference

LAL BAADSHAH
Eros Video (Electronics) Ltd - 5 March
India, Dir K.C. Bokadia
with Amitabh Bachchan, Shilpa Shetty, Manisha Koirala, Amrish Puri, Jayapradha
B.M.B. Productions
No S&S reference

The LAST DAYS
Downtown Pictures - 8 October
(PG) USA, Dir Jim Moll
with Irene Zisblatt, Renée Firestone, Alice Lok Cahana, Bill Basch, Congressman Tom Lantos, Dr Randolph Braham, Hans Munch
© Survivors of the Shoah Visual History Foundation
Steven Spielberg and Survivors of the Shoah Visual History Foundation present a Ken Lipper/June Beallor production,
this film was made possible by a generous grant from the Kenneth and Evelyn Lipper Foundation
in colour/black & white
87 minutes 12 seconds
S&S November 1999 p48

LAST NIGHT
FilmFour Distributors - 7 May
(15) Canada/France, Dir Don McKellar
with Don McKellar, Sandra Oh, Callum Keith Rennie, Sarah Polley, David Cronenberg
© Rhombus Media Inc
Rhombus Media presents a Rhombus Media production, produced with the participation of Telefilm Canada in association with La Sept ARTE and the Canadian Broadcasting Corporation, produced in association with Haut et Court with the participation of Canada Television and Cable Production Fund/Telefilm Canada - Equity Investment Program and the Canadian Film or Video Production Tax Credit Program
94 minutes 31 seconds
S&S July 1999 p44

The LAST YELLOW
Metrodome Distribution - 10 December
(15) UK/Germany, Dir Julian Farino
with Mark Addy, Charlie Creed-Miles, Samantha Morton, Kenneth Cranham, Alan Atherall
© Scala (Last Yellow) Ltd/Jolyon Symonds Productions/Hollywood Partners II GmbH
Scala Productions, Capitol Films and Hollywood partners present in association with the Arts Council of England and BBC Films a Scala/Jolyon Symonds production, developed with the support of the MEDIA programme of the European Union supported by the National Lottery through the Arts council of England
93 minutes 31 seconds
S&S January 2000 p55

LA WITHOUT A MAP
United Media - 17 September
(15)
UK/France/Finland/Luxembourg, Dir Mika Kaurismäki
with David Tennant, Vinessa Shaw, Julie Delpy, Vincent Gallo, Cameron Bancroft
© Los Angeles Without a Map Ltd
A Dan Films (London)/Euro
American Films (Paris)/Marianna Films (Helsinki) production in association with the Arts Council of England/Baltic Media/the Yorkshire Media Production Agency/the Finnish Film Foundation with the participation of British Screen and BSkyB, co-produced by CLT-UFA International, developed with the support of the European Script Fund and the Nordic Film & TV Fund, supported by the National Lottery through the Arts Council of England, finance provided by British Screen through its subsidiary the European Co-Production Fund (UK), part-funded by the European Regional Development Fund
107 minutes 4 seconds
Anamorphic [Technovision]
S&S October 1999 p50

La LEGGENDA DEL PIANISTA SULL'OCEANO/The LEGEND OF 1900
Entertainment Film Distributors Ltd - 17 December
(15) Italy, Dir Giuseppe Tornatore
with Tim Roth, Pruitt Taylor Vince, Mélanie Thierry, Bill Nunn, Peter Vaughan
© 1998 Medusa
FineLine Features Medusa Motion Pictures, a Medusa Film presentation produced by Sciarlò s.r.l., a Medusa Film production
c.170 minutes
Anamorphic [Technovision]
S&S January 2000 p56

LEVEL FIVE
ICA - shown at the ICA (London) from 23 April-6 May
(not submitted) France, Dir Chris Marker
with Catherine Belkhodja, Kenji Tokitsu, Nagisa Oshima, Junishi Ushiyama
Films de l'Astrophore/Argos-Films/Sept/Canal Plus
106 minutes
No S&S reference

LIFE
United International Pictures (UK) Ltd - 27 August
(15) USA, Dir Ted Demme
with Eddie Murphy, Martin Lawrence, Obba Babatundé, Ned Beatty, Bernie Mac
© Universal Studios
Universal Pictures and Imagine

Entertainment present a Brian Grazer production
108 minutes 32 seconds
S&S September 1999 p49

The LIMEY
FilmFour Distributors - 10 December
(18) USA, Dir Steven Soderbergh
with Terence Stamp, Lesley Ann Warren, Luis Guzmán, Barry Newman, Joe Dallesandro
© Artisan Pictures, Inc.
Artisan Entertainment presents
88 minutes 51 seconds
S&S January 2000 p57

LITTLE VOICE
Buena Vista International (UK) - 8 January
(15) UK/USA, Dir Mark Herman
with Brenda Blethyn, Michael Caine, Jim Broadbent, Ewan McGregor, Jane Horrocks
© Scala (Little Voice) Limited
Miramax Films and Scala present a Scala production
96 minutes 33 seconds
S&S January 1999 p48

LIVING OUT LOUD
Entertainment Film Distributors Ltd - 5 February
(15) USA, Dir Richard LaGravenese
with Holly Hunter, Danny DeVito, Queen Latifah, Martin Donovan, Elias Koteas
© New Line Productions,Inc
New Line Cinema presents a Jersey Films production
99 minutes 47 seconds
S&S February 1999 p47

LOLA RENNT/RUN LOLA RUN
Columbia Tristar Films (UK) - 22 October
(15) Germany, Dir Tom Tykwer
with Franka Potente, Moritz Bleibtreu, Herbert Knaup, Nina Petri, Armin Rohde
© X Filme Creative Pool GmbH
An X Filme Creative Pool GmbH with Westdeutschen Rundfunk WDR and Arte co-production in association with Filmstiftung Nordhein-Westfalen/Filmboard Berlin-Brandenburg/Filmförderungsanstalt/BMI
80 minutes 2 seconds
subtitles
S&S November 1999 p52

The LOST SON
United International Pictures (UK) Ltd - 25 June
(18) UK/France, Dir Chris Menges
with Daniel Auteuil, Nastassja Kinski, Katrin Cartlidge, Ciaran Hinds, Marianne Denicourt
© Scala (Lost Son) Ltd/Ima Films SA
The Film Consortium/Le Studio Canal+/Scala and Ima Films present in association with the Arts Council of England/FilmFour/Canal+/France 2 and France 3 a Scala/Ima production developed with support of the Media programme of the European Union, supported by the National Lottery through the Arts Council of England
102 minutes 27 seconds
S&S July 1999 p46

LOVED
Downtown Pictures - 26 February
(15) USA, Dir Erin Dignam
with William Hurt, Robin Wright Penn, Amy Madigan, Lucinda Jenney, Joanna Cassidy
© Love Productions, Inc.
Crosslight Ltd. in association with MDP Worldwide present in association with Clyde Is Hungry Films and Palisades Pictures
102 minutes 45 seconds
S&S November 1998 p56

The LOVE LETTER
United International Pictures (UK) Ltd - 1 October
(15) USA, Dir Peter Ho-Sun Chan
with Kate Capshaw, Blythe Danner, Ellen DeGeneres, Geraldine McEwan, Julianne Nicholson
© Dream Works LLC
Dream Works Pictures presents a Sanford/Pillsbury production
87 minutes 25 seconds
S&S October 1999 p51

LUCIA
Telescope Pictures Ltd - 1 October
(15) UK, Dir Don Boyd
with Ann Taylor, John Daszak, Andrew Greenan, John Osborn, Mark Holland
© Lexington Films Ltd.
LFL - Lexington Films
102 minutes 13 seconds
S&S December 1999 p50

LUCKY PEOPLE CENTER INTERNATIONAL
Jane Balfour Films Limited - 29 October
(12) Sweden/Denmark/Norway, Dir Johan Söderberg and Erik Pauser
with Alexander Brener,Toyoshige Sekiguchi, Björn Merker, Djossou Dotche, Djossou Hounsipké Edwige
© AB Memfis Film & Television
Produced by AB Memfis Film & Television in co-operation with Zentropa Productions/The Swedish Filminstitute [Peter Hald]/Swedish Television Documentary [Björn Arvas]/Stockholm Records/Film i Väst/TV2 Danmark[AnetteRømer]/The National Film Board of Denmark/NRK - Norwegian Television/Nordic Film & TV-Fund [Dag Alveberg] supported by Eurimages
some subtitles
80 minutes 49 seconds
S&S November 1999 p48

MAD COWS
Entertainment Film Distributors Ltd - 29 October
(15) UK, Dir Sara Sugarman
with Anna Friel, Joanna Lumley, Anna Massey, Phyllida Law, Greg Wise
© Flashlight (Mad Cows) Limited
Newmarket Capital Group, Capitol Films and Entertainment Film Distributors present a Flashlight production
90 minutes 35 seconds
S&S December 1999 p51

MADELINE
Columbia Tristar Films (UK) - 12 February
(U) USA/Germany, Dir Daisy von Scherler Mayer
with Frances McDormand, Nigel Hawthorne, Hatty Jones, Ben Daniels, Arturo Venegas
© Global Entertainment Production GmbH & Co. Film KG
TriStar Pictures presents a Jaffilms production, a Pancho Kohner/Saul Cooper production
89 minutes 1 second
S&S April 1999 p46

MANN
Yash Raj - 9 July
India, Dir Indra Kumar
with Aamir Khan, Manisha Koirala, Deepti Bhatnagar, Anil Kapoor, Sharmila Tagore
Maruti International
No S&S reference

*MANON DES SOURCES/MANON OF THE SPRINGS
Pathé Distribution - 11 June

(PG) France, Italy, Switzerland, Dir Claude Berri
with Yves Montand, Daniel Auteuil, Emmanuelle Béart, Hippolyte Girardot, Margarita Lozano
Renn Productions, Films A2, Raidue, D.D. Films, Antenne 2 with the assistance of Télévision Suisse Romande, Images Investissements, Investimage, Créations
120 minutes
MFB November 1987 p337

The MAN WHO DROVE WITH MANDELA
Jane Balfour Films Limited - 28 May
(not submitted) UK/USA/South Africa/Netherlands/Belgium, Dir Greta Schiller
with Corin Redgrave, Joseph Bale, Gavin Hayward, Robert Tsiesi, Ashley Brownlee
© Jezebel Productions and Beulah Films
Produced by Jezebel Productions in association with Beulah Films for the Corporation for Public Broadcasting (USA)/Channel 4 (UK), in association with The London Production Fund/The British Film Institute/SABC3 (South Africa)/AVRO (Netherlands)/VRT-Canvas (Belgium), this film was made possible in part by a grant from the South African Department of Arts, Culture, Science and Technology
82 minutes
S&S August 1999 p48

*The MAN WHO KNEW TOO MUCH
BFI Films - 20 August [NFT First Run 20-26 August]
(PG) UK, Dir Alfred Hitchcock
with Henry Oscar, S.J.Warmington, Frederick Piper, Frank Atkinson, Charles Paton, Clare Greet
Gaumont-British Picture Corporation
75 minutes 29 seconds
S&S September 1999 p50
MFB January 1935 p116

MAST
Eros Video (Electronics) Ltd - 15 October
India, Dir Ram Gopal Verma
with Urmila Matondkar, Aftaab Shivdasani, Dalip Tahil, Smita Jayakar
Varma Corporation Ltd.
No S&S reference

The MATCH
PolyGram Filmed Entertainment - 6 August
(15) UK/USA/Ireland, Dir Mick Davis
with Max Beesley, Isla Blair, James Cosmo, Laura Fraser, Richard E. Grant
© PolyGram Filmed Entertainment, Inc
PolyGram Filmed Entertainment presents a Propaganda Films/Allan Scott production in association with Irish Dreamtime
96 minutes 21 seconds
S&S August 1999 p49

The MATRIX
Warner Bros Distributors (UK) - 11 June
(15) USA/Australia, Dir The Wachowski Brothers
with Keanu Reeves, Laurence Fishburne, Carrie-Anne Moss, Hugo Weaving, Joe Pantoliano
© Warner Bros. (US/Canada/Bahamas/Bermuda) and Village Roadshow (BVI) Limited (all other territories)
Warner Bros. present in association with Village Roadshow Pictures/Groucho II Film Partnership a Silver Pictures production
super 35
136 minutes
S&S July 1999 p46

MEET JOE BLACK
United International Pictures (UK) Ltd - 15 January
(12) USA, Dir Martin Brest
with Brad Pitt, Anthony Hopkins, Claire Folani, Jake Weber, Marcia Gay Harden
© Universal City Studios, Inc
Universal Pictures presents a City Light Films production
180 minutes 37 seconds
S&S February 1999 p48

MESSAGE IN A BOTTLE
Warner Bros Distributors (UK) - 23 April
(12) USA, Dir Luis Mandoki
with Kevin Costner, Robin Wright Penn, Paul Newman, John Savage, Illeana Douglas
© Warner Bros/Bel-Air Entertainment LLC
Warner Bros presents in association with Bel-Air Entertainment a Tig production in association with Di Novi Pictures
131 minutes 17 seconds
S&S May 1999 p52

MICKEY BLUE EYES
PolyGram Filmed Entertainment - 20 August
(15) USA/UK, Dir Kelly Makin
with Hugh Grant, James Caan, Jeanne Tripplehorn, Burt Young, James Fox
© CR Films, LLC
Castle Rock Entertainment presents a Simian Films production
102 minutes 12 seconds
S&S September 1999 p50

A MIDSUMMER NIGHT'S DREAM
20th Century Fox (UK) - 24 September
(PG) USA/Germany, Dir Michael Hoffman
with Kevin Kline, Michelle Pfeiffer, Rupert Everett, Stanley Tucci, Calista Flockhart
© Twentieth Century Fox Film Corporation, Monarchy Enterprises B.V. and Regency Entertainment (USA), Inc
A Fox Searchlight Pictures and Regency Enterprises presentation in association with Taurus Film
120 minutes 30 seconds
Anamorphic [2.35 Research]
S&S October 1999 p.52

MIFUNE/MIFUNES SIDSTE SANG
Alliance Film Distributors - 1 October
(15) Denmark/Sweden, Dir [uncredited] Søren Kragh-Jacobsen
with Iben Hjejle, Anders W. Berthelsen, Jesper Asholt, Emil Tarding, Anders Hove
© Nimbus Film II ApS
Nimbus Film presents, produced by Nimbus Film in collaboration with Zentropa Entertainment, DRTV & SVT Drama, with support from Nordisk Film og TV Fond and Det Danske Filminstitut
subtitles
101 minutes 7 seconds
[opening title reads: DOGME 3]
S&S October 1999 p.52

MIGHTY JOE
Buena Vista International (UK) - 26 March
(PG) USA, Dir Ron Underwood
with Bill Paxton, Charlize Theron, Rade Serbedzija, Regina King, Peter Firth
© Disney Enterprises, Inc.
Walt Disney Pictures presents an RKO Pictures production in

association with The Jacobson
Company
114 minutes 10 seconds
[US release title: MIGHTY JOE
YOUNG]
S&S April 1999 p48

The MISADVENTURES OF MARGARET/Les MÉSAVENTURES DE MARGARET
The Feature Film Company - 23
April
(15) UK/France, Dir Brian Skeet
with Parker Posey, Jeremy Northam,
Craig Chester, Elizabeth McGovern,
Brooke Shields
© Mandarin/TF1 Films
Production/Lunatics & Lovers
TF1 International and Granada
present with the participation of the
European Co-production Fund
(UK) a Lunatics & Lovers/Granada
Film production in co-production
with Mandarin and TF1 Films
Production with the participation of
Canal+ in association with Film 50
92 minutes 25 seconds
S&S May 1999 p53

MIZU NO NAKA NO HACHIGATSU/AUGUST IN THE WATER
ICA - shown at the ICA (London)
on 2 April
(not submitted) Japan, Dir Sogo Ishii
with Rena Komine, Shinsuke Aoki,
Masaaki Takarai, Naho Toda, Reiko
Matsuo
Hill Villa Co.
117 minutes
No S&S reference

MOTEL SEONINJANG/MOTEL CACTUS
ICA - shown at the ICA (London)
30 July
(not submitted) Republic of Korea,
Dir Park Ki-Yong
with Lee Mi-Yun, Jin Heui-Kyeong,
Jung Woo-Sung, Park Shin-Yang,
Kim Seung-Hyun
Uno Films
91 minutes
No S&S reference

*MOUCHETTE
BFI Collections - 10 September
[NFT First Run 10-16 September]
(not submitted) France, Dir Robert
Bresson
with Nadine Nortier, Jean-Claude
Guilbert, Paul Hébert, Maria

Cardinal, Jean Vimenet
Argos-Films/Parc Film
90 minutes
MFB April 1968 p52

The MUMMY
United International Pictures (UK)
Ltd - 25 June
(12) USA, Dir Stephen Sommers
with Brendan Fraser, Rachel Weisz,
John Hannah, Arnold Vosloo, Kevin
J. O'Connor
© Universal Studios
Universal Pictures presents an
Alphaville production
124 minutes 43 seconds
S&S July 1999 p48

MUPPETS FROM SPACE
Columbia Tristar Film (UK) - 24
December
(U) UK/USA, Dir Tim Hill
with muppet performers Dave Goelz,
Steve Whitmire, Bill Barretta, Jerry
Nelson, Brian Henson
with Jeffrey Tambor, F.Murray
Abraham, Rob Schneider, Josh
Charles, Ray Liotta
© Jim Henson Pictures
A Jim Henson Pictures
presentation, Columbia Pictures
88 minutes 5 seconds
S&S January 2000 p58

The MUSE
Entertainment Film Distributors
Ltd - 10 December
(PG) USA, Dir Albert Brooks
with Albert Brooks, Sharon Stone,
Andie MacDowell, Jeff Bridges,
Mark Feuerstein
© October Films, Inc.
October Films presents
96 minutes 21 seconds
S&S January 2000 p58

MY FAVORITE MARTIAN
Buena Vista International (UK) -
28 May
(PG) USA, Dir Donald Petrie
with Jeff Daniels, Christopher Lloyd,
Elizabeth Hurley, Daryl Hannah,
Christine Ebersole
© Disney Enterprises, Inc
Walt Disney Pictures presents a
Jerry Leider/Robert Shapiro
production
93 minutes 32 seconds
S&S June 1999 p48

MY GIANT
Warner Bros Distributors (UK) -
12 February
(PG) USA, Dir Michael Lehmann
with Billy Crystal, Kathleen Quinlan,

Gheorghe Muresan, Joanna Pacula,
Zane Carney
© Castle Rock Entertainment
Castle Rock Entertainment
presents a Face production
103 minutes 29 seconds
S&S April 1999 p49

MYSTERY MEN
United International Pictures (UK)
Ltd - 24 December
(PG) USA, Dir Kinka Usher
with Hank Azaria, Claire Forlani,
Janeane Garofalo, Greg Kinnear,
William H.Macy
© Universal City Studios, Inc.
Universal Pictures and Lawrence
Gordon present a Golar/Lloyd
Levin/Dark Horse production
120 minutes 27 seconds
S&S February 2000 p50

NEVER BEEN KISSED
20th Century Fox (UK) - 27 August
(12) USA, Dir Raja Gosnell
with Drew Barrymore, David
Arquette, Michael Vartan, Molly
Shannon, John C.Reilly
© Twentieth Century Fox Film
Corporation
Fox 2000 Pictures presents a
Flower Films/Bushwood Pictures
production
107 minutes 18 seconds
S&S September 1999 p51

NIAGARA, NIAGARA
Feature Film Company - shown as
part of the 'American
Independence' tour from 12 March
US, Dir Bob Gosse
with Robin Tunney, Henry Thomas,
Michael Parks, Stephen Lang, John
MacKay
Niagara, Niagara LLC, Shooting
Gallery
93 minutes
No S&S reference

A NIGHT AT THE ROXBURY
United International Pictures (UK)
Ltd - 19 March
(15) USA, Dir John Fortenberry
with Will Ferrell, Chris Kattan, Dan
Hedaya, Molly Shannon, Richard
Grieco
© Paramount Pictures Corporation
Paramount Pictures presents in
association with SNL Studios a
Lorne Michaels and Amy
Heckerling production
81 minutes 49 seconds
S&S February 1999 p49

*The NIGHT OF THE HUNTER
BFI Collections - 2 April
(15) USA, Dir Charles Laughton
with Robert Mitchum, Shelley
Winters, Lillian Gish, James Gleason,
Evelyn Varden
Paul Gregory Productions
92 minutes
Black & white
MFB January 1956 p3

*The NINTH CONFIGURATION
Blue Dolphin Film & Video - 30
April
(15) USA, Dir William Peter Blatty
with Stacy Keach, Scott Wilson,
Jason Miller, Ed Flanders, Neville
Brand
© **The Ninth Configuration**
Company
117 minutes 37 seconds
S&S July 1999 p50
MFB March 1981 p53

Nô
Alliance Releasing (UK) - 9 April
(15) Canada, Dir Robert Lepage
with Anne-Marie Cadieux, Marie
Gignac, Richard Fréchette, Alexis
Martin, Éric Bernier
© **In Extremis Images Inc.**
Alliance Vivafilm presents an in
Extremis Images production,
produced with the financial
participation of Téléfilm
Canada/SODEC Société de
développement des entreprises
culturelles (Québec)/Crédit
d'impôt du Québec/Alliance
Vivafilm/Gouvernement du
Canada [programme de crédit
d'impôt pour production
cinématographique ou
magnétoscopique
canadienne]/Fonds de la
Radiodiffusion et des nouveaux
médias de Bell
84 minutes 41 seconds
subtitles
S&S April 1999 p50

*Le NOTTI DI CABIRIA/Les NUITS DE CABIRIA/NIGHTS OF CABIRIA
British Film Institute - 23 July
(PG) Italy/France, Dir Federico
Fellini
with Franco Fabrizi, Polidor, Maria
Luisa Rolando, Pina Gualandri,
Loretta Capitoli
© **Dino De Laurentiis**

Cinematografica S.p.A
Dino De Laurentiis
Cinematografica/Les Films
Marceau
black and white
subtitles
117 minutes 31 seconds
S&S October 1999 p53
MFB May 1958 p57

NOTTING HILL
PolyGram Filmed Entertainment -
21 May
(15) USA/UK, Dir Roger Michell
with Julia Roberts, Hugh Grant,
Hugh Bonneville, Emma Chambers,
James Dreyfus
© **PolyGram Filmed Entertainment**
Inc
PolyGram Filmed Entertainment
presents in association with
Working Title Films a Duncan
Kenworthy production from
Notting Hill Pictures
123 minutes 57 seconds
S&S June 1999 p49

*NRAN GOUYNE/The COLOUR OF POMEGRANATES
26 November
(PG) Soviet Union, Dir Sergei
Paradzhanov
with Sofiko Chiaureli, M.
Aleksanian, V. Galstian, G.
Gegechkori, O. Minassian
Armenfilm/Georgiafilm
Studios/Azerbaijanfilm
73 minutes
MFB November 1983 p291

*NUOVO CINEMA PARADISO
Metro Tartan Distributors - 17
December
(15) Italy/France, Dir Giuseppe
Tornatore
with Philippe Noiret, Jacques Perrin,
Antonella Attili, Enzo Cannavale, Isa
Danieli,
Cristaldi Film/Films
Ariane/Raitre/T.F.1 Films Production
(Paris)/Forum Pictures
123 minutes
MFB March 1990 p72

OCTOBER SKY
United International Pictures (UK)
Ltd - 10 December
(PG) USA, Dir Joe Johnston
with Jake Gyllenhaal, Chris Cooper,
William Lee Scott, Chris Owen,
Chad Lindberg
© **Universal City Studios, Inc.**
Universal Pictures presents a

Charles Gordon production
Anamorphic [Panavision]
107 minutes 25 seconds
S&S January 2000 p59

ONEGIN
Entertainment Film Distributors
Ltd - 19 November
(12) UK/USA, Dir Martha Fiennes
with Ralph Fiennes, Liv Tyler, Toby
Stephens, Lena Headey, Martin
Donovan
© **Onegin Productions Limited**
Seven Arts International presents a
Baby Productions film, developed
with the assistance of Protagonist
Film Corporation
106 minutes 9 seconds
S&S December 1999 p51

The OPPOSITE OF SEX
Columbia TriStar Films (UK) - 15
January
(18) USA, Dir Don Roos
with Christina Ricci, Martin
Donovan, Lisa Kudrow, Lyle Lovett,
Johnny Galecki
© **Rysher Entertainment, Inc.**
A Sony Pictures Classics release of
a Rysher Entertainment
presentation of a David
Kirkpatrick/Michael Bosman
production
100 minutes 54 seconds
S&S January 1999 p51

ORGAZMO
First Independent Films Ltd - 9
April
(18) USA, Dir Trey Parker
with Trey Parker, Dian Bachar,
Robyn Lynne, Michael Dean Jacobs,
Ron Jeremy
Kuzui Enterprises and MDP
Worldwide present an Avenging
Conscience production
94 minutes 24 seconds
S&S April 1999 p52

ORPHANS
Downtown Pictures - 23 April
(18) UK, Dir Peter Mullan
with Douglas Henshall, Gary Lewis,
Stephen McCole, Rosemarie
Stevenson, Frank Gallagher
© **Channel Four Television**
Corporation
Channel Four Films presents in
association with the Scottish Arts
Council National Lottery Fund and
the Glasgow Film Fund an Antoine
Green Bridge production for the
Glasgow Film Fund and Channel
4, development funded by the
Scottish Film Production Fund

101 minutes 35 seconds
S&S May 1999 p54

The OTHER SISTER
Buena Vista International (UK) -
19 November
(12) USA, Dir Garry Marshall
with Juliette Lewis, Diane Keaton,
Tom Skerritt, Giovanni Ribisi, Poppy
Montgomery
© Touchstone Pictures
Touchstone Pictures presents a
Mandeville Films production
130 minutes 7 seconds
Super 35 [2.35:1]
S&S December 1999 p52

OTHER VOICES OTHER ROOMS
Downtown Pictures - 11 June
(12) USA, Dir David Rocksavage
with Lothaire Bluteau, Anna
Thomson, David Speck, April Turner,
Frank Taylor
© The Golden Eye 1994
Partnership
A Golden Eye Films presentation
98 minutes 9 seconds
S&S July 1999 p51

OUT OF THE PRESENT
Downtown Pictures - 23 April
(U) Germany/France/Belgium/
Russia, Dir Andrei Ujica
with Anatoli Artsebarski, Sergei
Krikalev, Helen Sharman, Viktor
Afanasiev, Musa Monarov
Produced by Bremer Institut
Film/Fernsehen, co-produced by
WDR, La Sept/Arte, St. Petersburg
Documentary Film Studios and
Harun Farocki supported by
Filmstiftung Nordrhein-Westfalen,
Bundesministerium des Innern,
AKK Energia, Energia
Deutschland GmbH, sponsored by
Daimler-Benz Aerospace
subtitles
99 minutes 53 seconds
S&S March 1999 p45

The OUT-OF-TOWNERS
United International Pictures (UK)
Ltd - 5 November
(12) USA, Dir Sam Weisman
with Steve Martin, Goldie Hawn,
John Cleese, Mark McKinney, Oliver
Hudson
© Paramount Pictures Corporation
Paramount Pictures presents a Robert
Evans production in association with
Cherry Alley Productions and the
Cort/Madden Co.
92 minutes 14 seconds
S&S December 1999 p53

PAINTED ANGELS
Artificial Eye Film Company - 26
February
(12) Canada/UK, Dir Jon Sanders
with Brenda Fricker, Kelly McGillis,
Meret Becker, Bronagh Gallagher,
Lisa Jakub
© Prairie Doves Inc./Prairie Doves
UK Ltd
Cinepix Properties present a
Shaftesbury Films/Greenpoint
Films/Heartland Motion Pictures
production, produced with the
participation of British
Screen/SaskFILM/Saskatchewan
Opportunities
Corporation/Téléfilm Canada and
in association with BBC Films,
developed in association with First
Film Foundation/Diverse
Productions, developed with the
assistance of British Screen
Finance Ltd (London, England)
and with the support of The
European Script Fund, produced
with the assistance of The
Government of Canada - Canadian
Film or Video Production Tax
Credit program and The
Saskatchewan Future Skills
program and in association with
TMN - The Movie Network and
SuperChannel
109 minutes 41 seconds
S&S March 1999 p45

PAPERBACK HERO
PolyGram Filmed Entertainment -
3 September
(15) Australia, Dir Antony J.
Bowman
with Claudia Karvan, Hugh Jackman,
Angie Milliken, Andrew S.Gilbert,
Jeanie Drynan
© Australian Film Finance
Corporation Limited/the State of
Queensland and Paperback Films
Pty Limited
Australian Film Finance
Corporation presents a Paperback
Films production, a Lance
W.Reynolds production, developed
with the assistance of Archer Films
Entertainment, co-financed by the
Pacific Film and Television
Commission
96 minutes 30 seconds
S&S October 1999 p54

PARTING SHOTS
United International Pictures (UK)
Ltd - 14 May
(12) UK, Dir Michael Winner
with Chris Rea, Felicity Kendal, Bob

Hoskins, Ben Kingsley, Joanna
Lumley
© Michael Winner Ltd
Scimitar Films presents a Michael
Winner film
98 minutes 22 seconds
S&S June 1999 p50

PASSION IN THE DESERT
Entertainment Film Distributors
Ltd - 20 August
USA, Dir Lavinia Currier
with Ben Daniels, Michel Piccoli,
Paul Meston, Kenneth Collard
Roland Films
93 minutes
No S&S reference

PATCH ADAMS
United International Pictures (UK)
Ltd - 12 March
(12) USA, Dir Tom Shadyac
with Robin Williams, Monica Potter,
Daniel London, Philip Seymour
Hoffman, Bob Gunton
© Universal City Studios, Inc
Universal Pictures presents a Blue
Wolf, Farrell/Minoff, Bungalow 78
production
115 minutes 27 seconds
S&S March 1999 p46

PAYBACK
Warner Bros Distributors (UK) -
26 March
(18) USA, Dir Brian Helgeland
with Mel Gibson, Gregg Henry,
Maria Bello, David Paymer, Bill
Duke
© Warner Bros
Paramount Pictures presents an
Icon production
101 minutes 6 seconds
Super 35
S&S April 1999 p53

PECKER
Entertainment Film Distributors
Ltd - 5 February
(15) USA, Dir John Waters
with Edward Furlong, Christina
Ricci, Bess Armstrong, Mark Joy,
Mary Kay Place
Fine Line Features presents a Polar
Entertainment production
86 minutes 16 seconds
S&S February 1999 p50

PERDITA DURANGO
Metrodome Distribution Ltd - 26
February
(18) Spain/Mexico/USA, Dir Àlex de
la Iglesia
with Rosie Perez, Javier Bardem,
Harley Cross, Aimee Graham,

Screamin' Jay Hawkins
© Sogetel S.A./Lolafilms
S.A./Mirador S.A. de C.V.
An Andrés Vicente Gómez
production for
Sogetel/Lolafilms/Mirador S.A. de
C.V. in association with Canal+
(Spain)/Sogepaq S.A./IMCINE
(Mexico). A Sogetel S.A./Lolafilms
S.A./Mirador S.A. de
C.V./Occidental Media Corp co-
production
124 minutes 11 seconds
S&S March 1999 p48

PERFECT BLUE

Manga Entertainment - 1 June
(18) Japan, Dir Satoshi Kon
with the character voices of [English
version:] Ruby Marlowe, Wendee
Lee, Gil Starberry, Lia Sargent, Steve
Bulen [Japanese version:] Junko
Iwao, Rika Matsumoto, Tsuji
Shinpachi, Masaaki Okura, Yosuke
Akimoto
© Rex Entertainment Co Ltd.
Rex Entertainment Co Ltd. in
association with Kotobuki Seihan
Printing Co., Ltd/Asahi
Broadcasting Corporation/Fangs
Co., Ltd.
81 minutes 29 seconds
S&S August 1999 p50

PHÖRPA/The CUP

Alliance Releasing (UK) - 19
November
(PG) Australia, Dir Khyentse Norbu
with Orgyen Tobgyal, Neten
Chokling, Jamyang Lodro, Lama
Chonjor, Godu Lama
© Coffee Stain Productions Pty Ltd
Palm Pictures presents a Coffee
Stain Productions production
93 minutes 50 seconds
subtitles
S&S December 1999 p41

PI

Guild Film Distribution - 8
January
(15) USA, Dir Darren Aronofsky
with Sean Gullette, Mark Margolis,
Ben Shenkman, Pamela Hart,
Stephen Pearlman
© Protozoa Pictures, Inc
A Harvest Filmworks/Truth &
Soul/Plantain Films presentation
83 minutes 59 seconds
black and white
S&S January 1999 p52

PLACE VENDÔME

Artificial Eye Film Company - 6
August
(15) France/Belgium/UK, Dir Nicole
Garcia
with Catherine Deneuve, Jean-Pierre
Bacri, Emmanuelle Seigner, Jacques
Dutronc, Bernard Fresson
© Les Films Alain Sarde/TF1 Films
Production/Les Films de
l'Étang/Alhéna Films/Angel's
Company
Alain Sarde presents a Les Films
Alain Sarde/TF1 Films
Production/Les Films de
l'Étang/Alhéna Films/Angel's
Company, made with the support
of Eurimages, with the
participation of Canal+/Centre de
la Cinématographie and of Studio
Images 3
118 minutes 4 seconds
subtitles
S&S August 1999 p51

PLAYING BY HEART

Buena Vista International (UK) - 6
August
(15) USA, Dir Willard Carroll
with Gillian Anderson, Ellen Burstyn,
Sean Connery, Anthony Edwards,
Angelina Jolie
© Miramax Film Corp.
Miramax Films and Intermedia
Films present in association with
Morpheus a Hyperion production
121 minutes 3 seconds
S&S September 1999 p52

PLEASANTVILLE

Entertainment Film Distributors
Ltd - 12 March
(12) USA, Dir Gary Ross
with Tobey Maguire, Jeff Daniels,
Joan Allen, William H. Macy, J.T.
Walsh
© New Line Productions, Inc
New Line Cinema presents a
Larger Than Life production
124 minutes 20 seconds
S&S March 1999 p49

PLUNKETT & MACLEANE

PolyGram Filmed Entertainment -
2 April
(15) UK, Dir Jake Scott
with Robert Carlyle, Jonny Lee
Miller, Liv Tyler, Ken Stott, Michael
Gambon
© PolyGram Filmed
Entertainment, Inc.
PolyGram Filmed Entertainment
presents in association with the
Arts Council of England a
Working Title production
supported by the National Lottery
through the Arts Council of
England

101 minutes 11 seconds
S&S April 1999 p54

Le POLYGRAPHE/The POLYGRAPH

ICA - show at the ICA (London)
from 22 January
(not submitted) Canada
(Quebec)/France/Germany, Dir
Robert Lepage
with Patrick Goyette, Marie Brassard,
Peter Stormare, Maria de Medeiros,
Josée DeschÍnes
Téléfilm Canada/In Extremis
Images/Berlin-Brandenburg Film
Fund/Cinépix Film
Properties/Quebec Government/
Cinéa/Road Movies Dritte
Produktionen
97 minutes
No S&S reference

De POOLSE BRUID/The POLISH BRIDE

Artificial Eye Film Company - 16
July
(15) Netherlands, Dir Karim Traïdia
with Jaap Spijkers, Monic Hendrickx,
Rudi Falkenhagen, Roef Ragas,
Hakim Traïdia
© Motel Films/Ijswater
Films/VPRO
Ijswater Films and Motel Films
with VPRO in association with
Stichting Nederlands Fonds voor
de Film/Stichtin Co-
Produktiefonds Binnenlandse
Omroep/Stimuleringsfonds
Nederlandse Culturele
Omroepproducties
89 minutes 22 seconds
subtitles
S&S August 1999 p52

PRACTICAL MAGIC

Warner Bros Distributors (UK) -
22 January
(12) USA, Dir Griffin Dunne
with Sandra Bullock, Nicole Kidman,
Dianne Wiest, Stockard Channing,
Aidan Quinn
© Warner Bros.
(US/Canada/Bahamas/Bermuda)
© Village Roadshow Films (BVI)
Limited (all other territories)
Warner Bros. presents in
association with Village Roadshow
Pictures a Di Novi Pictures
production in association with
Fortis Films
104 minutes 4 seconds
S&S January 1999 p53

PRAISE

Barbican - shown at the Barbican 1

October
Australia, Dir John Curran
with Sacha Holder, Peter Fenton,
Marta Dusseldorp, Joel Edgerton,
Yvette Duncan
**Emcee Films/Australian Film
Finance Corporation/New South
wales Film and Television Offices**
97 minutes
No S&S reference

A PRICE ABOVE RUBIES
FilmFour Distributors - 14 May
(15) USA/France/UK, Dir Boaz
Yakin
with Renee Zellweger, Christopher
Eccleston, Allen Payne, Glenn
Fitzgerald, Julianna Margulies
© **Miramax Film Corp**
**Miramax Films presents in
association with Pandora Cinema
in association with Channel Four
Films a Lawrence Bender
production**
116 minutes 7 seconds
S&S June 1999 p51

La PROMESSE
**ICA - shown at the ICA (London)
on 26 March**
(not submitted)
Belgium/France/Luxembourg, Dir
Luc Dardenne and Jean-Pierre
Dardenne
with Jérémie Renier, Olivier
Gourmet, Assita Ouédraogo,
Rasmane Ouédraogo, Frédéric
Bodson
**ERTT (Tunisia)/Films du
Fleuve/RTBF/Dérives/Touza
Productions/Samsa Film**
90 minutes
No S&S reference

PROMETHEUS
FilmFour Distributors - 16 April
(15) UK, Dir Tony Harrison
with Michael Feast, Walter Sparrow,
Fern Smith, Jonathan Waistnidge,
Steve Huison
© **FilmFour Limited**
**FilmFour presents in association
with the Arts Council of England a
Holmes Associates Michael Kustow
production supported by the
National Lottery through the Arts
Council of England, a Holmes
Associates Michael Kustow
production for FilmFour**
130 minutes 9 seconds
S&S April 1999 p55

PSYCHO
**United International Pictures (UK)
Ltd - 8 January**

(15) USA, Dir Gus Van Sant
with Vince Vaughn, Julianne Moore,
Viggo Mortensen, William H. Macy,
Anne Heche
© **Universal City Studios, Inc**
**Universal Pictures presents an
Imagine Entertainment production**
103 minutes 50 seconds
S&S February 1999 p51

PUSHING TIN
**20th Century Fox (UK) - 29
October**
(15) USA, Dir Mike Newell
with John Cusack, Billy Bob
Thornton, Cate Blanchett, Angelina
Jolie, Jake Weber
© **Twentieth Century Fox Film
Corporation, Monarchy
Enterprises B.V. and Regency
Entertainment (USA), Inc.
Fox 2000 Pictures and Regency
Enterprises present a Linson Films
production**
123 minutes 43 seconds
Super 35 [2.35:1]
S&S November 1999 p49

PYAAR KOI KHEL NAHIN
Blue Star - 30 July
India, Dir Subhash Sehgal
with Sunny Deol, Mahima
Chaudhary, Apurva Agnihotri, Dalip
Tahil, Mohnish Bahl
Tristar Movies
No S&S reference

*Der RADFAHRER/The CYCLIST
**ICA - shown at the ICA (London)
from 26 February**
(not submitted) Iran, Dir Mohsen
Makhmalbaf
with Moharram Zeynalzadeh,
Esmail Soltanian
85 minutes
No S&S reference

The RAGE CARRIE 2
**Redbus Film Distribution - 19
November**
(15) USA, Dir Katt Shea
with Emily Bergl, Jason London,
Dylan Bruno, J. Smith-Cameron,
Zachery Ty Bryan
© **United Artists Pictures Inc.
United Artists Pictures presents a
Red Bank Films production 104
minutes 34 seconds**
S&S December 1999 p54

RAJAJI
UFDL - 21 May
India, Dir Vimal Kumar
with Raveena Tandon, Govinda,

Mohan Joshi, Aruna Irani, Divya
Dutta
Shivam Chitrya
No S&S reference

RANDOM HEARTS
**Columbia Tristar Films (UK) - 19
November**
(15) USA, Dir Sydney Pollack
with Harrison Ford, Kristin Scott
Thomas, Charles S. Dutton, Bonnie
Hunt, Dennis Haysbert
© **Global Entertainment
Productions GmbH & Co., Medien
KG
Columbia Pictures presents a
Rastar/Mirage Enterprises
production**
132 minutes 28 seconds
S&S December 1999 p55

RATCATCHER
Pathé Distribution - 12 November
(15) UK/France, Dir Lynne Ramsay
with William Eadie, Tommy
Flanagan, Mandy Matthews,
Michelle Stewart, Lynne Ramsay Jr
© **Pathé Fund Limited
Pathé Pictures and BBC Films
present in association with the Arts
Council of England and Lazennec
and Le Studio Canal+ a Holy Cow
Films production supported by the
National Lottery through the Arts
Council of England, developed in
association with BBC Scotland,
developed with the assistance of
Moonstone International**
93 minutes 24 seconds
S&S November 1999 p50

RAVENOUS
**20th Century Fox (UK) - 10
September**
(18) USA/UK, Dir Antonia Bird
with Guy Pearce, Robert Carlyle,
Jeremy Davies, Jeffrey Jones, John
Spencer
© **Twentieth Century Fox Film
Corporation
Fox 2000 Pictures presents an
Adam Fields/Heyday Films
production**
100 minutes 38 seconds
S&S September 1999 p53

The RED VIOLIN/II VIOLINO ROSSO
FilmFour Distributors - 9 April
(15) Canada/Italy/USA/UK, Dir
François Girard
with Carlo Cecchi, Jean-Luc Bideau,
Jason Flemyng, Sylvia Chang,
Samuel L. Jackson

© Red Violin Productions
Limited/Sidecar Films and TV
Srl/Mikado Film Srl
New Line International
Releasing/Channel Four
Films/Téléfilm Canada present a
Rhombus Media/Mikado
production in association with New
Line International
Releasing/Channel Four
Films/Canada Television and Cable
Production Fund/Téléfilm Canada
- Equity Investment
Program/Citytv/Bravo! New Style
Arts Channel and Sony Classical,
with the assistance of the Canadian
Film or Video Tax Credit Program

REGARDE LA MER/SEE THE SEA
ICA - shown at the ICA (London)
20 August
(not submitted) France, Dir François
Ozon
with Sasha Hails, Marina de Van,
Paul Raoux, Samantha
Fidélité Productions/Local
Films/Centre National de la
Cinématograph/Procirep
52 minutes
No S&S reference

RETURN TO PARADISE
Polygram Filmed Entertainment -
16 April
(15) USA, Dir Joseph Ruben
with Vince Vaughn, Anne Heche,
Joaquin Phoenix, David Conrad, Jada
Pinkett Smith
© PolyGram Filmed
Entertainment, Inc
© Propaganda Films
PolyGram Filmed Entertainment
presents a Propaganda Films
production in association with
Tetragram
111 minutes 34 seconds
S&S January 1999 p55

RIDE WITH THE DEVIL
Entertainment Film Distributors
Ltd - 5 November
(15) USA, Dir Ang Lee
with Skeet Ulrich, Tobey Maguire,
Jewel, Jeffrey Wright, Simon Baker
© Universal Studios
Universal presents a Good
Machine production
138 minutes 20 seconds
Anamorphic [2.35 Research]
S&S December 1999 p56

ROGUE TRADER
Pathé Distribution - 25 June
(15) UK/USA, Dir James Dearden

with Ewan McGregor, Anna Friel,
Yves Beneyton, Betsy Brantley,
Caroline Langrishe
© Granada Film Limited
Granada and Newmarket Capital
Group present a Granada
Film/David Paradine production
101 minutes 24 seconds
July 1999 p51

ROMANCE
Blue Light - 8 October
(18) France, Dir Catherine Breillat
with Caroline Ducey, Sagamore
Stévenin, François Berléand, Rocco
Siffredi, Reza Habouhossein
© Flach Film/CB Films/ARTE
France Cinéma
Jean-François Lepetit presents a
co-production of Flach Film/CB
Films/ARTE France Cinéma with
the participation of Centre
National de la Cinématographie
and with the support of la
Procirep, with the participation of
Canal+
98 minutes 51 seconds
subtitles
November 1999 p51

The RUGRATS MOVIE
United International Pictures (UK)
Ltd - 26 March
(U) USA, Dir Norton Virgien and
Igor Kovalyov
with the character voices of E.G.
Daily, Christine Cavanaugh, Kath
Soucie, Melanie Chartoff, Kath
Soucie
© Paramount Pictures/Viacom
International Inc
Paramount Pictures and
Nickelodeon Movies present a
Klasky/Csupo production
80 minutes 2 seconds
S&S April 1999 p56

RUNAWAY BRIDE
Buena Vista International (UK) - 8
October
(PG) USA, Dir Garry Marshall
with Julia Roberts, Richard Gere,
Joan Cusack, Hector Elizondo, Rita
Wilson
© Paramount Pictures and
Touchstone Pictures
Touchstone Pictures and
Paramount Pictures present an
Interscope Communications
production in association with
Lakeshore Entertainment
116 minutes 26 seconds
Super 35 [2.35:1]
S&S November 1999 p53

RUSHMORE
Buena Vista International (UK) -
20 August
(15) USA, Dir Wes Anderson
with Bill Murray, Olivia Williams,
Jason Schwartzman, Seymour Cassel,
Brian Cox
© Touchstone Pictures
Touchstone Pictures presents an
American Empirical
Pictures/Barry Mendel production
92 minutes 40 seconds
S&S September 1999 p54

SAFARI
Blue Star - 11 June
India, Dir Jyotin Goel
with Sanjay Dutt, Juhi Chawla,
Suresh Oberoi, Tanuja, Raza Murad
Goel Screencraft
No S&S reference

SANGHARSH
Spark - 3 September
India, Dir Tanuja Chandra
with Akshay Kumar, Preity Zinta,
Ashutosh Rana, Madan Jain,
Vishwajeet Pradhan
Vinesh Films P. Ltd
No S&S reference

SAR ANKHON PAR
GVI - 15 October
India, Dir Gyan Sahay
with Tara Deshpande, Anuj, Dilip
Joshi, Keith Stevenson, Charlie
Pinnacle Entertainments
No S&S reference

SARFAROSH
Eros Video (Electronics) Ltd - 30
April
India, Dir John Mathew Matthan
with Aamir Khan, Naseeruddin Shah,
Sonali Bendre, Mukesh Rishi,
Aakash Khurana
Cinematt Pictures
No S&S reference

SCHIZOPOLIS
Feature Film Company - shown as
part of the 'American
Independence' tour from 12 March
US, Dir Steven Soderbergh
with Steven Soderbergh, Betsy
Brantley, David Jensen, Mike
Malone, Eddie Jemison
Point 406
99 minutes
No S&S reference

*SCROOGE
Feature Film - 26 November
(U) UK, Dir Ronald Neame
with Albert Finney, Alec Guiness,

Edith Evans, Kenneth More, Michael Medwin
Waterbury Films
118 minutes
MFB January 1971 p13

The SECRET LAUGHTER OF WOMEN

Optimum Releasing - 26 November
(12) UK/Canada, Dir Peter Schwabach
with Colin Firth, Nia Long, Dan Lett, Joke Silva, Ariyon Bakare
© Secret Laughter of Women Ltd/Paragon Productions (Secret) Inc.
Paragon Entertainment Corporation/HandMade Films present with the participation of the European Co-production Fund (UK) and BSkyB in association with the Arts Council of England an Elba Films/Paragon Entertainment Corporation production, with the participation of the Government of Canada-Canadian Film and Video Production Tax Credit Program, developed with the support of the European Script Fund
99 minutes 6 seconds
S&S January 2000 p60

SEUL CONTRE TOUS/I STAND ALONE

Alliance Releasing (UK) - 19 March
(18) France, Dir Gaspar Noé
with Philippe Nahon, Blandine Lenoir, Frankye Pain, Martine Audrain, Zaven
© Gaspar Noé/Les Cinéma de la Zone
Produced by Les Cinémas de la Zone with the participation of Love Streams Production/Canal+/le Centre National de la Cinématographie and the financial support of La Procirep
92 minutes 31 seconds
S&S April 1999 p58

SEX LIFE IN L.A.

Dangerous to Know - 2 January
(not submitted) Germany, Dir Jochen Hick
with Matt Bradshaw, Tony Ward, Cole Tucker, Kevin Kramer, Patrick Morgan
© Galeria Alaska Productions/Jochen Hick
Galeria Alaska Productions present a film by Jochen Hick, funded by Hessische Filmförderung für Wissenschaft und Kunst

90 minutes
S&S February 1999 p52

SHAHEED-E-MOHABBAT BOOTA SINGH/MARTYR-IN-LOVE, BOOTA SINGH

Eros Video (Electronics) Ltd - 12 February
India, Dir Manoj Punj
with Gurdas Mann, Divya Dutta, Raghuvir Yadav, Arun Bakshi, Yograj Chedda
Sain Productions
130 minutes
No S&S reference

SHAHEED UDHAM SINGH

Venus - 24 December
India, Dir Chitrath Singh
with Raj Babbar, Barry John, Tom Alter, Shatrughan Sinha, Gurdas Mann
made in Hindi, Punjabi and English
No S&S reference

SHAKESPEARE IN LOVE

United International Pictures (UK) Ltd - 29 January
(15) USA, Dir John Madden
with Joseph Fiennes, Gwyneth Paltrow, Judi Dench, Ben Affleck, Colin Firth
© Miramax Films/Universal Pictures
Universal Pictures presents a Bedford Falls production
123 minutes 13 seconds
S&S February 1999 p5

*SHATRANJ KE KHILARI/The CHESS PLAYERS

Contemporary - 14 May [NFT First Run 14-27 May]
(PG) India, Dir Satyajit Ray
with Sanjeev Kumar, Saeed Jaffrey, Amjad Khan, Richard Attenborough, Shabana Azmi
Devki Chitra Productions
113 minutes
MFB March 1979 p53

SHE'S ALL THAT

FilmFour Distributors - 21 May
(12) USA, Dir Robert Iscove
with Freddie Prinze Jr, Rachael Leigh Cook, Matthew Lillard, Paul Walker, Jodi Lyn O'Keefe
© Miramax Film Corp.
A Tapestry Films/FilmColony production
95 minutes 30 seconds
S&S July 1999 p52

SHUANGLONG HUI/TWIN DRAGONS

Buena Vista International (UK) - 14 May
(12) Hong Kong/USA, Dir Tsui Hark and Ringo Lam Ling-Tung
with Jackie Chan, Maggie Cheung Man-Yuk, Teddy Robin Kwan, Anthony Chan Yau, Philip Chan Yan-Kin
© 1991 Paragon Films Ltd
Hong Kong Film Directors' Guild
89 minutes 11 seconds
S&S June 1999 p54

SIDE STREETS

First Independent Films Ltd - 23 April
(15) USA, Dir Tony Gerber
with Valeria Golino, Shashi Kapoor, Leon, Art Malik, Shabana Azmi
© Side Street Productions
A Merchant Ivory & Cornerstone Films production
130 minutes 50 seconds
S&S May 1999 p55

Die SIEBTELBAUERN/The INHERITORS

Metrodome Distribution Ltd - 28 May 1999
(15) Austria/Germany, Dir Stefan Ruzowitzky
with Sophie Rois, Simon Schwarz, Lars Rudolph, Tilo Prückner, Ulrich Wildgruber
© Dor Film
A Dor Film production in collaboration with ORF and BR, with the support of Österreichisches Filminstitut and Filmförderung des Landes Oberösterreich
94 minutes 11 seconds
subtitles
S&S March 1999 p42

The SIEGE

20th Century Fox (UK) - 8 January
(15) USA, Dir Edward Zwick
with Denzel Washington, Bruce Willis, Annette Bening, Tony Shalhoub, Sami Bouajila
© Twentieth Century Fox Corporation
Twentieth Century Fox presents a Lynda Obst production
116 minutes 1 second
S&S February 1999 p54

SILSILA HAI PYAR KA

Eros Video (Electronics) Ltd - 16 April
India, Dir Shrabani Deodhar
with Karishma Kapoor, Chandrachur

Singh, Aruna Irani, Shakti Kapoor, Saeed Jaffrey
N.N. Sippy Productions
No S&S reference

SIMON BIRCH
Buena Vista International (UK) - 25 June
(PG) USA, Dir Mark Stephen Johnson
with Ian Michael Smith, Joseph Mazzello, Ashely Judd, Oliver Platt, David Strathairn
© **Hollywood Pictures Company**
Hollywood Pictures present in association with Caravan Pictures a Roger Birnbaum/Laurence Mark production
113 minutes 52 seconds
S&S July 1999 p53

A SIMPLE PLAN
United International Pictures (UK) Ltd - 21 May
(15)
USA/UK/Japan/Germany/France, Dir Sam Raimi
with Bill Paxton, Billy Bob Thornton, Bridget Fonda, Gary Cole, Brent Briscoe
© **Paramount Pictures Corporation Mutual Film Company/British Broadcasting Corporation/Marubeni/Toho Towa/Tele-München/UGC-PH/Paramount Pictures present in association with Savoy Pictures, produced in association with British Broadcasting Corporation/Marubeni/Telemünchen/Toho-Towa/UGC-PH**
121 minutes 6 seconds
S&S June 1999 p52

SIMPLY IRRESISTIBLE
20th Century Fox (UK) - 22 October
(PG) USA/Germany, Dir Mark Tarlov
with Sarah Michelle Gellar, Sean Patrick Flanery, Patricia Clarkson, Dylan Baker, Christopher Durang
© **Monarchy Enterprises, B.V. and Regency Entertainment (USA), Inc.**
Regency Entertainment presents a Polar production in association with Taurus Film
95 minutes 39 seconds
Super 35 [2.35:1]
S&S November 1999 p54

SIRF TUM
Shernwali - 11 June
India, Dir Ahathian
with Sanjay Kapoor, Priya Gill, Mohnish Bahl, Johny Lever, Tej

Sapru
Narsimha Enterprises
No S&S reference

SITCOM
Alliance Releasing (UK) - 8 January
(18) France, Dir François Ozon
with Evelyne Dandry, François Marthouret, Marina de Van, Adrien de Van, Stéphane Rideau
© **Fidélité Productions/Le Studio Canal+**
Fidélité Productions presents in co-production with Le Studio Canal+, with the participation of Canal+
80 minutes 7 seconds
Subtitles
S&S January 1999 p56

The SIXTH SENSE
Buena Vista International (UK) - 5 November
(15) USA, Dir M.Night Shyamalan
with Bruce Willis, Toni Collette, Olivia Williams, Haley Joel Osment, Donnie Wahlberg
© **Spyglass Entertainment Group, L.P.**
Hollywood Pictures/Spyglass Entertainment present a Kennedy/Marshall/Barry Mendel production, the Kennedy/Marshall Company
107 minutes 24 seconds
S&S November 1999 p54

SKIN FLICK
Millivres Multimedia - 10 September
(not submitted) Germany/UK/Canada/Japan, Dir Bruce LaBruce
with Steve Master, Eden Miller, Tom International, Ralph Steel, Tim Vincent
© **Cazzo Film**
Cazzo Film in association with Millivres and Suzuki Akihiro/Stance Company
67 minutes
S&S November 1999 p55

SLAM
Metro Tartan Distributors - 9 April
(15) USA, Dir Marc Levin
with Saul Williams, Sonja Sohn, Beau Sia, Bonz Malone, Lawrence Wilson
© **Offline Entertainment Group**
An Offline Entertainment Group and Slam Pictures presentation
103 minutes 1 second
S&S April 1999 p59

SOLOMON AND GAENOR
FilmFour Distributors - 30 April
(15) UK, Dir Paul Morrison
with Ioan Gruffudd, Nia Roberts, Sue Jones Davies, William Thomas, Mark Lewis Jones
© **S4C and APT Film and Television Limited**
S4C and FilmFour with the Arts Council of England and the Arts Council of Wales present an APT Film and Television production in association with September Films for S4C and FilmFour supported by the National Lottery through the Arts Council of England and Wales
103 minutes 45 seconds
S&S May 1999 p56

SOORYAVANSHAM
Eros Video (Electronics) Ltd - 21 May
India, Dir E.V.V. Satyanarayana
with Amitabh Bachchan, Soundarya, Anupam Kher, Kader Khan, Bindu
Padmalaya Combines
No S&S reference

SOUR GRAPES
Warner Bros Distributors (UK) - 15 January
(15) USA, Dir Larry David
with Steven Weber, Craig Bierko, Matt Keeslar, Karen Sillas, Viola Harris
© **Castle Rock Entertainment**
A Castle Rock Entertainment presentation
91 minutes 52 seconds
S&S March 1999 p52

*SOUTH
BFI Collections - 23 July [NFT First Run 23-31 July]
(not submitted) UK, Dir Frank Hurley
with Ernest Shackleton
Imperial Trans-Antarctic Film Syndicate
c71 minutes
silent, black & white
[restoration 1998 by the NFTVA]
No S&S or MFB reference

SOUTH PARK BIGGER LONGER & UNCUT
Warner Bros Distributors (UK) - 27 August
(15) USA, Dir Trey Parker
with the character voices of Trey Parker, Matt Stone, Mary Kay Bergman, Isaac Hayes, Jesse Howell
© **Paramount Pictures Corporation and Warner Bros.**

Paramount Pictures and Warner Bros present a Scott Rudin and Trey Parker/Matt Stone production in association with Comedy Central
81 minutes 9 seconds
S&S September 1999 p55

SOUTHPAW
Downtown Pictures - 15 January
(15) Ireland/UK, Dir Liam McGrath
with Francis Barrett, Chick Gillen, Tom Humphries, Colum Flynn, Nicholas Cruz Hernandez
© Treasure Films
A Treasure Films production for Radio Telefis Éireann and Bord Scannán na hÉireann/the Irish Film Board and Channel 4, a Hillside Productions production for Treasure Films Ireland, produced with the support of investment incentives for the Irish film industry provided by the Government of Ireland
79 minutes 52 seconds
S&S March 1999 p53

STAR TREK INSURRECTION
United International Pictures (UK) Ltd - 1 January
(PG) USA, Dir Jonathan Frakes
with Patrick Stewart, Jonathan Frakes, Brent Spiner, LeVar Burton, Michael Dorn
© Paramount Pictures
Paramount Pictures presents a Rick Berman production
103 minutes 1 second
S&S February 1999 p55

STAR WARS EPISODE I THE PHANTOM MENACE
20th Century Fox (UK) - 16 July
(U) USA, Dir George Lucas
with Liam Neeson, Ewan McGregor, Natalie Portman, Jake Lloyd, Pernilla August
© Lucasfilm Ltd
A Lucasfilm Ltd production
132 minutes 43 seconds
S&S July 1999 p54

STEPMOM
Columbia Tristar Films - 29 January
(12) USA/Germany, Dir Chris Columbus
with Julia Roberts, Susan Sarandon, Ed Harris, Jena Malone, Liam Aiken
© Global Entertainment Productions GmbH & Co. Film KG

Columbia Pictures presents a Wendy Finerman production, A 1492 production
124 minutes 55 seconds
S&S February 1999 p56

The STICKY FINGERS OF TIME
Feature Film Company - shown as part of the 'American Independence' tour from 12 March
USA, Dir Hilary Brougher
with Nicole Zaray, Terumi Matthews, Belinda Becker, James Urbaniak, Leo Marks
Crystal Pictures/Good Machine
81 minutes
No S&S reference

STOP MAKING SENSE
Metrodome Distribution Ltd - 10 September
(PG) US, Dir Jonathan Demme
with David Byrne, Chris Frantz, Jerry Harrison, Tina Weymouth, Edna Holt
Talking Heads Films in association with Arnold Stiefel Company
88 minutes
MFB January 1985 p28

The STRAIGHT STORY
FilmFour Distributors - 3 December
(U) USA/France/UK, Dir David Lynch
with Richard Farnsworth, Sissy Spacek, Harry Dean Stanton, Everett McGill, John Farley
© The Straight Story, Inc.
Alain Sarde presents with Le Studio Canal+ and with the participation of FilmFour a Picture Factory production
111 minutes 26 seconds
S&S December 1999 p57

*STRANGERS ON A TRAIN
Contemporary - 13 August
(PG) US, Dir Alfred Hitchcock
with Farley Granger, Ruth Roman, Robert Walker, Leo G.Carroll, Patricia Hitchcock
Warner Bros.
100 minutes
MFB August 1951 p309

SUCH A LONG JOURNEY
Optimum Releasing - 15 October
(15) Canada/UK, Dir Sturla Gunnarsson
with Roshan Seth, Om Puri, Soni Razdan, Naseeruddin Shah, Sam Dastor
© Long Journey Inc, and Amy

International Artists Limited The Film Works and Amy International Artists present with the participation of Telefilm Canada/British Screen and the Harold Greenberg Fund, produced in association with Canada Television and Cable Production Fund/Telefilm Canada Equity Investment Program, Canadian Broadcasting Corporation/BSkyB/TMN - The Movie Network/UTV - United Television, developed with the assistance of British Screen Finance Limited/Telefilm Canada/the Harold Greenberg Fund and Ontario Film Development Corporation, produced with the participation of the Government of Canada/Canadian Film or Video Production Tax Credit Program and the Government of Ontario/Ontario Film and Television Tax Credit Program
113 minutes 20 seconds
S&S November 1999 p57

SWEET ANGEL MINE
Optimum Releasing - 17 September
(18) UK/Canada, Dir Curtis Radclyffe
with Oliver Milburn, Margaret Langrick, Anna Massey, Alberta Watson, John Dunsworth
© Mass Love Ltd and IMX Angel Flik Inc.
HandMade Films with the participation of British Screen/Telefilm Canada/the Nova Scotia Development Corporation in association with Statescreen Productions and Picture Palace, a Mass-Sam Taylor/Imagex production, developed with the assistance of British Screen Finance Ltd
88 minutes 14 seconds
S&S October 1999 p55

SWING
Entertainment Film Distributors Ltd - 7 May
(15) USA, Dir Nick Mead
with Hugo Speer, Lisa Stansfield, Tom Bell, Rita Tushingham, Alexei Sayle
© The Kushner-Locke Company and The Alpine Releasing Corporation
A Tapestry Films and The Kushner-Locke Company presentation

97 minutes 24 seconds
S&S June 1999 p52

SWITCHBLADE SISTERS
Downtown Pictures - 12 February
(18) USA, Dir Jack Hill
with Robbie Lee, Joanne Nail,
Monica Gayle, Asher Brauner, Chase
Newhart
© Centaur Pictures Inc
a Centaur Releasing presentation
86 minutes 5 seconds
S&S January 1999 p57

TAAL
Eros Video (Electronics) Ltd - 13
August
India, Dir Subhash Ghai
with Akshaye khanna, Aishwarya
Rai, Anil Kapoor, Amrish Puri, Alok
Nath
Mukta Arts
No S&S reference

TANGO
Metrodome Distribution Ltd - 9
July
(12) Argentina/Spain/France/
Germany, Dir Carlos Saura
with Miguel Àngel Solá, Cecilia
Narova, Mia Maestro, Juan Carlos
Copes, Carlos Rivarola
© Argentina Sono Film SACI,
Argentina/Alma Ata International
Pictures SL, Spain
Pandora Cinema presents an
Argentina Sono Film SACI/Alma
Ata International Pictures co-
production in association with
Terraplen Producciones/Astrolabio
Producciones/Adela Pictures/Beco
Films/Hollywood Partners/Saura
Films, a Juan C. Codazzi
production idea
115 minutes 27 seconds
subtitles
S&S August 1999 p52

TARZAN
Buena Vista International (UK) - 8
October
(U) USA, Dir Kevin Lima and Chris
Buck
with the character voices of Brian
Blessed, Glenn Close, Minnie Driver,
Tony Goldwyn, Nigel Hawthorne
© Edgar Rice Burroughs,
Inc/Disney Enterprises, Inc
Walt Disney Pictures presents
88 minutes 28 seconds
S&S November 1999 p58

TAXI
Metrodome Distribution Ltd - 26
November
(15) France, Dir Gérard Pirès

with Samy Naceri, Frédéric
Diefenthal, Marion Cotillard, Emma
Sjöberg, Manuela Gourary
© ARP/TF1 Films Production/Le
Studio Canal+
Luc Besson presents an ARP
production in co-production with
TF1 Films Production/Le Studio
Canal+, with the participation of
Canal+ and the financial support
of Cofimage 9 and of Studio
Images 4
89 minutes 45 seconds
Anamorphic [Technovision]
subtitles
S&S December 1999 p58

TE CON IL DUCE/TEA WITH MUSSOLINI
United International Pictures (UK)
Ltd - 2 April
(PG) Italy/UK, Dir Franco Zeffirelli
with Cher, Judi Dench, Joan
Plowright, Maggie Smith, Lily
Tomlin
© Medusa Film spa/Cineritmo
srl/Cattleya srl/Business Affair
Productions Ltd
A Medusa Film/Cattleya,
Cineritmo (Rome)/Film and
General Productions (London) co-
production
116 minutes 7 seconds
S&S April 1999 p60

TENSHI NO KUZU/ANGEL DUST
ICA - 8 January
Japan, Dir Sogo Ishii
with Kaho Minami, Takeshi
Wakamatsu, Etsushi Toyokawa,
Ryoko Takizawa
Euro Space, Twins Japan
117 minutes
No S&S reference

TEN THINGS I HATE ABOUT YOU
Buena Vista International (UK) - 9
July
(12) USA, Dir Gil Junger
with Julia Stiles, Heath Ledger,
Joseph Gordon-Levitt, Larisa
Oleynik, Larry Miller
© Touchstone Pictures
Touchstone Pictures presents a
Mad Chance/Jaret Entertainment
production
97 minutes 31 seconds
S&S July 1999 p55

TERRA ESTRANGEIRA/FOREIGN LAND
ICA - shown at the ICA (London)

from 12 February
(not submitted), Dir Walter Salles
with Fernanda Torres, Fernando
Alves Pinto, Luis Melo, Alexandre
Borges, Laura Cardoso
VideoFilmes Producoes Artisticas,
Animátografo-Producão de Filmes
110 minutes
No S&S reference

THAKSHAK
Venus - 3 December
India, Dir Govind Nihalani
with Ajay Devgan, Tabu, Amrish
Puri, Rahul Bose, Govind Namdeo
Udbhav
No S&S reference

The THEORY OF FLIGHT
Buena Vista International (UK) -
24 September
(15) South Africa/UK, Dir Paul
Greengrass
with Helena Bonham Carter, Kenneth
Branagh, Gemma Jones, Holly Aird,
Ray Stevenson
© Distant Horizon Ltd.
A Distant Horizon and BBC Films
presentation
101 minutes 15 seconds
S&S October 1999 p56

*O THIASSOS/The TRAVELLING PLAYERS
Greekfilm - 9 July
Greece, Dir Theo Angelopoulos
with Eva Kotamanidou, Aliki
Georgoulis, Stratos Pachis, Maris
Vassiliou, Petros Zarkadis
Georges Papalios Productions
230 minutes
MFB May 1976 p108-109+116

The THIN RED LINE
20th Century Fox (UK) - 26
February
(15) USA, Dir Terrence Malick
with Sean Penn, Adrien Brody, James
Caviezel, Ben Chaplin, George
Clooney
© Twentieth Century Fox Film
Corporation
A Fox 2000 Pictures presentation
from Phoenix Pictures in
association with George Stevens Jr,
a Geisler Roberdeau production
170 minutes 36 seconds
S&S March 1999 p53

*The THIRD MAN
Optimum Releasing - 16 July
(PG) UK, Dir Carol Reed
with Joseph Cotten, Valli, Orson
Welles, Trevor Howard, Paul
Hoerbiger

London Film Productions/British
Lion Film Corporation
104 minutes
MFB September 1949 p159

The 13TH WARRIOR
Buena Vista International (UK) - 3
September
(15) USA, Dir John McTiernan
with Antonio Banderas, Diane
Venora, Dennis Storhøi, Vladimir
Kulich, Omar Sharif
© Touchstone Pictures
Touchstone Pictures presents a
Crichton/McTiernan production
102 minutes 38 seconds
S&S September 1999 p57

*The 39 STEPS
Winstone Film Distributors - 5
March
(PG) UK, Dir Alfred Hitchcock
with Robert Donat, Madeleine
Carroll, Lucie Mannheim, Godfrey
Tearle, Peggy Ashcroft
Gaumont-British Picture
Corporation
87 minutes
MFB June 1935 p72

THIS YEAR'S LOVE
Entertainment Film Distributors
Ltd - 19 February
(18) UK, Dir David Kane
with Kathy Burke, Jennifer Ehle, Ian
Hart, Douglas Henshall, Catherine
McCormack
© Entertainment Film Distributors
Ltd
Entertainment Film Distributors
presents a Kismet Film production
in association with the Scottish Arts
Council National Lottery Fund
108 minutes 50 seconds
S&S March 1999 p55

The THOMAS CROWN AFFAIR
United International Pictures (UK)
Ltd - 20 August
(15) USA, Dir John McTiernan
with Pierce Brosnan, Rene Russo,
Denis Leary, Ben Gazzara, Frankie
Faison
© Metro-Goldwyn-Mayer Pictures
Inc.
Metro-Goldwyn-Mayer Pictures
presents an Irish Dream Time
production
113 minutes 20 seconds
S&S September 1999 p58

The TICHBORNE CLAIMANT
Redbus Film Distribution - 12

November
(PG) UK, Dir David Yates
with John Kani, Robert Pugh,
Stephen Fry, Robert Hardy, John
Gielgud
© Tom McCabe and Bigger Picture
Company
Tom McCabe presents a Bigger
Picture Company production in
association with Swiftcall
International Telephone Company
and the Isle of Man Film
Commission
98 minutes 11 seconds
S&S December 1999 p59

TITANIC TOWN
Alliance Releasing (UK) - 26
February
(15) UK/Germany/France, Dir Roger
Michell
with Julie Walters, Ciaran Hinds,
Ciaran McMenamin, Nuala O'Neill,
Lorcan Cranitch
© Titanic Town Ltd
BBC Films presents in association
with Hollywood Partners/Pandora
Cinema, supported by the Arts
Council of Northern Ireland
through its National Lottery Fund,
with the participation of British
Screen, a Company Pictures
production, developed with the
assistance of British Screen
Finance Limited
101 minutes 34 seconds
S&S January 1999 p58

TODO SOBRE MI MADRE/ALL ABOUT MY MOTHER
Pathé Distribution - 27 August
(15) Spain/France, Dir Pedro
Almodóvar
with Cecilia Roth, Marisa Paredes,
Candela Peña, Antonia San Juan,
Penelope Cruz
© El Deseo S.A./Renn
Productions/France 2 Cinéma
Agustín Almodóvar & Claude
Berri present an El Deseo
S.A./Renn Productions/France 2
Cinéma co-production
101 minutes 17 seconds
subtitles
S&S September 1999 p40

*TO HAVE AND HAVE NOT
BFI Collections - 8 January [NFT
First Run 8-14 January]
(PG) US, Dir Howard Hawks
with Humphrey Bogart, Walter
Brennan, Lauren Bacall, Marcel
Dalio, Hoagy Carmichael

Warner Bros.
100 minutes
MFB March 1945 p38

TOUCH OF EVIL
Artificial Eye Film Company - 18
June
(12) USA, Dir Orson Welles
with Charlton Heston, Janet Leigh,
Orson Welles, Joseph Calleia, Akim
Tamiroff
Universal Pictures Company
108 minutes
MFB June 1958 p73

Un 32 AOÛT SUR TERRE
Alliance Releasing (UK) - shown at
the ICA (London) 11-16 June
(not submitted) Quebec, Dir Denis
Villeneuve
with Pascale Bussières, Alexis Martin
Max Films Productions
88 minutes
No S&S reference

The TRENCH
Entertainment Film Distributors
Ltd - 17 September
(15) UK/France, Dir William Boyd
with Paul Nicholls, Daniel Craig,
Julian Rhind-Tutt, Danny Dyer,
James D'Arcy
© Somme Productions Ltd
A Blue PM/Skyline Films/Galatée
Films production with
participation of British Screen in
association with the Arts Council of
England and Bonaparte Films Ltd,
with support of Canal+, supported
by the National Lottery through
the Arts Council of
England/Bonaparte, finance
provided by British Screen through
the European Co-production Fund
(UK)
98 minutes 39 seconds
S&S October 1999 p57

TRUE CRIME
Warner Bros Distributors (UK) -
14 May
(15) USA, Dir Clint Eastwood
with Clint Eastwood, Isaiah
Washington, Denis Leary, Lisa Gay
Hamilton, Diane Venora
© Warner Bros.
Warner Bros. presents a Zanuck
Company/Malpaso production
127 minutes 23 seconds
S&S June 1999 p53

TWO GIRLS AND A GUY
20th Century Fox (UK) - 29
January
(18) USA, Dir James Toback

with Robert Downey Jr, Heather Graham, Natasha Gregson Wagner, Angel David, Frederique Van Der Wal
© Two Girls Inc
Fox Searchlight Pictures presents an Edward R. Pressman production, produced in association with Muse Productions
84 minutes 21 seconds
S&S February 1999 p57

UNIVERSAL SOLDIER THE RETURN
Columbia Tristar Films (UK) - 17 September
(18) USA, Dir Mic Rodgers
with Jean-Claude Van Damme, Michael Jai White, Heidi Schanz, Xander Berkeley, Justin Lazard
© TriStar Pictures, Inc.
TriStar Pictures presents a Baumgarten Prophet Entertainment/IndieProd Company/Long Road production
83 minutes
S&S November 1999 p59

URBAN LEGEND
Columbia Tristar Films (UK) - 26 February
(18) USA/France, Dir Jamie Blanks
with Jared Leto, Alicia Witt, Rebecca Gayheart, Joshua Jackson, Natasha Gregson Wagner
© Phoenix Pictures, Inc
Phoenix Pictures presents a Neal H. Moritz/Gina Matthews production in association with Canal + D.A.
99 minutes 33 seconds
S&S March 1999 p56

VAASTAV
Eros Video (Electronics) Ltd - 15 October
India, Dir Mahesh Manjrekar
with Sanjay Dutt, Namrata Shirodkar, Mohnish Bahl, Ektaa Kapoor, Reema Lagoo
Adishakti Films/Visions P. Ltd
No S&S reference

VAMPIRES/JOHN CARPENTER'S VAMPIRES
Columbia Tristar Films (UK) - 29 October
(18) USA, Dir John Carpenter
with James Woods, Daniel Baldwin, Sheryl Lee, Thomas Ian Griffith, Maximilian Schell
© Largo Entertainment, Inc.
Columbia Pictures and Largo Entertainment present a Storm

King production
107 minutes 48 seconds
Anamorphic [Panavision]
S&S December 1999 p60

VARSITY BLUES
United International Pictures (UK) Ltd - 10 September
(15) USA, Dir Brian Robbins
with James Van Der Beek, Jon Voight, Paul Walker, Ron Lester, Scott Caan
© Paramount Pictures Corporation
Paramount Pictures presents in association with MTV Films a Marquee Tollin/Robbins production in association with Tova Laiter Productions
104 minutes 46 seconds
S&S August 1999 p54

VÉNUS BEAUTÉ (INSTITUT)/VENUS BEAUTY
Gala Film Distributors - 18 June
(15) France, Dir Tonie Marshall
with Nathalie Baye, Bulle Ogier, Samuel LeBihan, Jacques Bonnaffé, Mathilde Seigner
© Agat Films & Cie/Arte Cinéma/Tabo Tabo
Agat Films & Cie/Gilles Sandoz present in co-production with Arte France Cinéma/Tabo Tabo Films with the participation of Canal+ & Sofica Sofinergie 4/Centre National de la Cinématographie
subtitles
106 minutes 43 seconds
S&S July 1999 p56

VERY BAD THINGS
PolyGram Filmed Entertainment - 29 January
(18) USA, Dir Peter Berg
with Christian Slater, Cameron Diaz, Daniel Stern, Jeanne Tripplehorn, Jon Favreau
© VBT Productions, Inc
PolyGram Filmed Entertainment presents in association with Initial Entertainment Group an Interscope Communications production in association with Ballpark Productions
100 minutes 25 seconds
S&S January 1999 p59

VIGO PASSION FOR LIFE
FilmFour Distributors - 4 June
(15)
UK/Japan/France/Spain/Germany, Dir Julien Temple
with Romane Bohringer, James Frain, Jim Carter, Diana Quick,

William Scott-Masson
© Channel Four Television Corporation and Little Magic/DML/Amuse/TV Tokyo
Channel Four Films presents in association with Little Magic Films an Impact Pictures/Nitrate Film/MACT production in association with Tornasol Films, SA/Road Movies Vierte Produktionen with the participation of Canal+ in co-operation with WDR/ARTE, an Impact Pictures/Nitrate Film/MACT production for Little Magic Films and Channel 4, developed with the support of the European Script Fund, produced with the help of Babs Thomas
103 minutes 2 seconds
S&S June 1999 p55

VIRTUAL SEXUALITY
Columbia Tristar Films (UK) - 2 July
(15) UK, Dir Nick Hurran
with Laura Fraser, Rupert Penry-Jones, Luke De Lacey, Kieran O'Brien, Marcelle Duprey
© Virtual Sexuality Productions, Ltd
The Bridge presents a Noel Gay Motion Picture Company production
92 minutes 17 seconds
S&S August 1999 p55

VIRUS
United International Pictures (UK) Ltd - 4 June
(18) USA, Dir John Bruno
with Jamie Lee Curtis, William Baldwin, Donald Sutherland, Joanna Pacula, Marshall Bell
© Universal City Studios, Inc
Universal Pictures and Mutual Film Company present a Dark Horse Entertainment/Valhalla Motion Pictures production
99 minutes 16 seconds
S&S June 1999 p56

La VITA È BELLA/LIFE IS BEAUTIFUL
Buena Vista International (UK) - 12 February
(PG) Italy, Dir Roberto Benigni
with Roberto Benigni, Nicoletta Braschi, Giustino Durano, Sergio Bustric, Lydia Alfonsi
© Melampo Cinematografica srl - Roma
Mario e Vittorio Cecchi Gori present/Roberto Benigni presents a production of Melampo

Cinematografica
116 minutes 25 seconds
subtitles
S&S February 1999 p46

WAKING NED
20th Century Fox (UK) - 19 March
(PG) UK/France/USA, Dir Kirk
Jones
with Ian Bannen, David Kelly,
Fionnula Flanagan, Susan Lynch,
James Nesbitt
© Tomboy Films (Ned Devine) Ltd
Tomboy Films present in
association with The Gruber
Brothers/Mainstream S.A.,
Bonaparte Films Ltd/the Isle of
Man Commission and Overseas
Filmgroup and with the
participation of Canal+
90 minutes 57 seconds
[US title: WAKING NED DEVINE]
S&S April 1999 p61

A WALK ON THE MOON
Miracle Communications - 19
November
(15) USA, Dir Tony Goldwyn
with Diane Lane, Viggo Mortensen,
Liev Schreiber, Anna Paquin, Tovah
Feldshuh
A Punch Production in association
with Village Roadshow
Pictures/Groucho Film Partnership
107 minutes 23 seconds
S&S December 1999 p61

WANDAFURU RAIFU/AFTER LIFE/WONDERFUL LIFE
ICA Projects - shown at the ICA
(London) 1 October
(not submitted) Japan, Dir Hirokazu
Koreeda
with Arata, Erika Oda, Susumu
Terajima, Taketoshi Naito, Kyoko
Kagawa
© TV Man Union, Inc/Engine Film,
Inc
118 minutes
S&S October 1999 p36

The WAR ZONE
FilmFour Distributors - 3
September
(18) UK/Italy, Dir Tim Roth
with Ray Winstone, Lara Belmont,
Freddie Cunliffe, Tilda Swinton,
Annabelle Apsion
© FilmFour Limited
FilmFour presents a Sarah
Radclyffe Productions/Portobello
Pictures production in association
with Fandango s.r.l. and Mikado

s.r.l., developed with the support of
the European Script Fund
98 minutes 57 seconds
S&S September 1999 p59

The WATERBOY
Buena Vista International (UK) -
30 April
(12) USA, Dir Frank Coraci
with Adam Sandler, Kathy Bates,
Fairuza Balk, Jerry Reed, Henry
Winkler
© Touchstone Pictures
Touchstone Pictures presents a
Robert Simonds/Jack Giarraputo
production
89 minutes 42 seconds
S&S May 1999 p57

WEST BEYROUTH/WEST BEIRUT
Metrodome Distribution Ltd - 23
July
(15)
France/Lebanon/Belgium/Norway,
Dir Ziad Doueiri
with Rami Doueiri, Mohammad
Chamas, Rola Al Amin, Carmen
Loubbos, Joseph Bou Nassar
© La Sept ARTE/3B Productions
La Sept ARTE 3B
Productions/Jean Bréhat & Rachid
Bouchareb & Douri Films present
a La Sept ARTE/Unité de
Programmes Fictions/Pierre
Chevalier & 3B productions
(France)/Douri Films (Liban)/Ciné
Libre (Belgium) [Eliane
Dubois]/Exposed Film productions
a.s. (Norway) [Bjørn Eivind
Aarskog] co-production with the
participation of Ministère Français
de la Culture & Ministère des
Affaires Etrangères/Centre
National de la Cinématographie
with the support of l'Agence de la
Francophonie/RTBF/NRK/Canal
Horizons
110 minutes 6 seconds
subtitles
S&S August 1999 p56

WILD WILD WEST
Warner Bros Distributors (UK) -
13 August
(12) USA, Dir Barry Sonnenfeld
with Will Smith, Kevin Kline,
Kenneth Branagh, Salma Hayek,
M.Emmet Walsh
© Warner Bros.
Warner Bros. presents a Peters
Entertainment/Sonnenfeld-
Josephson production in
association with Todman, Simon,
LeMasters Productions

105 minutes 49 seconds
S&S September 1999 p60

WING COMMANDER
20th Century Fox (UK) - 25 June
(PG) USA, Dir Chris Roberts
with Freddie Prinze Jr., Saffron
Burrows, Tchéky Karyo, David
Suchet, David Warner
No Prisoners/Digital Anvil in
association with Origin Systems,
Inc/Carousel Pictures Company
100 minutes
No S&S reference

The WINSLOW BOY
Columbia Tristar Films - 29
October
(U) USA, Dir David Mamet
with Nigel Hawthorne, Jeremy
Northam, Rebecca Pidgeon, Gemma
Jones, Matthew Pidgeon
© The Winslow Partnership,
L.L.C.
Sony Pictures Classics presents a
David Mamet film
104 minutes 24 seconds
S&S November 1999 p60

WINTERSCHLÄFER/WINTER SLEEPERS
City Screen Ltd - 2 July
(15) Germany/France, Dir Tom
Tykwer
with Floriane Daniel, Heino Ferch,
Ulrich Matthes, Marie-Lou Sellem,
Laura Tonke
© X Filme creative pool GmbH,
Berlin
X Filme creative pool in association
with Filmstiftung
NRW/FilmFernsehFonds
Bayern/Palladio
Film/WDR/MDR/art and BMI
present an X Filme creative pool
GmbH with Palladio
Film/Westdeutschen Rundfunk
WDR/Mitteldeutscher Rundfunk
MDR/arte co-production with
Filmstiftung
NR/FilmFernsehFonds
Bayern/Bundesministerium des
Innern
122 minutes 31 seconds
subtitles
S&S August 1999 p57

WITH OR WITHOUT YOU
FilmFour Distributors - 3
December
(18) UK, Dir Michael Winterbottom
with Christopher Eccleston, Dervla
Kirwan, Yvan Attal, Julie Graham,
Alun Armstrong
© FilmFour/Miramax Films

Revolution Films/presented by FilmFour and Miramax Films
90 minutes
No S&S reference

WITHOUT LIMITS
Warner Bros Distributors (UK) - 4 June
(12) USA, Dir Robert Towne
with Billy Crudup, Donald Sutherland, Monica Potter, Jeremy Sisto, Matthew Lillard
© Warner Bros.
Warner Bros. presents a Cruise/Wagner production
118 minutes 1 second
S&S July 1999 p57

The WORLD IS NOT ENOUGH
United International Pictures (UK) Ltd - 26 November
(12) UK/USA, Dir Michael Apted
with Pierce Brosnan, Sophie Marceau, Robert Carlyle, Denise Richards, Robbie Coltrane
© Danjaq LLC and United Artists Corporation
Albert R. Broccoli's Eon Productions Limited
128 minutes 1 second
Anamorphic [Panavision]
S&S January 2000 p62

WO SHI SHUI/WHO AM I?
Columbia Tristar Films (UK) - 11 June
(12) Hong Kong, Dir Jackie Chan and Benny Chan Muk-Sing
with Jackie Chan, Michelle Ferre, Mirai Yamamoto, Ron Smerczak, Ed Nelson
© Golden Harvest Pictures Limited
A Golden Harvest presentation, a Leonard Ho Production
107 minutes 54 seconds
S&S September 1999 p60

XIANGGANG ZHIZAO/MADE IN HONG KONG
ICA Projects - shown at the ICA from 25 June
(15) Hong Kong, Dir Fruit Chan Kuo
with Sam Lee Chan-Sam, Wenbers Li Tung-Chuen, Neiky Yim Hui-Chi, Amy Tam Ka-Chuen, Carol Lam Kit-Fong
© Nicetop Independent Limited
Presented by Shu Kei, produced by Nicetop Independent Ltd/Team Work Production House Ltd
108 minutes 33 seconds
subtitles

S&S August 1999 p47

*YA CUBA/SOY CUBA/I AM CUBA
Shown at the Barbican Cinema on 21 May
(not submitted) USSR/Cuba, Dir Mikhail Kalatozov
with Sergio Corrieri, José Gallardo, Raúl Garcia, Luz Maria Collazo, Jean Bouise
© Mosfilm
Mosfilm (USSR)/ICAIC (Cuba)
141 minutes
S&S August 1999 p45

*YELLOW SUBMARINE
United International Pictures (UK) Ltd - 3 September
(U) UK, Dir George Dunning
with the voices of John Clive, Geoffrey Hughes, Peter Batten, Paul Angelus, Dick Emery
King Features Entertainment/Subafilms/Apple Films/TV Cartoons
87 minutes
MFB September 1968 p136

YOU'RE DEAD...
Entertainment Film Distributors Ltd - 1 October
(15) USA/Germany, Dir Andy Hurst
with John Hurt, Rhys Ifans, Claire Skinner, Barbara Flynn, John Benfield
© Atlantic Streamline Filmproductions, Inc
Atlantic Streamline Filmproduction presents a Marco Weber production
97 minutes 16 seconds
Anamorphic [Arriscope]
S&S November 1999 p61

YOUR FRIENDS & NEIGHBOURS
PolyGram Filmed Entertainment - 12 February
(18) USA, Dir Neil LaBute
with Amy Brenneman, Aaron Eckhart, Catherine Keener, Nastassja Kinski, Jason Patric
© PolyGram Filmed Entertainment, Inc.
PolyGram Filmed Entertainment presents a Propaganda Films/Fleece production
99 minutes 54 seconds
S&S October 1998 p61

YOU'VE GOT MAIL
Warner Bros Distributors (UK) - 26 February
(PG) USA, Dir Nora Ephron

with Tom Hanks, Meg Ryan, Parker Posey, Jean Stapleton, Dave Chappelle
© Warner Bros.
Warner Bros. presents a Lauren Shuler Donner production
119 minutes 15 seconds
S&S March 1999 p57

ZULMI
Monohill - 16 April
India, Dir Kuku Kohli
with Akshay Kumar, Twinkle Khanna, Amrish Puri, Aruna Irani, Milind Gunaji
Chowdhary Enterprises
No S&S reference

SPECIALISED GOODS AND SERVICES

This section has been divided into four parts. The first part features services specialising in actors, audiences and casting. The second lists costume, make-up and prop services. The third section is a general section of specialised goods and services for the film, television and video industries including such items as film stock suppliers, effects units and music services. The final section combines legal and business services for the industry

Actors, Audiences and Casting

Actors Inc
14 Dean Street
London W1
Tel: 020 7437 4417
Philip Ball

Avalon Publicity Limited
4a Exmoor Street
London W10 6BD
Tel: 020 7598 7222
Fax: 020 7598 7223
email: edt@avalonuk.com
Edward Thomson
Provides audiences for TV productions

Bromley Casting (Film & TV Extras Agency)
77 Widmore Road
Bromley BR1 3AA
Tel: 020 8466 8239
Fax: 020 8466 8239
Website: www.showcall.co.uk
Providing quality background artists to the UK film and TV industry

Central Casting Inc
13-14 Dean Street
London W1
Tel: 020 7437 4211
Fax: 020 7 437 4221
M.Maco

Dolly Brook Casting Agency
52 Sandford Road
East Ham
London E6 3QS
Tel: 020 8472 2561/470 1287
Fax: 020 8552 0733
Russell Brook
Specialises in walk-ons, supporting artistes, extras and small parts for films, television, commercials, modelling, photographic, voice-overs, pop videos

Downes Agency
96 Broadway
Bexleyheath
Kent DA6 7DE
Tel: 020 8304 0541
Fax: 020 8301 5591
Agents representing presenters and actors experienced in the fields of presentations, documentaries, commentaries, narrations, television dramas, feature films, industrial videos, training films, voice-overs, conferences and commercials

Lip Service Casting
4 Kingly Street
London W1R 5LF
Tel: 020 7734 3393
Fax: 020 7734 3373
email: bookings@lipservice.co.uk
Website: www.lipservice.co.uk
Susan Mactavish
Voiceover agency for actors, and voiceover casting agency

Marcus Stone Casting
Georgian House
5 The Pavilions
Brighton BN2 1RA
Tel: 01273 670053
Fax: 01273 670053
Supplies television, film extras. Up to 1,000 extras available for crowd scenes

Costumes, Make-up and Props

Angels - The Costumiers
40 Camden Street
London NW1 0EN
Tel: 020 7387 0999
Fax: 020 7383 5603
email: angels@angels.uk.com
Website: www.angels.uk.com
Richard Green
Chairman: Tim Angel OBE
Contact: Jonathan Lipman
World's largest Costume Hire Company. Extensive ranges covering every historical period, including contemporary clothing, civil and military uniforms. Full in-house ladies and men's making service, millinery department, jewelery, glasses and watch hire. Branches also in Shaftesbury Avenue and Paris. Additional services:- experienced personal costumiers, designers office space, reference library and shipping department

Angels Wigs
40 Camden Street
London NW1 0EN
Tel: 020 7 387 0999
Fax: 020 7 383 5603
email: wigs@angels.uk.com
Ben Stanton
All types of styles of wigs and hairpieces in either human hair bespoke or synthetic ready-to-wear. Large stocks held, ready to dress, for hire including legal wigs. In house craftsmen to advise on style or period. Facial hair made to order for sale

Cabervans
Caberfeidh
Cloch Road
Gourock
Nr. Glasgow PA19 1BA
Tel: 01475 638775
Fax: 01475 638775
Make-up and wardrobe units, dining coaches, motorhomes 3 & 4 bay artistes caravans, generators, toilets. One stop transport source in Scotland

Hirearchy Classic and Contemporary Costume
45 Palmerston Road
Boscombe
Bournemouth
Dorset BH1 4HW
Tel: 01202 394465
Website: www.hirearchy.co.uk
Specialising in the hire of ladies and gents costumes from medieval to present day. Also accessories, make-up, wigs, militaria jewellery, textiles and luggage

Hothouse Models & Effects
10 St Leonard's Road
Park Royal
London NW10 6SY
Tel: 020 8961 3666
Fax: 020 8961 3777
email: jezclarke@hothousefx.co.uk
Website: www.hothousefx.co.uk
Jeremy Clarke
All models, props and effects for film and television

The Image Co
Pinewood Studios
Iver Heath
Buckinghamshire SL0 0NH
Tel: 01753 651700

John Prentice
Wardrobe costume badging service, prop and promotional clothing

Kevin Jones, Freelance Costume Designer & Assistant
32 Austen Walk
West Bromwich
West Midlands B71 1RD
Tel: (0121) 588 6801
Fax: (0121) 588 6801
Mobile: 07775 623738
London Tel: 020 8977 6416
Costume designer, Assistant, dresser for films, television, commercials, pop videos, promotions, product launches, fashion shows, theatre

Neal Scanlan Studio
Elstree Film Studios
Borehamwood
Hertfordshire WD6 1JG
Tel: 020 8324 2620
Fax: 020 8324 2774
Animatronics and special makeup effects

Robert Hale Flowers
Interior and Flower Designers
8 Lovell Street
York YO23 1BO

Tel: 01904 613044
Contact: Robert Hale
Suppliers and designers of interior flower decoration

Ten Tenths
106 Gifford Street
London N1 0DF
Tel: 020 7607 4887
Fax: 020 7609 8124
Props service specialising in vehicles (cars, bikes, boats and planes) ranging from 1901 to present day - veteran, vintage, classic, modern - with complementary wardrobe facilities

Film Services

Aerial Cameras Systems Ltd
Shepperton Studios
Shepperton
Middx TW17 0QD
Tel: 01932 564885

Agfa-Gevaert
Motion Picture Division
27 Great West Road
Brentford
Middx TW8 9AX
Tel: 020 8231 4301
Fax: 020 8231 4315
Major suppliers to the Motion Picture and Television Industries of Polyester based Colour Print Film and Optical Sound Recording Film

Any Effects
64 Weir Road
London SW19 8UG
Tel: 020 8944 0099
Fax: 020 8944 6989
Contact: Julianne Pellicci
Managing Director: Tom Harris
Mechanical (front of camera) special effects. Pyrotechnics: simulated explosions, bullet hits. Fine models for close up camera work. Weather: rain, snow, fog, wind. Breakaways: shatterglass, windows, bottles, glasses, collapsing furniture, walls, floors. Specialised engineering rigs

and propmaking service

Riky Ash 'Falling For You'
c/o 65 Britania Avenue
Nottingham NG6 0EA
Tel: 0115 849 3470
Television and Film Stuntman, Stunt Coordinator, Action Sequence Director with over 250 television and film credits. Extensive work for TV, feature films, commercials, non-broadcast video, promotions and advertising

Audio Interactive Ltd
Pinewood Studios
Iver Heath
Buckinghamshire SL0 0NH
Tel: 01753 651700
Dick Joseph
Sound for the Multimedia industry - two fully soundproofed production room, on-site composers and a library of 30,000 sound effects

Charlie Bennett Underwater Productions
114 Addison Gardens
West Kensington
London W14 0DS
Tel: 020 7263 952
email: chazben@aol.com
Ifafa, Main Street
Ashby Parva
Leicestershire LE17 5HU
Tel: 01455 209 405

Mobile: 07702 263 952
Contact: Charlie Bennett
Underwater services to the film and television industry, including experienced qualified diving personnel and equipment; underwater film and video, stills photography and scuba instruction. Advice, logistics and support offered on an international scale. Registered HSE Diving contractor

Bionic Productions Ltd
Pinewood Studios
Iver Heath
Buckinghamshire SL0 0NH
Tel: 01753 655885
Fax: 01753 656844
On-site computer playback, and computer hire

Bonded Services
Aerodrome Way
Cranford Lane
Hounslow
Middx TW5 9QB
Tel: 020 8897 7973
Fax: 020 8897 7979
Inventory management, worldwide freight, courier services, technical facilities including film checking and tape duplication, storage and distribution

Boulton-Hawker Films
Hadleigh
near Ipswich
Suffolk IP7 5BG
Tel: 01473 822235
Fax: 01473 824519
Wide range of educational videos and CD-ROMs. Subject catalogues on request

C I Travel
Shepperton Studios
Shepperton
Middx TW17 0QD
Tel: 01932 572323
Fax: 01932 568989
Transport and travel services

Camera Associates Ltd
Pinewood Studios
Iver Heath
Buckinghamshire SL0 0NH
Tel: 01753 631007
Dave Cooper
Film video and grip hire service. Workshop and repair service also available on the Pinewood lot

Cinetron Design
Shepperton Studios
Shepperton
Middx TW17 0QD

Tel: 01932 572611
Fax: 01932 568989

Concert Lights UK
c/o Elstree Film Studios
Borehamwood
Herts WD6 1JG
Tel: 020 8953 1600
Work on *Who Wants to be a Millionnaire?* for Celador Productions and a number of TV shows

Connections Communications Centre Ltd
Palingswick House
241 King Street, Hammersmith
London W6 9LP
Tel: 020 8741 1767
Fax: 020 8563 1934
email: @cccmedia.demon.co.uk
Website: www.cccmedia.
demon.co.uk
Jacqueline Davis
A registered charity producing promotional and educational videos for the voluntary sector. Currently in production *Travelling Forward* a 25 minute documentary commissioned by the Thalidomide Society

Cool Million
Mortimer House

46 Sheen Lane
London SW14 8LP
Tel: 020 8878 7887
Fax: 020 8878 8687
Dot O'Rourke
Promotional merchandising, launch parties and roadshows

De Wolfe Music
Shropshire House
2nd Floor East
11/20 Capper Street
London WC13 6JA
Tel: 020 7631 3600
Fax: 020 7631 3700
email: dewolfe_Music@
Compuserve.com
Warren De Wolfe, Alan Howe
World's largest production music library. Represents 25 composers for commissions, television and film scores. Offices worldwide, sound FX department, 3 x 24-track recording studies all with music to picture facilities, also digital editing

Diverse Design
Gorleston Street
London W14 8XS
Tel: 020 7603 4567
Fax: 020 7603 2148
email: danielcr@diverse.co.uk
Website: www.diverse.co.uk

Daniel Creasey (Head of Design)
Graphic design for television including titles, format and content graphics. Recent work: *The Knock, Cor Blimey, Reach for the Moon, Transworld Sport, Real Women 2, Dispatches, Badger, Lawyers, Behind the Crime, Hero of the Hour*

Dynamic Mounts International
Shepperton Studios
Shepperton
Middx TW17 0QD
Tel: 01932 572348
Fax: 01932 568989
Camera equipment

EOS Electronics AV
EOS House
Weston Square
Barry
South Glamorgan CF63 2YF
Tel: 01446 741212
Fax: 01446 746120
Specialist manufacturers of video animation, video time lapsing and video archiving equipment. Products: Supertoon Low Cost School Animation System, AC 580 Lo-band Controller, BAC900 Broadcast Animation Controller, LCP3 Compact Disc, Listening Posts

ETH Screen Music
17 Pilrig Street
Edinburgh EH6 5AN
Tel: 0131 553 2721
Harald Tobermann
Producer and publisher of original
music for moving images. Complete
creative team - composers, arrangers,
musicians

Eureka Location Management
51 Tonsley Hill
London SW18 1BW
Tel: 020 8870 4569
Fax: 020 8871 2158
Suzannah Holt
Finds and manages locations for film
and television in Britain and abroad.
Offices in London and Toronto

The Film Stock Centre Blanx
70 Wardour Street
London W1V 3HP
Tel: 020 7494 2244
Fax: 020 7287 2040
D John Ward
Independent distributor of major
manufacturers' motion picture film
stock, professional video tape,
Polaroid, audio tape, related
products. Impartial advice,
competitive prices, SOR, special
deals for low-budgets. Weekdays
9.00am to 6.30pm

Film Vault Search Service
16B Wynell Road
London SE23 2LN
Tel: 01865 361 000
Fax: 01865 361 555
email: mail@filmvault.co.uk
Website: www.filmvault.co.uk
Paul Cook
The largest deleted video search
service in the country. No charges for
deposit or 'search fees'. Every video
sold is checked against faults and is
professionally cleaned, comes with
the correct copyright, BBFC
certificate and full guarantee

Focus International Transport Ltd
Shepperton Studios
Shepperton
Middx TW17 0QD
Tel: 01932 572339
Fax: 01932 568989
Transport services

Harkness Hall Ltd
The Gate Studios
Station Road
Borehamwood
Herts WD6 1DQ
Tel: 020 8953 3611
Fax: 020 8207 3657
email: sales@harknesshall.com
Ian Sim, Robert Pickett
Projection screens and complete
screen systems, fixed and portable,
front or rear, flat, curved, flying,
roller etc. Curtain tracks, festoons,
cycloramas, raise and lower
equipment, stage equipment,
installation and maintenance

Heliphotos Aerial Photography
Elstree Aerodrome
Elstree
Hertfordshire
Tel: 020 8207 6042
Aerial photography

Kodak Limited
Professional Motion Imaging
PO Box 66
Hemel Hempstead
Herts HP1 1JU
Tel: 01442 61122
Fax: 01442 844458
A Kennedy
Suppliers of the full range of Kodak
colour negative and print films,
including the new family of Vision
colour negative films

MBS Underwater Video Specialists
1 Orchard Cottages
Coombe Barton
Shobrooke, Crediton
Devon
Tel: 01363 775 278
Fax: 01363 775 278
email: mbscm@mail.eclipse.co.uk
Website: www.eclipse.co.uk.mbs
Contact: Colin Munro
MBS provides underwater stills
photography and videography
services, specialising in underwater
wildlife shots. We can provide full
HSE registered dive teams for UK
based work, and cover all aspects of
diving safety and support, vessel
servicing and specialist underwater
equipment supply

Media Education Agency
5A Queens Parade
Brownlow Road
London N11 2DN
Tel: 020 8888 4620
David Lusted
Consultancy, lectures and teacher in-
service education (INSET) in film,

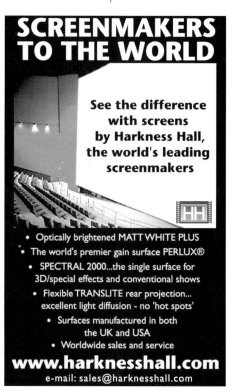

television and media studies. Contacts include academics, educationists, broadcasters, writers and actors

Midland Fire Protection Services

256 Foleshill Road
Coventry CV6 5AY
Tel: 024 7668 5252 (mobile) 07836 651408
Fax: 024 7663 7575
Robin Crane
Specialists in fire and rescue cover for location, studio and stage work. Special services, firefighters, action vehicles, fully equipped fire and rescue appliances, 5,000 gallons of water storage systems available, throughout the UK 24 hour service

Moving Image Touring Exhibition Service (MITES)

Foundation For Art & Creative Technology (FACT)
Bluecoat Chambers
Liverpool L1 3BX
Tel: 0151 707 2881
Fax: 0151 707 2150
email: mites@fact.co.uk
Website: www.mites.org.uk
Simon Bradshaw
Courses for artists, gallery curators, technicians and exhibitors concerned with the commissioning and presentation of moving image art works. Also development, advice, consultation services, an extensive exhibition equipment resource, DVD authority and production

Oxford Scientific Films (OSF)

Lower Road
Long Hanborough
Oxford OX8 8LL
Tel: 01993 881 881
Fax: 01993 882 808
email: osf_ltd@compuserve.com
45-49 Mortimer Street
London W1N 7TD
Tel: 020 7323 0061
Fax: 020 7323 0161
Independent production company specialising in blue-chip natural history documentaries for broadcast. 30 years of experience and innovation in specialist camera techniques

Pirate Motion Control

St Leonards Road
London NW10 6ST
Tel: 020 8930 5000
Fax: 020 8930 5001
email: help@pirate.co.uk

Website: www.pirate.co.uk
Michael Ganss
Motion Control Studio for 16mm film and video. 12 axis rig & 3 motion controlled lighting dimmer circuits. Call for showreel

ProDigital Audio Services

3 George Street
West Bay
Dorset DT6 4EY
Tel: 01308 422 866
Sound equipment, service and maintenance. Specialises in location sound equipment for the film and television industry - particularly DAT recorders

Radcliffes Transport Services

3-9 Willow Lane
Willow Lane Industrial Estate
Mitcham
Surrey CR4 4NA
Tel: 020 8687 2344
Fax: 020 8687 0997
Ken Bull
Specialist transport specifically for the film and television industry, both nationally and internationally. Fleet ranges from transit vans to 40' air ride articulated vehicles with experienced staff

The Screen Company

182 High Street
Cottenham
Cambridge CB4 8RX
Tel: 01954 250139
Fax: 01954 252005
Pat Turner
Manufacture, supply and installation of all types of front and rear projection screens for video, slide, film and OHP

Security Archives Ltd

1-8 Capitol Park
Capitol Way
London NW9 0EQ
Tel: 020 8205 5544
Fax: 020 8200 1130
Secure storage for film, video and audio tape in bomb-proof vaults with thermohydrographic controls and Halon fire suppression. 24hr collection and delivery, computerised, bar-coded management and tracking of clients' material

Snow-Bound

37 Oakwood Drive
Heaton
Bolton BL1 5EE
Tel: 01204 841285

Fax: 01204 841285
Suppliers of artificial snow and the machinery to apply it for the creation of snow/winter scenes. The product is life-like (not poly beads or cotton wool) adheres to any surface and is fire-retardent, non-toxic and safe in use, and eco-friendly

Stanley Productions

36 Newman Street
London W1P 3PD
Tel: 020 7636 5770
Fax: 020 7636 5660
Richard Hennessy
Europe's largest distributor of video tape and equipment. Full demonstration facilities with independent advice on suitable equipment always available

Studio Art

Elstree Film Studios
Borehamwood
Hertfordshire WD6 1JG
Tel: 020 8324 2600
Fax: 020 8324 2601
Danny Rogers
Specialist manufacturers of signs, neon, props and graphics for features and television

Visionworks Internet Ltd

13 Chartfield Avenue
London SW15 6DT
Tel: 020 8789 4254
Fax: 020 8785 0520
Website: www.visionworksinternet.com
Sandy Knight
Web design from basic level up to e-commerce.

Wrap it up

116a Acton Lane
Chiswick
London W4 5HH
Tel: 020 8995 3357 (Mobiles 07973 198154)
Wrap it up provides production services which include transcription, post production scripts, voice scripts and logging of rushes for production companies. Recent work: September Films - *Teenagers British lifestyles* - Transcription and Post Production Scripts. *Horizon* BBC - Transcription. *Dennis and Gnasher*, Tony Collingwood Productions - Voice Scripts

Zooid Pictures Limited

66 Alexander Road
London N19 5PQ
Tel: 020 7281 2407

Fax: 020 7281 2404
email: pictures@zooid.co.uk
Website: www.zooid.co.uk
Richard Philpott
For over 20 years, Zooid has been a one-stop media resources supplier and researcher for all copyright materials including film/video, stills, illustration, animation and sound, from archives, libraries, agencies, private collections and museums worldwide, for use in film, television, book publishing, CD-Rom, multimedia, presentations and on-line services. Zooid manage all aspects from first briefing through to licensing. Zooid use advanced digital technologies and license their management system, Picture Desk, to leading international publishers

Legal and Business Services

Ashurst Morris Crisp
Broadwalk House
5 Appold Street
London EC2A 2HA
Tel: 020 7638 1111
Fax: 020 7972 7990
email: film.tv@ashursts.com
Website: www.ashursts.com
Tony Ghee, Tasha Stanford, Andrea Fessler, Charlotte Douglas, Vanessa Bertelli
Leading City law firm with a young and progressive media and telecommunications team. Advice is provided on all aspects of the film and television industry, including corporate, employment, property and tax issues. Clients include leading national broadcasters, cable network operators and a number of small independents

Barclays Bank Media Banking Centre
27 Soho Square
London W1A 4WA
Tel: 020 7445 5773 or 020 7445 5777
Fax: 020 7445 5784
Geoff Salmon or Clare Gamble
Large business centre providing a comprehensive range of banking services to all aspects of the film and television industry

Deloitte & Touche
Hill House
1 Little New Street
London EC4A 3TR
Tel: 020 7936 3000
Fax: 020 7583 8517/1198
Gavin Hamilton-Deeley, Robert Reed
Advisors to film, television and broadcasting organisations. Business plans and financial models for companies, tax planning and business advice for individuals, and information on legal and regulatory developments affecting the sector

Film Finances
1-11 Hay Hill
Berkeley Square
London W1X 7LF
Tel: 020 7629 6557
Fax: 020 7491 7530
G J Easton, J Shirras, D Wilder, H Penallt Jones
Provide completion guarantees for the film and television industry

Henry Hepworth
Media Law Solicitors
5 John Street
London WC1N 2HH
Tel: 020 7242 7999
Fax: 020 7242 7988
A new specialist media and intellectual property practice with a distinctive high quality client base which is active across the entire spectrum of the copyright and intellectual property industries

The Media Law Partnership
187 Wardour Street
London W1V 3FA
Tel: 020 7479 7890
Fax: 020 7437 1558
email: mail@medialaw.uk.com
Adam Sutcliffe
Offers experience in all aspects of the negotiation and drafting of agreements for film production, film financing and international co-productions, with an emphasis on concise and effective documents, and a practical 'business affairs' approach to legal matters for all those involved in the film-making and distribution process

Nicholson Graham & Jones
110 Cannon Street
London EC4N 6AR
Tel: 020 7648 9000
Fax: 020 7648 9001
Selina Short, Communications
A City law firm and founder member
of the international GlobaLex
network in the UK, USA, Europe and
the Far East. The Intellectual
Property Group handles film and
television production, financing and
distribution, cable, satellite and
telecommunications work, book and
newspaper publishing, syndication,
advertising, merchandising,
sponsorship and sports law. Also
advise on technology transfer, patent,
trade mark, service mark, know-how
arrangements and franchising as well
as computer hardware and software
agreements and all intellectual
property copyright, moral and
performers' right issues

Olswang
90 Long Acre
London WC2E 9TT
Tel: 020 7208 8888
Fax: 020 7208 8800
email: olsmail@olswang.co.uk
Website: www.olswang.co.uk
One of the UK's leading
entertainment and media law firms. It
provides specialist advice in all
aspects of broadcasting, satellite,
cable, multimedia, IT &
telecommunications, media
convergence and music law, to the
European and US markets

Richards Butler
Beaufort House
15 St Botolph Street
London EC3A 7EE
Tel: 020 7247 6555
Fax: 020 7247 5091
email: law@richards-butler.com
Richard Philipps, Barry Smith,
Stephen Edwards, Martin Boulton
Richards Butler is an international
law firm which has been associated
with the media and entertainment
industry for over 60 years

STUDIOS

BBC Television Centre Studios
Wood Lane
London W12 7RJ
Tel: 020 8700 100 883
email: bbcresources.co.uk
Website: bbcresources.com
National Call Centre
8 full-facility television studios
TC1   10,250 sq ft
TC3   8,000 sq ft
TC4 and TC8   8,000 sq ft (digital and widescreen capable)
TC6   8,000 sq ft (digital)
TC2, TC5 and TC7   3,500 sq ft

Bray Studios
Down Place
Water Oakley
Windsor Road
Windsor SL4 5UG
Tel: 01628 622111
Fax: 01628 770381
Studio manager: Beryl Earl
STAGES
1 (sound) 955 sq metres
2 (sound) 948 sq metres
3 (sound) 238 sq metres
4 (sound) 167 sq metres
TELEVISION
Poirot 1999, Dirty Tricks, Ruth Rendall, Unconditional Love, Shiner

Capital FX
21A Kingly Court
London W1R 5LE
Tel: 020 7439 1982
Fax: 020 7734 0950
email: enquiries@capital.fx.co.uk
Website:www.capital.fx.co.uk
Graphic design and production, optical effects, film and laser subtitling

De Lane Lea Dean Street Studio
75 Dean Street
London W1V 5HA
Tel: 020 7439 1721/ 020 7432 3877 (direct line 24 hours)
Fax: 020 7437 0913
email: dll@delanelea.com
Website: www.delanelea.com
Studio manager: Dick Slade
STAGE
1 86 sq metres
40x23x18 SYNC

lighting rig, film and TV make-up rooms, one wardrobe, one production office, full fitted kitchen

Ealing Studios
Ealing Green
London W5 5EP
Tel: 020 8567 6655
Fax: 020 8758 8658
email: ealingstudios@iname.com
Website: www.ealingstudios.co.uk
Bookings Office
STAGES
1 (silent) - bluescreen/motion control = area 232m^2
2 (sound) - 864m^2
3A (sound) 530m^2
3B (sound) 530m^2
3A/B combined) 1,080m^2
4 (model stage silent) 390m^2
5 (sound) 90m^2
FILMS
East is East
Mansfield Town
Notting Hill
Guest House Paradiso
TELEVISION
Bob Martin (Granada); *The Royle Family* (Granada); *Cor Blimey* (Company Pictures); *Perfect World* (Tiger Aspect); *Other People's Children* (BBC Drama)

Halliford Studios
Manygate Lane
Shepperton
Middx TW17 9EG
Tel: 01932 226341
Fax: 01932 246336
Charlotte Goddard
STAGES
A 334 sq metres
B 223 sq metres

Holborn Studios
49/50 Eagle Wharf Road
London N1 7ED
Tel: 020 7490 4099
Fax: 020 7253 8120
email: reception@holborn-studios.co.uk
Website: www.holborn-studios.co.uk
Mike Hammond, Studio manager
STAGES
4 2,470 sq feet
6 2,940 sq feet
7 2,660 sq feet

18 roomsets 3,125 sq feet
Also eight fashion studios, set building, E6 lab, b/w labs, KJP in house, canal-side restaurant and bar. Productions; National Lottery Stills; Advertisements for Scratch cards; Saatchis - photographer Dave Stewart

Isleworth Studios
Studio Parade
484 London Road
Isleworth
Middx TW7 4DE
Tel: 020 8568 3511
Fax: 020 8568 4863
STAGES
A 292 sq metres
B 152 sq metres
C 152 sq metres
D 152 sq metres

Lamb Studio
Bell Media Group
Lamb House
Church Street
Chiswick Mall
London W4 2PD
Tel: 020 8996 9960
Fax: 020 8996 9966
email: paul@belmedia.demon.co.uk
Sound proofed, air-conditioned studio. Total floor area of 575 sq ft. Average ceiling height of 12ft. Free parking, production office, kitchen, make-up room. Easy access from central London, M4, M3 and M25. Ideal for talking heads, interviews, small dramas, pack shots, motion control, training. Post-production facilities also available

Leavesden Studios
PO Box 3000
Leavesden
Herts WD2 7LT
Tel: 01923 685 060
Fax: 01923 685 061
Studio Manager: Daniel Dark
STAGES
A 32,076 sq feet
B 28,116 sq feet
C 11,285 sq feet
D 11,808 sq feet
F 15,427 sq feet
G 14,036 sq feet
Flight Shed 1 35,776
Effects 15,367 sq feet

Back Lot   100 acres
180 degrees of clear and
uninterrupted horizon
Further 200,000 sq.ft of covered
space available
FILMS
GoldenEye, Mortal Kombat,
Annihilation; Sleepy Hollow, Star
Wars: Episode One -The Phantom
Menance, An Ideal Husband

Millennium Studios
Elstree Way
Herts WD6 1SF
Tel: 020 8236 1400
Fax: 020 8236 1444
Contact: Ronan Willson
'X' Stage: 327 sq metres sound stage
with flying grid and cyc. Camera
room, construction workshop,
wardrobe, dressing rooms, edit
rooms, hospitality suite and
production offices are also on site.
Recent productions: Carnival Films
'Bug' Series

Pinewood Studios
Pinewood Road
Iver Heath
Bucks SL0 0NH
Tel: 01753 651700
Fax: 01753 656844
Managing Director: Steve Jaggs
STAGES
A 1,685 sq metres
(Tank: 12.2m x 9.2m x 2.5m)
B 827 sq metres
C 827 sq metres
D 1,685 sq metres
(Tank: 12.2m x 9.2m x 2.5m)
E 1,685 sq metres
(Tank: 12.2m x 9.2m x 2.5m)
F 698 sq metres
(Tank: 6.1m x 6.1m x 2.5m)
G 247 sq metres
H 300 sq metres
J 824 sq metres
K 824 sq metres
L 880 sq metres
M 880 sq metres
N/P 767 sq metres
R 1,780 sq metres
S 1,780 sq metres
South Dock (silent)
1,547 sq metres
Albert R Broccoli 007 (silent) 4,223
sq metres (Tank: 90.5m x 22.3m x
2.7m Reservoir: 15.3m x 28.7m x
2.7m)
Large Process 454 sq metres
Small Process 164 sq metres (motion
control facilities available)
FX 335 sq metres
Exterior Lot 50 acres, comprising
formal gardens and lake, woods,

fields, cobbled streets, concrete
service roads and squares
Exterior Tank 67.4m narrowing to
32m wide, 60.4 long, 1.06m deep.
Capacity 764,000 gallons. Inner
Tank: 15.5m x 12.2m x 2.7m.
Backing 73.2m x 18.3m
Largest outdoor tank in Europe
FILMS
Mission: Impossible, The Fifth
Element, Event Horizon, Eyes Wide
Shut, Tomorrow Never Dies,
Entrapment, Still Crazy, Plunkett &
MacLeane, The World is not Enough
TELEVISION
Jonathan Creek, Little White Lies,
Hornblower, Last of the Summer
Wine, The Dark Room, Great
Expectations, Harbour Lights,
French & Saunders, The Tenth
Kingdom

Riverside Studios
Crisp Road
Hammersmith
London W6 9RL
Tel: 020 8237 1000
Fax: 020 8237 1011
Jon Fawcett
Studio One 529 sq metres
Studio Two 378 sq metres
Studio Three 112 sq metres
Plus preview cinema, various
dressing rooms, offices
TELEVISION
T.F.I. Friday, 'Collins & McConies
Movie Club', Channel 4 Sitcom
Festival, 'This Morning with Richard
Not Judy'

Rotherhithe Studios
119 Rotherhithe Street
London SE16 4NF
Tel: 020 7231 2209
Fax: 020 7231 2119
O Stockman, C Goodwin
STAGES
1 Rotherhithe 180 sq metres
Pre-production, construction, post-
production facilities, costume
making, props
FILMS
The Nutcracker Story (IMAX 3D)

Shepperton Studios
Studio Road
Shepperton
Middx TW17 0QD
Tel: 01932 562 611
Fax: 01932 568 989
Paul Olliver
STAGES
A 1,668 sq metres
B 1,115 sq metres
C 1,668 sq metres

D 1,115 sq metres
E 294 sq metres
F 294 sq metres
G 629 sq metres
H 2,660 sq metres
I 657 sq metres
J 1,394 sq metres
K 1,114 sq metres
L 604 sq metres
M 259 sq metres
T 261 sq metres
R 948 sq metres
S 929 sq metres
FILMS
Shakespeare in Love; Elizabeth,
Hilary & Jackie; Sliding Doors;
Notting Hill; Love's Labour's Lost;
End of the Affair

Stonehills Studios
Shields Road
Gateshead
Tyne and Wear NE10 0HW
Tel: 0191 495 2244
Fax: 0191 495 2266
Studio Manager: Nick Walker
STAGES
1 1,433 sq feet
2   750 sq feet
The North's largest independent
television facility comprising of
Digital Betacam Edit Suite with the
BVE 9100 Edit Controller, and
Abekas ASWR 8100 mixer, A57
DVE and four machine editing,
including two DVW 500s. Also three
Avid off-line suites, 2D Matador and
3D Alias graphics and a Sound
Studio comprising a Soundtracs 6800
24-track 32 channel desk and
Soundscape 8-track digital editing
machine
TELEVISION
Germ Genie, BBC 2; *The Spark,*
Border; Come Snow Come Blow,
Granada

Teddington Studios
Broom Road
Teddington
Middlesex TW11 9NT
Tel: 020 8977 3252
Fax: 020 8943 4050
email: sales@teddington.co.uk
Website: www.teddington.co.uk
Sales and Client Liaison
STUDIOS
1 653 sq metres
2 372 sq metres
3 120 sq metres
TELEVISION
This is Your Life; Des O'Connor
Tonight; Harry Hill; Brian Conley
Show; Alistair McGowan, My Hero,
Beast, Coupling

The Boilerhouse
8 Nursery Road
Brixton
London SW9 8BP
Tel: 020 7737 7777
Fax: 020 7737 5577
Clive Howard, Michael Giessler
100 sq metre studio, dry/wet stage,
special effect facilities, variable tank
systems, rain rigs. Productions:
Adidas, Cadbury Chocolate ads

Theed Street Studios
12 Theed Street
London SE1 8ST
Tel: 020 7928 1953
Fax: 020 7928 1952
Bill Collom
STAGE
A 151 sq metres
TELEVISION
Metropolis for BBC Continuing
Education; *Reality on the Rocks* for
C4; *Lost Civilisations* for Time Life

Three Mills Island Studios
Three Mill Lane
London E3 3DU
Tel: 020 7363 0033
Fax: 020 7363 0034
email: threemills@compuserve
Website: www.threemills.com

Edwin Shirley
STAGES
1   31'x 28'x 18'
2   33'x 28'x 18'
3   14'x 28'x 18'
4   87'x 77'x 23'7"
5   143'x 74' x 22'
6   101'x 77' x 27'
7   212' x 77'x 33'5"
8   84' x 49' x 31'
9   104' x 84' x 31'
10 121' x 46' x 23'
11 106' x 89' x 33'
12 157' x 50' x 33'

Twickenham Film Studios
St Margaret's
Twickenham
Middx TW1 2AW
Tel: 020 8607 8888
Fax: 020 8607 8889
Gerry Humphreys, Caroline Tipple
(Stages)
STAGES
1 702 sq metres
with tank 37 sq metres x 2.6m deep
2 186 sq metres
3 516 sq metres
2 x dubbing theatres; 1 x ADR/Foley
theatre; 40 x cutting rooms;
Lightworks, Avid 35/16mm

Wembley Studios
10 Northfield Industrial Estate
Beresford Avenue
Wembley
Middlesex HAO 1RT
Tel: 020 8903 4296
Fax: 020 8900 1353
STAGES
Studio 290 sq metres
Cyc 193 sq metres
Power: 900 amps 3 phase
Production offices, dressing rooms,
kitchen

Westway Studios
8 Olaf Street
London W11 4BE
Tel: 020 7221 9041
Fax: 020 7221 9399
Steve/Kathy
STAGES
1 502 sq metres (Sound Stage)
2 475 sq metres
3 169 sq metres
4 261 sq metres

TELEVISION COMPANIES

Below are listed all British terrestrial television companies, with a selection of their key personnel, and in some cases programmes. A more comprehensive listing of programmes, producers and cast members can be found via the web pages of each company. For details of feature films made for television see Production Starts

BBC Television

British Broadcasting Corporation
Television Centre
Wood Lane
London W12 7RJ
Tel: 020 8743 8000
Website: www.bbc.co.uk
Chairman: Sir Christopher Bland
Director-General: Greg Dyke
BBC Senior Management
Director Television: Mark Thompson.
Director Radio: Jenny Abramsky
Director BBC World Service: Mark Byford
Director News: Tony Hall
Director Drama, Entertainment and Children: Alan Yentob
Director Nations and Regions: Pat Loughrey
Director Finance, Property and Business Affairs: John Smith
Chief Executive BBC Resources Ltd: Margaret Salmon
Chief Executive BBC Worldwide: Rupert Gavin
Director Human Resources and Internal Communications: Gareth Jones
Director Distribution and Technology: Philip Langsdale
Director Marketing and Communications: Matthew Bannister
Director Learning: Michael Stevenson
Director Sport: Peter Salmon
Director Public Policy: Caroline Thomson
Director Strategy: Carolyn Fairbairn
Director New Media: Ashley Highfield

BBC Broadcast Programme Acquisition
Centre House
56 Wood Lane
London W12 7SB
Tel: 020 8225 6721
Fax: 020 8 749 0893
Controller, Programme Acquisition: Sophie Turner Laing
Senior Editor, Films: Steve Jenkins Selects and presents BBC TV's output of feature films on all channels
Business Development Executive: Paul Eggington
Contact for sub-licensing of material acquired by (but not produced by) the BBC

BBC East
St Catherine's Close
All Saint's Green
Norwich, Norfolk
Tel: 01603 619331
Head, Regional & Local Programmes: David Holdsworth

BBC East Midlands
East Midlands Broadcasting Centre,
London Road
Nottingham NG2 4UU
Tel: 0115 955 0500
Head of Regional & Local Progs: Liam McCarthy (Acting)

BBC London & South East
Elstree Centre
Clarendon Road
Borehamwood
Herts WD6 1JF
Tel: 020 8953 6100
Head of Regional & Local Programmes: Jane Mote

BBC North
BBC Broadcasting Centre
Woodhouse Lane
Leeds LS2 9PX
Tel: 0113 244 1188
Head of Regional & Local Programmes: Colin Philpott

BBC North East & Cumbria
Broadcasting Centre
Barrack Rd

Newcastle upon Tyne NE99 2NE
Tel: 0191 232 1313
Head of Regional & Local Programmes: Olwyn Hocking

BBC North West
New Broadcasting House
Oxford Road
Manchester M60 1SJ
Tel: 0161 200 2020
Head of Regional & Local Programmes: Martin Brooks

BBC Northern Ireland
Broadcasting House
Ormeau Avenue
Belfast BT2 8HQ
Tel: 028 90338224
Fax: 028 90338800
email: ni@bbc.co.uk

BBC Scotland
Broadcasting House
Queen Margaret Drive
Glasgow G12 8DG
Tel: 0141 338 2000
Fax: 0141 338 2660
email: enquiries.scot@bbc.co.uk

BBC South
Broadcasting House
Whiteladies Road
Bristol BS8 2LR
Tel: 0117 973 2211

BBC South West
Broadcasting House
Seymor Road
Mannamead
Plymouth PL3 5BD
Tel: 01752 229201
Head, Regional & Local Programmes: Eve Turner

BBC Wales
Broadcasting House
Llandaff
Cardiff CF5 2YQ
Tel: 029 2032 2000

BBC West
Broadcasting House
Whiteladies Road
Bristol BS8 2LR
Tel: 0117 973 2211
Head, Regional & Local Programmes: Leo Devine

BBC West Midlands
Pebble Mill
Birmingham B5 7QQ
Tel: 0121 414 8888
Head, Regional & Local Progs:
Laura Dalgleis

Independent Television Companies

Anglia Television
Anglia House
Norwich NR1 3JG
Tel: 01603 615151
Fax: 01603 631032
Website: www.anglia.tv.com
Chairman: David McCall
Managing Director: Graham Creelman
Director of Programmes: Malcom Allsop
Network programmes:
Sunday Morning
Trisha
Where the Heart is
Regional programmes:
Town and Country
Fair and Square
Inside and Out
Far and Wide
Day and Night
First Take
Kick-Off
Go Fishing with John Wilson

Border Television
The Television Centre
Carlisle CA1 3NT
Tel: 01228 525101
Fax: 01228 541384
email: ian@border.tv.com
Website: www.border-tv.com
Chairman: James Graham
Chief Executive: Paul Corley
Managing Director: Peter Brownlow
Head of Programme Acqusitions: Neil Robinson
Programmes include:
Lookaround
The Spark
Trailblazing

Carlton Television
101 St Martin's Lane
London WC2N 4AZ
Tel: 020 7240 4000
Fax: 020 7240 4171
Website: www.carlton.com
Chairman: Nigel Walmsley
Chief Executive: Clive Jones
Managing Director, Carlton Productions: Waheed Alli
Director of Programmes: Steve Hewlett
Chief Executive, Carlton Sales: Martin Bowley
Finance Director: Mike Green
Commercial Director: Tom Betts
Controller of Public Affairs: Hardeep

Kalsi
PRODUCTIONS
35-38 Portman Square
London W1H ONU
Tel: 020 7486 6688
Fax: 020 7486 1132
East Midlands
Carlton Studios
Lenton Lane
Nottingham NG7 2NA
Tel: 0115 863322
Fax: 0115 645552
Westcountry
Westcountry Television
Western Wood Way,
Language Science Park
Plymouth PL7 5BQ
Tel: 01752 333333
Fax: 01752 333444
Managing Director: Waheed Alli
Director of Programmes: Steve Hewlett
Controller, Business Affairs: Martin Baker
Director of Drama & Co-production: Jonathan Powell
Executive Producer, Drama: Rob Pursey
Executive Producer, Drama: Sharon Bloom
Controller of Children's & Young People's Programmes: Michael Forte
Executive Producer, Children & Young People's Programmes: David Mercer
Development Producer, Children's & Young People's Programmes: Jo Killingley
Controller of Entertainment: Mark Wells
Controller of Comedy: Nick Symons
Head of Development Entertainment: Graeme Smith
Controller, Factual Programmes: Polly Bide
Head of Current Affairs and Feautres: Mike Morley
Head of Regional Programmes, Carlton: Emma Barker
Head of Regional Programmes Central: Mike Blair
Director of Programmes, Westcountry: Jane McCloskey
Controller, Carlton Digital Programmes: Peter Lowe
BROADCASTING
Carlton Broadcasting
London
101 St Martin's Lane,
London WC2N 4AZ
Tel: 020 7240 4000
Fax: 020 7240 4171
London Television Centre
Upper Ground

London SE1 9LT
Tel: 020 7620 1620
Fax: 020 7827 7500
Central Broadcasting:
West Midlands
Central Court
Gas Street
Birmingham B1 2JP
Tel: 0121 643 9898
Fax: 0121 643 4897
East Midlands
Carlton Studios,
Lenton Lane
Nottingham NG7 2NA
Tel: 0115 986 3322
Fax: 0115 964 5552
South Midlands
Windrush Court
Abingdon Business Park
Abingdon OX1 1SA
Tel: 01235 554123
Fax: 01235 524024
Westcountry Television
Western Wood Way,
Language Science Park
Plymouth PL7 5BQ
Tel: 01752 333333
Fax: 01752 333444
Managing Director, Carlton
Broadcasting: Colin Stanbridge
Managing Director, Central
Broadcasting: Ian Squires
Managing Director, Westcountry
Television: Mark Haskell
Controller, Broadcasting: Coleena
Reid
Director of Finance: Ian Hughes
Head of Aquisitions: John Broadbent
Head of Presentation: Wendy
Chapman
Head of Presentation & Programme
Planning (Central): David Burge
Controller, News & Operations
(Central): Laurie Upshon
Controller, Sports (Central): Gary
Newbon
Editor, Central News West: John
Boileau
Editor, Central News East: Dan
Barton
Editor, Central News South: Phil
Carrodus
FACILITIES AND STUDIOS
Outside Broadcasting:
CARLTON 021
12-13 Gravelly Hill Industrial
Estate, Gravelly Hill
Birmingham B24 8HZ
Tel: 0121 327 2021
Fax: 0121 327 7021
Managing Director: Ed Everest
CARLTON SALES
London
101 St Martin's Lane

London WC2N 4AZ
Tel: 0171 240 4000
Fax: 0171 240 4171
Manchester
Elizabeth House, 3rd Floor
St Peter's Square
Manchester M2 3DF
Tel: 0161 237 1881
Fax: 0161 237 1970
Westcountry
Westcountry Television
Western Wood Way
Language Science Park
Plymouth PL7 5BQ
Tel: 01752 333311
Fax: 01752 333316
Birmingham
Central Court
Gas Street
Birmingham B1 2JT
Tel: 0121 643 9898
Fax: 0121 634 4414
Chief Executive: Martin Bowley
Managing Director: Steve Platt
Sales Director: Gary Digby
Deputy Sales Director: Chris Solden
Sales Administration Director: Ron
Coomber
Marketing Director: Fran Cassidy
Director of Sponsorship: David
Prosser
Client Sales Director: Caroline Hunt
CARLTON BROADCASTING
101 St Martin's Lane
London WC2N 4AZ
Tel: 0171 240 4000
Fax: 0171 240 4171
Chairman: Nigel Walmsley
Managing Director: Colin Stanbridge
CENTRAL BROADCASTING
Central Court
Gas Street
Birmingham B1 2JT
Tel: 0121 643 9898
Fax: 0121 616 1531
Carlton Studies
Lenton Lane
Nottingham NG7 2NA
Tel: 0115 986 3322
Fax: 0115 964 5552
Unit 9, Windrush Court
Abingdon Business Park
Abingdon OX1 1SA
Tel: 01235 554123
Fax: 01235 524024
Chairman: Nigel Walmsley
Managing Director: Ian Squires
Controller of News & Operations:
Laurie Upshon
Controller of Sport: Gary Newbon
Editor: Central News West: John
Boileau
Editor: Central News East: Dan
Barton

Editor: Central News South: Phil
Carrodus
WESTCOUNTRY
Language Science Park
Western Wood Way
Banham
Plymouth PL7 5BG
Tel: 01752 333333
Fax: 01752 333444
Chairman: Clive Jones
Managing Director: Mark Haskell
Director of Programmes: Jane
McClosky
Head of Presentation: Graham
Stevens
CARLTON STUDIOS
Lenton Lane
Nottingham NG7 2NA
Tel: 0115 9863322
Fax: 0115 9645552
Managing Director: Ian Squires
Director of Operations: Paul
Flanaghan
Production Controller: John Revill

Channel 5 Broadcasting
22 Long Acre
London WC2E
Tel: 020 7550 5555
Fax: 020 7550 5554
Website: www.channel5.co.uk
Britain's fifth terrestrial channel
launched at the end of March 1997
Chief Executive: David Elstein
Director of Programming: Dawn
Airey

Channel Four Television
124 Horseferry Road
London SW1P 2TX
Tel: 020 7396 4444
Fax: 020 7306 8353
Website:www.channel4.com
Executive Members
Chief Executive: Michael Jackson
Commercial Director: Andy Barnes
Director of Programmes: Tim
Gardam
Managing Director: David Scott
Director of Programmes: Tim
Gardam
Managing Director: David Scott
Director of Business Affairs: Janet
Walker
Director of Strategy and
Development: David Brook
Director and General Manager: Frank
McGettigan
Non–Executive Members
Chairman: Vanni Travers
Deputy Chairman: Barry Cox
Murray Grigor
Sarah Radclyffe
Usha Prashar, CBE
Andrew Graham

Robin Miller
Joe Sinyor

Channel Television
Television Centre, La Pouquelaye
St Helier
Jersey JE1 3ZD
Tel: 01534 816816
Fax: 01534 816817
Website: www.channeltv.co.uk
Television Centre, Bulwer Avenue
St Sampsons
Guernsey GY1 2BH
Tel: 01481 723451
Fax: 01481 710739
Chief Executive: John Henwood
Director of TV: Michael Lucas
Director of Productions: Phillipe
Bassett
Head of Programmes: Karen
Rankine
Head of Resource and Transmission:
Tim Ringsdore

GMTV
London Television Centre
Upper Ground
London SE1 9TT
Tel: 020 7827 7000
Fax: 020 7827 7001
email: malcolm.douglas@gmtv.co.uk
Website: www.gmtv.co.uk
Chairman: Charles Allen
Managing Director: Christopher
Stoddart
Director of Programmes: Peter
McHugh
Managing Editor: John Scammell
Editor: Gerry Melling
Head of Press & PR: Sue Brealey
Presenters: Eamonn Holmes, Fiona
Phillips, Lorraine Kelly, Penny
Smith, Matthew Lorenzo
6am-9.25am 7 days a week

Grampian Television
Queen's Cross
Aberdeen AB15 4XJ
Tel: 01224 846846
Fax: 01224 846800
Website: www.scottishmediagroup.
com
Chairman: Dr Calum A MacLeod
CBE

Granada Television
Granada Television Centre
Quay Street
Manchester M60 9EA
Tel: 0161 832 7211
Website: www.granadatv.com
36 Golden Square
London W1R 4AH
Tel: 020 7734 8080
Granada News Centre

Albert Dock, Liverpool L3 4BA
Tel: 0151 709 9393
Fax: 0151 709 3389
Granada News Centre
Bridgegate House
5 Bridge Place
Lower Bridge Street
Chester CH1 1SA
Tel: 01244 313966
Fax: 01244 320599
Granada News Centre
White Cross, Lancaster LA1 4XQ
Tel: 01524 60688
Fax: 01524 67607
Granada News Centre
Daisyfield Business Centre
Appleby Street
Blackburn BB1 3BL
Tel: 01254 690099
Fax: 01254 699299
Chief Executive: Charles Allen
Joint Managing Directors: Andrea
Wonfor, Jules Burns
Commercial Director: Katherine
Stross
Director of Production and
Resources: Brenda Smith
Director of Broadcasting: Julia
Lamaison
Sales Director: Mick Desmond
Director of Production: Max Graesser
Director of Public Affairs: Chris
Hopson
Technical Director: Roger Pickles
Controller of Drama: Sally Head
Controller of Entertainment and
Comedy: Andy Harris
Controller of Factual Programmes:
Dianne Nelmes
Controller of Programme Services
and Personnel: David Fraser
Head of Film: Pippa Cross
Head of Technical Operations: Chris
Hearn
Head of Entertainment: Bill Hilary
Head of Features: James Hunt
Head of Factual Drama: Ian McBride
Head of Regional Affairs: Rob
McLoughlin
Head of Planning and Marketing:
Colin Marsden
Head of Production Services: Jim
Richardson
Head of Music: Iain Rousham
Head of Regional Programmes: Mike
Spencer
Head of Design and Post Production:
Mike Taylor
Head of Current Affairs and
Documentaries: Charles Tremayne
Head of Transmission Operations:
Peter Williams
Head of Comedy: Antony Wood

HTV Wales
The Television Centre
Culverhouse Cross
Cardiff CF5 6XJ
Tel: 029 2059 0590
Fax: 029 2059 7183
Chairman HTV Wales: Gerald Davies
Managing Director - HTV Wales:
Henna Richards
Controller, Programming - HTV
Wales: Elis Owen
Human Resources and Site Services
Manager - HTV Wales
HTV West
The Television Centre
Bath Road
Bristol BS4 3HG
Tel: 0117 977 8366
Fax: 0117 972 2400
Chairman - HTV West: Louis
Sherwood
Managing Director - HTV West:
Jeremy Payne

Independent Television News
200 Gray's Inn Road
London WC1X 8XZ
Tel: 020 7833 3000
Fax: 020 7430 4700
Website: www.itv.co.uk
ITN is the news provider nominated
by the Independent Television
Commission to supply news
programme for the ITV network.
Subject to review, this licence is for a
ten year period from 1993. ITN also
provides news for Channel 4,
Channel 5 and for the Independent
Radio News (IRN) network. ITN is
recognised as one of the world's
leading news organisation whose
programmes and reports are seen in
every corner of the globe. In addition
to its base in London, ITN has
permanent bureaux in Washington,
Moscow, South Africa, the Middle
East, Hong Kong, and Brussels as
well as at Westminster and eight
other locations around the UK.

ITV Network Centre
200 Gray's Inn Road
London WC1X 8HF
Tel: 020 7843 8000
Fax: 020 7843 8160
Website: www.itv.co.uk
ITV is a federation of regional
broadcasters. National coverage is
achieved by 15 licensees,
broadcasting in 14 regional areas :
Anglia, Border, Carlton, Central,
Channel, Grampian, Granada, HTV,
LWT , Meridian, STV, UTV,

Westcountry, Tyne Tees, Yorkshire (London has two licencees, one for the weekday - Carlton and one for the weekend - LWT)

LWT (London Weekend Television)
The London Television Centre
Upper Ground
London SE1 9LT
Tel: 020 7620 1620
Fax: 020 7261 1290
Website: www.lwt.co.uk
Chairman: Charles Allen
Managing Director: Liam Hamilton
Controller of Arts: Melvyn Bragg
Controller of Drama: Jo Wright
Controller of Entertainment and Comedy: Nigel Lythgoe
Controller of Factual and Regional Programmes: Jim Allen
London's Burning
The South Bank Show
Blind Date
Reach for the Moon
The Knock
The Big Stage

Meridian Broadcasting
TV Centre
Northam Road
Southampton SO14 0PZ
Tel: 023 8022 2555
Fax: 023 8022 5050
Website: www.meridiantv.com
48 Leicester Square
London WC2H 7LY
Tel: 0171 839 2255
Fax: 0171 925 0665
West Point
New Hythe
Kent ME20 6XX
Tel: 01622 882244
Fax: 01622 714000
1-3 Brookway
Hambridge Lane
Newbury, Berks RG14 5UZ
Tel: 01635 522322
Fax: 01635 522620
Chairman: Clive Hollick
Managing Director: Mary Mcanally
Director of Corporate Affairs: Sue Robertson

S4C
Parc Ty Glas
Llanishen
Cardiff CF4 5DU
Tel: 029 2074 7444
Fax: 029 2075 4444
email: s4c@s4c.co.uk
Website: www.s4c.co.uk
Chairman: Elan Closs Stephens
Chief Executive: Huw Jones
Director of Productions: Huw Eirug

Director of S4C International: Wyn Innes
Testament - The Bible in Animation
9x30'
Co-production between S4C, BBC and Christmas Films. Produced by Cartwn Cymru, Right Angle and Christmas Films
Animated stories from the Bible
Saints and Sinners - The History of the Popes 6x50'
Co-production with RTE and La5
Production company: Opus 30
An insight into the power of the Papacy, of Popes past and present
Ancient Egypt 5x60'
Co-production with Discovery Communications and La 5
Production company: John Gwyn
An indepth journey through a dynasty that lasted 6,000 years
The Making of Maps 1x99'
Co-production with BBC + British Screen
Production company: Gaucho
Film set in Wales during the Cuban Missile Crisis of 1962 featuring the loss of childhood innocence
Famous Fred 1x30'
A co-production between S4C, Channel 4 and TVC
Production company -TVC
The fabulous furry adventures of Fred - the home-loving cat who turns into a rock star glamourpuss at night
Cameleon 1x120'
Production Company - Elidir Films
An idealistic, wayward young man joins the army in search of a more exciting life but goes absent without leave after it fails to meet his expectations
The Jesus Story 1 x 90' or 4x30'
Co-production with BBC + Christmas Films + British Screen
Animated full length feature film from the makers of 'Testament', Shakespeare The Animated Tales and 'Operavox The Animated Operas'
The Heather Mountain 1x80'
Production Company - Llun y Felin Productions
A feature film version of a classic Welsh story follows the story of a young girl growing up in North Wales at the turn of the Century
Wild Islands 24x30' or 8x50' + 50'
Raptor special
Co-production with STE + RTE
Production Company - Performance Films, Telesgop and Éamon de Buitléar
A unique insight into the wildlife and natural habitat of the national regions which make up Britain and Ireland

Scottish Television
Cowcaddens
Glasgow G2 3PR
Tel: 0141 300 3000
Fax: 0141 300 3030
Website: www.smg.plc.uk
3 Waterhouse Square
138-142 Holborn
London EC1N 2NY
Tel: 020 7882 1000
Fax: 020 7882 1005
Chairman: Don Cruickshank
Chief Executive: Andrew Flanagan
Managing Director, Television: Donald Esmlie
Managing Director, STE: Darrel James

Tyne Tees Television
The Television Centre
City Road
Newcastle Upon Tyne NE1 2AL
Tel: 0191 261 0181
Fax: 0191 261 2302
Chairman: Sir Ralph Carr-Ellison TD
Deputy Chairman: R H Dickinson
Managing Director: John Calvert
Director of Broadcasting: Peter Moth
Group Head of Engineering: John Nichol
Controller of News: Graeme Thompson
Controller of Programme Administration and Planning: Peter MacArthur
Controller of Operations: Margaret Fay
Head of Current Affairs: Sheila Browne
Head of Light Entertainment: Christine Williams
Head of Young Peoples Programmes: Lesley Oakden
Head of Sports: Roger Tames
Chain Letters
Production Company: Tyne Tees Television
Producer: Christine Williams
Director: Ian Bolt
Presenter: Ted Robbins

Ulster Television
Havelock House
Ormeau Road
Belfast BT7 1EB
Tel: 028 9032 8122
Fax: 028 9024 6695
Chairman: J B McGuckian
Managing Director: J D Smyth
General Manager: J McCann
Controller of Programming: A Bremner
Head of Public Affairs: M McCann
UTV Live at Six

Five days a week hour-long news and features programme. Includes a wide range of strands - environment, health, home, entertainments, local communities, consumer affairs and sport

Westcountry Television
Western Wood Way
Language Science Park
Plymouth PL7 5BG
Tel: 01752 333333
Fax: 01752 333444
Website: www.westcountry.co.uk
Westcountry Television is owned by Carlton
Managing Director: Mark Haskell
Director of Programmes: Jane McCloskey
Controller of News and Current Affairs: Brad Higgins
Controller of Features and Programme Development: Caroline Righton
Head of Broadcasting: Phil Barnes
Controller - Operations and Engineering: Mark Chaplin
Controller - Public Affairs: Mark Clare
Controller - Business Affairs: Peter Gregory

Yorkshire Television
The Television Centre
Leeds LS3 1JS
Tel: 0113 2 438283
Fax: 0113 2 445107
Global House
96-108 Great Suffolk Street
London SE1 OBE
Tel: 020 7578 4304
Fax: 020 7578 4320
Charter Square
Sheffield S1 3EJ
Tel: 0114 2 723262
Fax: 0114 275 4134
23 Brook Street
The Prospect Centre
Hull HU2 8PN
Tel: 01482 24488
Fax: 01482 586028
88 Bailgate
Lincoln LN1 3AR
Tel: 01522 530738
Fax: 01522 514162
Alexandra Dock Business Centre
Fisherman's Wharf
Alexandra Dock
Grimsby NE Lincs
DN21 1UL
Tel: 01472 357026
Fax: 01472 341967
8 Coppergate
York YO1 1NR
Tel: 01904 610066
Fax: 01904 610067
Director of Broadcasting: Mike Best
Controller, Features: Bridget Boseley
Controller of Factual Programmes: Chris Bryer
Controller of Commercial Affairs: Filip Cieslik
Head of International Facutal: Pauline Duffy
Head of Site Services: Peter Fox
Director of Production: David Fraser
Development Co-ordinator: Rachel Gilks
Executive Producer, Features and Factuals: Peter A. Gordon
Managing Director, Broadcasting: Richard Gregory
Group Head of Risk Management: John Hastings
PR & Regional Affairs Manager: Christine Hirst
Deputy Financial Controller - North East: Nick Holmes
Executive Producer, Schools Programmes: Chris Jelley
Head of News and Current Affairs: Clare Morrow
Controller of Drama, YTV: Carolyn Reynolds
Controller of Comedy Drama and Drama Features: David Reynolds
Controller of Drama: Keith Richardson
Head of Media Relations North: Sallie Ryle
Head of Engineering: John Nichol
Controller, Production Finance: Ian Roe
General Manager: Peter Rogers
Managing Editor of Factual Programmes: Helen Scott
Training and Development Manager: Sue Seager
Head of Personnel: Sue Slee
Controller of Comedy and Entertainment: Paul Spencer
Head of Sales and Planning: John Surtees
Deputy Controller of Children's, Granada Media Group
Director of Programmes: John Whinston
Programmes include:
Emmerdale
Heartbeat
A Touch of Frost
Bruce's Price is Right

VIDEO/DVD LABELS

These companies acquire the UK rights to all forms of audio-visual product and arrange for its distribution on videodisc, cassette or DVD at a retail level. Recent titles released on each label are also listed. A listing of all these available titles, and also those available for hire only, can be found in the trade catalogue *Videolog* (published by Trade Service Information) which is updated on a monthly basis. *Videolog* is used by most retailers - so check with your local store first - and may also be held by your local reference library

20:20 Vision Video UK
Horatio House
77-85 Fulham Palace Road
London W6 8JA
Tel: 020 8748 4034
Fax: 020 8748 4546
Little Women
Street Fighter
The Quick and the Dead

Arrow Film Distributors
18 Watford Road
Radlett
Herts WD7 8LE
Tel: 01923 858306
Fax: 01923 869673
Neil Agran
La Bonne Annee
Les Diaboliques
Europa Europa
Ginger and Fred
Montenegro
La Retour de Martin Guerre
Wages of Fear
Gulliver's Travels
Frank Sinatra: They Were Very Good Years
Leonardo DiCaprio: In His Own Words

Art House Productions
39-41 North Road
Islington
London N7 9DP
Tel: 020 7700 0068

Fax: 020 7609 2249
Richard Larcombe
Les Biches
Bicycle Thieves
Buffet Froid
Django
La Grande Bouffe
La Grande Illusion
The Harder They Come
Mephisto
Miranda
The Navigator
The Spirit of the Beehive
The Turning
Ultra

Artificial Eye Video
14 King Street
London WC2E 8HN
Tel: 020 7240 5353
Fax: 020 7240 5242
email: video@artificial-eye.com
Website: www.artificial-eye.com
Robert Beeson, Steve Lewis
Place Vendôme
Late August, Early September
A La Place Du Coeur
Alice et Martin
Time Regained
Rosetta
The Carriers are Waiting

BBC Video
Woodlands
80 Wood Lane
London W12 0TT
Tel: 020 8576 2236
Fax: 020 8743 0393
Blackadder
Dr Who
Match of the Day series
One Foot in the Grave
Pingu
Pole to Pole
Red Dwarf
Steptoe and Son

 bfi Video
21 Stephen Street
London W1T 1LN
Tel: 020 7957 8957
Fax: 020 7957 8968
Website: www.bfi.org.uk/bookvid
bfi Video, incorporating Connoisseur and Academy, distributes over 250 titles, including DVDs, covering every decade of cinema, from the

1890s to the present, across a broad range of genres. Complete catalogue and purchasing facilities available online.
Recent VHS releases include:
Kenneth Anger Volume 1-3
Dreams That Money Can Buy
Pink Narcissus
Club de femmes
Madchen in Uniform
les Enfants Terribles
Nanook of the North
Cinema of Transgression
South
The Lodger
The Ring
British Transport Films
Gallivant
A History of the British Avant Garde
Recent DVD releases include:
Seven Samurai
Yojimbo
Man With A Movie Camera
A Personal Journey With Martin Scorsese Through American Movies

Blue Dolphin Film & Video
40 Langham Street
London W1N 5RG
Tel: 020 7255 2494
Fax: 020 7580 7670
Joseph D'Morais
Video releases to date:
A Great Day in Harlem
A Fistful of Fingers
Invaders from Mars
Destination Moon
Flight to Mars
Mister Frost
The Square Circle
Loaded

Buena Vista Home Video
3 Queen Caroline Street
Hammersmith
London W6 9PE
Tel: 020 8222 1000
Fax: 020 8222 2795
Distribute and market Walt Disney, Touchstone, Hollywood Pictures and Henson product on video

Carlton Video Limited
The Waterfront
Elstree Road
Elstree
Herts WD6 3BS

Tel: 020 8207 6207
Fax: 020 8207 5789
Carlton Video releases sections from
Rank and Korda Collections. Also
features The Rohauer Collection,
Godzila - Japanese Originals
Up on the Roof
Made in Britain
Meantime
Prick Up Your Ears
Children's Programmes including:
*Tots TV, Bananas in Pyjamas, The
World of Peter Rabbit and Friends,
Old Bear and Friends, Rudolph the
Red-Nosed Reindeer, Annabelle's
Wish, Dream Street, Big Garage,
Jellikins, Kingdom of Rhymes, The
Fairies, Extreme Dinosaurs,
Timbuctoo, Potamus Park
TV Programmes: Inspector Morse,
Soldier Soldier, The Vice, Sharpe,
Cadfael, Goodnight Mister Tom, The
Scarlet Pimpernel, Kavanagh QC,
Frenchman's Creek, Cider With
Rosie, A Rather English Marriage,
The Jump*

CIC UK
Glenthorne House
5-17 Hammersmith Grove
London W6 0ND
Tel: 020 8563 3500
Fax: 020 8563 3501
A Universal/Paramount Company
Clear and Present Danger
The Flintstones
Forrest Gump
Jurassic Park
The Paper
River Wild
Schindler's List
The Shadow
True Lies

Columbia TriStar Home Video
Sony Pictures Europe House
25 Golden Square
London W1R 6LU
Tel: 020 7533 1200
Fax: 020 7533 1172
Devil in a Blue Dress
First Knight
Higher Learning
It Could Happen to You
Legends of the Fall
Little Women
Mary Shelley's Frankenstein
Only You
The Quick and the Dead
Street Fighter

Curzon Video
13 Soho Square
London W1V 5FB

Tel: 020 7437 2552
Fax: 020 7437 2992
Belle Epoque
Daens
Deadly Advice
Decadence
L'Enfer
Fausto
The Hour of the Pig
*How to be a Woman and Not Die in
the Attempt*
In Custody
Mina

Electric Pictures Video (Alliance Releasing)
184-192 Drummond Street
London NW1 3HP
Tel: 020 7580 3380
Fax: 020 7636 1675
Angel Baby
Arizona Dream
The Baby of Macon
Before the Rain
Belle de Jour
Blood Simple
Butterfly Kiss
The Celluloid Closet
Cold Fever
*The Cook, The Thief, His Wife and
Her Lover*
Death and the Maiden
Delicatessen
La Dolce Vita
Drowning by Numbers
The Eighth Day
The Flower of my Secret
I Shot Andy Warhol
Kansas City
Kika
Ladybird, Ladybird
Love and Human Remains
Orlando
Priest
Prospero's Books
Raise the Red Lantern
Red Firecracker, Green Firecracker
Ridicule
The Runner
Shanghai Triad
The Story of Qiu Ju
Trees Lounge
The White Balloon
The Young Poisoner's Handbook
Walking and Talking

Entertainment in Video
27 Soho Square
London W1V 5FL
Tel: 020 7439 1979
Fax: 020 7734 2483
Kingpin
Last Man Standing
Leaving Las Vegas
Living in Oblivion

Nixon
Seven
Twelfth Night
Up Close and Personal

First Independent Films
99 Baker Street
London W1M 1FB
Tel: 020 7317 2500
Fax: 020 7317 2502/2503
Above the Rim
Automatic
The Lawnmower Man II
Little Odessa
Mortal Kombat
Nostradamus
Rainbow
Sleep With Me

FoxGuild Home Entertainment
Twentieth Century House
31-32 Soho Square
London W1V 6AP
Tel: 020 7753 0015
Fax: 020 7434 1435
Website: www.fox.co.uk/
Airheads
Braveheart
Johnny Mnemonic
Judge Dredd
The Scout
The Shawshank Redemption
Stargate
Trapped in Paradise
Wes Craven's New Nightmare

Granada LWT International
London Television Centre
Upper Ground
London SE1 9LT
Tel: 020 7620 1620
Fax: 020 7928 8476
Brideshead Revisited
Cracker - series 1 & 2
Gladiators
Hale & Pace - Greatest Hits
Jeeves & Wooster - series 1 & 2
Jewell in the Crown
London's Burning - series 1 & 6
Nicholas and Alexandra
Rik Mayhall Presents... - series 1 & 2

guerilla films
35 Thornbury Road
Iselworth
Middlesex TW7 4LQ
Tel: 020 7758 1716
Fax: 020 7758 9364
email: david@guerilla.u-net.com
Website: www.guerilla-films.com
David Nicholas Wilkinson
Includes films by Eric Rohmer,
Barbet Shroeder, Jacques Rivette,
Monty Python

Imperial Entertainment (UK)
Main Drive, GEC Estate
East Lane
Wembley
Middx HA9 7FF
Tel: 020 8904 0921
Fax: 020 8904 4306/8908 6785
UK distributor of feature films
including Danielle Steele video titles

Le Channel Ltd
10 Frederick Place
Weymouth
Dorset DT4 8HT
Tel: 01305 780446
Fax: 01305 780446
Art videos about famous paintings of
the Western World. Palettes is a
collection of very high standard
videos about famous paintings of the
Western World. Adapted from the
French, the films have been
researched by leading art historians
and curators. Each Palette narrates
the creation of a painting, the story of
a painter, the progression of a Palette:
Claude; Leonardo; Monet Poussin,
Seurat, Vermeer

Lumiere Classics
167-169 Wardour Street
London W1V 3TA
Tel: 020 7413 0838
Fax: 020 7413 0838
Eating Roual
Eva

Lumiere Home Video
167-169 Wardour Street
London W1V 3TA
Tel: 020 7413 0838
Fax: 020 7734 1509
The Avengers
12 titles from Hammer
Hue and Cry
Laughter in Paradise
Bruce Lee
Mighty Max
Moby Dick
Mona Lisa (widescreen)

Mainline Pictures
37 Museum Street
London WC1A 1LP
Tel: 020 7242 5523
Fax: 020 7430 0170
Website: www.screencinemas.co.uk
Bandit Queen
The Diary of Lady M
A Flame in my Heart
Go Fish
Let's Get Lost
Luck, Trust & Ketchup
The Premonition

Ruby in Paradise
The Wedding Banquet
Lovers
Crazy Love
Metropolitan
Chain of Desire

Media Releasing Distributors
27 Soho Square
London W1V 5FL
Tel: 020 7437 2341
Fax: 020 7734 2483
Day of the Dead
Eddie and the Cruisers
Kentucky Fried Movie
Return of Captain Invincible
Distributed through Entertainment in
Video (qv)

Medusa Communications & Marketing Ltd
Regal Chambers, 51 Bancroft
Hitchin
Herts SG5 1LL
Tel: 01462 421818
Fax: 01462 420393
email: steve@medusa.com.co.uk
Steve Rivers
Video and DVD distributors for:
Playboy; Hong Kong Legends;
Medusa Pictures; Odyssey; Adult
Channel; Eastern Heros

Nova Home Entertainment
11a Winholme
Armthorpe
Doncaster DN3 3AF
Tel: 01302 833422
Fax: 08701 257917
email: nhe@novaonline.co.uk
Website: www.novaonline.co.uk/
homevideo
Contact: Andrew White, Maurice
White, Gareth Atherton
Sell-through video distributor, a
subsidiary of Nova Productions, with
a catalogue based on specialist and
local interest documentaries and
nostalgia programming. Recent titles
include: *Keith Beeden's Film
Archive; South Yorkshire Rail;
Sheffield Remembered; The
Doncaster Mansion House*

Odyssey Video
Regal Chambers
51 Bancroft
Hitchin
Hertfordshire, SG5 1LL
Tel: 01462 421 818
Fax: 01462 420 393
email: adrian_munsey@msn.com
Adrian Munsey
Ambush in Waco

Beyond Control
Burden of Proof
Honour Thy Father & Mother
Lady Boss
Lucky/Chances
Out of Darkness
A Place for Annie
Remember
War & Remembrance

Orbit Media Ltd
7/11 Kensington High Street
London W8 5NP
Tel: 020 7287 4264
Fax: 020 7727 0515
Website: www.orbitmedia.co.uk
Chris Ranger
Jordan Reynolds
Screen classics label, feature films
and documentaries

Out on a Limb
Battersea Studios
Television Centre
Thackeray Road
London SW8 3TW
Tel: 020 7498 9643
Fax: 020 7498 1494
Being at Home with Claude
Forbidden Love
My Father is Coming
No Skin Off My Ass
Seduction: The Cruel Woman
Virgin Machine

Picture Music International
20 Manchester Square
London W1A 1ES
Tel: 020 7486 4488
Fax: 020 7465 0748
Blur: Showtime
Cliff Richard: The Hit List
David Bowie: The Video Collection
Iron Maiden: The First Ten Years
*Kate Bush: The Line, The Cross and
The Curve*
Peter Gabriel: Secret World Live
Pet Shop Boys: Videography
Pink Floyd: Pulse
Queen; Box of Flix
Tina Turner: Simply the Best

Quadrant Video
37a High Street
Carshalton
Surrey SM5 3BB
Tel: 020 8669 1114
Fax: 020 8669 8831
Sports video cassettes

Screen Edge
28-30 The Square
St Annes-on-Sea
Lancashire FY8 1RF
Tel: 01253 712453

Fax: 01253 712362
email: king@visicom.demon.co.uk
Website: www.visionary.co.uk
Rhythm Thief
Der Todesking
Pervirella

SIG Video Gems Ltd
The Coach House
The Old Vicarage
10 Church Street
Rickmansworth
Herts WD3 1BS
Tel: 01923 710599
Fax: 01923 710549
Black Beauty (TV series)
The Great Steam Trains
Minder
Moonlighting
Professionals
Return of the Incredible Hulk
Rumpole of the Bailey
Ruth Rendell
Sweeney
UK Gold Comdey Compilation
UK Gold Action/Drama Compilation

Tartan Video
Atlantic House
5 Wardour Street
London W1V 3HE
Tel: 020 7494 1400
Fax: 020 7439 1922
email: alipkin@tartanvideo.co.uk
Website: www.tartanvideo.co.uk
Asher Lipkin
Cinema Paradiso
Man Bites Dog
Seventh Seal
The Umbrellas of Cherbourg
La Haine
The Dream Life of Angels
Kissed

Telstar Video Entertainment
The Studio
5 King Edward Mews
Byfeld Gardens
London SW13 9HP
Tel: 020 8846 9946
Fax: 020 8741 5584
A sell-through video distributor of
music, sport, special interest,
comedy, children and film
programmes
The Best Kept Secret in Golf
Foster & Allen: By Request
Harry Secombe Sings
Hollywood Women
John Denver: A Portrait
*Michael Crawford: A Touch of
Music in the Night*

Thames Video Home Entertainment
Pearson Television International
1 Stephen Street
London W1P 1PJ
Tel: 020 7691 6000
Fax: 020 7691 6079
*Mr Bean; Tommy Cooper;
Wind in the Willows; World at War;
Men Behaving Badly; The Bill; The
Sweeney*

THE (Total Home Entertainment)
National Distribution Centre
Rosevale Business Park
Newcastle under Lyme
Staffs ST5 7QT
Tel: 01782 566566
Fax: 01782 568552
email: jed.taylor@the.co.uk
Website: www.the.co.uk
Jed Taylor/Sue Nixon
Exclusive distributors for Visual
Corp, ILC, Quantum Leap, Mystique,
Prime Time, IMS, Wardvision,
Academy Media, Empire, RWP (over
6,000 titles)

Trumedia Ltd
PO Box 374
Headington
Oxford OX3 7NT
Tel: 01865 763097
Fax: 01865 763097
email: sales@trumedia.co.uk
Website: www.trumedia.co.uk
Bill Cotten
Literary video and audio resources
and DVD. Other videos: History of
Art; Foreign Language; History

Universal Pictures Visual Programming
Oxford House
76 Oxford Street
London W1N 0HQ
Tel: 020 7307 7600
Fax: 020 7307 7639
Carey Weich
A subsidiary of Universal Pictures
International, acquiring and
producing programmes for
worldwide television and video
distribution across popular culture
and childrens genre. Examples are:
*Cats, Joseph and The Amazing
Technicolour Dreamcoat, Lord of the
Dance, Maisy, Mr Bean and Barney*

Visionary Communications
28-30 The Square
St Annes-on-Sea
Lancashire FY8 1RF
Tel: 01253 712453

Fax: 01253 712362
email: king@visicom.demon.co.uk
Website: www.visionary.co.uk
Scorpio Rising
The Pope of Utah
Three Films' Burroughs'/Gysin
Destroy All Rational Thought
Cyberpunk
Angelic Conversation
In the Shadow of the Sun
The Gun is Loaded
Alice
Freaks
Island of Lost Souls
Mystery of the Wax Museum

WEBSITES

This section contains a small selection of useful websites which coincide with the sections in this book. For more detailed information visit the gateway film links section on the *bfi* website. www.bfi.org.uk

Archive and Film Libraries

FIAF
http://www.cinema.ucla.edu /FIAF

FIAT: International Federation of Television Archives
camilla.nb.no/fiat

France - La Vidéoteque de paris
http://www.vdp.fr/

National Film and TV Archive
www.bfi.org.uk/collections

Scottish Film and Television Archive
http://www.scottishscreen.com

East Anglian Film Archive
http://www.uea.ac.uk/eafa/

North West Film Archive
http://www.nwfa.mmu.ac.uk

Huntley Film Archives
http://www.huntleyarchives.com

Imperial War Museum Film and Video Archive
http://iwm.org.uk/lambeth/film.htm

Wessex Film and Sound Archive
http://www.hants.gov.uk/record-office/film.html

National Museum of Photography Film & Television
http://www.nmsi.ac.uk/nmpft

UK Film Archive Forum
http://www.bufvc.ac.uk/faf/faf.htm

British Association of Picture Libraries and Agencies (BAPLA)
http://www.bapla.org.uk

Awards

BAFTA
http://www.bafta.org/

Berlin
http://www.berlinale.de

Cannes
http://www.festival-cannes-fr

Edinburgh International Film Festival
http://www.edfilmfest.org.uk/

Emmys
http://www.emmys.org/

Emmys International
http://www.intlemmyawards.com/

European Film Awards
http://www.europeanfilmacademy.org

Golden Globes
http://www.hfpa.com

Golden Rose of Montreux
http://www.rosedor.ch

Golden Rasberry Awards
http://www.razzies.com/

Grierson Trust Awards
http://www.editor.net/griersontrustrman

Karlovy Vary
http://www.iffkv.cz/

Locarno
http://www.pardo.ch/

Oscars
http:// www.oscars.org/awards

Monte Carlo TV Festival
http://www.tvfestival.com/

Royal Television Society Awards
http://www.rts.org.uk/

Books

bfi Publishing
http://www.bfi.org.uk

Oxford University Press
http://www.oup.co.uk/

Routledge
http://www.routledge.com/

Booksellers

Blackwell's
http://www.blackwell.co.uk/bookshops

Cinema Store
http://www.atlasdigital.com/cinema store

Reel Posters
http://www.reelposter.com

Waterstones
http://www.waterstones.co.uk

Cable, Satellite and Digital

Cable/Satellite Guide
http://www.sceneone.co.uk/s1/TV

BSkyB
http://www.sky.co.uk

NTL
http://www.ntl.co.uk

ONDigital
http://www.ondigital.co.uk

SkyDigital
http://www.skydigital.co.uk

Telewest Communications
http://www.telewest.co.uk

Careers and Training

Film Education
http://www.filmeducation .org

Focal
http://www.focal.ch

Institut National de l'Audiovisual
http://www.ina.fr

National Film and Television School
http://www.nftsfilm-tv.ac.uk/

Skillset
http://www.skillset.org

Cinemas

Cinema Admissions
http://www.dodona.co.uk

Cinemas in the UK
http://www.aber.ac.uk/~jwp/cinemas

Apollo Cinemas
http://www.apollocinemas.co.uk

ABC Cinemas
http://www.abccinemas.co.uk

Caledonian Cinemas
http://www.caledoniancinemas.co.uk

Cineworld
http://www.cineworld.co.uk

Film Finder
http://www.yell.co.uk/yell/ff/

Fox Movies
http://www.foxmovies.com

Mainline
http://www.screencinemas.co.uk

Odeon
http://www.odeon.co.uk

Picturehouse
http://www.picturehouse-cinemas.co.uk

Scoot
http://www.cinema.scoot.co.uk

Showcase Cinemas
http://showcasecinemas.co.uk

UCI (UK) Ltd
http://www.uci-cinemas.co.uk

Warner Village
http://warnervillage.co.uk

Courses

The American Intercontinental University
http://www.aiulondon.ac.uk/

University of Bath
http://www.bath.ac.uk

Birkbeck College University of London
http://www.birkbeck.ac.uk/

University of Birmingham
http://www.birmingham.ac.uk

Bournemouth University
http://www.bournemouth.ac.uk

University of Bradford
http://www.bradford.ac.uk

Bristol Animation Course
http://www.mediaworks.org.uk/animate

University of Bristol
http://www.bristol.ac.uk

Brunel University
http://www.brunel.ac.uk

Canterbury Christ Church College
http://www.cant.ac.uk

Coventry University
http://www.alvis.coventry.ac.uk
Cyber Film School
http://www.cyberfilmschool.com

De Montfort University Bedford
http://www.dmu.ac.uk/Bedford

De Montfort University Leicester
http://www.dmu.ac.uk/Leicester

University of Derby
http://www.derby.ac.uk
University of East Anglia
http://www.uea.ac.uk

University of East London
http://www.bradford.ac.uk

University of Exeter
http://www.ex.ac.uk

University of Glasgow
http:// www.arts.gla.ac.uk/tfts/

Glasgow Caledonian University
http://www.gcal.ac.uk

Global Film School
http://www.globalfilmschool.com

Goldsmiths College
http://www.goldsmiths.ac.uk

Kent Institute of Art and Design
http://www.kiad.ac.uk

University of Kent
http://www.ukc.ac.uk

King Alfred's College Winchester
http://www.wkac.ac.uk

Kingston University
http://www.kingston.ac.uk

University of Leicester
http://www.le.ac.uk

University of Liverpool
http://www.liv.ac.uk

Liverpool John Moores University
http://www.livjm.ac.uk

London Guildhall University
http://www.lgu.ac.uk

London International Film School
http://www.lifs..org.uk

London School of Economics and Political Science
http://www.lse.ac.uk

University of Manchester
http://www.man.ac.uk

Middlesex University
http://www.mddx.ac.uk

Napier University
http://www.napier.ac.uk

National Film and Television School
http://www.nftsfilm-tv.ac.uk

University of Newcastle upon Tyne
http://www.ncl.ac.uk/ncrif

Northern School of Film and Television
http:// www.lmu.ac.uk

University of Northumbria at Newcastle
http://www.unn.ac.uk

Nova Camcorder School
http:// www.novaonline.co.uk

University of Portsmouth
http://www.port.ac.uk

University of Reading
http://www.reading.ac.uk

College of Ripon and York St John
http://www.ucrysj.ac.uk

Roehampton Institute
http://www.roehampton.ac.uk

Royal College of Art
http://www.rca.ac.uk/Design

University of Salford
http://www.salford.ac.uk

University of Sheffield
http://www.sheffield.ac.uk

Sheffield Hallam University
http://www.shef.ac.uk

South Bank University
http://www.sbu.ac.uk

Staffordshire University
http://www.staffs.ac.uk

University of Stirling:Film and Media Studies Department
http://www-fms.stir.ac.uk

The University of Sunderland
http://www.sunderland.ac.uk

University of Sussex
http://www.sussex.ac.uk

Thames Valley University
http://www.tvu.ac.uk

Trinity and All Saints College
http:// www.tasc.ac.uk

University of Wales College, Newport
http://www.newport.ac.uk

University College Warrington
http://www.warr.ac.uk

University of Warwick
http://www.warwick.ac.uk

University of Westminster
http://www.wmin.ac.uk

University of Wolverhampton
http://www.wolverhampton.ac.uk

Databases/film reviews

Animation World Network
http://www.awn.com

Baseline
http://www.pkbaseline.com

Box Office
http://www.entdata.com

Classic Movies
http://www.geocities.com/Hollywood/9766/

European Cinema On-Line Database
http://www.mediasalles.it

Hollywood Online
http://www.hollywood.com

InDevelopment
http://www.indevelopment.co.uk

Internet Movie Database
http://www.uk.imdb.com

The Knowledge
www.theknowledgeonline.com

Media UK Internet Directory
http://www.mediauk.com/directory

Mandy's International Film and TV
Production Directory
http://www.mandy.com

Movie Page
http://www.movie-page.com

Popcorn
http://www.popcorn.co.uk

Production Base
http://www.productionbase.co.uk

Spotlight
http://www.spotlightcd.com
http://www.players-guide.com

Distributors (Non-Theatrical)

Atom Films
http://www.alwaysindependentfilms.com

Central Office of Information
http:// www.coi.gov.uk/

CFL Vision
http://www.euroview.co.uk

Educational and Television Films
http://: www.etvltd.demon.co.uk

Vera Media
http://www.vera.media.co.uk

Distributors (Theatrical)

Alliance Releasing
http://www.alliance.

bfi
http://www.bfi.org.uk

Buena Vista
http://www.bvimovies.com

FilmFour
http://www.filmfour.com

Pathe Distribution´
http://www.pathe.co.uk

Twentieth Century Fox
http://www.fox.co.uk

UIP (United International Pictures)
http://www.uip.com

Universal Studios
http://universalstudios.com/

Warner Bros
http://www.warnerbros.com

Facilities

Abbey Road Studios
http://www.abbeyroad.co.uk/

Cinesite (Europe) Ltd
http://www.cinesite.com

Communicopia Ltd
http://www.communicopia.co.uk

Connections Communications Centre
http://www.cccmedia.demon.co.uk

Dubbs
http://www.dubbs.co.uk

Edinburgh Film Workshop Trust
http://www.efwt.demon.co.uk

The Film Factory at VTR
http://www.filmfactory.com

FrameStore
http://www.framestore.co.uk

Hillside Studios
http://www.ctvc.co.uk

Hull Time Based Arts
http://www.htba.demon.co.uk

Lee Lighting
http://www.lee.co.uk
PMPP Facilities
http://www.pmpp.dircon.co.uk

Salon Post-Productions
http://www.salon.ndirect.co.uk

Tele-Cine
http://www.telecine.co.uk

VTR Ltd
http://www.vtr.co.uk

Festivals

Film Festivals Servers
http://www.filmfestivals.com

Berlin
http://www.berlinale.de

Cannes
http://www.festival-cannes-fr

London Film Festival
http://www.lff.org.uk/

Film Societies

Film Societies
http://www.bffs.org.uk

Funding

Arts Council of England
http://www.artscouncil.org.uk/

Arts Council of Northern Ireland
http://www.artscouncil-ni.org/

Arts Council of Wales
http://www.ccc-acw.org.uk/

bfi
http://www.bfi.org.uk

British Council
http://www.britcoun.org/

The Film Council
http://www.filmcouncil.org.uk

Scottish Screen
http://www.scottishscreen.com

Sgrin, Media Agency for Wales
http://www.sgrinwales.demon.co.uk

UK Media
www.mediadesk.co.uk

Eastern Arts Board
http://www.eab.org.uk/

East Midlands Arts Board
http://www.arts.org.uk/directory/regions/east_mid/

English Regional Arts Boards
http://www.arts.org.uk

London Arts Board
http://www.arts.org.uk/directory/regions/london/

London Film and Video Development
Agency
http://www.lfvda.demon.co.uk/

Northern Arts Board
http://www.arts.org.uk/directory/regions/northern/

Northern Ireland Film Commission
http://www.nifc.co.uk/

North West Arts Board
http://www.arts.org.uk/directory/regions/north_west/

Scottish Arts Council
http://www.sac.org.uk/

Scottish Screen
http://www.scottishscreen.com/

Sgrîn
http://www.sgrinwales.demon.co.uk

Southern Arts Board
http://www.arts.org.uk/directory/regions/southern/

South East Arts Board
http://www.arts.org.uk/directory/regions/south_east/

South West Arts Board
http://www.swa.co.uk/

South West Media Development
Agency
http://www.swmediadevagency.co.uk/

West Midlands Arts Board
http://www.arts.org.uk/directory/regions/west_mid/

Yorkshire Arts Board
http://www.arts.org.uk/directory/regions/york/

International Sales

BBC Worldwide
http://www.bbc.worldwide.com

BRITE (British Independent
Television Enterprises)
http://www.brite.tv.co.uk

FilmFour International
http://www.filmfour.com

London Television Service
http://www.londontv.com

Pearson Television International
http://www.pearsontv.com

Twentieth Century Fox Television
http://www.fox.co.uk

Vine International Pictures
http://www.vineinternational.co.uk

Libraries

bfi National Library
www.bfi.org.uk/nationallibrary

British Library
www.bl.uk/

Library Association
http://www.la-hq.org.uk

Organisations

American Film Institute

http://www.afionline.org/

Arts Council of England
http://www.artscouncil.org.uk

BBC
http://www.bbc.co.uk

British Council - British films
http://www.britfilms.com

British Film Commission
http://www.britfilmcom.co.uk

British Film Institute
http://www.bfi.org.uk

BKSTS - The Moving Image Society
http://www.bksts.demon.co.uk

BUFVC(British Universities Film
and Video Council
http://www.bufvc.ac.uk

Department for Culture, Media and
Sport (DCMS)
http://www.culture.gov.uk/

Directors' Guild of Great Britain
http://www.dggb.co.uk

EDI
http://www.entdata.com

National Museum of Photography,
Film and Television
http://www.nmsi.ac.uk/nmpft/

New Producer's Alliance
http://www.npa.org.uk

PACT - Producers Alliance for
Cinema and Television
http://www.pact.co.uk

Scottish Screen
http://www.scottishscreen.com

Skillset
http://www.skillset.org

Organisations (Europe)

European Audio-visual Observatory
http:// www.obs.coe.int

EURIMAGES
http://www.culture.coe.fr/eurimages

**European Broadcasting Union
(EBU)**
http:// www.ebu.ch/
**EUTELSAT (European
Telecommunications Satellite
Organisation)**
http://www.eutelsat.org

Belgium - The Flemish Film Institute
http://www.vfi-filminsituutbe

Denmark - Danish Film Institute
http://www.dfi.dk

Finland - AVEK - The Promotion
Centre for Audio-visual Culture in

Finland
http://www.kopiostofi/avek
Finnish Film Archive
http://www.sea.fi
The Finnish Film Foundation
http://www.ses.fi/ses

France - Bibliothèque du Film (BIFI)
http://www.bifi.fr
TV France International
http://www.tvfi.com

Germany - Filmfˆrderungsanstalt
http://www.ffa.de

Iceland - Icelandic Film Fund
http://www.centrum.is/filmfund

Ireland - Bord Scann·n na
hÉ.ireann/Irish Film Board
http://www.iol.ie/filmboard

Film Institute of Ireland
http://www.iftn.ie/ifc

Poland - Polish Cinema Database
http://info.fuw.edu.pl/Filmy/

Portugal - Portuguese Film and
Audiovisual Institute
http://www.nfi.no/nfi.htm

Scottish Screen
http://www.scottishscreen.com

Press Contacts

6degrees.co.uk
http://www.6degrees.co.uk

Empire
http://www.empireonline.co.uk

Filmwaves
http://www.filmwaves.co.uk

Film Unlimited
http://filmunlimited.co.uk

Flicks
http://www.flicks.co.uk

Guardian online
http://www.guardian.co.uk/guardian

Inside Out
http://www.insideout.co.uk

Premiere
http://www.premieremag.com

Radio Times
http://www.radiotimes.beeb.com

Screen
http://www.arts.gla.ac

Screendaily
http://screendaily.com

Screen Digest
http://www.screendigest.com

Sunday Times
http://www.sunday-times.co.uk

Talking Pictures
http://www.filmcentre.co.uk

Television
http://www.rts.org.uk

Time Out
http://www.timeout.co.uk/

Total Film
http://www.futurenet.co.uk

UK Government press releases
http://www.open.gov.uk/

Uncut
http:// www.uncut.net

Variety
http://www.variety.com

Visimag
http://visimag.com

Preview Theatres

BAFTA
http://www.bafta.org

The Curzon Minema
http://www.minema.com

RSA
http://www.rsa.org.uk

The Screening Room
http://www.moving-picture.co.uk

Production Companies

Aardman Animations
http://www.aardman.com

British Film Commission
http://www.britfilmcom.co.uk

British Films Catalogue
http://www.britfilms.com/

FilmFour Productions
http://www.filmfour.com

Fox Searchlight Pictures
http://www.fox.co.uk

guerilla films
http://www.guerilla.u-net.com

Hammer Film Productions Limited
http://www.hammerfilms.com

imaginary films
http://www.imagfilm.co.uk

Mosiac Films Limited
http://www.mosaicfilms.com

New Producers Alliance
http://www.npa.org.uk

PACT
http://www.pact.co.uk

Zooid Pictures Limited
http://www.zooid.co.uk

Specialised Goods and Services

Ashurst Morris Crisp
http://www.ashursts.com

Bromley Casting (Film & TV Extras Agency)
http://www.showcall.co.uk
Hothouse Models & Effects
http://www.hothousefx.co.uk

MBS Underwater Video Specialists
http://www.eclipse.co.uk.mbs

Moving Image Touring Exhibition Service (MITES)
http://www.mites.org.uk

Olswang
http://www.olswang.co.uk

Studios

Capital FX
http://www.capital.fx.co.uk

Elstree Film Studios
http://www.elstreefilmstudios.co.uk

Hillside Studios
http://www.ctvc.co.uk

Millennium Studios
http://www.elstree-online.co.uk

Television Companies

625 Television Room
http://www.625.uk.com

TV Commissions
http://www.tvcommissions.com

TV Guides
http://www.link-it.com/TV
http://www.sceneone.co.uk/s1/TV

Episode Guides Page
http://epguides.com/

Anglia Television
http://www.anglia.tv.co.uk/

BBC
http://www.bbc.co.uk/

Border Television
http://www.border-tv.com/

Carlton Television
http://www.carltontv.co.uk/

Channel Four
http://www.channel4.com

Channel 4
http://www.channel4.co.uk

Granada Television
http://www.granada.co.uk

HTV
http://www.htv.co.uk/

London Weekend Television (LWT)
http://www.lwt.co.uk/

Meridian Broadcasting Ltd
http://www.meridan.tv.co.uk/

S4C
http://www.s4c.co.uk/

Scottish Television
http://www.stv.co.uk/

Ulster Television
http://www.utvlive.com

Video Labels

British Videogram Association
http://www.bva.org.uk

Blockbuster Entertainment
http://www.blockbuster.com

DVD rental
http://www.movietrak.com

MovieMail
http://www.moviem.co.uk

Movies Unlimited
http://www.moviesunlimited.com

Workshops

City Eye
http://www.city-eye.co.uk

Edinburgh Film Workshop Trust
www.efwt.demon.co.uk

Hull Time Based Arts
http://www.htba.demon.co.uk

The Lux Centre
http://www.lux.org.uk

Pilton Video
http://www.piltonvideo.co.uk

The Place in the Park Studios
http://www.screenhero.demon.co.uk

Real Time Video
http://www.rtvideo.demon.co.uk

Vera Media
http://www.vera-media.co.uk

Vivid
http://www.wavespace.waverider.co.uk/~vivid/

WORKSHOPS

The selection of workshops listed below are generally non-profit distributing and subsidised organisations. Some workshops are also active in making audio-visual products for UK and international media markets

Amber Side Workshop
5 Side
Newcastle upon Tyne NE1 3JE
Tel: 0191 232 2000
Fax: 0191 230 3217
Murray Martin
Film/video production, distribution and exhibition. Most recent productions include: *Letters to Katiya*, 1 hour documentary; *Eden Valley* 90 minute feature film; *The Scar* 115 minute feature film. The Workshops National Archive is based at Amber. Large selection of workshop production on VHS, a substantial amount of written material and a database. Access by appointment

Belfast Film Workshop
37 Queen Street
Belfast BT1 6EA
Tel: 028 90648387
Fax: 028 90646657
Alastair Hrron, Kate McManus
Film co-operative offering film/video/animation production and exhibition. Offers both these facilities to others. Made *Acceptable Levels* (with Frontroom); *Thunder Without Rain: Available Light*; a series on six Northern Irish photographers, various youth animation pieces and a series of videos on traditional music

Black Coral Training
130 Lea Valley Techno Park
Ashley Road
London N17 9LN
Tel: 020 8880 4861
Fax: 020 8880 4113
Black Coral Training is a non-profit making organisation specialising in 1-4 day foundation and intermediate level courses in: Production Management; Producing for low budget features; business skills for freelancers; digital sound editing;

movie magic. Multi-skilling for broadcast television; composing music for film & television; research for documentary; presenting and directing. Screenwriting courses include: Live script readings; script reading skills; TV script editing; developing comedy skills; writing a first short film; adapting a story into a short screenplay. All courses taught by industry professionals. Supported by Skillset, LFVDA and Middlesex University

Black Media Training Trust (BMTT)
Workstation
15 Paternoster Row
Sheffield S12 BX
Tel: 01142 492207
Fax: 01142 492207
Contact: Carl Baker
Film and video training. Commercial media productions facility and training resource within and for all Asian, African and African Caribbean communities for community development purposes. Also various commercial media consultancy and project services and facilities hire. Funded by National Lottery Single Regeneration Budget and church urban fund

Caravel Media Centre
The Great Barn Studios
Cippenham Lane
Slough SL1 5AU
Tel: 01753 534828
Fax: 01753 571383
Denis Statham
Training, video production, distribution, exhibition and media education. Offers all these facilities to others. Runs national video courses for independent video-makers

The Children's Film Unit
South Way
Leavesden
Herts WD2 7LZ
Tel: 01923 354656
Fax: 01923 354656
email: cfilmunit@aol.com
Website: www.btinternet.com/~cfu
Carol Rennie, Adminstrator
A registered educational charity, the CFU makes low-budget films for

television and PR on subjects of concern to children and young people. Crews and actors are trained at regular weekly workshops in Putney. Work is in 16mm and video and membership is open to children from 10 - 18. Latest films for Channel 4: *Emily's Ghost; The Higher Mortals; Willies War; Nightshade; The Gingerbread House; Awayday.* For the Samaritans: *Time to Talk.* For the Children's Film and Television Foundation: *How's Business*

City Eye
1st Floor, Northam Centre
Kent Street
Northam
Southampton SO14 5SP
Tel: 023 80634177
Fax: 023 80575717
email: info@city-eye.co.uk
Website: www.city-eye.co.uk
Richard McLaughlin
Film and video equipment hire. Educational projects. Production and post-production and multimedia services. Screenings. Community arts media development. Training courses all year in varied aspects of video, film, photography and radio. Committed to providing opportunities for the disadvantaged/under-represented groups. 50 per cent discount on all non-profit/educational work

Connections Communications Centre
Palingswick House
241 King Street
Hammersmith
London W6 9LP
Tel: 020 8741 1766
Fax: 020 8563 9134
email: connections@cccmedia. demon.co.uk
Website: www.cccmedia.demon.co.uk
Video production training for unemployed adults. NVQ assessment, 4 distinct modules including Basic Video production, crewing on Live Events, Avid Editing, Production opportunities. Introduction to Avid Editing for people in the multi-media industries who want to develop their digital editing skills. Fully wheelchair accessible

Cultural Partnerships
90 De Beauvoir Road
London N1 4EN
Tel: 020 7254 8217
Fax: 020 7254 7541
Heather McAdam, Lol Gellor, Inge Blackman
Arts, media and communications company. Offers various courses in digital sound training. Makes non-broadcast films, videos and radio programmes. Production-based training forms a vital part of the work. Studio facilities for dry/wet hire: fully air-conditioned and purpose built, 8000 sq ft multi-purpose studio. Analogue and Digital audio studios. Live audio studio

Depot Studios
Bond Street
Coventry CV1 4AH
Tel: 024 76525074
Fax: 024 76634373
email: info@covdepot.demon.co.uk
Contact: Deborah Martin-Williams, Anne Forgan, Den Hands
A video and sound recording facility run by Coventry City Council, providing training, equipment hire, support and information. A recently upgraded range of digital video and sound recording facilities available for hire, on a sliding scale. Projects and commissions also undertaken

Edinburgh Film Workshop Trust
56 Albion Road
Edinburgh EH7 5QZ
Tel: 0131 656 9123
email: post@efwt.demon.co.uk
Website: www.efwt.demon.co.uk
David Halliday
Scotland's only franchised workshop. Broadcast, non-broadcast and community integrated production. 24 years producing broadcast and non-broadcast film, video and animation

Exeter Phoenix
Media Centre
Bradninch Place
Gandy Street
Exeter
Devon EX4 3LS
Tel: 01392 667066
Fax: 01392 667596
email: media@exeterphoenix.org.uk
Video and multimedia training, access and activities. Media - 100, Betacam - SP, Digital - S (D9), Macintosh workstations, cinema, theatre and cafe

Film Fever Video Makers
13 All Saints Road
Ipswich
Suffolk IP1 4DG
Tel: 01473 250685
Small production Workshop offering occasional course in basic VHS and S-VHS production

Film House/Ty Ffilm
Chapter Arts Centre
Market Road
Canton
Cardiff CF5 1QE
Tel: 029 20409990

Film Work Group
Top Floor
Chelsea Reach
79-89 Lots Road
London SW10 0RN
Tel: 020 7352 0538
Fax: 020 7351 6479
Loren Squires, Nigel Perkins
Video and film post-production facilities. Special rates for grant-aided, self-funded and non-profit projects. Avid 'on line' (2:1) and 'off line' editing. 36 gigs storage. Digital Animation Workstations (draw, paint, image modification, edit).
3 machine Hi-Band SP and mixed Beta SP/Hi-Band with DVE
2 machine Lo-Band 'off line' with sound mixing. 6 plate Steenbeck

First Take
Merseyside Innovation Centre
131 Mount Pleasant
Liverpool L3 5TF
Tel: 0151 708 5767
Fax: 0151 707 0230
email: all@first-take.demon.co.uk
Website: www.first-take.demon.co.uk
Mark Bareham, Lynne Harwood
First Take is an independent production and training organisation. It is the foremost provider of video training and production services to the voluntary, community, arts, education and local authority sectors across the North West. Professional video training by BBC Assessors and broadcast quality productions

Four Corners Film Workshop
113 Roman Road
Bethnal Green
London E2 0QN
Tel: 020 8981 6111
Fax: 020 8983 4441
Holds film production courses in S8mm and 16mm and film theory

classes. A full programme runs all year round. Provides subsidised film and video equipment for low budget independent film-makers. Has a 40 seat cinema, S8mm, 16mm, Hi8 and U-Matic production and post-production facilities

Fradharc Ur
11 Scotland Street
Stornoway
Isle of Lewis PA87
Tel: 01851 703255
The first Gaelic film and video workshop, offering VHS and hi-band editing and shooting facilities. Production and training in Gaelic for community groups. Productions include: *Under the Surface, Na Deilbh Bheo; The Weaver; A Wedding to Remember; As an Fhearran*

Glasgow Media Access Centre
3rd Floor
34 Albion Street
Glasgow G1 1LH
Tel: 0141 553 2620
Fax: 0141 553 2660
email: admin@g-mac.co.uk
Website: www.g-mac.co.uk
Ian Reid, John Sackey, Rachel Seiffert, Cordelia Stephens
G-MAC is an open access training/access resource for film and video makers. Offers equipment hire and training courses at subsidised rates. Facilities include; BetaSP, MiniDV, DVCPro, S-VHS and VHS, cameras and edit suites (including 2 AVIDs and a Steenbeck) a multimedia computer and Super8mm and 16mm projectors. G-MAC runs two short film schemes: Screenworks for entry level filmmakers and Cineworks for animation, documentary and drama filmmakers who already have some experience. G-MAC produces, distributes and exhibits corporate and community based projects

Hull Time Based Arts
42 The High Street
Hull HU1 1PS
Tel: 01482 586340/216446
Fax: 01482 589952
email: lab@htba.demon.co.uk
Website: www.timebase.org
Jo Millett/Dan Van Heeswyk
HTBA promotes, produces and commissions timebased art: film, video, performance, sound. The Lab is HTBA's timebased media production training and hire facilities. Equipment

for hire includes two on-line Avid non-linear editing suites (Media Composer 9000 with uncompressed video, also Media Composer 1000), output to DVCPro, Beta SP, DVCam. Pro Tools suite, DVCPro, DVCam cameras and production facilities, video projectors also for hire. Range of training courses

Intermedia Film and Video
19 Heathcote Street
Nottingham NG1 3AF
Tel: 0115 955 6909
Fax: 0115 955 9956
email: info@intermedianotts.co.uk
Website: www.intermedianotts.co.uk
Ken Hay, Director
Intermedia is the media production development agency for the East Midlands, providing a range of services to support media producers working at all levels of the industry. We provide facilities, training, production advice and support and manage EMMI, the East Midlands Media Initiative, which is able to make development awards to media producers and provide co-financing for media production activities.

Jubilee Arts Co Ltd
84 High Street
West Bromwich
West Midlands B70 6JW
Tel: 0121 553 6862
Fax: 0121 525 0640
email: @jubart.demon.co.uk
Jubilee Arts is a unique multi-media community arts team, formed in 1974. Skills include photography, video, drama, audio visual, music/sound, computers, training and graphic design. We work with communities, using the arts as a tool to create opportunities for positive ways for people to express themselves. Jubilee Arts works in partnership with a wide range of groups, agencies and voluntary and statutory bodies

Leeds Animation Workshop (A Women's Collective)
45 Bayswater Row
Leeds LS8 5LF
Tel: 0113 248 4997
Fax: 0113 248 4997
Jane Bradshaw, Terry Wragg, Stephanie Munro, Janis Goodman, Milena Dragic
Production company making films on social issues. Distributing over 20 short films including - *A World of Difference, Did You Say Hairdressing?*

Waste Watchers, No Offence, Through the Glass Ceiling, Out to Lunch, Give us a Smile, All Stressed Up. They also offer short training courses

Lighthouse
9-12 Middle Street
Brighton BN1 1AL
Tel: 01273 384222
Fax: 01273 384233
email: info@lighthouse.org.uk
Website: www.lighthouse.org.uk
A training and production centre, providing courses, facilities and production advice for video and digital media. Avid off- and online edit suites. Apple Mac graphics and animation workstations. Digital video capture and manipulation. Output to/from Betacam SP. SVHS offline edit suite. Post Production and Digital Artists equipment bursaries offered three times a year

London Deaf Access Project
1-3 Worship Street
London EC2A 2AB
Tel: 020 7588 3522 (voice) Tel: 0171 588 3528 (text)
Fax: 020 7588 3526
email: Ldap@ndirect.co.uk
Translates information from English into British Sign Language (BSL) for Britain's deaf community, encourages others to do likewise and provides a consultancy/monitoring service for this purpose. Promotes the use of video amongst deaf people as an ideal medium for passing on information. Runs workshops and courses for deaf people in video production, taught by deaf people using BSL. Works with local authorities and government departments ensuring that public information is made accessible to sign language users. Titles include: *School Leavers, Access to Women's Services, Health issues*

London Screenwriters' Workshop
114 Whitfield Street
London W1P 5RW
Sandland Street
London WC1R 4PZ
Tel: 020 7387 5511
Alan Denman, Paul Gallagher
The LSW is an educational charity whose purpose is to help new and developing writers learn the craft of screenwriting for film and television. It offers writing workshops, industry seminars, a newsletter and a script reading service. It is open at very

reasonable cost to everyone. Membership £30.00 p.a

The Lux Centre
2-4 Hoxton Square
London N1 6NU
Tel: 020 7684 0101
Fax: 020 7684 1111
email: lux@lux.org.uk
Website: www.lux.org.uk
Lux (a merger of London Electronic Arts and London Film Makers' Co-op) is Britain's national centre for video and new media art. Offers a complete range of services including production based training, facility hire (production and post-production), distribution and exhibition of video and new media art and film

Media Arts
Town Hall Studios
Regent Circus
Swindon SN1 1QF
Tel: 01793 463224
Fax: 01793 463223
Ann Cullis, Shahina Johnson
Film & video production and training centre. Offers short courses and longer term media projects. First stop scheme offers funding for first time film/video makers. Also offers media education services, equipment hire, screenwriting advice and undertakes production commissions. Organises screenings and discussions

The Media Workshop
Peterborough Arts Centre
Media Department
Orton Goldhay
Peterborough PE2 0JQ
Tel: 01733 237073
Fax: 01733 235462
email: postmaster@p-arts.demon.co.uk
Video, multimedia and photography production, workshops and exhibitions. Offering DVCPRO, SVHS production/edit facilities and Media 100 non-linear editing. Also full multimedia authoring and design

Mersey Film and Video (MFV)
13-15 Hope Street
Liverpool L1 9BQ
Tel: 0151 708 5259
Fax: 0151 707 8595
email: mfv@hopestreet.u-net.com
Website: www.mfv.merseyside.org
Production facilities for: BETA SP, DVC PRO, MINI DV, multi-media stations, photoshop, Dolly and track,

Jibarm, Lights, Mica, DAT etc. Post Production Avid, MC1000, SVHS, BBC FX & music library. Guidance and help for production, scripting, funding, budgets,

Migrant Media
90 De Beauvoir Road
London N1 4EN
Tel: 020 7254 9701
Fax: 020 7241 2387
Ken Fero, Ivan Ali Fawzi, Soulyman Garcia
Media production training and campaigning for migrants and refugees. Focus on African and Middle Eastern communities. Networks internationally on media/political issues. Broadcast credits include: *After the Storm* (BBC); *Sweet France* (C4), *Tasting Freedom* (C4), *Justice For Joy* (C4)

Moving Image Touring Exhibition Services (MITES)
Foundation For Art & Creative Technology (FACT)
Bluecoat Chambers
Liverpool L1 3BX
Tel: 0151 707 2881
Fax: 0151 707 2150
email: mites@fact.co.uk
Website: mites.org.uk
Simon Bradshaw
Courses for artists, gallery curators, technicians and exhibitors

Nerve Centre
2nd Floor
Northern Counties Building
8 Customs House Street
Derry BT48 6AE
Tel: 01504 260562

The Old Dairy Studios
156b Haxby Road
York YO3 7JN
Tel: 01904 641394
Fax: 01904 692052
Digital video production facilities inc. Fast video system, 32 Track digital recording studio, audio visual facilities with Adobe Photoshop, Radio Production and Midi Composition Studios are available. Courses in video production and editing, sound engineering, radio production, midi composition and digital imaging. Working with people with disabilities, unemployed people, people aged between 12 and 25 as well as with members of the community in general

Oxford Film and Video Makers
The Stables
North Place
Headington
Oxford OX3 9HY
Tel: 01865 741682 or 01865 760074 (course enquiries)
Fax: 01865 742901
email: ofvm@ox39hy.demon.co.uk
Website: www.welcome.to/ofvm
Contact: Sue Evans, Office Administrator
Accredited training in video, experimental film and 16mm film. Also offering courses in scriptwriting, directing and digital editing. Subsidised training for the unemployed and community groups. Production support through the OFVM millennium video project and regular screenings organised at local cinemas and the major summer music festivals. Fast professional digital editing facility available for hire with or without editor

Picture This Moving Image
40 Sydney Row
Spike Island Studios
Bristol BS1 6UU
Tel: 0117 925 7010
Fax: 0117 925 7040
email: info@picturethis.demon.co.uk
Josephine Lanyon, Director
Picture This provides:
Training - a range of courses from beginner level to longer term training for under-represented groups. Short courses available in video, film and animation production and post production.
Awards and bursaries - opportunities for new work, with cash grants, advice and access to resources
Production and distribution - facilitate and commission productions for galleries, film festivals broadcasting agencies and cinemas
Membership scheme - support, information, and advice for individuals and groups
Facilities - access to film and video production and post production facilities ranging from 16mm film up to broadcast standard cameras and avid editing

Pilton Video
30 Ferry Road Avenue
Edinburgh EH4 4BA
Tel: 0131 343 1151
Fax: 0131 343 2820

email: office@
piltonvideo.freeserve.co.uk
Website: www.piltonvideo.co.uk
Hugh Farrell, Joel Venet, Eleanor Hill, Graham Fitzpatrick
Training and production facilities in the local community; documentary and fiction for broadcast. 4 non-linear edit suites

The Place in The Park Studios
Bellvue Road
Wrexham
North Wales LL13 7NH
Tel: 01978 358522
Fax: 01978 358522
email: knewmedia@screenhero.demon.co.uk
Website: www.screenhero.demon.co.uk
Richard Knew
Video/Film production access centre, offering subsidised facilities hire. Equipment includes Beta SP, Digital, Media 100,16mm and SVHS shooting and editing kit. The Place in The Park acts as a focal point/contact centre for independent film and video makers in the North Wales region and beyond

Platform Films and Video
3 Tankerton House
Tankerton Street
London WC1H 8HP
Tel: 020 7278 8394 Mobile: 0973 278 956
Fax: 020 7278 8394
Chris Reeves
Film/video production and distribution. Also equipment hire including complete Sony BVW400P shooting kit, Panasonic Hi-Fi sound VHS edit suite, Avid Media Composer 400, 9Gb, 20" monitors, Pro-Tools, title tool, Previs 2 fx, Sanyo 220 video projector

Real Time Video
The Arts and Media Centre
21 South Street
Reading RG1 4QU
Tel: 0118 901 5205
Fax: 0118 901 5206
email: info@rtvideo.demon.co.uk
Website: www.rtvideo.demon.co.uk
Clive Robertson
Community access video workshop, video production, training, exhibition and consultancy. Runs workshops and projects using video as development and self advocacy tool. Organises screenings and offers training in production, post-production,

computer graphics and community video practice. SVHS edit suite with video and audio-processing, and graphics available for hire (reduced rates for non-profit work)

Sankofa Film and Video
Spectrum House
Unit K
32-34 Gordon House Road
London NW5 1LP
Tel: 020 7692 0393
Fax: 020 7485 2869
Maureen Blackwood, Johann Insanally
Film production and 16mm editing facilities, training in film production and scriptwriting, screenings. Productions include: *The Passion of Remembrance, Perfect Image; Dreaming Rivers; Looking for Langston; Young Soul Rebels; In between; A Family Called Abrew; Des'ree EPK; Home Away From Home; Father Sons; Unholy Ghosts; Is it the design on the Wrapper? + Vacuum*

Sheffield Independent Film
5 Brown Street
Sheffield S1 2BS
Tel: 0114 272 0304
Fax: 0114 279 5225
email: admin.ympa@workstation.org.uk
Colin Pons
A resource base for independent film and video-makers in the Sheffield region. Regular training workshops; access to a range of film and video equipment; technical and administrative backup; office space and rent-a-desk; regular screenings of independent film and video. Regular producers sessions to help producers keep abreast of developments in the industry. Sister company Yorkshire Media Production Agency provides production loans of up to £200,000 or 25% of a film's budget

Signals Media Arts
Victoria Chambers
St Runwald Street
Colchester CO1 1HF
Tel: 01206 560255
Fax: 01206 369086
email: admin@signals.org.uk
Audrey Droisen
Film video and multimedia production centre and facility. Services in training, production, media education and equipment hire. Productions include: *Three Hours in High Heels is Heaven* (C4), *Coloured* (Anglia TV), *Cutting Up* (C4); *Garden of Eve* (Anglia TV) and *Fork*

in the Road

Swingbridge Video
Norden House
41 Stowell Street
Newcastle upon Tyne NE1 4YB
Tel/Fax: 0191 232 3762
email: swingvid@aol.com
Contact: Hugh Kelly
A producer of both broadcast and non-broadcast programmes, including drama and documentary formats and specialising in socially purposeful and educational subjects. Offers training and consultancy services to public sector, community and voluntary organisations. Also provides a tape distribution service. Productions include: *White Lies; An English Estate; Happy Hour; Where Shall We Go?; Sparks; Set You Free; Mean Streets* and many more

Trilith
Corner Cottage, Brickyard Lane
Bourton, Gillingham
Dorset SP8 5PJ
Tel: 01747 840750/840727
Trevor Bailey, John Holman
Specialises in rural television and video on community action, rural issues and the outlook and experiences of country born people. Also works with organisations concerned with physical and mental disability and with youth issues. Produces own series of tapes, undertakes broadcast and tape commissions and gathers archive film in order to make it publicly available on video. Distributes own work nationally. Recent work includes broadcast feature and work with farmers and others whose lives revolve around a threatened livestock market, and a production scripted and acted by people with disabilities. Another project enables young people to make programmes for local radio

Valley and Vale Community Arts Ltd
The Valley and Vale Media Centre,
Heol Dew, Sant Betws
Mid Glamorgan CF32 8SU
Tel: 01656 729246/871911
Fax: 01656 729185/870507
Video production, training, distribution and exhibition. Open access workshop offering training to community groups in production/post-production, Hi8, digital, Betacam SP and VHS formats, with linear and non-linear

(media 100) editing facilities

Vera Media
30-38 Dock Street
Leeds LS10 1JF
Tel: 0113 242 8646
Fax: 0113 242 8739
email: vera@vera-media.co.uk
Website: www.vera-media.co.uk
Alison Garthwaite, Catherine Mitchell
Video production - documentary, education, arts equality, public sector, health. Training (ESF/other) for women/mixed. Screenings. Participatory productions. Information resource. Runs membership organisation (NETWORKING) for women in film, video and television

Video Access Centre
25a SW Thistle Street Lane
Edinburgh EH2 1EW
Tel: 0131 220 0220 or 0131 477 4529
Fax: 0131 220 0017
email: fva-edinburgh@hotmail.com
Lara Celini
A membership-based association which provides resources and training for individuals and community groups to work with film and video. Courses are short and at basic or specialist level. Has VHS & SVHS, MiniDV camcorders, Sony DVCam. Super 8 and 16mm production facilities, runs bi-monthly newsletter and information service. Also non-linear editing facilities on AVID

Vivid
Birmingham's Centre for Media Arts Ltd
Unit 311F
The Big Peg
120 Vyse Street
Birmingham B18 9ND
Tel: 0121 233 4061
Fax: 0121 212 1784
email: info@vivid.org.uk
Website: www.vivid.org.uk
Yasmeen Baig Clifford
Marian Hall,
Training, resources and support for artists and media practitioners at all levels. Facilities include 16mm film production, Beta SX, DV Cam, Hi8 video production equipment, Avid, Video Machine and linear video editing, EOS animation, 5x4, medium format and 35mm photographic equipment and darkrooms, Power Macs and PCs running Photoshop, Premiere, director, dreamweaver, flash etc

Welfare State International (WSI)

The Ellers
Ulverston
Cumbria LA12 0AA
Tel: 01229 581127
Fax: 01229 581232

A consortium of artists, musicians, engineers and performers. Film/video production, hire and exhibition. Output includes community feature films *King Real* and the *Hoodlums* (script Adrian Mitchell) and work for television. Titles include: Piranha Pond (Border TV), RTS Special Creativity Award; Ulverston Town Map, community video; Community Celebration, Multinational Course leading to Lantern Procession (video) and Rites of Passage publications include: *The Dead Good Funerals* Book available from WSI. Recent Northern Arts Fellowships and exhibitions include Nick May, artist and filmmaker

West Yorkshire Media Services

Hall Place Studios
3 Queen Square
Leeds LS2 8AF
Tel: 0113 283 1906
Fax: 0113 283 1906
email: m.spadafora@lmu.ac.uk
Website: www.hallplacestudios.com
Maria Spadafora

18 month Certificate in Film and Video Production courses accredited by Leeds Metropolitan University. A free course that welcomes applications from women and people from minorities. Other courses and projects as per programme offers a thorough grounding in all aspects of film and video production

WFA

Media and Cultural Centre
9 Lucy Street
Manchester M15 4BX
Tel: 0161 848 9785
Fax: 0161 848 9783

Main areas of work include media access and training, including City and Guilds 770 National Certificate, with a full range of production, post-production and exhibition equipment and facilities for community, semi-professional and professional standards. Video production unit (BECTU). Distribution and sale of 16mm films and videos, booking and advice service, video access library. Cultural work, mixed media events. Bookshop/outreach work

ABBREVIATIONS

ABC
Association of Business Communicators

ABSA
Association of Business Sponsorship of the Arts

ACCS
Association for Cultural and Communication Studies

ACE
Arts Council of England/Ateliers du Cinéma Européen

ADAPT
Access for Disabled People to Arts Premises today

AEEU
Amalgamated Engineering and Electrical Union

AETC
Arts and Entertainment Training Council

AFC
Australian Film Commission

AFCI
Association of Film Commissioners International

AFECT
Advancement of Film Education Charitable Trust

AFI
American Film Institute/Australian Film Institute

AFM
American Film Market

AFVPA
Advertising Film and Videotape Producers' Association

AGICOA
Association de Gestion Internationale Collective des Oeuvres Audiovisuelles

AIM
All Industry Marketing for Cinema

AMCCS
Association for Media, Cultural and Communications Studies

AME
Association for Media Education

AMFIT
Association for Media Film and Television Studies in Higher and Further Education

AMPAS
Adcademy of Motion Picture Arts and Sciences (USA)

AMPS
Association of Motion Picture Sound

APC
Association of Professional Composers

APRS
The Professional Recording Association

AVEK
The Promotion Centre for Audio Visual Culture in Finland

BAFTA
British Academy of Film and Television Arts

BARB
Broadcasters' Audience Research Board

BASCA
British Academy of Songwriters, Composers and Authors

BATC
British Amateur Television Club

BBC
British Broadcasting Corporation

BBFC
British Board of Film Classification

BCS
British Cable Services

BECTU
Broadcasting Entertainment Cinematograph and Theatre Union

BFB
Black Film Bulletin

BFC
British Film Commission

BFFS
British Federation of Film Societies

BFI
British Film Institute

BIEM
Bureau Internationale des Sociétés gérant les Droits d'Enregistrement

BIPP
British Institute of Professional Photography

BKSTS
British Kinematograph Sound and Television Society

BNFVC
British National Film and Video Catalogue

BPI
British Phonographic Industry

BREMA
British Radio and Electronic Equipment Manufacturers' Association

BSAC
British Screen Advisory Council

BSC
British Society of Cinematiographers

Broadcasting Standards Commission

BSD
British Screen Development

BSkyB
British Sky Broadcasting

BSS
Broadcasting Support Services

BTDA
British Television Distributors Association

BUFVC
British Universities Film and Video Council

BVA
British Video Association

CAA
Cinema Advertising Association

CARTOON
European Association of Animation Film

CAVIAR
Cinema and Video Industry Audience Research

CD
Compact Disc

CDI
Compact Disc Interactive

CD ROM
Compact Disc

Read Only Memory

CEA
Cinematograph Exhibitors' Association

CEPI
Co-ordination Européene des Producteurs Indépendantes

CFTF
Children's Film and Television
Foundation

CFU
Children's Film Unit

C4
Channel 4

CICCE
Comitédes Industries
Cinématographiques et
Audiovisuelles des Communautés
Européenes et de l'Europe
Extracommunautaire

CILECT
Centre Internationale de Liaison des
Ecoles de Cinéma et de Télévision

CNN
Cable News Network

COI
Central Office of Information

CPBF
Campaign for Press and Broadcasting
Freedom

CTA
Cable Television Association/

Cinema Theatre Association

CTBF
Cinema and Television Benevolent
Fund

DAT
Digital Audio Tape

DBC
Deaf Broadcasting Council

DCMS
Department for Culture Media and
Sport

DBS
Direct Broadcasting by Satellite

DFE
Department for Education

DFI
Danish Film Institute

DGGB
Directors' Guild of Great Britain

DTI
Department of Trade and Industry

DVI
Digital Video Interactive

DVD
Digital Versatile Disc

EAVE
European Audiovisual Entrepreneurs

EBU
European Broadcasting Union

ECF
European Co-Production Fund

EDI
Euopaaisches Dokumentarfilm
Institut/Entertainment Data
International

EFA
European Film Academy

EFCOM
European Film Commissioners

EFDO
European Film Distribution Office

EGAKU
European Committee of Trade
Unions in Arts, Mass Media and
Entertainment

EIM
European Institute for the Media

EITF
Edinburgh International Television
Festival

EMG
Euro Media Garanties

ENG
Electronic News Gathering

EU
European Union

EUTELSAT
European Telecommunications
Satellite Organisation

FAA
Film Artistes' Association

FACT
Federation Against Copyright Theft

FAME
Film Archive Management and
Entertainment

FBU
Federation of Broadcasting Unions

FEITIS
Fédération Européene des Industries
Techniques de l'Image et du Son

FEMIS
Institut de Formation et
d'Enseignement pour les Métiers de
l'Unage et du Son

FEPACI
Fédération Pan-Africain des
Cinéastes

FESPACO
Festivale Pan-Africain des Cinémas
de Ougadougou

FEU
Federation of Entertainment Unions

FIA
International Federation of Actors

FIAD
Fédération Internationale des
Associations de Distributeurs de Films

FIAF
Fédération Internaionale des Archives
du Film

FIAPF
International Federation of Film
Producers Associations

FIAT
Fédération Internationale des
Archives de Télévision

FICC
Fédération Internationale des Ciné-
Clubs

FIFREC
International Film and Student
Directors Festival

FIPFI
Fédération Internationale des
Producteurs de Films Indépendants

FIPRESCI
Fédération Internationale de la Presse
Cinématographique

FOCAL
Federation of Commercial Audio
Visual Libraries

FTVLCA
Film and Television Lighting
Contractors Association

FX
Effects/special effects

HBO
Home Box Office

HDTV
High Definition Television

HTV
Harlech Television

HVC
Home Video Channel

IABM
International Association of
Broadcasting Manufacturers

IAC
Institute of Amateur
Cinematographers

ICA
Institue of Contemporary Arts

IDATE
Insitut de l'Audiovisuel et des
Télécommunications en Europe

IFDA
Independent Film Distributors'
Association

IFFS
International Federation of Film
Societies (aka FICC)

IFPI
International Federation of the
Phonographic Industry

IFTA
International Federation of Television Archives (aka FIAT)

IIC
International Institute of Communications

ILR
Independent Local Radio

INR
Independent National Radio

IPA
Institute of Practitioners in Advertising

ISBA
Incorporated Society of British Advertising

ISETV
International Secretariat for Arts, Mass Media and Entertainment Trade Unions

ISM
Incorporated Society of Musicians

ITC
Independent Television Commission

ITN
Independent Television News

ITV
Independent Television

ITVA
Independent Television Association

IVCA
International Vsual Communications Association

IVLA
International Visual Literacy Association

JICTAR
Joint Industries' Committee for Television Audience Research

LAB
London Arts Board

LFF
London Film Festival

LFVDA
London Film and Video Development Agency

LSW
London Screenwriters' Workshop

LVA
London Video Access

LWT
London Weekend Television

MBS
Media Business School

MCPS
Mechanical Copyright Protection Society

MEDIA
Mesures pour Encourager le Développement de l'Industrie Audiovisuelle

MENU
Media Education News Update

MFVPA
Music, Film and Video Producers' Association

MGM
Metro Goldwyn Mayer

MHMC
Mental Health Media Council

MIDEM
MarchéInternational du Disque et de l'Edition Musicale

MIFED
Mercato Internazionale del TV, film e del Documentario

MIPCOM
MarchéInternaional des Films et des Programmes pour la TV, la Vidéo, le C,ble et le Satellite

MIP-TV
MarchéInternational de Programmes de Télévision

MOMI
Museum of the Moving Image

MPA
Motion Picture Association of America

MPEAA
Motion Picture Export Association of American

MU
Musicians' Union

NAHEFV
National Association for Higher Education in Film and Video

NAVAL
National Audio Visual Aids Library

NCA
National Campaign for the Arts

NCC
National Cinema Centre

NCET
National Council for Educational Technology

NCVQ
National Council for Vocational Qualifications

NFDF
National Film Development Fund

NFT
National Film Theatre

NFTC
National Film Trustee Company

NFTS
National Film and Television School

NFTVA
National Film and Television Archive

NHMF
National Heritage Memorial Fund

NIFC
Northern Ireland Film Council

NMPFT
National Museum of Photography, Film and Television

NoW
Network of Workshops

NPA
New Producers Alliance

NSC
Northern Screen Commission

NTSC
National Television Standards Committee

NUJ
National Union of Journalists

NUT
National Union of Teachers

NVALA
National Viewers' and Listeners'Association

PACT
Producers Alliance for Cinema and Television

PAL
Programme Array Logic/

Phase Alternation Line

PPL
Phonographic Performance

PRS
Performing Right Society

RAB
Regional Arts Board

RETRA
Radio, Electrical and Television Retailers' Association

RFT
Regional Film Theatre

RTBF
Radio Television Belge de la CommunantéFranÁaise

RTS
Royal Television Society

S4C
Siandel Pedwar Cymru

S&S
Sight and Sound

SAC
Scottish Arts Council

SBFT
Scottish Broadcast & Film Training

SCALE
Small Countries Improve their
Audio-visual Level in Europe

SCTE
Society of Cable Television
Engineers

SECAM
Séquentiel couleur , mémoire

SFA
Short Film Agency

SFC
Scottish Film Council

SFD
Society of Film Distributors

SFPF
Scottish Film Production Fund

SFX
Special Effects

SIFT
Summary of Information on Film and
Television

SMATV
Satellite Mater Antenna Television

SOURCES
Stimulating Outstanding Resources
for Creative European Scriptwriting

TVRO
Television receive-only

UA
United Artists

UCI
United Cinemas International

UIP
United International Pictures

UNESCO
United Nations Educational,
Scientific and Cultural Organisation

UNIC
Union International des Cinémas

URTI
Université Radiophonique et
Télévisuelle Internationale

VCPS
Video Copyright Protection Society

VCR
Video Cassette Recorder

VHS
Video Home System

VLV
Voice of the Listener and Viewer

WGGB
Writers' Guild of Great Britain

WTN
Worldwide Television News

WTVA
Wider Television Access

YTV
Yorkshire Television

INDEX

C

H

I

M

Index of advertisers

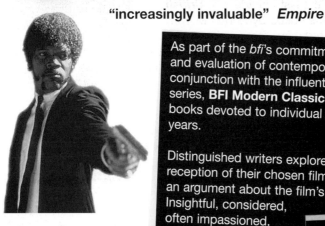